Binaural and Spatial Hearing in Real and Virtual Environments

Binaural and Spatial Hearing in Real and Virtual Environments

Edited by

Robert H. Gilkey

Wright State University, Dayton, Ohio

Timothy R. Anderson

Wright-Patterson Air Force Base, Ohio

Psychology Press
Taylor & Francis Group

New York London

First Published by
Lawrence Erlbaum Associates, Inc., Publishers
10 Industrial Avenue
Mahwah, New Jersey 07430-2262

Transferred to Digital Printing 2009 by Psychology Press
270 Madison Ave, New York NY 10016
27 Church Road, Hove, East Sussex, BN3 2FA

Cover design by Mairav Salomon-Dekel

Library of Congress Cataloging-in-Publication Data

Binaural and spatial hearing / edited by Robert H. Gilkey, Timothy R. Anderson.
p. cm.
Includes bibliographical references and index.
ISBN 0-8058-1654-2 (alk. paper)
1. Directional hearing. 2. Auditory perception. 3. Binaural hearing aids.
I. Gilkey, Robert H. II. Anderson, Timothy R.
QP469.B525 1996
612.8'5—dc20 95-48449
CIP

Publisher's Note
The publisher has gone to great lengths to ensure the quality of this reprint but points out that some imperfections in the original may be apparent.

Contributors

Timothy R. Anderson
AL/CFBA, Bldg. 441
2610 Seventh St.
Wright-Patterson AFB, OH 45433-7901

Daniel H. Ashmead
Department of Hearing
and Speech Sciences
Vanderbilt University Medical Center
Nashville, TN 37232-8700

Jennifer M. Ball
Department of Psychology
Wright State University
Dayton, OH 45435

Ranjan Batra
Department of Anatomy
University of Connecticut Health Center
Farmington, CT 06030

Leslie R. Bernstein
Surgical Research Center
Dept. of Surgery (Otolaryngology)
Center for Neurological Sciences
University of Connecticut Health Center
Farmington, CT 06030

Joan Besing
Department of Speech Pathology
and Audiology
University of South Alabama
2000 University Commons
Mobile, AL 36688

Jens Blauert
Lehrstuhl für Allgemeine
Elektrotechnik und Akustik
Ruhr-Universität Bochum
D-44780 Bochum
Germany

John F. Brugge
Department of Neurophysiology
and Waisman Center
University of Wisconsin
Madison, WI 53706

Thomas N. Buell
Naval Submarine Medical
Research Laboratory
Box 900, Naval Submarine
Base–New London
Groton, CT 06349-5900

Mahlon D. Burkhard
Sonic Perceptions Inc.
28 Knight St.
Norwalk, CT 06851

Robert A. Butler
Otolaryngology - Head and Neck Surgery
University of Chicago Medical Center
5841 South Maryland Ave., Box 412
Chicago, IL 60637

Joseph C. K. Chan
Department of Neurophysiology
University of Wisconsin
Madison, WI 53706
Current Address:
Division of Technology
City Polytechnic of Hong Kong
Kowloon, Hong Kong

Rachel K. Clifton
Department of Psychology
Tobin Hall, Box 37710
University of Massachusetts
Amherst, MA 01003

H. Steven Colburn
Department of Biomedical Engineering
Boston University
44 Cummington St.
Boston, MA 02215

Ruth A. Conley
Parmly Hearing Institute
Loyola University
Chicago, IL 60626

Theodore J. Doll
Electro-Optics, Environment, and Materials Laboratory
Georgia Tech Research Institute
Georgia Institute of Technology
Atlanta, GA 30332-0800

Richard O. Duda
Department of Electrical Engineering
San Jose State University
One Washington Square
San Jose, CA 95192

Nathaniel Durlach
Research Laboratory of Electronics
Rm. 36-709
Massachusetts Institute of Technology
Cambridge, MA 02139

Raymond H. Dye, Jr.
Parmly Hearing Institute
Loyola University
6525 N. Sheridan Rd.
Chicago, IL 60626

Mark A. Ericson
AL/CFBA, Bldg. 441
2610 Seventh St.
Wright-Patterson AFB, OH 45433-7901

Ralf Fassel
Drittes Physikalisches Institut
Universität Gottingen, Germany

Douglas C. Fitzpatrick
Department of Anatomy
University of Connecticut
Health Center
Farmington, CT 06030

Richard L. Freyman
Department of Communication Disorders
4 Arnold House
University of Massachusetts
Amherst, MA 01003

Robert H. Gilkey
Department of Psychology
Wright State University
Dayton, OH 45435
and AL/CFBA, Bldg. 441
2610 Seventh St.
Wright-Patterson AFB, OH 45433-7901

Michael D. Good
Scientific Research Laboratories
Ford Motor Company
P.O. Box 2035/MD3135
Dearborn, MI 48121

D. Wesley Grantham
The Bill Wilkerson Center and Vanderbilt University School of Medicine
Division of Hearing and Speech Sciences
1114 19th Avenue South
Nashville, TN 37212

Ervin R. Hafter
Department of Psychology
University of California
Berkley, CA 94720

Thomas E. Hanna
Naval Submarine Medical Research Laboratory
Box 900, Naval Submarine Base–New London
Groton, CT 06349-5900

William Morris Hartmann
Department of Physics
Michigan State University
East Lansing, MI 48824

Joseph E. Hind
Department of Neurophysiology
University of Wisconsin
Madison, WI 53706

Scott K. Isabelle
Armstrong Laboratory
AL/CFBA, Bldg. 441
2610 Seventh Street
Wright-Patterson AFB, OH 45433-7910

James Janko
Department of Psychology
Wright State University
Dayton, OH 45435

Philip X. Joris
Department of Neurophysiology
273 Medical Science Bldg.
University of Wisconsin Medical School
Madison, WI 53706

Doris J. Kistler
Waisman Center
University of Wisconsin, Madison
Madison, WI 53705

Janet Koehnke
Department of Speech Pathology
and Audiology
University of South Alabama
2000 University Commons
Mobile, AL 36688

Armin Kohlrausch
Institute for Perception Research
P.O. 513
NL-5600MB Eindhoven
The Netherlands

Birger Kollmeier
Fachbereich Physik
Universität Oldenburg
D-26111
Oldenburg, Germany

Gregory Kramer
Clarity/Santa Fe Institute
Nelson Lane
Garrison, NY 10524

Shigeyuki Kuwada
Department of Anatomy
University of Connecticut Health Center
Farmington, CT 06030

Hilmar Lehnert
Ruhr-Universität Bochum
D-44780 Bochum, Germany

Ruth Y. Litovsky
Department of Biomedical Engineering
Boston University
44 Cummington St.
Boston, MA 02215
and Eaton Peabody Laboratory
Massachusetts Eye and Ear Infirmary
243 Charles Street
Boston, MA 02114-3096

Richard L. McKinley
AL/CFBA, Bldg. 441
2610 Seventh St.
Wright-Patterson AFB, OH 45433-7901

Donald H. Mershon
Department of Psychology
North Carolina State University
Box 7801
Raleigh, NC 27695-7801

John C. Middlebrooks
Departments of Neuroscience
and Otolaryngology
Box 100244
University of Florida College of Medicine
Gainesville, FL 32610-0244
Current Address:
Kresge Hearing Research Institute
1301 East Ann Street
University of Michigan
Ann Arbor, MI 48109-0506

Israel Nelken
Department of Physiology
Hadassah Medical School
Hebrew University
Jerusalem, 91010 Israel

David R. Perrott
Department of Psychology
California State University
University Drive
Los Angeles, CA 90032-8227

Richard A. Reale
Department of Neurophysiology
and Waisman Center
University of Wisconsin
Madison, WI 53706

John J. Rice
Department of Biomedical Engineering
Johns Hopkins University
720 Rutland Ave.
Baltimore, MD 21205

Kourosh Saberi
Department of Psychology
University of California
Department of Psychology
Berkley, CA 94720
Current Address:
Research Laboratory of Electronics
36-767
Massachusetts Institute of Technology
Cambridge, MA 02139

Edgar A. G. Shaw
Institute for Microstructural Sciences
National Research Council
Ottawa, Ontario K1A OR6
Canada

Barbara Shinn-Cunningham
Research Laboratory of Electronics
Massachusetts Institute of Technology
Cambridge, MA 02139

Philip H. Smith
Department of Anatomy and Department of Neurophysiology
273 Medical Science Bldg.
University of Wisconsin Medical School
Madison, WI 53706

George A. Spirou
Department of Otolaryngology
Head and Neck Surgery
West Virginia University
Morgantown, WV 26506

Richard M. Stern
Department of Electrical and Computer Engineering and Biomedical Engineering Program
Carnegie Mellon University
Pittsburgh, PA 15213

Thomas Z. Strybel
Department of Psychology
California State University
Long Beach, CA 90840

Daniel J. Tollin
Department of Biomedical Engineering
Boston University
44 Cummington St.
Boston, MA 02215

Constantine Trahiotis
Department of Surgery (Otolaryngology)
Surgical Research Center and Center for Neurosciences
University of Connecticut Health Center
Farmington, CT 06030

Elizabeth Wenzel
NASA Ames Research Center
Mail Stop 262-2
Moffett Field, CA 94035

Frederic L. Wightman
Waisman Center and Department of Psychology
University of Wisconsin, Madison
Madison, WI 53705

Tom C. T. Yin
Department of Neurophysiology
273 Medical Science Bldg.
University of Wisconsin Medical School
Madison, WI 53706

William A. Yost
Parmly Hearing Institute
Loyola University of Chicago
6525 N. Sheridan Rd.
Chicago, IL 60626

Eric D. Young
Johns Hopkins School of Medicine
505 Traylor Bldg.
720 Rutland Ave.
Baltimore, MD 21205

Contents

1. G. Kramer
2. J. Blauert
3. E. Hafter
4. T. Moore
5. K. Saberi
6. R. McKinley
7. M. Ericson
8. M. Rickert
9. E. McPherson
10. R.W. Gatehouse
11. B. Simpson
12. L. Bernstein
13. B. Kollmeier
14. R. Bernacki
15. E. Young
16. S. Able
17. P. Joris
18. R. Butler
19. A. Wheeler
20. W. D'Angelo
21. W. Yost
22. J. Middlebrooks
23. M. Good
24. J. Chen
25. D. Davis
26. A. Kulkarni
27. D. Doan
28. D. Ashmead
29. D. W. Grantham
30. E. Shaw
31. B. Shinn-Cunningham
32. B. Rakerd
33. J. Weisenberger
34. G. Naylor
35. A. Musicant
36. M. Bakke
37. C. Trahiotis
38. R. Duda
39. S. Foster
40. F. Wightmann
41. D. Kistler
42. S. Isabelle
43. H. S. Colburn
44. F. Bilsen
45. S. Kuwada
46. R. Stern
47. E. Haas
48. K. Aboucharacra
49. J. Koehnke
50. D. Mershon
51. R. Lutfi
52. P. Zahorik
53. P. Allen
54. C. Schweitzer
55. W. Noble
56. J. Brugge
57. T. Strybel
58. T. Anderson
59. M. Oxley
60. N. Durlach
61. J. Ball
62. T. Buell
63. M. Burkhard
64. D. Perrott
65. J. Stewart
66. M. E. Jones
67. T. Yin
68. J. Hawks
69. W. Hartmann
70. R. Litovsky
71. R. Clifton
72. J. Cisneros
73. E. Wenzel
74. J. Janko
75. R. Gilkey

441
BIOCOMMUNICATIONS
LAB

Preface

The current popular and scientific interest in virtual environments has provided a new impetus for investigating binaural and spatial hearing. However, the many intriguing phenomena of spatial hearing have long made it an exciting area of scientific inquiry. The fact that a biological system is sensitive to a 10-μs interaural difference in time seems, at first glance, almost unimaginable. Striking perceptual effects can be achieved with relatively simple stimulus manipulations; for example, it is often possible to achieve an extremely compelling sense of presence in a remote environment, simply by listening binaurally to the output of microphones placed in the ear canals of a manikin head in that environment. Psychophysical and physiological investigations of spatial hearing seem to be converging on common explanations of underlying mechanisms. These understandings have in turn been incorporated into sophisticated yet mathematically tractable models of binaural interaction. Thus, binaural and spatial hearing is one of the few areas in which we are soon likely to find adequate physiological explanations of complex psychological phenomena, which can be reasonably and usefully approximated by mathematical and physical models.

In most situations, auditory spatial acuity is not match for visual or tactile spatial acuity; nevertheless, the auditory system has several strengths to recommend it as a spatial system. The auditory system can provide nearly continuous spatial information; it is not particularly dependent on light level, state of adaptation, or physical contact to function properly. We have no lids to cover our ears and seem to maintain some sense of the auditory spatial environment even during sleep. Although spatial misperceptions can occur with unusual stimuli, in unusual environments, when head movements are restricted, or when conflicting spatial information is provided from other sensory systems, most often the system operates reliably even in extremely complex acoustic environments. Finally, although spatial acuity for sounds arriving from the rear is not as good as for sounds arriving from the front, audition is a 360° sense; as such, it is well suited to act as a warning system and to direct the head and eyes toward important events in the environment.

During the past two decades, the field of binaural and spatial hearing has undergone significant intellectual growth and technological development. Prior to the 1980s, most research in this field was limited to headphone presentation of the stimuli with simple overall interaural differences in time and level. Such stimuli are only spatial in a very limited sense, with sounds typically being heard as lying within the head along the interaural axis. Studying spatial hearing with real sources arrayed in space around the subject was often difficult, time-consuming, and expensive. When such stimuli are presented in reverberant environments, the careful calibration and stimulus control that are standard in most psychophysical experiments can be difficult or impossible to achieve. On the other hand, presenting such stimuli in an anechoic environment requires a considerable capital outlay, which can cost from several hundred thousand to more than a million dollars (largely because of the cost of an anechoic chamber).

In 1989, Wightman and Kistler published the results of their rigorous and extensive measurements of head-related transfer functions (HRTFs, direction-specific transfer functions that describe the acoustic filtering of the torso, head, and pinnae). Stimuli filtered with these HRTFs and presented through headphones appear to arise from virtual locations outside the listeners head. Because Wightman and Kistler have generously made these functions available to other research laboratories, their work has had a significant impact on the field. Now it is possible for most laboratories to set up a relatively economical facility for studying spatial hearing. Moreover, these transfer functions have been incorporated into the Convolvotron from Crystal River Engineering and the Power DAC from Tucker-Davis Technologies. These commercially available devices are capable of generating moderately complex auditory virtual environments, which, when coupled with a head-tracking system, can produce very compelling spatial percepts.

During this time, the field was also re-evaluating the long-revered duplex theory of sound localization (Rayleigh, 1907). In particular, it was clear that the effects of the pinnae could not be ignored if one wished to account for the externalization of sounds (i.e., hearing them outside the head) and the ability to localize sounds in elevation. Physiological results questioned the traditional segregation of time-sensitive and intensity-sensitive cells in the brain stem. Scientists were beginning to investigate systematically the perception of moving and other time varying spatial stimuli. Phenomena such as echo suppression, which have often been thought of as relatively simple peripheral effects, were shown to have clear cognitive components. Models of binaural interaction were being questioned, on the one hand, because of their inability to predict the responses of subjects to simple stimuli in reproducible noise masking experiments and, on the other hand, because they did not address the richness of human perception in complex acoustic environments.

Because of the rapid developments in these and other areas of binaural and spatial hearing research and technology, we in the Armstrong Laboratory felt that it would be useful to hold a conference to allow researchers to interact, share ideas and data, and demonstrate new technologies. With financial support from the Air Force Office of Scientific Research and the Armstrong Laboratory, we were able to organize a 4-day conference that was held at Wright-Patterson Air Force Base, Ohio, from September 9–12, 1993. Thirty-seven speakers presented papers to an audience of more than 100 participants from around the world.

We also felt that it was important to chronicle the current state of knowledge in the field of binaural and spatial hearing, and we felt that the conference could provide an impetus for producing a book on the subject. Although a number of significant reviews on binaural and spatial hearing had been published during the pervious quarter century [Mills (1972), Durlach and Colburn (1978) Colburn and Durlach (1978), Blauert (1983), Gatehouse (1982), Yost and Gourevitch (1987), and Middlebrooks and Green (1991)], most of these works reviewed data from before 1984. Blauert's 1983 book had originally been published in German in 1974, Gatehouse (1982) was based on a conference at Guelph in

1979, and Yost and Gourovitch (1987) had developed from a special session at the 105th meeting of the Acoustical Society of America held in Cincinnati, Ohio, during 1983. Thus, only a single 25-page review article (Middlebrooks and Green, 1991) was available to summarize the explosive 10 years of research from 1984 to 1993. The present book is significant in that it reviews the important work during the past 10 to 15 years. In addition, it provides greater breadth and greater depth than most of the previous works, except perhaps the landmark volume by Blauert (1983).

ORGANIZATION OF THE BOOK

Although this book grew out of the Conference on Binaural and Spatial Hearing, it is meant to be more than a record of proceedings. The chapters are longer than typical proceedings papers and contain considerably more review material, including, in many cases, extensive bibliographies.

The chapters in the book are arranged into topical sections, which represent major thrusts in the recent literature. The authors of the first chapter in each section have been encouraged to take a broad perspective and review the current state of the literature. Subsequent chapters in each section tend to be somewhat more narrowly focused, and often emphasize the authors' own work. Thus, each section should provide overview, background, and current research on a particular topic.

The first section,"Sound Localization," describes psychophysical and physical investigations of the cues that determine the perception of direction in the free field. Wightman and Kistler (Chapter 1) discuss each of the three major classes of acoustic cues for sound localization: interaural time differences, interaural level differences, and "spectral cues." They consider a variety of situational factors that determine the importance of each of these cues, and present experimental results that indicate how each of these classes of cues contributes to the perceived direction. Shaw (Chapter 2) reviews nearly three decades of measurements describing the acoustic effects of the outer ear and discusses models of the physical systems that underlie these effects. Duda (Chapter 3) also discusses the physical cues introduced by the pinna but emphasizes interaural level differences introduced by the head and pinnae and shows that there is sufficient information in these interaural cues to approximate human localization performance. Middlebrooks (Chapter 4) and Butler (Chapter 5) describe the results of a variety of psychophysical experiments indicating that monaural cues can also be important determinants of localization judgments. These chapters provide a perspective on the current controversy in the field regarding the relative importance of monaural and interaural representations of spectral cues.

Although discussion of spectral cues dominates the first section of this book, it is clear that low-frequency interaural time differences dominate localization judgments (e.g., Wightman and Kistler, 1992). The study of interaural time cues and interaural intensity cues through lateralization and binaural masking experiments was the major focus of the binaural and spatial hearing literature during the 1950s, 1960s, and 1970s, and continues to be important today. In the section "Lateralization and Binaural Masking," Bernstein (Chapter 6) reviews recent trends in this literature and describes work from his laboratory on binaural sluggishness and the influence of interaural differences in the low-frequency envelope of high-frequency sounds, showing how these phenomena are related. Buell and Trahiotis (Chapter 7) examine the combined effects of interaural time differences, interaural intensity differences, and stimulus bandwidth on perceived lateral position. They find highly interactive effects that are not well described by simple time–intensity trading ratios. Dye (Chapter 8) examines how lateralization judgments in response to interaural intensity differences in a pure tone are influenced by interaural intensity differences at remote frequencies. The results indicate significant interactions even when the components are widely separated in frequency. Kohlrausch and Fassel (Chapter 9) review the literature on nonsimultaneous binaural masking and use their own data to help clarify the conflicting effects previously reported in the literature. Overall, this section provides a good overview of modern headphone-based studies of binaural interaction, which continue to provide the primary data for testing models of binaural processing (e.g., see Stern and Trahiotis, Chapter 24).

Although many experiments on sound localization are conducted in anechoic environments with sources placed at a fixed distance from the observer, most real-world listening environments are reverberant and sources differ in distance as well as direction. In the section "Echoes, Precedence, and Depth Perception," Hartmann (Chapter 10) provides a good overview of precedence and other effects related to the suppression of echoes. The results from his laboratory suggest that information is not only weighted according to which waveform arrives first, but also according to its plausibility in a given listening environment. Hafter (Chapter 11) reviews the work of his laboratory on a related phenomenon, binaural adaptation, but shows that it is likely to be mediated by a distinct mechanism. Clifton and Freyman (Chapter 12) review their work on the buildup of echo suppression, commonly known as the Clifton effect. They provide convincing evidence that unexpected changes in stimulation can lead to a release from echo suppression. Together, these three chapters provide a view of echo suppression that is both more complex and more cognitive than older views. Echoes and reverberation seem to be major cues that allow us to make judgments about distance. Mershon (Chapter 13) describes a number of interesting experiments on distance perception, while outlining a new methodology for recording distance judgments.

Surprisingly, over the long history of spatial hearing, there have been relatively few studies of motion. In the section "Motion Perception," Perrott and Strybel (Chapter 14) review these studies, provide an extensive bibliography on motion perception, and show that interest in motion perception (as revealed by the number of articles published) is increasing in recent years. They report on a number of studies from their laboratories that indicate that the perception of motion and the perception of direction are distinct and that in some situations motion can be perceived without a clear sense of the direction of movement. Grantham (Chapter 15) and Saberi and Hafter (Chapter 16) both examine the

Snapshot hypothesis of motion detection, using quite different experimental paradigms. Both sets of data question the adequacy of the Snapshot hypothesis as a general description for motion perception and indicate that information between the onset and offset of the stimulus can influence the perception of motion. Chapter 15 also contains an extended bibliography on the physiology of the auditory motion. Overall, these three chapters suggest that several distinct mechanisms may underlie motion perception. It is not clear that these mechanisms can be easily captured within existing models of binaural interaction.

Another important function of spatial hearing is to help segregate spatially separated sounds when multiple sources are simultaneously active . In the section "Sound Source Segregation and Free-Field Masking," Yost (Chapter 17) reviews 40 years of literature on this "cocktail party" problem. He concludes that there are a number of cues underlying the cocktail party effect and that spatial cues may not be the dominant ones. Good, Gilkey, and Ball (Chapter 18) consider the somewhat simpler situation of masked detection in the free field, but also find little evidence that free-field detection is strongly dependant on sound localization. Doll and Hanna (Chapter 19), in contrast, find that introducing spatial cues significantly increases the recognition of auditory targets. Although two of these three chapters suggest a relatively small role for spatial hearing (at least binaural hearing) in the cocktail-party effect, it is important to remember, as Yost points out, that relatively few studies come close to simulating a true cocktail party.

One of the most exciting aspects of spatial hearing is the close correspondence between psychophysical and physiological data. In the section"Physiology of Spatial Hearing," Kuwada, Batra, and Fitzpatrick (Chapter 20) provide a detailed overview of brain stem anatomy and physiology related to spatial hearing, including an extensive bibliography. Yin, Joris, Smith and Chan (Chapter 21) provide a good example of the close relation between psychophysical and physiological work on spatial hearing. They describe the Jeffress (1948) hypothesis for a place mechanism of interaural time discrimination, which was based on a small amount of psychophysical data and a substantial insight. They then chart the development of this idea through nearly half a century of physiological work and conclude that it is essentially correct. Brugge, Reale, and Hind (Chapter 22) review the anatomy and physiology of the auditory cortex as it relates to spatial hearing and describe their own measurements of the spatial receptive fields of single cells in primary auditory cortex. Young, Rice, Spirou, Nelken, and Conley (Chapter 23) consider how the head-related transfer function in the cat is affected by pinna position and how these acoustic changes influence the responses of cells in the cochlear nucleus. Although an entire volume could be written on recent work related to the physiology of spatial hearing, together, these four chapters provide a good overview of work being conducted at various levels of the auditory system and should serve as a significant bibliographic database for students interested in this area.

The interplay between models and data has long been emphasized in the binaural hearing literature. In the section "Models of Spatial Hearing," Stern and Trahiotis (Chapter 24) review models of binaural interaction (citing the major models and relevant papers) and describe the results from their own examinations of models based on arrays of Jeffress-type coincidence detectors. A major difficulty for models of binaural interaction is to predict the trial-by-trial responses of subjects to dichotic signals masked by reproducible noise. Colburn, Isabelle, and Tollin (Chapter 25) review the small literature on reproducible noise masking and describe their own efforts to model these data, indicating the classes of models that are likely to succeed and fail when applied to these data. Most models of binaural and spatial hearing are really models of headphone-based lateralization and detection; few models have attempted to predict three-dimensional sound localization. Janko, Anderson, and Gilkey (Chapter 26) use artificial neural networks to "interpret" both monaural representations and interaural representations of the putative acoustic cues for sound localization. They conclude that although some interaural information appears to be necessary in order to recover azimuth information reliably, the so-called "spectral cues" could be represented through either monaural or interaural channels.

An area that was neglected at the Conference on Binaural and Spatial Hearing was the development of spatial hearing. Litovsky and Ashmead (Chapter 27) graciously agreed to review this material in the section "Development of Spatial Hearing." They consider recent trends in the literature on the development of binaural and spatial hearing and then examine in greater depth psychophysical and physiological data related to the sensitivity to interaural cues and sound localization in the free field, the perception of distance, and the precedence effect.

The data and insights from laboratory studies of binaural and spatial hearing are leading to sophisticated technologies that can be applied to a number of real world problems. In the section "Applications," Blauert (Chapter 28) provides a broad overview of binaural technology and its applications. In his chapter, he considers physical, psychoacoustical, and psychological aspects of binaural hearing and suggests that although much of current binaural technology has been based on our understanding of the physical aspects, future applications are likely to depend more heavily on a deeper understanding of the psychological aspects of binaural hearing. Shinn-Cunningham, Lehnert, Kramer, Wenzel, and Durlach (Chapter 29) discuss issues associated with the design and application of auditory displays in general and then consider spatial auditory displays, in particular. They emphasize issues associated with implementing auditory displays within virtual environments and the possibility of presenting supernormal localization cues to users of auditory displays. Their chapter contains an extensive bibliography related to auditory displays, spatial hearing, and virtual environments. Burkhard (Chapter 30) describes procedures for making binaural measurements and shows how they produce superior results compared to single-microphone procedures in a variety of applications. One area where three-dimensional auditory displays have been of particular interest is in fighter cockpits. McKinley and Ericson (Chapter 31) review the history of the development of three-dimensional auditory displays within the Air Force and NASA, and then describe both laboratory and flight test data on the auditory localization cue synthesizer developed by the Air Force. One of the potential benefits of an auditory display is to increase the intelligibility of communication signals in noisy environments or when multiple simultaneous voices are present. Ericson and McKinley (Chapter 32) briefly review the literature on intelligibility level differences in the free field and then present results from several of their own experiments indicating substantial intelligibility gains when an auditory localization cue synthesizer is used to present different sounds from distinct virtual spatial locations. One of the most frequent problems reported by listeners with impaired hearing is difficulty hearing and understanding in noisy environments. It is often believed that this difficulty results, in part, from impaired spatial hearing capabilities. Koehnke and Besing (Chapter 33) compare measures of spatial hearing performance to standard audiological measures on the one hand and to expected performance with binaurally fitted hearing aids on the other hand. They conclude that even subjects with similar audiometric profiles can show great differences in binaural processing and in the benefits they receive from binaural amplification. Kollmeier (Chapter 34) reports on several promising signal processing strategies that have been developed in his laboratory to increase the noise suppression capabilities of binaural hearing aids and thereby increase speech intelligibility in "cocktail party" situations. While this section does not provide a complete review of the applications of binaural hearing technology, it does make clear the rich potential for this technology.

Overall, the book provides coverage of most of the major thrusts in modern research on binaural and spatial hearing. Other areas that could have received more discussion include the role of head movements and nonauditory cues in the perception of auditory space. Ideally, we would also have gone into greater depth on the important role of spatial hearing and spatial hearing technology in architectural acoustics and home entertainment.

ACKNOWLEDGMENTS

The Conference on Binaural and Spatial Hearing would not have been possible without the support of the Air Force Office of Scientific Research and the Armstrong Laboratory. John F. Tangney and Thomas J. Moore as representatives of these two institutions and as individuals have provided considerable financial, emotional, and intellectual support to both of us, not only during the preparation of the conference and book, but throughout much of our careers. Melinda McGuire of Wright State University, Chrissy Good, formerly of Wright State University, and Al Karl of Systems Research Laboratories were instrumental in organizing and implementing the conference. Several other people made significant contributions that helped make the conference a success: Mike Good, Jason Yow, Ed Jones, Jim Janko, Jan Weisenberger, Ellen Moore, Steve Bolia, Karen Hedrick, Emma Grove, Chuck Dempsey, Robert Van Patten, Kim McKenzie, and Dee Allen. We would also like to thank all of the conference speakers and others who gave up their time to come to the conference and participated in the numerous enlightening discussions. We were pleased that our European colleagues were able to attend the conference on relatively short notice. We note in particular the many insightful comments offered by Jens Blauert, which so much enriched the discussions.

A large number of people helped with the seemingly endless job of editing the book. We thank the authors for their hard work and patience. Melinda McGuire was once again central to this process. Sharon Adams, Brian Simpson, Dennis

Hale, and Jim Janko spent long hours over extended periods of time editing, formatting, and proofreading chapters. Janet Weisenberger, Scott Isabelle, Andy Noller, Jennifer Ball, Janae Dorn, and Theresa Subr also made significant contributions. We would also like to thank Dale Fox and Melissa Lush for the cover art, Barry Sanders for the conference photograph, and Cindy Sanders for the line drawing of the conference photograph.

—Robert H. Gilkey
—Timothy R. Anderson

REFERENCES

Blauert, J. (**1983**). *Spatial Hearing* (MIT Press,Cambridge, MA).

Colburn, H. S., and Durlach, N. I. (**1978**). "Models of binaural interaction," in *Handbook of Perception, Vol. IV, Hearing*, edited by E. C. Carterette and M. P. Friedman (Academic Press, New York), pp. 467–518.

Durlach, N. I., and Colburn, H. S. (**1978**). "Binaural phenomena," in *Handbook of Perception, Vol. IV, Hearing*, edited by E. C. Carterette and M. P. Friedman (Academic Press,New York), pp. 365–466.

Gatehouse, R. W. (Ed.) (**1982**). *Localization of Sound: Theory and Applications* (Ampora Press, Groton, CT).

Jeffress, L. A. (**1948**). "A place theory of sound localization," J. Comp. Physiol. Psychol. **41**, 35–39.

Middlebrooks, J. C., and Green, D. M. (**1991**). "Sound localization by human listeners," Annu. Rev. Psychol. **42**, 135–159.

Mills, A. W. (**1972**) "Auditory localization," in *Foundations of Modern Auditory Theory*, edited by J. V. Tobias (Academic Press, New York), pp. 301–348.

Rayleigh, Lord (J. W. Stutt, 3rd Baron of Rayleigh) (**1907**). "On our perception of sound direction," Philos. Mag. **13**, 214–232.

Wightman, F. L., and Kistler, D. J. (**1989a**). "Headphone simulation of free-field listening I: Stimulus synthesis," J. Acoust. Soc. Am. **85**, 858–867.

Wightman, F. L., and Kistler, D. J. (**1989b**). "Headphone simulation of free-field listening II: Psychophysical validation," J. Acoust. Soc. Am. **85**, 868–878.

Wightman, F. L., and Kistler, D. J. (**1992**). "The dominant role of low-frequency interaural time differences in sound localization," J. Acoust. Soc. Am. **91**, 1648–1661.

Yost, W. A., and Gourovitch, G. (Eds.). (**1987**). *Direcitonal Hearing* (Springer-Verlag, New York).

Part I

Sound Localization

Chapter 1

Factors Affecting the Relative Salience of Sound Localization Cues

Frederic L. Wightman
University of Wisconsin, Madison

Doris J. Kistler
University of Wisconsin, Madison

(Received October 1994; revised February 1995)

The apparent position of a sound source in auditory space is influenced by a number of acoustical cues, including interaural differences in time and level and the spectral cues provided by pinna filtering. The relative salience of these cues varies as a function of several factors such as the listener's *a priori* knowledge of source characteristics, source frequency content, the reliability and plausibility of the cues, and the consistency of the cues across the frequency spectrum. This chapter reviews the nature of the cues and the factors that affect their salience and describes the results of several experiments that were designed to isolate the contributions of one or more of the cues to the apparent position of a sound source.

INTRODUCTION

This chapter is about the relative salience of the acoustical cues to apparent sound source position. It consists of a rather loose collection of hypotheses and data. Most of the data come from our own experiments but some are from the work of others; some of the data are shown here for the first time, but many have been presented elsewhere. Our discussion focuses on the factors that influence the *apparent position* of a sound source. Very little attention is given here to the discriminability of sounds from different spatial positions or to the accuracy with which listeners can identify the true spatial origin of a sound source.

We begin with a brief review of the potential acoustical determinants of apparent position and follow with some educated guesses about which of these might be more or less salient in various listening conditions. We conclude by discussing the results of several experiments in which listeners indicated the apparent positions of sounds that had been modified to isolate the contributions of one or more of the potential cues.

I. ACOUSTICAL DETERMINANTS OF APPARENT POSITION

Given the extensive treatment of this topic elsewhere (e.g., Middlebrooks and Green, 1991; Wightman and Kistler, 1993; Shaw, Chapter 2, this volume; Duda, Chapter 3, this volume), most readers will be quite familiar with the acoustical determinants of apparent sound position, which we call localization cues. Thus, there is little need to review them here. However, at the risk of being repetitious, we discuss the cues from a slightly different perspective in order to emphasize a few simple points.

In our view, a potential acoustical localization cue is any physical aspect of the acoustical waveforms reaching a listener's ears that is altered by changes in the position of the sound source relative to that of the listener. For our purpose here we limit our discussion to the direction component of relative position and ignore the distance component. Given this limitation, a taxonomy of potential cues can be described as in Table I. The temporal–spectral distinction represented in Table I is artificial, given the isomorphism between a waveform and its spectrum. However, because the auditory mechanisms thought to subserve temporal and spectral processing are different, we find it useful to consider the two kinds of cues separately. The monaural–binaural distinction is included to emphasize the fact that changes in sound source position produce changes in the waveform at each ear individually (monaural), as well as changes in the relation between the waveforms at the two ears (binaural).

Consider the monaural cues first. The monaural temporal cue is the position-dependent change in the waveform at one ear caused by the change in the impulse response of the acoustical system consisting mostly of the head and pinna. The transfer function of this system is usually called the head-related transfer function or HRTF for short. Figure 1 shows the impulse response of the HRTF from a listener's left ear for two source positions. Note that there are substantial differences in the temporal fine structure of the two impulse responses. Some investigators suggest that this temporal fine structure, in particular the time differences among the major peaks, provides important information about sound source position that is extracted directly from the stimulus waveform by the auditory system (e.g., Batteau, 1967).

There are at least two reasons why such monaural temporal cues are not likely to be relevant for human sound localization. First, because the HRTF impulse responses are short, on the order of about 2 ms, the limited temporal resolving power of the auditory system, also about 2 ms, probably renders the temporal fine structure of the impulse responses undetectable (Green, 1971). Second, the

TABLE I. Potential acoustical localization cues.

	Temporal	*Spectral*
Monaural	Monaural phase *(Batteau)*	1. Overall level
		2. Monaural spectral cues
Binaural	Interaural time difference (ITD)	1. Interaural level difference (ILD)
		2. Binaural spectral differences

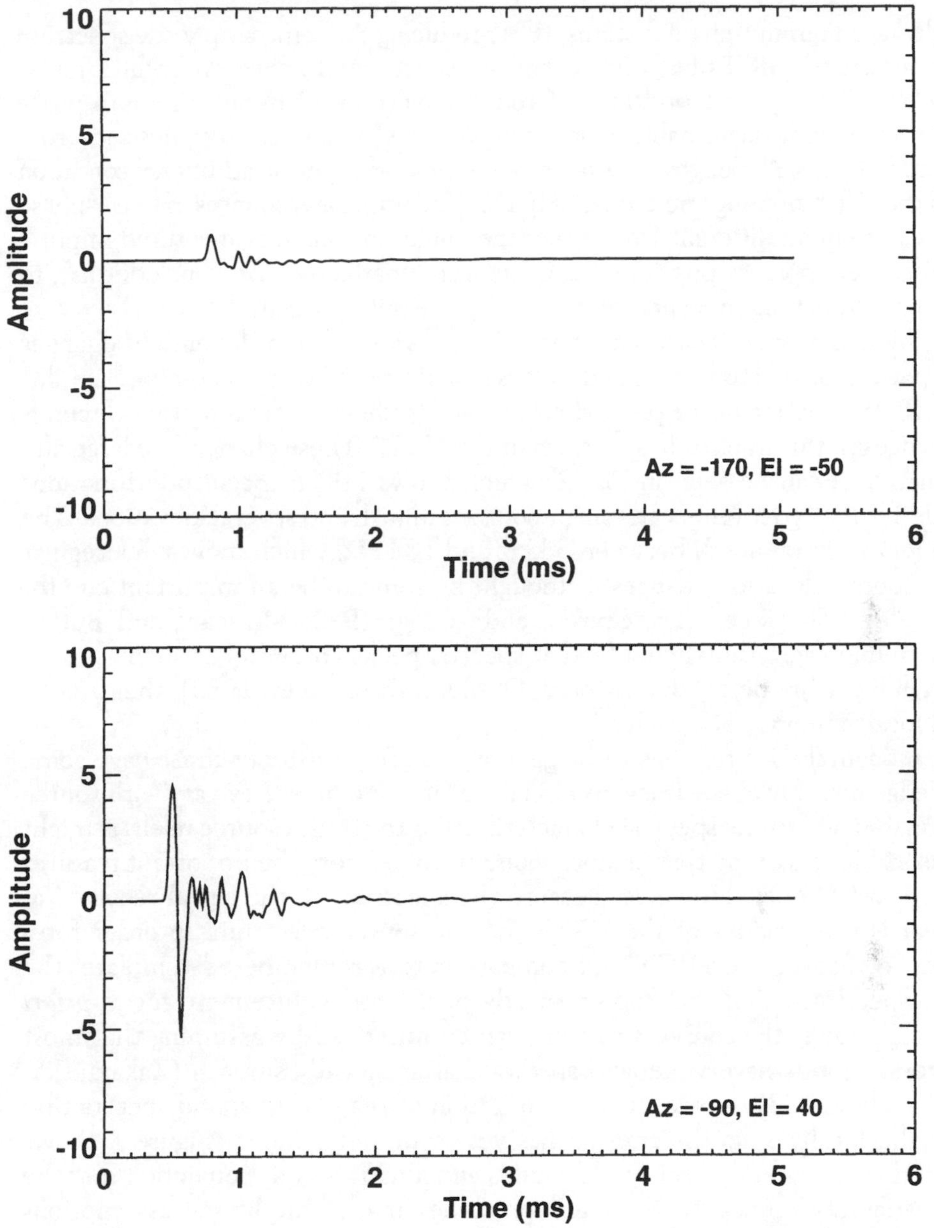

FIG. 1. Examples of HRTF impulse responses recorded from a listener's left ear for two source positions on the listener's left side.

results of a psychophysical experiment (Kistler and Wightman, 1992) suggest that changes in the temporal fine structure of the HRTF impulse responses do not produce subsequent changes in the apparent positions of sound sources. In this study, listeners judged the apparent positions of virtual sound sources presented via headphones (Wightman and Kistler, 1989a, 1989b). The virtual sources were synthesized using HRTFs that had been measured on the same listeners. In one condition of the experiment the HRTFs used to produce virtual sources were modeled as minimum-phase systems, thus producing the same amplitude spectrum as the measured HRTFs but different phase spectra and hence different impulse responses. The apparent positions of sources synthesized using minimum-phase HRTFs were indistinguishable from the positions of sources synthesized from measured HRTFs. Although it was not reported in that paper, an additional condition tested the effect of using linear-phase HRTFs. The impulse responses of linear-phase HRTFs were quite different from either the minimum-phase or measured impulse responses, yet apparent position judgments were unaffected. We conclude that, to a first approximation, monaural temporal cues are unimportant.

The monaural spectral cues are the well-known direction-dependent changes in the pattern of spectral peaks and valleys superimposed on an incoming stimulus by the filtering action of the pinna. In other words, they are the direction-dependent changes in the amplitude spectrum of the HRTF. These changes are large and systematic, as can be seen in Fig. 2, which shows HRTF magnitude functions recorded from two listeners at a single source azimuth and several elevations. The prominent spectral notch between 5 kHz and 10 kHz, which moves in a regular way as source elevation changes, is thought by some to be an important cue for source elevation (Rice, May, Spirou, and Young, 1992; Musicant and Butler, 1984). While there is little doubt that spectral peaks and notches such as those shown in Fig. 2 are detectable (Moore, Oldfield, and Dooley, 1989), their role in sound localization is not yet clear.

For monaural spectral cues to be generally useful, a listener must have some knowledge not only of the relevant HRTF features and how they vary with source position, but also of the spectral characteristics of the sound source itself. It might be reasonable to assume that listeners commit to memory the important features of their own HRTFs. However, because the spectrum of the signal received at each ear is the product of the HRTF and the source spectrum, in order for a listener to recover the HRTF and compare it to a remembered template, the source spectrum must be known in advance. The requirement for *a priori* knowledge about the source spectrum can be mitigated by assuming that most real-world sounds have wideband spectra that are locally smooth (Zakarauskas and Cynader, 1993). However, the proportion of real-world sound spectra that meets the locally smooth criterion has yet to be determined. Figure 3 shows amplitude spectra of six real-world sounds and illustrates our conviction that the wide variability among such sounds precludes many simplifying assumptions about their spectral characteristics.

There are two additional characteristics of the monaural spectral cues that might bear on their utility. First, they are highly idiosyncratic. Figure 4 illustrates this point by showing the directional features of the HRTFs from 10 listeners for one ear and a single source position. These "directional transfer functions" or DTFs are computed by dividing each HRTF by the rms average of the HRTFs from all directions measured. Note that in certain frequency regions the differences in the DTFs from one listener to another are as great as 20 dB. This suggests that the specific strategies used to obtain source position information from the spectral shape of HRTFs may vary from one listener to another. Second, the monaural spectral cues exist only at high frequencies, as might be expected given

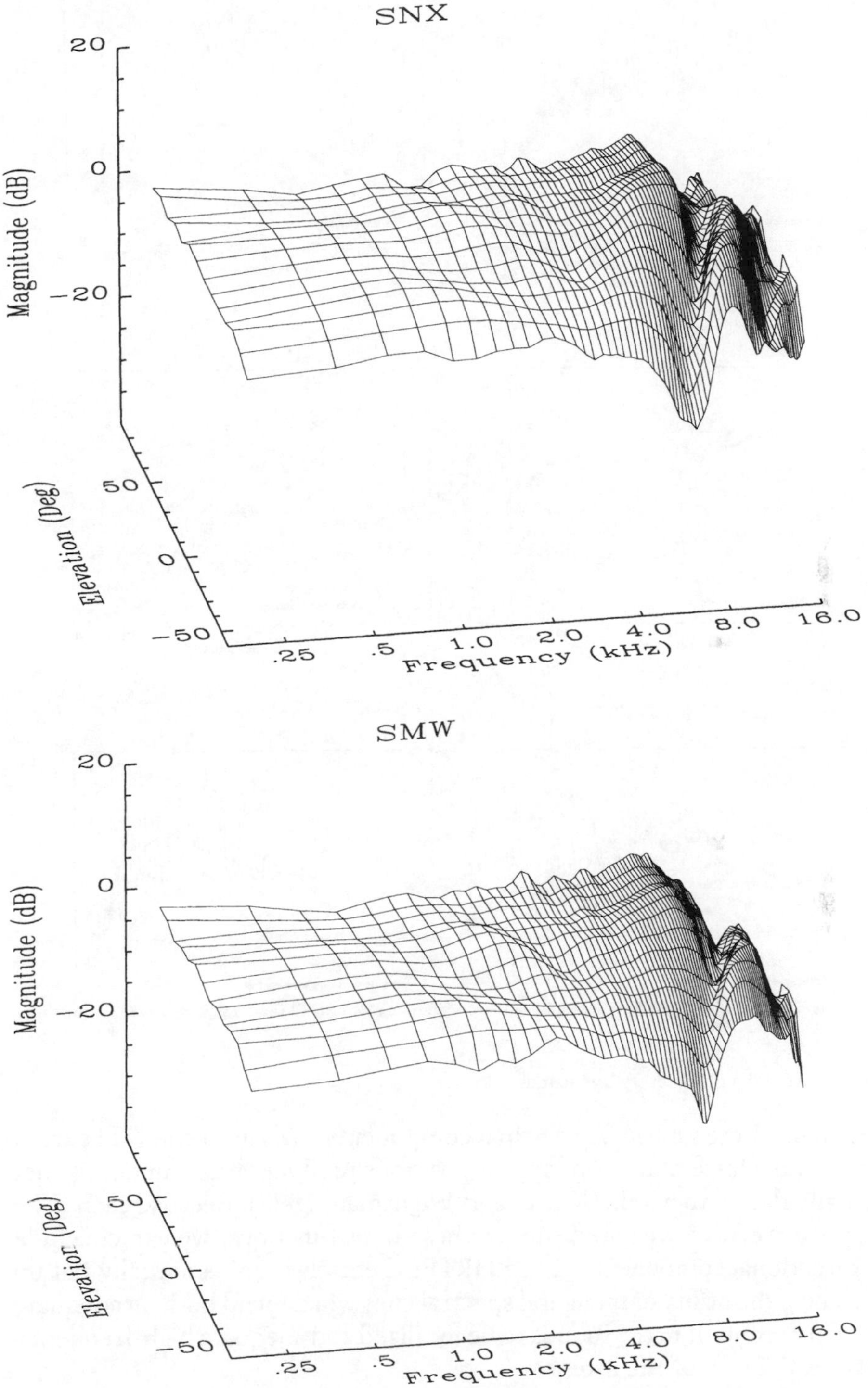

FIG. 2. DTFs (HRTFs divided by the rms of HRTFs from all directions) recorded from two listeners and sources at 90° azimuth.

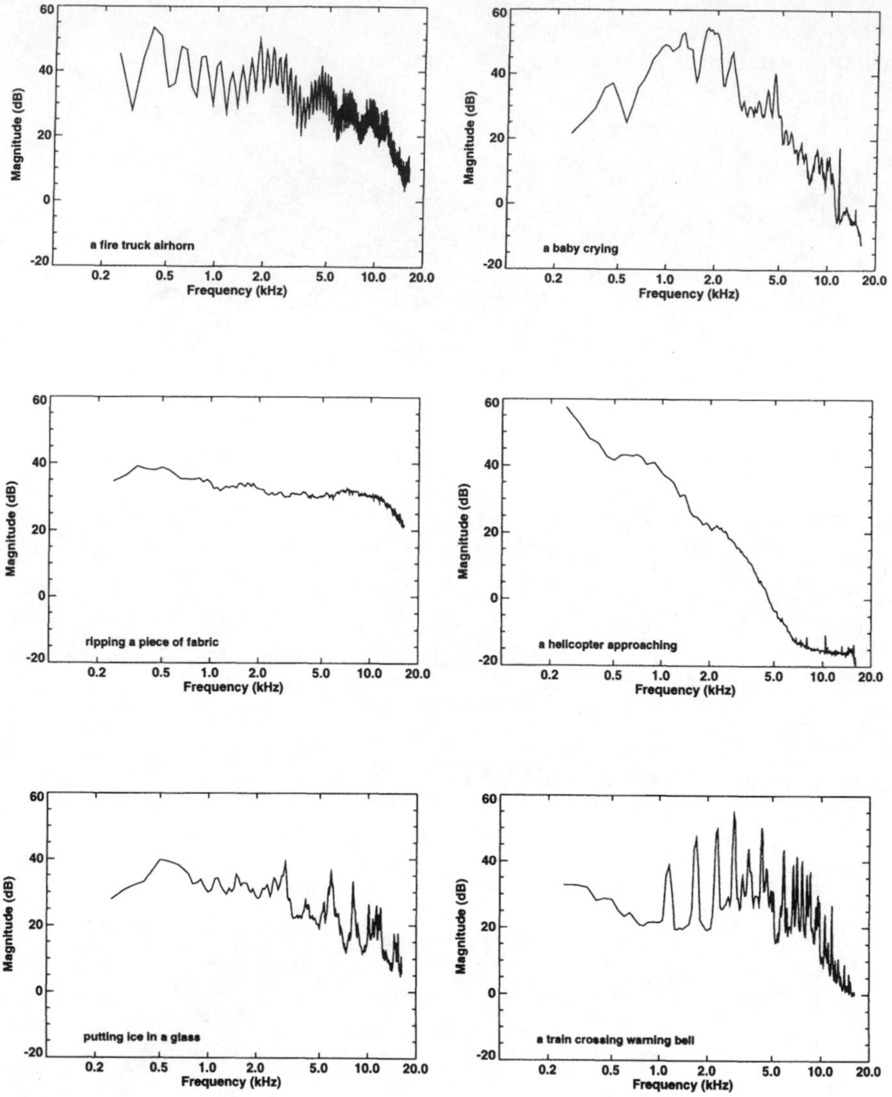

FIG. 3. Magnitude spectra of six "everyday" sounds.

the dimensions of the pinnae. A principal components analysis of the DTFs from 10 listeners and a large number of spatial positions produces basis functions that are essentially flat up to 5 kHz (Kistler and Wightman, 1992). Because each DTF can be represented as a weighted sum of these basis functions, we can conclude that the directional components of the HRTFs themselves are essentially flat up to 5 kHz. Thus, the utility of monaural spectral cues will depend both on adequate high-frequency content in the sounds to be localized and adequate high-frequency sensitivity on the part of the listener.

The binaural cues are presumed to be derived by some kind of differencing operation on the information retrieved from each ear. How this might be accomplished in the nervous system is not our concern here, so for the purposes of simplicity we assume the binaural cues are derived from a ratio of the HRTFs at the two ears. Because the spectrum of the sound source appears in both numerator and denominator of this ratio, it cancels. Thus the utility of the binaural cues does not depend critically on the characteristics of the source or on the listener's *a priori* knowledge of them.

Interaural time difference (ITD) is related to the phase of the HRTF ratio and is generally thought to be one of the most important localization cues. To a first approximation, the ITD is the same at all frequencies. Although the ITD in measured HRTFs is higher at low frequencies (below 1.5 kHz) than at high frequencies (Wightman and Kistler, 1989a), the observed low-frequency increase in the ITD is not as large as the 50% increase expected on theoretical grounds (Kuhn, 1977). Our view is that the larger ITD at low frequencies is perceptually irrelevant. Psychophysical evidence of this can be found in the results of the experiment reported by Kistler and Wightman (1992), in which listeners judged the apparent positions of sources in which the ITD was either natural or constant across frequency. The patterns of judgments in the two conditions were indistinguishable.

Figure 5 shows the ITD cue for two listeners. For these plots the ITD was estimated by computing the time delay at the maximum in the cross-correlation between left and right HRTF impulse responses at each spatial position. Note that the change in the ITD with changes in source position is smooth and roughly the same for the two listeners. Note also that the contours of constant ITD are roughly circular, in agreement with theoretical predictions made by assuming the head is a rigid sphere. The consequence of constant ITD contours is that a given ITD indicates not just one but a whole locus of potential source positions. We return to both of these details later.

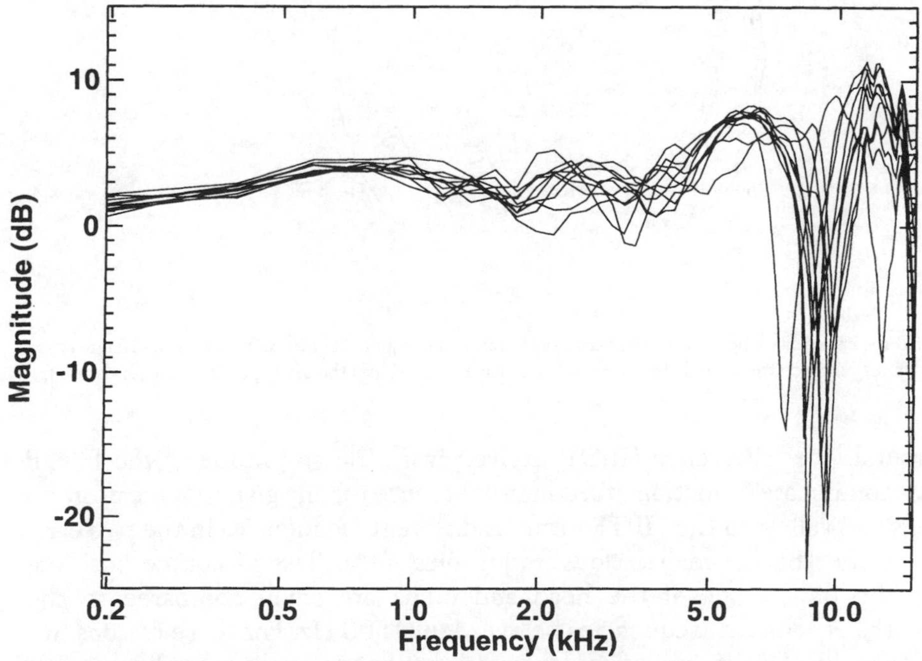

FIG. 4. DTFs recorded for a source located at 90° azimuth and 0° elevation from the right ear of 10 listeners.

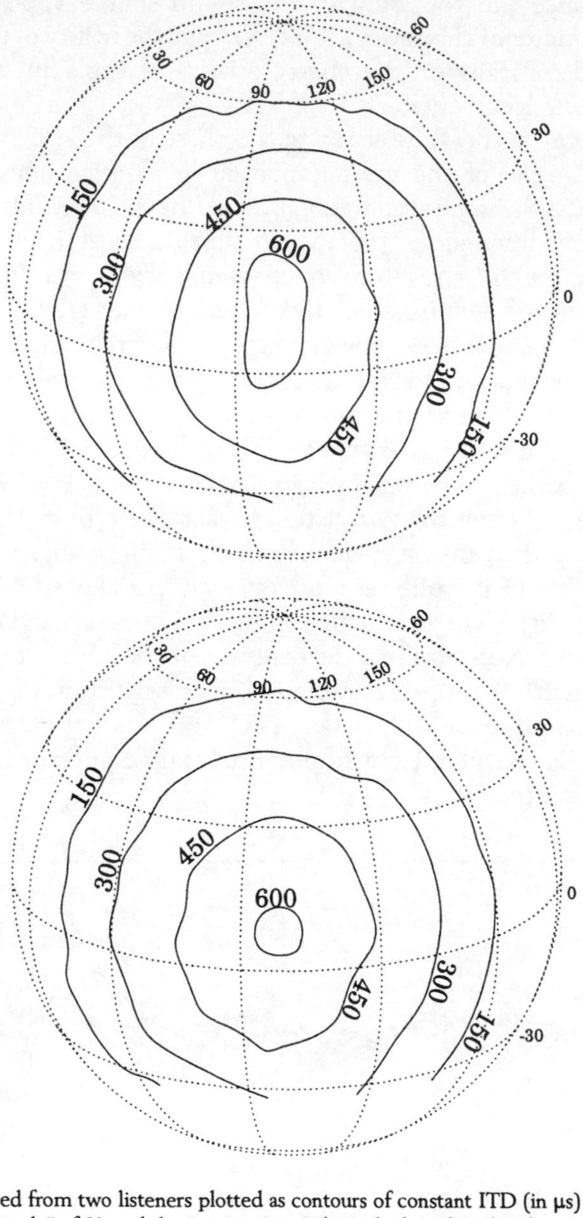

FIG. 5. ITD measured from two listeners plotted as contours of constant ITD (in μs) on a globe. Listeners are faced toward a "longitude" of 0°, and the "equator" or 0° latitude describes the plane passing through the ears.

Interaural level difference (ILD), derived from the amplitude of the HRTF ratio, is a complicated function of frequency because for any given source position the peaks and valleys in the HRTF occur at different frequencies in the two ears. Moreover, the ILD is small at low frequencies, regardless of source position, because the dimensions of the head and pinna are small compared to the wavelengths of sound at frequencies below about 1500 Hz. For these reasons, we suggest that the ILDs in individual frequency bands are much more likely to be useful localization cues than overall ILD. Figure 6 shows the ILDs in various

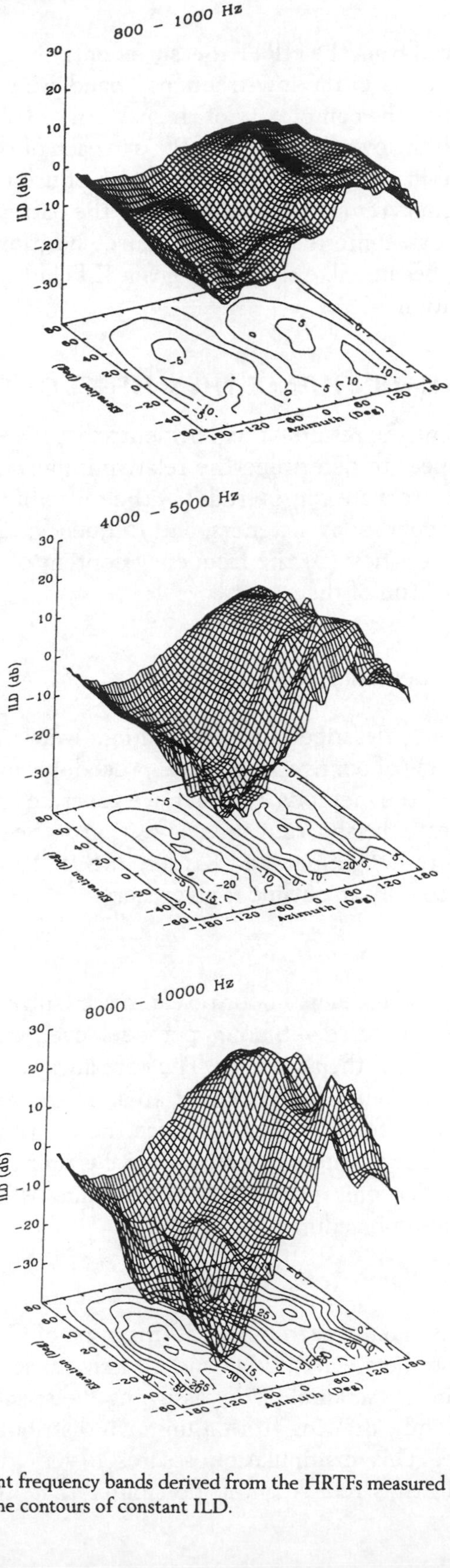

FIG. 6. ILDs in three different frequency bands derived from the HRTFs measured from a single listener. The "floor" of each panel shows the contours of constant ILD.

frequency regions derived from the HRTF measurements obtained from a typical listener. Note that the ILDs in the low-frequency band are small, regardless of source position. Note also the complexity of the pattern of ILDs in the high-frequency bands. Although the overall pattern of ILDs in each of the bands is similar, there is sufficient detail in each one so that extraction of useful localization cues would require that listeners remember the details of the pattern. Otherwise, the ILD can provide only coarse information about source position, and even that is likely to be ambiguous, because like the ITD a given ILD indicates a whole locus of potential source positions.

II. FACTORS THAT INFLUENCE THE SALIENCE OF THE CUES

In this section we present the results of experiments that reveal the stimulus or listener factors that appear to determine the relative importance or salience of the various cues. Four factors are considered: (1) the reliability or consistency of the cue across stimulus conditions, listeners, and frequency; (2) *a priori* knowledge of stimulus characteristics; (3) the frequency content of the stimulus; and (4) the plausibility or realism of the cue.

A. Methodological considerations

Most of the experiments described in this section were conducted in our laboratory, so a brief review of our psychophysical procedures may be useful here. The essential elements of the methods by which we generate and present stimuli and ask listeners to indicate the apparent spatial position of the sound source have been published elsewhere (Wightman and Kistler, 1989a, 1989b, 1992; Kistler and Wightman, 1992), so only an outline is given here.

1. Listeners

With few exceptions, the listeners in our research are University of Wisconsin undergraduate students who serve 4–6 hours per week over long periods of time and are paid an hourly rate for their services. They are always blindfolded before being led into the testing room, which is either an anechoic chamber or a small soundproof room. The blindfolds are kept in place the entire time the listeners are in the testing room. The listeners receive minimal training (2 hours at most) before data collection. The only purpose of the training is to familiarize the listeners with the response procedures.

2. Stimuli

The standard stimulus in our research is a 250-ms burst of Gaussian noise with a nominally flat spectrum between 200 Hz and 14 kHz. In some conditions the spectrum of the stimulus is "scrambled" by assigning the spectrum level within each critical band randomly, drawing from a uniform distribution with either a 20-dB or 40-dB range. This manipulation assures a very different stimulus spectrum on each trial, thus reducing the possibility that listeners will learn stimulus characteristics. In any one experiment stimuli are presented from a large number of real or virtual spatial positions all around the listener. The set of potential positions includes 24–36 azimuths (from −180° to +170°) and 6–10 elevations (from −50° to +60°). The stimuli are delivered through either small loudspeakers (Realistic Minimus 3.5) or headphones. The virtual source stimuli are synthesized using the standard FIR digital filtering techniques described in previous publications (e.g., Wightman and Kistler, 1989a).

3. *Responses*

Listeners report the apparent position of each stimulus verbally. Apparent azimuth and elevation are given in degrees, in accordance with standard single-pole world coordinates (the "North" and "South" poles are above and below the listener and the "equator" defines the horizontal plane that passes through the ears). Apparent distance is reported in feet. No feedback of any kind is given, except that when listeners appear to make a large sign error, for example, reporting a negative azimuth (left side) for a positive azimuth (right side) source, they are asked if they are sure they made the intended response. In any one condition, listeners make between 600 and 1000 responses at the rate of about 2 per minute.

4. *Data handling*

Because of the difficulties in dealing with front/back confusions we make no attempt here to generate summary statistics or measures of central tendency from our data. Thus, the figures show raw data; every response is represented on the figures. For ease of interpretation we represent the data in a three-pole coordinate system (Kistler and Wightman, 1992). The result is that each response (azimuth, ϕ, and elevation, θ) appears on three different plots. The azimuth component (ϕ) of each response is decomposed into a left/right component (λ) and a front/back component (Ψ) according to the following equations:

$$\lambda = \arcsin(\cos\theta\sin\phi)$$

$$\Psi = \arcsin(\cos\theta\cos\phi)$$

The elevation component of each response (θ) becomes the up/down component without transformation.

B. Cue reliability or consistency

There are several dimensions on which one might rate the "reliability" of a localization cue. Among them are the extent to which the cue depends on source characteristics, provides the same information in all bands across the frequency spectrum, is roughly the same from listener to listener, and is unambiguous. Our view is that a reliable cue will contribute more to the determination of apparent source position than a less reliable cue, and in situations in which cues conflict a reliable cue will be dominant.

Given the set of cues described earlier in this chapter and our criteria for reliability, the ITD cue would seem to score the highest. The ITD does not depend on source characteristics, provides roughly the same information in each frequency band, and the relationship between the ITD and source position is not highly idiosyncratic. However, as mentioned earlier, the cue is ambiguous because a given ITD indicates a range of potential source positions. This is an issue to which we return shortly.

A published experiment in which the ITD cue conflicted with the other localization cues revealed the dominance of the ITD cue (Wightman and Kistler, 1992). Listeners judged the apparent positions of virtual sources in which the ITD signaled one position and all other cues signaled another position. As long as the wideband noise stimulus contained low-frequency energy the listeners' judgments were completely determined by the ITD cue. In other words, listeners' judgments always indicated the position signaled by the ITD cue, even when, for example, all other cues pointed to a position on the opposite side of the head. When low frequencies were removed from the stimulus, by highpass filtering above about 1500 Hz, the dominance of the ITD cue was eliminated, and listeners' judgments seemed to be determined by the other cues, ILDs and the monaural spectral cues.

In the experiments on ITD dominance, as well as in several other experiments involving localization of both real and virtual sources, some listeners made frequent front/back confusions (Wightman and Kistler, 1989b, 1992; Kistler and Wightman, 1992). We believe that these front/back confusions reflect not only the ambiguity of the ITD cue but also the dominance of that cue. Although the ILD cues are also ambiguous, the contours of constant ILD and hence the confused positions are different in each frequency band. Thus, it seems unlikely that the source of front/back confusions is ILD ambiguity. In fact, one might argue that because the pattern of the ILDs across frequency is not ambiguous it could actually serve as a cue for resolving front/back confusions.

The pattern of ILDs across frequency is also a reliable localization cue in that it does not depend critically on stimulus characteristics. However, the facts that the ILDs are prominent only at high frequencies and are highly idiosyncratic (Fig. 6) may detract from their utility as localization cues. There is some evidence that the ILDs may be used primarily to resolve front/back confusions, as suggested earlier. In an unpublished conflicting cue experiment similar to the one already described (Wightman and Kistler, 1992), listeners localized virtual sources in which the pattern of ILDs was "zeroed," by using the leading ear's HRTF magnitude to synthesize both left and right ear stimuli. In addition, the spectrum of the noise stimulus was scrambled in this condition to prevent listeners from using monaural spectral cues. Because the ILD manipulation affected only the magnitude of the filters used to synthesize the virtual sources, the ITD cues were undisturbed. Figure 7 shows typical results from this condition along with baseline results from a condition in which all the cues were intact. Note that the consequences of setting the ILD cue to zero in all bands were to increase front/back confusions and to decrease the range of elevation judgments. The latter effect is observed in the data from only about half of the listeners. There is no hint of an overall bias of the judgments toward the median plane (0° on the

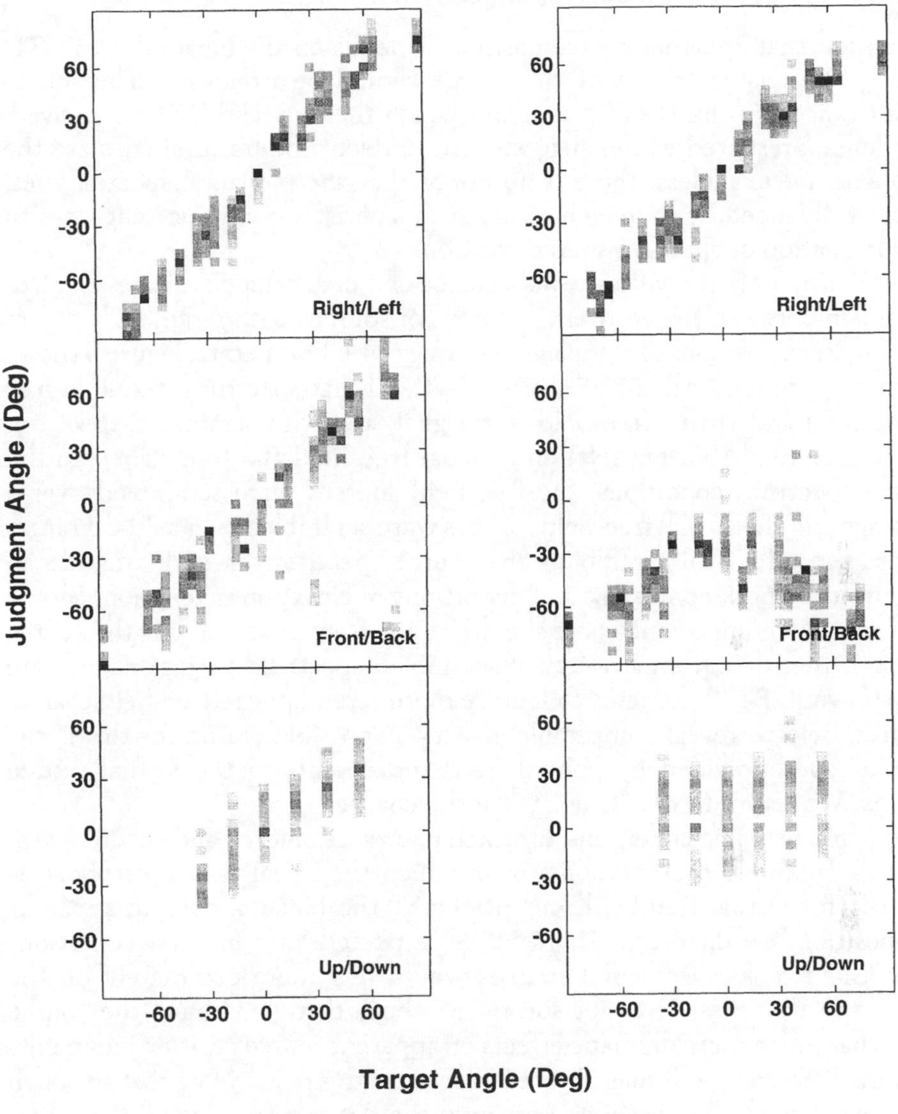

FIG. 7. Apparent position judgments from an experiment in which the ILD and ITD cues were set in conflict. The left panels show data from the condition in which cues were normal. The right panels show the results of setting the ILD to 0 dB at all frequencies. All responses are shown in each panel. The darkness of the data point indicates the proportion of possible judgments in that area. Front-to-back confusions are revealed in the "front/back" panels by negative judgments at positive target angles.

left/right plot) as would be expected if the ILD cue were contributing significantly to the apparent position judgments.

On our scale of cue reliability the monaural spectral cues are clearly the least reliable. They are highly idiosyncratic and their utility depends critically on a listener's *a priori* knowledge of source characteristics. The impact of a listener's knowledge or expectations about source characteristics is the topic of the next subsection.

C. The role of *a priori* knowledge of source characteristics

To the extent that apparent source position depends on the binaural cues (ITD and ILD), the characteristics of the source should be irrelevant. The source spectrum cancels in the HRTF ratio from which the ITD and ILD are derived. The evidence presented earlier suggests that, indeed, the binaural cues are the most salient. Nevertheless, there is no doubt that the monaural spectral cues, which are influenced by source characteristics, contribute in important ways to the determination of apparent source position.

One experiment that reveals the importance of monaural spectral cues involves a comparison between the apparent positions of sources with scrambled spectra and the apparent positions of comparable sources with flat spectra. Figure 8 shows typical results from a single listener presented with flat-spectrum stimuli in free field (top left) and virtual free field (top right), and with scrambled-spectrum stimuli in free field (bottom left) and virtual free field (bottom right). In the scrambled-spectrum conditions, the free-field sources were scrambled over a 40-dB range and the virtual free-field sources were scrambled over a 20-dB range. Note that the effects of scrambling the source spectrum on each trial are an increase in front/back confusions and distortions of elevation perception. If only binaural cues were important, there should be no effect of scrambling the source spectrum. Other data from a variety of scrambled-spectrum conditions indicate that, as shown in Fig. 8, it seems to require more scrambling in free field than in virtual free field to reveal comparable effects. A possible reason for this is the absence of cues provided by normal head movements in the virtual source conditions. We return to this issue later in the chapter.

In monaural listening conditions, in which one ear is plugged and covered with a muff (for free-field presentations) or in which the signal to one earphone is turned off (for virtual free-field presentations), the binaural cues to apparent source position are distorted. It might be expected that in such conditions listeners asked to localize sound sources would rely more completely on the monaural spectral cues. It is not surprising, then, that scrambling the source spectrum has much more dramatic effects on apparent source position judgments in monaural listening conditions. Figure 9 illustrates this point. Note that although some traces of source localizability remain in the flat-spectrum condition (judgments clustered around major diagonal), all evidence is gone in the scrambled-spectrum condition. The fact that all of the judgments in the monaural scrambled-spectrum condition are within 25° of the horizontal plane is curious and is a result we cannot readily explain.

D. Source frequency content

Accurate sound localization is possible only with wideband sound sources. For a source consisting of a sinusoid or a narrow band of noise, the apparent position and actual position are rarely coincident and often very far removed from one another. There are many reasons for our inability to localize narrowband sources. Narrowband stimuli provide an impoverished and typically ambiguous set of cues, because neither the pattern of ILDs across frequency nor the monaural spectral

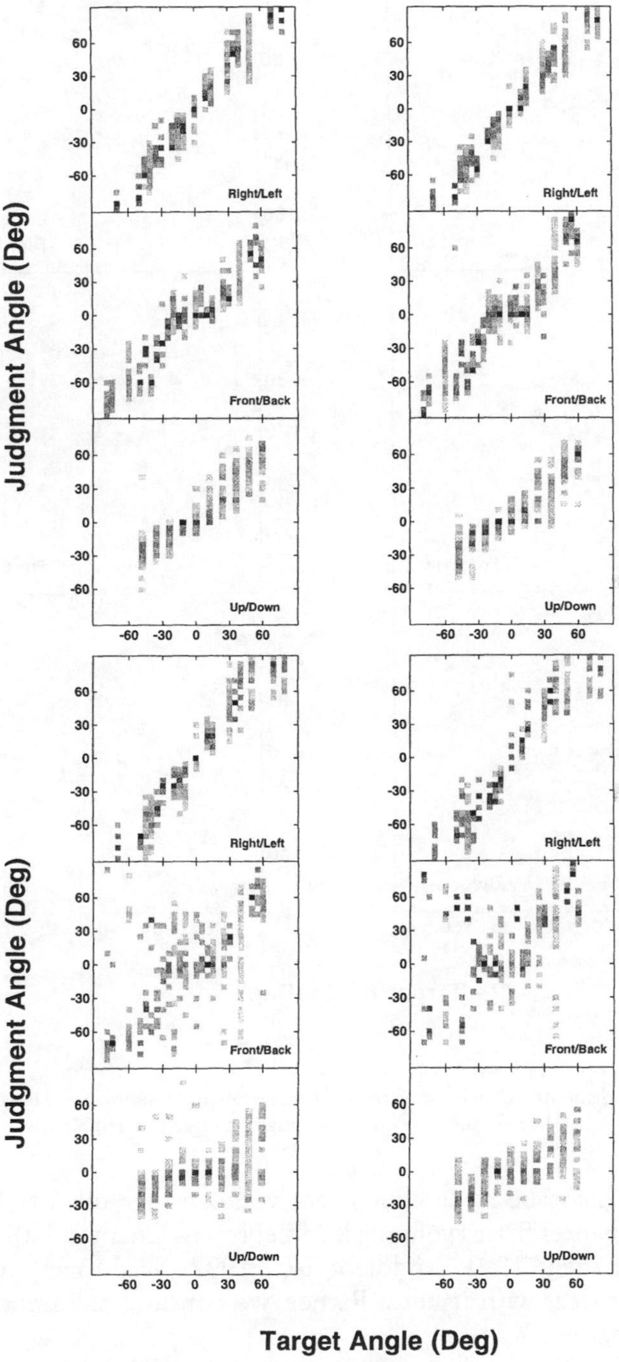

FIG. 8. Apparent position judgments with flat-spectrum stimuli (top panels) and scrambled-spectrum stimuli (bottom panels). The stimuli were presented either in free field (left) or virtual free field (right).

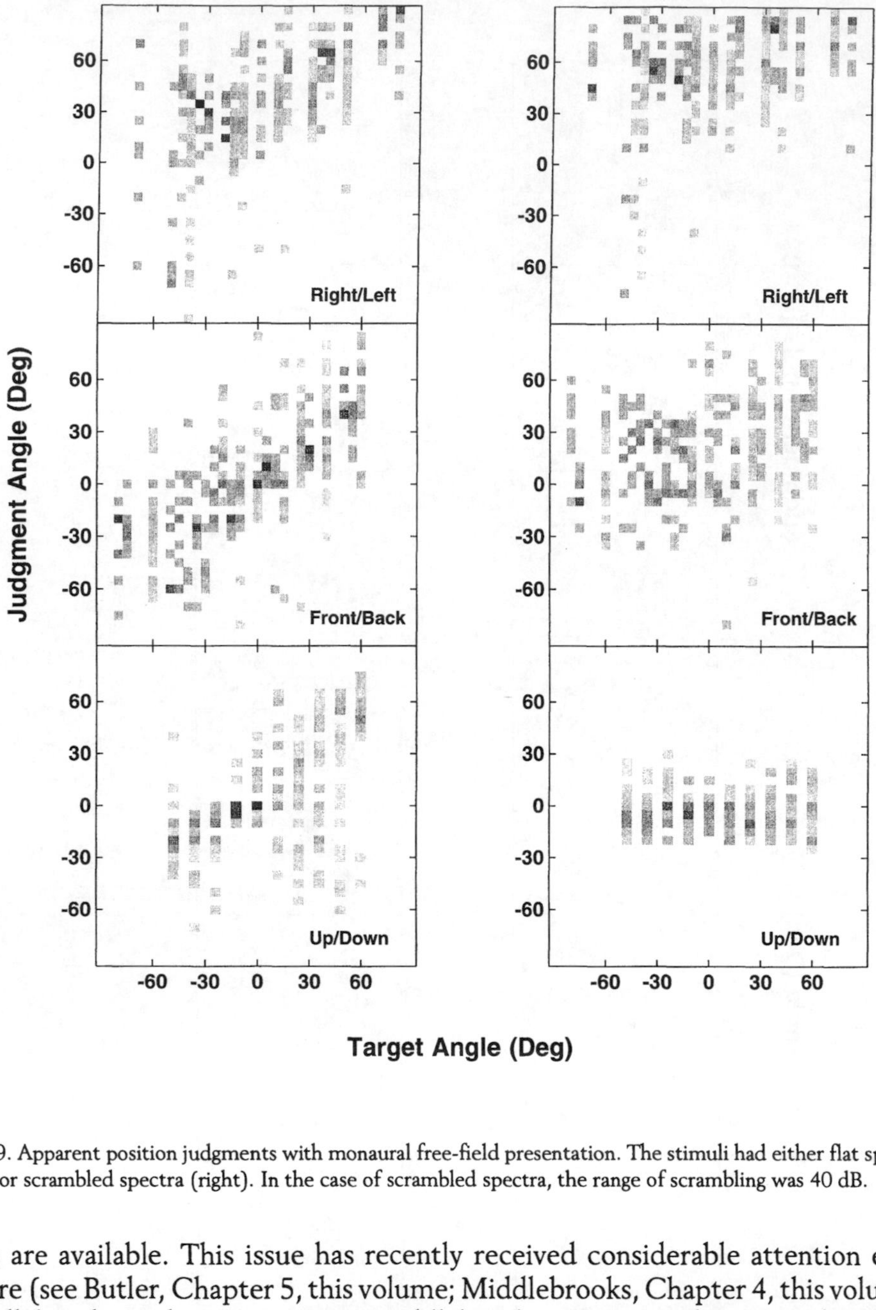

FIG. 9. Apparent position judgments with monaural free-field presentation. The stimuli had either flat spectra (left) or scrambled spectra (right). In the case of scrambled spectra, the range of scrambling was 40 dB.

cues are available. This issue has recently received considerable attention elsewhere (see Butler, Chapter 5, this volume; Middlebrooks, Chapter 4, this volume; Middlebrooks and Green, 1991; Middlebrooks, 1992; Wightman and Kistler, 1993), so we do not deal with it here. Rather, we consider the importance of specific frequency regions.

The experiment on ITD dominance discussed earlier (Wightman and Kistler, 1992) suggests that the salience of the ITD cues diminishes at high frequencies. On the other hand, the spectral cues (the ILDs in the various frequency bands and monaural spectral cues) might be expected to be more salient at high frequencies because it is there that these cues are acoustically more robust. An experiment in which listeners judged the apparent positions of filtered sound sources suggests that one way the high-frequency information is used is to resolve front/back confusions. Figure 10 shows apparent position judgments from a typical listener presented with wideband virtual sources (left) and sources with the frequencies from 5 kHz to 10 kHz removed with a bandstop filter. The most significant effect of the filtering seems to be an increase in front/back confusions. Although not shown here, the effect of lowpass filtering at 5 kHz is quite similar.

E. The role of cue realism or plausibility

The extent to which the constellation of localization cues presented to listeners matches their experience and expectation has significant effects on the apparent positions of sounds and on the relative weight assigned to the various cues. The results of several experiments we have conducted using virtual sound sources suggest that those cues that are unnatural or unusual are generally weighted less in the determination of apparent source position.

Some evidence on this point comes from experiments in which listeners hear sounds as if "through someone else's ears" (Wenzel, Arruda, Kistler, and Wightman, 1993). The virtual sources in these experiments are synthesized using HRTFs from a different listener than the one judging the apparent positions of those virtual sources. In such conditions one might expect that the ITD cues in the stimuli would match closely the ITD cues normally experienced by the listener (assuming comparable head sizes), but that the ILD and spectral cues would be very different. The most obvious consequence of listening "through someone else's ears" is a dramatic increase in front/back confusions (Wenzel *et al.*, 1993). We feel that this result reflects the fact that the spectral cues normally used to resolve front/back confusions are given less weight because they are unusual or unnatural.

In everyday listening, sound sources produce localization cues that are "consistent" across the frequency spectrum. In other words, because the sounds originate from a real source, the position indicated by the ITD, the ILD, and the monaural spectral cues is the same (with the natural ambiguities, of course) regardless of the frequency band considered. ITD, for example, is roughly the same at 500 Hz as it is at 5000 Hz. With real sources a situation could not occur in which the ILD in one frequency region indicated a source on one side of the head and the ILD in another frequency region indicated a source on the other side. Such sources can be easily synthesized, however, and a listener's judgments of their apparent positions can be revealing.

In our research on the cue realism issue, we studied the apparent positions of virtual stimuli in which cues in one frequency region conflict with cues in another frequency region. In one condition, for example, the ILD and spectral cues were the same throughout the frequency range (200 Hz–14 000 Hz) and indicated one of five possible directions on the horizontal plane. The ITD cue in each of four bands of equal width on a log scale (roughly 1.5 octaves wide) indicated a different

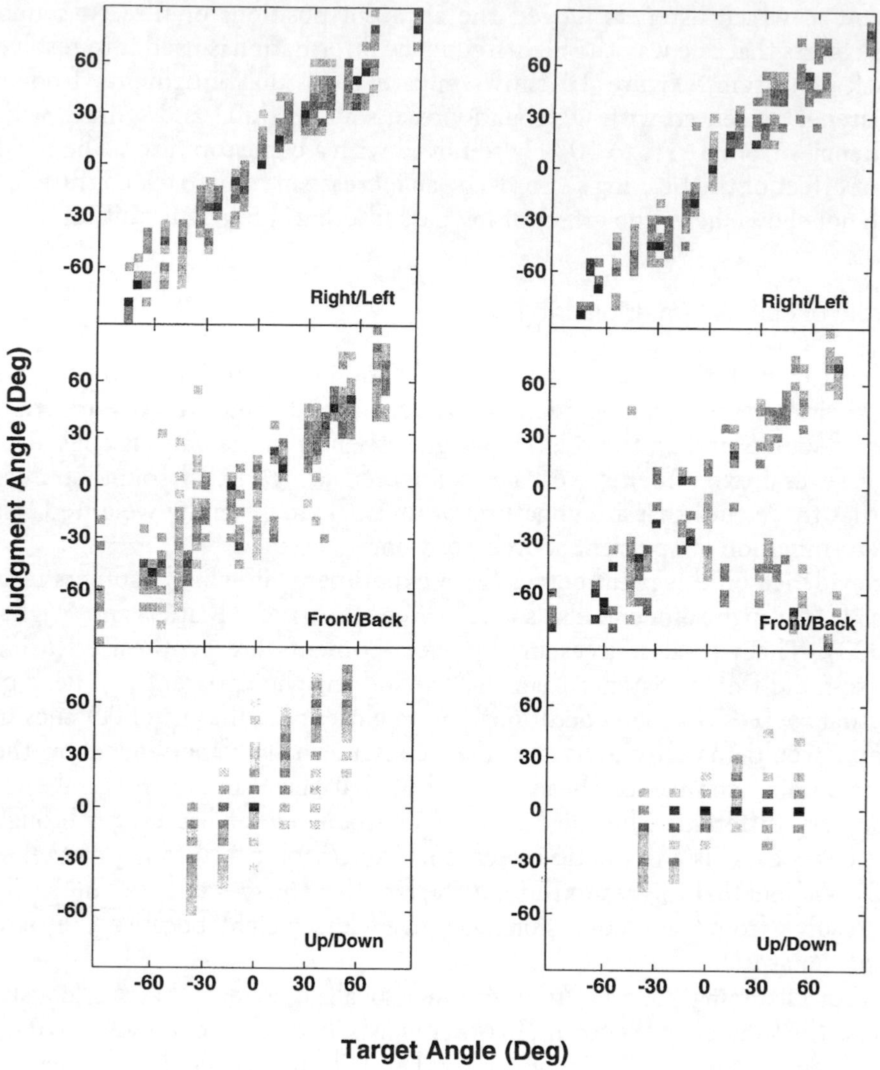

FIG. 10. Apparent position judgments with bandstop stimuli. The left panels show data from a baseline condition in which the wideband stimulus had a scrambled (on average flat) spectrum. The right panels show data from the condition in which the scrambled spectrum stimuli had energy between 5 kHz and 10 kHz removed by

direction. Thus, the ITD cue was "inconsistent" across the frequency range and the ILD and spectral cues were "consistent." In other conditions the ITD cue was consistent and the other cues inconsistent.

The results were the same for all 5 listeners tested and were unambiguous. The apparent position judgments always followed the consistent cue. Even if the ITD cue was inconsistent only in a single high-frequency band (above 5 kHz), listeners appeared to ignore the ITD altogether and put maximum weight on the ILD and spectral cues, which were consistent across the spectrum. This is an important result. It suggests not only that "realistic" cues are given greater weight than "unrealistic" cues but also that high-frequency ITD cues can be just as important as low-frequency ITD cues. In this condition, the fact that the high-frequency ITD cue was different from the low-frequency ITD cue was recognized and apparently led the listener to ignore both ITD cues.

III. ADDITIONAL CUES—RESOLUTION OF FRONT/BACK CONFUSIONS

Many of the experimental manipulations we described in this chapter have produced an increase in the frequency with which listeners make front/back confusions. Scrambling the source spectrum, removing the high-frequency energy from the source, and listening to unfamiliar spectral cues all increased the front/back confusion rate in our listeners. The obvious conclusion from these results is that the cues provided by source familiarity and high-frequency content are normally used by listeners to resolve confusions. However, there remains the problem that even in our free-field listening conditions, when the whole suite of cues is available, including normal ITDs, ILDs, and spectral cues, some listeners still make large numbers of front/back confusions. Figure 11 shows one example. Because there is no evidence that these individuals are handicapped by their localization errors in real life, we conclude that source familiarity and high-frequency content are not the only stimulus parameters that facilitate resolution of confusions and that in everyday listening additional cues must be used.

There are several differences between our free-field testing environment and everyday listening situations. The most obvious difference is that our environment lacks the echoes and reverberation present in nearly all everyday listening settings. We tested the influence of normal echoes by adding the first 20 reflections from a simple rectangular room to our normal virtual source stimuli. There was no change in front/back confusion rate.

The primary acoustical difference between sources in the front and sources in the rear appears in the frequency range between 3 kHz and 7 kHz. Figure 12 illustrates this difference by showing averaged DTF magnitude functions for front and rear sources. We reasoned that emphasizing the acoustical difference between front and rear sources might allow better front/rear distinction and lower confusion rate. To emphasize front/rear differences we squared the magnitude of the HRTFs used to synthesize virtual sources. Listeners' judgments of the apparent positions of the spectrally emphasized sources did not show any decrease in front/back confusion rate.

In all our previous work, involving both free-field and virtual-source conditions, listeners are asked not to move their heads. Thus, the usual changes in the localization cues that accompany head movements were not available. Because there are good reasons to believe that information from the changes in localization cues could be used to resolve confusions (e.g., Wallach, 1940), we have begun an experiment to assess the role of head movements. In this experiment, listeners localize virtual sources (2.5-s wideband noise bursts) in two conditions. In one,

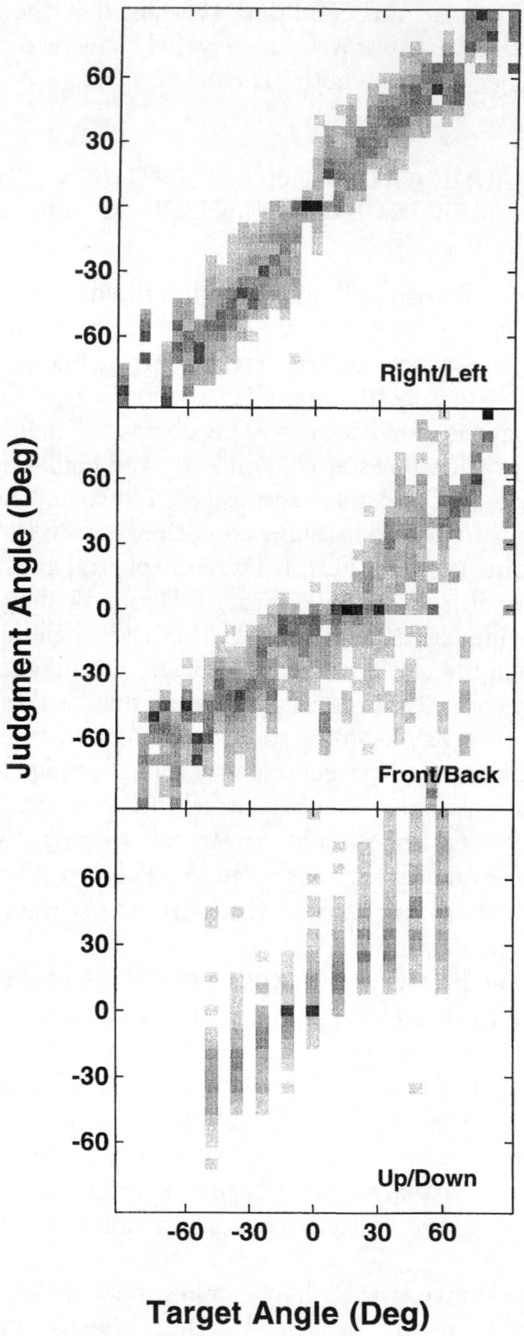

FIG. 11. Apparent position judgments from a single listener presented with flat-spectrum stimuli in free field. Note the large number of front/back confusions in the "front/back" panel.

the virtual stimuli are presented over headphones, and the listeners are asked not to move their heads during the test. This condition is identical to our usual virtual-source condition except that the stimulus is longer. In the second condition, using the same stimuli, listeners are encouraged to move their heads during stimulus presentation if they feel it would facilitate localization. A magnetic head tracker is used to sense head position and the virtual synthesis algorithm is modified according to the head tracker's reports in real time, using a Convolvotron (Foster, Wenzel, and Taylor, 1991), in order to simulate a stationary external source. Apparent position judgments are made verbally after each stimulus presentation. Preliminary results from a single listener are shown in Fig. 13. Note that in the head-stationary condition this listener makes frequent front/back confusions, as evidenced by the off-diagonal responses in the "front/back" panel. These data are from the same listener whose free-field judgments are shown in Fig. 11. In the head-movement condition, however, the front/back confusions are nearly eliminated.

The preliminary results of this experiment strongly suggest that among the additional cues we have considered, those provided by head movements can be important. It appears that head movements should be viewed as a natural and important component of the sound localization process. Future research designed to assess the salience of the other cues, ITD, ILD, and spectral cues will need to acknowledge the importance of the dynamic information provided by head movements and to appreciate the situations in which this information might be important.

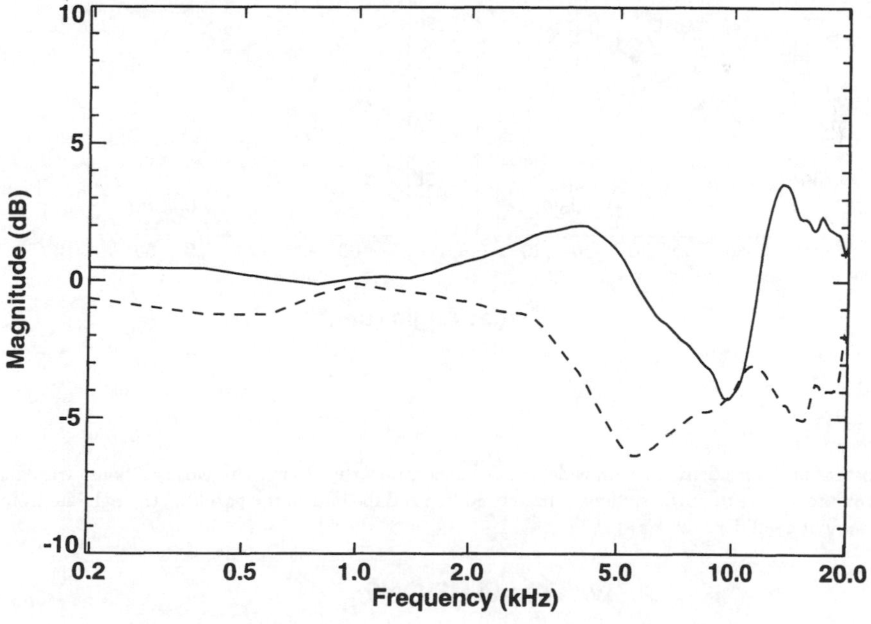

FIG. 12. Averaged DTF magnitude functions (12 listeners) for sources in the front (solid line, sources between –30° and 30° azimuth and –40° and 40° elevation), and for sources in the rear (dashed line, sources between –150° and 150° azimuth and –40° and 40° elevation).

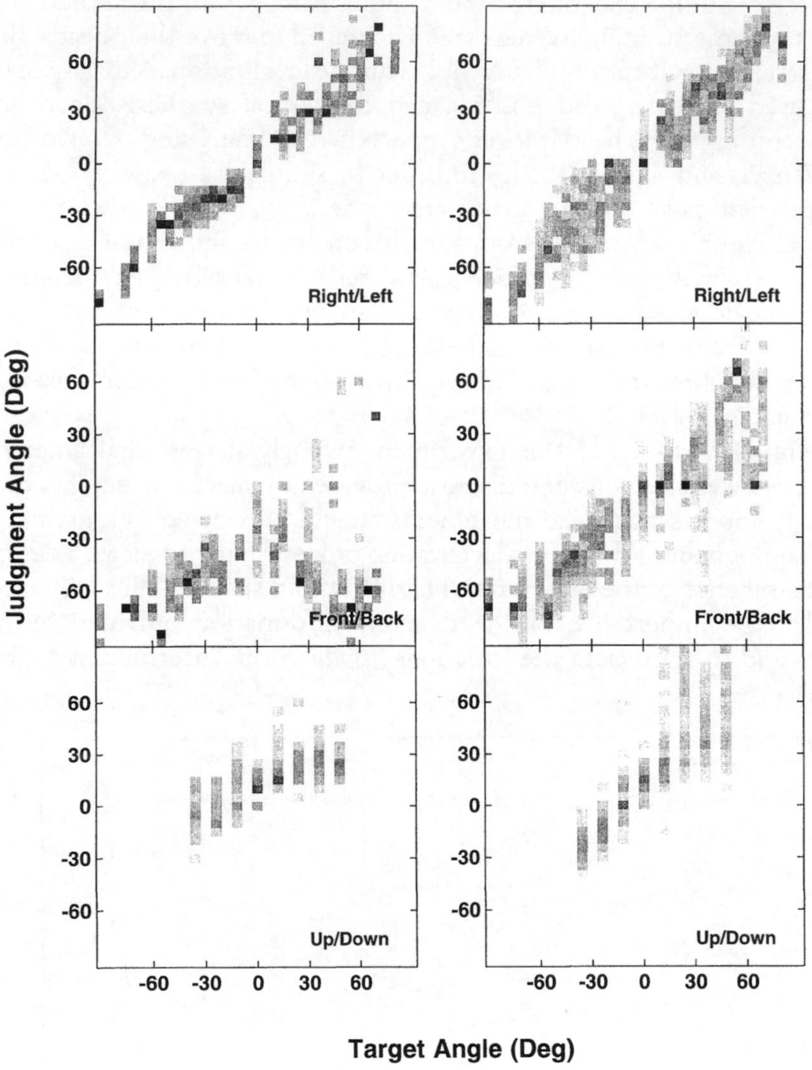

FIG. 13. Apparent position judgments with wideband flat-spectrum virtual sources in two conditions. The data in the panels on the left are from the stationary-head condition and the data in the panels on the right are from the head-movement condition.

IV. CONCLUSIONS

The main point we have tried to emphasize here is that the apparent position of a sound source is determined by much more than just the low-frequency ITDs and high-frequency ILDs highlighted in Lord Rayleigh's original duplex theory (Rayleigh, 1907). Many other cues are involved, such as monaural spectral cues, and the relative contributions of the cues seem to be determined by a variety of stimulus and listener factors, including stimulus dynamics, source familiarity, listener expectations, and cue plausibility. Although the general outline of a comprehensive theory of sound localization is beginning to emerge, many important questions remain unanswered and many details are missing. Modern technology has only recently given us the tools needed to address those questions and to fill in the details through systematic, controlled research. We can expect rapid progress in the years ahead.

ACKNOWLEDGMENTS

Preparation of this chapter was supported in part by a grant from the NIH (5-P01-DC00116-20) and a Cooperative Research Agreement with NASA (NCC2-542).

REFERENCES

Batteau, D. W. (**1967**). "The role of the pinna in human localization," Proc. R. Soc. London, Ser. B **168**, 158–180.

Foster, S. H., Wenzel, E. M., and Taylor, R. M. (**1991**). "Real time synthesis of complex acoustic environments," Proc. ASSP (IEEE) Workshop on Applications of Signal Processing to Audio and Acoustics, New Paltz, NY (IEEE, NY).

Green, D. M. (**1971**). "Temporal auditory acuity," Psych. Rev. **78**, 540–551.

Kistler, D. J., and Wightman, F. L. (**1992**). "A model of head-related transfer functions based on principal components analysis and minimum-phase reconstruction," J. Acoust. Soc. Am. **91**, 1637–1647.

Kuhn, G. F. (**1977**). "Model for the interaural time differences in the azimuthal plane," J. Acoust. Soc. Am. **62**, 157–167.

Middlebrooks, J. C. (**1992**). "Narrow-band sound localization related to external ear acoustics," J. Acoust. Soc. Am. **92**, 2607–2624.

Middlebrooks, J. C., and Green, D. M. (**1991**). "Sound localization by human listeners," Annu. Rev. Psychol. **42**, 135–159.

Moore, B. C. J., Oldfield, S. R., and Dooley, G. J. (**1989**). "Detection and discrimination of spectral peaks and notches at 1 and 8 kHz," J. Acoust. Soc. Am. **85**, 820–835.

Musicant, A. D., and Butler, R. A. (**1984**). "The influence of pinnae-based spectral cues on sound localization," J. Acoust. Soc. Am. **75**, 1195–1200.

Rayleigh, Lord (J. W. Strutt, 3rd Baron of Rayleigh) (**1907**). "On our perception of sound direction," Philos. Mag. **13**, 214–232.

Rice, J. J., May, B. J., Spirou, G. A., and Young, E. D. (**1992**). "Pinna-based spectral cues for sound localization in cat," Hear. Res. **58**, 132–152.

Wallach, H. (**1940**). "The role of head movements and vestibular and visual cues in sound localization," J. Exp. Psychol. **27**, 339–368.

Wenzel, E. M., Arruda, M., Kistler, D. J., and Wightman, F. L. (**1993**). "Localization using nonindividualized head-related transfer functions," J. Acoust. Soc. Am. **94**, 111–123.

Wightman, F. L., and Kistler, D. J. (**1989a**). "Headphone simulation of free-field listening I: Stimulus synthesis," J. Acoust. Soc. Am. **85**, 858–867.

Wightman, F. L., and Kistler, D. J. (**1989b**). "Headphone simulation of free-field listening II: Psychophysical validation," J. Acoust. Soc. Am. **85**, 868–878.

Wightman, F. L., and Kistler, D. J. (**1992**). "The dominant role of low-frequency interaural time differences in sound localization," J. Acoust. Soc. Am. **91**, 1648–1661.

Wightman, F. L., and Kistler, D. J. (**1993**). "Sound localization," in *Springer Handbook of Auditory Research, Vol. 3: Human Psychophysics*, edited by W. A. Yost, A. N. Popper, and R. R. Fay (Springer-Verlag, New York), pp. 155–192.

Zakarauskas, P., and Cynader, M. S. (**1993**). "A computational theory of spectral cue localization," J. Acoust. Soc. Am. **94**, 1323–1331.

Chapter 2

Acoustical Features of the Human External Ear

Edgar A. G. Shaw
Institute for Microstructural Sciences
National Research Council
Ottawa, Ontario
Canada

(Received April 1994; revised October 1994)

The sound pressures generated at the eardrums measure the response of a complex acoustical antenna system that couples the ears to the sound field. This system includes the head and external ears. The variations in response with source direction and frequency provide the physical basis for sound localization. Treating the head as a sphere and the ears as simple detectors provides useful values of interaural time difference but overlooks the effects of pinna diffraction and concha wave motion, which are significant at high frequencies. These effects have been studied in real human ears, replicas, and geometrical models using special sound sources close to the ear. Each human ear has distinctive patterns of response while sharing major features with other ears. These common characteristics are linked to the normal modes of the concha and can be reproduced in mode-matched physical models. When sounds are presented through earphones, the free-field characteristics of the ear are replaced by very different characteristics that are dependent on complex and unreliable interactions between the individual earphone and the individual ear. These interactions, which vary greatly with the class of earphone, pose challenges where there is a need to reproduce the subtleties of spatial hearing.

INTRODUCTION

The external ears, head, neck, and torso are components of a complex acoustical antenna system that couples the middle and inner ears to the external sound field. The response of this system can be measured in terms of the sound pressures generated at the two eardrums. In free-field listening, the variations in response with source direction and frequency, and the interaural differences in response, provide the physical basis for sound localization. These variations are associated with the wave characteristics of the various anatomical components.

So it is relevant to ask how sound pressure is transformed from the free field to the eardrum, how the transformation characteristics can be measured and modeled, and to what extent they may vary from individual to individual. The acoustical functions of the various anatomical components are also of interest because they are fundamental to the performance of the system and can provide information that is complementary to that gained from psychophysical studies.

When sounds are presented binaurally through earphones, the directionality of the ear is eliminated and an artificial system is created with acoustical characteristics that are dependent on the characteristics of the ear, the characteristics of the earphone, and the interaction between the two. This system generally provides an excellent channel for speech communication, but is put under considerable stress where there is a need to reproduce with fidelity the subtleties of spatial hearing.

I. FREE-FIELD RECEPTION

Under free-field conditions, the ear canal wall, the various parts of the pinna, and the surface of the head all present essentially rigid boundaries to airborne sound. Hence, the transformation of sound pressure from the free field to the eardrum is largely determined by diffraction and cavity resonance effects associated with these structures. These effects are defined by the geometry of the system, which, in humans, is substantially constant since the pinna is immoveable and the contributions from the torso are secondary (e.g., Shaw, 1974a; Kuhn, 1987).

A. Classical model: Spherical head

As a first approximation, the human head can be treated as a rigid sphere with simple pressure detectors, representing the ears, at opposite ends of a diameter. In this theoretical treatment, there is, by definition, symmetry about the interaural axis and it is common practice to choose a coordinate system based on this axis. In Fig. 1, for convenience, plane sound waves are shown approaching the head in the horizontal plane at azimuth θ.

Calculations of the interaural time difference (ITD), based on diffraction theory, then lead to the following asymptotic values at low and high frequencies:

$$\tau_{lf} = (a/c)(3 \sin\theta), \tag{1}$$

$$\tau_{hf} = (a/c)(\sin\theta + \theta), \tag{2}$$

where a is the radius of the head (~87.5 mm) and c is the velocity of sound in air (Kuhn, 1977). The high-frequency asymptote is identical with the frequency-independent value of ITD stemming from the geometrical argument that sound travels in a straight line to the left ear in Fig. 1, while following the curved surface of the head as it approaches the right ear, which lies in shadow. At intermediate frequencies (~0.5 to 2 kHz), there is a transition region with dispersion where it is necessary to distinguish between group or envelope delay and phase delay.

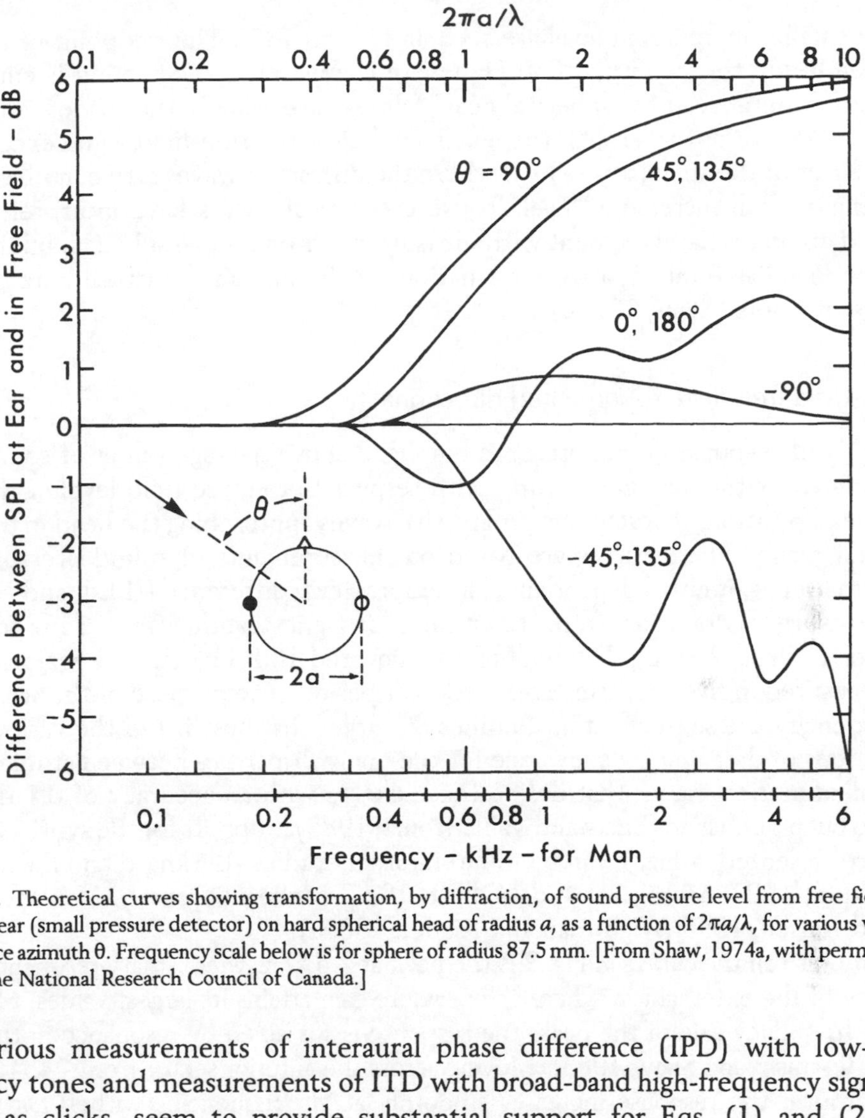

FIG. 1. Theoretical curves showing transformation, by diffraction, of sound pressure level from free field to simple ear (small pressure detector) on hard spherical head of radius a, as a function of $2\pi a/\lambda$, for various values of source azimuth θ. Frequency scale below is for sphere of radius 87.5 mm. [From Shaw, 1974a, with permission from the National Research Council of Canada.]

Various measurements of interaural phase difference (IPD) with low-frequency tones and measurements of ITD with broad-band high-frequency signals, such as clicks, seem to provide substantial support for Eqs. (1) and (2) as representative of average values (Shaw, 1974a; Kuhn, 1987). However, recent measurements of interaural envelope delay with bandlimited high-frequency signals have shown that the variations in delay, at any given azimuth, as a function of frequency, can be substantial. For signals of moderate bandwidth (0.22 octave), with center frequencies varying between 4 and 12 kHz, these variations are of the order of 100 μs rms. Much smaller variations are found when the bandwidth is increased to one octave (Middlebrooks and Green, 1990).

The graphs in Fig. 1 show the calculated sound pressure levels generated by diffraction at the left ear position for various values of θ as a function of $2\pi a/\lambda$, where λ is the wavelength of sound and a is the radius of the head. The auxiliary frequency scale is based on the conventional head radius of 87.5 mm. At normal incidence ($\theta = 90°$), the sound pressure level (SPL) rises steadily with increasing frequency approaching an asymptotic value 6 dB above the free-field level.

Slightly smaller increases in level are seen at 45° and 135°. The midpoint of the transition lies in the vicinity of 630 Hz where the wavelength of sound is equal to the circumference of the spherical head. When the ear lies in the shadow zone (e.g., $\theta = -45°$ and $\theta = -135°$), the levels fall below the free-field value except at the center of the zone ($\theta = -90°$), where the diffracted waves arrive in phase, producing a small increase in level. These theoretical curves have interpretive value and are in partial agreement with measurements on human subjects, but do not provide reliable quantitative information on the human acoustical antenna system as a whole (Shaw, 1974b).

B. Measured free-field response and directionality

The family of response curves presented in Fig. 2 shows average values of sound pressure level at the human eardrum, with respect to the free-field level at the center-head position, generated by progressive waves approaching the head in the horizontal plane. These curves are based on measurements of sound pressure transformation, azimuthal dependence, interaural level difference (ILD), and ear canal pressure distribution from 12 studies brought together in a common framework (Shaw, 1974b). The pool of data covered 100 subjects, the majority male, measured in five countries over a 40-year period. The purpose of the work was to identify the self-consistent families of curves that best fitted the various distributions of data making allowance for the many disparities between studies. Tables of numerical values that define these curves with an accuracy of 0.1 dB have also been published (Shaw and Vaillancourt, 1985). Support for the synthesis of data represented in Fig. 2 can be found in other studies (Burkhard and Sachs, 1975; Kuhn, 1987; Mehrgardt and Mellert, 1977; Møller, Sørensen, Hammershoi, and Jensen, 1995; Wightman and Kistler, 1989a).

Common to all the curves in Fig. 2 is the peak at 2.6 kHz, the primary resonance frequency of the external ear, where the pressure gain attains its largest values. On the high-frequency side of the peak, the response is sustained by resonance in the concha (Teranishi and Shaw, 1968). Moving across the anterior sector from −45° to +45° azimuth, the response increases smoothly at all frequencies with ILDs at azimuth 45° of magnitudes that are in keeping with elementary diffraction theory at high frequencies (see Fig. 1). Below 1 kHz, the ILDs are appreciably greater than the theoretical values, due, perhaps, to the proximity of the neck and torso (Shaw, 1974a). In the lateral sector, the most striking feature is the 5- to 10-dB decrease in response between azimuth 45° and azimuth 135° over the 2.5- to 6-kHz frequency band, which provides a physical foundation for localization in the lateral sector based on spectral coloration. This lack of symmetry with respect to the interaural axis is due to diffraction by the pinna flange (Teranishi and Shaw, 1968).

The shallow minimum between 1.0 and 1.3 kHz, which is present across the entire frontal sector, can be attributed to two unrelated phenomena. From 0° to 60° azimuth, there is interference between the direct wave and a reflected wave from the shoulder. Fortuitously, from −15° to −75°, at approximately the same frequency, there is shadow zone interference between diffracted waves reaching the ear from opposite sides of the head.

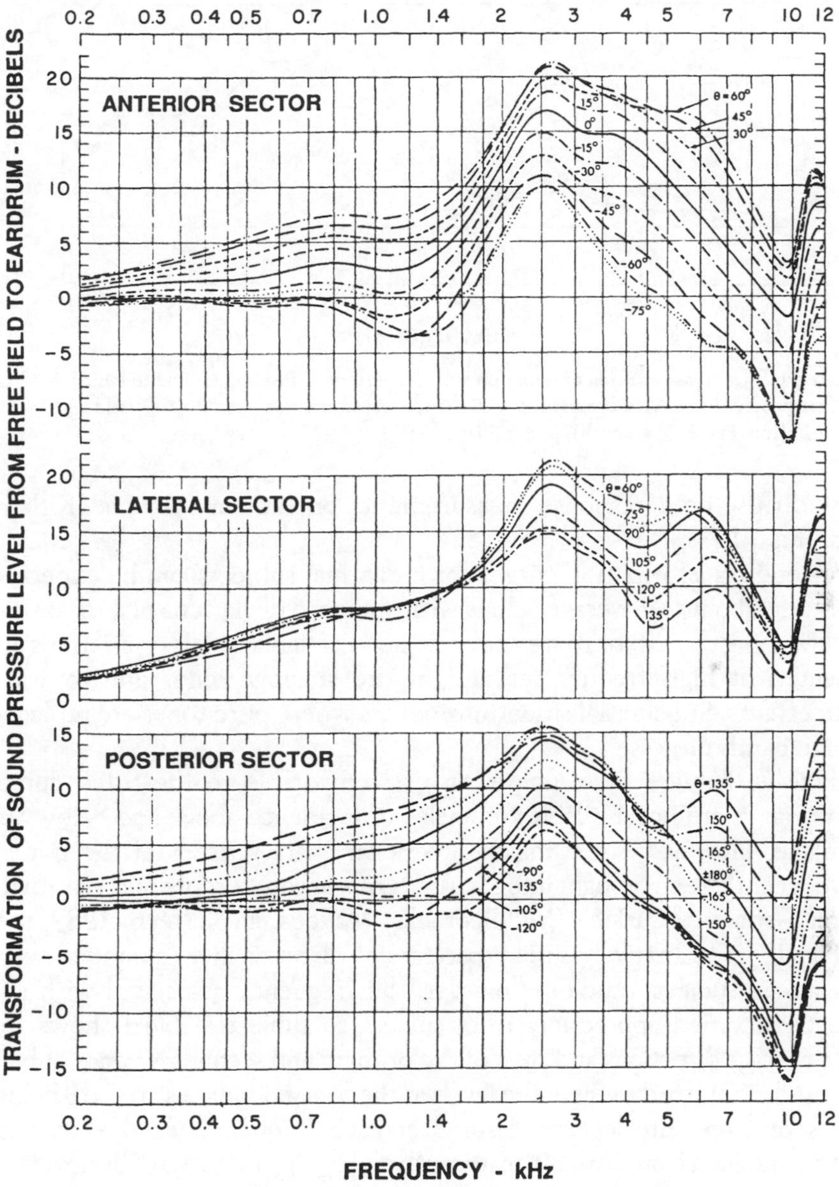

FIG. 2. Average transformation of sound pressure level from free field to human eardrum in the horizontal plane as a function of frequency at 15° intervals of source azimuth θ. Curves are based on synthesis of data from 12 studies. [From Shaw, 1974b, with permission from the National Research Council of Canada.]

The steady decline in response, seen in Fig. 2, between 6.5 and 9.5 kHz at all azimuths, reflects the relative insensitivity of the human ear in the horizontal plane within this particular frequency band. This insensitivity is highlighted in Fig. 3, which shows that the response in a diffuse sound field is substantially greater than the free-field response at 0° azimuth (frontal incidence) between 6 and 10 kHz. The diffuse-field curve is based on synthesized response data for an advanced model of the external ear and for replicas of several human ears (Shaw, 1980). It is also supported by theoretical considerations (Shaw, 1988), and is consistent

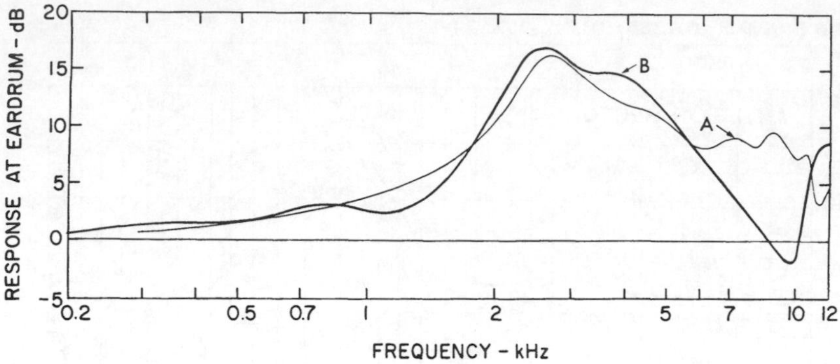

FIG. 3. Estimated average transformation of sound pressure level from diffuse sound field to human eardrum as a function of frequency (curve A) in comparison with average transformation from the free field with frontal incidence (curve B: from Fig. 2, 0° azimuth). [After Shaw, 1980.]

with recent diffuse-field response measurements on human subjects (Killion, Berger, and Nuss, 1987).

The pure-tone transformation curves for individual subjects can be expected to be distributed about the average values with standard deviations of 1 dB or less below 500 Hz rising to 5 dB or more above 5 kHz. Particularly large variations are to be expected at high frequencies and in the shadow zone, due to wave interference effects. Substantial smoothing occurs where pure tones are replaced by 1/3-octave bands of noise.

Comprehensive families of response curves, comparable to the fitted curves presented in Fig. 2, are not available for angles of incidence above and below the horizontal plane. However, some major directional characteristics of the human receiver have recently been brought into focus in terms of contours of equal sensitivity presented on a spherical surface (Middlebrooks, Makous, and Green, 1989; see, especially, Fig. 12). Qualitatively similar patterns of directionality (contours) were found with all six subjects studied; however, the frequency associated with any particular pattern varied appreciably from subject to subject. Table I shows the approximate average directions and sizes of the primary and secondary zones of high sensitivity found in this study, where the levels at the zone boundaries are 5 dB below the highest sound pressure levels measured at each frequency. At 4 kHz, high sensitivity is maintained from 0° to 80° in azimuth and from –50° to +70° in elevation.

TABLE I. Directions of high sensitivity in the human ear at various frequencies: Approximate angular positions of zone centers and angular magnitudes of zones based on Middlebrooks et al. (1989), Fig. 12.

	Frequency (kHz)							
Position	4	6	8[a]	8[b]	10	12[a]	12[b]	14
Azimuth	40°	60°	80°	30°	70°	10°	90°	15°
Elevation	10°	20°	30°	–40°	–20°	–10°	0°	10°
Magnitude	±40°az	±40°	±30°	±20°	±25°	±20°	±15°	±20°
	±60°el							

[a]Primary zone.
[b]Secondary zone.

At 6 kHz, there is a decrease in zone size and movement of the zone center to greater angles of azimuth and elevation. At 8 kHz, the pattern becomes bipolar with zones of high sensitivity above and below the horizontal plane. The pattern is also bipolar at 12 kHz but the zones of high sensitivity are now widely separated in azimuth and centered near the horizontal plane. These characteristics provide substantial spectral cues that are available for the localization of elevated sound sources.

C. The human acoustical receiver as a minimum phase system

It is evident that the transformation of sound pressure from the free field to the eardrum is not, in the strictest sense, a minimum phase process. In particular, as we have seen, multiple transmission paths associated with diffraction by the head and reflection from the shoulder leave visible imprints on the response curves. Nevertheless, in the processing of experimental data where simplicity and internal consistency may be paramount, it may be useful to regard the human acoustical receiver as a minimum phase system. In particular, there may be considerable merit in treating the magnitude spectrum as primary and combining it with a phase spectrum calculated from the Hilbert transform of the negative logarithm of the magnitude spectrum (Blauert, 1983; Kistler and Wightman, 1992; Middlebrooks and Green, 1990; Oppenheim and Schafer, 1975; Wightman and Kistler, 1989a).

II. ANATOMICAL FEATURES, PHYSICAL REPRESENTATIONS, AND MEASUREMENT TECHNIQUES

Some anatomical features of the human external ear are identified in Fig. 4. The canal is an irregular tubular structure with a sinuous central axis and a cross-sectional area that is sharply tapered in the region approaching and adjoining the eardrum, which, in fact, defines the shape of the canal at the inner end (Stinson and Lawton, 1989). For this reason, and because there is no clear boundary between the concha and the canal, it is difficult to assign a precise meaning to canal length. However, at frequencies below 8 kHz, the primary acoustical characteristics of the average canal are well represented by a simple cylindrical cavity 7.5 mm in diameter and 22.5 mm in length (volume 1 cm^3) terminated by a piston-like eardrum that is perpendicular to the axis (Shaw, 1974a). The concha, with a volume of approximately 4 cm^3, is a broad shallow cavity that is partially divided by the crus helias. The lower part, the cavum, is tightly coupled to the canal whereas the upper part, the cymba, is connected to the fossa. These structures clearly have specific acoustical attributes, which are discussed later, whereas the structures extending from the concha, such as the helix, the anti-helix, and the lobule, seem to function collectively as a simple flange (Teranishi and Shaw, 1968). In this respect, the human ear is markedly different from other mammalian ears in which the pinna extension is a significant conical structure under muscular control.

A. Simple physical models

Some major characteristics of the human external ear, such as the pressure gain due to resonance in the ear canal and concha and the directional asymmetry due to pinna diffraction, can readily be simulated with simple physical models. In one such model, the concha is represented by a broad inclined cylindrical cavity partially embedded in a rigid plane, the pinna flange by a rectangular plate, the ear canal proper by a narrow cylindrical cavity, and the eardrum by a simple acoustical network with appropriate damping (Teranishi and Shaw, 1968; Shaw, 1974a). This elementary model, with only four component parts, matches the free-field characteristics of the average ear very well up to 5 kHz but fails at higher frequencies. In particular, the transverse resonances in the cylindrical "concha" and the resultant directionality patterns are not at all like those observed in real ears.

B. Measurements of sound pressure in the ear

Five representative positions at which the input to the ear can be measured are shown in Fig. 5. The sound pressure at the eardrum is an accurate measure of the input to the middle ear except at the highest frequencies, where there are uncertainties associated with the dynamics of the eardrum and the acoustical characteristics of the canal (Stinson, 1985). To achieve an absolute accuracy of 1 dB at 10 kHz, it is necessary to use a microphone with a fine probe tube and place the orifice within 2 mm of the umbo. Measurements at other positions have comparative value provided that the directionality at the chosen position is essentially the same as that at the eardrum. Measurements that meet this requirement can, in principle, be made at any reproducible position in the canal provided that steps are taken to avoid errors due to the presence of transverse modes. Because the canal is small in diameter, these modes have high cutoff frequencies and correspondingly large attenuation constants (see, e.g., Rabbitt and Friedrich, 1991). These modes are generally low in amplitude 10 mm from the canal entrance, but can lead to errors in measurement at positions of minimum

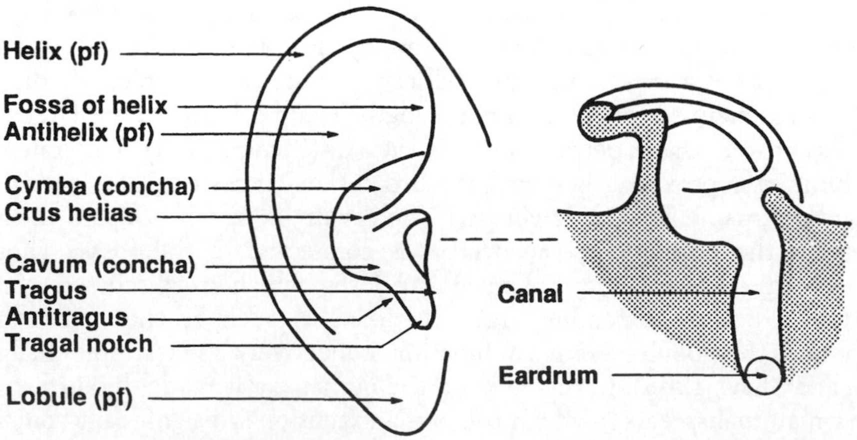

FIG. 4. Descriptive diagram of external ear.

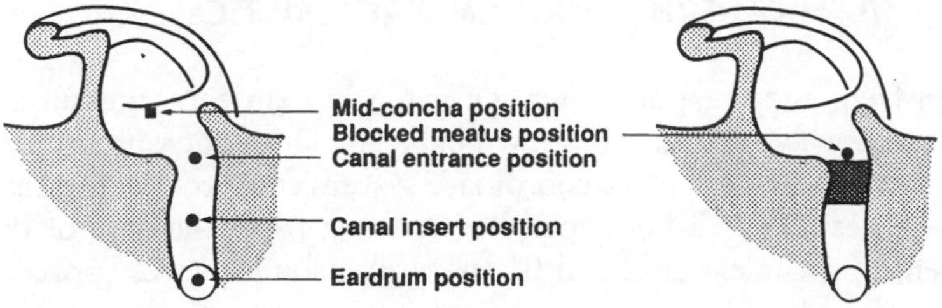

FIG. 5. Horizontal cross section of external ear showing five measurement positions.

pressure in the canal. The first pair of transverse modes have nodal surfaces passing through the centerline of the canal, which is, therefore, an acoustically desirable location for the microphone orifice.

Valuable comparative measurements of sound pressure can also be made with the microphone orifice placed at the center of a carefully fitted plug closing the entrance to the ear canal. This is the convenient and highly reproducible "blocked meatus" position first described by Yamaguchi and Sushi (1956). The validity of this type of measurement has been studied in experiments with an advanced physical model of the external ear (IRE) excited by the progressive-wave source described later. These experiments indicate that the transfer functions from the blocked meatus to the eardrum measured at many angles of incidence are, in this particular case, virtually indistinguishable below 8 kHz and lie within a 2–3 dB range up to 15 kHz (Shaw, 1982b). No experiments of comparable accuracy have been made with real human ears, but other data indicate that this result has broad validity. It should, however, be noted that measurements of sound pressure in the concha, other than blocked meatus measurements, are of limited value at frequencies greater than 5 kHz. The transformation of sound pressure from the free field to the blocked meatus has recently been measured at 97 angles of incidence in an experimental program encompassing 40 human subjects (Møller, Sørensen, Hammershoi, and Jensen, 1995).

C. Special sound source for high-frequency measurements

To obtain precise information on the high-frequency characteristics of the external ear, it is necessary to study real ears in isolation. The National Research Council (NRC) progressive-wave sound source was designed to operate sufficiently close to the ear that head diffraction effects are virtually eliminated while maintaining sufficient clearance to avoid significant interaction between the source and the ear (Shaw, 1975a, 1982a). A dynamic transducer, with a short waveguide designed to minimize wavefront irregularities, is mounted on an aluminum plate that is brought into close contact with the circumaural region of the head. The pinna extension passes through a circular opening in the plate, which is centered on the ear canal. This special sound source produces well-defined, moderately divergent progressive sound waves with smooth wavefronts that approach the ear at grazing incidence. The direction of the incident waves can be varied by changing the orientation of the source plate in the circumaural plane. The sound field at the ear is, therefore, similar in some important respects to that generated by plane waves approaching the head in the median plane.

III. HIGH-FREQUENCY CHARACTERISTICS

Families of high-frequency response curves for ten human ears, measured with the NRC progressive-wave source, are shown in Fig. 6. These measurements were made at eight angles of incidence in a coordinate system centered on the ear canal and oriented with respect to a horizontal line running from the base of the eye socket to the center of the ear canal. At 0°, therefore, sound waves approach the

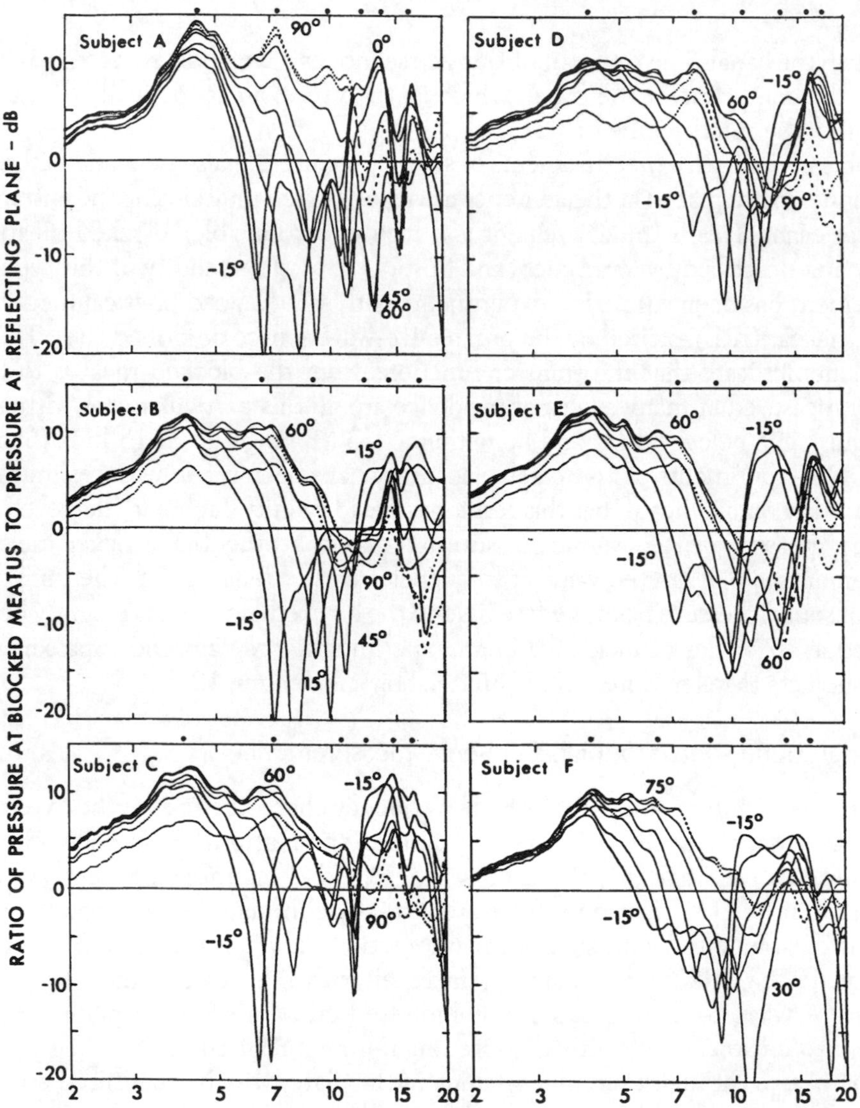

FIG. 6. Response curves for ten human ears (subjects A to J) measured at the blocked meatus position with progressive-wave source at eight angles of incidence in the circumaural plane (see diagram at J). Mean curves show average decibel levels. Solid points above graphs indicate individual and mean mode frequencies. Response curves for model ear IRE are also shown with mode frequencies indicated by arrows. [After Shaw, 1980, 1982b.] Figure 6 continues on p. 35.

ear from the front. At 90°, the approach is from above. The sound pressure was measured at the blocked meatus position with the probe tube orifice anchored to the center of a silicone rubber earplug carefully made to fit the individual ear. The measurements were normalized with respect to the sound pressure generated by the source at the center of a calibration plate representing the circumaural plane.

In every case, the response varies greatly with the angle of incidence, at frequencies greater than 5 kHz, and there are many idiosyncracies creating a wide variety of complex patterns that clearly distinguish one subject from another. In

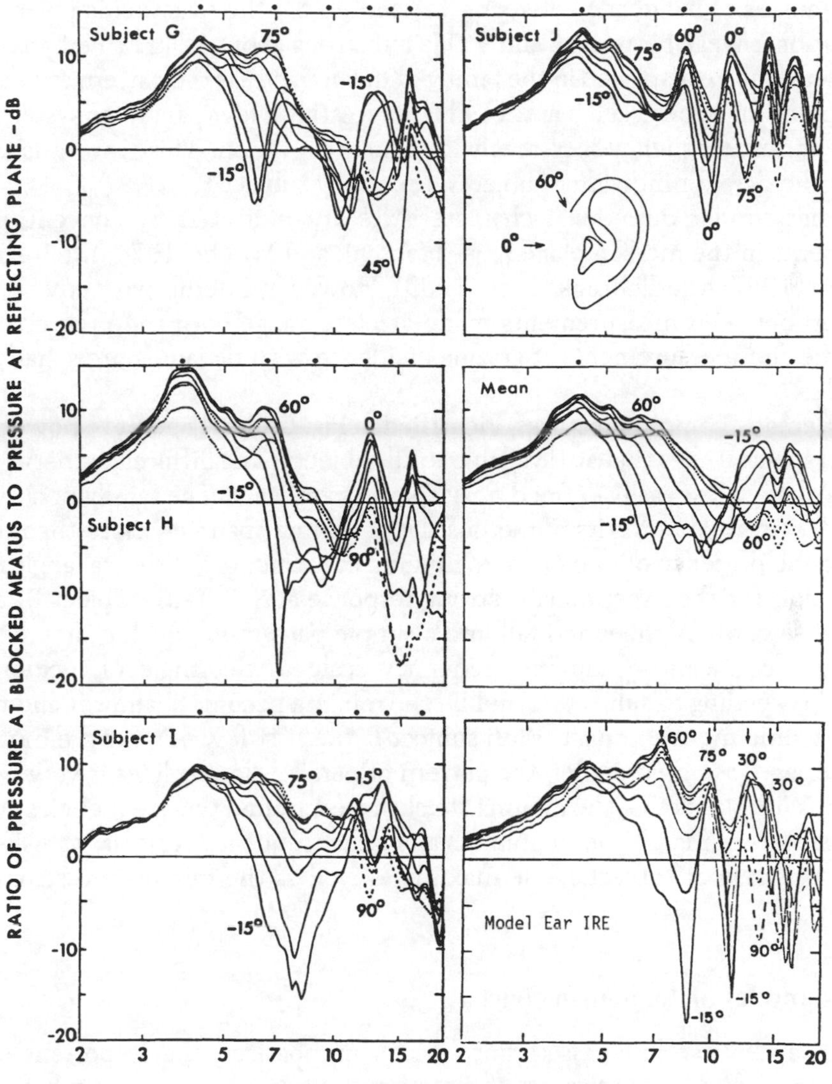

Fig. 6, to facilitate comparison, the ten sets of curves are presented as a sequence to be viewed in alphabetical order. The order of presentation was chosen to form an orderly progression in overall pattern within the 5- to 11-kHz band, where the intersubject differences are most sharply defined. It is, however, equally clear that all ten ears have much in common. These common characteristics are brought into focus in the 11th panel of Fig. 6, which shows mean curves constructed by averaging the ten sets of data. As can be seen, with sound waves approaching from high elevations (angles of incidence between 60° and 90°), the response is strong between 6 and 9 kHz but weak above 12 kHz. With sound waves approaching from the front (angles of incidence between −15° and +15°) the situation is reversed: The excitation is weak between 6 and 9 kHz but strong above 12 kHz. Perhaps the most striking feature displayed in the family of mean curves is the pattern of nearly parallel sloping lines, between 5 and 11 kHz, suggesting a low-pass filter system in which the cutoff frequency increases with source elevation. This feature is also present in the data for individual subjects, especially subject F.

Somewhat similar directional characteristics are indicated by conventional measurements in the median plane (e.g., Hebrank and Wright, 1974; Mehrgardt and Mellert, 1977; Middlebrooks *et al.*, 1989). However, a definitive study of the relationship between measurements made at close range with the progressive-wave source and measurements at grazing incidence with distant sources has yet to be made.

The systematic common features, identified in Fig. 6, clearly point to powerful broadband spectral cues that are available to all subjects. The differences between subjects, although less easily defined, may also be significant. The family of curves for subject A is notable for its numerous deep minima spanning more than one octave, for the presence of two or three minima in each curve at several angles of incidence, and for the exceptionally strong response at 90°. With subject B, the minima are fewer in number and fall into a simple pattern in which a "notch" in the response curve moves up the frequency scale as the angle of incidence increases. Proceeding to subjects C and D, the minima become shallower and the patterns become more compact. With subject F, the first few minima are muted in character and, as noted earlier, the pattern of parallel sloping lines is very well developed. With subject G, the minima are clustered around two frequencies and, with subject I, the "march" of the minima along the frequency scale has vanished. Finally, in the case of subject J, the maxima as well as the minima are strongly clustered.

A. Normal modes of the human concha

More than a century has passed since Mach emphasized the importance of high-frequency sounds as indicators of direction and argued that their timbre was affected by the pinna acting as an acoustical resonator (see Butler, 1975; Mach, 1959). The dimensions of the concha are consistent with this idea and the response curves presented in Fig. 6, which become highly divergent above 5 kHz, point specifically to transverse wave motion in the concha as the primary factor shaping the high-frequency directionality of the human ear. To pursue this idea experimentally, it was necessary to find ways of exciting the normal modes of the concha separately so that each could be properly identified and measured. This objective was not easily attained since the concha is a shallow open cavity with substantial radiation damping. As a consequence, its modes are broadly tuned and there is considerable overlapping of the tuning curves. Eventually, it was found that sufficient separation could generally be achieved by taking full advantage of the directional characteristics of the various modes.

The essential characteristics of the first six modes of the human concha under blocked meatus conditions are shown in Fig. 7 (Shaw, 1975a, 1980). The mode patterns, resonance frequencies, directions of maximum response, and response levels are average values based on data for the ten subjects featured in Fig. 6. In most cases, excitation was provided by the progressive-wave source, but on some occasions, a point source situated a few centimeters from the pinna was used. The sound pressure in the concha was measured with a probe microphone coupled to an oscilloscope. The normal modes were identified by searching for response maxima as the sound frequency and source position were varied. The pressure distributions across the base of the concha were then measured and the purity of each mode was tested by observing the residual values of sound pressure at the nodal surfaces. In most cases, minimum values no greater than 3% of the maximum values, with sharp reversals of phase across the nodal surfaces, were readily attained. Where necessary, the source position was readjusted to minimize the excitation of adjacent modes. The directions of maximum response were also noted and were confirmed and refined by referring to the families of response curves shown in Fig. 6. These curves were also used to estimate the levels of mode response.

The first mode (4.2 kHz) shown in Fig. 7 is a simple quarter-wavelength depth resonance with uniform sound pressure across the base of the concha (cf. Teranishi and Shaw, 1968). It is strongly excited from all directions. The other modes are essentially transverse and fall into two groups: a "vertical" pair (modes 2 and 3) and a "horizontal" triplet (modes 4, 5, and 6). Mode 2 has a single nodal surface near the crus helias separating pressure zones that are opposite in phase, one occupying the cavum and the other spreading through the cymba and fossa, as indicated by the signs (+ , –). This mode is best excited at a mean source angle of 68° (ten-subject range: 53° to 97°). Similarly, mode 3 is best excited at a mean source angle of 73° (range 57° to 105°), although its response is relatively weak in the majority of ears. This mode has two nodal surfaces, one slightly below the crus helias and the other at the junction between the cymba and fossa. In contrast, mode 4 (12.1 kHz) is strongly excited from the front at a mean source angle of –6° (range: –15° to +35°). It has three nodal surfaces and is characterized by positive pressure zones at the front of the cavum and cymba and negative zones at the rear and in the fossa. The pressure distributions for mode 5 (14.4 kHz) and mode 6 (16.7 kHz) are more complex with four and five nodal surfaces, respectively. However, in common with mode 4, both have pressure zones of alternating phase running horizontally through the cavum and both are strongly excited from the front with mean source angles of 8° for mode 5 (range: –7° to +15°) and 7° for mode 6 (range: –15° to +30°).

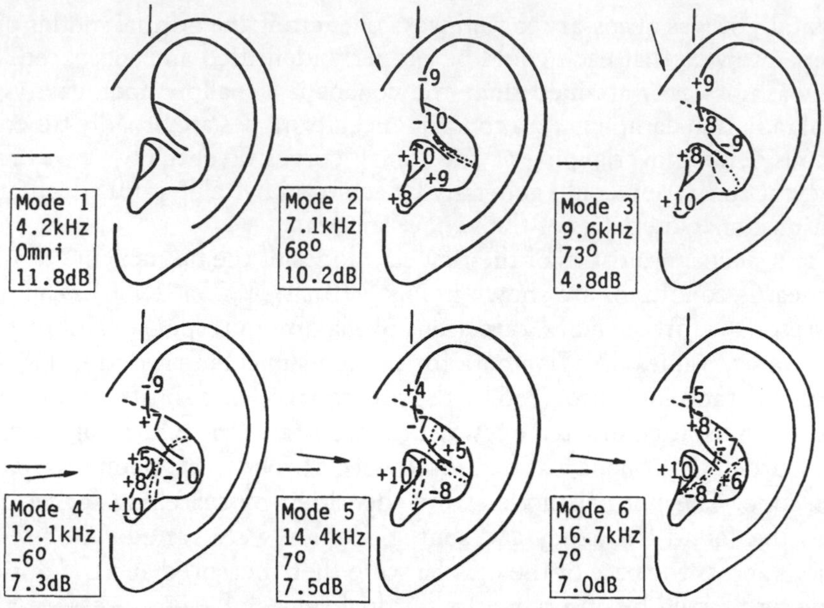

FIG. 7. Average characteristics of six modes under blocked meatus conditions based on data for ten subjects. Numerals indicate relative values of sound pressure, on a linear scale, measured at base of the concha. Signs (+/–) indicate relative phase (0°/180°). Broken and dotted lines show positions of nodal surfaces. Arrow indicates most favorable source direction. Data at left show mode number, mode frequency, most favorable source angle, and mode response. Mode 1 has uniform pressure across base of concha and is approximately omnidirectional. [After Shaw, 1975a.]

Mode 1 clearly has the characteristics of a monopole receiver, because its response is substantially omnidirectional and it has only one pressure zone. It is equally clear that the pressure distribution for mode 2 is essentially that of a vertical dipole. This is consistent with the free-field measurements made by Middlebrooks *et al.* (1989), who found two angular positions of high sensitivity in human subjects at 8 kHz, one above the horizontal plane and the other below (see Table I). On the other hand, apart from the negative zone in the fossa, the pressure distribution for mode 4 is essentially that of a horizontal dipole, which is also consistent with Middlebrooks *et al.*, who found two angular positions of high sensitivity at 12 kHz widely separated in azimuth and lying near the horizontal plane.

B. Physical models with matched modes

The normal modes of an acoustical system express the essential characteristics of the system in fundamental terms that may bring to light other significant characteristics. In particular, the analytical data presented in Fig. 7 provide a foundation for the systematic development of physical models that are acoustically similar to real human ears at high frequencies but markedly different in other respects. Such models are clearly of intrinsic interest and can also serve as investigative tools.

Panel A in Fig. 8 shows a family of response curves for a simple geometrical model in which the concha is represented by an inclined cylindrical cavity 22 mm in diameter and 10 mm in depth partially embedded in a rigid plane. This model is similar to that described by Teranishi and Shaw (1968), apart from the substitution of a plate of realistic shape to represent the pinna flange. The response curves were measured with the progressive-wave source described earlier and can be directly compared with the curves for human subjects presented in Fig. 6. This model is successful in the frequency range below 5 kHz, which is dominated by the depth mode of the concha (mode 1), but fails at higher frequencies. In contrast, panel B shows a comparable family of response curves for the more advanced model designated "IRE" (*inclined rectangular cavity*: Stage *E*). Here, the mode characteristics of the cavity representing the concha have been systematically modified to match those of the human ear. Some of the steps that were followed in the development of this model (Shaw, 1975a, 1980, 1982a) are indicated in Fig. 9.

There are two major deficiencies with the cylindrical concha: the absence of transverse modes below 11 kHz, and the lack of response at high angles of incidence. There is some improvement when the open cylinder is replaced by a cavity that is equal in volume (~3.8 cm^3) but rectangular in form as shown in Fig. 9b. The first-order transverse modes, both of which appear at 11 kHz with the cylindrical concha, are then resolved in the frequency domain and brought into alignment with the major and minor axes of the cavity, as seems to be required by the directionalities of the corresponding modes in the human ear. The first "horizontal" mode, which is comparable to mode 4 in Fig. 7, is readily tuned by adjusting the breadth of the cavity to 17 mm. However, it soon becomes apparent that any reasonable choice of cavity length places the first "vertical" mode at a frequency in the vicinity of 10 kHz, which is far greater than the average value of 7.1 kHz for mode 2 in the human ear. To bring the frequency down, it is necessary to erect a partial barrier, akin to the crus helias, that diverts the airflow to the rear of the cavity, thereby increasing its effective length. The triangular barrier shown in Fig. 9 reduces the resonance frequency of mode 2 by nearly 20% and enhances the sound pressure generated by that mode at the ear canal position. It also brings into play a second horizontal mode at approximately 14 kHz similar to mode 5 in Fig. 7.

At this stage of development, the model is still incomplete because it fails to produce a counterpart to mode 3. To correct this deficiency, it is necessary to provide an additional degree of freedom by adding a simple channel representing the fossa, as shown in Fig. 9d. This introduces a second vertical mode at approximately 10 kHz, as required, and further reduces the frequency of mode 2. The model now has just sufficient complexity to produce five modes with approximately the same mode frequencies, sound pressure distributions, most favorable angles of excitation, and levels of response at the blocked meatus as the corresponding modes of the human ear (modes 1 to 5 in Fig. 7).

Although the presence of a partial barrier is essential, its shape is not critical. The barrier used in the model ear IRE is rectangular in profile but shaped, as shown in Figs. 8 and 9e, to fit the circumference of the cylindrical canal (diameter

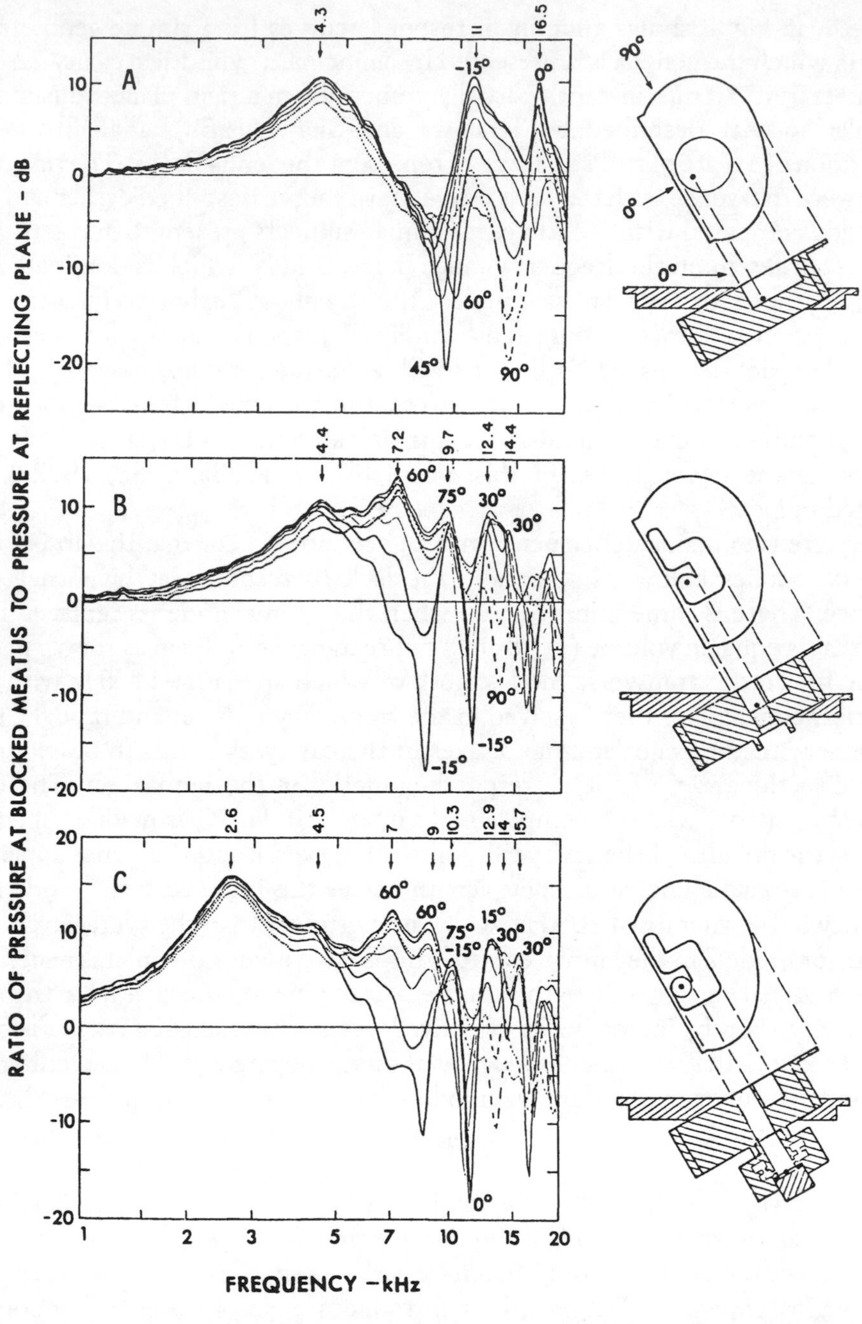

FIG. 8. Response curves for model ear at three stages of development measured with progressive-wave source at eight angles of incidence. Numerals indicate mode frequencies: (A) Cylindrical concha, blocked meatus position. (B) Model IRE, blocked meatus position. (C) Model IRE, eardrum position. Concha dimensions are given in Fig. 9. [After Shaw, 1980.]

7.5 mm; length ~25 mm). The final section of the canal is embodied in an experimental two-branch eardrum-impedance simulator, designated NRC Network D, that was developed at the National Research Council of Canada (Shaw, 1975a). A condenser microphone is placed at the eardrum position.

The blocked meatus response curves for the model IRE, shown in panel B of Fig. 8, are also presented in Fig. 6 in association with the ten sets of curves for human subjects. As can be seen, the directionality of the model ear is consistent with the common characteristics found in the ten human ears, and the distinctive features are generally within the bounds indicated by the intersubject differences.

Response curves for the model ear measured at the eardrum position are shown in panel C of Fig. 8. Opening the canal introduces additional degrees of freedom, which increase the number of resonances from five to eight, as indicated by the arrows above the graphs in panels B and C. In particular, the fundamental mode of the complete external ear comes into operation at 2.6 kHz. However, as noted earlier, the changes in response with angle of incidence measured at the eardrum position are almost identical with the changes measured at the blocked meatus. Hence, it can be inferred that the transverse pressure distributions in the concha, under free-field conditions, are substantially independent of the opening and closing of the ear canal.

The choice of a rectangular cavity as the foundation for the IRE model ear was inspired by the directionality observed in human ears. Later experiments indicated that other geometrical figures such as the circle, oval, semicircle, and triangle could also provide valid starting points for physical models with approximately human high-frequency characteristics. In every case, however, acceptable performance could only be achieved by placing a partial barrier, representing the crus helias, in the main cavity and adding a channel to represent the fossa.

C. Acoustical effects of pinna modification

In a classical psychophysical experiment, Bloch (1893) showed that the ability to localize sounds in the median plane was severely impaired when the upper parts of the pinnae were filled with cotton wool and the lobules were taped to the head. Similar findings have been reported by many others including Gardner and Gardner (1973), who found that localization accuracy progressively deteriorated as the cavities of the pinna were filled with a rubber compound. Physical measurements can shed much light on the acoustical effects of pinna modifications such as these.

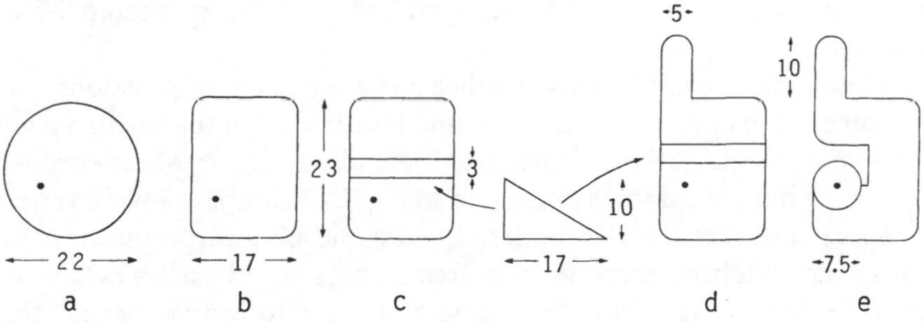

FIG. 9. Shapes of experimental cavities representing concha: (a) Cylinder (see Fig. 8A). (b) Rectangle. (c) Triangular barrier added to represent crus helias. (d) Channel added to represent fossa. (e) Model IRE: triangular barrier replaced by rectangular barrier enfolding entrance to canal (see Fig. 8B). Dots indicate blocked-meatus measurement positions. Dimensions: millimeters. Cavity depth: 10 mm.

In its original form, the manikin KEMAR was fitted with molded rubber pinnae made from impressions of the left and right ears of a carefully selected human subject (Burkhard and Sachs, 1975). Visually, these pinnae are so similar that each appears to mirror the other. It is therefore surprising to find that the families of blocked meatus response curves that they produce, when measured with the progressive-wave source, are markedly different (Shaw, 1982b). Indeed, the differences are sufficient that the patterns of response for the left and right pinnae might well be compared with those of subjects well separated in the Fig. 6 sequence.

When the tragal notch of KEMAR-L was bridged with a thin metal strip, the changes in response below 12 kHz were negligible apart from a small increase in the 4.4-kHz region (mode 1). Much more significant changes occurred when the fossa was filled with a malleable rubber compound. As noted earlier, the existence of mode 3 is dependent on the presence of the fossa, which also affects the frequency of mode 2. The fossa modification had a greater acoustical effect on KEMAR-L than on KEMAR-R, but in both cases the changes in response were at least as significant as the initial differences. A careful comparison of the two pinnae shows that KEMAR-L has more volume in the cymba, more volume near the tragal notch, less volume in the fossa, and a more slender connection between the fossa and cymba than KEMAR-R. These differences in geometry are qualitatively consistent with the patterns of response obtained with the fossa open and with the fossa closed (Shaw, 1982b).

Replica B, which is an imperfect copy of a human-ear replica studied earlier (Shaw and Teranishi, 1968), has an unusually broad and open concha, producing high-frequency response curves that are low in amplitude and well outside the performance range represented in Fig. 6. This pinna was modified by adding a crescent-shaped rubber "lip" that moved the rim of the concha inward by 5 mm at the rear tapering to 1 mm at the tragal notch and near the crus helias. With this modification, which decreased the open area of the concha by 20%, there were major increases in response at the mode frequencies and the sharpness of tuning became comparable with that of subject J in Fig. 6 (Shaw, 1982b). It can be inferred that the response of the external ear is strongly dependent on the "openness" of the concha. In particular, sharp tuning is to be expected where the concha volume is relatively large and the open area notably restricted by an inward-folding rim.

There have been many experimental studies and speculative discussions concerning the nature of the cues that underlie sound localization in the median plane (e.g., Hebrank and Wright, 1974; Butler and Belendiuk, 1977; Middlebrooks, 1992). The data for human subjects presented in Fig. 6 encompass a wide variety of patterns of response that are rich in detail and could be interpreted in many different ways. The wideband directional characteristics noted earlier, which are common to all subjects, are, however, robust. It is also worth noting that substantial acoustical differences may be present between pairs of pinnae that are very similar in appearance, as is the case with KEMAR-L and KEMAR-R. Such differences may be associated with minor aspects of pinna geometry such as the connection between the cymba and fossa. Considering that the pinna is a cartilaginous structure that is easily deformed, it seems highly probable that significant acoustical differences between pairs of pinnae are widespread if not universal. Further experimental work may be needed to determine whether interaural pinna disparity is, in fact, a significant factor in spatial hearing, as inferred by Searle, Braida, Davis, and Colburn (1976).

IV. EARS COUPLED TO EARPHONES

Realistic acoustic images external to the head can be created by sounds presented through earphones, provided that the waveforms generated at the two eardrums are carefully matched to those that would be generated in the free field (e.g., Blauert, 1983; Wightman, 1990). At present, this stringent requirement can only be met through the use of individual head-related transfer functions (HRTF). Probe microphones are first used to develop sets of data that define the transformation of sound pressure from the free field to the eardrums as functions of source direction. These sets of data are then used to make appropriate adjustments to the waveforms generated at the eardrums when the same subject is fitted with earphones. With this technique, which completely overrides the acoustical characteristics of the earphones, subjects are able to localize sounds presented through earphones at levels of accuracy that are only slightly inferior to those attainable in the free field (Wightman and Kistler, 1989a, 1989b). This method of treating earphone-presented sounds, although invaluable as a research tool, is probably too complex to be widely used in the creation of the diversity of virtual acoustical environments that now appear to be within reach (Acoustical Society of America, 1992). If this is so, then the intrinsic acoustical problems associated with earphone-presented sounds can hardly be avoided, elusive and troublesome though they may be.

When the external ear is coupled to an earphone, the free-field characteristics of the ear are replaced by very different characteristics that are dependent on the interaction between the individual earphone and the individual ear. The nature of this interaction varies greatly with the class of earphone, as can be seen in Fig. 10. In general, there is a low-frequency regime where the system can be described in terms of lumped acoustical elements and a high-frequency regime where wave effects are predominant (e.g., Shaw, 1974a). As the frequency increases, the transition between the two regimes can be said to commence when $\lambda/10$ becomes comparable with a characteristic dimension, ℓ, and can be considered complete

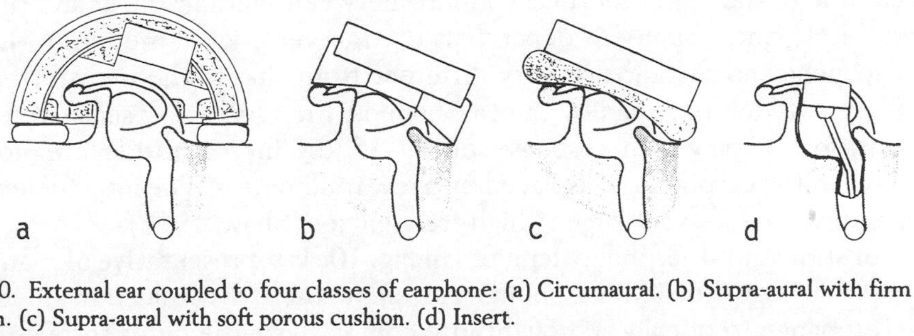

FIG. 10. External ear coupled to four classes of earphone: (a) Circumaural. (b) Supra-aural with firm airtight cushion. (c) Supra-aural with soft porous cushion. (d) Insert.

when $\lambda/4 \cong \ell$, where λ is the wavelength of sound. For practical purposes, the transition can be said to occur when $\lambda/6 \cong \ell$ or at a frequency $\nu \cong c/6\ell$, where c is the velocity of sound in air.

Contact with the pinna is avoided in the experimental circumaural earphone shown in Fig. 10a (Shaw and Thiessen, 1962). It comprises an outer cup sealed to the head by an airtight cushion and an inner cup, which supports a dynamic transducer and divides the enclosure into two parts connected by a ring of ports. Both cavities contain acoustically absorbent porous material. For this class of circumaural earphone, there are two characteristic dimensions, the cavity radius and the distance between the transducer and the eardrum. Both are approximately 40 mm, placing the transition frequency in the vicinity of 1.5 kHz. Below this frequency, the response is very well defined and the intersubject variations are small (Shaw, 1966). Between 1 and 5 kHz, the response measured at the eardrum tends to follow the primary resonance curve of the individual ear because the acoustical coupling between the ear and the transducer is comparatively weak. The response may, however, be greatly modified by the wave characteristics of the cavity that encloses the ear. As the frequency rises, the mode patterns in the cavity become increasingly complex and, above 5 kHz, the transverse modes of the concha also come into play, as in the free field. Unless the interactions between these wave systems are properly controlled, the intersubject and intrasubject variations in response between 5 and 10 kHz can be very large (Shaw, 1966; Møller, Hammershoi, Jensen, and Sørensen, 1995). The management of these factors presents formidable challenges in earphone design.

Close contact with the pinna is essential if the class of supra-aural earphone shown in Fig. 10b is to function as intended. This tightly coupled dynamic earphone, the TDH39/MX41AR, has a foam rubber cushion, which is sufficiently firm that it compresses the cartilaginous pinna, forming an imperfect seal. It is broadly representative of supra-aural earphones including conventional telephone receivers. In this case, the primary characteristic dimension is the distance between the face of the transducer and the eardrum, which is approximately 30 mm, placing the transition frequency in the vicinity of 2 kHz. Between 0.5 and 2 kHz, the response of this class of earphone is well defined and the intersubject and intrasubject variations in response are small. At lower frequencies, the response may vary by 5–15 dB depending on the airtightness of the seal and the rigidity of the cartilage. Between 1 and 5 kHz, the response measured at the eardrum is affected by, but does not follow, the primary resonance characteristics of the individual ear due to the tight acoustical coupling between the transducer and the ear. Beyond 5 kHz, the response is dependent on transverse wave motion in the compressed concha and fossa that is very different from that in the undistorted open ear. The excitation provided by the earphone is, therefore, very sensitive to earphone position. Changes in response of 10–15 dB in magnitude are not uncommon when the earphone is displaced by a few millimeters. The intersubject differences in response also are large at high frequencies (Shaw, 1966).

The class of supra-aural earphone depicted in Fig. 10c is representative of many current types of "high-fidelity" earphone. An unenclosed dynamic transducer with a low resonance frequency is brought into contact with the pinna through a soft porous cushion. Because most of the volume velocity generated by the transducer at low frequencies is vented through the cushion, the roll-off in response below 0.5 kHz is largely determined by the peripheral acoustic resistance of the cushion, which can, in principle, be kept under control and may be corrected by suitably shaping the transducer parameters. It would appear that the high-frequency characteristics of this earphone would also be highly dependent on the cushion parameters, especially the acoustic resistance presented to the transducer and the peripheral resistance and reactance bounding the enclosure. Informal reports suggest that the soft-cushion earphone may sometimes provide more reliable coupling than conventional supra-aural earphones. However, no systematic studies of the effects of the porous layer appear to have been undertaken, and it seems unlikely that the wave characteristics of this earphone are essentially different from those of conventional supra-aural earphones.

The characteristic dimension for the insert earphone shown in Fig. 10d is the distance between the tip of the ear mold and the center of the eardrum, which is approximately 12 mm, placing the transition frequency in the vicinity of 5 kHz. Assuming there is an airtight seal, the sound pressure generated at the eardrum, below the transition frequency, is determined by three elementary parameters: the volume of the inner portion of the ear canal ($\sim$500 mm^3), the input impedance at the eardrum, and the source impedance of the transducer. At higher frequencies, there is a simple standing wave system between the transducer and the eardrum. Below 1 kHz, the intersubject variations in response have a standard deviation of 1 dB rising to approximately 4 dB beyond 5 kHz (Sachs and Burkhard, 1972; see also Shaw, 1975b). The free-field resonance characteristics of the individual ears are, of course, eliminated when sounds are presented through insert earphones, but the response can be shaped with an electrical filter to match an appropriate standard curve such as the average diffuse-field response curve measured at the eardrum (see Fig. 3; e.g., Killion, 1993).

Finally, it should be noted that artificial ears and earphone couplers are designed to reproduce selected acoustical characteristics of the external ear, such as the input impedance presented to an earphone, but fail to deal with the complex wave effects that are predominant at high frequencies (e.g., Shaw, 1974a). These devices, although well adapted to the calibration of telephone receivers and audiometric earphones under standard conditions, shed no light on the special characteristics that may be desirable in earphones intended for use in the creation of virtual acoustical environments. Indeed, these characteristics have yet to be clearly defined. Perhaps they may include coupling with the external ear that (a) allows the response measured at the eardrum to follow the primary resonance curve of the individual ear and (b) minimizes the intersubject and intrasubject variations in response at other frequencies, especially above 5 kHz where the wave characteristics of the ear need to be taken into account. Undesirable spectral coloration could perhaps be minimized by choosing a reference curve based on the diffuse-field response measured at the eardrum.

REFERENCES

Acoustical Society of America (**1992**). "Virtual environments." Five special sessions, 124th Meeting of the ASA, J. Acoust. Soc. Am. **92**, 2331–2335, 2345–2347, 2375–2376, 2395–2396, 2437–2438.

Blauert, J. (**1983**). *Spatial Hearing* (MIT Press, Cambridge, MA).

Bloch, E. (**1893**). "Das binaurale Hören," Z. Ohrenheilk. **24**, 25–85. See: Butler, R. A. (1975).

Burkhard, M. D., and Sachs, R. M. (**1975**). "Anthropometric manikin for acoustic research," J. Acoust. Soc. Am. **58**, 214–222.

Butler, R. A. (**1975**). "Influence of the external and middle ear on auditory discriminations," in *Handbook of Sensory Physiology, Vol. V/2: Auditory System*, edited by W. D. Keidel and W. D. Neff (Springer-Verlag, Berlin), pp. 247–260.

Butler, R. A., and Belendiuk, K. (**1977**). "Spectral cues utilized in the localization of sound in the median sagittal plane," J. Acoust. Soc. Am. **61**, 1264–1269.

Gardner, M. B., and Gardner, R. S. (**1973**). "Problem of localization in the median plane: effect of pinnae cavity occlusion," J. Acoust. Soc. Am. **53**, 400–408.

Hebrank, J., and Wright, D. (**1974**). "Spectral cues used in the localization of sound on the median plane," J. Acoust. Soc. Am. **56**, 1829–1834.

Killion, M. C. (**1993**). Private communication. See also: Long (1993).

Killion, M. C., Berger, E. H., and Nuss, R. A. (**1987**). "Diffuse field response of the ear," J. Acoust. Soc. Am. **81**, Suppl. 1, S75.

Kistler, D. J., and Wightman, F. L. (**1992**). "A model of head-related transfer functions based on principal components analysis and minimum-phase reconstruction," J. Acoust. Soc. Am. **91**, 1637–1647.

Kuhn, G. F. (**1977**). "Model for the interaural time differences in the azimuthal plane," J. Acoust. Soc. Am. **62**, 157–167.

Kuhn, G. F. (**1987**). "Physical acoustics and measurements pertaining to directional hearing," in *Directional Hearing*, edited by W. A. Yost and G. Gourevitch (Springer-Verlag, New York), pp. 3–25.

Long, E. M. (**1993**). "Etymōtic Research ER-4 Earphones," Audio **77** (December), 78–81.

Mach, E. (**1959**). *The Analysis of Sensations*, translated by C. M. Williams and S. Waterlow (Dover Publications, New York), pp. 264–265. German editions: first (1885), fifth (1906).

Mehrgardt, S., and Mellert, V. (**1977**). "Transformation characteristics of the external human ear," J. Acoust. Soc. Am. **61**, 1567–1576.

Middlebrooks, J. C. (**1992**). "Narrow-band sound localization related to external ear acoustics," J. Acoust. Soc. Am. **92**, 2607–2624.

Middlebrooks, J. C., and Green, D. M. (**1990**). "Directional dependence of interaural envelope delays," J. Acoust. Soc. Am. **87**, 2149–2162.

Middlebrooks, J. C., Makous, J. C., and Green, D. M. (**1989**). "Directional sensitivity of sound pressure levels in the human ear canal," J. Acoust. Soc. Am. **86**, 89–108.

Møller, H., Hammershoi, D., Jensen, C. B., and Sørensen, M. F. (**1995**). "Transfer characteristics of headphones measured on human ears," J. Audio Eng. Soc. **43**, 203–216.

Møller, H., Sørensen, M. F., Hammershoi, D., and Jensen, C. B. (**1995**). "Head-related transfer functions of human subjects," J. Audio Eng. Soc. **43**, 300–321.

Oppenheim, A. V., and Schafer, R. W. (**1975**). *Digital Signal Processing* (Prentice Hall, Englewood Cliffs, NJ).

Rabbitt, R. D., and Friedrich, M. T. (**1991**). "Ear canal cross-sectional pressure distributions: Mathematical analysis and computation," J. Acoust. Soc. Am. **89**, 2379–2390.

Sachs, R. M., and Burkhard, M. D. (**1972**). Zwislocki Coupler Evaluation with Insert Earphones. Report 20022. Industrial Research Products, Inc., Elk Grove, IL.

Searle, C. L., Braida, L. D., Davis, M. F., and Colburn, H. S. (**1976**). "Model for auditory localization," J. Acoust. Soc. Am. **60**, 1164–1175.

Shaw, E. A. G. (**1966**). "Ear canal pressure generated by circumaural and supra-aural earphones," J. Acoust. Soc. Am. **39**, 471–479.

Shaw, E. A. G. (**1974a**). "The external ear," in *Handbook of Sensory Physiology, Vol. V/2: Auditory System*, edited by W. D. Keidel and W. D. Neff (Springer-Verlag, Berlin), pp. 455–490.

Shaw, E. A. G. (**1974b**). "Transformation of sound pressure level from the free field to the eardrum in the horizontal plane," J. Acoust. Soc. Am. **56**, 1848–1861.

Shaw, E. A. G. (**1975a**). "The external ear: New knowledge," in *Earmolds and Associated Problems, Proceedings of the Seventh Danavox Symposium*, edited by S. C. Dalsgaard, Scand. Audiol. (suppl. 5), pp. 24–50.

Shaw, E. A. G. (**1975b**). "Implications for hearing aid research," in *Earmolds and Associated Problems, Proceedings of the Seventh Danavox Symposium*, edited by S. C. Dalsgaard, Scand. Audiol. (suppl. 5), pp. 280–297.

Shaw, E. A. G. (**1980**). "The acoustics of the external ear," in *Acoustical Factors Affecting Hearing Aid Performance*, edited by G. A. Studebaker and I. Hochberg (University Park Press, Baltimore), pp. 109–124.

Shaw, E. A. G. (**1982a**). "1979 Rayleigh medal lecture: The elusive connection," in *Localization of Sound: Theory and Applications*, edited by R. W. Gatehouse (Amphora Press, Groton, CT), pp. 13–29.

Shaw, E. A. G. (**1982b**). "External ear response and sound localization," in *Localization of Sound: Theory and Applications*, edited by R. W. Gatehouse (Amphora Press, Groton, CT), pp. 30–41.
Shaw, E. A. G. (**1988**). "Diffuse field response, receiver impedance, and the acoustical reciprocity principle," J. Acoust. Soc. Am. **84**, 2284–2287.
Shaw, E. A. G., and Teranishi, R. (**1968**). "Sound pressure generated in an external-ear replica and real human ears by a nearby point source," J. Acoust. Soc. Am. **44**, 240–249.
Shaw, E. A. G., and Thiessen, G. J. (**1962**). "Acoustics of circumaural earphones," J. Acoust. Soc. Am. **34**, 1233–1246.
Shaw, E. A. G., and Vaillancourt, M. M. (**1985**). "Transformation of sound pressure level from the free field to the eardrum presented in numerical form," J. Acoust. Soc. Am. **78**, 1120–1123.
Stinson, M. R. (**1985**). "The spatial distribution of sound pressure within scaled replicas of the human ear canal," J. Acoust. Soc. Am. **78**, 1596–1602.
Stinson, M. R., and Lawton, B. W. (**1989**). "Specification of the geometry of the human ear canal for the prediction of sound-pressure level distribution," J. Acoust. Soc. Am. **85**, 2492–2503.
Teranishi, R., and Shaw, E. A. G. (**1968**). "External ear acoustic models with simple geometry," J. Acoust. Soc. Am. **44**, 257–263.
Wightman, F. L. (**1990**). "Creating three-dimensional auditory space with headphones," J. Acoust. Soc. Am. **87**, 421.
Wightman, F. L., and Kistler, D. J. (**1989a**). "Headphone simulation of free-field listening. I: Stimulus synthesis," J. Acoust. Soc. Am. **85**, 858–867.
Wightman, F. L., and Kistler, D. J. (**1989b**). "Headphone simulation of free-field listening. II: Psychophysical validation," J. Acoust. Soc. Am. **85**, 868–878.
Yamaguchi, Z., and Sushi, N. (**1956**). "Real ear response of receivers," J. Acoust. Soc. Jpn. **12**, 8–13 (in Japanese).

Chapter 3

Elevation Dependence of the Interaural Transfer Function

Richard O. Duda
San Jose State University

(Received December 1993; revised September 1994)

This chapter summarizes the results of experiments in estimating the azimuth and elevation of a sound source from the interaural intensity difference (IID). IID data were obtained for two cases—measurements of the KEMAR manikin made by the author, and measurements of a human (subject SLV) made at the University of Wisconsin. Results obtained for the two cases are very similar. For azimuths out to about 70 degrees, the scale of the IID surface is directly related to azimuth, and the shape of the surface is directly related to elevation. Maximum-likelihood estimates of azimuth and elevation using IID alone have an accuracy close to that of humans. However, when azimuth and elevation are estimated using a model based on SLV and inputs from KEMAR, performance is greatly degraded. This result confirms the importance of customizing head-related transfer functions to obtain veridical localization perception.

INTRODUCTION

The physical time and intensity cues for sound localization are expressed in the frequency domain by the well-known head-related transfer function (HRTF), which varies not only with the angular frequency ω, but also with the range (r), azimuth (θ), and elevation (ϕ) of the source (Blauert, 1983). In particular, the binaural cues for localization arise from the fact that the head-related transfer functions $H_L(\omega, r, \theta, \phi)$ for the left ear and $H_R(\omega, r, \theta, \phi)$ for the right ear are different. If $X(\omega)$ is the Fourier transform of the sound pressure waveform of the source and $X_L(\omega, r, \theta, \phi)$ and $X_R(\omega, r, \theta, \phi)$ are the Fourier transforms of the sound pressure levels at the left and right eardrums, respectively, then

$$X_L(\omega, r, \theta, \phi) = H_L(\omega, r, \theta, \phi)\, X(\omega) \qquad (1)$$

and

$$X_R(\omega, r, \theta, \phi) = H_R(\omega, r, \theta, \phi)\, X(\omega) \qquad (2)$$

The ratio $H = H_R/H_L$ is the so-called *interaural transfer function* (ITF). Its magnitude $A(\omega)$ (measured in dB) is the interaural intensity difference (IID), and the derivative of its phase is the interaural time difference (ITD) or, more precisely, the interaural group-delay time difference $Tg(\omega)$:

$$A(\omega) = 20\log_{10}\left|\frac{H_R(\omega)}{H_L(\omega)}\right| \tag{3}$$

and

$$T_g(\omega) = \frac{\partial}{\partial\omega}\angle\frac{H_R(\omega)}{H_L(\omega)} \tag{4}$$

If the source has a broadband spectrum, and if there are no other sound sources active, the ITF can be obtained from the ratio of the transforms of the signals reaching the two ears, which has the important property of being independent of the specific shape of the source spectrum:

$$H(\omega,r,\theta,\phi) = \frac{H_R(\omega,r,\theta,\phi)}{H_L(\omega,r,\theta,\phi)} = \frac{H_R(\omega,r,\theta,\phi)X(\omega)}{H_L(\omega,r,\theta,\phi)X(\omega)} = \frac{X_R(\omega)}{X_L(\omega)} \tag{5}$$

The ITF exposes binaural difference cues for sound localization. For a perfectly symmetric head, $H = 1$ for any point in the midsagittal plane. Thus, the ITF provides little or no information about the location of sources exactly in that plane. However, away from the midsagittal plane, the ITF provides very significant localization information.

Now it is well known that there are both monaural and binaural cues for sound localization.[1] It is commonly said that the main cues for azimuth are binaural (the ITD at low frequencies and the IID at high frequencies), whereas the main cues for elevation are monaural (e.g., spectral shape cues that result from pinna diffraction). This is a reasonable first approximation if the source is constrained to the horizontal plane when considering azimuth variation, and to the midsagittal plane when considering elevation variation. However, the general situation is more complex. In particular, whereas interaural cues for elevation are probably insignificant in the midsagittal plane, this is not the case even a few degrees away from this plane.[2]

---

[1]The classic book by Blauert (1983) provides a systematic and thorough exposition of the various sound localization cues; for an excellent review of subsequent research, see Middlebrooks and Green (1991).

[2]Middlebrooks, Makous, and Green (1989) showed that above 8 kHz the IID varies significantly with elevation, and observed that the IID could provide important cues for elevation. Carlile and Pralong (1994) illuminated this further with their study of perceptually relevant characteristics of the HRTF. To exploit the binaural cues, broadband signals are needed (Middlebrooks, 1992). Some researchers believe that so-called pinna disparities provide significant elevation cues even in the midsagittal plane (Butler, 1969; Searle *et al.*, 1975), whereas others doubt their importance (Herbrank and Wright, 1974; Morimoto and Nomachi, 1983). Our experimental measurements indicate that the pinna disparity cues exist but are relatively weak, and we focus our attention on points away from the midsagittal plane.

This chapter concerns the variation of the IID with frequency, azimuth, and elevation. We begin by examining experimental measurements taken using an interaural-polar-axis coordinate system. Using this coordinate system, we show that a Fourier series expansion helps to separate the azimuth-dependent and the elevation-dependent factors. We then use a maximum-likelihood procedure to provide "optimal" estimates of azimuth and elevation. Finally, we present experimental results to show that both azimuth and elevation can be extracted from the IID for a single broadband source in an anechoic environment with an accuracy comparable to human performance.

I. THE KEMAR ITF

A. The IID and the ITD

Although linear time-domain and frequency-domain methods are mathematically equivalent, experimental HRTF measurements are typically done using frequency-domain techniques (Mehrgardt and Mellert, 1977; Blauert, 1983; Pösselt *et al.*, 1986; Wightman, Kistler and Perkins, 1987; Middlebrooks, Makous and Green, 1989; Wightman and Kistler, 1989; Møller *et al.*, 1995). Although frequency-domain methods provide high signal-to-noise ratios, the presence of unavoidable room echoes introduces comb-filter ripples in the spectrum, and the "brick-wall" or other noncausal filters frequently used before inversion introduce precursor artifacts in the time domain. These artifacts make it difficult to interpret the short-time behavior of the impulse response. To avoid these problems, we decided to measure the head-related impulse response directly in the time domain (Duda, 1991). The measurements were made on a KEMAR manikin using the so-called standard or small pinnae (model DB-061) and equipped with Etymōtic Research ER-11 microphones. Pulses of 10 μs duration were used to drive a tweeter located 0.9 m from the center of the head. The tweeter was systematically positioned at some 231 different locations essentially evenly spaced over the right hemisphere. The microphone signals were sampled at 44.1 kHz and digitized with 16-bit precision. The responses to 20 pulses were averaged to form one record. Each record was limited to 128 samples, for a corresponding duration of about 2.9 ms. The ITF was estimated from ratio of the 128-point fast Fourier Transforms (FFTs) of the measured impulse responses, which yielded a frequency resolution of about 345 Hz.

The tweeter limited the lowest usable frequency to about 1.5 kHz, producing a high-pass filtered version of the actual response. Although this was a drawback, the resulting pulses had very short rise times and provided good localization information. Although free-field measurements were available to correct for the frequency response of the transducers, any common multiplicative compensation has no effect on the ratio of the HRTFs, and thus compensation was not needed for estimation of the ITF.

The location of the sound source was recorded using a single-pole, head-centered spherical coordinate system whose polar axis coincided with the interaural axis (see Fig. 1). In this coordinate system, a surface of constant elevation is a

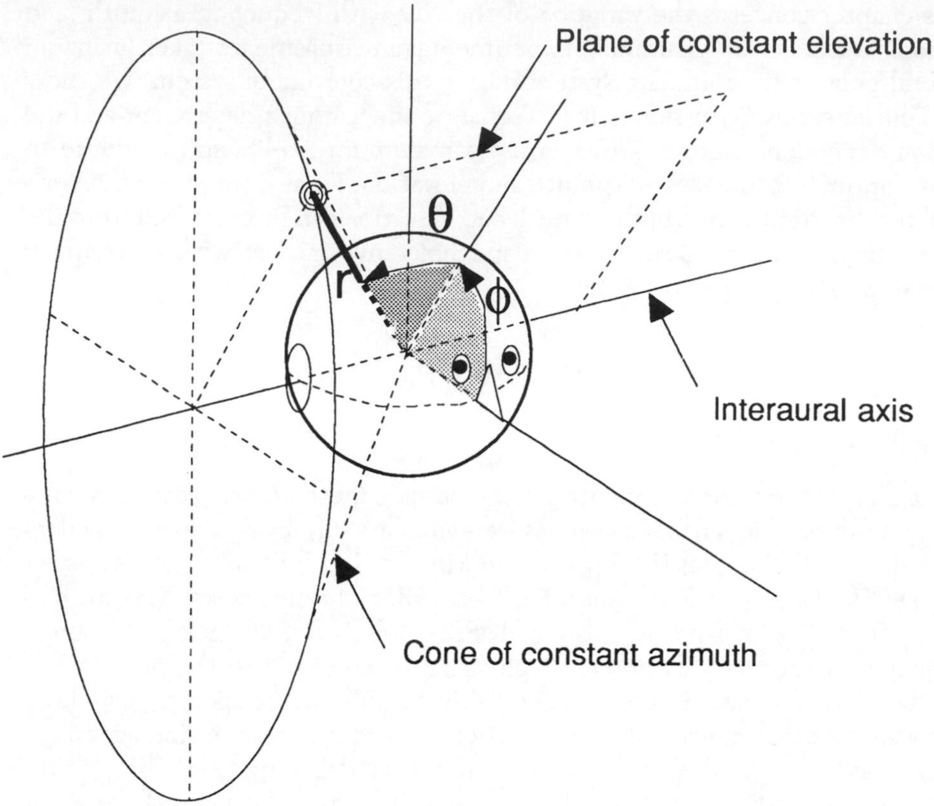

FIG. 1. The head-centered, interaural-polar spherical coordinate system used to specify the location of a sound source. With these coordinates, the interaural time difference is approximately constant on a cone of constant azimuth.

half-plane passing through the interaural axis, and a surface of constant azimuth is a cone whose axis is the interaural axis. The azimuth angle θ is restricted to the interval $-90° \leq \theta \leq 90°$, whereas the elevation angle ranges through a full 360° interval. With these coordinates, front/back reversal is related to elevation, not azimuth, with $\theta = 0°$, $\phi = 0°$ for a source directly ahead, and $\theta = 0°$, $\phi = 180°$ for a source directly behind. As Searle *et al.* (1975) and Morimoto and Aokata (1984) have noted, this coordinate system has the great advantage that the cones of constant azimuth are roughly the same as the loci of constant ITD, which are Woodworth's "cones of confusion." This property significantly simplifies the analysis of the measurements.

Figure 2 shows the IID and ITD for a typical case ($\theta = 30°$, $\phi = 0°$). These responses display several interesting features. First, the rapid decrease in both the left and right amplitude responses below 2 kHz is due to the limited low-frequency response of the tweeter. In principle, the tweeter limitations should have no effect on the interaural response. Indeed, this is true in the 1.8 kHz to 18 kHz frequency range where the signal levels are well above the noise. However, below about 1.8 kHz or above about 18 kHz, the signal levels drop to the point where noise becomes significant, and Eq. (5) is no longer valid. Thus, in the remainder of this chapter we window the spectrum, effectively ignoring the IID outside the 1.8-kHz to 18-kHz band.

In the frequency range between about 2 kHz and 6 kHz, the IID exhibits the steady increase that is characteristic of head shadow. However, there is a prominent peak around 7 kHz and a prominent notch around 11 kHz. The 7-kHz peak is clearly due to a notch in the left-ear response, and the 11-kHz notch is due to a notch in the right-ear response. As is well known, both of these notches are due to pinna diffraction. Although the magnitudes of some spectral extrema are quite large, the bandwidths can be too narrow to be perceptually significant.

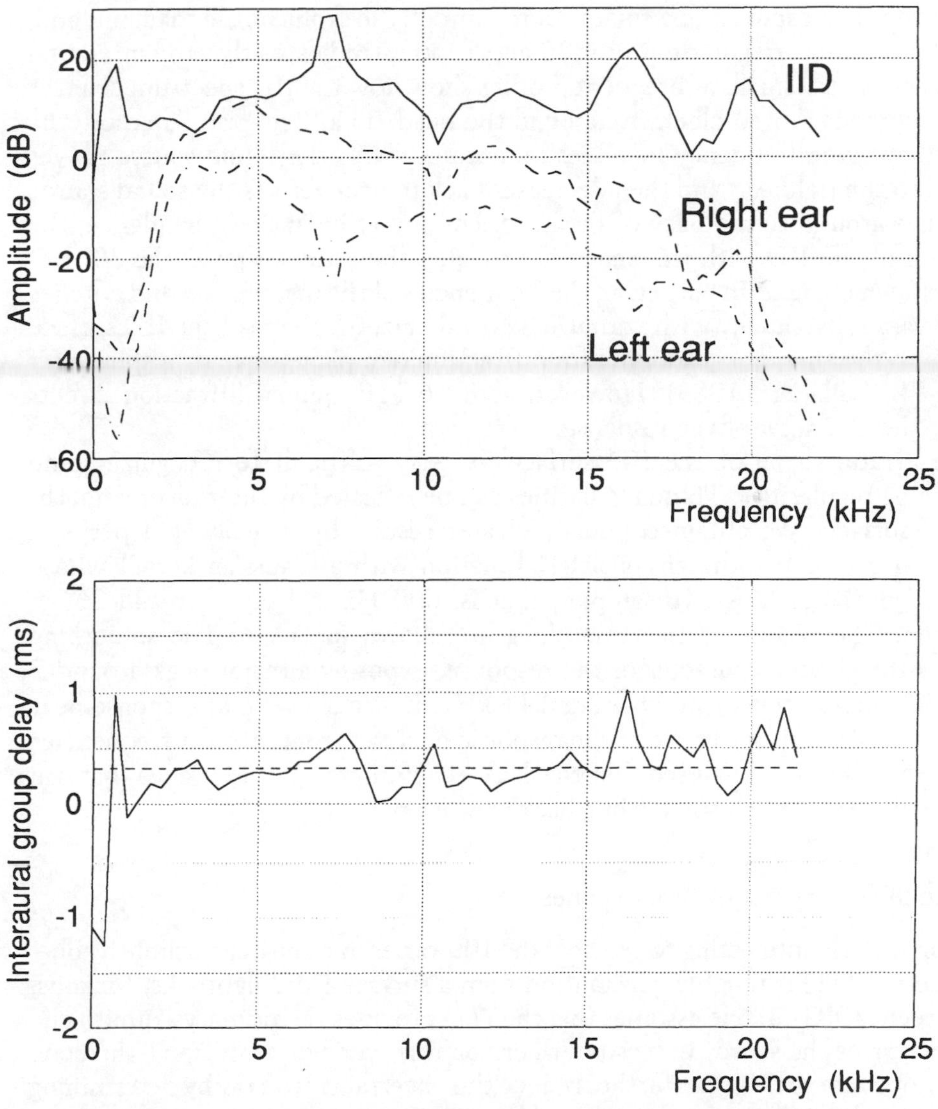

FIG. 2. Measured KEMAR amplitude and group-delay responses for 30° azimuth and 0° elevation. Note how the left-ear "pinna notch" produces a peak in the IID around 7 kHz. Note also that at frequencies below 1.8 kHz or above 18kHz, the signal levels are too low to obtain valid IID and ITD measurements.

In the 1.8-kHz to 18-kHz range, the ITD fluctuates between 0 and 1 ms, with an average around 0.35 ms. Although the differentiation process causes the ITD to be noisier than the IID, the fluctuations correlate with the locations of the peaks and notches in the IID spectrum. These general characteristics are seen at most of the other azimuths and elevations.

B. The IID in the Horizontal Plane

In general, both the IID and the ITD vary with ω and with the spherical coordinates r, θ, and ϕ. The variation of the IID in the horizontal plane for frequencies from 1.8 kHz to 18 kHz is shown in Fig. 3. The frequency profile at the bottom corresponds to a sound source directly in front of the manikin, and, except for minor irregularities near 10 and 17 kHz, indicates that the interaural difference is very small. Subsequent profiles show how the IID spectrum changes as the source is moved clockwise around the head. To a first approximation, the IID at any given frequency increases monotonically as the sound source moves around to the right ear, and then decreases back to near zero as the sound source continues around to the back of the head. For any given angle of incidence, the variation of the IID with frequency has roughly the same shape as the 30° IID curve shown in Fig. 2. In particular, the frequencies of the major peaks and notches do not vary substantially with azimuth. Below 6 kHz, the shape of the IID surface is close to the theoretical solution for diffraction of a plane wave by a sphere (cf Fig. 2.24 of Blauert, 1983). However, above 6 kHz, pinna diffraction effects change the character of the response.

The erratic shape of the IID surface makes it difficult to recognize some underlying regularities. These regularities can be revealed by filtering or smoothing the surface. We obtained visually clearer results by convolving a periodic extension of the two-dimensional IID function with a Gaussian kernel whose standard deviation was two samples, that is, 690 Hz in frequency and 26° in elevation. The results of this smoothing are shown in Fig. 4. The smoothing clarifies the general character of the response, exposing a major peak around 7 kHz and the subsequent notch around 11 kHz. It also shows that response near the back is not a mirror image of the response near the front, even at frequencies as low as 4 kHz. We shall see that this lack of symmetry provides cues that can help resolve the troublesome front/back confusion.

C. The IID on constant-azimuth cones

It is particularly interesting to see how the IID varies in a constant-azimuth cone, because the ITD is roughly constant on such a surface (Middlebrooks, Makous, and Green, 1989). If one assumes that the ITD provides the primary azimuth cue and constrains the source to be somewhere on this "cone of confusion," then one might hope that the IID can further reduce the uncertainty to a ray by determining the source elevation.

Figure 5 shows the smoothed IID values for a 40°-azimuth cone, with elevation values in 10° increments from –90° to +230°. For any fixed elevation, the IID

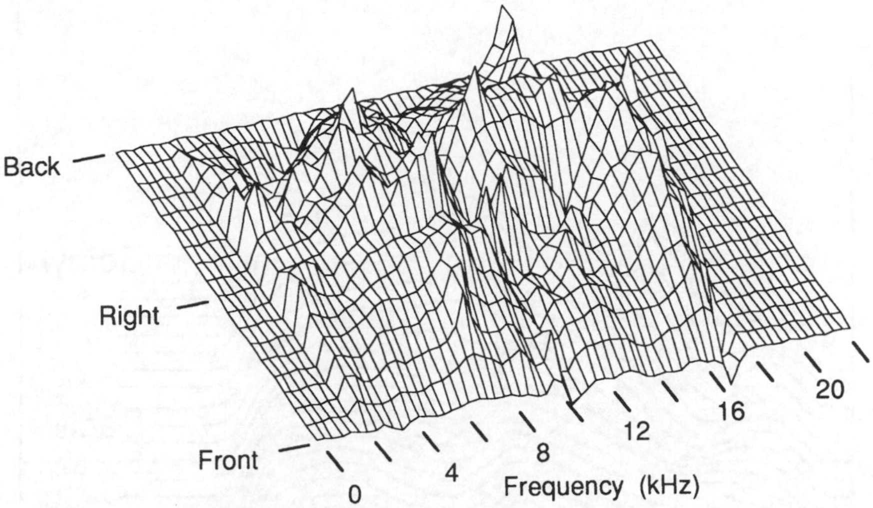

FIG. 3. Variation of the measured KEMAR IID as the source is moved in the horizontal plane. Peak amplitudes in this surface are approximately 35 dB. The symmetry of the KEMAR manikin is reflected in the virtual absence of interaural differences when the source is directly in front or directly in back.

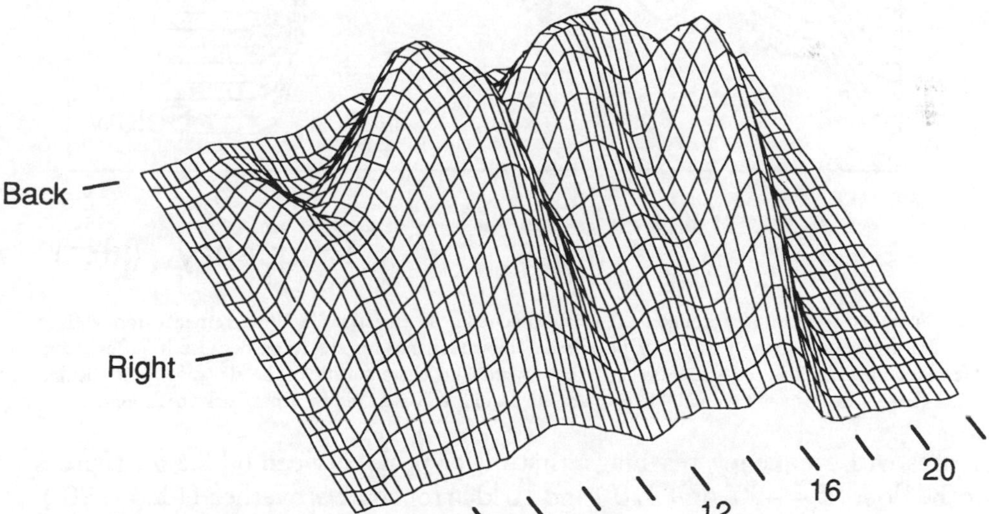

FIG. 4. Results of smoothing the KEMAR data in Fig. 3. Note that the frequencies for extrema do not vary significantly with azimuth. This is consistent with Eq. (11), which says that the IID varies approximately sinusoidally with azimuth. Except for a band of frequencies around 13 kHz, this is a useful approximation.

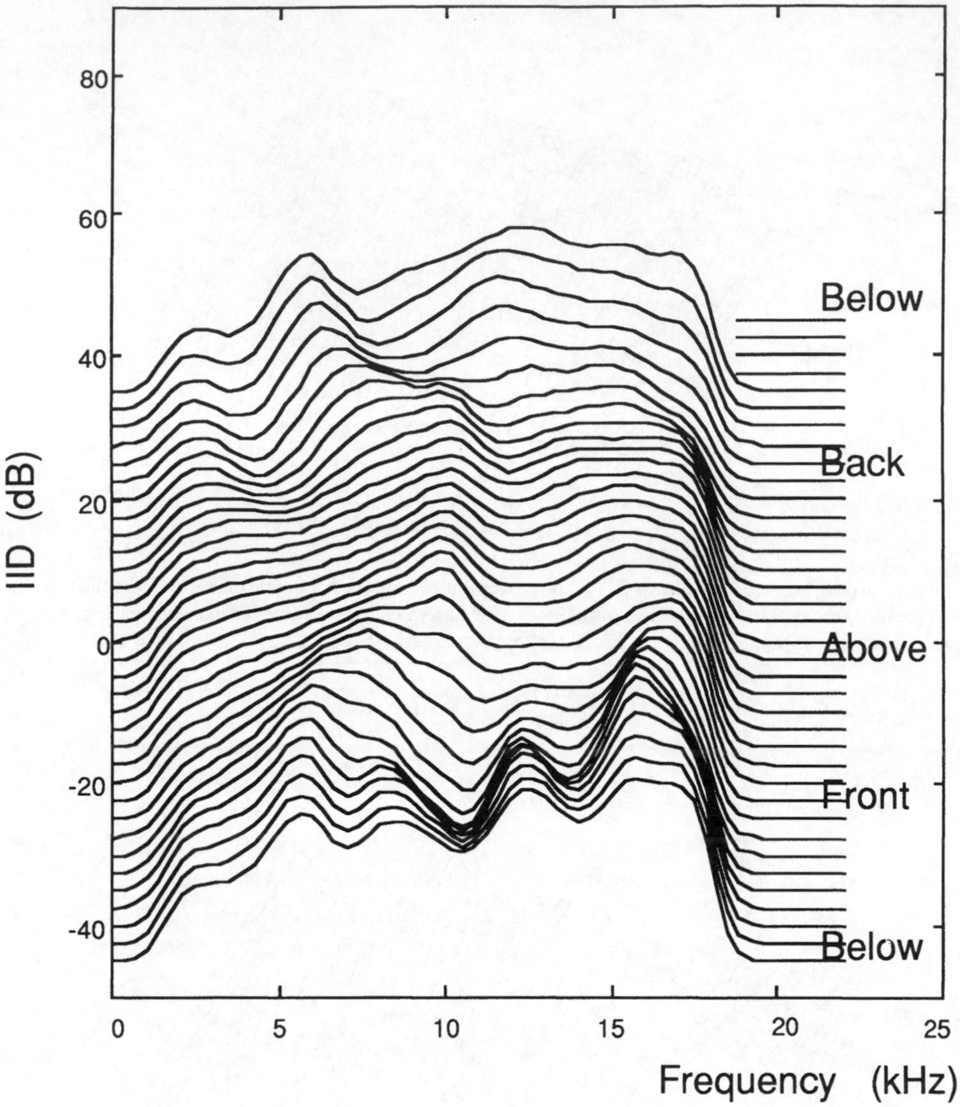

FIG. 5. Smoothed KEMAR IID around a 40°-azimuth cone for 33 elevations in 10° increments from –90° to +230°. The frequency of the first major peak is an ambiguous cue for elevation, because it suffers from front/back confusion. However, the entire shape of any profile is characteristic of the elevation. In particular, note that the relative response around 4 kHz or around 11 kHz serves to resolve front/back confusions.

increases with frequency, reaching a first major peak between 6 kHz for sources near the floor ($\phi = -90°$ or $+270°$) and 10 kHz for sources overhead ($\phi = +90°$). Although there is a clear correspondence between the frequency of this first major peak and the elevation angle, the correspondence is not one-to-one; there are two elevation angles for any value of peak frequency—one in the front and one in the back. Thus, other features are needed to resolve this front/back confusion.

Because the IID is not symmetric about $\phi = 90°$, there certainly is information available to make a front/back discrimination. In particular, some of this information exists at fairly low frequencies. The IID in the front is significantly larger than the IID in the back for frequencies around 4 kHz. In addition, the IID in the front is significantly smaller than the IID in the back for frequencies around 11 kHz. We have no evidence that the combination of the frequency of the first major peak and the relative responses around 4 and 11 kHz are the cues that humans actually use to determine elevation. However, it is clear that the shape of the IID spectrum—which is independent of the source spectrum—contains enough information to determine the elevation if the azimuth is known.

We conclude this qualitative examination of the KEMAR IID data by considering how the IID frequency/elevation surface varies with azimuth. Figure 6 shows a perspective view of that surface for $\theta = 40°$ that has been marked to show the "elevation ridge" and the 4-kHz and 11-kHz "front/back basins." Figure 7 shows the same view for azimuths ranging from 0° to 60°. Rather remarkably, the basic shape of all of these surfaces is roughly the same. Although the global maximum value of the IID varies directly with azimuth, the shape features (such as the frequency of the first major peak or the relative responses around 4 kHz and 11 kHz) appear to be very similar for all azimuths. We now use a Fourier series expansion to obtain a quantitative expression of these results.

II. FOURIER SERIES EXPANSION OF THE IID

Mathematically, the interaural amplitude response $A(\omega, \theta, \phi)$ is just a function of three variables, and its characteristics can be illuminated by any of a number of approximation techniques. Several researchers have employed a principal components analysis (or, equivalently, a Karhunen–Loève expansion) to obtain approximate representations (Martens, 1987; Kistler and Wightman, 1992; Chen, Van Veen, and Hecox, 1993). All of these studies examined the HRTF rather than the ITF. Where the first two studies addressed the expansion of the log amplitude spectrum, the third performed an expansion of the complex HRTF itself.[3]

Although principal components analysis is effective in addressing the random variations in the transfer functions, it does not explicitly account for geometrical characteristics. In particular, it is physically evident that $A(\omega, \theta, \phi)$ is periodic in θ and ϕ (or can be extended so as to be periodic), but principal components analysis does not exploit this periodicity. In contrast, through its use of periodic basis functions, a Fourier series expansion accounts for periodicity directly. Furthermore, the integration that is involved in finding the Fourier coefficients is also effective in reducing random irregularities.

In the coordinate system we use, we normally restrict the azimuth to the interval $(-\pi/2, \pi/2)$ and restrict the elevation to the interval $(-\pi/2, 3\pi/2)$.

---

[3]Physically, if we use a cascade model for H, we are led to a product representation $H \approx H_1 H_2 \cdots H_n$, so that $\log|H| \approx \log|H_1| + \log|H_2| + \cdots + \log|H_n|$. Thus, an expansion of the log amplitude implicitly corresponds to using a cascade model. Alternatively, if we use a multipath model for H, we are led to an additive representation $H \approx H_1 + H_2 + \cdots + H_n$, so that an expansion of the complex HRTF implicitly corresponds to using a multipath model. In reality, both cascade and multipath phenomena exist, and it would seem that an ideal representation should combine both methods. In this chapter, we work with the log amplitude spectrum, and thus tacitly use a cascade model.

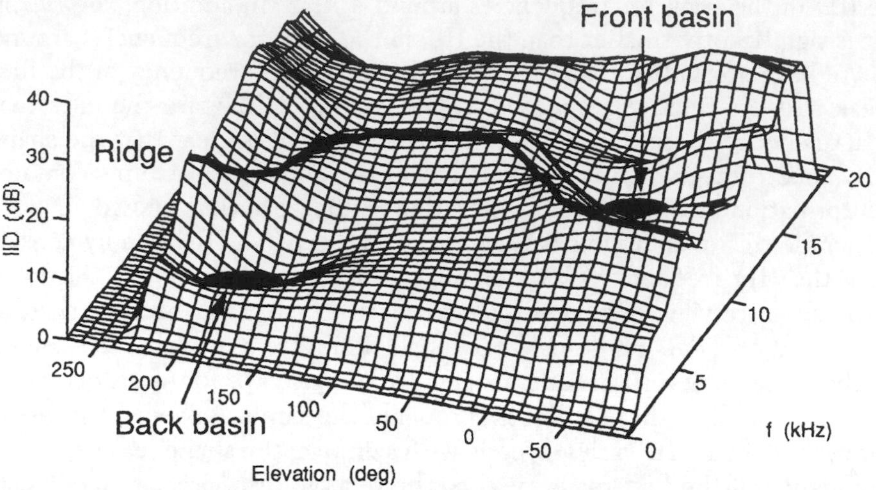

FIG. 6. Surface plot of the KEMAR IID for 40° azimuth. The "ridge" and "basin" features are conspicuous indicators of elevation.

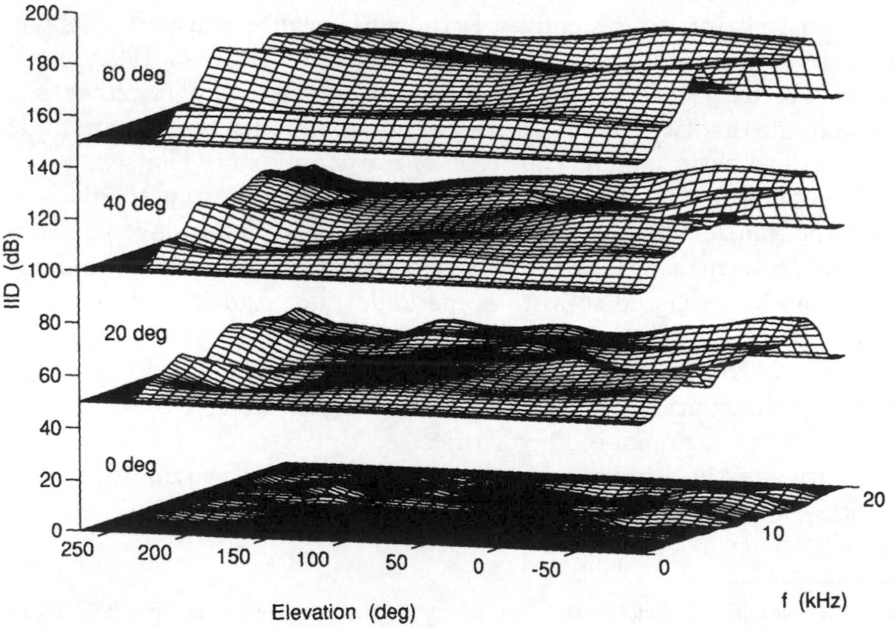

FIG. 7. KEMAR IID surface plots for four different azimuths. The IID surface for 0° azimuth is essentially flat. To a first approximation, although the scale of the IID surface changes with azimuth, its shape does not. (This approximation breaks down for azimuths near 90°, where the surface stretches out and becomes cylindrical.)

Although $A(\omega, \theta, \phi)$ is clearly periodic in ϕ, it has to be extended to be periodic in θ. When $\pi/2 < \theta < \pi$, it might seem natural to extend the domain of θ by using the value of A at the corresponding point on the sphere: $A(\omega, \theta, \phi) = A(\omega, \pi - \theta, \pi + \phi)$. However, this choice is not necessary. In fact, it is advantageous to extend A to produce a symmetric function. To be specific, the following symmetric extension A_e has the useful property that its Fourier expansion in terms of θ contains only even harmonics of the cosine terms and only odd harmonics of the sine terms:

$$A_e(\omega,\theta,\phi) = \begin{cases} A(\omega,-\pi-\theta,\phi), & \text{if } -\pi \le \theta < -\pi/2; \\ A(\omega,\theta,\phi) & \text{if } -\pi/2 \le \theta < \pi/2; \\ A(\omega,\pi-\theta,\phi), & \text{if } \pi/2 \le \theta < \pi \end{cases} \tag{6}$$

Because $A = A_e$ when $-\pi/2 \le \theta < \pi/2$, we obtain the following expansion:

$$A(\omega,\theta,\phi) = a_0 + \sum_{k\,\text{even}} a_k \cos k\theta + \sum_{k\,\text{odd}} b_k \sin k\theta \tag{7}$$

where

$$\begin{aligned} a_0(\omega,\phi) &= \frac{1}{\pi}\int_{-\frac{\pi}{2}}^{\frac{\pi}{2}} A(\omega,\theta,\phi)\, d\theta \\ a_k(\omega,\phi) &= \frac{2}{\pi}\int_{-\frac{\pi}{2}}^{\frac{\pi}{2}} A(\omega,\theta,\phi) \cos k\theta \, d\theta \quad , \quad k \text{ even and positive} \\ b_k(\omega,\phi) &= \frac{2}{\pi}\int_{-\frac{\pi}{2}}^{\frac{\pi}{2}} A(\omega,\theta,\phi) \sin k\theta \, d\theta \quad , \quad k \text{ odd and positive} \end{aligned} \tag{8}$$

Because these coefficients are periodic in ϕ, we could expand them in turn and obtain a double Fourier series representation. However, we stop at this point and consider the behavior of the coefficients $a_k(\omega, \phi)$ and $b_k(\omega, \phi)$.

In the important special case where the head is bilaterally symmetric, A is an odd function of θ, and all of the cosine terms drop out. In that case, Eqs. (7) and (8) simplify further to

$$A(\omega,\theta,\phi) = \sum_{k\,\text{odd}} b_k \sin k\theta \quad , \tag{9}$$

where

$$b_k(\omega,\phi) = \frac{4}{\pi}\int_{0}^{\frac{\pi}{2}} A(\omega,\theta,\phi) \sin k\theta \, d\theta \quad , \quad k \text{ odd and positive} \tag{10}$$

TABLE I. The average absolute error in a Fourier series approximation of the IID decreases monotonically with the number of terms in the expansion. Only a few terms are needed for a useful approximation.

Number of Terms	*Average Absolute Error (dB)*
0	11.2
1	1.7
2	0.6
3	0.4

By taking the first n terms in this series, we obtain a finite series approximation to $A(\omega, \theta, \phi)$. As Table I shows, not many terms are required for a useful approximation.

The case $n = 1$ provides the simplest approximation,

$$A(\omega,\theta,\phi) \approx b_1(\omega,\phi)\sin\theta \tag{11}$$

This provides a simple factoring of the effects of azimuth and elevation, in which the IID varies sinusoidally with azimuth, with an amplitude that is a function of frequency and elevation. To the extent that a single-term approximation is adequate, we can say that the scale of the IID surface is proportional to the sine of the azimuth, and the shape of the IID surface is directly related to elevation.[4] It must be admitted that this rough characterization cannot be valid at large azimuth angles. As θ approaches 90°, the cone of confusion narrows down to the interaural axis, and we get vanishingly small variations with elevation. Thus, if we were to include the $\theta = 90°$ surface in Fig. 7, it would display a cylindrical shape, showing no variation at all with elevation. However, this is not quite as serious a limitation as it may seem. For localization, the important error measure is the *location angle* φ between a ray to the sound source and a ray in the estimated direction to the sound source. If the ray to the sound source is determined by θ and ϕ, and if the ray to the estimated location is determined by $\hat{\theta}$ and $\hat{\phi}$, it is easy to show that

$$\cos\varphi = \cos(\theta - \hat{\theta}) - \cos\theta\cos\hat{\theta}\left[1 - \cos(\phi - \hat{\phi})\right] \tag{12}$$

Thus, if $\theta = \pm 90°$, errors in estimating elevation have no effect on the location error, which reduces to the azimuth error. When the azimuth is near $\pm 90°$, the location error is very insensitive to the elevation error, a fact that is supported by the small-error formula

$$\varphi^2 \approx (\theta - \hat{\theta})^2 + \cos^2\theta(\phi - \hat{\phi})^2 \tag{13}$$

---

[4]This is consistent with the psychoacoustic experiments reported by Morimoto and Aokata (1984) in support of their hypothesis that binaural disparity determines the azimuth and spectral cues determine elevation. However, we are referring to interaural rather than monaural spectral cues.

Finally, we note that KEMAR is more symmetric than most humans. When the IID is not an odd function of azimuth, we should include the cosine terms in the Fourier series expansion. However, when the median plane differences are sufficiently small, an attractive alternative is to use two separate expansions—one for points in the right hemisphere another for points in the left hemisphere. This allows us to retain the conceptual simplicity of single-term approximation given by Eq. (11), as long as we remember that we need a different $b_1(\omega, \phi)$ for positive θ than for negative θ.

III. ANALYSIS OF THE SLV DATA

A. The SLV measurements and coordinates

Wightman, Kistler, and their colleagues at the University of Wisconsin have measured the HRTF's for many human subjects (Wightman, Kistler, and Perkins, 1987; Kistler and Wightman, 1992). Their work has verified previous reports that indicated significant subject-to-subject variability of the HRTF. Dr. Wightman provided us with measurements for a subject identified as SLV, who was said to be particularly accurate at localizing sound sources in both azimuth and elevation. We applied the KEMAR signal processing techniques to the SLV data to see if the observations made for the KEMAR interaural transfer function were also valid for SLV.

The SLV data consisted of 265 measurements of the right-ear and left-ear impulse responses. The Wisconsin researchers used a spherical coordinate system with a vertical polar axis to specify the 265 sampled points. Spatial sampling was done in 24 vertical planes of constant vertical-polar azimuth, using uniform 15° increments. In each plane, 11 vertical-polar elevations were sampled from –48° to +72° in uniform 12° increments. In addition, one measurement was made directly overhead.

Our analysis required a coordinate transformation from a vertical-polar to an interaural-polar system. In theory, one should interpolate in both azimuth and elevation to resample the data. However, because there are different time delays associated with different points, one cannot simply interpolate between different impulse responses in the time domain. For example, if the impulse response were $h(t)$ at one sample point and $h(t - \Delta t)$ at an adjacent point, one would want $h(t - 0.5\Delta t)$ at the midpoint, not $0.5[h(t) + h(t - \Delta t)]$.

There are several possible solutions to this problem. One is to employ some kind of time-alignment procedure in the interpolation. Another, which can be used if one only cares about spectral magnitudes, is to interpolate amplitude responses, which are invariant to time shift. We used a version of this second method. For each desired interaural azimuth, we first selected a subset of points whose azimuths were within 5 degrees of that target value. (Although the impulse responses for these points often had roughly the same time delay, this was not guaranteed.) Because the resulting points had irregularly spaced elevation values, we interpolated the resulting $A(\omega, \theta, \phi)$ values. As with the KEMAR data, we windowed these results to remove signals below 1.8 kHz and above 18 kHz, and smoothed the data by convolution with a Gaussian kernel whose standard deviation was 2 samples.

B. The SLV IID on constant-azimuth cones

Figure 8 shows the resulting SLV IID responses for a 40° cone of constant azimuth. The major features are clearly qualitatively similar to the KEMAR results shown in Fig. 5. In both cases, there is a generally rising response with frequency, with greater oscillations at low elevation angles and a more uniform response at high elevations. The "elevation ridge" and the "front/back basins" also appear in each case. However, the SLV elevation ridge is less well defined, and the frequencies for the basins are different. In general, the IID features for KEMAR occur at somewhat higher frequencies than the corresponding features for SLV, although exceptions to this statement can be found.

The IID surfaces for several different azimuth angles are shown in Fig. 9. The IID for $\theta = 0°$ is not negligible, but is as much as 7.8 dB at some frequencies and elevations; it is not known whether this is due to pinna disparities, other deviations from bilateral symmetry in the head and torso, head misalignment, or other imbalances in the measurement process. As the azimuth is increased, the interaural intensity differences become much stronger and better defined. As with KEMAR, the general pattern is fairly stable for azimuth angles out to 60° or perhaps 70°. A Fourier series expansion again reveals the dominance of the first term and the adequacy of a two-term expansion. To a first degree of approximation, we can again say that the scale of the IID surface is proportional to the sine of the azimuth, and the shape of the IID surface is directly related to elevation. Thus, it seems possible in principle to recover both the azimuth and the elevation from the IID alone. We now turn to considering how accurately this can be done.

IV. A SYSTEM VIEW OF LOCALIZATION

A. Neural Network Localization Models

Consider the problem of localizing a single point source of sound $x(t)$ in the presence of interfering noise sources. Assume that the head-related impulse responses h_L and h_R and the distance r to the source are known, but that the signal $x(t)$ and its angular location are unknown. Then the problem is to estimate the azimuth and elevation using only the received sound pressures $x_L(t)$ and $x_R(t)$:

$$x_L(t) = \int_{-\infty}^{\infty} h_L(\tau, r, \theta, \phi) x(t - \tau)\, d\tau + n_L(t) \quad , \tag{14}$$

and

$$x_R(t) = \int_{-\infty}^{\infty} h_R(\tau, r, \theta, \phi) x(t - \tau)\, d\tau + n_R(t) \quad , \tag{15}$$

where $n_L(t)$ and $n_R(t)$ are the noise signals at the two ears.

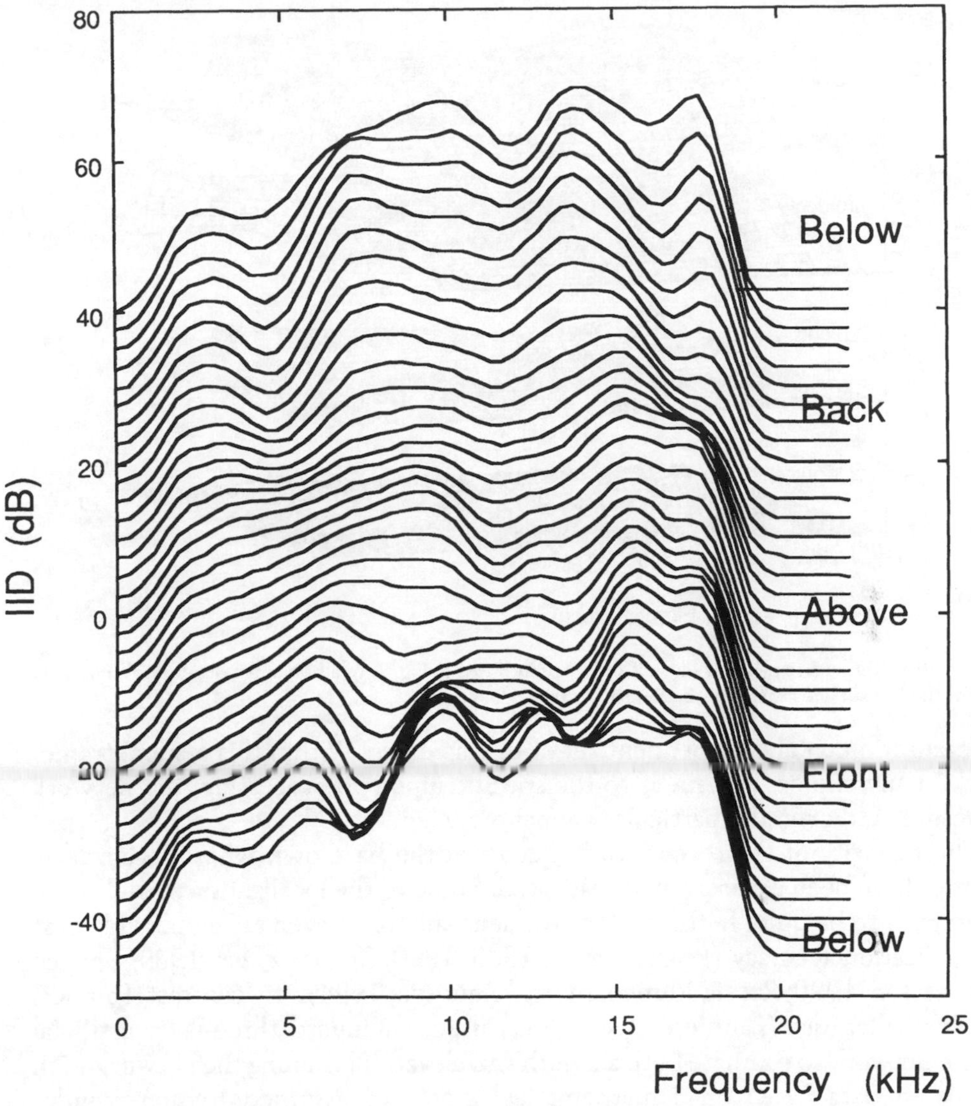

FIG. 8. Smoothed and interpolated IID data around a cone of 40° azimuth for subject SLV. This surface has the same general shape as the KEMAR surface shown in Fig. 5. However, the critical frequencies are generally higher for KEMAR than for SLV.

The classic Jeffress solution to this problem creates a spatial map of likely azimuth values using a fixed network of neural cross-correlators (Jeffress, 1948). Although the Jeffress model only considered ITD cues for azimuth, it has inspired most of the subsequent efforts. A common contemporary approach is to use a cochlear model or a signal processing technique such as the FFT to obtain a spectral representation of the signals, to use IID and/or ITD values for each spectral band as inputs to an adaptive neural network model, and to adapt the network to match the known azimuths and elevations for a set of training cases. A sufficiently large neural network can, in fact, be trained to match measured data, although care must be taken to have enough input cases to obtain reliable

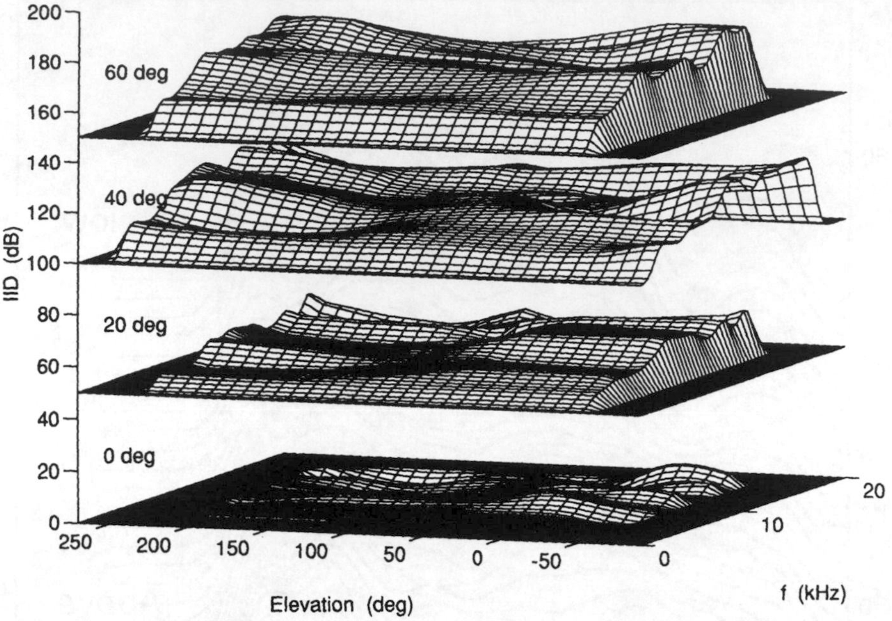

FIG. 9. SLV IID surface plots for four different azimuths. As in Fig. 7, to a first approximation, although the scale of the IID surface changes with azimuth, its shape does not.

generalization on an independent set of testing cases. Within this general framework, many choices remain as to the specific input preprocessing, the network structure, and even the particular animal modeled.

The majority of the recent studies concern the barn owl, whose localization abilities have been extensively investigated. Some of the localization models have attempted to be quite faithful to known neuroanatomy, even at the possible cost of localization accuracy (Pearson *et al.*, 1988, 1990; Spence *et al.*, 1989; Spence and Pearson, 1990; Rosen, Rumelhart, and Knudsen, 1994).[5] By contrast, Palmieri and his colleagues (Palmieri *et al.*, 1991) used a standard three-layer artificial neural network to estimate both azimuth and elevation, training the network with simulated data based on a mathematical model of assumed frequency-independent IID and ITD values. Unfortunately, the external ear structures of the barn owl produce IID cues that are much more directly related to elevation than is the case with humans, and these approaches do not carry over directly to human auditory localization.

Neti, Young, and Schneider (1992) used HRTF data for the cat to train a three-layer network having 128 values from a normalized amplitude spectrum for input, an 11×17 azimuth/elevation map for output, and a layer of 4–10 hidden units. Backman and Karjalainen (1993) used actual data from a Neumann dummy head, a bank of 24 critical-band filters, ITD and IID measurements, and a neural network with one hidden layer containing up to 8 hidden units feeding 4 outputs—the sines and cosines of the azimuth and elevation angles. Both of these

[5]Several researchers have demonstrated that these kinds of localization models can be realized as special analog very-large-scale integrated circuit (VLSI) chips, thereby enabling relatively inexpensive, real-time implementations (Lazzaro and Mead, 1989; Mead, Arreguit, and Lazzaro, 1991; Bhadkamkar and Fowler, 1993).

studies obtained excellent training results, but encountered serious problems with generalization on independent testing data. In an approach similar to ours, Nandy, Rao and Ben-Arie (1993) used the magnitude of the ITF derived from human HRTF data from the University of Wisconsin to estimate the azimuth of the source. Of the four azimuth-estimation procedures they investigated, the best results (an rms azimuth error of about 2.5°) were produced by a three-layer neural network with 128 spectral inputs, 15–30 hidden units, and 12 outputs. They solved the generalization problem by enlarging their limited set of training examples by adding noisy versions of the training data. Finally, Anderson, Gilkey, and Janko (1993) also used human HRTF data from the University of Wisconsin (subject SDO) and a bank of 22 1/4-octave filters to provide 45 monaural, IID and ITD inputs to a neural network with 50 hidden units and a 24 × 6 azimuth/elevation map for output. Like Nandy *et al.*, they solved the generalization problem by extensively enlarging their limited set of training examples through the addition of random noise, which represented the expected internal amplitude and time jitter.

B. Localization as a statistical estimation problem

Although neural network techniques are relatively simple to implement and can provide very good performance, there are also advantages to employing classical statistical procedures. In particular, Zakarauskas, Ozard, and Brower (1993) demonstrated that optimal statistical methods can provide superior localization performance. Because we wanted to know how well sound sources could be localized using IID information alone, we elected to take a statistical approach.

The assumption that θ and ϕ are random variables with a known prior density function $p(\theta, \phi)$ leads to a Bayesian formulation of the general localization problem: Given the prior density $p(\theta, \phi)$ and the data $x_L(t)$ and $x_R(t)$ as determined by Eqs. (14) and (15), find the posterior density $p(\theta, \phi | x_L, x_R)$.[6] In principle, this problem formulation allows us to use prior knowledge of the statistical characteristics of the source to exploit monaural as well as binaural cues. Unfortunately, it is very difficult to solve the general problem. We simplify the problem by restricting ourselves to source-independent binaural information, and by making several additional simplifying assumptions. In particular, we assume that $x(t)$, $n_L(t)$ and $n_R(t)$ can be Fourier transformed, and that the noise is small relative to the signal.[7] We then compute $X_L(\omega) = F\{x_L(t)\}$ and $X_R(\omega) = F\{x_R(t)\}$, and use only the information contained in the magnitude of the measured ratio

---

[6]One can interpret the neural maps of auditory space found in animals such as the barn owl (Knudsen, 1982; Carr and Konishi, 1990) as estimates of this posterior density. Localization models that estimate the posterior density have been developed by Martin (1995) and by Chau and Duda (1995).

[7]Existence of the Fourier transform is primarily a theoretical concern that arises if stationary random process models are used. In practice, we always work with finite, windowed segments of x_L and x_R for which the transform always exists, even though windowing introduces other errors that we overlook. The assumption that the noise is small relative to the signal is more problematic. In the frequency domain, it amounts to assuming that no problems arise in estimating H by the measured ratio $H_m = X_R(\omega)/X_L(\omega)$ because of small values for $X_L(\omega)$ or $X_R(\omega)$. This condition would certainly be violated if $x(t)$ were a pure tone or a narrow-band source. In practice, we are basically assuming that whatever $x(t)$ is, its spectrum is sufficiently broad that both $X_R(\omega)$ and $X_L(\omega)$ are above the noise levels at all frequencies considered. With narrow-band sources, one can restrict the range of frequencies considered to the range in which H can be reliably estimated, but there is still an unavoidable loss in localization accuracy.

$$\frac{X_R(\omega)}{X_L(\omega)} = \frac{H_R X + N_R}{H_L X + N_L} = \frac{H_R}{H_L} \frac{1+\frac{N_R}{H_R X}}{1+\frac{N_L}{H_L X}} \tag{16}$$

Substituting $A_m(\omega) = 20 \log_{10}|X_R/X_L|$ and $A(\omega, \theta, \phi) = 20 \log_{10}|H_R/H_L|$ we obtain

$$A_m(\omega) = A(\omega,\theta,\phi) + 20 \log_{10} \left| \frac{1+\dfrac{N_R}{H_R X}}{1+\dfrac{N_L}{H_L X}} \right| = A(\omega,\theta,\phi) + N \quad . \tag{17}$$

In other words, the measured IID $A_m(\omega)$ can be assumed to be the true IID $A(\omega, \theta, \phi)$ plus an additive random noise term N. By reducing the information used from everything in $x_L(t)$ and $x_R(t)$ to just the measured interaural spectrum $A_m(\omega)$, we simplify our problem to one of computing the conditional density $p[\theta, \phi | A_m(\omega)]$. By Bayes' rule

$$p[\theta,\phi | A_m(\omega)] = \frac{p(A_m | \theta,\phi) p(\theta,\phi)}{\int_{-\infty}^{\infty}\int_{-\infty}^{\infty} p(A_m | \theta,\phi) p(\theta,\phi)\, d\theta\, d\phi} \quad . \tag{18}$$

The key factor in this expression is $p(A_m | \theta, \phi)$. When the posterior density is unambiguously concentrated about a single point (θ, ϕ), we can employ a point estimate of the azimuth and elevation. A maximum likelihood estimate can be obtained by searching for values for θ and ϕ that maximize $p(A_m | \theta, \phi)$. Because $A_m = A + N$, if the values of N are normally distributed with zero mean, A_m is also normally distributed with mean A. For simplicity, we further assume that the values of N at different frequencies are statistically independent and have equal variance.[8] This assumption leads to the intuitively natural idea of estimating the azimuth and elevation of the source by finding values (θ, ϕ) that minimize the distance between the measured data $A_m(\omega)$ and the known IID function $A(\omega, r, \theta, \phi)$.

C. The Estimation Procedure

In implementing the maximum-likelihood procedure, we used a subset of the IID measurements to form a lookup table $A(\omega_i, \theta_j, \phi_k)$ of sampled raw spectral profiles indexed by azimuth and elevation. That is, for each j and k we stored a vector

[8]This is a rather doubtful assumption. The interfering signals that arise in normal environments are not like white Gaussian noise, and they are very likely to have considerably more energy at some frequencies than others. This means that the classification results that we present are suboptimal, and that even better localization accuracy may well be achievable.

giving the IID spectrum at frequencies $\omega_1, \omega_2, \cdots, \omega_n$, where n is the number of frequencies sampled. To obtain a "measured" IID, $A_m(\omega)$, we made a selection from the remainder of the measurements. Thus, we were tacitly assuming that the source signal $x(t)$ was an impulse. We estimated the azimuth and elevation for $A_m(\omega)$ by measuring the squared distance for every entry in the table and

$$\delta^2(\theta_i, \phi_j) = \sum_{i=1}^{n} \left| A_m(\omega_i) - A(\omega_i, \theta_j, \phi_k) \right|^2 \tag{19}$$

finding the angles θ_j and ϕ_k for which δ^2 is minimum.

Following the terminology used in neural network research, we call the subset used to form the lookup table the *training data* and the remainder the *testing data.* The performance of this "nearest neighbor" estimation procedure depends on how the training and testing data are selected. For example, one would obtain very poor performance if the size of the training set were very small, or if all of the training data came from low elevations and all of the testing data from high elevations. In most of our experiments, we used measurements with odd-indexed elevations for the training data, and measurements with even-indexed elevations for the testing data. Thus, the testing locations were uniformly distributed among the training locations.

Of course, because the (θ, ϕ) values for the testing data were always different from the (θ, ϕ) values for the training data, the angular error for this process, done as described, could never be smaller than the elevation and azimuth increments, which were on the order of 10°. To circumvent this problem, we augmented the lookup table by adding entries at interpolated elevation values. Thus, if the best match in every case turned out to be with one of these interpolated entries, it would be possible to have zero-error results.

The question of how best to measure localization error is somewhat subtle. Wenzel *et al.* (1993) discussed the distinctions between localization blur, front/back confusion, and up/down confusion, and described the use of appropriate spherical statistics for measuring localization performance. We decided to measure localization accuracy by the average absolute errors in azimuth, elevation, and location (denoted by e_θ, e_ϕ, and e_φ, respectively), without correction for front/back or up/down confusions. Although this leads to somewhat larger error values, it is a simple and conservative approach. In general, azimuth errors were almost always smaller than elevation errors, and the larger errors in elevation tended to dominate the location error. Although it might at first seem that e_φ could not be smaller than e_ϕ, elevation errors at large azimuth angles are not important (see Eq. 13), and we found that the average location error was usually slightly less than the average elevation error. This is important, because location error, not elevation error, is the most meaningful of the three error measures.

V. EXPERIMENTAL RESULTS

A. KEMAR data

The impulse responses for KEMAR were spatially sampled at 231 points. However, 69 points were in the median sagittal plane, where there were essentially no interaural differences. Were these points to be included in the training or testing sets, azimuth accuracy might be good, but large elevation errors would be made. In addition, 18 points in the frontal plane were measured at nonstandard angles. Exclusion of these special cases left the 144 points shown in Fig. 10. These 144 points fell on eight "circles of confusion," corresponding to azimuth angles from 10° to 80° in 10° increments. Because the surface of the sphere was roughly uniformly sampled, more points were sampled at small azimuths that at large azimuths. The training set was formed by taking every other point around a constant-azimuth circle. This led to the 72 training points and the 72 testing points shown in Fig. 10.

When the maximum-likelihood procedure described in Sec. IV.C was applied to the KEMAR data, the following average absolute errors were obtained: e_θ = 5.2°, e_ϕ = 12.0°, and e_φ = 11.3°. A scatter plot of the elevation estimates is shown in Fig. 11, and profile and frontal views of the individual location errors are shown in Fig. 12. The profile view reveals the presence of a few large front/back (mid/back) and up/down confusions, which tend to inflate the average errors. Although it is difficult to compare these results to "average" human performance, the average azimuth error seems somewhat larger than typical human abilities, but the average elevation error seems to be essentially comparable (Middlebrooks and Green, 1991). Thus, we see that the IID alone contains much of the information needed to localize sound sources if they are not in the median plane.

B. SLV data

The impulse responses for SLV were spatially sampled at 265 points, including 23 points in the median sagittal plane. Because there were significant interaural differences in the median plane, we decided to use all of the data, except for the one point directly overhead. The training set was formed by taking every other point around each longitudinal arc, which led to 144 training points interspersed by 120 testing points.

When the maximum-likelihood procedure described in Sec. IV.C was applied to the SLV data, the following average absolute errors were obtained: $e_{q\theta} =$ 4.5°, e_ϕ = 19.2°, and e_φ = 13.5°. However, even better performance was obtained by restricting the bandwidth to 12kHz: e_θ = 3.4°, e_ϕ = 17.2°, and e_φ = 11.5°. Apparently, the noise at high frequencies makes it hard to exploit any localization information that might be there. A scatter plot of the 12-kHz elevation estimates is shown in Fig. 13. Once again, there are a few large front/back and up/down confusions. Despite the apparently greater scatter, the average SLV performance is very close to the average KEMAR performance, and we again see that the IID alone contains much of the information needed to localize sound sources, even when we include points in the median plane.

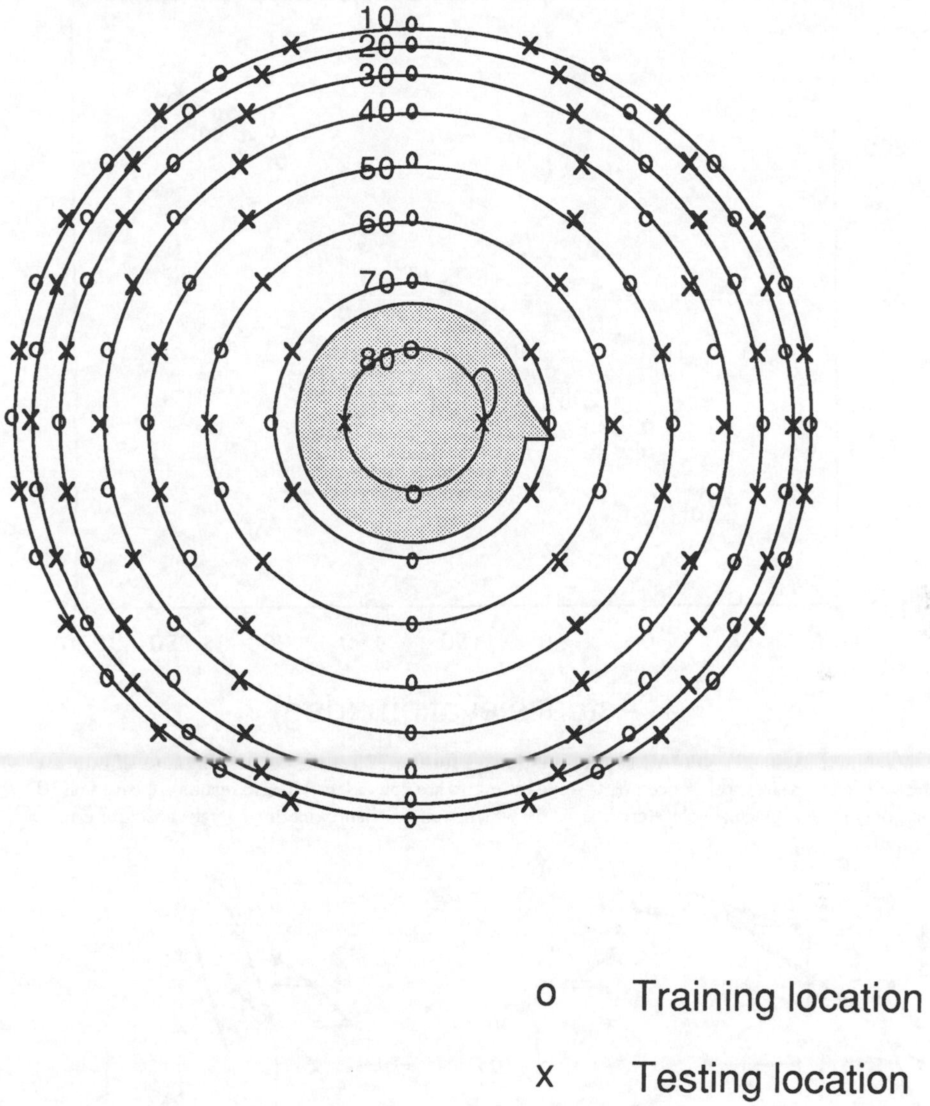

FIG. 10. A profile view of the spatial sampling for the KEMAR data. Concentric circles show azimuths of 10° to 80° in 10° increments. The 72 odd-indexed training elevations are indicated by o's, and the 72 even-indexed testing elevations by x's.

C. Training with SLV data and testing with KEMAR data

As we remarked earlier, the person-to-person variability of the HRTF is quite significant, and the degrading effect this has on so-called virtual acoustic displays has received increasing attention (Wenzel *et al.*, 1993). In our third experiment, we used all 264 SLV points to form the lookup table, and used them to classify all 144 of the KEMAR points. This simulates the situation in which SLV is trying to localize signals heard through KEMAR's external ears.

With this experiment, the errors were much higher, and high-frequency information was counterproductive (see Fig. 14). The best performance was achieved with a 6-kHz cutoff frequency: $e_\theta = 9.5°$, $e_\phi = 54.4°$, and $e_\varphi = 42.7°$.

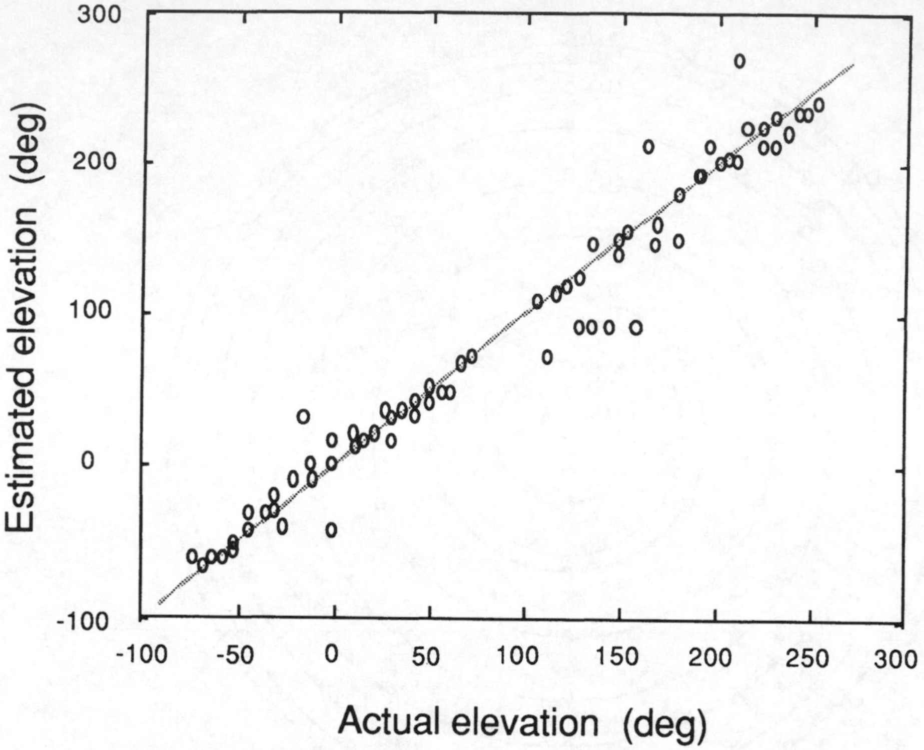

FIG. 11. Maximum likelihood KEMAR elevation estimates for the 72 testing points. (Because all estimates were quantized to the nearest reference point, some estimates are coincident.) These results are based on IID information only. The average absolute error is 12.0°, which is more than twice the average absolute error of 5.2° for azimuth.

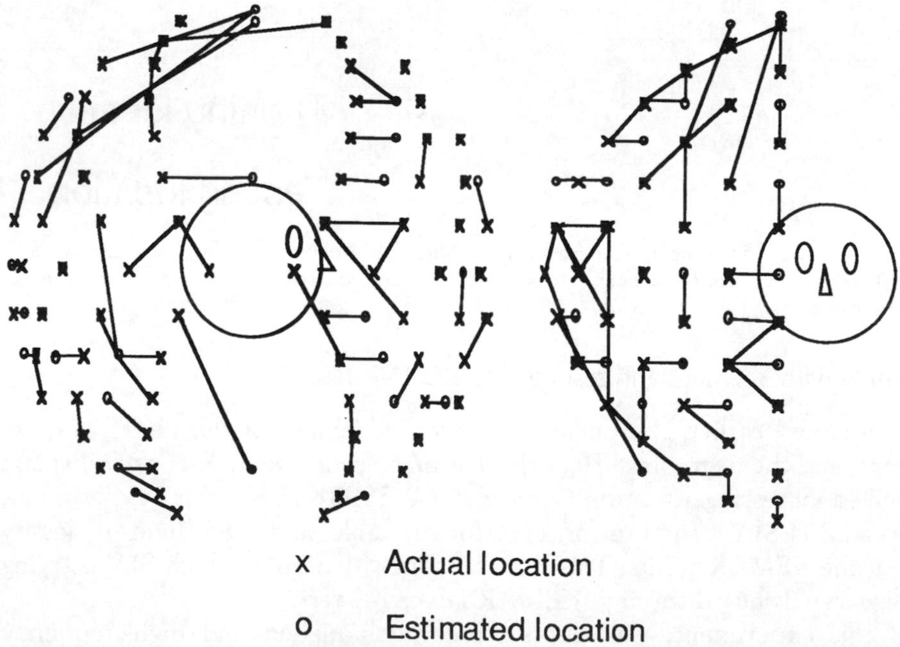

FIG. 12. Profile and frontal views of KEMAR localization errors. Note that elevation errors tend to be larger than azimuth errors, and that the midsagittal plane was excluded. The large errors tend to be front/back (or mid/back) confusions, although some up/down confusions are also present. Narrow-band sources produce more and much larger front/back errors.

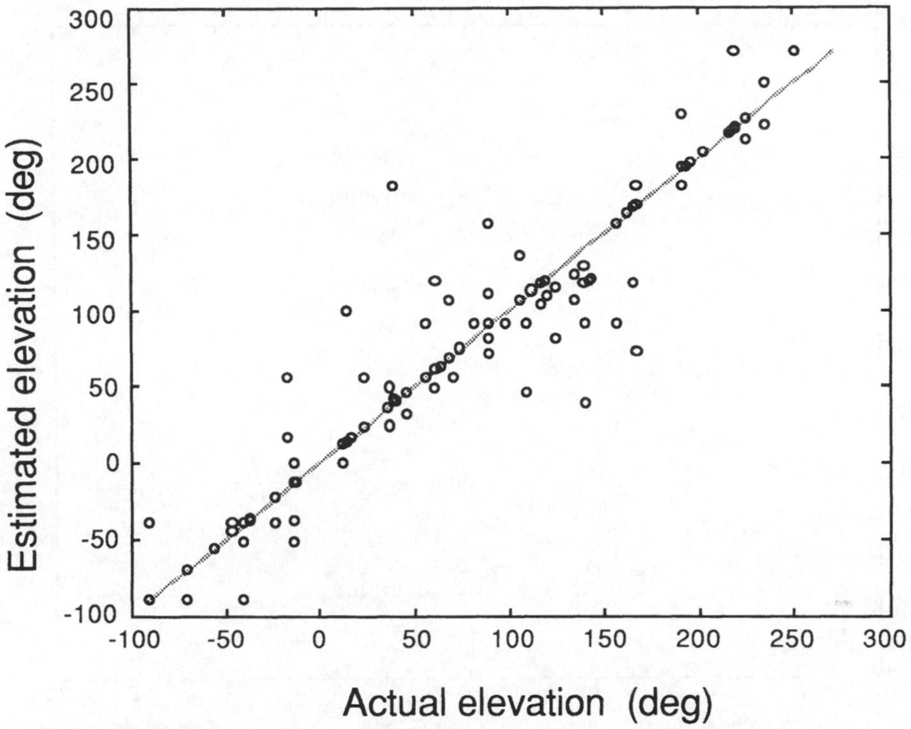

FIG. 13. Maximum likelihood SLV elevation estimates for the 120 testing points, which include points in the midsagittal plane. As in Fig. 13, these results are based on IID information only. The average absolute error is 17.2°, which is much larger than the average absolute error of 3.4° for azimuth. However, many of these errors occur near an azimuth of 90°, where they are unimportant. The average angular error in estimating a ray to the source is only 11.5°.

In general, the estimated elevation tends to be systematically larger than the actual elevation, a trend that is consistent with the fact that the IID features for KEMAR generally occur at higher frequencies than the corresponding IID features for SLV.

VI. DISCUSSION AND CONCLUSIONS

We have presented a new interpretation of the interaural intensity difference spectrum, and a straight-forward maximum-likelihood localization procedure that exploits the characteristics of that spectrum. Using an appropriate coordinate system, we have provided evidence that, to a first approximation, the scale of the IID spectrum determines azimuth, and the shape of the IID spectrum determines elevation. A central question was whether or not the IID spectrum contains enough information to localize a source in both azimuth and elevation. Although monaural cues are also important to humans for determining both azimuth and elevation, we showed that the binaural cues alone provide accuracy comparable to human abilities, and have the important advantage of being independent of the detailed shape of the source spectrum. The only requirement is that the signal energy exceeds the noise energy in the range of frequencies processed.

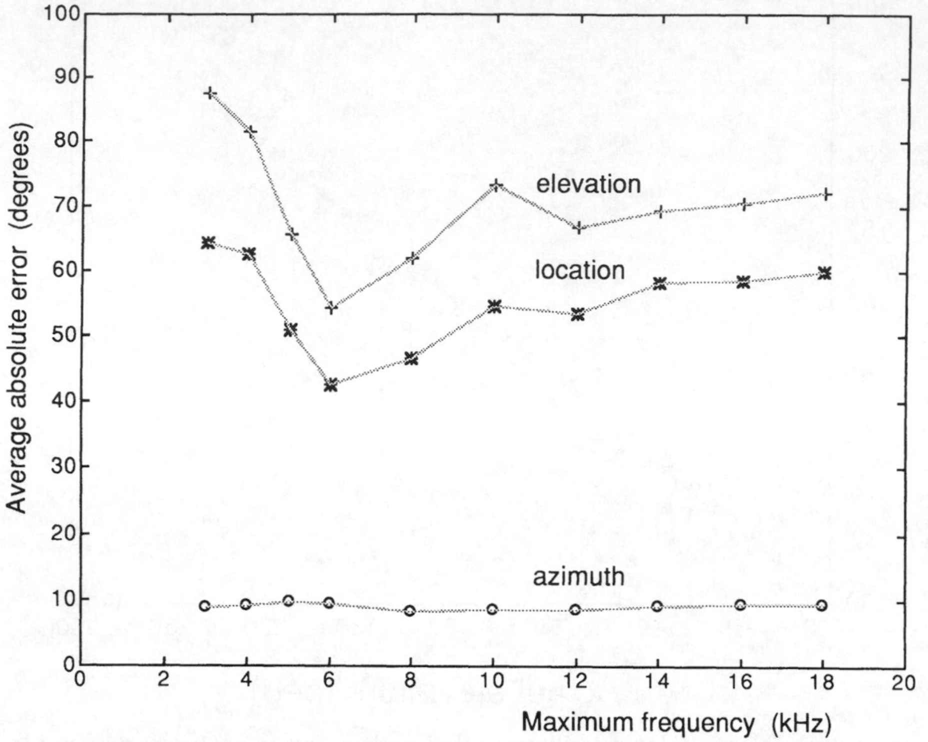

FIG. 14. In this experiment, the SLV IID functions were used to estimate the location of sounds filtered by the KEMAR HRTF's, which simulates SLV listening to signals heard through KEMAR's ears. While azimuth estimates were reasonable, elevation estimates were very poor. The best results were obtained when the signal bandwidth was limited to 6 kHz.

Of course, these results do not prove that the human auditory system is capable of extracting the information that is present in the IID spectrum. In particular, one might well be concerned that our maximum likelihood procedure could be exploiting spectral fine structure that falls within a critical band and is thus undetectable. In their study of the perceptually salient features of HRTF's, Carlile and Pralong (1994) used an auditory filter model to smooth such spectral fine structure. Following their general approach, we have recently shown that when an auditory model is substituted for our FFT analysis, localization accuracy is essentially unchanged (Lim and Duda, 1994). Thus, we believe that the results we have presented do not merely show what a statistical localization procedure can achieve, but are relevant to human performance.

Like most researchers in the field, we have investigated only the azimuth and elevation aspects of localization, and have worked with measurements taken at constant range. For sources that are sufficiently distant that the spherical wavefronts can be approximated as being planar, there is no useful range information in the IID data. Thus, one expects that our results will be essentially invariant to range for sources more than 2–3 meters from the head. However, the IID data changes radically for sources that are very close to the head, as exemplified by an insect buzzing in one's ear. Here the relationship between the ITD and IID cues for azimuth become very different than the relationship for distant sources, and the "discrepancy" between ITD and IID estimates should be a major cue for range.

In a practical sense, our results probably represent an upper bound on how well a sound source can be localized in azimuth and elevation using only IID information. We have tacitly assumed that there is only a single, broadband point source at known range in an anechoic environment. The more realistic problems of multiple, limited-bandwidth, extended sources at various ranges in reverberant environments will certainly require more sophisticated localization procedures. A full localization model should employ a cochlear model instead of FFT's for spectral analysis, include ITD measurements for more accurate azimuth localization, provide inhibition mechanisms to cope with echoes and reverberation, account for and exploit head motion, include range as well as azimuth and elevation estimates, and provide a spatial map rather than point estimates for source location. The simple model that we presented lacks these important characteristics. However, through its simplicity and reasonably effective performance, it offers a standard for evaluating more ambitious approaches.

ACKNOWLEDGMENTS

This work was supported by the National Science Foundation under grant IRI 9214233, with additional support from Apple Computer, Inc. The KEMAR measurements were made in an anechoic chamber in Dr. Eric Knudsen's laboratory in the Department of Neurobiology at Stanford University. The author greatly appreciates the cooperation and assistance provided by Dr. Knudsen and Steven Esterly. The author is indebted to Dr. Frederick Wightman of the University of Wisconsin for the SLV data, and to Richard F. Lyon of Apple Computer, Inc., and Dr. Malcolm Slaney of Interval Research Corporation for their enthusiasm, advice, and assistance. Finally, the author would like to express his appreciation to the editors for their helpful advice and suggestions.

REFERENCES

Anderson, T. R., Gilkey, R. H., and Janko, J. A. (**1993**). "Using neural networks to model human sound localization," Conference on Binaural and Spatial Hearing (Dayton, OH).

Backman, J., and Karjalainen, M. (**1993**). "Modelling of human directional and spatial hearing using neural networks," in *ICASSP 93 (Proc. IEEE Int. Conf. Acoustics Speech and Signal Processing)* (Minneapolis, MN), pp. I-125–I-128.

Bhadkamkar, N., and Fowler, B. (**1993**). "A sound localization system based on biological analogy," in *1993 IEEE International Conference on Neural Networks* (San Francisco), pp. 1902–1907.

Blauert, J. P. (**1983**). *Spatial Hearing* (MIT Press, Cambridge, MA).

Butler, R. A. (**1969**). "Monaural and binaural localization of noise bursts vertical in the median sagittal plane," J. Aud. Res. **3**, 230–235.

Carlile, S., and Pralong, D. (**1994**). "The location-dependent nature of perceptually salient features of the human head-related transfer functions," J. Acoust. Soc. Am. **95**, 3445–3459.

Carr, C. E., and Konishi, M. (**1990**). "A circuit for detection of interaural time differences in the brainstem of the barn owl," J. Neurosci. **10**, 3227–3246.

Chau, W., and Duda, R. O. (**1995**). "Combined monaural and binaural localization of sound sources," *Proc. Twenty-Ninth Annual Asilomar Conference on Signals, Systems and Computers* (IEEE, Asilomar, CA).

Chen, J., Van Veen, B. D., and Hecox, K. E. (**1993**). "Synthesis of 3D virtual auditory space via a spatial feature extraction and regularization model," in *VRAIS 93 (Proc. IEEE Virtual Reality Annual International Symposium)* (Seattle, WA), pp. 188–193.

Duda, R. O. (**1991**). "Short-time measurement of the KEMAR head-related transfer function," a report submitted to Richard F. Lyon, Apple Computer, Inc., Cupertino, CA.

Herbrank, J., and Wright, D. (**1974**). "Spectral cues used in the localization of sound sources in the median plane," J. Acoust. Soc. Am. **56,** 1829–1834.

Jeffress, L. A. (**1948**). "A place theory of sound localization," J. Comp. Physiol. Psychol. **41,** 35–39.

Kistler, D. J., and Wightman, F. L. (**1992**). "A model of head-related transfer functions based on principal components analysis and minimum-phase reconstruction," J. Acoust. Soc. Am. **91,** 1637–1647.

Knudsen, E. I. (**1982**). "Auditory and visual maps of space in the optic tectum of the owl," J. Neurosci. **2,** 1177–1194.

Lazzaro, J., and Mead, C. A. (**1989**). "A silicon model of auditory localization," Neural Comput. **1,** 47–57.

Lim, C., and Duda, R. O. (**1994**). "Estimating the azimuth and elevation of a sound source from the output of a cochlear model," *Proc. Twenty-Eighth Annual Asilomer Conference on Signals, Systems and Computers* (IEEE, Asilomar, CA), 399–403.

Martens, W. L. (**1987**). "Principal components analysis and resynthesis of spectral cues to perceived direction," *The International Computer Music Conference*, edited by J. Beauchamp (International Computer Music Association, San Francisco), pp. 274–281.

Martin, K. D. (**1995**). "Estimating azimuth and elevation from interaural differences," *Proc. 1995 IEEE ASSP Workshop on Applications of Signal Processing to Audio and Acoustics* (Mohonk Mountain House, New Paltz, New York).

Mead, C., Arreguit, X., and Lazzaro, J. (**1991**). "Analog VLSI model of binaural hearing," Neural Networks **2,** 230–236.

Mehrgardt, S., and Mellert, V. (**1977**). "Transformation characteristics of the external human ear," J. Acoust. Soc. Am. **61,** 1567–1576.

Middlebrooks, J. C. (**1992**). "Narrow-band sound localization related to external ear acoustics," J. Acoust. Soc. Am. **92,** 2607–2624.

Middlebrooks, J. C., and Green, D. M. (**1991**). "Sound localization by human listeners," Annu. Rev. Psychol. **42,** 135–159.

Middlebrooks, J. C., Makous, J. C. and Green, D. G. (**1989**). "Directional sensitivity of sound-pressure levels in the human ear canal," J. Acoust. Soc. Am. **86,** 89–108.

Møller, H., Sørenson, M. F., Hammershoi, D., and Jensen, C. B. (**1995**). "Head-related transfer functions of human subjects, J. Audio Engr. Soc. **43,** 300–321.

Morimoto, M., and Aokata, H. (**1984**). "Localization cues of sound sources in the upper hemisphere," J. Acoust. Soc. Jpn. **(E) 5,** 165–173.

Morimoto, M., and Nomachi, K. (**1983**). "Binaural disparity cues in median-plane localization," J. Acoust. Soc. Jpn. **(E) 3,** 99–103.

Nandy, D., Rao, K. R., and Ben-Arie, J. (**1993**), "Multiple auditory template matching using expansion," *Proc. 36th Midwest Symposium on Circuits and Systems* (Detroit, MI), pp. 899–902.

Neti, C., Young, E. D., and Schneider, M. H. (**1992**). "Neural network models of sound localization based on directional filtering by the pinna," J. Acoust. Soc. Am. **92,** 3140–3156.

Palmieri, F., Datum, M., Shah, A., and Moiseff, A. (**1991**). "Sound localization with a neural network trained with the multiple extended Kalman algorithm," in *Proc. Int. Joint Conf. on Neural Networks*, pp. I125–I131 (Seattle, WA).

Pearson, J. C., Gelfand, J. J., Sullivan, W. E., Peterson, R. M., and Spence, C. D. (**1988**). "Neural network approaches to sensory fusion," in *Proceedings of SPIE*, pp. 103–108.

Pearson, J. C., Spence, C. D., and Adolphs, R. (**1990**). "The computation of sound elevation in the barn owl: model and physiology," Soc. Neurosci. Abstr. **16,** 718.

Pösselt, C., Schröter, J., Opitz, M., Divenyi, P. L., and Blauert, J. (**1986**). "Generation of binaural signals for research and home entertainment," in *Proc. 12th Int. Congr. Acoust.*, Vol. I, B1–6 (Toronto).

Rosen, D., Rumelhart, D., and Knudsen, E. (**1994**). "A connectionist model of the owl's localization system," in *Advances in Neural Information Processing Systems—VI*, edited by J. D. Cowan, G. Tesauro, and J. Alspector (Morgan Kaufmann, San Mateo, CA), pp. 606–613.

Searle, C. L., Braida, L. D., Cuddy, D. R., and Davis, M. F. (**1975**). "Binaural pinna disparity: Another auditory localization cue," J. Acoust. Soc. Am. **57,** 448–455.

Spence, C. D., and Pearson, J. C. (**1990**). "The computation of sound source elevation in the barn owl," in *Advances in Neural Information Processing Systems—II*, edited by D. S. Touretzsky (Morgan Kaufmann, San Mateo, CA), pp. 10–17.

Spence, C. D., Pearson, J. C., Gelfand, J. J., Peterson, R. M., and Sullivan, W. E. (**1989**). "Neuronal maps for sensory-motor control in the barn owl," in *Advances in Neural Information Processing Systems—I*, edited by D. S. Touretzsky (Morgan Kaufmann, San Mateo, CA), pp. 366–374.

Wenzel, E. M., Arruda, M., Kistler, D. J., and Wightman, F. L. (**1993**). "Localization using nonindividualized head-related transfer functions," J. Acoust. Soc. Am. **94,** 111–123.

Wightman, F. L., and Kistler, D. J. (**1989**). "Headphone simulation of free-field listening. I: Stimulus synthesis," J. Acoust. Soc. Am. *85*, 858–867.

Wightman, F. L., Kistler, D. J., and Perkins, M. E. (**1987**). "A new approach to the study of human sound localization," in *Directional Hearing*, edited by W. A. Yost and G. Gourevitch (Springer Verlag, New York), pp. 26–48.

Zakarauskas, P., Ozard, J. M., and Brower, P. (**1993**). "Neural networks for independent range and depth discrimination in passive acoustic localization," IEEE Trans. Signal Processing **41,** 1394–1398.

Chapter 4

Spectral Shape Cues for Sound Localization

John C. Middlebrooks
University of Florida College of Medicine
(Received March 1994; revised September 1994)

Resonant cavities of the external ear transform the spectrum of an incident sound, thereby introducing potential cues to the location of the sound source. Human subjects apparently rely on spectral shape cues for localization in the vertical and front/back dimensions, but it is not clear whether spectra shape cues also aid in horizontal localization. We tested the ability of normal listeners to localize 1/6-octave-wide noise bursts that varied in azimuth and elevation. Subjects localized these sounds accurately in the horizontal dimension, whereas they made systematic errors in the vertical and front/back dimensions. The patterns of errors could be predicted by a model that compared stimulus spectra with the transfer functions of the external ears. The normal localization in the horizontal dimension could be accounted for by interaural difference cues. To confound interaural difference cues, we measured localization of broadband sounds under monaural conditions. Normal-hearing subjects who wore a plug in one ear showed a systematic localization bias toward the hearing ear, but a population of congenitally monaural patients showed reasonably accurate localization, both in horizontal and vertical dimensions. The results suggest that interaural differences, when present, are the predominant cue for horizontal localization. In the absence of such cues, however, spectral shape cues can provide useful cues to horizontal sound source location.

INTRODUCTION

Since Lord Rayleigh's studies conducted in the 19th century (Rayleigh, 1907), auditory researchers have known that listeners derive cues to the location of a sound source from interaural differences in the sound pressure and time of arrival of sounds. Listeners utilize interaural level differences (ILDs) at frequencies above about 3 kHz, the lowest frequency for which the listener's head casts a perceptible

* See Contributors' list for current address.

acoustic shadow. Listeners can utilize interaural delays either in the cycle-by-cycle phase of sounds (for frequencies below about 1.8 kHz) or in the envelopes of complex sounds (for carrier frequencies at which the listeners cannot follow the cycle-by-cycle phase). Neurophysiological studies in animals have identified neurons that are sensitive to ILDs (Rose, Gross, Geisler, and Hind, 1966; Boudreau and Tsuchitani, 1968), neurons that are sensitive to interaural delays in the phases of low-frequency tones (Goldberg and Brown, 1969), and neurons that are sensitive to delays in the envelopes of higher frequency complex sounds (Crow, Langford, and Moushegian, 1980; Yin, Kuwada, and Sujaku, 1984; Batra, Kuwada, and Stanford, 1989). Several physiological models of localization have emphasized interaural difference cues (e.g., Rose *et al.*, 1966; Middlebrooks, 1987).

Interaural difference cues vary systematically with the angle of displacement of a sound source from the midline plane and thus provide useful localization cues in the horizontal dimension. In contrast, interaural cues are relatively constant as a sound source is varied in vertical or front/back location, as long as the angle with the midline plane is kept constant. Thus, interaural cues are ambiguous in the vertical and front/back dimensions. Batteau (1967, 1968) proposed that reflections of the incident sound wave within the external ear might provide cues in these latter dimensions. He suggested that the time delay between the direct sound path and a reflection from an external ear structure would vary according to the angle of incidence of sound, and thus those delays might provide localization cues.

Since Batteau's time, research on external ear acoustics has tended to focus on spectral modifications, rather than on time delays *per se*. When a noise is delayed, then added back to itself, the resulting spectrum contains characteristic peaks and notches that vary in frequency according to the magnitude of the delay. One can think of the folds and cavities of the external ear as a system of resonators (Shaw, 1974; Shaw and Teranishi, 1968). Bioacoustical studies have shown that, indeed, the resonant properties of the external ear transform the spectrum of a sound source and that the spectral transformation varies according to the angle of incidence of sound. The component of the external ear transfer function that is specific to a particular source direction has been referred to as the *directional transfer function* (DTF; Middlebrooks and Green, 1990). Psychoacoustical studies have shown that certain experimental manipulations of the sound source spectrum result in systematic errors in localization, particularly in the vertical and front/back dimensions. This suggests that subjects normally utilize DTFs as cues to vertical and front/back source direction. The spatial information carried by DTFs is referred to here as "spectral shape cues." The psychophysical results, taken with the earlier results from studies of binaural hearing, have led to a general acceptance of the notion that interaural difference cues provide the principal cues to the horizontal dimension and that spectral shape cues provide the principal cues to vertical and front/back location (see Middlebrooks and Green, 1991, for review).

There are at least three lines of evidence suggesting that the influence of spectral shape cues might not be confined to the vertical and front/back dimensions, that is, that spectral shape cues might supplement the horizontal localization information that is available from interaural difference cues. First, visual inspection of plotted DTFs reveals that spectral features such as spectral peaks and notches seem to vary in frequency as much with the horizontal location of a source as with its vertical or front/back location (Shaw, 1974). This suggests that DTFs provide information about horizontal source location, although it does not indicate whether or not that information is utilized by subjects. Second, Butler and his colleagues have demonstrated that when a listener is asked to localize a narrowband sound presented in the horizontal plane, the reported horizontal location varies according to the center frequency (Butler and Flannery, 1980; Musicant and Butler, 1985). This has been seen most often under conditions in which the listener was wearing a plug in one ear, but Musicant and Butler also have demonstrated the phenomenon under binaural conditions. The results from Butler's group suggest that spectral shape cues can contribute to the horizontal localization judgment. Finally, there have been several reports of accurate localization of broadband sounds under monaural listening conditions, both in the case of normal listeners fitted with earplugs and in the case of patients who had a monaural hearing impairment. Spectral shape cues presumably are the only horizontal localization cues available to a monaural listener.

This chapter presents results of two psychophysical studies that are relevant to the issue of spectral shape cues for sound localization. In the first, normal binaural subjects localized narrowband filtered noise bursts that varied in center frequency. The sound sources varied in horizontal, vertical, and front/back location, and the subjects were free to respond at any location on the coordinate sphere. That study led to a computational model of localization based on ILD and spectral shape cues. The second study examined sound localization by patients who had long-standing (presumably congenital) profound hearing impairments in one ear. A subset of those patients demonstrated moderately accurate localization, even when the stimuli were presented on the side of the impaired ear. That result indicates that, at least under monaural conditions, spectral shape cues can effectively signal the horizontal location of a sound.

I. GENERAL METHODS

We presented free-field sound stimuli in a masonry block room that had inside dimensions of 2.6 × 3.1 × 4.3 m. The walls were lined with 3-in acoustical foam (Illbruck), which attenuates reflections of sounds that are higher than 500 Hz in frequency. The room contained a semicircular hoop, 1.2 m in radius, which rotated about a vertical axis (Fig. 1). The hoop could be positioned by a computer-controlled stepping motor. Sixteen dynamic loudspeakers (Radio Shack 3-in midrange tweeter, catalog no. 40-1289A) were mounted on the hoop in 10° steps from +90° (straight overhead) to –60°. Individual speakers could be activated by a computer-controlled multiplexer. Stimuli presented from the hoop-mounted stimuli lay on a 2.4-m-diameter virtual sphere. The human subject sat in a swivel chair that was positioned so that the center of the subject's interaural axis coincided with the center of the sphere.

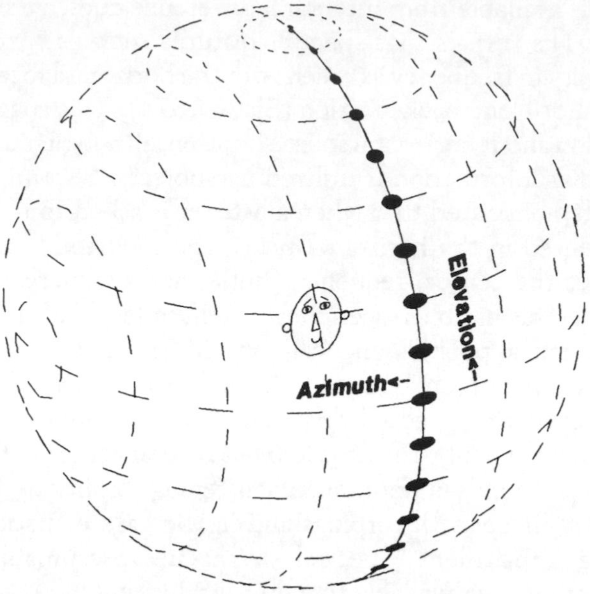

FIG. 1. Loudspeaker array and coordinate system. Sixteen loudspeakers were mounted on a semicircular hoop. They were spaced in 10° steps from –60° to +90° elevation. The hoop could rotate about the vertical axis that passed through the center of the subject's interaural axis. All sound sources fell on a 2.4-m-diameter virtual sphere. In this and all other related illustrations, the sphere is drawn as if looking in toward the subject. In this particular plot, the viewpoint is located at right 30° azimuth, +30° elevation. The dashed lines show contours of constant double pole azimuth and elevation in 20° increments. [From Middlebrooks, 1992; reprinted with permission]

Experiments were controlled by a microcomputer that was fitted with a 16-bit analog interface (Tucker-Davis Technologies); in our studies reported prior to 1992, the interface was a 12-bit system from Modular Instruments, Inc. Audio signals were generated and recorded at a 50-kHz sample rate. Waveforms were generated and analyzed using fast Fourier transform techniques on a Tucker-Davis digital signal processor. The responses of loudspeakers were calibrated using a Bruel and Kjaer sound level meter with a model 4133 microphone positioned in the center of the sound sphere. We derived for each loudspeaker an inverse response spectrum such that when a flat spectrum was combined with the inverse response, the spectrum measured in the center of the sphere had an root-mean-square deviation of less than 0.3 dB across a band of 1.5 to 18 kHz.

We specify stimulus and response locations in a double-pole coordinate system (Knudsen, 1982; Middlebrooks, Makous, and Green, 1989). The vertical location is given by the *elevation* coordinate, which is the angle formed by the sound source (or response location), the center of the subject's interaural axis, and the horizontal plane. Zero degrees elevation is on the horizontal plane and +90° is straight overhead. The horizontal location is given by the double pole *azimuth* coordinate, which is the angle formed by the sound source (or response location), the center of the interaural axis, and the midline plane. Azimuths behind the interaural axis are written as 180° minus the angle to the midline plane. Zero degrees azimuth is in front of the listener, +90° azimuth is straight to the listener's right, and ±180° azimuth is straight to the rear. Although the azimuth and elevation coordinates uniquely specify every point on the coordinate sphere, it is convenient for descriptive purposes to refer to a third, *front/back*, coordinate, which is the stimulus or response position relative to the vertical interaural plane.

We measured DTFs by presenting special broadband probe signals, "Golay codes" (see Zhou, Green, and Middlebrooks, 1992), from the hoop-mounted loudspeakers and recording with miniature microphones from the ear canals of human subjects. Stimuli were presented from 360 locations around the subject, spaced in increments of approximately 10° in azimuth and elevation. The spectrum of the signal recorded in the ear canal was shaped in part by the response properties of the microphone and by the standing wave pattern within the canal. In order to eliminate the contribution of those two factors, we subtracted from each spectrum a "common" spectrum that was formed by the average of log magnitude spectra elicited from all 360 source locations (Middlebrooks and Green, 1990). The result of this operation was a set of 360 DTFs for each ear. We convolved each DTF with a bank of bandpass filters. The filters had 3-dB bandwidths of 0.22 octave and center frequencies spaced logarithmically in 0.06-octave steps (Middlebrooks, 1992). The purposes of that filtering operation were to place the DTFs on a logarithmic scale and to approximate the filtering function of the cochlea.

In behavioral experiments, subjects localized broadband or narrowband noise bursts, 150 or 250 ms in duration. Across trials, stimulus levels roved between 50 and 60 dB above the threshold that was measured at 0° azimuth, 0° elevation. Each subject reported the apparent locations by orienting his or her head to face the remembered location of the sound; we told subjects to "point with your nose." The head orientation was measured with an electromagnetic device (Polhemus ISOTRAK). Behavioral trials were conducted in complete darkness. Each trial consisted of the following sequence. First, a broadband noise was turned on from a speaker fixed at 0° azimuth, 0° elevation. The subject oriented to that "centering" stimulus, then pressed a response key to indicate that he or she was in the starting position; activation of the response key terminated the centering stimulus. After a variable delay, the test stimulus, 250 ms in duration, was presented from a location unknown to the subject. The subject oriented to the test stimulus, then pressed the response key. Subjects' latencies to the onset of a head movement (as measured with the ISOTRAK) generally were longer than the duration of the test stimulus, so subjects received no dynamic auditory cues resulting from head movements.

II. RESULTS AND DISCUSSION

A. Directional transfer functions

Figure 2 shows some examples of DTFs from the right ear of one subject. The traces in Fig. 2A are from locations in the horizontal plane, varying in azimuth from 0° to right 160°. Those in Fig. 2B are from locations on the vertical midline

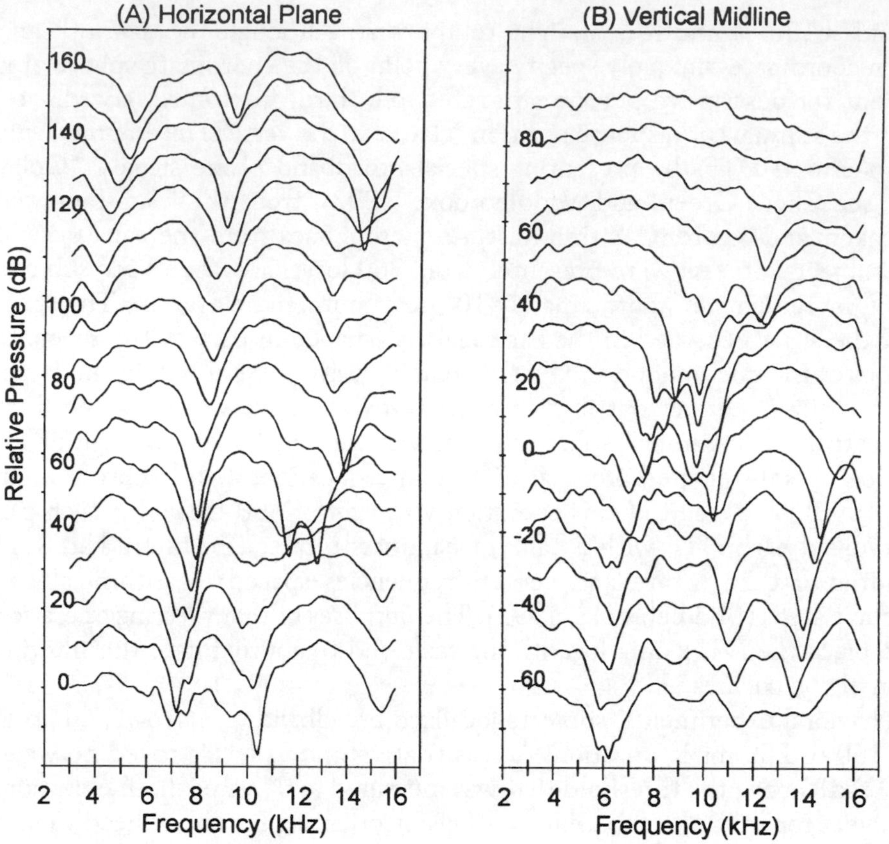

FIG. 2. Directional transfer functions (DTFs). These DTFs were recorded from the right ear of one subject. (A; left) DTFs for sound source locations in the horizonal plane (i.e., 0° elevation) at various azimuths. (B; right) DTFs for locations in the vertical midline plane (i.e., 0° azimuth) at various elevations. The number next to each DTF indicates the azimuth or elevation. The DTFs are separated vertically by 10-dB intervals. [From Middlebrooks, 1992; reprinted with permission]

in front of the subject; the elevations vary from –60° to +90°. The DTFs contain prominent spectral slopes, peaks, and notches that vary in frequency according to sound source location. Often the frequency of a particular spectral feature appeared to show a systematic location dependence. In Fig. 2A, for example, one can see a spectral notch that increases in center frequency from 7 kHz to 9.5 kHz as the sound source is moved around the subject from 0° to right 160° azimuth. The General Discussion considers specific spectral features that have been examined as possible spatial cues.

The DTFs in Fig. 2 show spectral cues in a familiar format, in which spectra are plotted for selected source locations. An alternative format is used in Fig. 3, which shows the amplitude gain of the external ear at selected frequencies as a function of source location. This format is useful in that it is comparable to the format used to display spatial receptive fields in neurophysiological experiments (e.g., Middlebrooks and Pettigrew, 1981). In the plots shown here, the coordinate sphere is drawn as if looking in toward the subject from a viewpoint 30° to the subject's right and 30° up. The shaded areas are the locations at which the magnitude of a sound of the specified frequency was within 5 dB of the greatest value recorded across all locations. The contour lines are labeled as dB down from the maximum. The pattern of ear directionality at individual frequencies contained either a single maximum (4, 6, 10, and 12 kHz) or two discrete maxima (8 and 12 kHz). The locations of maxima varied with frequency. The general pattern of directionality of the ear was preserved across subjects, with the proviso that a particular directional pattern that was seen at a given frequency for a particular subject might be seen at a different frequency for a different subject. The majority of the variance among subjects could be accounted for by a frequency multiplier, which, to a first approximation, appeared to scale with the size of the subject (Middlebrooks *et al.*, 1989).

B. Localization of broadband sounds

We tested the accuracy with which normal binaural subjects could localize broadband sounds (Makous and Middlebrooks, 1990; Middlebrooks, 1992; Slattery and Middlebrooks, 1994). The purpose of such measurements was to provide a baseline for human localization performance under near optimum conditions; of course, our measurements of localization performance are confounded to some extent by possible inaccuracies in the subjects' use of head orientation as a response measure (see Gilkey, Good, Ericson, Brinkman, and Stewart, 1995). Across three studies, the subjects ranged in age from 19 to 36 years. All had pure tone hearing sensitivity within 20 dB of audiometric zero. We used two types of

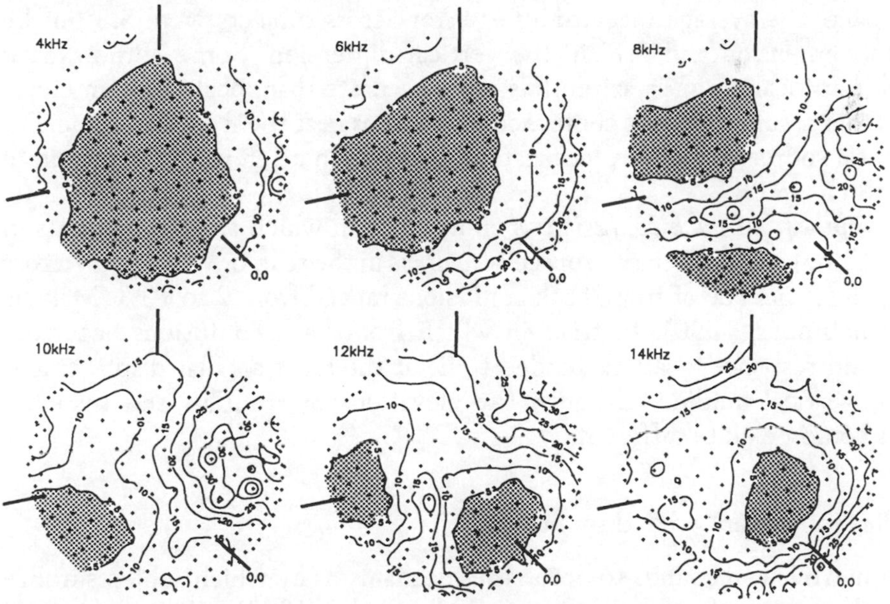

FIG. 3. Directional sensitivity of sound pressures in the ear canal. For each of the indicated six frequencies, the sound pressure in the ear canal is plotted as a function of sound source location. Sound pressure is expressed in dB down from the maximum that was recorded at each frequency. The stippled areas are the areas inside the 5-dB contours. The viewpoint is located at right 30° azimuth, +30° elevation. [From Middlebrooks *et al.*, 1989; reprinted with permission]

broadband stimuli. The first was a 150-ms sound burst synthesized with random phase and with a magnitude spectrum that was flat from 1.8 to 16 kHz and was at least 30 dB down outside of that band. The second was a 250-ms Gaussian noise burst bandpassed from 2 to 15 kHz. One might have expected that a listener would derive more accurate spectral shape cues for localization from a flat-spectrum source than from Gaussian noise, which exhibits trial-by-trial variation in spectrum. Nevertheless, we observed quantitatively similar localization performance when using either stimulus. Wightman and Kistler (1989) tested a more extreme condition of spectral variation by deliberately "scrambling" the spectra between trials in their broadband localization study; the spectral scramble might account in part for the larger localization errors observed in that study. Because our stimuli were high-passed above 1.8 or 2.0 kHz, the stimuli would not have provided usable cues from ITDs in cycle-by-cycle phase (Licklider, Webster, and Hedlun, 1950; Zwislocki and Feldman, 1956). For that reason, ILDs probably provided the major interaural difference cue in our situation.

Figure 4 shows an example of broadband localization performance. The upper half of the figure shows the view in toward the front of the subject, and the lower half shows the view in toward the subject from his right side. The filled circles indicate the locations of stimuli, and the open circles indicate the locations of the subject's responses. As one might expect, localization accuracy is best immediately in front of the subject, and sources in the front half of space consistently are localized more accurately than those behind the subject. The side view reveals that this particular subject showed an upward bias in his localizations of rear sound sources, but not all subjects exhibited such a bias. For sound sources in the front half of space, the average magnitudes of error across subjects were 5.8° in the horizontal dimension and 5.7° in the vertical dimension. Some authors have assumed that localization in azimuth is more accurate than localization in elevation, and that assumption was confirmed for sources near the frontal midline. For more lateral sources, however, localization in elevation often was more accurate than that in azimuth.

We define a *front/back confusion* as an instance in which a subject orients in the front half of space when the source actually is in the rear, or vice versa. Across subjects, the incidence of front/back confusions ranged from 2 to 10% (Makous and Middlebrooks, 1990). In trials in which front/back confusions occurred, stimulus and response locations tended to lie at the same angular displacement from the vertical midline, although the elevations of stimulus and response locations could be quite different.

C. Localization of narrowband sounds

We used narrowband sounds to probe the mechanisms by which subjects utilize spectral shape cues for localization (Middlebrooks, 1992). Normal binaural subjects localized narrowband-filtered Gaussian noise bursts. The narrowband filters had 3-dB bandwidths of 0.227 octave and center frequencies of 6, 8, 10, and 12 kHz. Subjects made conspicuous errors in localization in the vertical and front/back dimensions. A given subject tended to localize all sounds of a particular

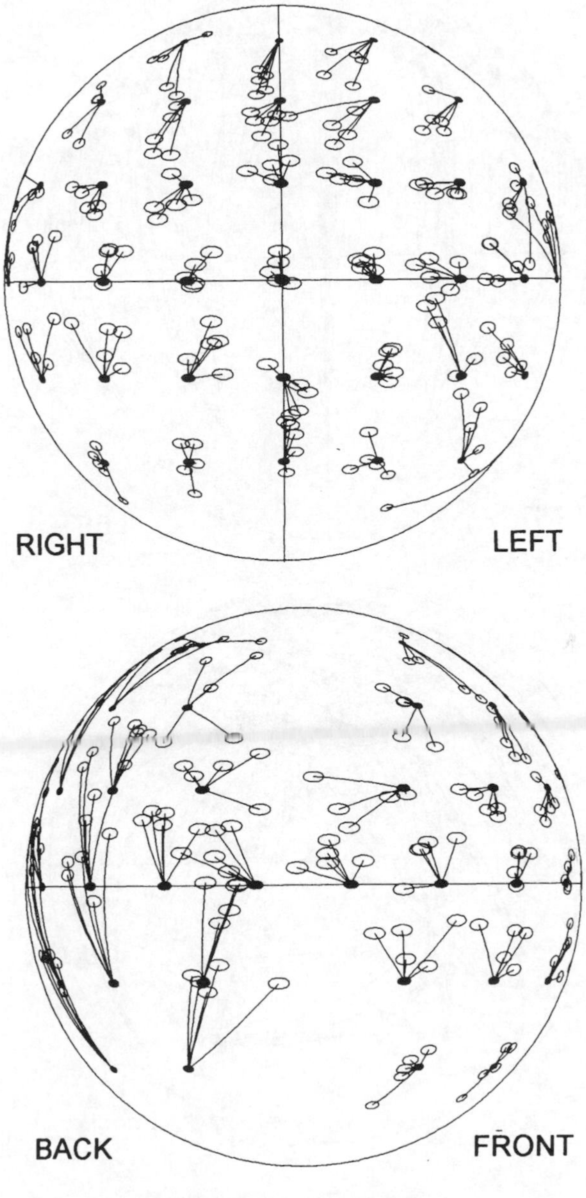

FIG. 4. Broadband sound localization. Broadband sounds were presented from the locations indicated by filled symbols. The subject's responses are represented by open symbols connected by arcs to the source locations. Each source location was tested five times. The viewpoints are located at 0° azimuth, 0° elevation (top plot) and right 90° azimuth, 0° elevation (bottom plot). [From Middlebrooks, 1992; reprinted with permission]

center frequency within a particular restricted vertical and front/back region. Figures 5 and 6 show one subject's localizations of 6-kHz and 8-kHz stimuli; in each figure, the upper half is a front view and the lower half is a view from the subject's right side. Responses to the 6-kHz stimulus consistently fell in a 20°-wide swath at high elevations in front of the subject (Fig. 5). In contrast, most responses

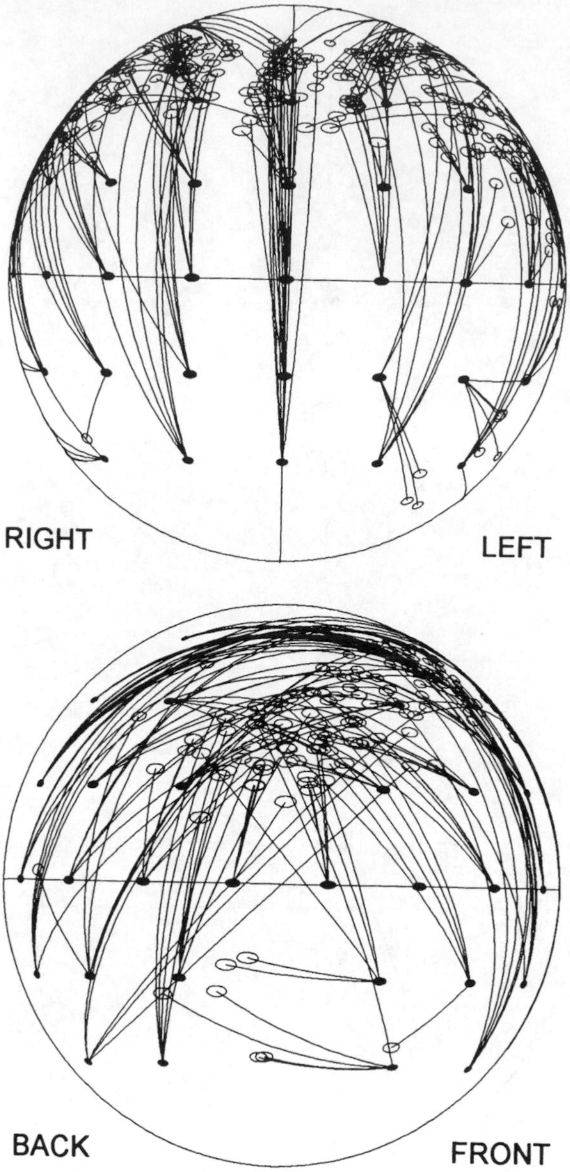

FIG. 5. Localization of a noise band centered at 6 kHz. The stimulus was Gaussian noise, bandpass filtered with a center frequency of 6 kHz and a 3-dB bandwidth of 0.227 octaves. The viewpoints and the format for representing stimulus and response locations are the same as in Fig. 4. [From Middlebrooks, 1992; reprinted with permission]

to the 8-kHz stimulus fell at low elevations, with responses to near-midline sources tending to lie in front and responses to lateral sources tending to lie in the rear (Fig. 6). This subject tended to localize all 10-kHz sources to the rear and all 12-kHz sources to the horizontal plane, front and rear.

Despite the systematic errors in localization in the vertical and front/back dimensions, localization of narrowband sounds in the horizontal dimension was

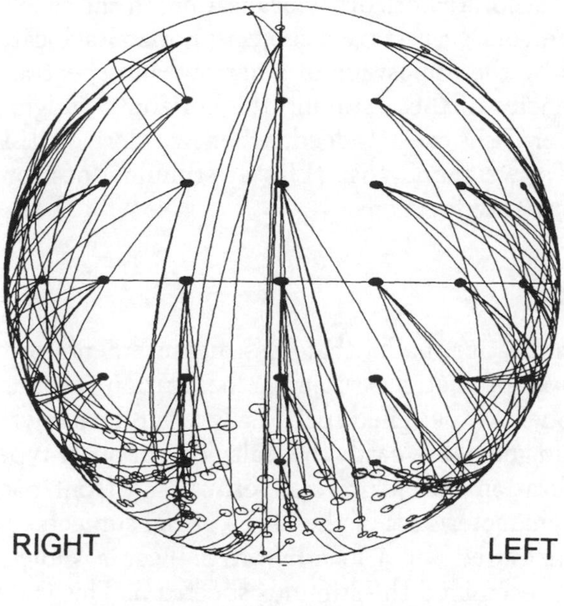

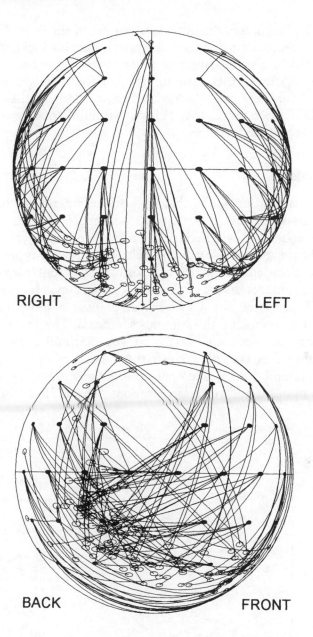

FIG. 6. Localization of a noise band centered at 8 kHz. The center frequency of the bandpass filter was 8 kHz. All other details are as in Fig. 5. [From Middlebrooks, 1992; reprinted with permission]

nearly as accurate as that for broadband sounds. When we express stimulus and response locations in terms of the angular displacement from the midline, irrespective of front/back location, the correlation coefficient (r) for stimulus versus response horizontal location ranged between 0.932 and 0.970 across all subjects and center frequencies. For comparison, the correlation coefficient for horizontal localization of broadband sounds ranged between 0.973 and 0.985 for the same subjects. The accurate horizontal localization, in the face of systematic vertical and front/back errors, suggests that subject's horizontal location judgment was largely unaffected by the imposition of a narrowband spectral peak. Given the high center frequencies of these stimuli, the horizontal judgment probably relied almost entirely on ILD cues. Indeed, when we derived ILDs from our measurements of DTFs, we found that ILDs at stimulus locations correlated closely with those at response locations.

D. A localization model

We have derived a quantitative model that uses measurements of the DTFs of subjects' external ears to predict the subjects' localization responses (Middlebrooks, 1992). The model was designed specifically around narrowband localization results, but it should generalize easily to localization of other types of stimuli.

In narrowband localization trials, subjects' vertical and front/back responses could be attributed to characteristics of the DTFs of the subjects' external ears. Generally, the DTF measured for a location at or near a subject's response contained features that resembled the stimulus spectrum. This is demonstrated in Fig. 7. In this example, when a 12-kHz narrowband stimulus was presented from –40°, +40° (forward, to the left, and up), the subject responded near –145°, –17° (back, to the left, and down). The figure shows the stimulus spectrum and DTFs measured at stimulus and response locations. The DTF at the response

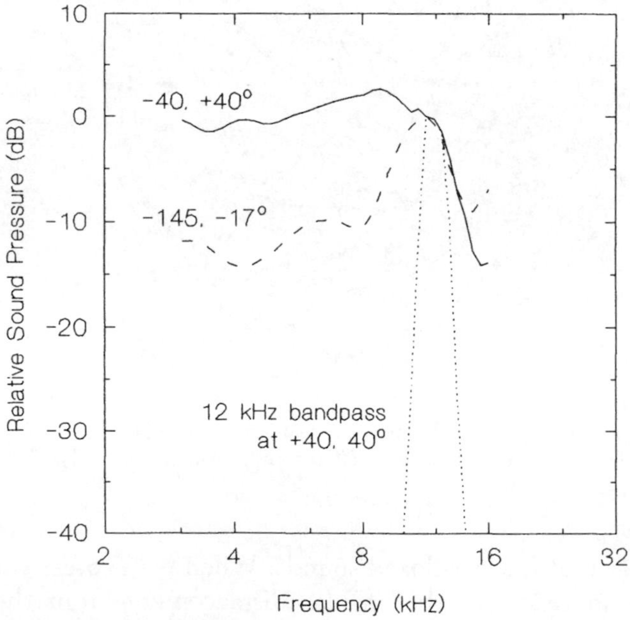

FIG. 7. Directional transfer functions. When a 12–kHz narrowband stimulus was presented from left 40°, +40° (front, left, and up), the subject whose DTFs are represented here consistently oriented near left 145°, –17° (back, left, and down). The DTFs recorded for those locations are indicated by solid and dashed lines. The dotted line is the stimulus spectrum added to the DTF at left 40°, +40°. [From Middlebrooks, 1992; reprinted with permission]

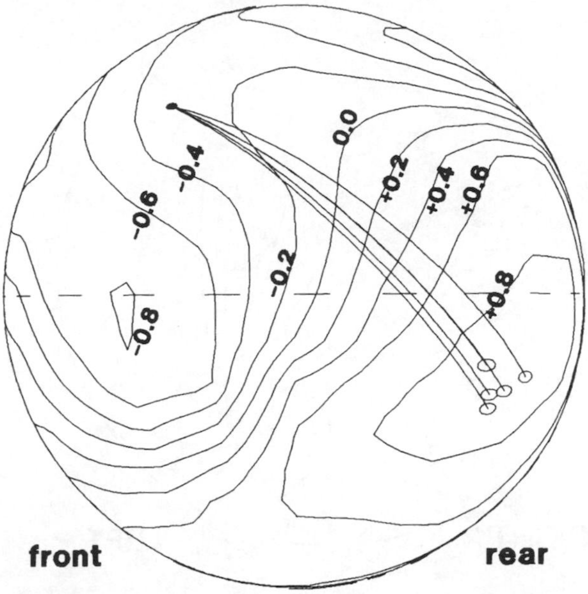

FIG. 8. Spatial distribution of spectral correlation for a noise band centered at 12 kHz. The viewpoint is from left 90°, 0°. The contours represent the correlation coefficient between the stimulus spectrum and DTFs at 1652 sites distributed evenly across the globe. The stimulus location at left 40°, +40° and five response locations are shown with symbols and arcs. [From Middlebrooks, 1992; reprinted with permission]

location contains a peak that coincides with the stimulus passband, whereas the DTF at the stimulus location peaks at a lower frequency. Frequency-by-frequency correlation coefficients were computed between each stimulus spectrum and each DTF in order to quantify their similarity. The results of this analysis are shown in Fig. 8 for the stimulus depicted in Fig. 7. The correlation coefficient was computed at each of 1652 equally spaced sites, and their values are represented by contours. The view is from the subject's left side. The DTFs for locations near the sound source (filled circle) had negative correlations with the stimulus, whereas those near the response locations (open circles) had correlations greater than +0.8.

We combined this correlation measure with a measure of the difference between the ILDs associated with stimulus and response locations. The result was a "similarity index" that scaled monotonically onto the predicted probability of a response at any particular location. For each stimulus location and center frequency, we computed the similarity index for each of 1652 locations around the subject, then shifted and scaled the index to have zero mean and unity variance. Figure 9 shows with contours the spatial distribution of similarity indices for one subject when a 6-kHz stimulus was presented from −20°, −40°. The behavioral responses straddle the contour that represents similarity indices equal to 1.5 standard deviations above the mean of the distribution.

As a measure of model performance across all behavioral trials, we ranked all of the 1652 similarity indices on each trial, then recorded the rank of the index that corresponded to response location. We then computed the median value of that rank for all trials by one subject at one stimulus center frequency. Figure 10

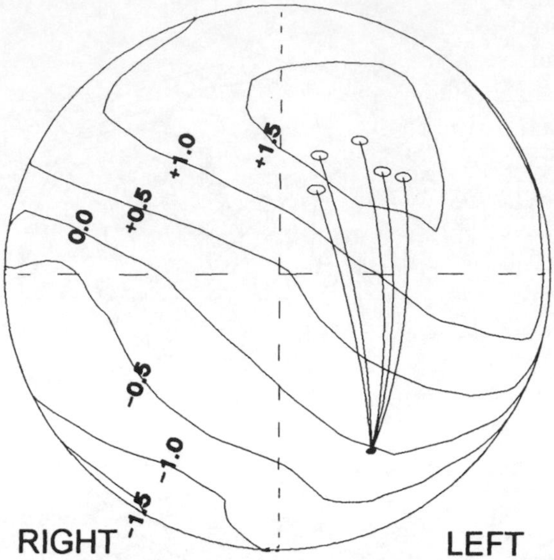

FIG. 9. Spatial distribution of similarity indices for a noise band centered at 6 kHz. The viewpoint is from 0°, 0° (i.e., straight in front). The contours represent the value of the *similarity index*, which represents the similarity of the stimulus spectrum and the ILD at the sound source location to the DTF and the ILD associated with each particular location. The DTF locations were distributed evenly across the globe. The stimulus location at left 20°, –40° and five response locations are shown with symbols and arcs. [From Middlebrooks, 1992; reprinted with permission]

shows the distribution of median ranks across all five subjects and four center frequencies. Random performance by the model would give a median rank of 50%. Instead, all median ranks that we measured were better than 20%, and the median of the distribution was 6.6%. A median rank of, say, 7%, means that if on each trial, one were to use the model to select 7% of the area of the coordinate sphere, the listener's response would fall within the selected area on half of the trials.

In our localization model, there is no explicit assignment of ILD or spectral shape cues to particular dimensions. Nevertheless, the narrowband localization results show that, at least under binaural conditions, horizontal localization is dominated by interaural cues and vertical localization and front/back localization require spectral cues. That conclusion comes from the observation that vertical and front/back localization, but not horizontal localization, are disrupted when spectral cues are altered by a narrowband filter. The narrowband localization experiment is an extreme case, because the filter not only shapes the stimulus spectrum in the frequency domain near the filter passband, but it also effectively eliminates spectral cues across frequency bands well above and below the filter passband. It might be that spectral cues contribute more to horizontal localization when such cues are available across a broader frequency range.

E. Monaural sound localization

One way to test the contribution of spectral shape cues to horizontal localization is to measure localization performance in the absence of binaural cues. Several studies have attempted to test monaural localization in that way by plugging one ear of normal binaural listeners (Fisher and Freedman, 1968; Oldfield and Parker, 1986; Butler, Humanski, and Musicant, 1990). That approach is successful in eliminating the normal spatial dependence of interaural difference cues, but it has the undesirable effect of introducing a potent, but erroneous, binaural cue that the sound source is always located on the side of the open ear. Under those experimental conditions, subjects tend to show a conspicuous lateral displacement of their localization judgments. We attempted to circumvent that problem by working with five patients who each had a long-standing, presumably congenital, hearing loss in one ear and normal hearing in the other ear (Slattery and Middlebrooks, 1994). We chose to work with monaural patients because the auditory systems of those patients presumably had no experience with normal binaural cues. We predicted that the patients might successfully utilize spectral shape cues for azimuth as well as for elevation.

The five monaural patients had complete unilateral sensorineural hearing loss in one ear across the 2- to 15-kHz frequency range of our localization stimulus. For each patient, the hearing loss was diagnosed prior to 3 years of age and was presumed to be congenital. In each patient, hearing thresholds in the unimpaired ear were within 20 dB of audiometric zero across the range of 250 Hz to 8 kHz. Seven control listeners in this study each had normal hearing in both ears. The control listeners were tested under binaural conditions and with one ear plugged. We tested localization in patients and controls with our standard free-field sound localization protocol, using 250-ms broadband noise bursts. Across trials, stimulus levels roved between 40 and 50 dB above threshold.

Figure 11 shows the localization performance of a control subject who wore a plug in his left ear. All of the responses were displaced toward the right, which is the side of the open ear. Nearly all of the responses fell to the right of the midline. This is the performance that one would expect of a subject who is making normal use of ILD cues for azimuth. When the left ear was plugged, the subject always experienced a greater sound pressure level in the right ear than in the left. A

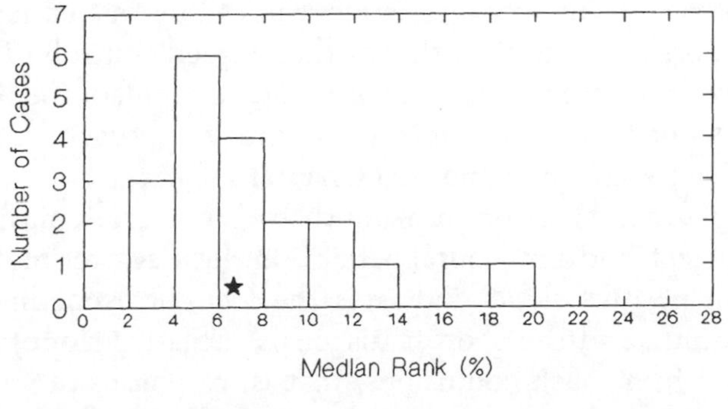

FIG. 10. Performance of the localization model. The success with which the localization model predicted a subject's behavior is represented by the *median rank*. The median rank can range from 0% to 100%, and 50% indicates chance performance. In the histogram shown here, each case represents one subject at one center frequency. The star indicates the median of this distribution. [From Middlebrooks, 1992; reprinted with permission]

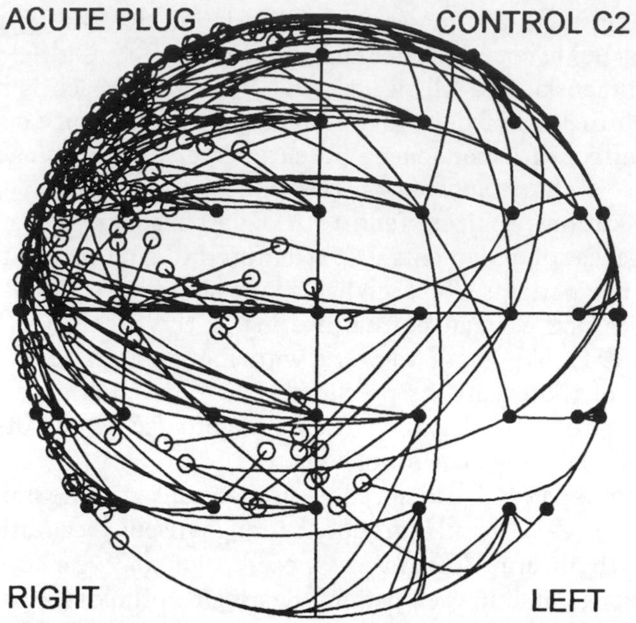

FIG. 11. Localization of broadband sound by a normal listener wearing a plug in the left ear. The viewpoint is straight in front. Note the consistent bias in responses toward the subject's right. Details of the plotting format are as in Fig. 5. [From Slattery and Middlebrooks, 1994; reprinted with permission]

rightward bias in sound pressure level normally signals that the sound source is on the right, so the subject's rightward responses were appropriate. We observed this behavior in all seven of the control subjects under unilateral plugged conditions and in two of the monaural patients.

Three of the monaural patients showed localization performance that was considerably better than that of the plugged controls or the other two patients in that they showed no systematic bias toward the hearing side. Figure 12 shows an example that is representative of these three patients. In the vertical dimension, localization was slightly better than the mean of the plugged controls, but the difference was not significant. Localization in azimuth by this patient, however, was substantially more accurate than that of the plugged controls. This patient's performance showed no systematic lateral bias, and nearly all of the responses fell within the correct quadrant. The subject's accuracy approached the range of accuracy that we have seen among normal binaural subjects.

Figure 13 compares localization in azimuth by a binaural control subject, a plugged control subject, and a monaural patient. In these scatter plots, the major diagonal (i.e., with positive slope) indicates the loci corresponding to perfect localization in azimuth, and the shorter diagonals (negative slope) indicate the locations of perfect front/back confusions, that is, responses in which the displacement from the vertical midline plane was correct but in which a front source was localized to the back or vice versa. Most of the responses of the binaural control (Fig. 13A) fell near the major diagonal, with a few front/back confusions. In contrast, the plugged control (Fig. 13B) always responded on the right side (i.e., positive azimuths). Responses to stimuli on that subject's right side showed some tendency to follow the major diagonal, but only in the sense that the subject tended to distinguish front from back correctly. The majority of responses to stimuli presented on the left were localized to the right and behind. The patient in Fig. 13C, who had no hearing in the right ear, showed greater scatter in responses than the normal control but showed none of the systematic bias shown by the plugged control. Performance was best within 40° of the front and rear midlines. Localization at the far right and far left was less accurate, but even far lateral sources tended to be localized within the correct quadrant, in contrast to the data from the plugged control. One possibility is that the patient represented in Fig. 13C exploited absolute stimulus level as a cue to sidedness, but our use of a stimulus that roved across a 10-dB range of levels should have confounded that cue to a large extent. The generally accurate localization performance of three of the five monaural patients that we tested suggested that they successfully exploited spectral shape cues for azimuth.

III. GENERAL DISCUSSION

The results of our narrowband localization experiments confirm previous observations that subjects make prominent errors in the vertical and front/back dimensions when required to localize strongly filtered sounds. Despite these errors, localization in azimuth was remarkably accurate. This suggests that when

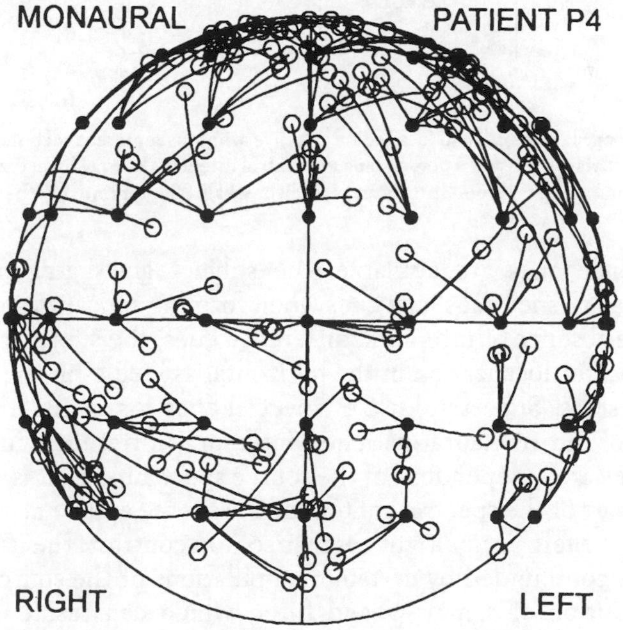

FIG. 12. Localization of broadband sound by a monaural patient. The patient had a complete hearing loss in the right ear. Although the scatter in responses is greater than for a normal binaural listener (e.g., Fig. 4), responses generally fell within the correct quadrant, and there was no consistent bias in responses. [From Slattery and Middlebrooks, 1994; reprinted with permission]

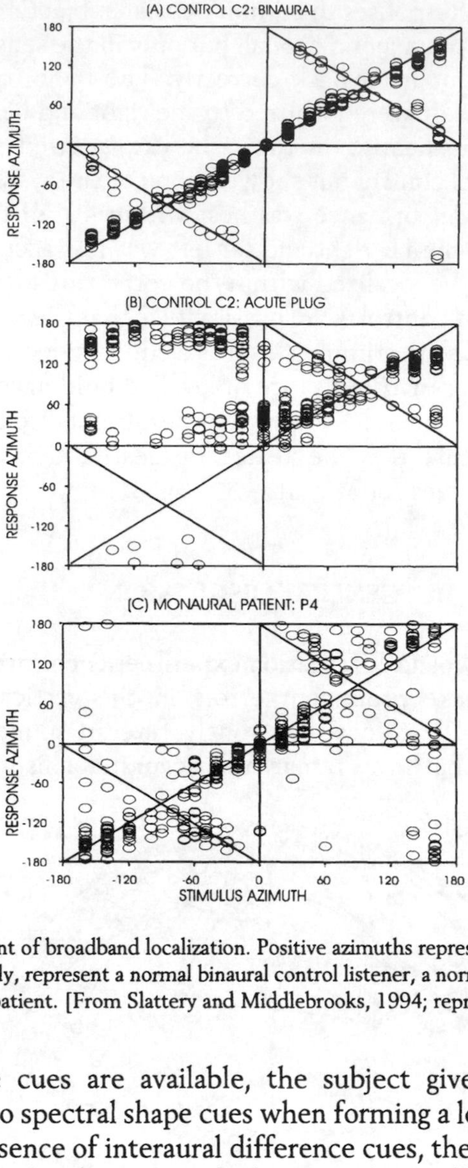

FIG. 13. Azimuth component of broadband localization. Positive azimuths represent each subject's right side. Parts A, B, and C, respectively, represent a normal binaural control listener, a normal listener wearing a plug in his left ear, and a monaural patient. [From Slattery and Middlebrooks, 1994; reprinted with permission]

interaural difference cues are available, the subject gives greater weight to interaural cues than to spectral shape cues when forming a localization judgment. Conversely, in the absence of interaural difference cues, the subject must rely on spectral shape cues for localization in the horizontal as well as in the vertical and front/back dimensions. Successful use of spectral cues for azimuth was demonstrated by some of our monaural patients. Interaural difference cues offer the advantage that they are independent of the source spectrum. That is, any spectral features that are part of the spectral content of the source appear at both ears and are eliminated by the left-versus-right comparison. In contrast, the use of spectral shape cues can be confounded by certain manipulations of the source spectrum, such as the imposition of a narrowband filter, which can result in erroneous localization responses.

We have described a simple quantitative model of localization that attempts to predict subjects' localization based on ILD and spectral shape cues; we disregarded interaural delays because the model was intended to account for our high-frequency localization results. The model assumes that the auditory system measures the ILD and the spectral shape at the tympanic membranes, then searches a library of ILDs and spectra to identify the most likely location of the sound source. There are two serious limitations to the spectral shape component of this model. The first is that the cross-correlation procedure that is used to recognize spectra, although mathematically convenient, is biologically implausible. It would require, in effect, that the auditory system store a complete copy of the external ear transfer function for each of some large number of sound locations. Certain artificial neural network architectures are more biologically plausible, are capable of the spectral recognition task, and would require much less storage. Neti, Young, and Schneider (1992) used such a network to model some neurophysiological localization results. Our model attempts to recognize spectra across a broad frequency range, whereas known neurophysiological mechanisms appear to work with local features of spectra.

The second limitation of our model is that it requires the listener to know the transfer function by which the stimulus has reached the tympanic membrane. Experimentally, one would compute an external ear transfer function by measuring the spectrum at the tympanic membrane and dividing by the known spectrum of the sound source. Under usual conditions of localization, however, the listener does not know the source spectrum precisely, so he or she must make certain assumptions about the source. In our model, the explicit assumption is that all source spectra are broad and flat. To a first approximation, that assumption is not unreasonable, because many natural sounds have broad flat spectra. Impulsive sounds, like the sound of a twig snapping or of one object striking another, are examples of natural sounds that have broad flat spectra. Moreover, we see that localization can fail when a source spectrum deviates too far from the "broad, flat" assumption, like when it is bandpassed or when it contains a prominent notch. Nevertheless, much of the information that is carried by sounds is coded in features of the spectra. A realistic model for extracting location cues from spectral shape cannot demand a flat source spectrum.

The transfer function of the external ear contains spectral slopes, peaks, and notches that are steeper or sharper than most information-bearing components of natural sounds. Certain investigators have championed particular spectral features as cues for sound localization. When a stimulus contains a spectral peak, as in the present study as well as in studies by Blauert (1969/1970) and by Butler and colleagues (Butler and Helwig, 1983; Butler, 1987), the localization judgments of subjects vary according to the center frequency of the peak. The response location tends to correspond to the area of space for which the external ear most effectively collects sound at the frequency of the peak. Butler described a model based on "covert peaks" in DTFs (Musicant and Butler, 1984). Elaborations of the Butler model are successful in predicting subjects' localization of narrowband stimuli (Musicant and Butler, 1984; Middlebrooks, 1992), but they are difficult to extend to the more general case of broadband localization and are difficult to relate to known biological mechanisms. Spectral notches also produce a potent illusion of source elevation (Bloom, 1977; Hebrank and Wright, 1974; Watkins, 1978). Poon and Brugge (1993) showed, in the cat, that a spectral notch is effectively coded by the frequency sensitivity of the auditory nerve. Young, Spirou, Rice, and Voigt (1992) identified neurons in the cat's dorsal cochlear nucleus that are sensitive to spectral notches that resemble notches that are present in DTFs from the cat's external ear.

Recent simulations by Zakarauskas and Cynader (1993) explored the spatial information that can be carried by spectral shape cues. Those investigators compared two models, one that transformed DTFs with a first-order finite difference operator and one that used a second-order finite difference operator. The first-order model emphasized spectral slopes in DTFs (the slopes of transfer function peaks and notches, for example) and required that the stimulus spectrum be locally flat. The second-order model emphasized changes in slope (e.g., the centers of peaks and notches) and required only that the spectrum have a locally constant slope. Experimental stimuli that contain spectral peaks or notches do not discriminate between these models because, for example, a narrowband notch contains two steep slopes as well as an abrupt change in slope. If we are to design detailed physiologically based models of localization mechanisms, we must identify the specific features of DTFs that constitute the most salient localization cues.

ACKNOWLEDGMENTS

I am pleased to acknowledge the contributions of Dr. David M. Green and Dr. William H. Slattery III to the research presented here. This research was supported by grants from the National Institute on Deafness and Other Communicative Disorders (NIDCD), the Office of Naval Research (ONR), and the Alfred P. Sloan Foundation.

REFERENCES

Batra, R., Kuwada, S., and Stanford, T. R. (**1989**). "Temporal coding of envelopes and their interaural delays in the inferior colliculus of the unanesthetized rabbit," J. Neurophysiol. **61**, 257–268.

Batteau, D. W. (**1967**). "The role of the pinna in human localization," Proc. Roy. Soc. Lond. B. **168**, 158–180.

Batteau, D. W. (**1968**). "Listening with the naked ear," in *The Neuropsychology of Spatially Oriented Behavior*, edited by S. J. Freedman (Dorsey Press, Homewood, IL), pp. 109–133.

Blauert, J. (**1969/1970**). "Sound localization in the median plane," Acustica **22**, 205–213.

Bloom, P. J. (**1977**). "Creating source elevation illusions by spectral manipulation," J. Audio Eng. Soc. **25**, 560–565.

Boudreau, J. C., and Tsuchitani, C. (**1968**). "Binaural interaction in the cat superior olive S segment," J. Neurophysiol. **31**, 442–454.

Butler, R. A. (**1987**). "An analysis of the monaural displacement of sound in space," Percept. Psychophys. **41**, 1–7.

Butler, R. A., and Flannery, R. (**1980**). "The spatial attributes of stimulus frequency and their role in monaural localization of sound in the horizontal plane," Percept. Psychophys. **28**, 449–457.

Butler, R. A., and Helwig, C. C. (**1983**). "The spatial attributes of stimulus frequency in the median sagittal plane and their role in sound localization," Am. J. Otolaryngol. **4**, 165–173.

Butler, R. A., Humanski, R. A., and Musicant, A. D. (**1990**). "Binaural and monaural localization of sound in two-dimensional space," Perception **19**, 241–256.

Crow, G., Langford, T. L., and Moushegian, G. (**1980**). "Coding of interaural time differences by some high-frequency neurons of the inferior colliculus: Responses to noise bands and two-tone complexes," Hear. Res. **3**, 147–153.

Fisher, H. G., and Freedman, S. J. (**1968**). "The role of the pinna in auditory localization." J. Aud. Res. **8**, 15–26.

Gilkey, R. H., Good, M. D., Ericson, M. A., Brinkman, J., and Stewart, J. M. (**1995**). "A pointing technique for rapidly collecting localization responses in auditory research," Behav. Res. Meth., Instr., Comp. **27**, 1–11.

Goldberg, J. M., and Brown, P. B. (**1969**). "Response of binaural neurons of dog superior olivary complex to dichotic tonal stimuli: Some physiological mechanisms of sound localization," J. Neurophysiol. **32**, 613–636.

Hebrank, J., and Wright, D. (**1974**). "Spectral cues used in the localization of sound sources on the median plane," J. Acoust. Soc. Am. **56**, 1829–1834.

Knudsen, E.I. (**1982**). "Auditory and visual maps of space in the optic tectum of the owl," J. Neurosci. **2**, 1177–1194.

Licklider, J. C. R., Webster, J. C., and Hedlun, J. M. (**1950**). "On the frequency limits of binaural beats," J. Acoust. Soc. Am. **22**, 468–473.

Makous, J. C., and Middlebrooks, J. C. (**1990**). "Two-dimensional sound localization by human listeners," J. Acoust. Soc. Am. **87**, 2188–2200.

Middlebrooks, J. C. (**1987**). "Binaural mechanisms of spatial tuning in the cat's superior colliculus," J. Neurophysiol. **57**, 688–701.

Middlebrooks, J. C. (**1992**). "Narrow-band sound localization related to external ear acoustics," J. Acoust. Soc. Am. **92**, 2607–2624.

Middlebrooks, J. C., and Green, D. M. (**1990**). "Directional dependence of interaural envelope delays," J. Acoust. Soc. Am. **87**, 2149–2162.

Middlebrooks, J. C., and Green, D. M. (**1991**). "Sound localization by human listeners," Annu. Rev. Psychol. **42**, 135–159.

Middlebrooks, J. C., Makous, J. C., and Green, D. M. (**1989**). "Directional sensitivity of sound-pressure levels in the human ear canal," J. Acoust. Soc. Am. **86**, 89–108.

Middlebrooks, J. C., and Pettigrew, J. D. (**1981**). "Functional classes of neurons in primary auditory cortex (A1) of the cat distinguished by sensitivity to sound location," J. Neurosci. **1**, 107–120.

Musicant, A. D., and Butler, R. A. (**1984**). "The psychophysical basis of monaural localization," Hear. Res. **14**, 185–190.

Musicant, A. D., and Butler, R. A. (**1985**). "Influence of monaural spectral cues on binaural localization," J. Acoust. Soc. Am. **77**, 202–208.

Neti, C., Young, E. D., and Schneider, M. H. (**1992**). "Neural network models of sound localization based on directional filtering by the pinna," J. Acoust. Soc. Am. **92**, 3140–3156.

Oldfield, S. R., and Parker, P. A. (**1986**). "Acuity of sound localization: a topography of auditory space. III. Monaural hearing conditions," Perception **15**, 67–81.

Poon, P. W. F., and Brugge, J. F. (**1993**). "Sensitivity of auditory nerve fibers to spectral notches," J. Neurophysiol. **70**, 655–666.

Rayleigh, Lord (J. W. Strutt, 3rd Baron of Rayleigh) (**1907**). "On our perception of sound direction," Philos. Mag. **13**, 214–232.

Rose, J. E., Gross, N. B., Geisler, C. D., and Hind, J. E. (**1966**). "Some neural mechanisms in the inferior colliculus of the cat which may be relevant to localization of a sound source," J. Neurophysiol. **29**, 288–314.

Shaw, E. A. G. (1974). "Transformation of sound pressure level from the free field to the eardrum in the horizontal plane," J. Acoust. Soc. Am. **56**, 1848–1861.

Shaw, E. A. G., and Teranishi, R. (**1968**). "Sound pressure generated in an external-ear replica and real human ears by a nearby point source," J. Acoust. Soc. Am. **44**, 240–249.

Slattery, W. H., III, and Middlebrooks, J. C. (**1994**). "Monaural sound localization: Acute versus chronic unilateral impairment," Hear. Res. **75**, 38–46.

Watkins, A. J. (**1978**). "Psychoacoustical aspects of synthesized vertical locale cues," J. Acoust. Soc. Am. **63**, 1152–1165.

Wightman, F. L., and Kistler, D. J. (**1989**). "Headphone simulation of free-field listening. II: Psychophysical validation," J. Acoust. Soc. Am. **85**, 868–878.

Yin, T. C. T., Kuwada, S., and Sujaku, Y. (**1984**). "Interaural time sensitivity of high-frequency neurons in the inferior colliculus," J. Acoust. Soc. Am. **76**, 1401–1410.

Young, E. D., Spirou, G. A., Rice, J. J., and Voigt, H. F. (**1992**). "Neural organization and responses to complex stimuli in the dorsal cochlear nucleus," Phil. Trans. Soc. Lond. B. **336**, 407–413.

Zakarauskas, P., and Cynader, M. S. (**1993**). "A computational theory of spectral cue localization," J. Acoust. Soc. Am. **94**, 1323–1331.

Zhou, B., Green, D. M., and Middlebrooks, J. C. (**1992**). "Characterization of external ear impulse responses using Golay codes," J. Acoust. Soc. Am. **92**, 1169–1171.

Zwislocki, J., and Feldman, R. S. (**1956**). "Just noticeable differences in dichotic phase," J. Acoust. Soc. Am. **28**, 860–864.

Chapter 5

Spatial Referents of Stimulus Frequencies: Their Role in Sound Localization

Robert A. Butler
University of Chicago
(Received December 1993; revised October 1994)

Stimulus frequency has a referent in space. When listening monaurally, the apparent location of a narrowband noise in the auditory hemifield ipsilateral to the functioning ear is governed by its frequency content, not its actual location. A spatial referent map of the different stimulus frequencies can be constructed. The pattern of the spatial map roughly is similar from one listener to the next. A seemingly related event occurs when measuring the physical acoustics of the external ear. Specifically, when recording sound pressure levels at the entrance to the ear canal for those stimuli originating in the same auditory hemifield, a pattern of maximum responses emerges. There is a place in space where, for example, a narrow noise band centered at 6.0 kHz generates a sound pressure level that is greater than it is for any other location in the hemifield. This is called the covert peak area for the 6.0-kHz centered noise. A map of a subject's covert peak area for differently centered narrow noise bands resembles his or her spatial reference map for these stimuli. It is proposed that the spatial distribution of the covert peak areas is the acoustical basis for the spatial referents of the different stimulus frequencies. The latter serves as the primary spectral cues for both monaural and binaural localization.

INTRODUCTION

The "duplex" theory of localization of sound in space, strongly supported by decades of research, has now been found wanting—wanting, in the sense that it may not adequately account for perceived elevation of sound. Certainly it cannot account for monaural localization of sound in space, but it was not designed to do so. What is required to handle these events is the availability of spectral cues. In the process of investigating the influence of spectral cues on perceived elevation as well as on monaural localization, one event kept recurring: namely, stimulus frequency has a referent in space. The purpose of this chapter is to first link spatial referents of stimulus frequency to acoustic measurements carried out at the entrance of the ear canal, and then to describe instances where impoverishment of selected spectral cues leads to disruption of localization of sound.

I. BEHAVIORAL MEASUREMENTS

Spatial referents (SRs) of stimulus frequency can be best demonstrated by rendering unusable the interaural differences in stimulus arrival time or stimulus level either through (1) presenting the stimulus in the median sagittal plane or (2) blocking one ear. When either of these procedures is carried out, the apparent location of a tonal stimulus or a narrowband of noise depends largely on the frequency content of the stimulus, not its actual location. The observation is not new. Pratt (1930) was the first to systematically study SRs. His listeners judged high-frequency tones presented in the median sagittal plane to originate above tones lower in frequency, irrespective of source elevation. Subsequently, Roffler and Butler (1968) elaborated on Pratt's work by, among other things, demonstrating the same phenomenon in children 4 and 5 years of age—an age before they use the words "high" and "low" to describe the perceptual experience of pitch. In view of the finding that tonal frequencies possess SRs, it would not be unexpected, although no one looked before Blauert (1969/1970), that narrowbands of noise differing in center frequency also possess SRs. Blauert had listeners report the location, in the median sagittal plane, of differently centered third-octave bands. Regardless of the actual position of the stimuli, those bands centering at 4 and 6 kHz appeared to come from in front, those centered at 8 kHz appeared to come from overhead, and those centered at 12 kHz appeared to come from behind. With a probe tube placed near the eardrum, a boost in sound pressure level at specific frequency segments coincided with the location judgments of these same frequencies; for example, the sound pressure level for 4 and 6 kHz was greater when the sound originated in front. Blauert referred to these differentially boosted frequency segments as "directional bands."

The SRs of stimulus frequencies, described earlier, have all the trappings of an auditory illusion. The sound appears to come from where it isn't. The first step toward building an argument that SRs, originally referred to as "judgmental biases," contribute to localization accuracy stemmed from the experiment of Belendiuk and Butler (1977). They puzzled over their finding that providing more spectral information in the stimulus did not necessarily result in improved monaural localization performance for sounds originating in the frontal segment of the horizontal plane (–15° to –75°). This result was contrary to that reported earlier by Butler and Planert (1976). The latter found that monaural localization accuracy in the median sagittal plane and in the horizontal plane increased with enhancement of stimulus bandwidth. What happened in the Belendiuk and Butler (1977) study was that a bandpass noise of a specific center frequency, stimulus

A, appeared to come from a certain location in the horizontal plane. Two other bandpass noises, stimulus B and stimulus C, differing in center frequency from stimulus A and from one another, were also employed. Stimulus B appeared to originate at the same location as stimulus A. Stimulus C appeared to originate from a different location. When stimulus A and stimulus B were presented simultaneously, monaural localization failed to improve over that recorded when either stimulus A or stimulus B was presented alone—the spectral cues were redundant. But when stimulus A and stimulus C were presented simultaneously, localization performance did, in fact, improve. Presumably, the SRs linked to the latter two stimuli were more widely distributed along the horizontal plane, thereby promoting accuracy in monaural localization. Observing that listeners could localize with reasonable accuracy an 11.0-kHz high-pass noise, we wondered whether the SRs of the components of this high-pass noise were distributed along the horizontal plane. If so, SRs would take on some meaning in the localization process; they would not be considered merely a laboratory curiosity. One listener was tested; the stimulus always originated at –45° azimuth. She reported that the 1.0-kHz-wide noise bands centered at 11.0 and 12.0 kHz appeared to come from –60° and –75° azimuth; that the 1.0-kHz-wide noise bands centered at 13.0 kHz appeared to come from –15° azimuth; and that a narrow band centered at 14.0 kHz appeared to come from –30° azimuth. This observation suggested that Belendiuk and Butler were on the right track and the finding served as the basis for the experiment of Butler and Flannery (1980). They presented 1.0-kHz-wide noise bands at center frequencies ranging from 4.0 through 14.0 kHz. The loudspeakers were positioned 15° apart, center-to-center, at azimuthal positions of –15°, –30°, –45°, –60°, –75°, and –90° azimuth. The stimulus was delivered in a haphazard order from –30°, –60°, and –90°. Listeners with their right ear blocked were asked to identify the loudspeaker delivering the sound. Figure 1 describes the pattern of location judgments for the 8 subjects. The perceived locations of the stimuli were dependent on their center frequency, not their actual location. Notice that as the center frequency was increased, the apparent location of the sound moved toward the side; then with further increases the apparent location of the sound switched to the front, and with still further increases in the center frequency the apparent location of the sound migrated again toward the side. For some listeners, the sound appeared to switch abruptly to the front when the center frequency reached 13.0 and 14.0 kHz. These disruptions in the migration of the apparent location of the sound when center frequency is increased are designated as breakpoints—events that have special importance for proficient localization performances. Specifically, for equal bandwidths, listeners' location judgments were more accurate if the frequency content of the stimulus spanned the breakpoint. When this happens, two adjacent components within the noise band possess widely different spatial referents, which somehow results in improved localization. Butler and Helwig (1983) followed up on these monaural studies by presenting various bandpass noise stimuli in the median sagittal plane under binaural listening conditions. They demonstrated that listeners less often chose a segment of the plane as the sound's source if that segment was not represented by SRs linked to the stimulus.

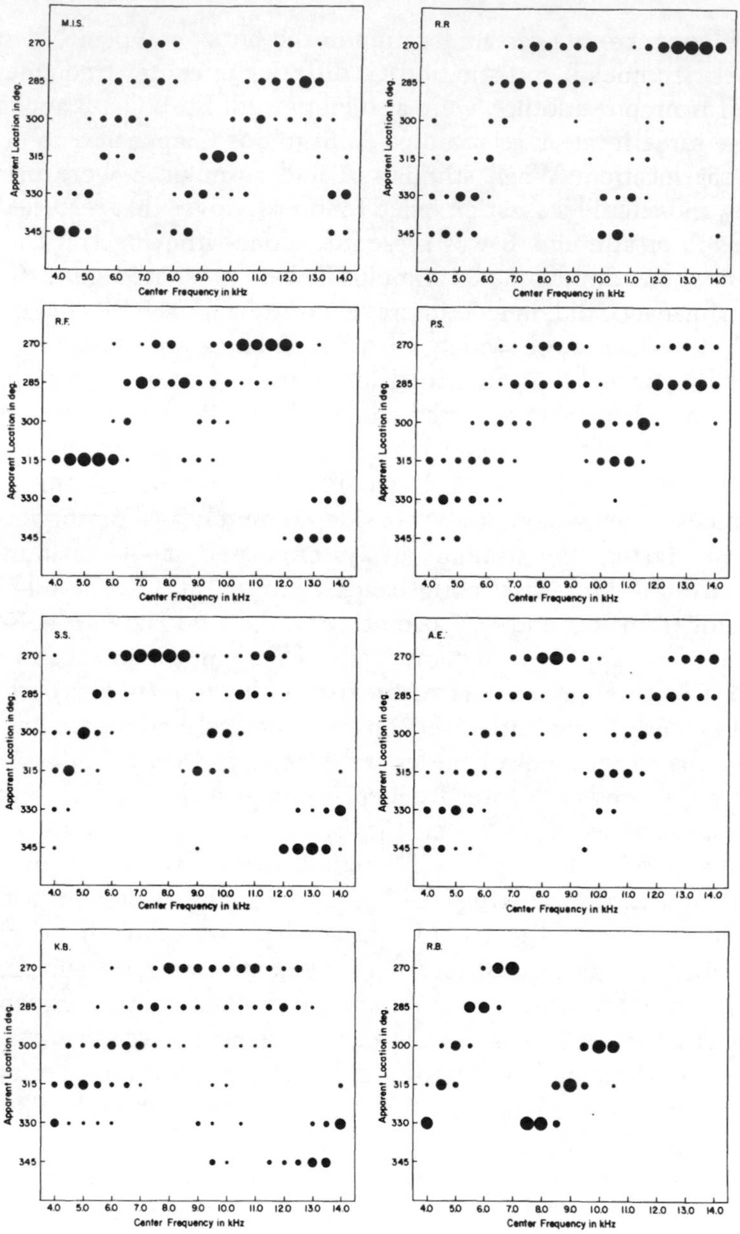

FIG. 1. Apparent location as a function of the center frequency of a 1.0-kHz wide noise burst. The area of the circles represents number of location judgments, with the largest circle in the figure indicating nine judgments and the smallest circle indicating one judgment. Subjects are identified by their initials. [From Butler and Flannery, 1980.]

II. ACOUSTIC MEASUREMENTS IN EAR CANAL

The SR of stimulus frequency is a behavioral event. By itself, it provides insight into the way in which spectral cues serve to promote monaural localization accuracy in the horizontal plane as well as monaural and binaural localization accuracy in the median sagittal plane. But in what way are SRs linked to the physical acoustics of the listening situation? This question has motivated much of the research carried out in the Psychoacoustics Laboratory at the University of Chicago. The research question is simple: What is the connection between the pattern of SRs for differently centered noise bands and the pattern of sound pressure levels, measured at the ear canal entrance, generated by these narrow noise bands presented from various locations in space? Blauert (1969/1970) made a significant start on this problem by his innovative research described at the beginning of this chapter. Others have elaborated on Blauert's findings. But before characterizing the physical event, that is, the pattern of sound pressure levels measured at the ear canal entrance, a word of background is in order. For any given tone or narrow band of noise presented in the free field, there is a place in space at which the sound pressure level, generated by the stimulus and measured just inside the entrance of the ear canal, is greater than that recorded when that same tone or narrow noise band comes from any other spatial location. This becomes evident when the amplitude of the ear canal microphone output is plotted against the location of the sound source with frequency serving as the parameter. Butler (1987) has referred to the highest point on the curve as the *covert peak*, because the location where a specific narrow band generates maximum output at the ear canal microphone is not always apparent when the microphone output is plotted against frequency with source location serving as the parameter. These two situations are illustrated in Fig. 2. Loudspeakers were positioned in the horizontal plane 15° apart, center-to-center. In the left-hand panel of the figure, the head related-transfer-function (HRTF) is plotted against azimuthal position of the sound source with center frequency of a 1.0-kHz-wide noise band serving as the parameter. With the center frequency fixed at 11.0 kHz (see dotted line), a peak in the function occurs when the source is positioned at 80° azimuth; the output of the ear canal microphone is greater when the 11.0-kHz

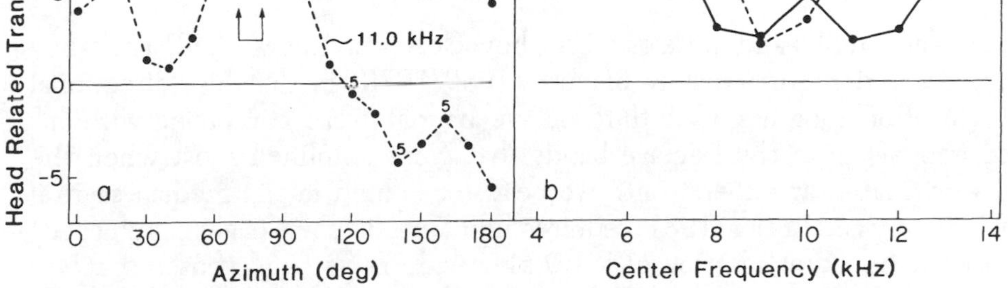

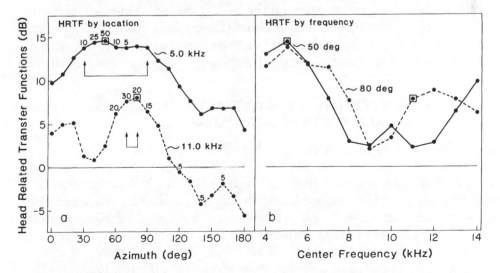

FIG. 2. Nature and determination of covert peaks. (a) HRTFs by source location for two fixed CFs. Each CF's absolute maximum energy (covert peak) is denoted by squares. (b) HRTFs by CF for those azimuthal locations at which each CF's maximum occurred. Again, the covert peaks are denoted by squares. [From Humanski and Butler, 1988.]

centered narrow noise originates from 80° azimuth than when it originates from any other location along the horizontal plane. When plotting HRTF against center frequency of the noise band, right-hand panel, the point on the curve for the center frequency of 11.0 kHz originating at 80° azimuth has lost its eminence, being several decibels down from the peak of the function. As evident from Fig. 2, the function relating HRTF to source location has no distinct peak. Given the error inherent in the measurement of a covert peak, the concept has been extended to include all source positions generating a sound pressure level, measured at the ear canal entrance, within 1 dB of the maximum. Rogers and Butler (1992) called this constellation of loudspeakers the *covert peak area* (CPA).

A CPA is equivalent to an isolevel contour—a term employed by those engaged in sound pressure measurements in animal pinnae and by Middlebrooks, Makous, and Green (1989) in their measurements on the human pinnae. The latter authors determined the directionality of sound pressure at the ear canal for broadband noise presented in two-dimensional space. Transforming the time waveform into the frequency domain, they plotted 5-dB isolevel contours for 4.0 through 14.0 kHz in 2.0-kHz steps. Generally speaking, with increasing frequency, the maximum sound pressure levels migrated from in front (4.0-kHz component) toward the rear and above (8.0-kHz component), although at 8.0 kHz the pattern split with one segment appearing below the horizontal plane and rearward. At the 10.0-kHz component, maximum sound pressure level was recorded when the sound source was toward the rear and below the horizontal plane. At the 12.0-kHz component, the pattern again split with one segment positioned toward the rear and spanning the horizontal plane, and the other segment being positioned in front and also spanning the horizontal plane where it remained for the 14.0-kHz component. Individual differences were observed, but the overall pattern of maximum sound pressure levels as a function of the various frequency components was similar among listeners. Of interest is the finding that pinna measurements in the cat also show migration of spatial maxima (CPAs) with changes in stimulus frequency. In addition, at places of abrupt transition in spatial maxima, the pattern splits into two locations of spatial maxima (Musicant, Chan, and Hind, 1990).

III. RELATION BETWEEN BEHAVIORAL MEASUREMENTS AND ACOUSTIC MEASUREMENTS

Given the data on SRs and those on CPAs, how closely are they linked? That they are linked was demonstrated by Blauert (1969/1970) in that his "directional bands" (location judgments of third-octave bands) were consonant with his boosted bands (those third-octave bands that were amplified most when the stimulus originated at either front, overhead, or behind in the median sagittal plane). Flannery and Butler (1981) required monaural listeners (right ear plugged) to report the apparent location of a 1.0-kHz wide noise band centered at 4.0 through 9.0 kHz. The stimuli always originated at –45° azimuth; loudspeakers were arrayed 15° apart from –15° to –90° azimuth. As described earlier, the apparent location of the stimuli was dependent on stimulus center frequency, not actual location. In other words the SRs of stimulus frequencies were obtained.

Next, sound pressure measurements were made at the listeners' ear canal entrance. A reasonably close relation was found between the SR of a particular frequency segment and the place in space (CPA) where that frequency segment generated the greatest sound pressure vis-à-vis other places along the horizontal plane. Later, Musicant and Butler (1984), equipped with a miniature microphone of a greater frequency response range, repeated the Flannery–Butler study. The center frequency of the 1.0-kHz wide frequency band extended to 14.0 kHz and the loudspeakers covered the entire left hemifield. Strong support was obtained for the purported linkage between SRs and CPAs. The Middlebrooks (1992) study more thoroughly delved into the linkage between behavioral and acoustical events central to auditory localization. He presented binaural listeners with broadband noise and 1/6-octave bandpass noise bursts centered at 6.0, 8.0, 10.0, and 12.0 kHz. Subjects were required to signify the origin of the source in two-dimensional space. Directional transfer functions were also obtained at the entrance of the ear canal and the "proximal stimulus," that present in the ear canal, was computed by combining the directional transfer function with the spectra of the narrow noise bands. A main finding was that the apparent location of the differently centered 1/6-octave bandpass noise was in the spatial region where a broadband noise emanating from that same spatial region would have produced the proximal stimulus spectrum—that is, that spectrum present at the ear canal entrance. Overall, the pattern of location judgments of the narrow noise bands was in accord with the pattern of sound pressure levels reported by Middlebrooks, Makous, and Green (1989). That is, what we have called CPAs were associated with the pattern of location judgments of differently centered 2.0-kHz-wide noise bands.

In the present chapter, a more detailed account of the linkage between CPAs and SRs is presented based on measurements of sound originating in two-dimensional space. When monaural listeners were asked to report the location of differently centered narrow noise bands, the apparent location or SR of these narrow noise bands changed in a relatively orderly way with variations in center frequency. The first set of data concerns monaural location judgments of a listener when the center frequency of a 1-kHz-wide noise band was changed from 4 to 14 kHz in steps of 0.5 kHz. Loudspeakers, 104 of them, were positioned in the left hemifield 15° apart, ranging from 0° to 180° in the horizontal plane, and from –45° to +60° in the vertical plane. Listeners used a simple code to report their location judgments. The columns of loudspeakers in the horizontal plane were numbered from 1 to 13, with 1 placed directly in front and 13 placed directly behind the listener. The rows of loudspeakers in the vertical plane were numbered from 1 to 8, with 1 placed at –45° elevation, and 8 placed at +60° elevation. Listeners were asked to report the horizontal position first, then the vertical position. They were instructed not to move their head; a headrest fostered compliance with the instructions. In this monaural localization task, the stimuli always came from –90° from midline (left hemifield) and 0° elevation.

Figure 3 illustrates the SR map for listener V.C. The mean SR for each center frequency ranging from 4.0 through 14.0 kHz in 0.5-kHz steps is plotted. For clarity of exposition, not all points in the display are identified by their center frequency, but the sequence of center frequencies is apparent. The discontinuities in the display

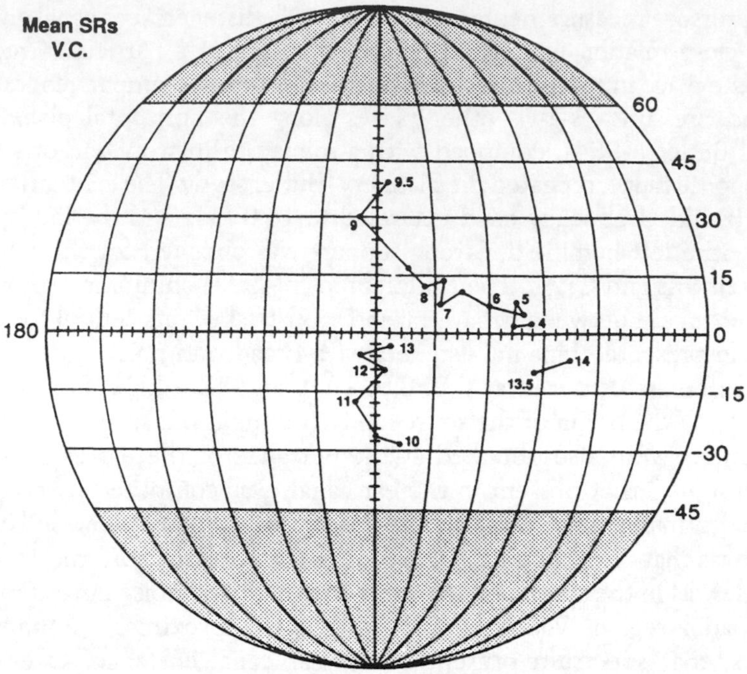

FIG. 3. Pattern of mean SRs as a function of the center frequency of a 1.0-kHz-wide noise band for listener V.C.

reflect an abrupt jump in the spatial referent plot to either a lower elevation or to a frontal location. These were the breakpoints that were referred to earlier.

Ear canal measurements were made at each differently centered 1.0-kHz wide noise band when the narrow noise was delivered from each of the 104 loudspeakers. The respective CPAs were identified and the mean values of the CPAs are plotted in Fig. 4 (listener V.C.) for the various center frequencies. It is instructive to compare the SR plot with the plot for CPAs. The patterns of the two events—a behavioral measure and a physical measure—show an overall similarity, but by no means do they map closely on one another. The largest differences occur at the breakpoints. The jump from above to below the horizontal plane occurred at a lower center frequency (9.0 kHz) for the CPA plot vis-à-vis the SR plot. The jump from side to front in the CPA plot also occurred at a center frequency (12.0 kHz) lower than the comparable jump shown in the SR plot. Figures 5 and 6 illustrate the plots of mean SRs and the mean location of the CPAs, respectively, for listener M.U. Again there is a similarity of patterns of migration as the center frequency was increased; the discontinuities were present, and the abrupt changes in the location of the mean CPAs again occurred at a lower center frequency than did the abrupt changes shown in the SR pattern. In fact, listener M.U. never indicated that noise bursts centered at 13.0 and 14.0 kHz appeared to come from the front, although the CPA for these center frequencies were positioned in front. The SR and CPA data for a third listener, Z.M. are shown in Figs. 7 and 8. For Z.M. there is a greater mismatch between her SR and the CPA patterns, but a similarity between the patterns of the two sets of measurements is readily recognizable.

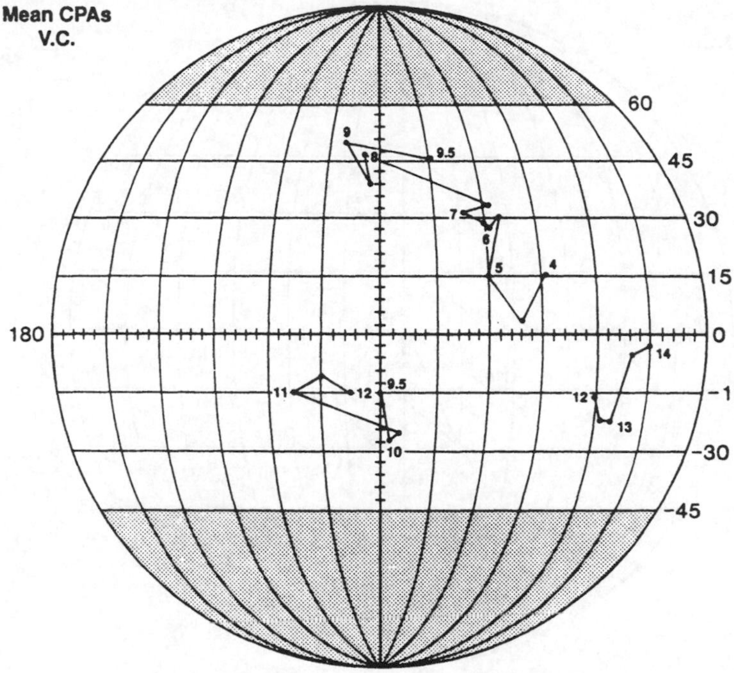

FIG. 4. Pattern of mean CPAs as a function of the center frequency of a 1.0-kHz-wide noise band for listener V.C.

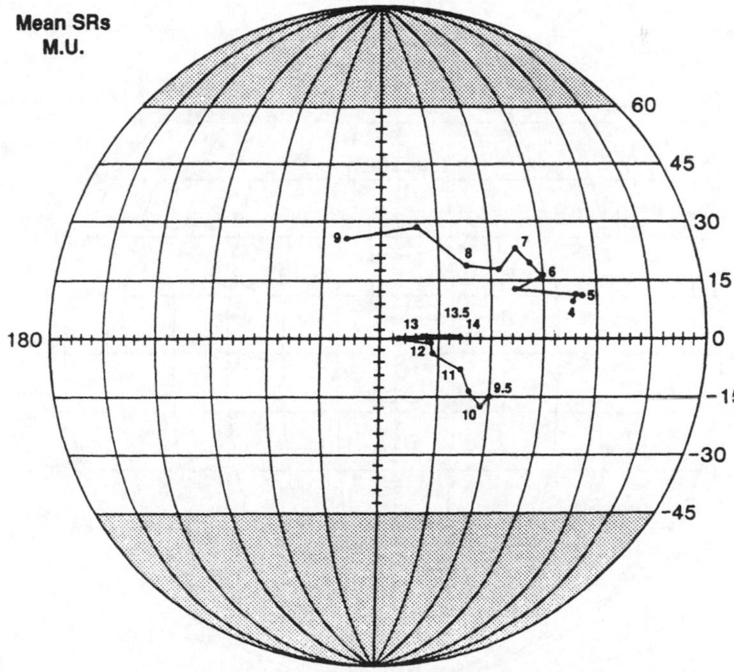

FIG. 5. Pattern of mean SRs as a function of the center frequency of a 1.0-kHz-wide noise band for listener M.U.

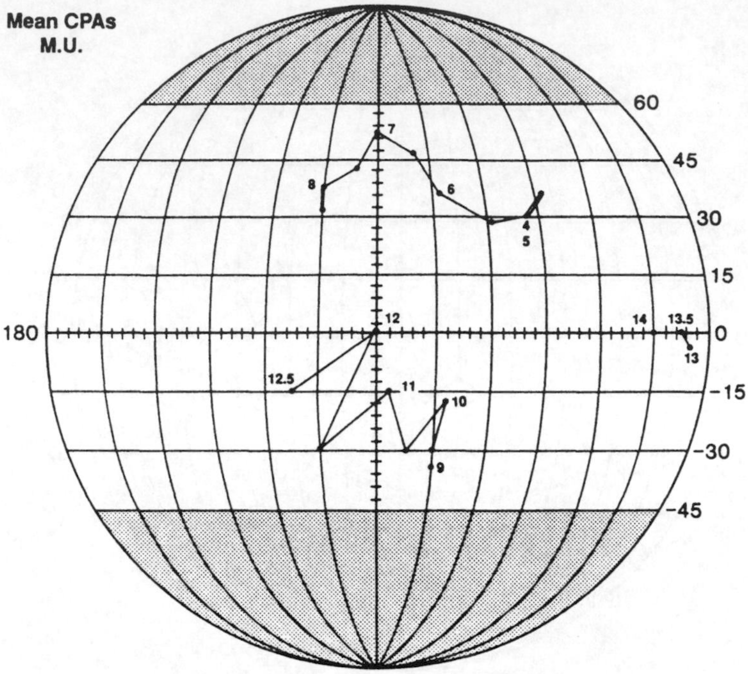

FIG. 6. Pattern of mean CPAs as a function of the center frequency of a 1.0-kHz-wide noise band for listener M.U.

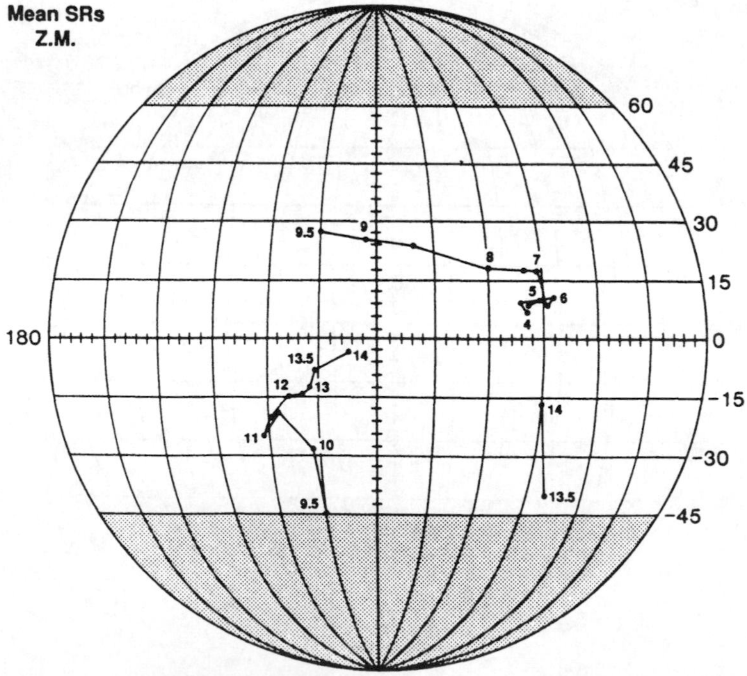

FIG. 7. Pattern of mean SRs as a function of the center frequency of a 1.0-kHz-wide noise band for listener Z.M.

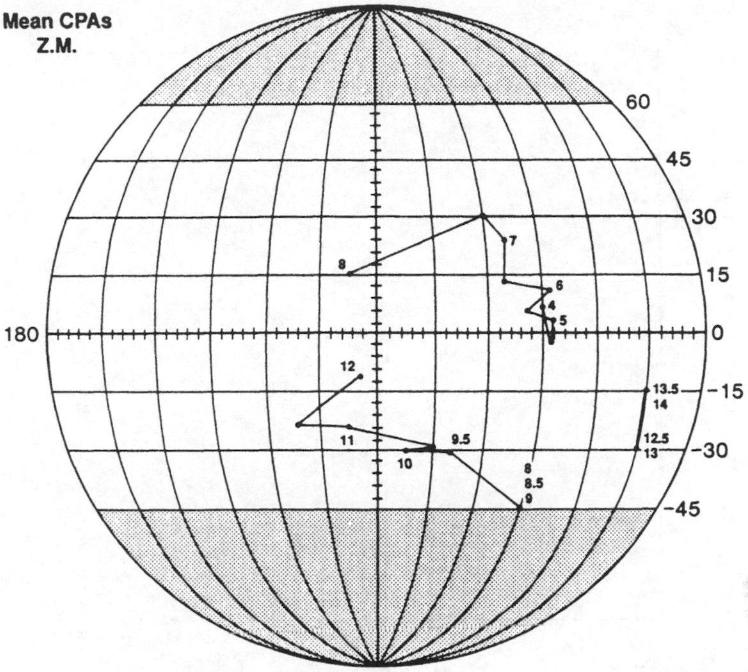

FIG. 8. Pattern of mean CPAs as a function of the center frequency of a 1.0-kHz-wide noise band for listener Z.M.

The overall relation between SRs and CPAs is more clearly shown by plotting mean location judgments, that is, the SRs, against mean location of the CPA with center frequency of the narrow noise band serving as the parameter. This is displayed for both the vertical plane and horizontal plane using data obtained on listeners V.C., M.U., and Z.M. (see Figs. 9 through 14). The relation between the two sets of data is reasonably orderly. The discontinuities that characterized the breakpoints in Figs. 3 through 8 are prominent as outliers in Figs. 9 through 14.

In a recent experiment (Butler and Musicant, unpublished observations), CPAs associated with two differently centered 2.0-kHz-wide noise bands, were selected so that one CPA was positioned above and the other below 0° elevation; none of the frequency segments involved the breakpoint; hence, none exhibited the discontinuity observed in the previous figures. The 104 loudspeakers were arrayed in the left hemifield. Subjects under binaural listening conditions were required to call out the location of the sound source. Figure 15 shows mean location judgment (i.e., the mean SRs) plotted against the CPAs in the vertical plane. In agreement with Middlebrooks (1992), perceived elevation of differently centered narrow noise band was in close accord with the spatial pattern of sound pressure levels generated by the noise bands and measured at the ear canal entrance.

IV. IMPLICATIONS FOR LOCALIZATION PROFICIENCY

In what way might the correspondence between the patterns of SRs and CPAs, based on monaural data, relate to accuracy in binaural localization of broadband noise? This is the core question. Butler and Musicant (1993) have made some

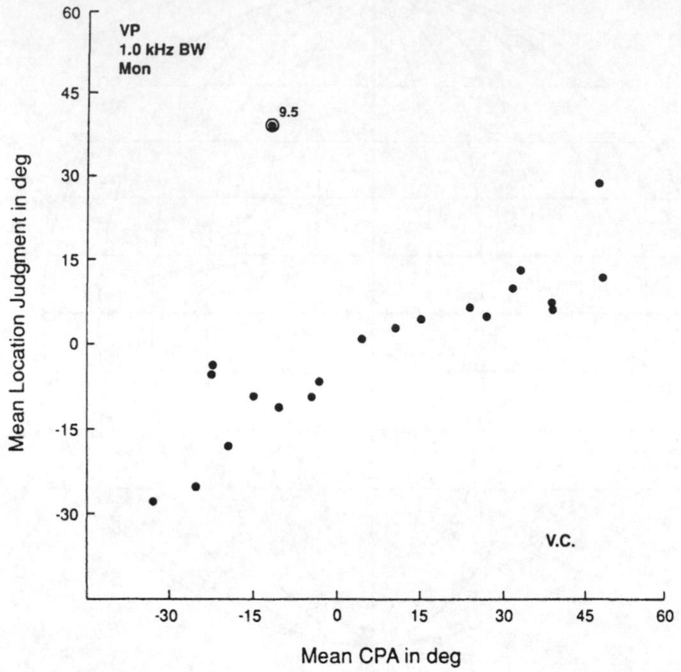

FIG. 9. Vertical plane (VP): Mean location judgment plotted against mean CPA with center frequency of 1.0-kHz-wide noise bands serving as the parameter. The outlier is identified by its center frequency. The listener is V.C.

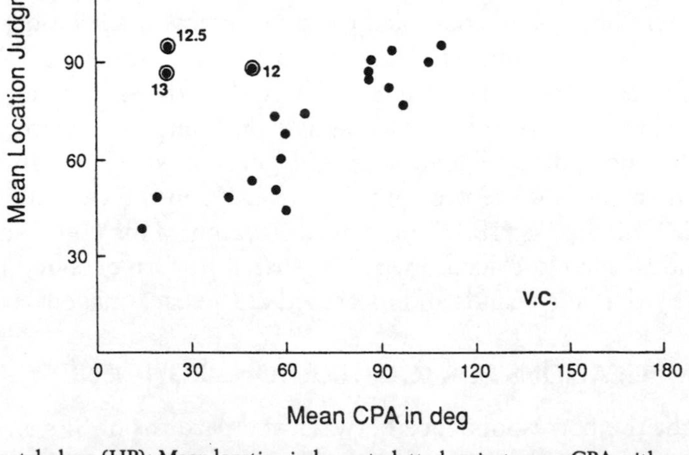

FIG. 10. Horizontal plane (HP): Mean location judgment plotted against mean CPA with center frequency of 1.0-kHz-wide noise bands serving as the parameter. The outliers are identified by their center frequency. The listener is V.C.

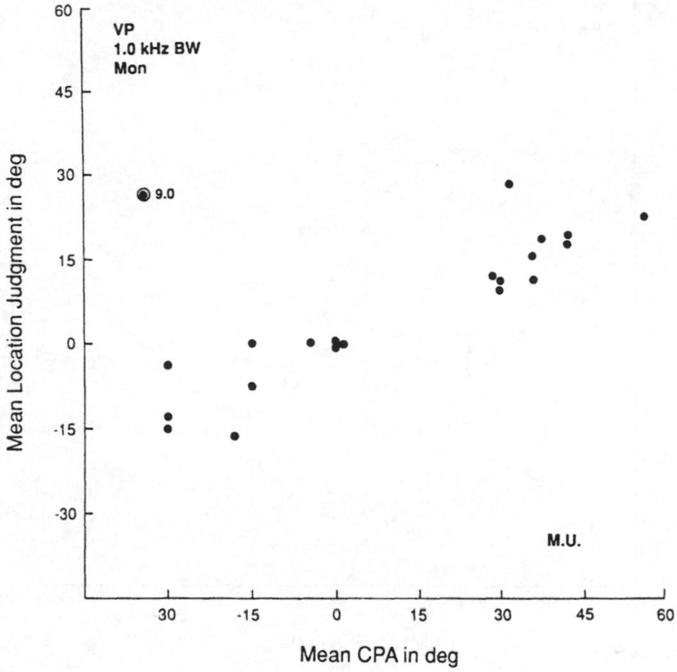

FIG. 11. Vertical plane plots for listener M.U.

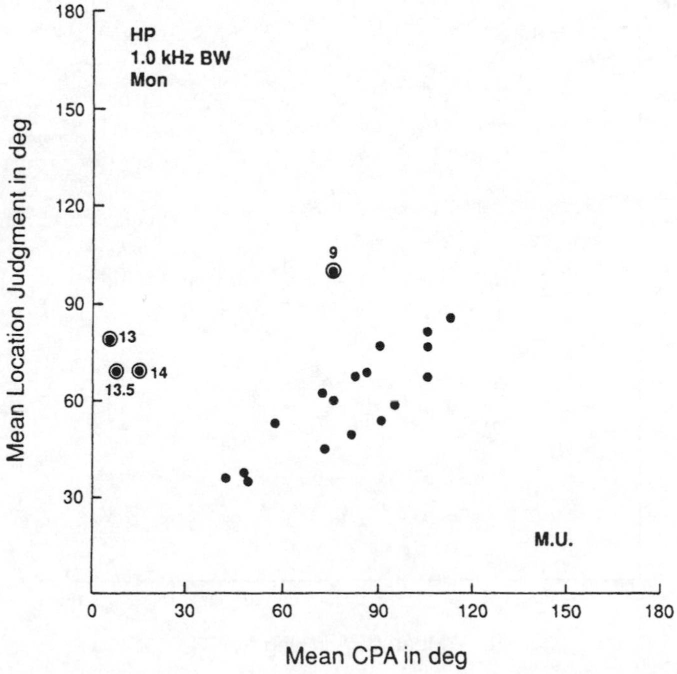

FIG. 12. Horizontal plane plots for listener M.U.

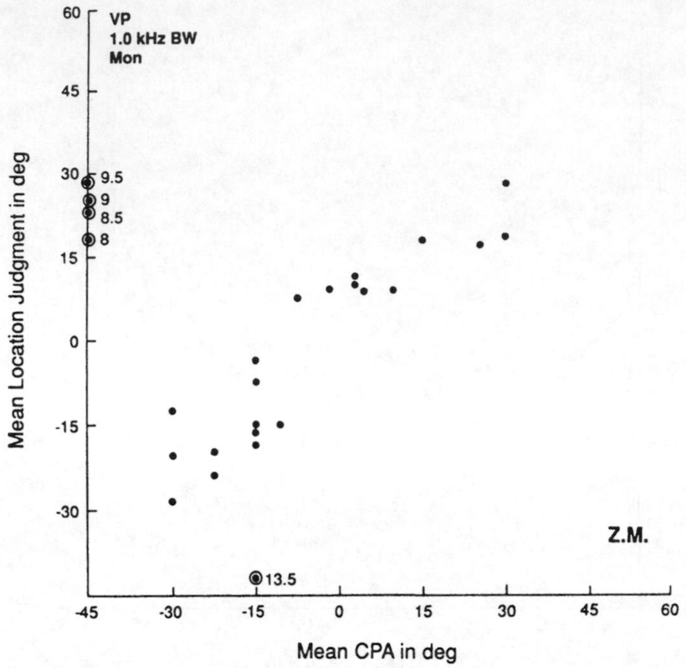

FIG. 13. Vertical plane plots for listener Z.M.

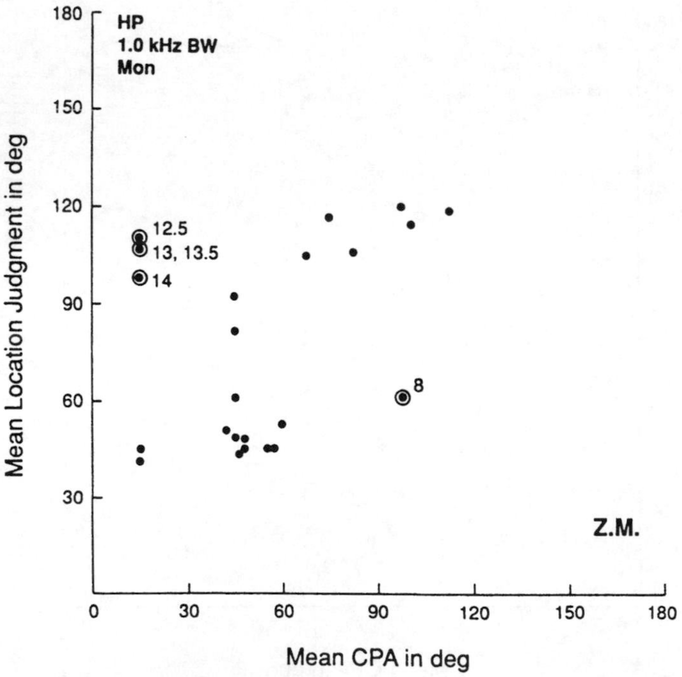

FIG. 14. Horizontal plane plots for listener Z.M.

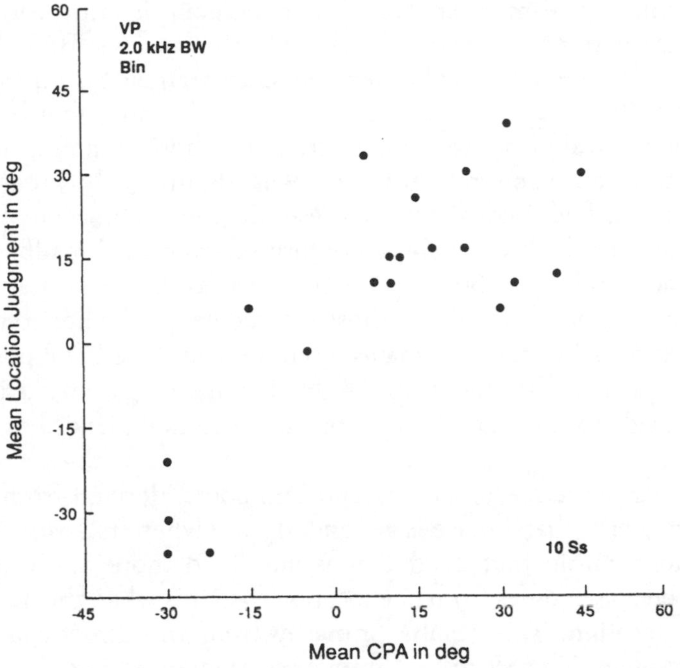

FIG. 15. Vertical plane (VP): Mean location judgments plotted against mean CPA with center frequency of 2.0-kHz-wide noise bands serving as the parameter. Ten binaural listeners localized two differently centered noise bands.

progress toward a satisfactory answer. They showed that specific deficits in performance on a binaural localization task can be reliably predicted from acoustic measurements made on only one pinna—the pinna ipsilateral to the sound source. They first determined the CPAs associated with differently centered 2-kHz-wide noise bands. Measurements were made at the left ear canal. Next, the frequency segment linked to a CPA was filtered from a broadband noise. They reasoned that notch-filtering a particular frequency segment, in effect, removed the SR linked to that segment. So when the filtered noise band was presented from the region of the now removed, or at least attenuated, spectral cue for the SR, the listener would no longer choose that region as the sound source. Eleven binaural listeners were tested. The 104 loudspeakers were arrayed in the left hemifield as described earlier. Localization performance on an unfiltered broadband stimulus served as the reference. The results clearly showed that subjects were significantly less likely ($p < 0.001$) to choose as the source of the filtered broadband noise that area in space occupied by the CPA of the filtered frequency segment compared to the unfiltered broadband noise. We inferred that selective filtering of the broadband noise lessened the influence of the SR connected to the filtered segment on binaural location judgments.

Another interesting finding emerged from this study. The data suggested that when the center frequency of the filtered frequency segment was near the breakpoint, localization accuracy was affected more adversely. Burlingame and Butler (unpublished observations) designed an experiment to directly test the idea that the frequency segment spanning the breakpoint is critical for binaural localization accuracy; remove it and localization performance suffers disproportionately compared to the removal of other frequency segments. And indeed, this is what we found. When the frequency segment (2 kHz wide) that bridged the breakpoint in the vertical plane was filtered from a broadband noise, the disruption of binaural localization performance was significantly greater ($p < 0.001$)—more errors, fewer correct responses—than when adjacent frequency segments, not spanning the breakpoint, were filtered from the broadband stimulus. The frequencies bridging the breakpoint tie together the spatial referents located above the horizontal plane with those located below the horizontal plane. Why this connection is important remains a puzzlement. The breakpoint at the higher center frequencies (around 12.0–14.0 kHz where a gap exists in the SR pattern from the side to the frontal sector of the horizontal plane) has not been investigated.

To conclude with some ideas, modest and immodest, derived from the data presented: When a broadband noise is generated somewhere in space, there is a frequency segment within that band that is amplified more at the ear canal entrance when the noise comes from one location than it is when the noise comes from any other location. This results primarily from the directional filtering properties of the pinna. The SR of that frequency segment is linked to the CPA associated with that same frequency segment. In other words, a behavioral response is linked to a physical measurement. I contend that the SR serves as one of the cues for the sound's location. Although it is primarily the pinna that modifies the spectrum of a broadband stimulus, thereby providing the spectral cues for localization, the pinna cannot differentially influence frequency segments within a noise band 1.0 or 2.0 kHz wide—bandwidths employed in the present experiments. So in effect, by presenting noise bands 1.0 and 2.0 kHz in width we bypassed the pinna. True, the pinna can differentially influence the loudness of the narrow noise bands, depending on their origin in space, but loudness is not a reliable cue for source location. By working with differently centered narrow noise bands, the pattern of the SRs is revealed. Presumably, the narrow noise bands stimulate restricted areas in the central auditory nervous system. In view of tonotopic organization of the auditory neural system, Butler (1974) suggested that one psychological correlate of a neural response confined to a specific frequency region in one or more of the tonotopic maps is a spatial experience—that sound comes from a restricted place in space. Should this suggestion prove difficult to accept, as apparently it has, I ask whether it is any more difficult to accept than is the idea that pitch perception is a correlate of stimulating a restricted neural region within one of the tonotopic maps by a specific frequency. Both ideas are conceptually equivalent. The latter has been incorporated into a prominent and historically rich psychological theory—the Place Theory.

The idea that frequency has a spatial referent, which may be implicated in localization, is not without experimental support at the animal level. Under the appropriate testing conditions, the removal of a cortical segment responsive to a set of frequencies results in the inability of the cat to localize these frequencies despite the fact that it can respond to them in other auditory tasks. The same cat can, however, localize frequencies whose cortical representation remained undisturbed (Jenkins and Merzenich, 1984). Neurophysiological research on mammals reveals multiple maps of frequency representation. Why so many? What is their function? Perhaps one might be involved primarily in sound localization.

ACKNOWLEDGMENTS

The author expresses his appreciation to Dr. Alan Musicant for his helpful suggestions on the preparation of this manuscript and more generally for his long-term participation in the sound localization studies carried out at the University of Chicago. This work was supported in part by NIH grant R0 1 NS25889-03.

REFERENCES

Belendiuk, K., and Butler, R. A. (1977). "Spectral cues which influence monaural localization in the horizontal plane," Percept. Psychophys. **22**, 353–358.

Blauert, J. (1969/1970). "Sound localization in the median plane," Acustica **22**, 205–213.

Butler, R. A. (1974). "Does tonotopicity subserve the perceived elevation of a sound?" Fed. Proc. **33**, 1920–1923.

Butler, R. A. (1987). "An analysis of the monaural displacement of sound in space," Percept. Psychophys. **41**, 1–7.

Butler, R. A., and Flannery, R. (1980). "The spatial attributes of stimulus frequency and their role in monaural localization of sound in the horizontal plane," Percept. Psychophys. **28**, 449–457.

Butler, R. A., and Helwig, B. A. (1983). "The spatial attributes of stimulus frequency in the median sagittal plane and their role in sound localization," Am. J. Otolarygol. **4**, 165–173.

Butler, R. A., and Musicant, A. M. (1993). "Binaural localization: Influence of stimulus frequency and the linkage to covert peak areas," Hear. Res. **67**, 220–229.

Butler, R. A., and Planert, N. (1976). "The influence of stimulus bandwidth on localization of sound in space," Percept. Psychophys. **19**, 103–108.

Flannery, R., and Butler, R. A. (1981). "Spectral cues provided by the pinna for monaural localization," Percept. Psychophys. **29**, 438–444.

Humanski, R. A., and Butler, R. A. (1988). "The contribution of the near and far ear toward localization of sound in the sagittal plane," J. Acoust. Soc. Am. **83**, 2300–2310.

Jenkins, W. M., and Merzenich, M. M. (1984). "Role of cat primary auditory cortex for sound-localization behavior," J. Neurophysiol. **52**, 819–847.

Middlebrooks, J. C. (1992). "Narrow-band sound localization related to external ear acoustics," J. Acoust. Soc. Am. **92**, 2607–2624.

Middlebrooks, J. C., Makous, J. C., and Green, D. M. (1989). "Directional sensitivity of sound-pressure levels in the human ear canal," J. Acoust. Soc. Am. **86**, 89–108.

Musicant, A. D., and Butler, R. A. (1984). "The psychophysical basis of monaural localization," Hear. Res. **14**, 185–190.

Musicant, A. D., Chan, J. C. K., and Hind, J. E. (1990). "Direction-dependent spectral properties of cat external ear: New data and cross-species comparisons," J. Acoust. Soc. Am. **87**, 757–781.

Pratt, C. C. (1930). "The spatial character of high and low tones," J. Exp. Psychol. **13**, 278–285.

Roffler, S. K., and Butler, R. A. (1968). "Localization of tonal stimuli in the vertical plane," J. Acoust. Soc. Am. **43**, 1260–1266.

Rogers, M. E., and Butler, R. A. (1992). "The linkage between stimulus frequency and covert peak areas as it relates to monaural localization," Percept. Psychophys. **52**, 536–546.

Part II

Lateralization and Binaural Masking

Chapter 6

Detection and Discrimination of Interaural Disparities: Modern Earphone-Based Studies

Leslie R. Bernstein
University of Connecticut

(Received January 1994; revised September 1994)

The major cues utilized by the binaural system to localize sounds in space and to detect the presence of sounds in noisy environments are interaural temporal disparities (ITDs) and interaural intensitive disparities (IIDs). Most of what is known about the binaural system's sensitivity to these cues under a variety of conditions has been gleaned from investigations that utilized earphones. The chief advantage of this method is that it allows for rather precise control over the stimuli and, most importantly, the interaural disparities that arrive at the two ears. This chapter focuses on two major topics of research that characterize modern, binaural, earphone-based studies: (1) temporal effects in detection and discrimination of ITDs and IIDs (binaural "sluggishness") and (2) sensitivity to ITDs within the envelopes of high-frequency, complex waveforms. Previous experimental findings in these two areas are discussed, integrated, and related to recent work conducted in our laboratory.

INTRODUCTION

It has been recognized for the last hundred years or so that the two major cues utilized by the binaural system to localize sounds in space and to detect the presence of sounds in noisy environments are interaural temporal disparities (ITDs) and interaural intensitive disparities (IIDs). The majority of what is known about the binaural system's sensitivity to these cues under a variety of conditions has been gleaned from investigations that utilized earphones (see Durlach and Colburn, 1978). The chief advantage of this method is that it allows for rather precise control over the stimuli and, most importantly, the interaural disparities that arrive at the two ears. Although several important topics of research can be identified that characterize modern, binaural, earphone-based studies of detection and discrimination of interaural disparities (several of which are discussed in other chapters within this volume), this discussion focuses on two of them and demonstrates how they relate to recent work conducted in our laboratory.

A. Temporal effects in detection and discrimination of ITDs and IIDs: Binaural sluggishness

The earliest studies of the binaural system's ability to process dynamic changes in ITDs were those that explored the phenomenon of "binaural beats" (e.g., Licklider, Webster, and Hedlun, 1950; Perrott and Nelson, 1969; Perrott and Musicant, 1977). Briefly, if a low-frequency tone is presented to one ear and one of slightly different frequency is presented to the other, then as the separation in frequency (Δf) is varied, listeners report several subjective effects. For Δf up to 5 Hz or so, listeners typically report the perception of a single, fused intracranial image that moves or "rotates" within the head at a rate of Δf. As Δf is increased, the perception of movement diminishes (as does that of a single fused image), being replaced by a fluctuation in loudness, which eventually gives way to the perception of "roughness." When Δf is increased beyond 30 Hz or so, listeners report two separate intracranial images with no apparent interaction.

While such investigations provided crucial insights, the data do not afford an objective, quantitative description of the ability of the binaural system to process dynamically varying interaural temporal disparities. This is so because either the data obtained were highly dependent on subjective response criteria and/or judgments might have been based on additional, confounding cues. The same is true of other studies in which performance was described as being based on the detection of time-varying ITDs (e.g., Blauert, 1972; McFadden, Russell, and Pulliam, 1972).

Grantham (1982, 1984) and Grantham and Wightman (1978, 1979) published an influential series of investigations aimed at providing such an objective, quantitative evaluation of listeners' sensitivity to dynamically varying interaural temporal disparities. These studies demonstrated rather convincingly that the binaural system is quite "sluggish" in that it appears to "smooth over," or average, rapid fluctuations in interaural disparities.

Grantham and Wightman (1978) employed a two-interval forced-choice task and measured listeners' abilities to discriminate between 440-ms bursts of broadband noise that were either diotic or contained an ITD that varied sinusoidally about an ITD of zero. As Grantham and Wightman noted, the sinusoidally varying ITD produced an intracranial image that, for low sinusoidal frequencies, seemed to "move" back and forth about the middle of the head. The main parameter of interest was the rate of sinusoidal variation, or "modulation frequency" of the ITD. The dependent variable was the maximum or "peak value" of the ITD necessary to discriminate the "moving" stimulus from the diotic one at each rate tested. Thus, Grantham and Wightman measured what may be thought of as a binaural modulation transfer function.

Figure 1 displays the results of this study separately for the three listeners tested. In the figure, the peak ITD necessary for 75% correct discrimination is plotted as a function of the frequency of the sinusoidally varying ITD. Focusing on frequencies of 50 Hz and below, the data indicate that the magnitude of the ITD required to discriminate the "moving" stimulus from the diotic stimulus increased monotonically as the frequency of the sinusoidally varying ITD was increased from 2.5 Hz. That is, the binaural system appears to display a *lowpass* characteristic with respect to the rate of change of ITD.

The data for frequencies of 50 Hz and above indicate that performance improved as the frequency of modulation was increased, an outcome that appears inconsistent with the characterization of the binaural system as lowpass with respect to dynamically changing ITDs. Grantham and Wightman (1978) noted that their listeners reported using very different cues in order to discriminate the "moving" from the diotic stimulus at these higher rates of modulation. Rather than basing their judgments on whether each stimulus seemed to move or to remain stationary, the listeners apparently based their judgments on the "width" or extent of the intracranial image produced by the stimuli. Although movement *per se* could no longer be perceived at these high rates of modulation, the noise that contained the sinusoidally varying ITD produced a diffuse and extended intracranial image that could be discriminated from the more punctate, stationary image produced by the diotic noise. In Grantham and Wightman's terms, the listeners' task was that of discriminating between a "line" and a "dot." On the basis of these data and those obtained in follow-up experiments, Grantham and

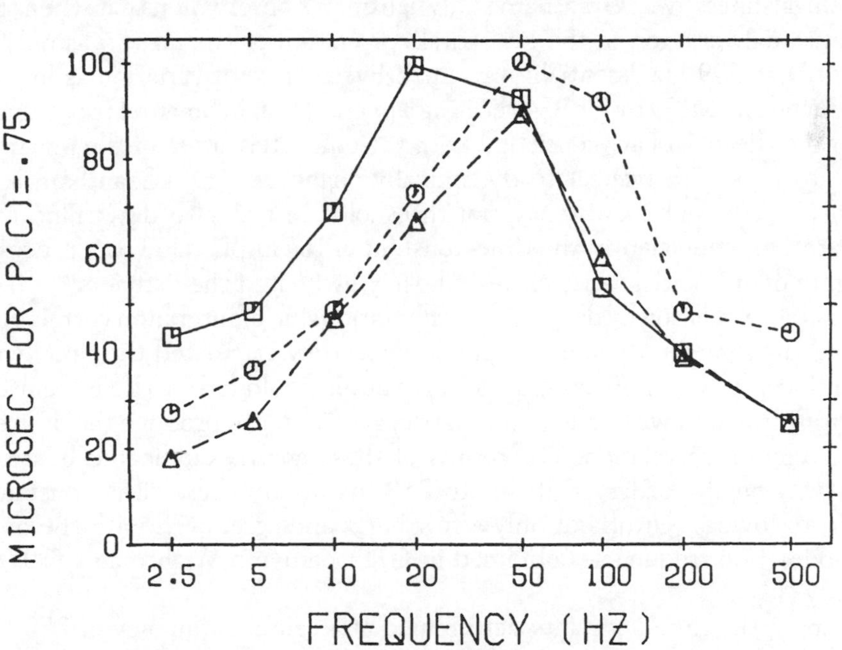

FIG. 1. "Peak" interaural temporal disparity required to discriminate broadband noise containing a sinusoidally varying ITD from diotic, broadband noise. Peak ITDs are plotted as a function of the frequency of the sinusoidally varying ITD. Data are presented separately for three listeners. [From Grantham and Wightman, 1978, with permission.]

Wightman (1978) argued that different cues may mediate the detectability of dynamically varying ITDs at low and high rates of modulation, respectively. This notion is discussed in more detail at the end of this section.

In a later study, Grantham and Wightman (1979) measured the magnitude of the binaural masking-level difference (MLD) when the masker was a ⅓-octave band of noise centered at either 250 Hz, 500 Hz, or 1000 Hz. The *interaural correlation* of the masker was varied sinusoidally between +1.0 and –1.0. The signal was a 16-ms, antiphasic tone (S_π) at the center frequency of the masker and was presented in the temporal center of a 1-s sample of the random masker. In the conditions of interest, the starting value of the interaural correlation of the masker was varied such that the S_π signal occurred at the instant the interaural correlation of the noise was equal to 1.0. The addition of the signal and masker in this manner corresponds to the N_0S_π configuration that yields the maximum binaural release from masking.

Grantham and Wightman (1979) compared thresholds of detection for the tones masked by a *static* value of interaural correlation equal to 1.0 with their counterparts when the masker's correlation was varied sinusoidally. The main parameter of interest was the rate of sinusoidal variation of the interaural correlation of the masking noise. As expected, for a static interaural correlation of 1.0, there was a large release from masking. For example, at 500 Hz an MLD of 15–17 dB was measured when the S_π tone was added to the noise with an interaural correlation of +1.0 (N_0S_π) as compared to when the tone was added to a noise with an interaural correlation of –1.0 ($N_\pi S_\pi$). A dramatic indication of binaural "sluggishness" was Grantham and Wightman's observation that when the rate of sinusoidal variation of the interaural correlation of the noise was only 4 Hz, the MLD at 500 Hz essentially vanished. Even a rate of variation as low as 0.5 Hz reduced the MLD by 4 dB, indicating a degradation in binaural processing.

Once again, these data are consistent with the characterization of the binaural system as lowpass with respect to dynamically changing ITDs. Grantham and Wightman (1979) used their behavioral thresholds in order to determine the lowpass cutoff or, equivalently, the time-constant of the implied lowpass process. For each rate of sinusoidal variation tested, they estimated the listeners' "effective" interaural correlation by determining the static value of interaural correlation that yielded the same behavioral threshold. Next, they calculated the time over which the sinusoidally varying interaural correlation would have to be integrated by a weighting function with an exponential decay in order to produce the desired effective interaural correlation. The results of these analyses indicated binaural time-constants on the order of 45 ms to 250 ms or so. These time-constants correspond to lowpass cutoffs of only a few hertz and agree well with the data for low modulation frequencies obtained in Grantham and Wightman's (1978) earlier study (Fig. 1).

Interestingly, the time-constants determined at a center frequency of 250 Hz were somewhat larger than those obtained at 500 Hz, indicating somewhat greater temporal resolution at the higher frequency. In a later study, Grantham (1982) measured listeners' ability to discriminate between interaurally uncorrelated bands of noise and bands of noise for which the interaural correlation was varied sinusoidally. In addition to obtaining lowpass "cutoffs" similar to those obtained in previous studies, temporal resolution appeared to improve with the center frequency of the noise.

Kollmeier and Gilkey (1990) utilized a task quite different from those just described and obtained binaural time-constants comparable to those reported by Grantham and Wightman (1979). In Kollmeier and Gilkey's procedure, a 20-ms, 500-Hz, S_π tone was presented against a 750-ms, broadband masker. A unique aspect of the masker in their "binaural" condition was that its interaural phase switched from N_π to N_0 after 375 ms. Threshold for detection of the signal was measured as a function of the time between the phase-transition of the masker and the *offset* of the signal. Thus, Kollmeier and Gilkey were able to measure the binaural system's response to a single, *transient* change in interaural phase. A diagram of the stimuli is presented in the left-hand portion of the upper part of Fig. 2. Note that if the signal were presented near the beginning of the masker, then the interaural configuration would be, effectively, $N_\pi S_\pi$, and no binaural release from masking would occur (thresholds would be highest). On the other hand, if the signal were presented near the end of the masker, then the interaural configuration would be, effectively, $N_0 S_\pi$ and the maximum binaural release from masking would occur (thresholds would be lowest).

The stimuli depicted in the right-hand portion of the upper part of Fig. 2 represent the stimulus configuration designed to estimate the "time-constant" of the "monaural" system. Rather than a phase-transition, the N_π masker was reduced in level by 15 dB after 375 ms. The value of 15 dB was chosen because it was expected to mimic the release from masking obtained by changing the interaural phase of the masker from N_π to N_0 in the binaural condition.

Representative data from a single listener are depicted in the lower portion of Fig. 2. Threshold is plotted as a function of the delay-time between the transition of the masker and the offset of the signal. The 0-dB point represents the threshold obtained for the $N_\pi S_\pi$ configuration when the phase and level of the masker were held constant over the 750-ms duration. Squares represent the data obtained in the "binaural" condition; triangles represent the data obtained in the "monaural" condition. The solid and dotted lines represent mathematical fits to the binaural and monaural functions, respectively. The data show that, for the binaural condition, the maximum release from masking is not achieved until the offset of the 20-ms signal occurs some 100 ms after the phase-transition. This suggests that although the phase-transition within the physical (masking) waveform occurs virtually instantaneously, the *effective* change occurs much more slowly within the binaural system. In fact, the time-constants derived by Kollmeier and Gilkey in their quantitative analyses of these data were comparable to those reported by Grantham and Wightman (1978). In contrast to the data from the binaural condition, the data from the monaural condition indicated substantially shorter time-constants.

Up to this point, only studies that have assessed the binaural system's sensitivity to dynamically changing ITDs have been discussed. Using a technique similar to that employed by Grantham and Wightman (1978), Grantham (1984) investigated listeners' sensitivity to dynamically changing IIDs. Grantham employed a

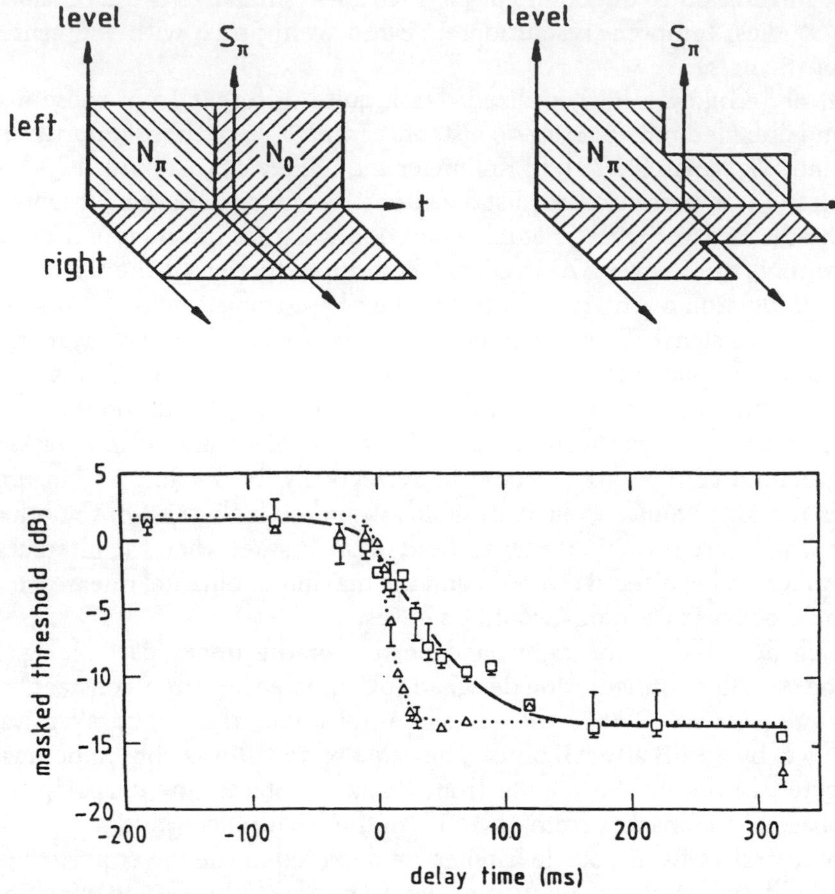

FIG. 2. Schematic of the stimuli (upper portion) and data (lower panel) from Kollmeier and Gilkey (1990). The upper left portion of the figure depicts the "binaural" condition in which a 20-ms, 500-Hz, $S\pi$ tone was presented against a 750-ms, broadband masker. The phase of the masker was "switched" from $N\pi$ to N_0 after 375 ms. The upper right portion of the figure depicts the "monaural" condition in which the level of the masker was reduced by 15 dB after 375 ms. The lower portion of the figure displays representative data from a single listener. In this graph, masked threshold is plotted as a function of the "delay time" between the relevant transition in the masker and the *offset* of the signal. The 0-dB point on the ordinate represents the threshold obtained in the $N\pi S\pi$ configuration when the phase and level of the masker were held constant over its 750-ms duration. Squares and triangles represent median thresholds obtained in the "binaural" and "monaural" conditions, respectively. Error bars represent interquartile ranges. The solid and dotted lines represent mathematical fits to the "binaural" and "monaural" functions, respectively. [From Kollmeier and Gilkey, 1990, with permission.]

two-interval, forced-choice task and measured listeners' ability to discriminate between a 1-s-long 0.4-octave-wide band of interaurally-uncorrelated noise that was sinusoidally modulated *in-phase* across the ears from one whose modulation was *phase-reversed* across the two ears. The phase-reversed condition produced an IID that varied sinusoidally at the frequency of the modulator. The depth of modulation controlled the magnitude or maximum value of the IID. For low rates and large depths of modulation, the phase-reversed condition produced an intracranial image that seemed to "move" back and forth about the middle of the head. Grantham measured the depth of modulation required to discriminate between the interaurally in-phase and phase-reversed modulation as a function of the frequency of modulation. In general, the data exhibited the expected lowpass characteristic. That is, greater depths of modulation (larger IIDs) were required as the frequency of modulation (rate of change of IID) was increased. However, for two of Grantham's listeners, the implied lowpass cutoff was an order of magnitude higher than that obtained in previous studies concerning dynamically changing ITDs (see earlier discussion). Furthermore, consistent with those earlier investigations, temporal resolution appeared to improve as the center frequency of the noise was increased from 500 Hz to 4000 Hz. For two of Grantham's listeners, the data indicated that little degradation in sensitivity occurred for rates of modulation up to 100 Hz! This outcome led Grantham to speculate that ITDs and IIDs may be smoothed or averaged via separate lowpass filters.

Taken together, the results of the representative studies cited here demonstrate that the binaural system is quite "sluggish" in that it appears unable to "follow" even moderately slowly varying interaural disparities. However, conceptualization and quantification of binaural sluggishness in a manner that explains most of the salient aspects of the behavioral data has not been accomplished. For the most part, binaural sluggishness has been modeled as a running average of the *values* of the interaural disparities that occur within a temporal window of finite duration (e.g., Grantham and Wightman, 1979; Gabriel, 1983; Kollmeier and Gilkey, 1990). Such averaging is, perhaps, most easily conceptualized in terms of an internal delay line or "cross-correlation" surface (e.g., Jeffress, 1948; Sayers and Cherry, 1957; Colburn, 1973, 1977). The surface is defined by ITD (i.e., τ) along the abscissa and "magnitude" or amount of activity along the ordinate. Here, the amount of activity refers to that of hypothetical neural units that respond to "coincidence" of neural firing from the two ears subsequent to the imposition of an internal delay. Given this conception, modeling binaural sluggishness as a running average of the *values* of the interaural disparities amounts to averaging, over time, the values *along the τ axis* of the cross-correlation surface. In fact, such a scheme accounts for much of the data just described and is even successful in accounting for the effects of binaural sluggishness in other binaural tasks such as N_0S_π detection and discrimination of interaural correlation (Gabriel, 1983; Zurek and Durlach, 1987).

For example, recall the experiment conducted by Grantham and Wightman (1978) in which the listener's task was to discriminate between bursts of broadband noise that were either diotic or that contained an ITD that varied sinusoidally about an ITD of zero. An averager of the sort described earlier would operate such that, as the frequency of sinusoidal variation of ITD was increased, more and more samples of the dynamically varying ITD would fall within the averaging window and the *effective* ITD would tend toward their mean of zero. Thus, if the frequency of the sinusoidal variation were increased, the peak ITD would have to be increased in order for the listener to discriminate a stimulus containing a sinusoidally varying ITD from one that was diotic. Figure 1 shows that for rates of modulation between 0 and 50 Hz, this was indeed the case.

However, as Fig. 1 also shows, when the rate of modulation was increased beyond 50 Hz, *smaller* peak ITDs were required. As discussed earlier, the listeners reported that, at these rates of modulation, although movement *per se* could no longer be perceived, the noise that contained the sinusoidally varying ITD produced a diffuse and extended intracranial image that could be discriminated from the more punctate, stationary image produced by the diotic noise. This outcome, along with the listeners' reports, appears to be inconsistent with a mechanism that averages, over time, the values of ITDs, that is, along the τ axis of the delay surface. Such averaging would result in the prediction that at high rates of modulation, the noise containing the sinusoidally varying ITD would have an effective, internal ITD of zero and thus be indiscriminable from a noise that was diotic.

On the other hand, the data obtained for rates of modulation above 50 Hz might be accounted for by assuming that the averaging takes place, not across the abscissa or τ axis of the delay surface, but across the ordinate that represents "amplitude" or amount of activity. That is, sluggishness might be thought of as resulting from a "persistence" of activity along the internal delay surface. Such a notion accounts for the general finding (e.g., Grantham and Wightman, 1978; Grantham, 1984) that as the rate of fluctuation of ITD is increased, the perception of movement *per se* is lost and the listener perceives an extended, stationary intracranial image.

Importantly, persistence of activity is precisely the manner in which Stern and Bachorski (1983) modeled binaural sluggishness. Their model represents an extension of Stern and Colburn's (1978) position-variable model. In that model, lateral position is estimated by computing the expected value of the centroid of activity along the cross-correlation surface. Stern and Bachorski modified the position-variable model by incorporating what amounts to lowpass filtering *the activity*, or output, of the neural "coincidence" units. In fact, this model was able to account quite well for the data obtained by Grantham and Wightman (1978) for rates of modulation below 50 Hz. For rates of modulation above 50 Hz, the model as described would predict that "peak ITD" would continue to increase, contrary to the data in Fig. 1.

However, recent discussions with Dr. Richard M. Stern revealed that computation of the *variance* of the centroid could provide a means for discriminating a diotic stimulus from one that contained a rapidly fluctuating ITD. The stimuli could be discriminated on this basis despite the fact that their "position estimates," as defined by the expected value of the centroid of activity, would be indistinguishable. For a diotic stimulus, the expected value of the centroid would be at the midline with a variance determined by random fluctuation in auditory-nerve activity. For a stimulus containing a sinusoidally varying ITD of given magnitude, as rate of modulation is increased from 0 Hz, estimates of lateral position would be expected to collapse toward the midline whereas the variance associated with each of those estimates would be expected to increase. Thus, at low rates of modulation, discrimination could be made on the basis of position, whereas at high rates, discrimination could be made on the basis of variance of activity. This notion is entirely consistent with the subjective reports of Grantham and Wightman's (1978) listeners. From this point of view, the data in Fig. 1 might reflect that the decrease in the salience of the perception of movement, *per se*, occurs simultaneously with an increase in the salience of the extended intracranial image as the rate of modulation is increased. Thus, as originally suggested by Grantham and Wightman, the data obtained at low and at high rates of modulation may simply reflect the use of two different decision variables.

In addition, it seems quite plausible that Stern and Bachorski's (1983) model that incorporates "persistence" of activity could also account for the effects of binaural sluggishness in other tasks, such as N_0S_π detection and discrimination of interaural correlation. Recall that these data can be accounted for quantitatively by a mechanism that assumes averaging, over time, of the *values* of interaural disparities. Note that discrimination in these tasks is often described as being based on changes in the variance or "width" of the distribution of dynamically varying interaural cues (e.g., Gabriel, 1983; Zurek and Durlach, 1987). Because any persistence of the relevant internal binaural display would affect this parameter directly, it seems reasonable to explore whether quantitative modeling based on this type of averaging might also account for these data. It is intriguing to speculate whether a relatively simple mechanism based on persistence of activity could account for virtually all of the behavioral data concerning binaural sluggishness. On the other hand, as Kollmeier and Gilkey (1990) suggested, sluggishness may arise independently at various stages throughout binaural processing. Different behavioral tasks may tap different sources to varying degrees and, ultimately, no single mechanism may be successful in accounting for the data.

B. Sensitivity to ITDs within the envelopes of high-frequency, complex waveforms

A second major experimental trend that characterizes modern earphone-based studies of binaural hearing is the exploration of the limits of traditional "duplex" theory (Rayleigh, 1907). The duplex theory holds that ITDs are utilized in order to localize sinusoidal signals below about 1500 Hz, whereas IIDs are used for localization above about 1500 Hz. The demonstrated insensitivity of listeners to ITDs of sinusoidal signals above 1500 Hz (e.g., Zwislocki and Feldman, 1956) is consistent with this notion.

Although listeners are insensitive to ITDs within high-frequency sinusoids, a number of early studies demonstrated that listeners are, indeed, sensitive to ITDs within complex waveforms such as sinusoidally amplitude-modulated (SAM) tones, filtered transients, and bands of noise when their spectral content is restricted to frequencies above 1500 Hz (e.g., Klumpp and Eady, 1956; Leakey, Sayers, and Cherry, 1958; David, Guttman, and van Bergeijk, 1959). Importantly, Klumpp and Eady (1956) demonstrated that sensitivity to ITDs within narrow bands of high-frequency noise rivals that obtained with low-frequency pure-tones; their listeners required only 20–40 μs or so to reach 75% correct detection. Leakey *et al.* (1958) made the rather astute observation that changes in lateral position produced by ITDs of high-frequency noises and SAM tones appeared to depend on the "correlated nature of the envelopes of the signals." Such observations suggest a dichotomy with regard to the processing of ITDs in low- and high-frequency waveforms. In the case of the former, such processing could be mediated by "cycle-by-cycle" disparities present in the *fine-structure* of the waveform or in the resolved components of certain complex stimuli. In the case of the latter, such processing could be mediated by envelope-based disparities.

More recently, there has been renewed interest in listeners' sensitivity to ITDs within high-frequency complex waveforms and in exploring the nature of this sensitivity in detail. These investigations employed a variety of stimuli including SAM tones, two-tone complexes, and bands of noise (e.g., Henning, 1974; McFadden and Pasanen, 1976; Nuetzel and Hafter, 1976, 1981). Figure 3 shows the results of representative data from Henning's (1974) study in which he measured listeners' sensitivities to ITDs within a SAM tone consisting of a 3900-Hz carrier modulated at 300 Hz. Henning delayed either the entire SAM tone (filled triangles) or only the modulator (open triangles). Delaying the entire waveform produces a delay of the fine structure or "cycle-by-cycle" changes within the waveform as well as its envelope. Listeners are, presumably, insensitive to ITDs within the fine-structure of such high-frequency waveforms. Delaying only the modulator results in a delay of only the envelope of the SAM tone. In addition, Henning measured performance when the ITD was presented within a pure tone of the same frequency (300 Hz) used to modulate the 3900-Hz carrier (Xs). Figure 3 shows that performance was virtually identical for all three stimuli, suggesting that (1) sensitivity to ITDs within the high-frequency SAM tone depends only on delays within the envelope of the stimulus, and (2) sensitivity to ITDs within the envelope of the high-frequency SAM tone is comparable to that obtained with a low-frequency pure tone.

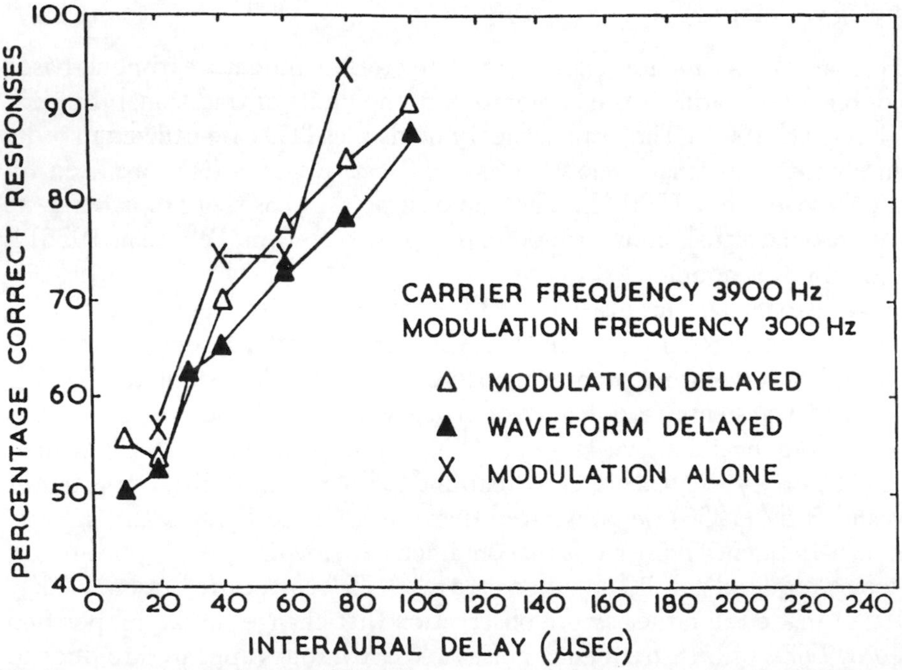

FIG. 3. Percent correct as a function of ITD. The parameter of the plot is the type of stimulus employed. Triangles represent thresholds obtained with a SAM tone consisting of a 3900-Hz carrier modulated (100%) at 300 Hz when only the modulator was delayed (unfilled) or when the entire waveform was delayed (filled). The Xs represent data obtained with a 300-Hz pure tone. [From Henning, 1974, with permission.]

Several lines of evidence from this study and the studies cited earlier suggest that sensitivity to ITDs within high-frequency complex waveforms is mediated by delays within the envelope of the waveform as processed within the high-frequency channels or basal portions of the cochlea. First, as discussed earlier, sensitivity to ITDs persists when only the envelope of the waveform is delayed (Henning, 1974; Nuetzel and Hafter, 1976). Second, excellent sensitivity to ITDs can be obtained in the presence of continuous lowpass noise (Henning, 1974; McFadden and Pasanen, 1976; Nuetzel and Hafter, 1976). Third, as demonstrated by McFadden and Pasanen (1976) for two-tone complexes, and by Nuetzel and Hafter (1981) for SAM tones, sensitivity to ITD declines as the depth-of-modulation of the waveform decreases. Fourth, there is no measurable sensitivity to ITD obtained when the delay occurs between the low-frequency, sinusoidally varying envelope of a high-frequency SAM complex in one ear and a pure tone at the frequency of modulation in the other ear (Nuetzel and Hafter, 1976).

Curiously, although listeners exhibit exquisite *sensitivity* to envelope-based ITDs within high-frequency complex waveforms, such delays appear to be relatively impotent in terms of affecting the lateral position of the intracranial image (Blauert, 1983; Bernstein and Trahiotis, 1985; Trahiotis and Bernstein, 1986). More recently, Wightman and Kistler (1992) obtained a similar result using stimuli that, when presented over earphones, were designed to simulate the free field.

In this and the previous section, an overview and experimental data were presented concerning binaural sluggishness and sensitivity to ITDs within the envelopes of high-frequency, complex waveforms. The following sections demonstrate how these two major topics in modern earphone-based studies of binaural hearing relate to recent work conducted in our laboratory. The experiments to be discussed were conducted and reported by Bernstein and Trahiotis (1992a, 1992b). Portions of the following discussion have been adapted from those publications.

I. EXPERIMENTAL RESULTS

A. Discrimination of interaural envelope correlation and binaural unmasking at high frequencies

Virtually all modern models of binaural hearing either explicitly or implicitly utilize cross-correlation as a central component of binaural interaction. Cross-correlation-based models have been used to describe and predict behavioral data gathered in a variety of binaural tasks, including (1) detection of tonal or spectrally complex signals embedded in noise in configurations that lead to a binaural release from masking; (2) detection, discrimination, and lateralization of stimuli that have been delayed interaurally; (3) discrimination of changes of interaural correlation *per se* for either narrowband or wideband stimuli; and (4) changes in relative compactness/diffuseness of binaural images produced in several environments including concert halls. The results of literally dozens of relevant experiments can be found in Blauert's (1983) comprehensive textbook, Durlach and Colburn's thoughtful review (1978), and Ando's recent monograph (1985). No doubt, the appeal of cross-correlation is due to its usefulness in providing a parsimonious description of many binaural stimuli of interest, its success as a process within mathematical, black-box models of binaural hearing, and its neuroanatomical and neurophysiological plausibility.

Recently, Gabriel (1983) and his colleagues (Gabriel and Colburn, 1981; Durlach, Gabriel, Colburn, and Trahiotis, 1986) described how well the MLD can be explained or accounted for by direct measures of listeners' sensitivity to changes in interaural correlation. For the direct measures, the changes in interaural correlation were produced by appropriate mixtures of independent sources of noise. Interestingly, the vast majority of data evaluated in this manner were gathered at low frequencies (i.e., at or below 1500 Hz or so) where listeners are known to be sensitive to ITDs conveyed via the fine-structure of the waveform.

A primary purpose of the experiments to be described was to begin to assess how well cross-correlation serves as a unifying concept for data obtained at high spectral frequencies where, as discussed earlier, listeners are known to be sensitive to ITDs conveyed via the envelope of the waveform (e.g., Henning, 1974; McFadden and Pasanen, 1976; Nuetzel and Hafter, 1976). Of particular interest was Colburn and Esquissaud's (1976) notion that the only difference in the binaural processing of high- and low-frequency stimuli results from the peripheral transduction of the acoustic waveform. Specifically, following complex peripheral transformations that result in essentially "bandpass" filtering, nerve fibers with low characteristic frequencies produce impulses synchronized to temporal features of the fine-structure of stimulation. Nerve fibers with relatively high characteristic frequencies synchronize principally to the envelope. As discussed by Colburn and Esquissaud, neural impulses synchronized to temporal features of the waveform, be they fine-structure-based or envelope-based, could serve as inputs to more central mechanisms that process information from both ears.

Of primary interest was whether sensitivity to changes in interaural correlation could underlie the large binaural unmasking of high-frequency signals that occurs for narrowband maskers (Metz, von Bismark, and Durlach, 1967; McFadden and Pasanen, 1978; Zurek and Durlach, 1987). To that end, both detection (in the well-known N_0S_π binaural masking-level difference configuration) and correlation-discrimination (from a reference correlation of 1.0) experiments were performed with the same listeners. The goal was to determine whether both sets of data could be accounted for by sensitivity to changes in the interaural correlation of only the envelope of the stimuli.

B. Tone-in-noise detection

Listeners' detection thresholds for 4-kHz tones were measured utilizing the interaural configurations N_0S_0 and N_0S_π. Several bandwidths of noise (50 Hz to 3200 Hz, in octave steps) centered on 4 kHz were used, each presented at a spectrum level of 50 dB SPL. The noise maskers were presented for 145 ms (including 10-ms $\cos^2$ rise/decay ramps). Signals were similarly gated, had a total duration of 125 ms, and were temporally centered within the pulsed maskers. Each band of masking noise was generated via a digital implementation of so-called "quadrature multiplication."

The stimuli were presented in a two-cue, two-alternative temporal forced-choice adaptive task. The first and fourth intervals contained only the masking noise and served as cues. The tonal signal was presented with equal *a priori* probability in either the second or third interval. The level of the signal was varied adaptively in order to estimate 70.7% correct (Levitt, 1971).

Thresholds for detection (E/N_0 in dB) in the N_0S_0 and N_0S_π configurations are shown in Fig. 4 as a function of the bandwidth of the masking noise. Panels a–c contain the data from individual listeners and panel d displays the same data averaged across listeners. Open and closed squares represent the N_0S_0 and N_0S_π thresholds, respectively. Asterisks depict representative N_0S_π thresholds derived from Zurek and Durlach (1987, Fig. 2). In panels a–c, the error bars represent ±1 standard error of the mean of ten estimates of threshold. In panel d, the error bars represent ±1 standard error of the mean based on the three listeners' data.

As expected from previous investigations utilizing essentially the same stimuli (e.g., Metz *et al.*, 1967; Zurek and Durlach, 1987; Sever and Small, 1979), thresholds for the N_0S_0 and N_0S_π configurations increased with increases in the bandwidth of the masking noise, but at different rates. Consequently, the

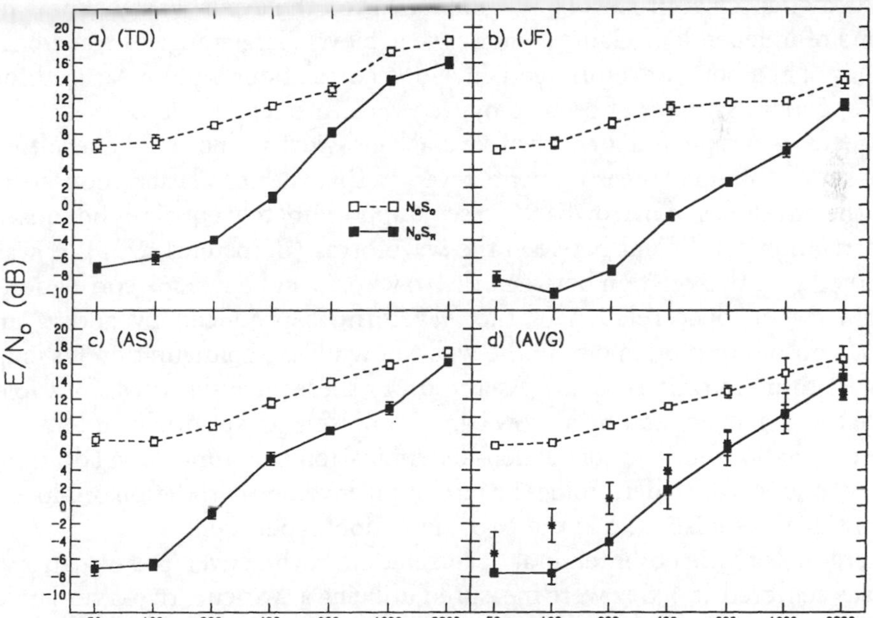

FIG. 4. Thresholds of detection in the N_0S_0 (open squares) and N_0S_π (closed squares) configurations as a function of the bandwidth of the masking noise. Panels (a), (b), and (c) display the data for the three listeners, respectively. Each point represents the mean of ten estimates of threshold. Panel (d) displays the data averaged across the three listeners. The asterisks depict data from Zurek and Durlach (1987, Fig. 2). Error bars represent ±1 standard error of the mean. [From Bernstein and Trahiotis, 1992a, with permission.]

masking-level difference, which was on the order of 14 dB or so at the narrowest bandwidths, decreased to 2 dB or so as the bandwidth of the masking noise was increased to 3200 Hz. Note that for all three listeners, N_0S_π thresholds continued to increase at a fairly constant rate for bandwidths up to at least 1600 Hz. This indicates that each listener's effective (e.g., internal or "critical") bandwidth was at least 1600 Hz wide.

C. Direct discrimination of interaural correlation

As stated earlier, the primary purpose of these experiments was to begin to assess how well cross-correlation of the envelope serves as a unifying concept for data obtained at high spectral frequencies. This experiment was designed to assess whether sensitivity to the interaural correlation of the envelope similar to that observed in the detection experiment just described would be observed for each of our listeners, respectively, in a correlation-discrimination task.

For the correlation-discrimination experiment, it was necessary to generate bands of noise with specified interaural correlations between their envelopes. However, no algorithms were available that specified how to achieve a desired envelope correlation. Algorithms were available that permitted the computation of a desired interaural waveform correlation (Licklider and Dzendolet, 1948; Jeffress and Robinson, 1962) by combining or "mixing" independent Gaussian noises. Via digital signal-processing, we implemented the available algorithms to "mix" pairs of independent Gaussian noises to achieve a large range of waveform correlations. Then both waveform and envelope correlations were measured for many independent samples of each computed waveform correlation.

This process was repeated for each of several bandwidths of noise. The resulting extensive set of empirical measurements revealed that the correlation coefficient between the envelopes of narrowband noises is approximately equal to the square of the correlation coefficient between the waveforms (Bernstein, 1991). It was also observed that this relation between the waveform and envelope correlations also obtains when decorrelation of the waveform is produced by adding an antiphasic sinusoid to diotic noise in the well-known N_0S_π configuration (as long as the signal-to-noise ratio is small). As a result of these analyses, it was possible to achieve the goal of generating narrow bands of noise with specifiable interaural envelope correlations for the correlation-discrimination experiment. In addition, the analyses allowed us to determine the interaural envelope correlation produced by a given signal-to-noise ratio in the N_0S_π detection experiment.

Listeners' sensitivities to interaural decorrelation of the envelopes of narrowband noises centered at 4 kHz were measured utilizing a two-cue, two-alternative temporal forced-choice paradigm similar to that employed in experiment 1. The first and fourth intervals of each trial contained diotic noise and served as cues. The listener's task was to detect an interaurally decorrelated noise that was presented with equal *a priori* probability in either the second or third interval. The value of the interaural correlation of the envelope presented during the "signal" interval was fixed over a block of trials. For each bandwidth of noise (50

Hz to 1600 Hz in octave steps), three or four values of the interaural correlation of the envelope were used to obtain a psychometric function.[1] By interpolation, the values of the interaural correlation of the envelope (r_{ENV}) corresponding to 71% correct in a two-alternative task, that is, the level of performance that defined threshold in experiment 1, were obtained.

The three panels of Fig. 5 display the thresholds of discriminability for interaural decorrelation (asterisks) of the envelope as a function of bandwidth for each listener separately. The data are plotted both in terms of the discriminable interaural correlation of the envelope (r_{ENV}, left ordinate) and the corresponding difference between the discriminable interaural correlation and that of the diotic cues for which $r_{ENV} = 1.0$, (Δr_{ENV}, right-hand ordinate). For comparison, the N_0S_π thresholds (squares) from Fig. 4 have been transformed to interaural correlation of the envelope and are replotted.

The correlation-discrimination thresholds for all three listeners are quite similar and exhibit little, if any, change as a function of the bandwidth of the noise. The data for the narrower bandwidths indicate that the derived (N_0S_π detection) and directly measured thresholds are quite similar. For bandwidths greater than 200–400 Hz, the disparity between the directly measured difference thresholds and the derived ones increases, especially for listeners TD and AS. At a bandwidth of 1600 Hz, the differences in the data drawn from the two different paradigms are quite large.

The data collected in the N_0S_π detection task are consistent with the notion that some type of "rate limitation" operates to degrade performance for bandwidths greater than 200–400 Hz. Note that when the bandwidth of the masker in the N_0S_π configuration is increased, both the rate of fluctuation of the envelope and the rate of fluctuation of the dynamically varying ITDs and IIDs increase. Thus, the decline in performance observed for the N_0S_π detection data may have been due to an inability to process or "follow" the rapidly fluctuating envelope (within a monaural channel) and/or an inability to process or "follow" (due to binaural sluggishness) the rapidly fluctuating interaural cues on which detection of the S_π signal is based.

On the other hand, the data collected in the direct discrimination paradigm imply that the listener simply requires a constant decorrelation within an internal or effective filter in order to discriminate, regardless of the bandwidth of the noise. At the outset, this outcome seemed paradoxical because in this paradigm as well, increasing the bandwidth of the noise leads to increases in both the rate of fluctuation of the envelope and the rate of fluctuation of the dynamically varying ITDs and IIDs.

One possibility was that listeners might have employed some strategy in the direct discrimination task that effectively circumvented any rate limitation that might hinder performance. One such ploy, suggested to us by Dr. Pat Zurek, would have the listeners shift the center of their internal "filters" or critical bands away from the 4-kHz region. This would result in a narrower effective internal

[1]A bandwidth of 3200 Hz was not employed in this task because that bandwidth is too great, relative to the center frequency of 4 kHz, to yield a "well-defined" envelope.

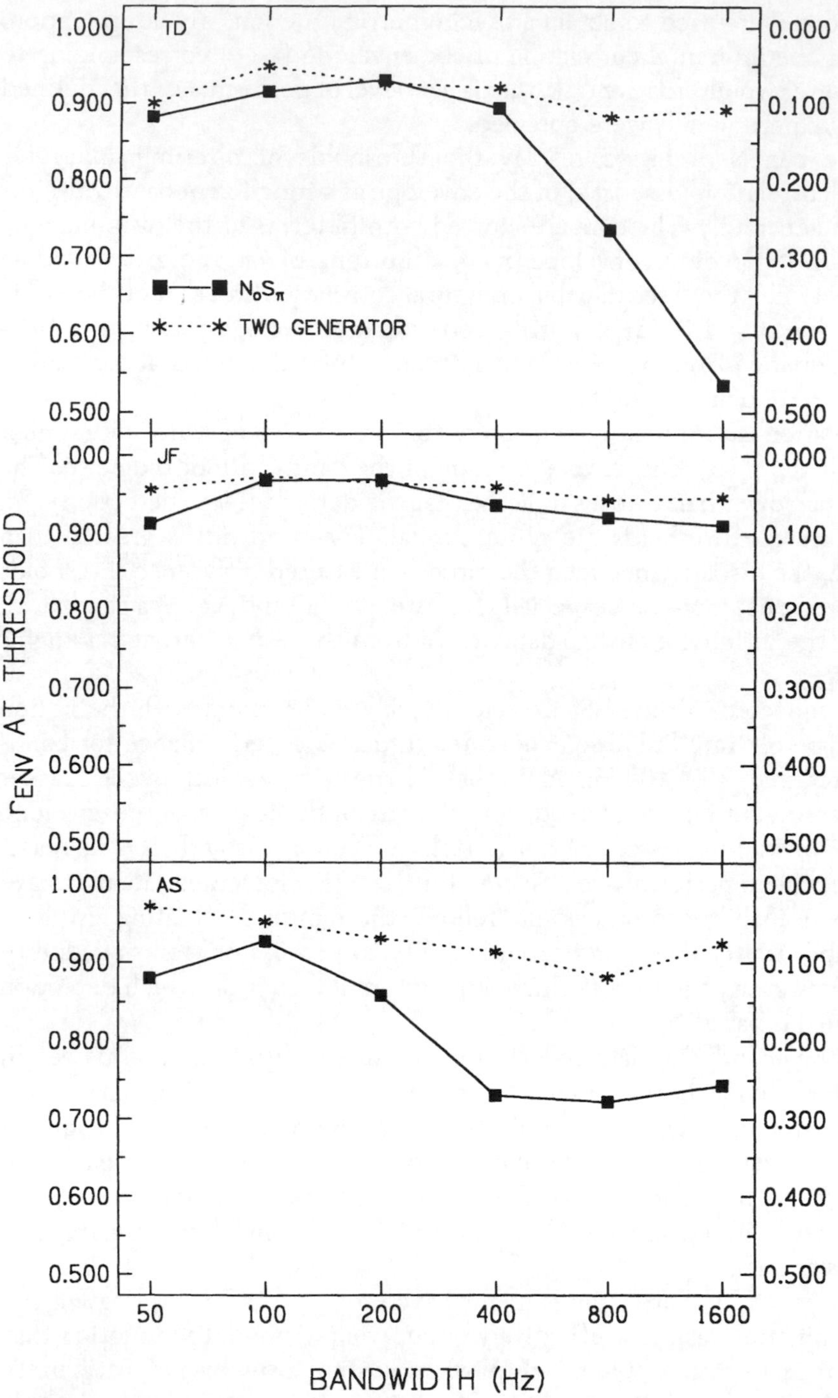

FIG. 5. Interaural correlation of the envelope (r_{ENV}, left-hand ordinate) as a function of the bandwidth of the masking noise in the correlation-discrimination task (asterisks) and in the N_0S_π detection task (squares). The N_0S_π thresholds from Fig. 4 have been transformed and replotted. The right-hand ordinate (Δr_{ENV}) is the corresponding change in interaural correlation (from 1.0) and is simply $1 - r_{ENV}$. The three panels display the data for the three listeners, respectively. [From Bernstein and Trahiotis, 1992a, with permission.]

bandwidth of the noise with a concomitant decrease in the rate of fluctuation in the envelope and/or in the interaural cues. It is important to note that the interaural correlation of the envelope, *per se*, would be unaffected by such a strategy. When pairs of independent noise waveforms are mixed to produce a desired envelope correlation, the correlation is homogeneous across the entire bandwidth of the resulting stimulus. The strategy of shifting the center frequency of the "internal" filter away from the 4-kHz region would not be useful in the N_0S_π detection task because such "off-frequency" listening would result in attenuation of the S_π signal. It is the addition of the S_π signal to the diotic (N_0) masker that produces the decorrelation presumed necessary for detection.

D. Discrimination of interaural correlation in bands of noise with "split-correlation"

A third experiment was designed to determine whether listeners were, indeed, able to "shift the center frequency" of their internal filters in order to attend to binaural cues within select spectral regions of the widest bands of noise. The direct correlation discrimination described earlier was essentially repeated with the decorrelation of the envelope restricted to *only the lower* or *only the upper* half of a 1600-Hz-wide band of noise centered at 4 kHz. This bandwidth was chosen because, as shown in Fig. 5, it yielded the greatest discrepancy between the direct-discrimination and the N_0S_π detection data.

Suppose a listener were able to discriminate between a diotic and a slightly decorrelated noise when the interaural correlation of the envelope changes from 1.0 to about 0.95 (as shown in Fig. 5). If half the spectral width of the noise were diotic, and the listener were unable to attend exclusively to the opposite half that contained the decorrelation, then the amount of the decorrelation would have to be sufficient to reduce the correlation of the envelope to 0.95 as measured *over the entire bandwidth of the noise*. In this case, the interaural correlation of the envelope in the decorrelated half would have to be equal to 0.90 because the interaural correlation over the entire band is equal to the average of the correlation in the two halves. In contrast, if the listener were able to attend exclusively to that portion of the spectrum that contained the decorrelation of the envelope, then the correlation would only have to be reduced to 0.95 to be discriminable from diotic.

The results for three listeners are presented in Table I. Here, the decorrelation of the envelope at threshold computed over only that portion of the spectrum that was not diotic is tabulated. The first column of the table shows the thresholds required when the entire 1600-Hz band was decorrelated. As indicated in the second column of the table, when only the envelope of the lower 800-Hz-wide subband was decorrelated, all three listeners' thresholds were virtually identical to the thresholds obtained when the envelope of the entire 1600-Hz band was decorrelated. In sharp contrast, the rightmost column of the table reveals that all three listeners were extremely insensitive to decorrelations of the envelope restricted to the upper half of the band of noise.

TABLE I. Thresholds of decorrelation of the envelope computed over only the portion of the 1600-Hz bandwidth that was not diotic. [From Bernstein and Trahiotis, 1992a, with permission.]

	Spectral region of decorrelation		
		"Split correlation"	
	Entire 1600-Hz band (3200–4800 Hz)	*Lower 800 Hz (3200–4000 Hz)*	*Upper 800 Hz (4000–4800 Hz)*
TD	0.89	0.90	0.62
AS	0.90	0.93	0.47
SM	0.95	0.94	0.79

The fact that diotically presented information below, but not above, the spectral region conveying the interaural decorrelation degrades performance is consistent with the notion that the listeners' internal filters are highly asymmetric, possessing much sharper high-frequency than low-frequency "skirts" (i.e., consistent with the shape of first-order neural tuning curves). Such filter shapes when centered below the center frequency of the noise would allow for substantial rejection of the upper portion of the spectrum of the noise due to the sharp high-frequency skirt. In contrast, due to the relatively shallow low-frequency skirt, if such a filter were centered above the center frequency of the noise, relatively poor rejection of the lower half of the spectrum would be produced.

In addition, data were collected when the upper 800-Hz-wide subband, for which performance had been degraded, served as the lower subband of a new band of noise centered at 4800 Hz. Once more, the upper 800-Hz-wide subband was diotic. Under these conditions, listeners were again quite sensitive to the interaural decorrelation of the lower subband of the noise. Importantly, these data suggest that the poor performance depicted in Table I for the upper subband of noise was not due to any inability to process binaural information in that spectral region *per se*.

Taken together, the data collected with the "split-correlation" conditions strongly suggest that listeners were, indeed, able to "shift the center frequency of their internal filter" and attend to the binaural cues within select spectral regions, that is, the lower portions of our widest bands of noise. Recall that the listeners were precluded from using such a strategy in the traditional N_0S_π detection paradigm because any attenuation of the tonal signal at 4 kHz as a result of "shifting the center of an internal filter" would work against them. This finding affords a reconciliation of the differences in the decorrelation of the envelope required in the detection and discrimination tasks as depicted in Fig. 5.

E. The nature of the rate limitation

One important question regarding the data just presented concerns the nature of the proposed "rate limitation" responsible for the decline in sensitivity in the N_0S_π detection task as the bandwidth of the masker is increased beyond 200–400 Hz. As mentioned earlier, two explanations seem plausible. The reduction in sensitivity could be due to an inability to "follow" the increasingly rapid fluctuations of the envelope that occur as bandwidth is increased. Alternatively, the reduction in sensitivity could be due to an inability to "follow" the increasingly rapid fluctuations in the interaural disparities that occur as bandwidth is increased, a notion based on binaural sluggishness and discussed by Zurek and Durlach (1987).

In order to understand in some detail how binaural sluggishness would affect sensitivity in the N_0S_π detection task, it is useful to note that MLDs for high-frequency signals are commonly attributed to the detection of IIDs (Durlach, 1964). For a tone masked by Gaussian noise in the N_0S_π configuration, the distribution of IIDs is symmetric around a mean of zero and fluctuates at a rate proportional to the bandwidth of the effective masker. Importantly, as discussed at length earlier, the binaural system appears to average or "smooth over" rapid fluctuations in interaural disparities. When the bandwidth of a masker is increased, the increased rate of fluctuation of the interaural cues causes the number of independent samples entering into the binaural "averaging window" to be increased. The result is that the *variability* of independently determined values of the average, which Zurek and Durlach suggested serves as a cue to the listener, *decreases*. Therefore, increasing the bandwidth of the masker could lead to an increase in the N_0S_π threshold (a decrease in the magnitude of the MLD) because it would allow a greater number of samples of IID to be averaged, given a constant integration time.

Note that the rate of fluctuation of the IIDs in the N_0S_π configuration is approximately lowpass at half the bandwidth of the masker (Zurek and Durlach, 1987). Figure 5 shows that the decline in sensitivity in the N_0S_π detection task was observed for bandwidths between about 200 and 400 Hz. Assuming a rate limitation based on binaural sluggishness, these data imply that sensitivity declines when the rate of fluctuation of the IIDs exceeds 150 Hz or so. Recall that Grantham (1984) found that listeners were able to maintain sensitivity to dynamically varying IIDs within high-frequency signals up to essentially this same rate.

Although binaural sluggishness appears to be a plausible and parsimonious explanation for the decline in sensitivity observed for the N_0S_π thresholds in Fig. 5, those data do not preclude other explanations such as a monaural limitation in the ability to encode the increasingly rapid fluctuations of the envelope that occur as bandwidth is increased. Unfortunately, typical measures of N_0S_π tonal thresholds taken as a function of the bandwidth of the masker do not permit an independent assessment of the mechanism(s) that potentially degrade(s) sensitivity. This is so because rate of fluctuation of the interaural cues, rate of fluctuation of the envelope, rate of fluctuation of the fine-structure, interaural correlation, and bandwidth of the masker are all confounded.

What was needed was a unique method of constructing stimuli that would permit independent manipulation of the rate of fluctuation of IIDs, the bandwidth of the masker, and the decorrelation of the envelope of high-frequency masking noise. Such stimuli were employed in a separate experiment designed to reveal whether, and/or the degree to which, each of the formerly confounded factors affect detectability for several bandwidths of high-frequency masking noise.

In this experiment, the signal to be detected can be thought of as an interaurally phase-reversed (S_π) sinusoid added to *only the envelope* of the high-frequency band of noise that served as the masker. The frequency of the sinusoid determined the rate of fluctuation of the IIDs independent of the bandwidth of the masker. The amplitude of the sinusoidal signal determined the maximum IID and the interaural correlation of the signal-plus-noise envelope. Masker bandwidths between 50 and 1600 Hz were employed. Importantly, any particular bandwidth of noise was only tested with signal frequencies that precluded the generation of sidebands beyond the nominal bandwidth of the masking noise.

The results of this study indicated that the detectability of the signal was relatively unaffected by the rate of fluctuation of IIDs for rates between 5 and 160 Hz! Furthermore, interaural correlation of the envelope accounted rather precisely for the listeners' sensitivity, as long as the rate of fluctuation of IIDs was about 160 Hz or less. For these rates, there was no increase in the amount of decorrelation required for detection as bandwidth was increased. This aspect of the data indicates that listeners were "processing" the entire stimulus bandwidth and thus precludes any monaural inability to process rapid fluctuations of the envelope for the bandwidths tested.

In contrast, rates of fluctuation of the IID greater than 160 Hz resulted in substantial degradations of performance. The rates of fluctuation of the binaural cues that produced degraded performance in this study coincided precisely with the rates of the binaural cues produced by the bandwidths that yielded degraded performance in the N_0S_π detection study discussed earlier (Fig. 5). These rates also coincide with those found by Grantham to represent the highest rates of fluctuation of dynamically varying IID to which sensitivity can be maintained.

II. CONCLUSION

Overall, the data from the experiments discussed here support the notion that decorrelation of the envelope can account for performance in both N_0S_π detection and correlation discrimination experiments at high frequencies. Furthermore, the data are entirely consistent with those of Grantham (1984) and the theoretical analysis provided by Gabriel (1983) that suggests that sensitivity to interaural decorrelation of high-frequency, complex waveforms may be mediated by interaural *intensitive* disparities, as opposed to interaural envelope-based *temporal* disparities.

REFERENCES

Ando, Y. (1985). *Concert Hall Acoustics* (Springer-Verlag, Berlin).

Bernstein, L. R. (1991). "Measurement and specification of the envelope correlation between two narrow bands of noise," Hear. Res. **52**, 189–194.

Bernstein, L. R., and Trahiotis, C. (1985). "Lateralization of sinusoidally amplitude-modulated tones: Effects of spectral locus and temporal variation," J. Acoust. Soc. Am. **78**, 514–523.

Bernstein, L. R., and Trahiotis, C. (1992a). "Discrimination of interaural envelope correlation and its relation to binaural unmasking at high frequencies," J. Acoust. Soc. Am. **91**, 306–316.

Bernstein, L. R., and Trahiotis, C. (**1992b**). "Detection of antiphasic sinusoids added to the envelopes of high-frequency bands of noise," Hear. Res. **62**, 157–165.
Blauert, J. (**1972**). "On the lag of lateralization caused by interaural time and intensity differences," Audiology **11**, 265–270.
Blauert, J. (**1983**). *Spatial Hearing* (MIT Press, Cambridge, MA).
Colburn, H. S. (**1973**). "Theory of binaural interaction based on auditory-nerve data I. General strategy and preliminary results on interaural discrimination," J. Acoust. Soc. Am. **54**, 1458–1470.
Colburn, H. S. (**1977**). "Theory of binaural interaction based on auditory-nerve data II. Detection of tones in noise," J. Acoust. Soc. Am. **61**, 525–533.
Colburn, H. S., and Esquissaud, P. (**1976**). "An auditory-nerve model for interaural time discrimination of high-frequency complex stimuli," J. Acoust. Soc. Am. Suppl. 1, **59**, S23.
David, E. E., Guttman, N., and van Bergeijk, W. A. (**1959**). "Binaural interaction of high-frequency complex stimuli," J. Acoust. Soc. Am. **31**, 774–782.
Durlach, N. I. (**1964**). "Note on binaural masking-level differences at high frequencies," J. Acoust. Soc. Am. **36**, 576–581.
Durlach, N. I., and Colburn, H. S. (**1978**). "Binaural phenomena," in *Handbook of Perception, Vol. IV, Hearing*, edited by E. C. Carterette and M. P. Friedman (Academic Press, New York), pp. 365–466.
Durlach, N. I., Gabriel, K. J., Colburn, H. S., and Trahiotis, C. (**1986**). "Interaural correlation discrimination: II. Relation to binaural unmasking," J. Acoust. Soc. Am. **79**, 1548–1557.
Gabriel, K. J. (**1983**). "Binaural interaction in hearing impaired listeners," Doctoral dissertation, MIT, Cambridge, MA.
Gabriel, K. J., and Colburn, H. S. (**1981**). "Interaural correlation discrimination: I. Bandwidth and level dependence," J. Acoust. Soc. Am. **69**, 1394–1401.
Grantham, D. W. (**1982**). "Detectability of time-varying interaural correlation in narrowband noise stimuli," J. Acoust. Soc. Am. **72**, 1178–1184.
Grantham, D. W. (**1984**). "Discrimination of dynamic interaural intensity differences," J. Acoust. Soc. Am. **76**, 71–76.
Grantham, D. W., and Wightman, F. L. (**1978**). "Detectability of varying interaural temporal differences," J. Acoust. Soc. Am. **63**, 511–523.
Grantham, D. W., and Wightman, F. L. (**1979**). "Detectability of a pulsed tone in the presence of a masker with time-varying interaural correlation," J. Acoust. Soc. Am. **65**, 1509–1517.
Henning, G. B. (**1974**). "Detectability of interaural delay in high-frequency complex waveforms," J. Acoust. Soc. Am. **55**, 84–90.
Jeffress, L.A. (**1948**). "A place mechanism of sound localization," J. Comp. Physiol. **41**, 35–39.
Jeffress, L. A., and Robinson, D. E. (**1962**). "Formulas for the coefficient of interaural correlation for noise," J. Acoust. Soc. Am. **34**, 1658–1659.
Klumpp, R. G., and Eady, H. R. (**1956**). "Some measurements of interaural time difference thresholds," J. Acoust. Soc. Am. **28**, 859–860.
Kollmeier, B., and Gilkey, R. H. (**1990**). "Binaural forward and backward masking: Evidence for sluggishness in binaural detection," J. Acoust. Soc. Am. **87**, 1709–1719.
Leakey, D. M., Sayers, B. McA., and Cherry, C. (**1958**). "Binaural fusion of low- and high-frequency sounds," J. Acoust. Soc. Am. **30**, 222–223.
Levitt, H. (**1971**). "Transformed up-down methods in psychoacoustics," J. Acoust. Soc. Am. **49**, 467–477.
Licklider, J. C. R., and Dzendolet, E. (**1948**). "Oscillographic scatterplots illustrating various degrees of interaural correlation," Science **107**, 121–124.
Licklider, J. C. R., Webster, J. C., and Hedlun, J. M. (**1950**). "On the frequency limits of binaural beats," J. Acoust. Soc. Am. **22**, 468–473.
McFadden, D., and Pasanen, E. G. (**1976**). "Lateralization at high frequencies based on interaural time differences," J. Acoust. Soc. Am. **59**, 634–639.
McFadden, D., and Pasanen, E. G. (**1978**). "Binaural detection at high frequencies with time-delayed waveforms," J. Acoust. Soc. Am. **63**, 1120–1131.
McFadden, D., Russell, W. E., and Pulliam, K. (**1972**). "Monaural and binaural masking patterns for a low-frequency tone," J. Acoust. Soc. Am. **51**, 534–543.
Metz, P. J., von Bismark, G., and Durlach, N. I. (**1967**). "Further results on binaural unmasking and the EC model. II. Noise bandwidth and interaural phase," J. Acoust. Soc. Am. **43**, 1085–1091.
Nuetzel, J. M., and Hafter, E. R. (**1976**). "Lateralization of complex waveforms: Effects of fine-structure, amplitude, and duration," J. Acoust. Soc. Am. **60**, 1339–1346.
Nuetzel, J. M., and Hafter, E. R. (**1981**). "Discrimination of interaural delays in complex waveforms: Spectral effects," J. Acoust. Soc. Am. **69**, 1112–1118.
Perrott, D. R., and Musicant, A. D. (**1977**). "Rotating tones and binaural beats," J. Acoust. Soc. Am. **61**, 1288–1292.
Perrott, D. R., and Nelson, M. A. (**1969**). "Limits for the detection of binaural beats," J. Acoust. Soc. Am. **46**, 1477–1481.

Rayleigh, Lord (J. W. Strutt, 3rd Baron of Rayleigh) (**1907**). "On our perception of sound direction," Philos. Mag. **13**, 214–232.
Sayers, B. McA., and Cherry, E. C. (**1957**). "Mechanism of binaural fusion in the hearing of speech," J. Acoust. Soc. Am. **29**, 973–987.
Sever, J. C., and Small, A. M. (**1979**). "Binaural critical masking bands," J. Acoust. Soc. Am. **66**, 1343–1350.
Stern, R. M., and Bachorski, S. J. (**1983**). "Dynamic cues in binaural perception," in *Hearing—Physiological Bases and Psychophysics*, edited by R. Klinke and R. Hartmann (Springer-Verlag, New York), pp. 209–215.
Stern, R. M., and Colburn, H. S. (**1978**). "Theory of binaural interaction based on auditory-nerve data. IV. A model for subjective lateral position," J. Acoust. Soc. Am. **64**, 127–140.
Trahiotis, C., and Bernstein, L.R. (**1986**). "Lateralization of bands of noise and sinusoidally amplitude-modulated tones: Effects of spectral locus and bandwidth," J. Acoust. Soc. Am. **79**, 1950–1957.
Wightman, F.L., and Kistler, D.J. (**1992**). "The dominant role of low-frequency interaural time differences in sound localization," J. Acoust. Soc. Am. **91**, 1648–1661.
Zurek, P. M., and Durlach, N. I. (**1987**). "Masker-bandwidth dependence in homophasic and antiphasic tone detection," J. Acoust. Soc. Am. **81**, 459–464.
Zwislocki, J., and Feldman, R. S. (**1956**). "Just noticeable differences in dichotic phase," J. Acoust. Soc. Am. **28**, 860–864.

Chapter 7

Recent Experiments Concerning the Relative Potency and Interaction of Interaural Cues

Thomas N. Buell
Naval Submarine Base—New London, Groton, Connecticut

Constantine Trahiotis
University of Connecticut

(Received August 1994; revised August 1995)

The extent of laterality of intracranial images is determined by interaural intensitive differences, interaural temporal differences in the gating and ongoing portions of the signal, and in some cases, the bandwidth of the signal. This chapter reviews several of our earphone-based experiments designed to determine the relative potency of these various cues using an acoustic pointing procedure. Unlike the classic work in this area, the present results reveal highly interactive effects with certain combinations of these cues. The outcomes underscore the importance of a "pattern analysis" stage within modern cross-correlation models of binaural hearing.

INTRODUCTION

The purpose of this chapter is to discuss two of our recent investigations regarding how the intracranial position of acoustic images is affected by combinations of interaural cues. Our general strategy has two components. The first is to measure the position of intracranial images while parametrically manipulating a large set of variables. The second is to account for the large set of data by appealing to modern cross-correlation-based models of binaural hearing. The cross-correlator is composed of (physiologically realistic) elements that are "tuned" both to frequency and to interaural temporal delay. An important feature of the more modern models is that they include a stage of "pattern analysis" that serves to integrate and to weigh, across frequency, activity that occurs within the cross-correlation mechanism. Such an approach has been used successfully to describe how the intracranial position of acoustic images is determined not only by interaural differences, but also by the bandwidth of the stimulus (e.g., Stern, Zeiberg, and Trahiotis, 1988; Trahiotis and Stern, 1989).

We focus on studies designed to help elucidate (1) how interaural temporal differences (ITDs) and interaural intensitive differences (IIDs) interact and (2) the relative potency of gating and/or ongoing interaural time delays presented singly, in consonance, or in opposition. New data were required because the classic literature regarding these two issues has come either from experiments that focused on the relative discriminability of the cues or from experiments that did not systematically vary the bandwidth of the stimuli.

To illustrate the importance of bandwidth, first consider the intracranial locus of the acoustic image produced by a very narrow band of noise centered at 500 Hz and having an ongoing ITD of 1500 μs. The listener hears a "tonal" stimulus lateralized well toward the lagging ear. Second, consider the effect of increasing bandwidth while keeping the ITD constant. When the bandwidth is 100 Hz or so, the sound is lateralized at or near midline. Finally, when the bandwidth is further increased to about 400 Hz or so, the sound is heard as a "noise" with an intracranial image that is fully lateralized toward the ear leading in time.

Let us see how the lateralization of such acoustic images may be explained by appealing to a cross-correlation mechanism that includes pattern analysis. The general notion is that the intracranial position of a stimulus can be predicted from the activity within a complex, neurally based cross-correlation model. Figure 1 schematizes the peaks of the patterns of activity produced within a two-dimensional cross-correlation surface, wherein interaural delay is plotted along the

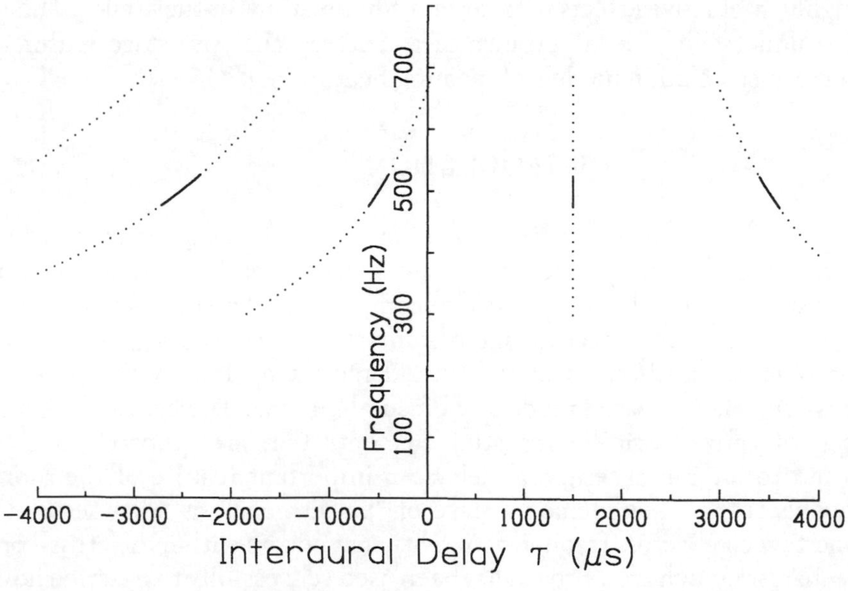

FIG. 1. Patterns of activity for a two-dimensional cross-correlation surface whose axes are defined by frequency and interaural delay. Only the maxima of the activity are plotted. The solid lines and dotted lines represent the activity for narrowband stimuli and broadband stimuli, respectively. Note that the "straight" trajectory is at the true delay of 1500 μs.

abscissa and frequency is plotted along the ordinate. The relative salience of activity within the cross-correlation surface is captured by weighing more heavily (1) peaks of activity occurring at the relatively smaller interaural delays (denoted as "centrality") and (2) peaks of activity occurring at interaural delays that are relatively consistent across a range of frequencies (denoted as "straightness"). The weighing of activity according to centrality and straightness is a form of pattern analysis.

When the bandwidth of the signal is relatively small (e.g., the stimulus indicated in Fig. 1 by the solid portion of the trajectories), the signal is heard toward the ear lagging in time. According to the model, this occurs because lateralization is dominated by the more central trajectory at an ITD of –500 μs. Because of the periodic nature of the inputs, multiple maxima will occur at integer multiples of the periods of the spectral components of the signal. That is, peaks of the cross-correlation function will occur not only at the external or "true" interaural delay, but also at the delays corresponding to these "slipped cycles" of the input.

When the bandwidth is suitably large (as depicted by dotted portions of the trajectories), the stimulus is lateralized toward the ear leading in time. According to the model, this happens because lateralization is now dominated by the straight trajectory, which indicates a consistent ITD across frequency and is located at the true ITD of 1500 μs. We use the term *true ITD* because an external sound source, at a particular azimuth, produces interaural delays, as a function of frequency, that are relatively constant (Kuhn, 1977).

There is strong confirmation that lateralization is determined by straightness and centrality. The relative amounts of straightness can be manipulated by imposing appropriate combinations of interaural time delay (ITD) and interaural phase delay (IPD) on the bands of noise. When this is done, the positions of the acoustic images change and the new positions are well described by the model (Stern *et al.*, 1988; Trahiotis and Stern, 1989; Stern and Trahiotis, 1992; Stern and Trahiotis, Chapter 24, this volume).

I. COMBINATIONS OF INTERAURAL INTENSITIVE AND TEMPORAL DIFFERENCES

Currently IIDs are thought to effect lateralization by weighing, point-for-point along the ITD dimension, activity occurring within the cross-correlation function (e.g., Sayers and Cherry, 1957; Stern and Colburn, 1978; Blauert, 1980; Lindemann, 1986). We were especially interested in assessing how IIDs and ITDs would interact in an experimental context that would allow us to manipulate the relative amounts of straightness and centrality of the stimuli. We felt that investigating time/intensity interactions within the pattern analysis approach would generate sets of data that would be novel and might clarify how, and possibly where, IIDs act within the internal cross-correlation mechanism.

To that end, we measured laterality with IIDs applied to several bandwidths of noise, with each band of noise having an ITD of 1500 μs. In more general terms, the stimuli were chosen to reveal how well lateralization of complex stimuli could be described by taking into account straightness, centrality, and the "weighing" properties of IIDs.

An acoustic pointing task was employed that required listeners to vary the interaural intensitive difference (IID) of a 200-Hz-wide band of noise centered at 500 Hz (the pointer) so that it matched the intracranial position of a second, experimenter controlled, stimulus (the target). The IID adjusted by the listener served as a metric of the intracranial position of the target. Each sequence of stimuli consisted of three presentations of the target (each separated by 200 ms), a pause of 300 ms, three presentations of the pointer (each separated by 200 ms), and a pause of 600 ms. The procedure was described in detail in Bernstein and Trahiotis (1985), Trahiotis and Stern (1989), and Buell, Trahiotis, and Bernstein (1991). Targets were Gaussian noises with a center frequency of 500 Hz and with bandwidths of either 50, 100, 200, or 400 Hz. Further details concerning the stimuli can be found in Buell, Trahiotis, and Bernstein (1994).

Figure 2 contains the data obtained with a particular combination of ITD and IID. The reader is cautioned that "IIDs" are plotted along both the ordinate and the abscissa. The IID of the pointer required to match the intracranial position of the target is plotted as a function of the IID of the target. The parameter is the bandwidth of the target. The data are means computed across the five listeners and the error bars represent ±1.0 standard error. Only the averages across listeners are presented because they accurately depict the form of the data for any given listener, both within and across conditions.

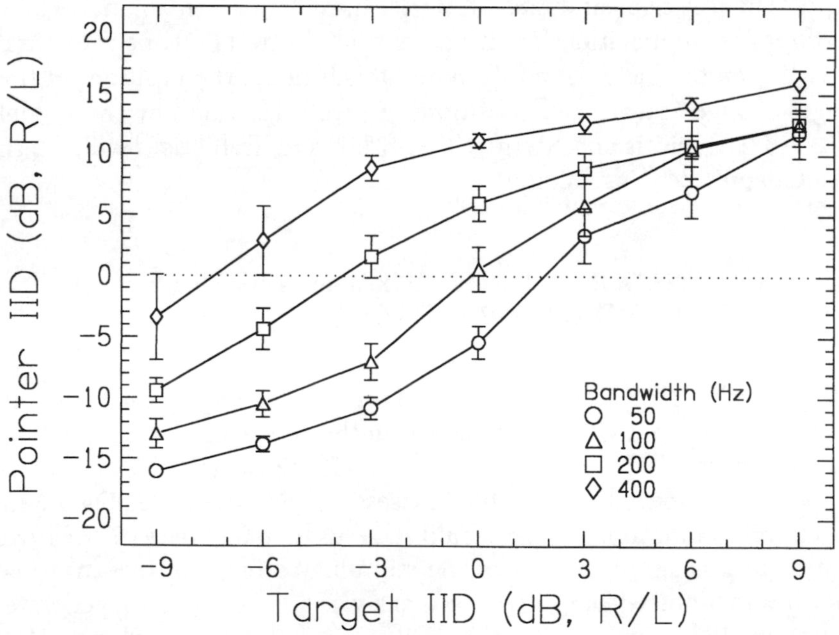

FIG. 2. Pointer IID (interaural intensitive difference) required to match the position of a band of noise (the target) as a function of target IID. The parameter is the bandwidth of the target. Targets were interaurally delayed 1500 μs. Data points represent the means across five listeners and the error bars depict ±1.0 standard error of the mean. The dotted line indicates matches that correspond to intracranial images at the midline. [After Buell *et al.*, 1994.]

For ease of exposition, the data are discussed directly in terms of the lateral position of the intracranial images produced by the targets, rather than in terms of the values of the IID inserted in the pointer by the listeners.

Beginning with data collected with an IID of 0 dB, it is apparent that increasing the bandwidth of the target from 50 Hz to 400 Hz produced large shifts in the intracranial position of the target. The target with the 50-Hz bandwidth was perceived toward the left ear, which "lagged" in time. With increasing bandwidth, the target moved toward the (leading) right ear. Thus, as discussed earlier, the stimuli with broader bandwidths contained enough "straightness" to counteract the more "central" trajectory at –500 μs.

When the IID of the targets was increased to 3 dB favoring the right (leading) ear, all of the targets were heard on the right-side of the head, regardless of bandwidth. Note that the target with the narrowest bandwidth had a disproportionately large shift in its intracranial position. An 8-dB change in the amount of IID of the pointer was required in order to match the change in position produced by a target IID of 3 dB. That is, only a 3-dB change in the IID of the target moved the intracranial locus of the noise from well toward the left ear to a position slightly toward the right ear. Further increases of IID resulted in proportionate (dB-for-dB) changes in the amount of IID of the pointer for a match to be made.

Likewise, a 3-dB IID favoring the left ear (shown as –3 dB in Fig. 2) also produced a substantial, greater than dB-for-dB, shift toward that ear. Under this condition, a 6-dB or so change in IID of the pointer was used by the listener to make a match. Overall, changes in IID of the 50-Hz-wide targets resulted in either disproportionately large (for targets with small IIDs) or proportionate (for targets with large IIDs) changes in the IID of the pointer required to make a match.

The greater than dB-for-dB relation between IID of the pointer and IID of the target was also evident in the matches made to the targets with wider bandwidths. These greater than dB-for-dB outcomes reflect a systematic interaction of IIDs with bandwidth. We noticed a similar greater than dB-for-dB outcome when we replotted data from Domnitz and Colburn (1977) concerning the lateralization of 500-Hz tones having certain combinations of ITDs and IIDs. The finding that IIDs are sometimes "super potent" is interesting, and it is comforting to know that it holds true for both bands of noise and tonal stimuli. It is tempting to assume that the greater than dB-for-dB effects are evidence that IIDs can act directly on, and thereby modify, the patterns of activity within the cross-correlation surface. In this manner, IIDs could act "early" in the process, before the straightness/centrality weighting. Despite this detailed discussion concerning the interactive effects of IID with bandwidth, it should be stressed that such interactive effects are secondary. The primary manner by which an IID is manifest appears to be as a scalar weight applied "later" in the process. Presently, we are unable to be more explicit about the specific manners by which IIDs may operate. Unfortunately, the models are realistic and contain many parameters whose combined effects must be carefully evaluated.

II. COMBINATIONS OF GATING AND ONGOING INTERAURAL DELAYS

It is well known that several types of interaural delay can affect the lateral position of binaural signals. Delays can occur within the gating (onset/offset) and/or within ongoing portions of the signal. A major purpose of a recent study from our laboratory (Buell *et al.*, 1991) was to measure lateralization with gating and ongoing delays, using tonal stimuli with the cues that were presented either in concert, in isolation, or in opposition. An acoustic pointing task was used, so that the relative potencies of the various interaural delays could be determined for intracranial positions appreciably away from midline. Prior studies either employed "centering" tasks, which necessarily focused on images near the midline, or binary left/right judgments that preclude a fine-grain analysis.

To illustrate the outcomes, we discuss data collected with 500-Hz or 1000-Hz tones having a total duration of 100 ms (including rise/decay times of 5 ms). The delays were of (1) the entire waveform; (2) only the gating portions (onset and offset delayed, fine structure presented diotically); (3) only the ongoing portions (onset and offset simultaneous, fine structure presented dichotically); or (4) both onset/offset portions and ongoing portion where the two types of delay were placed in opposition. All stimuli were digitally generated and presented at 75 dB SPL.

Figure 3 contains the data averaged across the five listeners. Only the averages across listeners are presented because they accurately depict the form of the data for any given listener, both within and across conditions. The ordinate is the IID of the pointer required to match the intracranial position of the interaurally

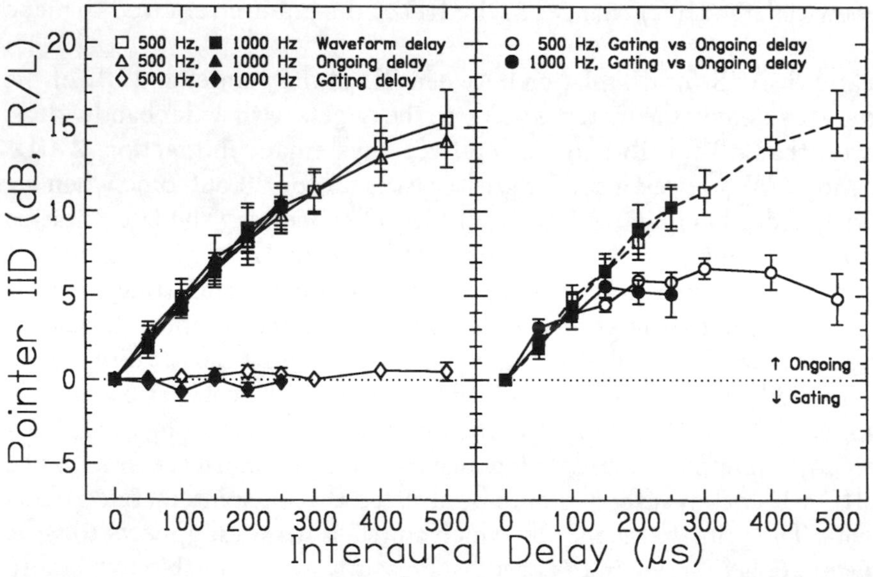

FIG. 3. Pointer IID plotted as a function of the interaural delay of the target. Each point represents the mean of six matches made by each listener averaged across the five listeners. Error bars indicate ±1 standard error of the mean. The parameter indicates the frequency of the target (500 and 1000 Hz) and the type of interaural delay (waveform, ongoing, and gating are in the left panel and gating vs. ongoing and waveform are in the right panel). [After Buell *et al.*, 1991.]

delayed target. The left-hand panel contains the data obtained with the waveform delays, the ongoing delays, and the gating delays. The right-hand panel contains the data obtained when gating and ongoing delays were placed in opposition. In each panel, the data collected with each combination of frequency and type of delay are plotted separately and the error bars represent ±1.0 standard error.

Beginning with the left-hand panel, note that substantial and similar extents of laterality were produced by equal values of waveform delay and ongoing delay. Also note that lateralization is not affected by delays restricted to the gating portion of the signal (the data indicated by the diamonds). Even with gating delays of up to 500 μs, images were always heard at the midline. This pattern of data would be expected if lateralization were determined primarily, but not necessarily exclusively, by interaural delays in the ongoing portions of the signals.

Indeed, the right-hand panel of Fig. 3 contains data (circles) showing that gating delays can be effective. These data were obtained with gating delays and ongoing delays that were equal in magnitude, but favored opposite ears. Note that the intracranial images produced with these opposing cues are still heard toward the leading ear, but closer to the midline than are the images produced by the waveform delay (squares).

Although not shown here, the same overall pattern of results was found for signal durations ranging from 15 ms to 200 ms. In passing, note the complete overlap of the data collected with the 500-Hz and 1000-Hz targets. The overlap shows that interaural time delay and not interaural phase delay, *per se*, is the critical variable for lateralization.

The last experiment to be discussed was designed to capitalize on the fact that ongoing interaural delays corresponding to phase shifts of near 180° are ambiguous, typically not producing a single intracranial image with a well-defined locus. We expected that the addition of a gating delay, be it consistent or opposing, might "tip the scale" and resolve such an ambiguity.

The four panels in Fig. 4 depict data collected with the previously described four types of interaural delay, respectively. The target was a 1000-Hz tone and the interaural delays were large, ranging from ¼ period (250 μs) to ½ period (500 μs). Within each panel, the IIDs of the pointer representing individual matches are displayed for each listener and interaural delay. The data from each of the five listeners are slightly offset along the abscissa. The data include matches made for target durations of either 100 ms or 200 ms because, as was discussed earlier, the results were quite homogeneous.

When the ongoing delay (panel b) was 400 or 500 μs, the distribution of pointer IIDs was relatively large. These delays, corresponding to interaural phase shifts of 144° or 180°, respectively, have previously been shown to produce multiple or ambiguous intracranial images (e.g., Sayers, 1964).

The data obtained with the waveform delay, which can be thought of as a result of a gating delay and an ongoing delay that is both consistent and of equal magnitude, are presented in panel a. Note that the addition of the gating delay produced consistency as to the sidedness of the image. This outcome should be compared to that shown in panel b, where there was only an ongoing delay. That is, the distribution of judgments with the waveform delay always indicated images toward the "leading"

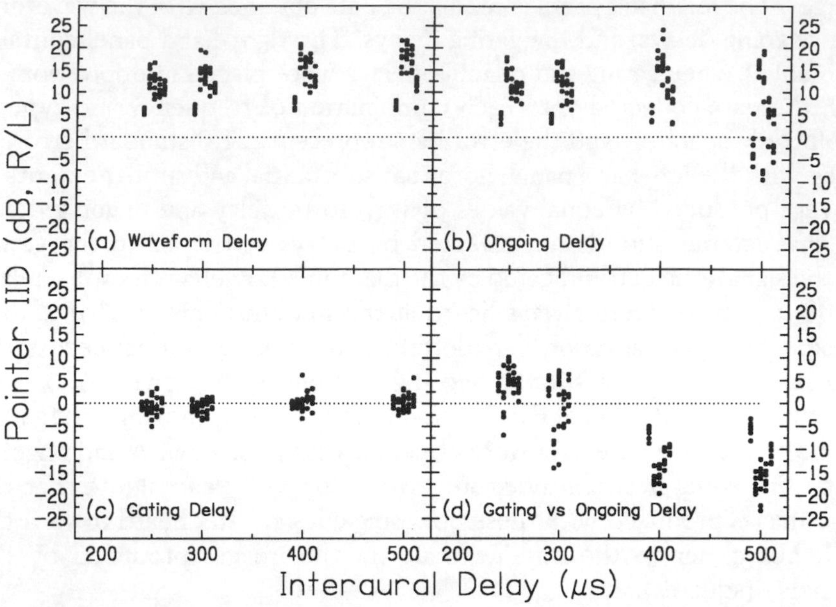

FIG. 4. Pointer IID required to match the position of interaurally delayed tones. The individual points represent the individual matches for each of the 1-kHz targets. The type of delay is indicated in each panel and the data for each of the five listeners are offset horizontally. In panel d (gating vs. ongoing) the ongoing portion of the waveform "leads" at the right ear. [From Buell *et al.*, 1991.]

ear. A similar outcome was reported by Shackelton, Bowsher, and Meddis (1991) using a short-duration, bandpassed signal centered at 800 Hz.

When an ongoing delay of 500 μs (corresponding to a phase shift of 180°) was combined with a gating delay that favored the opposite ear (panel d), images were heard exclusively on the side favored by the gating delay. This pattern of results suggests that gating delays can be quite effective when the ongoing delays are ambiguous (i.e., not clearly favoring one ear or the other). In other words, gating delays appear effectively to "resolve" potentially ambiguous phase shifts.

Panel c contains the data collected with only a gating delay. Consistent with the data shown in Fig. 3, the distribution of intracranial images remained tightly clustered about the midline. The reader is reminded that positions at the midline underscore the potency of the diotic, ongoing, cycle-by-cycle portion of the waveform.

In summary, the lateral positions of intracranial images produced by low-frequency tonal targets are strongly dominated by interaural delays conveyed by the ongoing, cycle-by-cycle portion of the waveform. Interaural gating delays, *per se*, are relatively ineffectual save for their important role when ongoing delays provide ambiguous information.

We believe that these lateralization data can be explained by merging arguments first put forth by Yost, Wightman, and Green (1971), McFadden and Pasanen (1976), and Yost (1977) with a "pattern analysis" within the cross-correlation surface. Their main idea was that gating the tonal signals introduced a "spread" or "splatter" of energy, which also conveyed binaural information. In terms of our cross-correlation surface, the splatter of energy at the onset of the tonal signal would activate units across a range of characteristic frequencies. Of course, each of these units would be tuned to a specific interaural delay. In this manner, adding a gating delay could effectively produce "straightness" even though the signal, on a long-term basis, is otherwise narrowband. The resulting activity in the cross-correlator conveying straightness would be relatively short-lived and would reflect the "ringing" time of the relatively narrowly tuned low-frequency units.

It is reasonable to speculate that the spread of energy to the lower frequencies would be especially important because that binaural information is conveyed via the fine structure in a cycle-by-cycle manner. The energy spread to the higher frequencies would be less important, because that binaural information would only be conveyed via the envelope. This is so because the auditory system cannot encode the higher frequencies in a phase-locked manner.

We attempted to test directly the salience of energy spread to the higher frequencies from gating the signal. We listened to a 1-kHz tone that had a gating delay of 500 μs favoring the left ear and an ongoing phase-delay of 180°. This was done both before and after lowpass filtering the stimuli at 1500 Hz. We always heard images lateralized toward the left ear, even when the energy above 1500 Hz (produced by gating the signal) was removed by filtering.

Overall, our general findings indicate that interaural delays conveyed in an ongoing (cycle-by-cycle) manner at low frequencies are more potent than interaural delays conveyed by short-lived, high-frequency, envelope-based interaural timing information produced by gating. In other studies it has been shown that the ongoing envelope delays in high-frequency, complex signals typically produce relatively small extents of laterality (e.g., Blauert, 1983; Trahiotis and Bernstein, 1986). Taken together, it appears that low-frequency, fine-structure-encoded timing information appears to be the "dominate" temporal cue. This summary is consistent with Blauert's (1983) early findings and discussion as well as the recent analyses of Wightman and Kistler (1992) and Zurek (1993).

In closing, we wish to emphasize our primary finding that ongoing interaural delays are, in the main, much more potent than gating delays in determining lateral position. Gating delays, on the other hand, are relatively ineffective, save for stimulus conditions that render the ongoing delays more or less ambiguous. These general statements hold true over a wide range of signal duration and apply to rise/decay times as short as 5 ms.

This is not to say that listeners are "deaf" to interaural gating delays. Perrott and Baars (1974) measured sensitivity to ITDs conveyed by onset and/or offset differences for interaurally correlated and interaurally uncorrelated noises. Although their listeners were sensitive to these differences, they stated that "neither onset nor offset transients affected the apparent locus of the 100- and 1000-ms pulses. In the latter conditions the subjects reported they were detecting a transient in one earphone, separate from the acoustic image heard during the ongoing period of the pulse" (Perrott and Baars, 1974, p. 1292). Interestingly, we also heard such "compound" images when we listened to large, conflicting ITDs presented in stimulus conditions like those utilized by Tobias and Schubert in their classic investigation (Tobias and Schubert, 1959). The perception of such anomalous, ancillary, transient images produced by large onset or offset delays, in our view, should not detract from the dominance of the acoustic image determined by the ongoing delay.

ACKNOWLEDGMENTS

This work was supported by a grant from the National Institutes of Health (DC00234) and Air Force Office of Scientific Research (AFOSR) grant 89-0030. The views expressed in this chapter are those of the authors and do not reflect the official policy or position of the Department of the Navy, Department of Defense, or the U. S. government.

REFERENCES

Bernstein, L. R., and Trahiotis, C. (**1985**). "Lateralization of low-frequency, complex waveforms: The use of envelope-based temporal disparities," J. Acoust. Soc. Am. **77**, 1868–1880.

Blauert, J. (**1980**). "Modelling of interaural time and intensity difference discrimination," in *Psychophysical, Physiological, and Behavioural Studies in Hearing,* edited by G. van den Brink and F. A. Bilsen (Delft University Press, Delft), pp. 421–424.

Blauert, J. (**1983**). *Spatial Hearing* (MIT, Cambridge, MA).

Buell, T. N., Trahiotis, C., and Bernstein, L. R. (**1991**). "Lateralization of low-frequency tones: Relative potency of gating and ongoing interaural delays," J. Acoust. Soc. Am. **90**, 3077–3085.

Buell, T. N., Trahiotis, C., and Bernstein, L. R. (**1994**). "Lateralization of bands of noise as a function of combinations of interaural intensitive differences, interaural temporal differences, and bandwidth," J. Acoust. Soc. Am. **95**, 1482–1489.

Domnitz, R. H., and Colburn, H. S. (**1977**). "Lateral position and interaural discrimination," J. Acoust. Soc. Am. **61**, 1586–1598.

Kuhn, G. F. (**1977**). "Model for the interaural time differences in the azimuthal plane," J. Acoust. Soc. Am. **62**, 157–167.

Lindemann, W. (**1986**). "Extension of a binaural cross-correlation model by contralateral inhibition. I. Simulation of lateralization for stationary signals," J. Acoust. Soc. Am. **80**, 1608–1622.

McFadden, D., and Pasanen, E. G. (**1976**). "Lateralization at high frequencies based on interaural time differences," J. Acoust. Soc. Am. **59**, 634–639.

Perrott, D. R., and Baars, B. J. (**1974**). "Detection of interaural onset and offset disparities," J. Acoust. Soc. Am. **55**, 1290–1292.

Sayers, B. McA. (**1964**). "Acoustic-image lateralization judgments with binaural tones," J. Acoust. Soc. Am. **36**, 923–926.

Sayers, B. McA., and Cherry, C. (**1957**). "Mechanism of binaural fusion in the hearing of speech," J. Acoust. Soc. Am. **29**, 973–987.

Shackelton, T. M., Bowsher, J. M., and Meddis, R. (**1991**). "Lateralization of very short duration tone-pulses of low-and high-frequencies," Q. J. Exp. Psychol. **43A**, 503–516.

Stern, R. M., and Colburn, H. S. (**1978**). "Theory of binaural interaction based on auditory-nerve data. IV. A model for subjective lateral position," J. Acoust. Soc. Am. **64**, 127–140.

Stern, R. M., and Trahiotis, C. (**1992**). "The role of consistency of interaural timing over frequency in binaural lateralization," in *Auditory Physiology and Perception*, edited by Y. Cazals, L. Demany, and K. Horner (Pergamon Press, New York), pp. 547–554.

Stern, R. M., Zeiberg, A. S., and Trahiotis, C. (**1988**). "Lateralization of complex binaural stimuli: A weighted image model," J. Acoust. Soc. Am. **84**, 156–165.

Tobias, J. V., and Schubert, E. D. (**1959**). "Effective onset duration of auditory stimuli," J. Acoust. Soc. Am. **31**, 1595–1605.

Trahiotis, C., and Bernstein, L. R. (**1986**). "Lateralization of bands of noise and sinusoidally amplitude-modulated tones: Effects of spectral locus and bandwidth," J. Acoust. Soc. Am. **79**, 1950–1957.

Trahiotis, C., and Stern, R. M. (**1989**). "Lateralization of bands of noise: Effects of bandwidth and differences of interaural time and phase," J. Acoust. Soc. Am. **86**, 1285–1293.
Wightman, F. L., and Kistler, D. J. (**1992**). "The dominant role of low-frequency interaural time differences in sound localization," J. Acoust. Soc. Am. **91**, 1648–1661.
Yost, W. A. (**1977**). "Lateralization of pulsed sinusoids based on interaural onset, ongoing, and offset temporal differences," J. Acoust. Soc. Am. **61**, 190–194.
Yost, W. A., Wightman, F. L., and Green, D. M. (**1971**). "Lateralization of filtered clicks," J. Acoust. Soc. Am. **50**, 1526–1530.
Zurek, P. M. (**1993**). "A note on onset effects in binaural hearing," J. Acoust. Soc. Am. **93**, 1200–1201.

Chapter 8

The Relative Contributions of Targets and Distractors in Judgments of Laterality Based on Interaural Differences of Level

Raymond H. Dye, Jr.
Loyola University, Chicago

(Received January 1994; revised September 1994)

This study examined the ability of listeners to lateralize 753-Hz targets on the basis of interaural differences of level (IDLs) in the presence of a distractor component (253, 353, 553, 953, 1253, 1753, and 2753 Hz) that also contained an IDL. The durations of the two-tone complexes were 200 ms. The IDLs of the target and distractor ranged from –7 to +7 dB in 1.5-dB steps, with each combination of target and distractor IDLs presented once in a block of 100 trials. Relative target weights were computed from the slopes of the best linear boundaries between left and right responses. Two of the four listeners gave more weight to the target than the distractor when the frequency separation (Δf) was large. The other two listeners weighted the target and distractor equally when Δf was large. Three of the four listeners showed a low-frequency dominance when the target and distractor were within a few hundred Hertz of one another, such that the lower frequency was weighted more heavily regardless of whether it was assigned the role of the target or distractor. The fact that a high-frequency dominance has been reported for judgments based on interaural differences of time (Dye, 1993) indicates that the mechanisms underlying spectral asymmetries in binaural processing are likely to be central rather then peripheral in origin.

INTRODUCTION

When threshold interaural delays are measured for a target component presented against a background of diotic components (distractors), thresholds are elevated relative to those obtained for targets presented in isolation (Dye, 1990; Trahiotis and Bernstein, 1990; Buell and Hafter, 1991; Woods and Colburn, 1992; Stellmack and Dye, 1993; Buell and Trahiotis, 1993). This phenomenon has been called binaural interference because it can occur even when the target and distractors are spectrally remote from one another (McFadden and Pasanen, 1976).

The explanations of binaural interference that have been put forth so far argue that the binaural auditory system has difficulty associating interaural differences with the particular spectral regions from which they arise. This has been formulated as either nonoptimal weighting of binaural information across the frequency domain (Buell and Hafter, 1991; Dye, 1990; Woods and Colburn, 1992) or summation of the outputs of narrowband cross-correlators tuned to different frequencies (Shackleton, Meddis, and Hewitt, 1992). In addition to the elevated interaural thresholds caused by diotic distractors, spectrally synthetic processing has been inferred from the fact that listeners in interference studies generally report hearing fused intracranial images of the spectrally complex signals, even though only a restricted spectral region of the complex is actually interaurally delayed (Dye, 1990; Buell and Hafter, 1991; Woods and Colburn, 1992).

Recently, we have employed a two-dimensional stimulus-classification (2D-SC) procedure that provides a means of assessing the extent to which the perceived laterality of targets is influenced by binaural information arising from distractors (Dye, Yost, Stellmack, and Sheft, 1994). The initial study focused on the effect of duration on the ability to lateralize a 753-Hz target on the basis of interaural delay in the presence of a 553-Hz distractor. The target was presented with one of ten interaural delays, five leading at the left ear and five leading at the right ear. On each test trial, the target was presented along with a distractor component, which also took on one of the same ten interaural delays. Each of the ten target delays was paired with each of the ten distractor delays once and only once during a block of 100 trials (presented in a random order). Listeners were asked to classify the target, ignoring the distractor, as "left" or "right" of the intracranial midline. Each trial consisted of two intervals, with the first presenting a diotic sample of the target alone to help mark the intracranial midline and cue the listener to the frequency of the target. The second constituted the test interval, presenting one of the 100 possible combinations of target and distractor interaural delay as described above.

Each condition was repeated 10 times, creating a composite matrix of "left" and "right" responses plotted as a joint function of target delay (on the abscissa) and distractor delay (on the ordinate). The dependence of judgments based on target delay on the distractor was assessed by finding the slope of the best linear boundary between left and right responses. Vertical boundaries are associated with *spectrally analytic* processing of target interaural delay, lateralization judgments that are independent of the distractor delay. Boundaries with slopes near –1.0 are associated with *spectrally synthetic* processing, lateralization judgments that are correlated with the distractor delay. The results showed that the majority of the listeners (six of nine) became increasingly analytic as the duration of the signals increased from 25 to 400 ms. Two listeners were analytic and one was synthetic at all durations that were tested.

The focus of the current study is on the ability of listeners to classify targets based on interaural differences of level (IDLs) in the presence of concurrent distractors presented with IDLs. Although binaural interference has been more extensively studied with interaurally delayed signals, diotic distractors have also been found to interfere with processing of IDLs (Dye and Stellmack, 1990; Heller and Richards, 1991), even when targets and distractors are far apart in frequency. Because sensitivity to IDLs does not change appreciably with frequency (with the exception of a slight loss near 1 kHz; Grantham, 1984; Yost and Dye, 1988), the frequency difference between the target and distractor can be varied over a large range without affecting the sensitivity to the cue. The frequency of the distractor was varied from 253 Hz to 2753 Hz while the target was fixed at 753 Hz, so that the effect of the frequency difference between the target and distractor could be assessed. The duration of the signals was fixed at 200 ms, a duration at which most listeners in Dye et al. (1994) were analytic in their processing of interaural delays.

I. EXPERIMENTAL METHODS

A. Procedure

Each trial consisted of two intervals, with the first providing a diotic presentation of a 753-Hz cue tone that served to indicate the intracranial midline and the target frequency. The second interval presented the test signal, which was a two-tone complex comprised of the 753-Hz target and a distractor component (253, 353, 553, 953, 1253, 1753, or 2753 Hz). The two intervals that comprised a trial were separated by 300 ms. Data were gathered in blocks of 100 trials, with the target and distractor each presented at ten different IDLs that were symmetrically placed about 0 dB. Each possible pairing of target and distractor IDLs was presented once, in a random order, during each block of trials. Subjects were instructed to indicate, by pressing one of two keys on a response terminal, whether the target component appeared to the left or right of the intracranial midline as marked by the cue tone presented during the first interval. Feedback was provided to listeners on a trial-by-trial basis.

The durations of the signals were 200 ms, with the target and distractor gated simultaneously with 10-ms rise-decay times. The IDLs of the target and distractor components ranged from −7 dB to +7 dB in 1.5-dB steps, with negative values indicating components that were more intense at the left ear and positive values indicating components that were more intense at the right ear. The level of each component prior to the introduction of IDLs was 53 dB SPL. Within a block of 100 trials, the distractor frequency was fixed. Matrices of left–right judgments were generated for each block of trials, with target IDL plotted on the abscissa and distractor IDL plotted on the ordinate. Each condition was repeated 20 times and left–right judgments were collapsed across repetitions, yielding composite matrices based on 2000 judgments.

Before each block of 100 trials, subjects were allowed to listen to a series of practice trials, which were like those to be presented during the experimental session (with target and distractor interaural differences of level varying from trial to trial). Listeners were instructed to adjust the position of the headphones during practice trials so that the diotic cue tone (first interval) sounded intracranially centered. When ready, the listeners initiated test trials. Data were collected in sessions that lasted approximately 1.5 h, during which each listener made 600–900 left–right judgments.

B. Analysis of left–right responses

The slope and y intercept of the best-fitting linear boundaries between left and right responses were extracted from each composite matrix of responses. An algorithm that minimizes the summed Euclidean distances between the boundary and misclassified responses ("left" responses to the right of the boundary, "right" responses to the left of the boundary) was used to find the best linear boundaries.

Assume that the IDLs of the target and distractor are related by separate functions to the percepts (perceived laterality) arising from each,

$$X_j = f(IDL_{Ti}), \quad Y_j = f(IDL_{Dj}), \tag{1}$$

where X_i is the percept associated with the ith interaural difference of level of the target and Y_j is the percept associated with the jth interaural difference of level of the distractor. Assume that the decision variable used by listeners is a weighted combination of the percepts arising from the target and the distractor dimensions, with w_T and w_D representing the weights given to the target and the distractor perceptual dimensions, respectively. Signals that are more intense at the left ear produce negative values of the percept and signals more intense at the right ear produce positive values. Listeners respond

$$\text{"Right" if } (w_T X_i + w_D Y_j) > C \qquad \text{"Left" if } (w_T X_i + w_D Y_j) < C, \tag{2}$$

where C is the decision criterion used for making left and right responses on the basis of the decision variable. Solving for Y_j yields

$$Y_j = (-w_T / w_D) X_i + c / w_D, \tag{3}$$

and the slope of the linear boundary between left and right responses is the ratio of the weights given to the two perceptual dimensions ($m = -w_T/w_D$). Often it will be convenient to normalize the weights so that $w_T + w_D = 1.0$, so

$$w_T = m / (m - 1) \text{ and } w_D = 1 / (1 - m). \tag{4}$$

The y intercept multiplied by w_D provides an estimate of the decision criterion, C. Analytic performance is associated with w_T's near 1.0. Synthetic performance is associated with w_T's near 0.5, reflecting equal weighting of the target and distractor. Target weights less than 0.5 indicate greater weight being given to the distractor than to the target.

C. Stimulus generation and presentation

Signals were generated and presented by a Masscomp minicomputer interfaced with 16-bit digital-to-analog converters with output rates set to 20 kHz per channel. The signals were lowpass filtered by a pair of matched Rockland (Series 2000) filters set to 7.5 kHz (for signal reconstruction). The levels of the signals were adjusted with variable attenuators (Tech Lab, Inc.) before being passed on to Crown stereo amplifiers, which were used to drive Sony MDR-V6 headphones. Listeners were seated in a sound-attenuating chamber and responses were recorded on Toshiba 1000 notebook computers interfaced with the Masscomp. Interaural differences of level were created by incrementing one channel by one half of the IDL and decrementing the other channel by one half of the IDL.

D. Subjects and training

All four observers were undergraduates at Loyola University and were paid an hourly wage for their participation. All listeners had extensive prior experience in lateralization experiments. Three of the listeners were in their early twenties and one (subject 1) was in his mid-thirties. Prior to data collection, all listeners received at least 2 weeks of training (making 5000–6000 judgments), during which they lateralized 753-Hz tones in isolation as well as in the presence of various distractor components.

II. RESULTS

Figure 1 shows composite histograms of the probability of a left response as a joint function of the target and distractor IDLs. The top panel depicts hypothetical results from a perfectly analytic listener for whom judgments are independent of the distractor delay ($w_T = 1.0$). The bottom panel shows hypothetical results from a perfectly synthetic listener who weighs information from the two components equally ($w_T = 0.5$). Both the analytic and synthetic listeners are depicted as deterministic responders making judgments under conditions of minimal perceptual noise.

Figures 2–5 present data obtained from four different listeners. Each figure presents composite histograms obtained from one subject, with each panel in a figure depicting the result of 20 replications with a particular distractor frequency. The left column shows conditions in which the distractor is lower in frequency than the target; the right column shows conditions in which the distractor is higher in frequency than the target. The lower left panel in each figure shows plots of the derived target weights as a function of distractor frequency. In no case did the best-fitting linear boundary computed from the composite histograms have an intercept that deviated substantially from 0.0, so values of C (the criterion used for making left–right judgments) are not reported here.

Subject 1's data (Fig. 2) are perhaps the most straightforward to describe. Starting with the results obtained with the largest frequency differences on the

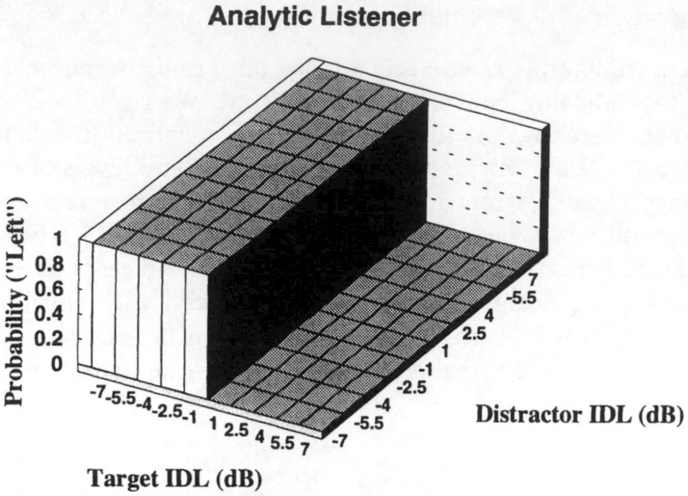

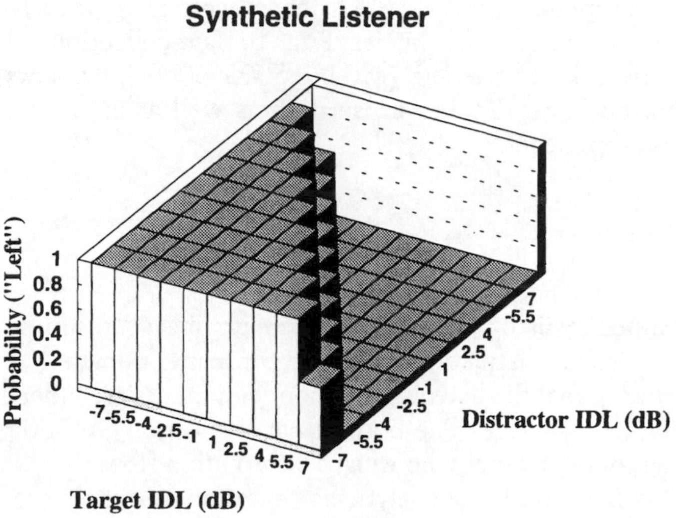

FIG. 1. The probability of a left response as a joint function of target IDL and distractor IDL is plotted for two hypothetical observers. The top panel depicts ideal performance for a listener who is perfectly analytic. The bottom panel shows ideal performance for a listener who is synthetic and combines information from the target and distractor, weighing the two equally. For cases in which the target and distractor IDLs are equal in magnitude but opposite in sign, the synthetic listener guesses and the probability of a left response is 0.5.

low- and high-frequency side of the target, note that this listener appears to make judgments of target laterality based on IDLs that are independent of the distractor IDL. As the distractor is brought to within about 200 Hz of the target from either the low- or high-frequency side, the influence of the distractor on laterality judgments increases such that the target and the distractor components contribute equally at the smallest Δfs. Consistent with the impression obtained from the histograms, it can be seen that the target weights for subject 1 are substantially greater than 0.5 when the distractors are spectrally remote from the target but approach 0.5 as Δf is decreased.

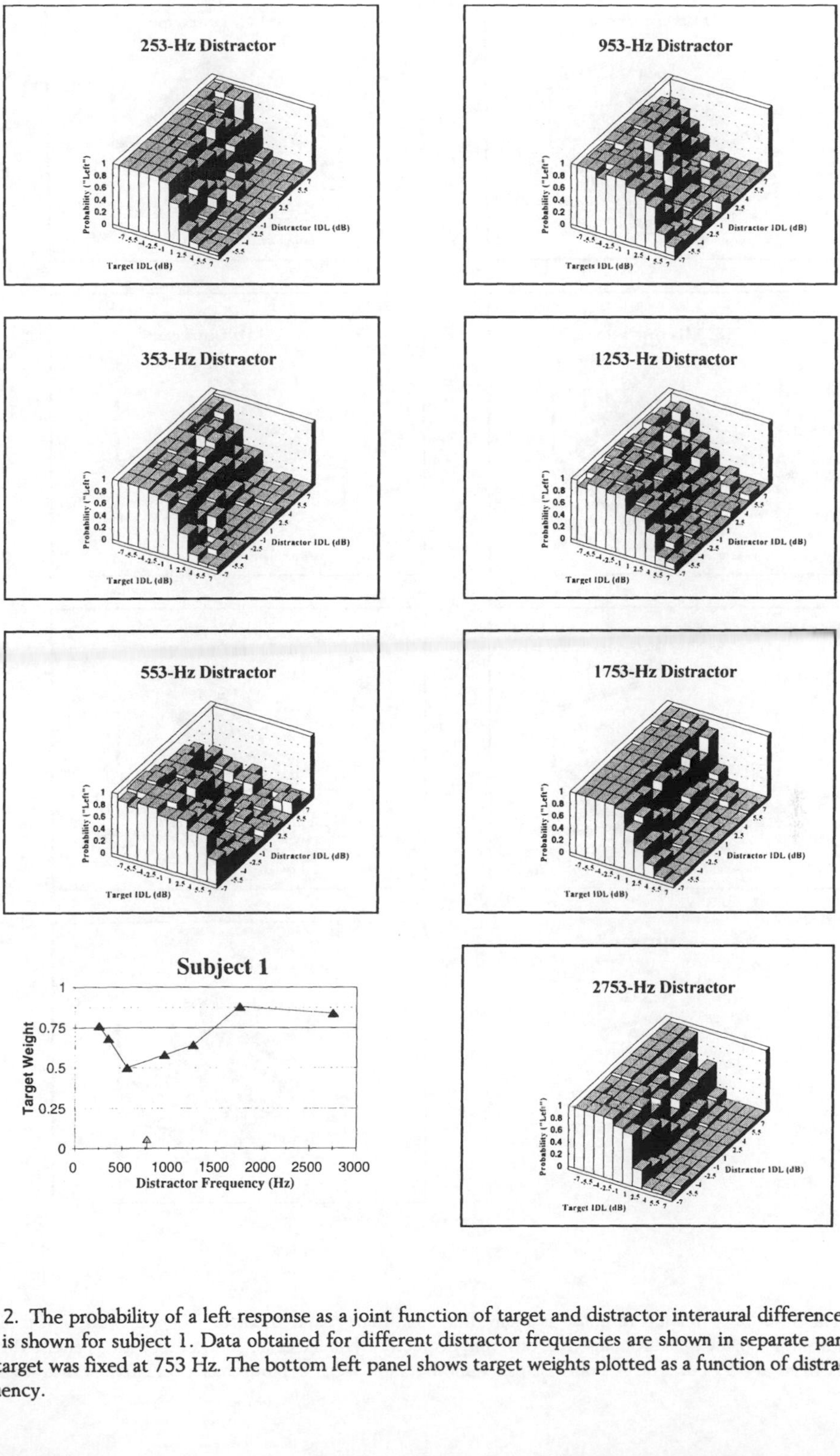

FIG. 2. The probability of a left response as a joint function of target and distractor interaural differences of level is shown for subject 1. Data obtained for different distractor frequencies are shown in separate panels. The target was fixed at 753 Hz. The bottom left panel shows target weights plotted as a function of distractor frequency.

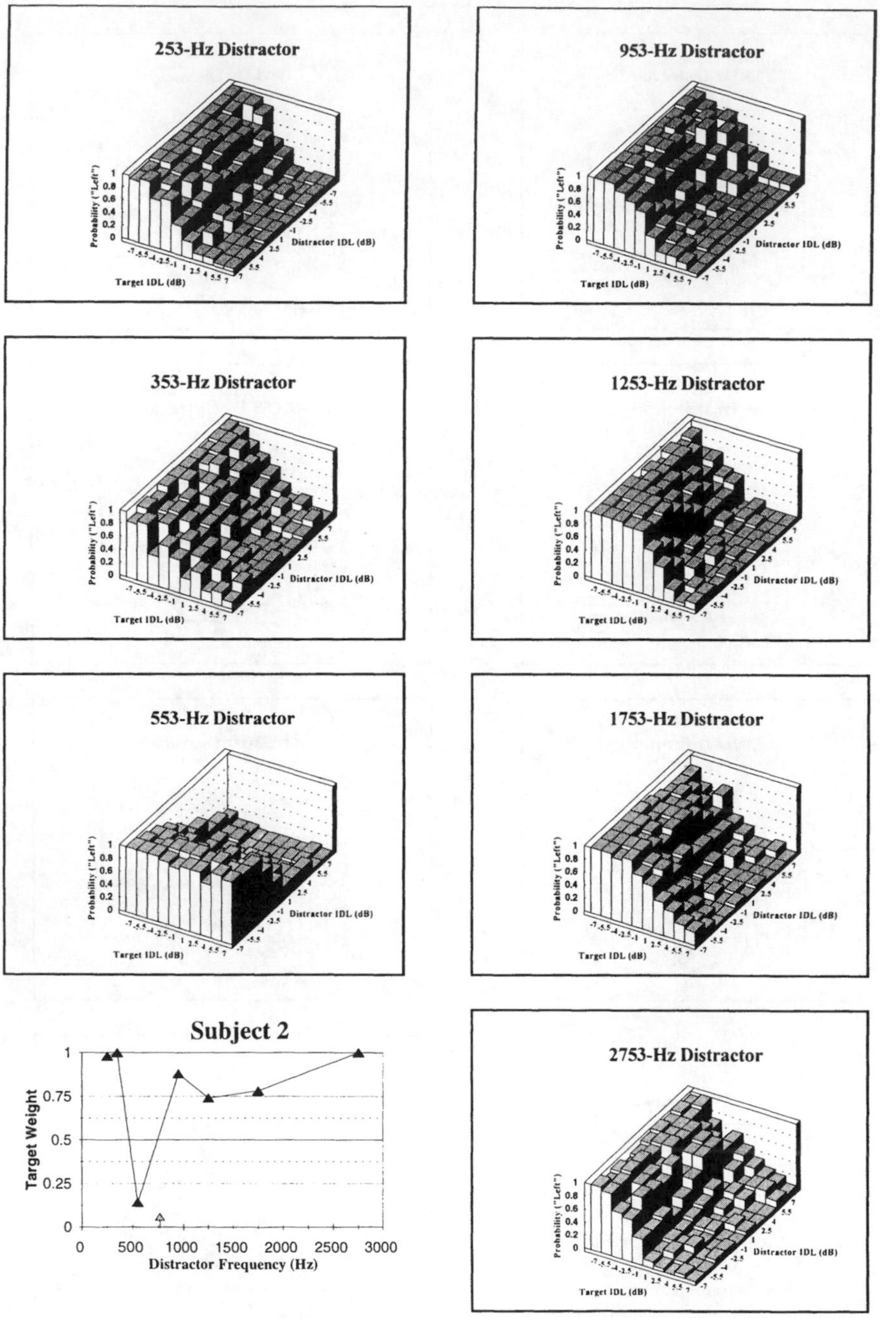

FIG. 3. The probability of a left response as a joint function of target and distractor interaural differences of level is shown for subject 2. Data obtained for different distractor frequencies are shown in separate panels. The target was fixed at 753 Hz. The bottom left panel shows target weights plotted as a function of distractor frequency.

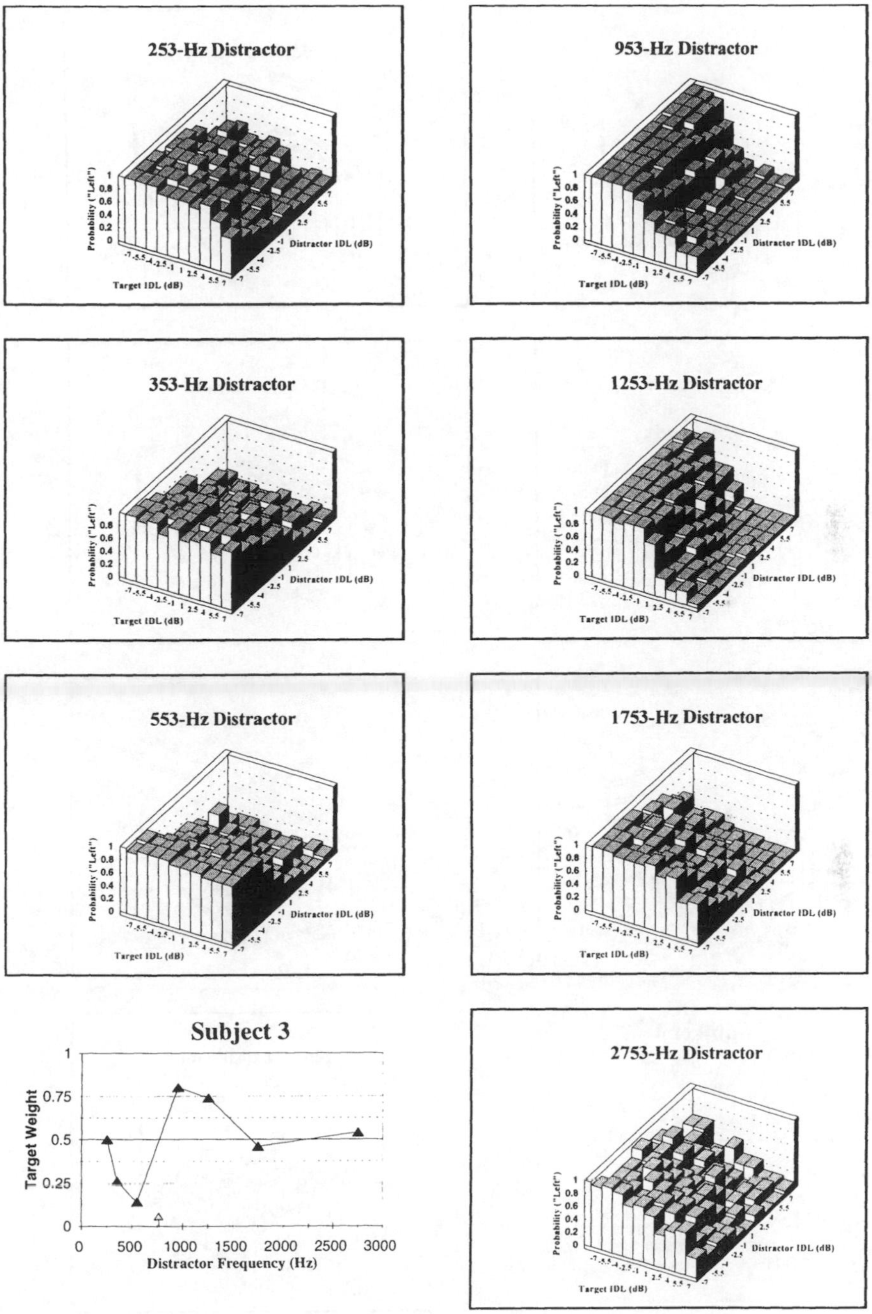

FIG. 4. The probability of a left response as a joint function of target and distractor interaural differences of level is shown for subject 3. Data obtained for different distractor frequencies are shown in separate panels. The target was fixed at 753 Hz. The bottom left panel shows target weights plotted as a function of distractor frequency.

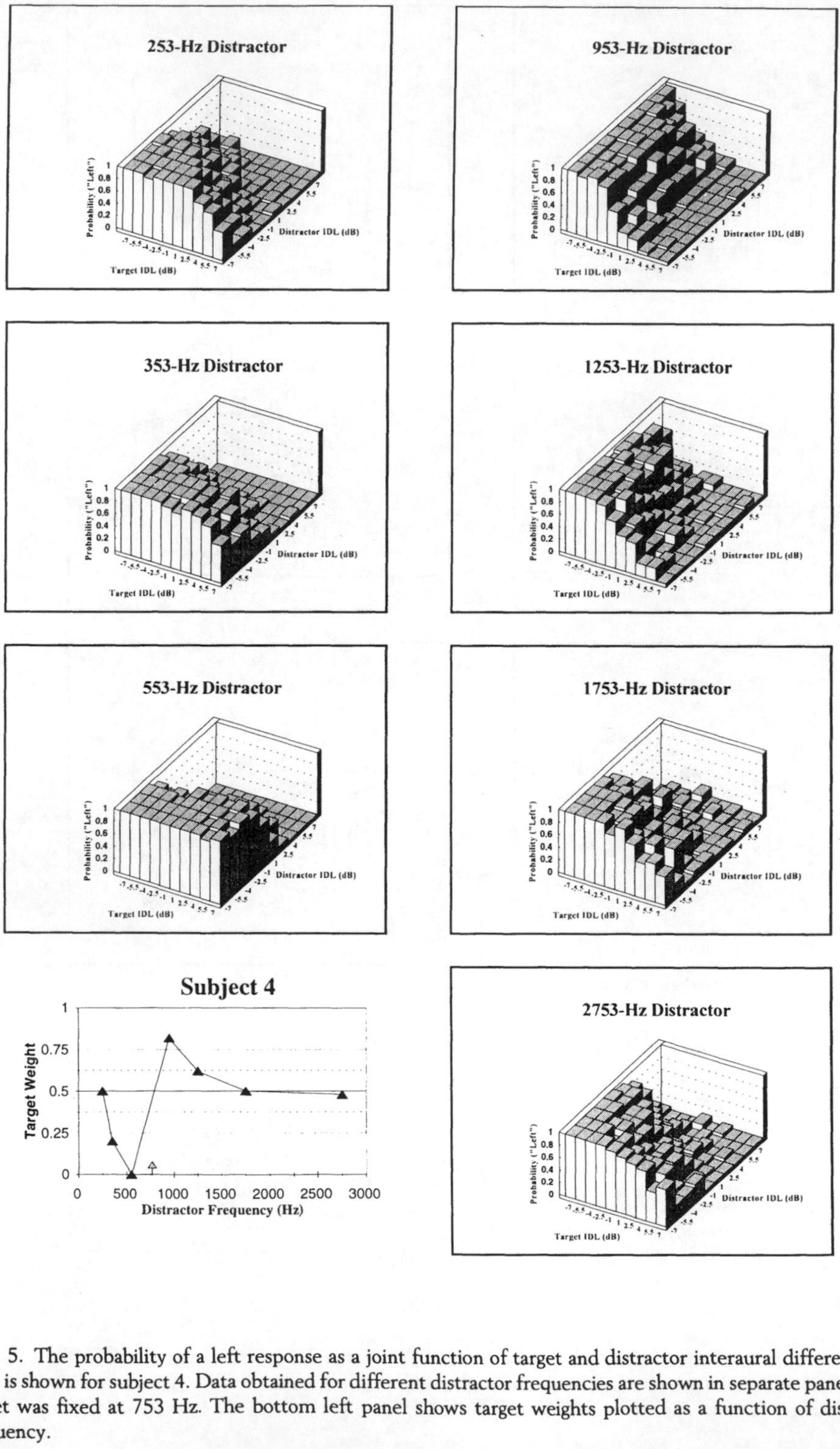

FIG. 5. The probability of a left response as a joint function of target and distractor interaural differences of level is shown for subject 4. Data obtained for different distractor frequencies are shown in separate panels. The target was fixed at 753 Hz. The bottom left panel shows target weights plotted as a function of distractor frequency.

Subject 2's data (Fig. 3) are similar to subject 1's in that she appears to judge the laterality of the target independent of the distractor at wide frequency separations. The greatest difference between this listener and the first occurs when the distractor is 553 Hz. Subject 2 appears to make judgments that are predominately a function of the distractor IDL, as though the lower frequency dominates. Also note that the influence of the distractor on laterality judgments for this listener appears to be greater with the distractor at 1253 or 1753 Hz than when it is 953 Hz, consistent with the notion that the lower component dominates when the target and distractor are within a few hundred Hertz of each other. The derived target weights for this subject approach 1.0 at the widest frequency separations, but reflect low-frequency dominance for narrower Δfs, with the 753-Hz target receiving less weight than the 553-Hz distractor but more weight than the 953-Hz distractor.

The histograms for subjects 3 and 4 (Figs. 4 and 5) are quite different from those of the first two listeners. For 253- and 2753-Hz distractors, these listeners appear to be quite synthetic, showing little ability to judge the target laterality independent of the distractor IDL, even when the target and distractor are spectrally remote. As Δf is narrowed by decreasing the higher frequency distractor, the influence of the distractor actually appears to diminish for subjects 3 and 4, whereas raising a lower frequency distractor to 553 Hz (to decrease Δf) causes it to dominate in judgments of laterality (much like subject 2). Again, the impression is of dominance of the lower frequency over the higher frequency when the components are within 400–500 Hz of one another. Plots of target weights for subjects 3 and 4 show the lower of the two components to be weighted more heavily as Δf decreases to 400–500 Hz (regardless of which component is designated as the target).

III. DISCUSSION

Before discussing the changes in target weight with distractor frequency that were observed, a word of caution must be given regarding what can logically be deduced from target weights indicative of synthetic or analytic binaural processing. Neither the pattern of left and right responses nor the derived target weights can allow one to address questions concerning the number of intracranial images that result from presentation of the composite signals; this is true whether performance indicates analytic or synthetic binaural processing. When considering *analytic* processing one thinks of a listener forming separate intracranial images associated with the target and distractor components, maintaining information about the spectral composition of each image. The image associated with the distractor is simply ignored, and judgments are based solely upon the intracranial image of the target. However, a second possibility exists, specifically that the listener forms single intracranial images based on the composite stimulus, but that the interaural cues of the target dominate those of the distractor in determining the laterality of the composite image. *Synthetic* performance refers to judgments based on the target interaural differences that are correlated with the value of the distractor delay. Synthetic binaural processing occurs when there is either a failure to form separate intracranial images or a failure to maintain information about the spectral composition of separate images for the target and distractor. The first type of synthetic processing is synonymous with the binaural spectral fusion that has been postulated to account for binaural interference (Dye, 1990; Buell and Hafter, 1991; Woods and Colburn, 1992) in which the interaural differences conveyed in different spectral regions are averaged. The second type represents the possibility that separate intracranial images are formed for the target and distractor, but that listeners respond according to which side of intracranial space is associated with the more lateralized image without regard to the spectral composition of the images. Both accounts of synthetic performance are equally plausible, and the current paradigm is again unable to distinguish between them.

Although the analytic–synthetic distinction has been useful in conceptualizing the original question of how binaural information is combined across the frequency domain, it provides an inadequate account of the results contained in the current study. The analytic–synthetic distinction fails to meaningfully describe those conditions in which distractors are weighted more heavily than targets. Target weights near 0.0 show that the listener is entirely unable to utilize binaural cues carried by the target, and thus "analytically" utilizes distractor information. While the use of "analytic" under those conditions seems peculiar, it is no less reasonable than referring to the performance of subjects 3 and 4 as "analytic" when higher frequency distractors were within 200 Hz of the 753-Hz target and low-frequency dominance was evident. Because of the inadequacy of the two terms in the present context, they will be dropped in favor of the neutral reporting of relative target weights to characterize performance.

A. Individual differences

The results showed rather large individual differences between the four listeners who participated in the study. When the target and distractor were spectrally remote, two (subjects 1 and 2) appeared to be able to make judgments based on the target IDL that were independent of the IDL carried by the distractor. Under the same conditions, the other two listeners (subjects 3 and 4) gave equal weight to the target and to the distractor components. Although the magnitudes of these individual differences may seem surprising, they are not out of line with those that have been observed for interaural differences of time (Dye *et al.*, 1994). Dye *et al.* varied the duration of the target (753-Hz) and distractor (553-Hz) components over a range from 25 to 400 ms and found listeners who gave equal weighting to the target and distractor at all durations and other listeners who effectively ignored the distractor at all durations.

One of the greatest advantages of the 2D-SC paradigm employed in this study is that it provides a means for characterizing individual differences that are often found in studies of lateralization. Studies of binaural interference compare performance between conditions in which the target is presented alone and in the presence of some number of distractors. Although individual differences in the amount of interference were reported in many of the studies done to date (Dye, 1990; Buell and Hafter, 1991; Woods and Colburn, 1992; Stellmack and Dye,

1993), little can be learned regarding the bases of those differences from traditional interaural time- or level-detection paradigms. For instance, binaural spectral fusion was put forth as an explanation of interference effects (Dye, 1990; Buell and Hafter, 1991; Woods and Colburn, 1992). One would expect the 2D-SC task to yield target weights near 0.5 if the explanation based on binaural spectral fusion were accurate. On the other hand, the deleterious effect of diotic components on the detection of target interaural differences could be due to a loss in the "spatial resolution" of the binaural system. If this were the case, the presence of distractors might result in an intracranial image of the target that is broader, more variable in location, and/or closer to the midline, yet spatially and spectrally resolved from the distractor. The 2D-SC task employed here would yield target weights close to 1.0, because target judgments would be independent of the interaural parameters of the distractor. The 2D-SC task allows one to more directly examine the extent to which the target is spatially/spectrally resolved from the distractor and to characterize, rather than simply measure, individual differences in this ability.

B. Low-frequency dominance in the processing of interaural differences of level

Three of the four listeners (subjects 2, 3, and 4) showed evidence of low-frequency dominance in the processing of interaural differences of level. Subject 2, a listener who is able to lateralize according to target IDLs at the widest frequency separations, made left–right judgments consistent with the distractor when it was 200 Hz below the 753-Hz target. When the distractor was 200 Hz higher in frequency than the target (distractor = 953 Hz), this listener's results yielded target weights that exceeded those measured at distractor frequencies that were even higher (1253 and 1753 Hz) and thus more spectrally remote from the target. The findings for this listener are consistent with dominance of the lower frequency component, at least when the target and distractor were within 200 Hz of one another.

Subjects 3 and 4 showed low-frequency dominance over even larger ranges of Δf than subject 2. Subjects 3 and 4 yielded target weights that were well below 0.5 even when the distractor was 400 Hz below the target. Both yielded target weights above 0.5 when the distractor was as much as 500 Hz above the target, even though the target and distractor were weighted equally when the distractor exceeded the target by 1000 and 2000 Hz. On the basis of this finding, one is led to the conclusion that subjects 3 and 4 were unable to spectrally/spatially resolve the target from the distractor regardless of Δf, but that the interaural cues of the lower frequency dominated when Δf was less than 400 Hz.

As a way of taking a closer look at this low-frequency dominance in judgments based on interaural differences of level, additional data were gathered from subject 1, subject 3, and a fifth subject for conditions in which the target and distractor frequencies were set to 753 Hz and 853 Hz. Conditions were run in which 753 Hz served as the target (853 Hz as the distractor) and 853 Hz as the target (753 Hz as the distractor). The goal was to examine the extent to which placing a component in the role of target had any significant impact on the weight given to it in judgments of laterality when the frequency separation between the target and distractor was small. If the weight given to a component is a function of its relative frequency, then the target weights obtained under the two conditions should sum to 1.0, indicating that a particular component receives the same weight regardless of whether it serves as a target or distractor. The obtained target weights are shown in Table I. It appears that placing a component in the role of the target had no impact on its contribution to judgments of laterality based on interaural differences of level—the weight given to a particular frequency did not change as its role in the paradigm changed from target to distractor. Note that subject 1, the listener who showed no appreciable low-frequency dominance for $\Delta f = 200$ Hz, shows a slight low-frequency dominance under these conditions ($\Delta f = 100$ Hz), because the higher frequency (853-Hz) target yielded a weight of less than 0.5.

It should be pointed out that weights are not assigned solely on the basis of the spectral relationship between the target and the distractor when the frequency separations are large. The two listeners (subjects 1 and 2) who gave weights near 1.0 to the target when the frequency separations were large, did so regardless of whether the 753-Hz or 2753-Hz component served as the target. Subject 1 yielded target weights of 0.84 when the 753-Hz component served as the target and 0.91 when the 2753-Hz component served as the target. Subject 2 yielded target weights of 1.00 in both cases, demonstrating that the designation of a component as the target, and not its spectral relationship with the distractor, determined its contribution to judgments of laterality based on interaural differences of level when Δfs were large.

The mechanisms by which the binaural auditory system might differentially weight information arising from different spectral regions are not well understood. Bilsen and Raatgever (1973) and Raatgever (1980) found that the spectral region in the vicinity of 600–700 Hz is dominant with regard to the processing of interaural delay, but no comparable study has been undertaken of interaural level processing. Buell and Hafter (1991) suggested that the auditory system might give greater weight to information arriving over channels possessing the greatest sensitivity to interaural differences. The optimal rule for a multichannel observer is to weigh each channel by the inverse of the variance associated with that channel, $1/\sigma^2$. However, there is no *a priori* reason to suspect that any differential weighting across the frequency domain should occur, because sensitivity to interaural differences of level is nearly constant over the range of frequencies used in this study (Grantham, 1984; Yost and Dye, 1988).

The fact that low-frequency dominance occurred when components were relatively close in frequency raises the possibility that it might be due to peripheral within-channel interactions. The dominance of lower frequencies is consistent

TABLE I. Target weights associated with the best linear boundaries between left and right responses for three observers. Interaural differences of level ranging from −7 to +7 dB in 1.5-dB steps served as the cue. The target frequency was 753 or 853 Hz, as was the distractor frequency.

Target	*Distractor*	*Subject 1*	*Subject 3*	*Subject 5*
753 Hz	853 Hz	0.61	0.77	0.91
853 Hz	753 Hz	0.44	0.26	0.00

with the "upward spread" that is observed in masking patterns when signals are of at least moderate level (Zwicker and Feldtkeller, 1967). This type of spectral asymmetry is usually attributed to the mechanical properties of the cochlea (the increase in bandwidth with frequency and the asymmetry of peripheral tuning; see Moore and Glasberg, 1983, 1987). Although it would be incorrect to argue that the lower frequency component "masks" the higher frequency, because both components are presented at suprathreshold levels and are far enough apart in frequency to be heard separately (Plomp and Steeneken, 1968), the salience of the lower frequency component might exceed that of the higher frequency when the two are presented together.

If upward spread of activation were responsible for the low-frequency dominance observed in the current study, it is surprising that it was in evidence for two listeners (subjects 3 and 4) when the Δfs were as large as 400–500 Hz, given that the estimated width of the auditory filter at 750 Hz (as measured by the equivalent rectangular bandwidth) is about 100 Hz (Patterson, 1974; Moore and Glasberg, 1983). In order to account for the range of Δfs over which low-frequency dominance was observed, one must invoke critical bandwidths that are even wider than the already broad binaural critical bandwidths that have been discussed elsewhere (e.g., Hall, Tyler, and Fernandes, 1983).

The fact that different listeners show this low-frequency dominance to such different degrees and over such different ranges of frequency casts doubt on arguments based solely on cochlear mechanics. Although individual differences are prominent in estimates of auditory filter shape and bandwidth (Moore and Glasberg, 1987), it seems unlikely that they are of sufficient magnitude to account for the difference in low-frequency dominance between subject 1 and subjects 3 and 4. Most damning to explanations based on peripheral mechanisms is the finding that the spectral asymmetry found in the processing of interaural delays as assessed with the two-dimensional stimulus-classification paradigm is opposite in direction to that found for interaural differences of level (Dye, 1993). Figure 6 shows target weights obtained for 100-ms signals that consisted of a 753-Hz target and a variable frequency distractor. For interaural delays, the weights associated with the higher of the two components tend to be greater. Note that the range of frequency variation was considerably less than in the IDL study, because the range of frequencies over which good sensitivity to interaural delay is maintained is more constricted.

The mechanisms that underlie spectral asymmetries in the processing of interaural differences of time and level require further study. The fact that spectral dominance is by the lower frequency for interaural differences of level and by the higher frequency for interaural differences of time indicates that the mechanisms are likely to be central, beyond the point of binaural interaction, rather than peripheral.

IV. SUMMARY

Results from a two-dimensional stimulus-classification paradigm showed large individual differences in the extent to which laterality judgments based on IDLs of a target component were dependent on the distractor IDL. Two listeners made

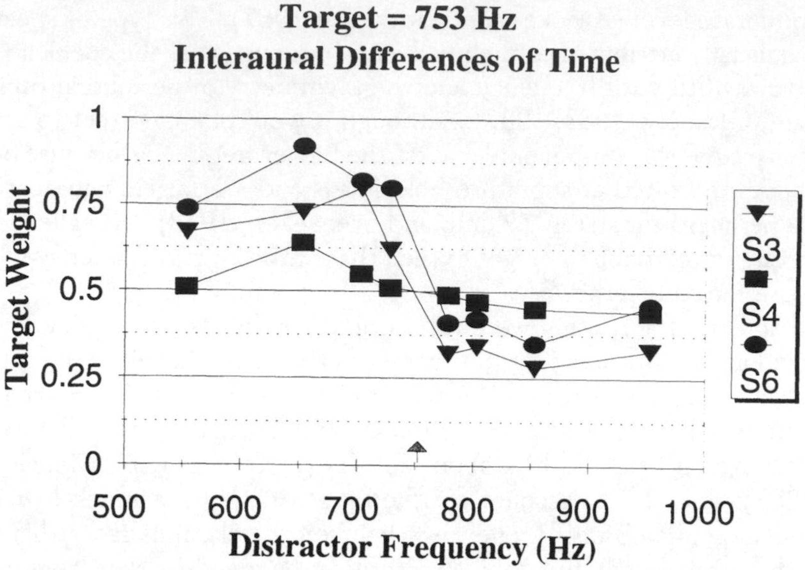

FIG. 6. Target weights are plotted as a function of the distractor frequency for three listeners. The target frequency (753 Hz) is marked by the gray arrow on the abscissa. Target and distractor interaural delays ranged from −45 to +45 μs in 10-μs steps. Note that the range of distractor frequencies is much narrower than that used in the current study of judgments based on IDLs. Subjects 3 and 4 also participated in the IDL study; subject 6 did not. [From Dye, 1993.]

judgments that were largely independent of distractor IDL, with left–right judgments partitioned by best-linear boundaries that were nearly vertical. The remaining two listeners weighed target and distractor information equally even at the widest target-distractor Δ*f*s.

Listeners showed a low-frequency dominance in their weighting of interaural level information when the distractor and target were within several hundred Hertz of each other, such that the weights associated with the lower frequency exceeded those of the higher frequency regardless of which component was designated as the target. This low-frequency dominance in judgments based on IDL also showed large individual differences both in its magnitude and in the range of Δ*f*s over which it occurred. Although low-frequency dominance is consistent with "upward spread of activation," the fact that judgments based on interaural differences of time (Dye, 1993) show a high-frequency dominance indicates that the mechanisms underlying spectral asymmetries in binaural processing are likely to be central rather than peripheral.

Two-dimensional stimulus-classification tasks, like the one employed in the current study, are likely to be useful in the future study of the combination of binaural information across the frequency domain. They provide a more direct measure of the extent to which interaural information arising from various spectral components is combined, which can only loosely be inferred from measures of binaural interference. Furthermore, the estimated target weights provide a quantitative estimate of the degree to which a particular component contributes to judgments of laterality. Perhaps the greatest advantage of the 2D-SC paradigm is its ability to characterize individual differences in the ability of listeners to both spatially and spectrally resolve a target component in the presence of distractors.

ACKNOWLEDGMENTS

I would like to thank my colleagues at the Parmly Hearing Institute (William Yost, Stan Sheft, Mark Stellmack, William Shofner, Richard Fay, Sheryl Coombs, Jud Crawford, J. D. Trout, and Tony Grange) for many hours of discussion of classification procedures. I wish to thank Scott Larson and Gail Gumauskas for their help with data collection. This work was supported by a program project grant from the National Institutes of Health.

REFERENCES

Bilsen, F. A., and Raatgever, J. (**1973**). "Spectral dominance in binaural lateralization," Acustica **28**, 131–132.

Buell, T. N., and Hafter, E. R. (**1991**). "Combination of binaural information across frequency bands," J. Acoust. Soc. Am. **90**, 1984–1990.

Buell, T. N., and Trahiotis, C. (**1993**). "Interaural temporal discrimination using two sinusoidally amplitude-modulated, high-frequency tones: Conditions of summation and interference," J. Acoust. Soc. Am. **93**, 480–487.

Dye, R. H. (**1990**). "The combination of interaural information across frequencies: Lateralization on the basis of interaural delay," J. Acoust. Soc. Am. **88**, 2172–2184.

Dye, R. H. (**1993**). "The relative contributions of targets and distractors in laterality judgments," J. Acoust. Soc. Am. **93**, S2349.

Dye, R. H., and Stellmack, M. A. (**1990**). "Detection of interaural differences of level in multitone complexes," J. Acoust. Soc. Am. **88**, S97.

Dye, R. H., Yost, W. A., Stellmack, M. A., and Sheft, S. (**1994**). "Stimulus classification procedure for assessing the extent to which binaural processing is spectrally analytic or synthetic," J. Acoust. Soc. Am. **96**, 2720–2730.

Grantham, D. W. (**1984**). "Interaural intensity discrimination: Insensitivity at 1000 Hz," J. Acoust. Soc. Am. **75**, 1191–1194.

Hall, J. W., Tyler, R. S., and Fernandes, M. A. (**1983**). "Monaural and binaural auditory frequency resolution measured using bandlimited noise and notched-noise masking," J. Acoust. Soc. Am. **73**, 894–898.

Heller, L. M., and Richards, V. M. (**1991**). "Differential lateralization interference for interaural time and interaural level differences," J. Acoust. Soc. Am. **89**, S1995.

McFadden, D., and Pasanen, E. G. (**1976**). "Lateralization at high frequencies based on interaural time differences," J. Acoust. Soc. Am. **59**, 634–639.

Moore, B. C. J., and Glasberg, B. R. (**1983**). "Suggested formulae for calculating auditory-filter bandwidths and excitation patterns," J. Acoust. Soc. Am. **74**, 750–753.

Moore, B. C. J., and Glasberg, B. R. (**1987**). "Formulae describing frequency selectivity as a function of frequency and level, and their use in calculating excitation patterns," Hear. Res **28**, 209–225.

Patterson, R. D. (**1974**). "Auditory filter shape," J. Acoust. Soc. Am. **55**, 802–809.

Plomp, R., and Steeneken, H. J. M. (**1968**). "Interference between two simple tones," J. Acoust. Soc. Am. **43**, 883–884.

Raatgever, J. (**1980**). "On the binaural processing of stimuli with different interaural phase relations," Doctoral dissertation, Delft University of Technology, The Netherlands.

Shackleton, T. M., Meddis, R., and Hewitt, M. J. (**1992**). "Across frequency integration in a model of lateralization," J. Acoust. Soc. Am. **91**, 2276–2279.

Stellmack, M. A., and Dye, R. H. (**1993**). "The combination of interaural information across frequencies: The effect of number and spacing of components, onset asynchrony, and harmonicity," J. Acoust. Soc. Am. **93**, 2933–2947.

Trahiotis, C., and Bernstein, L. R. (1990). "Detectability of interaural delays over select spectral regions: Effects of flanking noise," J. Acoust. Soc. Am. 87, 810–813.
Woods, W. S., and Colburn, H. S. (1992). "Test of a model of auditory object formation using intensity and interaural time difference discrimination," J. Acoust. Soc. Am. 91, 2894–2902.
Yost, W. A., and Dye, R. H. (1988). "Discrimination of interaural differences of level as a function of frequency," J. Acoust. Soc. Am. 83, 1846–1851.
Zwicker, E. and Feldtkeller, R. (1967). *Das Ohr als Nachrichtenempfanger* (Verlag, Stuttgart).

Chapter 9

Binaural Masking Level Differences in Nonsimultaneous Masking

Armin Kohlrausch
Institute for Perception Research (IPO), Eindhoven, The Netherlands

Ralf Fassel
Universität Göttingen, Germany

(Received December 1993; revised September 1994)

This chapter investigates the extent to which binaural unmasking occurs with nonsimultaneous presentation of masker and signal, particularly in forward masking. The majority of previous studies that addressed this question found that there is a substantial binaural masking level difference (BMLD) in forward masking even for fairly long signal delays, but that the amount decreases with increasing temporal separation between masker and signal. The existence of a BMLD at long delays is difficult to explain by theories of binaural interaction. A few studies, on the other hand, reported a substantial BMLD only for short delays between masker offset and signal. To further examine these conflicting findings, forward-masking curves were measured for a 10-ms 500-Hz signal in the conditions N_0S_0 and N_0S_π. The masker was a bandpass frozen noise (20 Hz–1 kHz) with a duration of either 20 or 300 ms. In an additional condition, a series of frozen-noise pulses of 20-ms duration and 30-ms interpulse separation was used as the masker. A comparison of the results from the two interaural conditions showed a significant BMLD in simultaneous conditions and for the first 10–20 ms of the forward-masking curve but not for longer signal delays. Thus, the BMLD in forward masking was restricted to the short period after masker offset that corresponds to the decay time of the basilar-membrane filter at low frequencies.

INTRODUCTION

This chapter is concerned with binaural masking level differences (BMLDs) for nonsimultaneous presentation of masker and signal. Nonsimultaneous masking is one of several procedures used to investigate temporal properties of the hearing system. In nonsimultaneous masking, the audibility of a (usually) short signal is measured as a function of its temporal separation from the masker. Depending on whether the signal is presented before or after the masker, the terms backward or forward masking are used to define the temporal relation between masker and signal. Because forward masking is more prominent, in terms of the amount of masking as well as in terms of its temporal extent, we concentrate on this condition.

Monaural experiments on forward masking have revealed the following results. After the offset of a long masker, thresholds are elevated for a period up to 200 ms. This period of 200 ms appears to be fairly independent of the masker level (Stein, 1960). Therefore, the forward-masking curve becomes steeper with increasing masker level. In contrast to simultaneous masking, forward masking depends strongly on the masker duration. The shorter the masker, the steeper the slope of the forward-masking curve and the shorter the period of elevated thresholds after masker offset (Zwicker, 1984). The first part of the forward-masking curve is influenced by the signal's frequency: the lower the frequency, the shallower the slope. Beyond about 30 ms after masker offset, forward masking is independent of frequency (Langhans, 1991). The phase relation between the signal and a (deterministic) masker does not seem to influence forward-masked thresholds (Yost, Grantham, Lutfi, and Stern, 1982; Langhans, 1991).

It is assumed that at least two processes play a role in forward masking (Duifhuis, 1973). The first is the ringing of the basilar-membrane filter, which extends the masker beyond its physical offset. Because the duration of ringing is inversely related to the bandwidth of the inner-ear filter at the signal frequency, this effect will be stronger at lower frequencies. This process dominates forward masking immediately after masker offset.

The second process is thought to be due to neuronal aftereffects. This process might be excitatory (being some kind of slow decay of neuronal excitation) or suppressive (like temporal adaptation). Duifhuis (1973) assumed a time constant of 75 ms for this process.

I. NONSIMULTANEOUS MASKING IN BINAURAL CONDITIONS

In this section we summarize results from other studies that investigated nonsimultaneous masking in a variety of binaural conditions. The following signal-masker conditions were applied in these studies:

1. A noise masker followed by a short tonal signal.
2. A noise masker followed by a click of duration less than 1 ms.
3. A tonal masker followed by a short tonal signal of equal frequency.

In reviewing forward-masking data from different studies, there exists a manifest problem. The temporal distance between masker and signal is specified with reference sometimes to the onset of the signal and sometimes to its offset. Because it is generally believed that the end of the signal is the most relevant part in detection, we always express the temporal position of the signal as the delay between masker offset and signal offset, even if a different measure was used in the original articles. If not stated explicitly, we use the term BMLD for the difference in masked threshold between the conditions N_0S_0 (noise and signal diotic) and N_0S_π (noise diotic, signal interaurally phase inverted).

The largest amount of data is available for condition 1, but only a few studies measured thresholds for a large number of signal delays. Small, Boggess, Klich, Kuehn, Thelin, and Wiley (1972) determined BMLDs for a signal at 250 Hz and a duration of 10 ms (rectangularly gated) for five nonsimultaneous conditions. The masker was a 500-ms wideband noise with a spectrum level of 46 dB SPL. The BMLD decayed from 10.5 dB in simultaneous masking to 7 dB at a delay of 20 ms, to around 3 dB at delays of 30 and 40 ms, and to 0 dB at a delay of 60 ms.

Zwicker and Zwicker (1984a) used uniform masking noise of 300 ms to mask 10-ms signals at 400 Hz. Eight different signal delays including one simultaneous condition were used. In the course of forward masking, the BMLD decreased continuously from the simultaneous value of 12 dB. For a delay of 20 ms, it was 8 dB; for a delay of 50 ms, it was 4 dB; and for a delay of 100 ms, it was 3 dB. In a different condition, a series of five noise pulses of 10 ms duration and an interpulse distance of 10 ms were used to mask a 2-ms 800-Hz signal. In simultaneous masking, a BMLD of 10–12 dB was obtained. For a delay of 10 ms (measured from the offset of the last pulse), the BMLD was reduced to 6 dB; for delays of 20 ms or more, the BMLD was only 1–2 dB.

Yama (1992) determined the BMLD for a 10-ms 250-Hz signal as a function of the delay and the masker level. For the two highest masker levels, the data showed a similar decrease to that observed by Zwicker and Zwicker (1984a): From 15.9 dB in simultaneous masking, the BMLD decreased to about 7.5 dB at a delay of 25 ms, to 5 dB at a delay of 50 ms, and to about 2 dB at a delay of 110 ms.

A number of other studies determined the BMLD for only one signal delay. Lakey (1976) measured the BMLD for a 500-Hz signal, 8 ms in duration, that followed a wideband noise masker with a fixed delay of 18 ms. The experimental parameter was the noise duration. For durations beyond 100 ms, the BMLD ranged from 6.7 to 9.2 dB. For shorter durations, the BMLD was not larger than 3.9 dB and disappeared for durations shorter than 5 ms.

Yost and Walton (1977) obtained BMLDs for various interaural conditions (N_0S_m, N_0S_π, $N_\pi S_0$). The signal was a 500-Hz tone of 20-ms duration that had a delay of 30 ms with respect to the broadband noise. In all three conditions, the BMLD in forward masking was about half the value in simultaneous masking, being 9, 7, and 4 dB for N_0S_π, $N_\pi S_0$ and N_0S_m, respectively.

Yama (1982) obtained BMLDs for a 500-Hz signal of 10-ms duration at a delay of 22.5 ms. The experimental parameter was the masker bandwidth. For the wideband masker the BMLD was around 2 dB for two subjects and 9 dB for a third subject. At intermediate bandwidths (around 50 Hz), the BMLD increased up to about 20 dB, mainly due to relatively poor performance in the N_0S_0 reference condition.

In another paper, Yama (1985) measured BMLDs for a 15-ms signal at a delay of 25 ms. The experimental parameter was signal frequency. For the three subjects and the two lowest signal frequencies of 250 and 500 Hz, the BMLD varied between –2.5 and +7.5 dB, with an average of 3.2 dB.

A very specific paradigm was applied by Punch and Carhart (1973). Thresholds were measured for fairly long 500-Hz signals, which in the forward-masking condition were extended in duration beyond the offset of the masker. The BMLD was reduced from the simultaneous value of 11.3 dB to about 5 dB at 15 ms and to no more than about 3 dB for delays of 25 ms or more.

In summary, the majority of these studies found a substantial BMLD (>3 dB) for delays of up to 50 ms. A minority of studies found substantial BMLDs occurred only for delays up to 20 ms.

In condition 2 (click following a broadband noise), Berg and Yost (1976) measured the BMLD for five delays between 0 and 40 ms. Directly at masker offset, the BMLD was about 12 dB, and it decreased continuously to about 6 dB at the longest delay.

In a similar condition, Yost (1985) observed large intersubject differences. Click BMLDs were measured for delays of 1, 15, and 30 ms for three masker levels and for clicks that were lowpass filtered at 1.5 or 5 kHz. Substantial BMLDs were obtained for two of the three subjects. The values were higher for clicks filtered at 1.5 kHz and decreased with increasing delay. For the highest masker level, the average BMLD for the two subjects was about 5.5 dB at a delay of 15 ms and 4 dB at a delay of 30 ms.

Finally, Hanna, Robinson, Shiffrin, and Gilkey (1982) measured BMLDs for clicks following a 300-ms masker with a delay of 20 ms or following a 10-ms masker with a delay of 5 ms. Lowpass filters of 1 and 5 kHz were used to limit the click spectrum. BMLDs were less than 1 dB except for the 1-kHz pulse with a 5-ms delay. For this condition, the BMLD increased with increasing masker level up to about 9 dB.

In summary, the click data give an unclear picture as to the maximal delay that results in a substantial BMLD. BMLDs in forward masking seem to be smaller for clicks than for tone pulses.

In condition 3 (tonal masker and target), Yost *et al.* (1982) investigated the influence of the interaural phase difference, between the stimuli at the two ears, as well as the influence of the monaural phase difference, between the masker and the signal. The 20-ms signal at 500 Hz followed the masker immediately; thus the delay in our definition was 20 ms. The (monaural) phase angle between masker and signal had little effect on thresholds in forward masking. The interaural phase of the signal, on the other hand, did influence the thresholds in forward masking and the BMLD, averaged across three monaural phase values and four subjects, amounted to 5.1 dB. This experiment directly points to the major problem in explaining a BMLD in forward masking.

Many BMLD effects in simultaneous masking are compatible with the assumption of a vectorial addition of masker and signal, which describes the interaural differences of time and/or amplitude that lead to lower binaural thresholds (Colburn and Durlach, 1978). Applied to BMLDs in nonsimultaneous masking, this view requires that information about the relative phase between masker and signal is preserved beyond the offset of the masker (cf. Lakey, 1976). However, as the results of Yost *et al.* (1982) and also of Langhans (1991) showed, such a preservation of phase is not observed in monaural forward-masking experiments.

Nevertheless, several authors (e.g., Small *et al.*, 1972; Zwicker and Zwicker, 1984a) assumed that, somehow, phase information is preserved beyond the physical offset of the masker. This could happen either because of a temporal overlap of the neuronal excitation of masker and signal or, even less specifically, because of the fact that "from the periphery more information about the time structure of a masker is transmitted towards higher levels than can be derived from the post-masking thresholds" (Zwicker and Zwicker, 1984a, p. 227).

Another argument used to explain BMLDs in forward masking is the influence of the masker level on the BMLD. In simultaneous masking, the BMLD decreases with decreasing masker level (e.g., Yost, 1988). In forward masking, both the masked threshold in the N_0S_0 reference condition and the BMLD decrease. Several authors (e.g., Zwicker and Zwicker, 1984a; Yama, 1992) emphasized this similarity in the discussion of possible causes for a BMLD in nonsimultaneous masking.

However, there exists no satisfying theoretical framework as to why a substantial binaural advantage should exist in nonsimultaneous masking. In the next section, a model for nonsimultaneous thresholds in monaural conditions that incorporates a quantitative formulation of adaptation-like processes is described. Based on this model, two different hypotheses are derived with respect to binaural thresholds in forward masking that form the basis for the current measurements.

II. MODELLING FORWARD MASKING

Püschel (1988) proposed a model that allows the prediction of thresholds in nonsimultaneous conditions. This model is described in detail elsewhere (Kohlrausch, Püschel, and Alphei, 1992; Dau, Püschel, and Kohlrausch, 1996), and we emphasize only some properties relevant for the present study.

In the model, signals are first filtered with a linear basilar-membrane model (Strube, 1985). The output signals are half-wave rectified and lowpass filtered at 1 kHz. In this stage, which simulates the transformation in the inner hair cell, an absolute threshold for the target is introduced by adding a noise floor with appropriate level.

The central part of the model contains a series of five feedback loops (Fig. 1) that mimic the adaptive properties of the auditory periphery. In each individual element, the input I is attenuated by a value that corresponds to the lowpass filtered version of the output. For stationary signals, the output O of an individual stage is equal to the square root of the input. For the series of five elements that was used by Püschel, the range of (stationary) input values is compressed almost logarithmicly. The output O of this stage forms the basis for the decision whether audible changes are introduced by the test signal or not. This detection part can consist of a simple integrator (Püschel, 1988) or of an optimal processor stage (Dau *et al.*, 1996).

Input variations that occur quickly compared to the time constant of a specific element are transformed linearly, because the output of the lowpass filter that

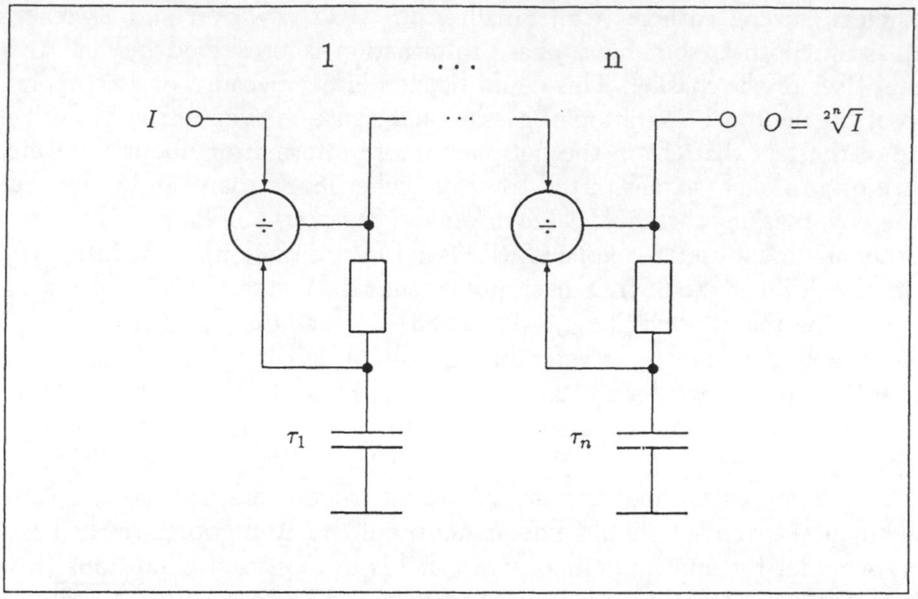

FIG. 1. Series of five feedback loops with different time constants τ_i (Püschel, 1988). In each single element, the lowpass-filtered output is fed back to form the denominator of the dividing element. The divisor is the momentary charging state of the lowpass filter, determining the attenuation applied to the input. The time constants are distributed linearly between 5 and 500 ms.

controls the attenuation of the input signal cannot follow the input changes. This sluggishness of the lowpass filters forms the basis for the course of thresholds in forward masking. If a masker that has charged the feedback loops is turned off, the lowpass filters will discharge at a speed determined by their time constants. These are chosen for the five stages from the range 5 to 500 ms. A short signal presented after the masker offset will be attenuated according to the momentary charging state of the feedback loops. In order to cause a sufficient change in the output O of the model, the signal must have a high input level if it is presented immediately after masker offset, because the attenuation of the feedback loops is greatest at that point. For a greater delay of the signal, the feedback loops are somewhat discharged; therefore, the attenuation is smaller and the signal's input level can also be smaller. Thus, in this model, forward masking is not caused by a slowly decreasing excitation of the masker, but rather by a decreasing amount of "temporal suppression."

When a short masker is used, only the feedback loops with short time constants are charged significantly. Because these feedback loops need less time to discharge after masker offset, the range of temporal suppression will be shorter compared to that for a long masker and the forward-masking curve decreases more quickly.

Because the amount of suppression is derived from an integrated value, the model predicts that no phase-sensitive interaction between masker and signal should occur in (monaural) forward masking.

III. PREDICTING FORWARD MASKING IN BINAURAL CONDITIONS

Based on this quantitative model of forward masking and on the observation that forward masking curves are steeper for higher masker levels, it is possible to derive predictions about the amount of binaural unmasking in forward masking conditions. These predictions will differ depending on the assumed succession of adaptation and binaural processing. We first derive the prediction for the hypothesis that binaural interaction *precedes* adaptation.

In a binaural masking condition, the effectiveness of the masker is reduced by an internal interaction between the right and left channels. This interaction leads to lower simultaneous masked thresholds and to a lower dynamic range of forward masking compared to a diotic reference condition. This reduction of masker effectiveness can be described by a subtraction of the two channels as in the EC theory (Durlach, 1972) or by a separation of the internal representation of masker and signal as in crosscorrelation models (e.g., Colburn, 1977).

The adaptation stage that follows the binaural interaction stage will adapt to different masker levels in diotic and dichotic conditions. Due to the lower "effective" masker level in a dichotic condition, the forward masking curve will start at a lower threshold value and will decay more slowly than the diotic curve. Therefore, the first hypothesis predicts that the two curves will approach each other in the course of forward masking resulting in a *continuously decreasing* value of the BMLD in forward masking.

This prediction is illustrated by the following two figures. Figure 2 shows forward-masking data for N_0S_0 (circles) and N_0S_π (squares) conditions from Zwicker and Zwicker (1984a). The *x* axis indicates the signal delay. The simultaneous BMLD (data point for delay 0 ms) is about 12 dB. Figure 3 shows predicted forward-masking curves using the above model for two (monaural) maskers that differ in level by 12 dB. Although the slope of the model prediction is steeper than that of the data, the difference between the two curves in each figure decreases very similarly with increasing delay.

Because according to this view a BMLD in forward masking is a direct consequence of the different effective masker levels in diotic and dichotic conditions, we can derive the following prediction: If the levels of the corresponding maskers are adjusted to yield equal *simultaneous* thresholds, forward-masking curves in diotic and dichotic conditions should decay with identical slope. This prediction is tested in our first experiment.

The second hypothesis assumes that binaural interaction *follows* adaptation. According to this hypothesis, the right and left channels are first adapted separately to the masker level and undergo binaural interaction afterward. The amount of adaptation is thus the same for a diotic and a dichotic condition. As long as masker and signal overlap temporally, binaural interaction will lead to lower thresholds. This overlap is, however, restricted to simultaneous conditions and to the first milliseconds of the forward-masking curve, where ringing of the basilar membrane dominates. As soon as adaptation processes dominate, diotic and

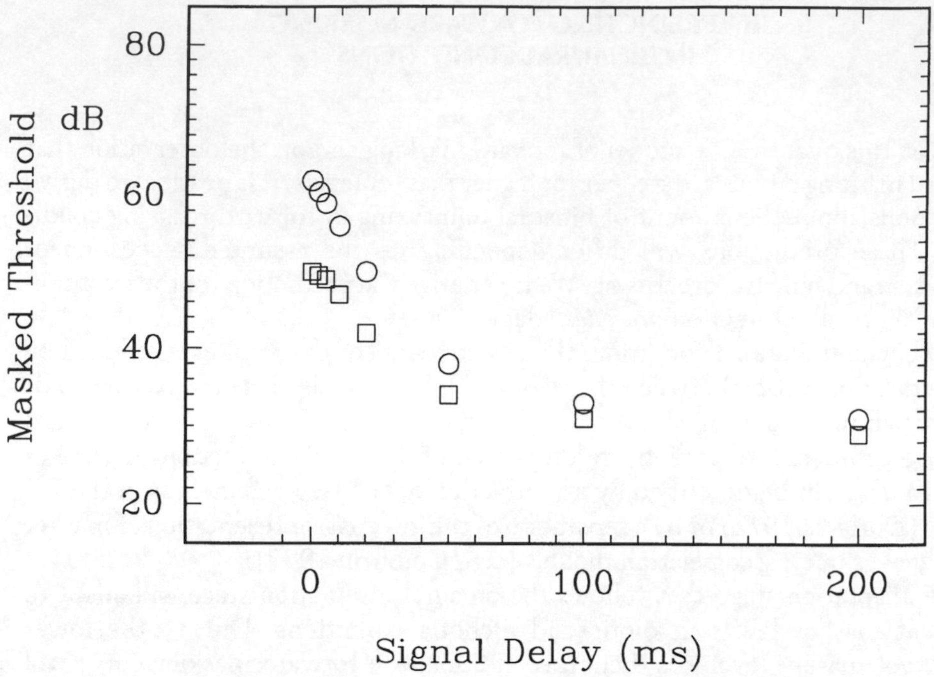

FIG. 2. Measured forward-masking curves in the condition N_0S_0 (circles) and N_0S_π (squares). The signal was a 400-Hz tone pulse of 10 ms duration. The masker was a uniform-masking noise with a critical-band level of approximately 56 dB and a duration of 300 ms. The absolute threshold for the subjects is 25 dB. [After Zwicker and Zwicker, 1984a.]

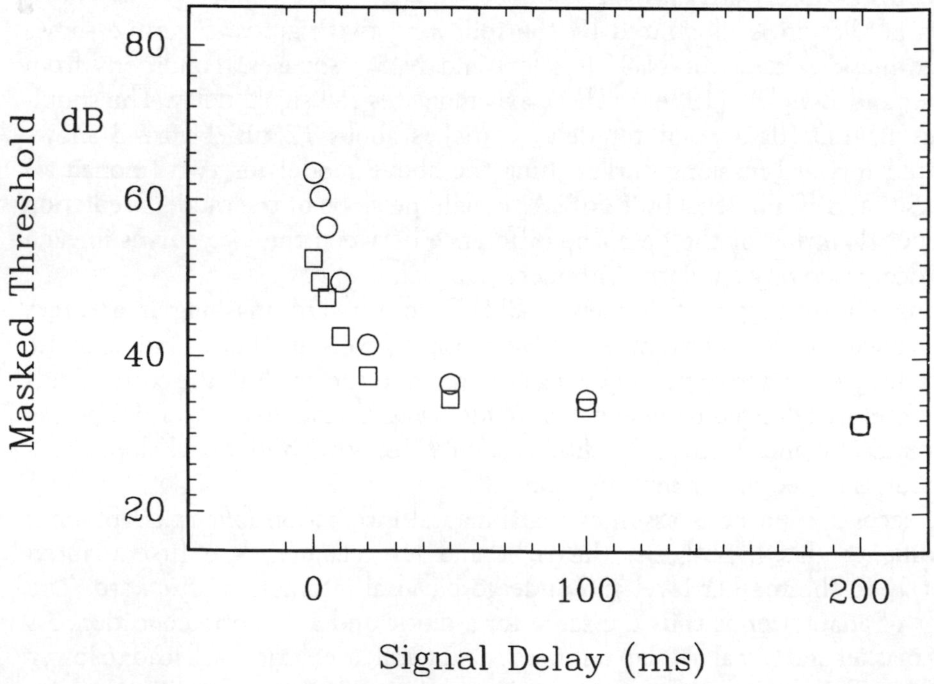

FIG. 3. Calculated forward-masking curves for the condition N_0S_0 for two different masker levels. The signal was a 400-Hz signal with a 10-ms Hanning envelope. The masker was running noise with a lowpass spectrum (0–1 kHz) and with a sound pressure level of 62 dB (circles) or 50 dB (squares). The absolute threshold was adjusted to 31 dB.

dichotic thresholds should be identical; at least, they should not differ by more than the difference in absolute threshold for an S_0 and an S_π signal. Because the amount of adaptation is affected by the masker duration, N_0S_0 and N_0S_π curves should both decay faster after a short masker than after a long masker.

These two hypotheses make clearly different predictions about the BMLD in forward masking. The majority of data from the literature agrees with the first hypothesis. But there are also papers (e.g., Hanna *et al.*, 1982) that provide data in support of the second hypothesis.

IV. METHOD

Thresholds were measured using a three-interval, forced-choice procedure with adaptive level tracking (Levitt, 1971). A two-down one-up rule with a step size for level changes of 1 dB was applied. At the beginning of each run, the step size was 10 dB and it was reduced after each upper reversal of the signal level. When the step size reached 1 dB—typically after 20 trials—evaluation of thresholds started and was extended over the next 10 reversals. The median level from these last 10 reversals was used as threshold value. Thresholds for a complete forward-masking curve were usually obtained within one session of about 30–60 minutes duration. In total, four subjects participated in the experiments. They were all members of the psychoacoustic research group in Göttingen and had many hours of prior training in forward-masking conditions.

Stimuli were generated digitally and converted to analog signals by means of a two-channel D/A (digital-to-analog) converter at a sample rate of 20 kHz. Masker and signal were delivered via different channels of the converter and their levels were separately adjusted by two analog attenuators. After lowpass filtering at 5 kHz (two filters in series with a total slope of 96 dB/octave), the stimuli were presented to the subjects via headphones (Beyer DT 880M with diffuse-field equalizer).

The signal was a 500-Hz tone pulse shaped with a 10-ms Hanning envelope. The masker was a fixed noise sample (frozen noise) with a flat bandpass spectrum between 20 and 1000 Hz. It was generated in the frequency domain by choosing equal amplitudes and random phases for the corresponding spectral components. The overall level was varied between 55 and 85 dB SPL. The duration of the masker was 20 or 300 ms. The waveform of the short masker was identical to the last 20 ms of the long masker. In a third measurement, a series of noise pulses was gated out of the long masker. The pulses had a duration of 20 ms and an interpulse distance of 30 ms. All onsets and offsets of the maskers were gated rectangularly. Thresholds were obtained for the two conditions N_0S_0 and N_0S_π. In the figures, masked thresholds are indicated in dB SPL as a function of the delay between masker and signal offset. The data are usually based on one adaptive run; otherwise, the means and standard deviations of the results from repeated runs are indicated in the figures.

V. EXPERIMENTAL RESULTS

A. Experiment I: Forward-masking curves for equal levels of simultaneous masking

This first experiment was performed to test the prediction of the first hypothesis that forward-masking curves are identical if the levels of the diotic and the dichotic maskers are adjusted to yield equal simultaneous thresholds. Forward-masking curves were measured for a masker duration of 300 ms and masker levels of 85, 70, and 55 dB. Because the average BMLD across subjects amounted to 15 dB, it was possible to compare diotic and dichotic forward-masking curves that had approximately equal simultaneous thresholds (e.g., a masker of 85 dB in a dichotic condition to a masker of 70 dB in a diotic condition). Figures 4 to 6 show examples of those curve pairs for subjects AK and RF. In Fig. 4, the masker for N_0S_0 was presented with a level of 70 dB and the masker for N_0S_π had a level of 85 dB. In Figs. 5 and 6, the masker levels were both 15 dB less, being 55 dB for N_0S_0 and 70 dB for N_0S_π. The N_0S_0 data are always indicated by the circles, the N_0S_π data by the squares.

In simultaneous masking, the two curves overlap. Due to the use of a frozen-noise masker, the threshold values at a specific signal delay depend on the phase-sensitive interaction between masker and signal that obviously affects diotic

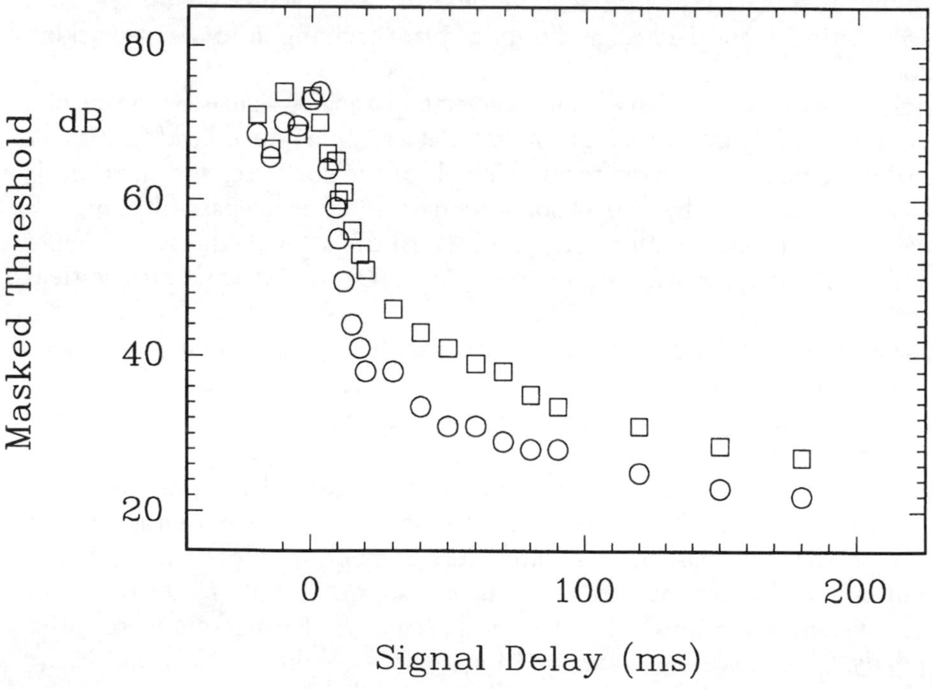

FIG. 4. Comparison of forward-masking data for the conditions N_0S_0 (circles) and N_0S_π (squares). The masker was a 300-ms frozen noise with a bandpass spectrum (20 Hz–1 kHz) and a level of 70 dB for the condition N_0S_0 and 85 dB for the condition N_0S_π. The signal was a 500-Hz pulse with a Hanning envelope of a total duration of 10 ms. The signal delay is defined as the time difference between masker and signal offsets. Results are for subject AK.

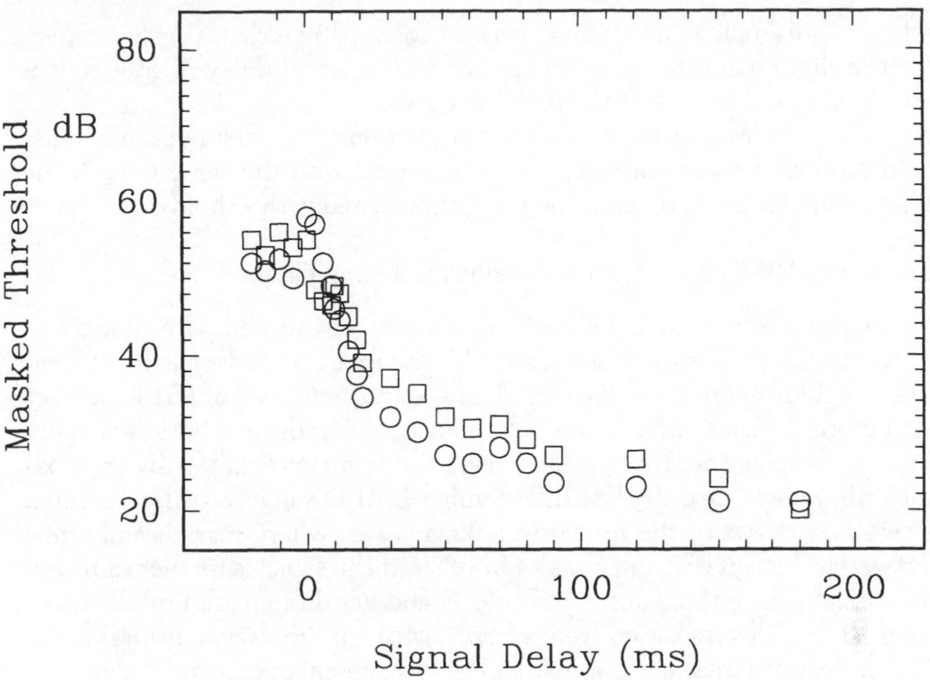

FIG. 5. Same as Fig. 4 for masker levels of 55 dB (N_0S_0) and 70 dB (N_0S_π).

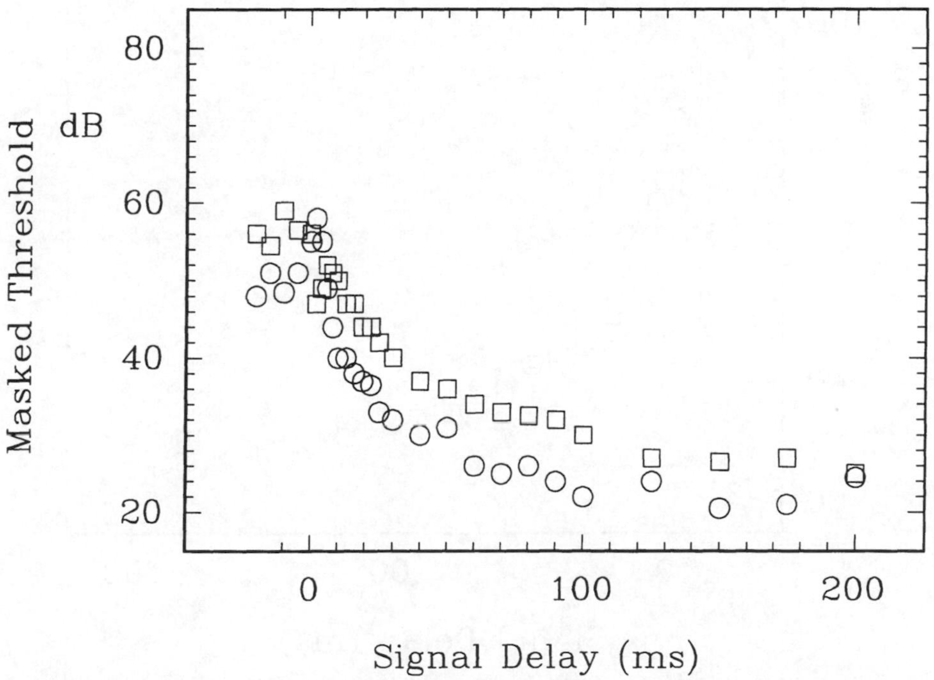

FIG. 6. Same as Fig. 5 for subject RF.

and dichotic thresholds in a different way. In forward masking, the two curves diverge. The diotic curve is much steeper and for a signal delay of 50 ms, it is about 10 dB below the value of the dichotic curve.

These data thus clearly disagree with the prediction of the first hypothesis that diotic and dichotic forward-masking curves decrease with the same slope if the masker levels are adjusted to yield the same simultaneous thresholds.

B. Experiment II: BMLDs in forward masking for a long masker

In order to test the second hypothesis, it is necessary to compare diotic and dichotic thresholds for identical masker levels. The first comparison is performed for maskers of 300-ms duration. Figure 7 shows results for a level of 85 dB (subject AK). As before, squares indicate dichotic and circles indicate diotic data. For simultaneous masking (negative signal delays) the two curves differ by approximately 15 dB, indicating a clear BMLD. Similar BMLD values are also obtained for the two first points of the forward-masking curve, where masker and signal partially overlap (delays of 2 and 5 ms). However, if the signal is further removed from the masker, the BMLD decreases quickly and has disappeared for delays of more than 10 ms. This transition from a large BMLD in simultaneous masking to no BMLD in forward masking is shown in Fig. 8 on an enlarged time scale.

The same result is obtained at a 15-dB lower masker level (Figs. 9 and 10). Again, the BMLD decreases rapidly for delays between 5 and 15 ms. In the N_0S_0 curve for subject RF (Fig. 10), a "bump" is apparent around a delay of 20 ms. In the region of this bump, the BMLD is a little bit larger (maximum 4 dB) than it

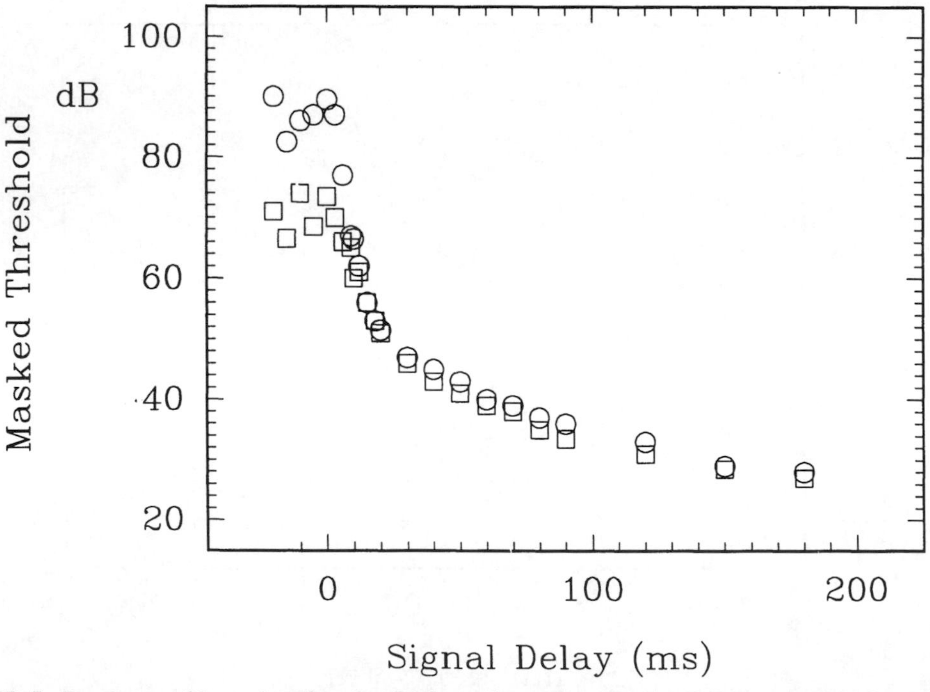

FIG. 7. Comparison of forward-masking data for the conditions N_0S_0 (circles) and N_0S_π (squares). The masker was a 300-ms frozen noise with a bandpass spectrum (20 Hz–1 kHz) and a level of 85 dB for both conditions. Results are for subject AK.

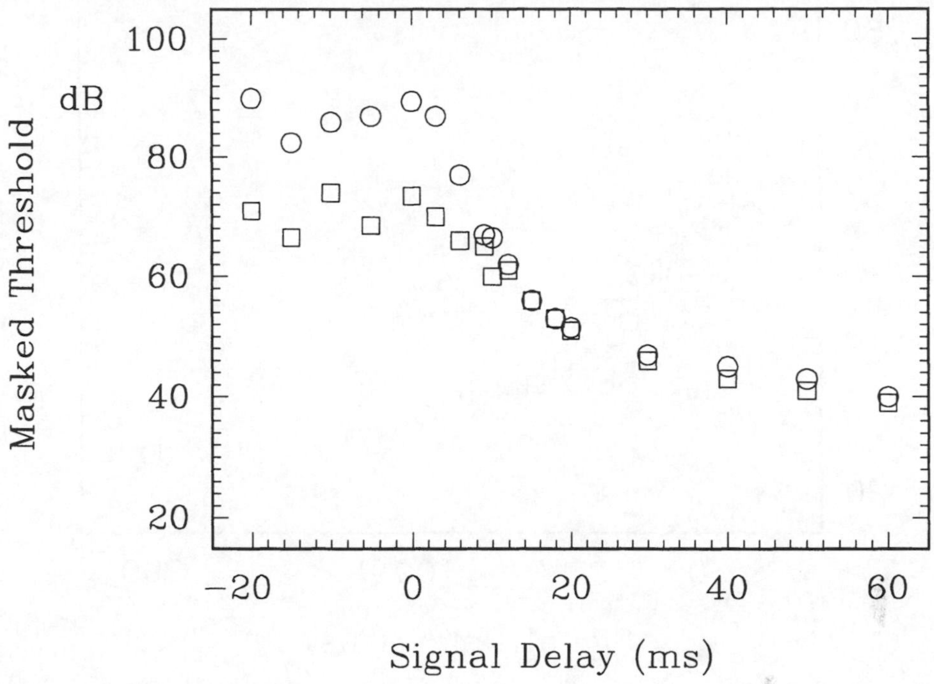

FIG. 8. Detail of Fig. 7 shown on an enlarged time scale.

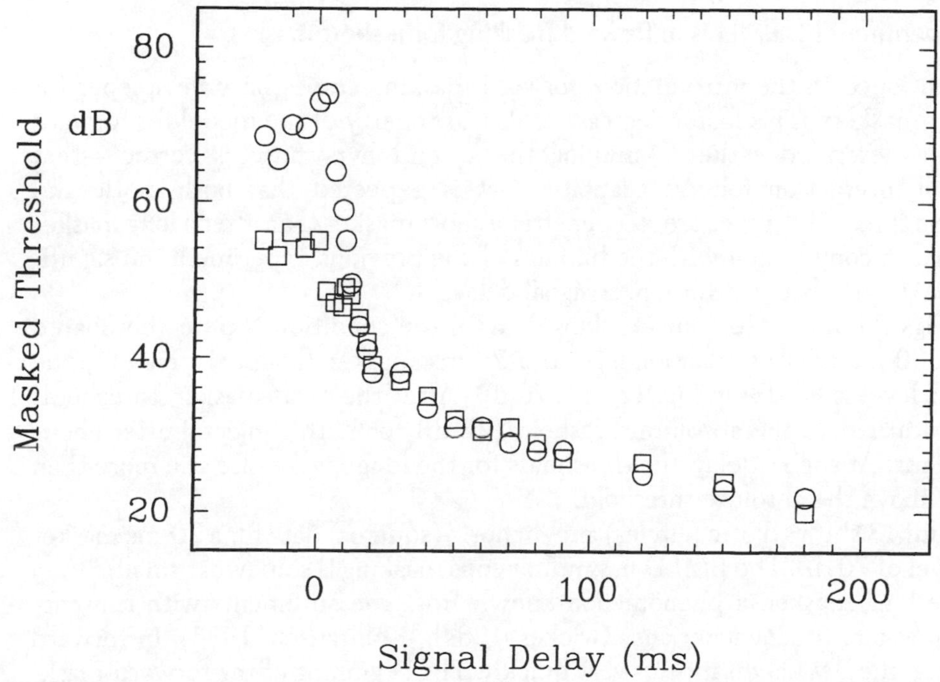

FIG. 9. Same as Fig. 7 for a masker level of 70 dB.

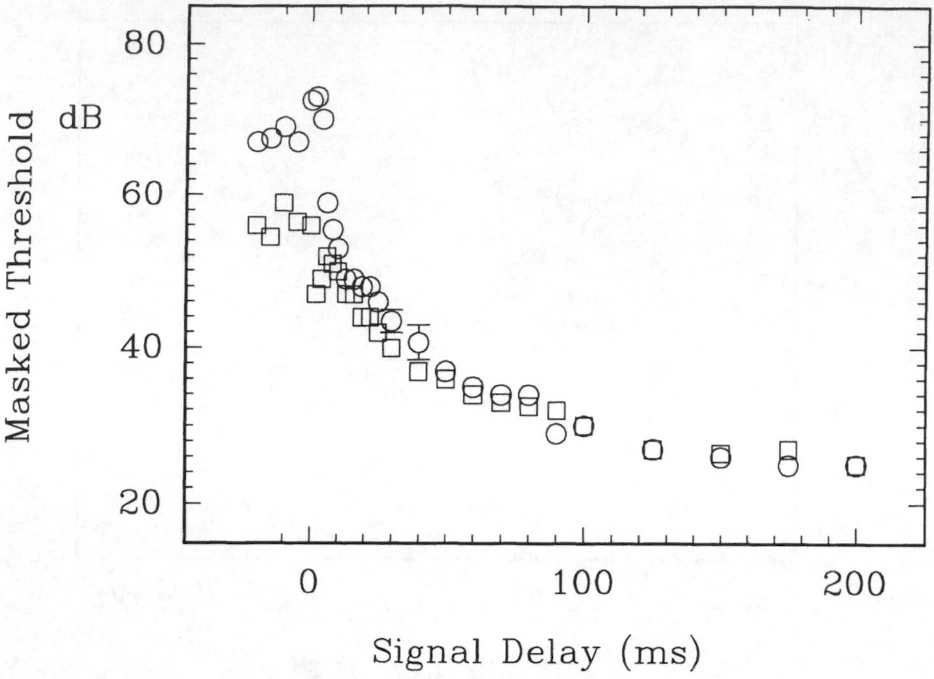

FIG. 10. Same as Fig. 9 for subject RF.

is for earlier or later signal positions. In summary, these results do not show a significant and consistent BMLD for signal delays of more than 20 ms.

C. Experiment III: BMLDs in forward masking for a short masker

As mentioned in the introduction, forward-masking curves become steeper for shorter maskers. This faster decrease is also a property of the model for forward masking described earlier. Assuming the second hypothesis is correct—that binaural interaction follows adaptation—it is expected that both diotic and dichotic threshold curves are steeper after a short masker than after a long masker and that in conjunction with the findings of the previous experiment, no significant BMLD is observed for longer signal delays.

In Figs. 11 and 12 forward-masking data for the condition N_0S_0 are compared for a 300-ms masker (diamonds) and a 20-ms masker (stars). In Fig. 11, the masker level is 85 dB; in Fig. 12, it is 70 dB. After the short masker, thresholds have returned to the absolute threshold (22 dB for both subjects) after about 60–70 ms. At such a delay, the thresholds for the long masker are still more than 10 dB above the absolute threshold.

Figure 13 shows diotic (circles) and dichotic (squares) data for a 20-ms masker at a level of 70 dB. The BMLD in simultaneous masking is somewhat smaller than for the long masker, a phenomenon known from measurements with running-noise maskers (cf. Zwicker and Zwicker, 1984b; Kohlrausch, 1986). In forward masking, the BMLD disappears very quickly. The beginning of the forward-masking curve from Fig. 13 is plotted on an enlarged time scale in Fig. 14. Figures 15 and 16 show data for the same masker level for two other subjects.

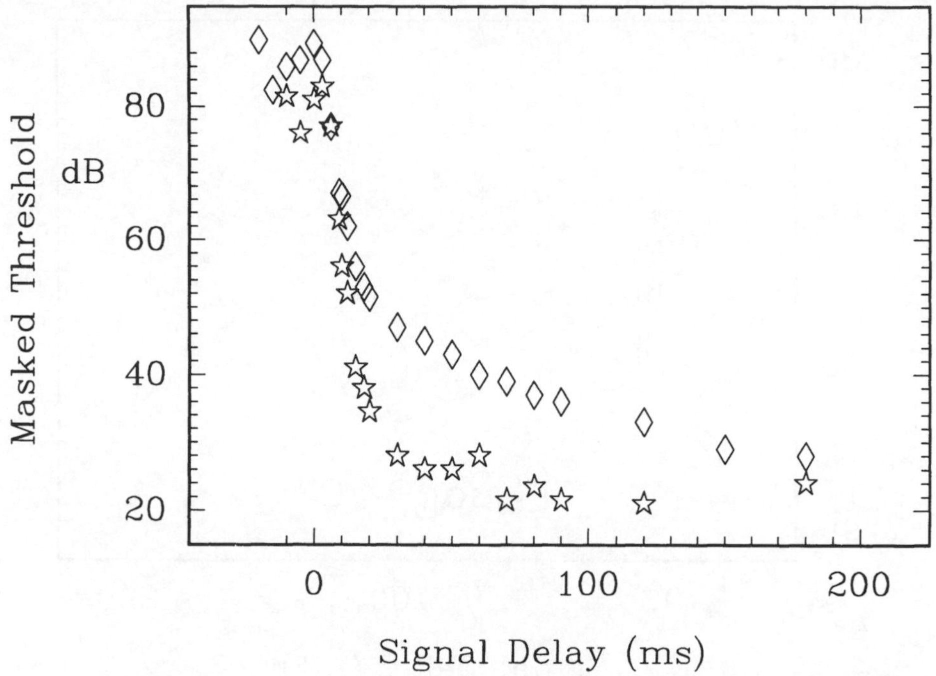

FIG. 11. Forward-masking curves in the condition N_0S_0 for two different durations of the frozen-noise masker: 300 ms (diamonds) and 20 ms (stars). The waveform of the short masker was identical to the last 20 ms of the long masker. The masker level was 85 dB. Results are for subject AK.

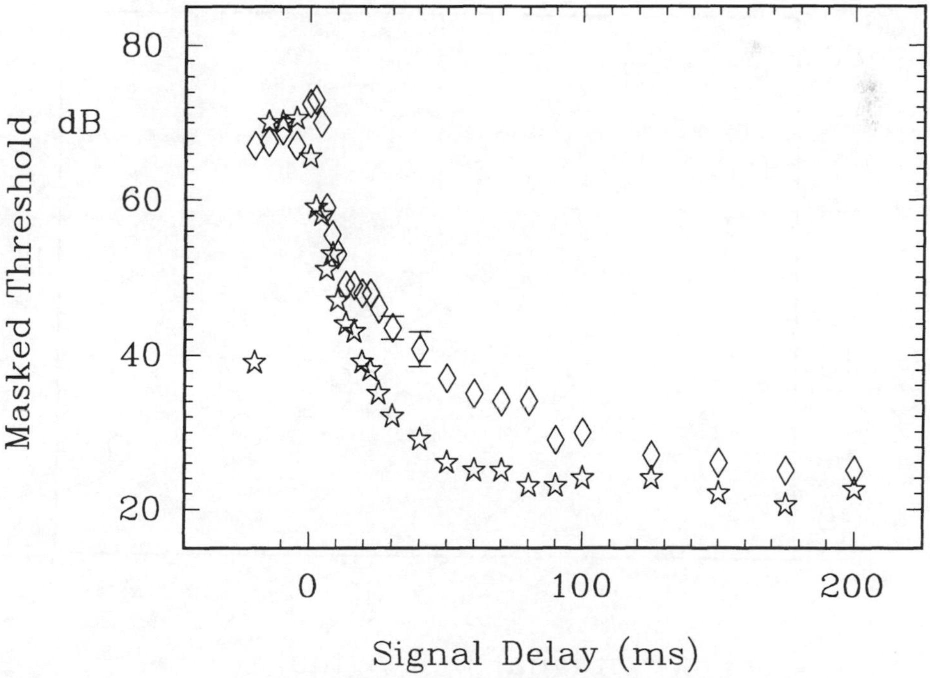

FIG. 12. Same as Fig. 11 for a masker level of 70 dB. Results are for subject RF.

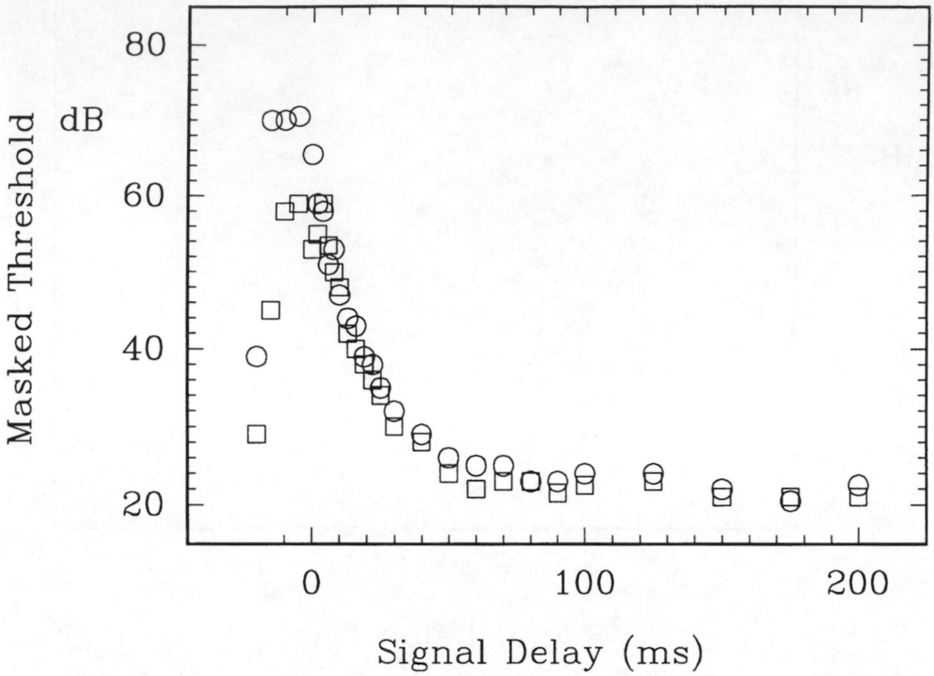

FIG. 13. Comparison of forward-masking data for the conditions N_0S_0 (circles) and N_0S_π (squares). The masker was a 20-ms frozen noise with a bandpass spectrum (20 Hz–1 kHz) and a level of 70 dB for both conditions. Results are for subject RF.

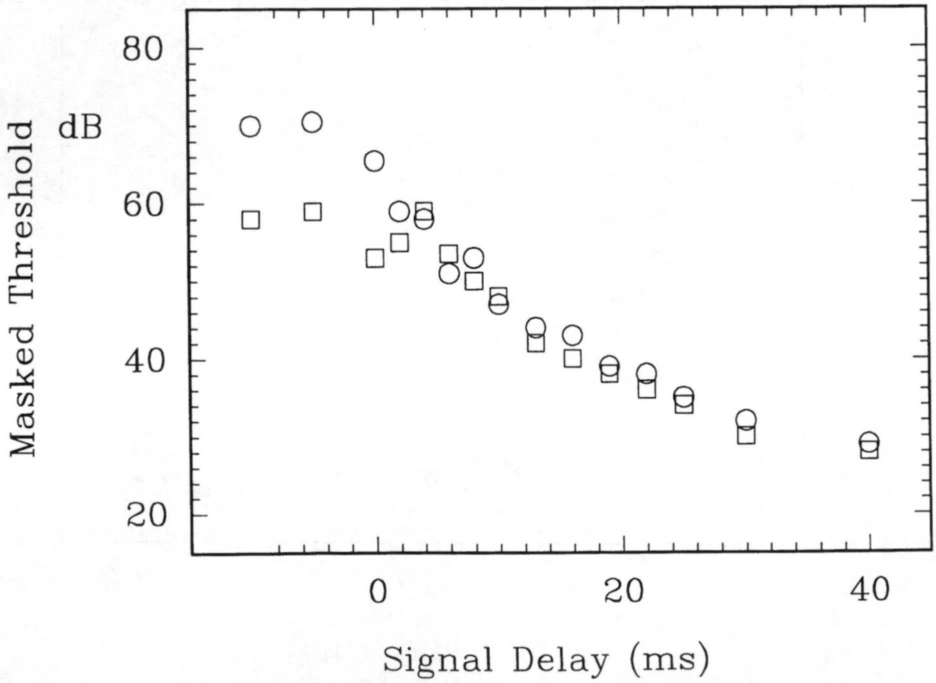

FIG. 14. Detail of Fig. 13 shown on an enlarged time scale.

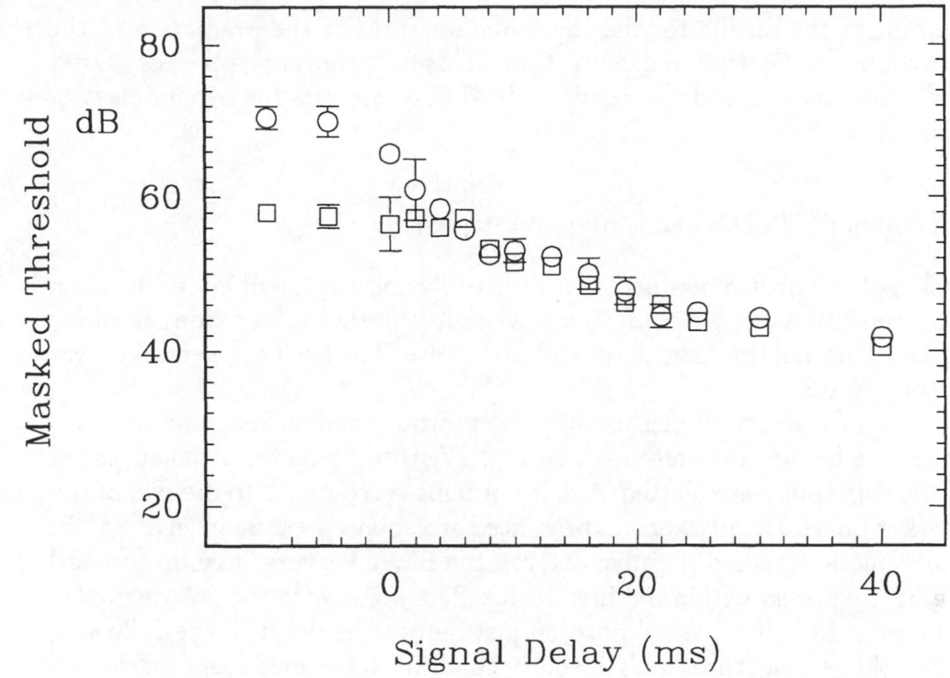

FIG. 15. Same as Fig. 14 for subject DP.

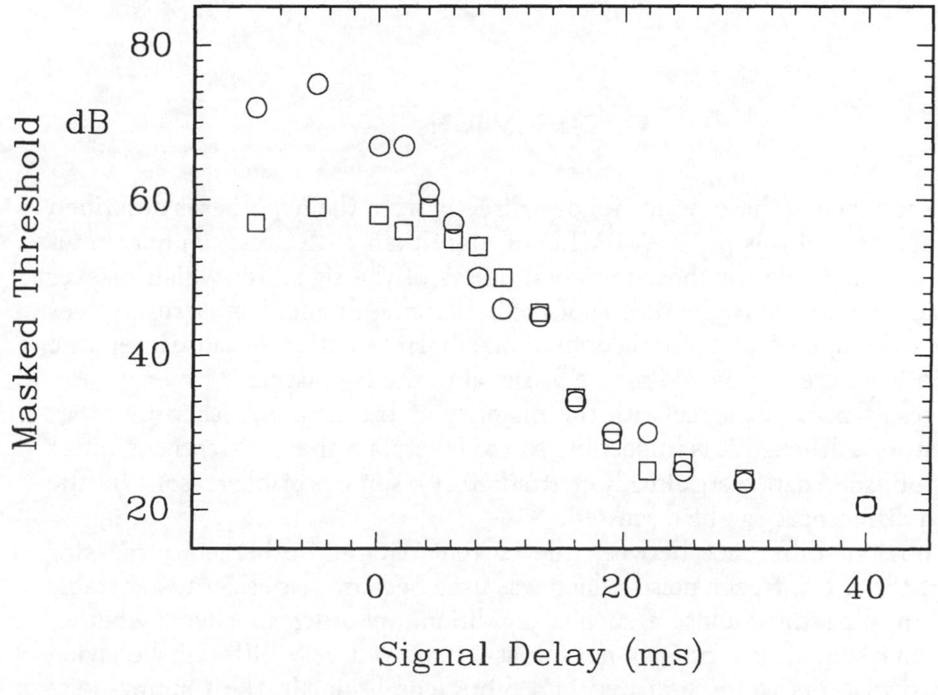

FIG. 16. Same as Fig. 14 for subject SM.

In summary, the results for the short masker support the prediction of the second hypothesis. Diotic and dichotic thresholds for a short masker decay faster than for a long masker and the resulting BMLD disappears for signal delays of about 10 ms or more.

D. Experiment IV: BMLDs in a noise-pulse sequence

The masker of this final experiment consisted of six noise pulses of 20-ms duration that were separated by pauses of 30 ms. Masked thresholds were measured for signals placed around the first, third, and fifth pulse. The level of the masker was either 70 or 85 dB.

The results were very similar for all pulse positions and subjects, so only two representative figures are presented. In Fig. 17, thresholds for a signal placed around the third pulse are plotted. A delay of 0 ms corresponds to the end of the third masker pulse. The masker was presented at a sound pressure level of 85 dB. For simultaneous masking (negative delays), the BMLD is very large. In forward masking, it disappears within the first 10 ms. The point with the greatest delay in this figure represents a signal position just before the onset of the following pulse. For this signal, thresholds in both conditions are increased (backward masking) and a BMLD of 8 dB is measured.

Figure 18 shows a corresponding result for the fifth pulse that extends from 230 to 250 ms. Due to a lower masker level (70 dB), the forward-masking curve decays less steeply than in the previous figure. The results with respect to the BMLD in simultaneous, forward, and backward masking are the same as in Fig. 17.

VI. DISCUSSION

The consequence of these results follows directly from the hypotheses described at the beginning of this paper. A BMLD of more than 3 dB occurs in nonsimultaneous masking only for those temporal delays of the signal for which masker and signal overlap due to the ringing of the basilar membrane. Such a result does not pose any major problem for theories of binaural interaction, because interaural differences are created by adding the S_π signal to the N_0 masker.

This result does not agree with the majority of the data published by other investigators. Although it is impossible to really explain these differences (after all, the published data were already contradictory), some possible reasons for the observed differences can be discussed.

One obvious difference between the current data and other noise-masking studies is the use of frozen noise, which was used because it is easier to get stable forward-masked thresholds in such a condition. In order to check whether forward masking after a running-noise masker showed very different behavior, these two maskers were compared in a diotic condition. In the running-noise measurement, a long noise buffer was calculated and in every interval of the

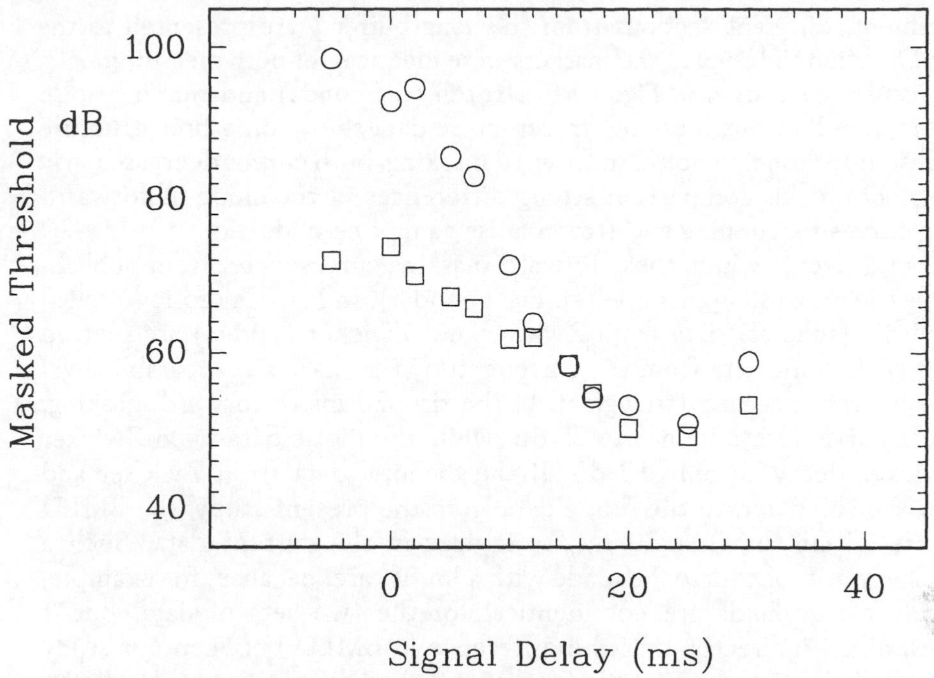

FIG. 17. Comparison of masking data for the conditions NoSo (circles) and NoSπ (squares). The masker was a frozen noise consisting of six pulses with a duration of 20 ms and an interpulse distance of 30 ms. It had a bandpass spectrum (20 Hz–1 kHz) and a level of 85 dB for both conditions. A 0-ms signal delay corresponds to the offset of the third masker pulse. Results are for subject AK.

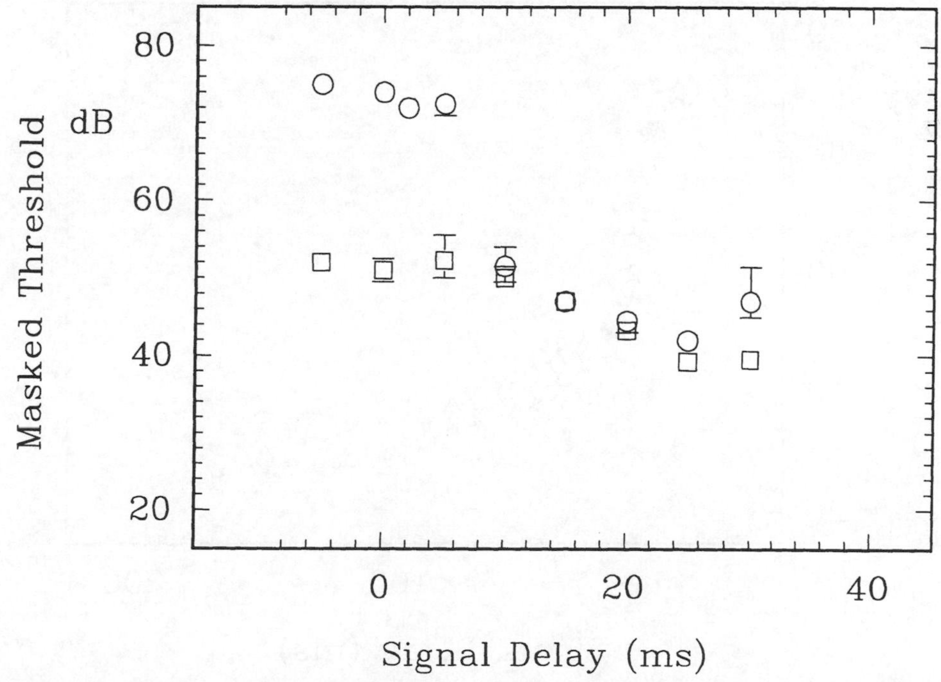

FIG. 18. Similar to Fig. 17 for a signal placed after the fifth pulse in the masker that had a level of 70 dB. Results are for subject RF.

measurement, different sections from this long buffer were presented as the masker. Duration and level of the maskers were identical for both measurements.

The results are shown in Fig. 19 for frozen (diamonds) and running noise (stars). In simultaneous masking, frozen-noise data show some fine structure that is absent for running noise. In forward masking, both curves decrease fairly smoothly. From this comparison strong differences in the slope of forward-masking curves for running and frozen noise cannot be deduced.

Another aspect in which these forward-masking curves differ from published data is the much steeper slope (cf. Figs. 2 and 3). In Fig. 20, diotic (circles) and dichotic (squares) data from Zwicker and Zwicker (1984a) are plotted together with diotic data from the current study that have a comparable level range in forward masking (triangles). In the first 20 ms of forward masking, our diotic curve decays by nearly 25 dB, while the diotic data from Zwicker and Zwicker decay by only 12 dB. If the dichotic data from Zwicker and Zwicker are compared to the diotic data from the present study, the BMLD disappears within the first 20 ms, as it does in the current data. Such a comparison must, of course, be made with a lot of care, because, for example, the absolute thresholds are not identical for the two sets of data. But it indicates, albeit indirectly, that the difference in BMLD between our study and that of Zwicker and Zwicker is probably due to differences in the diotic, rather than in the dichotic, thresholds.

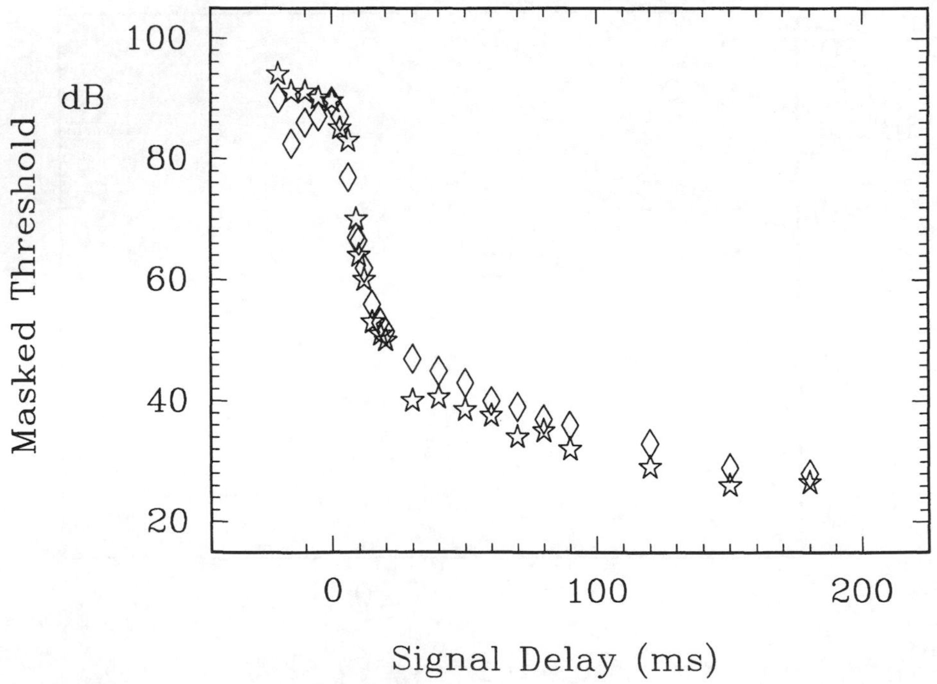

FIG. 19. Comparison of forward-masking data for a frozen (diamonds) and a running noise (stars). Both maskers had a level of 85 dB and a duration of 300 ms. Results are for subject AK.

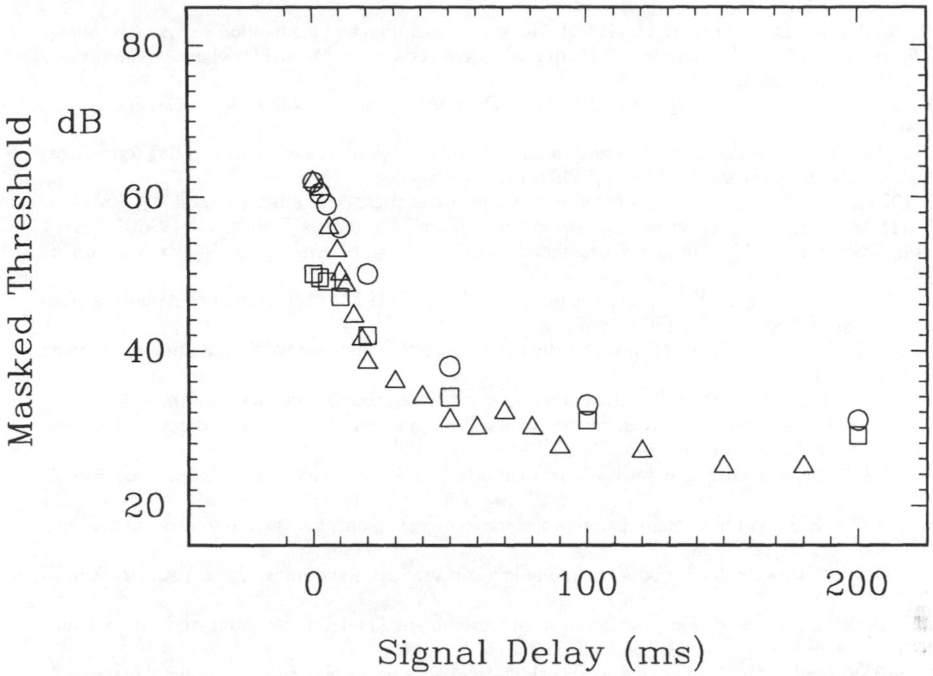

FIG. 20. Comparison of NoSo (circles) and NoSπ data (squares) from Zwicker and Zwicker (1984a) (cf. Fig. 2) with NoSo data from the current measurements (triangles).

ACKNOWLEDGMENTS

We would like to thank Torsten Dau (now at the University of Oldenburg, Germany) for performing the model simulations shown in Fig. 3. Shari Campbell, Robert Gilkey, and Timothy Anderson provided very helpful comments on earlier drafts of this paper. This study was supported by a grant from the Deutsche Forschungsgemeinschaft (Schr 38/24).

REFERENCES

Berg, K., and Yost, W. A. (**1976**). "Temporal masking of a click by noise in diotic and dichotic listening conditions," J. Acoust. Soc. Am. **60,** 173–177.

Colburn, H. S. (**1977**). "Theory of binaural interaction based on auditory-nerve data. II. Detection of tones in noise," J. Acoust. Soc. Am. **61,** 525–533.

Colburn, H. S., and Durlach, N. I. (**1978**). "Models of binaural interaction." in *Handbook of Perception,* edited by E. C. Carterette and M. P. Friedman (Academic Press, New York), Vol. IV, pp. 467–518.

Dau, T., Püschel, D., and Kohlrausch, A. (**1996**). "A quantitative model of the 'effective' signal processing in the auditory system: I. Model structure," J. Acoust. Soc. Am. **99,** 3615–3622.

Duifhuis, H. (**1973**). "Consequences of peripheral frequency selectivity for nonsimultaneous masking," J. Acoust. Soc. Am. **54,** 1471–1488.

Durlach, N. I. (**1972**). "Binaural signal detection: Equalization and cancellation theory," in *Foundations of Modern Auditory Theory,* edited by J. V. Tobias (Academic Press, New York), Vol. II, pp. 369–462.

Hanna, T. E., Robinson, D. E., Shiffrin, R. M., and Gilkey, R. H. (**1982**). "Forward masking of diotic and dichotic clicks by noise," J. Acoust. Soc. Am. **72,** 1171–1177.

Kohlrausch, A. (**1986**). "The influence of signal duration, signal frequency and masker duration on binaural masking level differences," Hear. Res. **23,** 267–273.

Kohlrausch, A., Püschel, D., and Alphei, H. (**1992**). "Temporal resolution and modulation analysis in models of the auditory system," in *The Auditory Processing of Speech*, edited by M. E. H. Schouten (Mouton De Gruyter, Berlin), pp. 85–98.

Lakey, J. R. (**1976**). "Temporal masking-level differences: The effect of mask duration," J. Acoust. Soc. Am. **59,** 1434–1442.

Langhans, A. (**1991**). "Psychoakustische Messungen und Modellvorstellungen zur Wahrnehmung reproduzierbarer und statistisch fluktuierender Signale," PhD thesis, University of Göttingen.

Levitt, H. (**1971**). "Transformed up-down procedures in psychoacoustics," J. Acoust. Soc. Am. **49,** 467–477.

Püschel, D. (**1988**). "Prinzipien der zeitlichen Analyse beim Hören," PhD thesis, University of Göttingen.

Punch, J., and Carhart, R. (**1973**). "Influence of interaural phase on forward masking," J. Acoust. Soc. Am. **54,** 897–904.

Small, A. M., Boggess, J., Klich, R., Kuehn, D., Thelin, J., and Wiley, T. (**1972**). "MLDs in forward and backward masking," J. Acoust. Soc. Am. **51,** 1365–1367.

Stein, H. J. (**1960**). Das Absinken der Mithörschwelle nach dem Abschalten von weißem Rauschen," Acustica **10,** 116–119.

Strube, H. W. (**1985**). "A computationally efficient basilar-membrane model," Acustica **58,** 207–214.

Yama, M. F. (**1982**). "Differences between psychophysical 'suppression effects' under diotic and dichotic listening conditions," J. Acoust. Soc. Am. **72,** 1380–1383.

Yama, M. F. (**1985**). "Binaural analysis in forward masking: Effects of signal frequency," J. Acoust. Soc. Am. **78,** 2141–2145.

Yama, M. F. (**1992**). "Effects of temporal separation and masker level on binaural analysis in forward masking," J. Acoust. Soc. Am. **91,** 327–335.

Yost, W. A. (**1985**). "Click stimuli do produce masking-level differences, sometimes," J. Acoust. Soc. Am. **77,** 2191–2192.

Yost, W. A. (**1988**). "The masking-level difference and overall masker level: Restating the internal noise hypothesis," J. Acoust. Soc. Am. **83,** 1517–1521.

Yost, W. A., and Walton, J. (**1977**). "Hierarchy of masking-level differences obtained for temporal masking," J. Acoust. Soc. Am. **61,** 1376–1379.

Yost, W. A., Grantham, D. W., Lutfi, R. A., and Stern, R. M. (**1982**). "The phase angle of addition in temporal masking for diotic and dichotic listening conditions," Hear. Res. **7,** 247–259.

Zwicker, E. (**1984**). "Dependence of post-masking on masker duration and its relation to temporal effects in loudness," J. Acoust. Soc. Am. **75,** 219–223.

Zwicker, E., and Zwicker, U. T. (**1984a**). "Binaural masking-level differences in non-simultaneous masking," Hear. Res. **13,** 221–228.

Zwicker, U. T., and Zwicker, E. (**1984b**). "Binaural masking-level difference as a function of masker and test-signal duration," Hear. Res. **13,** 215–219.

Part III

Echoes, Precedence, and Depth Perception

Chapter 10

Listening in a Room and the Precedence Effect

William Morris Hartmann
Michigan State University

(Received May 1994; revised October 1994)

The precedence effect makes its appearance in several guises: as a localization phenomenon, as the Haas effect, and as dereverberation and decoloration. To understand the diverse psychophysical and physiological experiments that have been done on this multifaceted effect requires a central model of considerable flexibility. The precedence effect and variations on the precedence effect, the Franssen illusion, the Clifton effect, and the case of overlapping tones, represent competitions between successive stimulus sounds and among their localization cues. Experiments with steady-state and transient signals suggest that the cues are weighted by a plausibility evaluation prior to a localization calculation. More generally, the concept of localization strengths as weighting factors in an optimum processor model of localization offers promise for a comprehensive theory of the precedence effect.

INTRODUCTION

When a sound is produced in a room it propagates outward from the source in all directions and is then reflected from all the surfaces in the room. A listener in the room who hears the sound is therefore exposed to multiple copies of it. There is first the direct sound, which arrives by a straight-line path. It is followed by reflected sound waves, which can be classified as early reflections, reverberation, and echoes.

Early reflections, by definition, arrive at the listener within the first 20 ms of the direct sound. In large-room situations where early reflections are few in number, architectural acousticians may attempt to deal with these individually. They may be concerned with the strength of an early reflection from the side wall or about diffusing an early reflection from the ceiling. Reverberation is an amalgam of later arriving reflections. These reflections have normally been multiply scattered from many surfaces in the room. Because there is such a profusion of later reflections, they are never treated individually, only statistically. It is not usual to be concerned about the directional properties of reverberation either. Finally, an echo is a late-arriving reflection that is so strong, or so isolated in time from other reflections, that it stands out as a discrete event in the midst of reverberation. Although the "echo" is defined perceptually rather than physically, one can predict that a strong discrete reflection that follows the direct sound by 50 ms or more will lead to an echo.

Given the complexity that a room imparts even to a simple sound, it is natural to wonder what the listener hears in a room and how he or she hears it. The model of the perceptual process is that there is a form of competition between the direct sound and the various reflections that follow it. The most important element of the model is known as the *precedence effect*, which says, basically, that the direct sound wins the competition because it arrives first. But although the precedence effect identifies the winner, there remains a diversity of opinion about what the nature of the competition actually is. Some viable options are given next.

I. THE PRECEDENCE EFFECT

What is commonly known as the precedence effect among psychoacousticians was defined in a classic paper by Wallach, Newman, and Rosenzweig (WNR) (1949), which links the precedence effect firmly with the localization of the sound. When the precedence effect operates, the combination of direct and reflected sounds is heard as a single entity, and the perceived location of the entity corresponds to the direction of the direct sound. As a result, the source is correctly localized in space, despite reflections that come from many different directions. The earliest arriving sound wins the localization contest even if the reflected sound is somewhat more intense than the earliest sound, as much as 10 dB more intense. This is true whether the late-arriving competitor consists of many reflections or a single large reflection. In this view, the precedence effect does not totally eliminate the effect of a reflection. Reflections add a sense of "space filling" and loudness to the sound as a whole, but the reflections are fused with the direct sound.

An alternative viewpoint comes under the classification of the Haas effect (Haas, 1951), which mainly links the precedence effect with the perception of speech in a reverberant environment. It is observed that early reflections do not interfere with speech communication so long as the reflections arrive soon enough after the direct sound. In fact, reflections aid communication by increasing the sound intensity level. The emphasis that Haas gave to speech perception is interesting because speech is enormously sensitive to reverberation characteristics, particularly in contrast to music perception. Small changes in reflection delay time or reverberance are instantly noted when listening to speech, whereas even large changes may be barely noticed in the case of music. This distinction has recently been made widely apparent by the availability of audio ambience synthesizers, which has encouraged informal experimenting by audiophiles.

The integration of a direct sound with a reflected sound, à la Haas, was neatly described by Green (1976): If one stands in a room 1 m from a reflecting wall and creates an impulsive sound, by clicking two rocks together, there is a reflection from the wall that arrives 6 ms after the direct sound. One never hears that kind of reflection. On the other hand, if a listener wears headphones and hears two clicks in one ear separated by 6 ms, the listener immediately hears two well-separated clicks. The suppression of the reflection that takes place in the room, but not with headphones, can be called the precedence effect.

A third viewpoint concerns an effect that might be called "de-reverberation." Unlike the localization precedence effect studied by WNR, there is no standard defining experiment for de-reverberation, but the idea is simply that we are not normally much aware of reverberated sound, even though the energy in the reverberated sound may be several times larger than the energy in the direct sound. The effect is demonstrated in the compact disc distributed by the Acoustical Society of America (Houtsma, Rossing, and Wegenaars, 1987), by the simple expedient of playing recordings both forward and backward. Only when the recording is played backward is one aware of how intense and prolonged the reverberated sound actually is.

Perhaps the most impressive demonstration of de-reverberation is to listen to a conversation in an ordinary room, to record that conversation on tape through a microphone placed near the listener, and then to play back the tape, either through headphones or loudspeakers. The tape recording reveals reverberated sound that interferes with the direct sound, making comprehension difficult, and it reveals coloration of the speech caused by room resonances. One realizes that these disruptive characteristics of the recording were not present a few moments earlier when listening to the original conversation in person. De-reverberation and "de-coloration" somehow depend upon receiving the sound field immediately with one's ears attached to one's head in the usual way.

The de-reverberation process is particularly interesting because it appears that individuals who wear hearing aids may not be able to do it very well. Amplification-assisted people have great difficulty comprehending speech in reverberant environments. It is widely believed that de-reverberation depends importantly on binaural hearing. Koenig (1950) demonstrated that binaural listening improves clarity for signals recorded in a reverberant environment. A complementary informal exercise shows that de-reverberation in a natural room environment can be made less effective by plugging one ear. However, there is also significant monaural de-reverberation. (The ASA compact disc demonstration is not rendered ineffective by monaural presentation.) At this time, there is a need for good experiments to assess the relative importance of the binaural and monaural contributions to this effect.

The three faces of the precedence effect that have just been described have in common the fact that the direct sound wins the perceptual competition over later arriving sound. It is natural to suppose that a common process is responsible.

A. The time constants

If the three faces of the precedence effect manifest a common process, then one might expect them to exhibit similar time constants. In fact, however, the time constants are quite different.

The temporal character of the localization precedence effect was described by von Békésy (1960) and by Blauert (1974). Consider a stimulus consisting of two clicks of equal intensity. The two clicks come from different directions in space, and the second click represents the reflection. If the second click arrives within 1 ms of the first, it is perceptually integrated with the first, and the integrated entity is perceived to have a location that is an average of the locations of first and second clicks. This is the regime known as *summing localization*. Within this regime there is an orderly weighting: the greater the delay, the less the weight given to the second click in the averaging. (Note: The upper limit of summing localization duration is sometimes found to be as low as 0.5 ms instead of 1 ms.)

For delay values between 1 and 4 ms, the localization precedence effect is maximal. However, the effect is not absolute. As Haas noted, the second sound always contributes a sense of spaciousness. There also remains some localization averaging. Even for a delay of 2 ms, where the precedence effect is most effective, the perceived location is biased slightly in the direction of the second source. The bias can actually be seen in the original data of WNR. (The next section will make good use of this effect.) Further, the second source always leads to some localization blur (Blauert and Lindemann, 1986). Blur is observed as increased variability in listener judgments of location. The blur may not be large when the precedence effect is strong, but the presence of a reflected sound always leads to more variability than would be obtained with a source in an anechoic environment. Although it may be true that some aspects of listening are enhanced by reflected sound in a room (Benade, 1976), localization precision is not one of them.

Finally, in the range of delays from 5 to 10 ms, the precedence effect starts to fail. In a two-click experiment the second click emerges as a distinct entity. For experiments with sources in the azimuthal plane (typical for these studies) the second click is independently localized, leading to large variability in localization judgments. The listener becomes confused as to which source to localize and is quite aware of this confusion.

The time constants found in the Haas effect are rather different. Reflected sounds normally become a problem for speech comprehension only when they are delayed by 50 ms or more. Therefore, 50 ms is normally considered to be the maximum delay for the Haas effect. The balancing experiments done by Haas show that the ability of a leading source to suppress a lagging source is maximal for a delay of 10–20 ms. That means that as the reflection delay increases, the Haas effect becomes strongest when the localization precedence effect, as studied with clicks in an experiment of the WNR type, has already disappeared.

The time constants for de-reverberation are enormously longer, extending to several seconds, which is the reverberation time of typical concert halls. Interestingly, it does seem likely that de-reverberation does not extend to the enormous reverberation times of vast spaces with highly reflective surfaces. In Notre Dame

(Paris) and the Taj Mahal (Agra), where the reverberation time approaches 10 s, one is quite aware of the reverberation. But a de-reverberation time constant of 1 s or more is still several orders of magnitude longer than the WNR limit of 5 ms.

The difference in time scales for the three faces of the precedence effect may mean that there are three precedence effects, mediated by three different processes. Alternatively, one may be able to preserve a model of a single precedence effect, as long as one incorporates flexibility whereby the manner of processing of the signal depends on the signal itself. This conclusion is the first indication that the precedence effect, if it is a single process, must be a rather complex one.

B. Extended sounds

In an experiment of the WNR type, the stimulus is a click plus its reflection. It is common to have the click and reflection come from opposite sides of the listener to establish a clear localization competition. For example, there might be a loudspeaker to the listener's left and a single reflecting surface on the right. All other surfaces of the room would be anechoic.

It is supposed that all the events in the WNR experiment are instantaneous. As a result, there are four distinct events, shown in Fig. 1. For the geometry described earlier, there is first the arrival of the direct sound at the left ear, then the arrival of the direct sound at the right. After the gap, the reflected sound first arrives at the right ear then at the left. When the precedence effect operates, the reflected sound is suppressed by the direct sound, and the four events are perceived as a single click, localized on the left.

In daily life, however, the great majority of sounds are extended in time. They are typically longer than the delay between the two ears, and longer than the gap between direct and reflected sounds. As a result, there is wave interference between direct and reflected sound. The signal generated by the interference can lead to an entirely new location cue, not necessarily related to either the location of the source or the direction of the reflection. Therefore, the case of overlapping sounds leads to some ambiguity concerning the nature of the competition involved in the precedence effect. It is not clear *what* is preceded. Is it the cue generated by the interference, or is it the reflected sound itself in contrast to the direct

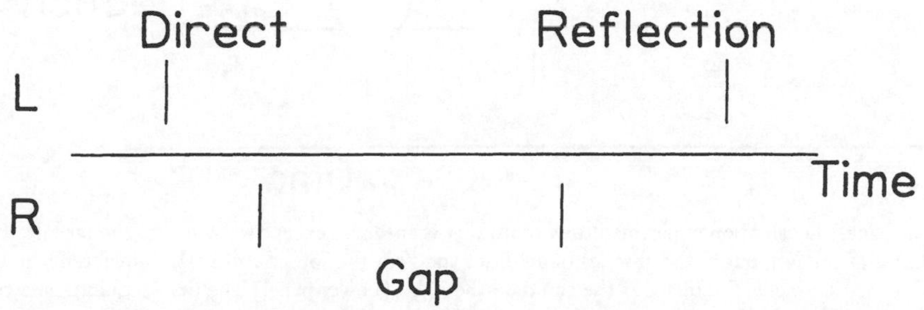

FIG. 1 The classic WNR experiment: The first two pulses (to left and right ears) make the direct sound. After the gap, the second two pulses (to right and left ears) make the reflection.

sound? In the interests of understanding what is actually going on, this ambiguity needs to be resolved.

The configuration that studies the precedence effect for overlapping sources is shown in Fig. 2. The source is to the left, and the reflecting wall is even further to the left. Therefore, the time lines show the envelopes for both the source and the reflection leading at the left ear as expected. However, it is quite possible to position the reflecting surface so that the steady-state signal, created by the interference between the direct sound and the reflection, has an ongoing phase that leads in the right ear. Such a steady-state cue suggests a virtual source on the right, as shown by the little cloud in the figure.

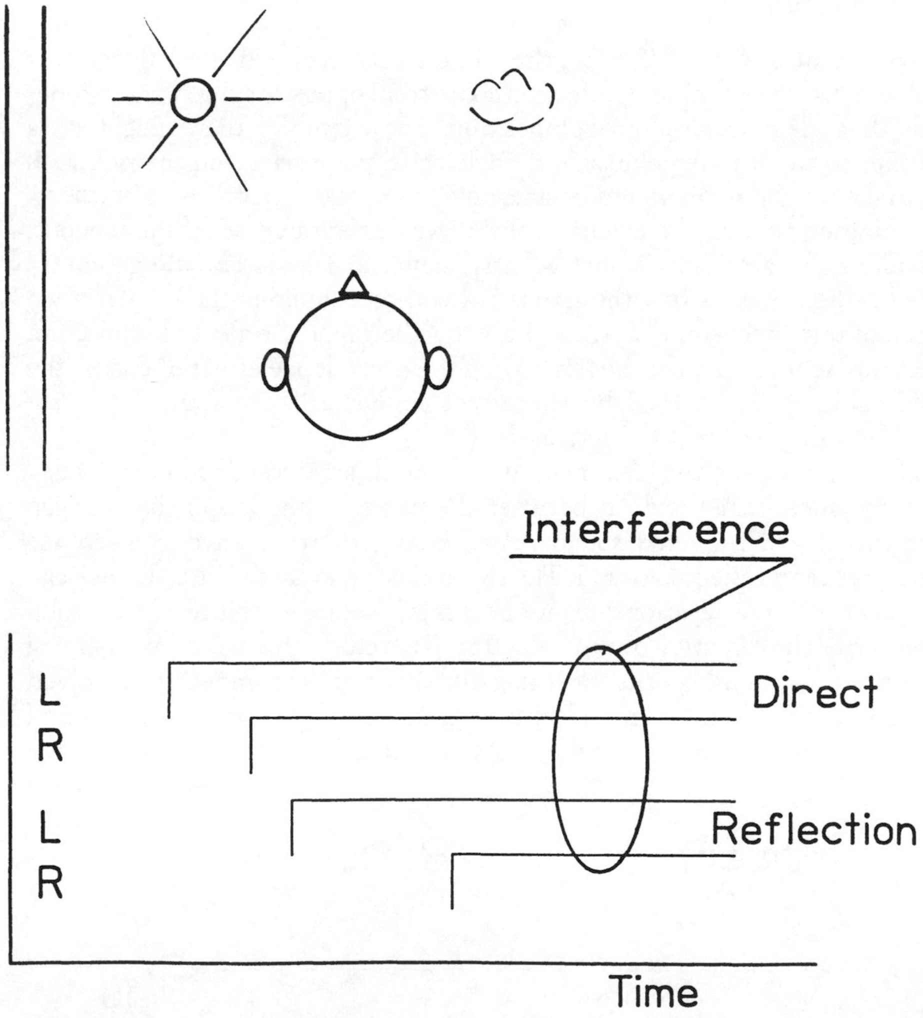

FIG. 2 (Upper panel) Localization experiment in a room that is anechoic except for a wall at the far left. The source of sound is at the left, but in the absence of an onset transient the source-reflection interference in the steady-state fine structure puts the image at the cloud on the right. (Lower panel) The time sequence showing amplitude envelopes for extended signals with abrupt onset transients, given the geometry of the upper panel. The envelope for the reflection tends to pull the image to the left, but the interference in the fine structure tends to pull the image to the right.

What then is the nature of the competition? If the envelope onsets are critical, then the competition is between a direct sound to the left and a reflection that is further to the left. Any departure from a perfect precedence effect should be revealed as a bias in the leftward direction from the direct source location. If, however, the the steady-state portion of the sound is critical, then the competition is between a direct sound to the left and the transition to the steady-state field that points to the right. Departures from a perfect precedence effect should appear as a bias to the right of the direct source location. Experiments using this kind of ambiguous geometry and 50-ms pulses of 500-Hz tones show that the bias is, in fact, to the right (Rakerd and Hartmann, 1985). That means that the competition is with the transition to the steady-state field and not with the envelope of the reflection.

Although these experiments with precedence effect in the overlapping case were resolved in favor of the transition to steady-state cues, it is possible that other conditions could lead to a different result. In particular, with a high-frequency sine tone, the steady-state portion of the sound would have no useable interaural time difference cue. It's not clear what would happen then. However, recognizing the significance of the competition between onset and the transition to the ongoing sound field is important because most naturally occurring sources are broadband and lead to ongoing sound fields with useable interaural time localization cues. It is likely that in such cases the correct way to think about the precedence effect is again as a competition between onsets and transitions to ongoing cues.

II. THE PLAUSIBILITY HYPOTHESIS

For about a century, it has been known that sounds in the azimuthal plane are localized on the basis of interaural time differences (ITD) and interaural intensity differences (IID). Rivalry experiments have shown that, depending on the stimulus, these two factors are differentially weighted. The ITD is dominant for low-frequency sounds (<800 Hz), and the IID is dominant for high-frequency sounds. The relative weights of the ITD and the IID are generally described by a trading ratio with units of μs/dB. The sense of the unit is that an image that has been diverted from the midline by an IID of 1 dB can be returned to midline by an ITD of Δt μs favoring the other side. The trading ratio is then Δt μs/dB. The actual experiment used to determine a trading ratio may differ from the simple midline test, but it typically reflects a competition between time and intensity differences that is approximately equivalent to that test.

About a decade ago it was discovered that the trading ratio could be manipulated by room acoustics and visual cues (Rakerd and Hartmann, 1985). The experiment required listeners to identify the source of a 500-Hz sine tone in a room with a single reflection. The tone had no onset transient, and the steady-state ITD and IID cues that remained were badly distorted by interference from the reflected sound. Not surprisingly, listeners made large errors in sound localization. What was striking about the data, however, was that different listeners made the same errors. To try to understand these data, we made measurements of ITD and IID using an artificial head. What finally emerged from the comparison of listener localization judgments and physical measurements was that listeners appeared to assign reduced weights to interaural time differences that were unreasonably large. This was the origin of the plausibility hypothesis.

The idea can be understood with the aid of Fig. 3. The source array in the experiments spanned an angle of 10.5° to the left of midline and 10.5° to the right. In a free field, the maximum ITD for a source at the extremes of the array would be ±140μs. That value is shown by the long dashed vertical line in Fig. 3. Because the listener could see the sources in the array, the listener was justified in regarding any time delay outside that range as more or less implausible and discounting it. Actual time-intensity trading ratios determined from listener judgments are given in Fig. 3. The figure shows that the less plausible the ITD cue, the less weight it was given. All the trading ratio values in the implausible region were larger than the trading ratio of 5μs/dB determined for the same listeners in the same task under anechoic conditions. It should be noted that although one may talk about the plausibility evaluation as though it were a conscious decision on the part of the listener, the operation is actually quite automatic and outside consciousness.

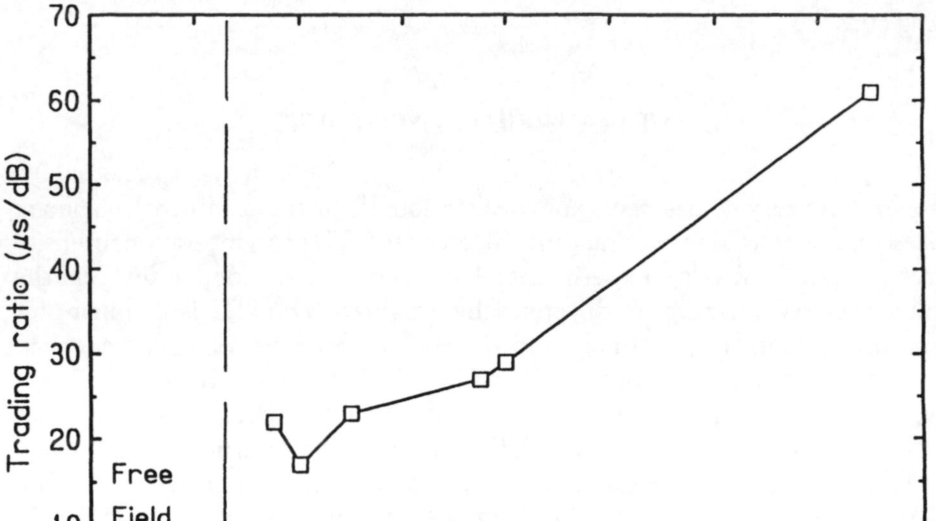

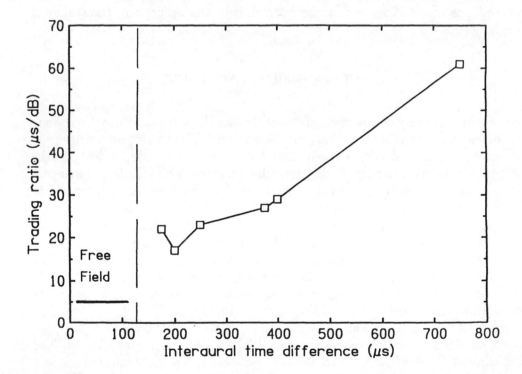

FIG. 3 The time-intensity trading ratio discovered in localization experiments using a sine tone in an anechoic room and in a room with one wall. In free field the interaural time differences (ITDs) are less than 140°, and the trading ratio is small. With a wall the ITDs are large and implausible, and the trading ratio increases dramatically. These data led to the plausibility hypothesis.

A. Plausible implausibilities

The plausibility hypothesis, as it has been developed to date, is rather insistent that it is ITD cues that are subject to a plausibility evaluation. There is no comparable discounting of IID cues. Initial evidence on this point came from the 1985 experiments where it was discovered that localization judgments for 500-Hz tones tracked IIDs as large as 10 dB. Because of head diffraction, a listener never hears a 10 dB difference in a 500-Hz tone in a free field, unless the source is very close to the head, and yet such an implausible difference was apparently not discounted. Corroborating evidence was found in headphone experiments by Yost (1981), which showed that the dependence of lateralization on the IID is essentially independent of frequency. This is a rather remarkable result. In daily life, the binaural system regularly makes use of large IIDs at high frequency, but only finds large IID at low frequency for sources that are close to the head. In the end, however, the headphone experiments showed that all this daily experience does not matter.

To test this idea further Hartmann and Fontana (1991) performed extensive experiments with contrived stimuli having plausible ITD cues and implausible IID cues. The results showed what might be called an inverse plausibility hypothesis. The experiment used a digital recording of sounds reproduced by headphones so that interaural intensity differences could be readily changed. The recording was made with a dummy head in an anechoic room, where there were a dozen real sources in an azimuthal array. During the experiment, the subject sat where the dummy head had been so that he could see the sources. The stimuli, therefore, had ITDs that were correct for each source, but variable IID. Typical data are shown in Fig. 4, which plots perceived location versus actual source location for a single listener. The data show that the listener ignored IIDs of 5 dB. Other listeners ignored IIDs as large as 10 or 15 dB, but grossly implausible differences (>15 dB) always strongly affected localization judgments. This experimental result is completely opposite to the effect known as plausibility hypothesis, which asserts that the most implausible cues get the least weight. The conclusion is that the plausibility process discounts ITD cues and not IID cues.

The discounting of ITD cues in favor of IID cues postulated by the plausibility hypothesis needs to be reconciled with recent data from Wightman and Kistler (1992) suggesting that cases of conflict between IID and ITD cues are resolved in favor of the ITD. In fact, those data do not pose a problem for the plausibility hypothesis because the ITD cues were plausible in that particular experimental context. It seems likely that if the experiments were repeated with implausible cues different results would be obtained.

It is natural to wonder what, precisely, is the basis for evaluating the plausibility of ITD cues. There are a number of possible ways to determine that an ITD is implausible: The ITD might be greater than 800 μs, which is approximately the maximum possible value achievable in an anechoic room. Alternatively, the ITD might exceed the values that are expected for sources of sound in the listener's context. In a source identification experiment, the context is the range of the source array that the listener can see or otherwise knows. An ITD may be judged

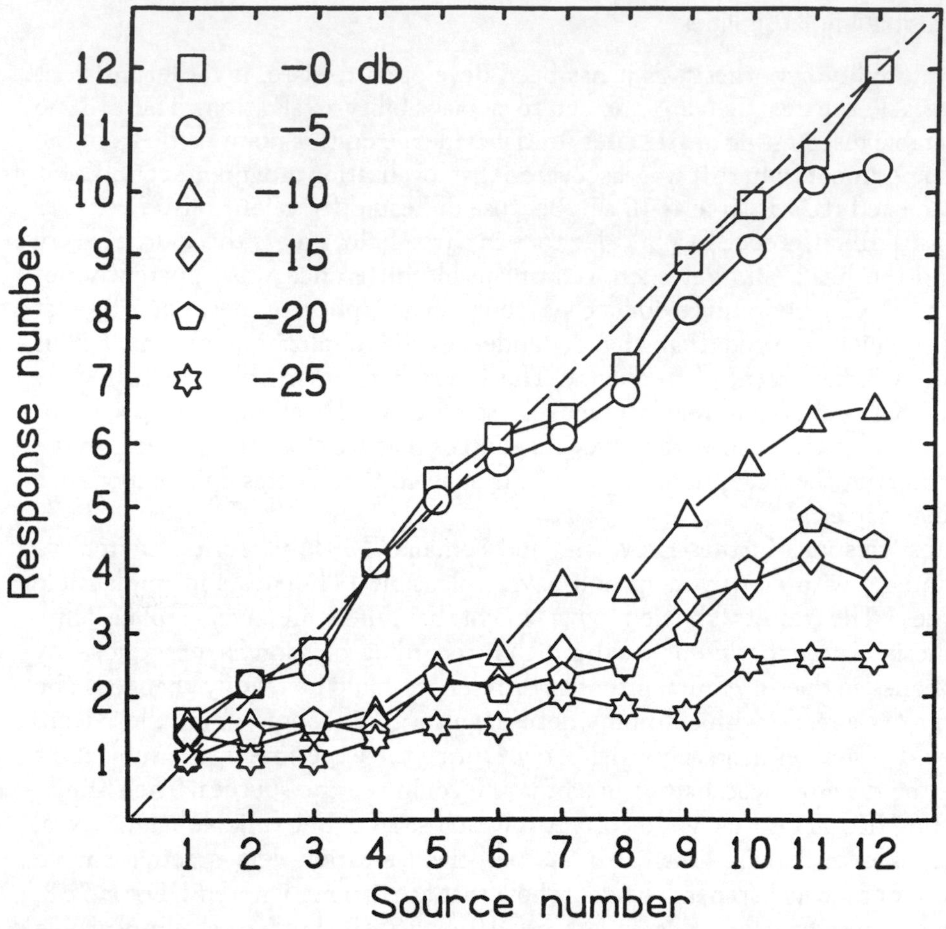

FIG. 4 Source localization judgements for twelve sources, spaced by 3°, in an anechoic room, given correct (plausible) ITDs but artificial IIDs. The IIDs were altered by attenuating the signal to the right ear by the amount shown in the legend. For large (implausible) IIDs, the signal image is pulled far to the left (small response numbers), supporting the assertion that the plausibility hypothesis does not operate on IID cues.

implausible if it is unstable against small movements of the head, or if it varies rapidly with signal frequency. Possibly, an ITD is implausible if it disagrees with the observed IID (Gaik, 1993). Even when the ITD has a reasonable value, it might be judged implausible if the frequency is high enough to put the interaural phase difference close to 180°. All of these discrepant factors are possible candidates for implausibility. Knowing which are actually operative in particular circumstances is something that will require a great deal more work.

B. Plausibility and the precedence effect

Up to this point, the discussion of plausibility hypothesis has said nothing about the precedence effect or about transient sounds. In fact, a major role for the processing of ITD cues in transient sounds is logically necessary for the existence of the mechanism of the plausibility hypothesis. The reason is as follows: The plausibility hypothesis says that plausibility, for steady-state sounds, is evaluated with respect to free-field cues. On its face, this suggestion would seem to make very little sense. Listeners have almost no experience with steady-state sounds in free field. Hence, it would seem that they have little opportunity to develop criteria for evaluating plausibility. To cope with this logical difficulty, one must suppose that listeners learn about plausible cues from exposure to transients and then apply that experience to steady-state sounds. It follows that the plausibility hypothesis should apply to transient sounds as well. Supporting evidence for that position was not long in coming; it appeared in a reevaluation of the Franssen effect.

Franssen's illusion (Franssen, 1960) is created with two loudspeakers in a typical stereophonic configuration in a room. A 500-Hz sine tone is turned on abruptly at one of the two speakers, say the left. Immediately this tone is faded out while a complementary tone rises at the right loudspeaker. After a few seconds, the tone at the right loudspeaker decays to silence. A listener hearing these events is quite convinced that the left speaker is the only one that ever sounded, even though it was the right speaker that was on for most of the time.

Because the leading source is found to dominate, the Franssen illusion resembles the precedence effect. Franssen's explanation of his effect (Franssen, 1962) was precisely along the lines of classical explanations of the precedence effect. It consisted of a model of binaural hearing in which excitation arriving at the leading ear inhibited later excitation arriving first at the other ear. This model was subsequently developed further by Lindemann (1986).

A variation on Franssen's experiment was presented by Berkley (1983, 1987). It began just like the original, but Berkley simply never turned off the second source. The listener, now listening to the right speaker only, remained convinced that it was the left speaker (where the onset transient had been) that continued to sound. The illusory image, generated by the onset transient on the left, seemed to persist indefinitely. The problem posed by Berkley's experiment, although the significance was apparently not recognized at the time, is that there is no way that the illusion could be caused by a process as elementary as peripheral inhibition. The effect persists too long. What appears to be the case is that the steady-state sound has no real power to generate a sensation of localization. This, we imagine to be a result of a plausibility evaluation.

Good evidence in favor of the plausibility hypothesis was discovered simply by moving the Franssen experiment into an anechoic room (Hartmann and Rakerd, 1989). There, the Franssen illusion was a complete failure. This is shown in Fig. 5, where the anechoic condition corresponds to a ratio of total power to direct power of unity ($T/D = 1$). There localization performance is perfect, in contrast to four other room conditions where localization d' is usually less than 1.

The explanation for the failure of the Franssen effect is that in the anechoic room the steady-state sound creates plausible interaural time differences and therefore generates a strong localization sensation. By contrast, in an ordinary room the ITDs are implausible and they are subconsciously discounted as localization cues. Localization is then based on the only remaining plausible cue, namely the onset transient. It is not hard to generalize this conclusion and to predict that

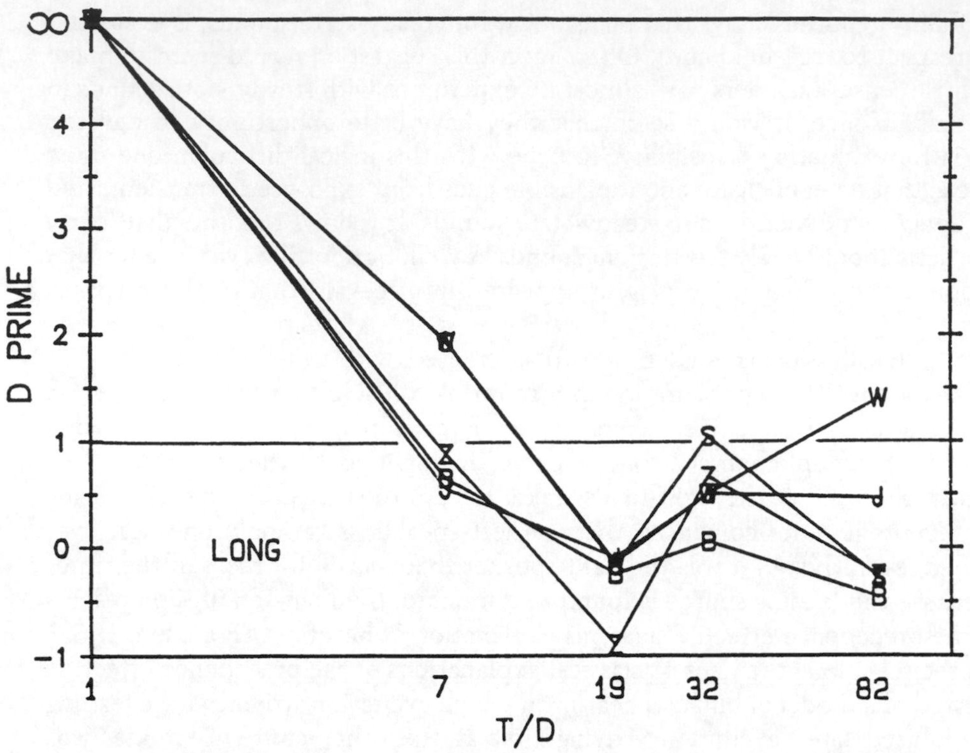

FIG. 5 Correct responses in a Franssen experiment, expressed as d', given different values of the ratio of total sound power to direct sound power (T/D). For an anechoic room the ratio is 1. Four other values were (from left to right): large room at 10 f, large room at 20 f, reverberation room at 10 f, and reverberation room at 20 f. Data for 5 listeners are shown separately.

the Franssen illusion will fail under any circumstances in which the steady-state part of a sound can be accurately localized by itself. For example, broadband noise can be localized in a room even without an onset transient (Hartmann, 1983). It was found that the Franssen illusion does indeed fail when the pure tone signal is replaced by white noise (Hartmann and Rakerd, 1989).

C. Echoes from the past

One of the original experiments by Wallach, Newman, and Rosensweig provides further evidence in support of the plausibility hypothesis, although, as we shall see, the plausibility hypothesis is not a unique explanation for the results. The WNR experiment was a competition between a leading click and a lagging click. The particular stimulus is shown in Fig. 6a. For the leading click there is no interaural time difference at all ($ITD_1 = 0$). The lagging click arrives after a gap of 2 ms, which is a delay that leads to a fused sound. The lagging click leads in the right ear by ITD_2. (If ITD_2 is negative, the lagging click leads in the left ear.)

Listeners were asked to decide whether the entire stimulus was to the left or to the right of midline. If the precedence effect operates perfectly then the symmetrical leading click would dominate entirely, the image would be centered,

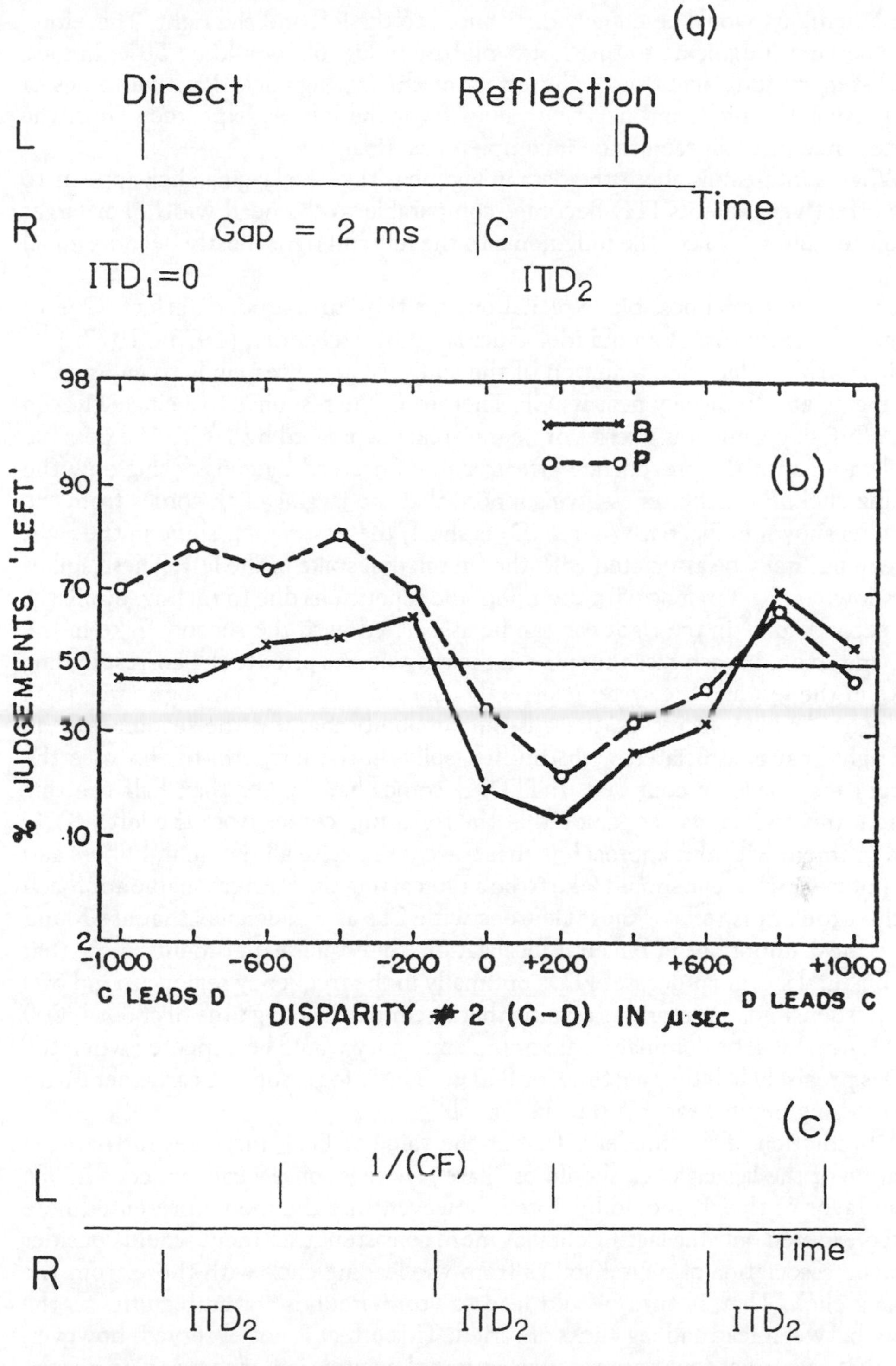

FIG. 6 (a) The sequence of pulses from a special experiment by WNR. (b) Percent judgements to the left given the sequence in (a), revealing a bias caused by the reflection. Data for two listeners are shown separately. (c) Tentative explanation for the turn-arounds in (b) based on a ringing response in the auditory nerve. As shown here, the interaural time difference for the reflected sound (ITD_2) is somewhat shorter than half the ring time of the auditory filter, leading to a bias to the right as expected.

and judgments would be equally distributed to the left and the right. Therefore, the "percent judgments to the 'left,'" plotted in Fig. 6b, would be 50%. In fact, the listeners' judgments show the effect of the lagging click. Positive values of ITD_2 favor the right, and negative values favor the left, as expected. Thus, the precedence effect is seen to be incomplete, as usual.

What is interesting about the data in Fig. 6b is that the lagging click appears to lose effectiveness as its ITD becomes comparable to the head width. For larger absolute values of ITD_2, the judgments to the left and right mostly become equal again.

There are several possible explanations for this "turn-around" effect. One of them is an extension of an old idea elucidated by McFadden (1973a, 1973b). It begins with the fact that a neuron of the auditory nerve responds to an impulse by ringing at a frequency near its CF. Therefore, the response to a single click in the WNR experiment is a series of neural spikes separated by 1/CF. The possible implications for the precedence effect can be imagined by considering only the lagging click. For definiteness, we suppose that the lagging click comes from the right, as shown in Fig. 6a. When ITD_2 is short, the first neural spike in the right ear can naturally be associated with the first neural spike in the left. These spikes are shown in Fig. 6c along with their periodic repetitions due to ringing. Similarly, the second spike in the right ear can be associated with the second spike in the left, and so on. In each case the spike in the right occurs prior to the corresponding spike in the left and the system correctly concludes that the lagging source is on the right. As ITD_2 increases, there is the possibility that it is the second spike in the right that is associated with the first spike in the left, etc. In this case the system may become confused. If ITD_2 is somewhat greater than half the ring period, the system may conclude that the reflection comes from the left.

A problem with this approach is that the clicks excite all the neural fibers and it is not clear what one should take to be a typical ring time. A reasonable approach to the problem is to take those neurons with CFs at frequencies that are found to be most important in binaural localization. Sine-tone experiments show that the binaural system processes ITDs optimally in the frequency region around 600 Hz. It is sensible, therefore, to assume that circuits with a ring time of about 1/600 Hz (1.7 ms) will be dominant. Maximum ambiguity would be expected when the ITD is precisely half the ring time, or 850 μs. This is in reasonable agreement with the crossing points near ±700 μs in Fig. 6b.

A prediction of this model is that as the value of ITD_2 increases further, the location of the lagging click should oscillate. There is some weak evidence in Fig. 6b in favor of this. It should be noted, however, that the model presented here has considered only the lagging click. A more consistent treatment would consider also the association of neural spikes from the leading click with those from the lagging click. That, in turn, would lead to "turn-arounds" or ambiguities as the delay between lead and lag clicks is varied. This effect is not observed, however, and that fact must count as evidence against the extension of the ringing-neuron model to the precedence effect.

An alternative explanation of the "turn-around" effect is a form of plausibility hypothesis. As the ITD approaches 700 or 800 μs it becomes comparable to the maximum possible delay for a free-field source, the so-called Hornbostel–Wertheimer constant. Delays longer than this may be found implausible and discounted. The effect of that would be to reduce the ability of the reflection to bias the judgments, and the responses should return to the midline (50%). The plausibility hypothesis by itself would not predict that responses oscillate.

III. LOCALIZING THE LOCALIZER

Much of the psychoacoustical experimenting that has been done on the precedence effect has been directed toward the discovery of the site within the nervous system where the precedence operation takes place. Given a neural wiring that is reasonably well understood, the question of "how it works" is closely connected to the question of "where it happens." The search gets off to an excellent start because physiologists have so successfully identified the initial encoding of binaural differences in the superior olive: IIDs are registered in the lateral superior olive. ITDs are registered in the medial superior olive (MSO). The process in the MSO resembles the delay line and cross-coincidence network suggested by Jeffress (1948). (See Yin and Chan, 1990, for a recent article with standard references.) There is even significant progress on the representation of localization information at the cortical level (Middlebrooks, Clock, Xu, and Green, 1994).

But it has been clear for some time that localization is not the same as precedence effect. As noted in the review article by Zurek (1987), unilateral ablation of the auditory cortex in cats can disrupt the precedence effect, leaving unimpaired the ability to localize single sound sources (Cranford and Oberholtzer, 1976; Whitfield, Diamond, Chiveralls, and Williamson, 1978). Further, although newborn human infants can localize single sounds, as evidenced by a head-turn reflex, they do not show a precedence effect. Competing sounds that would lead to a localizable image after 6 months of postnatal cortical development, as evidenced by a head turn in the direction of the leading sound source, do not lead to a head-turn reflex prior to that time (Clifton, Morrongiello, Kulig, and Dowd, 1981; Clifton, Morrongiello, and Dowd, 1984).

More recently, experiments with adult subjects (Clifton, 1987; Clifton, Freyman, Litovsky, and McCall, 1994) show that the precedence effect can be disrupted by a dramatic change in the stimulus. The central auditory system appears to require some high-level preparation in order to exhibit the precedence effect (see chapter 12, this volume, by Clifton and Freyman.) This is important because it addresses one of the most powerful arguments in favor of a low-level precedence effect, namely, that it is fast. Clifton's effect shows that it is advance preparation (and not especially fast neural response) that is responsible for the speed seen in precedence effect. This conclusion can be contrasted with the fact that the auditory periphery does need to respond rapidly to maintain precise timing in order to code the ITD localization cues in the first place. The time constants associated with establishing the precedence effect as revealed by Clifton are similar to the times measured in the study of what is known as "binaural sluggishness" (e.g., Grantham and Wightman, 1978). It would be interesting to see if the latter has the number-of-events character that the Clifton effect seems to have. All of this work strongly implicates the central nervous system in the precedence effect. Further, the process of the plausibility hypothesis, especially as regards the Franssen effect as described earlier, would also seem to involve high-level processing, probably including visual input and memory.

In assigning a site to the precedence effect, it is also interesting to review the experiments of Wyttenbach and Hoy (1993) on the field cricket. Experiments with competing ultrasonic pulses from left and right sides, as shown in Fig. 7, show a well-developed precedence effect, with summing localization (gap $\Delta t <$ 2 ms) and release from precedence ($\Delta t >$ 75 ms). Anatomically, the cricket has a low-level binaural comparison stage in the prothorax, the so-called 501 circuit, which may be regarded as the analog of the superior olive complex in mammals. However, Wyttenbach and Hoy showed that this is not the origin of precedence. Their conclusion is that even if one happens to be a field cricket, one still needs a brain in order to get a precedence effect.

What then is one to make of models of the binaural system like those of Franssen (1962) and Lindemann (1986)? These models incorporate the precedence effect into the low-level delay line and cross-coincidence network that has now been identified with the superior olive. One must conclude that it is not possible for such models to be both autonomous and uniquely responsible for

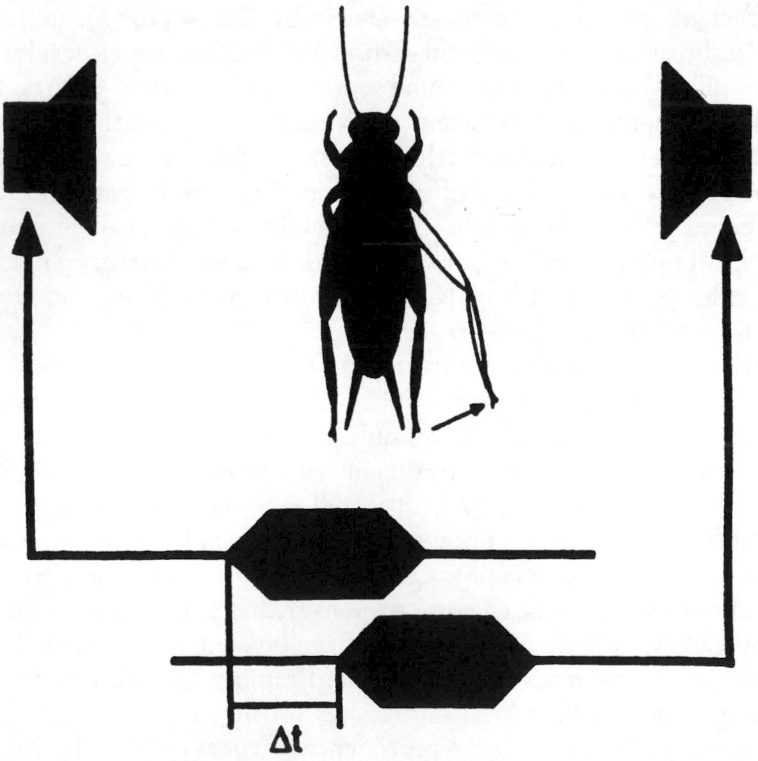

FIG. 7 Precedence effect in the field cricket as studied by Wyttenbach and Hoy (1993) by monitoring leg muscle reflex to ultrasonic pulses.

precedence. At the least, they need to have input from higher levels of the auditory system. Alternatively, processes similar to those of the low-level models may be supplemented with higher level processes. In either case, it no longer seems fruitful to build a self-contained peripheral model and to test it against observed precedence-effect psychophysical data.

A particular limitation of the models that incorporate precedence into an interaural neural delay line is that they apply only to cases in which localization is determined by binaural differences. But precedence is not restricted to sources in the horizontal plane (Blauert, 1969/1970). Recent work by Rakerd and Hartmann (1992) showed that the precedence effect operates very similarly for sources confined to the median sagittal plane, where binaural difference cues are minimal. The data from a variety of precedence-like tasks show that the differences between the planes are quantitative and not qualitative. One answer to these data is to model the precedence effect at an even lower stage, as suggested by the cochlear nucleus experiments of Wickesberg and Oertel (1990); another answer is to put it higher; a third is to distribute the processing. Perhaps here, as so often seems to be the case, we find the brain imitating itself in all its ramifications.

The accumulation of evidence over the past 20 years, as described earlier, has led to a consensus among psychoacousticians that the precedence effect manifests considerable involvement of the central auditory system (Zurek, 1987; Hafter, 1987; Hafter, Saberi, Jensen, and Briolle, 1992). This recognition challenges us to maintain our course of scientific reductionism without falling into teleological traps, such as auditory scene analysis. Recent work by Divenyi (1992) is promising in this respect. First, Divenyi showed experimentally that a leading tone pulse can generate considerable precedence effect for a lagging tone pulse of greatly different frequency. The significance of this result is that the leading and lagging pulses are not fused into a single auditory image, yet the precedence effect occurs (Blauert and Divenyi, 1988). Said differently, there appears to be precedence effect for localization, yet the Haas effect is not present. By contrast, teleological models tend to predict that precedence and fusion go together because of their emphasis on images that are logically consistent.

Divenyi's work also suggested the concept of localization strength, called *localizability*. What is important here is the idea that the localization strength can be independent of localization direction. To clarify the distinction, we note that the WNR experiment, in which a leading pulse pointing slightly to the left of midline is balanced by a lagging pulse that points to the right by a much larger angle, involves localization direction only. It does not involve localization strength, which is related to the compellingness of the small- and large-angle images.

Relatively little is known about the determinants of localization strength. We know that ITD loses its effectiveness at higher frequency (the particular example used by Divenyi) and that sounds made with competing ITD and IID can be ambiguous, hence low in strength. In general, a localization cue that is implausible has low strength. To quantify this concept, one might begin with localization blur, as measured by the standard deviation of localization decisions, as an inverse measure of strength. As applied to the precedence effect, this perceptual model says that strongly localizable signals suppress signals with weaker localizability, or at least they suppress the directional character of such signals. The strength parameter, included in the model according to an optimum processor theory, can become an important new quantitative construct. In Divenyi's example, precedence itself (strength of the first wavefront) becomes only one of many possible contributions to the strength.

IV. CONCLUSION

The precedence effect, above all, illustrates competition between sounds, essentially a competition for attention. It takes several forms, described earlier as localization precedence effect (WNR), Haas effect, and de-reverberation. Because of the differences among these effects, especially their time scales, a unified explanation requires that the precedence effect reflect a complicated process of the central nervous system. Physiological observations, as well as the psychophysics of the plausibility hypothesis and the Clifton effect, reinforce the idea that precedence phenomena arise centrally and are subject to many inputs, including vision and memory. A promising new approach to competitions like those of the precedence effect adds the concept of localization strength to the theory of localization. Strongly localizable sounds win out over weaker, and precedence is an important part of that.

To conclude, we sketch how the strength concept can approach Green's dilemma, with which this essay began. The problem is that two clicks, 6 ms apart, are perceptually segregated when heard monaurally by headphones but are fused when heard in a room. The explanation based upon strength might begin by noting that in the headphone presentation the leading click has strength due to its precedence, but the lagging click has considerable strength too because it is strongly localizable. In a room, by contrast, the lagging click that is reflected from the wall is less strongly localizable, perhaps because its interaural time and intensity cues are different in different frequency channels or because these cues do not agree with any plausible source, or because they are only part of a volley of reflected cues which do not point to any one plausible location. Obviously even this simple application needs a lot of work. And there is still more work needed to discover whether the concept of localization strength will help us understand the precedence effect in all its diverse forms.

ACKNOWLEDGMENTS

The author is grateful to Dr. Brad Rakerd for many discussions over many years. Dr. Rachel Clifton, Dr. Richard Duda, and Dr. Robert Gilkey made helpful comments on an earlier version of this chapter.

REFERENCES

Békésy, G., von. (1960). *Experiments in Hearing* (McGraw-Hill, New York), reprinted (Acoustical Society of America, Woodbury, NY).

Benade, A. H. (1976). *Fundamentals of Musical Acoustics* (Oxford, New York).

Berkley, D. A. (**1983**). "Room acoustics and listening," J. Acoust. Soc. Am. (abstr.) **73**, S17.

Berkley, D. A. (**1987**). "Hearing in rooms," in *Directional Hearing*, edited by W. A. Yost and G. Gourevitch (Springer, New York), pp. 249–260.

Blauert, J. (**1969/1970**). "Sound localization in the median plane," Acustica **22**, 205–213.

Blauert, J. (**1974**). *Spatial Hearing*, English translation by J. S. Allen (MIT Press, Cambridge, MA, 1983).

Blauert, J., and Divenyi, P. L. (**1988**). "Spectral selectivity in binaural contralateral inhibition," Acustica **66**, 267–274.

Blauert, J., and Lindemann, W. (**1986**). "Auditory spaciousness: Some further psychoacoustic analyses," J. Acoust. Soc. Am. **80**, 533–542.

Clifton, R. K. (**1987**). "Breakdown of echo suppression in the precedence effect," J. Acoust. Soc. Am. **82**, 1834–1835.

Clifton, R. K., Freyman, R. L., Litovsky, R. Y., and McCall, D. (**1994**). "Listeners' expectations about echoes can raise or lower echo thresholds," J. Acoust. Soc. Am. **95**, 1525–1533.

Clifton, R. K., Morrongiello, B. A., and Dowd, J. M. (**1984**). "A developmental look at an auditory illusion: The precedence effect," Dev. Psychobiol. **17**, 519–536.

Clifton, R. K., Morrongiello, B. A., Kulig, J. W., and Dowd, J. M. (**1981**). "Newborn's orientation towards sound: Possible implications for cortical development," Child Dev. **52**, 833–838.

Cranford, J., and Oberholtzer, M. (**1976**). "Role of neocortex in binaural hearing in the cat II: The precedence effect in sound localization," Brain Res. **111**, 225–239.

Divenyi, P. L. (**1992**). "Binaural suppression of nonechoes," J. Acoust. Soc. Am. **91**, 1078–1084.

Franssen, N. V. (**1960**). "Some considerations on the mechanism of directional hearing," Thesis, Technische Hogeschool, Delft, The Netherlands.

Franssen, N. V. (**1962**). *Stereophony*, English translation (Philips Technical Library, Eindhoven, The Netherlands, 1964).

Gaik, W. (**1993**). "Combined evaluation of interaural time and intensity differences: Psychoacoustic results and computer modeling," J. Acoust. Soc. Am. **94**, 98–110.

Grantham, D. W., and Wightman, F. L. (**1978**). "Detectability of varying interaural temporal differences," J. Acoust. Soc. Am. **63**, 511–523.

Green, D. M. (**1976**). *An Introduction to Hearing* (Lawrence Erlbaum Associates, Hillsdale, NJ).

Haas, H. (**1951**). "Uber den Einfluss des Einfachechos auf die Horsamkeit von Sprache," Acustica **1**, 49–58. English translation "The influence of a single echo on the audibility of speech," J. Audio Eng. Soc. **20**, 146–159 (1972).

Hafter, E. R., Buell, T. N., and Richards, V. M. (**1988**). "Onset coding in lateralization: It's form, site and function" in *Auditory Function*, edited by G. W. Edelman, E. Gall, and W. M. Cowen (Wiley, New York), pp. 647–676.

Hafter, E. R., Saberi, K., Jensen, E. R., and Briolle, F. (**1992**). "Localization in an echoic environment," in *Auditory Physiology and Perception*, edited by Y. Cazals, L. Demany, and K. Horner, (Pergamon, Oxford), pp. 555–561.

Hartmann, W. M. (**1983**). "Localization of sound in rooms," J. Acoust. Soc. Am. **74**, 1380–1391.

Hartmann W. M., and Fontana, P. (**1991**). "Azimuthal localization and the asymmetry of the plausibility hypothesis," J. Acoust. Soc. Am. (abstr.) **90**, 2266.

Hartmann, W. M., and Rakerd, B. (**1989**). "Localization of sound in rooms IV—The Franssen effect," J. Acoust. Soc. Am. **86**, 1366–1373.

Houtsma, A. J. M., Rossing, T. D., and Wegenaars, W. M. (**1987**). Auditory Demonstrations (compact disc, Acoustical Society of America, Eindhoven, The Netherlands).

Jeffress, L. A. (**1948**). "A place theory of sound localization," J. Comp. Physiol. Psychol. **41**, 35–39.

Koenig, W. (**1950**). "Subjective effects in binaural hearing," J. Acoust. Soc. Am. **22**, 61–62.

Lindemann, W. (**1986**). "Extension of a binaural cross-correlation model by contralateral inhibition II. The law of the first wavefront," J. Acoust. Soc. Am. **80**, 1623–1630.

McFadden, D. (**1973a**). "Precedence effects and auditory cells with long characteristic delays," J. Acoust. Soc. Am. **54**, 528–530.

McFadden, D. (**1973b**). "A note on auditory neurons having periodic response functions to time-delayed, binaural stimuli," Physio. Psychol. **1**, 265–266.

Middlebrooks, J. C., Clock A. E., Xu, L., and Green, D. M. (**1994**). "A panoramic code for sound location by cortical neurons," Science **264**, 842–844.

Rakerd, B., and Hartmann, W. M. (**1985**). "Localization of sound in rooms II: The effect of a single reflecting surface," J. Acoust. Soc. Am. **78**, 524–533.

Rakerd, B., and Hartmann, W. M. (**1992**). "Precedence effect with and without binaural differences—Sound localization in three planes," J. Acoust. Soc. Am. (abstr.) **92**, 2296.

Wallach, H., Newman, E. B., and Rosenzweig, M. R. (**1949**). "The precedence effect in sound localization," Am. J. Psych. **62**, 315–337.

Whitfield, I. C., Diamond, I., Chiveralls, K., and Williamson, T. (**1978**). "Some futher observations on the effects of unilateral cortical ablation on sound localization in the cat," Exp. Brain Res. **31**, 221–234.

Wickesberg, R. E., and Oertel, D. (**1990**). "Delayed, frequency-specific inhibition in the cochlear nuclei of mice: A mechanism for monaural echo suppression," J. Neurosci. **10**, 1762–1768.

Wightman, F. L., and Kistler, D. J. (**1992**). "The dominant role of low-frequency interaural time differences in sound localization," J. Acoust. Soc. Am. **91**, 1648–1661.
Wyttenback, R. A., and Hoy, R. R. (**1993**). "Demonstration of the precedence effect in an insect," J. Acoust. Soc. Am. **94**, 777–784.
Yin, T. C. T., and Chan, J. C. K. (**1990**). "Interaural time sensitivity in medial superior olive of cat," J. Neurophysiol. **64**, 465–488.
Yost, W. A. (**1981**). "Lateral position of sinusoids presented with interaural intensive and temporal differences," J. Acoust. Soc. Am. **70**, 397–409.
Zurek, P. M. (**1987**). "The precedence effect," in *Directional Hearing* edited by W. A. Yost and G. Gourevitch (Springer, New York), pp. 85–106.

Chapter 11

Binaural Adaptation and the Effectiveness of a Stimulus Beyond Its Onset

Ervin R. Hafter
Department of Psychology
University of California, Berkeley

(Received February 1995; revised June 1995)

The binaural precedence effect is often spoken of as evidence of neural suppression of echoes. This chapter reviews a detection-based technique designed to measure the amount of binaural information actually derived from successive portions of a signal. The work shows that, for high stimulus rates (tonal frequencies or rates of modulation), the effectiveness of each part of a stimulus is less than the part that precedes it. The process responsible for this loss in binaural information is dubbed binaural adaptation. It is well described with compressive power functions whose exponents decline as the stimulus rate is increased. It has been found with a variety of stimuli such as pure tones, noise, sinusoidal amplitude modulation, and trains of clicks. Experiments cited here discuss the level of auditory processing at which binaural adaptation takes place; these point to monaural channels in the auditory periphery, prior to binaural interaction. Other experiments describe a rapid recovery from binaural adaptation in response to a variety of extraneous acoustical triggers. Together, these results are contrasted with binaural precedence, which is argued to be a more cognitive process residing in a more central part of the auditory system. The general conclusion is that these two processes rely on separate mechanisms.

I. BINAURAL PRECEDENCE

Listeners in a complex acoustic environment gather the appropriate auditory components into groups that define the auditory figure and ground. Bregman (1990) calls this auditory scene analysis. Because the primary code for azimuthal localization is the interaural time-difference (ITD) (Wightman and Kistler, 1992), it is not surprising that components should be grouped on the basis of a common ITD (Trahiotis and Stern, 1989). This process is complicated by reverberation, where delayed copies of the signal produced by reflection produce interaural differences that vary from that of the primary pathway alone. Fortunately, the perceived direction of the signal in this case is essentially that of the source. In a classical study of this phenomenon, Wallach, Newman, and Rosenzweig (1949) used earphones to present pairs of dichotic clicks separated by a brief interclick interval (ICI). Their subjects responded with the lateral position of the fused image as a function of ITDs in the first and second click, producing judgments that showed the first click to have a much stronger effect than the second. The special importance of the leading portion of a stimulus for lateralization has been called "binaural precedence" or the "law of the first wavefront" (Blauert, 1983). A variety of paradigms have produced the same general conclusion; that is, although differences in the ITD of the initial and ongoing portions of a signal may spread or blur the lateral extent of the image, the onset is dominant. (For discussion and review of these phenomena, see Hartmann, Chapter 10, this volume.)

Although precedence is often cited as evidence of "echo suppression," doing so requires an important caveat. This is easily demonstrated by standing equidistant between the stereo loudspeakers in one's living room. Move away from the midline and the apparent azimuth of the fused sound moves toward the nearer speaker and when the difference between the two wavefronts exceeds about 1–2 ms, precedence makes the entire stimulus seem to come from the nearer speaker. Then disconnect the more distant speaker. This produces a change in loudness and often spaciousness and timbre, showing that nondirectional features of the delayed stimulus remain accessible, despite the directional dominance of the first wavefront. Indeed, psychophysical studies using restricted stimuli have shown that directional features of the secondary signal may also register. Saberi and Perrott (1990) presented a pair of clicks from a centered speaker followed by a second click presented from a speaker set to one side. With practice, subjects became good at identifying the side of the second click. Similarly, when Hafter, Saberi, Jensen, and Briolle (1991) asked subjects in a "virtual" acoustic field to point to the directions of clicks presented from various directions, they found that in the presence of single reflective surfaces, the judgments were close to the azimuths of the primary sources, but biased toward the directions of the reflector.

II. MEASURING THE POST-ONSET LOSS OF SPATIAL INFORMATION

In a study using earphones, Hafter, Dye, and Gilkey (1979) measured the detectability of ITDs carried only in the ongoing (non-onset) portions of continuous low-frequency tones by totally masking the tones' onsets and offsets with noise. They found that when the durations of the tones were sufficiently long, performance was as good as without the masker. However, one might speculate that this result could occur if the offset of the masker noise triggered onset-like behavior similar to that which occurs in response to the true onset when the signal is presented in quiet. Such notions are hard to evaluate with traditional measures of precedence, which provide neither a precise definition of the portion of the stimulus constituting its onset nor a measure of the course of information retrieval from the portions that follow. As an improved approach to the study of the latter, Houtgast and Plomp (1968) studied the detectability of ITDs presented in low-frequency stimuli of various durations. Signal-detection theory (Green and Swets, 1974) asserts that performance is limited by *noise* in the domain of the signal; when the signal is an interaural delay, this means random variation in the ITD to be detected. For stimuli presented in quiet, the limiting noise is assumed to be internal to the listener; in this case that would be random "jitter" added to responses of neurons carrying the temporal code. According to detection theory, the information transmitted by a signal is inversely proportional to the variance of the limiting noise and so directly related to the detectability index, d'^2 (Lindsay, Taylor, and Forbes, 1968). From this, Houtgast and Plomp (1968) reasoned that if all parts of the stimulus were equally effective, d' should improve with the square-root of duration. Instead, they found that the growth of performance with duration was slower than optimal, indicating that the latter parts of their signals were less effective than the onsets. Following this line of reasoning, Ricard and Hafter (1973) found similar results using tones of up to 500 Hz, as did Nuetzel and Hafter (1976) using sinusoidal amplitude modulation (SAM). Interestingly, when Houtgast and Plomp (1968) presented signals against a moderate background of random noise, the square-root relation prevailed, so that external noise actually improved the effectiveness of the ongoing ITD. This idea was later incorporated in a model that attributed masking-level differences (MLDs) to ITD, regardless of the signal's frequency (Hafter, 1977).

III. ITDS CARRIED IN THE STIMULUS ENVELOPE

The relation between sensitivity to ITD and the signal's frequency has been of interest since Rayleigh's (1907) classic "duplex theory" argued that ITDs are the appropriate cue for localizing low frequencies whereas interaural level differences (ILDs) serve for high frequencies. Many observations with pure tones have supported this model, but evidence emerging in the 1970s (e.g., Henning, 1974; McFadden and Pasanen, 1976; Nuetzel and Hafter, 1976) showed that listeners could detect ITDs carried in the envelopes of amplitude-modulated high-frequency carriers as long as the modulation frequency was not too high. Thus, the traditional theory had to be modified to say that the upper limit for detection of ITD is determined less by the stimulus frequency than by its rate, where *rate* refers to the rate of occurrence of whatever feature of the signal carries the interaural information. In search of a better understanding of the relation between rate and the post-onset loss of binaural sensitivity, my colleagues and I (Ricard and Hafter, 1973; Nuetzel and Hafter, 1976; Hafter, Dye, and Nuetzel, 1980) began a series of experiments to determine the interaction between rate and duration. By simply extending the logic of Houtgast and Plomp (1968), we measured the relation between detection and duration and teased apart the empirical functions to assess the amount of useful binaural information carried by each portion of the stimulus. Following preliminary work using tones and SAM as stimuli, we settled on trains of clicks. Every click in the train was bandpass filtered with a high center frequency, generally 4000 Hz. Parametric evaluation was done with trains consisting of *n* clicks presented at a click rate determined by the ICI. The use of trains of clicks offers several advantages:

1. It is easy to exert independent control over the rate of information and duration of the signal.
2. The minimum duration, that is, the single click ($n = 1$), is a useful standard against which to compare longer trains.
3. Unlike the case with tones and SAM, a change in rate is not accompanied by a change in the slope of the stimulus waveform or envelope.
4. High-frequency clicks avoid the low-frequency auditory filters whose relatively narrow bandwidths can produce a periodicity of their own (ringing) and so limit the use of complex stimuli.

IV. OPTIMAL PROCESSING

We define *optimal processing* as the case in which the information derived from each successive click in the train equals that derived from the first click. If so, the process is said to exhibit statistical *stationarity* so that the mean and variance are the same for all clicks, regardless of their positions in the train. By convention, threshold is defined as the signal needed to produce a d' of 1.00. Thus, with a single click ($n = 1$), the threshold (ΔITD_1) equals the standard deviation of the internal temporal noise added to the auditory representation of that click. For n greater than 1, optimal processing produces a threshold of

$$\Delta ITD_n = \frac{\Delta ITD_1}{n^{0.5}} . \tag{1}$$

Figure 1a shows the effect of such processing. The shape of the square root of *n* function is concave, typical of those found for the effects of duration on sensory thresholds. Unfortunately, it is difficult to use for testing models because many functions are concave and look alike to the eye. Thus, we prefer the logarithmic form

$$\log \Delta ITD_n = \log \Delta ITD_1 - 0.5 \log n \tag{2}$$

shown in Fig. 1b, which provides a straight line whose slope is –0.5 and whose intercept is the threshold for a single click. Stationarity is implied whenever the slope of a log-threshold versus log-duration plot is –0.5. For further convenience,

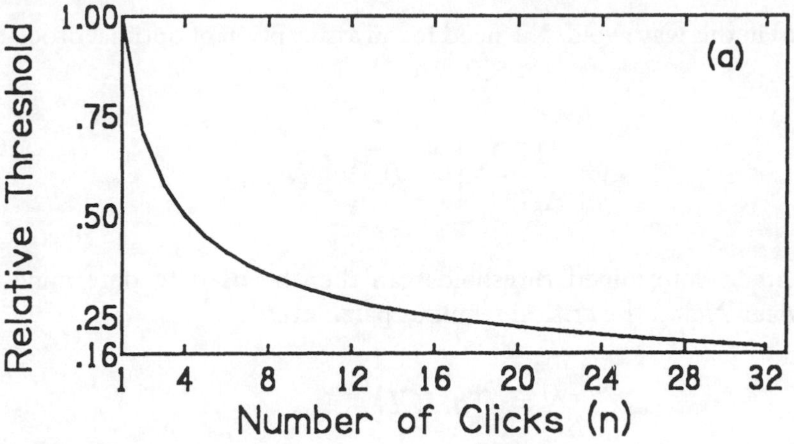

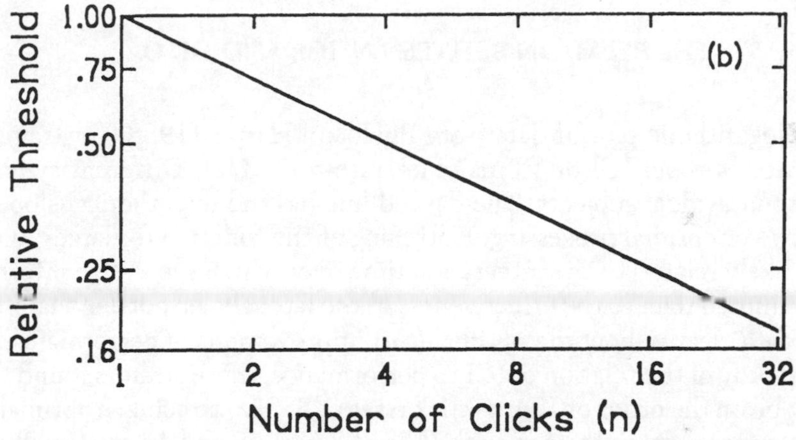

FIG. 1. Hypothetical functions describing optimal processing of the information in trains of *n* clicks. Relative thresholds are the threshold for *n* clicks (ΔITD_n) divided by the threshold for 1 click (ΔITD_1). The units for panel (a) are linear, and for panel (b), logarithmic.

one may plot performance in units of *relative threshold* ($\Delta ITD_n/\Delta ITD_1$), making the intercept 1.0, regardless of the units of the stimulus. This allows for direct comparisons between results from different kinds of signals such as ITDs and ILDs.

V. MEASUREMENT IN TERMS OF A HYPOTHETICAL NEURAL RESPONSE, *N*

In order to describe the effect of stimulus rate on post-onset processing we have sought to measure the individual effectiveness of each successive part (click) of the ongoing stimulus as a function of the ICI. For this we consider the magnitude of a hypothetical variable, N, defined as the number of informative neural events evoked by the entire train of n clicks. For simplicity, N is scaled so that $N = 1$ when $n = 1$.

Defining N in this way avoids the need for an assumption of optimal processing to assert:

$$\log\left[\frac{\Delta \mathrm{ITD}_n}{\Delta \mathrm{ITD}_1}\right] = -0.5 \log N \ , \tag{3}$$

Experimentally determined thresholds can then be used to determine the relation between N and the critical stimulus parameters:

$$N = f[n, ICI] \quad . \tag{4}$$

VI. THE RELATION BETWEEN *N*, ICI, AND DITD

Figure 2 is a logarithmic plot of data from Buell and Hafter (1988) for trains of clicks presented with an ICI of 13 ms (click rate = 77 Hz). Different symbols correspond to individual subjects. The dashed line has the hypothetical slope of –0.5, indicative of optimal processing. Flattening of the function for larger values of n is more likely related to the integration time over which successive information can be summed than to the effectiveness of the later clicks; putting that issue aside, these data clearly show the optimal ($\sqrt{n}$) improvement in performance. In a parametric study of the relation of ICI to performance, these authors found that the ICI must be on the order of 12 ms (click rates of 85 Hz) to achieve optimality.

Figure 3 compares data obtained with ICIs of 2.5, 4, 9, and 14 ms (Buell and Hafter, 1988). Again, the dashed line has the slope of –0.5 expected from optimal processing. Typical of results with this paradigm (e.g., Hafter and Dye, 1983), results with long ICIs follow the $\sqrt{n}$ prediction (unless the total duration of the train exceeds the integration time). Solution of Eq. (4) for an ICI ^{3} 12 ms produces $N = n$. However, results with the shorter ICIs are fit well by straight lines whose intercepts are 1.0 but whose slopes are shallower than the $\sqrt{n}$ line. That is,

$$\log\left[\frac{\Delta ITD_n}{\Delta ITD_1}\right] = -0.5k \log n \qquad 0 \le k \le 1, k = f(\mathrm{ICI}). \tag{5}$$

Figure 4 offers a schematic representation of Eq. (5) drawn for k values (from top to bottom) of 0.2, 0.4, 0.6, 0.8, and 1.0. In these cases, solving Eq. (4) for N shows the relation to be a compressive power function:

$$N = n^k \qquad 0 \le k \le 1, k = f(ICI) \ , \tag{6}$$

whose exponent, k, declines with ICI. We see that it offers an excellent description of the data in Fig. 3.

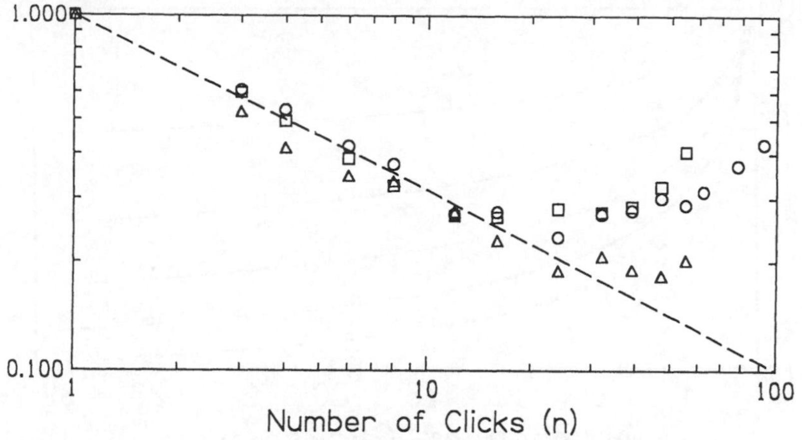

FIG. 2. Log relative thresholds for ITD plotted versus log*n*. The dashed line has a slope of –0.5, indicative of optimal processing. The ICI is 13 ms. Various symbols represent individual subjects. [Data are from Buell and Hafter, 1988.]

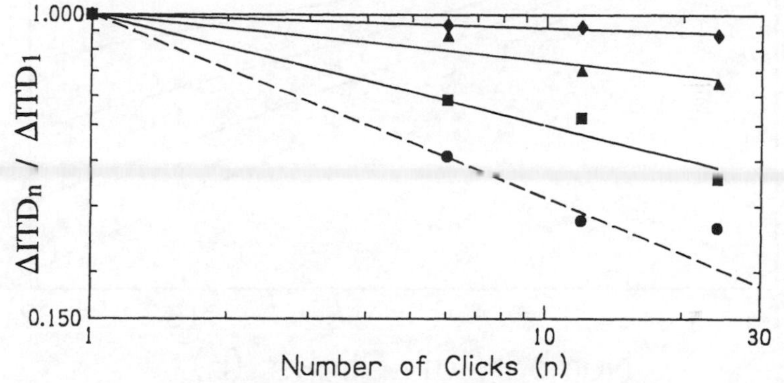

FIG. 3. Log relative thresholds for ITD plotted versus log*n*. The dashed line has a slope of –0.5, indicative of optimal processing. The ICIs are 2.5 ms (diamonds), 4 ms (triangles), 9 ms (squares), and 14 ms (circles). [Data are from a single subject in Buell and Hafter, 1988.]

VII. MECHANISMS THAT MIGHT BE AFFECTED BY HIGH CLICK RATES

A. Those described by essentially stationary statistics

Figure 4 reinforces our confidence in the use of log-log plots for visualizing the effects of duration on thresholds. The linearly plotted functions are all concave, regardless of k. Thus, had performance been obtained with only a single click rate, the loss of effectiveness of clicks later in the train would have been less apparent. Moreover, given the decline in performance over the course of the train, the log-log plot is the more useful for discriminating between various models of a loss of information due to high stimulus rates. To illustrate, Hafter and Dye (1983) considered three biological processes that might limit the auditory responsiveness

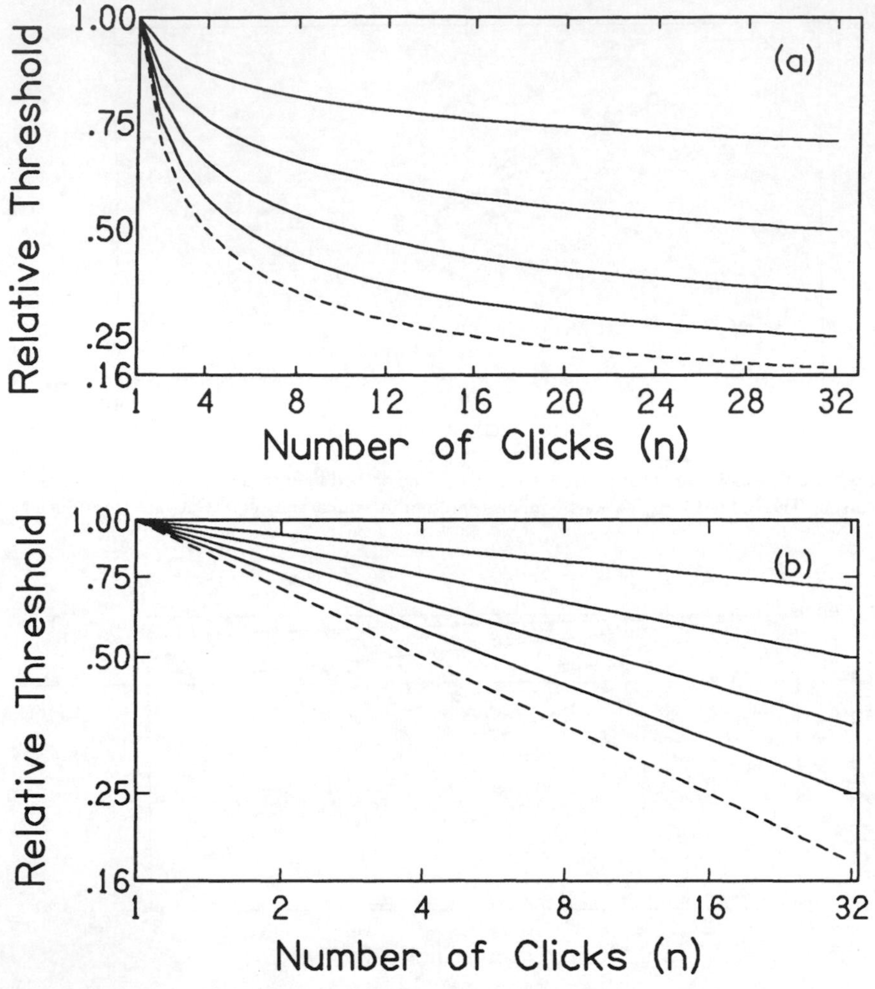

FIG. 4. Hypothetical values of the relative threshold generated by the compressive power process described in Eq. (5). The parameter is the exponent (k), ranging from 0.2 at the top to 1.0 at the bottom as described in the text. Dashed lines represent optimal ($\sqrt{n}$) processing. The units for panel (a) are linear, and for panel (b), logarithmic.

to successive clicks presented at high rates: (1) neural refractoriness, which reduces the response to successive clicks when the rate is high by preventing neurons that have just responded from refiring; (2) reduction of the effective depth of modulation, and thus the accuracy of timing at high rates due to attenuation of the stimulus sidebands by the auditory filters (Nuetzel and Hafter, 1981); and (3) nonzero correlations between successive samples of the internal noise due to such factors as surges in cochlear blood flow and respiration, which affect detection-theoretic assumptions about independence. Figure 5 shows a hypothetical plot of less-than-optimal performance given restrictions set by the first of these, neural refractoriness. With an ICI shorter than the absolute refractory period of an auditory neuron, the responsiveness of that neuron to n clicks should be reduced by a percentage, p, with p being an inverse function of ICI. Because the response to the first click in the train should be unaffected by refractoriness, this predicts the relation $N = [1 + p(n - 1)]$. Figure 5 plots this model for values of p (from top to bottom) of 0.2, 0.4, 0.6, 0.8, and 1.0. As seen here, such linear operations do not affect stationarity; thus, while overall thresholds may increase due to refractoriness, the slopes of the functions of duration approach the optimum value of –0.5 for large n. Hafter and Dye (1983) showed that all three of the mechanisms listed earlier, refractoriness, bandwidth limitation, and serial correlation, can be modeled by this approximation to Eq. (4) ($N \approx pn$). Thus, each is described by stationary statistics, which means that while overall performance may decline with ICI, clicks in the train beyond the first are equally effective. Thus, none of the stationary models explain data described by Eq. 6. Again one can see the value of plotting data in this way, noting that visual inspection of the concave linear plots in Figs. 4 and 5 finds them to be similar, whereas the two sets of logarithmic plots clearly diverge with larger values of n.

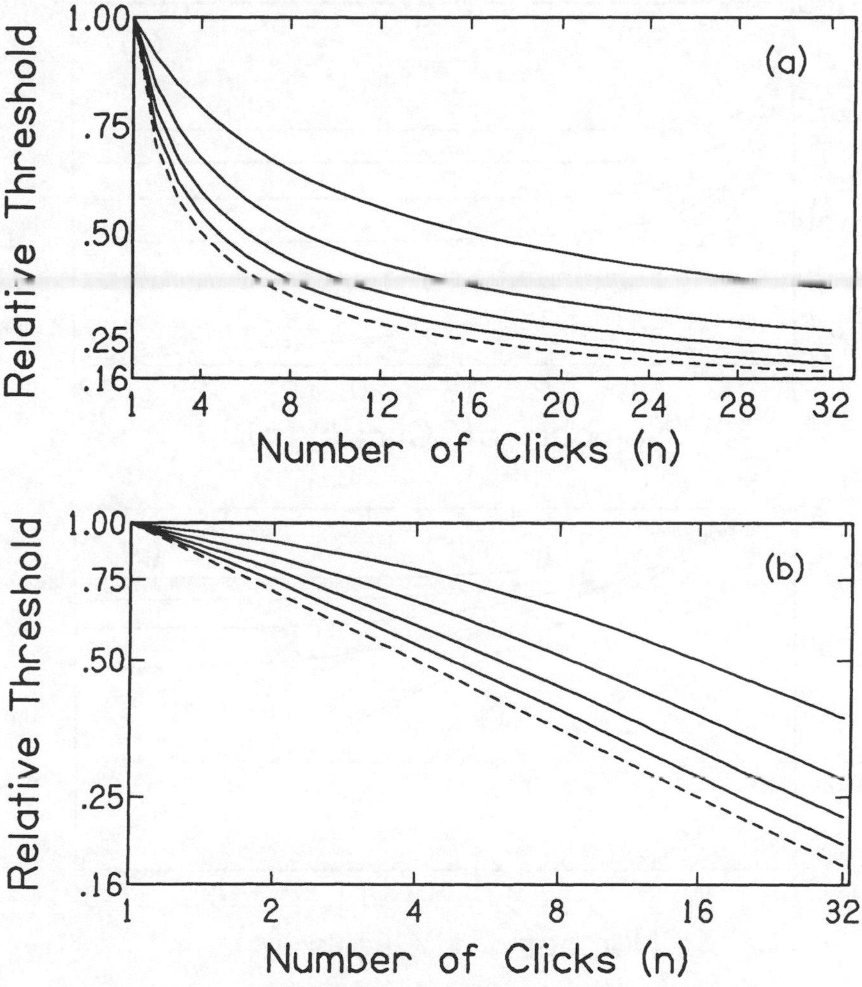

FIG. 5. Hypothetical values of the relative threshold generated by various essentially stationary process described in Section VII.A. The parameter is the proportion (p), ranging from 0.2 at the top to 1.0 at the bottom as described in the text. Dashed lines represent optimal ($\sqrt{n}$) processing. The units for panel (a) are linear, and for panel (b), logarithmic.

B. A short-term depletion of neural resources

Finally, a different type of concept offered for the effects of high stimulus-rates suggests that repeated stimulation produces a form of fatigue that reduces the effectiveness of the ongoing train by depleting a limited neural resource. This can be modeled by letting the total neural response to each click in the train be a fixed fraction (α) of the remaining resource and assuming that each response reduces the resource by an amount proportional to α. This predicts that N should be proportional to the sum from 1 to n of α^{n-1} with $\alpha \leq 1$. For comparison, Fig. 6 shows linear and logarithmic plots of this prediction for values of a (from top to bottom) of 0.6, 0.7, 0.8, 0.9, and 1.0. Again, the logarithmic curves are the most informative, this time turning upward with larger n's, indicating the presence of virtually no useful information in the later clicks.

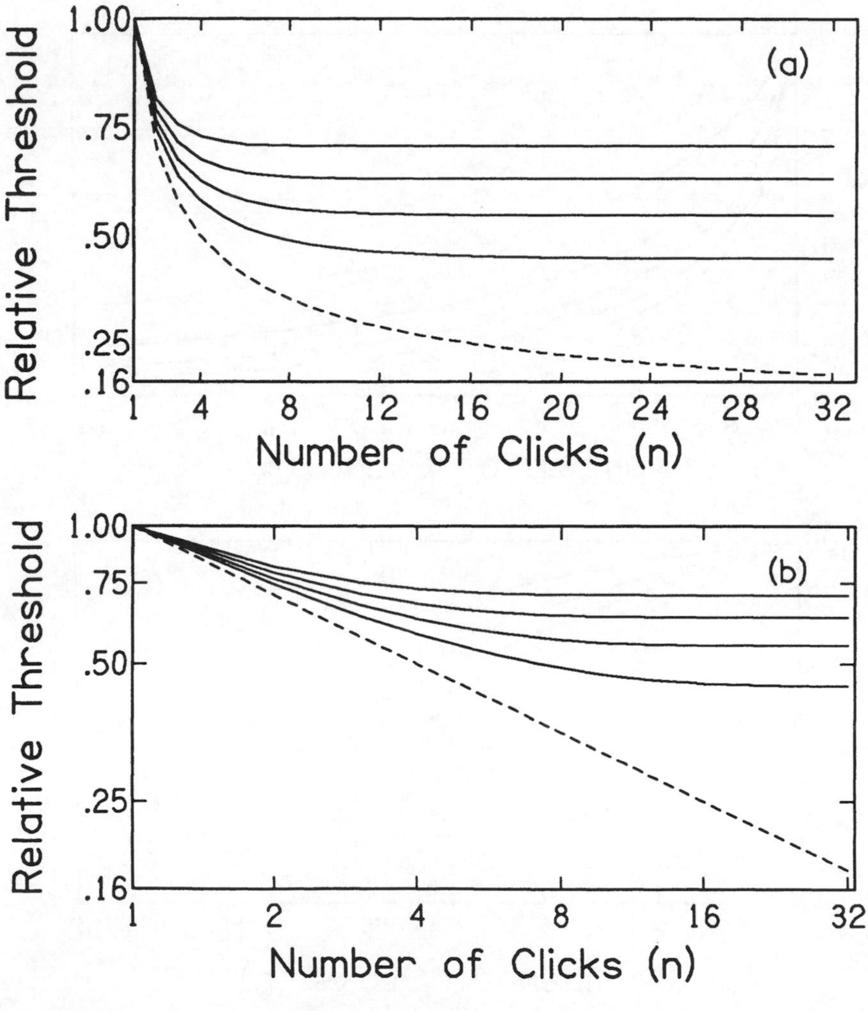

FIG. 6. Hypothetical values of the relative threshold generated by a depletion process described in Section VII.B. The parameter represents values of α ranging from 0.6 at the top to 1.0 at the bottom as described in the text. Dashed lines represent optimal ($\sqrt{n}$) processing. The units for panel (a) are linear, and for panel (b), logarithmic.

VIII. BINAURAL ADAPTATION

Because predictions from the hypothetical processes described earlier (refractoriness, bandwidth limitations, serial correlation, and cumulative neural fatigue) do not characterize the data described by Eq. (6), we have been led to postulate a different mechanism. This process, which we call *binaural adaptation* (Hafter, Buell, and Richards, 1988), reduces the effectiveness of the interaural information in a signal after its onset by an amount dependent on the stimulus rate. One way to visualize the effects of a compressive power function on threshold is in terms of the relative effectiveness of the *j*th click in a train. Calculating the difference function for Eq. (6) gives this as

$$N_j = j^k - (j-1)^k \quad . \tag{7}$$

Based on this, a hypothetical cumulative neural response to trains of *n* clicks (ΣN_j) can be computed for various values of *n* and ICI in Fig. 7. At one extreme, long ICIs produce $k = 1.0$, predicting a "tonic" response in which every click is equally effective. At the other extreme, very short ICIs produce $k = 0$ and so essentially a "phasic" response in which only the first click in the train is effective. For ICIs in between, we find a family of curves in which the effectiveness of successive clicks depends on rate. In retrospect, we have found this relation to be ubiquitous, covering a variety of stimuli including low-frequency tones, noise, and SAM (Yost and Hafter, 1987). Before going on to speculate on the potential biological underpinnings of binaural interaction, it is important to emphasize that its discovery and description derived entirely from psychophysical and not physiological observations.

IX. THE RELATION BETWEEN ADAPTATION AND STIMULUS LEVEL

The discrimination of ITD improves considerably in response to increases in the stimulus level, presumably due to such factors as a gain in the internal signal-to-noise ratio and an increase in the number of entrained neural firings (Dye and Hafter, 1984). However, the overall level of the clicks has no effect on binaural adaptation. This was shown by measuring the effects of ICI using trains of clicks set to either 20, 40, or 60 dB SPL. Although magnitudes of the binaural thresholds were strongly affected by level, there was no interaction between level and the slopes of the log-threshold versus log-*n* functions. This independence from level is in accord with neurophysiological measures of monaural adaptation in primary auditory neurons, which suggest that adaptation is an additive rather than multiplicative factor (Smith and Zwislocki, 1975).

X. THE NEURAL SITE OF BINAURAL ADAPTATION

Obviously, psychophysical measurement cannot replace the direct observations of neuroanatomy and neurophysiology. However, we have found that the ability

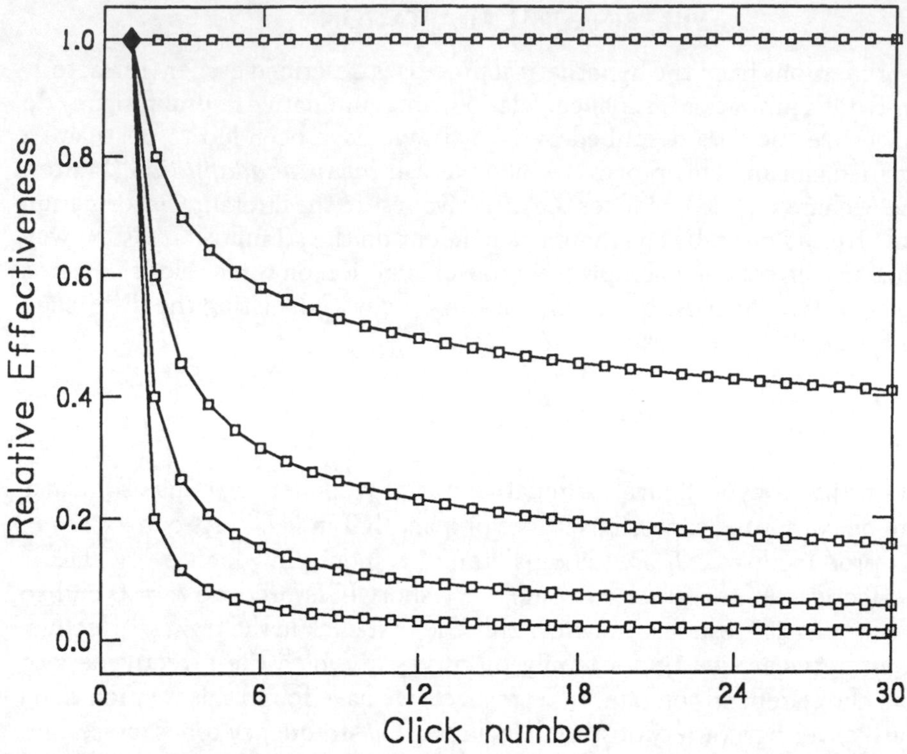

FIG. 7. Hypothetical values of the relative effectiveness of the successive clicks in a train as a function of the slope (k) of the compressive power function. Values of k for the various curves are, from the top, 0.2, 0.4, 0.6, 0.8, and 1.0.

to measure the amount of adaptation (k) in response to ICI has allowed us to relate adaptation to other stimulus features whose neural processing is better understood. The logic of this kind of functional anatomy says that when binaural interaction acts without regard to a stimulus feature thought to be processed at level x or below, it implies that the mechanism of adaptation lies at a level no later than x in the auditory pathway.

A. Binaural adaptation found with ILDs

Since the introduction of the duplex theory, investigators have speculated on the existence of separate neural channels for interaural time and level. The fact that ILDs are readily detected in high-frequency tones, whereas ITDs can only be used in low-frequency tones or in the low-frequency envelopes of AM signals, might lead one to speculate that binaural adaptation affects only the coding of ITD. However, Hafter, Dye, and Wenzel (1983) measured sensitivity to ILD utilizing the same basic paradigm as with ITD and found results that were virtually indistinguishable from those with ITD; that is, the effectiveness of the ILD in each successive click fell as described by compressive power functions like those described by Eq. (6). This suggests that a single process is responsible for binaural adaptation with both interaural differences. Related to this, Hafter, Dye, Wenzel, and Knecht (1990) measured discriminability with clicks that contained various combinations of ITD and ILD. They found that not only did the two interaural differences add linearly to performance, but there was no interaction between the effects of adaptation and the particular mixture of ITD and ILD.

Two very different theories about the site of binaural adaptation might account for its common effect on discrimination of ITD and ILD. One would place the mechanism of adaptation well out into the auditory periphery, prior to binaural interaction, arguing that adaptation in the left channel is totally independent of what is happening in the right channel, and vice versa. At the other extreme, one could argue that the mechanism for adaptation is at a very high level of neural processing, where specific activity reflects a location in auditory space, regardless of whether that location depends on interaural differences of time or level. The following experiments were designed to distinguish between these two points of view.

B. Binaural adaptation within separate frequency channels

The primary function of the peripheral auditory system is to segregate the responses to sound into separate channels according to acoustic frequencies. Thus, Trahiotis and Stern's (1989) demonstrations that lateralization of wideband stimuli reflects a combination of interaural information from across the spectrum suggests that the perceived location of a wideband stimulus reflects coding in the central auditory system, certainly higher than the early binaural interactions of the superior olivary complex (Moushegian, Rupert, and Gidda, 1975). Together, these notions have a prediction for the site of binaural adaptation. If it were at a more central level of processing, one would expect its effects to reflect adaptation to the whole stimulus, without regard for its separate frequencies. On the other hand, if the site is more peripheral, then adaptation would be expected to reflect only the interactions between clicks of the same frequency. Hafter and Wenzel (1983) addressed this issue by (1) measuring performance with trains of clicks whose center frequencies (CFs) were either 4 kHz or 6 kHz and finding that both frequency regions produced functions like those in Fig. 4b, and (2) presenting trains in which the CFs of successive clicks alternated between 4 kHz and 6 kHz to see if the effective ICI was that between successive clicks or between clicks with the same CF. If each frequency channel carries its own mechanism of adaptation, then performance should be like that found with a single CF but twice the ICI. That is, if 4-kHz clicks interact only with 4-kHz clicks, and so forth, a train with alternating CFs and an ICI of 5 ms should produce a slope of the log-threshold versus log-n functions comparable to that found with a single CF and an ICI of 10 ms. The data clearly show that the effective ICI is the longer one, that binaural adaptation does not cross frequency boundaries, supporting the idea that binaural adaptation has multiple sites divided according to frequency channels. Further support for this observation comes from tests with simultaneously presented clicks with different CFs (Wenzel and Hafter, 1983; Wenzel, 1984). There, although overall performance improved with stimulus bandwidth, the slopes of the log-threshold versus log-n functions were unchanged, again indicative of separate mechanisms within each frequency-band and so supportive of a peripheral site for binaural adaptation.

C. Binaural adaptation with differing interaural cues

In an extension of the alternating-CF paradigm described earlier, Hafter and Wenzel (1983) presented clicks that alternated in their interaural differences rather than CFs. Thus, if the first click contained an ITD, the second contained an ILD, and so forth. Results were precisely the opposite of those found with differing CFs. Here, the slopes of the log-threshold versus log-*n* functions were the same as those with ITD or ILD alone, reflecting the ICI between adjacent clicks, regardless of the type of interaural information. As before, these data too support the idea of a monaural (prebinaural) site where the amount of adaptation is unrelated to what is happening in the other ear.

D. Binaural adaptation with signals having two different perceived locations

Although the experiments cited point to a peripheral site, they do not completely rule out the possibility of adaptation at a central location where units encode specific spatial localizations, regardless of the bases for that code. For that reason, Hafter and Buell (1984; Hafter *et al.*, 1988) presented trains in which clicks differed according to their individual perceived locations. Specifically, a two-interval, forced choice paradigm was used to measure discrimination of right-leading versus left-leading clicks in a condition in which the test clicks to be compared were preceded by uninformative clicks that led always to the right ear. These uninformative clicks appeared at the beginning of the train in each interval; their ITD was extremely large (500 μs), which by itself would produce an image far to the right side of the head. Test clicks were chosen to make the two intervals just noticeably different from one another; if heard alone, they would produce images just to the left or right of center. If adaptation were based on processing in higher order neurons encoded by perceived location, adapting to the uninformative clicks would have no effect on the responses to test clicks. Conversely, for a peripheral adaptation, prior to binaural interaction, the system would adapt to the uninformative clicks and show poor performance in response to the test clicks that follow. This is what happened.

All of the experiments cited so far seem to point to a peripheral site, prior to binaural interaction. Rate-dependent adaptation has not been reported for activity in the auditory nerve fibers (Kiang, Watanabe, Thomas, and Clark, 1965), although no one has actually looked for it; thus we cannot rule it out absolutely. However, the lack of an affect of overall level on adaptation makes the VIIIth nerve seem an unlikely place. Thus, we have postulated the cochlear nucleus (CN) as the most probable site for binaural interaction. The following sections add support for this proposal.

XI. ADAPTATION AFFECTS LOCALIZATION BUT NOT PITCH

Having argued that binaural adaptation results from processing in the monaural channels of the CN, we must address the issue of how an adapted auditory system even hears stimuli with high stimulus rates. Why don't they simply fade away during adaptation; how are spectral changes able to trigger recovery from that adaptation? Toward addressing these issues, Hafter and Richards (1988) tested for adaptation in a purely monaural discrimination task using trains of high-frequency clicks (CF = 3.5 kHz) presented only to one ear. Stimuli differed only in their click rates (1/ICI), requiring discrimination to be based on differences in the perceived "periodicity pitch." As before, the parameters of interest were *n* and ICI. By definition, there is no periodicity with a single click, and periodicity pitch is quite weak with only a few clicks. However, slopes of the log-threshold versus log-*n* functions can be examined over the larger values of *n*. Figure 8 shows a sample of such data from three subjects (from Hafter and Richards, 1988) for click-rates of 167, 250, and 400 Hz. These correspond to ICIs of 6, 4, and 2.5 ms, respectively. The dotted lines have the optimal slopes of –0.5. Past experience has shown that an ICI of 2.5 ms produces extremely shallow slopes in plots of log DIDT versus log *n*. The essentially parallel relation between the obtained functions in Fig. 8 and the optimal lines implies quite a different relation between discrimination of periodicity pitch and click-rate. Given this, our conjecture that binaural adaptation takes place at or before the CN must be expanded to include the idea of separate, parallel branches or pathways for carrying the information used for lateralization and pitch.

XII. RESTARTING BINAURAL PROCESSING AFTER ADAPTATION

A. The effects on adaptation of a gap in the train

A full description of the workings of sensory adaptation requires explication of how the system recovers from adaptation at the appropriate time. For this reason, Hafter and Buell (1990) presented click trains broken into clusters by temporal gaps, with the idea being to ascertain how long a gap must be in order to allow processing of the part of the train following the gap. An example of the experimental paradigm is described in Fig. 9. Accordingly, performance is first tested with unbroken trains such as those in (a) and (b) using dichotic clicks separated

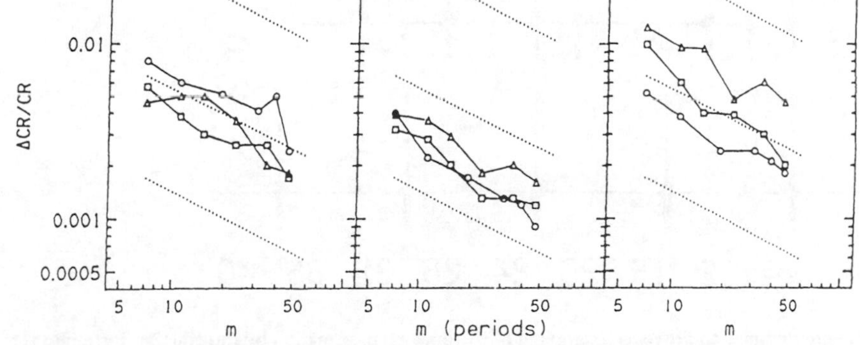

FIG. 8. Log relative thresholds for click rate (CR) plotted versus log*n*. The dotted lines have slopes of –0.5, indicative of optimal processing. The ICIs are 2.5 ms (squares), 4 ms (circles), and 6 ms (circles). [Reproduced from three subjects in Hafter and Richards, 1988.]

by a short ICI, here 2.5 ms. Hypothetical thresholds for these unbroken conditions are plotted in Fig. 10 as solid squares, fitted with a solid line whose shallow slope indicates binaural adaptation. Tests are then conducted with trains divided by temporal gaps as in the example shown as (c), where a single 7.5-ms gap separates a train of 12 clicks into two clusters of 6 clicks each. The logic of this experiment says that if the duration of the total stimulus does not exceed the integration time for detection, a sufficient gap in the center should produce recovery from adaptation, resulting in a threshold based on the two equal clusters. In the example shown, the predicted threshold for two equal clusters of 6 clicks ($DIDT_{2,6}$) would be $1/\sqrt{2}$ times that for an unbroken train of 6 clicks alone; similarly, the threshold for a train of 24 clicks broken into four clusters of 6 clicks ($DIDT_{4,6}$) should be $1/\sqrt{4}$ times that for the unbroken train of 6 clicks. These predictions are shown in Fig. 10 by the open squares labeled (c) and (c'), respectively. The logarithmic form of this relation,

$$\log \Delta ITD_{2,6} = \log \Delta ITD_{1,6} - 0.5 \log 2 \,. \tag{8}$$

shows the optimal slope of –0.5. This is shown by the dotted line drawn through the points for $\Delta ITD_{1,6}$, $\Delta ITD_{2,6}$, and $\Delta ITD_{4,6}$. Note that we expect no further

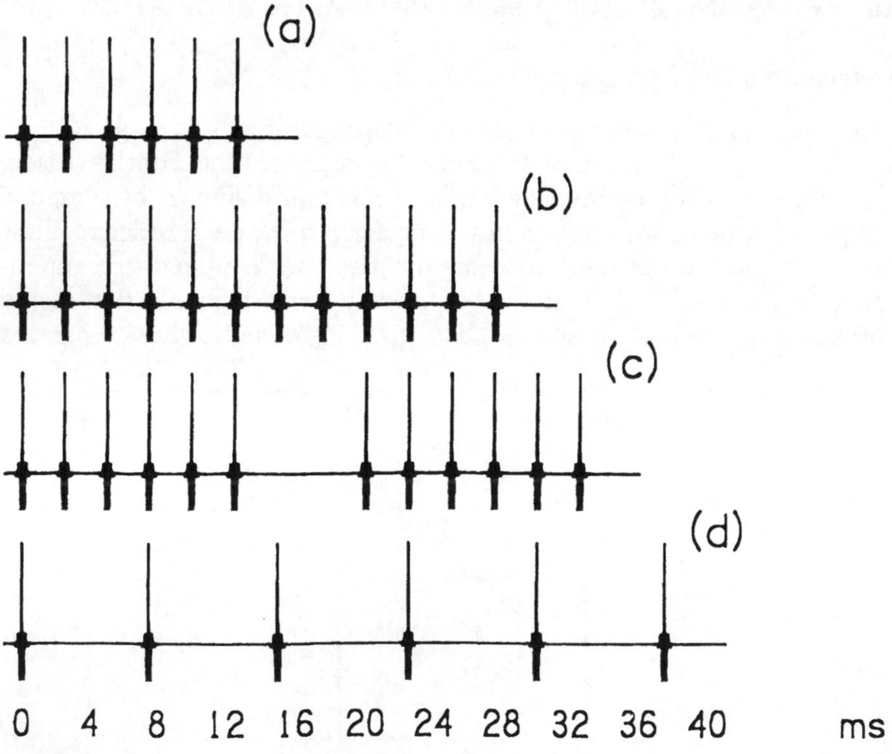

FIG. 9. A paradigm designed to provoke resampling of the binaural information by introducing a gap into the train. The conditions are (a) a train of 6 clicks with an ICI of 2.5 ms, (b) a train of 12 clicks with an ICI of 2.5 ms, (c) a train of 12 such clicks with a gap of 7.5 ms inserted at its center, and (d) a train of 6 clicks with an ICI of 7.5 ms and no gap in its center.

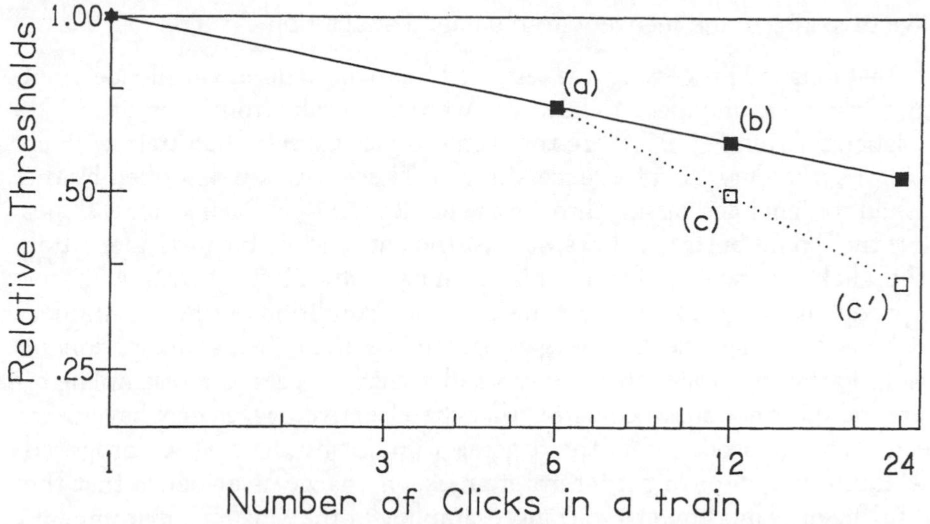

FIG. 10. Hypothetical plot (see text) of log relative threshold versus log$n$ for conditions (a), (b), and (c) described in Fig. 8, as well as an additional point (c¢) indicating thresholds for a train of 24 clicks with an ICI of 2.5 ms and three gaps placed after the 6th, 12th, and 18th click.

reduction with the broken trains as a result of binaural adaptation, because it has already been taken into account in the separate thresholds for the single train of 6 clicks.

Data from an experiment of this kind are shown in Fig. 11 (adapted from Hafter and Buell, 1990). Thresholds obtained with unbroken trains with ICIs of 2.5 ms and n = 6, 12, 24, or 48 are plotted as solid squares and fitted with solid lines. The open diamonds and squares are from trains with either one or three gaps of either 5 or 7.5 ms, respectively; gap size had no significant effect. Dotted lines through the solid squares have the optimal slope of –0.5, and we see that results from the broken trains approach the predicted, optimal values. The magnitudes of the changes in threshold with gaps are summarized in Fig. 12, plotted as the thresholds found for a particular point divided by the predicted (from the fitted solid line) thresholds for the appropriate comparison conditions. The individual bars within groups show results for individual subjects. Unbroken trains are shown by solid bars; trains broken by gaps are shown as open bars. Thus, for example, the leftmost set of solid bars shows the individual thresholds for 6 clicks divided by the thresholds for 12 clicks, whereas the open bars show the thresholds for a train of 6 clicks divided by the threshold for two sets of 6 clicks, separated by a gap. Optimal summation should produce a gain of $\sqrt{2}$ for trains broken by a single gap and $\sqrt{4}$ for trains broken by three gaps. Because of the strong adaptation with a 2.5-ms ICI, the unbroken trains show little improvement with n, but the improvements with trains broken into two clusters are well described by the predicted $\sqrt{2}$; with four clusters the gain was typically less than the optimal $\sqrt{4}$, perhaps showing that binaural adaptation may also act on regular sequences of groups. Nevertheless, the results are close enough to optimal to clearly demonstrate that the binaural system responded to gaps by resampling the ongoing interaural differences.

B. Active triggering of the recovery from binaural adaptation

The fact that binaural processing was restarted following a period of silence is not surprising. What was unexpected, however, were the results from a condition like the one labeled (d) in Fig. 9, where the stimulus was an unbroken train with an ICI of 7.5 ms, the duration of a successful gap. These data are described by the long-dashed straight lines passing through the point for $n = 1$. Their shallow slopes show that the 7.5 ms between clicks was insufficient to avoid binaural adaptation when the click rate was uniform. This seeming contradiction, with a 7.5-ms spacing producing recovery from adaptation in one condition but not in another, suggests that the response to the gap was more than just a dissipation of adaptation. Rather it implies that the gap had actively triggered a resampling of the interaural information. Speculating that the effective trigger may have been the spectral change produced in the ongoing stimulus by the gap, we proposed that the auditory system might interpret any such change as evidence that the signal is sufficiently modified to warrant resampling of the binaural environment. To test this, Hafter and Buell (1990) examined several potential spectral triggers, including brief bursts of noise or tones of various frequencies, and even a "temporal squeeze," in which the separation between clicks at the center was decreased relative to the ongoing ICI. Generally, these other triggers produced results much like those in Figs. 11 and 12, supporting the idea that spectral change promotes active recovery from adaptation.

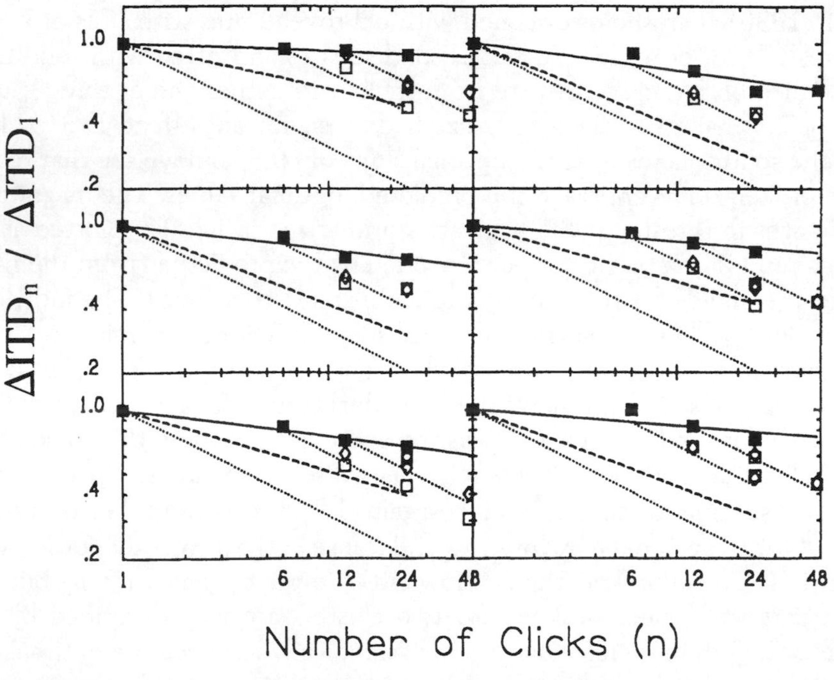

FIG. 11. Results of introducing gaps into trains of $n = 12$, 24, or 48 clicks with ICIs of 2.5 ms. The dotted line has a slope of –0.5, indicative of optimal processing. Solid squares and solid lines show data with unbroken trains, that is, no gaps. Diamonds and open squares show data with gaps of either 5 or 7.5 ms placed so as to divide the trains into equal halves or quarters. The long-dashed lines present results with unbroken trains (no gaps) and an ICI of 7.5 ms. [Reproduced from Hafter and Buell, 1990.]

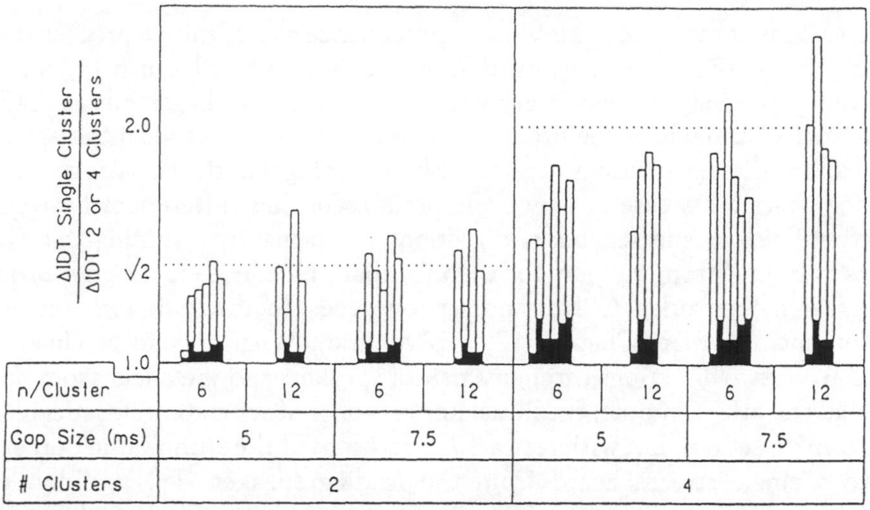

FIG. 12. The gain in performance produced by gaps. Solid bars show the improvements due to doubling or quadrupling unbroken (without gaps) trains. Open bars show the effects of breaking longer trains into two or four equal clusters of 6 or 12 clicks. Dotted lines indicate the appropriate predictions for restarting: $\sqrt{2}$ for doubling and $\sqrt{4}$ for quadrupling. [Reproduced from Hafter and Buell, 1990.]

XIII. BINAURAL ADAPTATION AND PRECEDENCE

At first reading, the loss of post-onset information for binaural detection (Houtgast and Plomp, 1968; Hafter and Dye, 1983; Hafter *et al.*, 1983) seems a good candidate for the mechanism underlying precedence. However, the triggered recovery from adaptation has led us (Hafter *et al.*, 1988) to argue that although binaural adaptation and precedence may interact, they are based on different processes. Imagine hearing a signal in a reverberant environment where stimuli in the primary (direct) and secondary (echoic) pathways overlap in time. If an extraneous signal occurs during the overlap and triggers recovery from adaptation, one expects the binaural system to resample the interaural information. However, the newly sampled interaural differences must reflect levels and phases of the sum of primary and secondary waveforms. Do extraneous signals produce a change in the apparent direction? Although the answer to this is not certain, we think not. That is to say, precedence still seems to hold in multisource environments, showing that resampling does not destroy perception of the directions of the individual sources. In support of this, Blauert, Canévet, and Voinier (1989) reported an inability to produce the "restarting" phenomenon in a direct measure of precedence.

In another vein, binaural adaptation appears to be a peripheral neural process that takes little time to begin and dissipates quickly in response to stimulus change. Conversely, precedence seems to reflect higher order processing whereby echoes are differentiated from new signals by comparisons of both physical and global features of the echo to memories of those features in the stimulus onset. Thus, precedence can act over delays in the tens of milliseconds for complex stimuli such as speech and music (Blauert, 1983), whereas binaural adaptation lasts no more than 12 ms at the most. This view of precedence as a cognitive process sees it as being more similar to sensory dominance (e.g., ventriloquism) than to fundamental processing in the primary sensory system. Accordingly, just as in the case of ventriloquism where the brain reconciles differences between the apparent visual and auditory directions of a source by assuming that the visual is correct, precedence describes a case in which the brain reconciles differences between the apparent primary and secondary directions of a signal by assuming that the primary is correct. Strong support for the idea that precedence is a higher order process is seen in the work of Clifton and her colleagues (for discussion and review, see Clifton and Freyman, Chapter 12, this volume). When a train of clicks is presented from two directions through a pair of speakers and the clicks from one speaker lead the others in time, the initial impression is of separate trains received from the two directions, but with repeated repetitions of the stimuli, the percept fuses into a single stream heard from the leading speaker. This buildup of precedence over time is what one might expect of a cognitive process that uses repeated observations to match physical features in the primary and secondary waveforms. Additional support for the argument that precedence is a higher order process can be found in Zurek (1987) and Blauert (1983).

Finally, with respect to the argument that binaural adaptation is not precedence because it acts at a low level in the auditory system, one should address Lindemann's (1986a, 1986b) model of precedence based on lateral inhibition in a Jeffress (1948) cross-correlator. This view puts precedence at a reasonably peripheral site at the initial level of binaural interaction. However, when the response to increased stimulus rate was tested in Lindemann's model (Lindemann, 1984), there was no evidence of binaural adaptation, again supporting the idea that binaural adaptation is more peripheral and precedence is more central.

XIV. SUMMARY

When interaural differences of time or level are presented at too high a stimulus-rate, their effectiveness for discrimination declines following the stimulus onset. We call this *binaural adaptation*. If rate is defined as the frequency of a pure tone or the envelope frequency of amplitude modulation, the course of binaural adaptation is described by a compressive power function whose exponent is inversely related to rate. This means that each portion of the stimulus is less effective than the one it follows. This adaptation is seen for rates above about 85–100 per second.

In seeking to describe the level of neural processing responsible for binaural adaptation, we have examined the interaction between adaptation and such stimulus factors as its frequency region, the type of its interaural information, and its apparent lateral position. Results suggest that adaptation takes place in CN, prior to the first stages of binaural interaction.

Questions about why peripheral adaptation does not cause the stimulus to fade away or how the system hears the spectral changes needed to trigger recovery from adaptation were addressed by asking listeners to discriminate changes in the periodicity pitch induced by changing the ICI in a train of clicks. The lack of adaptation in that experiment, even for high click rates, suggests the presence of separate channels for the two functions in CN. This is reminiscent of the long held view of visual cortex that there are separate "processing pathways, a 'ventral stream' for object vision and a 'dorsal stream' for spatial vision" (Ungerleider and Haxby, 1994). The dichotomy proposed here for pitch and lateralization suggests a similar organization in audition, albeit at a more peripheral level of processing.

Rapid recovery from binaural adaptation can be triggered in response to a change in the ongoing spectrum. This provokes resampling of the interaural differences, adding further evidence to the conclusion that binaural adaptation is fundamentally different from binaural precedence.

The overall working model from this work is that separate channels in the brain stem divide the auditory signal into two categories: (a) who made the sound, and (b) where did it come from. The former is essentially tonic, providing information for continuous monitoring of the ongoing pitch. The latter is more like a sample-and-hold circuit, keeping primarily onset information about the location of the source unless a change in the ongoing spectrum warrants resampling.

ACKNOWLEDGMENTS

This work was supported by a grant from the National Institute of Deafness and Communication Disorders. Great thanks are due to Eric Jensen and Chris Stecker, who read the manuscript and made many helpful comments.

REFERENCES

Blauert, J. (1983). *Spatial Hearing* (MIT Press, Cambridge, MA).

Blauert, J., Canévet, G., and Voinier, T. (1989). "The precedence effect: No evidence for an 'active' release process found," J. Acoust. Soc. Am. **85**, 2581–2586.

Bregman, A. S. (1990). *Auditory Scene Analysis* (MIT Press, Cambridge, MA).

Buell, T. N., and Hafter, E. R. (1988). "Discrimination of interaural differences of time in the envelopes of high-frequency signals: Integration times," J. Acoust. Soc. Am. **84**, 2063–2066.

Dye, R. H., Jr., and Hafter, E. R. (1984). "The effects of intensity on the detection of interaural differences of time in high-frequency trains of clicks," J. Acoust. Soc. Am. **75**, 1593–1598.

Green, D. M., and Swets, J. A. (1974). *Signal Detection Theory* (Krieger, Huntington, NY).

Hafter, E. R. (1977). "Lateralization model and the role of time-intensity trading in binaural masking: Can the data be explained by a time-only hypothesis?," J. Acoust. Soc. Am. **62**, 633–635.

Hafter, E. R., and Buell, T. N. (1984). "Onset effects in lateralization denote a monaural mechanism," J. Acoust. Soc. Am. **76**, S91(A).

Hafter, E. R., and Buell, T. N. (1990). "Restarting the adapted binaural system," J. Acoust. Soc. Am. **88**, 806–812.

Hafter, E. R., Buell, T. N., and Richards, V. M. (1988). "Onset-coding in lateralization: Its form, site and function," in *Auditory Function: Neurobiological Bases of Hearing*, edited by G. Edelman, W. E. Gall and W. M. Cowan (Wiley, New York), pp. 648–676.

Hafter, E. R., and Dye, R. H., Jr. (1983). "Detection of interaural differences in time in trains of high-frequency clicks as a function of interclick interval and number," J. Acoust. Soc. Am. **73**, 644–651.

Hafter, E. R., Dye, R. H., and Gilkey, R. H. (1979). "Lateralization of tonal signals which have neither onsets nor offsets," J. Acoust. Soc. Am. **65**, 471–477.

Hafter, E. R., Dye, R. H., Jr., and Nuetzel, J. M. (1980). "Lateralization of high-frequency stimuli on the basis of time and intensity," in *Psychological, Physiological and Behavioral Studies of Hearing*, edited by G. van den Brink and F. A. Bilsen (Delft University Press, Delft, Holland), pp. 394–401.

Hafter, E. R., Dye, R. H., Jr., and Wenzel, E. (1983). "Detection of interaural differences in intensity in trains of high-frequency clicks as a function of interclick interval and number," J. Acoust. Soc. Am. **73**, 1708–1713.

Hafter, E. R., Dye, R. H., Jr., Wenzel, E., and Knecht, K. (1990). "The combination of interaural time and intensity in the lateralization of high-frequency complex signals," J. Acoust. Soc. Am. **87**, 1702–1708.

Hafter, E. R., and Richards, V. M. (**1988**). "Discrimination of the rate of filtered impulses," Percept. Psychophys. **43**, 405–414.

Hafter, E. R., Saberi, K., Jensen, E. R., and Briolle, F. (**1991**). "Localization in an echoic environment," in *Auditory Physiology and Perception*, edited by Y. Cazals, L. Demany, and K. Horner (Pergamon, Oxford), pp. 555–561.

Hafter, E. R., and Wenzel, E. (**1983**). "Lateralization of transients presented at high rates: site of the saturation effect," in *Hearing—Physiological Basis and Psychophysics*, edited by R. Klinke and R. Hartmann (Springer-Verlag, Berlin-Heidelberg, West Germany), pp. 202–208.

Henning, G. B. (**1974**). "Detectability of interaural delay in high-frequency complex waveforms," J. Acoust. Soc. Am. **55**, 84–90.

Houtgast, T., and Plomp, R. (**1968**). "Lateralization threshold of a signal in noise," J. Acoust. Soc. Am. **44**, 807–812.

Jeffress, L. A. (**1948**). "A place mechanism of sound localization," J. Comp. Physiol. Psych. **41**, 35–39.

Kiang, N. Y. S., Watanabe, T., Thomas, E. C., and Clark, L. F. (**1965**). "Discharge patterns of single fibers in the cat's auditory nerve," Research monograph 35 (MIT Press, Cambridge, MA).

Lindemann, W. (**1984**). Informal experiments based on calculations of the Lindemann model, conducted at the University of the Ruhr in conjunction with E. R. Hafter.

Lindemann, W. (**1986a**). "Extension of a binaural cross-correlation model by contralateral inhibition. I. Simulation of lateralization for stationary signals," J. Acoust. Soc. Am. **80**, 1608–1622.

Lindemann, W. (**1986b**). "Extension of a binaural cross-correlation model by contralateral inhibition. II. The law of the first wavefront," J. Acoust. Soc. Am. **80**, 1623–1630.

Lindsay, P. H., Taylor, M. M., and Forbes, S. M. (**1968**). "Attention and multidimensional discrimination," Percept. Psychophys. **4**, 113–117.

McFadden, D., and Pasanen, E. G. (**1976**). "Lateralization at high frequencies based on interaural time differences," J. Acoust. Soc. Am. **59**, 634–639.

Moushegian, G. A., Rupert, A. L., and Gidda, J. S. (**1975**). "Functional characteristics of superior olivary neurons to binaural stimuli," J. Neurophys. **38**, 1037–1048.

Nuetzel, J. M., and Hafter, E. R. (**1976**). "Lateralization of complex waveforms: effects of fine structure, amplitude and duration," J. Acoust. Soc. Am. **62**, 1339–1346.

Nuetzel, J. M., and Hafter, E. R. (**1981**). "Discrimination of complex waveforms: spectral effects," J. Acoust. Soc. Am. **69**, 1112–1118.

Rayleigh, Lord (J. W. Strutt, 3rd Baron of Rayleigh) (**1907**). "On our perception of sound direction," Philos. Mag. **13**, 214–232.

Ricard, G. L., and Hafter, E. R. (**1973**). "Detection of interaural time differences in short-duration-low-frequency tones," J. Acoust. Soc. Am. **53**, 335(A).

Saberi, K., and Perrott, D. R. (**1990**). "Lateralization thresholds obtained under conditions in which the precedence effect is assumed to operate," J. Acoust. Soc. Am. **87**, 1732–1737.

Smith, R. L., and Zwislocki, J. J. (**1975**). "Short-term adaptation and incremental responses of single auditory-nerve fibers," Biological Cybernetics **17**, 169–182.

Trahiotis, C., and Stern, R. M. (**1989**). "Lateralization of bands of noise: effects of bandwidth and differences of interaural time and phase," J. Acoust. Soc. Am. **86**, 1285–1293.

Ungerleider, L. G., and Haxby, J. V. (**1994**). "'What' and 'where' in the human brain," Curr. Opin. Neurobiol. **4**, 157–165.

Wallach, H., Newman, E. B., and Rosenzweig, M. R. (**1949**). "The precedence effect in sound localization," Am. J. Psychol. **52**, 315–336.

Wenzel, E. (**1984**). "Lateralization of high-frequency clicks based on interaural time: Additivity of information across frequency," Unpublished doctoral dissertation, University of California, Berkeley.

Wenzel, E., and Hafter, E. R. (**1983**). "Lateralization of clicks based on interaural time: additivity of information across frequency," J. Acoust. Soc. Am. **74**, S85(A).

Wightman, F. L., and Kistler, D. J. (**1992**). "The dominant role of low-frequency interaural time differences in sound localization," J. Acoust. Soc. Am. **91**, 1648–1661.

Yost, W. A., and Hafter, E. R. (**1987**). "Lateralization," in *Directional Hearing*, edited by W. Yost and G. Gourevitch (Springer-Verlag, New York), pp. 49–84.

Zurek, P. M. (**1987**). "The precedence effect," in *Directional Hearing*, edited by W. A. Yost and G. Gourevitch (Springer-Verlag, New York), pp. 85–105.

Chapter 12

The Precedence Effect: Beyond Echo Suppression

Rachel K. Clifton
University of Massachusetts

Richard L. Freyman
University of Massachusetts

(Received January 1994; revised December 1994)

Echo threshold is known to be affected by qualities of sound such as duration and onset rise time. We know that clicks or brief noise bursts have lower echo thresholds than complex sounds such as speech or music. Recently a series of studies in our laboratory has shown that echo threshold (defined as the shortest delay at which the echo is perceived as a separate sound at its location) is also affected by ongoing stimulation. That is, echo threshold changes from moment to moment as a function of the auditory context. Echo threshold can be either lowered or raised, depending on prior stimulation heard by the listener. Lower thresholds can be induced by rapidly switching the location of lead and lag sounds, and by changes in the echo that signify an unusual change in room acoustics. Higher thresholds can be induced by repeating the same lead–lag pairs for several presentations. Several experiments are described in which echo thresholds shifted as a function of ongoing stimulation. We interpret these results in terms of listeners' changing expectations about echoes. It is proposed that echoes provide information about room acoustics, which the listener picks up during the ongoing sound and uses to form expectations about what will be heard. These expectations subsequently affect echo threshold.

INTRODUCTION

Just a few years ago the precedence effect seemed like a straightforward auditory phenomenon based on hard-wired echo suppression, but data presented in this chapter compel us to entertain the possibility that listeners' expectations influence this perceptual process. The precedence effect can be simply described and is easily produced in any laboratory equipped with sound-generating and -controlling devices. To produce the effect one sets up two loudspeakers with one output leading the other by several milliseconds. Listeners report hearing one sound, not two, with the source located at the leading site. At short delays between the original sound and the delayed sound, the latter exerts little directional influence on the perceived location of the original sound. Delayed sounds produced in the laboratory can be used to simulate the reflections that occur in an ordinary room caused by sound bouncing off the floor, ceiling, walls, and objects in the room. These reflections "color" the original sound and reinforce its loudness, but are not recognized by the listener as separate sounds. At long delays echoes are perceived as separate sounds at their true locations. Throughout this chapter we use the term *echo suppression* to refer to the listener's failure to hear the echo as a separate auditory event at its true location. We are following Blauert's definition (1983, pp. 224–225) of echo threshold as the shortest delay between lead and lag onsets at which the echo is perceived as a separate sound, no longer fused with the original sound. When delays are below echo threshold the echo continues to influence the quality and timbre of the sound, so it is incorrect to think that echo suppression means the echo is not "heard."

Until about a decade ago the status of the precedence effect was that of a phenomenon discovered back in the 19th century that had received sporadic flurries of interest now and then, resulting in a modest literature. Reviews of the literature appeared, starting with Gardner (1968), followed by Mills (1972) and Green (1976), with the most extensive consideration by Blauert (1983). The precedence effect was viewed primarily as the result of a "handy" echo suppression mechanism, an inhibitory process that enabled the listener to sort out the true sound source from auditory chaos. The most recent literature review by Zurek (1987) described the various methods of studying the precedence effect and summarized results up through the mid-1980s. At that time, Zurek (1987) noted that the precedence effect "has not yet been woven into existing theories of binaural hearing." This is still true today. Early work concentrated mostly on the effect of the time delay between onsets and relative intensity of lead and lag sounds as the critical variables. This work supported the conceptualization of the precedence effect as mechanistic and dependent on stimulus properties alone. Little or no consideration was given as to how listeners' expectations or experiences with echoes might alter their perception (including the suppression) of echoes. In other words, the precedence effect was investigated with the assumption that the listener was a passive receiver.

Our view of the precedence effect goes beyond mechanistic echo suppression to emphasize the active role of perceptual processes in determining how sound is localized. Several researchers have hinted about cognitive aspects of the precedence effect, but without spelling this out in detail. The first hint came from Thurlow and Parks (1961) in an investigation of echo thresholds using click trains. In a postsession interview many subjects reported that echo suppression took 1 or 2 s to "build up." Thurlow and Parks (1961) speculated that listeners' changing thresholds were due to "a central build-up of an inhibitory effect" (p. 11). Hafter, Buell, and Richards (1988) proposed that the precedence effect is "a case of sensory rivalry" (p. 670). Echoes present the listener with conflicting information about a sound's direction, a conflict that is usually resolved in favor of the first arriving wavefront. They made an analogy between precedence and ventriloquism, with echoes being "captured" at the leading sound's location just as the voice gets captured by vision in ventriloquism. Rakerd and Hartmann (1985) and Hartmann and Rakerd (1989) proposed a "plausibility hypothesis" that relied on subjects' evaluation of cues to explain results of time–intensity trade experiments. Their subjects appeared to weight interaural time cues less when they were extreme values, that is, beyond the range that would be plausible for their head size. In such cases listeners weighted interaural intensity cues more heavily in their localization judgments, more or less discounting the "implausible" interaural time differences (ITDs).

Blauert and Col (1992) tried several manipulations of the precedence effect, such as suddenly switching the lead and lag sound locations or injecting a click from a single loudspeaker into a train of precedence-effect clicks (i.e., lead–lag click pairs). They concluded that, in addition to the peripheral signal processing involved in the precedence effect, listeners also employ "more central, top-down activities" to evaluate the information about reflections. They proposed a "pattern recognition process" as a reasonable possibility, which would enable the suppression of irrelevant attributes. Perrott and colleagues (Perrott, Strybel, and Manligas, 1987; Perrott, Marlborough, Merrill, and Strybel, 1989) conducted several experiments that are directly relevant. They found that listeners were sensitive to information about spatial location in echoes even when the echoes were below threshold. In these experiments the lead sound was from the center speaker and the lag could be either to the right or left of center. The sound's apparent location was pulled toward the lag sound's location and the listener could detect the switch in locations of the lag sound. Perrott *et al.* (1989) argued that there is no such thing as echo suppression because even when listeners cannot "hear" the echo, they remain sensitive to the directional information contained in the sound. Saberi and Perrott (1990) claimed that the precedence effect could be "unlearned," based on the experience of their highly practiced listeners after hours in the sound booth. They concluded that the information in the echo is always available to the listener, but that the strength of the precedence effect is related to the nervous system's organization of that information. Thus, if the task is to detect a change in the echo, the listener can eventually learn to pay attention to that auditory information. Blauert and Col (1992) also noted the effects of laboratory experience on listeners, in that echoes became more audible when subjects were instructed to listen selectively to the reflected sound. All of these observations point to the possibility that listeners' perception of echoes shift as a function of their experience or task instructions. There are short-term changes that can occur within a single brief trial, and there are long-term changes that persist when a subject becomes highly practiced at discriminating echoes. These observations challenge the view that the precedence effect is strictly hard-wired and rests on simple inhibition of information contained in the delayed sounds.

I. HOW TO PRODUCE A CHANGE IN ECHO THRESHOLD

Our research on this topic began with the observation that if the output of lead and lag loudspeakers was suddenly switched, echo suppression was released so that the listener heard sound from both locations (Clifton, 1987). This breakdown in suppression was short-lived, however, lasting only a few seconds until once again sound was localized solely at the leading loudspeaker. The stimulus in this study was a click train, and fast click rates led to faster reinstatement of suppression than slower rates. These observations have significant implications for understanding how processes underlying the precedence effect works. First, the breakdown in echo suppression following a switch in location suggests that coding of the echo's location relative to the listener and/or to the lead sound's location is involved in establishing echo threshold. Second, the gradual reinstatement of echo suppression implies that repeated exposure to echoes builds up a model of the echo as a reflection of the original sound as opposed to a new sound. Following the switch in lead and lag locations, the nervous system appears to momentarily relax echo suppression, gather more information, then reestablish suppression in light of incoming information. We feel that exploration of the conditions under which echo suppression changes will provide new insights into how the brain processes auditory information to construct our perception of the auditory environment.

The buildup in echo suppression that takes place during an ongoing train of clicks or noise bursts has been the focus of our research. We have investigated several variables of the train itself, including delay between lead and lag loudspeaker onsets, click rate, number of clicks, total duration of click train, presence or absence of the echo during the train, and variations of the sound within the train. We have developed the hypothesis that listeners build up certain expectations about what "reasonable" echoes are on the basis of information in the ongoing train. Disconfirmation of expectations leads to a breakdown or lowering of echo threshold. Several experiments are described that detail how listeners' expectations can be manipulated.

First, let us describe what the listener does in our experimental situation. The listener sits in the center of an anechoic chamber with loudspeakers, one located to the left and one located to the right. A train of identical clicks or noise bursts comes from both loudspeakers, and the delay between speaker onsets is manipulated. If the delay is short (e.g., 2 ms), the listener will localize sound from the leading loudspeaker only. If the delay is long, above echo threshold (e.g., 15 ms), the listener will localize sound from both loudspeakers throughout the train. However, if the delay is close to threshold (e.g., 6–10 ms), the listener will initially localize sound from both lead and lag loudspeakers, but as the train progresses the sound becomes localized solely at the leading loudspeaker. The lagging sound still exerts an effect on timbre and loudness, but it is no longer localized as a separate sound at its location. We think the echo threshold or breakdown point is important because it reflects a decision-making process. By measuring the shift in echo threshold as a function of ongoing stimulation we can quantify this decision process.

We have assessed listeners' perception of echoes in two ways. In Clifton (1987) and Clifton and Freyman (1989), listeners depressed a key whenever they heard sound localized at the lagging loudspeaker during the click train. Although this response worked well, subjects had to make continual decisions throughout the trial about the presence or absence of an echo. In later experiments (Freyman, Clifton, and Litovsky, 1991) we simplified the task such that the response required from the subject on each trial was more clearly delineated. Subjects listened to a click train and made a decision concerning the presence or absence of an echo only at the end, for the final click pair or *test click*, as we termed it. The test click was demarcated from the train by a brief (750 ms) pause. For comparison we presented an isolated click pair, and the shift in threshold was measured by the extent to which echo threshold differed for the isolated click pair versus that same click pair preceded by a click train. This methodology was adapted from a report by Wolf (1988), and has allowed us to assess the effect of many variables on echo threshold. Finally, in some experiments we have made the listener's task more objective by setting up an array of loudspeakers with the lead at 45° on the listener's left, and three lag loudspeakers at 35°, 45°, and 55° on the right (see Fig. 1). During the train the delayed sound comes from the middle lag loudspeaker; then during the test stimulus, it switches right or left. The listener presses either the right or the left button to indicate the perceived location of the lag sound after the switch. The rationale behind this task is that if subjects can hear the echo, they can localize it, but if it is below echo threshold they will be at chance in selecting the lag sound's location.

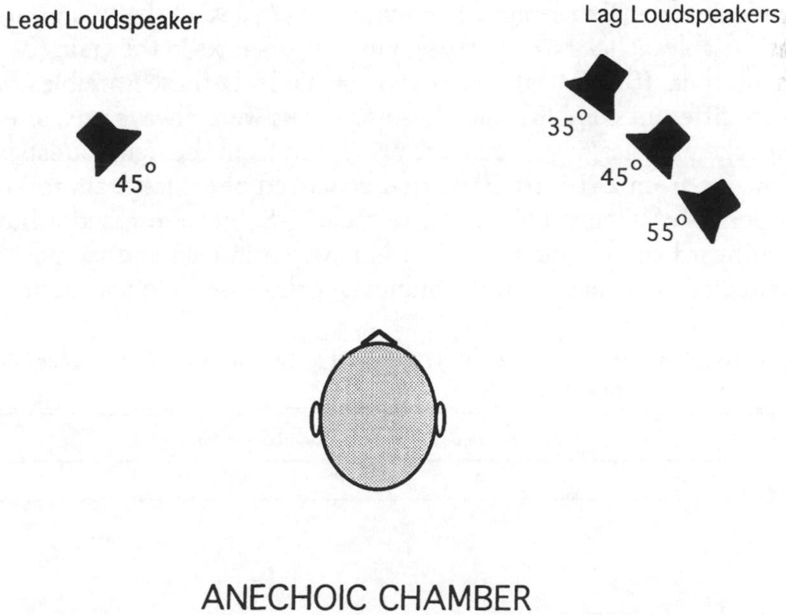

FIG. 1. Schematic display of the loudspeaker arrangement in the anechoic chamber.

A. Effect of delay, click rate, and switch in lead-lag location on echo threshold

Clifton and Freyman (1989) investigated how delay and click rate would affect echo threshold after a switch in location of the leading and lagging sounds. Subjects listened to a click train in which lead and lag sound positions were switched at some point in the train, followed by 12 s of the train continuing in the new locations. Echo perceptibility was assessed following the switch by having subjects hold down a button as long as they heard an echo at the lagging loudspeaker. We found that the "fade out" of the echo after the switch was a function of the delay. If the delay between leading and lagging clicks was short (4 ms or less), then subjects reported hearing the echo for only 1 or 2 s; if the delay was long (5–9 ms) they heard the echo up to 5 or 6 s. However, the effect of delay was complicated by click rate. Click trains were presented at three rates: 1/s, 2/s, and 4/s. The echo faded out after the switch as a function of rate, with the slowest rate resulting in the perception of echoes for as long as 10 s. In this study click rate was confounded with number of clicks and click train duration, so it was unclear what caused the effect. Subjects also reported hearing the echo at the beginning of the train, with the sound fading before the switch reinstated it; thus, buildup occurred anytime that a repeating train was presented. This finding enabled us to design studies to investigate changes in echo threshold without having to switch the location of lead and lag sounds; it was sufficient to present a train and then change some aspect of the train that was hypothesized to affect echo threshold.

B. Effect of click rate versus number of clicks in the train

In order to explicate the critical variable that would most influence echo threshold, we designed a study (Experiment 1, Freyman *et al.*, 1991) that manipulated three relevant variables: click rate (1–16/s), number of clicks in the train (3–17), and duration of train (0.5–8.0 s). As shown in Table I, these variables were presented in 16 different combinations. Leading clicks were always presented to the left loudspeaker, and lagging clicks were presented from the right loudspeaker with delays ranging from 2–14 ms. Each trial consisted of a click train followed by a 750-ms period of silence before the test click. Subjects pressed a button whenever they heard the lagging test click. No switch in lead and lag positions during the train was made in this study. Subjects' echo threshold was defined as

TABLE I. Stimulus conditions in Freyman *et al.* (1991). Values in the body of the table are the corresponding click train durations in seconds.

	Number of clicks in conditioning train			
Rate (clicks/s)	3	5	9	17
1	2	4	8	—
2	1	2	4	8
4	0.5	1	2	4
8	—	0.5	1	2
16	—	—	0.5	1

the delay between leading and lagging click onsets at which the echo was reported on 50% of trials. Four subjects completed the detailed testing on 16 combinations of number, rate, and duration, as well as isolated click pairs. The major shift in echo threshold took place within the initial 7–9 clicks in the train, with some additional elevation in threshold out to 17 clicks. All subjects were consistent in that the number of clicks in the preceding train was the most critical variable influencing the magnitude of the shift in echo threshold. Click rate and duration of the train had little influence independent of number of clicks (see Figs. 2 and 3). This means that at very fast rates the subject is not aware of the "buildup," because it occurs very quickly. At slow rates (1/s) subjects can at first hear the lagging click, but then it appears to "fade away." We ran an additional condition of a very fast rate (50/s) lasting 0.5 s with the same result: increased echo threshold compared to an isolated click pair. Thus, even very brief click trains with fast rates produced a buildup in echo suppression. Most complex sounds such as speech or noise contain multiple rapid impulses, so that buildup in echo suppression occurs so quickly as not to be noticeable to the listener. Only impulses that are spread out over time, as in a slow click train, lead to the sensation of an echo, present at first, that fades with repetition.

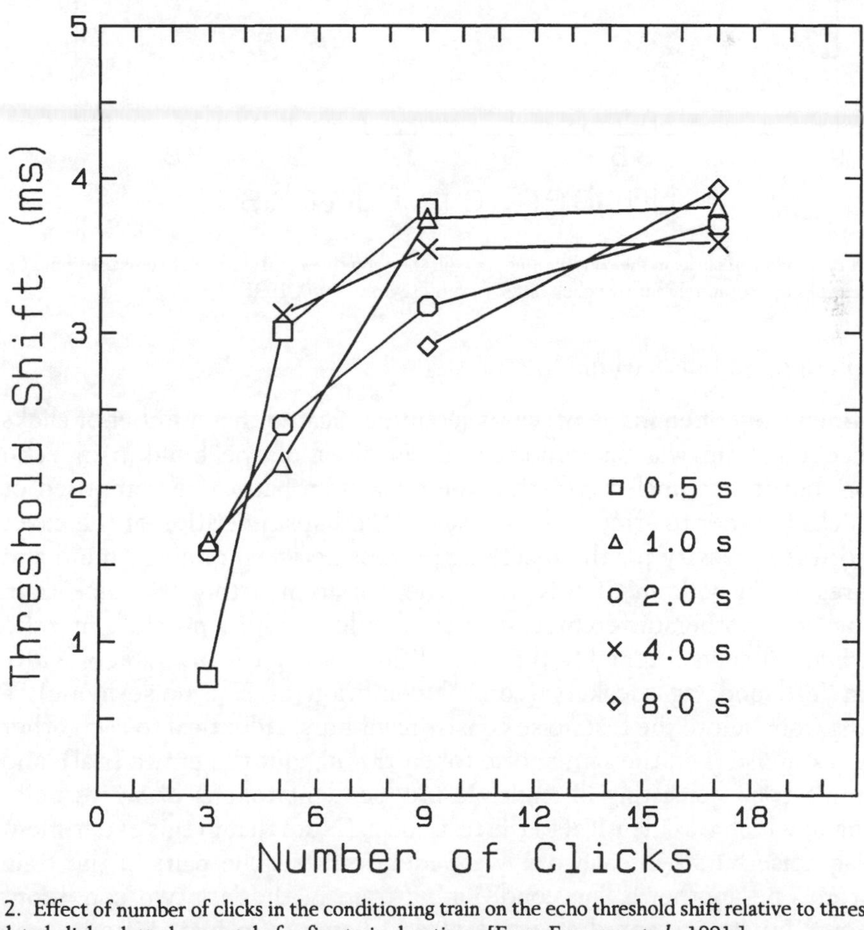

FIG. 2. Effect of number of clicks in the conditioning train on the echo threshold shift relative to threshold for an isolated click, plotted separately for five train durations. [From Freyman *et al.*, 1991.]

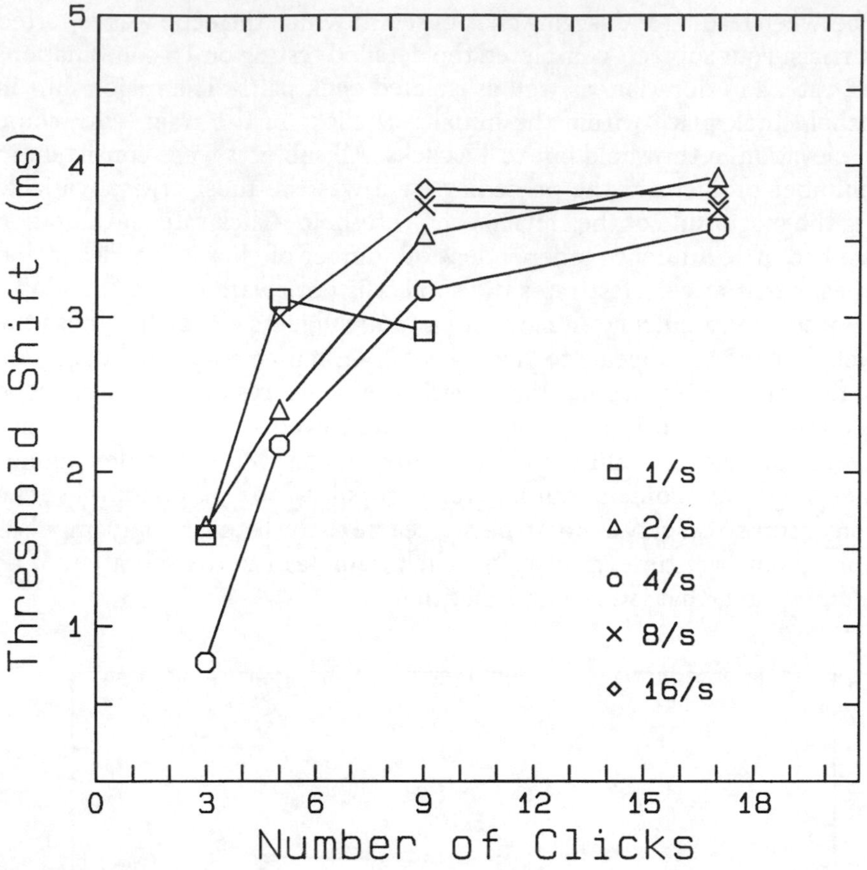

FIG. 3. Effect of number of clicks in the conditioning train on the echo threshold shift relative to threshold for an isolated click, plotted separately for five click rates. [From Freyman *et al.*, 1991.]

C. Variation of noise bursts within the train

The experiment described in the previous section indicated that number of clicks in the preceding train was an important determiner of the buildup of echo suppression, but it was unclear whether the click train had to be composed of identical clicks in order to affect echo threshold. Perhaps repetition of the exact same sound was necessary for the matching process between original sound and echo that results in buildup. If this were true, variation within the click train followed by yet another different test click should produce no shift in echo threshold. Four subjects listened to three conditions: a single 4-ms burst of white noise from lead and lag speakers (control condition of test noise alone); a conditioning train before the test noise consisting of bursts identical to each other and to the test noise (i.e., the same noise token throughout the entire trial); and a conditioning train consisting of multiple independent tokens of white noise bursts, none of which was identical to the test noise. (Note that in this experiment lead and lag noise bursts in each pair were identical, but the pairs in the train differed from one another.) The conditioning train in the last two conditions consisted of 9 bursts presented at a rate of 4/s. Large (3–6 ms) shifts in echo threshold for the test noise were observed for both conditioning trains, compared to the isolated noise burst. Negligible differences were found between the results for the single- and multiple-token noise train conditions, suggesting that stimuli during the train need not be exact replicas of each other or the test stimulus in order for echo threshold to be elevated (Experiment 2, Freyman *et al.*, 1991).

D. Presence of the echo during the train affects echo threshold

A third experiment investigated whether it was necessary for the echo click to be present during the click train (Experiment 3, Freyman *et al.*, 1991). That is, must stimuli be presented from both lead and lag loudspeakers during the conditioning train in order to produce a shift in echo threshold? This experiment began to address the issue of precisely what produces the change in echo suppression observed during the click train. Four experimental conditions were run using the 4-ms multiple-token white noise stimuli from the previous experiment, with the 4/s rate, and a test noise burst from both loudspeakers on which subjects based their decision concerning the echo. Preceding the test noise burst, subjects were presented with:

1. Lead-only condition, in which only the left leading loudspeaker was active during the conditioning train.
2. Lag-only condition, in which only the right lagging loudspeaker was active.
3. Precedence-effect condition, in which both lead and lag were presented during the train.
4. Control condition (NC), where the test noise burst was presented without a conditioning train preceding it.

For this study we developed the more objective methodology in which listeners must judge whether the echo shifted right or left during the test stimulus. When listeners report whether or not they perceive an echo from the lagging loudspeaker, the task is subjective because there is no way to check their answer: The lagging sound is actually present on every trial. Incorporating trials with no lagging noise does not provide a solution because these trials are easily distinguishable due to qualitative changes in the perception of the leading noise when "fused" with the lagging noise, as described earlier. The subjective task poses a particular problem when detectability of the echo is considerably different during the noise train than during the test noise (as in the Lead-only and Lag-only conditions, where the train has only one loudspeaker active but the test noise has both). We were concerned that subjects, faced with these qualitatively different stimuli, would have difficulty maintaining a constant criterion for reporting the presence or absence of echoes across the four conditions. To circumvent this potential criterion problem, subjects chose which of two loudspeakers emitted the echo on the test burst, instead of reporting whether or not they heard an echo. The experimental set-up was that shown in Fig. 1. For the Lead-only condition the signal during the train was presented from the leading loudspeaker, and for the Lag-only condition from the center (45°) lag loudspeaker. For the Precedence-effect condition, the signals during the train were presented from the lead loudspeaker on the left and the center lag loudspeaker at 45° on the right. During the test noise, the lead signal was presented from the left loudspeaker as always, and the lag signal was presented from either the 35° or 55° lag loudspeaker. The subject's task was to press a left or right button to indicate whether the lag sound originated from the left or right lagging loudspeaker.

Figure 4 displays echo thresholds for the four discrimination conditions. Thresholds were derived from the psychometric functions by interpolating to find the delay corresponding to a *d*' of 1.5. The Lead-only condition produced the lowest thresholds (6.8 ms), followed by Lag-only (9.4 ms), NC isolated click (11.2 ms), and Precedence-effect (14.9 ms). The fact that the Precedence-effect threshold was higher than the NC threshold for every subject indicated that the buildup of echo suppression during a stimulus train, observed previously with the subjective task, was also measurable with the discrimination paradigm. The most exciting finding was that the Lead- and Lag-only conditions produced no build-up in echo threshold. Clearly, the echo must be present during the conditioning train in order to produce the increased threshold. If anything, trains coming from only one loudspeaker appeared to enhance discrimination performance, particularly for the Lead-only condition. Subjects reported that the echo seemed to "pop out" after the click train from a single loudspeaker.

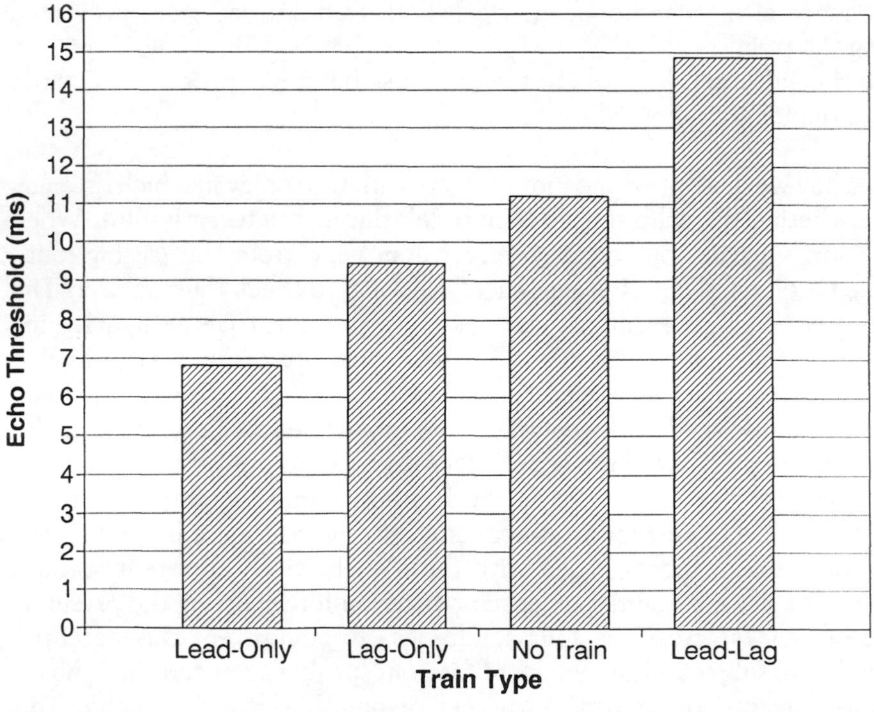

FIG. 4. Echo thresholds, defined as the delay required for a *d*' of 1.5 on the lag loudspeaker discrimination task. The Lead-only and Lag-only conditions had a preceding noise train from only the leading or lagging loudspeaker, respectively; the Precedence-effect condition had a train from both leading and lagging loudspeakers; and the NC condition presented the test noise with no preceding train. [After Freyman *et al.*, 1991.]

What would happen if the echo were present intermittently during the click train? Blauert and Col (1992) tried such a manipulation with interesting results. They presented click trains in which the echoes were switched off, either randomly or regularly. These interruptions in the lag sound caused subsequent echoes to become more audible. This finding is similar to our results with echoless trains, which contrasted highly with the test burst containing an echo. In both cases the absence of the echo appeared to lower inhibition, resulting in lower echo thresholds when an echo was subsequently presented. In a related study Blauert and Col (1992) extended the switch manipulation of Clifton (1987) by switching lead and lag locations not once, but continually during the train. That is, a train of clicks was presented in which the location of lead and lag clicks reversed after each click pair. Would such alternation in echo location prevent echo suppression? At first subjects heard both the lead and lag sounds following each switch, but after several repetitions they heard only the lead sound jumping back and forth. Furthermore, as subjects experienced this moving sound source repeatedly, the time taken to suppress the echo shortened. The initial presentation of the oscillating sounds produced the longest period of audible echoes. These results support the view that (1) "unexpected" echoes tend to have lower echo thresholds, and (2) listeners' perceptions change as they experience new lead–lag combinations. In effect, listeners appear to use the flow of auditory information to sort out their perceptual world. In Bregman's terms they engage in "auditory scene analysis" in an effort to make sense of the myriad of auditory cues (Bregman, 1990).

To summarize thus far, redundant information in the form of an ongoing train appears to raise echo threshold by several milliseconds (Clifton and Freyman, 1989; Freyman *et al.*, 1991; Thurlow and Parks, 1961). Threshold is raised as a direct function of the number of stimulus bursts in the train (Freyman *et al.*, 1991); asymptote is reached fairly quickly (within 9 to 12 bursts), suggesting that a finite amount of incoming information is sufficient to stabilize perception. Rate of bursts does not appear to affect buildup in echo threshold, at least over the range of rates studied (1/s–50/s). When new information arrives in the form of unexpected echoes, the system seems to reset echo threshold back to the unadapted level. New information can be in the form of an echo in a train that previously had no echo (Freyman *et al.*, 1991), a sudden switch in location of the lead–lag stimuli (Blauert and Col, 1992; Clifton, 1987), and occasional omission of the echo in an ongoing train (Blauert and Col, 1992). The question is: What constitutes new information and what constitutes redundant information? Clifton, Freyman, Litovsky, and McCall (1994) proposed the following hypothesis: *Changes in echoes that are apt to be experienced in everyday life will not disrupt echo suppression, but changes that are improbable will disrupt the process.* This hypothesis assumes that listeners have expectations about what "reasonable" echoes would be in a particular situation; these expectations are built up from moment to moment as auditory information comes in. As noted before, this assumes that listeners have expectations about what "reasonable" echoes are. When we present a stimulus train to the listener, we are building up expectations about the characteristics of echoes in that situation. If an "unexpected" echo arrives, then the buildup in echo suppression collapses, so that echo threshold returns to an unadapted level. As adults we have had experiences in a wide variety of acoustic environments. This backlog of experience affects our interpretation of the transitory auditory information specific to the current ongoing acoustic environment. The acoustic characteristics of delayed sounds inform the listener about the reflecting surfaces in the room; this is a rapid, automatic, and unconscious process.

To test this hypothesis we manipulated echoes in four ways, two of which were expected to disrupt echo suppression and two of which were not expected to. All manipulations involved changes in lead–lag combinations that presented new information, but only information relevant to reflecting surfaces was expected to affect echo threshold.

E. Changes between train and test stimuli that lower echo threshold: Delay

In the first experiment (see Clifton *et al.*, 1994, for details) we presented the stimulus train with one delay between lead–lag pairs; then on the test burst we either lengthened or shortened the delay. This manipulation simulates a sudden change in the distance of reflecting surface, either away from the listener (if the delay is lengthened) or toward the listener (if the delay is shortened).

We expected delay between lead and lag to be a critical acoustic parameter because it carries important information about the spatial location of the reflecting surface. A variation in delay between train and test noise bursts would indicate that the reflecting surface had suddenly changed in distance from the listener. This should break any echo suppression built up during the ongoing train.

The loudspeaker array was as shown in Fig. 1, and the subjects' task was as described previously, with direction of the test burst echo moving left or right after the train. Each subject was screened for echo threshold on a single isolated test noise, then run with delays that surrounded a delay slightly above the isolated echo threshold. For example, if a subject's echo threshold for a single test noise pair was 6 ms, then 7 ms was chosen for the test noise delay. This was kept constant through the rest of the session, and the delay of the conditioning train was made longer and shorter in different blocks of trials.

The results for this study are shown in Fig. 5. Each subject's discrimination of the test noise echo in isolation is indicated by the open diamond. The buildup in echo threshold is shown by the lower d' for the test noise echo at the same delay when preceded by a train at the same delay. This data point is located directly below the diamond in the solid curve. We expected V-shaped functions in the d' values, centered at this delay where preceding train and test noise delays were matched. Matching delays would produce the most difficult discrimination because any buildup during the train would be maintained by the identical test noise delay. As the preceding delay differed from the test delay, discrimination should be easier (and d' higher) if delay is being encoded as an important parameter of the echo to be suppressed. This hypothesis was upheld in that a shift

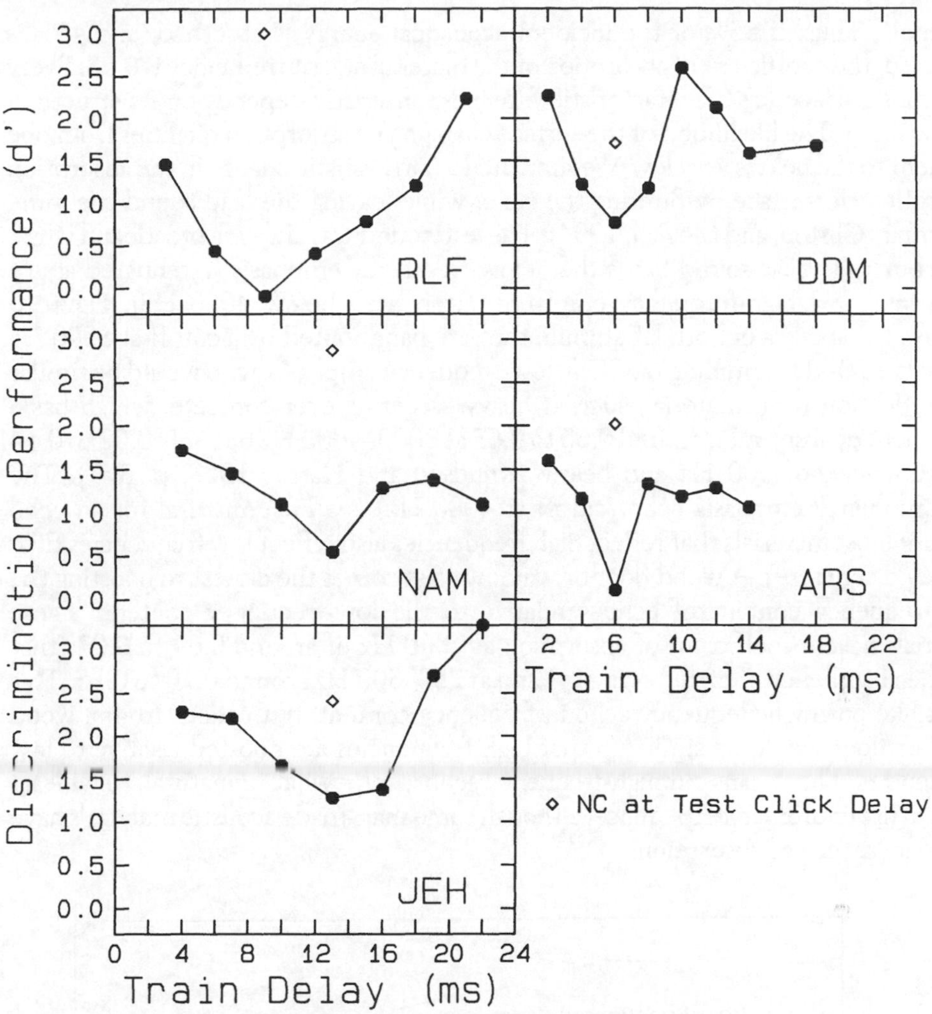

FIG. 5. Performance of five subjects on a task where delay of the test noise burst was held constant and delay of the preceding train of noise bursts was varied. Discriminability of the echo when not preceded by the train is indicated by the isolated open diamond. Immediately below each diamond is the condition in which a train of the same delay as the test bursts preceded it. Other points on the line are conditions when the train delay was either shorter or longer than the test burst delay. [From Clifton *et al.*, 1994.]

in delay, which simulates the reflecting surface jumping either toward or away from the subject, diffused the echo suppression that had developed during the conditioning train.

F. Changes between train and test stimuli that lower echo threshold: Filtering characteristics of the reflecting surface

Another change that would produce an "improbable" echo is a change in the frequency content of the echo that would signify that the coefficient of absorption of the reflecting surface had changed. The coefficient of absorption at a particular frequency is defined by Knudsen and Harris (1978, p. 77) as "the fractional part of the energy of an incident sound wave that is absorbed (not reflected) by the material." Thus, if 55% of the incident acoustical energy is absorbed, and 45% is reflected, the coefficient of absorption of the material at that frequency is 0.55. Every reflecting surface has a characteristic filter response that depends on its structural composition. The likelihood of the surface changing its absorption qualities from one moment to the next is very low. We simulated a fairly drastic change in the absorption of a reflective surface by filtering the echo, while leaving the lead sound the same (Freyman, Clifton, and McCall, 1994). The lead sound was always a broadband white noise burst. The lag sound had either a low-frequency emphasis (attenuated above 2000 Hz) or a high-frequency emphasis (attenuated below 4000 Hz). Figure 6 displays the spectra of both lag stimuli; they are bandlimited by a cutoff at 8500 Hz due to the 20-kHz sampling rate. The low-frequency emphasis echo would be similar to a reflection from material, such as heavy carpeting over concrete, which has a coefficient of absorption around 0.60 to 0.65 at 2000–4000 Hz but only 0.02 to 0.14 at frequencies of 500 Hz and below (Knudsen and Harris, 1978, p. 377). The high-frequency emphasis echo (cutoff at 4000 Hz) is a bit unnatural for an echo because most materials that reflect high frequencies also reflect low frequencies (like brick and concrete). A wood floor or window glass comes the closest to boosting the high-frequency content of echoes relative to the low-frequency content. These materials have a coefficient of absorption at 4000 Hz of around 0.04 to 0.07 (that is, little absorbency of high frequency) and at 250–500 Hz around 0.10 to 0.25. This is not like our high-frequency echo in frequency content, but echoes from a wood panel or floor would be similar in that high frequencies are boosted relative to low frequencies. This means our high-frequency echo is somewhat "unnatural," or at least unusual in our ordinary experience, although some man-made acoustic materials have a similar pattern of absorption.

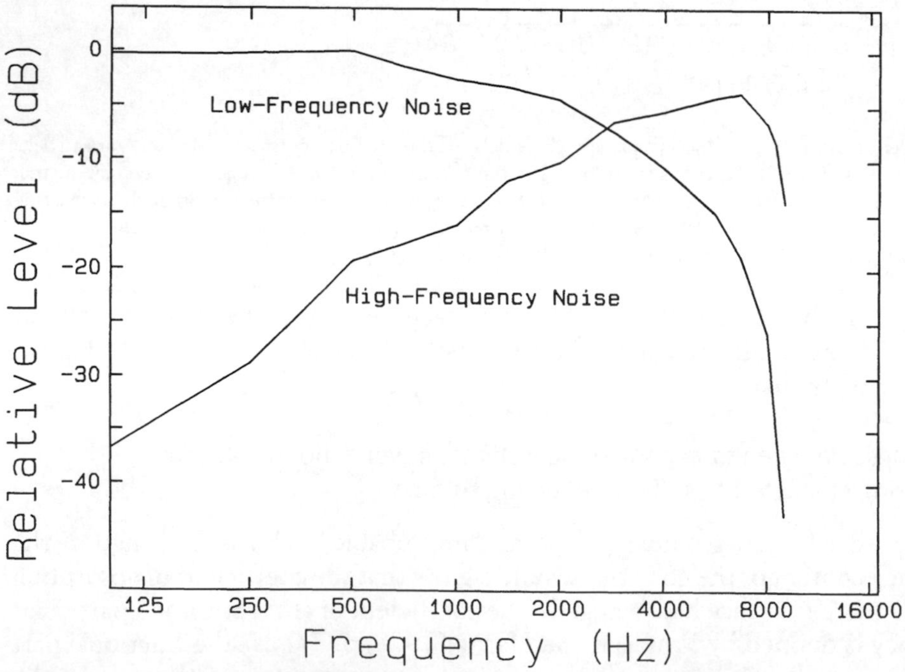

FIG. 6. Spectra of filtered noise bursts.

The full design of this experiment is shown in Table II. Each subject was screened with the two isolated test noise bursts (-BL and -BH) to find a range of delays that spanned the steepest slope of each subject's psychometric function. We attempted to present the subject with delays that would yield d' values varying from $d' < 1.0$, which would indicate that the subject had difficulty in discriminating the echo's directional shift, to $d' > 2.0$, which would indicate that the subject heard the echo's shift with ease. During a particular run, delays were always the same for train and test. This design allowed a comparison between the same test noise (e.g., -BL, the broadband lead paired with the lowpass lagging sound) when it was preceded by the same combination during the train (BL-BL) or a different combination (BH-BL).

If our hypothesis is correct, listeners should have greater difficulty in hearing the echo when the test noise is preceded by itself because echo threshold will increase during the train and remain high for the test noise. If the test noise is preceded with a train containing a different echo, whatever increase in echo threshold that developed during the train will be broken by the unexpected test noise echo. Discrimination performance for the unexpected test noise should be similar to that when the test noise is presented with no train. Figures 7 and 8 display the data for two subjects under conditions in which the test noise burst was always -BL, that is, the lead was broadband and lag was lowpass filtered. Each data point in the figure is a mean of 90 trials. The three conditions shown here differ in what preceded the -BL test noise burst. The effect of the train on echo threshold is shown by the lower d' values for BL-BL than -BL. On the other hand, the effect of the high-frequency echo in the train does not carry over to the low-frequency test noise echo (BH-BL). Whatever buildup that occurred during the train seems to be broken when the echo changes, confirming our hypothesis. As would be expected with any precedence-effect stimuli, discrimination got better as delay got longer in every condition, but the conditions remained separated in the direction the hypothesis predicts. We collected data on four more subjects and they showed the same pattern as in Figs. 7 and 8.

The story is a bit complicated, however. There is an asymmetry in our data in that the BH echo was more difficult to hear and possibly more difficult to localize

TABLE II. Experimental conditions in Freyman et *al.* (1994).

	Train		*Test*	
Condition	*Lead*	*Lag*	*Lead*	*Lag*
BL-BL	Broadband	Lowpass	Broadband	Lowpass
BH-BL	Broadband	Highpass	Broadband	Lowpass
-BL	—		Broadband	Lowpass
BH-BH	Broadband	Highpass	Broadband	Highpass
BL-BH	Broadband	Lowpass	Broadband	Highpass
-BH	—		Broadband	Highpass

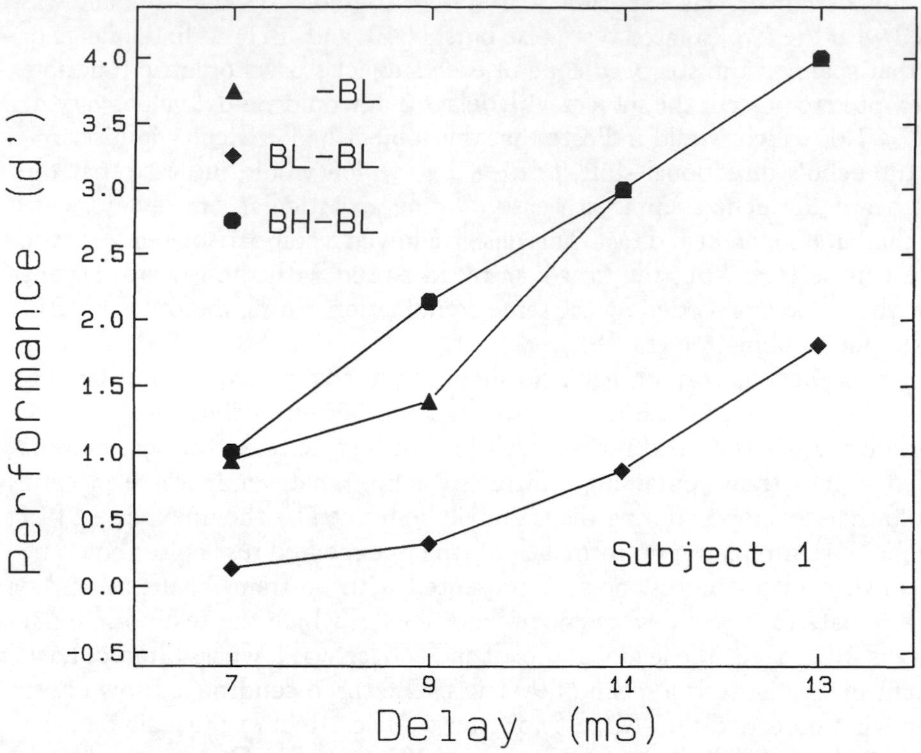

FIG. 7. Discrimination of the echo by subject 1 when the low-frequency test noise was presented alone (-BL), preceded by a similar train (BL-BL), and preceded by a different high-frequency train (BH-BL).

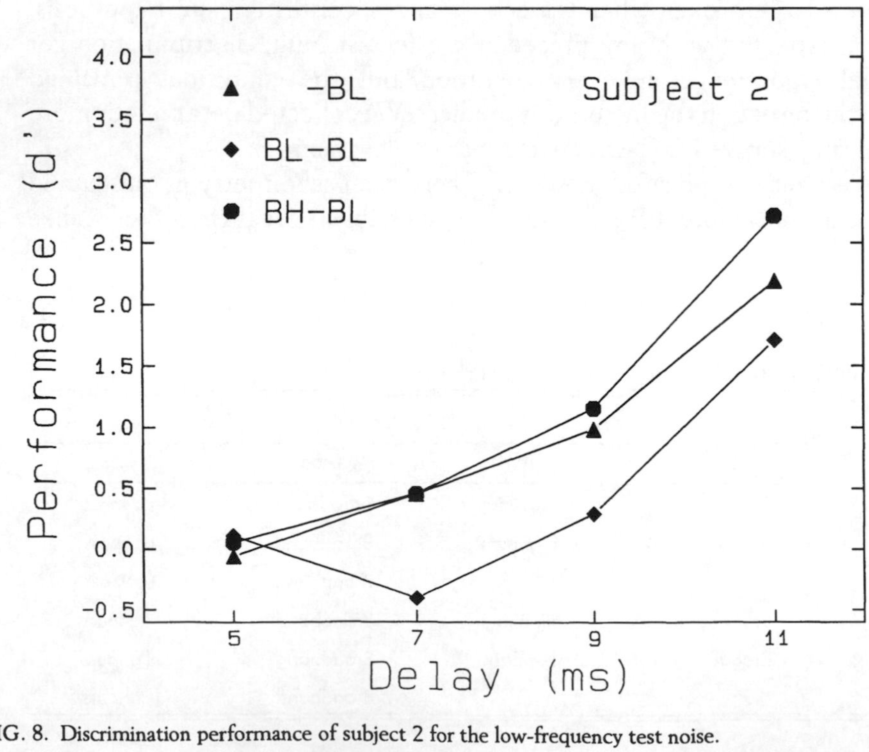

FIG. 8. Discrimination performance of subject 2 for the low-frequency test noise.

than the BL echo. Figures 9 and 10 show discrimination performance for subjects 1 and 2 when the test noise echo was the highpass version of the lead. In all three conditions, subjects had trouble discriminating the BH echo, and there was no improvement when delay increased. Subject 2 reported that he could hear the echo (and his performance is above chance some of the time), but he had trouble localizing the directional shift of the test noise. Subject 1 said that she had great difficulty ever hearing the echo, even in the -BH condition. To get perfectly symmetrical results, we would have to pick a high-frequency echo that was as easy to localize and to hear above the broadband lead sound as the low-frequency echo. In addition, longer delays for the BH echo might be necessary in order to get good performance. Some piloting out to 20–25 ms did not help performance very much, leading us toward a tentative conclusion that the BH echo was difficult to localize. Although symmetrical effects of filtering the echo would be simpler to explain than the asymmetry we found, the results of the BL condition strongly confirmed our hypothesis. In both studies that featured a change in the echo that was "improbable" (either in the delay between lead and lag sound or the frequency content of the echo), we found that listeners' echo threshold was reduced to that of the echo presented in isolation.

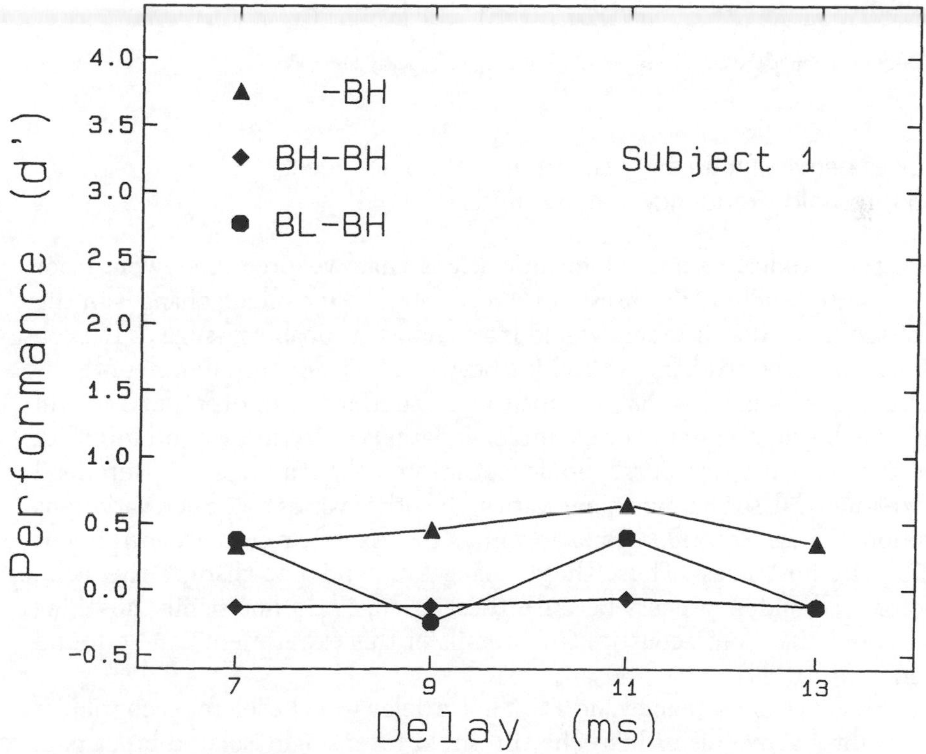

FIG. 9. Discrimination of the echo by subject 1 when the high-frequency test noise was presented alone (-BH), preceded by a similar train (BH-BH), and preceded by a different low-frequency train (BL-BH).

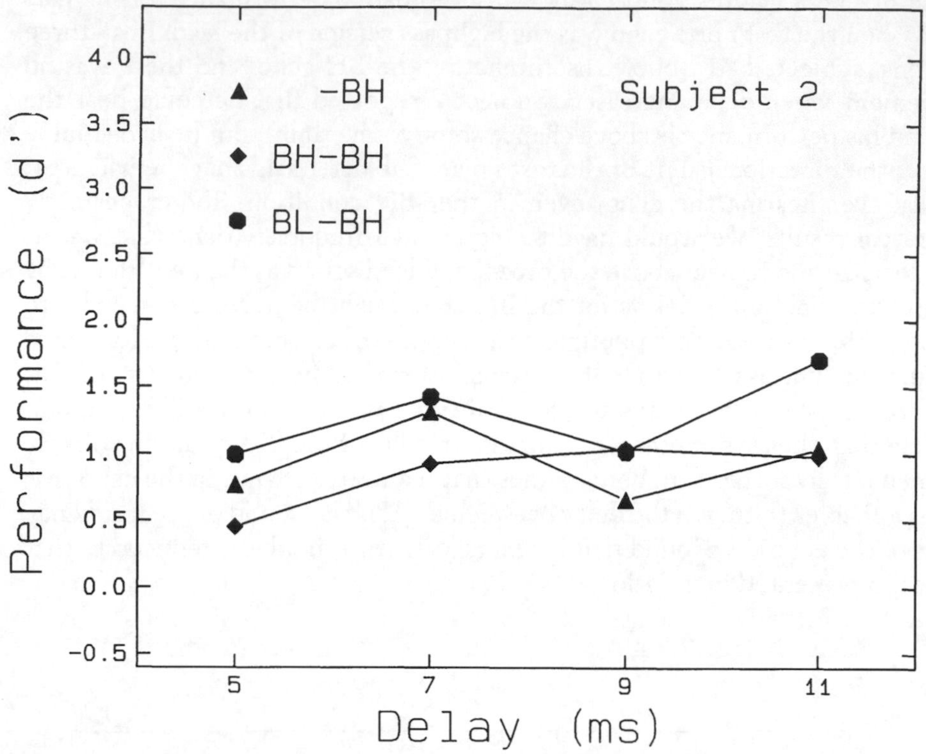

FIG. 10. Discrimination of the echo by subject 2 for the high-frequency test noise.

C. Changes between train and test stimuli that do not affect echo threshold: Frequency of noise bursts

The next two studies examined manipulations that we predicted would not produce a disruption in echo threshold. We wanted to introduce changes in the train–test sequence that listeners would interpret as "probable changes." In such cases, there should be no change in buildup between train and test. Our hypothesis says that changes in echoes that are apt to be experienced in everyday life will not disrupt echo suppression. For example, variations in frequency and intensity between the train and test burst should not affect echo suppression. Here lead and lag are identical, so that when one varies, the other varies too. Such variations are common in ongoing sounds. In fact, sounds that exactly repeat are infrequent in natural circumstances. Thus, these changes should not disrupt the echo suppression or buildup process because these changes do not signify anything different about the room acoustics (full details of this experiment can be found in Clifton *et al.*, 1994).

Again, subjects were screened and a test noise delay was chosen for each subject that was slightly above his or her echo threshold for a single isolated burst pair. This meant that if there was no effect of the conditioning train, subjects should hear the echo easily on the test noise burst. On the other hand, if threshold increased after the train, the test echo should be difficult to hear. The stimuli were narrowband noise bursts, with 300-Hz bandwidth; the low-frequency noise burst was 300–600 Hz (450 Hz center) and the high-frequency noise burst was 800–1100 Hz (950 Hz center). We attempted to have stimulus sets with similar echo thresholds by choosing high and low frequencies that were fairly close together.

Results are shown in Figs. 11 and 12 for the low-frequency test noise and the high-frequency test noise, respectively. Data are plotted for four subjects, with averaged data in the far right columns. The three conditions shown in each figure are NCL or NCH (low- or high-frequency test burst presented alone), HL or LH (low- or high-frequency test burst preceded by a different train), and LL or HH (the test burst preceded by a similar low-or high-frequency burst). Recall that lead and lag sounds were identical, so that a change from train to test was a change in both lead and lag sounds. For both low- and high-frequency test noise bursts, the echo in the isolated test burst was easier to discriminate than when it was preceded by a train of either frequency. An analysis of variance with follow-up tests found no difference between performance when the test noise was preceded by a similar train (LL/HH) or a different train (HL/LH). We concluded that a change in frequency between train and test noises did not disrupt the buildup in echo suppression.

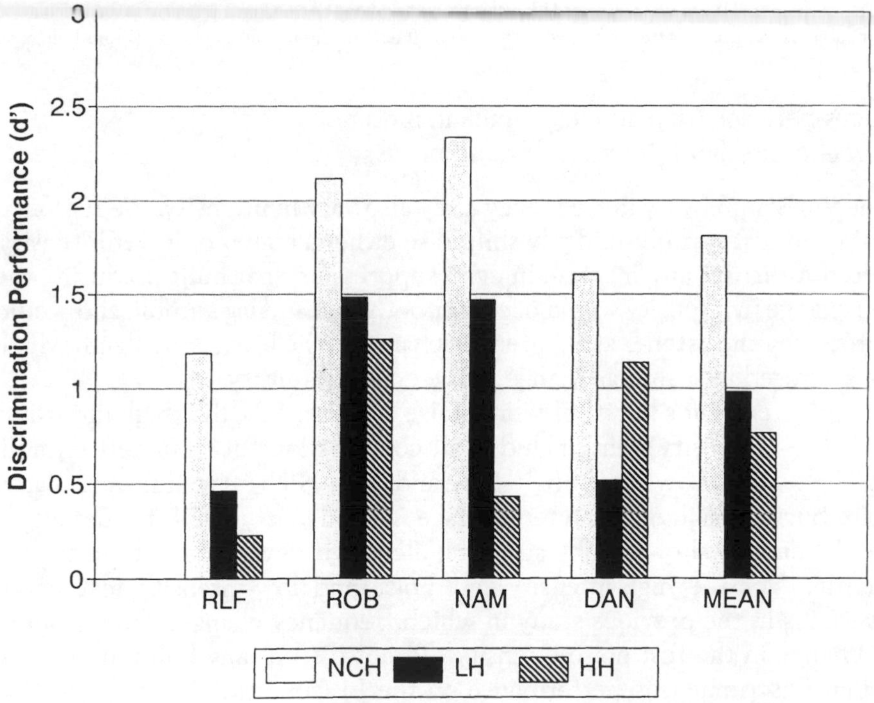

FIG. 11. Discrimination performance of subjects for the high-frequency test burst when the preceding train of noise bursts was lower (LH) or was the same (HH), compared to when the test burst was presented in isolation (NCH). Four subjects' data are plotted, along with the averaged data in the far right column. [From Clifton *et al.*, 1994.]

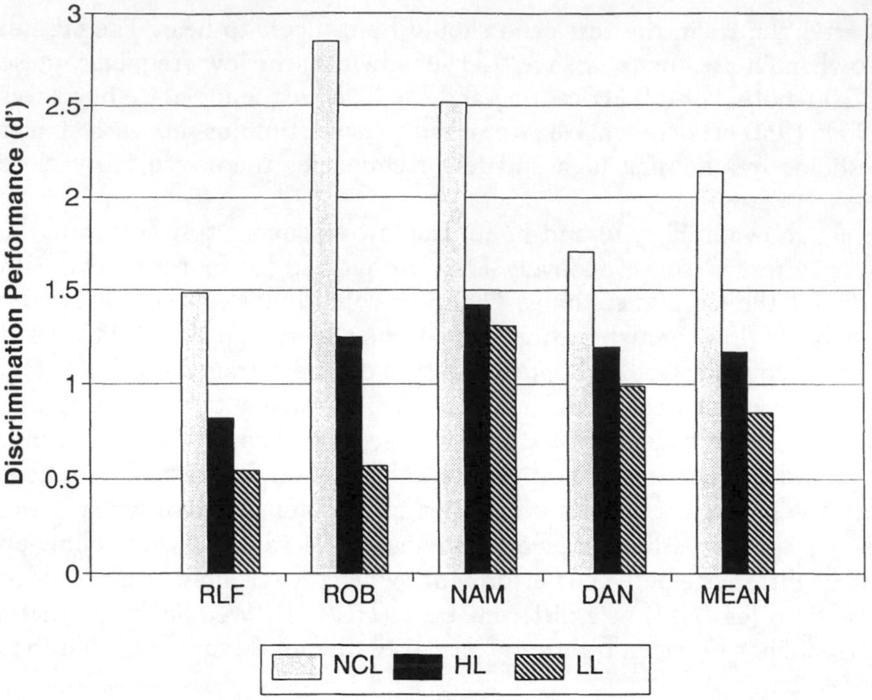

FIG. 12. Discrimination performance of subjects for the low-frequency test bursts when the preceding train of noise bursts was higher (HL) or was the same (LL), compared to when the test burst was presented in isolation (NCL). Four subjects' data are plotted, along with the averaged data in the far right column. [From Clifton *et al.*, 1994.]

H. Changes between train and test stimuli that do not affect echo threshold: Intensity of noise bursts

Just as ongoing stimuli vary in frequency, they also vary in intensity. We reasoned that if train and test stimuli suddenly shifted to either a higher or lower intensity, this would not disrupt any increase in echo suppression that built up during the train. The change in intensity would occur for both lead and lag stimuli, and would be interpreted by the listener as an intensity change in the lead sound itself, which would be mirrored by a similar change in the echo's intensity.

The stimuli were 4-ms bursts of white noise at either 50 dBC (high intensity) or 40 dBC (low intensity), and included all combinations of train–test stimuli, including High–High, Low–Low, High–Low, and Low–High, as well as the isolated single noise burst at high or low intensity (see Clifton *et al.*, 1994, for details).

Figures 13 and 14 show 6 subjects' data, along with averaged data in the far right columns, for the high-intensity test noise and low-intensity test noise, respectively. As in the previous study in which frequency changed from train to test, the change in the test noise intensity did not disrupt any build up in echo suppression. Discrimination performance on the LL condition is similar to that on the HL condition, and performance on the HH condition is similar to that on the LH condition. Finally, both types of train–test sequences had worse performance than when the isolated high or low burst was presented, indicating the effect of the train on the test noise echo.

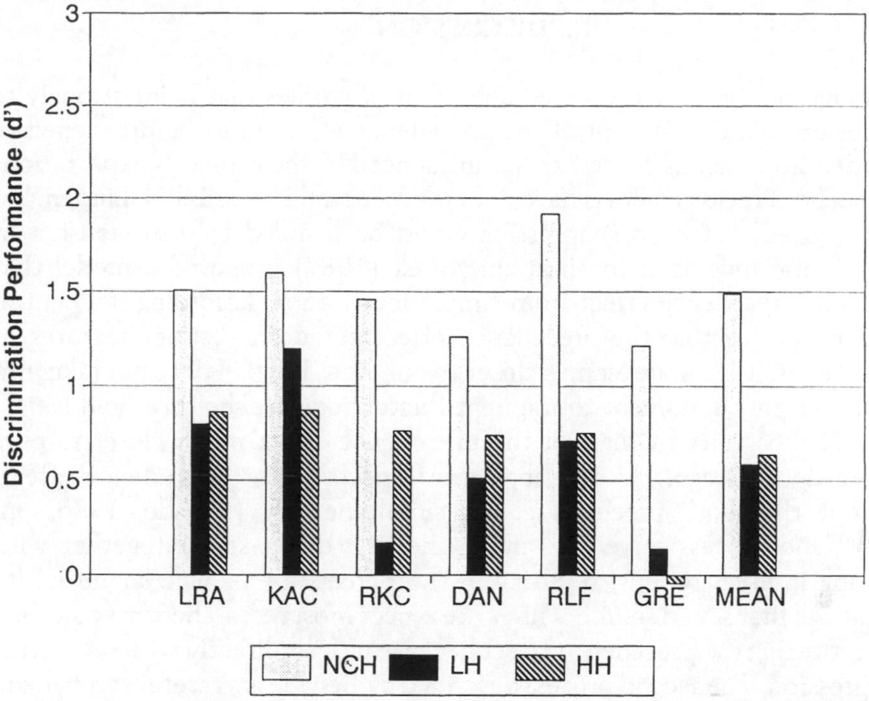

FIG. 13. Discrimination performance of subjects for the high-intensity test bursts when the preceding train of noise bursts was lower (LH) or was the same (HH), compared to when the test burst was presented in isolation (NCH). Six subjects' data are plotted with the averaged data in the far right column. [From Clifton *et al.*, 1994.]

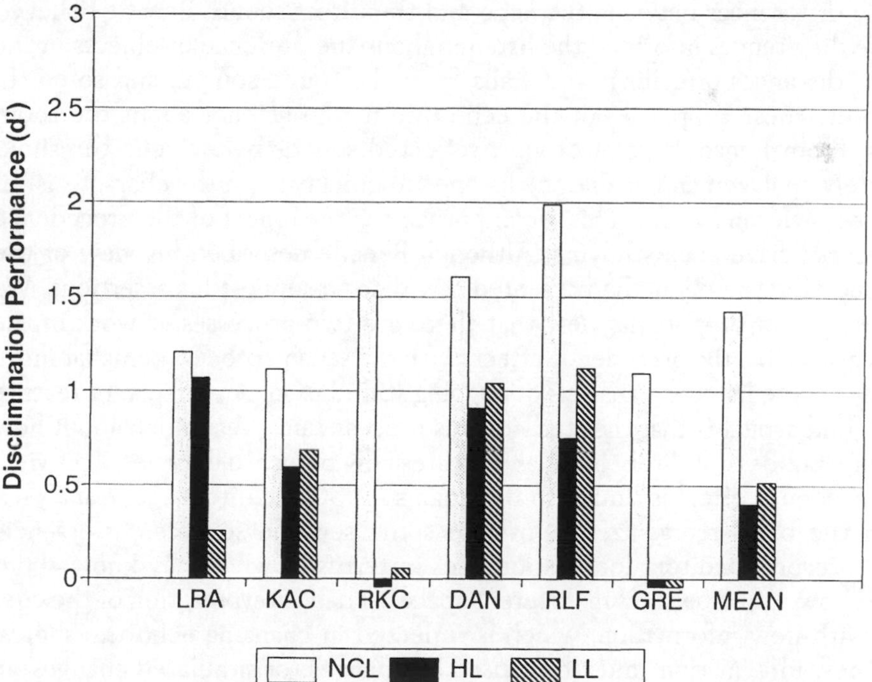

FIG. 14. Discrimination performance of subjects for the low-intensity test bursts when the preceding train of noise bursts was higher (HL) or was the same (LL), compared to when the test burst was presented in isolation (NCL). Six subjects' data are plotted with the averaged data in the far right column. [From Clifton *et al.*, 1994.]

II. DISCUSSION

In this chapter we have presented a number of studies that point strongly to the conclusion that the concept of the precedence effect must be broadened to include a decision-making process that is influenced by the listener's expectations about the echo. Previous models have not entertained this possibility. Lindemann (1986) proposed that echo suppression could be handled by an extension of cross-correlation models of localization. Zurek (1987) proposed a model that separated the precedence effect from simple localization, according it a central locus and proposing that the precedence effect acted on abstract features of localization cues. This model comes closer to our view, but still does not take into account the listener's moment-to-moment fluctuations in echo threshold.

Benade (1976) voiced a view of the precedence effect much closer to ours almost two decades ago. He described two aspects of the precedence effect, pointing out that both processes go on simultaneously (Benade, 1976, pp. 208–210). One process served to "melt" the first direct sound together with later-arriving indirect sounds, resulting in the percept of a single sound entity localized at the first sound source. This is the aspect most researchers have studied when investigating the precedence effect because it deals directly with measuring echo suppression. The second process described by Benade is a careful comparison of frequency and time components in the later-arriving sound with their counterparts in the original waveform. Although the delayed sound is not heard as a separate entity, the listener is nevertheless highly sensitive to frequency and amplitude differences between the echo and the direct sound. Benade believed that these differences informed the listener about the presence of objects in the room, the distances of ceilings and walls from the sound source, and so on. In other words, these properties of the echo inform the listener about the room acoustics. From Benade's point of view reflected sounds below echo threshold are minutely analyzed and enable the listener to quickly learn the characteristics of sound behavior in a room. This second process is the aspect of the precedence effect that we have been studying. Although Benade described his view of the precedence effect in detail, he presented few data to support his assertions. We feel that our data support his view that there are two processes at work in the phenomenon called the precedence effect, with the second process being far more influenced by the listener's analysis of ongoing stimulation. An important feature of this second aspect is that the study of this process can reveal much about how the brain responds to auditory input and creates new perceptual scenes. This view of the precedence effect is similar to Bregman's (1990) "auditory scene analysis" in which the brain reorganizes input into some sensible scheme. In essence, listeners interpret auditory localization cues in terms of what they know about space and how sound behaves in different spaces. Their interpretation of the cues changes with new information, which is reflected in changing echo thresholds, but the "new information" must be caused by changes (or simulated changes) in room acoustics in order to affect echo threshold. The work presented here is a start toward testing these ideas, and may lead to a more complete model of the precedence effect.

ACKNOWLEDGMENTS

Research reported in this chapter was supported by a grant from the National Institute on Deafness and Other Communication Disorders, DC 01625, to R. L. Freyman and R. K. Clifton, and by a Research Scientist Award from the National Institute of Mental Health (MH00332) to R. K. Clifton. We wish to thank Ruth Litovsky and Daniel McCall for their invaluable help on this project.

REFERENCES

Benade, A. H. (**1976**). *Fundamentals of Musical Acoustics* (Oxford University Press, London).

Blauert, J. (**1983**). *Spatial Hearing* (MIT Press, Cambridge, MA).

Blauert, J., and Col, J. P. (**1992**). "Irregularities in the precedence effect," in *Auditory Physiology and Perception*, edited by Y. Cazals, K. Horner, and L. Demany (Pergamon Press, Oxford), pp. 531–538.

Bregman, A. S. (**1990**). *Auditory Scene Analysis: The Perceptual Organization of Sound* (MIT Press, Cambridge, MA).

Clifton, R. K. (**1987**). "Breakdown of echo suppression in the precedence effect," J. Acoust. Soc. Am. **82**, 1834–1835.

Clifton, R. K., and Freyman, R. L. (**1989**). "Effect of click rate and delay on breakdown of the precedence effect," Percept. Psychophys. **46**, 139–145.

Clifton, R. K., Freyman, R. L., Litovsky, R. Y., and McCall, D. D. (**1994**). "Listeners' expectations about echoes can raise or lower echo threshold," J. Acoust. Soc. Am. **95**, 1525–1533.

Freyman, R. L., Clifton, R. K., and Litovsky, R. Y. (**1991**). "Dynamic processes in the precedence effect," J. Acoust. Soc. Am. **90**, 874–884.

Freyman, R. L., Clifton, R. K., and McCall, D. D. (**1994**). "Listeners' sensitivity to information about room acoustics in echoes," J. Acoust. Soc. Am. **95**, 2898.

Gardner, M. B. (**1968**). "Historical background of the Haas and/or precedence effect," J. Acoust. Soc. Am. **43**, 1243–1248.

Green, D. (**1976**). *Introduction to Hearing* (Lawrence Erlbaum Associates, Hillsdale, NJ).

Hafter, E. R., Buell, T. N., and Richards, V. M. (**1988**). "Onset-coding in lateralization: Its form, site, and function," in *Auditory Function: Neurobiological Bases of Hearing*, edited by G. M. Edelman, W. E. Gall, and W. M. Cowan (John Wiley, New York), pp. 647–676.

Hartmann, W. M., and Rakerd, B. (**1989**). "Localization of sound in rooms IV: The Franssen effect," J. Acoust. Soc. Am. **86**, 1366–1373.

Knudsen, V. O., and Harris, C. M. (**1978**). *Acoustical Designing in Architecture* (American Institute of Physics, Acoustical Society of America, New York).

Lindemann, W. (**1986**). "Extension of a binaural cross-correlation model by contralateral inhibition II: The law of the first wavefront," J. Acoust. Soc. Am. **80**, 1623–1630.

Mills, A. (**1972**). "Auditory localization" in *Foundations of Modern Auditory Theory, Vol. II*, edited by J. V. Tobias (Academic Press, New York), pp. 303–348.

Perrott, D. R., Marlborough, K., Merrill, P., and Strybel, T. A. (**1989**). "Minimum audible angle thresholds obtained in conditions in which the precedence effect is assumed to operate," J. Acoust. Soc. Am. **85**, 282–288.

Perrott, D. R., Strybel, T. A., and Manligas, C. L. (**1987**). "Conditions under which the Haas/precedence effect may or may not occur," J. Aud. Res. **27**, 59–72.

Rakerd, B., and Hartmann, W. M. (**1985**). "Localization of sound in rooms II: The effects of a single reflecting surface," J. Acoust. Soc. Am. **78**, 524–533.

Saberi, K., and Perrott, D. R. (**1990**). "Lateralization thresholds obtained under conditions in which the precedence effect is assumed to operate," J. Acoust. Soc. Am. **87**, 1732–1737.

Thurlow, W. R., and Parks, T. E. (**1961**). "Precedence-suppression effects for two click sources," Percept. Motor Skills **13**, 7–12.

Wolf, S. (**1988**). "Untersuchungen zum gesetz der ersten wellenfront," *Fortschritte der Akustik-DAGA '88* (DPG-GmbH, Bad Honnef), pp. 605–608.

Zurek, P. M. (**1987**). "The precedence effect," in *Directional Hearing*, edited by W. A. Yost and G. Gourevitch (Springer-Verlag, New York), pp. 85–105.

Chapter 13

Phenomenal Geometry and the Measurement of Perceived Auditory Distance

Donald H. Mershon
North Carolina State University

(Received December 1993; revised November 1994)

The theory of phenomenal geometry describes the notion that spatial experiences are dependent on three primary perceptual variables: perceived direction, perceived distance, and perceived self-motion. From knowledge of these primary variables, one may predict (by application of the laws of geometry) such derived variables as apparent target displacement or motion. Conversely, measures of appropriate "derived" variables can be used to estimate the magnitude of an underlying primary variable. Although originally developed by Gogel (1990) within the context of his research on visual space perception, the theory is not intrinsically limited to visual experiences. Discrete auditory targets may also be described in terms of their apparent directions and distances. The perception of one's own movement (or lack of movement) is, of course, independent of target modality. This chapter provides a discussion of the application of the concepts of phenomenal geometry to auditory spatial experiences, with a specific concern for the possible usefulness of the theory in constructing techniques for the "indirect" (nonverbal) measurement of perceived auditory distance. Some initial studies, involving a variety of different distance cues, are discussed.

INTRODUCTION

The general topic of this chapter is the perception of auditory distance. That is, I am concerned with those factors that determine whether a source of sound will seem near to or far away from a listener. Unlike the research described in many of the other chapters in this book, our research is usually concerned with sounds presented from loudspeakers, for durations typically measured in seconds (rather than milliseconds), within fairly normal rooms. Our listeners are typically naive with respect to experimental goals and commonly make only a few observations each.

My more specific goal in this chapter is to describe the basics of an approach that integrates such percepts of distance with the more traditional judgments of auditory direction into a single theory of auditory spatial experience. I hope to show how this theoretical approach, known as phenomenal geometry (see Gogel, 1990; Gogel and Tietz, 1992), may suggest some new and useful procedures for measuring perceived auditory distance.

Although the study of perceived auditory distance has been a frequently neglected topic within the field of auditory localization, there are recent signs of increased interest from a variety of laboratories (Ashmead, LeRoy, and Odom, 1990; Guski, 1990; Litovsky and Clifton, 1991; Petersen, 1990). Certainly it is not difficult to demonstrate the importance of understanding how we perceive the distances of sounds. As Speigle and Loomis (1993) discussed, errors in distance perception can lead to unintended changes in appearance—despite accurate information about directional change. Figure 1 illustrates this point. If an auditory target is perceived to be closer than its true distance ($D' < D$), one may perceive that the physically stationary target is moving away from the listener as the listener walks forward. A target perceived as being farther than its true position ($D' > D$) may be experienced as moving toward the listener. Such errors have consequences for the effective implementation of virtual reality environments.

Many sorts of acoustic information have been suggested as providing cues for the auditory perception of the distance to a source (Blauert, 1983; Coleman, 1963; Mershon and Bowers, 1979; von Bekesy, 1960). Although many of these cues are available to a stationary listener, there has also been some interesting work on possible dynamic cues (Speigle and Loomis, 1993; Ashmead, Davis, and Northington, 1995). Only a summary of the most relevant factors is provided in this presentation.

First, remember that information concerning distance is provided by the pattern of reflections/reverberation in most interior spaces (Mershon, Ballenger, Little, McMurtry, and Buchanan, 1989). Specifically, the "reverberation cue" refers to the tendency to compare directly arriving sound and reverberant

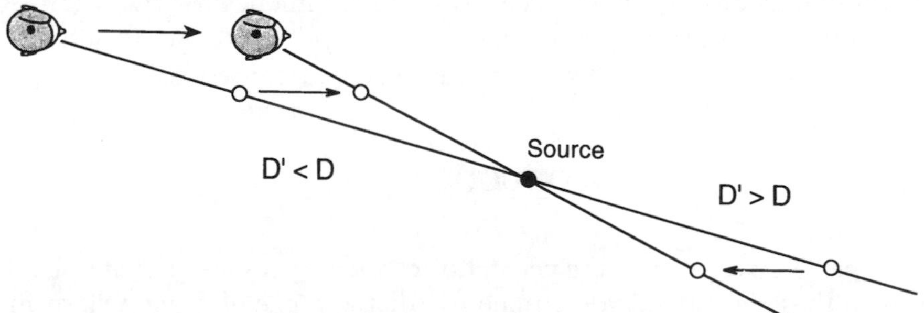

FIG. 1. Top view of a moving listener, showing the expected effects of errors in perceived distance (D') on apparent source displacement during forward motion. Each open circle represents an apparent position of the source; the filled circle (at an initial physical distance D) marks the source's true location. Note that the small dot positioned at the center of the listener's head in this figure and in subsequent figures merely indicates an appropriate value for zero distance. All sounds in these experiments are perceptually externalized.

(diffusely reflected) sound. Typically, the greater the relative amount of direct sound energy, the closer the source will appear. Thus, purposely minimizing reverberation in an interior space usually leads to the perception that sources are fairly close. An extreme case occurs in an anechoic environment—where even sources across a large chamber may seem very near (Mershon and King, 1975).

Second, remember that *changes* in sound level and/or in high-frequency spectral content can produce *changes* in the apparent distance to a source (Coleman, 1962, 1968; Little, Mershon, and Cox, 1992; Strybel and Perrott, 1984). As would be expected from the normal spread of sound energy with distance, decreases in sound level are usually accompanied by the perception of increased distance. As would be expected from the normal consequences of selective attenuation by passage through the air, decreases in high-frequency content also lead to the perception that a sound source is at an increased distance. When such changes in sound level and/or spectral content are introduced artificially, they will cause a change in perceived distance, even when the physical distances to the source are too small to produce any significant change in natural attenuation (Little *et al.*, 1992).

A. The theory of phenomenal geometry

The theory of phenomenal geometry was developed by Walter C. Gogel (Gogel, 1990; Gogel and Tietz, 1992). Although his interest has always been the perception of visual space, the concepts that underlie the theory are not at all limited to vision. In our laboratory, we have been investigating their application to auditory space perception.

To understand Gogel's theoretical viewpoint, it is critical to recognize that phenomenal geometry applies to the interrelationships among *perceived* spatial experiences. Although it is sometimes appropriate (for simplicity) to assume that a perceptual quantity is equal to some corresponding physical extent (e.g., that apparent direction is perceived correctly in a given situation), the theory itself is specified entirely in perceptual terms.

The basic idea of phenomenal geometry is that three perceptual quantities are primary variables in determining spatial experience. These are the perceived direction of the target, the perceived distance of the target, and one's own sense of self-motion (or lack thereof). It is perhaps worth noting that each of these primary variables can be related to more-or-less independent sources of information—either environmentally based cues or information provided by the individual listener. To be very clear, we recognize that many separate factors may influence perceived direction. Many other factors may influence perceived distance or perceived self-motion. We are interested in how the three resulting percepts are related to each other and to certain additional spatial experiences.

Application of the laws of geometry to these primary perceptual variables specifies a variety of derived spatial experiences. I should perhaps point out here that, following Gogel (1990), we have been using Euclidean geometry to examine these interrelationships. Although alternative geometries may ultimately turn out to be more appropriate, it is difficult to assess such alternatives (especially for auditory space) without first developing the general framework of the theory, as well as better techniques for measuring the variables involved.

Figure 2 shows a simple situation involving the relationship between the perception of auditory distance and the appearance of target displacement that may occur during a lateral head movement. (We assume here that the perception of azimuth and the sense of head movement are both accurate.) During the lateral head movement, the source always remains physically stationary at the position shown. To the extent that the source appears correctly in distance, one should expect no apparent displacement of the source. If, however, the source appears closer than its true distance, phenomenal geometry predicts that it should seem to move in the same direction as the head. The extent of such apparent displacement will be related to the magnitude of the error in perceived distance. (In this, as in other figures, extents indicated with a prime notation, e.g., D', denote perceptual quantities; those without a prime denote physical quantities.) Concomitant source displacement will also occur when the source is perceived as being farther than its physical distance, but now the direction of apparent displacement will be opposite to that of the head.

I. GENERAL METHOD

Let us consider briefly the characteristics of the environment in which our research has been conducted and some of the typical procedures. The testing room itself has been described in detail elsewhere (Mershon *et al.*, 1989). Basically, it consists of a room 7.2 m × 7.2 m with an average ceiling height of 3.7 m. The walls are paneled with removable, absorbent squares (60 cm on a side). The floor is covered with carpet, which can also be removed. These manipulations allow a modification of the T_{60} reverberation time by a factor of more than 4:1 (i.e., from 1.65 s to 0.36 s for the range of frequencies usually employed). A system of overhead speakers provides a low constant background noise (at a sound level of approximately 50 dBA) to mask extraneous sounds.

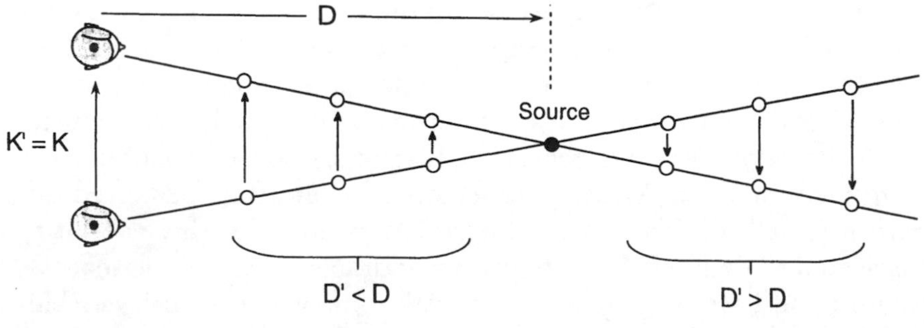

FIG. 2. The effects of errors in perceived distance on apparent source displacement during a lateral head movement. The pairs of open symbols represent the apparent displacements expected for errors of various magnitude (and sign). For simplicity, perceived head displacement (K') is assumed to equal actual head displacement (K).

Each listener is typically blindfolded before being led into the testing room and positioned directly in front of an acoustically absorbent backdrop. This backdrop is designed to minimize immediate reflections from behind the listener. The sound source is any one of several different loudspeakers, which may be positioned in front of the listener and along the listener's midline. For most experiments, the experimenter remains in the room. The experimenter can initiate appropriate stimuli and record most responses, remotely from the listener's position.

A. Generation of stimuli

Stimuli for the first of the reviewed experiments were generated using appropriate modules from Coulbourn Instruments. Later experiments involved stimuli created and/or modified using software from digidesign, including their SoftSynth and Sound Designer II applications. These applications were run on an Apple Macintosh-SE computer equipped with a Sound Accelerator DSP board, also from digidesign. Spectral filtering of the stimuli for the second experiment was carried out entirely in software. With the addition of an appropriate analog–digital (A-D) converter, environmental stimuli (such as the voices used in the third experiment) could be digitally recorded onto the computer's hard disk with 16-bit resolution. All stimuli to be presented as target sounds were eventually amplified using a Crown DL-2 preamplifier and Crown PS-200 amplifier before being sent to an appropriate loudspeaker. [Identification of the loudspeaker(s) used for each of the studies is given with the specific experimental description.] The low-level background noise was generated by a Matrix Corp. signal generator and amplified by a Toshiba preamplifier and amplifier.

B. Response measures

Experiments on perceived auditory distance have included many different types of measures. Our own earlier work used the most common measure—direct verbal reports in feet and/or inches. Other researchers have sometimes used motoric responses—such as asking the listener to walk to the perceived position of a previously heard sound (Loomis, Hebert, and Cicinelli, 1990; Ashmead *et al.*, 1995). Both of these procedures, however, involve what may be called a "direct" response (Gogel, Loomis, Newman, and Sharkey, 1985). That is, the listener is asked directly about the dimension of interest.

Direct techniques are subject to several "cognitive corrections," which may not accurately reflect the perceptual properties of the situation. For example, a listener may modify his or her verbal report on the basis of some nonauditory estimate of typical room sizes in the building. Alternatively, a familiar sound that is perceived to be too quiet (i.e., to be quieter than the listener believes that it should be) may be reported as being farther away than it actually seems. Carlson and Tassone (1962) investigated a similar cognitive relationship between visual size and distance. Specifically, they found that people often held an implicit belief that "small" and "far away" were necessarily associated. They suggested that this sort of "perspective bias" could result in systematic shifts in verbal reports of spatial experience, especially if the bias were inadvertently emphasized by the instructions to the observer. Gogel (1976) showed explicitly that verbal reports were subject to cognitive modifications that did not necessarily reflect genuine perceptual change.

In contrast to the foregoing procedures, so-called "indirect" techniques take advantage of the interrelationships specified by phenomenal geometry. These techniques are not subject to the same sorts of cognitive adjustments as are direct judgments. Instead, they involve asking the listener about some other aspect of his or her spatial experience and using the response to calculate a value for perceived distance. Converging evidence supports the interpretation that such techniques (at least for visual stimuli) can reflect a unitary underlying perceptual extent (Gogel *et al.*, 1985). The following experiments demonstrate some of the possible ways to learn about perceived auditory distance without asking for a direct judgment of distance.

II. THREE EXPERIMENTS

A. A study of apparent alignment

Our first study (Mershon and Hutson, 1991) was based on the expectation that the effects of errors in perceived distance produce apparent displacements, which are indistinguishable from the effects of genuine physical displacement. That is, we created an experimental situation in which listeners' judgments of genuine physical changes would be modified by combining them with the perceptual changes introduced during a lateral head movement.

Two 12.7-cm (5-in) diameter loudspeakers were used, one positioned 38 cm above the other and both at a physical distance of 3 m. The lower speaker was fixed in the listener's midline. The upper speaker could be horizontally displaced, relative to the lower one, by as much as 38 cm to the left or right. For any set of trials, each of 11 possible relationships, including the center case of actual alignment of the two speakers, was randomly presented once (see Fig. 3).

For each presentation, listeners made judgments of the apparent alignment (i.e., the apparent degree of "offset") of the two speakers. For some sets of judgments, the test room had minimal absorbency. We called such a condition the "live" room. For other sets of judgments, all wall panels and carpeting were in place, creating an acoustically "dead" (although not anechoic) environment.

Each trial proceeded as follows. A 2-s burst of broadband noise (0.5–8 kHz) from the lower (fixed) loudspeaker occurred first. Then, following a brief pause, there was a similar burst from the upper loudspeaker. Each burst was 70 dBA, as measured at the normal position of the listener's head. Note that listeners were asked to make judgments about the relationship of these two discrete target sounds, not about a continuously moving source.

Most importantly, the listener either remained stationary for both bursts (condition S-H), or the listener executed a previously trained lateral head movement of 60 cm between the bursts (condition M-H). Such head movements involved a simple lateral shift in the position of the entire body. The previous

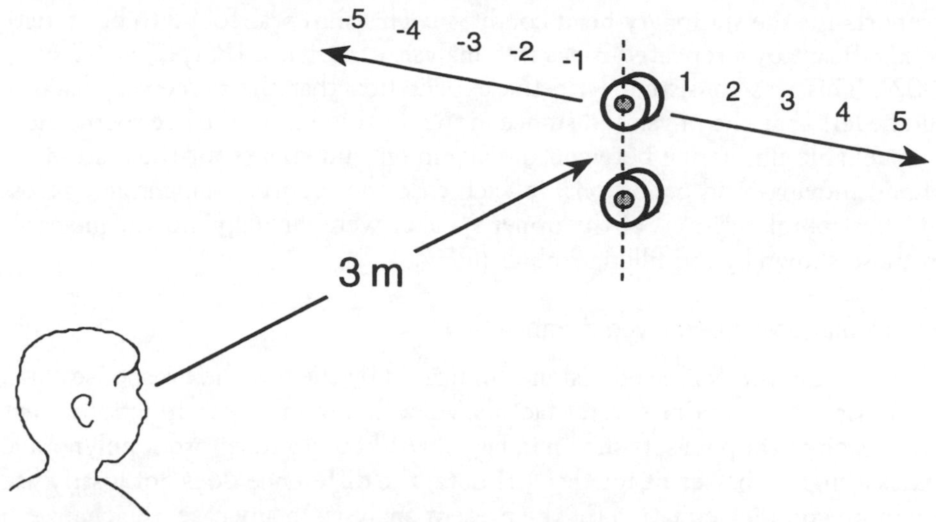

FIG. 3. Loudspeaker configuration in the study by Mershon and Hutson (1991). In the center (or "zero") position, the moveable upper loudspeaker was positioned directly above the lower loudspeaker at a center-to-center separation of 38 cm. [From Mershon and Hutson, 1991, reprinted by permission of the Psychonomic Society, Inc.]

training emphasized the need to move the head in a straight line, while avoiding any tilting or rotation. (Listeners generally mastered the body movements necessary to accomplish this motion with little difficulty. The experimenter visually monitored such movements during the relevant conditions.)

Judgments of apparent alignment were reported with a haptically manipulated, upright, freely rotatable rod. Basically, the listener rotated the rod around its center, in order to indicate the perceived relationship of the speakers. (We suggested that the listener imagine that the top and bottom of the rod represented the two loudspeakers and swing the rod accordingly.) If the top speaker appeared to be to the left of the lower speaker, the tilt of the rod would produce a value less than 90°. If the top speaker appeared to be to the right of the lower one, the value would be greater than 90°.

The two conditions of reverberation were expected to produce differences in the perceived distance to the sounds. The dead-room condition was expected to result in the perception that sounds were closer than their physical distance. The live room was not expected to have such an effect. Thus, for the dead room only, there would be a shift of all judgments to the left (toward lower numbers) when the listener made a lateral head movement between the two noise bursts. No leftward shift should occur for the stationary-head condition, nor should there be any leftward shift in the live room (in which perceived distances were approximately veridical).

1. Basic results

As can be seen in Fig. 4, Mershon and Hutson (1991) found that the mean alignment judgments in the dead room all shifted leftward (that is, to lower numbers), when the head was moved between the noise bursts—compared to the reports for the stationary-head condition. This shift was found to be statistically significant by a repeated-measures analysis of variance [$F(1,27) = 12.69$, $p < .002$]. This was consistent with the expectation that the perceived distance would be less than the physical distance in the dead room. In the live room, there was no reliable difference between the alignment judgments for the stationary-head and moving-head conditions; in each case the reports of alignment across the 11 horizontal positions of the upper speaker were virtually indistinguishable from those shown by the filled symbols in Fig. 4.

2. Calculations of perceived distance

To determine the perceived distance indicated by the obtained response shift, it is necessary to consider several factors. As a first step, linear functions were fitted to each of the data sets shown in Fig. 4. (Although a third-order polynomial provides a slightly better fit for the S-H data, the difference does not justify use of the more complex equation for the present analysis. In any case, the change in the calculated value for D' would be minimal.) To demonstrate the next steps, one may follow the dashed line in Fig. 5: The alignment judgment for the zero loudspeaker position was noted for the S-H condition; the position that produced this same alignment response for the M-H condition was determined from the regression functions. (As can be seen in Fig. 5, the difference between the two conditions amounted to a change of 2.56 positions. Given a separation of 7.6 cm between neighboring loudspeaker positions, this represents a shift of 19.46 cm.) The perceived distance indicated by this shift in alignment judgments may be obtained by applying Eq. (1):

$$D' = K'\,D / (\text{shift} + K'), \qquad (1)$$

where, for the present experiment, K' is assumed to equal K (= 60 cm) and the physical distance, D = 300 cm. From the above values, we can calculate that D' was approximately 226 cm.[1]

The preceding calculations, however, leave two questions. First, what would be the consequence of errors in estimating K' (the felt movement of the head)? Second, what would be the consequence of variations in the perceived vertical separation of the loudspeakers? Clearly, if the perceived vertical separation (V') were not equal to the physical vertical separation (V), it could affect the orientation judgments and, hence, the calculation of D'.

a. Effects of errors in K and/or K'. Inasmuch as any estimate of D' is dependent on the accuracy of the lateral head movement (or, more precisely, on the value of K'), *it is instructive to determine the consequences if* K (or K') were not equal

[1]This calculation of D' varies slightly from the 253 cm originally reported by Mershon and Hutson (1991). The earlier calculation used the average slope and average intercept values from 28 individual response functions; current calculations are all based on linear functions fitted directly to the group data shown in Fig. 4. This procedural change simplifies some of the later calculations, but does not otherwise affect the arguments presented.

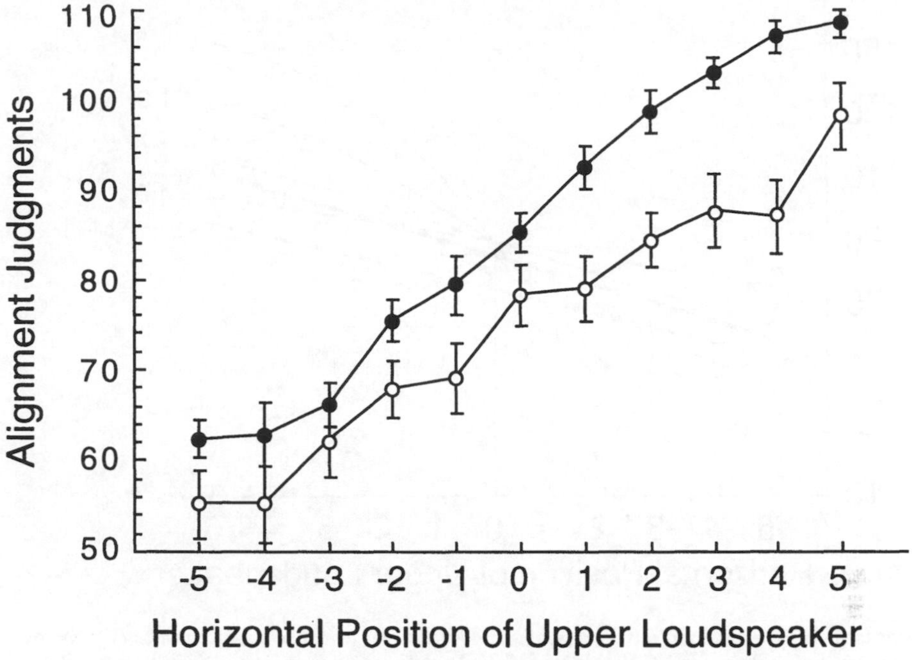

FIG. 4. Data from Mershon and Hutson (1991): Alignment judgments reported by listeners in the dead room. Filled data points represent results from the condition with a stationary head; open data points represent results from the condition in which the head moved laterally between presentations of the two sounds. Ideally, a report of 90° should have indicated that the two loudspeakers seemed directly above one another; that the actual response for the zero position in the stationary-head condition was slightly less than 90° was probably due to differences in the ease of clockwise versus counterclockwise hand rotation. All data are given as means (±1 standard error), $n = 28$. [From Mershon and Hutson, 1991, reprinted by permission of the Psychonomic Society, Inc.]

to the nominal 60 cm. Appropriate calculations indicate that errors of ±20% in K would result in changing the value of D' from a low of 214 cm (for $K = 48$ cm) to a high of 236 cm (for $K = 72$ cm). Given the training and the continued monitoring by the experimenter, it is unlikely that errors of this size could have occurred unnoticed in K. The validity of the basic $K' = K$ assumption was not tested, but again, errors as great as ±20% in the felt-movement of the head seem unlikely. Thus, regardless of whether or not listeners were completely accurate in their head movements (or in their perceptions of that movement), the results clearly support the interpretation that $D' < D$.

b. Effects of errors in V' relative to V. The perception of vertical position is generally not as accurate as the perception of azimuth (Middlebrooks and Green, 1991). In the present experiment, it is certainly possible that listeners incorrectly perceived the vertical separation of the loudspeakers. To what extent is this a concern for the interpretation of the data?

If poor vertical localization simply increases the variability of the judgments, with the average perception of separation remaining approximately veridical, little harm will be done. On the other hand, if poor localization implies the existence

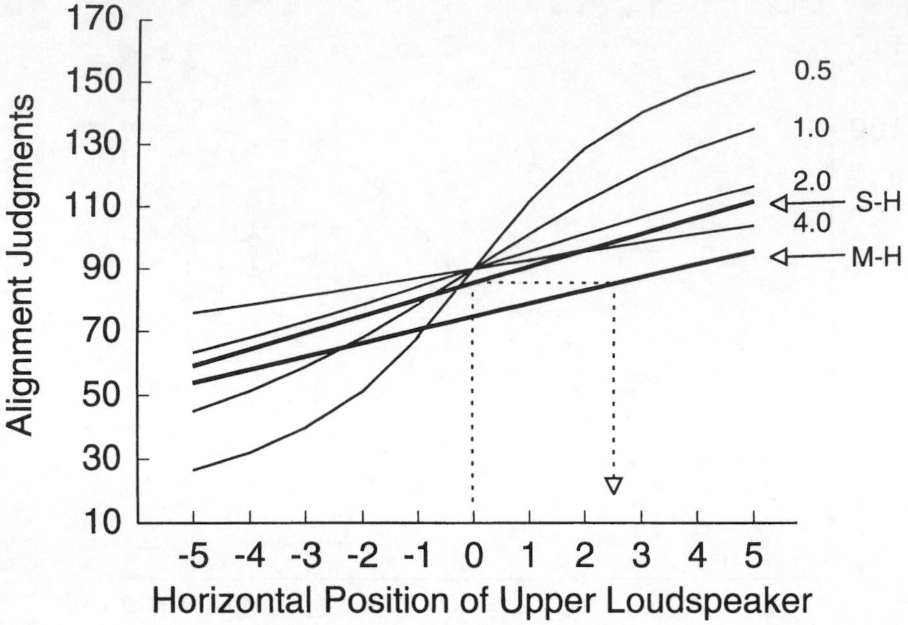

FIG. 5. Effects of errors in perceived vertical separation (V'), *relative to actual vertical separation* (V). Narrow lines show theoretical functions for various values of V'/V. Thick lines show linear functions fitted to the data (shown in Fig. 4) for the stationary-head (S-H) and moving-head (M-H) conditions. The dashed line reflects the process of using the horizontal separation between S-H and M-H curves to determine the position (in the moving-head condition) for which the upper loudspeaker seemed directly above the lower loudspeaker. The extent of this shift (indicated by the downward arrow) was used in calculating D'.

of a systematic ("constant") error, then it may be necessary to account explicitly for such error in later calculations.

One may note that there is a "correct" orientation response for each of the horizontal positions of the upper loudspeaker (positions −5 and +5, for example, would be correctly reported by slants of 45° and 135° on the response device, respectively). This assumes that $V' = V$.

If V' were less than V, the same set of loudspeaker positions would yield slants that vary over a more extreme range (and the function relating alignment judgments to position would become distinctly nonlinear). If V' were greater than V, the functions would be more nearly linear and would show decidedly lower slopes. Figure 5 shows some theoretical curves (narrow lines) for values of V'/V from 0.5 to 4.0.

We made no *a priori* assumptions about the veridicality of V'. Nevertheless, assuming that the relative horizontal positions are correctly perceived, it is possible to determine something about V' by comparing the obtained data to the theoretical functions. In particular, the slopes of the functions fitted to the data should indicate the approximate magnitude of any systematic errors in V'. Note therefore that both of the data curves show slopes that "should" occur if V' were overperceived (i.e., if $V'/V \approx 2$). Note also that the slope for the M-H function is slightly lower than that for the S-H function. This means that some of the lateral shift observed between the S-H and M-H conditions may involve a small change in V', rather than an error in D'. This possibility is considered next.

If there were in fact no error in D', then the two data functions might differ in slope, but they should cross at zero and no horizontal shift would be measured by the procedure described above (and shown graphically in Fig. 5). The failure of the data functions to cross indicates that there is some error in D'. A part of the overall shift, however, may be due to a change in V', and that part should not be used in calculating D'. To provide a more definitive value for D', therefore, we determined that the shift between the S-H and M-H conditions due to the D' error alone is 15.5 cm. Using Eq. (1), such a shift corresponds to $D' = 238$ cm. Reconsideration of the possible effects of errors in head movement yields the further result that $227 < D' < 247$ cm, for errors in K of $\pm 20\%$.

3. Discussion

The preceding results clearly indicate that the indirectly measured value of perceived distance was consistent with expectations based on our past research with the dead-room condition, even after allowing for possible errors in K' or V'. The robustness of the finding that distance is underperceived in such rooms supports the usefulness of indirect measures based on phenomenal geometry. However, there is still one other factor to consider: the possibility that listeners experienced significant errors in their perceptions of azimuth. Although we believe this to be unlikely, it must be conceded that calculations of D' could change if listeners made directional errors.

Interpretations based solely on directional error are, however, difficult to entertain, because such errors would have had to be conveniently present in one situation, but not present in a comparable situation. Thus, if the process of moving one's head had introduced systematic errors in apparent direction, why did not the same response shift show up for the moving-head condition in the live room? On the other hand, if there were directional errors caused by the complex reflections of sound in the live-room environment, why was the effect of head movement only obvious in the dead room?

Despite the preceding arguments in favor of an interpretation based on the underperception of distance, our second experiment was explicitly designed to consider both directional and distance errors. Figure 6 shows the fundamental problem to be considered. If errors in apparent direction occur (for whatever reason) simultaneously with errors in perceived distance, then the amount of apparent displacement of a target source during head movement is determined by both types of error. Specifically, one must consider any error in perceived distance in relation to the intersection of the lines of perceived direction, rather than in relation to the lines of actual direction. In the example shown in Fig. 6, the apparent displacement of the source would be reduced by the combined errors in perceived direction. Opposite errors in perceived direction would result in reports of greater perceived displacement.

B. An investigation of apparent displacement

In our next study (Cox, 1992; Cox and Mershon, 1996) we measured both the apparent concomitant displacement of a source due to a head movement and the

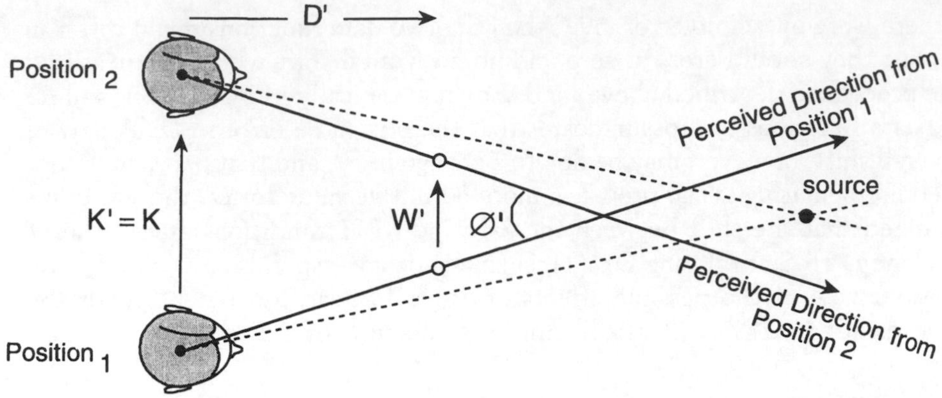

FIG. 6. The expected effects of simultaneous errors in both perceived distance and perceived direction upon apparent source displacement (*W'*) during a lateral head movement. The figure is not shown precisely to scale; *D'* would usually be larger than *K'*.

apparent direction of the target from each of the two extreme head positions. Apparent displacement was measured using a device with two vertical posts. The posts could be separated horizontally along a channel positioned directly in front of the listener, approximately at waist level. Haptic separation of the posts indicated the magnitude of any perceived source displacement. The listener indicated verbally whether such displacement occurred with the head's motion or opposite to it. Apparent direction was indicated by having the listener position another, single post (just below chest height) to seem directly in line between his or her head and the position of the sound source. In this experiment (and the final one) only the dead-room condition was used.

In order to alter the perceived distance of target stimuli under the constant conditions of reverberation, we varied both sound level and spectral content, concurrently. The basic stimulus was a 750-ms burst of broadband noise, rolled off rapidly under 1 kHz. The high-frequency content was manipulated by changing the cutoff value for additional lowpass filtering. A stimulus with a sound level of 62 dBA and a lowpass cutoff at 9.0 kHz was chosen as a standard. Remember that a sound should seem closer to the listener as its sound level and its high-frequency content increase. A sound should seem farther as its sound level and high-frequency content decrease. (The values for the standard and for the four other stimuli are shown in Table I, labeled according to these expectations.) All stimuli were presented to the listener from a Heil air-motion transformer (the tweeter section from an ESS loudspeaker system).

Each trial began with five presentations of the Standard. (These presentations were intended to create a stable initial percept of distance.) Each trial ended with five presentations of the "target" stimulus. For the Mid-Near and Mid-Far targets, only the Standard and the target stimulus were used. For the Near and Far targets, three additional presentations of either the Mid-Near or the Mid-Far stimulus, respectively, were used between the standard and the target stimulus, to create a smoother transition in apparent distance. The systematic changes in the signal characteristics were expected to produce clear shifts in auditory depth for each of the nonstandard stimuli. The final two presentations of any target were always the ones to be judged.

During one phase of the experiment, listeners reported the apparent direction of these final two sounds, from one or the other extreme head position. During another phase of the experiment, listeners reported the apparent lateral displacement of these final stimuli. That is, they listened to the first of the final bursts from one head position. They then quickly moved to the other head position, and were presented with the second of the final bursts. Listeners returned to a center position and reported any perceived displacement, using the device previously described.

Phenomenal geometry (Gogel, 1990) states that the perceived distance (D') of a target source may be calculated from the judgments of apparent displacement (W') according to Eq. (2):

$$D' = (K' - W')/2\tan(\phi'/2). \qquad (2)$$

where D', K', and W' are measurements of linear extent; W' is considered positive, if the source seems to move with the head, and negative if the source seems to move opposite to the head. The angle ϕ' indicates the angle of intersection of the lines of apparent direction, determined by the listener's directional judgments; K' represents the extent of perceived self-motion (here again assumed to equal the actual head movement, K).

The overall results of this experiment are shown in Fig. 7. Although the differences in the calculated values of D' were not great, there was a significant shift in the values of perceived distance in the manner expected from the manipulation of sound level and spectral content (Page test for ordered alternatives, $L^* = 1.93$, $p = .0268$; Hollander and Wolfe, 1973). What makes these data so interesting, however, is that at no time were the listeners asked to report (or even to consider) the distances to the sounds. The values shown are entirely as calculated from the combined displacement and directional judgments.

Furthermore, unlike the experiment by Mershon and Hutson (1991), the effects of any errors in apparent direction have already been incorporated in the calculations. The systematic variation is thus more clearly tied to the intentional manipulations of perceived distance, supporting the predictions from phenomenal geometry.

TABLE I. Characteristics of the stimuli in research by Cox (1992). Sound levels (dBA) were measured at the normal position of the listener's head.

Stimulus	*Sound level*	*Lowpass filter (kHz)*
Near	67.5	11.0
Mid-Near	65.0	10.0
Standard	62.0	9.0
Mid-Far	60.0	8.0
Far	57.5	7.0

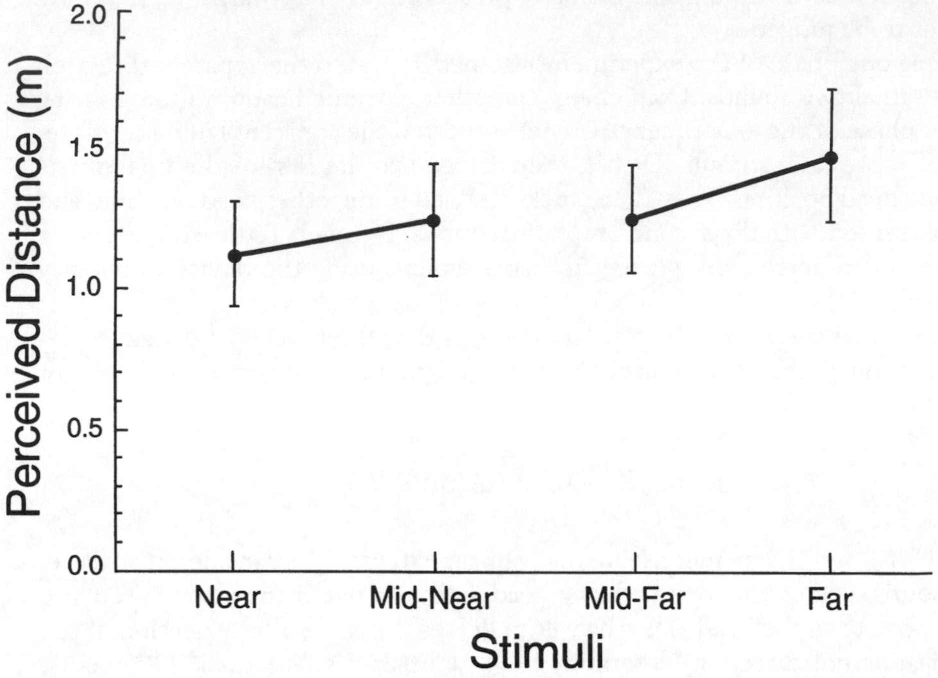

FIG. 7. Data from Cox (1992): Perceived distance values calculated from combined displacement and directional judgments for the four experimental stimuli (sound levels and lowpass cutoff values for the stimuli can be found in Table I). All data are given as means (±1 standard error), $n = 29$.

C. A study of off-median pointing

Finally, I briefly describe a somewhat different (and certainly less arduous) task, which is also based on phenomenal geometry and which also promises to provide a possible indirect technique for measuring perceived auditory distance. We have termed this new procedure the "off-median pointing task" (Mershon and Castle, 1996). Among its advantages are that it requires much less instruction to the listener than the concomitant displacement task, because the response involves primarily pointing to the apparent location of the target sound, with no necessity for specially timed body movement. Unlike traditional measures of directional pointing, however, the listener is asked to adjust a pointer whose center-of-rotation is not centered on the listener, but which is instead positioned to the side of the listener.

Figure 8 shows the off-median task. As should be clear from the drawing, different apparent distances of the target sound should result in different rotations of the pointer. The pointer itself is not visible to the listener; it is controlled haptically by the listener's preferred hand. A preliminary study shows that most listeners can be highly reliable in aiming the pointer toward a specified target, despite the unusual aspects of the situation (Mershon and Castle, 1996).

Again, unless there is a specific wish to do so, no mention need be made of distance in instructing the listener. The listener may simply be requested to point the marker rod at the apparent source of the sound. (It is, of course, important either to be certain that the sound appears directly in front of the listener or to obtain an additional measurement using a standard listener-centered pointing response.) Additionally, it is important to know the apparent distance between the listener and the center of rotation of the marker rod. In our initial studies, we have assumed that this "baseline" separation (*B*) is small enough that available haptic information provides a nearly veridical percept.

To examine the usefulness of the off-median pointing task, we chose first to investigate some stimuli that we had recently been studying with traditional verbal reports (Mershon and Philbeck, 1996).

Past experiments have been pretty consistent in showing that different types of recorded speech are reported as seeming to be at systematically different distances, even when played back to listeners at essentially equivalent sound levels. To be specific, whispered speech is described as seeming closer than conversational speech, which itself seems closer than shouted speech (Gardner, 1969; McGregor, Horn, and Todd, 1985; Mershon and Philbeck, 1996).

We therefore applied our off-median pointing task to the measurement of such sounds (i.e., to samples of prerecorded male or female voices uttering the phrase "How does my voice seem?" in each of the three speech styles). No mention of distance was made to our listeners during the instructions. Instead, listeners were instructed using a drawing that indicated the basics of the task. In the drawing, potential target positions were scattered randomly at a variety of distances and in different directions within approximately ±30° of frontal space, relative to the listener's median plane.

The Polk-5 loudspeaker system employed for this experiment was always located in the median plane and at a physical distance of 2.5 m. Because the appropriate basis for "equalizing" varied speech samples is not clear, we intentionally biased the conditions against finding the expected difference in perceived

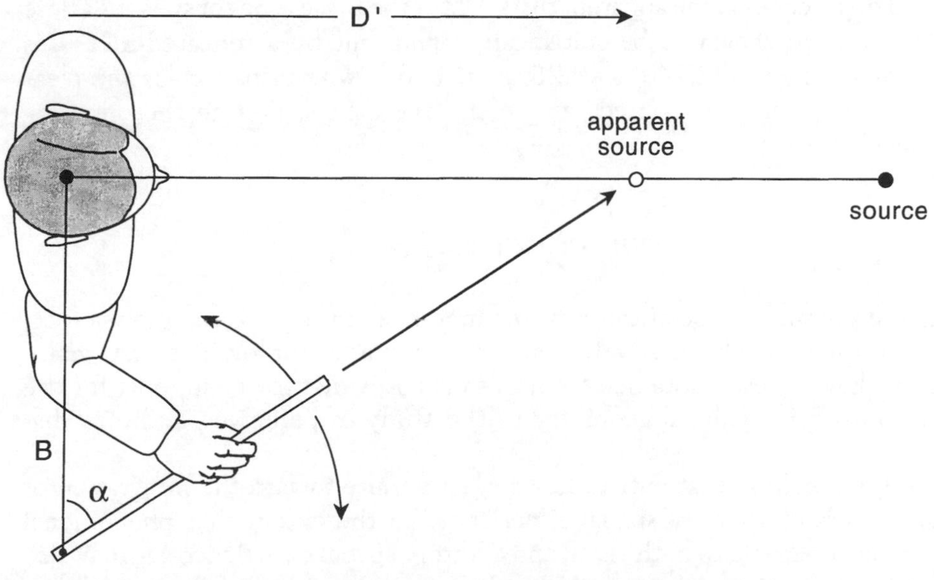

FIG. 8. Overhead view of the off-median pointing task. The listener is shown adjusting the pointer to alignment with a sound that appears to originate from a location closer than the actual source.

distance. Thus, the shouted speech was actually presented at an average level about 6 dB greater than the levels for the whispered or conversational speech samples. This may have brought the shouted speech samples slightly closer in perceived distance than might otherwise have been the case, but insured that, if the shouts were reported to be farther, it could not be a consequence of an inadvertent sound-level cue.

As suggested by the presentation in Fig. 8, a first approximation for the apparent distance of each target sound is given by Eq. (3):

$$D' = B(\tan\alpha), \tag{3}$$

where D' and B are in common units of linear extent. Note, however, that Eq. (3) is a mixed equation in which both physical and perceptual quantities are included. Thus, it implicitly involves the assumption that the perceived length (B') of the baseline of the off-median triangle is correct ($B' = B$), and that the angular settings of the marker rod (α) correctly reflect the corresponding, haptically perceived directions (α') for each judgment. A full test of the predictions of phenomenal geometry would require the verification of these assumptions and/or the substitution of appropriate values of B' and α' for B and α, respectively. The resulting equation would then be specified entirely in terms of the critical perceptual variables. Until such validation can be completed, it would be prudent to consider that off-median reports can indicate relative perceived distances under a constant set of conditions, but not to assume that the absolute values of auditory perceived distance are necessarily correct.

Figure 9 shows the results of the described experiment. The off-median task (even without the mention of distance) was fully capable of distinguishing the expected differences in the apparent distances of the three types of speech. These differences were shown to be statistically significant by a repeated-measures analysis of variance [$F(2,140) = 4.26$, $p = .016$]. Note in particular the clear difference between the shouted sample and the others, despite the opposing sound-level cue.

III. CONCLUSIONS

We plan to pursue the use of this new off-median pointing task in our research, because it appears to be relatively easy for listeners to employ. The systematic results we have already obtained from this task provide further support for the application of phenomenal geometry to the study of perceived auditory distance.

Indeed, we believe that our studies suggest a route toward the integration of several aspects of auditory spatial experience. To the extent that phenomenal geometry is applicable to both visual and auditory spatial experiences, it may also represent a theoretical structure within which spatial experiences in general may be considered.

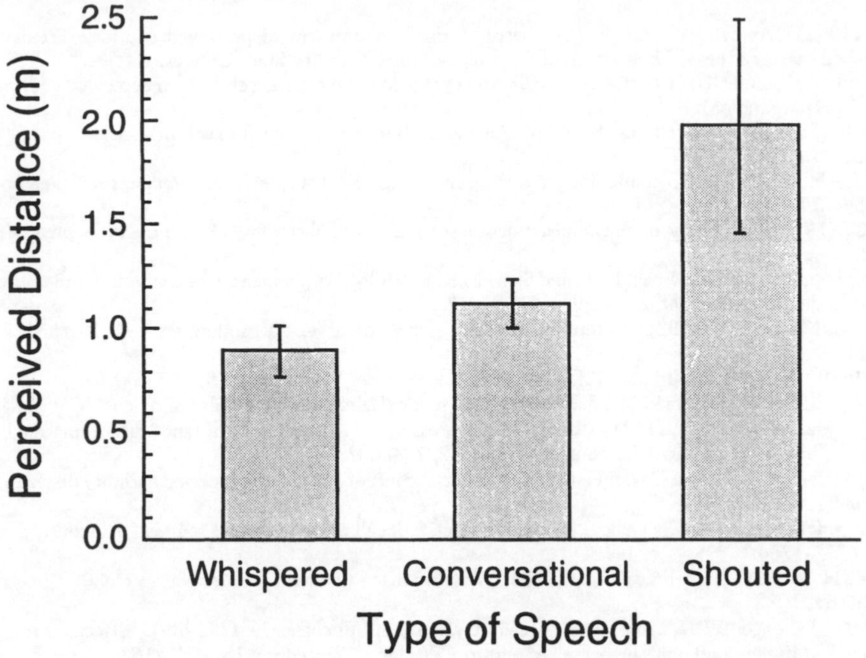

FIG. 9. Data from Mershon and Castle (1996): Perceived distances calculated for the three different types of speech, as determined from the off-median pointing task. All data are given as means (±1 standard error), n = 72.

ACKNOWLEDGMENTS

Development of the laboratory in which the described studies were conducted was supported by National Science Foundation research grant ECS-8023787. Additional equipment was provided by the College of Education and Psychology, North Carolina State University. The author thanks Bill Hutson, Patrick Cox, and Lesley Castle for their collaboration on the three experiments reviewed in this chapter, and David Bright for his assistance with the preparation of the figures.

REFERENCES

Ashmead, D. H., Davis, D. L., and Northington, A. (**1995**). "Contribution of listeners' approaching motion to auditory distance perception," J. Exp. Psych.: Hum. Percept. Perform. **21**, 239–256.

Ashmead, D. H., LeRoy, D., and Odom, R. D. (**1990**). "Perception of the relative distances of nearby sound sources," Percept. Psychophys. **47**, 326–331.

Bekesy, G., von. (**1960**). *Experiments in Hearing* (McGraw-Hill, New York).

Blauert, J. (**1983**). *Spatial Hearing* (MIT, Cambridge, MA).

Carlson, V. R., and Tassone, E. P. (**1962**). "A verbal measure of the perspective attitude," Am. J. Psychol. **75**, 644–647.

Coleman, P. D. (**1962**). "Failure to localize the source distance of an unfamiliar sound," J. Acoust. Soc. Am. **3**, 345–346.

Coleman, P. D. (**1963**). "An analysis of cues to auditory depth perception in free space," Psychol. Bull. **60**, 302–315.

Coleman, P. D. (**1968**). "Dual role of frequency spectrum in determination of auditory distance," J. Acoust. Soc. Am. **44**, 631–632.

Cox, P. H. (1992). "Applying phenomenal geometry to the measurement of perceived auditory distance," Unpublished master's thesis, Department of Psychology, North Carolina State University.
Cox, P. H., and Mershon, D. H. (1996). "Using an indirect method for measuring changes in perceived auditory distance," (in preparation).
Gardner, M. B. (1969). "Distance estimation of 0° or apparent 0°-oriented speech signals in anechoic space," J. Acoust. Soc. Am. **45**, 47–53.
Gogel, W. C. (1976). "An indirect method of measuring perceived distance from familiar size," Percept. Psychophys. **20**, 419–429.
Gogel, W. C. (1990). "A theory of phenomenal geometry and its applications," Percept. Psychophys. **48**, 105–123.
Gogel, W. C., Loomis, J. M., Newman, N. J., and Sharkey, T. J. (1985). "Agreement between indirect measures of perceived distance," Percept. Psychophys. **37**, 17–27.
Gogel, W. C., and Tietz, J. D. (1992). "Determinants of the perception of sagittal motion," Percept. Psychophys. **52**, 75–96.
Guski, R. (1990). "Auditory localization: Effects of reflecting surfaces," Perception **19**, 819–830.
Hollander, M., and Wolfe, D. A. (1973). *Nonparametric Statistical Methods* (John Wiley and Sons, New York).
Litovsky, R. Y., and Clifton, R. K. (1991). "Use of sound-pressure level in auditory distance discrimination by 6–month-old infants and adults," J. Acoust. Soc. Am. **92**, 794–802.
Little, A. D., Mershon, D. H., and Cox, P. H. (1992). "Spectral content as a cue to perceived auditory distance," Perception **21**, 405–416.
Loomis, J. M., Hebert, C., and Cicinelli, J. G. (1990). "Active localization of virtual sounds," J. Acoust. Soc. Am. **88**, 1757–1764.
McGregor, P., Horn, A. G., and Todd, M. A. (1985). "Are familiar sounds ranged more accurately?" Percept. Mot. Skills **61**, 1082.
Mershon, D. H., Ballenger, W. L., Little, A. D., McMurtry, P. L., and Buchanan, J. L. (1989). "Effects of room reflectance and background noise on perceived auditory distance," Perception **18**, 403–416.
Mershon, D. H., and Bowers, J. N. (1979). "Absolute and relative cues for the auditory perception of egocentric distance," Perception **8**, 311–322.
Mershon, D. H., and Castle, L. (1996). "A simple, non-verbal procedure for measuring perceived auditory distance," in preparation.
Mershon, D. H., and Hutson, W. E. (1991). "Toward the indirect measurement of perceived auditory distance," Bull. Psychonom. Soc. **29**, 109–112.
Mershon, D. H., and King, E. L. (1975). "Intensity and reverberation as factors in the auditory perception of egocentric distance," Percept. Psychophys. **18**, 409–415.
Mershon, D. H., and Philbeck, J. W. (1996). "Auditory perceived distance of familiar speech sounds," under revision.
Middlebrooks, J. C., and Green, D. M. (1991). "Sound localization by human listeners," Annu. Rev. Psychol. **42**, 135–159.
Petersen, J. (1990). "Estimation of loudness and apparent distance of pure tones in a free field," Acustica **70**, 61–65.
Speigle, J. M., and Loomis, J. M. (1993). "Auditory distance perception by translating observers," in *Proc. IEEE Symposium on Research Frontiers in Virtual Reality*, San Jose, CA (IEEE, New York), pp. 92–99.
Strybel, T. Z., and Perrott, D. R. (1984). "Discrimination of relative distance in the auditory modality: The success and failure of the loudness discrimination hypothesis," J. Acoust. Soc. Am. **76**, 318–320.

Part IV

Motion Perception

Chapter 14

Some Observations Regarding Motion Without Direction

David R. Perrott
California State University, Los Angeles
Thomas Z. Strybel
California State University, Long Beach
(Received September 1993; revised September 1994)

If the number of publications on a given topic is a valid index of interest, then phenomena associated with motion in the auditory modality have enjoyed considerable attention over the last third of the century. However, of the nearly 80 papers published on this general topic in the last 30 years, less than 20 of these were based on experiments in which a sound source actually moved during the listening interval. In effect, most of the psychophysical and all of the physiological research published during this period utilized stimuli that only "simulated" some aspect of a sound source in motion relative to the listener. In this chapter, the various motion and motion simulation paradigms are discussed with particular attention given to the most commonly employed of these, the sequential presentation of discrete acoustic events (e.g., Altman and Viskov, 1977). Results from our laboratories, using the latter technique, are also presented. This work, conducted over the last 8 years, has led to a most curious observation, namely, that the temporal aspects of the stimulus sequence appear to be the sole determinant of whether or not motion is experienced with this paradigm. Conversely, we find that it is the spatial distribution of the discrete events, far more than the temporal, that seems to underlie the subject's ability to correctly identify the direction of travel. Under some conditions one can even observe "motion without direction." The implications of these and other observations are discussed.

INTRODUCTION

When our first experiment examining motion in the auditory modality was initiated at California State University, Los Angeles, in the fall of 1968, published research on the human capacity to appreciate whether or not a sound source was in motion was nearly nonexistent. Only one study (Pierce, 1901) could be found in which the sound source actually moved during the listening interval. However, there were six published papers that described auditory "autokinesis," reports of motion made by listeners even though the sound source was stationary throughout the presentation (Bernardin and Gruber, 1957; Fisher, 1961, 1966; Anderson and Moss, 1964; Cautela and McLaughlin, 1965). Between these two extremes (actual motion and the autokinetic illusion of motion), there were several papers (in some the reports of motion were only mentioned incidentally) that considered the conditions under which the experience of motion could be invoked: (1) when two sound sources were activated in succession (Burtt, 1917; Kester, 1926; Klemm, 1920; Matheisen, 1931; Scholz, 1924; Trimble, 1928; Wittmann, 1925) and (2) in a lateralization task, when the interaural time difference of a lowpass noise was varied in discrete steps over the listening interval (Wilcott and Gales, 1954; Wilcott, 1955). A number of papers had also been published on the binaural beat phenomenon during the first half of the century (e.g., Halverson, 1927; Lane, 1925; Licklider and Webster, 1950; Peterson, 1916; Stewart, 1917; Valentine, 1928). In these papers, it was common to report that for some tonal stimuli (generally tones lower than 1000 Hz), small interaural frequency differences resulted in a "rotating tone" (i.e., the auditory image moved more or less continuously). Unlike the autokinetic task mentioned earlier, in all of the latter paradigms at least some of the information that would normally be present if a sound source were moved was available to the listener. Presentations in which the stimulus sequence contains at least one aspect of the information normally present during motion of an active sound source are referred to as motion simulation paradigms.

In preparing this chapter, it seemed reasonable to access the trends, if any, in research on this topic over the intervening years (a "snapshot" of the current literature). Papers not readily available to the authors in their complete form (at least 20 conference reports, for example) were not included. The solid line in Fig. 1 presents the cumulative number of papers presenting new data on motion perception in the auditory modality from 1901 to the present (both psychophysical and physiological experiments are included). It is fair to say that the auditory motion literature has been increasing at a steady rate since 1968. The lowest curve in Fig. 1 (open squares) represents the cumulative total of publications that reported results acquired when a sound source was actually moved relative to the listener. Beginning with the publication by Harris and Sergeant (1971), this literature has been growing at a rate of one paper per year. The auditory autokinetic literature (X symbols), which was vigorously expanding during the 1960s, abruptly terminated in the mid-1970s (the last published report was by Russell and Nobel, 1974). In contrast, the results from "simulation" paradigms (filled triangles) have been accumulating at a rate of nearly three per year for the last two decades.

The implications of these data seem quite clear. Paradigms that mimic some stimulus aspects that are present when sound sources move, relative to a listener, presently account for most of the existing "motion" literature. The difference in the rate of new publications suggests that our knowledge of how the auditory spatial channel processes motion will become increasingly dependent on data derived from such simulation paradigms.

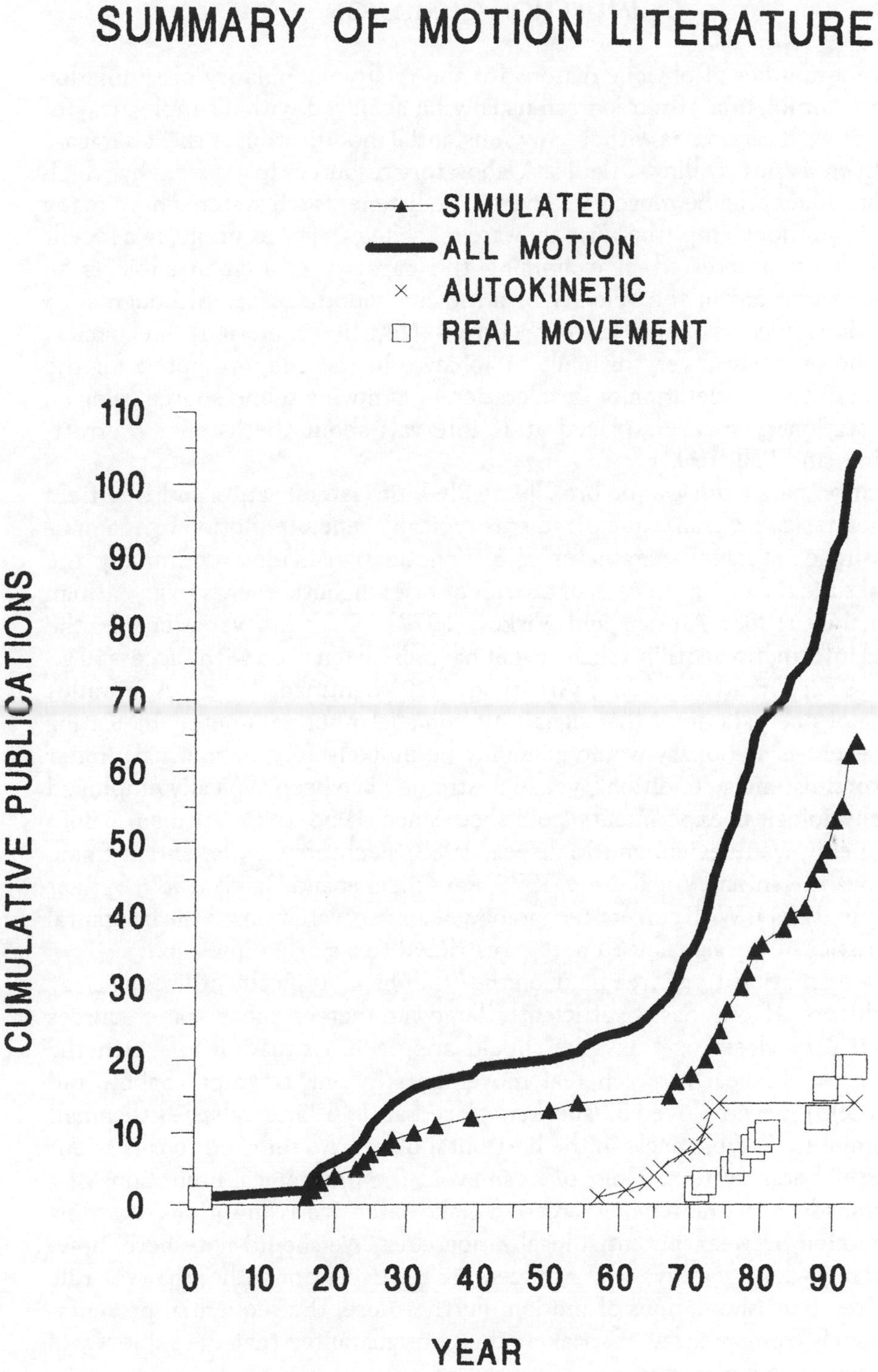

FIG. 1. Number of motion publications by category.

I. SIMULATION OF MOTION

There are a number of obvious reasons for the relative popularity of simulation paradigms. Simulation of motion can usually be achieved with a simple array of speakers or with earphones without any substantial modification of the laboratory facility. Even if one is willing to dedicate laboratory resources to a system by which audio transducers can be moved relative to the listener, such systems have many inherent limitations simply because they are mechanical. For example, in a recent paper we were interested in examining the capacity of human subjects to appreciate variations in the velocity of a moving sound source. Although such manipulations were possible on our current (fourth generation) mechanical system, they were still very difficult to achieve. In the end, we opted for the simulation of the acceleration or deceleration of a moving sound source using an array of stationary speakers placed at 1° intervals about the listener (Perrott, Costantino, and Ball, 1993).

Simulation paradigms can be broadly divided into lateralization and free-field localization tasks. Lateralization paradigms typically generate motion by manipulating a single interaural parameter of a dichotic signal, most commonly the interaural time difference of each of a series of brief dichotic events (e.g., Altman and Romanov, 1988; Altman and Viskov, 1977). Dynamic variations in the interaural information within a single event have also been used with success (e.g., Blauert, 1972; Grantham, 1984; Grantham and Wightman, 1978). A stimulus consisting of one parameter that signals motion and other parameters indicating that the event is stationary would generally be unlikely (even abnormal) under most natural listening conditions, yet such stimuli have been typically employed in the physiological experiments published since 1968 (e.g., Altman, 1968; Altman, Belov, Vaitulevich, and Maltseva, 1983; Bechterev, Syka, and Altman, 1975; Kuwada, Yin, and Wickesberg, 1979; Rauschecker and Harris, 1989; Spitzer and Semple, 1991). With current technology, of course, variations in the interaural characteristics of the signal need not be restricted to a single dimension.

Simulated motion in the free field, on the other hand, typically utilizes an array of transducers. If one has a sufficiently large number of these static sources positioned very close together, one should approach a situation in which the simulation would nearly match real movement. In one attempt (Saberi and Perrott, 1990), we employed 32 speakers placed at 0.46° intervals, less than half of the minimum audible angle in the horizontal plane. We referred to this as our "solid-state" boom system. Thus, one can avoid the mechanical limitations of a moving transducer without being forced to make extensive assumptions regarding the interaction between potential localization cues. We should note here, however, that high-density arrays of transducers are the exception rather than the rule in most free-field simulations of motion. Furthermore, the sequential presentation of signals from an array of speakers does not guarantee that the subject will hear the sound as moving.

Of course, with any simulation, one must be concerned with fidelity, or how closely the paradigm mimics the real event. In most of the auditory simulation literature this step has been ignored, and with good reason. A moving sound produces a variety of potential binaural and monaural cues. An effective, high-fidelity simulation of motion should contain all of the information required by the auditory system. The difficulty in creating such a simulation is that presently we do not know which cues are actually used or their relative contributions. In essence, the adequacy of any auditory motion simulation paradigm is unknown.

In the visual motion perception literature, one seldom encounters the idea of motion simulation, and real motion is seldom used (for a review of this topic see Anstis, 1986). Indeed, over the last five decades there has been a systematic attempt to identify the conditions under which motion is perceived, particularly the "minimum" conditions using the simplest possible stimulus that creates the perception of motion. What is required is that one must systematically ask the subject whether or not "motion" is present. Unfortunately, in many auditory simulation experiments this question is either not asked or it is obtained informally. Thus, a subject may be required to indicate whether a click train moved left or right, but it is the discrimination of the direction of the event sequence that is considered and not whether motion is actually experienced. In these experiments it is even possible that motion is not heard on many trials, and that the perception of motion maybe unrelated to the subject's ability to detect the direction of motion. For example, performance on the direction identification task may be the result of the listener relying on static cues (e.g., starting and/or ending points of the movement sequence) to determine the "direction" of motion. In the next section, we present the results of a number of experiments that were conducted over the last 8 years. In every experiment, the subjects were asked to indicate whether or not motion was heard and the direction (or order) of the event sequence.

II. AUDITORY APPARENT MOTION

In the visual literature, the term *apparent motion* is employed to describe the illusion of motion that may result when two or more stationary events are presented sequentially (Boring, 1942). Aside from the fact that such stroboscopic effects are critical in the generation of motion in most visual media, the apparent motion paradigm has also been the primary research vehicle employed in the visual literature. Interestingly, the first simulated motion experiment in the auditory modality (Burtt, 1917) was in fact a systematic replication of the now classic visual apparent motion experiments of Wertheimer (1912).

Figure 2 presents what we believe to be an interesting view of the existing auditory motion simulation literature. If one ignores the various terms that have been employed over the last 76 years, most of the simulation experiments (open squares) used the sequential presentation of two or more auditory events.[1] These are in essence apparent motion experiments. In the experiment reported by

[1]Figure 2 considers only research whose purpose was the simulation of motion. There are also some number of papers that did not deal specifically with auditory motion perception, but inadvertently created the experience of motion (as reported by the subjects) through the sequential presentation of acoustic events (e.g., Perrott, 1984; Perrott and Pacheco, 1989).

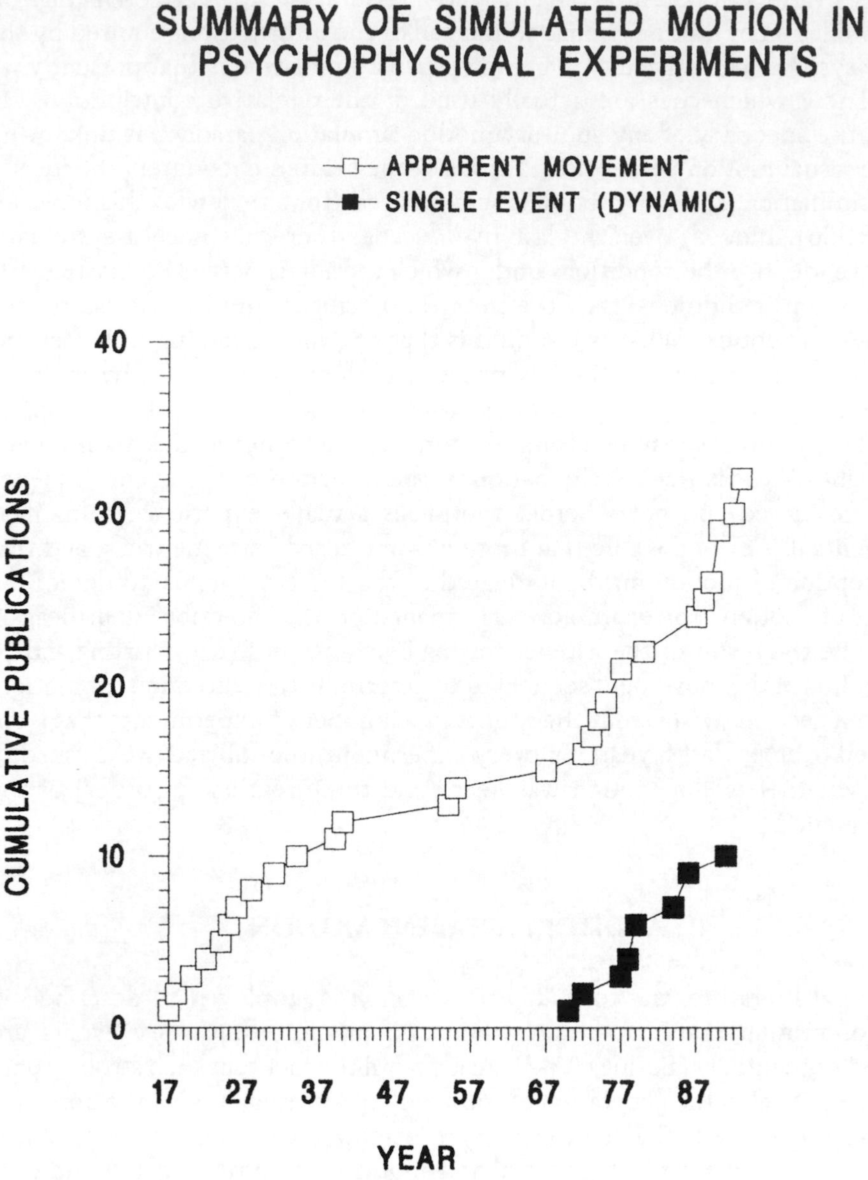

FIG. 2. Number of simulated motion publications by category.

Altman and Viskov (1977), for example, a series of clicks was presented sequentially. Although the total number of acoustic events presented on a given trial could be quite large, at least relative to most apparent motion experiments, the number of events has never been a defining feature of apparent or stroboscopic motion. In fact, the "minimum" number of dichotic clicks required for the perception of motion is two—the number used in most apparent motion experiments (Viskov, 1975). A small number of other simulation experiments (filled squares) that employed dynamic variations in the binaural signal, in particular some of the work reported by Grantham (e.g., Grantham, 1986; Grantham and Wightman, 1978), cannot be so easily classified. Grantham (1986), for example, created sound images whose location was determined by dynamically varying the intensity of the signals generated by each of two speakers.

As illustrated in Fig. 3, in the simplest of apparent movement paradigms, only two speakers are activated sequentially. Typically the delay between the onset of the first event and the onset of the second (the interstimulus onset interval or ISOI) is manipulated within the test session using the method of constant stimuli. Both the ISOI and the duration of the sounds are important in determining

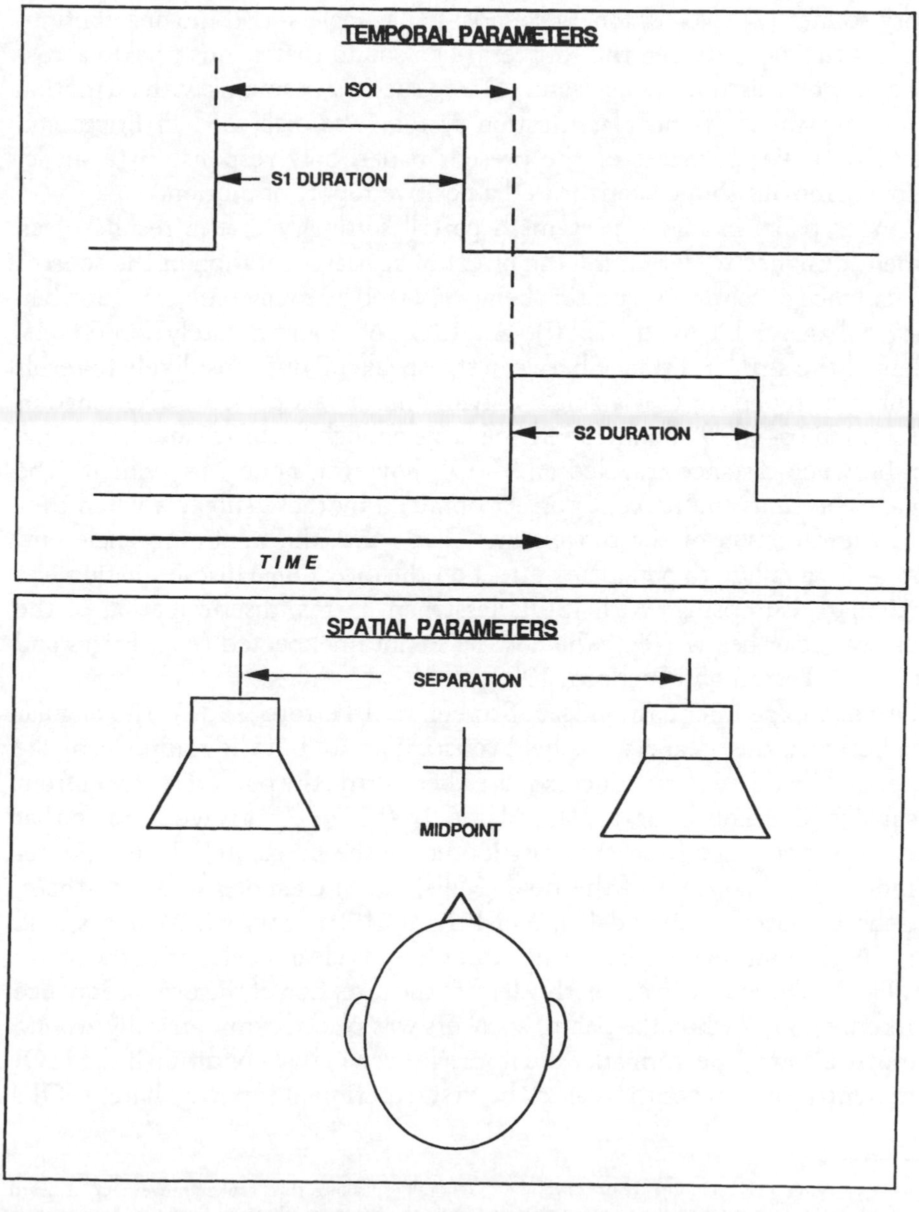

FIG. 3. Stimulus parameters in the perception of auditory apparent motion.

whether or not motion is heard. In most of the experiments that are reported here, the duration of each of the two events was set at 50 ms. The optimal ISOI for continuous motion under these conditions lies between 30 and 60 ms. In effect, the two events may be completely successive with a 10-ms gap between the offset of the first event and the onset of the second (i.e., 60-ms ISOI) or they may actually overlap for 20 ms (i.e., 30-ms ISOI).

Unlike the typical minimum audible movement angle (MAMA) task that we employ in our laboratory (simulated or real motion), the subject is asked to indicate whether or not motion was heard as well as the direction of the event sequence. Usually five response categories are available to the subject: (1) a single stationary sound; (2) two stationary sounds; (3) a single sound moving continuously across the gap between the sources; (4) a sound that seems to skip across the space or move discontinuously; and (5) two successive sounds with no motion heard. Development of this classification system was discussed in Briggs and Perrott (1972). For purposes of the present paper, only response 3 (a single, continuously moving sound) constituted a positive report of motion.[2]

The upper panel in Fig. 4 presents a partial summary of the results of an experiment designed to determine the effect of spatial separation of the sources on the incidence of continuous motion being reported by 8 naive subjects (Strybel, Manligas, Chan, and Perrott, 1990). An ISOI of approximately 30–60 ms, regardless of the angular distance between the speakers, was most likely to result in the subjects reporting that a single moving image was present. The range of angles sampled (6–160°) should have been large enough for us to detect a simple relation between distance traveled and ISOI; however, none was evident. The lower panel presents the percent correct obtained by these subjects when they reported the direction of the movement. Given that the minimum angle employed was 6°, a failure to obtain any effect on the directional discrimination was not particularly surprising. With ISOIs less than 25 ms, discrimination of the direction was at or below 70%, which was also not unexpected (e.g., Briggs and Perrott, 1972; Perrott and Pacheco, 1989).

In the next experiment (Manligas, Strybel, and Perrott, 1987), the angular distance between the speakers was held constant at 40° but the midpoint of the arc subtended by the two transducers was either astride the point directly in front of the subject (0° azimuth) or displaced laterally 45° or 90°. It is well known that localization performance for events distributed on the horizontal plane is poorer in the more lateral portions of the field (Mills, 1958; Chandler and Grantham, 1992; Saberi, Dostal, Sadralodabai, and Perrott, 1991; Strybel, Manligas, and Perrott, 1992). Some evidence for the latter effect is clearly evident in the lower panel of Fig. 5. The ability to correctly identify the direction of the event sequence was markedly poorer when the pair of speakers was placed symmetrically around 90° azimuth, although performance did improve even in that condition if the ISOI was sufficiently long. In contrast, as in the first experiment reported here, ISOI's

[2]Response category 4 is also indicative of movement. Generally speaking, this "broken movement" is heard at ISOIs of 60–200 ms. In most of the research reported here, the functions obtained for continuous motion can also describe the broken motion function.

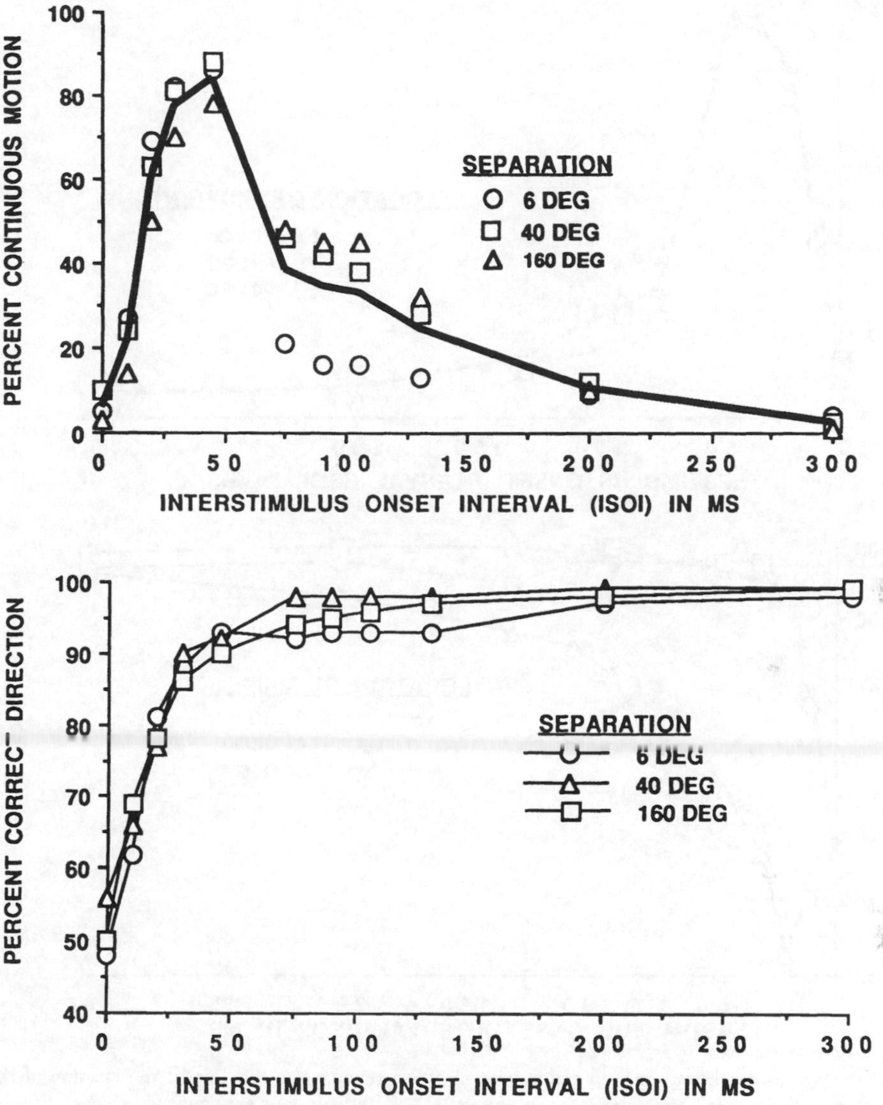

FIG. 4. Percentage of continuous motion and correct direction reports as a function of ISOI for separations of 6° to 160°, centered at 0° azimuth. Eight naive listeners were used in this experiment. Stimuli were two 50-ms broadband noise bursts. [After Strybel *et al.*, 1990.]

of 30–60 ms were still optimal for the reports of continuous motion, regardless of the locus of the midpoint of the speaker array (see upper panel of Fig. 5).

Strybel and Neale (1994) also found the optimal ISOIs for continuous movement were approximately 30–60 ms, when a pair of 50-ms noise pulses was employed, regardless of whether or not monaural or binaural conditions were imposed upon the listeners (see upper left panel of Fig. 6). Localization performance was at chance for the three naive and three experienced subjects tested monaurally (see the lower left panel), which was not surprising considering that the bandwidth of the noise stimulus (2–4 kHz) employed was not favorable for

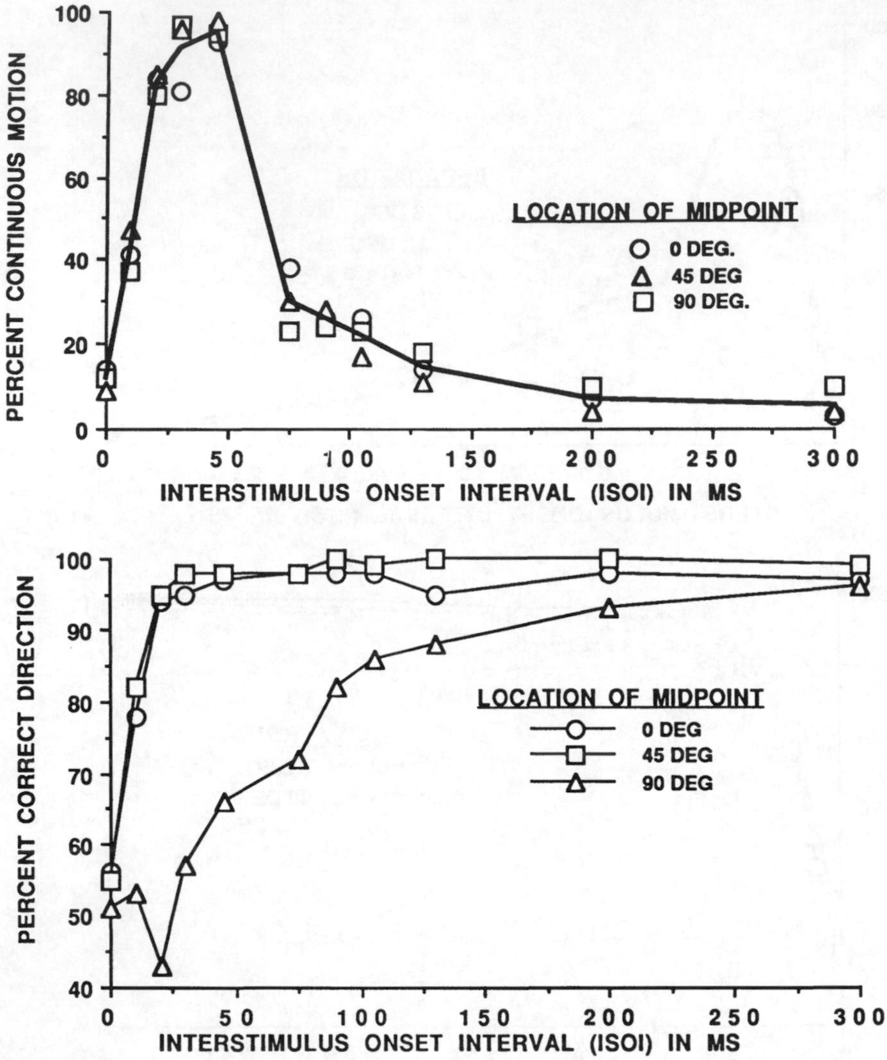

FIG. 5. Percentage of continuous motion and correct direction reports as a function of the location of the midpoint between the sources. Separation was constant at 40°. Data from four experienced listeners. Stimuli were two 50-ms broadband noise bursts. [After Manligas *et al.*, 1987.]

monaural static localization. These results clearly show that motion can be heard (upper left panel) in the absence of an accurate assessment of the direction of that motion (lower left panel). The upper right-hand panel simply presents the same experiment performed with 300-ms noise pulses. It has been shown previously (e.g., Briggs and Perrott, 1972) that longer ISOIs are required to produce optimal conditions for apparent motion when longer events are employed. Obviously, the latter rule also can be applied to monaural stimuli.

If the temporal constraints required to produce continuous motion when two speakers are activated in sequential order are the same whether or not the subject listens binaurally or monaurally, it should come as no great surprise that the orientation of the array relative to the listener would have little impact. In Fig. 7, taken from Strybel and Neale (1994), the results obtained when the speakers were arrayed on the horizontal or vertical plane are presented. In addition, tests were also conducted with one speaker located at 0° azimuth and the second at 180° (front/back configuration). As in all of the previous experimental data presented here, the optimal ISOI for motion is the same regardless of the orientation of the speaker array. As expected, discrimination of the direction of motion was far superior for sources oriented on the horizontal than the vertical (Saberi and Perrott, 1990). Performance on the front/back dimension was found to be similar to that observed on the vertical. Note that in this experiment, a more limited range of ISOIs (0–70 ms) was used and continuous motion was reported for the same range of ISOIs.

Thus far the research that we have described here suggests that only the temporal characteristic of the event sequence determine whether or not motion is experienced; notably, the apparent motion generated by the successive presentation of two brief noise pulses occurs regardless of the spatial distribution of the sources. Similarly, the mode of listening (monaural vs. binaural) seems to have no systematic impact on the apparent motion function (i.e., the range of ISOI's is the same in both cases). The impression of motion that results when two 50-ms auditory events are presented with an ISOI in the range 30–60 ms seems nearly universal.

In our search for other variables that may determine whether or not motion is experienced, we reasoned as follows: If the ability to perceive motion in the environment were to have any adaptive value, then motion should not be

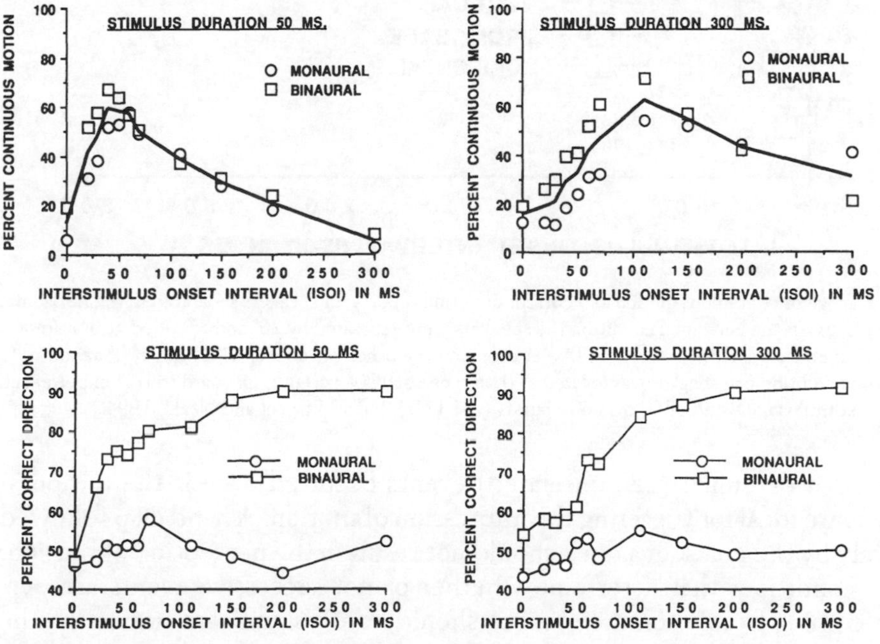

FIG. 6. Percentage of continuous motion and correct direction reports under monaural and binaural listening conditions as a function of ISOI and stimulus duration. The separation was constant at 40°. In the binaural listening condition, the speakers were centered about 0° azimuth. In the monaural condition, the speakers were centered about 90°. The stimulus consisted of random noise with a bandwidth of 2–4 kHz. Data are from six subjects (three naive and three experienced listeners). [After Strybel and Neale, 1994.]

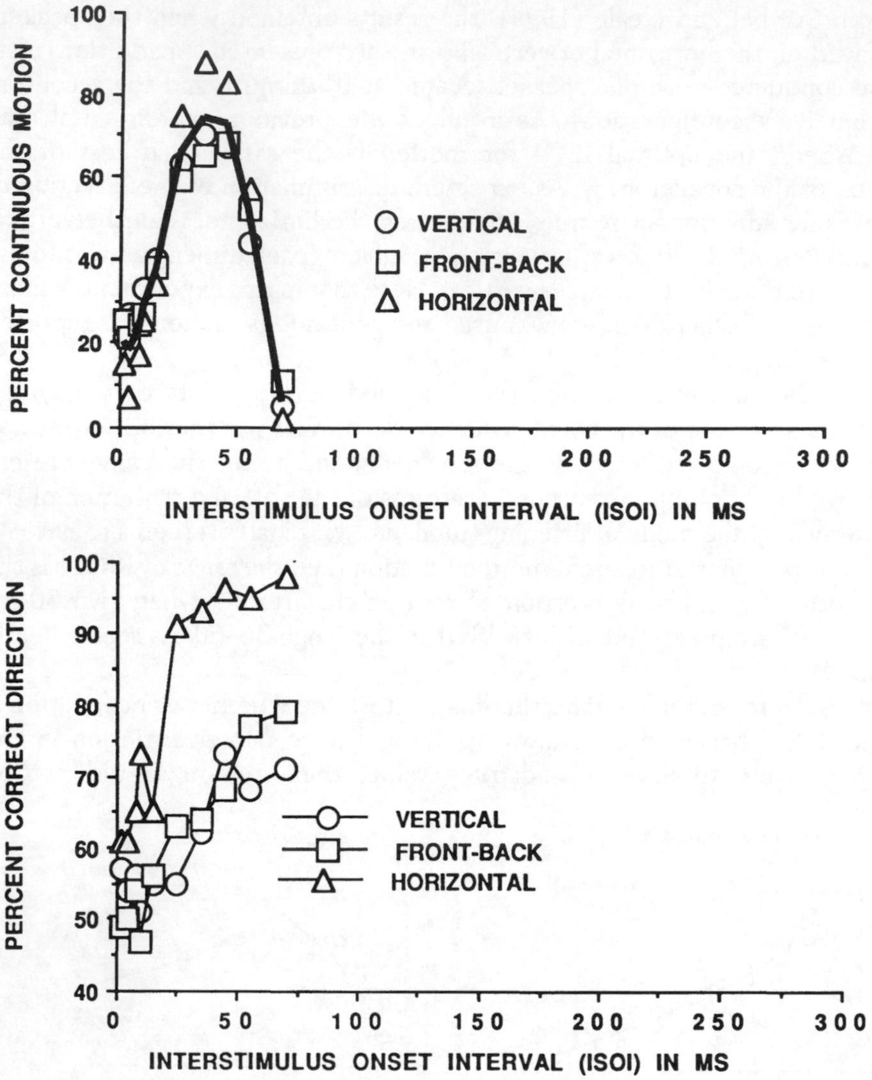

FIG. 7. Percentage of continuous motion and correct direction reports for speakers separated in the horizontal and median planes. In the horizontal condition the speakers were separated by 20° and centered at 0° azimuth. In the vertical condition, one speaker was at 0° elevation and the other 20° above, with both at 0° azimuth. In the front/back condition one speaker was located at 0° and one at 180° azimuth. Data are from 5 experienced listeners. The stimulus consisted of 50-ms noise bursts (2–8 kHz). [After Strybel and Neale, 1994.]

experienced if dissimilar (i.e., unrelated) events occurred even if the temporal sequence were ideal for triggering the impression of motion. A hand clap followed successively by the quack of a duck should not result in the perception of motion. In effect, conditions that determine whether or not successive events are perceived as coming from a common source should have a significant impact on the apparent motion function.

The test conditions were identical with those described earlier but with the following changes: (1) only ISOIs of 10, 40, and 90 ms were employed; (2) one of the events (first or second pulse) was a 1-kHz tone; and (3) the other event was a tone that varied, from trial to trial, from 0.7 to 4 kHz. From the previous experiments, we expected that the ISOI of 40 ms would result in continuous motion reports, at least with two identical tones. Neither the 10-ms nor the 90-ms ISOI should be effective in producing continuous motion.

The results of this manipulation are presented in Fig. 8. The horizontal axis now indicates the frequency of the disparate tone. In the upper panel, as expected, the optimal condition for the report of motion was evident at an ISOI of 40 ms.

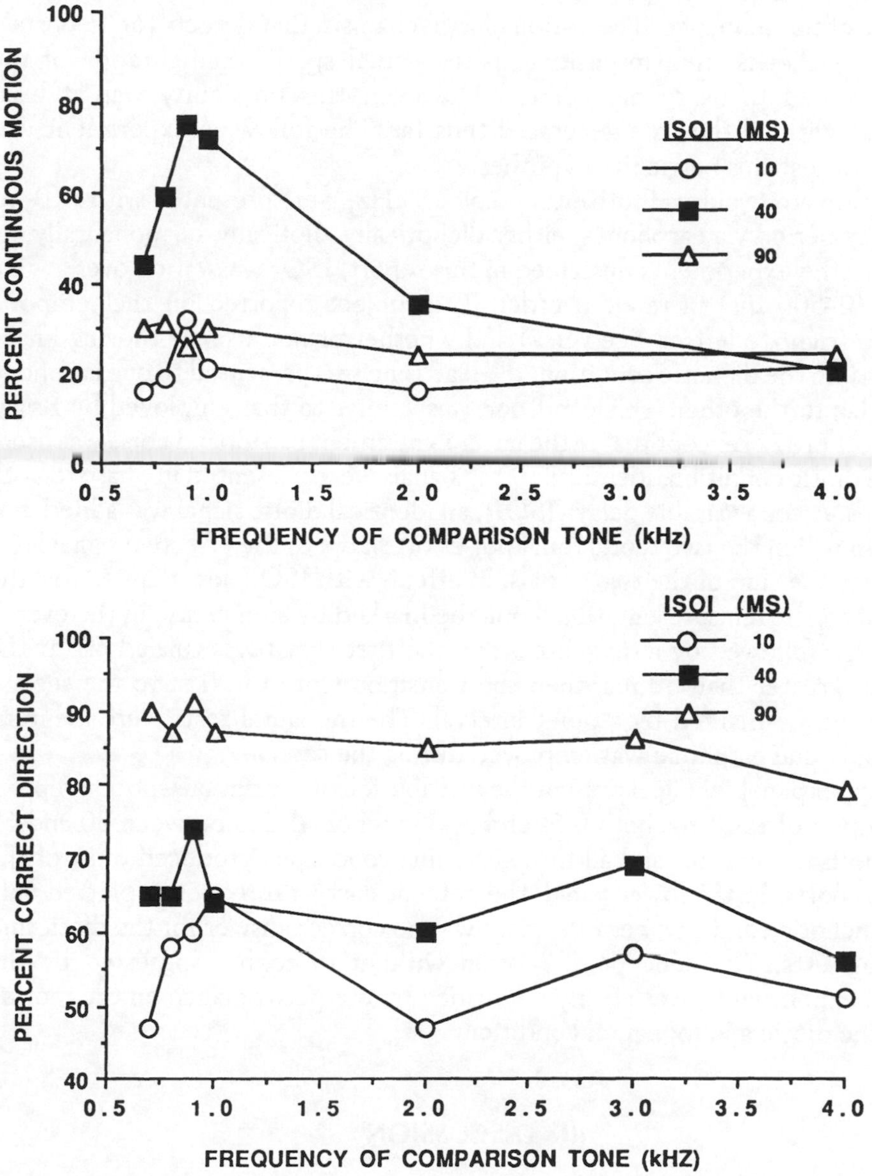

FIG. 8. Percentage of continuous motion and correct direction reports for sine waves differing in frequency. The speakers separated by 20° in the horizontal plane (with the midpoint at 0° azimuth). Data are from 3 experienced listeners and 1 naive listener.

However, unlike the results reported earlier in this chapter, ISOI was no longer the sole determinant of whether or not the 50-ms events would be appreciated as moving. A frequency difference of more than 100 Hz in the two successive events abruptly reduced the likelihood of motion being reported. Localization performance, on the other hand, appeared to be relatively unaffected by the latter variable.

The continuous motion that is reported when human subjects are presented two auditory events in succession, if the sounds are spectrally similar (as noted in the last experiment), appears to be determined exclusively by the temporal structure of the sequence. The notion of a mechanism that detects (or "reports") motion but that is itself insensitive to the actual spatial configuration of the events seemed to us to be unlikely. However, this possibility was at least consistent with all the data generated thus far. The following experiment was initiated to test this particular hypothesis.

Two 50-ms tone pulses (both either 0.5 or 5 kHz) were presented with a 10-ms rise–decay period via earphones, either dichotically, diotically, or monaurally. As in most of the experiments described in this report, ISOI was varied over a wide interval (0–500 ms) in random order. The subject reported on the temporal sequence (right to left or vice versa) and whether or not a single moving image was heard. In the dichotic condition, the lead tone was presented to one earphone and the lag to the other. This condition was similar to that employed by Briggs and Perrott (1972) except that in the latter experiment broadband noise was used.

In the diotic condition, identical 50-ms signals were presented in phase to both earphones. After a variable delay (ISOI), an identical diotic signal was added. For periods in which the two diotic tonal pulses overlapped, the effective signal level was simply the sum of the two signals. In effect, with ISOIs less than 50 ms, the period of concurrent presentation would be marked by an increase in the overall signal level, followed by a decrease when the first signal was turned off. If the ISOI was greater than 50 ms, then the transition from the first to the second event would be marked by a quiet interval. The monaural tests were identical except only one earphone was employed during the session.

The upper panels of Fig. 9 present the distribution of continuous motion reports as a function of ISOI for both 0.5- and 5-kHz tones. ISOIs between 30 and 60 ms for both frequencies and all three listening conditions produced most of the motion reports. In the lower panel, the percent correct direction is plotted only for the dichotic condition because there was no correct answer for the diotic and monaural tests. The concept of motion without direction, suggested by the previous experiments, was clearly confirmed by the performance on the motion task in the diotic and monaural conditions.

III. DISCUSSION

Many psychophysical experiments have focused on the spatial consequences of motion. Thus, one might ask the subject to discriminate direction of motion, distance traveled, or velocity of the moving sound. All such tasks would require

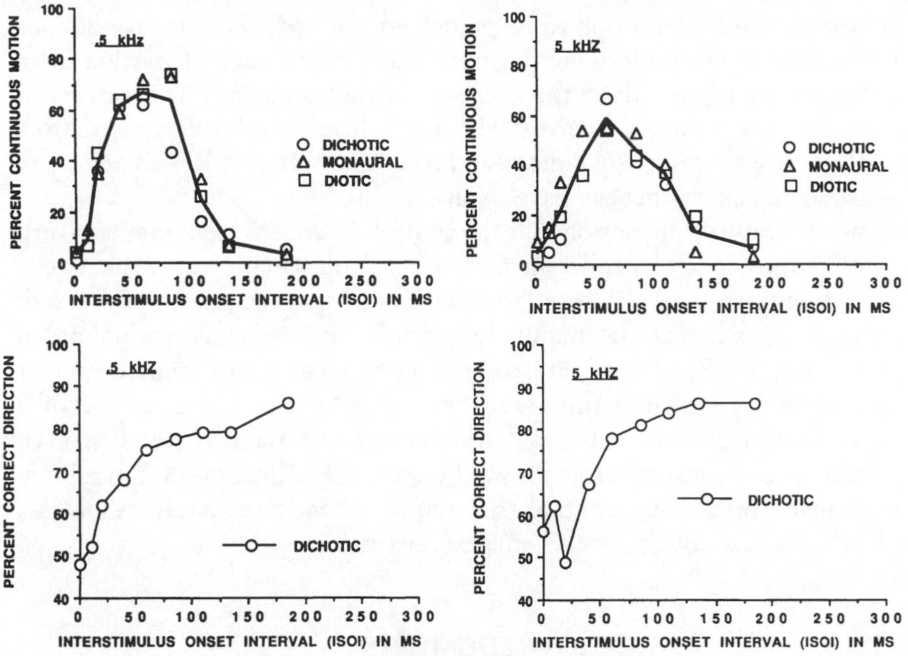

FIG. 9. Percentage of continuous motion and correct direction reports under dichotic, diotic and monaural listening conditions. The stimuli were sine waves of 0.5 and 5 kHz and were the same on each trial. Data are from 4 experienced listeners. [After Kodimer and Strybel, 1991.]

resolving the spatial information in the sequence. It is not surprising that such tasks produce results similar in a general way to those reported in the static paradigm (e.g., Perrott and Tucker, 1988). However, these are spatial discrimination tasks performed with moving sources and not tasks designed specifically to ascertain whether or not the subject detects motion. If, in the experiments reported here, our conclusions regarding auditory motion perception were based solely on the ability to discriminate the direction or distance traveled or the velocity of the displacement, this discussion of auditory motion perception would be substantially different.[3]

The sequence of experiments reported here was initiated in the mid-1980s to determine how the binaural localization mechanism was able to extract information so as to determine that a sound source was in motion relative to the listener under the simplest conditions that we could devise. The specific conclusion that we can draw is that a change in the apparent location of the sound image (or sound

[3]Auditory motion perception, especially when determination of the direction of travel is important, is likely governed by a variety of cues. Dynamic variations in interaural time and intensity differences, for example, probably play a significant role in motion. A monaural component, one that detects changes in amplitude brought about by a moving sound, is also likely. Zakarauskas and Cynader (1991), for example, demonstrated mathematically how the first time derivative of the spectrum level could be used to signal the velocity of a constant intensity moving sound. For a sound moving around the head, the spectrum level at each ear is proportional to the head pinna directivity function. For sounds moving on other trajectories, spectrum level, interaural intensity differences, and their first time derivatives can signal the velocity of the source. At the present time, we are unable to determine how these monaural and binaural cues might be integrated in listening situations when all motion cues are present.

source) is not required for motion to be perceived. Indeed, there is no evidence of any spatial constraints underlying the perceptual experience of motion in an apparent motion paradigm. Given the presence of motion using a tonal stimulus under monaural conditions, it seems likely that a brief amplitude modulation, within a well-defined temporal window (and frequency channel), is an adequate trigger for the mechanism that we have explored.[4,5]

In the visual literature, the notion that the central nervous system may perform an analysis of sensory input by reducing the complex information available at the retina into a finite series of discrete "features" has been frequently discussed. Neural elements sensitive to motion of the stimulus are certainly not unknown (e.g., Westheimer, 1988). The ability to appreciate change in stimulation over time, as noted in the research presented here, is a critical characteristic of a "motion detection mechanism." It is only the lack of a spatial constraint that we find surprising. The latter observation is, we believe, a significant problem for any theory of auditory motion perception that requires that the system resolves a "change" in the location of the sound image over time.

ACKNOWLEDGMENTS

This research was supported in part by a grant from the National Science Foundation (BNS-9025118).

REFERENCES[6]

Ahissar, M., Ahissar, E., Bergman, H., and Vaadia, E. (**1992**). "Encoding of sound-source location and movement: Activity of single neurons and interactions between adjacent neurons in the monkey auditory cortex," J. Neurophysiol. **67**, 203–215.

Altman, J. (**1968**). "Are there neurons detecting direction of sound source motion?," Exp. Neurol. **22**, 13–25.

Altman, J. (**1984**). "Role of higher parts of the auditory system in the localization of a moving sound source," Neurosci. Behav. Physiol. **14**, 200–205.

Altman, J. (**1988**). "Information processing concerning moving sound sources in the auditory centers and its utilization by brain integrative and motor structures," in *Auditory Pathway: Structure and Function*, edited by J. Syka and R. Masterton (Plenum Press, New York), pp. 349–354.

---

[4]The role of amplitude modulation in auditory motion perception is also suggested in the work of Reinhardt-Rutland (1988, 1992). Reinhardt-Rutland (1992) showed that a changing loudness aftereffect could be produced by an adapting stimulus consisting of simulated moving sound. Motion was simulated by dynamically varying interaural intensity differences, so that the sound amplitude was increasing in one ear and simultaneously decreasing in the other. After the adaptation period, the ear receiving the increasing intensity tone would perceive a steady tone as decreasing in loudness, and the ear receiving the decreasing intensity would perceive the steady tone as increasing. There was no changing-loudness aftereffect for binaural steady-state stimuli presented after the adaptation period. Furthermore, Reinhardt-Rutland (1988) showed that there was very little interaural transfer of a changing loudness aftereffect produced by an increasing or decreasing tone presented monaurally.

[5]There are similar reports in the visual apparent motion literature. In these experiments, the position of a visual figure did not change (objectively), yet motion was reported when the luminance of either the figure or background was changed (Boring, 1942; Anstis, 1967; Gregory and Heard, 1983; Mather, 1984; Derrington, 1985; Masterbroek and Zaagman, 1988). In fact, Anstis (1967) observed that visual apparent motion was reported with only an adaptation-produced apparent change in brightness.

[6]Reference list includes all references used to construct Figs. 1 and 2.

Altman, J., Belov, I., Vaitulevich, S., and Maltseva, N. (1983). "Characteristics of human auditory evoked potentials during lateralization of a moving acoustic image," Neurosci. Behav. Physiol. **13**, 412–418.

Altman, J., and Kalmykova, I. (1986). "Role of the dog's auditory cortex in discrimination of sound signals simulating sound source movement," Hear. Res. **24**, 243–253.

Altman, Y., Nikitin, N., and Shakhshaev, S. (1989). "Sound image lateralization under conditions of immersion hypokinesia," Sens. Syst. **3**, 306–312.

Altman, J., and Romanov, V. (1988). "Psychophysical characteristics of the auditory image movement perception during dichotic stimulation," Int. J. Neurosci. **38**, 369–379.

Altman, J., and Vaitulevich, S. (1990). "Auditory image movement in evoked potential," Electroencephalogr. and Clin. Neurophysiol. **75**, 323–333.

Altman, J., and Viskov, O. (1977). "Discrimination of perceived movement velocity for fused auditory image in dichotic stimulation," J. Acoust. Soc. Am. **61**, 816–819.

Anderson, D., and Moss, C. (1964). "The auditory autokinetic effect," Am. J. Psychol. **77**, 502–503.

Anstis, S. (1967). "Visual adaptation to a gradual change in intensity," Science **155**, 710–712.

Anstis, S. (1986). "Motion perception in the frontal plane," in *Handbook of Perception and Human Performance: Sensory Processes and Perception*, edited by K. R. Boff, L. Kaufman, and J. P. Thomas (Wiley, New York), Vol. 1, Chapter 16.

Bechterev, N., Syka, J., and Altman, J. (1975). "Responses of cerebellar units to stimuli simulating sound source movement and visual moving stimuli," Experientia **31**, 819–821.

Bernardin, A., and Gruber, H. (1957). "An auditory autokinetic effect," Am. J. Psychol. **70**, 133–134.

Blauert, J. (1970). "Zur Tragheit des Richungshorens bei Laufzeit-und Intensitatsstereophonie," Acustica **23**, 287–293.

Blauert, J. (1972). "On the lag of lateralization caused by interaural time and intensity differences," Audiology **11**, 265–270.

Boring, E. (1942). *Sensation and Perception in the History of Experimental Psychology* (Appleton, New York).

Briggs, R., and Perrott, D. R. (1972). "Auditory apparent movement under dichotic listening conditions," J. Exp. Psychol. **92**, 83–91.

Burtt, H. (1917). "Auditory illusions of movement: A preliminary study," J. Exp. Psychol. **2**, 63–75.

Cautela, J., and McLaughlin, D. (1965). "The influence of suggestion on the audioautokinetic effect," J. Psychol. **60**, 117–122.

Chandler, D., and Grantham, D. W. (1992). "Minimum audible movement angle in the horizontal plane as a function of stimulus frequency and bandwidth, source azimuth, and velocity," J. Acoust. Soc. Am. **91**, 1624–1636.

Derrington, A. M. (1985). "Apparent motion from luminance change: Sequence discriminators see it too," Vision Res. **25**, 2003–2004.

Dooley, G. (1986). "The perception of auditory dynamic stimuli," Doctoral dissertation, Department of Experimental Psychology, University of Cambridge, Cambridge, UK.

Ehrenstein, W. (1984). "Richtungsspezifische Adaptation des Raum-und Bewegungshorens," in *Sensory Experience, Adaptation and Perception*, edited by L. Spillman and B. Wootenen (Lawrence Erlbaum Associates, Hillsdale, NJ).

Ehrenstein, W., and Hellweg, F. (1976). "Richtungs-spezifische akustische Nachwirkungen nach vorangegangener Schallrotation," Pfluegers Arch. Suppl. R49, **195**, 365.

Fisher, G. (1961). "Autokinesis in the spatial senses," Bull. Br. Psychol. Soc. **44**, 16–17.

Fisher, G. (1966). "Autokinesis in vision, audition and tactile-kinesthesia," Percept. Mot. Skills **22**, 470–475.

Fobes, J., and Perrott, D. R. (1972). "Auditory autokinesis: Effects of signal frequency and intensity," Psychonom. Sci. **26**, 317–318.

Fobes, J., and Perrott, D. R. (1973). "Auditory autokinesis as a function of intramodal fields," J. Exp. Psychol. **97**, 13–15.

Gatehouse, R., and Frankie, G. (1980). "The development of an auditory concept of speed." J. Genet. Psychol. **136**, 221–229.

Gauthier, G., and Hofferer, J. (1976). "Eye movements in response to real and apparent motions of acoustic targets," Percept. Mot. Skills **42**, 963–971.

Grantham, D. W. (1984). "Discrimination of dynamic interaural intensity differences," J. Acoust. Soc. Am. **76**, 71–76.

Grantham, D. W. (1986). "Detection and discrimination of simulated motion of auditory targets in the horizontal plane," J. Acoust. Soc. Am. **79**, 1939–1949.

Grantham, D. W. (1989). "Motion aftereffects with horizontally moving sound sources in the free field," Percept. Psychophys. **45**, 129–136.

Grantham, D. W. (1989). "Auditory motion perception via successive 'snapshot' analysis," in *Sound Localization by Human Observers: Symposium Proceedings* (National Academy of Sciences, Washington, DC), p. 35.

Grantham, D. W. (1992). "Adaptation to auditory motion in the horizontal plane: Effect of prior exposure to motion detectability," Percept. Psychophys. **52**, 144–150.

Grantham, D. W., and Robinson, D. (1977). "Role of dynamic cues in monaural and binaural signal detection," J. Acoust. Soc. Am. **61**, 542–551.

Grantham, D. W., and Wightman, F. (**1978**). "Detectability of varying interaural temporal differences," J. Acoust. Soc. Am. **63**, 511–523.
Grantham, D. W., and Wightman, F. (**1979**). "Detectability of a pulsed tone in the presence of a masker with time-varying interaural correlation," J. Acoust. Soc. Am. **65**, 1509–1517.
Grantham, D. W., and Wightman, F. (**1979**). "Auditory motion aftereffects," Percept. Psychophys. **26**, 403–408.
Gregory, R. L., and Heard, P. F. (**1983**). "Visual dissociations of movement, position, and stereo depth: Some phenomenal phenomena," Q. J. Exp. Psychol. **35A**, 217–237.
Halliday, R., and Callaway, E. (**1978**). "Time shift evoked potentials (TSEPs): Method and basic results," Electroencephalogr. Clin. Neurophysiol. **45**, 118–121.
Halverson, H. (**1922**). "Binaural localization of phase and intensity," Am. J. Psychol. **33**, 178–212.
Halverson, H. (**1927**). "The upper limits of auditory localization," Am. J. Psychol. **38**, 97–106.
Harris, J. D. (**1972**). "A florilegium of experiments on directional hearing," Acta Otolaryngol. Suppl. 298, 5–260.
Harris, J. D., and Sergeant, R. (**1971**). "Monaural/binaural minimum audible angle for a moving sound source," J. Speech Hear. **14**, 618–629.
Hisata, T. (**1934**). "Experimentelle Untersuchungen ueber die-'Scheinbewegungen' in akustischen Gebeit," Jpn. J. Psychol. **9**, 25–26.
Hornbostel, E. von (**1923**). "Beobachtungen uber ein- und zweiohriges Horen," Psychol. Forsch. **4**, 64–114.
Kester, P. (**1926**). "Uber Lokalisations-und Bewegungs-Erscheinungen bei Gerauschpaaren," Psychol. Forsch. **8**, 75–113.
Klemm, O. (**1918**). "untersuchungen uber die Lokalisation von Schallreizen. 3. Mitteilung: Uber der Anteil des beidohrigen horens," Arch. Ges. Psychol. **38**, 71–114.
Klemm, O. (**1920**). "Untersuchungen uber die Lokalisation von Schallreizen. 4 Mitteilung: Uber den Einfluss des binauralen Zeitunterschiedes auf die Lokalisation," Arch. Ges. Psychol. **40**, 116–146.
Kodimer, M., and Strybel, T. Z. (**1991**). "Auditory apparent motion under dichotic, diotic and monaural listening conditions," Presented at the annual meeting of the Western Psychological Association, San Francisco, CA.
Kolers, P. (**1979**). "A difference between auditory and visual apparent movement," Bull. Psychonom. Soc. **13**, 303–304.
Kuwada, S., Yin, T., and Wickesberg, R. (**1979**). "Response of cat inferior colliculus neurons to binaural beat stimuli: Possible mechanisms for sound localization," Science **228**, 1331–1333.
Lackner, J. (**1977**). "Induction of illusory self-rotation and nystagmus by a rotating sound-field," Aviation Space Environ. Med. **48**, 129–131.
Lakatos, S. (**1993**). "Temporal constraints on apparent motion in auditory space," Percept. Psychophys. **54**, 139–144.
Lane, C. (**1925**). "Binaural beats," Phys. Rev. **26**, 401–412.
Licklider, J., and Webster, J. (**1950**). "On the frequency limits of binaural beats," J. Acoust. Soc. Am. **22**, 468–473.
Manligas, C., Strybel, T., and Perrott, D. (**1987**). "Auditory apparent motion at different locations in space," presented at the Spring meeting of the Western Psychological Association, Long Beach, CA.
Masterbroek, H. A. K., and Zaagman, W. H. (**1988**). "Apparent movements induced by luminance modulations: A model study," Perception **17**, 667–679.
Mateef, S., and Hohnsbein, J. (**1988**). "Dynamic auditory localization: Perceived position of a moving sound source," Acta Physiol. Pharmacolo. **14**, 32–38.
Matheisen, A. (**1931**). "Apparent movements in auditory perception," Psychol. Monogr. **41**, 74–131.
Mather, G. (**1984**). "Luminance change generates apparent movement: Implications for models of directional specificity in the human visual system," Vision Res. **24**, 1399–1405.
Mills, A. (**1958**). "On the minimum audible angle," J. Acoust. Soc. Am. **30**, 237–246.
Moore, C., Cranford, J., and Rahn, A. (**1990**). "Tracking of a 'moving' fused auditory image under conditions that elicit the precedence effect," J. Speech Hear. Res. **33**, 141–148.
Mosseff, A., and Haresign, T. (**1992**). "Response of auditory units in the barn owl's inferior colliculus to continuously varying interaural phase differences," J. Neurophysiol. **67**, 1428–1436.
Mukhamedrakhimov, R. (**1989**). "Role of the hippocampus in the short-term retention of moving and unmoving sound image localization in human beings," Sens. Syst. **3**, 150–158.
Odenthal, D. (**1963**). "Perception and neural representation of simultaneous dichotic pure tone stimuli," Acta Physiol. Pharmacol. Neerl. **12**, 453–496.
Ohmura, H. (**1987**). "Intersensory influences on the perception of apparent movement," Jpn. Psychol. Res. **29**, 1–9.
Perrott, D. R. (**1974**). "Auditory apparent movement," J. Aud. Res. **14**, 163–169.
Perrott, D. R. (**1984**). "Binaural resolution of the size of an acoustic array: Some experiments with stereophonic arrays," J. Acoust. Soc. Am. **76**, 1704–1712.
Perrott, D. R. (**1988**). "Are there motion detectors in the auditory system?," in *Sound Localization by Human Observers: Symposium Proceedings* (National Academy of Sciences, Washington, DC), p. 36.
Perrott, D. R., and Briggs, R. (**1973**). "Effects of the apparent motion of the masker upon the binaural masking function," J. Aud. Res. **13**, 328–332.

Perrott, D. R., Brooks, R., and Fobes, J. L. (1973). "The instability of auditory perceptual experience II: Reports of spontaneous shifts in pitch, loudness and locus," J. Aud. Res. **13**, 220–223.
Perrott, D. R., Buck, V., Waugh, W., and Strybel, T. (1979). "Dynamic auditory localization: Systematic replications of the auditory velocity function," J. Aud. Res. **19**, 277–285.
Perrott, D. R., Costantino, B., and Ball, J. (1993). "Discrimination of moving events which accelerate or decelerate over the listening interval," J. Acoust. Soc. Am. **93**, 1053–1057.
Perrott, D. R., and Fobes, J. (1971). "Autokinesis as a binaural localization phenomenon: Effects of signal bandwidth," J. Exp. Psychol. **87**, 1972–1975.
Perrott, D. R., and French, D. (1969). "Apparent movements of sounds: Auditory autokinesis," Psychonom. Sci. **17**, 207–208.
Perrott, D. R., and Marlborough, K. (1989). "Minimum audible movement angle: Marking the end points of the path traveled by a moving sound source," J. Acoust. Soc. Am. **85**, 1773–1775.
Perrott, D. R., Mason, R., and Fobes, J. (1973). "The instability of auditory perceptual experience I: Auditory autokinesis," J. Aud. Res. **13**, 80–86.
Perrott, D. R., and Musicant, A. (1977). "Minimum auditory movement angle: Binaural localization of moving sound sources," J. Acoust. Soc. Am. **62**, 1463–1466.
Perrott, D. R., and Musicant, A. (1977). "Rotating tones and binaural beats," J. Acoust. Soc. Am. **61**, 1288–1292.
Perrott, D. R., and Musicant, A. (1981). "Dynamic minimum audible angle: Binaural spatial acuity with moving sound sources," J. Aud. Res. **21**, 287–295.
Perrott, D. R., and Nelson, M. (1969). "Limits for the detection of binaural beats," J. Acoust. Soc. Am. **46**, 1477–1481.
Perrott, D. R., and Pacheco, S. (1989). "Minimum audible angle thresholds for broadband noise as a function of the delay between the onset of the lead and lag signals," J. Acoust. Soc. Am. **85**, 2669–2672.
Perrott, D. R., Strybel, T., and Manligas, C. (1987). "Conditions under which the Haas-precedence effect may or may not occur," J. Aud. Res. **27**, 59–72.
Perrott, D. R., and Tucker, J. (1988). "Minimum audible movement angle as a function of signal frequency and the velocity of the source," J. Acoust. Soc. Am. **83**, 1522–1527.
Peterson, J. (1916). "The nature and probable origin of binaural beats," Psychol. Rev. **23**, 333–351.
Pierce, A. (1901). *Auditory and Visual Space Perception* (Longmans, Green and Company, New York).
Rauschecker, J., and Harris, L. (1989). "Auditory and visual neurons in the cat's superior colliculus selective for the direction of apparent motion stimuli," Brain Res. **490**, 56–63.
Reinhardt-Rutland, A. H. (1988). "Interaural transfer of a changing sound level in a tone," J. Gen. Psychol. **115**, 69–73.
Reinhardt-Rutland, A. H. (1992). "Changing-loudness aftereffect following simulated movement: Implications for channel hypotheses concerning sound level change and movement," J. Gen. Psychol. **119**, 113–121.
Rosenblum, L., Carello, C., and Pastore, R. (1987). "Relative effectiveness of three stimulus variables for localizing a moving sound source," Perception **16**, 175–186.
Russell, G., and Nobel, W. (1974). "Effects of signal frequency on auditory autokinesis," J. Exp. Psychol. **103**, 173–174.
Saberi, K., Dostal, L., Sadralodabai, T., and Perrott, D. R. (1991). "Minimum audible angles for horizontal, vertical and oblique orientations," Acustica **75**, 57–61.
Saberi, K., and Perrott, D. R. (1990). "Minimum audible movement angle as a function of sound source trajectory," J. Acoust. Soc. Am. **88**, 2639–2644.
Scholz, W. (1924). "Experimentelle Untersuchungen uber die phanomenale Grosse von Raumstrecken, die durch Sukzessiv-Darbietung zweier Reize begrenzt werden," Psychol. Forsch. **5**, 219–272.
Sovijarvi, A., and Hyvarinen, J. (1974). "Auditory cortical neurons in the cat sensitive to the direction of sound source movement," Brain Res. **73**, 455–471.
Sovijarvi, A., Hyvarinen, J., and Koskinen, K. (1973). "Specific neurons in the auditory cortex of the cat for detecting the direction of sound source movement," Scand. J. Clin. Lab. Invest. **31**, suppl. 130, 18.
Spitzer, M., and Semple, M. (1991). "Interaural phase coding in auditory midbrain: Influence of dynamic stimulus features," Science **254**, 721–724.
Stewart, G. (1917). "Binaural beats," Phys. Rev. **9**, 502–508.
Stream, R., Whitson, E., and Honrubia, V. (1980). "Visual tracking of auditory stimuli," J. Aud. Res. **20**, 233–243.
Strybel, T., Manligas, C., Chan, O., and Perrott, D. R. (1990). "A comparison of the effects of spatial separation on apparent motion between the auditory and visual modalities," Percept. Psychophys. **47**, 439–448.
Strybel, T., Manligas, C., and Perrott, D. R. (1989). "Auditory apparent motion under binaural and monaural listening conditions," Percept. Psychophys. **45**, 371–377.
Strybel, T., Manligas, C., and Perrott, D. R. (1992). "Minimum audible movement angle as a function of the azimuth and elevation of the source," Hum. Fac. **34**, 267–275.
Strybel, T., and Neale, W. (1994). "The effect of burst duration, interstimulus onset interval, and loudspeaker arrangement on auditory apparent motion in the free field," J. Acoust. Soc. Am. **96**, 3463–3475.
Strybel, T., Witty, A., and Perrott, D. R. (1992). "Auditory apparent motion in the free field: The effects of stimulus duration and separation," Percept. Psychophys. **52**, 139–143.

Stumpf, E., Toronchuk, J. M., and Cynader, M. (**1992**). "Neurons in cat primary auditory cortex sensitive to correlates of auditory motion in three-dimensional space," Exp. Brain Res. **88**, 158–168.

Takahashi, T., and Keller, C. (**1992**). "Simulated motion enhances neuronal selectivity for a sound localization cue in background noise," J. Neurosci. **12**, 4381–4390.

Toronchuk, J., Stumpf, E., and Cynader, M. (**1992**). "Auditory cortical neurons sensitive to correlates of auditory motion: Underlying mechanisms," Exp. Brain Res. **88**, 169–180.

Trimble, O. (**1928**). "Some temporal aspects of sound localization," Psychol. Monographs **38**, 172–225.

Valentine, W. (**1928**). "Notes on the binaural beat," Comp. Psychol. **7**, 357–368.

Van Eyl, F. (**1972**). "Effects of acoustics on auditory and visual autokinesis," Psychonom. Sci. **29**, 205–206.

Viskov, O. (**1975**). "The perception of the fused auditory image movement," Hum. Physiol. **1**, 371–376.

Wallach, H. (**1939**). "On sound localization," J. Acoust. Soc. Am. **10**, 270–274.

Wallach, H. (**1940**). "The role of head movements and vestibular and visual cues in sound localization," J. Exp. Psychol. **27**, 339–367.

Waugh, W., Strybel, T., and Perrott, D. R. (**1979**). "Perception of moving sounds: Velocity discrimination," J. Aud. Res. **19**, 103–110.

Weber, B., and Milburn, W. (**1967**). "The effects of arhythmically moving auditory stimuli on eye movements in normal young adults," J. Aud. Res. **7**, 259–266.

Wernick, J., and Starr, A. (**1968**). "Binaural interaction in the superior olivary complex of the cat: An analysis of field potential evoked by binaural-beat stimuli," J. Neurophysiol. **35**, 428–441.

Wertheimer, M. (**1912**). "Experimentelle Studien uber das Sehen von Bewegung," Z. Psychol. **61**, 161–265.

Westheimer, G. (**1988**). "Vision: Space and movement," in *Stevens' Handbook of Experimental Psychology, Vol. I*, edited by R. C. Atkinson, R. J. Herrnstein, G. Lindzey, and R. D. Luce (John Wiley & Sons, New York), pp. 165–193.

Wilcott, R. (**1955**). "Variables affecting the angular displacement threshold of simulated auditory movement," J. Exp. Psychol. **49**, 68–72.

Wilcott, R., and Gales, R. (**1954**). "Comparison of the masked thresholds of a simulated moving and stationary auditory signal," J. Exp. Psychol. **47**, 451–456.

Wittmann, J. (**1925**). "Beitrage zur Analyse des Horens bie dicotischer Reizaufnahme," Arch. Gems. Psychol. **51**, 21–122.

Yin. T., and Kuwada, S. (**1983**). "Binaural interaction in low-frequency neurons in inferior colliculus of the cat: II. Effects of changing rate and direction of interaural phase," J. Neurophysiol. **50**, 1000–1019.

Zakarauskas, P., and Cynader, M. (**1991**). "Aural intensity for a moving source," Hear. Res. **52**, 233–244.

Chapter 15

Auditory Motion Perception: Snapshots Revisited

D. Wesley Grantham
Vanderbilt University School of Medicine

(Received January 1994; revised September 1994)

Auditory spatial resolution in the horizontal plane was measured in a number of conditions involving both dynamic and static signal presentation. In the case of dynamic signal presentation, a single wideband noise signal was presented, and the subject had to say whether it was moving or stationary; in the case of static signal presentation, two stationary noise bursts were presented in succession, and the subject had to say whether they came from the same or from different spatial positions. The critical parameters of interest in both cases were the spatial extent or separation of the source(s) and the velocity of the movement or displacement. For a velocity of 20°/s, subjects used more information in the moving target than that obtained only at stimulus onset and offset; that is, a simple "snapshot" mechanism was not entirely adequate to explain performance. For targets moving at 60°/s, however, performance was as good when only endpoint information was available as when the target was present during its entire trajectory. These results suggest that if there is a specialized mechanism in the auditory system sensitive to horizontal motion, it apparently operates only over a restricted range of velocities and becomes ineffective as velocity increases to 60°/s.

INTRODUCTION

It is not well understood how the human auditory system processes the motion of horizontally moving sound sources. On the one hand, it has been suggested that there are mechanisms in the auditory system that are specifically responsive to moving targets ("motion detectors") (Perrott, Costantino, and Ball, 1993). An alternative argument is that the perception of horizontally moving sounds does not invoke special motion mechanisms, but rather is based on an observer's discrimination of the spatial positions and the temporal sequence associated with a trajectory's endpoints (the so-called "snapshot hypothesis") (Grantham, 1986). The current experiments were designed to shed more light on this interpretive issue.

A. Static and dynamic measures of auditory spatial resolution in the horizontal plane

Before considering the relative merits of the snapshot hypothesis and the motion-detection hypothesis, it is instructive to consider auditory spatial resolution as measured with stationary versus moving targets. The first case is exemplified by the minimum audible angle (MAA) experiment. In this experiment two brief (e.g., 20-ms) stationary sounds (markers) are presented in sequence, and the subject must say whether the second is to the left or right of the first. The angular separation between the two markers for which subjects achieve some given criterion level of performance is defined as the MAA. Typically, the best MAA is about 1° of arc for low-frequency tones or noises presented directly in front of a subject (Mills, 1958; Harris and Sergeant, 1971; Grantham, 1986; Perrott and Pacheco, 1989; Hartmann and Rakerd, 1989; Chandler and Grantham, 1992).

In contrast to the statically measured MAA, a dynamic measure of auditory spatial resolution can be made with horizontally moving sounds. In a typical experiment, a single sound is presented from a loudspeaker that is moving either left-to-right or right-to-left in front of the observer. The smallest angular excursion required for a subject to just discriminate the direction of travel is called the minimum audible movement angle (MAMA). Under the best circumstances (slow-moving targets presented from directly in front of the subject), the MAMA is 2–5° (Harris and Sergeant, 1971; Grantham, 1986; Chandler and Grantham, 1992). Thus, when measured under optimum conditions, the MAMA has typically been reported to be at least twice as large as the MAA.

B. The snapshot hypothesis

Having described static (MAA) and dynamic (MAMA) measures of auditory spatial resolution, we now turn to a description of the snapshot hypothesis. According to a simple version of the snapshot hypothesis, a subject, when presented with a horizontally moving target, extracts spatial samples at two discrete temporal points during the target's presentation and bases his or her judgments on the spatial difference between them. Just as in a static MAA task, performance is limited by the actual spatial separation of the two samples, and by the internal noise associated with the spatial sampling process; the latter, in turn, is a function of such stimulus parameters as intensity, frequency content, and velocity.

Based on the consistency and success of the spatial extent cue (as opposed to the velocity cue) in explaining performance in a number of motion detection and discrimination tasks, Grantham (1986) hypothesized that subjects did indeed *infer* direction or extent of motion from a spatial comparison of the "snapshots" taken at the endpoints of moving trajectories. Grantham's argument in favor of the snapshot hypothesis was based partially on parsimony: Given subjects' spatial resolution thresholds under static conditions (the MAAs), there was no need to invoke specialized motion mechanisms to explain their performance in the tasks involving moving targets.

To the extent that the markers in an MAA task are equivalent to the internal "snapshots" sampled during exposure to a moving target, the snapshot hypothesis predicts that performance in the MAMA and MAA tasks would be the same: In both cases the subject would base his or her decisions on the spatial attributes of two discrete samples. Thus, an initial test of the existence and utility of a snapshot mechanism would be a direct comparison of the MAMA and the MAA.

One must be cautious, however, in comparing the MAMA and the MAA, because both are sensitive to temporal parameters. The MAMA is optimum when measured with slow-velocity targets; it increases approximately linearly with velocity (Perrott and Musicant, 1977; Grantham, 1986; Chandler and Grantham, 1992). Similarly, the MAA is optimum for long interstimulus intervals (ISIs) and increases as ISI is decreased (Grantham, 1985; Perrott and Pacheco, 1989). The widely cited best MAA (1°) is obtained with a long ISI (e.g., 1 s, Mills, 1958), and may not be the appropriate value to compare to some of the more recently measured MAMAs. A fair comparison between the two measures can be made only when duration is held constant.

In an unpublished study reported at the Austin meeting of the Acoustical Society of America, Grantham (1985) compared the MAMA to the MAA for a 500-Hz tone under conditions in which the total duration of the trials was held constant for the two conditions. Duration in the case of the MAMA referred to the duration of the single moving target; in the case of the MAA it referred to the total time from the onset of the first 20-ms marker to the offset of the second 20-ms marker. Subjects had to say whether the order of the markers (MAA task) or the direction of target motion (MAMA task) was left-to-right or right-to-left. Data are shown in Fig. 1, which plots threshold angle (MAMA or MAA) as a function of duration for four subjects. It can be seen that for durations greater than 100–150 ms performance was not different in the two conditions (for the briefer durations, the MAMA was consistently elevated). The coincidence of these functions over much of the range of duration is consistent with the view that discrimination of direction in the MAMA task is accomplished by a snapshot mechanism in which the subject samples and spatially discriminates the endpoints of the moving target.[1]

C. Specialized motion detectors

As an alternative to a snapshot processor, there may be mechanisms in the auditory system that respond *directly* to the motion of auditory targets. A number of studies have demonstrated that single units at various stages in the cat and monkey

[1]The elevated MAMA thresholds at the shortest durations might be due to the inaccuracy of snapshots of moving targets' endpoints at such brief durations and fast velocities. For example, if there is a built-in temporal jitter in the execution of snapshots, the resulting *spatial* jitter in the imaged positions would increase with velocity, thus yielding higher thresholds according to a simple statistical sampling model.

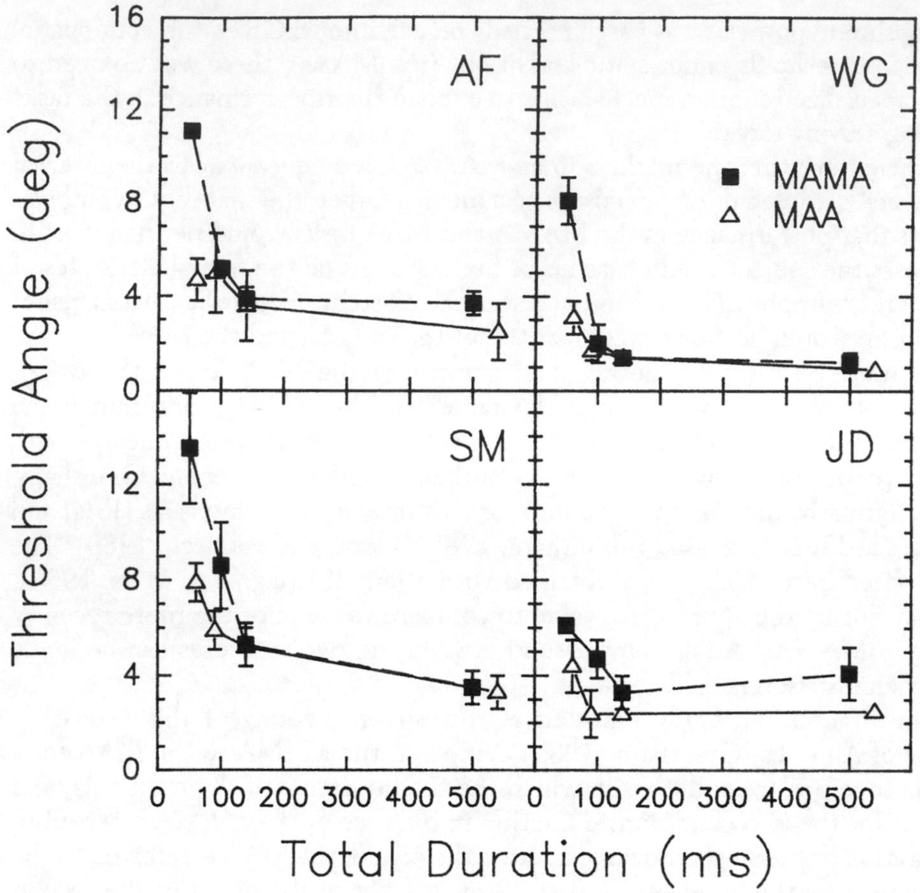

FIG. 1. Threshold in degrees as a function of the total duration of stimulus presentation. For the MAMA task (filled squares), duration was the presentation time of the single moving target. For the MAA task (open triangles), duration was the time from onset of the first marker until offset of the second marker. Medians and semi-interquartile ranges for three to six replications are shown separately (in the four panels) for the four subjects. Where no error bars are shown, the semi-interquartile ranges were smaller than the size of the datapoint. [After Grantham, 1985.]

auditory systems do respond directly to the direction or velocity of moving auditory targets (e.g., Altman, Syka, and Shmigidina, 1970; Ahissar, Ahissar, Bergman, and Vaadia, 1992; Yin and Kuwada, 1983). In contrast to a snapshot mechanism, a motion mechanism might respond to auditory targets that move in specific directions or at particular velocities, without necessarily being sensitive to the spatial characteristics associated with the target (e.g., its endpoint positions). One psychophysical result that might support the existence of such a mechanism would be the finding that a MAMA is smaller than a corresponding MAA.

In apparent contrast to the results from Grantham (1985), Perrott and Marlborough (1989) reported just such a result: They found that the MAMA for broadband noise was consistently smaller than the minimum detectable angle measured when a moving loudspeaker was activated for 10 ms only at the end points of its trajectory. This latter condition, called the "marked endpoints" (ME) condition, is analogous to the MAA conditions discussed previously, in that subjects heard two successive markers and had to respond whether the second was to the left or right of the first. Velocity was held constant in both conditions at 20°/s. The data are plotted in Fig. 2: the MAMA is about 1°, while the ME threshold is 1.5–1.7°, more or less independent of stimulus level.

This result is not consistent with a simple snapshot view of motion perception, which would predict similar performance in these two tasks (i.e., it would predict that the same information would be available in both cases). Apparently, subjects were able to use more information in the moving sounds than that contained in 10-ms samples at the endpoints.

D. Reevaluation of the snapshot hypothesis

One explanation for Perrott and Marlborough's results is that the snapshot hypothesis is incorrect; for the stimuli and conditions they employed, subjects somehow benefited from the midportions of the moving target as well as its endpoints. However, an alternate explanation is that a snapshot analysis is correct and was performed on the moving targets, but that the information in the 10-ms ME condition represented a poor and degraded simulation of the auditory system's snapshots. Thus, the ME thresholds were elevated because they represented poor snapshots.

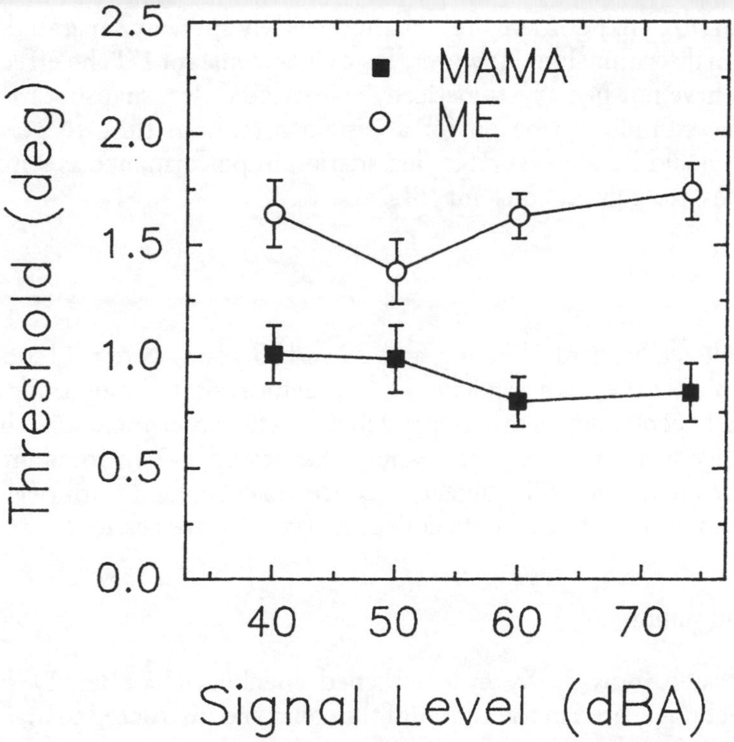

FIG. 2. Threshold in degrees as a function of signal level. Filled squares: MAMA task; open circles: marked endpoint (ME) task. [Adapted, with permission, from Perrott and Marlborough, 1989.]

Perrott and Marlborough did control for one aspect of the quality of the "simulated" snapshots by varying stimulus level. Their finding that thresholds were independent of level in both conditions effectively ruled out the possibility that ME thresholds were elevated because the total energy or loudness was less in that condition than in the MAMA condition.

However, another possibility is that the ME thresholds were elevated because the markers were so brief (10 ms). In other words, perhaps the snapshot mechanism requires a longer stimulus on-time than 10 ms to perform optimally, and the ME condition led to poorer performance because it did not faithfully simulate the best conditions for sampling the endpoints. This possibility could explain why Grantham (1985), who used 20-ms markers, found no difference between the two conditions, whereas Perrott and Marlborough found the ME condition to be degraded relative to the MAMA condition.

The following experiment investigated the effect of marker duration in auditory spatial resolution.

I. EXPERIMENT 1: THE EFFECT OF MARKER DURATION ON THE MAA

It is known that the MAA increases as interstimulus interval (ISI) decreases (Grantham, 1985; Perrott and Pacheco, 1989). The closer together in time the two markers in an MAA experiment are, the more widely spatially separated they must be to remain discriminable. However, for a given constant ISI the effects of *marker* duration have not been systematically investigated. If a snapshot mechanism requires the stimulus to be on for a certain minimum time to perform optimally, there should be a measurable degradation in performance as stimulus duration decreases, for a given constant ISI.

A. Subjects

Two adults with clinically normal hearing, ages 29 and 33 years, were paid subjects in this experiment. Neither had participated in previous spatial resolution tasks, although both had been subjects in other psychoacoustic experiments. Each was tested three to five times per week in sessions that lasted 1–2 h; frequent rest intervals were provided. For each subject, practice was provided until performance had stabilized prior to formal data collection (two to five sessions).

B. Apparatus and stimuli

Subjects were tested individually in a darkened anechoic chamber. During a session the subject was seated in the center of the room and instructed to maintain a steady upright, forward orientation without tilting the head either to the side or forward. No bite bar was provided, although a head rest served to minimize head movements.

The subject faced the center of a horizontal arc of 55 stationary (JBL-8110H) loudspeakers, positioned at ear level 1.8 m distant from the subject and spanning 164°. Only 11 loudspeakers of this array, separated from each other by 2° and subtending an arc from –4° to +16°, were employed in this experiment.

The stimulus was a wideband (100–8200 Hz) noise burst with a 5-ms rise–decay time. Marker duration was either 50 ms (the LONG condition) or 10 ms (the SHORT56 condition; see Fig. 3). Nominal stimulus level in these two cases was 56 dB SPL. A third condition was employed in which marker duration was 10 ms and nominal level was 63 dB SPL (SHORT63 condition). This condition was included to allow an assessment of the effects of stimulus duration for equal-energy stimuli.

Most previous investigations of the MAA have held ISI constant (say at 1 s) and have derived psychometric functions by varying the angular separation between the two markers. In the present experiment, angular separation was varied, but in such a way as to keep *velocity* constant. Note in Fig. 3 that angular separation is shown as 6°, and total duration between onset of the first marker and offset of the second marker is 300 ms; thus, the velocity is 6°/300 ms = 20°/s. When presenting a smaller separation (say 4°), the total duration was decreased (to 200 ms in this example), thus maintaining velocity constant at 20°/s. In this experiment functions were derived for velocities of 20°/s and 60°/s. The slower velocity entails timing parameters for which spatial resolution in dynamic tasks approaches an optimum level, whereas at the faster velocity spatial resolution is noticeably impaired (Chandler and Grantham, 1992).

For each presentation of a marker, a stimulus was randomly sampled from a catalog of 30 tokens of the desired duration stored on the disk. These tokens had been pregenerated such that levels in the 24 adjacent critical bands were independently jittered over a 20-dB range (e.g., see Wightman and Kistler, 1992); this spectral scrambling was designed to prevent subjects from learning individual loudspeaker characteristics.

C. Procedure

A trial consisted of two noise burst markers presented sequentially from the stationary loudspeaker(s). Both were either 10 ms or 50 ms in duration, depending on the condition under investigation (see Fig. 3). The first (reference) marker occurred from a random location between –4° and +4° azimuth. The second marker was presented either from the same loudspeaker as the first (a "nonsignal trial"), or from a loudspeaker to the right of the first (a "signal" trial). The *a priori* probability of each type of trial was 0.50. The subject responded by button press to indicate whether the second pulse appeared to be in the same location or a location to the right of the first pulse. Immediate feedback was given.[2]

[2]Note that this "same–different" paradigm is different from the more commonly employed "left–right" paradigm described in the introduction. The former procedure was employed here to be consistent with the MAMA procedure (described in the following experiment), which for technical reasons could not mix leftward and rightward motion across trials.

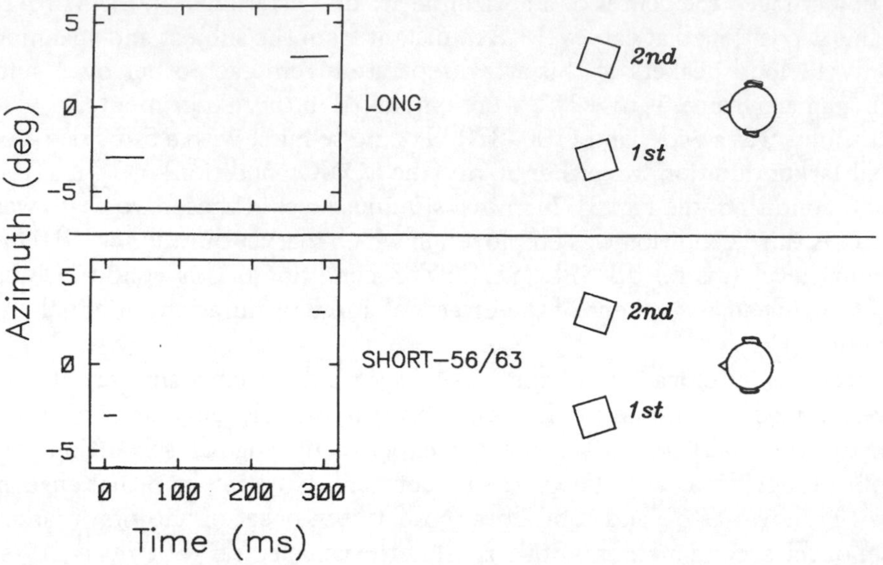

FIG. 3. The left side illustrates the temporal and spatial sequence for a "signal" trial in the conditions employed in experiment 1; the right side depicts top view of a subject's experience in each case. Upper panel: LONG condition (marker duration: 50 ms); lower panel: SHORT56 and SHORT63 conditions (marker duration: 10 ms).

A blocked procedure was employed, such that the spatial separation of the two pulses on a signal trial was fixed at a value of 2–12°. Blocks consisted of 50 trials; spatial separations were chosen to obtain two- or three-point psychometric functions with *d'* in the range from 0.30 to 3.50.

Conditions were run in a pseudo-random order, with velocity, duration/level condition, and spatial extent varied from block to block. Each combination of these parameters was run three to six times, not all on the same day. Summary data points were taken as the mean of the separate *d'* values computed for individual blocks.

D. Results and discussion

Performance as a function of angular extent is plotted in Fig. 4. The upper two panels show the data for subject LC, and the lower two for subject XY. Data for the two velocities are displayed separately in the left and right panels; the parameter is the duration/level condition. It is clear from the figure that there are no consistent differences in resolution among the three conditions.

It appears that 50-ms markers did not provide any more information or enable any finer spatial discrimination than 10-ms markers, even with the equal-intensity comparison (LONG vs. SHORT56). Thus, these data suggest that the brevity of the ME in Perrott and Marlborough's experiment was not a factor in the comparatively poorer performance in this condition than in the MAMA condition. MAMAs were lower than ME thresholds evidently because subjects were able to make use of information in the midportion of the moving targets in addition to that provided by the stimulus endpoints.

These data also suggest that the difference in marker durations between the studies by Grantham (1985), 20 ms, and by Perrott and Marlborough (1989), 10 ms, was not the source of the different results in the two experiments.

II. EXPERIMENT 2: REPLICATION AND EXTENSION OF PERROTT AND MARLBOROUGH (1989)

In an attempt to understand the apparently conflicting results of Grantham (1985) and of Perrott and Marlborough (1989), the next experiment sought to replicate the results of the latter study using the modes of stimulus presentation employed in both studies.

The various modes of stimulus presentation are illustrated in the left side of Fig. 5, which plots the timing of a "left–right" trial in the three relevant conditions (the right side illustrates the corresponding experience of the subject in each case). The upper panel shows the MAMA condition, which was the same in the two experiments: A single moving stimulus was presented that was activated

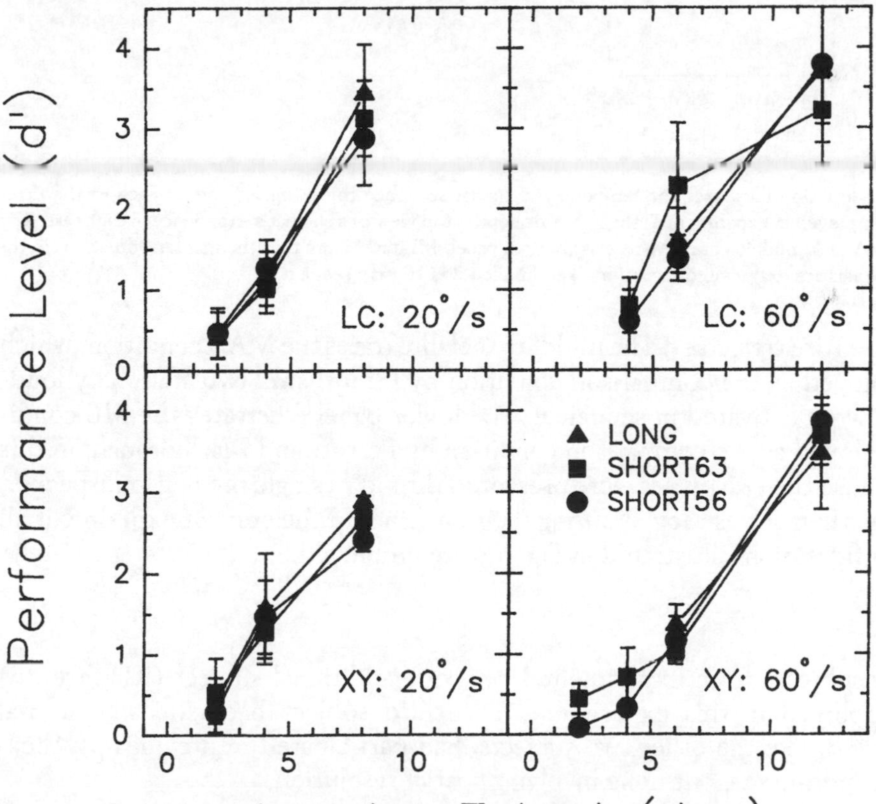

FIG. 4. Performance (d') as a function of angular separation of markers on signal trials for the three conditions tested in experiment 1. The upper two panels show data for subject LC, and the lower two panels for subject XY. Data are shown separately for velocities of 20°/s (left panels) and 60°/s (right panels). Means and standard deviations are shown as computed across three to six replications.

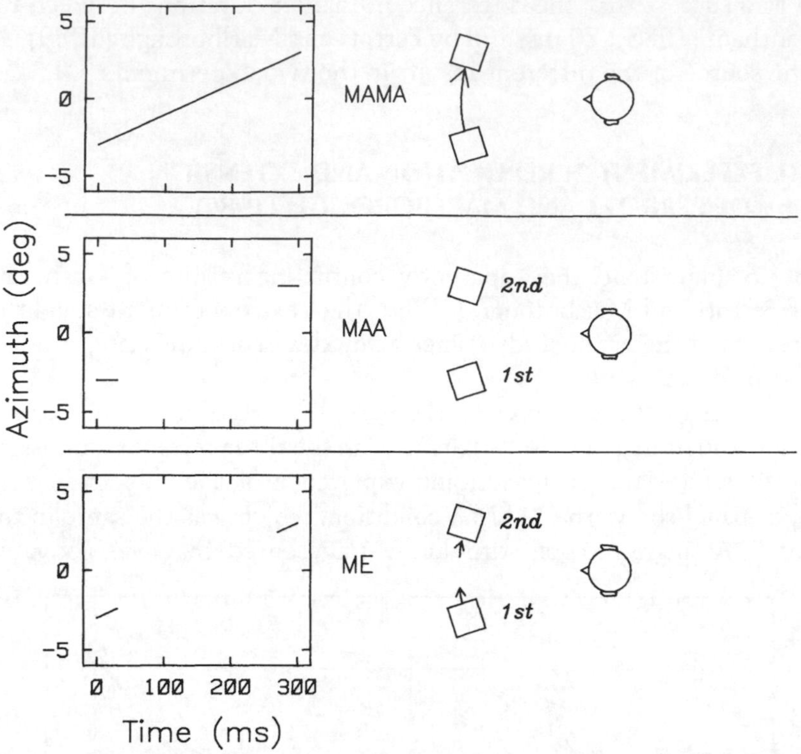

FIG. 5. The left side illustrates the temporal and spatial sequence for a "signal" trial in each of the three conditions employed in experiment 2; the right side depicts top view of a subject's experience in each case. Top panel, MAMA task; middle panel, MAA task; bottom panel, ME task. Note that the markers' durations in the lower two panels are exaggerated (actual marker duration was 10 ms); see text.

during its entire trajectory. The middle panel illustrates the MAA condition, which was employed as the comparison condition by Grantham: Two stationary loudspeakers were activated in sequence. The lower panel illustrates the ME condition, employed as the comparison condition by Perrott and Marlborough; in this case, because the two pulses were presented through a single moving loudspeaker, the pulses themselves moved during their on-time. In the current experiment all three configurations illustrated in Fig. 5 were employed.

A. Subjects

The two subjects from experiment 1 plus one additional subject (KH, age 28) were employed in this experiment. The third subject had clinically normal hearing, and, like the other two subjects, had participated in previous psychoacoustic experiments, but none involving spatial resolution.

B. Apparatus and stimuli

Testing site and apparatus were identical to those described earlier for experiment 1. In addition to the 55-loudspeaker array described previously, two movable loudspeakers were employed. These two loudspeakers were suspended from opposite ends of an overhead boom; they could move 360° around the listener at the same height as (and just within the arc of) the stationary speakers (see Chandler and Grantham, 1992, for a photograph).

The stimulus was the same wideband (100–8200 Hz) noise burst described previously, presented at a nominal level of 56 dB SPL. For two of the three conditions (described later) noise bursts were 10 ms in duration; for the third (moving) condition, the duration of the burst was determined by the angular extent traversed. Rise–decay time was 5 ms. As described earlier, each presentation of a noise burst was drawn from a sample of 30 tokens, each spectrally scrambled in a different way to prevent subjects from learning individual loudspeaker characteristics.

C. Procedure

Three conditions were employed.

1. The MAA condition was the SHORT56 condition from experiment 1: A trial consisted of two 10-ms noise markers presented sequentially from the stationary loudspeaker(s). The second burst was presented either from the same loudspeaker as the first (nonsignal trial), or from a loudspeaker to the right of the first (signal trial).
2. In the MAMA condition, a trial consisted of a single noise presentation. The noise was presented either from a loudspeaker moving at a constant positive (left-to-right) velocity (signal) or from a stationary loudspeaker (nonsignal).
3. In the ME condition, a trial consisted of two sequential 10-ms noise bursts; they were presented either from a single stationary loudspeaker (nonsignal) or from a single moving loudspeaker while it was passing in front of the subject (signal).

Signal trials for each condition are illustrated in Fig. 5; nonsignal trials were identical in duration to signal trials, but contained stimuli that did not move or change positions. The *a priori* probability of each type of trial was 0.50.

For all trials the onset position of the first marker (or for the single stimulus in the MAMA condition) was jittered from trial to trial over an 8° range to discourage subjects from using onset or offset position to perform the task. In all cases, the subject had to respond whether the second pulse was in the same location or a location to thc right of the first pulse (in the MAMA condition, whether the single presentation was stationary or moved to the right). Immediate feedback was given.

A blocked procedure was employed, such that the spatial separation of the two pulses on a signal trial (or the extent spanned by the moving stimulus in the MAMA condition) was fixed within a block at a value of 2–12°. Blocks consisted of 50 trials; spatial separations were chosen to obtain two- or three-point psychometric functions with d' in the range from 0.30 to 3.50.

Stimulus velocities of 20°/s and 60°/s were employed. As mentioned earlier, these velocities were chosen as conditions that would result in near-optimum and suboptimum spatial resolution, respectively. For the MAMA and ME conditions, the chosen velocity determined the velocity of the moving loudspeaker employed for the signal trials. For the MAA condition, the "velocity" determined the ISI; for example, for a separation of 6° and a velocity of 20°/s, the total duration was set to 6/20 = 300 ms (ISI = 280 ms).

It should be noted that varying velocity to obtain a range of performance is equivalent to varying total duration (higher velocities correspond to shorter durations and result in poorer performance). Here, in order to hold velocity constant, variations in angular separation or extent were always accompanied by variations in total duration.

Conditions were run in a pseudo-random order, with velocity, condition type, and spatial extent varied from block to block. Each combination of these parameters was run three to six times, not all on the same day. Summary data points were taken as the mean of the separate d' computed for individual blocks.

D. Results and discussion

The results are shown in Fig. 6 (velocity = 200/s) and Fig. 7 (velocity = 600/s); in both cases d' is plotted as a function of the angular extent employed on signal trials (i.e., either the separation of the two markers or the distance traversed by the single moving target). Data are shown separately for the three subjects, with the means across subjects shown in the lower right panels. Within the three subject panels, error bars indicate standard deviations around the means computed over the three to six replications; in the lower right panels, error bars indicate standard deviations computed across subjects.

The data indicate that the differences among the three conditions of presentation were small for both the slower velocity (Fig. 6) and faster velocity (Fig. 7) displacements. There was a tendency for MAA performance to be better than MAMA performance and for MAMA performance to be better than ME performance (see the mean psychometric functions in the lower right panels of Figs. 6 and 7).

Derived thresholds reveal that the small differences noted in the psychometric functions were consistent across subjects. Thresholds were computed by applying a linear regression to each of the psychometric functions and taking the angular extent required for $d' = 1.0$ (see Table I). The ranking of thresholds, which was the same for all three subjects, reflected the aforementioned hierarchy: for 20°/s, mean MAA = 3.4°, mean MAMA = 4.8°, and mean ME threshold = 5.6°; for 60°/s, mean MAA = 5.9°, mean MAMA = 7.8°, and mean ME threshold = 8.0°.

1. Comparison with previous measures of spatial resolution

a. The MAMA. Table I indicates that the mean MAMA at 20°/s was 4.8° and the mean MAMA at 60°/s was 7.8°. These values are slightly smaller than, but still in the same range as, those reported by Chandler and Grantham (1992) (5.7° at 20°/s; 8.2° at 45°/s; the latter investigators did not employ a 60°/s target). On the other hand, the 20°/s MAMA in this experiment was somewhat larger than that reported by Perrott and Marlborough (1989) (they reported a MAMA of

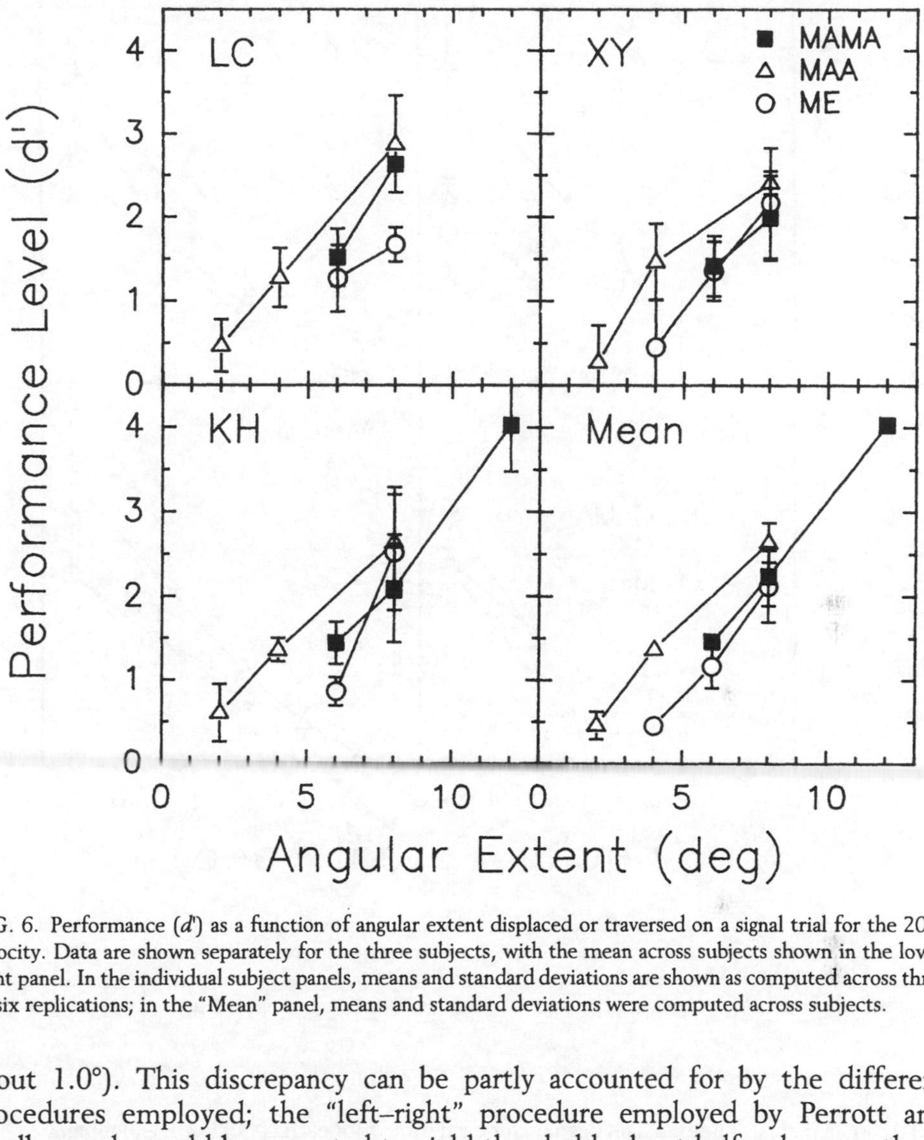

FIG. 6. Performance (d') as a function of angular extent displaced or traversed on a signal trial for the 20°/s velocity. Data are shown separately for the three subjects, with the mean across subjects shown in the lower right panel. In the individual subject panels, means and standard deviations are shown as computed across three to six replications; in the "Mean" panel, means and standard deviations were computed across subjects.

about 1.0°). This discrepancy can be partly accounted for by the different procedures employed; the "left–right" procedure employed by Perrott and Marlborough would be expected to yield thresholds about half as large as those obtained here with a "same–different" procedure (see analysis by Hartmann and Rakerd, 1989). The remainder of the discrepancy may be attributable to procedural and stimulus differences; for example, the smaller radius of loudspeaker movement employed by Perrott and Marlborough (0.9 m, as opposed to 1.75 m in the present study) may have led to differential weighting of available cues and consequent lower thresholds.

b. The MAA. The estimated 20°/s MAA in this experiment (3.4°) is also somewhat larger than that reported for wideband noise in previous studies (about 1.0°, Perrott and Pacheco, 1989; Chandler and Grantham, 1992). However, it should be recalled that the psychometric function in the present case is somewhat uncoventional. Because "velocity" is held constant at 20°/s, variation in angular

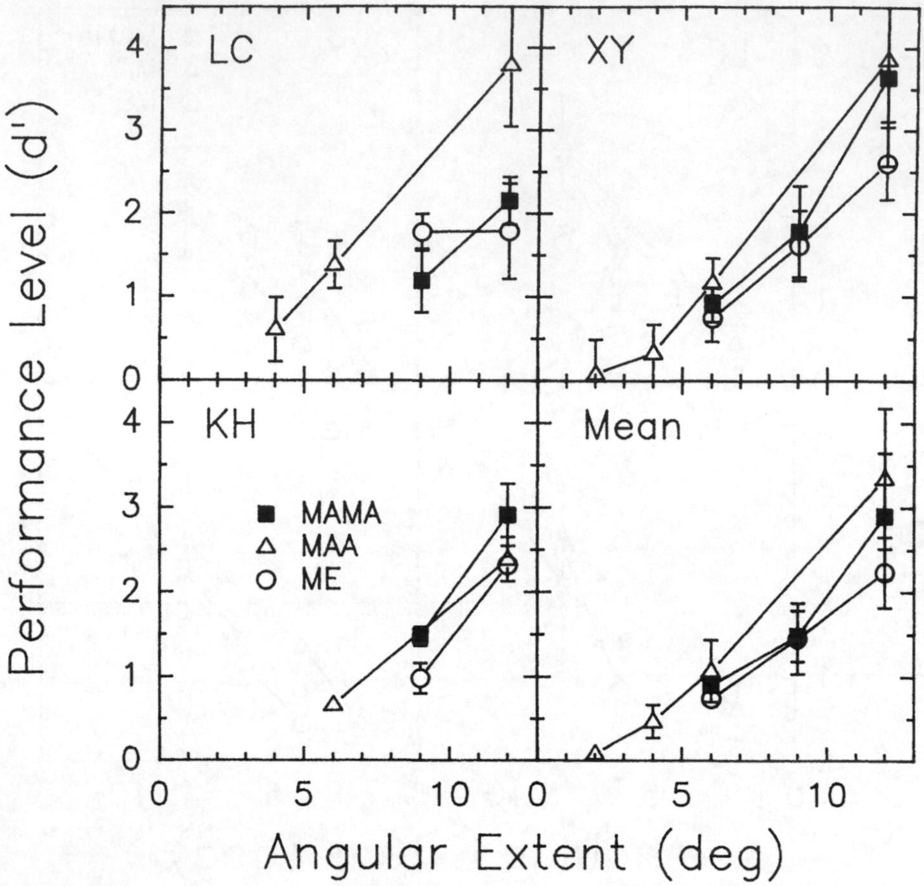

FIG. 7. Performance (d') as a function of angular extent displaced or traversed on a signal trial for the 60°/s velocity. Data are shown separately for the three subjects, with the mean across subjects shown in the lower right panel. In the individual subject panels, means and standard deviations are shown as computed across three to six replications; in the "Mean" panel, means and standard deviations were computed across subjects.

TABLE I. Estimated angular threshold (in degrees) for each subject for each condition in experiment 2.

		Condition		
Velocity	*Subject*	*MAA*	*MAMA*	*ME*
20°/s	LC	3.5	4.8	5.4
	XY	3.6	4.4	5.4
	KH	3.0	5.1	6.1
	Mean	3.4	4.8	5.6
60°/s	LC	5.0	8.7	—[a]
	XY	5.6	6.7	6.9
	KH	7.2	8.1	9.1
	Mean	5.9	7.8	8.0

[a]Threshold could not be estimated due to irregular psychometric function.

extent along the abscissa in Fig. 6 is accompanied by a variation in interstimulus interval; for example, a 7° extent corresponds to a total duration of 7/20 = 350 ms (ISI = 330 ms), whereas a 2° extent corresponds to a duration of 100 ms (ISI = 80 ms). This manner of plotting the functions would result in steeper psychometric functions, and thus higher threshold estimates, than the more conventional method of holding ISI constant when plotting performance versus angular extent.

c. ME threshold. The only known previous report of a ME threshold is that of Perrott and Marlborough (1989). These investigators reported a threshold of about 1.5°, compared to the value of 5.6° obtained here. Again, the different procedures employed in the two experiments would account for some of this discrepancy; had they used a "same–different" procedure, presumably they would have obtained a threshold of about 3.0°.

2. Implications for the snapshot hypothesis

The primary question addressed in this experiment was whether information in the midportion of a horizontally moving target is useful in making spatial judgments, or whether the information at the moving target's endpoints is sufficient to perform optimally. Accordingly, spatial resolution with moving targets was compared directly to spatial resolution with 10-ms end point markers, thus replicating some of the features of experiments conducted by Grantham (1985) and by Perrott and Marlborough (1989). As described in the introduction, the former study concluded that the midportion was not necessary for optimal spatial resolution, whereas the latter concluded that it was necessary.

The direction of results in the present study is consistent with the results of both previous studies. The MAMAs were slightly lower than the ME thresholds (replicating Perrott and Marlborough); however, the MAMAs were *not* lower than the MAAs (replicating Grantham).[3]

This unexpected outcome makes it necessary to decide which of the two "marker" conditions (MAA or ME) is the more appropriate simulation of the output of a snapshot processor. Once confronted with this decision, the choice seems clear: Because any sampling operation performed by the auditory system on a moving target would presumably not be not instantaneous, it would have to involve the processing of dynamic stimuli. The ME stimulus would therefore represent a more faithful simulation of obtained snapshots than would the MAA stimulus, whose markers are static. Given this choice of reference condition, it is clear that a snapshot hypothesis is not entirely adequate to explain the MAMA performance for 20°/s moving targets.

The caveat to be kept in mind regards the *magnitude* of the effects. Although Perrott and Marlborough obtained a clear and consistent advantage of the MAMA over the ME threshold (by a factor of 1.5), the advantage in the present study

---

[3]The fact that the present study found the MAMAs in fact to be consistently *higher* than the MAAs, while Grantham (1985) found them to be not different, may be attributed to stimulus differences (wideband noise vs. 500 Hz tones).

was only 1.17 at 20°/s, and only 1.03 at 60°/s. Thus, under the conditions employed here, the contribution from a moving target's midportion to spatial resolution judgments was minimal at best. The larger and more consistent difference found by Perrott and Marlborough may have been due to certain stimulus differences between the two studies (in particular, the smaller radius of moving targets employed in their study, which may have introduced different cues or different weighting of available cues; see Blauert, 1983, pp. 116ff).

A reasonable conclusion from this work is that the human auditory system possesses both types of mechanisms—a snapshot processor that operates for more rapidly moving events, and a motion-sensitive mechanism (or, alternatively, a multi-snapshot mechanism that samples several times during exposure to motion) that is tuned to slower velocity (and perhaps more near-field) events. One might suppose further that the two mechanisms evolved separately based on different environmental pressures. The snapshot mechanism may have developed as a consequence of discrete, impulsive acoustic information (e.g., the successive twig snaps generated by moving predator or prey), whereas the motion-sensitive system may have developed as a consequence of the changing apparent position of more continuous acoustic stimulation (rustling leaves or vocalizations) associated with a predator/prey/companion's motion.

3. The MAA as the most sensitive measure of spatial resolution

As implied in the previous paragraphs, the modest but consistent advantage of the MAA over the ME thresholds (by a factor of 1.7 at 20°/s and 1.3 at 60°/s) was a surprise. The two conditions are apparently indistinguishable (i.e., subjects do not report the markers to be moving in the ME condition). The threshold differences certainly cannot be accounted for by the small differences in angular distances between the marker centroids in the two cases (0.2° at 20°/s; 0.6° at 60°/s). If real, these threshold differences indicate a possible interference effect associated with the dynamic presentation of a marker.

One possible explanation is that even though subjects do not perceive the motion of the markers, the apparent *positions* of the ME markers might be affected by the dynamic stimulus presentation. If, for example, the apparent position of the first marker is biased in the direction of motion, whereas that of the second marker is for some reason not consistently biased, the apparent distance between the two markers would on the average be less than that in a comparable MAA condition, and performance would be correspondingly worse. Although there is no evidence to support this notion for such brief pulses, it is possibly relevant that the apparent position of the onset of a moving target is indeed displaced in the direction of motion whereas the apparent position of its offset is not consistently displaced in either direction (Perrott and Musicant, 1977). An alternative hypothesis that would explain the superiority of the MAA performance is that, independent of any bias in localizing the markers, the variability associated with localizing moving markers is greater than that associated with localizing stationary markers. Such increased response variability would lead to a predicted decrement in d', as was observed.

IV. SUMMARY AND CONCLUSIONS

The present experiments were conducted to investigate certain aspects of spatial sampling, as might be carried out by the auditory system in making judgments about stationary or moving targets in the horizontal plane. In the first experiment, it was found that spatial resolution did not depend on marker duration (between 10 and 50 ms) in an MAA task if the total duration of a trial (from onset of first marker to offset of second marker) was held constant. In terms of a sampling or snapshot mechanism, a stimulus duration of 10 ms is as good as a duration of 50 ms, implying that accuracy of localization ("snapshot focus") is not dependent on stimulus duration over this range. Perrott and Marlborough's (1989) finding that the MAMA was consistently lower than the ME threshold evidently cannot be attributed to the brevity of the markers in the latter condition.

In the second experiment auditory spatial resolution in the horizontal plane was measured in three different stimulus configurations at two different velocities. When the velocity was slow (20°/s), spatial resolution as measured with a continuously moving target (the MAMA condition) was slightly better than that measured with brief pulses presented only at the end points of the moving loudspeaker's trajectory (the ME condition). These results are in the same direction as those of Perrott and Marlborough (1989), and suggest that a simple, two-snapshot (onset/offset) processor is not entirely adequate to describe subjects' performance with horizontally moving targets. However, the advantage observed in the present study was much smaller than that obtained by Perrott and Marlborough. Evidently subjects were able to use information in the intermediate portions of the moving target to assist in spatial judgments, but under the stimulus conditions employed in this study, the contribution from the midportion was minimal.

At the faster velocity (60°/s), where performance was degraded in all conditions, there was no longer any advantage of the moving target over the ME presentation. A snapshot hypothesis is consistent with the results at this faster velocity. These results, taken together with those of Perrott and Marlborough (1989), suggest that both a snapshot mechanism and a motion-sensitive mechanism might exist in the human auditory system. The motion-sensitive system (or a multi-snapshot mechanism) apparently operates only over a restricted range of velocities and becomes ineffective as velocity increases to 60°/s. Whether such a mechanism would become more effective at slower velocities than 20°/s remains to be investigated.

Spatial resolution as measured with stationary pulses (the MAA condition) was slightly but consistently superior to that in both of the dynamic conditions. This finding is consistent with the notion that auditory spatial resolution is best under static conditions; the MAMA can approach, but not exceed the MAA (Chandler and Grantham, 1992). The consistent advantage of the MAA over the ME condition was somewhat of a surprise, because the two tasks are phenomenologically indistinguishable. The difference might be explained by assuming that there is a larger bias and/or a greater amount of response variability associated with localizing dynamically presented markers than that associated with localizing static markers. According to this notion, although marker *duration* apparently has little or no effect on localization accuracy (experiment 1), the *manner* of marker presentation (static vs. dynamic) does have an effect on accuracy.

Although the differences among the three conditions tested in experiment 2 were small, they are consistent with the following description of dynamic auditory processing:

1. For slowly moving targets in the horizontal plane, the midportions of a moving sound can contribute to an observer's spatial resolution judgments. Under these circumstances, a simple snapshot hypothesis is inadequate to describe performance. For more rapidly moving targets, on the other hand, there is no evidence that information in the trajectory's midportions is useful.
2. Even under the best circumstances, the contribution of a moving target's midportion toward spatial resolution is minimal. It is possible that targets presented more in an observer's near field (thus, perhaps, evoking a greater contribution of dynamic spectral information; as in Perrott and Marlborough, 1989) provide more adequate stimulation of a motion-sensitive system than the targets employed here.
3. Due perhaps to bias effects and/or increased response variability, spatial resolution in the horizontal plane involving dynamic stimuli (both MAMA and ME conditions) is degraded relative to that measured with static stimuli (the MAA). The latter condition appears consistently to yield the most sensitive measure of horizontal-plane spatial resolution. However, this fact is apparently not, as had heretofore been assumed, sufficient grounds to reject the operation of a motion-sensitive mechanism within the auditory system, however minimally it might contribute to performance.

ACKNOWLEDGMENTS

The author thanks Dr. Daniel H. Ashmead and the editors of this volume, Drs. Timothy R. Anderson and Robert H. Gilkey, for helpful comments and suggestions on an earlier version of this manuscript. This research was supported by National Institute on Deafness and Other Communication Disorders grant DC00185.

REFERENCES

Ahissar, M., Ahissar, E., Bergman, H., and Vaadia, E. (**1992**). "Encoding of sound-source location and movement: Activity of single neurons and interactions between adjacent neurons in the monkey auditory cortex," J. Neurophysiol. **67**, 203–215.

Altman, J. A., Syka, J., and Shmigidina, G. N. (**1970**). "Neuronal activity in the medial geniculate body of the cat during monaural and binaural stimulation," Exp. Brain Res. **10**, 81–93.

Blauert, J. (**1983**). *Spatial Hearing: The Psychophysics of Human Sound Localization*, translated by J. S. Allen (MIT, Cambridge, MA).

Chandler, D. W., and Grantham, D. W. (**1992**). "Minimum audible movement angle in the horizontal plane as a function of stimulus frequency and bandwidth, source azimuth, and velocity," J. Acoust. Soc. Am. **91**, 1624–1636.

Grantham, D. W. (**1985**). "Auditory spatial resolution under static and dynamic conditions," J. Acoust. Soc. Am. Suppl. 1 77, S50.
Grantham, D. W. (**1986**). "Detection and discrimination of simulated motion of auditory targets in the horizontal plane," J. Acoust. Soc. Am. **79**, 1939–1949.
Harris, J. D., and Sergeant, R. L. (**1971**). "Monaural/binaural minimum audible angles for a moving sound source," J. Speech Hear. Res. **14**, 618–629.
Hartmann, W. M., and Rakerd, B. (**1989**). "On the minimum audible angle—A decision theory approach," J. Acoust. Soc. Am. **85**, 2031–2041.
Mills, A. W. (**1958**). "On the minimum audible angle," J. Acoust. Soc. Am. **30**, 237–246.
Perrott, D. R., Costantino, B., and Ball, J. (**1993**). "Discrimination of moving events which accelerate or decelerate over the listening interval," J. Acoust. Soc. Am. **93**, 1053–1057.
Perrott, D. R., and Marlborough, K. (**1989**). "Minimum audible movement angle: Marking the end points of the path traveled by a moving sound source," J. Acoust. Soc. Am. **85**, 1773–1775.
Perrott, D. R., and Musicant, A. D. (**1977**). "Minimum auditory movement angle: Binaural localization of moving sound sources," J. Acoust. Soc. Am. **62**, 1463–1466.
Perrott, D. R., and Pacheco, S. (**1989**). "Minimum audible angle thresholds for broadband noise as a function of the delay between the onset of the lead and lag signals," J. Acoust. Soc. Am. **85**, 2669–2672.
Wightman, F. L., and Kistler, D. J. (**1992**). "The dominant role of low-frequency interaural time differences in sound localization," J. Acoust. Soc. Am. **91**, 1648–1661.
Yin, T. C. T., and Kuwada, S. (**1983**). "Binaural interaction in low-frequency neurons in inferior colliculus of the cat. II. Effects of changing rate and direction of interaural phase," J. Neurophysiol. **50**, 1000–1019.

Chapter 16

Experiments on Auditory Motion Discrimination

Kourosh Saberi[1] and Ervin R. Hafter
University of California, Berkeley

(Received February 1994; revised October 1994)

Temporal aspects of dynamic sound localization were examined in four experiments. Motion was simulated by dynamically changing the interaural delay of a train of high-frequency-filtered, Gaussian clicks. Determining the direction of motion could not be explained by a model that relies entirely on the onset–offset positions of the moving stimulus. The data suggest a lowpass filtering of interaural delay information with a time constant estimated at 60–130 ms. Results from discrimination and descriptive studies of motion are compared.

INTRODUCTION

There is a paucity of research on dynamic sound localization. The reason for this is both the experimental difficulty associated with the physical movement of sound sources[2] and the theoretical complexity of modeling results related to time-varying signals (Stern and Bachorski, 1983). Consequently, there has been little agreement on how the auditory system encodes sound-source movement (Perrott and Musicant, 1977; Perrott, 1989; Grantham, 1986, 1989a; Stern and Bachorskin, 1983; Toronchuk, Stumpf, and Cynader, 1992). The considerable work done in the area of stationary sound localization has provided solid models of binaural hearing (Jeffress, 1948; Colburn and Durlach, 1978; Stern, Xu, and Tao, 1991; Searle, Braida, Davis, and Colburn, 1976), which have found physiological support in the past decade (Carr and Konishi, 1990; Yin and Chan, 1990). Although models of stationary localization provide useful substrates for the study

[1]Current address: Research Laboratory of Electronics, 36-767, Massachusetts Institute of Technology, Cambridge, MA 02139.

[2]Changing the direction and velocity of movement of a loudspeaker between or within trials without introducing extraneous sounds can prove difficult. Few laboratories are equipped with the requisite apparatus. Many have consequently opted to examine dynamic processes by presenting carefully controlled dichotic stimuli through headphones.

of dynamic processes, the psychophysical and perceptual differences between dynamic and stationary localization require recognition in modeling dynamic processing.

One area of discrepancy between results from experiments on stationary and dynamic localization concerns the rapidity with which independent bits of information are processed (Blauert, 1972, 1983; Hafter, Buell, and Richards, 1988). If interaural delays are dynamically changing, the binaural system requires a greater time for sustaining independent processing than if interaural delays are kept constant. Hafter *et al.* (1988) have shown that when the interclick interval (ICI) in a train of high-frequency clicks is about 12 ms, performance based on information derived from n clicks is superior to that based on one click by $n^{0.5}$, denoting optimum summation of interaural information across the n clicks. Increasing the ICI beyond 12 ms does not result in further improvements in performance. As shown later in this chapter, when interaural delays vary between successive clicks, the binaural system cannot make optimum use of interaural information even with an ICI of 130 ms—a value that is more than 10 times greater than that which is sufficient for stationary sources.

The following four experiments were designed to study the temporal aspects of dynamic processing. The first experiment examines the detectability of direction of motion as the interaural delay of a dichotic click train is linearly increased. The second experiment addresses the question of whether the motion mechanism is an onset–offset detector. The third experiment examines the contribution of the ongoing signal to the detection process (as compared to the contribution of the onset and offset of the signal). Finally, the fourth experiment explores the idea of "lag of lateralization" (Blauert, 1972), more commonly referred to as binaural sluggishness (Grantham and Wightman, 1978).

I. EXPERIMENT I

A change in interaural delay may be associated with a change in the lateral distance traveled by a source. The first experiment provides a baseline where an observer's ability to determine the direction of movement of an auditory image is examined as a function of the magnitude of linear change in interaural delay.

A. Design

Signals were trains of dichotic clicks whose temporal envelopes were Gaussian and centered at the cosine phase of a 6-kHz carrier. The trains, presented through electrostatic headphones (STAX-SR5), were used to simulate the dynamic changes in the interaural time difference (ITD) of an intermittent sound source in lateral motion. Figure 1 shows the stimulus configuration. The ITD of each click increased by a constant amount ($\Delta\tau = 10$ μs) relative to the click immediately preceding it. The starting ITD was randomly selected from a predetermined set of values. The ICI was 13 ms jittered by 10% between trials to eliminate monaural pitch cues. On each trial of a single-interval design, the ITDs either

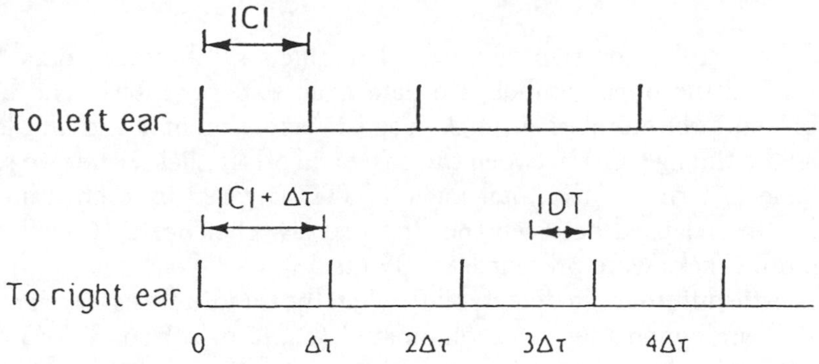

FIG. 1. Stimulus configuration used in experiment I.

progressively increased or decreased. The subject's task was to determine the direction of movement of the auditory image (right or left). The number of clicks in the train was an experimental parameter.

B. Results

Figure 2 shows the results of this experiments for two subjects. The ordinate is a measure of detectability (d') and the abscissa represents the number of clicks. Because the change in ITD between successive clicks and the ICI were constant, one may consider the abscissa to be representative of a scale monotonically related to the distance. Thus, larger numbers of clicks represent a greater distance of simulated lateral movement. Not surprisingly, as the number of clicks increased, the detectability of direction of movement improved. It is noteworthy that subjects had difficulty in correctly identifying the direction of movement when the click train consisted of only six to nine clicks. The duration of the train with only six to nine clicks was 65 to 104 ms. We return to this latter observation shortly.

II. EXPERIMENT II

A. Design

Experiment II was designed to compare the ability of observers to detect the direction of movement when the information required for performing such a task was limited to the onset and offset positions of movement. The stimulus configuration was identical to that used in experiment I except that the middle clicks were eliminated. The temporal relations between the first and last clicks, however, were maintained as before. That is, in this two-click design (onset–offset), the ITD and ICI of the first and last clicks were determined as if the middle clicks were present.

B. Results

Figure 3 shows results for two subjects. The filled symbols are data from experiment I and the open symbols are data from experiment II. The upper abscissa represents the number of clicks used in experiment I and the lower abscissa plots the timing (ICI) between the onset and offset clicks. The two scales are comparable in terms of the total range of ITD covered by each train. For example, the time elapsed between the first and last clicks of a 16-click train when the middle clicks were present was 195 ms.

There was little difference in detectability when the middle clicks were present (experiment I) and when they were eliminated (onset–offset condition). One might presume from these data that the mechanism for the detection of motion relies heavily on information provided by the onset and offset positions of the moving source, and from this argue that the interaural configurations of the middle pulses were inconsequential. Experiment III was designed to address this question.

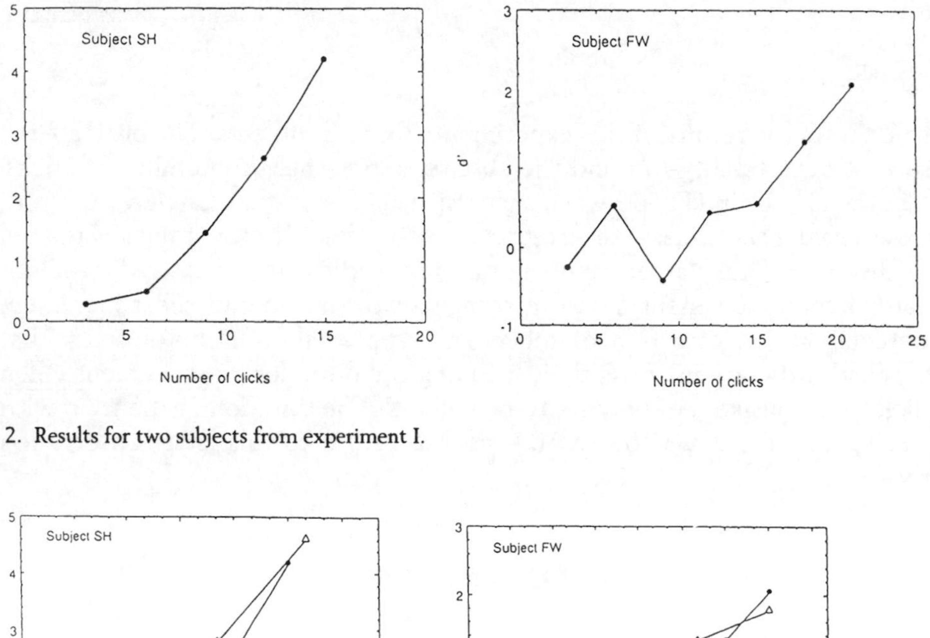

FIG. 2. Results for two subjects from experiment I.

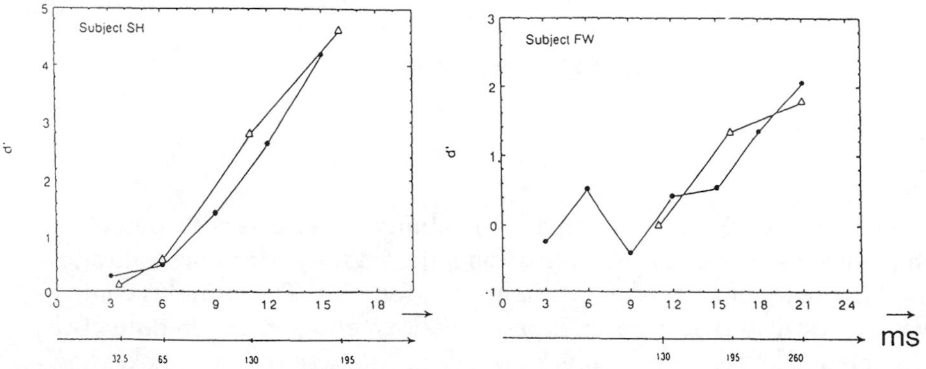

FIG. 3. Results for two subjects from experiment II (open symbols). The filled symbols are data from experiment I and are plotted for comparison. The upper abscissa refers to the number of clicks used in experiment I and the lower abscissa refers to the interclick interval between the two clicks used in experiment II.

III. EXPERIMENT III

A. Design

The purpose of this experiment was to test the idea suggested by the results of experiment II that the mechanism of motion detection is an onset–offset detector. The effective onset duration of an auditory stimulus has been estimated at 2–4 ms (Tobias and Schubert, 1959). Based on these estimates, we consider only the first click in the train to be representative of onset information. The ITDs of the middle pulses were varied according to one of three conditions. In case A, the ITDs of the middle pulses were the same as the ITD of the onset click. One may think of this as presenting the middle clicks from the same location as that of the onset click, while presenting the last click at the same position (ITD) used in experiments I and II. Note that if one accepts the hypothesis devised from the results of experiment II, the middle clicks simply repeat the position of the first click. If the binaural system were a simple onset–offset detector, performance should be identical to that obtained in experiment II. In case B, the ITD of the middle clicks matched the ITD of the offset click. Predictions are similar in both cases. In case C, the interaural delay of the first half of the click train was set to that of the onset click whereas the interaural delay of the second half of the train was set equal to that of the offset click. It should be noted that the ICI between the two center clicks was the same as any other pair of successive clicks (i.e., 13 ms).

B. Results

Results for cases A and B of this experiment are plotted for a single subject in Fig. 4. As in previous figures, the filled symbols are data from experiment I; the open symbols are data from experiment III. The left and right panels plot results for cases A and B, respectively. Comparison of these data to Fig. 3 shows that the interaural configuration of the middle pulses substantially affected performance. In both cases, detectability of the direction of motion dropped to near chance even with as many as 20 clicks (a difference of close to 3 d' units compared with experiments I and II). The results of case C for two subjects are plotted in Fig. 5 (open symbols). As before, the filled symbols are data from experiment I. Here, performance is generally comparable to those observed in experiments I and II.

The results of the three cases of experiment III show that the interaural configuration of the middle pulses affected the discrimination of direction of motion. One intuitive explanation that is congruent with our observations is that the auditory system averages successive estimates of the interaural delay to arrive at centroid ITD values. This would be similar to lowpass filtering of the interaural information. For example, consider the stimulus configuration used in cases B and C of experiment III. A simplified version of these two conditions are plotted for four-click stimuli in Fig. 6. What would our predictions be for these cases if the integration time of the averaging process was long enough to encompass two clicks? A single interaural delay would be calculated for each averaging window.

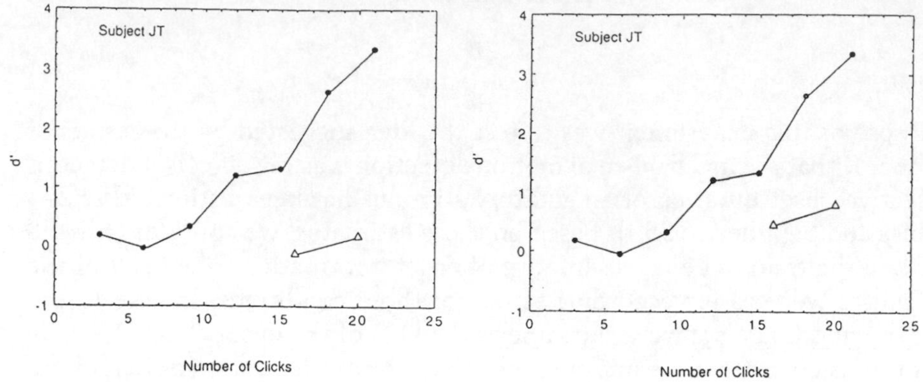

FIG. 4. The left and right panels show results for one subject from cases A and B of experiment III respectively. The filled symbols are data from experiment I and the open symbols from experiment III.

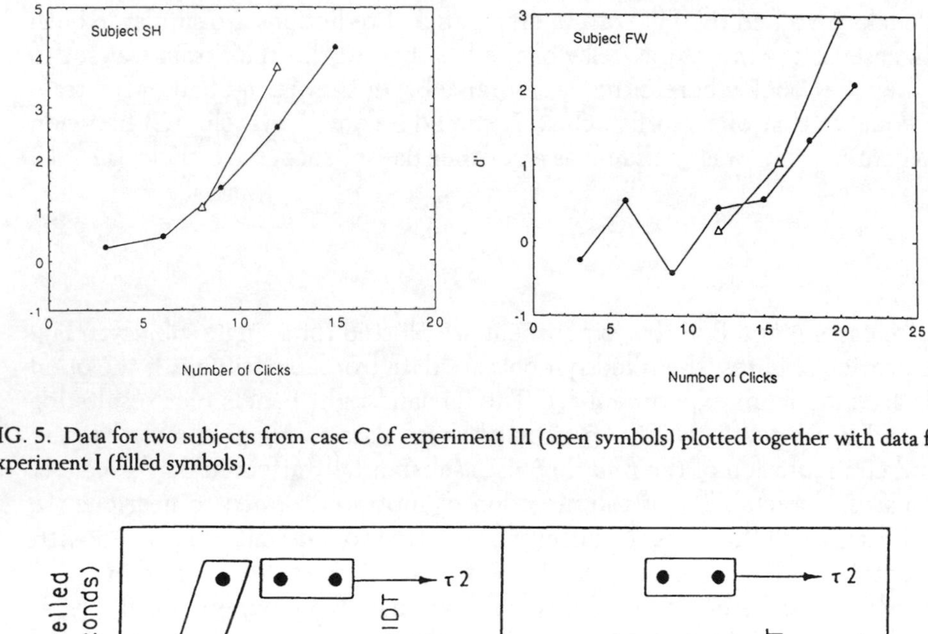

FIG. 5. Data for two subjects from case C of experiment III (open symbols) plotted together with data from experiment I (filled symbols).

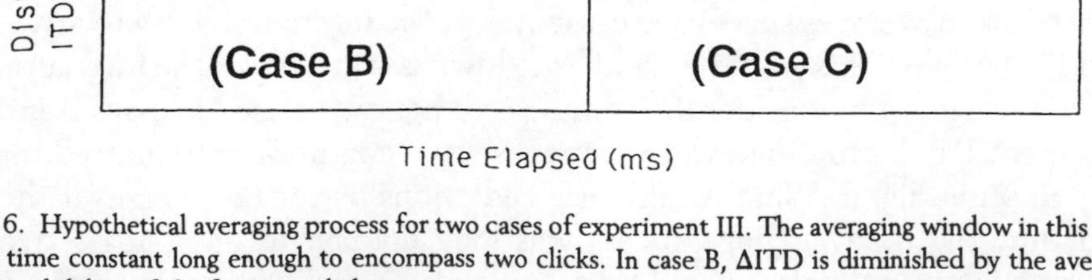

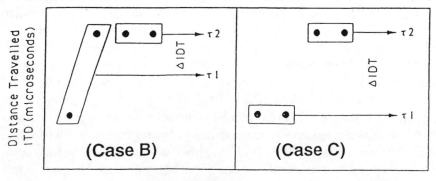

FIG. 6. Hypothetical averaging process for two cases of experiment III. The averaging window in this example has a time constant long enough to encompass two clicks. In case B, ΔITD is diminished by the averaging of interaural delays of the first two clicks.

In case B (left panel), τ_1 and τ_2, representing the two interaural-delay centroids, provide a change in the centroids of interaural delay (ΔITD) that is smaller than that provided by the difference in the interaural-delay centroids seen in case C. The reason for this is that in case B, the onset weighting is diminished by averaging. Of course, the diagram of Fig. 6 is purely hypothetical and given only to illustrate the preceding argument. The averaging window may encompass more than two clicks. We assume that the time constant of averaging is fixed, but subject to temporal noise, and independent of the number of clicks.

From this perspective, the data from experiment I offer one way to estimate the time-constant over which centroids for the onset and offset positions are calculated. The value so obtained is between 60 and 130 ms. To do this, we note (Figs. 2 and 4) that performance was close to chance when all of the clicks fell within a window of this size, implying that for these shorter trains, all of the clicks were averaged to produce a single centroid at the stimulus onset. As such, there was no cue for detecting the direction of motion. In order to obtain further information with regard to the hypothesis of averaging across clicks, experiment IV was designed to reexamine experiment II in a way that would allow disassociation of ICI from the change in ITD responsible for motion.

IV. EXPERIMENT IV

A. Design

Several studies have suggested that the binaural system responds more slowly to changing interaural delays than to ITDs that are held constant (Blauert, 1972; Grantham and Wightman, 1978).[3] Experiments I, II, and III support these observations. Experiment IV utilized a two-click design as in experiment II, only here we varied both the interclick interval (corresponding to the rate of change in interaural delay) and the magnitude of change in interaural delay between the two clicks (corresponding to the spatial distance separating the "locations" of the two clicks). The purpose was to examine spatiotemporal interactions in dynamic localization. The signals and task were identical to those used in experiment II (onset–offset experiment) with the exception that four different values of ICI (32.5, 65, 130, 260 ms) were paired with each of four values of ΔITD (25, 50, 100, 200 μs) in a factorial design.

B. Results

Figure 7 displays results for subject SH from experiment IV. Clearly, increasing the ΔITD, which may be considered as increasing the distance between the positions of the two clicks, improved performance. Previous studies have shown that when the task is to discriminate an ITD that remains constant throughout

[3]The binaural system's ability to track changing interaural level differences is not as poor as its ability to track ITDs (Blauert, 1972).

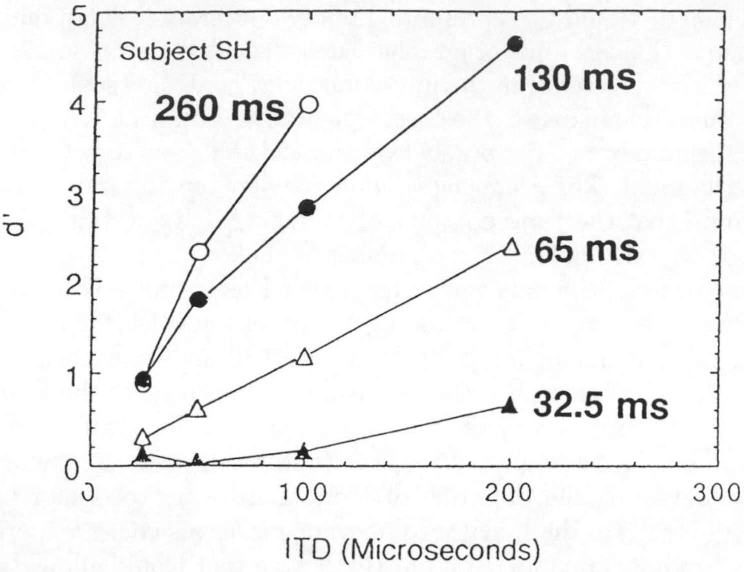

FIG. 7. Results from experiment IV (two-click design) for one subject. The abscissa represents the change in interaural delay from first to second clicks. The parameter is ICI. Filled triangles (32.5 ms), open triangles (65 ms), filled circles (130 ms), and open circles (260 ms).

the train, shortening the ICI leads to a reduction in the effectiveness of each successive click in the train, a process that has been called "binaural adaptation" (Hafter and Dye, 1983). However, if the ICI exceeds about 12 ms the effectiveness of each click is independent of the one immediately preceding it (Hafter *et al.*, 1988). In stark contrast to that result are the data with dynamically changing ITDs. Here we find improvement in the ability to detect the direction of motion when the ICI is increased from 130 to 260 ms, suggesting a lowpass filtering process that enacts an averaging of the individual parts of the stimulus over a duration on the order of 5 to 10 times as long as with the static case. The seeming long time constant of integration for motion is reminiscent of studies on the "lag of lateralization" (Blauert, 1972) or "binaural sluggishness" (Grantham and Wightman, 1978). The latter authors have suggested that the speed with which the binaural system may track interaural delays is limited by an internal noise introduced during the process of taking the time derivative of interaural delays—that is, at the stage where information about position is transformed into changing position. We note that this seeming long time constant for motion is in the range of that estimated earlier from experiment I.

V. DISCUSSION

A. Lowpass filtering of interaural delay information

The time constant of the binaural system is estimated at between 100 to 700 ms depending on psychophysical task, procedures, and stimuli employed (McFadden and Sharpley, 1972; Tobias and Zerlin, 1959; Grantham and Wightman, 1978).

This implies that if the time that separates binaural events exceeds this constant, at least one observation may be made during every time window and each may be considered as a discrete event. The more intricate questions in the binaural literature, however, are related to the processes that occur within this time window. One view, which we have examined, is that the binaural system detects information derived only from the onset and offset positions of a moving sound source when the duration of movement is less than about a quarter of a second. The results of experiment III do not favor this idea, showing that the interaural delay of the ongoing signal may affect the detectability of the direction of source movement. Instead, the results of the current study have supported a lowpass filtering model of changing interaural information during source movement. An estimate of 60–130 ms is suggested for the time constant of the lowpass process. Over two decades ago, Blauert (1972) referred to "lag of lateralization" as the observation that the percept of movement diminishes as the source velocity is increased. He took this as evidence that the binaural system requires a minimum time period to process information received from a source whose interaural information is changing. The assumed lowpass filtering of dynamically changing ITDs shown here is clearly in accord with this "lag" and the "binaural sluggishness" of Grantham and Wightman (1978).

B. Discrimination and descriptive studies of motion and implications for stationary models

Descriptive studies of binaural beats also support the idea that the binaural system lowpass filters or averages changing interaural information. A transition from movement to pulsation is reported as the interaural frequency difference, equal to the beat rate, increases beyond 2–5 Hz (Licklider, Webster, and Hedlun, 1950; von Bekesy, 1960), suggesting that the binaural system cannot track the movement of a signal whose interaural delay is rapidly changing. It is instructive to compare results obtained from these descriptive studies of motion (Licklider *et al.*, 1950; von Bekesy, 1960; Perrott and Briggs, 1972) and those obtained from discrimination experiments (Grantham, 1986; Perrott and Marlborough, 1988). Although discrimination tasks can delineate important features of dynamic processing (e.g., whether the motion mechanism is an onset–offset detector), they cannot fully explore or explain many perceptual aspects of auditory motion. Thus, researchers who have used discrimination tasks have tended to favor stationary models of motion. These models contend that the putative mechanism for coding moving auditory stimuli relies on information derived from successive sampling of positions in space. In most psychophysical motion-discrimination tasks, the observer is required to discriminate either between right and left movements or between a moving and a stationary source. Subjects' performance is then summarized by some measure of detectability, for example, d' or threshold for movement. Such experimental designs, by definition, require that subjects detect at least two locations. Subjects' percepts are not of interest but rather their ability to detect a change in location. Consequently, discrimination tasks are an inadequate test of the validity of stationary models, because by definition they cannot subject the theory to being proven false.

Stationary models, embodied in snapshot theory[4] (Grantham, 1986, 1989a), implicitly contend that the spatial information between successive samples of a moving auditory stimulus is lost. As the sampling period of the supposed snapshot mechanism is shortened, however, given the noise inherent in sensory systems, stationary theories become indistinguishable from those that are based on continuous information processing. Thus, snapshot theory may at best be of marginal utility if it cannot demonstrate a quantization of spatial information such that the information between long successive snapshots is lost.

In descriptive studies, qualitative reports of the moving source are solicited, for example, the binaural beat studies described earlier (Licklider *et al.*, 1950; von Bekesy, 1960) or those on apparent motion and the auditory phi phenomenon (Burtt, 1917; Strybel, Manligas, Chan, and Perrott, 1990). These latter studies have shown that when two transient and spatially separated sounds occur within short temporal intervals (<100 ms), a single image is perceived that traverses continuously through the spatial extent between the two sound sources. Our subjects reported similar percepts in experiment IV. It is noteworthy that in the latter type of studies the observer has no *a priori* knowledge of the location of the second sound until it has occurred, and therefore the percept of continuous motion must be generated retroactively; this is a phenomenon not easily explained by the simple static coding of stationary positions. In addition, other behavioral studies, such as those on adaptation (Grantham and Wightman, 1979; Grantham, 1989b, 1992), have examined the effects of prolonged exposure to moving stimuli. Behavioral responses to test stimuli favored a direction opposite to that of the adapting stimulus, suggesting an adaptation of neural elements tuned to motion.

C. Physiological studies of auditory motion

There are several animal studies on the physiology of motion detectors that may be of interest. While one should exercise caution in extending results from animal physiology to human psychophysics, the physiological literature does lend some support to a motion mechanism in at least some species. A listing of these articles is provided in Appendix I. Seventeen articles involved single-cell recording (Table I).[5] All but one article reported neural elements that may be classified as motion detectors. The criterion for classifying a unit as a motion-detector is usually one of the following: (1) it responds to an auditory stimulus moving in one direction and is either inhibitory or responds less vigorously in the opposite direction, or (2) it responds to a moving auditory stimulus but is nonresponsive to a stationary sound-source. The receptive fields of these units are usually sharper at the higher auditory centers relative to the lower centers (Altman, 1978). Some studies have reported on units with preferred velocities at the level of the cortex (Stumpf,

[4]To our knowledge, the term snapshot was originally coined in the hearing literature by Masters, Moffat, and Simmons (1985) in describing how the bat uses discrete sonar pulses in tracking moving prey.

[5]Some articles were excluded due to insufficient information.

Table I. Summary of studies on animal physiology of auditory motion. The entries in the upper table represent the number of articles concerned with each area. The entries in the lower table represent the number of units studied in each article. For each entry, the left number represents the number of units sensitive to motion (see text) out of the total number of units studied (right number). For example, in the one motion study of the medial geniculate body, 11 out of 50 cells studied were classified as motion detectors (c = cat, g = gerbil, m = monkey). Not all articles in the upper table provided detailed information on the number of units studied.

Articles on the physiology of auditory motion detection

Superior Olive	*Inferior Colliculus*	*Superior Colliculus*	*Medial Geniculate Body*	*Cerebellum*	*Cortex*	*Other (Gross Potentials Reviews and models*
1	5	4	1	1	5	6

Total # of Articles: 23

Reported number of motion-detector units

Superior Olive	*Inferior Colliculus*	*Superior Colliculus*	*Medial Geniculate Body*	*Cerebellum*	*Cortex*
0/21	10/79 (c)	26/39 (c)	11/50 (c)	12/29 (c)	12/50 (c)
	113/145 (g,c)	10/136 (c)			63/180 (m)
	14/100 (c)				61/80 (c)
	52/114 (c)				8/25 (c)

Toronchuk, and Cynader, 1992). Others have reported on units in the superior colliculus responsive to both auditory and visual movement (Wickelgren, 1971). These latter units have the same preferred direction in both modalities. The measurement of gross potentials in human observers has also implicated a physiological mechanism tuned to motion (Ruhm, 1976; Halliday and Callaway, 1978; Altman and Vaitulevich, 1990).

SUMMARY

Although the detectability of the direction of movement of a linearly moving sound stimulus is nearly equivalent to the detectability of a sound source that marks the starting and ending positions of movement, it cannot be concluded that the motion mechanism is a simple onset–offset detector. The equivalence of performance for these two stimulus conditions may be explained if one assumes an averaging or lowpass filtering of interaural information. In support of this latter contention, altering the interaural configuration of the ongoing signal (i.e., middle pulses) demonstrates an adverse effect on detectability. Additional data show that decreasing the ICI between two clicks from 260 to 130 ms degrades the detectability of interaural information, further supporting a temporal lowpass process.

REFERENCES

Altman, J. A. (1978). "Sound localization: Neurophysiological mechanisms," in *Translations of the Beltone Institute for Hearing Research (no. 30)*, edited by J. Tonndorf (Beltone Publications, Chicago).

Altman, J. A., and Vaitulevich, S. F. (1990). "Auditory image movement in evoked potential," Electroencephalogr. Clin. Neurophysiol. **75**, 323–333.

Bekesy, G., von. (1960). *Experiments on Hearing* (McGraw-Hill, New York), p. 392.

Blauert, J. (1972). "On the lag of lateralization caused by interaural time and intensity differences," Audiology **11**, 265–270.

Blauert, J. (1983). *Spatial Hearing* (MIT Press, Cambridge, MA).

Burtt, H. E. (1917). "Auditory illusions of movement—A preliminary study," J. Exp. Psychol. **2**, 63–75.

Carr, C. E., and Konishi, M. (1990). "A circuit for detection of interaural time differences in the brain stem of the barn owl," J. Neurosci. **10**, 3227–3246.

Colburn, H. S., and Du.lach, N. I. (1978). "Models of binaural interaction," *Handbook of Perception, Vol. IV, Hearing*, edited by E. C. Carterette and M. P. Friedman (Academic Press, New York), pp. 467–518.

Grantham, D. W. (1986). "Detection and discrimination of simulated motion of auditory targets in the horizontal plane," J. Acoust. Soc. Am. **79**, 1939–1949.

Grantham, D. W. (1989a). "Auditory motion perception via successive 'snapshot' analysis," *Sound Localization by Human Observers—Symposium Proceedings* (National Academy of Sciences, Washington, DC), p. 35.

Grantham, D. W. (1989b). "Motion aftereffects with horizontally moving sound sources in the free field," Percept. Psychophys. **45**, 129–136.

Grantham, D. W. (1992). "Adaptation to auditory motion in the horizontal plane: Effect of prior exposure to motion on motion detectability," Percept. Psychophys. **52**, 144–150.

Grantham, D. W., and Wightman, F. L. (1978). "Detectability of varying interaural temporal differences," J. Acoust. Soc. Am. **63**, 511–523.

Grantham, D. W., and Wightman, F. L. (1979). "Auditory motion aftereffects," Percept. Psychophys. **26**, 403–408.

Hafter, E. R., Buell, T. N., and Richards, V. M. (1988). "Onset-coding in lateralization: Its form, site, and function," in *Auditory Function*, edited by G. M. Edelman, W. E. Gail, and W. M. Cowan (Wiley, New York), pp. 647–676.

Hafter, E. R., and Dye, R. H. (1983). "Detection of interaural differences of time in trains of high-frequency clicks as a function of interclick interval and number," J. Acoust. Soc. Am. **73**, 1708–1713.

Halliday, R., and Callaway, E. (1978). "Time shift evoked potentials (TSEPs): Method and basic results," Electroencephalogr. Clin. Neurophysiol. **45**, 118–121.

Jeffress, L. A. (1948). "A place theory of sound localization," J. Comp. Psysiol. **41**, 35–39.

Licklider, J. C. R., Webster, J. C., and Hedlun, J. M. (1950). "On the frequency limits of binaural beats," J. Acoust. Soc. Am. **22**, 468–473.

Masters, W. M., Moffat, A. J. M., and Simmons, J. A. (1985). "Sonar tracking of horizontally moving targets by the big brown bat *Eptesicus fuscus*," Science **228**, 1331–1333.

McFadden, D. M., and Sharpley, A. D. (1972). "Detectability of interaural time differences as a function of signal duration," J. Acoust. Soc. Am. **52**, 574–576.

Perrott, D. R. (1989). "Are there motion detectors in the auditory system?," *Sound Localization by Human Observers—Symposium Proceedings* (National Academy of Sciences, Washington, DC), p. 36.

Perrott, D. R., and Briggs, R. M. (1972). "Auditory apparent movement under dichotic listening conditions," J. Exp. Psychol. **92**, 83–91.

Perrott, D. R., and Marlborough, K. (1988). "Minimum audible movement angle: Marking the end points of the path traveled by a moving sound source," J. Acoust. Soc. Am. **85**, 1773–1775.

Perrott, D. R., and Musicant, A. D. (1977). "Minimum audible movement angle: Binaural localization of moving sound sources," J. Acoust. Soc. Am. **62**, 1463–1466.

Ruhm, H. B. (1976). "Brain response to intracranial auditory motion," J. Acoust. Soc. Am. **60**, S16.

Searle, C. L., Braida, L. D., Davis, M. F., and Colburn, H. S. (1976). "Model for auditory localization," J. Acoust. Soc. Am. **60**, 1164–1175.

Stern, R. M., and Bachorski, S. J. (1983). "Dynamic cues in binaural perception," in *Hearing—Physiological Bases and Perception*, edited by R. Klinke and R. Hartmann (Springer-Verlag, Berlin), pp. 209–215.

Stern, R. M., Xu, X., and Tao, S. (1991). "A coincidence-based model that describes straightness weighting in binaural perception," *Abstracts of the 14th meeting of the Association for Research in Otolaryngology*, St. Petersburg, FL.

Strybel, T. Z., Manligas, C. L., Chan, O., and Perrott, D. R. (1990). "A comparison of the effects of spatial separation on apparent motion in the auditory and visual modalities," Percept. Psychophys. **47**, 439–448.

Stumpf, E., Toronchuk, J. M., and Cynader, M. S. (1992). "Neurons in cat primary auditory cortex sensitive to correlates of auditory motion in three-dimensional space," Exp. Brain Res. **88**, 158–168.

Tobias, J. V., and Schubert, E. D. (1959). "Effective onset duration of auditory stimuli," J. Acoust. Soc. Am. **31**, 1595–1605.

Tobias, J. V., and Zerlin, S. (1959). "Lateralization threshold as a function of stimulus duration," J. Acoust. Soc. Am. **31**, 1591–1594.
Toronchuk, J. M., Stumpf, E., and Cynader, M. S. (1992). "Auditory cortex neurons sensitive to correlates of auditory motion: underlying mechanism," Exp. Brain. Res. **88**, 169–180.
Wickelgren, B. G. (1971). "Superior colliculus: some receptive field properties of bimodally responsive cells," Science **173**, 69–72.
Yin, T. C., and Chan, J. C. K. (1990). "Interaural time sensitivity in the medial superior olive of the cat," J. Neurophysiol. **64**, 465–487.

APPENDIX I: PHYSIOLOGICAL ARTICLES ON MOTION

Ahissar, M., Ahissar, E., Bergman, H., and Vaadia, E. (1992). "Encoding of sound-source location and movement: Activity of single neurons and interactions between adjacent neurons in the monkey auditory cortex," J. Neurophysiol. **67**, 203–215.
Altman, J. A. (1968). "Are there neurons detecting direction of sound source motion?," Exp. Neurol. **22**, 13–25.
Altman, J. A. (1971). "Neurophysiological mechanisms of sound-source localization," in *Sensory Processes at the Neuronal and Behavioral Levels*, edited by G. V. Gersuni (Academic Press, New York), pp. 221–244.
Altman, J. A. (1975). "Neurophysiological mechanisms in auditory localization," in *Soviet Research Reports, Vol. 1*, edited by C. D. Woody (Brain Information Service Publications, University of California, Los Angeles), pp. 1–36.
Altman, J. A. (1978). "Sound localization: Neurophysiological mechanisms," in *Translations of the Beltone Institute for Hearing Research (no. 30)*, edited by J. Tonndorf (Beltone Publications, Chicago).
Altman, J. A. (1981). "Psychophysical and neurophysiological data on sound source perception," in *Neuronal Mechanisms of Hearing*, edited by J. Syka and L. Aitkin (Plenum Press, New York), pp. 289–299.
Altman, J. A. (1988). "Information processing concerning moving sound sources in the auditory centers and its utilization by brain integrative and motor structures," in *Auditory Pathway: Structure and Function*, edited by J. Syka and R. B. Masterton (Plenum Press, New York), pp. 349–354.
Altman, J. A., and Kalmykova, I. V. (1986). "Role of the dog's auditory cortex in discrimination of sound signals simulating sound source movement," Hear. Res. **24**, 243–253.
Altman, J. A., Syka, J., and Shmigidina, G. N. (1970). "Neuronal activity in the medial geniculate body of the cat during monaural and binaural stimulation," Exp. Brain Res. **10**, 81–93.
Altman, J. A., and Vaitulevich, S. F. (1990). "Auditory image movement in evoked potential," Electroencephalogr. Clin. Neurophysiol. **75**, 323–333.
Bechterev, N. N., Syka, J., and Altman, J. A. (1975). "Responses of cerebellar units to stimuli simulating sound source movement and visual moving stimuli," Experientia **15**, 819–821.
Gordon, B. S. (1972). "The superior colliculus of the brain," Sci. Am. **227**, 72–81.
Halliday, R., and Callaway, E. (1978). "Time shift evoked potentials (TSEPs): Method and basic results," Electroencephalogr. Clin. Neurophysiol. **45**, 118–121.
Kuwada, S., Yin, T.C.T., and Wickesberg, R. E. (1979). "Response of cat inferior colliculus neurons to binaural beat stimuli: Possible mechanisms for sound localization," Science **206**, 586–588.
Morrell, F. (1972). "Visual systems view of acoustic space," Nature **238**, 44–46.
Rauschecker, J. P., and Harris, L. R. (1989). "Auditory and visual neurons in the cat's superior colliculus selective for the direction of apparent motion stimuli," Brain Res. **490**, 56–63.
Ruhm, H. B. (1976). "Brain response to intracranial auditory motion," J. Acoust. Soc. Am. **60**, S16.
Sovijarvi, A., Hyvarinen, J., and Koskinen, K. (1973). "Specific neurons in the auditory cortex of the cat for detecting the direction of sound source movement," Scand. J. Clin. Lab. Invest., Suppl. 130, **31**, p. 18.
Sovijarvi, A. R. A., and Hyvarinen, J. (1974). "Auditory cortical neurons in the cat sensitive to the direction of sound source movement," Brain Res. **73**, 455–471.
Spitzer, M. W., and Semple, M. N. (1991). "Interaural phase coding in auditory midbrain: Influence of dynamic stimulus features," Science **254**, 721–723.
Stumpf, E., Toronchuk, J. M., and Cynader, M. S. (1989). "Auditory cortex neurons sensitive to correlates of auditory motion in three-dimensional space," Soc. Neurosci. Abstr. **15**, 110.
Stumpf, E., Toronchuk, J. M., and Cynader, M. S. (1992). "Neurons in cat primary auditory cortex sensitive to correlates of auditory motion in three-dimensional space," Exp. Brain Res. **88**, 158–168.
Syka, J., and Straschill, M. (1970). "Activation of superior colliculus neurons and motor responses after electrical stimulation of the inferior colliculus," Exp. Neurol. **28**, 384–392.
Toronchuk, J. M., Stumpf, E., and Cynader, M. S. (1992). "Auditory cortex neurons sensitive to correlates of auditory motion: Underlying mechanism," Exp Brain Res, **88**, 169–180.
Viskov, O. V. (1975). "Principles governing formation of perception of motion of a subjective acoustic image," Hu. Physiol. (transl. of Fiziol. Chelov.) **1**, 359–365.
Wickelgren, B. G. (1971). "Superior colliculus: some receptive field properties of bimodally responsive cells," Science **173**, 69–72.
Yin, T. C. T., and Kuwada, S. (1983). "Binaural interaction in low-frequency neurons in inferior colliculus of the cat. II. Effects of changing rate and direction of interaural phase," J. Neurophysiol. **50**, 1000–1019.

Part V

Sound Source Segregation and Free-Field Masking

Chapter 17

The Cocktail Party Problem: Forty Years Later

William A. Yost
Loyola University of Chicago

(Received December 1993; revised August 1994)

Forty years ago, Collin Cherry [J. Acoust. Soc. Am. **25**, 975–979 (1953)] described the "cocktail party problem," and he suggested that spatial hearing was a major method used by the auditory system to separate sound sources in a multisource acoustic environment. This chapter provides a review of spatial hearing studies that involve more than one sound source or potential sound sources in an attempt to determine the role spatial hearing plays in sound source segregation. Almost all of the data involve only two sound sources, and the results indicate that spatial hearing may not be the major cue used for sound source segregation. However, there are very few studies that have investigated the cocktail party problem in real-world listening conditions, especially when there are more than two sound sources.

INTRODUCTION

In 1953 Cherry (pp. 975–976) wrote,

> How do we recognize what one person is saying when others are speaking at the same time (the "cocktail party problem")? On what logical basis could one design a machine ("filter") for carrying out such an operation? A few of the factors which give mental facility might be the following: (a) The voices come from different directions. (b) Lip-reading, gestures, and the like. (c) Different speaking voices, mean pitches, mean speeds, male and female, and so forth. (d) Accents differing. (e) Transition-probabilities (subject matter, voice dynamics, syntax).

The cocktail party effect has become an often referenced auditory phenomenon. In recent years the cocktail party problem has been reconstituted as sound source determination (see Yost, 1992a, 1992b) or sound source segregation (see Bregman, 1990), and Fig. 1 provides a schematic view of the problem. That is,

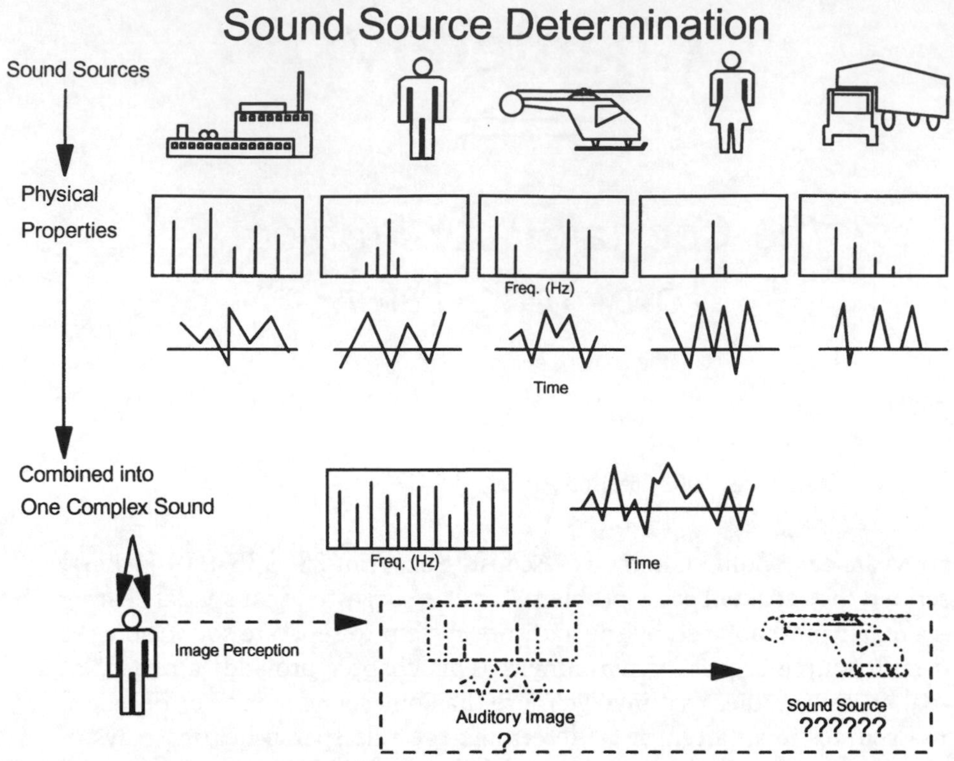

FIG. 1. The steps in sound source determination in a multisource acoustic environment. Five sound sources are shown, each with its schematized temporal and spectral representations. These individual waveforms are combined into a single complex sound field, which forms the auditory stimulus. The auditory system then codes this complex sound field input prior to its decomposition into a scene of auditory images, where each image indicates the presence of one of the sound sources (one of the images, that corresponding to the helicopter, is shown).

how do we determine the sources of sound in multisource acoustic environments? As seen in the quotation, Cherry suggested some variables that might contribute to a solution to this problem. Over the years, several authors (see Yost, 1992a, 1992b, for a review) have added to Cherry's original list of possible solutions (see Table I).

Cherry felt that spatial separation was a major contributor to solving the cocktail party problem. Thus, I refer to the use of spatial cues as an aid in sound source determination or segregation as the cocktail party problem. It is important to recognize that spatial cues are just one of a set of possible cues (see Table I) that may be used to determine the sources of sound. Consider listening to a monaural recording of an orchestra over monaural headphones. Although you might not determine the location of the instruments, you have no difficulty determining what most of the instruments are. Thus, spatial cues are not both necessary and sufficient for sound source determination. The question this chapter attempts to answer is, What role does spatial hearing play in sound source determination? My review of the literature suggests that we know surprisingly little about this question.

TABLE I. Seven physical attributes of sound that might be used as a basis for sound source determination.

1. Spectral separation
2. Spectral profile
3. Harmonicity
4. Spatial separation
5. Temporal separation
6. Temporal onsets and offsets
7. Temporal modulations

Figure 2 presents the cocktail party problem in the terms of selective or divided attention (see Jones and Yee, 1993, for a review of auditory attention). Figures 1 and 2 suggest two questions: What is known about our ability to attend to one or more sources in a multisource environment, and what role does binaural hearing play in this ability? Everyday experience suggests that we can attend to more than one sound source, and that we often know the spatial location of the sources. However, what are the data that describe this ability, what do we know about how we do this task, and how important is binaural hearing in aiding us in attending to one or more sources?

I. SELECTIVE ATTENTION

The experiments Cherry designed to study the cocktail party problem are selective attention procedures using headphones as shown in Fig. 3. Cherry contrasted the ability of listeners to attend to two different spoken passages when they were mixed and presented together to the same ear versus when one passage was delivered to one ear and the other passage was delivered to the other ear. Cherry's results, as well as those from many other studies (see Jones and Yee, 1993), show that when one message is delivered to one ear and a different message to the other ear, listeners can easily attend to one or the other of the messages. Almost all of the information in the attended message can be determined, but very little about the unattended message can be recalled. Little of either message can be determined when the messages are mixed and presented monaurally.

Thus, Cherry saw his selective attention data as suggesting that spatially separating the two messages (one to one ear and the other to the opposite ear) did aid in attending to a set of two concurrently occurring messages. Cherry (1953) then became interested in whether other forms of separation (e.g., filtering) could serve as a solution to the cocktail party problem. Filtering the two messages into two bands was better than not filtering the speech, but performance was much poorer than when the sounds were split between the two ears. Cherry and Taylor (1954) were also very interested in what aspects of the unattended message could be processed. This question is one of the major ones in the study of selective and divided attention (see Treisman and Gelade, 1980).

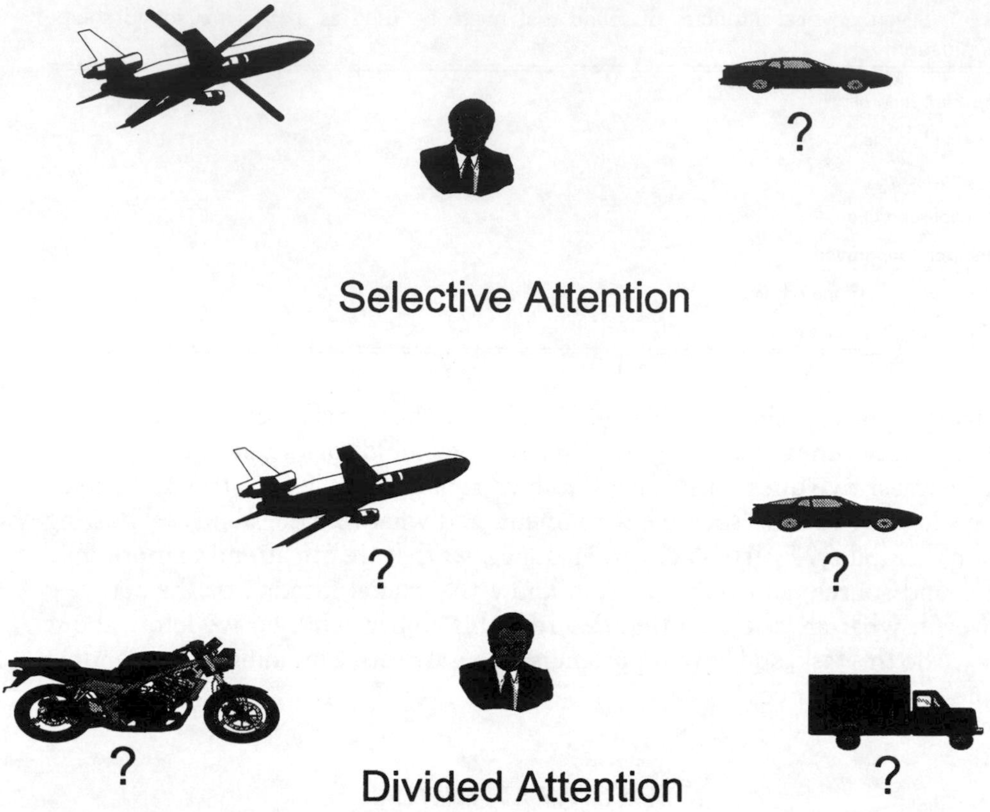

FIG. 2. Schematic diagram of the selective and divided attention paradigms. In selective attention, the listener is asked to attend to one particular sound source (e.g., the car in the top figure) and to ignore other sources, whereas in divided attention all of the sound sources are to be attended to. Most of the work in hearing has been devoted to measures of selective attention with the stimuli being presented over headphones.

Broadbent (1958; Broadbent and Ladefoged, 1959) performed similar studies and he championed a channel or stage theory approach to explain performance based on conditions in which different messages were delivered to the two ears. However, the study of auditory selective attention moved away from the study of binaural variables toward research on temporal factors (see Jones and Yee, 1993). The paradigm shown in Fig. 3 has become known as the "dichotic listening" paradigm and is used to study hemispheric specialization (see Lauter, 1983). The studies of dichotic listening are not designed to address issues related to the cocktail party problem, and the stimulus conditions often deviate significantly from those one would encounter in a real multisource acoustic environment.

Theories of selective attention are almost entirely based on visual input (see Jones and Yee, 1993, for a review), where the critical features of the visual scene have been well defined and quantified. The classic major theoretical view of attention is that attention is a stage or a number of stages of information processing, involving filters (information channels) through which relevant features flow to higher processes. Other theories do not postulate stages of processing and avoid the concept of filtering. These theories see attention as dynamic and interactive with other cognitive processes. A key ingredient linking the many theories of attention is the idea that objects have features and that attention is devoted to processing these features. These theories are difficult to apply to sound, because auditory science has not developed a lexicon of auditory features to parallel those used in vision, especially concerning spatial or binaural perceptual features.

Although Cherry saw his work as documenting the importance of binaural separation as part of the solution to the cocktail party problem, his paradigm deviates significantly from a real-world cocktail party. Hence, the relevance of the selective attention literature to selective and divided attention in the real world is called into question. That is, it isn't clear to what extent one's ability to attend to a message delivered over headphones to one ear while the other ear receives a competing message actually corresponds to the real world where both ears would receive each message.

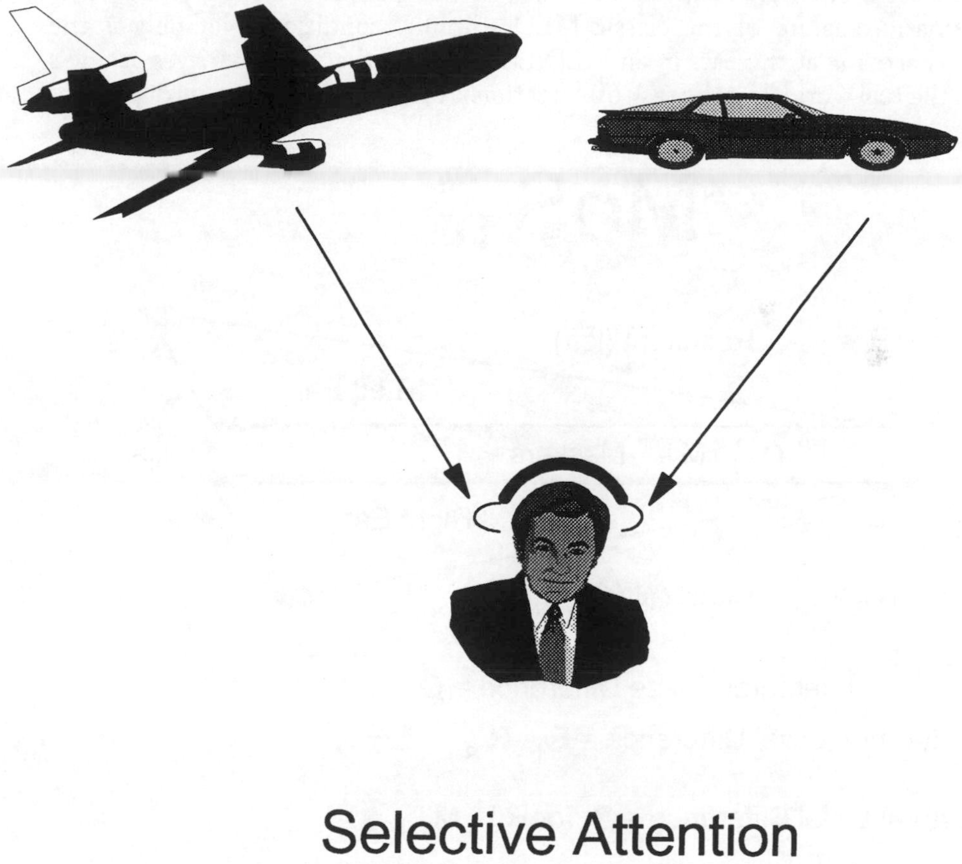

FIG. 3. Schematic depiction of the selective attention task with headphones as used by Cherry (1953) in his original study of the cocktail party problem.

II. MASKING-LEVEL DIFFERENCES

A few years before Cherry coined the term cocktail party effect, Licklider (1948) and Hirsh (1948) showed that the ability to detect a signal in a background of noise was easier if the signal was presented with a different interaural time configuration than that of the noise masker. If one assumes that interaural differences constitute the basic spatial cues for azimuthal localization, then this result indicates that signal detection is improved if the signal has a different set of spatial cues than the masker (Green and Yost, 1975; Durlach and Colburn, 1978; and McFadden, 1975, review the major corpus of the masking-level difference or MLD literature). For instance, a signal presented with a 180° interaural phase shift (S_π) and masked by a diotic noise (N_0) has a masked threshold that is often 15–18 dB lower than one obtained when both the signal and masker are presented diotically (that is, the N_0S_π threshold is 15–18 dB lower than the N_0S_0 threshold). Again, however, the classic MLD paradigm deviates significantly from listening to two sources in the real world. In the real world signals rarely arrive at the two ears interaurally phase-reversed as they do in the classic noise diotic-signal antiphasic—N_0S_π—MLD procedure. Figure 4 provides a schematic diagram of the classic MLD stimulus condition. Not only is the stimulus arriving at the ears in an MLD task not like that which arrives at one's ears in the real world, but the task of detection is different from recognizing voices at a cocktail party.

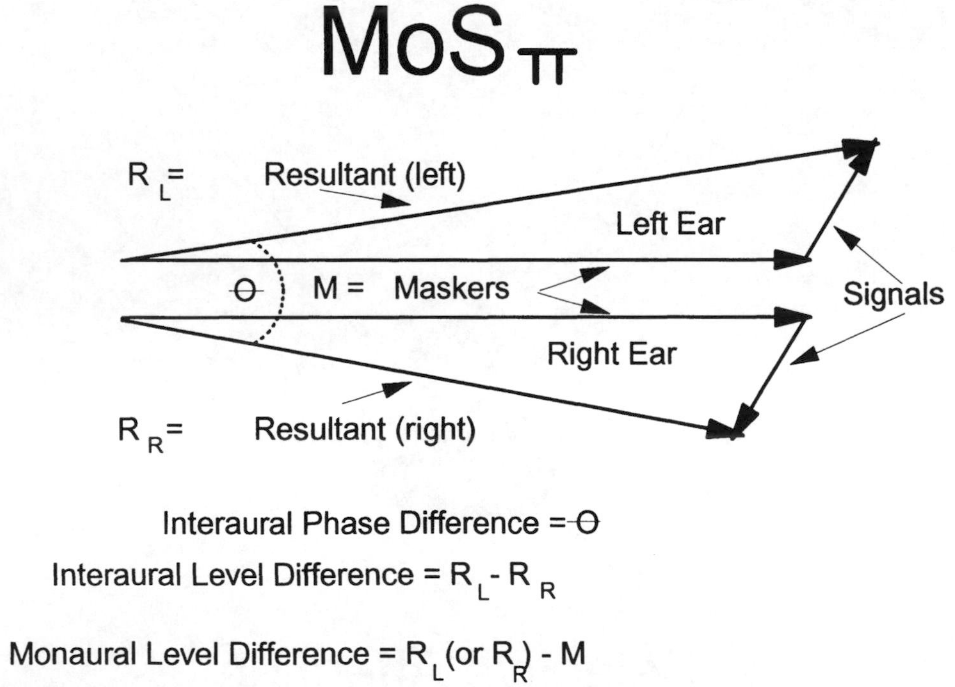

FIG. 4. Vector diagram representing the addition of an interaurally out-of-phase signal to a diotic masker. The waveform reaching the listener's ears consists of interaural phase and amplitude differences, which must form the basis for signal detection. That is, the information arriving at the ears is not separated into two sources: signal and masker. The binaural auditory system must process the interaural information in order to improve detection in this N_0S_π condition.

The large detection MLDs of 15–18 dB (or larger if the masker is a narrowband noise with a low center frequency; e.g., see Hall and Harvey, 1989) have often been pointed to as evidence for the role of binaural analysis in solving the cocktail party problem. Nevertheless, the data from discrimination or recognition studies do not show such a large binaural advantage when signals and maskers are presented with different sets of interaural variables (because the MLD refers to a difference in masked thresholds, I use binaural advantage to refer to studies that include suprathreshold measures other than detection). Figure 5 summarizes results from four types of discrimination or recognition tasks: frequency discrimination, intensity discrimination, speech intelligibility, and loudness judgments. In each of these studies, the judgments were made in two conditions as a function of signal-to-noise ratio. In the diotic condition, the same signal and noise were presented to both ears, whereas in the dichotic condition the signal was presented with a 180° interaural phase difference and the noise was presented diotically.

The data plotted in Fig. 5 were obtained by taking the decibel difference between the diotic and dichotic psychometric functions (this difference is labeled the binaural advantage, in decibels) at each of several different levels of performance. The scale below the figure indicates what 0 dB SL refers to in terms of E/N_0 (the ratio of signal energy to noise spectrum level) or speech-to-noise (broadband speech power to broadband noise power) ratio. For instance, for the study of frequency discrimination (delta F), the listener was presented two tones in a background of broadband diotic noise, one at 250 Hz and one at 253 Hz in the diotic and dichotic conditions. Percent discrimination [P(C)] for determining the 3-Hz difference in frequency was measured for each condition as a function of the signal-to-noise ratio. At each of several different levels of performance [P(C)] the decibel difference between the diotic and dichotic functions (the binaural advantage, in decibels) was plotted as a function of the signal-to-noise ratio of the diotic signal (normalized to sensation level as indicated on Fig. 5). The data for intensity discrimination (delta I; Henning, 1973) involved discriminating a 2-dB difference in intensity at 250 Hz, the speech recognition task (Carhart, Tillman, and Johnson, 1967; see also Levitt and Rabiner, 1967) was to identify words from a closed set of NU-6 words, and the loudness task (Townsend and Goldstein, 1973) was to make magnitude estimates of the judged loudness of a 250-Hz tone presented in a background of noise in the two binaural conditions.

The data of Fig. 5 clearly show that as the signal-to-noise ratio increases the binaural advantage decreases. Put another way, as the signal becomes easier to detect, the advantage of spatially separating the signal from the noise disappears. Thus, only at low signal-to-noise ratios where the signal is not easily detected is there a binaural advantage. Therefore, these binaural advantage data suggest that spatially separating signals from noise for suprathreshold sounds may not make the signals more easy to discriminate or recognize. However, as indicated earlier, the conditions under which these data were collected are not at all like those that occur for sound sources in our everyday world.

A number of investigators have determined the detectability and recognition of signals coming from a loudspeaker at one location in an anechoic room when noise was coming from a loudspeaker at a different location in the room (Plomp,

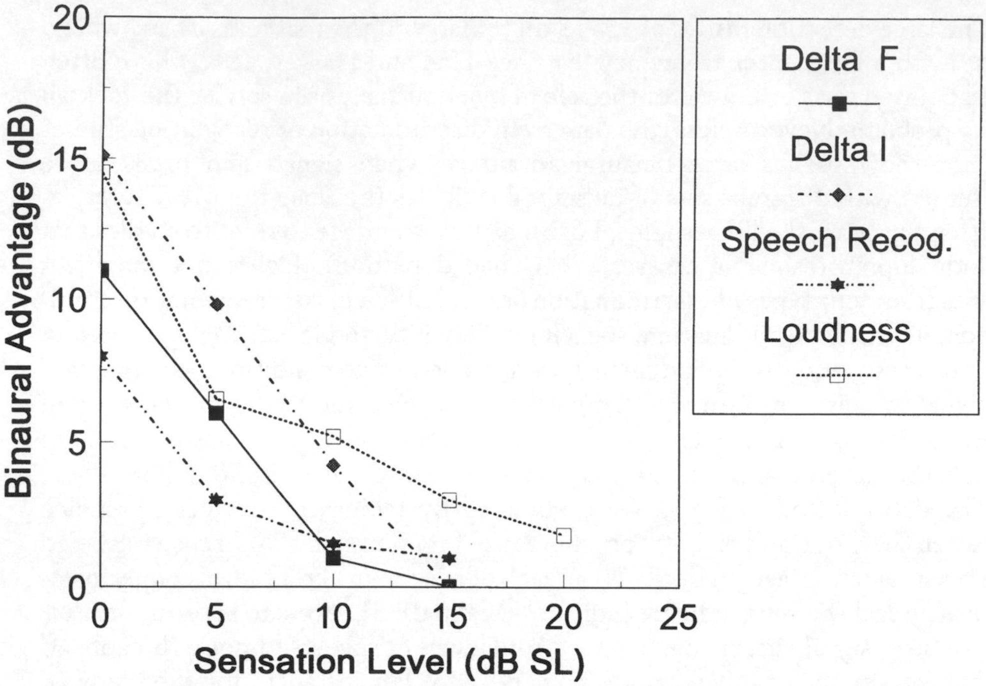

0 dB SL = 10 dB E/No = -15 dB Speech/Noise

FIG. 5. Summary of the results from four studies of suprathreshold measures of the binaural advantage afforded to signal discrimination or recognition. The binaural advantage (in dB) for discriminating, recognizing, or making a loudness judgment is plotted as a function of the signal-to-noise ratio, normalized as indicated on the bottom of the figure. The binaural advantage is the decibel difference between psychometric functions associated with the signal interaurally in phase and the signal interaurally out of phase. This difference was measured at several different performance levels. Additional explanation is provided in the text, but the main point of this figure is that there is a very small binaural advantage for suprathreshold measures of performance when the signal-to-noise ratio is high, that is, when the signal is easy to detect. Data are from Carhart, Tillman, and Johnson (1967), Henning (1973), and Townsend and Goldstein (1973).

1976; Plomp and Mimpen, 1981; Saberi, Dostal, Sadraladabi, Bull, and Perrott, 1991; Santon, 1987; Thompson and Webster, 1963, 1964; see also Kollmeier, Chapter 34, this volume, and Good, Gilkey, and Ball, Chapter 18, this volume). This type of study is sometimes referred to as a free-field MLD study. Figure 6 displays results from two representative studies: one in which signal detection was determined (Saberi *et al.*, 1991), and one in which word recognition was measured (Plomp, 1976). As can be seen, when the signal and noise masker were spatially separated the signal was easier to detect and words were easier to recognize than when the signal and masker were close together in space. However, the improvement in word recognition is less than that obtained for signal detection. The data of Saberi *et al.* (1991) have been corrected for the fact that when the head is held stationary, signal detection varies as a function of the location of the sound source relative to the fixed head. The thresholds for detecting a sound in quiet were therefore subtracted from those shown in Fig. 6. Thus, the data of Fig. 6 represent a good estimate of the role binaural processing plays in detecting and recognizing a signal spatially separated from a masker.

In the study by Plomp (1976) the reverberation characteristics of the room were also varied and the data shown in Fig. 6 represent the best condition, when there was minimal reverberation. The word recognition advantage associated with spatial separation decreases when there is a considerable reverberation.

Thus, the results from the masking-level difference literature show that spatially separating signals and maskers can lead to a 15–18 dB improvement in signal detectability over headphones and 10–12 dB in a free field. The binaural advantage for signal recognition or discrimination over headphones is very small for signals that are easily detected when they are presented over headphones, but can be 4–6 dB when signals are presented in the free field with minimal reverberation. However, in the real world, which contains reverberation, the advantage in recognition of separating the signal and the masker is probably very small.

III. LATERALIZATION AND LOCALIZATION

With a few exceptions that are described later, the selective attention and MLD literature exhausts the studies of detection, discrimination, and recognition of signals that are spatially separated from maskers. If spatial separation is a con-

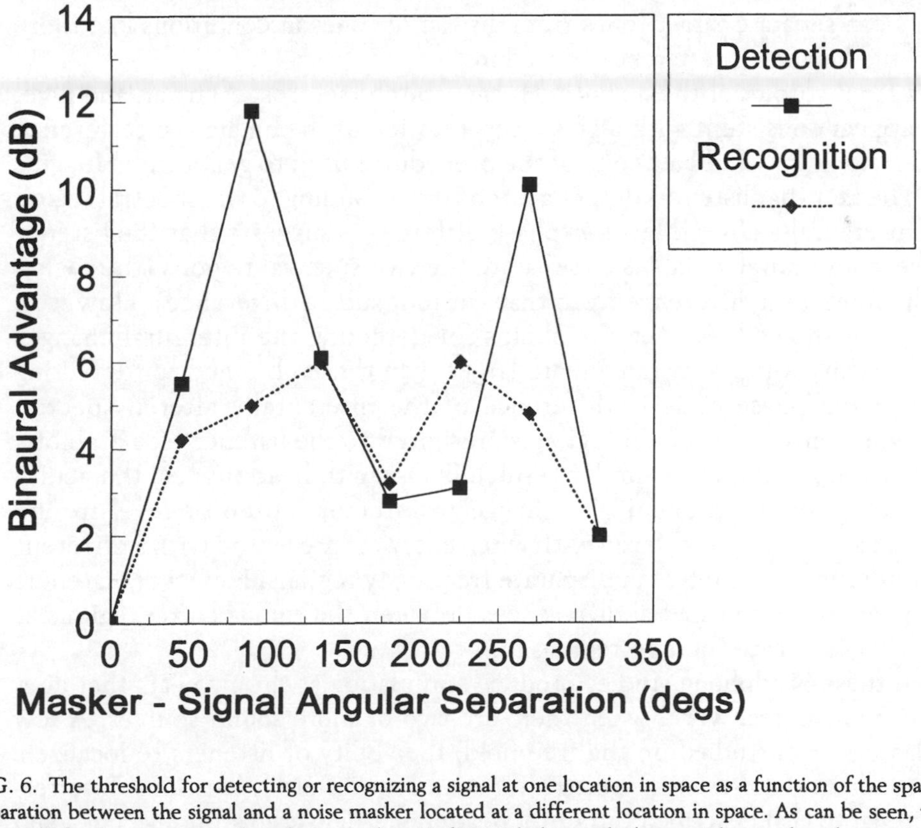

FIG. 6. The threshold for detecting or recognizing a signal at one location in space as a function of the spatial separation between the signal and a noise masker located at a different location in space. As can be seen, the threshold for detecting a signal can be as much as 12 dB (12 dB binaural advantage) lower when the signal and masker are separated by 90°. The advantage for speech recognition (recognition curve) is smaller, being approximately 6 dB when there is little reverberation.

tributor to a solution to the cocktail party problem, then we might gain additional insights by understanding performance of human listeners in tasks of auditory localization when there are two or more sound sources.

In recent years several investigators (see Stellmack and Dye, 1993; Dye, Chapter 8, this volume; Bernstein, Chapter 6, this volume; Buell and Trahiotis, Chapter 7, this volume) have studied the ability of listeners to detect a change in the interaural time or level difference of a target tone in the presence of one or more additional tones with different interaural parameters. These studies show that there can be a considerable elevation in interaural time or level thresholds for the target, even when the additional tones (distractor tones) differ in frequency from the target tone by more than a critical band. Thus, these "binaural interference" studies suggest that the acuity for processing spatial information in one spectral region can be interfered with by information in remote spectral regions. One interpretation of these results is that listeners cannot use the interaural differences between the distractor and the target to separate the target from the distractor. As such, this interpretation casts doubt on the ability of spatially separated signals to aid in sound source segregation, and to form a solution for the cocktail party problem. Dye (Chapter 8, this volume) argues that elevated thresholds, while suggesting a loss in acuity, may not mean a loss in sound source segregation. His data, using a new psychophysical procedure, show that many listeners can separate target tones from distractor tones in conditions like those used in the binaural interference procedure.

Data from studies of the dichotic Huggins pitch (see Yost, Harder, and Dye, 1987) appear consistent with Dye's interpretation of the binaural interference procedure. Figure 7 indicates one of the procedures used to generate a Huggins pitch. The fact that listeners detect a pitch corresponding to the spectral region of the interaurally altered level or phase differences suggests that the listener uses these interaural variables to separate the two spectral regions (the region with the interaural difference from that without such a difference). However, Yost (1991) showed that the thresholds for detecting the interaural changes in the Huggins stimulus paradigm are larger than those obtained for detecting the interaural phase or level difference of the interaurally altered spectral region when only this spectral region is presented to the listener (see Trahiotis and Bernstein, 1990, for a similar result). Thus, with headphones, the acuity for detecting or discriminating a change in interaural time or level in one spectral region can be interfered with when energy is presented with a different set of interaural parameters in disparate frequency regions. However, listeners still appear to use the spatial differences between the two spectral regions as a means to segregate the two regions.

Again these headphone studies produce stimulation at the two ears that does not occur in the real world when there are two or more sound sources. A few investigators have studied, in the free field, the ability of listeners to localize a target sound in the presence of distractor sounds at different locations. Interference similar to that described earlier for headphone-delivered stimuli occurs, and in some cases the presence of a sound at one location leads to a mislocalization of a sound presented at a different location.

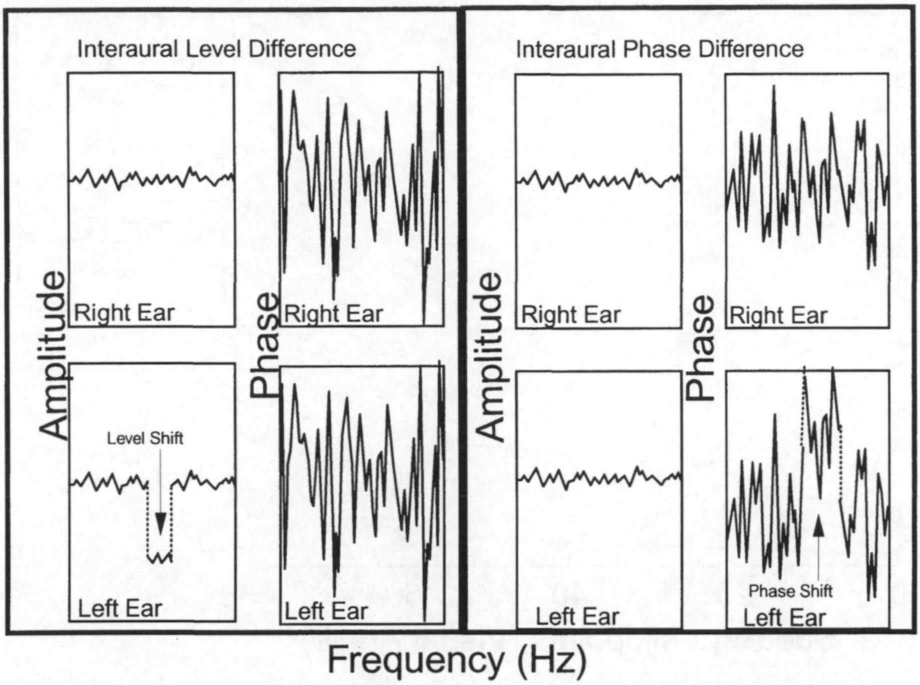

FIG. 7. A schematic of the stimulus conditions used to generate Huggins pitch. Either an interaural phase difference or an interaural level difference is introduced to a narrow region of the spectrum of a broadband noise stimulus. Under the appropriate conditions the pitch of this narrowband interaurally altered region is perceived as a different auditory image from that of the noise background. Huggins pitch suggests that interaural differences that are different in different spectral regions can help separate auditory images that might result from different sound sources.

Figure 8 depicts results from a study by Perrott (1984), which suggested an interference effect measured in the free field. In this study the listener was presented two tones simultaneously over two loudspeakers; one tone was 500 Hz and the other was 515, 543, 572, or 601 Hz. The listener had to indicate whether the higher frequency tone was produced by the left or right loudspeaker. The angular separation between the two speakers required for threshold discrimination (MAA) was determined as a function of the midpoint of the two loudspeaker arrays relative to the location of the listener. Figure 8 shows the minimal audible angle (MAA) required for threshold discrimination as a function of the midpoint angle for two frequency separations (43 and 101 Hz). The data are compared to the classic MAA for discriminating the change in loudspeaker location for a single 500-Hz tone presented first to one loudspeaker and then to the other loudspeaker (Mills, 1958). As can be seen, when both loudspeakers are simultaneously stimulated there is an increase in the threshold MAA as compared to conditions in which only one loudspeaker at a time is stimulated. That is, there appears to be interference of spatial acuity when two sounds are simultaneously presented at different locations. However, the task in the Perrott (1984) study is different than that used by Mills (1958). Therefore, although the differences shown in Fig. 8 are large, they may be partially due to the procedural differences.

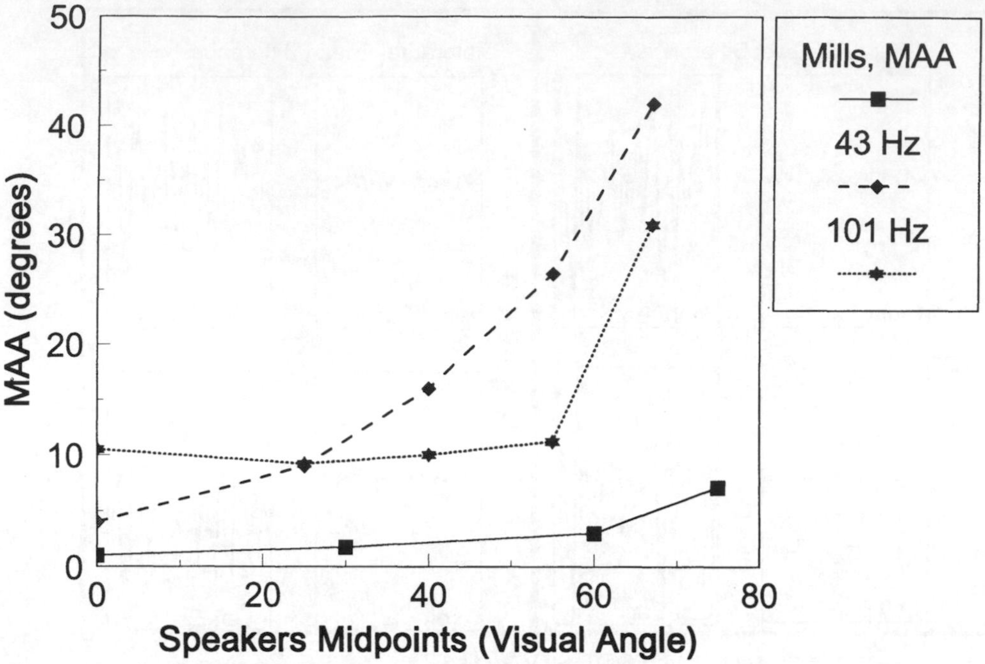

FIG. 8. Data from a study by Perrott (1984) in which listeners were asked to indicate if the right loudspeaker of two simultaneously stimulated loudspeakers contained the high-frequency sound. This judgment was determined as a function of the angular separation between the loudspeakers and the frequency difference (43 or 101 Hz). The minimal audible angle (MAA) required for the listeners to just discriminate the speaker location based on the frequency difference is plotted as a function of the location of the midpoint of the two loudspeakers and for the two frequency differences. The data are compared to the MAA data of Mills (1958), in which only one loudspeaker at a time was stimulated with the same tonal frequency and listeners were asked to discriminate the difference in location. The MAA is larger when two sound sources are simultaneously presented than when only one sound source at a time is presented.

Figure 9 shows data from a study by Thurlow and Marten (1962) in which listeners indicated the position of a short duration target source (using a light pointer) when other longer duration sound sources were present. In their study, 2000-Hz highpass noise was delivered alternately, without any temporal gaps, between two loudspeakers and listeners were asked to judge the location of the short-duration target. In Fig. 9 one of the analyses performed by Thurlow and Marten is displayed, in which the noise bursts were alternated between the two loudspeakers at 2 or 14 times per second and the angle of separation between the loudspeakers was varied from condition to condition. These data show the influence of alternation rate and angular separation on the error in target location. The listeners misperceived the target's location in that it was "attracted" to the location of the other sound source. Thus, the location of a sound source at one location in space was disrupted by the presence of another sound source stimulated at about the same time. However, if the target and distractor sounds were not spatially separated they probably would have been perceived as one sound and the target would have been nearly impossible to identify.

The precedence or law of the first wavefront effect (see Blauert, 1987; Hartmann, Chapter 10, this volume; Blauert, Chapter 28, this volume; Clifton and Freyman, Chapter 12, this volume; Hafter, Chapter 11, this volume) is a classic example of the influence the sound from one point in space has on the perception of a sound at a different location. The precedence effect deals with stimulus situations in which the perception of the sound's source remains relatively constant even when the sound is reflected off nearby surfaces such that these reflective surfaces act as possible new sources for the sound. In these situations the reflected sound is strongly correlated with the originating sound, and the later arriving reflection appears to be suppressed by the earlier arriving original sound (see Clifton and Freyman, Chapter 12, and Hartmann, Chapter 10, this volume, for exceptions). However, even in this "precedence effect" the acuity for determining the location of the original sound source is decreased when there are sufficient echoes from reflections (Hartmann, 1983; Rakerd and Hartmann, 1985, 1986). In reflective environments, the location of the source is still that associated with the first waveform reaching the listener's ears, but the accuracy with which the listener can locate this source is reduced as compared to situations when there are no echoes.

As the sound from reflective sources becomes decorrelated (in Blauert's terms incoherent) from that of the original source, the listener perceives both sources as the precedence effect breaks down. Divenyi (1992) has studied the precedence

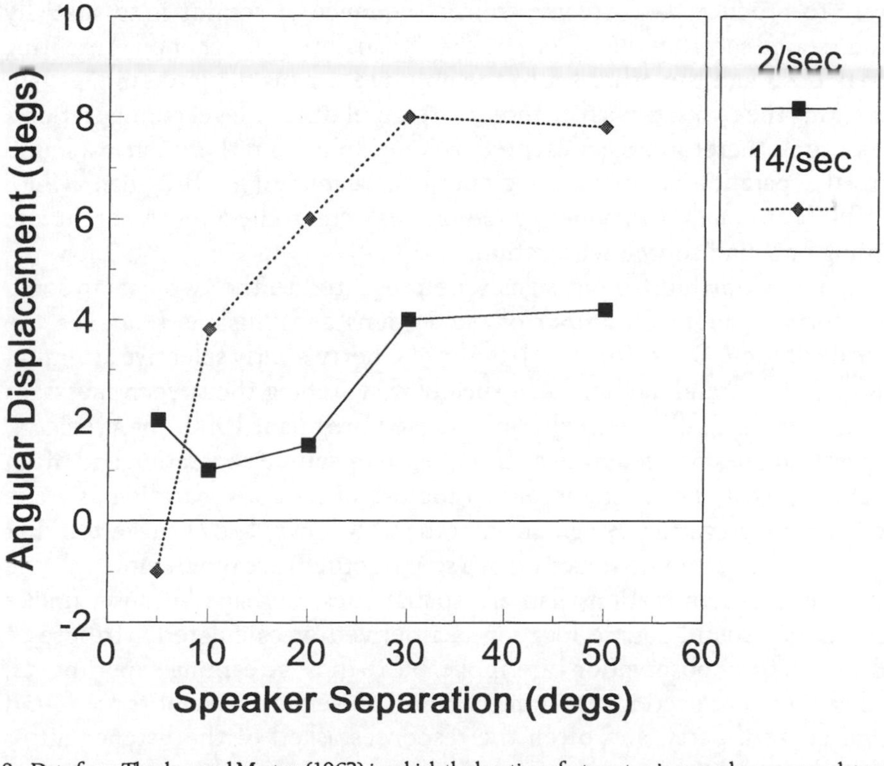

FIG. 9. Data from Thurlow and Marten (1962) in which the location of a target noise sound source was determined when the noise was quickly switched between the target source and a distractor source. The error in location of the target is plotted as a function of the angular separation between the two sources and the rate of switching the sound between the two sources (twice per second or 14 times per second). When the noises are almost simultaneously presented the location of the target is misperceived toward the direction of the distractor.

effect under conditions in which the original and reflective sources were spectrally incoherent. When the source and its echo are spectrally different, the location of both the original source and the echo is perceived; however, the location of neither is as accurately determined as when each is presented as a separate source.

Thus, in a variety of localization conditions the acuity for determining the location of one source is compromised when other sources (or echoes of the original source) are present at different locations. In the literature, the extent to which such a loss in acuity reduces the role of spatial hearing as a solution for the cocktail party problem has not been addressed.

IV. STREAMING AND STREAM SEGREGATION

When two or more sounds are presented in sequence, the perception of the stream of sound is often that of two or more simultaneously occurring streams as if there were two or more sources each producing a sequence of sounds. Bregman (1990) and his coworkers have documented many conditions that lead to these "streaming" effects, and Bregman has articulated a number of principles governing streaming as one of the means of performing auditory scene analysis (Bregman, 1990).

One way to produce two streams from a sequence of sounds is to spatially separate one sound set from the other set. This is usually done either by presenting one set to one ear and the other set to the opposite ear (as depicted in Fig. 10), or by presenting the two sets with different interaural time or level configurations. These conditions, therefore, are presented over headphones rather than in a sound field. Spatial separation is not a strong cue for streaming (see Bregman, 1990; Kubovy, 1987), although it may help another weak cue to be a more potent cue for streaming or sound source segregation.

Experiments in which different signals are presented to the two ears in some alternating form generate a number of perceptions and illusions (e.g., see the Deutsch scale illusion, Deutsch, 1974). Some of Cherry's early selective attention experiments (Cherry and Taylor, 1954) involved switching the speech messages between the ears. In all of these experiments (see Bregman, 1990, for a review), spatial separation does not generate a strong sense of source separation and often leads to illusions that are contradictory to the use of spatial separation as a cue for sound source segregation. Bregman and others (Kubovy, 1987) suggested that other cues (e.g., the harmonic structure of a sound source) are much more reliable for sound source determination than are spatial cues, perhaps because, unlike frequency coding, sound source location is a derived or calculated attribute of sound. Although these observations are applicable to most streaming experiments, the stimulus situations used in streaming studies are very atypical of those found at a natural cocktail party, and often the responses asked of the listener differ from those that might occur at a cocktail party or in a multisource acoustic environment. Thus, caution should be exercised in drawing strong conclusions about the role of spatial hearing as a solution to the cocktail party problem based on the data and arguments derived from streaming experiments.

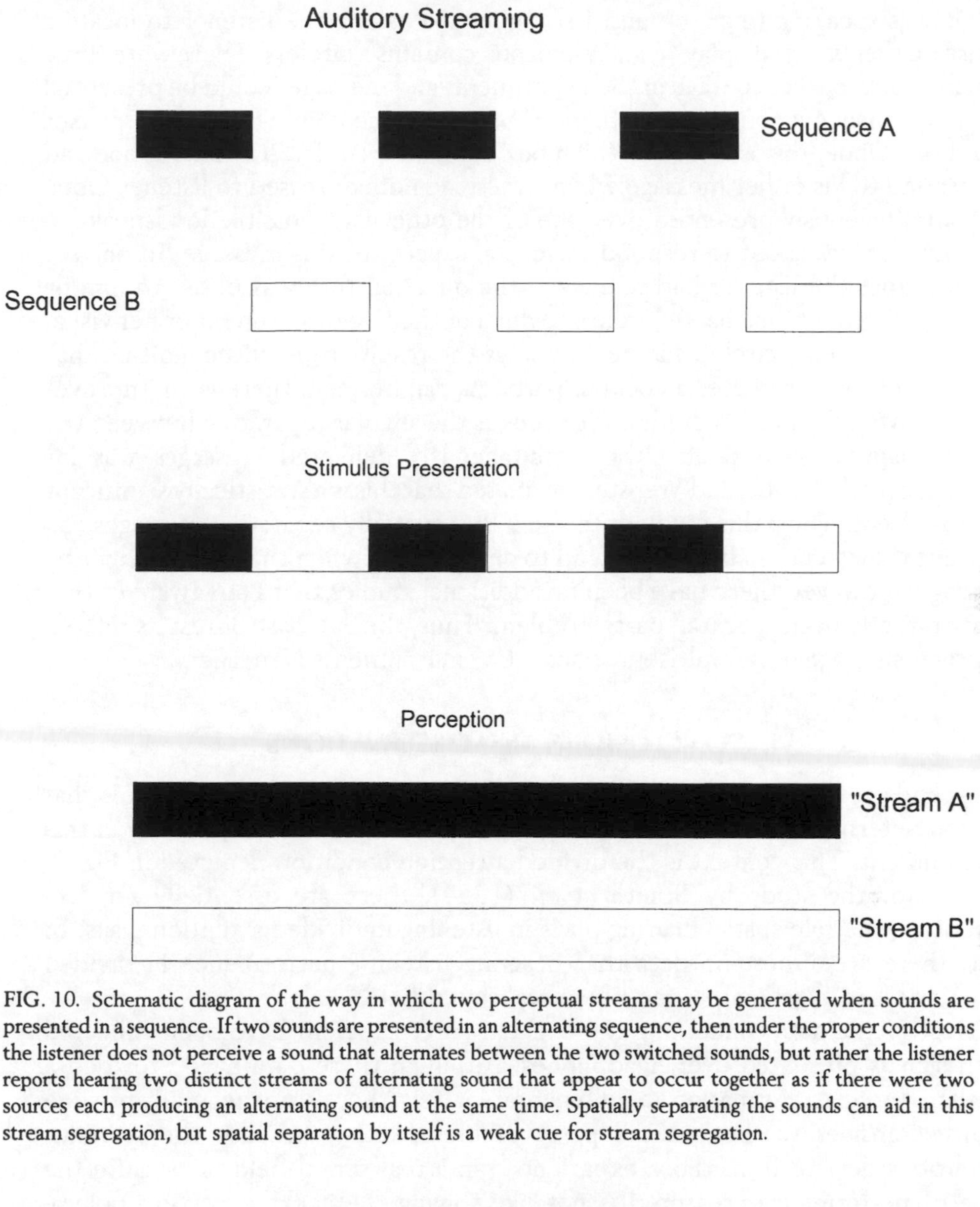

FIG. 10. Schematic diagram of the way in which two perceptual streams may be generated when sounds are presented in a sequence. If two sounds are presented in an alternating sequence, then under the proper conditions the listener does not perceive a sound that alternates between the two switched sounds, but rather the listener reports hearing two distinct streams of alternating sound that appear to occur together as if there were two sources each producing an alternating sound at the same time. Spatially separating the sounds can aid in this stream segregation, but spatial separation by itself is a weak cue for stream segregation.

V. A COCKTAIL PARTY EXPERIMENT

Although the data described so far are relevant to how we use spatial information in a cocktail party situation, they do not speak directly to sound source processing in multisource acoustic environments. Spieth, Curtis, and Webster (1954) performed an experiment directly related to the cocktail party problem soon after Cherry coined the term. In this study listeners were asked to code one message from a set of simultaneous messages delivered from different loudspeakers at various places in the test room. The message contained four parts: (1) a word identifying the listener (e.g., Oboe or King), (2) a word identifying which loudspeaker was being stimulated (e.g., Able), (3) a number indicating which talker was speaking (e.g., 1), and (4) a question asking the listener to locate a figure on their visual display (e.g., Which box contains a circle?). There were three possible loudspeaker sources in the experiment, and messages could be presented simultaneously over any two of them. Thus, a message coming over one speaker could be "Oboe, this is Able 1. Which box contains a circle?" Listener Oboe had to respond to his or her message when a message not addressed to listener Oboe was simultaneously presented over one of the other two possible loudspeakers. The listener was asked to respond to several aspects of this message. In one set of conditions the listener had to answer the question that was posed to him or her (e.g., listener Oboe had to indicate which of the five boxes on his or her visual display contained a circle). Figure 11 shows the results from this condition that most closely approximates a cocktail party. As can be seen, there is an improvement of over 25% in correct identifications as the angular separation between the two loudspeakers containing the simultaneously delivered messages was increased; Spieth, Curtis, and Webster calculated that this is a statistically significant improvement. Thus, this study does show that spatially separating messages can improve the listener's ability to attend to one message when there is a competing message. However, there have been no additional studies that I am aware of that relate directly to the cocktail party problem. Thus, the database of results related to processing signals in multisource acoustic environments is meager.

VI. CONCLUSIONS AND OBSERVATIONS

We spend most of our time in multisource sound fields, and our intuition is that we can determine the sources of many, if not most, of the sound sources in this environment. This context is the divided attention condition depicted in Fig. 2. Except for the study by Spieth *et al.* (1954), there are essentially no data describing the role spatial hearing plays in listening in divided attention tasks. In fact, there are almost no data that describe listening performance in divided listening tasks in general, especially in real sound fields.

Most of the data concerning the cocktail party problem have been collected with signals presented over headphones. Although these data have provided a wealth of crucial information about binaural analysis, they do not generally provide a direct answer to the cocktail party problem, either because the stimulus conditions deviate from those experienced in a real sound field or because the type of performance measured is not like solving the cocktail party problem. When conditions studied with headphones are conducted in sound fields, the size of the effects measured with headphones is often reduced. The sound-field data that do exist indicate that detection of a signal at one location can be improved if the signal is moved further away from a masker source. However, this binaural advantage is reduced for signal recognition and discrimination. In addition, there are almost no data for conditions involving more than two sources.

If, as Table I suggests, there are various cues that can be used to solve the cocktail party problem, then, even if spatial hearing may not be a major cue, the problem can still be solved by use of some of these other cues. However, the data concerning the role of these other cues in sound source determination and

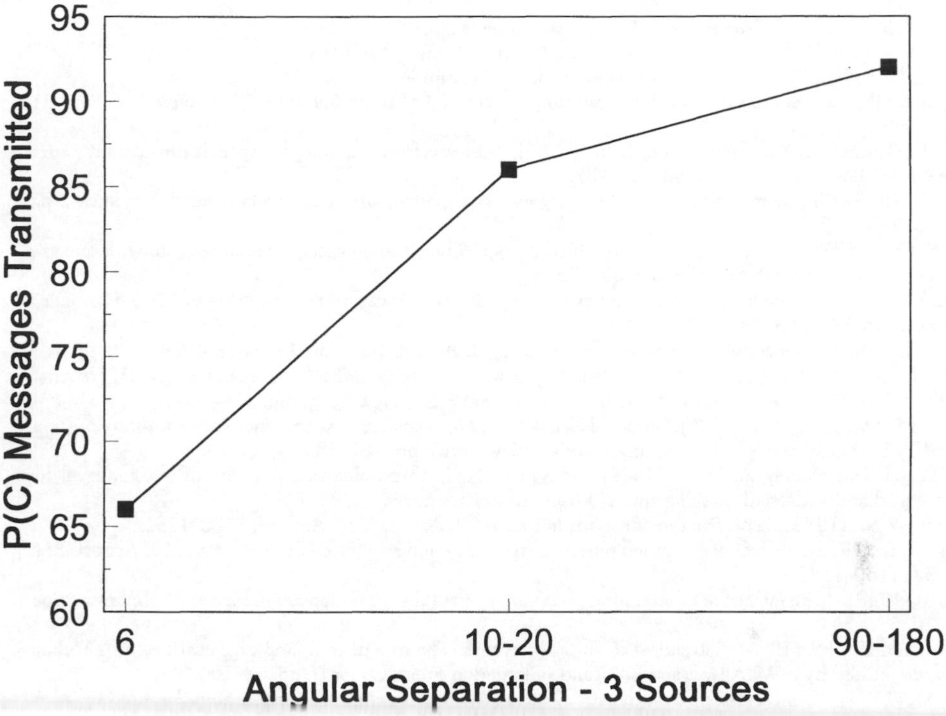

FIG. 11. The results of part of the study by Spieth, Curtis, and Webster (1954). The task for the listener was to listen to two simultaneously presented messages that could come from two of three possible locations. One of the messages contained instructions for the listener to locate a particular object on a visual display. The data show the percent correct performance in finding the appropriate object as a function of the spatial separation between the two loudspeakers containing the two simultaneously presented messages. This is an example of spatial cues aiding signal recognition as proposed in the cocktail party effect.

segregation are just as meager as those for spatial hearing, especially regarding performance in real sound fields.

Sound source determination and the cocktail party effect are a major component of hearing (see Yost, 1992a, 1992b) and of our everyday lives. Thus, we need to have a better database describing how human listeners perform in complex sound fields and the role played by the various cues in determining this performance. That is, it seems crucial that after 40 years we find better answers to Cherry's (1953, pp. 975–976) questions, "How do we recognize what one person is saying when others are speaking at the same time (the 'cocktail party problem')? On what logical basis could one design a machine ('filter') for carrying out such an operation?"

ACKNOWLEDGMENTS

I am grateful to the faculty of the Parmly Hearing Institute, especially Toby Dye and Stan Sheft, for their guidance in preparing this chapter.

The chapter was written with support from the National Institute on Deafness and Other Communication Disorders and the Air Force Office of Scientific Research.

REFERENCES

Blauert, J. (**1987**). *Spatial Hearing* (MIT Press, Cambridge, MA).

Bregman, A. S. (**1990**). *Auditory Scene Analysis* (MIT Press, Cambridge, MA).

Broadbent, D. E. (**1958**). *Perception and Communication* (Pergamon, London).

Broadbent D. E., and Ladefoged, P. (**1959**). "Auditory perception of temporal order," J. Acoust. Soc. Am. **31**, 1539–1544.

Carhart, R., Tillman, T. W., and Johnson, K. R. (**1967**). "Release from masking for speech through interaural time delay," J. Acoust. Soc. Am. **42**, 124–138.

Cherry, C. (**1953**). "Some experiments on the recognition of speech, with one and two ears," J. Acoust. Soc. Am. **25**, 975–979.

Cherry, E. C., and Taylor, W. K. (**1954**). "Some further experiments upon recognition of speech, with one and with two ears," J. Acoust. Soc. Am. **26**, 554–559.

Deutsch, D. (**1974**). "Lateralization by frequency for repeating sequences of dichotic 400– and 800–Hz tones," J. Acoust. Soc. Am. **63**, 184–191.

Divenyi, P. L. (**1992**). "Binaural suppression of nonechoes," J. Acoust. Soc. Am. **91**, 1078–1084.

Durlach, N. I., and Colburn, H. S. (**1978**). "Binaural phenomena," in *Handbook of Perception, Vol. IV, Hearing,* edited by E. C. Carterette and M. P. Friedman (Academic Press, New York), pp. 365–466.

Green, D. M., and Yost, W. A. (**1975**). "Binaural analysis," in *Handbook of Sensory Physiology: Auditory System,* edited by W. Keidel and W. Neff (Springer-Verlag, New York), pp. 461–480.

Hall, J. W. III, and Harvey, A. D. G. (**1989**). "N_0S_0 and N_0S_π thresholds as a function of masker level for narrowband and wideband masking noise," J. Acoust. Soc. Am. **76**, 1699–1703.

Hartmann, W. M. (**1983**). "Localization of sounds in rooms," J. Acoust. Soc. Am. **74**, 1380–1391.

Henning, G. B. (**1973**). "Effect of interaural phase on frequency and amplitude discrimination," J. Acoust. Soc. Am. **54**, 1160–1178.

Hirsh, I. J. (**1948**). "The influence of interaural phase on interaural summation and inhibition," J. Acoust. Soc. Am. **20**, 536–544.

Jones, M., and Yee, W. (**1993**). "Attending to auditory events: The role of temporal organization," in *Thinking in Sound,* edited by S. McAdams and E. Bigand (Clarendon Press, Oxford), pp. 69–106.

Kubovy, M. (**1987**). "Concurrent pitch segregation," in *Auditory Processing of Complex Sound,* edited by W. A. Yost and C. S. Watson (Lawrence Erlbaum Associates, Hillsdale, NJ), pp. 299–313.

Lauter, J. L. (**1983**). "Stimulus characteristics and relative ear advantages: A new look at old data," J. Acoust. Soc. Am. **74**, 1–17.

Levitt, H., and Rabiner, L. R. (**1967**). "Predicting binaural gain in intelligibility and release from masking for speech," J. Acoust. Soc. Am. **42**, 820–829.

Licklider, J. C. R. (**1948**). "Influence of interaural phase relations upon the masking of speech by white noise," J. Acoust. Soc. Am. **20**, 150–159.

McFadden, D. M. (**1975**). "Masking and the binaural system," in *The Nervous System,* edited by E. L. Eagles (Raven Press, New York), Vol. 3, pp. 137–146.

Mills, A. W. (**1958**). "On the minimum audible angle," J. Acoust. Soc. Am. **30**, 237–243.

Perrott, D. (**1984**). "Concurrent minimum audible angle: A re-examination of the concept of auditory spatial acuity," J. Acoust. Soc. Am. **75**, 1201–1206.

Plomp, R. (**1976**). "Binaural and monaural speech intelligibility of connected discourse in reverberation as a function of azimuth of a single competing sound source (speech or noise)," Acustica **34**, 200–211.

Plomp, R., and Mimpen, A. M. (**1981**). "Effect of the orientation of the speaker's head and the azimuth of a noise source on the speech-reception threshold for sentences," Acustica **48**, 325–328.

Rakerd, B., and Hartmann W. M. (**1985**). "Localization of sounds in rooms, II. The effect of a single reflecting surface," J. Acoust. Soc. Am. **78**, 524–533.

Rakerd, B., and Hartmann, W. M. (**1986**). "Localization of sounds in rooms, III. Onset and duration effects," J. Acoust. Soc. Am. **80**, 1695–1706.

Saberi, K., Dostal, L., Sadraladabai, T., Bull, V., and Perrott, D. A. (**1991**). "Free-field release from masking," J. Acoust. Soc. Am. **90**, 1355–1370.

Santon, F. (**1987**). "Detection d'un son pur dans un bruit masquant suivamt l'angle d'incidence du bruit. Relation avec le seuil de reception de la parole," Acustica **63**, 222–228.

Spieth, W., Curtis, J. F., and Webster, J. C. (**1954**). "Responding to one of two simultaneous messages," J. Acoust. Soc. Am. **26**, 391–396.

Stellmack, M. A., and Dye, R. H. (**1993**). "The combination of interaural information across frequencies: The effects of number and spacing of components, onset asynchrony, and harmonicity," J. Acoust. Soc. Am. **93**, 2933–2947.

Thompson, P. O., and Webster, J. C. (**1963**). "The effect of talker-listener angle on word intelligibility," Acustica **13**, 319–323.

Thompson, P. O., and Webster, J. C. (**1964**). "The effect of talker-listener angle on word intelligibility. II. In an open field," Acustica **14**, 44–47.

Thurlow, W. R., and Marten, A. W. (**1962**). "Perception of steady and intermittent sounds with alternating noise burst stimuli," J. Acoust. Soc. Am. **34**, 1853–1858.

Townsend, T. H., and Goldstein, D. P. (**1973**). "Suprathreshold binaural unmasking," J. Acoust. Soc. Am. **51**, 621–624.

Trahiotis, C., and Bernstein, L. R. (**1990**). "Detectability of interaural delays over select spectral regions: Effects of flanking noise," J. Acoust. Soc. Am. **87**, 810–813.

Treisman, A. M., and Gelade, G. (**1980**). "A feature-integration theory of attention," Cog. Psych. **12**, 97–136.

Yost, W. A. (**1991**). "Thresholds for segregating a narrow-band from broadband noise based on interaural phase and level differences," J. Acoust. Soc. Am. **89**, 838–844.

Yost, W. A. (**1992a**). "Auditory image perception and analysis," Hear. Res. **56**, 8–19.

Yost, W. A. (**1992b**). "Auditory perception and sound source determination," Current Directions Psychol. Sci. **1**(6), 15–19.

Yost, W. A., Harder, P. J., and Dye, R. H. (**1987**). "Complex spectral patterns with interaural differences: Dichotic pitch and the 'central spectrum,' " in *Auditory Processing of Complex Sounds*, edited by W. A. Yost and C. S. Watson (Lawrence Erlbaum Associates, Hillsdale, NJ), pp. 190–201.

Chapter 18

The Relation Between Detection in Noise and Localization in Noise in the Free Field

Michael D. Good[1]
Honeywell Inc., Minneapolis, Minnesota

Robert H. Gilkey
Wright State University, Dayton, Ohio

Jennifer M. Ball
Wright State University, Dayton, Ohio

(Received October 1994; revised December 1994)

The results from two experiments on detection in noise are compared to those from two experiments on localization in noise. In the detection experiments, large increases in detectability are observed when the signal is horizontally separated from the masker (up to 16 dB), or vertically separated from the masker (up to 9 dB), in the free field. In most cases, these increases in detectability can be explained by monaural processing alone, and thus these results do not imply the use of binaural sound localization mechanisms. In the localization experiments, the accuracy of localization is shown to depend, in a complex manner, on both the signal-to-noise ratio and the location of the masker; although more detectable signals are usually localized more accurately, this is not always the case. Overall, the results of the two sets of experiments fail to show a clear and direct relation between detection and localization.

INTRODUCTION

Cherry (1953) suggested that the ability to "hear out" a signal in the presence of other interfering sounds (i.e., the "cocktail party effect") is dependent on the spatial distribution of the stimuli. That is, to the degree that a signal can be

[1]This work was performed when the first author was a graduate student in the Department of Psychology at Wright State University, Dayton, OH 45435.

localized to a particular spatial location that is different from the locations of the interfering sounds, the listener can attend to the particular spatial location where the signal might occur and ignore the other locations. In contrast to this view, modern views on spatial hearing suggest that fairly detailed information about the arrival time and spectral shape of the stimuli reaching the tympanic membranes is needed for accurate sound localization; therefore, it is reasonable to expect that a signal might have to be presented at a level well above "detection threshold" (where such detailed information could be consistently resolved) in order for its location to be determined reliably.

This chapter considers the relation between two sets of experiments that have been conducted in our laboratory in order to illuminate the seemingly paradoxical relation between these two views. The first set considers the detectability of signals as a function of their spatial relation to a masker (experiment 1 is from Gilkey, Good, and Ball, 1996); the second set of experiments considers how the accuracy of localization judgments is influenced by the presence of a masker (experiments 3 and 4 are from Good and Gilkey, 1996a, 1996b). The chapter should be considered an interim report on a program of research that is investigating the ability of subjects to detect, localize, and recognize a variety of signals in the presence of interfering acoustic stimuli.

I. EXPERIMENT 1: MASKED DETECTION IN THE FREE FIELD[2]

The influence on detection of the "spatial parameters" of the signal and the masker has been most extensively examined with headphone presentation of stimuli (for a review of early work, see Durlach and Colburn, 1978; for more recent efforts, see Bernstein, Chapter 6, this volume; Kohlrausch and Fassel, Chapter 9, this volume; and Yost, Chapter 17, this volume). These headphone studies have shown that when the interaural parameters of a low-frequency signal are different from those of the masker, the detectability of the signal can be increased by 15 dB or more, relative to the case when the interaural parameters of the signal and masker are the same. This change in signal detectability is known as the masking level difference (MLD). As the signal frequency is increased, the magnitude of the MLD decreases to about 3 dB (for frequencies above 2–3 kHz). This frequency dependence has led to the development of models that emphasize the role of low-frequency interaural time differences (ITDs) in determining the magnitude of the MLD (see Colburn and Durlach, 1978, and Stern and Trahiotis, Chapter 24, this volume, for reviews of models of binaural hearing).

Although most studies of free-field masking have examined the detectability and intelligibility of speech in noise (e.g., Bronkhorst and Plomp, 1988; Ebata, Sone, and Nimura, 1968; Kock, 1950; Plomp, 1976), there is a recent literature that has emphasized masking of nonspeech signals (e.g., Doll, Hanna, and Russotti, 1992; Gilkey and Good, 1995; Saberi, Dostal, Sadralodabai, Bull, and Perrott, 1991). For example, Gilkey and Good (1995) examined the detectability of a

[2] This experiment has previously been reported by Gilkey, Good, and Ball (1996).

click-train signal in a continuous Gaussian noise masker. Both the signal and the masker were bandlimited into low-, mid-, or high-frequency regions. To a first approximation, the reductions in masking they observed with horizontal separations were similar in magnitude to the values of the MLD observed under comparable headphone conditions (i.e., maximum reductions of about 18 dB); therefore, the observed reductions might reasonably be expected to be based on the changes in interaural parameters that occur when the signal is horizontally separated from the masker. However, they also observed large reductions in masking (up to 8 dB) when the signal was vertically separated from the masker within the median plane. Unlike performance for horizontal separations, these reductions are difficult to explain by an analysis of interaural differences; that is, there are minimal differences between the interaural parameters of the stimuli when they are vertically separated within the median plane (at least for frequencies below about 5 kHz). Although the overall pattern of results was similar to that observed by Saberi *et al.* for broadband stimuli, Gilkey and Good found that the largest reductions in masking occurred for their high-frequency (>5 kHz) signal. Based on the data of Yost and Dolan (1978), they argued that it was unlikely that ITDs would lead to masking reductions of this magnitude at high frequencies. On the other hand, after comparing the physical measurements of Feddersen, Sandel, Teas, and Jeffress (1957) to the psychoacoustic measurements of Egan (1965), they argued that the increase in the interaural level difference (ILD) from their mid-frequency signals to their high-frequency signals was unlikely to have yielded the larger masking reductions that they observed at high frequencies. Thus, some other mechanism was indicated. Gilkey and Good suggested that their subjects might have listened in narrowband frequency regions, where pinna filtering had increased the effective signal-to-noise ratio (SNR).

Experiment 1 replicates the measurements of Gilkey and Good (1995), using a pulsed masker instead of a continuous masker. Previous research on the effect of masker fringe on the magnitude of the MLD (e.g., Gilkey, Simpson, and Weisenberger, 1990; McFadden, 1966; Robinson and Trahiotis, 1972; Yost, 1985) suggests that smaller reductions in masking might be observed for a pulsed masker. In addition, the pulsed-masker results from this free-field experiment will be compared to the pulsed-masker results from a headphone study (experiment 2), in order to evaluate the relative contribution of monaural and binaural cues for determining the detectability of masked signals.

A. Method

Three female subjects, with normal hearing, participated in the experiment. The subjects ranged in age from 21 to 24 years. The experiment was conducted in the Auditory Localization Facility at Wright-Patterson Air Force Base. Within this facility is a large anechoic chamber that houses a 4.3-m diameter geodesic sphere. During the experiment, the subjects were seated with their heads positioned in the center of the sphere and held a bite-bar to minimize head movements. The subjects listened to sounds presented through a subset of the 277 speakers mounted along the surface of the sphere.

The 165-ms signal was a train of 25-μs pulses, which were repeated at a rate of 100 Hz. The masker was a 250-ms Gaussian noise. In separate conditions, both the signal and the masker were filtered into low-, mid-, or high-frequency regions. Within any particular block of trials both the signal and masker occupied the same frequency region. The signal was bandpass-filtered from 0.387 to 0.938 kHz (the low-frequency condition), from 1.72 to 4.70 kHz (the mid-frequency condition), or from 5.20 to 14.0 kHz (the high-frequency condition), and the masker was bandpass-filtered from 0.238 to 1.33 kHz (the low-frequency condition), from 1.14 to 7.10 kHz (the mid-frequency condition), or from 3.53 to 19.1 kHz (the high-frequency condition).

Using a cued, two-alternative, forced-choice (cued-2AFC) adaptive staircase procedure (Levitt, 1971), the threshold SNR for 79.4% correct performance was measured as a function of the spatial separation between the signal and masker within the horizontal plane or within the median plane. Under separate conditions, the masker could originate from one of three spatial locations: directly in front of the subject (0° azimuth, 0° elevation), directly to the left of the subject (–90° azimuth, 0° elevation), or directly above the subject (0° azimuth, 90° elevation). Depending on the condition, the signal could originate from a subset of spatial locations within either the horizontal plane or the median plane. At least two threshold estimates were obtained under each condition for each subject.

B. Results and discussion

The mean data are shown in Fig. 1 for the cases in which the signal and masker are spatially separated within the horizontal plane. The estimated threshold SNR is plotted as a function of the azimuth of the signal. The arrow along the abscissa indicates the spatial location of the masker (i.e., data points directly above the arrow denote the case in which the signal and the masker were presented from the same speaker). The parameter of the curves represents the frequency region of the stimuli. The left panel of the figure shows data for the case in which the masker was directly in front of the subject (0° azimuth, 0° elevation). As can be seen, when the signal was separated from the masker in azimuth, there were substantial reductions in masking in all three frequency regions. Maximum reductions in masking were about 10 dB, 4 dB, and 10 dB, for the low-, mid-, and high-frequency conditions, respectively. The largest reductions were observed when the signal and masker were separated by 45° to 135°. The right panel shows data for the case when the masker was directly to the left of the subject (–90° azimuth, 0° elevation). As the signal was separated from the masker in azimuth, there were reductions in masking of 7 dB, 9 dB, and 16 dB, for the low-, mid-, and high-frequency conditions, respectively. For this case, the largest reductions were observed when the signal and masker were on opposite sides of the head.

The data for conditions in which the signal and masker were vertically separated within the median plane are shown in Fig. 2. The estimated SNR is plotted as a function of the elevation of the signal. Again, the parameter of the curves represents the frequency of the stimuli. The left panel of the figure shows data for the case in which the masker was directly in front of the subject (0° azimuth,

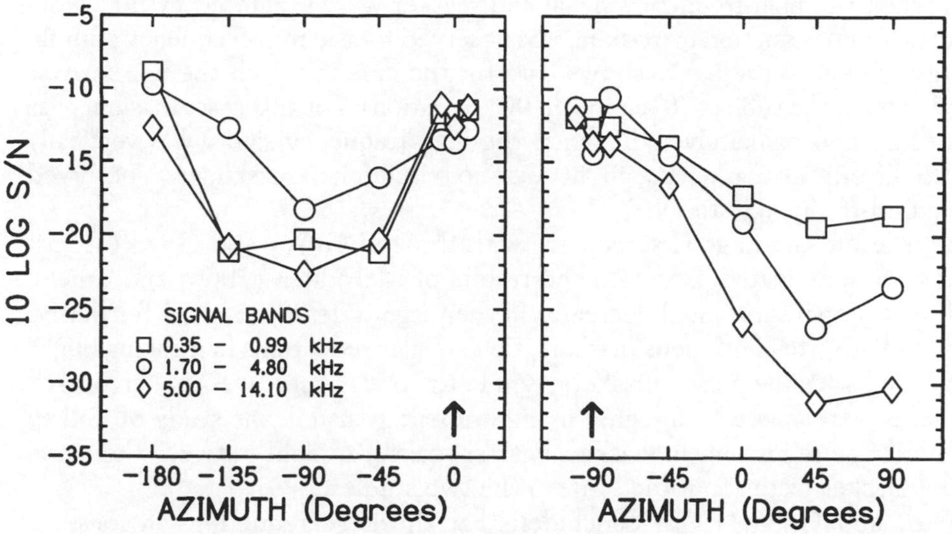

FIG. 1. Threshold SNR as a function of the azimuth of the signal within the horizontal plane. The position of the masker is indicated by the arrow in each panel. The data have been averaged across three subjects. Each of the three curves in each panel shows the results for one of the three signal bands. The left panel shows data for the case when the masker is located in front of the subject (0° azimuth, 0° elevation). The right panel shows data for the case when the masker is located to the left of the subject (–90° azimuth, 0° elevation). (After Gilkey, Good, and Ball, 1996.)

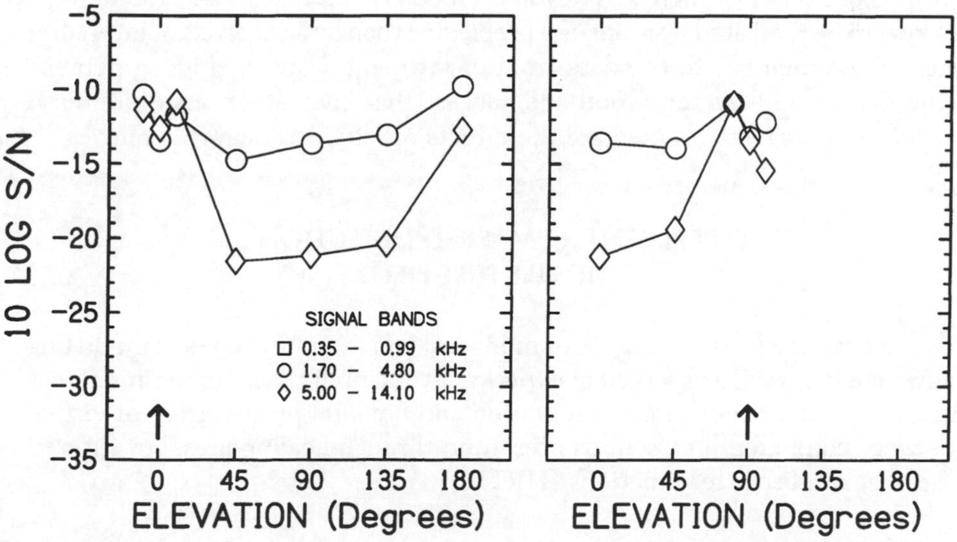

FIG. 2. Threshold SNR as a function of the elevation of the signal within the median plane. The left panel shows data for the case when the masker is located in front of the subject (0° azimuth, 0° elevation). The right panel shows data for the case when the masker is located above the subject (0° azimuth, 90° elevation). Other details are as in Fig. 1. (After Gilkey, Good, and Ball, 1996.)

0° elevation). For this condition, the maximum reduction in masking was about 9 dB, when the high-frequency signal and masker were separated by 90°. Note that little or no reduction in masking was observed for the mid-frequency stimuli. The right panel of the figure shows data for the case in which the masker was directly above the subject (0° azimuth, 90° elevation). For this case, masking was reduced by approximately 8 dB when the high-frequency signal was vertically separated from the masker. Again, little or no reduction in masking was observed for the mid-frequency stimuli.

These results are in good agreement with those of Gilkey and Good (1995). It had been anticipated, based on the results of McFadden (1966) and others, which had shown substantial decreases in the magnitude of the MLD for pulsed maskers relative to continuous maskers, that smaller reductions in masking might be observed with the pulsed maskers used in the present study. Although overall thresholds were about 2 dB higher in experiment 1 than in the study of Gilkey and Good, the reductions in masking with spatial separations between the signal and the masker were about the same in the two studies.

Gilkey and Good (1995) concluded that the large reductions in masking observed at high frequencies, particularly those associated with vertical separations between the signal and the masker, were unlikely to be based on ITDs or ILDs. Instead, they pointed out that when the signal and masker are presented from different directions, the spectral effects introduced by the pinna will be different for the two stimuli, and therefore there will be narrowband regions where the effective SNR is increased substantially, compared to the SNR when both the signal and masker are presented from the same speaker. Thus, by focusing on these narrow spectral regions, the observer could achieve reductions in masking similar to those observed here. Gilkey and Good argued that these effects were more likely to be mediated by monaural processing than by an analysis of interaural parameters. As mentioned, the data from experiment 1 are in close agreement with the data of Gilkey and Good and suggest that cues other than interaural difference cues are likely to mediate the effects observed at high frequencies.

II. EXPERIMENT 2: MASKED DETECTION IN A VIRTUAL FREE FIELD

In order to evaluate further the role of monaural and interaural cues in mediating the reduction in masking observed in experiment 1, a preliminary experiment was undertaken in which monaural presentation and binaural presentation of virtual sounds were compared [i.e., sounds presented through headphones, but filtered with head-related transfer functions (HRTFs)].

A. Method

Three male subjects, with normal hearing, and one female subject, with a mild unilateral hearing loss (≤25 dB HL) between 2 and 6 kHz, participated in the experiment. The subjects ranged in age from 21 to 28 years. During the experiment the subjects were seated in individual single-walled sound booths at the Signal Detection Laboratory of Wright State University and listened to sounds presented through headphones. HRTFs from subject SDO of Wightman and Kistler (1989) were used to synthesize sounds that appeared to originate from "virtual" locations corresponding to a subset of the "real" locations considered in experiment 1.

The 200-ms signal was a train of 20-μs pulses, repeated at a rate of 100 Hz. The signal was convolved with the HRTFs that corresponded to the intended spatial location and was bandpass-filtered from 0.35 to 0.99 kHz (the low-frequency condition), from 1.70 to 4.81 kHz (the mid-frequency condition), or from 5.00 to 14.1 kHz (the high-frequency condition). The 250-ms Gaussian noise masker[3] was convolved with the appropriate HRTFs and bandpass-filtered from 0.25 to 1.40 kHz (the low-frequency condition), from 1.20 to 6.80 kHz (the mid-frequency condition), or from 3.35 to 20.0 kHz (the high-frequency condition). The signal and masker waveforms were mixed with an analog mixer and presented through insert headphones (Etymotic Research, ER-2).

As in experiment 1, a cued-2AFC adaptive staircase procedure was used to estimate the threshold SNR (for 79.4% correct performance) as a function of the spatial separation between the virtual sounds. Under separate conditions, the masker could originate from one of two virtual spatial locations: directly in front of the subject (0° azimuth, 0° elevation) or directly to the left of the subject (–90° azimuth, 0° elevation). The signal could originate from selected virtual locations within either the horizontal plane or the median plane. At least three threshold estimates were obtained under each condition for each subject.

B. Results and discussion

The results of experiment 2 are compared to those of experiment 1 in Figs. 3–5. In these figures, the reduction in masking when the signal and masker are presented from spatially separated virtual locations, compared to when they were presented from the same virtual location, is shown for several combinations of frequency region and mode of presentation. Each cluster of bars shows the results for one of the three stimulus frequency regions; within each cluster, the single-slashed bars show the results obtained in experiment 2 for monaural headphone presentation (performance is shown for the ear with the greatest reduction in masking), the double-slashed bars show the results obtained in experiment 2 for binaural headphone presentation, and the open bars show the results obtained in experiment 1 for free-field presentation. The results have been averaged across subjects and the error bars show ±1.0 standard error across subjects.

[3]Prior to the experiment, 1000 white Gaussian noise waveforms were generated and stored on a computer disk. It was intended that on each trial three waveforms would be sampled, without replacement, for filtering and presentation during the three intervals of the cued-2AFC trial. However, due to a programming error, one particular noise sample had an extremely high probability (nearly 1.0) of being presented in the second interval (the first observation interval). Subsequent measurements suggest that this error did not affect the form of the results.

Figure 3 shows the results for horizontal separations between the signal and the masker when the masker is presented from directly in front of the subjects (0° azimuth, 0° elevation) and the signal is presented from the same speaker or from directly to the left of the subjects (–90° azimuth, 0° elevation). Despite the fact that different subjects participated in the two experiments and that the subjects in experiment 2 were not listening through their own HRTFs, there is good agreement between free-field (open bars) and binaural headphone presentations (double-slashed bars). In the low-frequency condition, binaural (either free-field or headphone) presentation is superior to monaural headphone presentation, suggesting that binaural processing may be required to achieve the masking reductions observed in the free field. In contrast, under the mid- and high-frequency conditions, monaural headphone presentation (for the ear with the best performance) is comparable to binaural presentation, suggesting that binaural processing is not necessarily required in order to achieve the reductions in masking observed in the free field.

Figure 4 shows the results for horizontal separations between the signal and the masker when the masker is presented from directly to the left of the subjects (–90° azimuth, 0° elevation) and the signal is presented from the same speaker or

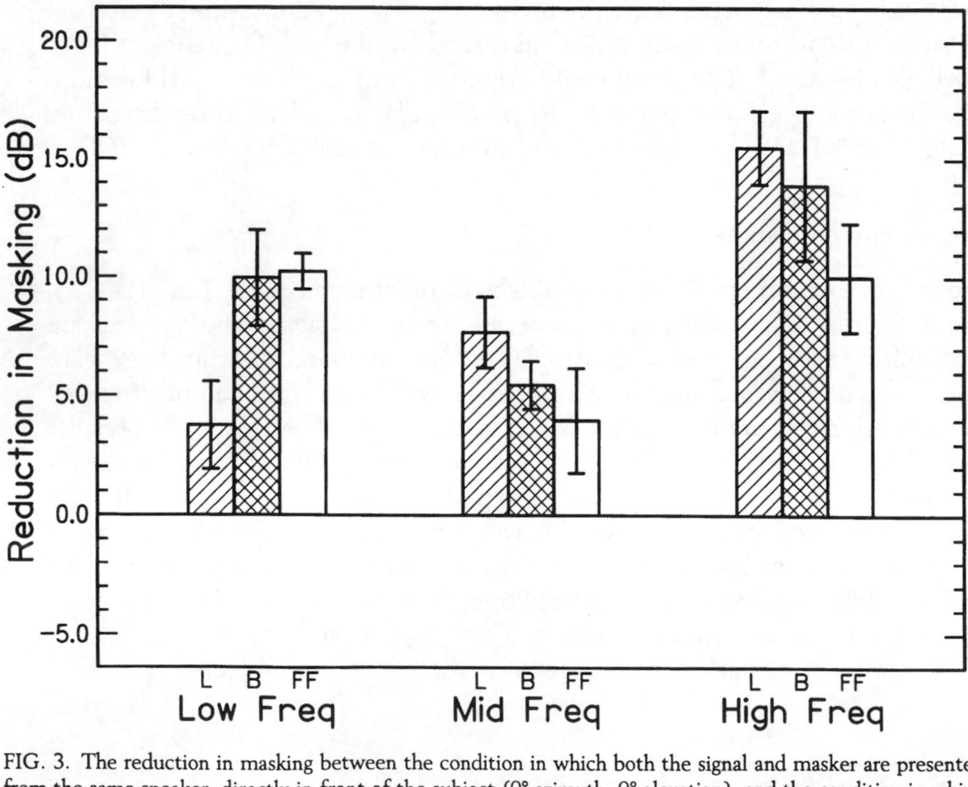

FIG. 3. The reduction in masking between the condition in which both the signal and masker are presented from the same speaker, directly in front of the subject (0° azimuth, 0° elevation), and the condition in which the signal is presented from directly to the left of the subject (–90° azimuth, 0° elevation) and the masker is presented from directly in front of the subject (0° azimuth, 0° elevation). The single-slashed bars show performance for the left-ear monaural headphone presentation mode (L), the cross-hatched bars show performance for the binaural headphone presentation mode (B), and the open bars show performance for the free-field presentation mode (FF). The error bars represent ±1 standard error across subjects.

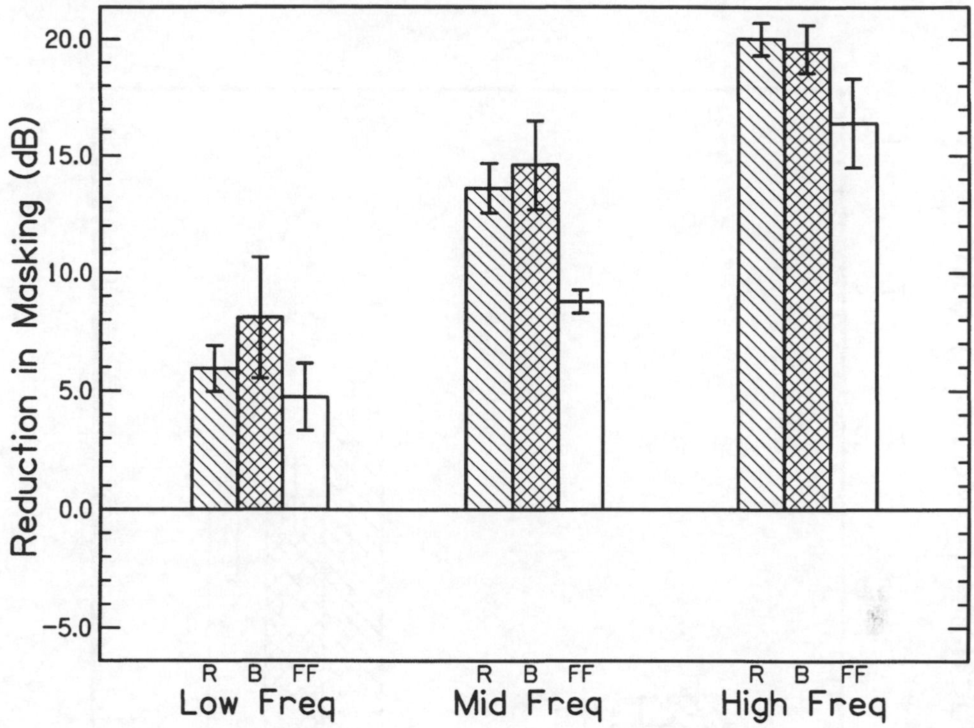

FIG. 4. The reduction in masking between the condition in which both the signal and masker are presented from the same speaker, directly to the left of the subject (–90° azimuth, 0° elevation), and the condition in which the signal is presented from the right of the subject (45° azimuth, 0° elevation) and the masker is presented from directly to the left of the subject (–90° azimuth, 0° elevation). The single-slashed bars show performance for the right-ear monaural headphone presentation mode (R). Other details are as in Fig. 3.

from a speaker to the right of the subjects (45° azimuth, 0° elevation). Again, there is good agreement between the free-field presentation mode of experiment 1 and the binaural headphone presentation mode of experiment 2. In this case, there is also good agreement between monaural headphone presentation and binaural headphone presentation in all three frequency regions, indicating that binaural processing may not be required to achieve these levels of masking reduction.

Figure 5 shows the results for vertical separations between the signal and the masker when the masker is presented from directly in front of the subjects (0° azimuth, 0° elevation) and the signal is presented from the same speaker or from above the subjects (0° azimuth, 54° elevation).[4] Again, there is good agreement between free-field presentation and binaural headphone presentation. At both frequencies, the monaural headphone presentation is also comparable, indicating relatively little impact of binaural processing.

---

[4]In the free-field conditions of experiment 1, detection performance was not measured for a speaker location at 54° elevation; therefore, the performance shown in Fig. 5 has been interpolated between the performance estimated with the speaker at 45° elevation and the performance estimated with the speaker at 90° elevation.

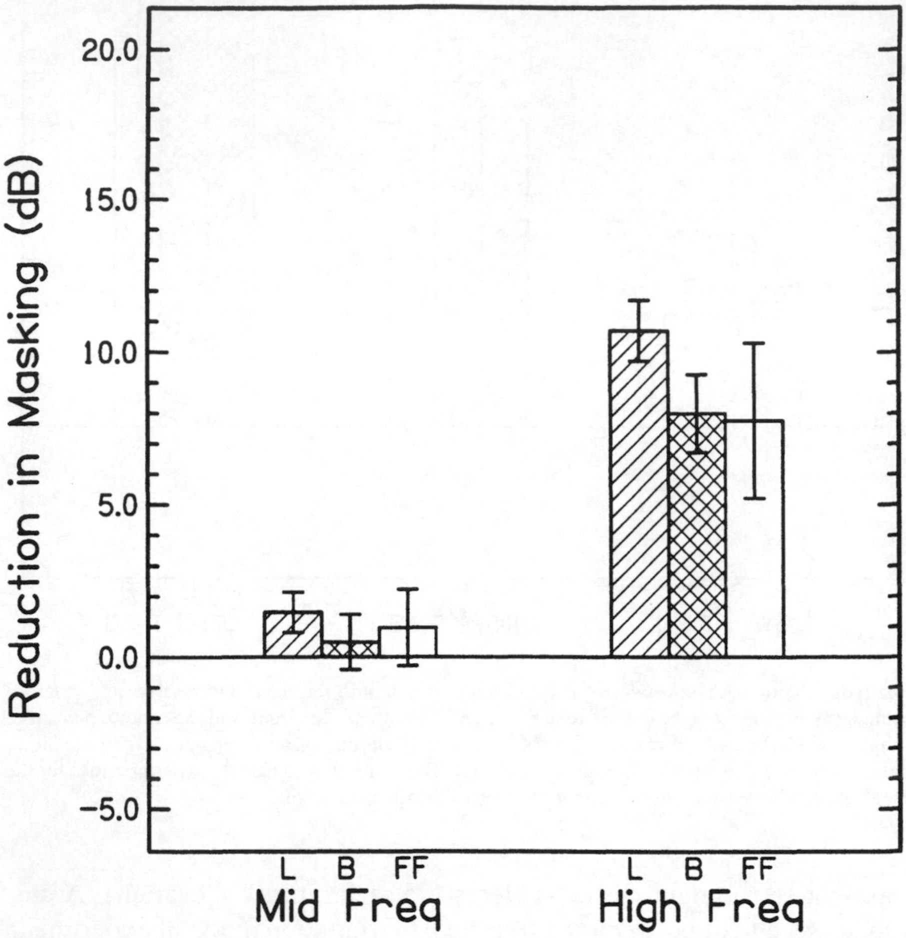

FIG. 5. The reduction in masking between the condition in which both the signal and masker are presented from the same speaker, directly in front of the subject (0° azimuth, 0° elevation), and the condition in which the signal is presented from above the subject (0° azimuth, 54° elevation) and the masker is presented from directly in front of the subject (0° azimuth, 0° elevation). Other details are as in Fig. 3.

III. THE RELATION OF FREE-FIELD MASKED DETECTION TO SOUND LOCALIZATION

The results of experiments 1 and 2 indicate a role for binaural information in mediating detection judgments at low frequencies, at least for the case when the masker is in front and the signal is to the side. Although these results do not deny the possibility of binaural involvement in other situations, the overall pattern of results suggests that, in general, binaural processing is not required in order to realize substantial reductions in masking when the signal is spatially separated from the masker.

The Lateralization Model (Hafter, 1971) extended the work of Jeffress (Jeffress, Blodgett, Sandel, and Wood, 1956; Jeffress, 1972) and attempted to relate the results from binaural masking experiments to the results from lateralization experiments. The idea was that if the signal-plus-noise stimulus was lateralized to a different spatial position from the noise-alone stimulus, the subject could use this change in spatial position as a cue for detection. For example, in the N_0S_π condition (noise diotic, signal 180° out of phase interaurally), the noise-alone stimulus is lateralized in the center of the subject's head, but the signal-plus-noise stimulus is likely to be lateralized away from the midline. Other authors suggest that the random fluctuations inherent in the masker cause the interaural differences in the signal-plus-noise stimulus to fluctuate randomly within a trial, leading not to a punctate lateralization percept, but rather to either a moving stimulus or a diffuse spatial percept, which can be discriminated from the noise-alone stimulus based on perceived spatial extent (see for example, Zurek and Durlach, 1987).

Hafter, Bourbon, Blocker, and Tucker (1969) directly compared lateralization and detection judgments for the N_0S_π condition. They found that when a signal was presented at a level below detection threshold, the distribution of lateralization judgments was concentrated near the midline. In contrast, when the signal was presented above detection threshold a bimodal distribution resulted; most lateralization judgments were located either to the left or to the right, away from the midline. They applied signal detection analysis to the distribution of lateralization judgments and determined that detection performance near that for the human subjects could be achieved based on lateralization cues alone.

A logical extension of the Lateralization Model, from headphone-based research to free-field masking, would suggest that when the spatial percept on signal-plus-noise trials is different from the spatial percept on noise-alone trials, the subject can use this spatial difference as a detection cue. Similarly, the argument of Cherry (1953), implying that the subject is able to focus on a particular spatial location in order to hear the signal, requires the use of spatial information to achieve optimal detection performance. To the degree that spatial hearing is binaural, the fact that comparable performance is often observed under monaural conditions (experiment 2) implies that neither of these spatial mechanisms (i.e., a lateralization-like model or focused attention) is required for the reductions in masking observed in the free field (experiment 1). That is, it does not appear that the impact of the signal in experiment 1 was to change the spatial position or to increase the spatial extent of the percept associated with the masker. It also does not appear that the subjects focused on a particular location associated with the signal, in order to "hear it" better (although they may have focused on a particular ear). Remember, however, that in the case where a low-frequency signal was presented from the side and the masker was presented from the front, there did appear to be an advantage of binaural listening, suggesting that spatial mechanisms may play a role in this case. Also, note that monaural hearing is not necessarily nonspatial, as indicated by Butler (Chapter 5 in this volume) and by Middlebrooks (Chapter 4 in this volume). Thus, although it seems unlikely, it may be that even in the monaural listening conditions of experiment 2, subjects detected the signal based on a spatial change.

IV. EXPERIMENT 3: LOCALIZATION ACCURACY AS A FUNCTION OF SIGNAL-TO-NOISE RATIO[5]

Although the results of experiments 1 and 2 suggest that free-field detection is not strongly dependent on the subject's ability to localize the sounds, it seems unlikely that the reverse would be the case. That is, it seems that a signal that is difficult to detect should be difficult to localize.

Despite the fact that it will often be important for the users of auditory displays to localize sounds in quite noisy environments, relatively few studies have examined sound localization in noise. Jacobsen (1976) measured the minimum audible angle (MAA) in the free field for pure-tone signals masked by noise. The masker was presented from directly in front of the subjects and the task was to determine if the signal originated from the left or from the right of the masker. Jacobsen observed that when the SNR was 10–15 dB above masked threshold, the MAAs for both his 500-Hz and 3000-Hz signals were comparable to those observed when no masker was present (<3°). However, when the SNR was only 3 dB above masked threshold, the MAA for his 3000-Hz signal was considerably larger (>6°) than that observed in the quiet. On the other hand, the MAA for his 500-Hz signal was only slightly larger than that observed in the quiet. These results suggest that quite good localization performance may be possible at signal levels that are very near threshold.

Perrott (1984), using a paradigm similar to that of Jacobsen (1976), investigated the ability of subjects to localize concurrent sounds. Although he did not envision his experiment as a masking task and considered only tonal stimuli, not noise, his results indicate that the accuracy of localization judgments was degraded when multiple stimuli were presented simultaneously. On each trial, two pure tones were simultaneously presented, one from each of two spatially separated speakers. The standard tone was always 500 Hz. The test tone ranged in frequency from 515 to 601 Hz. The subject's task on each trial was to determine whether the test tone had been presented from the left or from the right of the standard. At the smallest frequency separation (15 Hz), the subjects were unable to reach the 75% correct criterion, even for the widest speaker separation (180°). With wider frequency separations, the MAA between the two sources went from less than 10°, for sources in front, to more than 30°, for sources to the side. These values of MAA are larger than would be expected based on the data of Mills (1972) for sources that did not overlap in time [in a second experiment, Perrott (1984) was able to demonstrate dramatic performance increases when the amount of temporal overlap between the standard and test stimuli was reduced]. Moreover, these values of MAA are also large compared to the values that Jacobsen (1976) reported for a 500-Hz signal masked by a simultaneous noise. This is a somewhat surprising result given that Perrott's stimuli are likely to have been clearly audible (i.e., well above threshold). However, the test tone and standard in Perrott's study were more similar perceptually than the signal and masker in Jacobsen's study. Therefore, subjects may have heard a "fused" image or reported the location of

---

[5]This experiment has previously been reported by Good and Gilkey (1996a).

the wrong sound in Perrott's study. However, it is difficult to have confidence in this *post hoc* explanation.

Experiments 3 and 4 were designed to examine how the presence of noise influences localization performance. In contrast to the experiments of Jacobsen (1976) and Perrott (1984), our subjects were required to make an absolute judgment about the true location of a sound that could arrive from any of a large number of possible spatial locations. The influences of both SNR and masker location were considered.

A. Method

One female and two male subjects, with normal hearing, participated in the experiment. The subjects ranged in age from 23 to 25 years. The experiment was conducted in the Auditory Localization Facility at Wright-Patterson Air Force Base. During the experiment, the subjects were seated with their heads in the center of the geodesic sphere of speakers and held a bite-bar to restrict head movements.

The 268-ms signal was a train of 25-μs pulses, which were repeated at a rate of 100 Hz. The signal was bandpass-filtered from 0.53 to 11.0 kHz. The 468-ms Gaussian noise masker was bandpass-filtered from 0.41 to 14.2 kHz.

Localization performance was examined for a quiet condition and 9 masked conditions, with SNRs ranging from –13 dB to +14 dB relative to the detection threshold when the signal and masker were presented from the same speaker. In the masked conditions, the masker was always located directly in front of the subjects (0° azimuth, 0° elevation). On each trial, the signal was randomly chosen from a set of 239 speaker locations completely surrounding the subject in azimuth (–172° to +180°) and ranging in elevation from –45° to 90°. Either the signal was presented alone (quiet condition), or the masker and the signal were presented together (masked conditions). After the observation interval, the subjects had an unlimited amount of time to respond. Localization judgments were measured using the God's Eye Localization Pointing (GELP) technique. In this technique, subjects use an electromagnetic stylus to point to the position on a 20.3-cm spherical model of auditory space that corresponds to the perceived direction of the signal (see Gilkey, Good, Ericson, Brinkman, and Stewart, 1995, for details). Six localization judgments were obtained for each speaker, under each condition, from each subject.

B. Results and discussion

The effect of the noise on the accuracy of localization judgments can be seen most clearly by plotting the data in the "three-pole" coordinate system (see, e.g., Kistler and Wightman, 1992). In this system, the azimuth component of each location is decomposed into two dimensions: the left/right (L/R) dimension (the angle between the location vector and the median plane) and the front/back (F/B) dimension (the angle between the location vector and the frontal plane). The elevation component of each location is represented in the up/down (U/D) dimension (the angle between the location vector and the horizontal plane).

Partial results for subject MG are shown in Fig. 6 for the L/R dimension in the upper three panels, for the F/B dimension in the center three panels, and for the U/D dimension in the lower three panels. The left three panels show the results for the quiet condition. As noted by the close proximity of the data to the positive-slope diagonal, judgments are fairly accurate in all three dimensions.

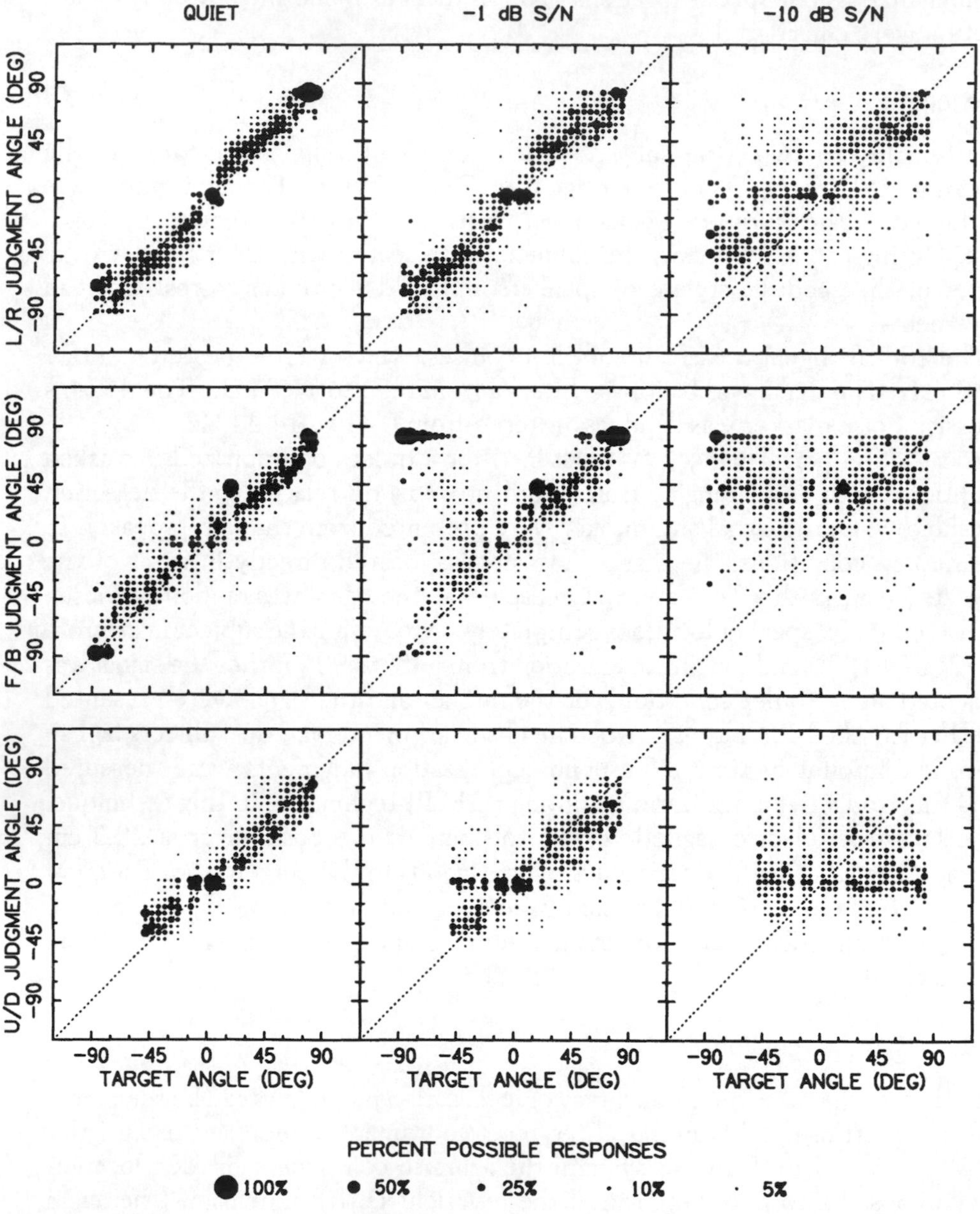

FIG. 6. Performance in the left/right (L/R), front/back (F/B), and up/down (U/D) dimensions is shown for one subject (MG) at each of three SNRs (relative to the same speaker detection threshold) examined in experiment 3. In each panel, the judgment angle is plotted as a function of the target angle. Targets are grouped into 5° wide bins. The size of each symbol represents the percentage of the total number of judgments in each target-angle bin that fall within each 5° wide judgment-angle bin. (After Good and Gilkey, 1996a.)

However, the spread in the judgments around the positive-slope diagonal increases as the SNR is lowered. The middle three panels show the results obtained at a SNR that is 1.0 dB below the same-speaker detection threshold. Performance in the L/R and U/D dimensions is still fairly accurate, but there is clearly more spread around the positive-slope diagonals, indicating that the subjects are making larger localization errors. Performance in the F/B dimension appears to be more strongly influenced by this reduction in SNR, as indicated by the greater spread of the data in this dimension and the large number of back-to-front reversals (judgments falling in the upper-left quadrant). The right three panels show the results at an SNR 10 dB below the same-speaker detection threshold. At this level, the relation between the judgment angle and the target angle is considerably weaker. Judgment angles in the F/B and U/D dimensions are essentially independent of the actual target angle. Careful inspection of these figures indicates that localization judgments are "biased" toward the location of the masker at low SNRs; that is, the masker is at 0° L/R, 90° F/B, and 0° U/D, and more judgments lie near 0° in the L/R and U/D dimensions, whereas more judgments lie near 90° in the F/B dimension. It is not clear whether this "bias" reflects a response bias or a systematic change in the perceived location of the signals.

The results shown in Fig. 6 are summarized in Fig. 7 by plotting the root mean square (rms) error in each dimension as a function of SNR. The results have been averaged across subjects. The rms error in each dimension increases as SNR is lowered. However, the rms error in the L/R dimension was quite small and did not appear to be strongly influenced by the noise until the SNR was very low. Values of rms error in the U/D dimension were slightly larger than those in the L/R dimension, but showed a similar trend as the SNR was lowered. In contrast, values of rms error in the F/B dimension were quite large and increased rapidly with reductions in SNR.

The results of this experiment indicate that the ability to determine the direction of a signal decreased nearly monotonically, in all three dimensions, as the SNR was lowered. However, the rate of degradation in performance varied across the dimensions. Kistler and Wightman (1992) suggested that judgments in the L/R dimension are based primarily on an analysis of ITDs and ILDs. Furthermore, they suggest that judgments in the F/B and U/D dimensions are likely to be based on an analysis of the spectral details of the stimuli reaching the ears. Thus, the differences in rms error across the three dimensions may be due to the masker differentially affecting these cues.

V. EXPERIMENT 4: LOCALIZATION ACCURACY AS A FUNCTION OF MASKER LOCATION[6]

Although the differences observed across dimensions in experiment 3 may have resulted from differences in underlying mechanisms, it is difficult to have confidence in this conclusion because only one masker location was investigated.

[6]This experiment has previously been reported by Good and Gilkey (1996b).

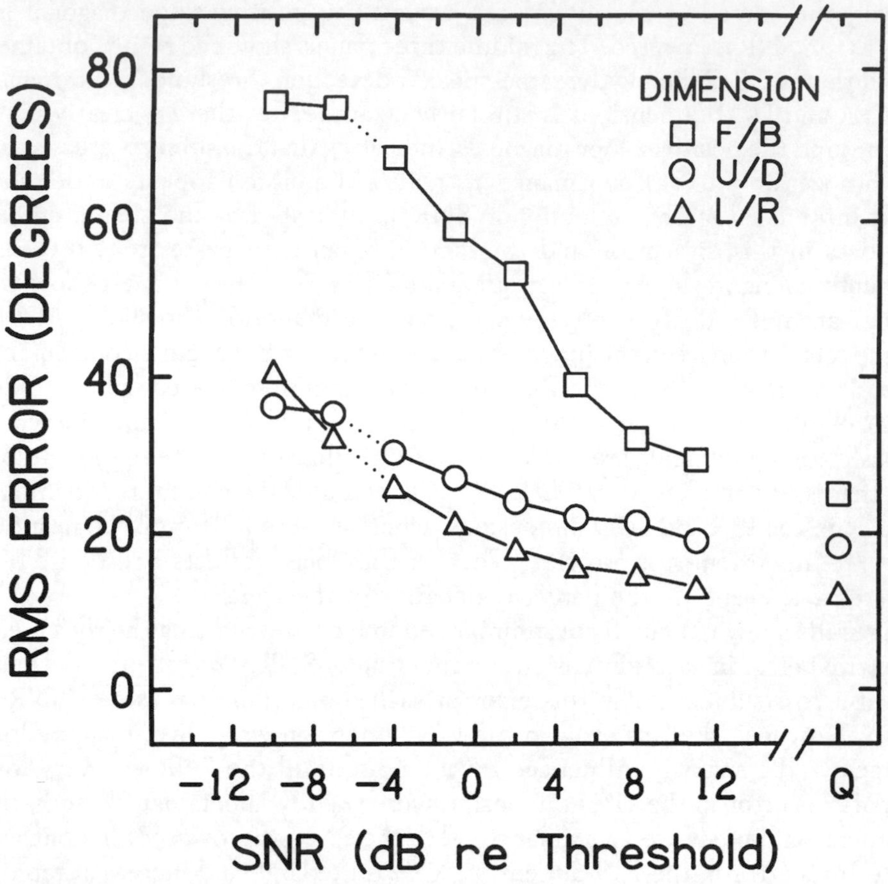

FIG. 7. Root mean square error in each dimension is plotted as a function of SNR (relative to the same speaker detection threshold). The data have been averaged across the three subjects. (After Good and Gilkey, 1996a.)

We noted, in passing, that the responses appear to be biased toward the direction of the masker at low SNRs. That is, responses are biased toward 0° L/R, 90° F/B, and 0° U/D. If responses are biased toward ±90° in a particular dimension, values of rms error will tend to be large, because there are very few actual locations near ±90° and many locations quite far away from ±90°. In contrast, if responses are biased toward 0° in a particular dimension, values of rms error will be smaller, because many of the speakers are located near 0°. Thus, the observed differences in rms error across dimensions may merely reflect the effects of bias and may not reflect differences in the underlying processes. Experiment 4 was undertaken to determine the effect of the masker position on localization accuracy, and thereby to help to clarify this issue.

A. Method

The apparatus, stimuli, and procedures were very similar to those employed in experiment 3. However, in this experiment the masker could originate from one of five possible spatial locations: directly in front of the subject (0° azimuth, 0°

elevation), directly to the left of the subject (–90° azimuth, 0° elevation), directly to the right of the subject (90° azimuth, 0° elevation), directly behind the subject (180° azimuth, 0° elevation), or directly above the subject (0° azimuth, 90° elevation). Localization judgments were measured for two SNRs at each of the five masker locations. The two SNRs were chosen individually for each subject based on their localization performance in experiment 3. The higher of the two SNRs would be expected to yield good performance in the L/R and U/D dimensions and moderate performance in the F/B dimension. The lower of the two SNRs would be expected to lead to moderate performance in the L/R and U/D dimension and poor performance in the F/B dimension. The actual SNRs presented for the three subjects are shown in Table I.

All other methodological details were as in experiment 3, except that in this experiment digital techniques were used to flatten and equalize the responses of the speakers; the speakers were not equalized in experiment 3. Due to the limits of our equalization technique, the bandwidths of the signal and the masker were reduced somewhat relative to experiment 3. The signal bandwidth was 0.48 kHz to 10.1 kHz and the masker bandwidth was 0.40 kHz to 12.0 kHz.

B. Results and discussion

Values of rms error in each dimension are shown in Table II for each combination of masker location and SNR. For comparison, values of rms error are shown for the quiet condition in Table III. Although the same subjects performed in both experiments, the experiments were separated by several months and there were slight stimulus differences. Performance for subject CG and JY in experiment 4 was, in general, worse than that measured in experiment 3.

As in experiment 3, rms error increases as SNR is reduced. Also notice that the magnitude of the rms error in each dimension depends on the masker location, but that the effects of the masker location are different for the three dimensions. In the L/R dimension, rms error tends to be largest when the masker is to the left or to the right. In the F/B dimension, it tends to be largest when the masker is in front of or behind the subject. In the U/D dimension, rms errors are largest when the masker is above the subject. Thus, the results of experiment 4 suggest that the values of rms error observed for the F/B dimension in experiment 3 were, at least in part, dependent on the location of the masker.

Relatively good performance can be observed in the L/R dimension even at the low SNR; this results, at least in part, from the fact that the subjects can usually determine whether the signal was presented from the left or right hemisphere

TABLE I. Signal-to-noise ratios (in dB re same-speaker detection threshold) used in experiment 4.

Subject	*Signal-to-Noise Ratio*	
	High	*Low*
MG	–3.0	–13.0
CG	1.0	–10.0
JY	5.0	–6.0

TABLE II. Values of rms error (in degrees) observed in the masked conditions of experiment 4.

		Left/right dimension masker location					*Front/back dimension masker location*					*Up/down dimension masker location*				
Subject	*SNR*	*Front*	*Back*	*Above*	*Right*	*Left*	*Front*	*Back*	*Above*	*Right*	*Left*	*Front*	*Back*	*Above*	*Right*	*Left*
MG	High	16	16	18	27	26	41	40	39	38	41	21	23	40	23	26
	Low	25	27	41	40	42	69	65	44	42	42	33	34	70	29	32
CG	High	16	18	18	24	24	52	48	43	46	48	27	25	29	26	26
	Low	27	25	42	38	39	74	66	64	50	47	32	32	49	32	31
JY	High	17	16	16	19	20	41	35	39	40	43	29	29	31	30	30
	Low	27	27	30	33	34	68	44	44	41	43	34	36	59	32	34

TABLE III. Values of rms error (in degrees) observed for the quiet condition of experiment 4.

	Dimension		
Subject	*Left/right*	*Front/back*	*Up/down*
MG	11	18	13
CG	14	45	25
JY	15	36	25

(the percentage of correct left-hemisphere/right-hemisphere judgments is typically well above 80 even at the low SNR, except when the masker is presented from above the subject). In contrast, at the low SNR subjects are typically able to judge correctly whether the signal arose from the front or rear hemisphere much less than 70% of the time.[7] Finally, note that subjects tend to show bias toward the direction of the masker; however, the pattern of responses is not simply related to masker location (see Good and Gilkey, 1996b, for a more detailed description of these data.)

VI. RELATION OF LOCALIZATION ACCURACY TO DETECTABILITY

The results of experiments 3 and 4 show that localization accuracy can be severely degraded by the presence of masking noise. The exact impact of the noise depends on both the SNR and the location of the masker. Depending on the masker location, performance in either the F/B or the U/D dimension can be severely disrupted at the high SNR. In contrast, performance in the L/R dimension can be good even at the low SNR.

A. Comparison to experiments on lateralization in noise

Although there have been few experiments that have examined localization in noise, there is a modest literature of studies that have examined lateralization (headphone-based discrimination of interaural differences) in the presence of noise. The accuracy of lateralization judgments has been shown to depend not only on the SNR, but also on the interaural parameters of the noise.

Egan and Benson (1966) and Robinson and Egan (1974) directly compared detection and lateralization performance. They presented a monaural signal masked by a binaural noise and, in separate blocks, asked the subject either to determine whether the signal was present (detection) or to determine which ear had received the signal (lateralization). If the task was to detect a low-frequency signal, performance was about 10 dB better when the masker was diotic (N_0) than

[7]Because on any given trial it was much more likely that the signal was presented from the upper hemisphere, it is difficult to generate a comparable number for the U/D dimension.

when the masker was interaurally uncorrelated (N_u); that is, there was a substantial MLD. If the task was to lateralize a low-frequency signal, performance was only about 4–5 dB better with the N_0 masker than with the N_u masker. Said differently, in the N_0 masker, a signal needed to be about 6 dB above detection threshold (75% correct) in order to be lateralized accurately (75% correct), whereas in the N_u masker this difference was only about 1 dB.[8] Egan and Benson argued that lateralization performance in diotic noise was poor compared to detection because of the presence of a salient interaural time cue, which was reliable for detection, but ambiguous for lateralization. When Robinson and Egan made comparable measurements in an N_0 masker, but used a 3000-Hz signal (i.e., in a frequency region where interaural time cues would be expected to be less salient), the detection threshold was only about 1 dB better than the lateralization threshold.

The work of Egan and his colleagues can be thought of as describing the ability of subjects to discriminate whether a signal came from the extreme left or from the extreme right. Most studies of lateralization in noise have required subjects to discriminate small interaural time differences for images that, in the quiet, would be located near the midline. For example, Houtgast and Plomp (1968) investigated the sensitivity of subjects to ITDs in the presence of a noise that was interaurally delayed by 400 μs. In a two-interval task, subjects were required to determine if the sequence of signal ITDs was left-leading-to-right-leading or right-leading-to-left-leading between the two observation intervals. Subject performance was evaluated both in the quiet and in the presence of noise. They found that at low SNRs ITD thresholds were large and did not return to quiet levels until the SNR was 10–30 dB above detection threshold.

Cohen (1981) examined the ability of subjects to lateralize a 250-Hz tone as a function of the SNR and the interaural parameters of the background noise. She found that ITD discrimination was much better with an N_0 masker than with a masker that was interaurally phase inverted (N_π). In general, performance with an N_u masker fell between that observed with the N_0 and N_π maskers. That is, lateralization accuracy was not directly related to detectability; although the signals (which were nearly in phase interaurally, S_0) were the most detectable in the N_π masker, they were also the most difficult to lateralize in that masker. In some cases, ITD thresholds were substantially elevated even though the signal was more than 30 dB above the $N_\pi S_0$ detection threshold.

Ito, Colburn, and Thompson (1982) measured lateralization performance based on ITDs, under a variety of masker conditions. They also found that masked lateralization performance was best with the diotic masker. Indeed, for some subjects, performance in the quiet was only a few microseconds better than in the diotic noise condition. In addition, they showed that performance was not systematically related to the perceived location of the masker.

---

[8]These results were complicated by the fact that the slope of the psychometric function for lateralization in the diotic noise was quite shallow compared to the other three psychometric functions. So, for example, in order for a signal to be lateralized with 99% correct accuracy in diotic noise, it would have to be presented at a level 10 dB or more above the level that led to 99% correct detection performance.

Stern, Slocum, and Phillips (1983) performed a similar experiment, but considered lateralization based on ILDs, as well as lateralization based on ITDs. Lateralization performance was measured in the presence of maskers with a variety of interaural configurations. They also found that lateralization performance was best in the presence of the diotic masker, even though the signal was much more detectable in the presence of maskers with other interaural configurations.

Although experiments 3 and 4 were not specifically designed to generate data comparable to those from other experiments on localization and lateralization in noise, such a comparison might be instructive. In experiment 3, the masker was always presented from directly in front of the subject and thus, was approximately diotic. When the signal came from the same speaker, the condition was approximately comparable to an N_0S_0 condition presented through headphones. Egan and Benson (1966) and Robinson and Egan (1974) found that subjects were able to determine which ear received a low-frequency monaural pure-tone signal when it was approximately 3–4 dB below the N_0S_0 threshold. A monaural signal would correspond loosely to a signal coming from an extreme left or extreme right speaker location in experiment 3. Therefore, to compare our data to those of Egan and Benson and Robinson and Egan, we computed the proportion of the trials on which the signal was presented from an extreme position (greater than +75° L/R or less than –75° L/R) for which subjects' localization judgments indicated that they were able to determine the correct hemisphere (left or right). These results are shown in the left panel of Fig. 8. As can be seen, subjects are able to judge accurately the hemisphere from which the signal originated, even at SNRs 3–12

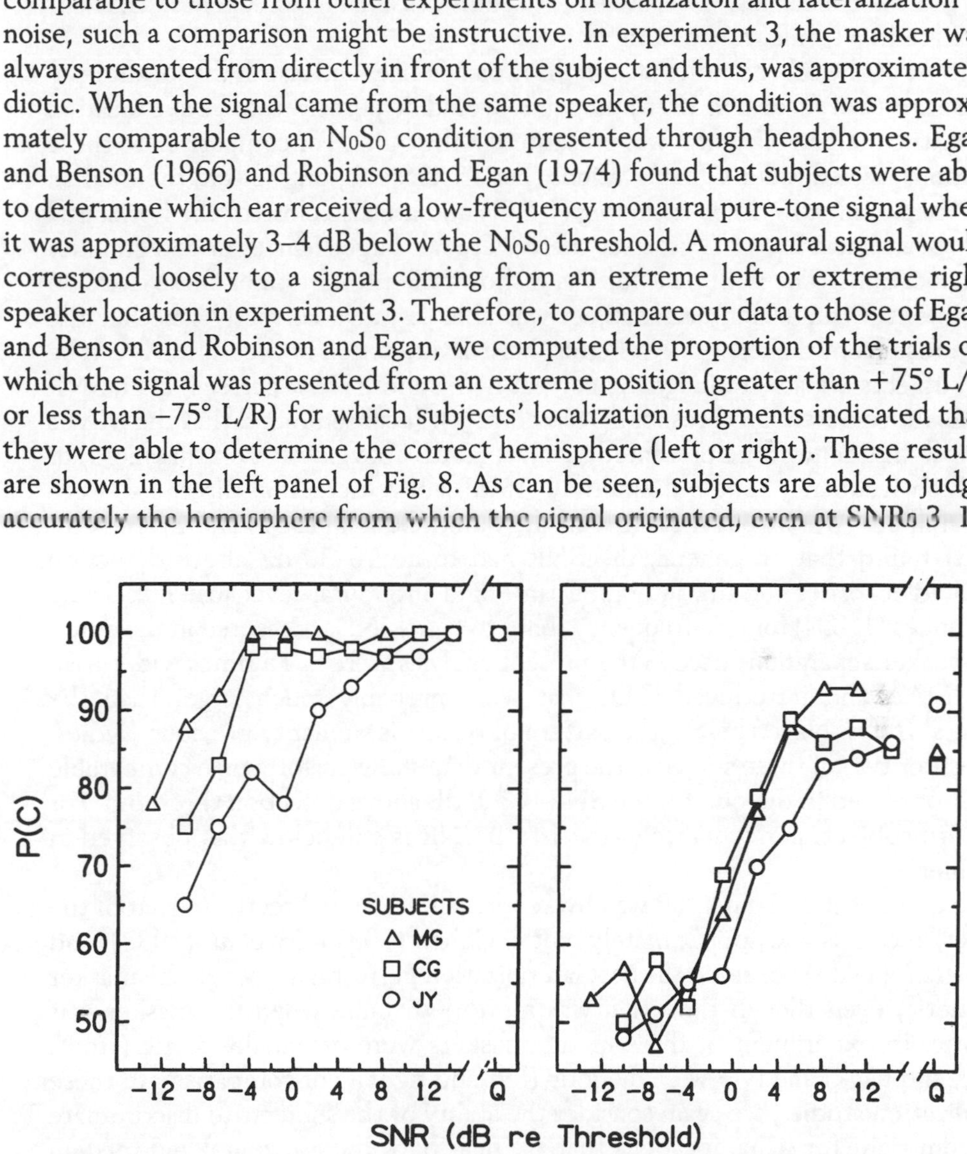

FIG. 8. The percentage of correct left-hemisphere/right-hemisphere judgments from experiment 3 is plotted as a function of the SNR (relative to the same-speaker detection threshold). The left panel shows the results for signal locations at the extreme left or extreme right (beyond ±75° L/R). The right panel shows the results for signal locations close to, but not on, the median plane (between ±15° L/R, excluding 0° L/R) and close to the horizontal plane (between ±25° U/D). The three curves in each panel show individual results for three subjects.

dB below the same speaker detection threshold. Based on the data of Shaw (1974), we know that the intensity of the signal at the eardrums will change when the signal is moved. For example, we would expect the signal at the left eardrum to be about 0–10 dB more intense (depending on frequency) when it is presented from the left side than when it is presented from the front (i.e., the same speaker as the masker). It is therefore not clear which of our nominal SNRs would be expected to lead to performance comparable to the performance observed by Egan and his colleagues; nevertheless, it seems reasonable to conclude that our results are in a similar range to theirs.

In most of the other studies of lateralization in noise (and also in the localization in noise study of Jacobsen, 1976) the signal would be perceived to be at a location close to the median plane if it was presented in the quiet. For comparison to these conditions, we consider signal locations that are close to, but not on, the median plane (between ±15° L/R, excluding 0° L/R) and are also close to the horizontal plane (between ±25° U/D) so that there were not large changes in detectability across locations. The right panel of Fig. 8 shows the proportion of these cases, in experiment 3, for which each subject was able to judge correctly whether the signal arose from the left or right hemisphere as a function of the SNR. As can be seen, subjects are able to judge the correct hemisphere (79% correct) at an SNR 2–7 dB above detection threshold (79% correct). Jacobsen found that the MAAs for a low-frequency tone presented at a level 3 dB above detection threshold, or for a high-frequency tone presented 10–15 dB above detection threshold, were comparable to the MAAs measured in the quiet. Cohen (1981) and Stern *et al.* (1983) found that, in general, the SNR had to be 10–30 dB above detection threshold in order for the interaural time and interaural level just noticeable differences (JNDs) for low-frequency tones to equal JNDs measured in the quiet. The speaker separations used in the present analysis were 2–15 times wider than quiet MAA and introduced ITDs that were probably much larger than the subjects' JNDs. Nevertheless, the pattern of results is similar to previous studies. That is, for two of three subjects, the present data show performance comparable to that observed in the quiet when SNR is 3–8 dB above detection threshold. For the third subject, performance at the 14 dB SNR is still below that observed in the quiet.

In experiment 3, the masker was always presented from directly in front of the subject, and thus was approximately diotic. Cohen (1981), Ito *et al.* (1982), and Stern *et al.* (1983) observed the best lateralization performance when the masker was diotic, even though the signal was more detectable when the masker was dichotic. In experiment 4, three of the maskers were essentially diotic (front, above, and back) and two were dichotic (left and right). For comparison to these lateralization studies, we again consider the ability of the subjects to discriminate left from right for signal locations that are near both the horizontal and median planes (i.e., between ±15° L/R, excluding 0° L/R, and between ±25° U/D). Because the signals are likely to be more detectable when the masker is presented from above the subject than when the masker is presented from the front or from the back, we do not include the condition when the masker is above in this analysis (i.e., the masker above condition is not comparable to the other median plane conditions). Thus, we compare performance for conditions where the masker is "diotic" and the signals should be relatively difficult to detect (masker in front and masker behind) to conditions where the masker is "dichotic" and the signals should be relatively easy to detect (masker right and masker left). At the low SNR all of the subjects had a higher proportion of correct left-hemisphere/right-hemisphere judgments when the masker was "dichotic" than when the masker was "diotic" (MG: 0.62 vs. 0.55; CG: 0.69 vs. 0.50; JY: 0.73 vs. 0.65). That is, the results were in the opposite direction to those found in lateralization studies (note that this may result because at this level our "diotic" signals were roughly 6–13 dB below detection threshold). At the high SNR two of the three subjects performed better in the "diotic" conditions (MG: 0.66 vs. 0.77; CG: 0.72 vs. 0.93; JY: 0.82 vs. 0.81). Although this analysis does not indicate a clear and direct relation between detectability and localization accuracy, it also does not show clear agreement with the pattern of results observed in lateralization studies.

It is important to stress that these comparisons between localization performance and lateralization are extremely rough. The overall patterns of results show fair, but not complete, agreement between the two sets of data and suggest that the accuracy of localization judgments (in the L/R dimension), like that of lateralization judgments, may be only loosely dependent on the detectability of the signal.

B. Localization accuracy at constant sensation level

Another view of the relation between localization accuracy and detectability can be obtained by using the free-field detection data (from experiment 1) to determine sets of conditions in experiment 3 where the signals were at approximately equal sensation levels. Plotting these data within a single graph allows one to compare localization accuracy at different spatial locations, without some of the confounding effects of changes in detectability (also see Sec. VI.C).

For this analysis, we consider the localization judgments of subjects to targets within the horizontal or median planes (from experiment 3), because these are the cases for which we have detection data in experiment 1. We make the additional assumption that detection performance would be approximately bilaterally symmetric, such that we can consider localization responses at both positive and negative azimuth. The results for azimuth and elevation are shown in Figs. 9 and 10, respectively. Each panel in the figures combines data from several different conditions of experiment 3 (i.e., several different SNRs); these data were selected based on the detection thresholds from experiment 1. For example, the localization data plotted at 58° azimuth in Fig. 9 were obtained as follows. We found the maximum detection threshold (across the three frequency regions) for the average subject at 45° azimuth and at 90° azimuth from the left panel of Fig. 1. We then interpolated to estimate the detection threshold at 58°. The point plotted in the 11-dB sensation level (SL) panel was taken from the SNR condition in experiment 3 that was closest to 11 dB above the interpolated value; the point plotted in the 8-dB SL panel was taken from the SNR condition in experiment 3 that was closest to 8 dB above the interpolated value; and so on. Thus, all the data

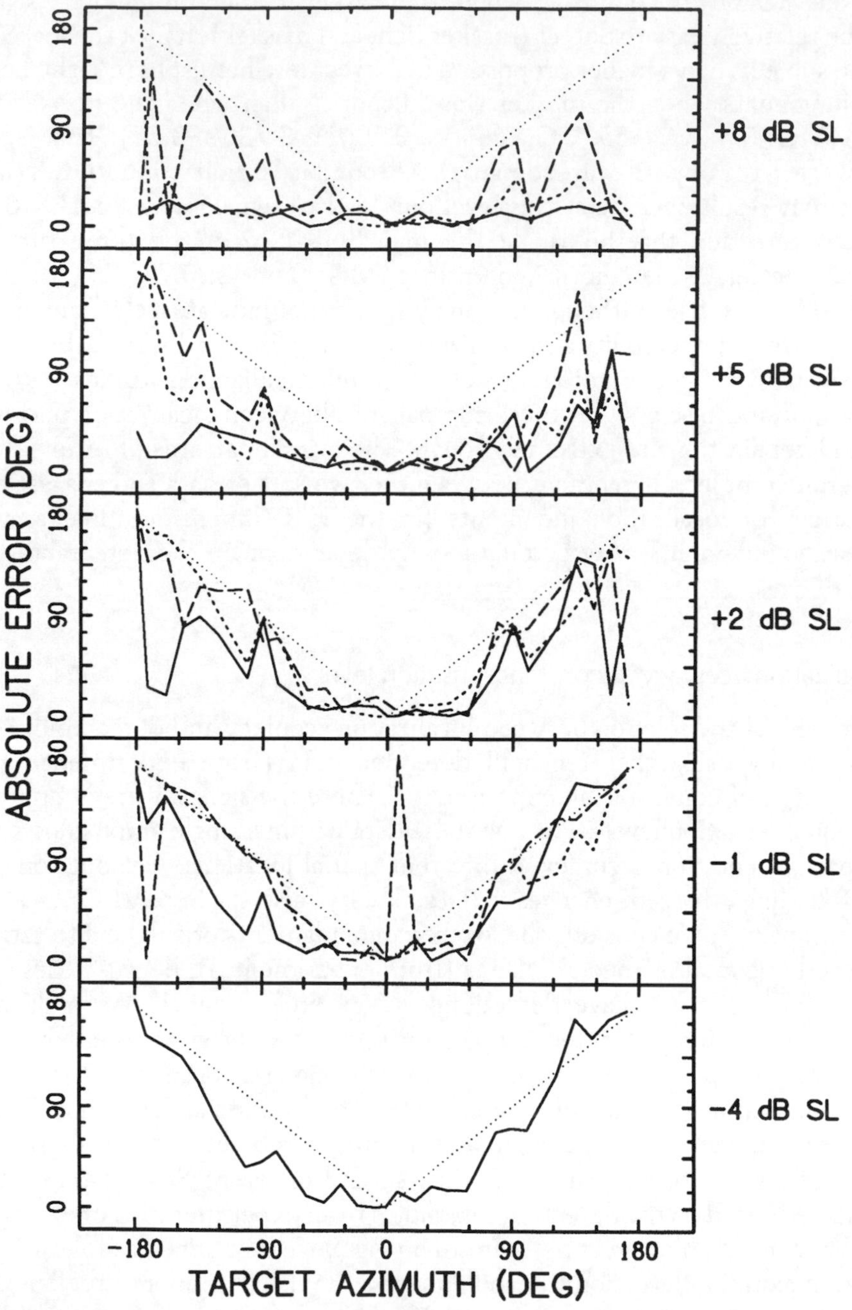

FIG. 9. The horizontal component of the absolute error in the judgment centroids is plotted for each of the three subjects (solid lines, MG; short-dashed lines, CG; long-dashed lines, JY) as a function of the azimuth of the target within the horizontal plane. The thin dotted line indicates the results that would be obtained if the subject always responded with an azimuth of 0°. Each panel shows localization performance for signals that are roughly equally detectable (see text for details). Note that at the lowest sensation level data are shown only for subject MG.

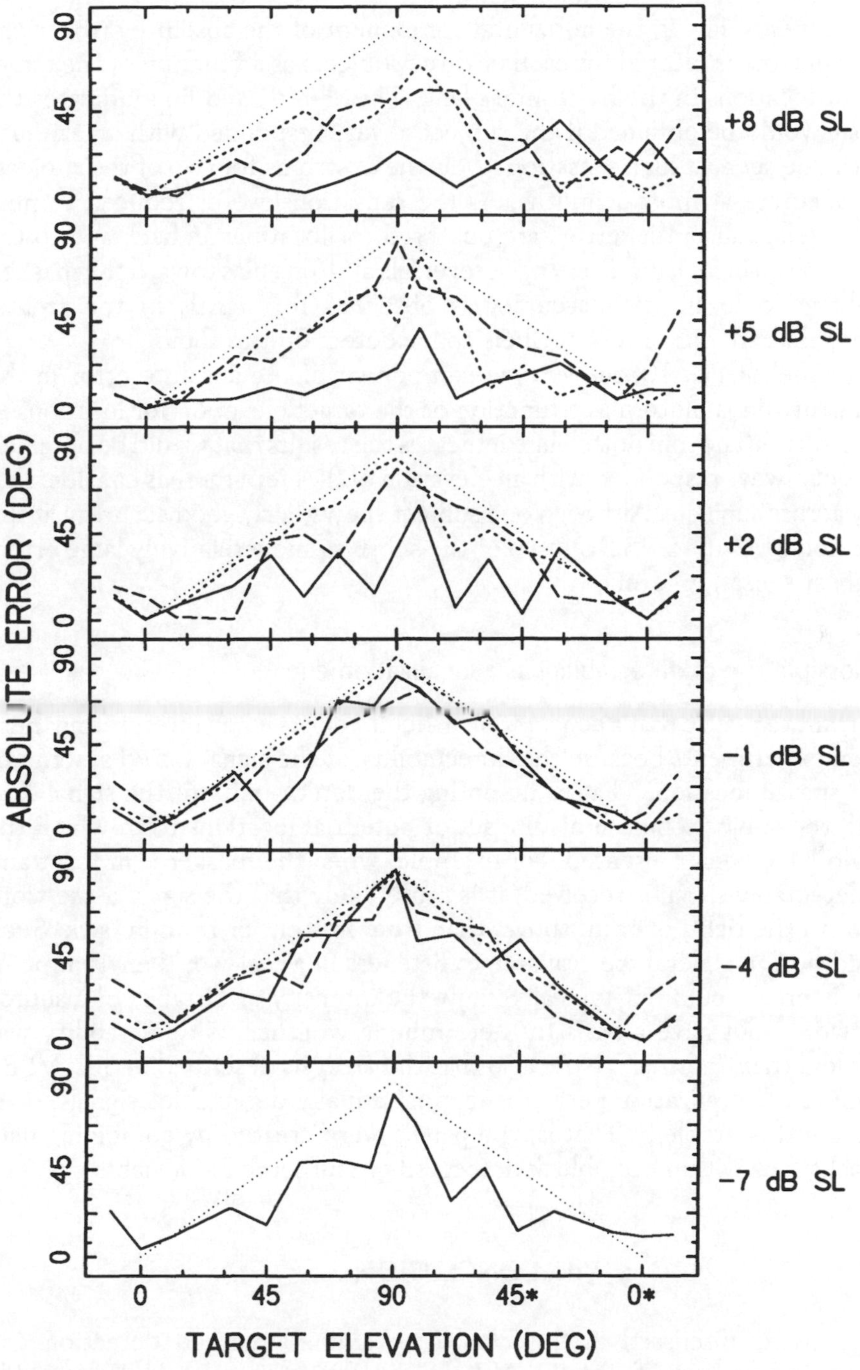

FIG. 10. The vertical component of the absolute error in the judgment centroids is plotted as a function of the elevation of the target within the median plane for each subject. The thin dotted line indicates the results that would be obtained if the subject always responded with an elevation of 0°. Other details are as in Fig. 9.

within a given panel were collected on trials where the signals were presented at approximately the same sensation level.

In each panel of Fig. 9, the horizontal component of the absolute error in the judgment centroid is plotted for each of three subjects as a function of the target azimuth for locations in the horizontal plane. The thin dotted line indicates the results that would be obtained if the subject always responded with an azimuth of 0°. As can be seen, at high sensation levels the centroids for two of the subjects are quite accurate at most azimuths. As the sensation level is reduced to near threshold levels, substantial errors are observed for locations in back and to the side, indicating an increase in front/back reversals and/or a bias toward the masker. Reasonably good localization accuracy is observed for signals in the frontal hemisphere that are only a few decibels above detection threshold.

In each panel of Fig. 10, the vertical component of the absolute error in the judgment centroid is plotted as a function of the target elevation for locations in the median plane. The thin dotted line indicates the results that would be obtained if the subject always responded with an elevation of 0°. Here there is considerable variability across subjects. Although one subject shows fairly good accuracy at the high sensation levels (>5 dB SL), two of the subjects show relatively large errors at the highest sensation level.

C. The possible use of detectability as a localization cue

It is important to realize that a conceptual difficulty exists when interpreting these localization experiments because the detectability of the signal varied systematically with spatial location. That is, by noting the detectability of the signal on a given trial, the subject could limit the set of potential locations from which the signal could have been presented. For example, when the masker is in front and a highly detectable signal is received, it is more likely that the signal arose from the left, from the right, or from above, than from in front or from in back. Such cues would not, in general, be available to listeners in a real-world environment. That is, a listener would not typically know the intensity or distance of a source and thus would not have a basis for determining whether its detectability was greater or less than "normal." Note also that the analysis described in Sec. VI.B., which compared localization performance for "equally detectable" signals, does not eliminate this problem. That is, the panels were created by combining data across blocks, but within each block detectability still served as a viable cue.

VII. CONCLUSION

The experiments discussed in this chapter examined masked detection and masked localization in the free field. Although at the outset it seemed reasonable to expect that there might be a strong relation between these two phenomena, the results indicate that masked detection does not depend critically on the accurate localization of the signal. We note, however, that the fact that monaural detection performance is, in general, as good as binaural detection performance does not necessarily mean that observers do not use spatial cues when listening in noisy environments.

The accuracy of localization judgments is clearly affected by the presence of masking noise. The impact of the noise is complex and depends on both the SNR and the position of the masker relative to the subject. Contrary to our original expectations, relatively good localization performance could be observed in cases where the signals were very near detection threshold.

Finally, it should be noted that the fact that behavioral measures of masked detection and masked localization do not appear to be strongly related does not necessarily mean that these behaviors are mediated by different underlying mechanisms. Indeed, as indicated by the analyses of Egan and Benson (1966), Robinson and Egan (1974), Ito *et al.* (1982), and Stern *et al.* (1983), the apparent lack of relation between binaural detection and binaural lateralization is well predicted by models of binaural processing.

ACKNOWLEDGMENTS

This work was supported by grants from the Air Force Office of Scientific Research (AFOSR-91-0289) and the National Institute of Deafness and Other Communicative Disorders (DC-00768). Additional support was provided by the Armstrong Laboratory, Crew Systems Directorate, Biodynamics and Biocommunications Division, Bioacoustics and Biocommunications Branch; and by Wright State University.

The authors wish to thank John Brinkman, Doug Brungart, Mark Ericson, Lawrence Jacknin, Richard McKinley, and John Stewart for technical assistance; Sharon Adams, Christine Good, and Melinda McGuire for help in preparing this chapter; and Timothy Anderson, Donald Robinson, and Janet Weisenberger for reading and commenting on an earlier draft of this chapter.

REFERENCES

Bronkhorst, A. W., and Plomp, R. (1988). "The effect of head-induced interaural time and level differences on speech intelligibility in noise," J. Acoust. Soc. Am. **83**, 1508–1516.

Cherry, E. C. (1953). "Some experiments on the recognition of speech, with one and with two ears," J. Acoust. Soc. Am. **25**, 975–979.

Cohen, M. F. (1981). "Interaural time discrimination in noise," J. Acoust. Soc. Am. **70**, 1289–1293.

Colburn, H. S., and Durlach, N. I. (1978). "Models of binaural interaction," in *Handbook of Perception, Vol. IV, Hearing*, edited by E. C. Carterette and M. P. Friedman (Academic Press, New York), pp. 467–518.

Doll, T. J., Hanna, T. E., and Russotti, J. S. (1992). "Masking in three dimensional auditory displays," Hum. Factors **34**, 255–265.

Durlach, N. I., and Colburn, H. S. (1978). "Binaural phenomena," in *Handbook of Perception, Vol. IV, Hearing*, edited by E. C. Carterette and M. P. Friedman (Academic Press, New York), pp. 365–466.

Ebata, M., Sone, T., and Nimura, T. (1968). "Improvement of hearing ability by directional information," J. Acoust. Soc. Am. **43**, 289–297.

Egan, J. P. (1965). "Masking-level differences as a function of interaural disparities in intensity of signal and of noise," J. Acoust. Soc. Am. **38**, 1043–1049.

Egan, J. P., and Benson, W. (1966). "Lateralization of a weak signal presented with correlated and with uncorrelated noise," J. Acoust. Soc. Am. **40**, 20–26.

Feddersen, W. E., Sandel, T. T., Teas, D. C., and Jeffress, L. A. (1957). "Localization of high-frequency tones," J. Acoust. Soc. Am. **29**, 988–991.

Gilkey, R. H., and Good, M. D. (1995). "Effects of frequency on free-field masking," Hum. Factors, 37, 835–843.

Gilkey, R. H., Good, M. D., and Ball, J. M. (1996). "A comparison of 'free-field' masking for real and for virtual sounds," J. Acoust. Soc. Am. (in revision).

Gilkey, R. H., Good, M. D., Ericson, M. A., Brinkman, J., and Stewart, J. M. (1995). "A pointing technique for rapidly collecting localization responses in auditory research," Behavior Res. Methods, Instr., Comput. 27, 1–11.

Gilkey, R. H., Simpson, B. D., and Weisenberger, J. M. (1990). "Masker fringe and binaural detection," J. Acoust. Soc. Am. 88, 1323–1332.

Good, M. D., and Gilkey, R. H. (1996a). "Sound localization in noise: I. The effect of signal-to-noise ratio," J. Acoust. Soc. Am., B99, 1108–1117.

Good, M. D., and Gilkey, R. H. (1996b). "Sound localization in noise: II. Effects of masker location," (in preparation).

Hafter, E. R. (1971). "Quantitative evaluation of a lateralization model of masking-level differences," J. Acoust. Soc. Am. 50, 1116–1122.

Hafter, E. R., Bourbon, W. T., Blocker, A. S., and Tucker, A. (1969). "A direct comparison between lateralization and detection under conditions of antiphasic masking," J. Acoust. Soc. Am. 46, 1452–1457.

Houtgast, T., and Plomp, R. (1968). "Lateralization threshold of a signal in noise," J. Acoust. Soc. Am. 44, 807–812.

Ito, Y., Colburn, H. S., and Thompson, C. L. (1982). "Masked discrimination of interaural time delays with narrow-band signal," J. Acoust. Soc. Am. 72, 1821–1826.

Jacobsen, T. (1976). "Localization in noise," Tech. Rep. 10, Technical University Acoustics Laboratory, Lybny, Denmark.

Jeffress, L. A. (1972). "Binaural signal detection: Vector theory," in *Foundations of Modern Auditory Theory, Vol. II*, edited by J. V. Tobias (Academic Press, New York), pp. 351–368.

Jeffress, L. A., Blodgett, H. C., Sandel, T. T., and Wood, C. L. III. (1956). "Masking of tonal signals," J. Acoust. Soc. Am. 28, 416–426.

Kistler, D. J., and Wightman, F. L. (1992). "A model of head-related transfer functions based on principal components analysis and minimum-phase reconstruction," J. Acoust. Soc. Am. 91, 1637–1647.

Kock, W. E. (1950). "Binaural localization and masking," J. Acoust. Soc. Am. 22, 801–804.

Levitt, H. (1971). "Transformed up-down methods in psychoacoustics," J. Acoust. Soc. Am. 49, 467–477.

McFadden, D. (1966). "Masking-level differences with continuous and with burst masking noise," J. Acoust. Soc. Am. 40, 1414–1419.

Mills, A. W. (1972). "Auditory localization," in *Foundations of Modern Auditory Theory, Vol. II*, edited by J. V. Tobias (Academic Press, New York), pp. 303–348.

Perrott, D. R. (1984). "Concurrent minimum audible angle: A re-examination of the concept of auditory spatial acuity," J. Acoust. Soc. Am. 75, 1201–1206.

Plomp, R. (1976). "Binaural and monaural speech intelligibility of connected discourse in reverberation as a function of azimuth of a single competing sound source (speech or noise)," Acustica 34, 200–211.

Robinson, D. E., and Egan, J. P. (1974). "Lateralization of an auditory signal in correlated noise and in uncorrelated noise as a function of signal frequency," Percept. Psychophys. 15, 281–284.

Robinson, D. E., and Trahiotis, C. (1972). "Effects of signal duration and masker duration on detectability under diotic and dichotic listening conditions," Percept. Psychophys. 12, 333–334.

Saberi, K., Dostal, L., Sadralodabai, T., Bull, V., and Perrott, D. R. (1991). "Free field release from masking," J. Acoust. Soc. Am. 90, 1355–1370.

Shaw, E. A. G. (1974). "Transformation of sound pressure level from the free field to the eardrum in the horizontal plane," J. Acoust. Soc. Am. 56, 1848–1861.

Stern, R. M., Slocum, J. E., and Phillips, M. S. (1983). "Interaural time and amplitude discrimination in noise," J. Acoust. Soc. Am. 73, 1714–1722.

Wightman, F. L., and Kistler, D. J. (1989). "Headphone simulation of free-field listening. I: Stimulus synthesis," J. Acoust. Soc. Am. 85, 858–867.

Yost, W. A. (1985). "Prior stimulation and the masking-level-difference," J. Acoust. Soc. Am. 78, 901–907.

Yost, W. A., and Dolan, D. (1978). "Masking-level differences for repeated filtered transients," J. Acoust. Soc. Am. 63, 1927–1930.

Zurek, P. M., and Durlach, N. I. (1987). "Masker-bandwidth dependence in homophasic and antiphasic tone detection," J. Acoust. Soc. Am. 81, 459–464.

Chapter 19

Directional Cuing Effects in Auditory Recognition

Theodore J. Doll
Georgia Institute of Technology

Thomas E. Hanna
Naval Submarine Base–New London, Groton, Connecticut

(Received May 1994; revised November 1994)

It has been suggested that virtual auditory displays (VADs) be used to enhance the intelligibility of warnings, advisories, and speech communications in noisy environments. It is often assumed that the benefit gained by giving the signals distinct perceptual locations is related to the masking level difference (MLD). This study suggests another possible reason: Signals with distinct locations may be preattentively processed in parallel because auditory location cues lead the listener to perceptually organize them as separate "objects." This research investigated auditory display techniques that might enable sonar operators to monitor multiple channels concurrently. On each test trial, short bursts representing underwater events were presented at a rate of either 1 or 2 bursts/s. The subject's task was to determine whether a previously learned target burst was among those presented and, in some conditions, to also identify the relative location of the target. The bursts were presented at virtual locations based on the full head-related transfer function ("3-D sound" cues), at comparable locations based on interaural time and intensity differences only, diotically with visual location cues, or diotically with no location cues. 3-D sound cues enhanced recognition relative to diotic presentation, but visual and time/intensity cues did not. Because the bursts were relatively widely separated in time, explanations in terms of the MLD seem unlikely. Rate of presentation did not interact with 3-D versus diotic presentation, suggesting that the segregation of sound sources accompanying 3-D sound cues is not based on a limited-capacity mechanism (i.e., focal attention). Contrary to the recognition results, visual cues produced better localization performance than did 3-D sound cues or time/intensity cues. These results suggest that with 3-D sound cues the bursts are perceptually organized as objects and preattentively processed in parallel, whereas with visual cues they must be serially processed in focal attention. The importance of attentional processes in recognition performance with virtual auditory displays is discussed.

INTRODUCTION

One of the many potential applications suggested for virtual auditory displays (VADs) is that they be used to enhance the recognition of warnings, advisories, and speech communications by giving various messages different apparent spatial locations (e.g., Begault and Wenzel, 1993; Doll, Gerth, Engelman, and Folds, 1986). To date, however, there have been few studies of recognition performance with VADs.

This type of application would exploit the well-known cocktail party effect (Cherry, 1953). Yost (1991) defined the cocktail party effect as the use of spatial location as a means to form auditory images, or determine (recognize or identify) a sound source. One might expect that the literature on the long-standing cocktail party effect would provide insights as to how to best design VADs so as to facilitate recognition. As Yost noted, however, relatively little is known about how the cocktail party effect works. He stated, "Despite numerous references to the cocktail party effect in the auditory literature, virtually no experimental data exist which describe listeners' ability to determine actual sound sources in actual listening environments" (1991, p. 16). Although many studies of speech recognition in free or diffuse sound fields have been reported, they are more demonstrations of the cocktail party effect than explanations of how it works (e.g., Carhart, Tillman, and Greetis, 1969; Ebata, Sone, and Nimura, 1967; Plomp, 1977; Plomp and Mimpen, 1981; Thompson and Webster, 1963).

There has, however, been extensive study of the experimental analog of the cocktail party effect, dichotic listening. The early dichotic listening experiments showed that when a listener shadows a message in one ear, the listener remembers almost nothing of material played to the other, unattended ear (e.g., Cherry, 1953). Broadbent (1958) accounted for these and other findings with his Filter Theory, according to which perception is like a limited-capacity communication channel that can process only a limited amount of information per unit time. Streams of information coming into the organism are initially held in a short-term store, and a selective filter operates to pass only one stream at a time on to the limited capacity perceptual system. Attention to more than one channel requires switching and serial application of the limited capacity system.

Filter Theory had to be modified when it was shown that listeners recognize their names and occasionally respond to the meaning of items on the unattended channel (Moray, 1959; Treisman, 1960). After decades of attention experiments and theoretical development, a two-process theory emerged, the basic tenets of which are widely accepted. Several different names for, and characterizations of, the two processes were coined by various authors. For example, Norman and Bobrow (1975) distinguished between "data-driven" and "conceptually-driven" processes in perception. "Data-driven" refers to "bottom-up" processing, which is determined only by the sensory input, whereas "conceptually-driven" refers to "top-down" processing, which is under conscious control. Neisser (1967) contrasted these two processes as analytical and constructive. According to him, a preattentive mechanism processes all sensory inputs automatically and in parallel, without conscious attention. This part of perception is analytical. That is, the preattentive mechanism breaks down sensory input into constituent features (e.g., signal-to-noise ratios in each critical band). In contrast, focused attention is constructive, that is, sensory inputs are supplemented by preexisting knowledge and expectations to produce percepts. A number of authors (Neisser, 1967; Treisman and Gelade, 1980) used the term "focal" or "focused" attention to characterize this conscious, serial, and limited capacity part of perception.

It is not clear whether the cocktail party effect is a product of preattentive processing or focal attention. It is probable that both processes are involved. The directional qualities of different conversations may cause them to be processed as different "streams" by the preattentive mechanism, as suggested by Moore (1982) and Kahneman and Henik (1981). On the other hand, any one of the conversations may be selected for constructive processing by the focal attention mechanism, or the mechanism may be multiplexed among them.

The distinction between preattentive processing and focal attention may have important implications for the design of VADs. Giving auditory inputs different apparent locations may cause them to be perceptually organized as different preattentive streams. This means that at least the initial processing of such inputs would not be subject to capacity or workload limitations. Even if further processing by the focal attention mechanism were necessary, the earlier parallel processing should facilitate recognition of the inputs.

On the other hand, the fact that auditory inputs have different apparent locations might not affect preattentive processing, but may simply provide a way for the focal attention mechanism to select one input for processing at any given time, while excluding others. That is, directional cues might enhance the selective "filter" in Broadbent's (1958) theory. Each input would then have to be processed serially, and capacity limitations would play a role. This would mean that there is some amount of mental workload involved in recognizing each input, and would make performance more vulnerable to variables that stress the limited capacity mechanism, such as the rate of presentation.

The research presented here investigated display techniques that might enable listeners to concurrently monitor multiple channels, thereby increasing the amount of information per unit time that can be processed. Several techniques for perceptually separating, or calling attention to, auditory inputs were examined.

Of course, VADs are only one means of cuing items in an auditory display. Visual cues offer another means. Accompanying each auditory input with a unique visual stimulus would be expected to enhance focal attention to that input by providing a cue that helps the listener select one input and ignore others. Unlike auditory location cues, however, visual cues are not necessary to obtain the cocktail party effect, and would not be expected to cause the inputs to be segregated into different auditory streams.

The signals were short bursts representing underwater events previously collected with sonar systems. The signal presentation rate was varied to determine under what cuing conditions auditory recognition performance is based on a limited capacity mechanism.

It was also of interest to determine whether there is a trade-off between the fidelity of auditory location cues and their effectiveness in facilitating recognition. The auditory cuing conditions therefore included one in which only interaural time and intensity differences were used (i.e., the bursts were lateralized), and another in which the full head-related transfer function (HRTF) was simulated. The signals were also presented diotically, both with and without visual cues. There was also a condition with both visual cues and the full HRTF.

I. METHOD

A. Stimuli and experimental conditions

The stimuli were 21 sound bursts, which were divided into seven subsets of three bursts each. The three members of each subset were exemplars of a common type of underwater event. The events included a variety of impact-type sounds from different objects and materials, some more reverberant than others. The duration of each burst ranged from tens to hundreds of milliseconds, and each was centered approximately within a 1-s interval. The recorded events had been sampled at 12.5 kHz with 12 bits of linear encoding of amplitude and lowpass filtered at 5 kHz.

On each test trial, four nonoverlapping bursts were presented binaurally over a Sennheiser HD430 headset. Subjects indicated whether one of the four bursts on each trial was a member of a subset that they had previously learned to recognize as "target" bursts. Subjects indicated their response by pressing boxes on a CRT/touch screen. In some conditions, there were just two response boxes, marked "yes" and "no," arranged one above the other in a single column. In other conditions, four columns of yes/no boxes were displayed horizontally across the screen. In this case, subjects indicated the relative direction (extreme left, left center, right center, or extreme right) of the target burst, as well as its presence or absence, by pressing either the "yes" or "no" box in the corresponding columnar position. In this condition, subjects had a choice of four different "no" boxes that could be pressed if they believed that no signal had been presented. They were told to press the "no" box corresponding to the direction from which the target was most likely to have come in the event that they were mistaken and one had been presented.

One-half of the subjects received subset 1 as targets (see Fig. 1), and the remaining subjects received subset 2 as targets (see Fig. 2). Figure 3 shows one burst from each of the five subsets that served as nontargets for both groups. The nontarget set also included subset 1 or 2 (whichever was not the target set for that group). Target bursts were chosen based on a previous study of confusions between the bursts (Hanna, 1990). The two subsets chosen as targets were those that were most frequently confused with the other bursts.

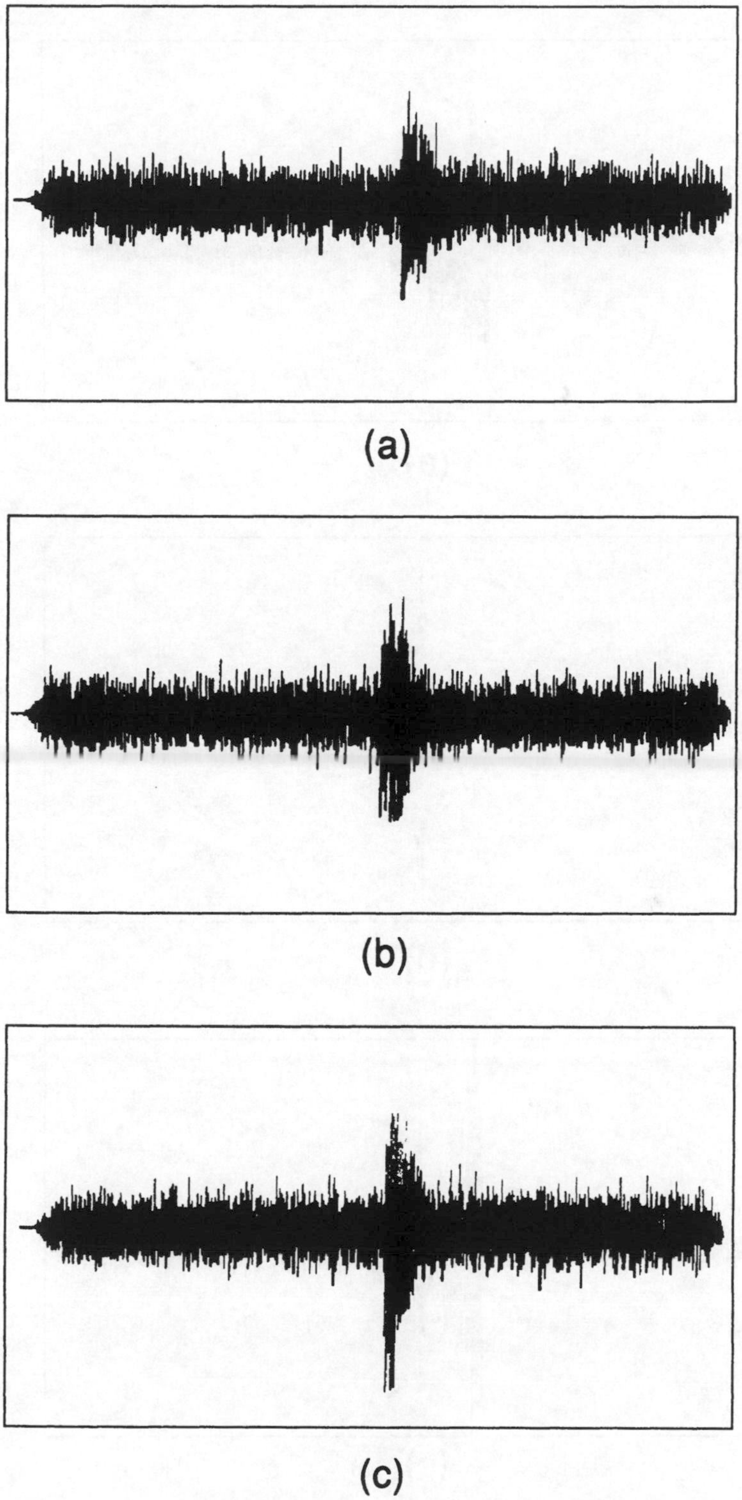

FIG. 1. Subset 1 of three bursts (a–c), used as targets for one-half the subjects and as nontargets for the remaining subjects.

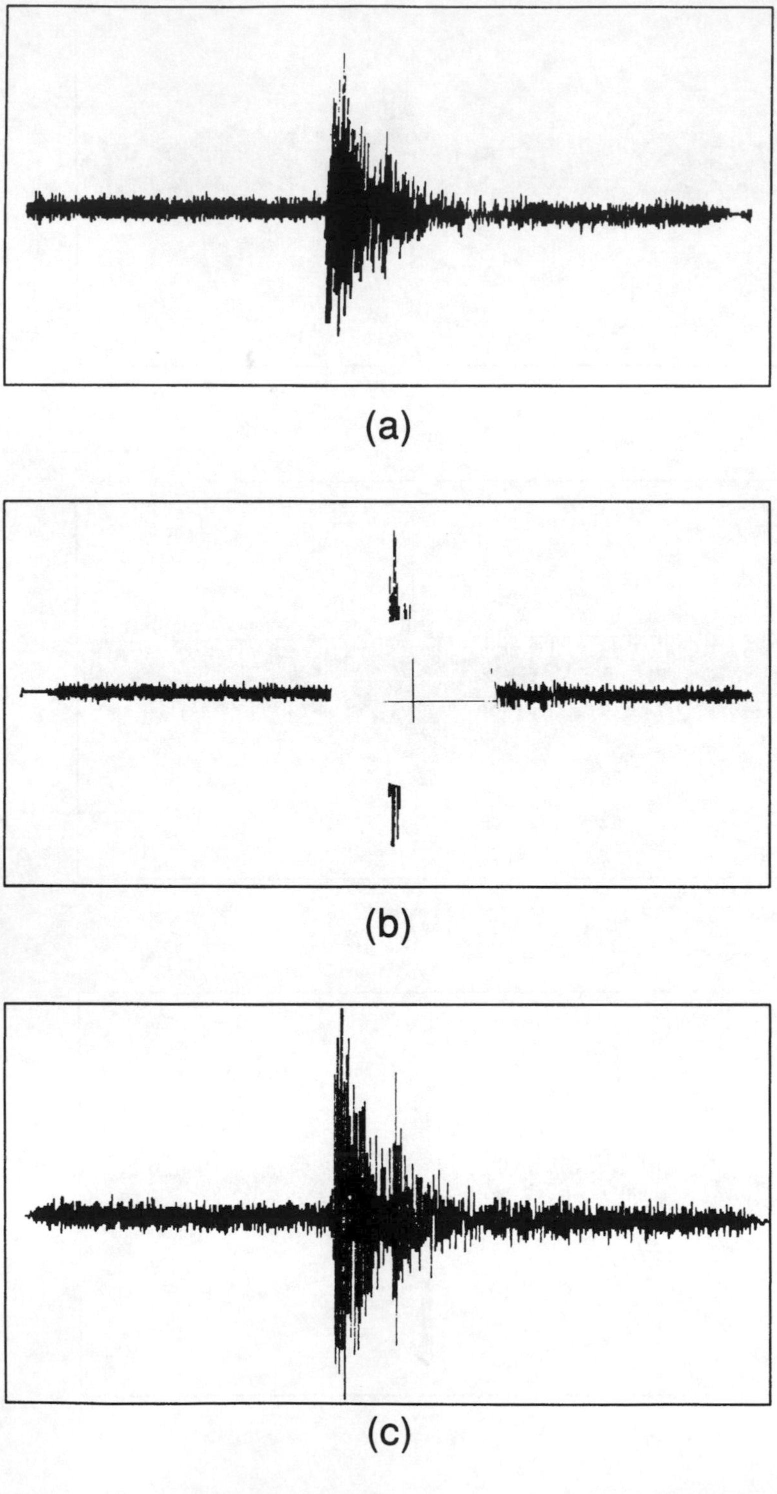

FIG. 2. Subset 2 of three bursts (a–c), used as targets for one-half the subjects and as nontargets for the remaining subjects.

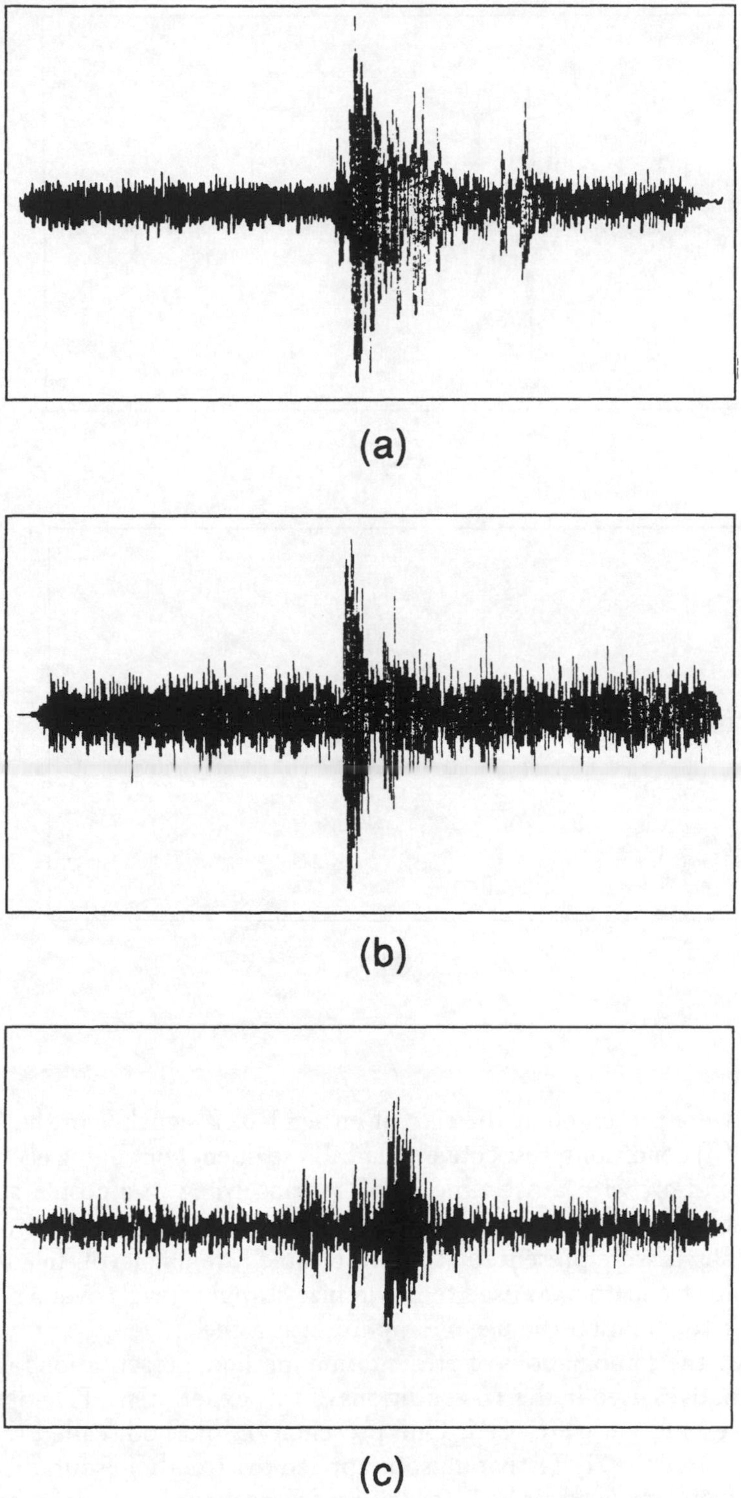

FIG. 3. Five bursts (a–e), one from each of the five subsets that served as nontargets for both groups of subjects.

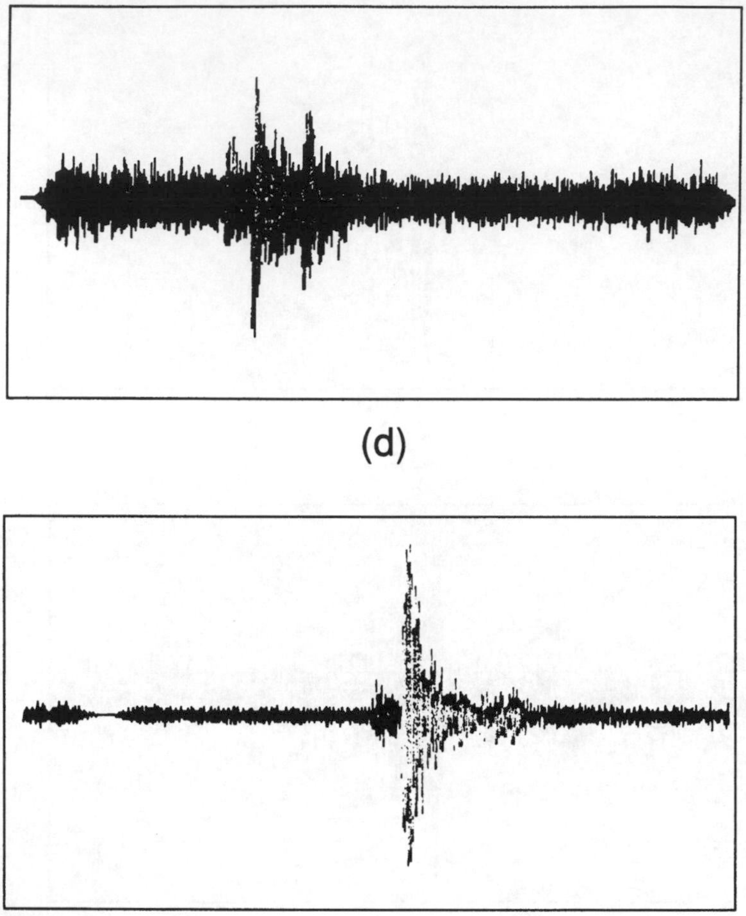

(d)

(e)

FIG. 3. Continued.

The bursts were presented at the rate of either 1 or 2 signals/s in the "slow" (S) and "fast" (F) conditions, respectively. The 1-s segment containing each burst was gated on and off with a rise time of 50 ms according to a cosine squared function. Bursts were equated for loudness in preliminary testing with five pilot subjects. The bursts were presented at a comfortable listening level. In addition, a programmable attenuator was used to randomize stimulus levels over a range of ±3 dB in order to minimize the use of amplitude as a cue.

Table I shows the combinations of presentation method, presentation rate, and response alternatives used in the 10 conditions of this experiment. Five different methods of presentation were used. One presentation method, called the 3-D condition, simulated the HRTF that must be applied to a free-field source in order to match the signals received at the listener's eardrums. Each burst was presented at a different apparent direction (azimuths of ±90° and ±30° and elevations of 0° relative to the listener's interaural axis). Azimuth was measured counterclockwise from directly in front of the observer. All the presentation methods were produced by appropriately programming the Convolvotron system produced by Crystal River Engineering Co. The 3-D condition employed the HRTFs for subject SDO (Wightman and Kistler, 1989).

In a second, "time-intensity" (TI) presentation method, the bursts were lateralized to four equally spaced locations analogous to those used in the 3-D condition. In this case, directional cues consisted of fixed (frequency-independent) interaural time and amplitude differences. Interaural time and amplitude differences were determined in pilot testing with 3 subjects with normal bilateral hearing. The interaural time differences were ±0.77ms, and ±0.20 ms, for the ±90° and ±30° azimuth positions, respectively. Interaural amplitude differences were ±20 dB and ±6 dB for the ±90° and ±30° azimuth positions, respectively.

A third (control) presentation method consisted of diotic or "one channel" (1C) presentation. A fourth (1CQ) presentation method involved presenting a visual cue with each diotic burst. The fifth presentation method (3DQ) consisted of presenting a visual cue in combination with 3-D presentation of the bursts. In the 1CQ and 3DQ conditions, the relative direction of each burst was indicated by displaying question marks (?) in both the "yes" and "no" boxes of one column on the CRT/touch screen. The question marks came on 0.25 s after the initiation of the 1-s segment for the corresponding signal, and remained on for 0.3 s.

B. Subjects and procedure

The subjects were nine women and three men, aged 20 to 49 years (mean 29), with normal hearing (≤20 dB HL at octave frequencies from 250 Hz to 4 kHz and at 6 kHz, and ≤20 dB interaural difference at any test frequency). Six subjects were randomly assigned to each of the two groups.

TABLE I. Experimental conditions.

Condition name	*Presentation method*	*Presentation rate (signals/s)*	*Response alternatives*
1CF1	"1 Channel" (diotic)	2	1Y/N
1CS1	"1 Channel" (diotic)	1	1Y/N
3DF1	"3-D" (full HRTF)	2	1Y/N
3DS1	"3-D" (full HRTF)	1	1Y/N
3DF4	"3-D" (full HRTF)	2	4Y/N
3DS4	"3-D" (full HRTF)	1	4Y/N
TIF1	"TI" (time-intensity)	2	1Y/N
TIF4	"TI" (time-intensity)	2	4Y/N
1CF4Q	"1 Channel" (diotic) + visual cues (Q)	2	4Y/N
3DF4Q	"3-D" (full HRTF) + visual cues (Q)	2	4Y/N

Note: F denotes fast presentation (2 signals/s); S denotes slow presentation (1 signal/s); 1 or 4 following F or S denotes the number of pairs of yes/no response alternatives.

On each test trial, either one or zero target bursts and three or four nontarget bursts were randomly selected from the pool of 3 targets and 18 nontargets, respectively. A target was presented randomly on one-half of the test trials. In those conditions in which the bursts were accompanied by directional cues (those with 3-D, TI, or Q in the condition name; see Table I), the four directional cues were activated in random order.

Each subject participated in nine 2-h sessions, and no more than one session per day. The first three sessions were devoted to practice. Pilot testing revealed that this amount of practice was sufficient to bring subjects to nearly asymptotic recognition performance. In the first practice session, the task was demonstrated, following which the subject performed four blocks of test trials of gradually increasing difficulty. Difficulty was controlled by the choice of nontargets. In the easier blocks, nontargets were those that had been found to be least often confused with the targets in an earlier study (Hanna, 1990). In the second and third practice sessions, the demonstration was repeated and the subject performed 10 blocks of test trials, randomly selected from among the experimental conditions. In each of the subsequent six experimental sessions, each subject performed one block in each of the 10 experimental conditions.

Each block was 60 test trials in length. The response boxes were displayed on the CRT/touch screen at all times. Blocks were initiated after the subject responded to the message "press any box to begin." The message "please enter your response now" was displayed immediately after the four signals had been presented, and any earlier response was ignored. Feedback was provided 0.5 s after the response, and consisted of a plus (+) for correct or minus (–) for incorrect displayed for 0.5 s in the box that the subject had pressed. The next test trial began 0.5 s after the end of the feedback.

II. RESULTS

The data were tabulated in terms of both recognition performance and localization performance. A correct recognition was any "yes" response, given that a target had been presented, regardless of whether the "yes" also indicated the correct relative location of the target. Correct localization consisted of responding in the correct relative location when a target was presented, regardless of whether the response was "yes" or "no."

A. Recognition performance

Recognition sensitivities (d' values) were first calculated for each subject for each condition at two levels of practice (first three experimental sessions vs. the last three). Prior to submitting the d' values to analysis of variance (ANOVA), the extent to which they conform to the normal distribution was evaluated. The d' values were pooled within each of three major categories of condition (visual cues, 3-D, and diotic/time-intensity). The resulting histograms, shown in Fig. 4, reveal that the distributions are quite "mound-shaped" for each type of condition. In

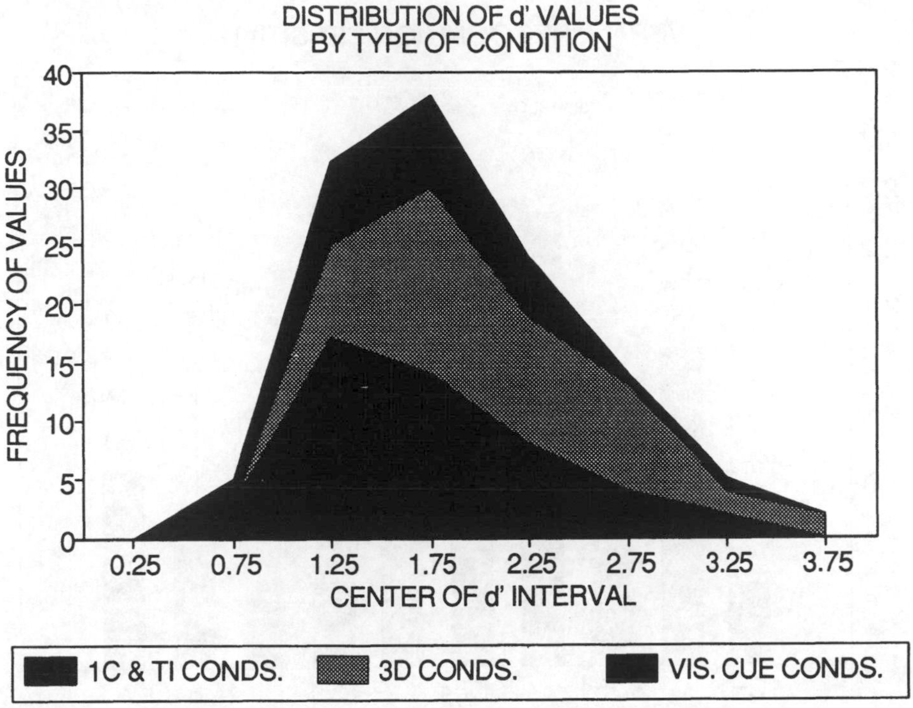

FIG. 4. Distribution of individual-subject average sensitivity (d') values for recognition performance by type of condition: all diotic and time/intensity conditions pooled (1C and TI), all 3-D sound conditions, and all visual cue conditions.

view of the robustness of ANOVA to departures from the normal distribution assumption, it was judged safe to use ANOVA.

An ANOVA with two repeated measures (Condition and Practice) and one between-Ss measure (Group) was used to examine the overall main effects of these variables and their interactions. In order to evaluate and correct for possible heterogeneity of variances and covariances, the parameter lambda was calculated using the procedure outlined by Myers (1972, p. 178). The resulting lambda value was 0.42, indicating moderate heterogeneity. To control the probability of Type 1 error, lambda was used to adjust the degrees of freedom in the ANOVA as outlined by Myers (p. 177).

The ANOVA revealed a significant effect of Presentation Method [$F(3, 37) = 12.95, p < .001$]. The effect of Practice was not significant, even with the greater unadjusted degrees of freedom [$F(1,10) = 17.19, p > .05$]. The effect of Group was also not significant, indicating no difference between the two subsets of target bursts [$F(1, 10) = 5.71, p > .05$]. None of the interactions were significant. The data were therefore pooled over Practice and Group for subsequent planned comparisons.

Figure 5 shows mean d' values for each condition. (The abbreviations used for condition names in this section are explained in Table I). The most important effect is the difference between the 3-D and diotic (1C) conditions. The mean d' for the 3DS1 and 3DF1 conditions was significantly greater than that for the 1CS1 and 1CF1 conditions [$F(1, 41) = 7.67, p < .01$]. The 3-D conditions (3DF1

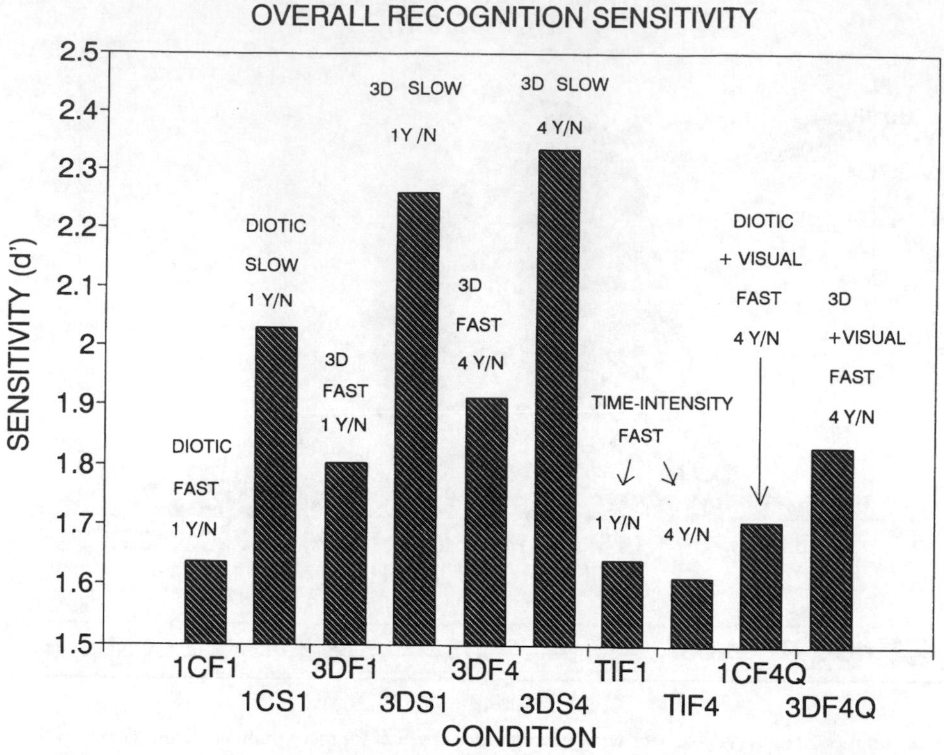

FIG. 5. Recognition sensitivity averaged over subjects as a function of condition (see Table I for explanation of condition codes).

and 3DF4) were also superior to the TI conditions (TIF1 and TIF4) [$F(1, 41) = 10.41$, $p < .01$]. Although not tested, it appears that performance in the TI conditions was no better than that in the fast diotic condition (1CF1).

Three planned comparisons examined the effects of visual cues. Surprisingly, visual cues with diotic presentation did no better than diotic presentation alone (1CF4Q vs. 1CF1) [$F(1, 41) = 0.48$, $p > .05$]. Second, visual cuing with 3-D presentation did no better than 3-D presentation alone (in fact, recognition was poorer in 3DF4Q than in 3DF4) [$F(1, 41) = 0.64$, $p > .05$]. Consistent with these effects, 3-D presentation produced significantly better recognition than diotic presentation with visual cues (3DF4 vs. 1CF4Q) [$F(1, 41) = 4.15$, $p < .05$]. Thus, 3-D sound cues produced better recognition than did visual cues.

There is also a striking effect of presentation rate in Fig. 5. The mean d' for the slow (S) presentation conditions was significantly greater than that for the corresponding fast (F) conditions [$F(1, 41) = 53.01$, $p < .001$]. (In this contrast, the mean of the 3DS4, 3DS1, and 1CS1 conditions was compared to the mean of the 3DF4, 3DF1, and 1CF1 conditions.)

More important, however, there was a notable lack of interaction between type of auditory presentation (3-D vs. diotic) and presentation rate [$F(1, 41) = 0.20$, $p > .05$]. Note in Fig. 5 that the difference between the 1CS1 and 1CF1 conditions was almost identical to the difference between the 3DS1 and 3DF1 conditions.

Two additional planned comparisons examined the effects (1) of the number of response alternatives, and (2) of the interaction of presentation rate with number of response alternatives. First, the number of response alternatives did not significantly affect recognition performance [$F(1, 41) = 0.79, p > .05$]. This contrast compared the means of the 3DS1, 3DF1, and TIF1 conditions to those of the 3DS4, 3DF4, and TIF4 conditions. Second, the effect of presentation rate on recognition did not differ significantly as a function of number of response alternatives (3DS1–3DF1 vs. 3DS4–3DF4) [$F(1, 41) = 0.06, p > .05$].

B. Localization performance

As with the recognition data, the extent to which the data conform to the normal distribution was evaluated prior to submitting them to ANOVA. Because the overall percentage of correct localizations was relatively similar across conditions, the data were pooled for the purposes of this evaluation. The resulting histogram, shown in Fig. 6, reveals that the distribution of scores does not depart radically from normality, and it was judged appropriate to use ANOVA. An ANOVA with two repeated measures (Condition and Practice) and one between-S's measure (Group) was used to examine the overall main effects of these variables and their interactions. The procedure outlined by Myers (1972) was again used to evaluate, and correct for, possible heterogeneity of variances and covariances. The resulting lambda value, 0.65, was used to adjust the degrees of freedom in the ANOVA.

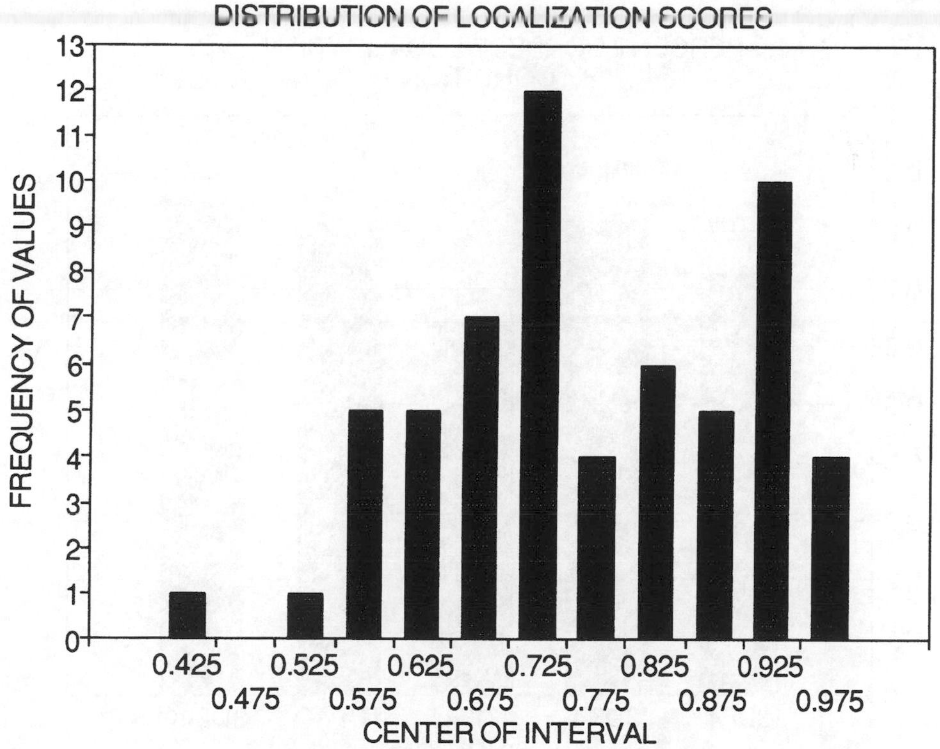

FIG. 6. Distribution of individual-subject average percent correct localization scores pooled over all conditions in which localization data was collected (conditions with four Y/N response alternatives—see Table I).

The ANOVA revealed a significant effect of Condition [$F(2, 26) = 17.07, p < .001$]. Again, the effect of Practice was not significant, even with the greater unadjusted degrees of freedom [$F(1, 10) = 0.54, p > .05$]. The effect of Group was also not significant, indicating no difference between the two subsets of target bursts [$F(1, 10) = .01, p > .05$]. None of the interactions were significant. The data were therefore pooled over Practice and Group for subsequent planned comparisons.

Figure 7 shows the mean percentage of correct localizations for each condition. The most notable aspect of these results is that, unlike recognition, visual cuing generally facilitated performance. For example, visual cues with diotic presentation produced significantly better localization than did 3-D presentation (1CF4Q vs. 3DF4) [$F(1, 29) = 6.67, p < .05$]. Second, localization was better with the combination of visual cues and 3-D sound than with 3-D sound alone (3DF4Q vs. 3DF4) [$F(1, 29) = 24.76, p < .001$].

As with recognition performance, the slower rate of presentation led to better performance in the 3-D sound conditions (3DS4 vs. 3DF4) [$F(1, 29) = 13.06, p < .01$]. And again, 3-D presentation produced better performance than did the TI condition [$F(1, 29) = 9.29, p < .01$].

The fact that 3-D sound cues produce better recognition, but visual cues produce better localization, suggests a simple two-process model of listeners' performance. The two processes are recognition and localization. The target burst must first be recognized in order to be localized. However, given recognition,

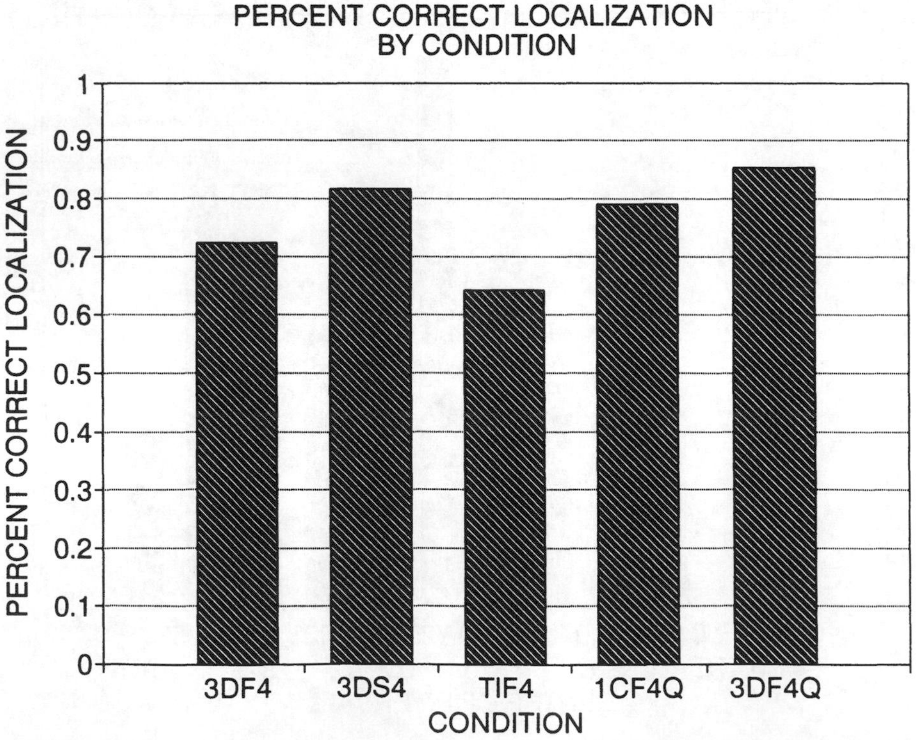

FIG. 7. Percent correct localization averaged over subjects as a function of condition (see Table I for explanation of condition codes).

localization is not assured. 3-D sound cues apparently facilitate recognition more than do visual cues, but do less well in terms of supporting localization. On the other hand, visual cues seem to produce less benefit in terms of recognition, but given that the target was recognized, they do a better job of supporting localization.

This two-process hypothesis was further tested as follows. If the visual cuing supports better localization, given that the signal is correctly recognized, then measured localization performance in the visual cuing conditions should be closer to that of an ideal observer than is localization performance in the 3-D sound conditions. For the ideal observer, it is possible to predict sensitivity (d') to the presence of a target on any individual channel (spatial location) from overall sensitivity to the presence of a target on the ensemble of all four channels (Nolte and Jaarsma, 1967). Given these estimates of individual channel d' values, one can compute the probability that the channel with the target (plus random Gaussian noise) will produce a greater value of "targetness" than any of the nontarget (noise only) channels, and therefore be chosen as the correct alternative (i.e., correctly localized) (Green and Dai, 1991). That is, one can predict the percentage of correct localizations that an ideal observer would make for any given level of recognition performance.

Figures 8 through 12 show plots of measured versus predicted percentage of correct localizations for the five conditions. If the listeners' localization performance were optimal, within the limits of their ability to recognize the targets, then the points would lie on a line with a slope of 1.0 and intercept of 0.0, that is, the positive diagonal. Inspection of the figures reveals that the points are closest to the diagonal in the visual cuing conditions (1CF4Q and 3DF4Q) and further from the diagonal in the 3DF4, TIF4, and 3DS4 conditions.

The standard error of estimate for predicting measured from predicted values was computed for each condition. These statistics, shown in Table II, quantify the vertical deviation of the measured values from the positive diagonal. A Newman-Kuels multiple F test was conducted to compare the standard errors of estimates among conditions. The results, shown in the bottom of Table II, reveal that measured localization in both the 3DF4Q and 1CF4Q conditions deviates significantly less from the ideal observer predictions than does localization in the 3DF4, 3DS4, and TIF4 conditions. Thus, this analysis confirms that visual cues provide better localization than do 3-D sound cues, given that the signal was correctly recognized. However, as noted earlier, 3-D sound cues produce better recognition performance than do visual cues.

An interesting ancillary finding apparent from Table II is that localization of the signals, given that they were recognized, was no better with 3-D sound cues than when the signals were simply lateralized (TI condition).

III. DISCUSSION AND CONCLUSIONS

The present results show that accompanying each of a series of acoustic bursts with 3-D sound cues facilitates recognition of a predefined target burst relative to both diotic presentation of the burst and a condition in which the bursts were lateralized. It should be noted that the auditory events were relatively widely

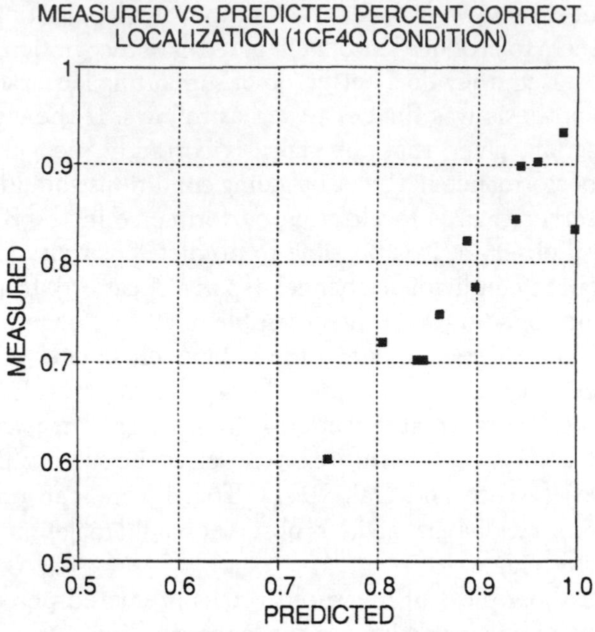

FIG. 8. Measured percent correct localization in the 1CF4Q (visual cue + diotic, fast) condition versus value predicted for ideal observer, given the percent correct recognition for that condition.

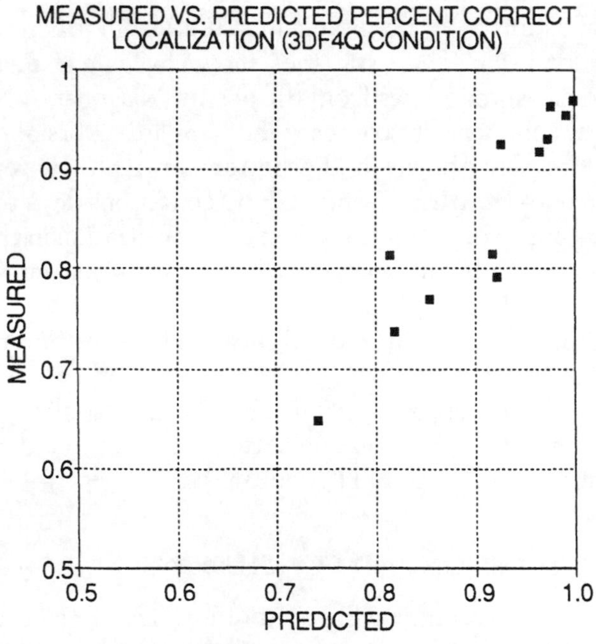

FIG. 9. Measured percent correct localization in the 3DF4Q (visual cue + 3-D sound, fast) condition versus value predicted for ideal observer, given the percent correct recognition for that condition.

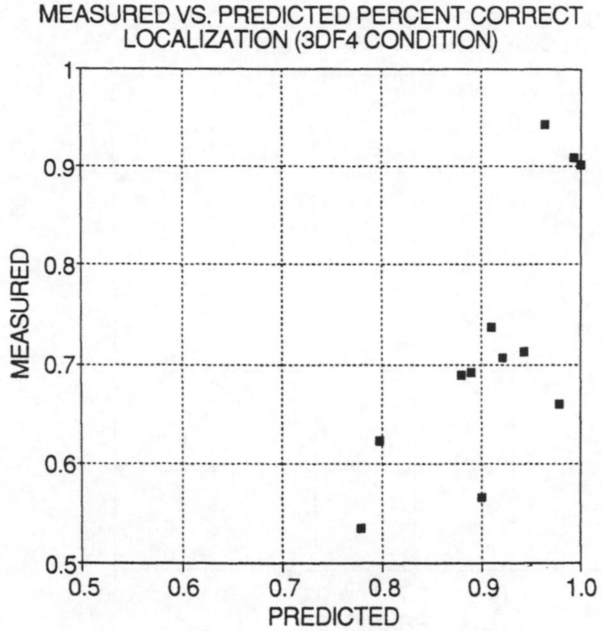

FIG. 10. Measured percent correct localization in the 3DF4 (3-D sound, fast) condition versus value predicted for ideal observer, given the percent correct recognition for that condition.

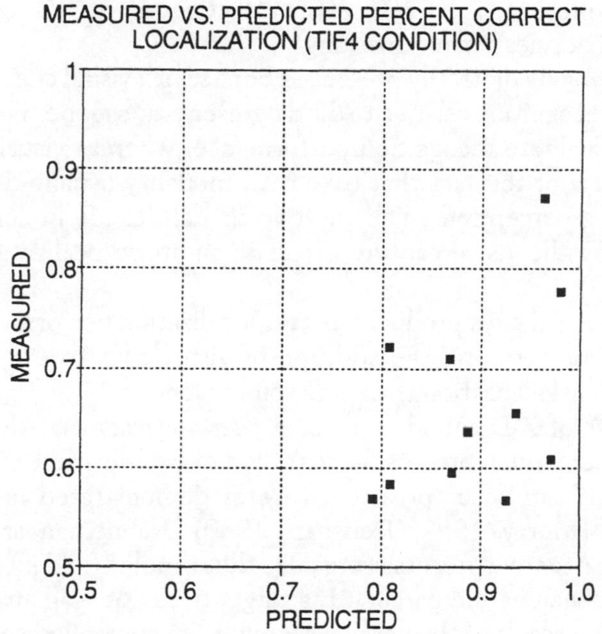

FIG. 11. Measured percent correct localization in the TIF4 (time/intensity, fast) condition versus value predicted for ideal observer, given the percent correct recognition for that condition.

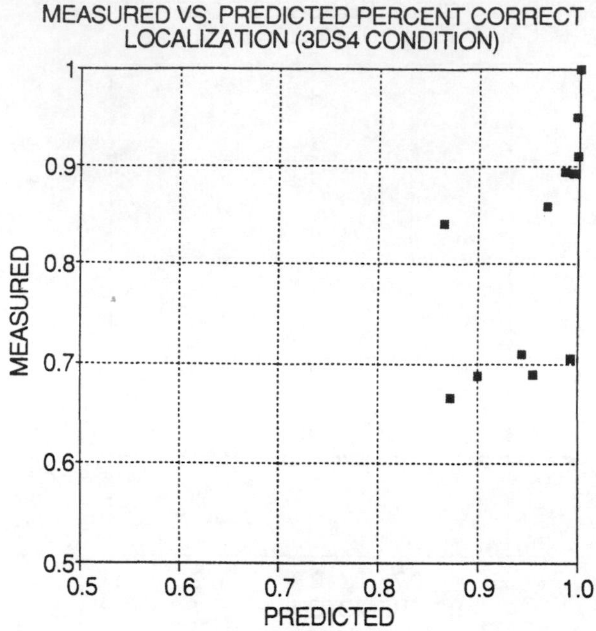

FIG. 12. Measured percent correct localization in the 3DS4 (3-D sound, slow) condition versus value predicted for ideal observer, given the percent correct recognition for that condition.

separated in time, especially at the slower of the two presentation rates, and no other noise source was presented. Therefore, the effectiveness of 3-D sound cues cannot be attributed to a release from masking.

In contrast, accompanying diotically presented bursts with visual cues does not significantly facilitate recognition relative to diotic presentation alone. The finding that 3-D sound cues facilitate recognition performance, whereas visual cues do not, is surprising in view of the fact that the visual modality usually dominates audition in determining perception when the two modalities are in conflict (as shown, for example, by the visual capture effect in auditory localization; Pick, Warren, and Hay, 1969).

On the other hand, visual cues produced better localization performance than did 3-D sound cues. Furthermore, the addition of visual cues to a 3-D sound display resulted in better localization than 3-D sound alone.

The differing effects of 3-D sound and visual cues suggests that they affect different parts of the perceptual process. Recognition of well-learned and certain other meaningful items can occur preattentively, as demonstrated in dichotic listening experiments (Moray, 1959; Treisman, 1960). Kahneman and Henik (1981) argued that preattentive processes organize the stimulus field into perceptual objects, which are searched in parallel. If a target does not "call attention to itself" (i.e., pop out) as a result of the parallel search, then controlled search may follow (p. 188). The fact that 3-D cues facilitate recognition suggests that they may facilitate the preattentive organization of the bursts into perceptual objects, which are then searched in parallel. The fact that visual cues did not enhance recognition relative to diotic presentation suggests that they do not result in the bursts being organized as perceptual objects, and therefore the bursts must be searched in a controlled, serial manner (i.e., in focal attention).

It is likely that most recognition tasks involve some amount of processing by both mechanisms—preattentive and focal. In conditions where preattentive processing is more extensive, less processing in focal attention may be required. The present results are consistent with the idea that preattentive processing predominates in the recognition of auditory bursts accompanied by 3-D sound cues, whereas focal attention predominates in the same task with visual cues.

Unlike recognition, which can occur preattentively, localization requires focal attention, by definition (i.e., in order to localize a signal, we must pay attention to it). The fact that visual cues produced better localization performance than did 3-D sound cues suggests that visual cues play a greater role in focal attention. That is, visual cues may provide a more effective means for selecting one input and ignoring others than do 3-D sound cues.

An ancillary finding of the present study is that, given that the bursts were correctly recognized, 3-D sound cues produced no better localization of the bursts than did lateralization (time-intensity cues).

The notable lack of interaction between the rate of presentation and 3-D versus diotic presentation further reinforces the view that 3-D sound cues produce only a weak effect, if any, on focal attention. Focal attention is a limited-capacity mechanism. Therefore, increasing the rate of presentation of bursts should have produced a greater performance decrement in the 3-D condition than in the diotic condition if 3-D sound cues involve focal attention. It is, of course, possible that even the fast presentation rate in the present study was not sufficient to cause an overload of the limited-capacity focal attention mechanism.

An ecological rationale can be offered to explain why 3-D sound cues affect preattentive processing of auditory signals and visual cues do not. We learn from a very early age to associate the direction and distance of sound sources with certain spectral features and binaural differences. On the other hand, visual cues are not paired with sound source locations in any consistent manner. The associations of spectral features and interaural differences (i.e., HRTFs) with

TABLE II. Standard errors of estimate for comparing measured to predicted localization performance, and *F* tests comparing variances of estimate between conditions.

	Presentation method				
	3DF4	*3DS4*	*TIF4*	*1CF4Q*	*3DF4Q*
	Standard errors of estimate				
	0.082	0.092	0.091	0.037	0.038
Presentation method	*F ratios for comparisons of variances of estimate*				
3DS4	0.802				
TIF4	0.820	1.022			
1CF4Q	5.049*	6.296*	6.158*		
3DF4Q	4.592*	5.726*	5.601*	0.910	

Note: Asterisk denotes significant differences ($p < .05$ or better).

sound source locations are extremely well learned, and allow the listener to segregate auditory signals into parallel perceptual streams.

To summarize, the present study shows that imparting a 3-D quality to acoustic bursts enhances recognition performance. This finding is very similar to the cocktail party effect. However, in this case it is clear that the effects of 3-D cues were not due to release from masking, because the bursts were well separated in time. An alternative explanation is that 3-D cues produce a reorganization of perception, such that the bursts become perceptual "objects" and can be searched in parallel, without conscious attention (i.e., preattentively). The present study is consistent with the work of Clifton and her colleagues in suggesting that auditory information is represented in terms of the listeners' hypotheses about the nature of objects and events around them (e.g., Clifton and Freyman, Chapter 12, this volume.)

These findings have important implications for the design of VADs. They suggest that 3-D sound cues in VADs can do more than enhance focal attention. They may also produce a reorganization of perception that allows information to be processed in parallel, without conscious effort. Because many of the situations in which VADs may be applied involve high workload, any techniques that encourage preattentive, parallel processing could be extremely valuable. The present results also make it clear that 3-D sound cues provide a more effective means of enhancing performance in tasks involving the recognition of auditory bursts than do visual cues. Although the stimuli in this study were limited to sonar signals, it is likely that the findings will also apply to other types of auditory information, such as speech communications.

These findings suggest that attentional processes play an important role in determining the effectiveness of VADs. Heretofore, very few studies of VADs have considered attentional processes. Most recent studies of virtual and free-field auditory displays have used localization or detection as measures of sound source segregation (e.g., Divenyi and Oliver, 1989; Doll, *et al.*, 1986; Doll and Hanna, 1995; Doll, Hanna, and Russotti, 1992; Gilkey and Good, 1995; Gilkey, Good, and Ball, 1996; Loomis, Hebert, and Cicinelli, 1990; McKinley and Ericson, 1988; Perott and Saberi, 1990; Saberi, Dostal, Sadralodabai, Bull, and Perrott, 1991; Wightman and Kistler, 1989). The present results show that although segregation may be necessary for effective VADs, it does not capture all the factors that provide benefits with VADs. It is also important to optimize other aspects of information processing, especially perceptual organization and preattentive processing.

ACKNOWLEDGMENTS

This research was supported jointly by Naval Medical Research and Development Command Work Unit No. 65856NM0100.001-5001 and a Navy-ASEE Summer Faculty Fellowship held by the first author at the Naval Submarine Medical Research Laboratory. The authors are grateful to Lee Shapiro, Linda Merrill, and John Wojtowicz for their support. Thanks are also due to Dr. Tom Buell for his helpful suggestions. The opinions or assertions expressed here are not to be construed as official or reflecting the views of the U. S. Department of the Navy or Department of Defense.

REFERENCES

Begault, D. R., and Wenzel, E. M. (**1993**). "Headphone localization of speech," Hum. Factors **35**, 361–376.

Broadbent, D. E. (**1958**). *Perception and Communication* (Pergamon Press, London).

Carhart, R., Tillman, T. W., and Greetis, E. S. (**1969**). "Perceptual masking in multiple sound backgrounds," J. Acoust. Soc. Am. **46**, 694–703.

Cherry, E. C. (**1953**). "Some experiments on the recognition of speech with one and with two ears," J. Acoust. Soc. Am. **25**, 975–979.

Divenyi, P. L., and Oliver, S. K. (**1989**). "Resolution of steady-state sounds in simulated auditory space," J. Acoust. Soc. Am. **85**, 2042–2052.

Doll, T. J., Gerth, J. M., Engelman, W. R., and Folds, D. J. (**1986**). "Development of simulated directional audio for cockpit applications," Report No. AAMRL-TR-86-014 (Armstrong Laboratory, Wright-Patterson Air Force Base, OH).

Doll, T. J., and Hanna T. E. (**1995**). "Spatial and spectral release from masking in three-dimensional auditory displays," Hum. Factors **37**, 341–355.

Doll, T. J., Hanna, T. E., and Russotti, J. S. (**1992**). "Masking in three-dimensional auditory displays,"Hum. Factors **34**, 255–265.

Ebata, M., Sone, T., and Nimura, T. (**1967**). "Improvement of hearing ability by directional information," J. Acoust. Soc. Am. **43**, 289–297.

Gilkey, R. H., and Good, M. D. (**1995**). "Effects of frequency on free-field masking," Hum. Factors.

Gilkey, R. H., Good, M. D., and Ball, J. M. (**1996**). "A comparison of free-field masking for real and virtual sounds," J. Acoust. Soc. Am. (in revision).

Green, D. M., and Dai, H. (**1991**). "Notes and comment: Probability of being correct with 1 of M orthogonal signals," Percept. Psychophys. **49**, 100–101.

Hanna, T. E. (**1990**). "Contributions of envelope information to classification of brief sounds," NSMRL Report No. 1165 (Naval Submarine Medical Research Laboratory, Groton, CT).

Kahneman, D., and Henik, A. (**1981**). "Perceptual organization and attention," in *Perceptual Organization*, edited by M. Kubovy and J. R. Pomerantz (Lawrence Erlbaum Associates, Hillsdale, NJ), pp. 245–316.

Loomis, J. M., Hebert, C., and Cicinelli, J. G. (**1990**). "Active localization of virtual sounds," J. Acoust. Soc. Am. **88**, 1757–1764.

McKinley, R. L., and Ericson, M. A. (**1988**). "Digital synthesis of binaural auditory localization azimuth cues using headphones," J. Acoust. Soc. Am. Suppl. **83**, 18.

Moore, B. C. J. (**1982**). *An Introduction to the Psychology of Hearing* (Academic Press, New York), 2nd ed.

Moray, N. P. (**1959**). "Attention in dichotic listening: Affective cues and the influence of instructions," Q. J. Exp. Psychol. **11**, 56–60.

Myers, J. L. (**1972**). *Fundamentals of Experimental Design* (Allyn and Bacon, Boston), 2nd ed.

Neisser, U. (**1967**). *Cognitive Psychology* (Appleton-Century-Crofts, New York).

Nolte, L. W., and Jaarsma, D. (**1967**). "More on the detection of one of m orthogonal signals," J. Acoust. Soc. Am. **41**, 497–505.

Norman, D. A., and Bobrow, D. G. (**1975**). "On data-limited and resource-limited processes," Cognitive Psychol. **7**, 44–64.

Perrott, D. R., and Saberi, K. (**1990**). "Minimum audible angle thresholds for sources varying in both elevation and azimuth," J. Acoust. Soc. Am. **87**, 1728–1731.

Pick, H. L., Warren, D. H., and Hay, J. C. (**1969**). "Sensory conflict judgments of spatial direction," Percept. Psychophys. **6**, 203–205.

Plomp, R. (**1977**). "Acoustical aspects of cocktail parties," Acustica **38**, 186–191.

Plomp, R., and Mimpen, A. M. (**1981**). "Effect of the orientation of the speaker's head and the azimuth of the noise source on the speech-reception threshold for sentences," Acustica **48**, 325–328.

Saberi, K., Dostal, L., Sadralodabai, T., Bull, V., and Perrott, D. (**1991**). "Free-field release from masking," J. Acoust. Soc. Am. **90**, 1355–1370.

Thompson, P. O., and Webster, J. C. (**1963**). "The effect of talker-listener angle on word intelligibility," Acustica **13**, 319–323.

Treisman, A. (**1960**). "Contextual cues in selective listening," Q. J. Exp. Psychol. **12**, 242–248.

Treisman, A., and Gelade, G. (**1980**). "A feature-integration theory of attention," Cognitive Psychol. **12**, 97–136.

Wightman, F. L., and Kistler, D. J. (**1989**). "Headphone simulation of free-field listening II: Psychophysical validation," J. Acoust. Soc. Am. **85**, 868–878.

Yost, W. A. (**1991**). "Auditory image perception and analysis: The basis for hearing," Hear. Res. **56**, 8–18.

Part VI

Physiology of Spatial Hearing

Chapter 20

Neural Processing of Binaural Temporal Cues

Shigeyuki Kuwada, Ranjan Batra, and Douglas C. Fitzpatrick
Department of Anatomy, University of Connecticut Health Center, Farmington, Connecticut 06030

(Received June 1994; revised November 1994)

The first part of this chapter provides an overview of early anatomical and physiological studies and of conceptual models related to sound localization. The remainder is concerned with the processing of interaural time differences (ITDs), a major cue for locating sounds along the azimuth. We first focus on the circuitry and response properties of neurons in the superior olivary complex (SOC), the initial site of ITD processing. The ITD sensitivity of the neurons there is in accord with the basics of the coincidence model for neurons that receive excitatory inputs from both ears, a schema proposed by Jeffress in 1948. One modification to this model is the extension to cells that receive excitatory inputs from one ear and inhibitory inputs from the other ear. Such cells are also found in the SOC and show ITD sensitivity. We then discuss ITD processing in auditory structures above the SOC. Some response properties seen at the SOC are reflected at these higher sites, but several transformations are also evident. For example, ITD tuning appears to be progressively sharpened. This might be akin to narrowing of the receptive field for sound location. Neural circuits that could provide a sharpening mechanism for ITD tuning are described and future directions are discussed.

INTRODUCTION

The localization of external stimuli is a major function of the visual and auditory systems. The mechanisms by which this task is accomplished are both different and similar in the two systems. In the visual system, spatial information is mapped onto the receptor surface, the retina, and the receptor topography is preserved in the central nervous system. For this reason, damage to one eye does not severely impede the ability to locate an object in space. In contrast, the receptors in the auditory system are specialized to encode the frequency of the sound, not its location. Functions such as pitch and loudness perception can be performed by one ear alone, but accurate sound localization requires central comparisons of neural signals evoked by the acoustic inputs to the two ears. In a similar manner, some aspects of visual depth perception involve central comparison of neural signals evoked by a visual object creating disparate retinal images in the two eyes (Wagner and Frost, 1993).

Three cues are used by humans to localize a sound. For localizing sound sources along the vertical plane, spectral changes created by the pinnae are the primary cue (Butler and Belendiuk, 1977). For localizing sources along the horizontal plane (azimuth), interaural level differences (ILDs) and interaural time differences (ITDs) are the primary cues. Most investigations of sound localization have focused on the role of the azimuthal cues, ITD and ILD. According to the duplex theory first postulated by Lord Rayleigh (1907), the ILD resulting from the sound shadow cast by the head is the primary cue for localizing high-frequency tones, whereas the ITD between the arrival of the sound at the two ears is the cue used to localize low-frequency tones. The basis for this distinction is best understood in terms of the degree to which the head shadows sounds of different frequencies. For high-frequency signals, the wavelength is small compared to the size of the head, and the head becomes an obstacle to the propagating sound wave, creating an ILD. The magnitude of the ILD increases as the sound moves laterally along the azimuth. At lower frequencies, where the wavelength is larger than the size of the head, sound waves diffract around the head, and no ILD is created. At these frequencies, the ITD is the most important cue. Like the ILD, the magnitude of the ITD increases as the sound moves laterally.

Although the duplex theory is valid for pure tones, it does not hold for complex, high-frequency signals. Human listeners can detect changes in ITDs of the low-frequency envelopes of high-frequency sounds (Henning, 1974; McFadden and Pasanen, 1976; Nuetzel and Hafter, 1976). This finding is important because many naturally occurring sounds have envelopes. Thus, ITDs can be a cue for localizing both low- and high-frequency signals.

The intention of this chapter is first to provide a brief history of sound localization, especially those parts concerning neural organization and models of neural function. This is followed by a discussion of contemporary views on the neural mechanisms and circuitry underlying ITD processing in the mammalian nervous system. The primary focus is the processing of ITDs of low-frequency signals and envelopes of high-frequency signals. Comparisons of ITD sensitivity are made between structures along the ascending auditory pathway, followed by a discussion of the neural circuits that could account for changes in ITD processing. For other reviews see Erulkar (1972), Altman (1978), Brugge and Geisler (1980), Yin and Kuwada (1984), Aitkin (1986), Irvine (1986, 1992), Kuwada and Yin (1987), Yin and Chan (1988), Brugge (1992), Clarey, Barone, and Imig (1992), and Carr (1993).

I. HISTORICAL PERSPECTIVE ON SOUND LOCALIZATION

A. Early anatomical and physiological studies

According to Rosenzweig (1961), the first experiments on sound localization in humans were conducted by Giovanni Battista Venturi (1796) in Italy. Venturi was perhaps the first to recognize that interaural cues were important for localization and he proposed that differences in ILDs were the primary cue. David Ferrier (1890) in England began his studies in 1873 and was probably the first to discover that the spatial sound field was contralaterally represented in the cortex. He electrically stimulated the auditory cortex of dogs and noted that the animal moved its ear and often the head or eyes to the side contralateral to the stimulation. Luigi Luciani of Italy and his colleagues (Luciani and Tamburini, 1879; Luciani, 1884; Luciani and Seppilli, 1886) used systematic cortical ablations to extend Ferrier's findings. They found that after a unilateral cortical lesion animals could detect sounds in the contralateral sound field, but could not locate such sounds. In contrast, the animals could both detect and locate sounds ipsilateral to the lesioned site. These early findings have passed the test of time and the idea that sound location is represented contralaterally is well established for structures above the superior olivary complex (SOC; Neff and Diamond, 1958; Strominger and Oesterreich, 1970; Thompson and Masterton, 1978; Jenkins and Masterton, 1982; Kavanagh and Kelly, 1987).

The major auditory nuclei, their inputs, and their projections were relatively well known in the early 1900s. Ramon y Cajal (1909) provided an extensive description of these nuclei, their constituent cell types, and many of the interconnections. However, functional properties were poorly understood. For example, Cajal believed that the nuclei of the superior olive were acoustic reflex centers and that their primary projection was to the reticular formation where they made connections with motor nuclei. Malone (1923) reinforced this notion by reporting that cells in the superior olive were cytologically similar to motor neurons. Papez (1930) refuted the idea that the superior olive was a reflex center because all the fibers arising from the superior olive appeared to enter the lateral lemniscus and ascend to higher centers. Moreover, no fibers could be found entering the reticular formation, dorsal to the superior olive as postulated by Cajal. Viewed from a current perspective, both Cajal and Papez were correct. The main output of the superior olive enters the lateral lemniscus and synapses in higher auditory centers. However, some axons from the superior olive that enter the lateral lemniscus travel to the caudal pontine reticular nucleus, a structure implicated in the acoustic startle reflex (Lingenhohl and Friauf, 1994).

The nomenclature of the nuclei of the SOC has an interesting history. Cajal, based on the brainstem of the cat and rabbit, named the lateral S-shaped segment the superior olivary nucleus and the smaller, medial cell group the accessory nucleus. In contrast to these species, however, primates were found to have an ill-defined lateral group and a prominent medial group, thus posing a problem with Cajal's terminology (Stotler, 1953). Consequently, the lateral S-shaped segment was named the lateral superior olive (LSO) and the medial segment became the medial superior olive (MSO).

Direct inputs from the cochlear nucleus to the ipsilateral LSO were described over 100 years ago (von Monakow, 1890; Held, 1893; Cajal, 1909). Indirect inputs from the cochlear nucleus to the contralateral LSO follow a two-step pathway: cochlear nucleus to contralateral medial nucleus of the trapezoid body (MNTB) and MNTB to ipsilateral LSO. The first leg of this pathway was described by Held (1893). The second leg, MNTB to LSO, was inferred by Rasmussen

(1946) based on degeneration after lesions of the trapezoid body. The tracts from cochlear nucleus to MNTB and from MNTB to LSO have therefore been referred to as Held's tract and Rasmussen's tract, respectively (Glendenning, Hutson, Nudo, and Masterton, 1985). Stotler (1953) was the first to show that MSO neurons were innervated by the axons arising in the cochlear nuclei of both sides (see Yin, Joris, Smith, and Chan, Chapter 21, this volume).

B. Early models

Although it was established rather early that the cortex is important for sound localization (Ferrier, 1890; Luciani, 1884), and that ITDs are used for locating low frequencies and ILDs for locating high frequencies (Thompson, 1878; Rayleigh, 1907), the development of explicit neural models of sound localization is relatively recent. In 1930 von Bekesy (see von Bekesy, 1960) proposed a neural scheme whereby the inputs from both ears converged onto a group of cells. Localization was signaled by the proportion of cells excited by a particular ear. The impulses that arrived first and the number of active fibers signalled the ear that was stimulated first and with the greatest intensity. Woodworth (1938) proposed a similar model, and van Bergeijk (1962, 1964) refined the ideas of von Bekesy and Woodward into a neural model using Stotler's (1953) anatomical finding that the MSO received inputs from both cochlear nuclei. Contrary to our present knowledge (see Fig. 2A), van Bergeijk's model assumed that the contralateral input to the MSO was excitatory and the ipsilateral input was inhibitory. In van Bergeijk's (1964) words:

> If excitation gets there first, the neuron will be excited, and inhibition cannot supersede. Conversely, if inhibition arrives first, subsequent excitation is ineffective, and the neuron remains inactive. The input fibers are assumed to be graded with respect to sensitivity. The wave of activity arriving at the accessory nuclei from each ear, then, will have a certain width (number of active fibers). The wave will penetrate for a certain length into each of the nuclei, until it "collides" with the wave from the other ear, travelling in the opposite direction. The Δt between the ears determines how far each of the excitatory waves penetrates in the respective nuclei, ΔI determines how much wider one wave is than the other. Thus, we define in the model, two rectangular areas whose length are determined by Δt, and whose widths are determined by ΔI. The surfaces thus defined are proportional to the number of active cells in each nucleus. The model then finally assumes that some higher center counts the active cells in each nucleus and on the basis of the difference in activity decides whether the image is in the center (no difference) or off to one side. (p. 8)

Although early single-unit studies (Galambos, Schwartzkopff, and Rupert, 1959; Hall, 1965) provided some support for van Bergeijk's model, the notion that the MSO receives excitatory inputs primarily from the contralateral ear and inhibitory inputs primarily from the ipsilateral ear, as well as the idea of count comparison as a neural mechanism for localization, has not received strong experimental support.

Jeffress (1948) proposed a neural circuit quite different in principle from those of von Bekesy, Woodward, and van Bergeijk. He postulated a group of cells that received excitatory inputs from both ears. Each cell responded optimally when the inputs from each side arrived simultaneously. He conceived that each pair of inputs would be matched in conduction time to a particular interaural delay, i.e., the axons from each side could act as delay lines (see Yin *et al.*, Chapter 21, this volume). For example, if both ears were stimulated simultaneously and the ipsilateral input arrived some 100 μs before the contralateral input, then this cell would be maximally activated by delaying the signal to the ipsilateral ear by 100 μs relative to stimulation of the contralateral ear. This is achieved by moving the sound source to a position in the contralateral field. An array of such neurons, each tuned to a different ITD, could code for different locations in space. He also felt that a similar circuit might process ILDs, because stimulus intensity affects neural latency. Jeffress reasoned that an obvious location for such interactions would be the SOC, but based on Kemp and Robinson's (1937) finding that binaural interactions were not evident in the lateral lemniscus, he suggested that the locus might be in a structure above the lateral lemniscus, perhaps the medial geniculate body (MGB). In a later article titled "Medial Geniculate Body—A Disavowal," Jeffress (1958) acknowledged his error and postulated that the interactions occur in the MSO. Rosenzweig (1961) provided some evidence that the rudiments of Jeffress's model were proposed by Bowlker as early as 1908:

> We may suppose that the transmission of sound impulses through some specialized part of the auditory apparatus or brain takes a definite time from each ear, and that the point where the impulses meet is the focus that gives rise to the sensation of a sound image (p. 327)

As discussed by Yin *et al.* (Chapter 21, this volume), the neural mechanisms and circuitry for processing ITDs in the SOC are surprisingly close to those postulated by the Jeffress model.

II. ONSET AND ONGOING ITDs

Before proceeding further, it is important to distinguish between two types of ITD, onset and ongoing. The onset ITD is the initial difference produced by the sound reaching the ears at different times, whereas the ongoing ITD is that produced by ongoing differences in the pattern of pressure variations at the two ears. Figure 1 illustrates the response of a neuron that was sensitive to ongoing ITDs, but not onset ITDs. In one stimulus condition, a pure-tone stimulus to one ear was systematically delayed relative to that to the other ear, creating both onset and ongoing ITDs (filled circles). In another condition, the ongoing delay was adjusted to remain constant, independent of the gating delay (open squares). Thus, this second stimulus contained only onset ITDs. The stimulus with both onset and ongoing cues resulted in a series of peaks and troughs as a function of ITD. This cyclic delay function has a period equal to that of the stimulating tone (1300 Hz, 769 μs). In contrast, the response to the stimulus with only onset ITDs showed no ITD sensitivity. This indicates that the neuron's sensitivity was to the ongoing ITDs.

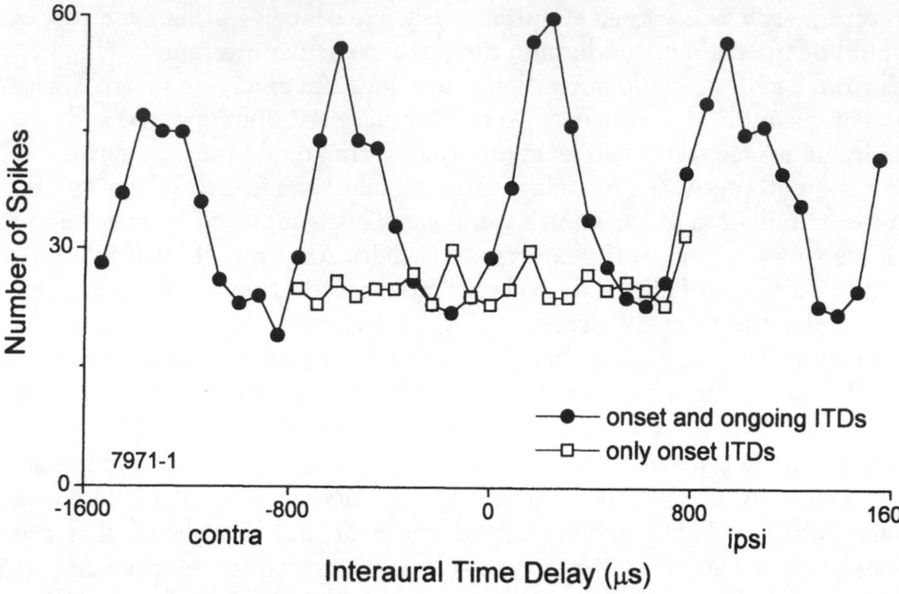

FIG. 1. A neuron sensitive to ongoing ITDs, but not onset ITDs. Tones were presented to both ears via a sealed sound system. When the stimulus contained both onset and ongoing ITDs (filled symbols), the response varied cyclically with the interaural delay. When only onset ITDs were varied and the ongoing ITDs were held constant (accomplished by controlling the starting phase of the tone), no variations in the response occurred (open symbols). Each point reflects the responses to 4 presentations of a 500-ms tone, repeated every 800 ms (1300 Hz, 60 dB SPL). (After Kuwada and Yin, 1983, Fig. 6A.)

The neural evidence for sensitivity to ongoing ITDs is abundant and has been observed at all levels of the auditory pathway [e.g., SOC: Goldberg and Brown, 1969b; Moushegian, Rupert, and Gidda, 1975; Crow, Rupert, and Moushegian, 1978; Langford, 1984; Yin and Chan, 1990; dorsal nucleus of the lateral lemniscus (DNLL): Brugge, Anderson, and Aitkin, 1970; inferior colliculus (IC): Rose, Gross, Geisler, and Hind, 1966; Geisler, Rhode, and Hazelton, 1969; Stillman, 1971; Kuwada, Yin, and Wickesberg, 1979; Kuwada, Stanford, and Batra, 1987; Yin and Kuwada, 1983; Spitzer and Semple, 1993; auditory thalamus: Aitkin and Webster, 1972; Aitkin, 1973; Ivarsson, De Ribaupierre, and De Ribaupierre, 1988; Stanford, Kuwada, and Batra, 1992; and auditory cortex: Brugge, Dubrovsky, Aitkin, and Anderson, 1969; Reale and Brugge, 1990]. Neural sensitivity to onset ITDs has been studied by only a few investigators (e.g., Harnischfeger, 1980; Caird and Klinke, 1983, 1987; Kelly and Phillips, 1991). Such investigations are complicated by the fact that even transient stimuli can give rise to ongoing ITDs (Carney and Yin, 1989). For example, a brief click can evoke a synchronous discharge in auditory nerve fibers tuned to low frequencies, presumably because brief sounds can "ring" the basilar membrane. The discharge to transient sounds is often synchronized to the fiber's best frequency (Kiang, Watanabe, Thomas, and Clark, 1965).

Psychophysical measurements show that in humans the ongoing ITDs are much more potent than onset ITDs in determining the position of a lateralized image (Tobias and Schubert, 1959; Yost, 1977; Buell, Trahiotis, and Bernstein, 1991).

III. CONTEMPORARY PERSPECTIVES ON ITD PROCESSING IN THE SOC

A. Anatomy of the SOC

The anatomy of the binaural pathways presented next is an overview of the major nuclei that play a role in ITD processing. For more detailed treatments of this topic, see reviews by Harrison and Feldman (1970), Cant (1992), Oliver and Heurta (1992), Ryugo (1992), Schwartz (1992), and Winer (1992).

A schematic representation of the principal nuclei involved in processing ITDs from the cochlear nucleus to the cortex is shown in Fig. 2. The SOC is the site where the outputs of the two cochlear nuclei first interact. This interaction occurs in two major nuclei: the MSO and LSO.

The MSO is shaped like a sausage with its long axis in the rostrocaudal direction. It has a disproportionately large area devoted to low frequencies (Osen, 1969; Guinan, Norris, and Guinan, 1972). Low to high frequencies are represented in the dorsoventral axis, and thus a horizontal slice through its long axis would contain an isofrequency band.

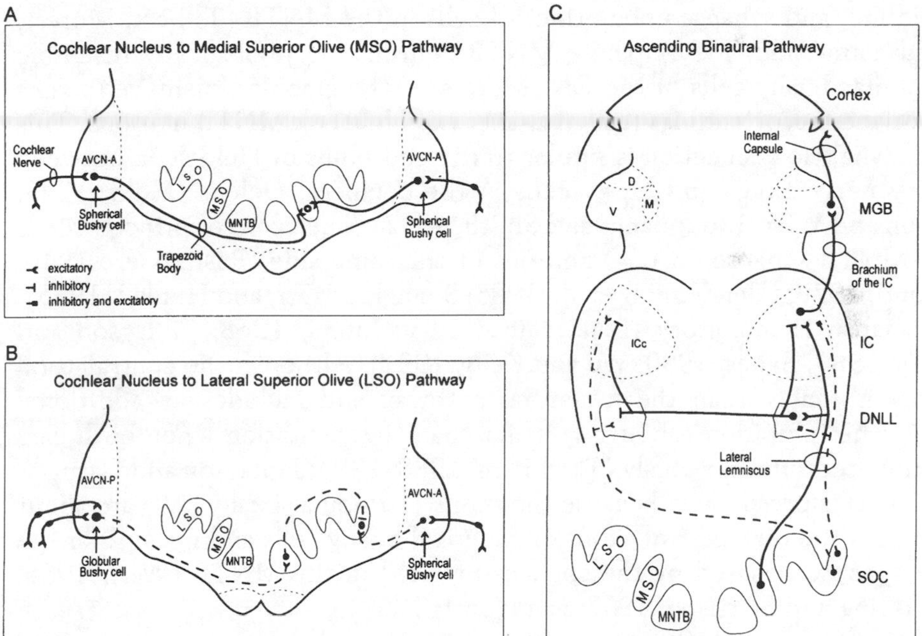

FIG. 2. Anatomy of the ascending, binaural pathway involved in processing cues for ITDs. (A) Schema of pathways from the two cochlear nuclei to medial superior olive (MSO). Projections are depicted as solid lines. (B) Schema of pathways from the two cochlear nuclei to the lateral superior olive (LSO). Projections are depicted as dashed lines. (C) Schema of the ascending binaural pathway from the superior olivary complex (SOC) to the primary auditory cortex. Projections from the LSO to the DNLL and inferior colliculus (IC) are shown as dashed lines, and other projections are depicted as solid lines. Other abbreviations: AVCN-A (anterior part of the anteroventral cochlear nucleus); AVCN-P (posterior part of AVCN); MNTB (medial nucleus of the trapezoid body); ICc (central nucleus of the IC); MGB (medial geniculate body); D (dorsal); V (ventral); M (medial).

The pathway from the cochlear nucleus to the MSO is diagrammed in the upper left panel (Fig. 2A). The spherical bushy cells located in the anterior part of the anteroventral division of the cochlear nucleus (AVCN-A) receive large calyceal-type endings (end bulbs of Held) from auditory nerve fibers. This synapse appears to faithfully transmit the temporal information conveyed by auditory nerve fibers to spherical bushy cells (Pfeiffer, 1966; Kiang, Morest, Godfrey, Guinan, and Kane, 1973; Morest, Kiang, Kane, Guinan, and Godfrey, 1973; Rhode, Oertel, and Smith, 1983). The axons of spherical bushy cells leave the cochlear nucleus and enter the ventral acoustic stria (trapezoid body) (Harrison and Warr, 1962; Cant and Casseday, 1986) to innervate both MSOs. This circuitry fits one of the features of the Jeffress model, namely, that neurons in the MSO receive similar innervation from both sides.

The pathway from the cochlear nucleus to the LSO is diagrammed in the lower left panel (Fig. 2B). The ipsilateral pathway is similar to that for the MSO, while the contralateral pathway is different. Axons of the spherical bushy cells in AVCN-A travel via the trapezoid body to synapse in the LSO of the same side (Harrison and Warr, 1962; Warr, 1966). The contralateral input begins with the axons of globular bushy cells in the posterior part of the contralateral AVCN (AVCN-P). These axons enter the trapezoid body, cross the midline, and synapse upon principal cells in the MNTB (Tolbert, Morest, and Yurgelun-Todd, 1982). These MNTB neurons morphologically resemble the globular bushy cells of the CN. Moreover, the globular bushy cell axons make calyceal-type endings (called chalices of Held) on MNTB neurons. This type of synaptic connection is similar to the end bulbs of Held seen between auditory nerve fibers and bushy cells in the cochlear nucleus (Held, 1893; Harrison and Warr, 1962; Banks and Smith, 1992). The axons of principal cells in the MNTB synapse on LSO neurons of the same side (Rasmussen, 1946; Elverland, 1978; Glendenning et al., 1985; Spangler, Warr, and Henkel, 1985). This synapse is inhibitory (Boudreau and Tsuchitani, 1968; Finlayson and Caspary, 1989; Sanes, 1990; Wu and Kelly, 1991). Although the contralateral pathway is longer than the ipsilateral pathway and includes an additional synapse, the inhibition can arrive earlier than the excitation when both ears are stimulated simultaneously (Tsuchitani, 1988, 1994; Finlayson and Caspary, 1989). This is presumably because the axons of globular bushy cells are about three times the diameter of axons of spherical bushy cells and because of the secure synapse ensured by the chalices of Held in the MNTB (Warr, 1966, 1972; Irving and Harrison, 1967; van Noort, 1969).

In the LSO, low to high frequencies are represented along a lateral to medial gradient and the area devoted to high frequencies is disproportionately large (Tsuchitani and Boudreau, 1966; Guinan *et al.*, 1972). This bias toward high frequencies is the reason that the LSO has traditionally been considered a center for the initial processing of ILDs. However, its circuitry has many of the elements of the MSO circuit, that is, bushy cells and calyceal-type synapses, suggesting that the LSO circuitry is also designed to process timing information. Consistent with this reasoning, low-frequency cells sensitive to ITDs in the fine structure (e.g., of tones) and high-frequency cells sensitive to ITDs in envelopes have been encountered in the LSO (Caird and Klinke, 1983; Joris and Yin, 1995; Finlayson and Caspary, 1991; Kuwada and Batra, 1991).

The circuitry of the MSO and LSO is more complex than that reflected in Figs. 2A and 2B. In addition to the excitatory inputs from both sides (Fig. 2A), there is also evidence for inhibitory inputs to the MSO neurons from the lateral and medial nuclei of the trapezoid body (Schwartz, 1984; Saint Marie, Ostapoff, and Morest, 1989; Kuwabara and Zook, 1991; Brunso-Bechtold, Henkel, and Linville, 1992; Cant and Hyson, 1992). Electrical stimulation involving these inhibitory tracts evoked inhibition in nearly all cells in the gerbil MSO, and it was usually able to block synaptically evoked action potentials (Grothe and Sanes, 1993). Inhibitory inputs from each side were first proposed in a neural model of ITD processing to account for the observation that for many neurons the discharge rate at unfavorable ITDs falls below the firing rate for monaural stimulation alone (Sujaku, Kuwada, and Yin, 1981; Sujaku, 1984).

The LSO circuit (Fig. 2B) has, in addition, a small, direct projection from the contralateral cochlear nucleus to the LSO (Goldberg and Brown, 1969a; Warr, 1972, 1982; Glendenning *et al.*, 1985). The function of this direct projection is unknown, but if it is excitatory, an LSO neuron receiving such inputs might take on MSO properties.

B. A neural schema of ITD processing in the SOC

In the following, we present a neural schema, based on the Jeffress model, to explain the ITD sensitivity of MSO and LSO neurons. An essential assumption is that the inputs from each ear convey the temporal patterns of the corresponding sound waveform. Such temporal preservation has been observed in the auditory nerve fibers. When the sound is a low-frequency tone, the discharge of a fiber is synchronized to a particular phase of the tone. This response feature is called "phase-locking." Auditory nerve fibers phase-lock only to frequencies up to ~2500 Hz in cats (Johnson, 1980; Weiss and Rose, 1988). Auditory nerve fibers cannot phase-lock to higher frequencies, but can do so to the envelopes of high-frequency tones if they are amplitude modulated (e.g., Joris and Yin, 1992). Envelope following in cats extends to ~1400 Hz (Joris and Yin, 1992).

The temporal features of a sound are conveyed to the SOC by the circuitry described in the previous section (Figs. 2A and B). The phase-locking of a neuron in the MSO of a cat to a 700-Hz tone is illustrated in Fig. 3A, which is adapted from Galambos *et al.* (1959). It is perhaps the first demonstration of phase-locking in the SOC. Figure 3B depicts the phase-locking of an LSO neuron in the rabbit to the 200-Hz envelope of a sinusoidally amplitude-modulated tone delivered to the ipsilateral ear. Note that an action potential does not occur for every cycle of the envelope. This is a common feature for both low-frequency tones and envelopes (Moushegian, Rupert, and Langford, 1967; Rose, Brugge, Anderson, and Hind, 1967; Frisina, Smith, and Chamberlin, 1990a, 1990b). Thus, both the MSO and LSO receive information about the temporal pattern of the stimulating waveforms, a necessary ingredient for ITD processing.

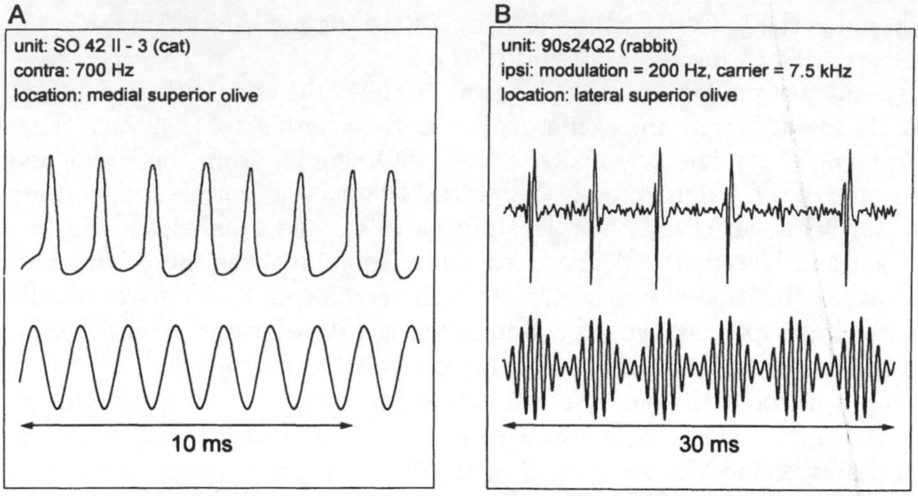

FIG. 3. Example of phase-locked responses to a low-frequency pure tone and to the envelope of a sinusoidally amplitude modulated (SAM) tone. (A) An extracellular recording from a neuron in the MSO of the cat that fired synchronously to each cycle of a 700-Hz tone. Intensity: –115 dB (re: 0.1 V). (B) An extracellular recording from a neuron in or near the LSO of the unanesthetized rabbit that fired synchronously to the envelope of a SAM tone delivered to the ipsilateral ear (modulation = 200 Hz, modulation depth = 80%; carrier = 7500 Hz, 60 dB SPL). (Adapted from Galambos *et al.*, 1959, Fig. 5.)

Figure 4 schematically illustrates how a model MSO neuron that receives excitatory inputs from each side might process ITDs. The inputs from the ipsilateral and contralateral cochlear nuclei convey phase-locked discharges. For purposes of the model, these discharges can be phase-locked either to low-frequency tones or to low-frequency envelopes of high-frequency signals. Figure 4A depicts the condition where the ITD is adjusted such that the phase-locked action potentials from both sides (left traces) arrive simultaneously at the MSO neuron. When only one input is active (middle traces), each action potential produces a subthreshold (arrow) excitatory postsynaptic potential (EPSP) in the binaural neuron. Under binaural conditions the EPSPs from the two inputs sum, resulting in a depolarization that exceeds the neuron's discharge threshold (right traces). Thus, this binaural cell fires maximally when the inputs arrive simultaneously. When the ITD is adjusted such that the phase-locked action potentials from each side arrive exactly out of phase, the EPSPs created by each input do not sum and the neuron fires minimally or not at all (Fig. 4B). Thus, the cell acts like a coincidence detector.

Let us now examine the response of a model LSO neuron that receives excitatory input from the ipsilateral side and inhibitory input from the contralateral side. In contrast to the model MSO neuron, when the phase-locked inputs arrive coincidentally at the LSO neuron (Fig. 4C, left traces), the inhibitory input cancels the excitatory input and the response is maximally suppressed (Fig. 4C, right traces). When the inputs arrive out of phase (Fig. 4D, left traces), the EPSPs are not canceled, creating the condition for an excitatory discharge. To summarize, coincident input onto MSO neurons results in maximal excitation, whereas such input onto LSO neurons creates maximal suppression.

Because ITD-sensitive neurons show a sequence of peaks and troughs when the ITD is varied (Fig. 1), it is not possible from this single delay curve to determine whether coincidence evokes maximum excitation or suppression. However, this matter can be resolved by measuring responses at several stimulus frequencies. Figure 5 illustrates the responses of model MSO and LSO neurons to different stimulating frequencies. For the model MSO neuron (Fig. 5A, left panel), responses at different stimulating frequencies all show a maximum at a common ITD, in this case, when the ipsilateral stimulus is delayed by 200 μs relative to the contralateral stimulus. In contrast to the MSO neuron, the ITD functions for the model LSO neuron display a minimum at a common ITD, in this case, when the ipsilateral stimulus is delayed by 200 μs (Fig. 5B, left panel).

Rose *et al.* (1966) coined the phrase "characteristic delay" (CD) after observing that low-frequency neurons in the IC discharged maximally or minimally at a common ITD, irrespective of the stimulating frequency. They argued that the CDs reflected a difference in the anatomical delays required to activate the binaural cell. By offsetting the difference in anatomical delays with an ITD, the

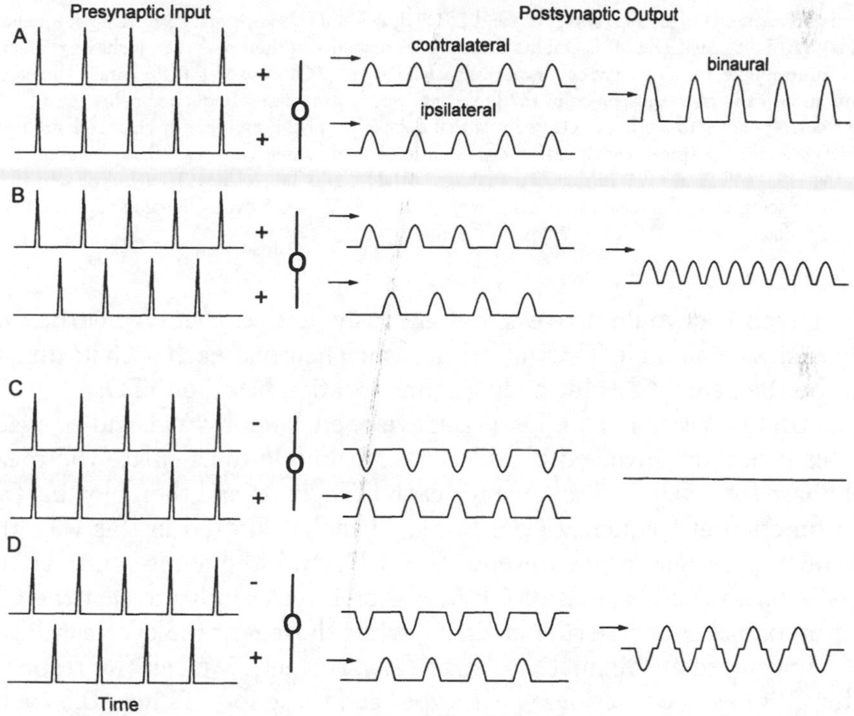

FIG. 4. Neural schema of ITD processing for model MSO and LSO neurons. The MSO neuron (A and B) receives excitatory (+) inputs from each side, and the LSO neuron (C and D) receives excitatory inputs from the ipsilateral side and inhibitory inputs (–) from the contralateral side. Left column: Schematic of phase-locked action potentials evoked by contralateral (upper trace) and ipsilateral (lower trace) stimulation. Depicted are action potentials that arrive in-phase (A and C) or out-of-phase (B and D) at the model cell. Middle column: Postsynaptic potentials resulting from contralateral and ipsilateral inputs. Right column: Summed postsynaptic responses to binaural stimulation. Threshold for action potentials is indicated by arrows and is lower in the LSO cell (C and D) than for the MSO cell (A and B). When inputs arrive coincident in time (A and C), the cell with only excitatory inputs (A) discharges maximally, whereas the cell with an inhibitory input (C) does not discharge at all.

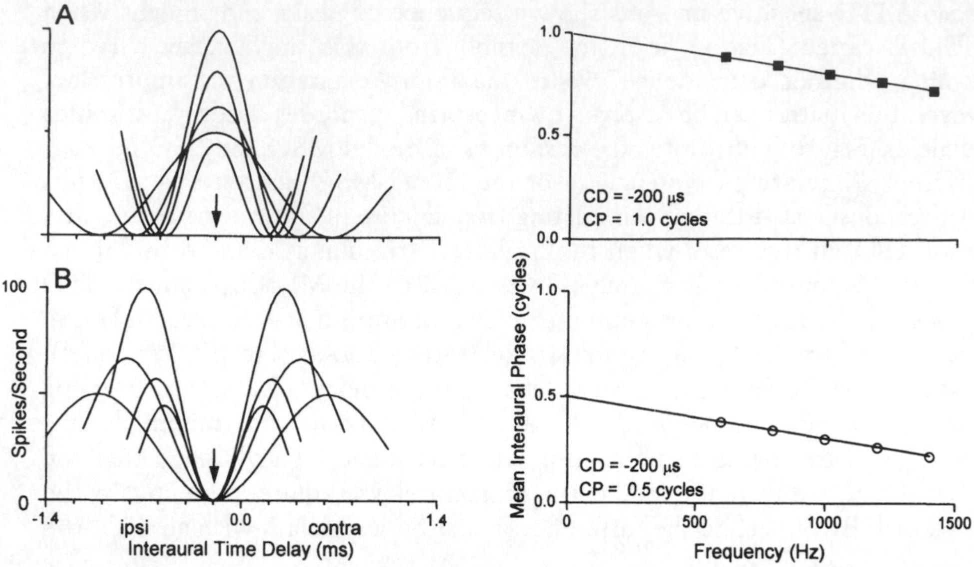

FIG. 5. Simulated responses of an ideal MSO (A) and LSO (B) cell to ITDs at several stimulating frequencies (600–1400 Hz). (A) Left panel: The MSO cell has delay curves that align at their peak, i.e., it shows peak-type sensitivity. In this example, the alignment occurs at ipsilateral delay of 200 μs (arrow). Right panel: The plot of the mean interaural phase of the responses in the left panel versus stimulating frequency is linear and has a negative slope corresponding to a CD of 200-μs ipsilateral delay. The phase intercept or characteristic phase (CP) = 1.0 cycles; a value consistent with a peak-type response. (B) Left panel: The ideal LSO cell has the same properties as the MSO cell except that its delay curves align at the troughs, i.e., it shows trough-type sensitivity. Right panel: Same features as the ideal MSO cell except that the CP = 0.5 cycles, a value consistent with trough-type ITD-sensitivity.

inputs from each ear would arrive simultaneously at the binaural neuron and maximally excite or inhibit it. Thus, an array of such neurons, each with its unique CD, could be the neural basis for coding sound location based on ITDs.

The quantitative analysis of CDs was developed later by Yin and Kuwada (1983). This procedure involved using vector arithmetic to calculate the mean interaural phase for maximal discharge for each ITD curve, and then plotting this phase as a function of frequency (Fig. 5, right panels). Plotted in this way, the slope of the regression line represents the CD, and the *y*-intercept is the characteristic phase (CP). Values of CP near 0 or 1 cycles indicate that the CD occurred at maximal discharge (upper right), while those near 0.5 cycles indicate that the CD occurred at minimal discharge (lower panel). We call the response patterns for CPs near 0 or 1 cycles "peak-type" and those for CPs near 0.5 cycles "trough-type" (Batra, Kuwada, and Stanford, 1993).

How realistic are the responses suggested by the neural schema (Figs. 4 and 5)? At the first stage of binaural processing, that is, the SOC, the predictions are quite accurate. The early studies established that neurons near or within the MSO could display ITD sensitivity to dichotic clicks (Galambos *et al.*, 1959; Moushegian, Rupert, and Whitcomb, 1964a; Hall, 1965) and to dichotic tones (Moushegian, Rupert, and Whitcomb, 1964b; Moushegian *et al.*, 1967). A major breakthrough regarding ITD mechanisms was provided by Rose *et al.* (1966), who, by their demonstration that neurons in the IC had CDs, were the first to provide physiological evidence for the Jeffress delay line. Another major breakthrough was the demonstration by Goldberg and Brown (1969b) that neurons in the MSO acted like the Jeffress coincidence detectors; that is, the phase at which a neuron responded to stimulation of each ear could be used to accurately predict the ITD at which the neuron fired maximally. Yin and Chan (1990) provided the most extensive data on ITD-sensitive neurons in the MSO (also see Yin *et al.*, Chapter 21, this volume). Consistent with the neural schema, they showed that MSO neurons act like coincidence detectors and display a CD at maximal discharge. Moreover, most of the neurons were excited by monaural stimulation of either ear (see Fig. 5A). The distribution of CDs was biased toward ipsilateral delays, a finding consistent with the known anatomical arrangement where the ipsilateral input to the MSO has a shorter path length than the contralateral input. Such delays would be produced by sounds in the contralateral field. This bias toward ipsilateral delays is also suggested in the recordings from the SOC of kangaroo rats (Crow *et al.*, 1978). Yin and Chan (1990) also provided the first demonstration of a high-frequency cell in the MSO that was sensitive to the ITDs of envelopes. Consistent with the neural schema, this cell was excited by monaural stimulation of either ear and discharged maximally at the same ITD across modulation frequencies.

For neurons in the LSO that are tuned to high frequencies, ITD sensitivity has been demonstrated to the envelopes of SAM tones in both the cat (Joris and Yin, 1995) and the rabbit (Kuwada and Batra, 1991). Consistent with the neural schema for LSO neurons (Figs. 4C, 4D, and 5B), they have minimum discharge at a common ITD across modulation frequencies.

The first study to show ITD sensitivity in the LSO to low-frequency tones was that by Caird and Klinke (1983). Finlayson and Caspary (1991) extended this finding by demonstrating that most low-frequency neurons in the lateral limb of the LSO are sensitive to ITDs. We have also recorded from low-frequency neurons in or near the lateral limb of the LSO that have minimal discharge at a common ITD across frequencies (Kuwada and Batra, 1991, and personal observations).

IV. PROCESSING OF ITDs AT LEVELS ABOVE THE SOC

A. Anatomy

The anatomical circuitry of the primary sites of binaural interaction, that is, the MSO and LSO, was described earlier (Figs. 2A and 2B). Here we describe the pathways by which ITD sensitivity is carried from the SOC to the midbrain, thalamus, and cortex.

The MSO projects to the ipsilateral inferior colliculus (IC; Fig. 2C) (Roth, Aitkin, Andersen, and Merzenich, 1978; Adams, 1979; Glendenning and Masterton, 1983). The MSO projections terminate in the central nucleus of the IC (ICc; Rockel and Jones, 1973; Morest and Oliver, 1984). The MSO projection is thought to be excitatory (Schwartz and Yu, 1986; Helfert, Bonneau, Wenthold, and Altshuler, 1989; Glendenning, Baker, Hutson, and Masterton, 1992). In contrast, the LSO projects almost equally to both the ipsilateral and contralateral ICc (Roth *et al.*, 1978; Adams, 1979; Glendenning and Masterton, 1983; Henkel and Brunso-Bechtold, 1993). The contralateral LSO projection is thought to be excitatory, while the ipsilateral projection is probably mixed; that is, some neurons may be excitatory, while others may be inhibitory (Saint Marie *et al.*, 1989; Glendenning *et al.*, 1992).

There appears to be a mediolateral gradient of LSO neurons projecting ipsilaterally or contralaterally to the IC. However, the direction of this gradient varies with the species examined. Glendenning *et al.* (1992) found that in the cat most neurons in the medial limb (high-frequency part) of the LSO project to the contralateral ICc, whereas most neurons in the lateral limb (low-frequency part) project to the ipsilateral ICc. In the ferret, however, the medial limb of the LSO projects predominantly to the ipsilateral ICc and the lateral limb to the contralateral ICc (Henkel and Brunso-Bechtold, 1993).

Information regarding ITDs can also reach the ICc from other sources. Both the MSO and LSO provide inputs to the DNLL that appear similar to those they send to the ICc (Glendenning, Brunso-Bechtold, Thompson, and Masterton, 1981; Shneiderman, Oliver, and Henkel, 1988). Almost all neurons in the DNLL are immunoreactive to γ-aminobutyric acid (GABA) and glutamic acid decarboxylase (Adams and Mugnaini, 1984; Penney, Conley, Schmechel, and Diamond, 1984) and thus are likely to provide inhibitory inputs to their projection sites. The major targets of the DNLL are the contralateral DNLL and the ICc of both sides (Shneiderman *et al.*, 1988; Hutson, Glendenning, and Masterton, 1991; Li and Kelly, 1992; Faingold, Anderson, and Randall, 1993). Thus, neurons in the ICc can receive ascending inputs from ITD-sensitive neurons in the ipsilateral MSO, from the LSO of both sides, and from the DNLL of both sides. In addition, neurons in the ICc may receive ITD-sensitive inputs from the contralateral IC via the commissure of the IC and also by intrinsic connections within an IC. Intrinsic sources appear to be substantial, because most, if not all, neurons in the IC have extensive intrinsic axon collaterals (Oliver, Kuwada, Yin, Haberly, and Henkel, 1991). Finally, descending influences may also provide the IC with ITD information. The primary auditory cortex provides a direct input to the dorsal cortex of the IC (Diamond, Jones, and Powell, 1969; Rockel and Jones, 1973; Andersen, Snyder, and Merzenich, 1980), and ITD-sensitive neurons have been recorded in the dorsal cortex (Yin and Chan, 1988; Oliver *et al.*, 1991).

The IC projects to the auditory thalamus via the brachium of the IC. The auditory thalamus consists of the MGB and the lateral part of the posterior thalamic group. The MGB is comprised of ventral, dorsal, and medial divisions (Morest, 1964). Although all divisions receive some inputs from the ICc, the ventral division receives its primary input from the ipsilateral ICc in the form of strong, topographic projections (Moore and Goldberg, 1963; Calford and Aitkin, 1983; Oliver, 1984). The ICc also provides the primary input to the lateral part of the posterior thalamic group (Moore and Goldberg, 1963; Tarlov and Moore, 1966; Andersen, Roth, Aitkin, and Merzenich, 1980; Kudo and Niimi, 1980; Phillips and Irvine, 1983; Imig and Morel, 1985). The posterior group and the ventral MGB have reciprocal connections with the primary auditory cortex. Thus, corticofugal projections could help to shape the ITD sensitivity of neurons in the auditory thalamus.

B. Preservation of ITD sensitivity at higher auditory stations

All four ITD response types (low and high frequency; peak types and trough types) predicted by the model of ITD sensitivity (Figs. 4 and 5) and seen in the SOC are also present in the IC (Yin and Kuwada, 1984; Yin, Kuwada, and Sujaku, 1984; Kuwada *et al.*, 1987; Stanford *et al.*, 1992; Batra *et al.*, 1993). An example of each type, for neurons in the IC, is shown in Fig. 6. For the sake of comparison, only the ITD functions between 400 and 1000 Hz (tone or modulation frequency) are displayed (left column). The middle column is the composite curve derived by averaging the ITD functions on the left. The right column displays the plots of mean interaural phase of the response versus stimulus frequency (see Fig. 4) using all the tested frequencies. Note that for peak-type neurons (Figs. 6A and

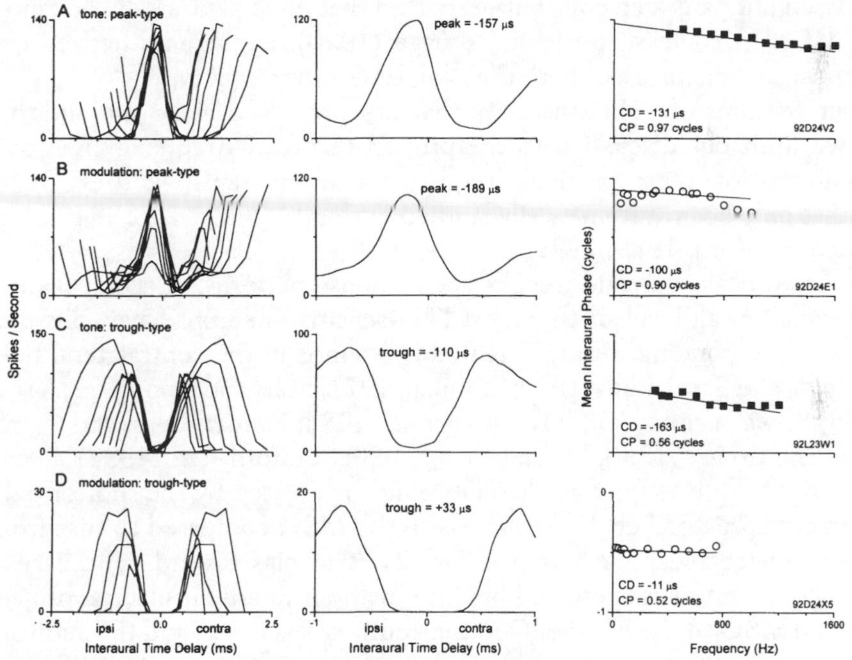

FIG. 6. Examples of four types of ITD sensitivity observed in the inferior colliculus of the unanesthetized rabbit: peak-type (A, B) and trough-type (C, D) evoked by low-frequency pure tones (A, C) and envelopes of high-frequency SAM tones (B, carrier = 4500 Hz; D, carrier = 4000 Hz). Left column: Delay curves plotted on a common ITD axis. To facilitate comparisons between response types, only ITD curves evoked by frequencies between 400 and 1000 Hz (pure tone or modulation frequency) are displayed. The curves were generated by delivering slightly disparate frequencies, that is, tones or envelopes that differ by 1 Hz to the two ears. This produces a continuous cyclic variation in the interaural phase difference at a rate of 1 Hz (see Kuwada *et al.*, 1979). Middle column: Composite curves generated by averaging the ITD curves in the left column. The peak and trough delays were calculated by fitting a parabolic arc to the top (peak) or bottom (trough) 30% of the composite curve. Right column: Plots of mean interaural phase of the response versus stimulating frequency. The line is a weighted, least-squares fit to all frequencies tested that evoked ITD-sensitive responses. The slope of the line is the characteristic delay (CD), and the phase intercept is the characteristic phase (CP).

6B) the peak widths for pure tone and envelope sensitivity are very similar (Batra *et al.*, 1993). An interesting parallel to this finding is that human acuity for detecting changes in the ITDs of low-frequency tones is similar to that for ITDs of low-frequency envelopes of SAM tones with high-frequency carriers (Henning, 1974). The troughs of trough-type neurons (Figs. 6C and 6D) are wider than the peaks of peak-type neurons (Batra *et al.*, 1993). We have also observed the same four types in the DNLL (personal observations) and auditory thalamus (Stanford *et al.*, 1992, and personal observations). The presence of the four types of ITD sensitivity at each level suggests that, at least in part, they remain segregated from the SOC to the thalamus.

Only a few studies in the auditory cortex have examined ITD sensitivity (Brugge *et al.*, 1969; Brugge and Merzenich, 1973; Benson and Teas, 1976; Orman and Phillips, 1984; Reale and Brugge, 1990), and none have assessed ITD sensitivity of high-frequency cells to envelopes. Comparisons between the available studies are difficult because of small sample sizes, species differences, analytic and procedural differences, and anesthetic effects. For example, Benson and Teas (1976), in the unanesthetized but paralyzed chinchilla, reported that most neurons did not show peak-type CDs. In contrast, Reale and Brugge (1990), in the anesthetized cat, found ITD-sensitive neurons of both the peak type and trough type.

For other features of ITD sensitivity that are preserved along the auditory pathway, we limit our discussion to the properties of low-frequency neurons, because information regarding high-frequency neurons sensitive to ITDs of envelopes has only been systematically studied in the IC (Yin *et al.*, 1984; Batra, Kuwada, and Stanford, 1989, 1993).

In addition to peak-type and trough-type response patterns, a second feature that is preserved at all levels is that most ITD-sensitive neurons have CDs that favor delays corresponding to those created by sounds in the contralateral field (Altman, Syka, and Shmigidina, 1970; Stillman, 1971; Starr and Don, 1972; Crow *et al.*, 1978; Kuwada *et al.*, 1987; Ivarsson *et al.*, 1988; Palmer, Rees, and Caird, 1990; Reale and Brugge, 1990; Yin and Chan, 1990; Stanford *et al.*, 1992). Recall that in the MSO the bias for contralateral sounds is created by the shorter path length from the ipsilateral cochlear nucleus to the MSO compared to that from the contralateral cochlear nucleus (see Fig. 2). The bias toward contralateral sounds at higher centers is preserved because of the primarily ipsilateral projections from the MSO to the IC, the IC to the auditory thalamus, and the auditory thalamus to the auditory cortex. A third feature that is preserved at different levels is that the large majority of CDs fall within the estimated range of ITDs available to the animal (e.g., cat, ±400 μs; rabbit, ±300 μs). Thus, the preference for ITDs corresponding to sounds in the contralateral field that is created in the SOC is preserved in the IC, auditory thalamus, and auditory cortex, as is a preference for ITDs within the animal's physiological range.

C. Transformations of ITD sensitivity at higher auditory stations

Several aspects of sensitivity to ITDs appear to change as one ascends to higher levels. To begin with, the information used to construct ITD-sensitive neurons in the SOC is gradually eliminated. This information is reflected in the phase-locking of neurons to tones and envelopes (see Fig. 3). At the level of the SOC, most, if not all, ITD-sensitive neurons phase-lock (Yin and Chan, 1990, and personal observations). From there, phase-locking is systematically reduced. At the level of the IC and auditory thalamus, about 25% and 10% of the neurons phase-lock, respectively (Rouiller, de Ribaupierre, and de Ribaupierre, 1979; Kuwada, Yin, Syka, Buunen, and Wickesberg, 1984; Stanford *et al.*, 1992). At the level of the cortex, virtually none of the neurons phase-lock (Brugge *et al.*, 1969). The quality of phase-locking (synchronization coefficient) is also systematically reduced. Thus, at levels above the SOC, even if a neuron does phase-lock, its synchrony is usually poor. This result suggests that the primary processing of ITDs occurs in the SOC.

Another change is that the bandwidth of ITD tuning appears to increase. At the level of the SOC, most low-frequency, ITD-sensitive neurons respond over about a 1.0-1.5 octave range (personal observations), whereas in the IC the majority of neurons show ITD sensitivity over a 1.5–3.0 octave range (Stanford *et al.*, 1992). The increased bandwidth between the SOC and IC suggests convergence of ITD inputs with different best frequencies in the IC. No further increase in bandwidth is apparent between the IC and auditory thalamus (Stanford *et al.*, 1992).

One consequence of increased bandwidth is that a neuron can show ITD sensitivity to both low- and high-frequency signals. Figure 7 illustrates the responses of two such neurons recorded in the IC of the unanesthetized rabbit. The first neuron had peak type ITD sensitivity both to low-frequency tones (Fig. 7A; 500–1500 Hz) and to envelopes of SAM tones (Fig. 7B; 500–1050 Hz) with a high-frequency carrier (4375 Hz), whereas the second neuron had trough-type ITD sensitivity to both low-frequency tones (Fig. 7E; 500–1300 Hz) and envelopes (Fig. 7F; 500–800 Hz, carrier = 5000 Hz). Averaging the ITD curves across tone and modulation frequencies for each neuron produces the composite curves in Figs. 7C and 7G. Note that the composite curve in Fig. 7C has a peak within the rabbit's estimated physiological range (±300 μs), while the curve in Fig. 7G has a trough in this range. Such responses suggest that some neurons have the capability to encode, in a consistent way, the ITDs of both the fine structure of low-frequency signals and the envelopes of high-frequency signals. Such cells may be ideally suited for coding the location of signals with wide spectra.

Another transformation is the emergence of ITD functions that have an asymmetrical shape with a steep change in slope near zero ITD. Although such functions are seen in the SOC, they become more prevalent at higher centers. Figure 8 presents the composite curves of four neurons that had such "sawtooth" delay function: two from the IC (left panels) and two from the auditory thalamus (right panels). The steep slopes indicate that small changes in ITD can markedly affect the response, in a manner akin to the properties of edge detectors in the visual system. For the two neurons that show the steepest slope (lower left panel, Fig. 8B, and upper right panel, Fig. 8C), a 20-μs shift in ITD creates about a 10% change in discharge rate.

Sawtooth delay curves usually have ITD curves at different frequencies that align on the medial slope, rather than at the peak or trough. Consequently, their

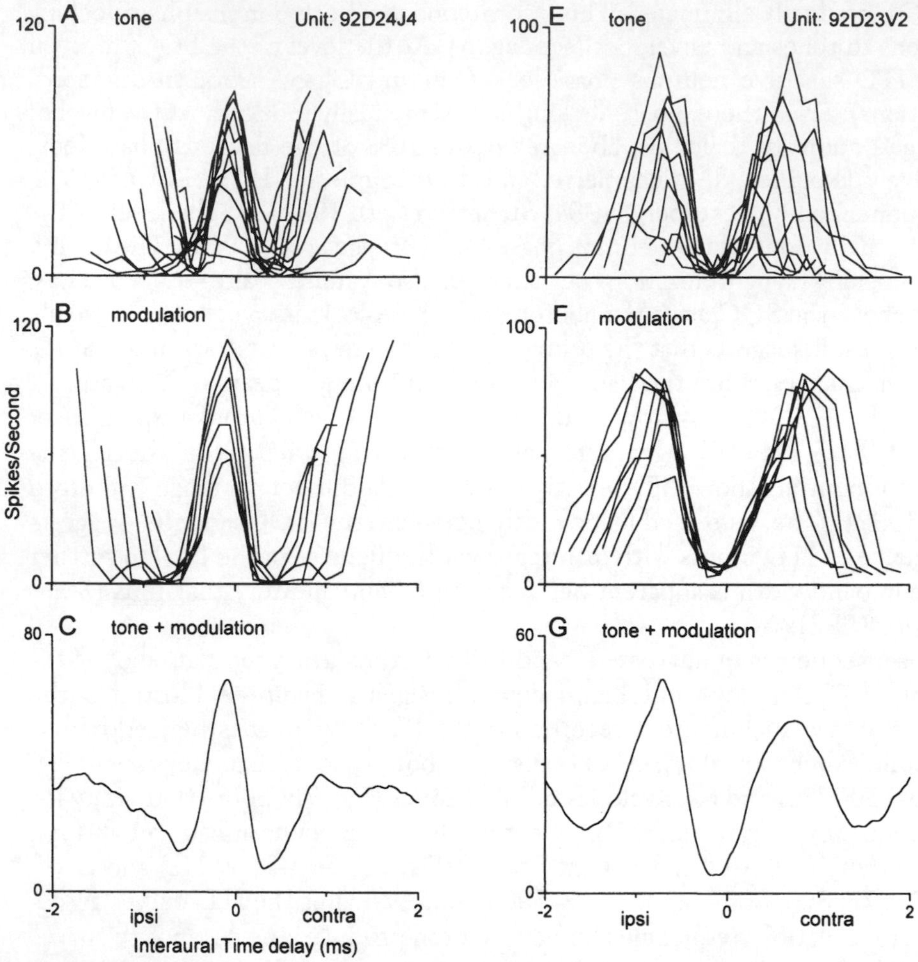

FIG. 7. Responses of two neurons (left and right column) recorded in the IC of the unanesthetized rabbit that displayed ITD sensitivity both to low-frequency tones (A and E) and to modulations of SAM tones with high-frequency carriers (B, carrier = 4375 Hz; F, carrier = 5000 Hz). Frequency range: (A) 500–1500 Hz, (B) 550–1050 Hz, (E) 500–1300 Hz, and (F) 500–800 Hz. Composite delay curves in C and G were created by averaging curves in A, B, and E, F, respectively.

CPs are generally intermediate between 0 and 0.5 cycles, instead of lying near one or the other value. Sawtooth neurons, by virtue of their steeply sloped ITD functions, could encode the position of a sound source with high accuracy.

How might such sawtooth delay functions be created? Figure 9 presents a neural circuit that could produce such responses. The ITD curves for the ipsilateral MSO (Fig. 9A) and contralateral DNLL (Fig. 9B) are modeled after responses recorded in these nuclei in the unanesthetized rabbit. The higher discharge rate for the DNLL response is a characteristic of DNLL neurons (personal observation). The DNLL receives its input from the ipsilateral MSO and has a strong projection to the contralateral IC. Thus, creating the sawtooth response in the IC (Fig. 9C) could involve convergence between excitatory inputs from the ipsilateral MSO and inhibitory inputs from the contralateral DNLL (Fig.

9D). The sawtooth shape of the ITD response occurs as a result of the overlap between the excitatory and inhibitory inputs.

Another transformation that occurs at higher levels of the auditory pathway is the increased sharpness of tuning to ITDs (Stanford *et al.*, 1992). If we view the ITD curve as the response of a neuron while a source moves along the azimuth, then the width of the excitatory region is equivalent to a neuron's azimuthal receptive field. Viewed in this way, the widths of the receptive fields systematically decreased at successively higher stations in the ascending auditory pathway (e.g., from SOC to IC to auditory thalamus).

Figure 10 presents a neural circuit that could provide the sharpening in ITD sensitivity seen between the SOC and IC. This circuit involves the convergence of an excitatory peak-type input from the ipsilateral MSO, and an inhibitory trough-type input from the ipsilateral LSO onto an IC neuron. Both the MSO and LSO inputs are assumed to have the same CD. This convergence would produce a sharper peak-type response compared to that of the MSO alone. Because the inputs have the same CD, the response in the IC is symmetrical as a function of ITD, a common feature of peak-type neurons in the IC. The proposed neural circuit is consistent with the known anatomy. Recall that some of the neurons in the LSO that project to the ipsilateral IC stain positively for glycine, and thus presumably make inhibitory synapses onto IC neurons (Saint Marie *et al.*, 1989; Glendenning *et al.*, 1992). Consistent with the sharpening

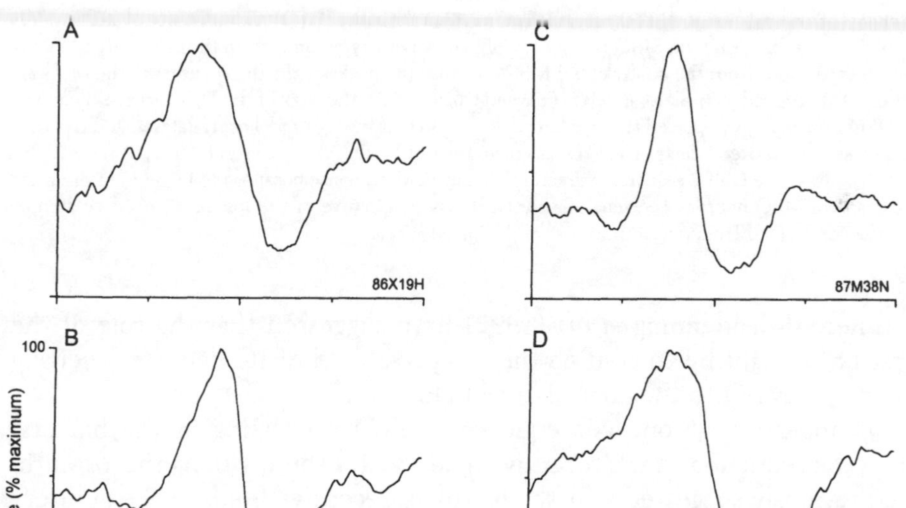

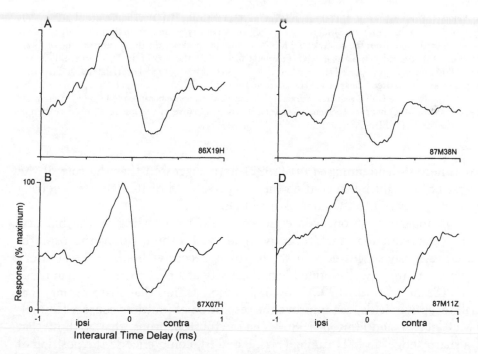

FIG. 8. Sawtooth-shaped composite delay curves. Examples of two units each from the IC (A and B) and MGB (C and D) recorded in the unanesthetized rabbit. The composite curves of these neurons are asymmetrical and sawtooth in shape, unlike the peak-type and trough-type responses (see Fig. 5), and most often have their steep slope within the animals physiological range (rabbit: ~±300 μs). Their CPs are generally intermediate between those of peak-type and trough-type responses. (After Stanford *et al.*, 1992, Fig. 7.)

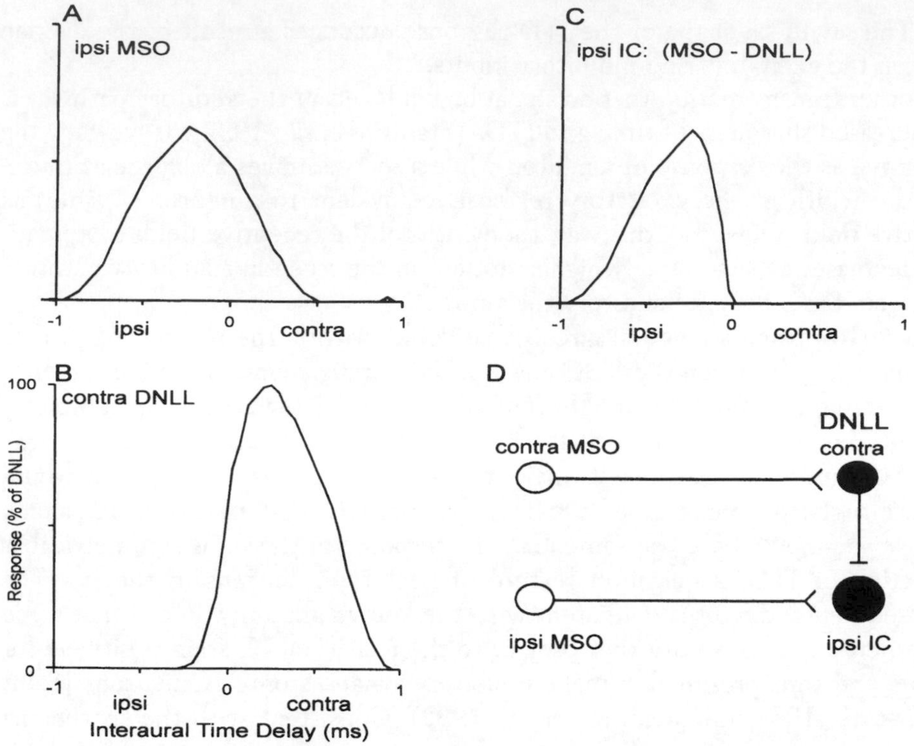

FIG. 9. Schema of a neural circuit that may create sawtooth neurons in the IC (D). Convergence of an excitatory peak-type input from the ipsilateral MSO (A) and an inhibitory peak-type input from the contralateral DNLL (B) that receives its input from the contralateral MSO. Because the peaks of the delay curves in the MSO are biased toward ITDs created by ipsilateral delays (Yin and Chan, 1990), the peak of the ITD curve of the model ipsilateral MSO neuron (A) was placed at an ipsilateral delay, and that for the model contralateral DNLL neuron (B) was placed at a contralateral delay. The ITD curves for the ipsi MSO (A) and contra DNLL (B) are modeled after actual responses. The DNLL response is greater than the MSO response because DNLL neurons discharge at higher rates than MSO neurons (personal observation). The ITD curve of the ipsi IC (C) was created by subtracting the contra DNLL curve (B) from that of the ipsi MSO (A).

proposed here, Glendenning *et al.* (1992) have suggested that the role of the ipsilateral LSO might be to confine the receptive field of IC neurons receiving inputs from the MSO to the contralateral field.

Thus, it appears that one consequence of ITD processing in the binaural pathway is the reduction of the receptive field size for sounds along the azimuth. We have previously suggested that the narrower receptive fields in the auditory thalamus create more well-defined loci of activity at a particular ITD than those in the IC (Stanford *et al.*, 1992). Population models find that sharp tuning, that is, small receptive fields, can improve the resolution of multiple sources (Rumelhart, McClelland, and Hinton, 1986). The sawtooth neurons, that is, those that show a sharp "edge" in ITD tuning (Figs. 8 and 9), could encode the position of a sound source with great accuracy by having a sharp delineation between the excited and non-excited populations. It could thus be that the sharpening of peaks (Fig. 10) and edges (Figs. 8 and 9) serve two different localization functions: The populations of neurons with narrow, symmetrical ITD-tuning would be most useful for resolving multiple-sound sources, whereas the population of asymmetrical, "edge-detector" neurons would be most useful for achieving accurate localization of a single sound source.

V. CONCLUSIONS

The mechanisms of ITD processing at the primary site of binaural interaction, the SOC, appear to be reasonably well understood and to follow the rules set out by Jeffress in his classic 1948 paper. One modification to this model is the inclusion of cells that receive excitatory inputs from one ear and inhibitory inputs from the other ear. These cells also exhibit ITD sensitivity, but were not included in the original Jeffress model, which considered only cells that received excitatory inputs from both ears. Beyond the primary site, our results suggest that ITD tuning may be systematically sharpened at successive stations along the auditory pathway. Future research is needed to determine the circuits involved in this sharpening process and also what aspects of the ITD functions are used by the nervous system to code the location of the sound. The region over which steep changes in the neural activity occurs as a function of ITD, rather than the point of maximal spike output, may be the relevant region encoded. Another pressing question is whether

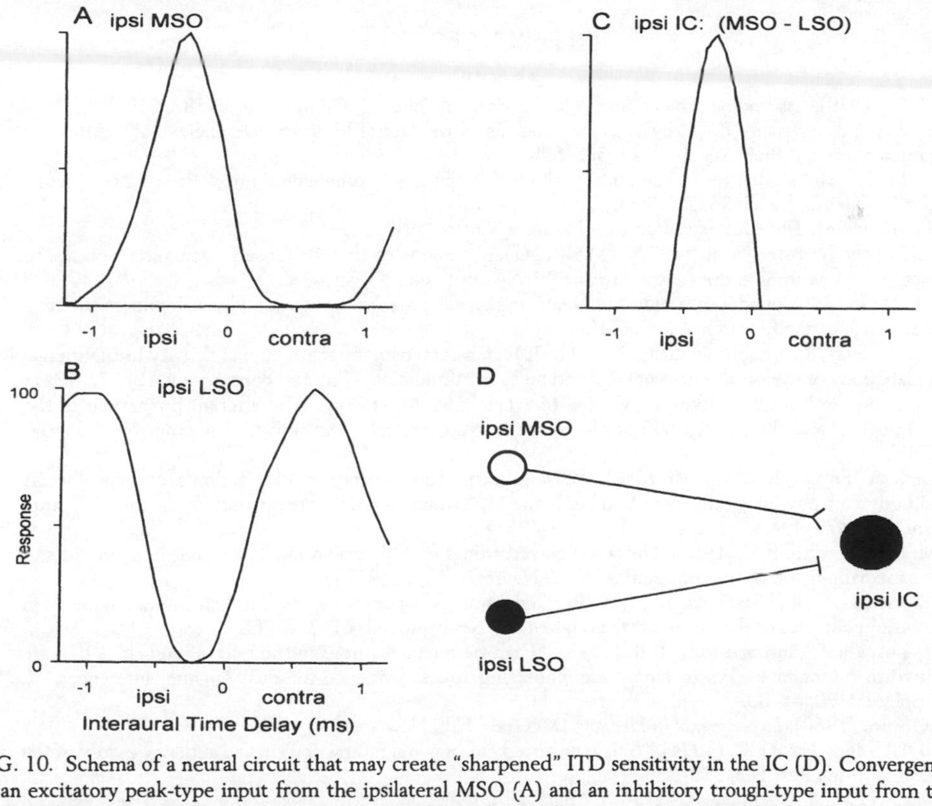

FIG. 10. Schema of a neural circuit that may create "sharpened" ITD sensitivity in the IC (D). Convergence of an excitatory peak-type input from the ipsilateral MSO (A) and an inhibitory trough-type input from the ipsilateral LSO (B), both with the same CD, would produce a sharper, peak-type response (C) compared to that of the MSO alone (A). The ITD curves for MSO (A) and LSO (B) are modeled after actual responses. The ITD curve in the ipsi IC (C) was derived by subtracting the ipsi LSO (B) from the ipsi MSO (A).

there is a topographic array of ITD units coding different locations in space. At present, there is a suggestion of such topography in the MSO (Yin and Chan, 1990), but it has yet to be demonstrated in the ascending auditory pathways beyond the SOC.

Most neural studies of ITD sensitivity have employed an anesthetized preparation. Anesthesia is known to affect the ITD sensitivity of IC neurons (Kuwada, Batra, and Stanford, 1989). Thus, to properly address issues of neural mechanisms and ITD representation, recordings need to be made in an unanesthetized preparation. Because attentional factors could also influence ITD sensitivity, especially at higher levels (i.e., thalamus and cortex) it would be ideal to record from neurons in an animal trained to attend to the stimulus, perhaps by making appropriate behavioral responses to acoustic signals at different spatial locations.

ACKNOWLEDGMENTS

We thank Drs. Christina Benson, Laurie Heller, Larry Hurd, and Douglas Oliver for their helpful comments. Supported by National Institute of Health grants NS 18027 and DC 01366.

REFERENCES

Adams, J. C. (**1979**). "Ascending projections to the inferior colliculus," J. Comp. Neurol. **183**, 519–538.

Adams, J. C., and Mugnaini, E. (**1984**). "Dorsal nucleus of the lateral lemniscus: A nucleus of GABAergic projection neurons," Brain Res. Bull. **13**, 585–590.

Aitkin, L. M.(**1973**). "Medial geniculate body of the cat: Responses to tonal stimuli of neurons in the medial division," J. Neurophysiol. **36**, 275–283.

Aitkin, L. M. (**1986**). *The Auditory Midbrain* (Humana, Clifton, NJ).

Aitkin, L. M., and Webster, W. R. (**1972**). "Medial geniculate body of the cat: Organization and responses to tonal stimuli of neurons in the ventral division," J. Neurophysiol. **35**, 356–380.

Altman, J. A. (**1978**). "Sound localization," in *Neurophysiological Mechanisms*, edited by J. Tonndorf (Beltone Institute for Hearing Research, Chicago, IL).

Altman, J. A., Syka, J., and Shmigidina, G. N. (**1970**). "Characteristic of the neuronal activity in the medial geniculate body of the cat during monaural and binaural stimulation," Physiol. Bohemoslov. **19**, 177–184.

Andersen, R. A., Roth, G. L., Aitkin, L. M., and Merzenich, M. M. (**1980**). "The efferent projections of the central nucleus and the pericentral nucleus of the inferior colliculus in the cat," J. Comp. Neurol. **194**, 649–662.

Andersen, R. A., Snyder, R. L., and Merzenich, M. M. (**1980**). "The topographic organization of corticocollicular projections from physiologically identified loci in the AI, AII, and anterior cortical fields of the cat," J. Comp. Neurol. **191**, 479–494.

Banks, M. I., and Smith, P. H. (**1992**). "Intracellular recordings from neurobiotin-labeled cells in brain slices of the rat medial nucleus of the trapezoid body," J. Neurosci. **12**, 2819–2837.

Batra, R., Kuwada, S., and Stanford, T. R. (**1989**). "Temporal coding of envelopes and their interaural delays in the inferior colliculus of the unanesthetized rabbit," J. Neurophysiol. **61**, 257–268.

Batra, R., Kuwada, S., and Stanford, T. R. (**1993**). "High-frequency neurons in the inferior colliculus that are sensitive to interaural delays of amplitude-modulated tones: Evidence for dual binaural influences," J. Neurophysiol. **70**, 64–80.

Bekesy, G. von. (**1960**). *Experiments in Hearing* (McGraw-Hill, New York).

Benson, D. A., and Teas, D. C. (**1976**). "Single unit study of binaural interactions in the auditory cortex of the chinchilla," Brain Res. **103**, 313–338.

Boudreau, J. C., and Tsuchitani, C. (**1968**). "Binaural interaction in the cat superior olive S segment," J. Neurophysiol. **31**, 442–454.

Bowlker, T. J. (**1908**). "On the factors serving to determine the direction of sound," Phil. Mag. **15**, 318–332.

Brugge, J. F. (**1992**). "An overview of central auditory processing," in *Springer Handbook of Auditory Research, Vol. 2, The Mammalian Auditory Pathway: Neurophysiology*, edited by A. N. Popper and R. R. Fay (Springer-Verlag, New York), pp. 1–33.

Brugge, J. F., Anderson, D. J., and Aitkin, L. M. (**1970**). "Responses of neurons in the dorsal nucleus of the lateral lemniscus of cat to binaural tonal stimulation," J. Neurophysiol. **33**, 441–458.

Brugge, J. F., Dubrovsky, N. A., Aitkin, L. M., and Anderson, D. J. (**1969**). "Sensitivity of single neurons in the auditory cortex of cat to binaural tonal stimulation: Effects of varying interaural time and intensity," J. Neurophysiol. **32**, 1005–1024.

Brugge, J. F., and Geisler, C. D. (**1980**). "Auditory mechanisms of the lower brainstem," Annu. Rev. Neurosci. **1**, 363–394.

Brugge, J. F., and Merzenich, M. M. (**1973**). "Responses of neurons in the auditory cortex of macaque monkey to monaural and binaural stimulation," J. Neurophysiol. **36**, 1138–1158.

Brunso-Bechtold, J. K., Henkel, C. K., and Linville, C. (**1992**). "Ultrastructural development of the medial superior olive (MSO) in the ferret," J. Comp. Neurol. **324**, 539–558.

Buell, T. N., Trahiotis, C., and Bernstein, L. R. (**1991**). "Lateralization of low-frequency tones: Relative potency of gating and ongoing interaural delays," J. Acoust. Soc. Am. **90**, 3077–3085.

Butler, R. A., and Belendiuk, K. (**1977**). "Spectral cues utilized in the localization of sound in the medial saggital plane," J. Acoust. Soc. Am. **61**, 1264–1269.

Caird, D., and Klinke, R. (**1983**). "Processing of binaural stimuli by cat superior olivary complex neurons," Exp. Brain Res. **52**, 385–399.

Caird, D., and Klinke, R. (**1987**). "Processing of interaural time and intensity differences in the cat inferior colliculus," Exp. Brain Res. **68**, 379–392.

Cajal, S. R. (**1909**). "Nerf acoustique: Sa branche cochleene ou nerf cochléaire," in *Histologie de Système Nerveux de l'Homme et des Vertébrés* (Maloine, Paris), Vol. I, p. 774. (Reprinted Madrid, Sonsejo Superior de Investigaciones Cientificas, 1952.)

Calford, M. B., and Aitkin, L. M. (**1983**). "Ascending projections to the medial geniculate body of the cat: Evidence for multiple, parallel auditory pathways through thalamus," J. Neurosci. **3**, 2365–2380.

Cant, N. B. (**1992**). "The cochlear nucleus: Neuronal types and their synaptic organization," in *Springer Handbook of Auditory Research, Vol. 1, The Mammalian Auditory Pathway: Neuroanatomy*, edited by D. B. Webster, A. N. Popper, and R. R. Ray (Springer-Verlag, New York), p. 66.

Cant, N. B., and Casseday, J. H. (**1986**). "Projections from the anteroventral cochlear nucleus to the lateral and medial superior olivary nuclei," J. Comp. Neurol. **247**, 447–470.

Cant, N. B., and Hyson, R. L. (**1992**). "Projections of the lateral nucleus of the trapezoid body to the medial superior olive in the gerbil," Hear. Res. **58**, 26–34.

Carney, L. H., and Yin, T. C. (**1989**). "Responses of low-frequency cells in the inferior colliculus to interaural time differences of clicks: Excitatory and inhibitory components," J. Neurophysiol. **62**, 144–161.

Carr, C. E. (**1993**). "Processing of temporal information in the brain," Annu. Rev. Neurosci. **16**, 223–243.

Clarey, J. C., Barone, P., and Imig, T. J. (**1992**). "Physiology of the thalamus and cortex," in *Springer Handbook of Auditory Research, Vol 2, The Mammalian Auditory Pathway: Neurophysiology*, edited by A. N. Popper and R. R. Fay (Springer-Verlag, New York), p. 232.

Crow, G., Rupert, A. L., and Moushegian, G. (**1978**). "Phase locking in monaural and binaural medullary neurons: Implications for binaural phenomena," J. Acoust. Soc. Am. **64**, 493–501.

Diamond, I. T., Jones, E. G., and Powell, T. P. S. (**1969**). "The projection of the auditory cortex upon the diencephalon and brain stem in the cat," Brain Res. **15**, 305–340.

Elverland, H. H. (**1978**). "Ascending and intrinsic projections of the superior olivary complex in the cat," Exp. Brain Res. **32**, 117–134.

Erulkar, S. D. (**1972**). "Comparative aspects of spatial localization of sound," Physiol. Rev. **52**, 237–360.

Faingold, C. L., Anderson, C. A. B., and Randall, M. E. (**1993**). "Stimulation or blockade of the dorsal nucleus of the lateral lemniscus alters binaural and tonic inhibition in contralateral inferior colliculus neurons," Hear. Res. **69**, 98–106.

Ferrier, D. (**1890**). *The Croonian Lectures on Cerebral Localization* (Smith, Elder, London).

Finlayson, P. G., and Caspary, D. M. (**1989**). "Synaptic potentials of chinchilla lateral superior olivary neurons," Hear. Res. **38**, 221–228.

Finlayson, P. G., and Caspary, D. M. (**1991**). "Low-frequency neurons in the lateral superior olive exhibit phase-sensitive binaural inhibition," J. Neurophysiol. **65**, 598–605.

Frisina, R. D., Smith, R. L., and Chamberlin, S. C. (**1990a**). "Encoding of amplitude modulation in the gerbil cochlear nucleus: I. A heirarchy of enhancement," Hear. Res. **44**, 99–122.

Frisina, R. D., Smith, R. L., and Chamberlin, S. C. (**1990b**). "Encoding of amplitude modulation in the gerbil cochlear nucleus: II. Possible neural mechanisms," Hear. Res. **44**, 123–142.

Galambos, R., Schwartzkopff, J., and Rupert, A. (**1959**). "Microelectrode study of superior olivary nuclei," Am. J. Physiol. **197**, 527–536.

Geisler, C. D., Rhode, W. S., and Hazelton, D. W. (**1969**). "Responses of inferior colliculus neurons in the cat to binaural acoustic stimuli having wide band spectra," J. Neurophysiol. **32**, 960–974.

Glendenning, K. K., Baker, B. N., Hutson, K. A., and Masterton, R. B. (1992). "Acoustic chiasm V: Inhibition and excitation in the ipsilateral and contralateral projections of LSO," J. Comp. Neurol. **319**, 100–122.
Glendenning, K. K., Brunso-Bechtold, J. K., Thompson, G. C., and Masterton, R. B. (1981). "Ascending auditory afferents to the nuclei of the lateral lemniscus," J. Comp. Neurol. **197**, 673–703.
Glendenning, K. K., Hutson, K. A., Nudo, R. J., and Masterton, R. B. (1985). "Acoustic chiasm II. Anatomical basis of binaurality in the lateral superior olive of the cat," J. Comp. Neurol. **232**, 261–285.
Glendenning, K. K., and Masterton, R. B. (1983). "Acoustic chiasm: Efferent projections of the lateral superior olive," J. Neurosci. **3**, 1521–1537.
Goldberg, J. M., and Brown, P. B. (1969a). "Functional organization of the dog superior olivary complex: An anatomical and electrophysiological study," J. Neurophysiol. **31**, 639–656.
Goldberg, J. M., and Brown, P. B. (1969b). "Response properties of binaural neurons of dog superior olivary complex to dichotic tonal stimuli: Some physiological mechanisms of sound localization," J. Neurophysiol. **32**, 613–636.
Grothe, B., and Sanes, D. H. (1993). "Bilateral inhibition by glycinergic afferents in the medial superior olive," J. Neurophysiol. **69**, 1192–1196.
Guinan, J. J., Norris, B. E., and Guinan, S. S. (1972). "Single auditory units in the superior olivary complex II: Locations of unit categories and tonotopic organization," Internat. J. Neurosci. **4**, 147–166.
Hall, J. L. II (1965). "Binaural interaction in the accessory superior-olivary nucleus of the cat," J. Acoust. Soc. Am. **37**, 814–823.
Harnischfeger, G. (1980). "Brainstem units of echolocating bats code binaural time differences in the microsecond range," Naturwissenschaften **67**, 314–316.
Harrison, J. M., and Feldman, M. L. (1970). "Anatomical aspects of the cochlear nucleus and superior olivary complex," in *Contributions to Sensory Physiology*, edited by W. D. Neff (Academic Press, New York), Vol. 4, p. 95.
Harrison, J. M., and Warr, W. B. (1962). "A study of the cochlear nuclei and ascending auditory pathways of the medulla," J. Comp. Neurol. **119**, 341–380.
Held, H. (1893). "Die zentrale Gehorleitung.," Arch. Anat. Physiol. **17**, 201–248.
Helfert, R. H., Bonneau, J. M., Wenthold, R. J., and Altshuler, R. A. (1989). "GABA and glycine immunoreactivity in the guinea pig superior olivary complex," Brain Res. **6**, 269–286.
Henkel, C. K., and Brunso-Bechtold, J. K. (1993). "Laterality of superior olive projections to the inferior colliculus in adult and developing ferret," J. Comp. Neurol. **331**, 458–468.
Henning, G. B. (1974). "Detectability of ITD in high-frequency complex waveforms," J. Acoust. Soc. Am. **55**, 84–90.
Hutson, K. A., Glendenning, K. K., and Masterton, R. B. (1991). "Acoustic chiasm. IV: Eight midbrain decussations of the auditory system in the cat," J. Comp. Neurol. **312**, 105–131.
Imig, T. J., and Morel, A. (1985). "Tonotopic organization in lateral part of posterior group of thalamic nuclei in the cat," J. Neurophysiol. **53**, 836–851.
Irvine, D. R. F. (1986). "The auditory brainstem," in *Progress in Sensory Physiology*, edited by D. Ottoson (Springer-Verlag, Berlin, Heidelberg, New York), Vol. 7.
Irvine, D. R. F. (1992). "Physiology of the auditory brainstem," in *Springer Handbook of Auditory Research, Vol. 2, The Mammalian Auditory Pathway: Neurophysiology*, edited by A. N. Popper and R. R. Fay (Springer-Verlag, New York), p. 153.
Irving, R., and Harrison, J. M. (1967). "The superior olivary complex and audition: a comparative study," J. Comp. Neurol. **130**, 77–86.
Ivarsson, C., De Ribaupierre, Y., and De Ribaupierre, F. (1988). "Influence of auditory localization cues on neuronal activity in the auditory thalamus of the cat," J. Neurophysiol. **59**, 586–606.
Jeffress, L. A. (1948). "A place code theory of sound localization," J. Comp. Physiol. Psych. **41**, 35–39.
Jeffress, L. A. (1958). "Medial geniculate body: A disavowal," J. Acoust. Soc. Am. **30**, 802–803.
Jenkins, W. M., and Masterton, R. B. (1982). "Sound localization: Effects of unilateral lesions in central auditory system," J. Neurophysiol. **47**, 987–1016.
Johnson, D. H. (1980). "The relationship between spike rate and synchrony in responses of auditory-nerve fibers to single tones," J. Acoust. Soc. Am. **68**, 1115–1122.
Joris, P. X., and Yin, T. C. T. (1992). "Responses to amplitude-modulated tones in the auditory nerve of the cat," J. Acoust. Soc. Am. **91**, 215–232.
Joris, P. X., and Yin, T. C. T. (1995). "Envelope coding in the lateral superior olive. I. Sensitivity to interaural time differences," J. Neurophysiol. **73**, 1043–1062.
Kavanagh, G. L., and Kelly, J. B. (1987). "Contributions of auditory cortex to sound localization by the ferret (*Mustela putorius*)," J. Neurophysiol. **57**, 1746–1766.
Kelly, J. B., and Phillips, D. P. (1991). "Coding of interaural time differences of transients in auditory cortex of *Rattus norvegicus*: Implications for the evolution of mammalian sound localization," Hear. Res. **55**, 39–44.
Kemp, E. H., and Robinson, E. H. (1937). "Electric responses of the brain stem to bilateral auditory stimulation," Am. J. Physiol. **120**, 316–322.

Kiang, N. Y. S., Morest, D. K., Godfrey, D. A., Guinan, J. J., and Kane, E. C. (**1973**). "Stimulus coding at caudal levels of the cat's auditory nervous system: I. Response characteristics of single units," in *Basic Mechanisms of Hearing*, edited by A. R. Moller (Academic Press, New York), p. 455.

Kiang, N. Y. S., Watanabe, T., Thomas, E. C., and Clark, L. F. (**1965**). *Discharge Patterns of Single Fibers in the Cat's Auditory Nerve* (MIT, Cambridge, MA).

Kudo, M., and Niimi, K. (**1980**). "Ascending projections of the inferior colliculus in the cat: An autoradiography study," J. Comp. Neurol. **191**, 545–566.

Kuwabara, N., and Zook, J. M. (**1991**). "Classification of the principal cells of the medial nucleus of the trapezoid body," J. Comp. Neurol. **314**, 707–720.

Kuwada, S., and Batra, R. (**1991**). "Sensitivity to interaural time differences (ITD) in the superior olivary complex (SOC) of the unanesthetized rabbit," Soc. Neurosci. Abstr. **17**, 450.

Kuwada, S., Batra, R., and Stanford, T. R. (**1989**). "Monaural and binaural response properties of neurons in the inferior colliculus of the unanesthetized rabbit: Effects of sodium pentobarbital," J. Neurophysiol. **61**, 269–282.

Kuwada, S., Stanford, T. R., and Batra, R. (**1987**). "Interaural phase-sensitive units in the inferior colliculus of the unanesthetized rabbit: Effects of changing phase," J. Neurophysiol. **57**, 1338–1360.

Kuwada, S., and Yin, T. C. T. (**1983**). "Binaural interaction in low-frequency neurons in the inferior colliculus of the cat. I. Effects of long interaural delays, intensity, and repetition rate on interaural delay function," J. Neurophysiol. **50**, 981–999.

Kuwada, S., and Yin, T. C. T. (**1987**). "Physiological studies of directional hearing," in *Directional Hearing*, edited by W. A. Yost and G. Gourevitch (Springer-Verlag, New York), pp. 146–176.

Kuwada, S., Yin, T. C. T., Syka, J., Buunen, T. J. F., and Wickesberg, R. E. (**1984**). "Binaural interaction in low-frequency neurons in inferior colliculus of the cat IV. Comparison of monaural and binaural response properties," J. Neurophysiol. **51**, 1306–1325.

Kuwada, S., Yin, T. C. T., and Wickesberg, R. E. (**1979**). "Response of cat inferior colliculus neurons to binaural beat stimuli: Possible mechanisms for sound localization," Science **206**, 586–588.

Langford, T. L. (**1984**). "Responses elicited from medial superior olivary neurons by stimuli associated with binaural masking and unmasking," Hear. Res. **15**, 39–50.

Li, L., and Kelly, J. B. (**1992**). "Binaural responses in rat inferior colliculus following kainic acid lesions of the superior olive: Interaural intensity difference functions," Hear. Res. **61**, 73–85.

Lingenhohl, K., and Friauf, E. (**1994**). "Giant neurons in the rat reticular formation: A sensorimotor interface in the elementary acoustic startle circuit," J. Neurosci. **14**, 1176–1194.

Luciani, L. (**1884**). "On the sensorial localisations in the cortex cerebri," Brain **7**, 145–160.

Luciani, L., and Seppilli, G. (**1886**). *Die Funktions-Localisations auf der Grosshirnrinde* (translated by M. O. Fraenkel) (Denicke's, Leipzig).

Luciani, L., and Tamburini, A. (**1879**). *Ricerche sperimentali sui centri psico-sensori corticali* (Reggio Emilia, Calderini).

Malone, E. F. (**1923**). "The cell structure of the superior olive in man," J. Comp. Neurol. **35**, 205.

McFadden, D., and Pasanen, E. (**1976**). "Lateralization at high frequencies based on ITDs," J. Acoust. Soc. Am. **59**, 634–639.

Monakow, C. von. (**1890**). "Striae acusticae und untere Schliefe," Arch. Psychiatr. Nervenkrankh. **22**, 1–29.

Moore, R. Y., and Goldberg, J. M. (**1963**). "Ascending projections of the inferior colliculus in the cat," J. Comp. Neurol. **121**, 109–136.

Morest, D. K. (**1964**). "The neuronal architecture of the medial geniculate body of the cat," J. Anat. **98**, 611–630.

Morest, D. K., Kiang, N. Y. S., Kane, E. C., Guinan, J. J., and Godfrey, D. A. (**1973**). "Stimulus coding at caudal levels of the cat's auditory nervous system: II. Patterns of synaptic organization," in *Basic Mechanisms of Hearing*, edited by A. R. Moller (Academic Press, New York), p. 479.

Morest, D. K., and Oliver, D. L. (**1984**). "The neuronal architecture of the inferior colliculus in the cat: Defining the functional anatomy of the auditory midbrain," J. Comp. Neurol. **222**, 209–236.

Moushegian, G., Rupert, A. L., and Gidda, J. S. (**1975**). "Functional characteristics of superior olivary neurons to binaural stimuli," J. Neurophysiol. **38**, 1037–1048.

Moushegian, G., Rupert, A., and Langford, T. L. (**1967**). "Stimulus coding by medial superior olivary neurons," J. Neurophysiol. **30**, 1239–1261.

Moushegian, G., Rupert, A., and Whitcomb, M. A. (**1964a**). "Brain-stem neuronal response patterns to monaural and binaural tones," J. Neurophysiol. **27**, 1174–1191.

Moushegian, G., Rupert, A., and Whitcomb, M. A. (**1964b**). "Medial superior-olivary-unit response patterns to monaural and binaural clicks," J. Acoust. Soc. Am. **36**, 196–202.

Neff, W. D., and Diamond, I. T. (**1958**). "The neural basis of auditory discrimination," in *Biological and Biochemical Basis of Behavior*, edited by H. F. Harlow and C. N. Woolsey (University of Wisconsin Press, Madison), p. 101.

Nuetzel, J. M., and Hafter, E. R. (**1976**). "Lateralization of complex waveforms: Effect of fine structure, amplitude, and duration," J. Acoust. Soc. Am. **60**, 1339–1346.

Oliver, D. L. (**1984**). "Neuron types in the central nucleus of the inferior colliculus that project to the medial geniculate body," Neuroscience **11**, 409–424.

Oliver, D. L., and Heurta, M. F. (**1992**). "Inferior and superior colliculi," in *Springer Handbook of Auditory Research, Vol. 1, The Mammalian Auditory Pathway: Neuroanatomy*, edited by D. B. Webster, A. N. Popper, and R. R. Fay (Springer-Verlag, New York), p. 168.

Oliver, D. L., Kuwada, S., Yin, T. C. T., Haberly, L., and Henkel, C. K. (**1991**). "Dendritic and axonal morphology of HRP-injected neurons in the inferior colliculus of the cat," J. Comp. Neurol. **303**, 75–100.

Orman, S. S., and Phillips, D. P. (**1984**). "Binaural interaction of single neurons in posterior field of cat auditory cortex," J. Neurophysiol. **51**, 1028–1039.

Osen, K. K. (**1969**). "The intrinsic organization of the cochlear nuclei in the cat," Acta Oto-Larngol. **67**, 352–359

Palmer, A. R., Rees, A., and Caird, D. (**1990**). "Interaural delay sensitivity to tones and broad band signals in the guinea-pig inferior colliculus," Hear. Res. **50**, 71–86.

Papez, J. W. (**1930**). "Superior olivary nucleus, its fiber connections," Arch. Neurol. Psychiatry **24**, 1–20

Penney, G. R., Conley, M., Schmechel, D. E., and Diamond, I. T. (**1984**). "The distribution of glutamic acid decarboxylase immunoreactivity in the diencephalon of the opposum and rabbit," J. Comp. Neurol. **228**, 38–56.

Pfeiffer, R. R. (**1966**). "Classification of response patterns of spike discharges for units in the cochlear nucleus: Tone burst stimulation," Exp. Brain Res. **1**, 220–235.

Phillips, D. P., and Irvine, D. R. F. (**1983**). "Some features of binaural inputs to single neurons in physiologically defined area AI of cat cerebral cortex," J. Neurophysiol. **49**, 383–395.

Rasmussen, G. L. (**1946**). "The olivary peduncle and other fiber projections of the superior olivary complex," J. Comp. Neurol. **84**, 141–219.

Rayleigh, Lord (J. W. Strutt, 3rd Baron of Rayleigh) (**1907**). "On our perception of sound direction," Phil. Mag. **3**, 456–464.

Reale, R. A., and Brugge, J. F. (**1990**). "Auditory cortical neurons are sensitive to static and continuously changing interaural phase cues," J. Neurophysiol. **64**, 1247–1260.

Rhode, W. S., Oertel, D., and Smith, P. H. (**1983**). "Physiological response properties of cells labeled intracellularly with horseradish peroxidase in cat ventral cochlear nucleus," J. Comp. Neurol. **213**, 448–463.

Rockel, A. J., and Jones, E. G. (**1973**). "The neuronal organization of the inferior colliculus of the adult cat. I. The central nucleus," J. Comp. Neurol. **147**, 22–60.

Rose, J. E., Brugge, J. F., Anderson, D. J., and Hind, J. E. (**1967**). "Phase-locked response to low-frequency tones in single auditory nerve fibers of the squirrel monkey," J. Neurophysiol. **30**, 769–793.

Rose, J. E., Gross, N. B., Geisler, C. D., and Hind, J. E. (**1966**). "Some neural mechanisms in the inferior colliculus of the cat which may be relevant to localization of a sound source," J. Neurophysiol. **29**, 288–314.

Rosenzweig, M. R. (**1961**). "Development of research on the physiological mechanisms of auditory localization," Psychol. Bull. **58**, 376–389.

Roth, G. L., Aitkin, L. M., Andersen, R. A., and Merzenich, M. M. (**1978**). "Some features of the spatial organization of the central nucleus of the inferior colliculus of the cat," J. Comp. Neurol. **182**, 661–680.

Rouiller, E. M., de Ribaupierre, Y., and de Ribaupierre, F. (**1979**). "Phase-locked responses to low frequency tones in the medial geniculate body," Hear. Res. **1**, 213–226.

Rumelhart, D. E., McClelland, J. L., and Hinton, G. E. (Eds.). (**1986**). *Parallel Distributed Processing: The Microstructure of Cognition, Vol. 1: Foundations* (MIT Press, Cambridge, MA).

Ryugo, D. K. (**1992**). "The auditory nerve: peripheral innervation, cell body morphology, and central projections," in *Springer Handbook of Auditory Research, Vol. 1, The Mammalian Auditory Pathway: Neuroanatomy*, edited by D. B. Webster, A. N. Popper, and R. R. Fay (Springer-Verlag, New York), p. 23.

Saint Marie, R. L., Ostapoff, E. M., and Morest, D. K. (**1989**). "Glycine-immunoreactive projection of the cat lateral superior olive: Possible role in midbrain ear dominance," J. Comp. Neurol. **279**, 382–396.

Sanes, D. H. (**1990**). "An in vitro analysis of sound localization mechanisms in the gerbil lateral superior olive," J. Neurosci. **10**, 3494–3506.

Schwartz, I. R. (**1984**). "Axonal organization in the cat medial superior olivary nucleus," in *Contributions to Sensory Physiology*, edited by W. D. Neff (Academic Press, New York), Vol. 8, p. 99.

Schwartz, I. R. (**1992**). "The superior olivary complex and lateral lemniscal nuclei," in *Springer Handbook of Auditory Research, Vol. 1, The Mammalian Auditory Pathway: Neuroanatomy*, edited by D. B. Webster, A. N. Popper, and R. R. Fay (Springer-Verlag, New York), p. 117.

Schwartz, I. R., and Yu, S. M. (**1986**). "An anti-GABA antibody labels subpopulations of axon terminals and neurons in the gerbil cochlear nucleus and superior olivary complex," Soc. Neurosci. Abstr. **12**, 780.

Shneiderman, A., Oliver, D. L., and Henkel, C. K. (**1988**). "Connections of the dorsal nucleus of the lateral lemniscus: An inhibitory parallel pathway in the ascending auditory system?" J. Comp. Neurol. **276**, 188–208.

Spangler, K. M., Warr, W. B., and Henkel, C. K. (**1985**). "The projections of principal cells of the medial nucleus of the trapezoid body in the cat," J. Comp. Neurol. **238**, 249–262.

Spitzer, M. W., and Semple, M. N. (**1993**). "Responses of inferior colliculus neurons to time-varying interaural phase disparity: Effects of shifting the locus of virtual motion," J. Neurophysiol. **69**, 1245–1263.

Stanford, T. R., Kuwada, S., and Batra, R. (**1992**). "A comparison of the interaural time sensitivity of neurons in the inferior colliculus and thalamus of the unanesthetized rabbit," J. Neurosci. **12**, 3200–3216.

Starr, A., and Don, M. (**1972**). "Responses of squirrel monkey (Samiri sciureus). medial geniculate units to binaural click stimuli," J. Neurophysiol. **35**, 501–517.

Stillman, R. D. (**1971**). "Characteristic delay neurons in the inferior colliculus of the Kangaroo rat," Exp. Neurol. **32**, 404–412.

Stotler, W. A. (**1953**). "An experimental study of the cells and connections of the superior olivary complex of the cat," J. Comp. Neurol. **98**, 401–432.

Strominger, N. L., and Oesterreich, R. E. (**1970**). "Localization of sound after section of the brachium of the inferior colliculus," J. Comp. Neurol. **138**, 1–18.

Sujaku, Y. (**1984**). "A simplified discrete-time model of neurons sensitive to changes of interaural phase," J. Acoust. Soc. Jpn. **5**, 175–183.

Sujaku, Y., Kuwada, S., and Yin, T. C. T. (**1981**). "Binaural interaction in the cat inferior colliculus: Comparisons of the physiological data with a computer simulated model," in *Neuronal Mechanisms of Hearing*, edited by J. Syka and L. Aitkin (Plenum Press, New York), p. 233.

Tarlov, E. C., and Moore, R. Y. (**1966**). "The tecto-thalamic connections in the brain of the rabbit," J. Comp. Neurol. **126**, 403–422.

Thompson, G. C., and Masterton, R. B. (**1978**). "Brain stem auditory pathways involved in reflexive head orientations to sound," J. Neurophysiol. **41**, 1183–1202.

Thompson, S. P. (**1878**). "Phenomena of binaural audition," Phil. Mag. **6**, 383–391.

Tobias, J. V., and Schubert, E. D. (**1959**). "Effective onset duration of auditory stimuli," J. Acoust. Soc. Am. **31**, 1595–1605.

Tolbert, L. P., Morest, D. K., and Yurgelun-Todd, D. A. (**1982**). "The neuronal architecture of the anteroventral cochlear nucleus of the cat in the region of the cochlear nerve root: Horseradish peroxidase labelling of identified cell types," Neuroscience **7**, 3031–3052.

Tsuchitani, C. (**1988**). "The inhibition of cat lateral superior olive unit excitatory responses to binaural tone bursts. I. The transient chopper response," J. Neurophysiol. **59**, 164–183.

Tsuchitani, C. (**1994**). "The brain stem evoked response and medial nucleus of the trapezoid body," Otolaryngol. Head Neck Surg. **110**, 84–92.

Tsuchitani, C., and Boudreau, J. C. (**1966**). "Single unit analysis of stimulus frequency and intensity by cat superior olive S-segment cell discharge," J. Neurophysiol. **42**, 794–805.

van Bergeijk, W. A. (**1962**). "Variation on a theme of Bekesy: A model of binaural interaction," J. Acoust. Soc. Am. **34**, 1431–1437.

van Bergeijk, W. A. (**1964**). "Physiology and psychophysics of binaural hearing," Int. Audiol. **3**, 174–175.

van Noort, J. (**1969**). *The Structure and Connections of the Inferior Colliculus. An Investigation of the Lower Auditory System* (Van Gorcum, Assen).

Venturi, J. B. (**1796**). "Considerations sur la connaissance de l'etendue que nous donne le sens de l'ouie," Mag. Encycl. J. Lett. Arts **3**, 29–37.

Wagner, H., and Frost, B. (**1993**). "Disparity-sensitive cells in the owl have characteristic disparity," Nature **364**, 796–798.

Warr, W. B. (**1966**). "Fiber degeneration following lesions in the anterior ventral cochlear nucleus of the cat," Exp. Neurol. **14**, 435–474.

Warr, W. B. (**1972**). "Fiber degeneration following lesions in the multipolar and globular cell areas in the ventral cochlear nucleus of the cat," Brain Res. **40**, 247–270.

Warr, W. B. (**1982**). "Parallel ascending pathways from the cochlear nucleus: neuroanatomical evidence for functional specialization," in *Contributions to Sensory Physiology*, edited by W. D. Neff (Academic Press, New York), Vol. 7, p. 1.

Weiss, T. F., and Rose, C. (**1988**). "A comparison of synchronization filters in different auditory receptor organs," Hear. Res. **33**, 175–180.

Winer, J. A. (**1992**). "The functional architecture of the medial geniculate body and the primary auditory cortex," in *Springer Handbook of Auditory Research, Vol. 1, The Mammalian Auditory Pathway: Neuroanatomy*, edited by D. B. Webster, A. N. Popper, and R. R. Fay (Springer-Verlag, New York), p. 222.

Woodworth, R. S. (Ed.). (**1938**). *Experimental Psychology* (Holt, New York).

Wu, S. H., and Kelly, J. B. (**1991**). "Physiological properties of the mouse superior olive: membrane characteristics and postsynaptic responses studied in vitro," J. Neurosci. **65**, 230–246.

Yin, T. C. T., and Chan, J. C. K. (**1988**). "Neural mechanisms underlying interaural time sensitivity to tones and noise," in *Auditory Function*, edited by E. M. Edelman, W. E. Gall, and W. M. Cowan (John Wiley & Sons, New York), p. 385.

Yin, T. C., and Chan, J. C. (**1990**). "Interaural time sensitivity in medial superior olive of cat," J. Neurophysiol. **64**, 465–488.

Yin, T. C. T., and Kuwada, S. (**1983**). "Binaural interaction in low-frequency neurons in inferior colliculus of the cat. III. Effects of changing frequency," J. Neurophysiol. **50**, 1020–1042.

Yin, T. C. T., and Kuwada, S. (**1984**). "Neuronal mechanisms of binaural interaction," in *Dynamic Aspects of Neocortical Function*, edited by G. M. Edelman, W. E. Gall, and W. M. Cowan (Wiley, New York), p. 263.

Yin, T. C. T., Kuwada, S., and Sujaku, Y. (**1984**). "Interaural time sensitivity of high-frequency neurons in the inferior colliculus," J. Acoust. Soc. Am. **76**, 1401–1410.

Yost, W. A. (**1977**). "Lateralization of pulsed sinusoids based on interaural onset, ongoing, and offset temporal differences," J. Acoust. Soc. Am. **61**, 190–194.

Chapter 21

Neuronal Processing for Coding Interaural Time Disparities

Tom C. T. Yin, Philip X. Joris
University of Wisconsin

Philip H. Smith
University of Wisconsin

Joseph C. K. Chan[1]
University of Wisconsin

(Received February 1994; revised May 1995)

Sensitivity to interaural time disparities (ITDs) is known to be one of the important cues for sound localization. This chapter reviews the physiological and anatomical mechanisms by which ITDs are encoded in the mammalian central auditory system. All of the essential attributes of the model first put forth by Jeffress in 1948 have been confirmed in recent studies of the medial superior olive (MSO). The model posits three assumptions: Cells in the MSO receive afferent inputs from the anteroventral cochlear nucleus that carry timing information about the acoustic stimulus, the binaural cells behave like coincidence detectors, or cross-correlators, and the anatomical projections of afferents to the MSO from the contralateral cochlear nucleus take the form of neuronal delay lines. The result of these assumptions is that a spatial map of ITDs is created along the rostral–caudal axis of the MSO. Evidence supporting the three assumptions and the resulting spatial map are presented.

INTRODUCTION

As indicated from other chapters in this book, there are ample psychophysical data attesting to the importance of interaural time disparities (ITDs) in spatial hearing. This chapter reviews the physiological and anatomical mechanisms by

[1]Current address: City Polytechnic of Hong Kong

which ITDs are first encoded in the mammalian central auditory system. We limit our discussion primarily to data from the cat and to the circuitry in the lower auditory brainstem nuclei. Although there is a great deal of information on the psychophysics of perceptual functions outside of the realm of sound localization, for example, pitch perception or intensity discrimination, much less is known about the neuronal circuitry underlying these other percepts. Thus, the choice of the topic of sound localization is a fortuitous match of psychophysics and physiology.

I. THE JEFFRESS MODEL

Our story begins almost 50 years ago with the publication of a short paper by Jeffress (1948), which set forth a theoretical model by which ITDs could be encoded. Remarkably, the essential attributes of this model have been borne out in almost all respects, even though many of the mechanisms were not evident at the time it was proposed. Figure 1 shows a diagram of the Jeffress model. Basically, the model makes three assumptions: (1) excitatory afferents into the binaural nucleus carry information about the timing of the acoustic stimuli, (2) the binaural cells behave like coincidence detectors, that is, they respond maximally when the inputs from the two sides arrive in coincidence, and (3) the anatomical projections of afferents to the nucleus take the form of neuronal delay lines as shown in Fig. 1. Because of the conduction delays imposed on the afferents, the inputs from the contralateral side to cell 1 will arrive slightly earlier than the contralateral inputs to cell 2. Conversely, inputs from the ipsilateral side will arrive at cell 2 earlier than at cell 1. Thus, if we assume that the path lengths from the two sides to cell 1 are equal and that the acoustic input to the two ears is such that the ears are activated simultaneously (e.g., if the sound source were on the midsagittal plane), then cell 1 will be maximally excited. If an acoustic delay is imposed, then the conduction delay that just compensates for that delay will determine which cell is maximally excited. For example, if the sound source is moved into the contralateral sound field so that there is an acoustic delay to the ipsilateral ear, then the point of maximal activation will move toward cell 2 because the

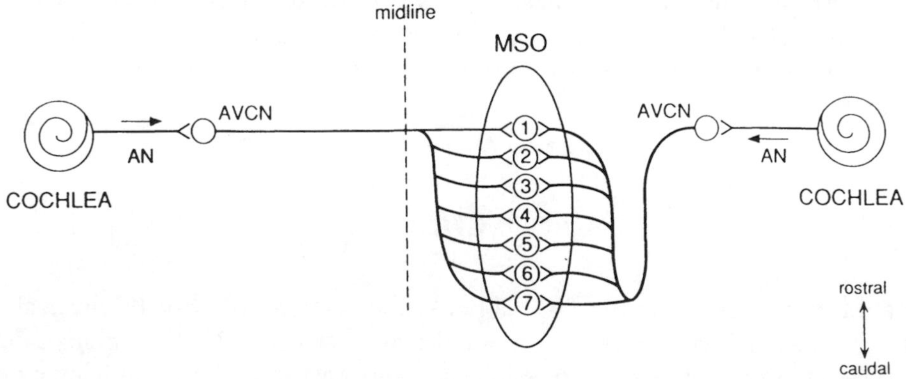

FIG. 1. Schematic diagram of the Jeffress model. Excitatory afferents to the binaural cells come from both sides by way of neural delay lines. The time of arrival of the input to the nucleus from each side is proportional to the length of each axon. The binaural cells are assumed to be coincidence detectors.

contralateral input to cell 2 will arrive later and the ipsilateral input will arrive earlier. As the acoustic delay is increased further, the point of maximal activation will move toward cell 7. The result will be a spatial map of ITDs across the axis of the nucleus from cells 1 to 7.

Several aspects of the model are noteworthy. First, it should be appreciated that by virtue of the fast conduction of neural impulses (5–40 m/s for myelinated axons) and short distances traveled in the brain, it is still possible to use conduction delays to cancel out the short acoustic delays. In humans the maximum ITD is about 800 μs (Kuhn, 1977), whereas in the cat it is about 300–400 μs (Roth, Kochhar, and Hind, 1980). Second, while Jeffress envisioned the delay lines on afferents from both the ipsilateral and contralateral sides, it is possible for the model to work if there is only a delay line on one side, provided that the afferents from the other side arrive synchronously. Third, it should be kept in mind that the spatial map of ITDs proposed by the model must be superimposed on the tonotopic organization found in all major auditory structures.

Before reviewing the anatomical and physiological evidence for the Jeffress model, it is appropriate to emphasize the importance of this model in the formulation of theoretical models of binaural interaction (see Stern and Trahiotis, Chapter 24, this volume). Almost all modern theories of binaural processing that have derived from psychophysical studies rely on a coincidence, or cross-correlation, element to compare the inputs to the two ears (Blauert, 1983; Colburn and Durlach, 1978; Licklider, 1959; Lindemann, 1986).

A. Medial superior olive (MSO)

At the time that Jeffress (1948) first proposed his model, there was not enough information known to place his model in the appropriate auditory nucleus. Since that time, numerous anatomical and physiological studies of the auditory brainstem nuclei have led to a general consensus that the initial site for encoding ITDs lies in the medial superior olive (MSO) of the superior olivary complex. The purpose of this chapter is to review the evidence that supports the Jeffress model and places it in the MSO.

Several anatomical and physiological features suggest that the MSO would be an appropriate candidate for encoding ITDs. First, the MSO is the first site at which excitatory inputs from the two ears converge. Because there is a potential loss of timing information at each synapse, it is reasonable to expect that the encoding of ITDs would be found early in the central auditory system. Second, the cytoarchitecture of the MSO and its afferents is unusual and seems to be optimized for comparing inputs from each side. MSO principal cells are bipolar with two primary dendrites that extend in opposite directions. The inputs from the two ears are segregated on the two dendrites: Each dendrite receives inputs from the cochlear nucleus of one side (Fig. 2; Cajal, 1909; Stotler, 1953). Third, the frequency representation of the MSO shows a preponderance of low-frequency cells (Guinan, Norris, and Guinan, 1972), which matches the expectation from psychophysical studies that ITDs are the primary cue for encoding sound location at low frequencies. By contrast, both of the other major superior olivary

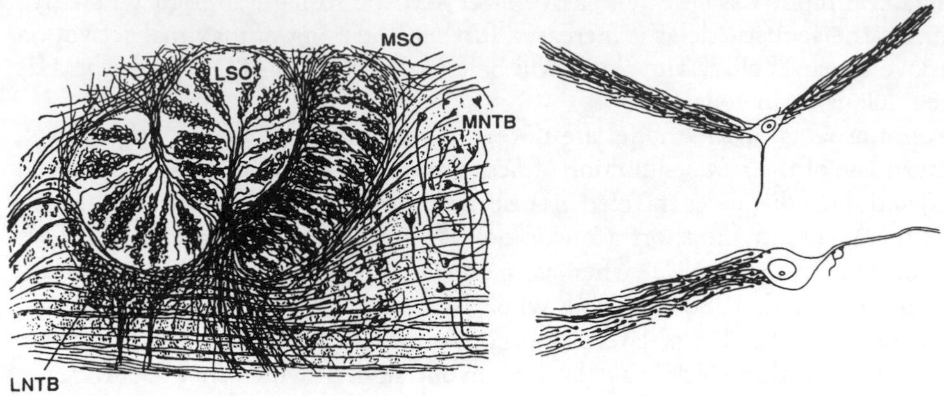

FIG. 2. (Left) Drawing of the afferents into the left superior olivary complex following Golgi staining. (From Cajal, 1909.) Note the dense plexus of terminals from the right and left side to the MSO. Abbreviations: LNTB, lateral nucleus of the trapezoid body; MNTB, medial nucleus of the trapezoid body; MSO, medial superior olive; LSO, lateral superior olive. (Right, upper) Drawing of the afferents onto the dendrites and soma of a cell in the normal MSO. (Right, lower) Similar drawing following a lesion of the right cochlear nucleus and degeneration of all afferents from that side. (From Stotler, 1953.)

nuclei, the lateral superior olive (LSO) and medial nucleus of the trapezoid body (MNTB), which are implicated in encoding interaural level differences, have frequency representations biased toward high frequencies.

Physiological studies have shown that MSO cells are indeed sensitive to ITDs (Goldberg and Brown, 1969; Crow, Rupert, and Moushegian, 1978). Unfortunately, the well-known difficulty in recording from cells in the MSO has limited the available data. For example, in the Guinan *et al.* (1972) sampling study of the superior olivary complex, only 2.5% (11/432) of the recordings were thought to arise from the MSO. Part of the reason for the difficulty in studying the MSO electrophysiologically is the presence of large field potentials, which arise from the summed phase-locked activity of the afferents to the MSO or from the large dendrites of MSO cells themselves. In addition, in the cat, the standard mammalian preparation, the MSO is a thin sheet of cells oriented such that the typical electrode approach traverses the narrow axis of the nucleus. The classic studies of Goldberg and Brown (1968, 1969) were done in the dog because its MSO is not as thin and is folded in the dorsal–ventral dimension. Despite the paucity of data supporting (or refuting) the Jeffress model, it is still the most commonly accepted model for binaural processing (see Stern and Trahiotis, Chapter 24, this volume). For this reason we thought it worthwhile to reexamine the Jeffress model by systematically studying each of the three assumptions basic to the model, as well as its conclusions. Surprisingly, perhaps, almost all facets of the model were upheld in our findings.

B. Phase locking of afferents

To understand the unique nature of phase locking of afferents to the MSO, it is first necessary to consider the properties of auditory nerve fibers. It is well known that the low-frequency components of the temporal features of an acoustic stimulus are preserved in the discharge patterns of auditory nerve fibers in the form of phase-locked activity. This is usually studied by delivering pure tones and generating cycle histograms (Fig. 3) that are synchronized to each cycle of the input stimulus. The abscissa of the histogram then represents one cycle of the stimulus, and the degree to which the fiber tends to respond at a particular phase angle is reflected in the peakedness of the histogram. The vector strength or synchronization coefficient R, which varies between 0 and 1.0, is usually used to measure phase locking (Goldberg and Brown, 1969). A perfectly phase-locked fiber responds only at one particular phase angle of the tone, and the cycle histogram will contain spikes in only a single bin ($R = 1$). If the fiber has no preferred phase angle, then the cycle histogram will be flat with equal entries in all bins ($R = 0$).

Auditory nerve fibers are of two types. In the cat, 90–95% are large myelinated fibers, type I (Spoendlin, 1969), which innervate a single inner hair cell along the organ of Corti (Kiang, Rho, Northrup, Liberman, and Ryugo, 1982; Liberman, 1982), whereas the remaining are small unmyelinated fibers, type II, which innervate multiple outer hair cells. All recordings from auditory nerve fibers have likely been from type I. In accordance with the frequency selectivity of the basilar membrane (von Bekesy, 1960), type I auditory nerve fibers only respond over a narrow range of frequencies for low-intensity stimuli. The characteristic frequency (CF) of each fiber is the frequency at which its threshold is lowest. Early physiological recordings of auditory nerve fibers showed phase-locking only to low-frequency tones, with synchronization decreasing above 1 kHz and becoming

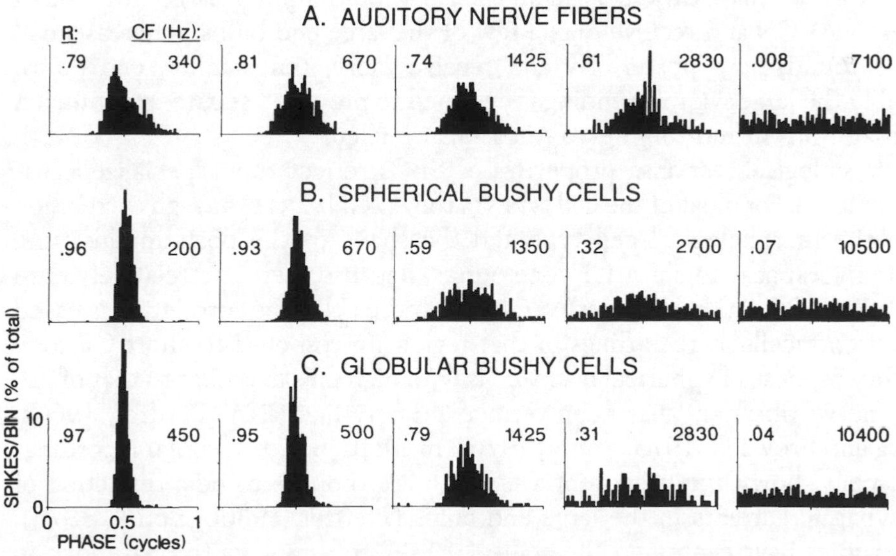

FIG. 3. Cycle histograms of (A) auditory nerve fibers, (B) spherical, and (C) globular bushy cells. The CFs of the cells are arranged from low on the left to high on the right. In each column, the CFs are approximately matched. The synchronization coefficient R and CF are given for each histogram. Each histogram has 64 bins and is plotted with the ordinate normalized to the number of spikes and shifted on the phase axis to have a mean phase of 0.5. (From Joris, Carney, Smith, and Yin, 1994.)

insignificant above 4–5 kHz (Kiang, Watanabe, Thomas, and Clark, 1965; Johnson, 1980). Most high-frequency auditory nerve fibers also have low-frequency tails (Kiang and Moxon, 1974) and will phase-lock to low-frequency tones of high intensity.

Although most studies of temporal processing of auditory nerve fibers have used tones, the same properties are also reflected in their responses to more complex stimuli, such as noise (Ruggero, 1973), clicks (Kiang *et al.*, 1965), or speech sounds (Sachs and Young, 1979). For example, when stimulated with a broadband noise, the low-CF fibers will synchronize to the low-frequency components of the noise, which can be demonstrated by computing the reverse correlation function (de Boer and de Jongh, 1978; Carney and Yin, 1988). As expected from tonal responses, the reverse correlation is only effective for low-frequency fibers; that is, the response is only synchronized to the low-frequency components of the input noise.

Anatomical studies have shown that the projection to the MSO from the cochlear nucleus derives from cells in the anteroventral cochlear nucleus (AVCN) known as bushy cells, from the appearance of their dendritic trees in Golgi preparations (Brawer, Morest, and Kane, 1974). Bushy cells in the AVCN have been further subdivided into spherical and globular, based on their location and appearance in Nissl stained sections (Osen, 1969). Spherical bushy cells (SBCs) project to the MSO (Warr, 1966; Cant and Casseday, 1986) and receive much of their synaptic input from the auditory nerve by way of the large specialized synaptic endings known as end bulbs of Held (Held, 1893; Cajal, 1909; Brawer and Morest, 1975; Cant and Morest, 1979). There is a gradient with position in the AVCN in the size of the SBCs and their end bulb inputs: Large SBCs lie in the anterior AVCN and receive only a few of the large end bulbs, whereas small SBCs are found more posteriorly and receive more, but smaller, end bulbs. Presumably the large synaptic ending is designed to provide a secure transmission of information from auditory nerve to cochlear nucleus.

The physiological response properties of SBCs reflect their specialized anatomical features. For most of the cell types in the AVCN, there is a high correlation between the morphological cell type and the shape of the poststimulus time histogram in response to short CF tone bursts. Because there is a relatively pure population of SBCs in the anterior AVCN, for these cells this correlation is based chiefly on extracellular recordings in that region. In response to short CF tone bursts, the response of spherical bushy cells with high CFs is similar to that of the auditory nerve fibers and has been termed primary-like (PL) (Pfeiffer, 1966a; Goldberg and Brownell, 1973; Bourk, 1976). In addition, extracellular recordings from PL cells show large prepotentials, which are thought to be a reflection of the presynaptic currents in the large end bulbs (Pfeiffer, 1966b; Bourk, 1976). Several studies have examined the ability of SBCs of low CFs to phase lock to tones, and conventional wisdom holds that cochlear nucleus cells are able to phase lock as well as, but not better than, auditory nerve fibers (Lavine, 1971; Goldberg and Brownell, 1973; Bourk, 1976; van Gisbergen, van Grashuis, Johannesma, and Vendrik, 1975; Kettner, Feng, and Brugge, 1985; Palmer, Winter, and Darwin, 1986).

For the other cell types in the AVCN, extracellular recordings provide a less reliable measure of the correlation of cell type with physiological response, because the different cell types are intermixed in the nucleus. Consequently, the technique of intracellular recording followed by morphological staining of a small number of individual cells (Rhode, Oertel, and Smith, 1983; Rhode, Smith, and Oertel, 1983; Smith and Rhode, 1985, 1987, 1989) has provided critical verification of this correlation. Globular bushy cells (GBCs), located in the posterior AVCN and nerve root region, are associated with the primary-like-with-notch (PL_N) response at high sound pressure levels. The PL_N response is very similar to the PL except that the initial onset spike is so well timed that poststimulus time histograms show a large onset peak followed by a short (1–2 ms) period without spikes due to refractoriness, creating a notch in the histogram. Stellate cells, located throughout the cochlear nucleus, have a well-timed and very regular discharge rate, known as the chopper pattern, whose interval is unrelated to the stimulus frequency. The small number of AVCN cells that have been studied intracellularly have not included SBCs nor many low-frequency cells.

In order to study the bushy cell population more thoroughly, we recorded from the trapezoid body, which carries the axons of all of the major cell types of the AVCN projecting to the superior olive. We were surprised to find that the low-frequency fibers of bushy cells show an enhanced synchronization to CF tones, relative to auditory nerve fibers. Figure 3 shows a comparison of cycle histograms of auditory nerve, spherical, and globular bushy cells (top to bottom) from low to high (left to right) CFs (Joris, Carney, Smith, and Yin, 1994). For each histogram the CF and synchronization coefficient R are given. For CFs < 1 kHz the R values of both SBCs and GBCs are greater than 0.90, which is the upper limit seen in auditory nerve fibers. The bushy cells are classified on the basis of their axonal projection pattern: The SBC axons travel in the dorsal component of the trapezoid body and innervate the MSO bilaterally, whereas the GBC axons run in the ventral component of the trapezoid body and innervate the contralateral medial nucleus of the trapezoid body (Smith, Joris, Carney, and Yin, 1991; Smith, Joris, and Yin, 1993). In Fig. 4, the distribution of the maximum R values for the entire population of 176 fibers with significant phase locking is compared to values found in auditory nerve fibers by Johnson (1980). About two-thirds (41/63) of the fibers with CF < 1.0 kHz have values greater than those ever seen in the auditory nerve. Interestingly, the population plot of Fig. 4 shows that the bushy cell synchronization drops below that seen in the auditory nerve at frequencies above about 2 kHz. In addition to enhanced synchronization, both cell types show a greater degree of entrainment at low frequencies than auditory nerve fibers; that is, they tend to respond to each cycle of the stimulating tone. At frequencies below 700 Hz, the cochlear nucleus cells can respond one-for-one to each cycle of the tone (Joris, Carney, Smith, and Yin, 1994). In addition, many cells with high CFs that can be driven in their low-frequency tail also exhibit enhanced synchronization to low-frequency tones of high SPLs (Joris, Smith, and Yin, 1994).

Another way to measure synchronization to tones, which may be more easily compared with psychophysical data, is to compute the amount of time jitter in the individual modes of the poststimulus time histograms. The minimum standard

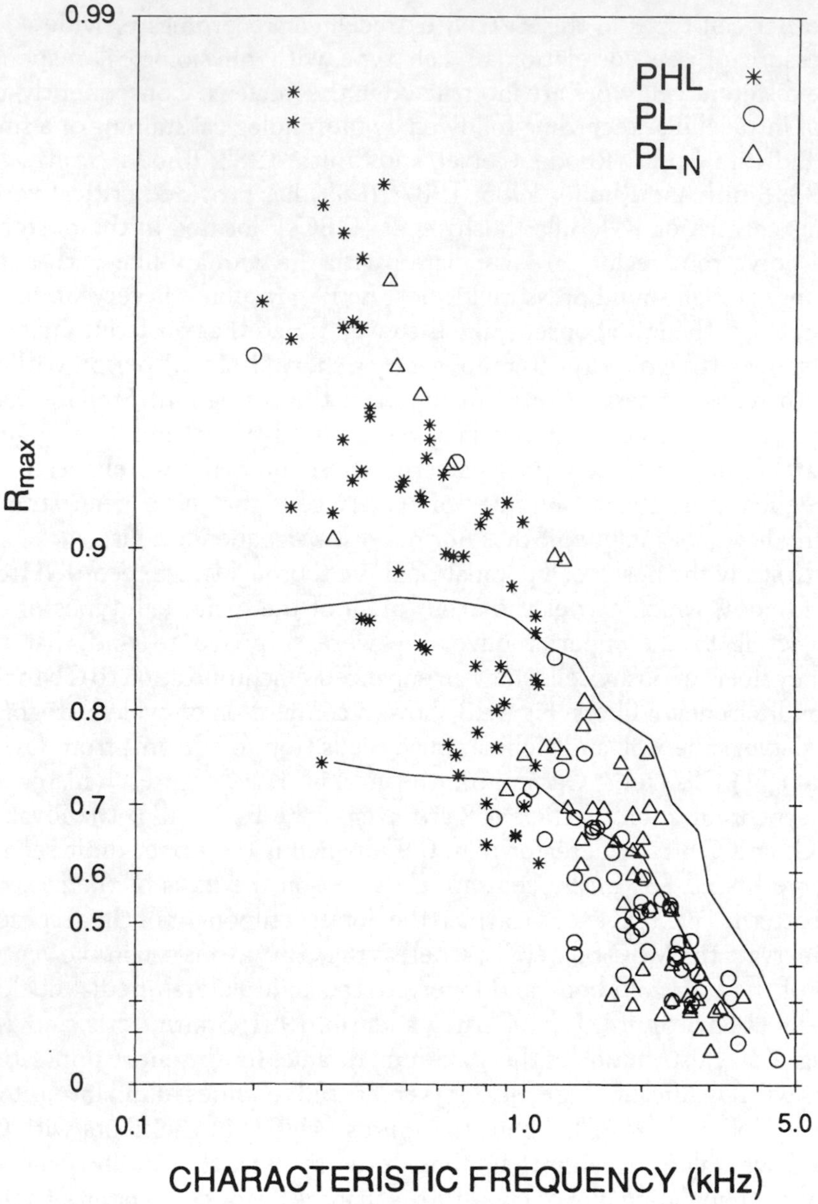

FIG. 4. Comparison of the maximum synchronization in auditory nerve and trapezoid body fibers. Solid lines indicate the range of values reported for auditory nerve fibers by Johnson (1980). Symbols indicate responses from trapezoid body fibers: PL, primary-like responses from SBCs; PL_N, a primary-like-with-notch response from GBCs; and PHL, a phase-locked response. The latter category is necessary for those fibers with a CF less than about 1.0 kHz for which we have no anatomical data and are unable to distinguish PL from PL_N responses. The ordinate is plotted on a logarithmic $(1 - R_{max})$ scale to provide an equal variance axis (Johnson, 1980). (From Joris, Carney, Smith, and Yin, 1994.) Reprinted with permission.

deviation we found in the bushy cells is ~28 μs, whereas for auditory nerve fibers the minimum is ~94 μs. When stimulating in the tail of high-frequency bushy cells, the minimal standard deviation can be as small as 20 μs, which may represent a limit on the temporal resolution of the cat's auditory system in response to tones.

As described earlier, GBCs and SBCs with high CFs can be discriminated on physiological grounds: The post stimulus time histograms of GBCs at high stimulus levels are PL_N, while those of SBCs are PL. This distinction cannot be made for fibers with CF < 1 kHz because the individual modes of phase-locking obscure the notch. As a result both GBCs and SBCs exhibit phase-locked (PHL) poststimulus time histograms at these low frequencies. Randomizing the phase of the tone stimulus does not provide an effective means for this discrimination (Smith *et al.*, 1993). Therefore, to determine whether the response is from a SBC or GBC of low CF requires additional information, usually anatomical.

Thus, our recordings in the trapezoid body reveal that the coding of temporal features of the acoustic stimulus carried by the auditory nerve fibers is not only preserved but enhanced by the bushy cells of the cochlear nucleus, although over a somewhat more limited frequency range. These physiological specializations reflect the well-known anatomical specializations in the synaptic arrangements of auditory nerve fibers onto bushy cells and probably contribute to the auditory system's ability to resolve ITDs on a microsecond time scale.

C. Coincidence detection and cross correlation in the MSO

Although there has been only weak support for many aspects of the Jeffress model, it has been widely accepted for many years largely because there is good evidence that MSO cells behave like the coincidence detectors required in the model's second assumption (Goldberg and Brown, 1969). Coincidence was tested by comparing the interaural phase required for optimal binaural response with the phase predicted from monaural stimulation of each ear. Such analysis requires cell responses that show sensitivity to interaural phase and phase locking to monaural stimulation of each ear. Goldberg and Brown (1969) were the first to demonstrate such evidence of coincidence in the MSO of the dog; Fig. 5 illustrates similar responses obtained from the MSO of the cat (Yin and Chan, 1990). The cycle histograms derived from monaural stimulation of each ear (Fig. 5, right) show that the cell phase locks well for the CF tones of 1000 Hz. The values ϕ_c and ϕ_i indicate the mean phase angle of inputs from the contralateral and ipsilateral ears, respectively, as computed from vector averaging. The coincidence model predicts that the maximal binaural response should occur when an ITD is introduced such that the peaks of the two inputs arrive in-phase. In the example shown in Fig. 5, the difference between the mean phase angles ($\phi_c - \phi_i = 1.02 - 0.87$) is 0.15, which means that the maximal binaural response should occur when the ipsilateral input is delayed by 0.15 cycles. The binaural response as a function of ITD is shown in Fig. 5 (left). The central peak of the delay curve occurs when the ipsilateral ear is delayed by 100 μs, or 0.10 cycles, and the mean interaural phase (ϕ_d) of the ITD curve averaged over the four cycles shown is 0.09, both of which are close to the value predicted from the monaural responses. The analysis shown in Fig. 5 was done at the CF of the cell. The model predicts that it should also hold at all other frequencies at which the cell responds, which was indeed the case. Similar analysis for 14 other MSO cells showed a high correlation ($r = 0.83$, slope $= 1.09$, $n = 179$) between the mean interaural phase and the phase

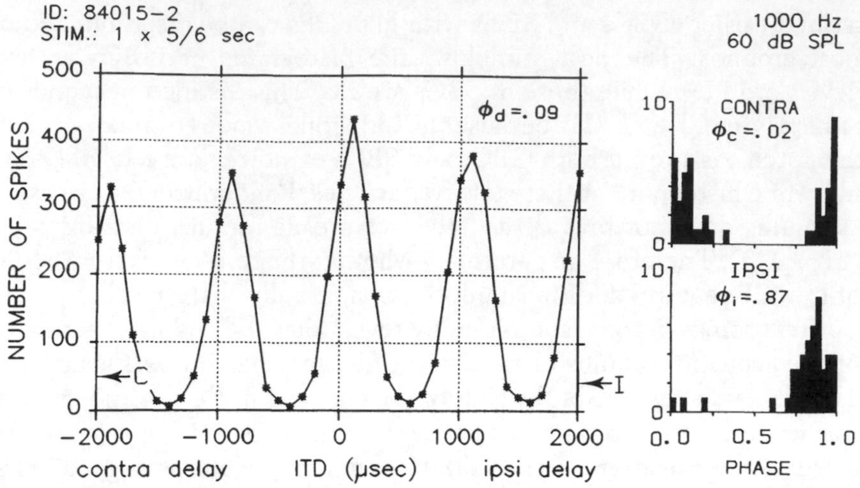

FIG. 5. Interaural time delay curves (left) and monaural period histograms (right) for a cell in the MSO. The mean interaural phase is given by ϕ_d, and the mean monaural phases by ϕ_c and ϕ_i for contralateral and ipsilateral responses, respectively. The arrows labeled C and I indicate the monaural response rates for contralateral and ipsilateral stimulation, respectively. (From Yin and Chan, 1990.) Reprinted with permission.

predicted from the monaural responses at many different frequencies and SPLs. Note that a basic assumption in this analysis is that the relative time of arrival of the inputs to the MSO cell can be inferred from the timing of the output spikes from the MSO cell.

Although it is straightforward to test the coincidence model with pure tones, where the interaural phase is well specified, it is less clear how to test it with more complex stimuli, for example, Gaussian noise where the interaural phase is randomly varying. For these complex stimuli, it is useful to consider the functionally equivalent cross-correlation model. Almost all modern theories of binaural processing rely on a cross-correlator as the comparator element for the signals from the two ears (see Stern and Trahiotis, Chapter 24, this volume). We used broadband-noise signals to study the way ITDs of complex stimuli are represented and to verify the cross-correlation model. Figure 6A shows responses of a cell in the MSO to ITDs of eight different tones plotted on the same ITD axis. If we assume that the cell linearly sums all spectral components equally, then the cell's response to a broadband-noise curve should be equal to the average of all the tonal responses. We call this the tonal composite curve. Figure 6B shows that the responses of the same cell to ITDs of broadband noise is very similar to that of the tonal composite curve, suggesting that the responses to the broadband noise can be predicted from its tonal responses using linear spectral summation. Comparable responses were seen in the other cells tested. When there were deviations, it was usually that the shapes of the curves near the peak were similar, but that the secondary peaks of the noise curves were more pronounced than in the composite tonal responses.

Three experiments provided additional verification of the cross-correlation, or coincidence, model. First, when uncorrelated noises were presented to the two ears, sensitivity to ITDs was eliminated. Second, if we used a computer to cross-correlate the monaural responses to noise to the left and right ears, the result was similar to the response of the cell to binaural responses to the same noise. Third, in recordings from cells in the inferior colliculus (IC), the target of axons from the MSO, the degree of modulation of the ITD curves was a systematic and monotonic function of the degree of decorrelation of noises to the two ears (Yin, Chan, and Carney, 1987). Thus, we believe there is strong evidence that the binaural comparator cell in the MSO behaves like the coincidence, or cross-correlation, detector proposed by Jeffress (1948).

D. Neuronal delay lines on afferents to MSO

In order to study the form of the afferent projection to the MSO by the SBCs of the cochlear nucleus on each side, it is necessary to label the fibers for anatomical examination. We chose to impale and label individual fibers, each of which had

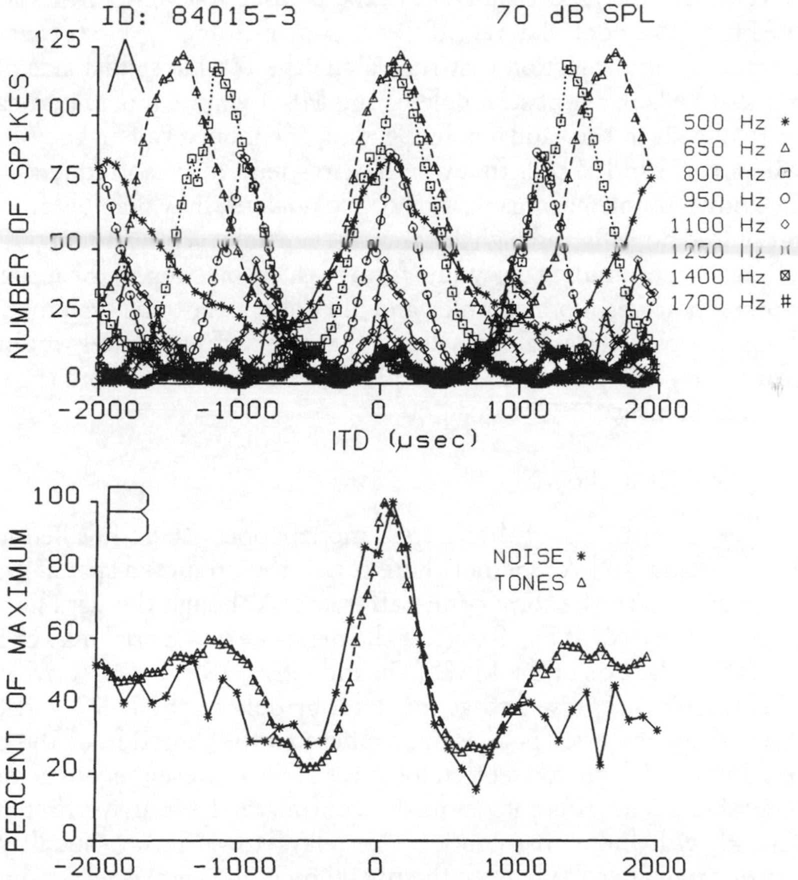

FIG. 6. (A) Interaural time delay curves for an MSO cell to eight different stimulation frequencies, all plotted on a common time scale. (B) ITD curves for the same cell in response to broadband noise stimulation (asterisk) or derived from the tonal responses in A by computation of the composite curve (Δ). (From Yin and Chan, 1990.) Reprinted with permission.

been characterized physiologically to verify the physiological response properties of these afferents. By impaling single axons of trapezoid body fibers near the midline, we could record their responses to CF tones and then inject them with an intracellular marker for morphological analysis. Our findings (Smith *et al.*, 1991, 1993) confirmed several features of trapezoid body fibers. First, for high-CF fibers as described earlier, there was good correlation between physiological response type, as judged by the shape of the poststimulus time histogram to short CF tones, and morphological cell type, as judged by the axonal projection pattern into the superior olivary complex. GBCs project to the MNTB with a large calyceal ending and have PL_N or PHL histograms; SBCs project bilaterally to the MSO and have PL or PHL histograms. Second, there is an orderly segregation of axons of bushy cells in the trapezoid body: The large GBC axons travel in the ventral half, while the medium-diameter SBC axons run in the dorsal component (Warr, 1966; Brownell, 1975). Third, the spontaneous discharge of SBCs was significantly higher than that of GBCs.

Two important features, most apparent in the parasagittal view, of the projection of one SBC to the contralateral MSO are shown in Fig. 7. First, there is a lattice-like form of the projection that runs along the rostral–caudal axis of the nucleus such that cells in the rostral pole of the MSO will be innervated earlier by this axon than cells in the caudal pole. Second, the innervation in the MSO is confined to a narrow band of cells that would correspond to an isofrequency strip based on the known tonotopic organization of the nucleus, in which low frequencies are represented dorsally and high frequencies ventrally (Guinan *et al.*, 1972). We did not find a corresponding delay-line form in the projection to the ipsilateral MSO. This projection was more complex and did not appear to be systematically arranged along the rostral–caudal axis. Recall that the Jeffress model would still function with a delay line on only one side, provided the afferents from the other side arrive synchronously.

E. Spatial map of ITDs in the MSO

Because all three assumptions of the Jeffress model appear to be fulfilled in the cat's MSO, it is natural to ask whether there is also the predicted spatial map of ITDs that corresponds to the form of the afferents. Although the data here are admittedly sparse, the data of Fig. 8 suggest the presence of a spatial map of ITDs along the rostral-caudal axis of the MSO (Yin and Chan, 1990). The form of this map, with ITDs near 0 represented at the anterior pole of the MSO and ITDs near +400 μs at the posterior pole, is appropriate to the direction of the delay lines on the afferents. In our convention, positive ITDs represent acoustic delays of the ipsilateral ear. The afferents from the contralateral ear arrive first at the rostral pole and with increasing conduction delays toward the caudal MSO. Therefore, as one moves caudally from the rostral pole, the increasing conduction delay of the contralateral input can be compensated by increasing acoustic delay to the ipsilateral ear, and thus cells become progressively more responsive to ITDs > 0. If the orientation of the delay line were in the opposite direction, that is, with increasing delays from caudal to rostral for the contralateral axon, then the spatial map of ITDs would have to be in the opposite direction.

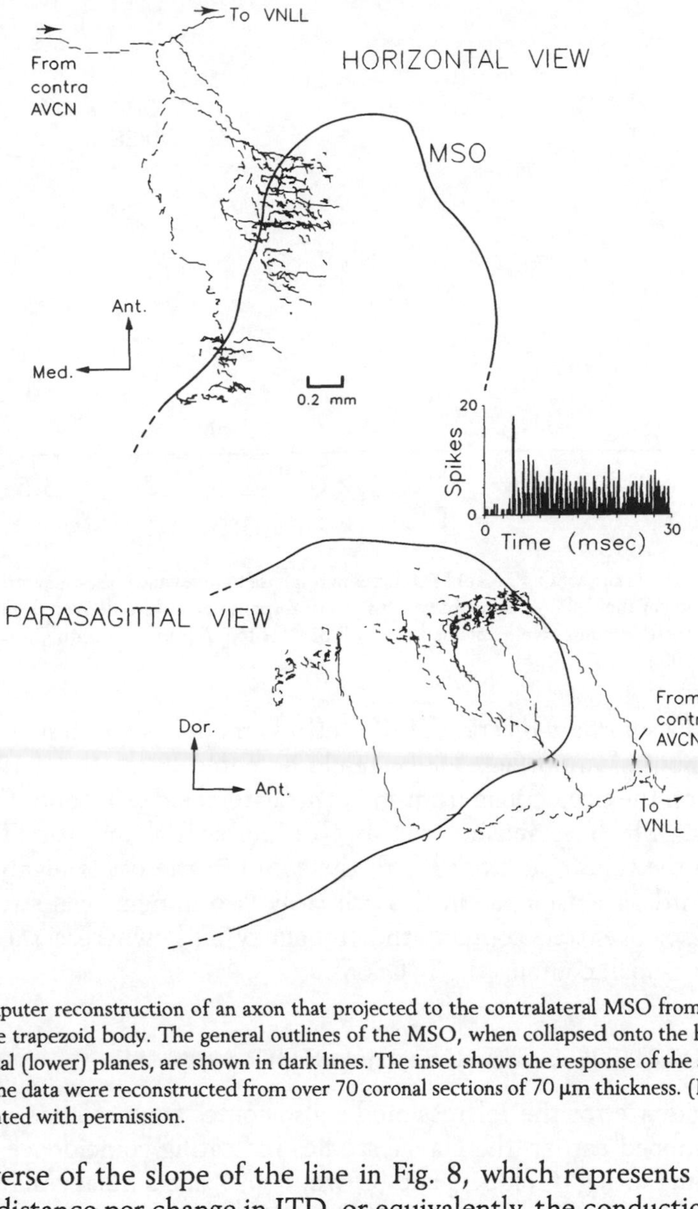

FIG. 7. Computer reconstruction of an axon that projected to the contralateral MSO from a SBC labeled in its axon in the trapezoid body. The general outlines of the MSO, when collapsed onto the horizontal (upper) and parasagittal (lower) planes, are shown in dark lines. The inset shows the response of the axon to a CF tone (1350 Hz). The data were reconstructed from over 70 coronal sections of 70 μm thickness. (From Smith *et al.*, 1993.) Reprinted with permission.

The inverse of the slope of the line in Fig. 8, which represents the required change in distance per change in ITD, or equivalently, the conduction velocity of the afferents, is about 8.8 m/s. Taking into consideration that the axons branch into many smaller collaterals near their terminals, with a resultant slowing of conduction, this estimate of conduction velocity is in the range of that expected for myelinated fibers.

The spatial map of ITDs in the MSO does not include negative ITDs. Thus, the MSO on one side only represents the contralateral sound field. The ipsilateral sound field is, of course, represented by the MSO on the other side. This physiological result is consonant with the behavioral finding that lesions of the lateral lemniscus or MSO on one side only produce deficits in sound localization in the contralateral sound field (Jenkins and Masterton, 1982).

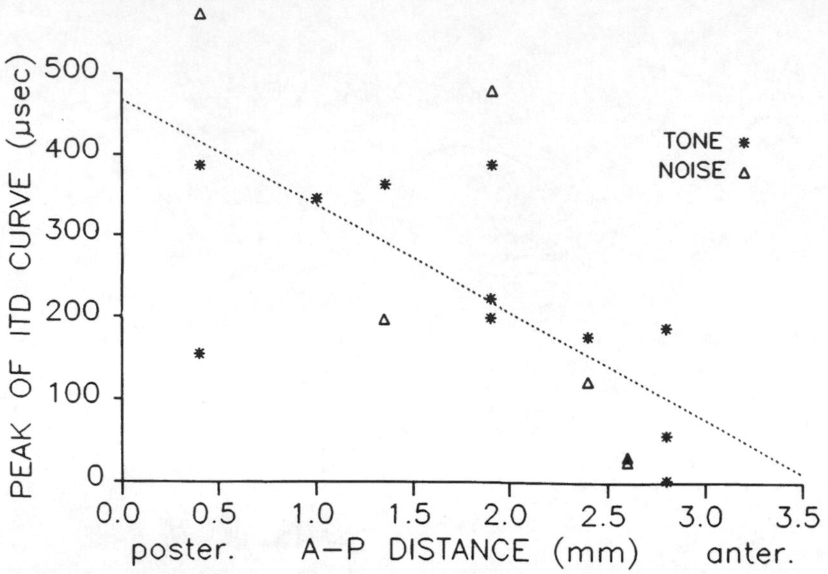

FIG. 8. Spatial map of ITDs in the MSO. Peaks of ITD curves in response to tones and noise are plotted against the rostral–caudal position of the cell on a standard nucleus. Tonal response data were derived from peaks of the composite curves. These responses were obtained at 60 dB SPL for tones, from cells with CF < 500 Hz. (From Yin and Chan, 1990.)

Figure 9 shows a summary diagram of the Jeffress model as we think it exists in the cat. A number of important points should be noted. First, the delay lines are only present on the projections from the contralateral side. Second, the axis of the delay line, which establishes the axis of the spatial map of ITDs, is perpendicular to the tonotopic axis. Third, the MSO in the cat is highly compressed in the third dimension, so in this primarily two-dimensional structure, one dimension, dorsoventral, contains the frequency axis, whereas the other dimension, rostrocaudal, contains the ITD axis.

II. EVIDENCE FOR THE JEFFRESS MODEL IN OTHER ANIMALS

Corroborating evidence for the Jeffress model also comes from studies in other animals. As mentioned earlier, the classic studies indicating coincidence in the MSO were done in the dog (Goldberg and Brown, 1969), and similar results were found for a small number of cells in the MSO of the kangaroo rat (Crow *et al.*, 1978). Studies in nucleus laminaris, the avian homologue of the MSO, have also provided some supportive evidence. In the chick, anatomical data on the projection from nucleus magnocellularis, which appears to contain cells similar to the bushy cells of AVCN, to nucleus laminaris also take the form of a delay line on the contralateral, but not the ipsilateral, side (Young and Rubel, 1983). There are no recordings from nucleus laminaris *in vivo*, but recordings made from brain slices also support a coincidence mechanism (Joseph and Hyson, 1993) as well as neural conduction delays (Overholt, Rubel, and Hyson, 1992). Likewise, in the barn owl, a model preparation for studying mechanisms of sound localization, there is evidence for coincidence from recordings of afferents to, and output axons of, nucleus laminaris (Carr and Konishi, 1990). The anatomical projection to laminaris from nucleus magnocellularis in the barn owl also looks like that seen in the cat and chick with a prominent delay line on the contralateral, but not the ipsilateral, side. However, curiously, the apparent map of ITDs does not run along the axis of this prominent delay line, leaving open the question of why the delay line on the contralateral side exists in the owl.

III. COMPLICATIONS TO THE MODEL

Thus far, we have shown data that basically support the original Jeffress model in almost all respects. There are, however, a number of additional observations that have yet to be incorporated into the model. One major factor is the question of inhibitory inputs to the MSO. There is strong anatomical and physiological evidence for inhibitory inputs to MSO cells. Immunocytochemical and electron microscopic studies of the MSO indicate the presence of inhibitory terminals synapsing on principal cells (Clark, 1969; Lindsey, 1975; Schwartz, 1984; Adams and Mugnaini, 1990; Brunso-Bechtold, Henkel, and Linville, 1992). Axons from the MNTB, known to provide inputs to the lateral superior olive that use the inhibitory neurotransmitter glycine, also send inhibitory collaterals to the MSO (Smith, Joris, Banks, and Yin, 1989; Kuwabara and Zook, 1991; Banks and Smith,

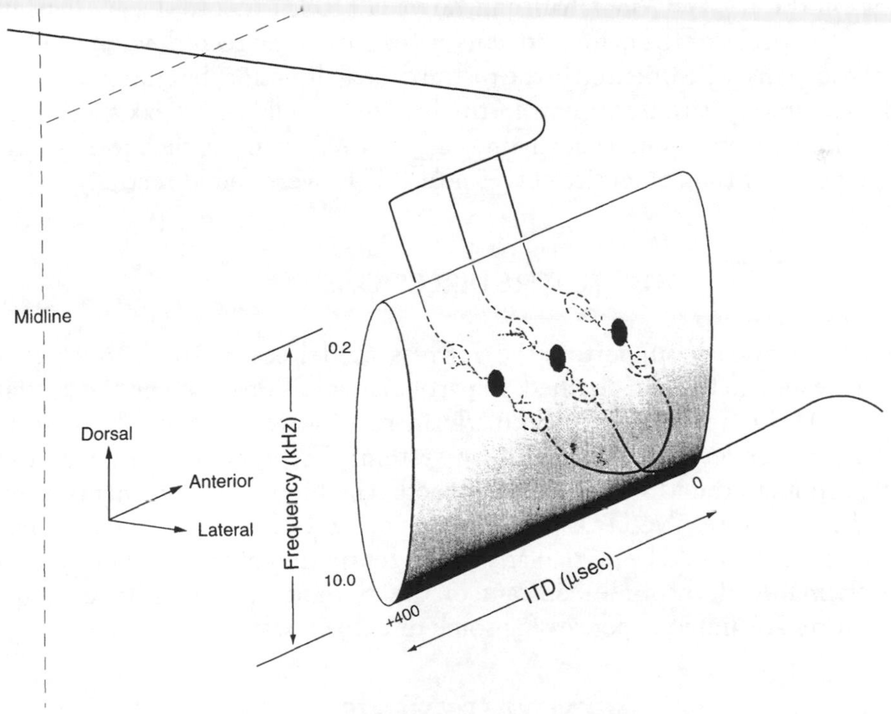

FIG. 9. Three-dimensional schematic diagram of the innervation of the right MSO in the cat. A single contralateral fiber and an ipsilateral fiber are shown innervating a row of MSO cells that lie in the same isofrequency lamina. The approximate ranges of the frequency and ITD axes are shown.

1992). Some cells of the lateral nucleus of the trapezoid body, which also appear glycinergic (Wenthold, Huie, Altschuler, and Reeks, 1987; Saint Marie, Ostapoff, Morest, and Wenthold, 1989), send a projection to the MSO (Cant and Hyson, 1992). Intracellular physiological recordings from the MSO in brain slices have demonstrated the presence of inhibitory postsynaptic potentials following shocks to the trapezoid body fibers (Grothe and Sanes, 1993; Smith, 1995). Extracellular recordings from MSO have also suggested that inhibitory processes may be active during auditory stimulation, based on the response at unfavorable ITDs (Yin and Chan, 1990) or to clicks (Rupert, Moushegian, and Whitcomb, 1966; Moushegian, Rupert, and Langford, 1967). However, a computer model of the MSO has shown that it is not necessary to postulate inhibitory processes in order to model the diminished response at unfavorable ITDs (Colburn, Han, and Cullota, 1990), which leaves unresolved the functional significance of the inhibitory inputs.

A logical consequence of the spatial map of ITDs in the MSO is the expectation that the map would be retained at higher levels in the auditory CNS. As mentioned earlier, many studies have shown that the phase sensitivity set up in the MSO is preserved in the discharge rate of IC cells (Rose, Gross, Geisler, and Hind, 1966; Kuwada and Yin, 1987). However, there is little evidence of a spatial map in any of the auditory nuclei above the level of the IC. In the IC there are only a few reports of such a spatial map: Aitkin, Pettigrew, Calford, Phillips, and Wise (1985) found evidence for a map of azimuthal space from free-field recordings in the IC, and Yin, Chan, and Kuwada (1983) reported a gradient in the ITD of the peaks of the composite curves from dichotic recordings in the IC. Both of these maps were oriented in the rostral caudal direction, but unfortunately seemed to be in opposite directions. In the free field, cells with peak sensitivity near the midline were found caudally in the IC, whereas in the dichotic experiments the peaks of the composite curves near 0 ITD were found rostrally.

IV. FUTURE DIRECTIONS

Although the evidence supporting the Jeffress model seems solid, much still remains to be elucidated and clarified. In particular, additional data on the spatial map in the MSO are needed, particularly in relation to whether the map is retained at higher levels of the auditory system. The functional role of the inhibitory inputs to the MSO is not understood. The biophysical mechanisms by which the cells can resolve ITDs on the order of tens of microseconds are not well understood. It would be particularly useful for models of the binaural system to have estimates of the time constant of the running cross-correlation. Our present efforts are aimed at addressing some of these questions.

ACKNOWLEDGMENTS

This work was supported by grants from the National Institute of Health (DC00116) and National Science Foundation (BNS-8901993).

REFERENCES

Adams, J. C., and Mugnaini, E. (**1990**). "Immunocytochemical evidence for inhibitory and disinhibitory circuits in the superior olive," Hear. Res. **49**, 281–298.

Aitkin, L. M., Pettigrew, J. D., Calford, M. B., Phillips, S. C., and Wise, L. Z. (**1985**). "Representation of stimulus azimuth by low-frequency neurons in inferior colliculus of the cat," J. Neurophysiol. **53**, 43–59.

Banks, M. I., and Smith, P. H. (**1992**). "Intracellular recordings from neurobiotin-labeled cells in brain slices of the rat medial nucleus of the trapezoid body," J. Neurosci. **12**, 2819–2837.

von Bekesy, G. (**1960**). *Experiments in Hearing* (McGraw-Hill, New York).

Blauert, J. (**1983**). *Spatial Hearing. The Psychophysics of Human Sound Localization* (MIT Press, Cambridge, MA).

de Boer, E., and de Jongh, H. R. (**1978**). "On cochlear encoding: Potentialities and limitations of the reverse-correlation technique," J. Acoust. Soc. Am. **63**, 115–134.

Bourk, T. R. (**1976**). *Electrical Responses of Neural Units in the Anteroventral Cochlear Nucleus of the Cat*, Ph.D. Thesis (MIT Press, Cambridge, MA).

Brawer, J. R., and Morest, D. K. (**1975**). "Relations between auditory nerve endings and cell types in the cat's anteroventral cochlear nucleus seen with the Golgi method and Nomarski optics," J. Comp. Neurol. **160**, 491–506.

Brawer, J. R., Morest, D. K., and Kane, E. C. (**1974**). "The neuronal architecture of the cochlear nucleus of the cat," J. Comp. Neurol. **155**, 251–300.

Brownell, W. E. (**1975**). "Organization of the cat trapezoid body and the discharge characteristics of its fibers," Brain Res. **94**, 413–433.

Brunso-Bechtold, J. K., Henkel, C. K., and Linville, C. (**1992**). "Ultrastructural development of the medial superior olive (MSO) in the ferret," J. Comp. Neurol. **324**, 539–558.

Cajal, R. Y. (**1909**). *Histologie du systeme nerveux, Vol. 1* (Instituto Ramon Y Cajal, Madrid, Spain).

Cant, N. B., and Casseday, J. H. (**1986**). "Projections from the anteroventral cochlear nucleus to the lateral and medial superior olivary nuclei," J. Comp. Neurol. **247**, 457–476.

Cant, N. B., and Hyson, R. L. (**1992**). "Projections from the lateral nucleus of the trapezoid body to the medial superior olivary nucleus in the gerbil," Hear. Res. **58**, 26–34.

Cant, N. B., and Morest, D. K. (**1979**). "Organization of the neurons in the anterior division of the anteroventral cochlear nucleus of the cat. Light microscopic observations," Neuroscience **4**, 1909–1923.

Carney, L. H., and Yin, T. C. T. (**1988**). "Temporal coding of resonances by low-frequency auditory nerve fibers: Single-fiber responses and a population model," J. Neurophysiol. **60**, 1653–1677.

Carr, C. E., and Konishi, M. (**1990**). "A circuit for detection of interaural time differences in the brainstem of the barn owl," J. Neurosci. **10**, 3227–3246.

Clark, G. M. (**1969**). "The ultrastructure of nerve endings in the medial superior olive of the cat," Brain Res. **14**, 293–305.

Colburn, H. S., and Durlach, N. I. (**1978**). "Models of binaural interaction," in *Handbook of Perception, Vol. IV, Hearing*, edited by E. C. Carterette and M. P. Friedman (Academic Press, Inc., New York), pp. 467–518.

Colburn, H. S., Han, Y. A., and Cullota, C. P. (**1990**). "Coincidence model of MSO responses," Hear. Res. **49**, 335–346.

Crow, G., Rupert, A. L., and Moushegian, G. (**1978**). "Phase locking in monaural and binaural medullary neurons: Implications for binaural phenomena," J. Acoust. Soc. Am. **64**, 493–501.

Goldberg, J. M., and Brown, P. B. (**1968**). "Functional organization of the dog superior olivary complex: An anatomical and electrophysiological study," J. Neurophysiol. **31**, 639–656.

Goldberg, J. M., and Brown, P. B. (**1969**). "Response of binaural neurons of dog superior olivary complex to dichotic tonal stimuli: Some physiological mechanisms of sound localization," J. Neurophysiol. **32**, 613–636.

Goldberg, J. M., and Brownell, W. E. (**1973**). "Discharge characteristics of neurons in the anteroventral and dorsal cochlear nuclei of cat," Brain Res. **64**, 35–54.

Grothe, B., and Sanes, D. H. (**1993**). "Bilateral inhibition by glycinergic afferents in the medial superior olive," J. Neurophysiol. **69**, 1192–1196.

Guinan, J. J., Jr., Norris, B. E., and Guinan, S.S. (**1972**). "Single auditory units in the superior olivary complex. II: Location of unit categories and tonotopic organization," Int. J. Neurosci. **4**, 147–166.

Held, H. (**1893**). "Die centrale Gehörleitung," Arch. Anat. Physiol., Anat. Abt., 201–248.

Jeffress, L. A. (**1948**). "A place theory of sound localization," J. Comp. Physiol. Psychol. **41**, 35–39.

Jenkins, W. M., and Masterton, R. B. (**1982**). "Sound localization: Effects of unilateral lesions in central auditory system," J. Neurophysiol. **47**, 987–1016.

Johnson, D. H. (**1980**). "The relationship between spike rate and synchrony in responses of auditory-nerve fibers to single tones," J. Acoust. Soc. Am. **68**, 1115–1122.

Joris, P. X., Carney, L. H., Smith, P. H., and Yin, T. C. T. (**1994**). "Enhancement of neural synchronization in the anteroventral cochlear nucleus. I: Responses to tones at the characteristic frequency," J. Neurophysiol. **71**, 1022–1036.

Joris, P. X., Smith, P. H., and Yin, T. C. T. (**1994**). "Enhancement of neural synchronization in the anteroventral cochlear nucleus. II. Responses in the tuning curve tail," J. Neurophysiol. **71**, 1037–1051.
Joseph, A. W., and Hyson, R. L. (**1993**). "Coincidence detection by binaural neurons in the chick brain stem," J. Neurophysiol. **69**, 1197–1211.
Kettner, R. E., Feng, J., and Brugge, J. F. (**1985**). "Postnatal development of the phase-locked response to low frequency tones of auditory nerve fibers in the cat," J. Neurosci. **5**, 275–283.
Kiang, N. Y. S., and Moxon, E. C. (**1974**). "Tails of tuning curves of auditory-nerve fibers," J. Acoust. Soc. Am. **55**, 620–630.
Kiang, N. Y. S., Rho, J. M., Northrup, C. C., Liberman, M. C., and Ryugo, D. K. (**1982**). "Hair-cell innervation by spiral ganglion cells in adult cats," Science **217**, 175–177.
Kiang, N. Y. S., Watanabe, T., Thomas, E. C., and Clark, L. F. (**1965**). *Discharge Pattern of Single Fibers in the Cat Auditory Nerve* (MIT Press, Cambridge, MA).
Kuhn, G. F. (**1977**). "Model for the interaural time differences in the azimuthal plane," J. Acoust. Soc. Am. **62**, 157–167.
Kuwabara, N., and Zook, J. M. (**1991**). "Classification of the principal cells of the medial nucleus of the trapezoid body," J. Comp. Neurol. **314**, 707–720.
Kuwada, S., and Yin, T. C. T. (**1987**). "Physiological mechanisms of directional hearing," in *Directional Hearing*, edited by W. A. Yost and G. Gourevitch (Springer-Verlag, Berlin), pp. 146–176.
Lavine, R. A. (**1971**). "Phase-locking in response of single neurons in cochlear nuclear complex of the cat to low-frequency tonal stimuli," J. Neurophysiol. **34**, 467–483.
Liberman, M. C. (**1982**). "Single-neuron labeling in the cat auditory nerve," Science **216**, 1239–1241.
Licklider, J. C. R. (**1959**). "Three auditory theories," in *Psychology: A Study of a Science*, edited by S. Koch (McGraw-Hill, New York), pp. 41–144.
Lindemann, W. (**1986**). "Extension of a binaural cross-correlation model by contralateral inhibition. I. Simulation of lateralization for stationary signals," J. Acoust. Soc. Am. **80**, 1608–1622.
Lindsey, B. G. (**1975**). "Fine structure and distribution of axon terminals from the cochlear nucleus on neurons in the medial superior olivary nucleus of the cat," J. Comp. Neurol. **160**, 81–103.
Moushegian, G., Rupert, A. L., and Langford, T. L. (**1967**). "Stimulus coding by medial superior olivary neurons," J. Neurophysiol. **30**, 1239–1261.
Osen, K. K. (**1969**). "Cytoarchitecture of the cochlear nuclei in the cat," J. Comp. Neurol. **136**, 453–484.
Overholt, E. M., Rubel, E. W., and Hyson, R. L. (**1992**). "A circuit for coding interaural time differences in the chick brain stem," J. Neurosci. **12**, 1698–1708.
Palmer, A. R., Winter, I. M., and Darwin, C. J. (**1986**). "The representation of steady-state vowel sounds in the temporal discharge patterns of the guinea pig cochlear nerve and primarylike cochlear nucleus neurons," J. Acoust. Soc. Am. **79**, 100–113.
Pfeiffer, R. R. (**1966a**). "Classification of response patterns of spike discharge for units in the cochlear nucleus: Tone burst stimulation," Exp. Brain Res. **1**, 220–235.
Pfeiffer, R. R. (**1966b**). "Anteroventral cochlear nucleus: Wave forms of extracellularly recorded spike potentials," Science **154**, 667–668.
Rhode, W. S., Oertel, D., and Smith, P. H. (**1983**). "Physiological response properties of cells labeled intracellularly with horseradish peroxidase in cat ventral cochlear nucleus," J. Comp. Neurol. **213**, 448–463.
Rhode, W. S., Smith, P. H., and Oertel, D. (**1983**). "Physiological response properties of cells labeled intracellularly with horseradish peroxidase in cat dorsal cochlear nucleus," J. Comp. Neurol. **213**, 426–447.
Rose, J. E., Gross, N. B., Geisler, C. D., and Hind, J. E. (**1966**). "Some neural mechanisms in the inferior colliculus of the cat which may be relevant to localization of a sound source," J. Neurophysiol. **29**, 288–314.
Roth, G. L., Kochhar, R. K., and Hind, J. E. (**1980**). "Interaural time differences: Implications regarding the neurophysiology of sound localization.," J. Acoust. Soc. Am. **68**, 1643–1651.
Ruggero, M. A. (**1973**). "Response to noise of auditory nerve fibers in the squirrel monkey," J. Neurophysiol. **36**, 569–587.
Rupert, A., Moushegian, G., and Whitcomb, M. A. (**1966**). "Superior-olivary response patterns to monaural and binaural clicks," J. Acoust. Soc. Am. **39**, 1069–1076.
Sachs, M. B., and Young, E. D. (**1979**). "Encoding of steady-state vowels in the auditory nerve: Representation in terms of discharge rate," J. Acoust. Soc. Am. **66**, 470–479.
Saint Marie, R. L., Ostapoff, E. M., Morest, D. K., and Wenthold, R. J. (**1989**). "Glycine immunoreactive projection of the cat lateral superior olive: Possible role in midbrain ear dominance," J. Comp. Neurol. **279**, 382–396.
Schwartz, I. R. (**1984**). "Axonal organization in the cat medial superior olivary nucleus," in *Contributions to Sensory Physiology*, edited by W.D. Neff (Academic Press, New York), pp. 99–129.
Smith, P. H. (**1995**). "Structural and functional differences distinguish principal from non-principal cells in the guinea pig MSO slice," J. Neurophysiol. **73**, 1653–1667.
Smith, P. H., Joris, P. X., Banks, M. I., and Yin, T. C. T. (**1989**). "Physiology and anatomy of principal cells in the cat MNTB," Soc. Neurosci. Abstr. **15**, 746.
Smith, P. H., Joris, P. X., Carney, L. H., and Yin, T. C. T. (**1991**). "Projections of physiologically characterized globular bushy cell axons from the cochlear nucleus of the cat," J. Comp. Neurol. **304**, 387–407.

Smith, P. H., Joris, P. X., and Yin, T. C. T. (**1993**). "Projections of physiologically characterized spherical bushy cell axons from the cochlear nucleus of cat: Evidence for delay lines to the medial superior olive," J. Comp. Neurol. **331**, 245–260.

Smith, P. H., and Rhode, W. S. (**1985**). "Electron microscopic features of physiologically characterized, HRP-labeled fusiform cells in the cat dorsal cochlear nucleus," J. Comp. Neurol. **237**, 127–143.

Smith, P. H., and Rhode, W. S. (**1987**). "Characterization of HRP-labeled globular bushy cells in the cat cochlear nucleus," J. Comp. Neurol. **266**, 360–376.

Smith, P. H., and Rhode, W. S. (**1989**). "Structural and functional properties distinguish two types of multipolar cells in the ventral cochlear nucleus," J. Comp. Neurol. **282**, 595–616.

Spoendlin, H. (**1969**). "Innervation patterns in the organ of Corti of cat, " Acta Otolaryngol. **67**, 239–254.

Stotler, W. A. (**1953**). "An experimental study of the cells and connections of the superior olivary complex of the cat," J. Comp. Neurol. **98**, 401–432.

van Gisbergen, J. A. M., Grashuis, J. L., Johannesma, P. I. M., and Vendrik, A. J. H. (**1975**). "Spectral and temporal characteristics of activation and suppression of units in the cochlear nuclei of the anaesthetized cat," Exp. Brain Res. **23**, 367–386.

Warr, W. B. (**1966**). "Fiber degeneration following lesions in the anterior ventral cochlear nucleus of the cat," Exp. Neurol. **14**, 453–474.

Wenthold, R. J., Huie, D., Altschuler, R. A., and Reeks, K. A. (**1987**). "Glycine immunoreactivity localized in the cochlear nucleus and superior olivary complex," Neurosci. **22**, 897–912.

Yin, T. C. T., and Chan, J. C. K. (**1990**). "Interaural time sensitivity in medial superior olive of cat," J. Neurophysiol. **64**, 465–488.

Yin, T. C. T., Chan, J. C. K., and Carney, L. H. (**1987**). "Effects of interaural time delays of noise stimuli on low-frequency cells in the cat's inferior colliculus. III. Evidence for cross-correlation," J. Neurophysiol. **58**, 562–583.

Yin, T. C. T., Chan, J. C. K., and Kuwada, S. (**1983**). "Characteristic delays and their topographical distribution in the inferior colliculus of the cat," in *Mechanisms of Hearing*, edited by W.R. Webster and L.M. Aitkin (Monash University Press, Victoria), pp. 94–99.

Young, S. R., and Rubel, E. W. (**1983**). "Frequency-specific projections of individual neurons in chick brainstem auditory nuclei," J. Neurosci. **3**, 1373–1378.

Chapter 22

Auditory Cortex and Spatial Hearing

John F. Brugge, Richard A. Reale, Joseph E. Hind
University of Wisconsin Medical School

(Received July 1994; revised May 1995)

Behavioral and physiological studies implicate auditory cortex as playing a pivotal role in spatial hearing. Here we describe a new approach to simulation of free-field sound sources and its application to studies of neural mechanisms of spatial hearing. We synthesized a set of signals (clicks) for earphone delivery whose waveforms and amplitude spectra, measured at the eardrum, mimic those of sounds arriving from a free-field source. A full array of these signals forms a "virtual acoustic space." Primary auditory cortical neurons exhibit "virtual space receptive fields" (VSRFs) similar to those obtained under open-field conditions. VSRFs of AI cells can be placed into five categories based on size and location at stimulus levels 20–30 dB above threshold. VSRFs are shaped, in part, by binaural interactions. These fields are not homogeneous throughout with respect to discharge strength or spike timing. For certain cells a restricted region in virtual acoustic space exists for which latency is shortest and firing level is highest. This is referred to as the "effective virtual space receptive field" and is interpreted as a focus of activity that may signal stimulus direction. Simulated linear movement of a sound source revealed that some cells are motion sensitive.

INTRODUCTION

Fundamental questions in the study of sensory perception relate to how the brain forms mental images, or scenes, of the world using the information provided by the senses. The problem faced by the brain is to assemble the various elements of the sensory input as transmitted in the peripheral nerve array in such a way that the representation of the world is accurate. This is the "scene analysis problem," and in recent years it has received increasing attention as it relates to hearing (Hartmann, 1988; Bregman, 1990; Handel, 1990; Yost, 1991). How the brain solves the scene analysis problem in hearing is not known. Among the attributes that contribute to forming an auditory image is spatial location, and evidence points to auditory cortex as playing a role in the localization process.

Auditory cortex usually refers to that collection of temporal fields receiving major ascending input via the auditory lemniscal routes, as well as those areas reached over more diffuse, nonlemniscal pathways. The organization of auditory cortex has been studied in a wide variety of mammalian orders. In those mammals in which the temporal regions have been mapped electrophysiologically, a tonotopically organized primary auditory field, AI, is recognized. It is usually surrounded by other auditory fields, which may or may not exhibit tonotopic order. Auditory cortical organization is probably best understood in the cat where it has undergone close scrutiny for some 50 years, beginning with the evoked-potential mapping studies of Woolsey and Walzl (1942). Figure 1 illustrates the spatial arrangement of the known auditory fields in cat. Those served by the lateral lemniscal pathways include the primary (AI) and second (AII) auditory areas, and the anterior (A), posterior (P), ventral (V), and ventral posterior (VP) auditory fields. Insular (IN) and temporal (T) auditory areas are identified, although little is known of their organization. Cortical auditory areas are richly and topographically interconnected, and they can be distinguished from one another on the bases

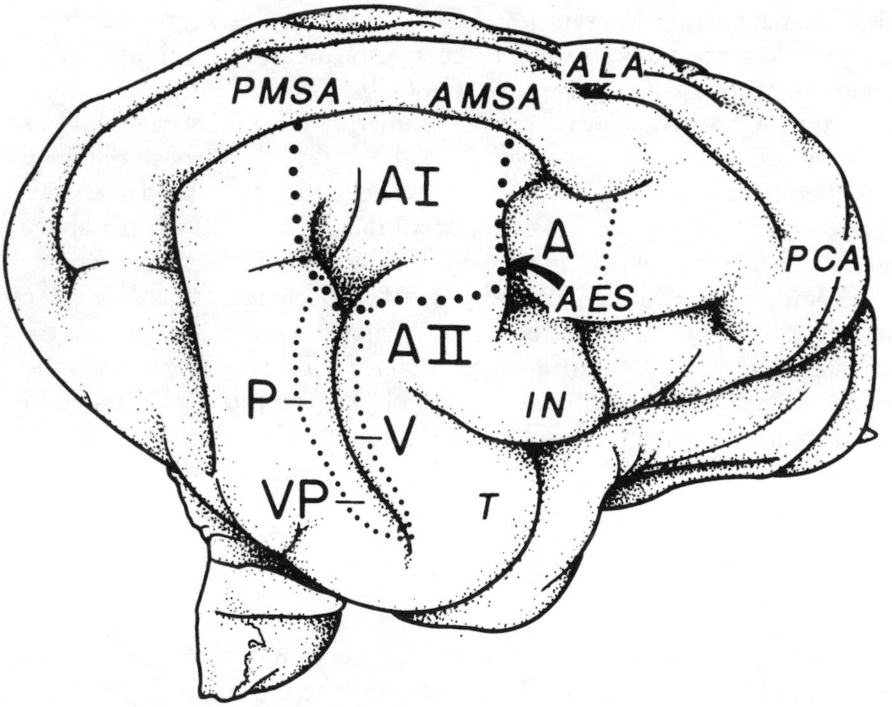

FIG. 1. Lateral view of the cat brain showing the locations of auditory fields identified electrophysiologically. Major lemniscal auditory fields include the primary (AI) and second (AII) auditory area, and the anterior (A), posterior (P), ventral (V), and ventral posterior (VP) auditory fields. Insular (IN) and temporal (T) auditory areas are identified, although little is known of their organization. Association cortex includes an area on the middle suprasylvian sulcus possibly made up of anterior (AMSA) and posterior (PMSA) fields, areas around the anterolateral (ALA) and the posterior cruciate (PCA) sulci, and a polysensory area (AES) located deep in the anterior ectosylvian sulcus.

of cytoarchitecture, connectivity patterns, functional maps, and neuronal coding properties. The functional architecture of the auditory forebrain, including cortical connections with the thalamus and striatum, has been reviewed extensively in recent years (Brugge and Reale, 1985; Aitkin, 1990; Clarey, Barone, and Imig, 1992; Winer, 1992).

Areas of the cortex that have been variously called "polysensory," "nonspecific," and "associational" may be considered part of a second (and possibly third) ascending auditory system sometimes called a "diffuse" or "lemniscal adjunct" system (Irvine and Phillips, 1982). Neurons in these cortical fields typically show poor frequency selectivity, blurred tonotopy, and considerable convergent input from other sensory systems. In the cat, these areas have been localized electrophysiologically to anterior ectosylvian (AES), suprasylvian (PMSA and AMSA), anterolateral (ALA), and pericruciate cortex (PCA). One of them, field AES (so named because of its location deep in the anterior ectosylvian sulcus), is of particular interest for studies of sound localization, for it is the only known auditory field that sends projections to the superior colliculus (Meredith and Clemo, 1989), where a map of auditory space has been shown to exist (Middlebrooks, 1988). Recently, Middlebrooks, Clock, Xu, and Green (1994) presented electrophysiological evidence for a mechanism whereby AES neurons may encode information about the direction of a sound source. Evidence from electrophysiological (Newman and Lindsley, 1976; Vaadia, Benson, Hienz, and Goldstein, 1986) and behavioral (Wegener, 1964) studies in the monkey has also implicated prefrontal cortex as playing a role in auditory localization.

Perhaps some of the first experiments that sought the location of auditory cortex also revealed a spatial hearing function for it. During focal electrical stimulation of the superior temporal gyrus of the monkey, Ferrier (1876) observed "sudden retraction or pricking of the opposite ear, wide opening of the eyes, dilation of the pupils, and turning of head and eyes to the opposite side." He went on to make similar observations in rabbits, cats, dogs, and jackals, concluding that this area was auditory cortex because "these phenomena resemble the sudden start and look of astonishment or surprise which are caused when a loud sound is made in the ear opposite the hemisphere which is being irritated." Much later Penfield and his colleagues reported the results of more than 1200 operations to relieve cerebral seizures in which exploratory electrical stimulation of the cerebral cortex was carried out in patients under local anesthesia (see Penfield and Perot, 1963, for a summary of results). When small currents were applied to regions of the temporal lobe surrounding Heschl's gyrus, the site of the primary auditory field in humans, the patient immediately reported hearing sounds that were often recognized as familiar and coming from the past, and some of them were perceived as coming from behind or out in the room or from a particular source (e.g., a radio). When the electrode was moved to Heschl's gyrus, the auditory sensation was usually a crude one consisting of a tone, buzz, or knocking sound with no indication that it had a spatial location.

Lesions of auditory cortex can create major impairments in performance of tasks requiring sound localization (Neff, 1968; Neff, Diamond, and Casseday, 1975; Heffner and Masterton, 1975; Heffner, 1978; Heffner and Heffner, 1990).

The results of such lesion-behavior studies have not been totally consistent, possibly because they were influenced by any number of experimental factors, including the size and location of the lesion, the natures of the tasks and tests, and the species under study (Elliott and Trahiotis, 1972).

Human patients that have undergone temporal lobectomy, usually to relieve the symptoms of epilepsy, consistently fail to localize accurately the source of a sound in the acoustic hemifield opposite the side of the lesion. Sanchez-Longo, Forster, and Auth (1957) reported this after simply using a tuning fork at the bedside, and later systematic studies of temporal lobectomized patients confirmed this observation (Sanchez-Longo *et al.*, 1957; Sanchez-Longo and Forster, 1958). Poirier, Lassonde, Villemure, Geoffroy, and Lepore (1994) reported recently that none of the three unilaterally hemispherectomized patients they studied was able to point accurately to a fixed sound source or to the beginning and end of a moving stimulus when the signal was in the opposite hemifield.

Under normal conditions and without learning, adult cats (and other mammals) tend to orient to a sudden and novel sound by executing a rapid and accurate head movement in the direction of the sound source. This ability to make a simple and natural response to sound is impaired, although not eliminated, by large bilateral auditory cortical lesions, especially when these lesions include the insular and temporal areas (Thompson and Welker, 1963; Thompson and Masterton, 1978; Beitel and Kaas, 1993). Systematic study of behavioral deficits caused by lesions at all levels of the auditory neuroaxis has led to the conclusion that the direction and accuracy of a head movement toward the source of an unexpected sound are mediated at cortical and subcortical levels by activity arising over both lemniscal and nonlemniscal auditory pathways (Thompson and Masterton, 1978; Beitel and Kaas, 1993).

Extensive unilateral or bilateral ablation of auditory cortex has little effect on the animal's ability to make a simple discrimination between a sound occurring to the left of the animal and one occurring to the right (Jenkins and Masterton, 1982; Kavanagh and Kelly, 1988; Heffner and Heffner, 1990). This is not surprising perhaps, for such a discrimination can be made on cues that are not necessarily "spatial" in nature. On the other hand, such lesions can have a devastating effect on sound-localizing ability when the animal is required to move to the sound source to obtain a food reward (Neff, Fisher, Diamond, and Yela, 1956; Strominger, 1969a, 1969b; Heffner and Heffner, 1990). As was the case for orienting behavior, a unilateral lesion impairs the animal's ability to perform such a task when the sound occurs in the opposite acoustic hemifield (Jenkins and Masterton, 1982). This failure to approach a sound source is not a motor deficit *per se*, for it can readily be demonstrated that animals with such lesions can perform similar motor acts under different conditions.

Whitfield and his colleagues (Whitfield, Cranford, Ravizza, and Diamond, 1972; Whitfield, 1977) trained cats in a Y-maze to discriminate between trains of pulses delivered from sources on the left or right. Various stimulus configurations were employed in an attempt to isolate the sensory and perceptual elements associated with the behavior. Unilateral destruction of cortex confined to AI, AII, and the posterior ectosylvian field (as defined by Woolsey, 1960, 1961, and which includes those parts of fields P and VP on the gyral surface) was sufficient to disrupt performance in the acoustic hemifield where an "apparent" source would be found based on whether the left or right stimulus train was time-delayed. These authors found that lesioned animals did not consistently move in the wrong direction in the maze, but they simply ran at random. Whitfield (1977) interpreted this result to mean that to the cat with such an auditory cortical lesion the sound source did not have a wrong direction—it had no direction. Wegener (1964) in his studies of decorticate monkeys came to a similar conclusion, that auditory cortical lesions disrupt the organization of auditory space. Thus, although the mechanisms that underlie these behavioral response patterns are not known, it seems that auditory cortical lesions create a deficit in the perception of "acoustic space" in which the ability to detect the spatial attributes of the sound is impaired or is no longer related to mechanisms that underlie the execution of the motor patterns necessary to move toward the sound (see also Heffner and Masterton, 1975; Heffner, 1978; Heffner and Heffner, 1990; Beitel and Kaas, 1993).

In order to address the question of which cortical field(s) contribute to localization behavior, attempts have been made to confine lesions to one or a few of the known auditory cortical fields (e.g., Strominger, 1969a). Unfortunately for such studies, the location of auditory fields with respect to brain surface landmarks varies considerably from one animal to the next even within the same species; thus localization of lesions using such anatomical features is subject to certain error. Jenkins and Merzenich (1984) circumvented this problem by first mapping cortex with microelectrodes, thereby identifying the boundaries and tonotopic organization of field AI. They then created a lesion confined not only to AI but to a narrow strip of cortex within it representing a small range of characteristic frequencies. They found that under conditions in which the lesioned cat was trained to choose the location of one of seven sound sources in the horizontal plane, localization performance was significantly impaired for brief tones in the contralateral auditory hemifield at frequencies roughly corresponding to those whose representations were destroyed by the lesion. Taken together, results of lesion-behavior studies indicate that AI (and perhaps other fields as well) is necessary for normal binaural sound-localization performance and that major mechanisms reside in the cerebral hemisphere on the side opposite from the field in which the sound arises. Furthermore, in AI at least, processing of sound direction is carried out along frequency-specific channels.

I. AUDITORY CORTICAL NEURONS ENCODE SOUND-LOCALIZATION CUES OF INTERAURAL TIME AND INTENSITY

Most electrophysiological studies of sound localization mechanisms in animals have employed closed-field stimulation through sealed and calibrated earphone systems, thereby allowing independent control of the stimulus at each ear. The experimental paradigm has typically been limited to observing the effects of changes in interaural time difference (ITD) and interaural level difference (ILD) of simple sounds such as clicks and pure tones (for reviews, see Yin and Kuwada, 1984; Kuwada and Yin, 1987).

Using this approach, it is now well established that auditory cortical neurons are sensitive to ITD and ILD cues used by listeners to localize sound sources. In primary auditory cortex of cat (Brugge, Dubrovsky, Aitkin, and Anderson, 1969; Reale and Brugge, 1990), monkey (Brugge and Merzenich, 1973), and chinchilla (Benson and Teas, 1976), neurons have been found to be sensitive to small static changes in ITD (or interaural phase) when stimulus frequency is below about 3 kHz. In the cat, this sensitivity is also exhibited by neurons in the posterior (Orman and Phillips, 1984) and anterior (Brugge *et al.*, 1969) auditory fields. Moreover, when low-frequency tones of slightly different frequency are delivered to two ears, thereby creating a binaural beat, AI neurons exhibit sensitivity to shifting interaural phase. AI neurons may also exhibit a "characteristic delay," thereby detecting an interaural time difference independent of the frequency content of the source signal (Reale and Brugge, 1990).

For cortical neurons responding to high stimulus frequency, spike count and spike timing are a function of sound level at the two ears and of interaural level differences created by the acoustical filtering properties of the ears, head, and torso (Brugge *et al.*, 1969; Phillips and Irvine, 1981, 1983; Semple and Kitzes, 1993a, 1993b). Neurons with these properties are generally believed to be involved in mechanisms underlying a listener's ability to use ILD for high-frequency sound localization. Semple and Kitzes (1993a, 1993b), in their systematic study of interaural level sensitivity of high-frequency AI neurons, found that the discharge of a great majority of cells depended on both the ILD and the overall stimulus level. This resulted in an excitatory focus over a limited range of SPL at each ear. Each neuron was "tuned" broadly to a different SPL combination such that there was considerable overlap in the response domains of different cells. Most neurons exhibited excitatory foci with SPL combinations favoring the contralateral ear or when the binaural SPLs were the same. The free-field results of Imig, Irons, and Samson (1990), showing that the response of many recorded AI neurons is a joint function of azimuth and stimulus level, are consistent with these dichotic studies. Thus, Semple and Kitzes (1993b) postulated that tuning by single AI neurons to binaural SPL and the pattern of activity generated within a population of such neurons could provide an accurate cortical representation of both spatial direction and incident-sound intensity.

Interaural time and level sensitivities exhibited by cortical neurons may be largely the result of binaural interactions taking place in the brainstem and midbrain, for they mirror those shown by cells in the medial and lateral superior olivary nuclei, the dorsal nucleus of the lateral lemniscus, and the central nucleus of the inferior colliculus (Aitkin, 1985; Irvine, 1985). The question naturally arises with respect to the possible emerging properties that forebrain circuits might impose on this sensitivity. One answer may lie with proportions. It has been found, for example, that binaural level sensitivity is more widespread among AI neurons (Semple and Kitzes, 1993a) than in neurons of the central nucleus of the inferior colliculus (Semple and Kitzes, 1987). Another may lie with the fact that ILD and ITD sensitivity has been characterized mainly in animals under anesthesia. In unanesthetized but untrained animals, ILD and ITD sensitivities also are clearly recognized but are superimposed on changes in excitability related to the state of the animal (Brugge and Merzenich, 1973). In trained animals, however, it can be shown that the sensitivity and discharge properties of at least some auditory cortical neurons are highly dependent on the behavioral context in which a stimulus appears (Benson, Hienz, and Goldstein, 1981; Gottlieb, Vaadia, and Abeles, 1989).

II. SENSITIVITY OF CORTICAL NEURONS TO THE DIRECTION OF SOUND SOURCES IN SPACE

It is well known that a human subject receiving dichotic stimuli over headphones involving only ITD and ILD cues tends to perceive a sound source located within or close to the head (Plenge, 1974); discrimination of ITD or ILD cues is usually designated as lateralization, to distinguish it from localization of a sound source in three-dimensional space (Yost and Hafter, 1987). To create a realistic, out-of-the-head listening experience, more complex cues must be included, such as those introduced by pinna directionality and by reflections from objects in the acoustical environment. Thus, although closed-field experiments employing only ITD and ILD have been useful in illuminating neural mechanisms of binaural interaction that may underlie sound localizing ability, the results do not reflect the complex manner in which these quantities actually vary when a sound source changes direction in the open field. Thus, in order to understand cortical mechanisms involved in localization behavior it is imperative that a way be found to study the interactions of spatial attributes of a sound in a controlled and systematic way.

Several laboratories have taken a direct approach to studying mechanisms of sound localization in cat AI by creating an open-field acoustic environment, utilizing either a single movable sound source or an array of closely spaced speakers within an anechoic space (Middlebrooks and Pettigrew, 1981; Imig *et al.*, 1990; Rajan, Aitkin, Irvine, and McKay, 1990; Rajan, Aitkin, and Irvine, 1990). Under these conditions, a large percentage of AI neurons has been found to be sensitive to sounds originating in restricted regions of acoustic space: They exhibit spatial receptive fields.

Middlebrooks and Pettigrew (1981) found that about half of their sample of AI cells was selective for sound-source direction. These they divided into two populations: hemifield neurons, which responded only to sound presented in the contralateral auditory hemifield, and axial neurons, which had spatial receptive fields that coincided with the acoustical axis of the contralateral pinna. In all cases reported, spatial receptive fields were relatively large in relation to the auditory spatial acuity of the cat (Martin and Webster, 1987). Furthermore, although the two populations tended to show preferential cortical distribution, there was no indication of a systematic map of acoustic space in AI. Similar studies, but of a more quantitative nature, were carried out by Imig *et al.* (1990), Rajan, Aitkin, Irvine, and McKay (1990), and Rajan, Aitkin, and Irvine (1990). These studies estimated the population of direction-dependent cells at between 76% and 82%. Most of these neurons (31–35%) preferred sounds at azimuths in the contralateral hemifield, with the remainder split about equally between cells preferring ipsilateral and frontal locations. Imig *et al.* (1990) also found neurons whose spike output was a nonmonotonic function of sound pressure level, and these cells exhibited the highest directionality for azimuth (horizontal plane). The azimuthal functions presented in the Imig and Rajan studies are also broad, in agreement with the earlier Middlebrooks and Pettigrew results.

Open-field approaches using a movable speaker or a speaker array, although creating "natural" transformations of the sound reaching the eardrums, have several limitations. First, there is the obvious difficulty of eliminating reflections and diffraction caused by the surfaces of the room and necessary apparatus, especially at the higher frequencies to which many animals, including the cat, are sensitive. This becomes important for accurate measurement of the spatial cues introduced by the head and external ears alone. Second, in studies using a single movable speaker, the time required to reposition the source after each trial usually determines the number of locations that can be sampled in a given amount of time and thus limits the spatial solid angle that can be explored, as well as the degree of spatial resolution that can be achieved. This is a crucial problem in studying single neurons, which remain in contact with a recording electrode for limited periods of time. With a speaker array, experiments are limited to the fixed position of the array (usually horizontal). Third, it is difficult, if not impossible, to manipulate independently and parametrically each of the different cues known to be used in sound localization, including ITD, ILD, spectrum, and the relative amounts of direct and reflected sound in a typical listening environment. All of these limitations can be overcome by the use of appropriately synthesized dichotic stimuli presented separately to each ear via insert earphones.

III. VIRTUAL ACOUSTIC ENVIRONMENT

Since the pioneering work of Sutherland (1965, 1968) on the head-mounted three-dimensional virtual visual display, attempts have been made to produce virtual acoustic displays, that is, sounds that, when presented over headphones, simulate a free-field listening experience (for reviews see Blauert, 1983; Wenzel, 1992). Wightman, Kistler, and Perkins (1987) and Wightman and Kistler (1989a, 1989b) used digital signal processing techniques to produce such signals, arguing that if the acoustical waveforms at a listener's eardrums are the same under headphone and open-field listening conditions, then the auditory experience under these two conditions should also be the same. Indeed, localization by human listeners was shown by Wightman and colleagues to be as accurate using these headphone stimuli as it was under open-field conditions. This approach now provides a valuable experimental tool by which "localization," as opposed to "lateralization," of a sound source can be studied under highly controlled acoustic conditions.

We have implemented a "virtual acoustic space" (VAS) for the cat using a strategy similar to that of Wightman and Kistler (1989a); transient stimuli that mimic the sounds arriving at the cat's eardrums from different open-field directions are delivered through calibrated earphones (Brugge, Reale, Hind, Chan,

Musicant, and Poon, 1994). This approach now enables us to synthesize and control dichotically those sound-pressure waveforms present near the tympanums that contain salient localization cues generated by an open-field sound source and thus provides an opportunity to study parametrically neural mechanisms of directional hearing.

A. Virtual acoustic space—Direction-dependent acoustic transformation of time, level, and spectrum

Sound arriving at the tympanic membranes of a listener in a open sound field varies with source direction, in part due to reflection and diffraction caused by the torso and head but also because of the directional transmission characteristics of the external ear or pinna (see Shaw, 1974a, for a review). The combined influence of these acoustical factors can be evaluated in terms of a "free-field to eardrum transfer function" (FETF), which expresses, for a given source direction and over a specified range of frequencies, the transformations of amplitude and phase that occur from sound pressure measured in the free field in the absence of a subject to the pressure measured near the eardrum when the subject is introduced into the sound field. In psychoacoustics the term "head-related transfer function" (HRTF) is used even though it is clear that structures in addition to the head contribute to the acoustical properties. Estimation of the FETF involves both systematic free-field measurements and appropriate compensation for the undesirable spectral characteristics of the sound delivery and measurement systems. The FETFs derived from measurements in both cat and human are characterized by peaks and notches, some of which vary systematically in frequency with changes in source direction (Shaw, 1974b; Musicant, Chan, and Hind, 1990; Rice, May, Spirou, and Young, 1992). Along with ITD and ILD, these direction-dependent changes in spectral features in the FETF are believed to provide cues used in localizing a source of sound in space, especially under conditions of monaural listening (Musicant and Butler, 1984) or when the sound is on the midsaggital plane (Blauert, 1969; Hebrank and Wright, 1974; Butler and Belendiuk, 1977).

B. FETF estimation

In a VAS approach, the sound-pressure waveforms that would be present near the right and left tympanums are computed using the appropriate pair of FETFs corresponding to the specified direction and are then delivered through compensated earphones in the closed field. The success of the VAS–earphone procedure depends first on accurately estimating an FETF from two open-field measurements. One represents the free-field recording made without the presence of the animal, and the second represents the recording made near the animal's eardrum for the specified sound-source direction. In our experiments, these raw data are used to model the FETF as a finite-impulse-response (FIR) filter (Chen, Wu, and Reale, 1994). The coefficients of the FIR filter are determined using a least-squares error criterion. The least-squares FIR filter is implemented entirely in the time domain and thereby avoids the usual problems associated with division, which are inherent in a frequency-domain estimation. An FETF estimated by a least-squares FIR filter is veracious; its impulse response can be used to synthesize signals that were recorded near the eardrum in the open field with a very high fidelity. Figures 2A and 2B illustrate, respectively, a waveform recorded near the eardrum and the corresponding waveform synthesized using the FETF from the same sound-source direction. Comparing 3632 sample pairs yields a correlation coefficient that typically exceeds 0.99 (Fig. 2C).

The FETFs used in our neurophysiological studies were derived from a detailed set of direction-dependent recordings made near the tympanum of anesthetized cats in an anechoic room by Musicant and colleagues (1990). In that study, a

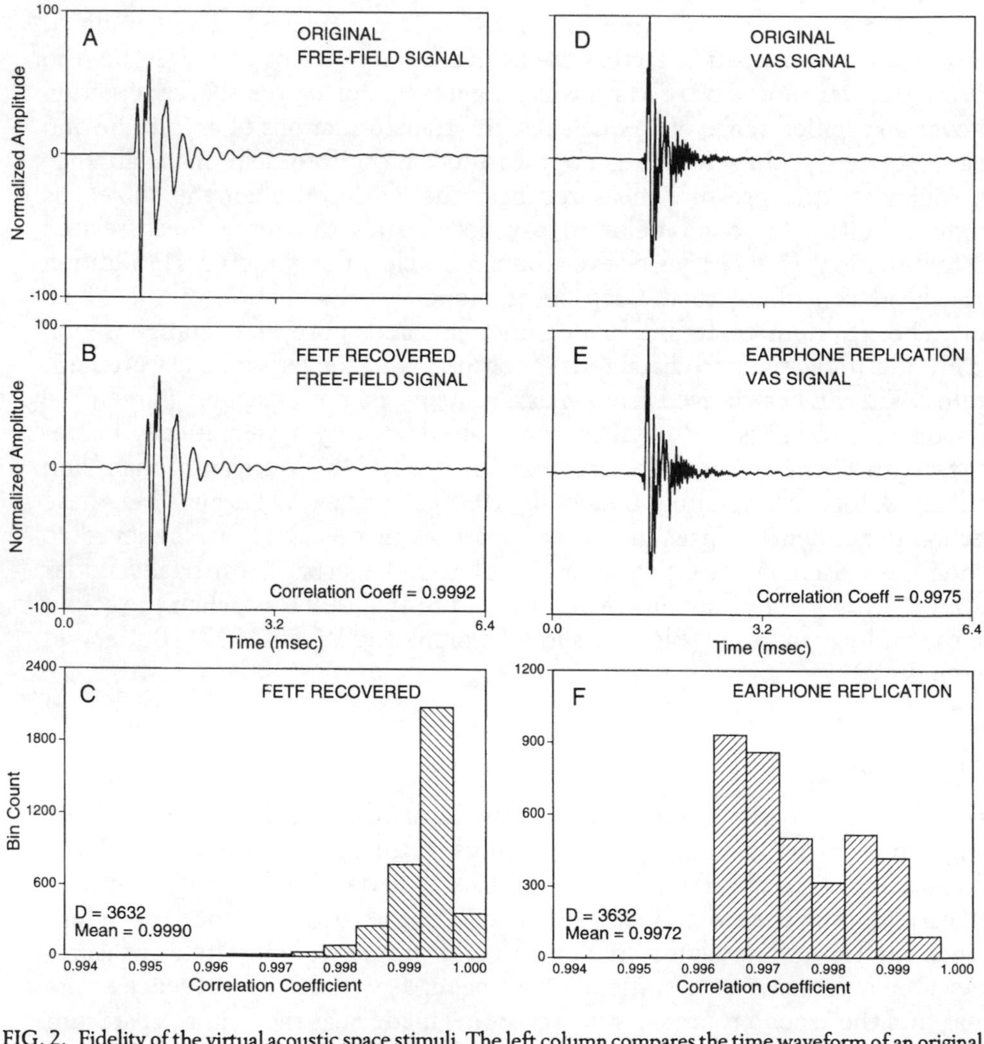

FIG. 2. Fidelity of the virtual acoustic space stimuli. The left column compares the time waveform of an original free-field signal recorded by a probe microphone near the eardrum (A) to the signal computed (or recovered) with the FETF (B) for the same sound-source direction. Histogram (C) shows the distribution of correlation coefficients for 3632 sample comparisons. The right column compares an original time waveform of a signal synthesized with the VAS (D) to the waveform delivered through the compensated insert earphone system (E). Histogram (F) shows distribution of correlation coefficients for 3632 sample comparisons.

rectangular pulse was used to excite the free-field loudspeaker, whose direction was varied systematically in a spherical coordinate system, in steps as fine as 4.5°, covering 360° in azimuth (horizontal direction) and 126° in elevation (vertical direction). The animal's interaural axis was centered within the sphere, with 0° azimuth directly in front and 180° directly behind the cat. Miniature microphones (Knowles EA 1934), which had been fitted with probe tubes and surgically implanted in the wall of the ear canal, were used to record the pressure waveforms near the eardrums. Recordings were made near the right and left eardrums for each position at which the loudspeaker was located. Figure 3 shows the animal's head centered within an imaginary sphere having a coordinate system the same as that used in obtaining both ear canal pressure measurements and the neuronal responses to VAS stimulation. For logistical reasons it has not been possible to obtain FETFs and carry out electrophysiological recording in the same animal, although results from human psychophysical studies (Wightman and Kistler, 1989b; Pralong and Carlile, 1994) indicate that such an approach is feasible. Instead, we constructed a VAS from a set of 3632 FETFs derived for one of the cats in the Musicant *et al.* (1990) study summarized earlier. This VAS was used to synthesize stimuli for all other experimental cats undergoing single-neuron recording.

C. Insert earphone sound delivery

The VAS earphone procedure also requires appropriate compensation for the undesirable spectral characteristics of the closed-field earphone sound delivery and measurement systems. Ideally, the frequency response of both sound systems would be characterized by a spectrum that has flat magnitude and linear phase characteristics. Although a specially designed insert earphone sound system (Chan, Musicant, and Hind, 1993) is employed, neither the earphone nor the measuring probe microphone typically used in neurophysiological studies has such ideal characteristics. In the past, this problem was partially remedied by a simple inverse filtering technique. This technique can be an unstable process, however, and it generally requires ad hoc filter-design rules specific to the system being compensated. Instead, we have adopted the least-squares FIR filter as an alternative method to compensate the nonideal sound delivery and measurement systems (Chen *et al.*, 1994). As was the case in FETF estimation, subjective compromises in the filter's design were not necessary when a least-squares FIR filter was applied to the task of compensation. Similarly, least-squares FIR filters proved excellent in compensating closed-field sound systems. Figures 2D and 2E show, respectively, a comparison between an original VAS signal and the corresponding waveform delivered by a compensated earphone. As can be seen the waveforms are nearly identical, and for the entire sample set the correlation was nearly perfect (Fig. 2F).

D. Virtual space receptive fields

Previous free-field studies have illustrated spatial tuning curves (Middlebrooks and Pettigrew, 1981) and azimuthal functions (Imig *et al.*, 1990; Rajan, Aitkin,

Irvine, and McKay, 1990; Rajan, Aitkin, and Irvine, 1990) exhibited by AI neurons. A spatial tuning curve shows the boundaries of responsiveness of a cortical neuron, but nothing about the information-bearing content of neuronal discharge within it. Azimuthal functions, on the other hand, provide quantitative information about the neuronal discharges within a spatial tuning curve, but do so along a single dimension and only for discharge rate. Using the VAS approach, we have been able to study in a systematic and quantitative way both the discharge time and rate over the full extent of a spatial receptive field.

Data have been obtained from more than 200 neurons located in the high-frequency representation of area AI in cats under sodium barbiturate anesthesia. In these experiments we were also able to test a neuron's responsiveness to pure tones. Fewer than 5% of recorded AI cells failed to respond to tones; the

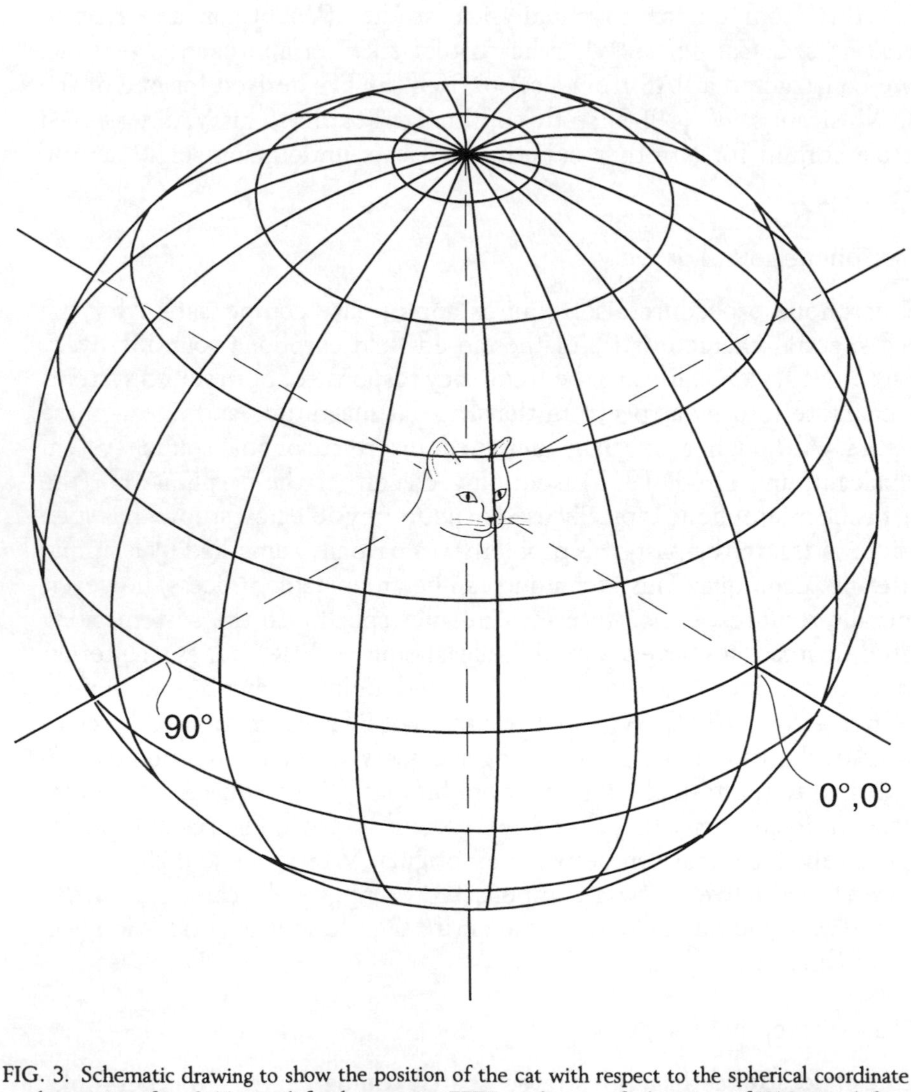

FIG. 3. Schematic drawing to show the position of the cat with respect to the spherical coordinate system used to position free-field stimuli for determining FETFs and to specify directions of VAS stimuli for mapping spatial sensitivity of single neurons.

characteristic frequencies of responsive neurons ranged from 9.0 to 25.5 kHz. The data presented here were obtained using click stimuli (e.g., Fig. 2E) that were computed for each of the 1816 virtual-space directions. Stimuli from all directions, or from some subset of them, were presented in random order at a rate of about 5/s. Stimulus intensity could be attenuated over a range of 127 dB from the maximal stimulus level available. Stimuli were attenuated equally at the two ears. Primary auditory cortical neurons responded to an effective VAS stimulus with a time-locked single spike or burst of two to three spikes. The onset latency varied from neuron to neuron and, for any given neuron, from one location to another. Nearly 80% of cells responded to the synthesized clicks, and of those, more than 90% responded to both clicks and tones. Around 20% of neurons responded to tones presented monaurally or binaurally but failed to respond to clicks at any virtual-space direction.

For most neurons, clicks were effective in influencing a neuron's discharge only at selected virtual-space directions. The aggregation of these effective directions forms what we refer to as a "virtual space receptive field" (VSRF). The VSRF data shown in Fig. 4 were obtained at an intensity of about 20dB above the lowest threshold for the given neuron. We chose this stimulus level for the purpose of comparing the VSRF results with data obtained by others on the responses of AI neurons to free-field sounds (Middlebrooks and Pettigrew, 1981; Imig *et al.*, 1990; Rajan, Aitkin, Irvine, and McKay, 1990; Rajan, Aitkin, and Irvine, 1990). Data

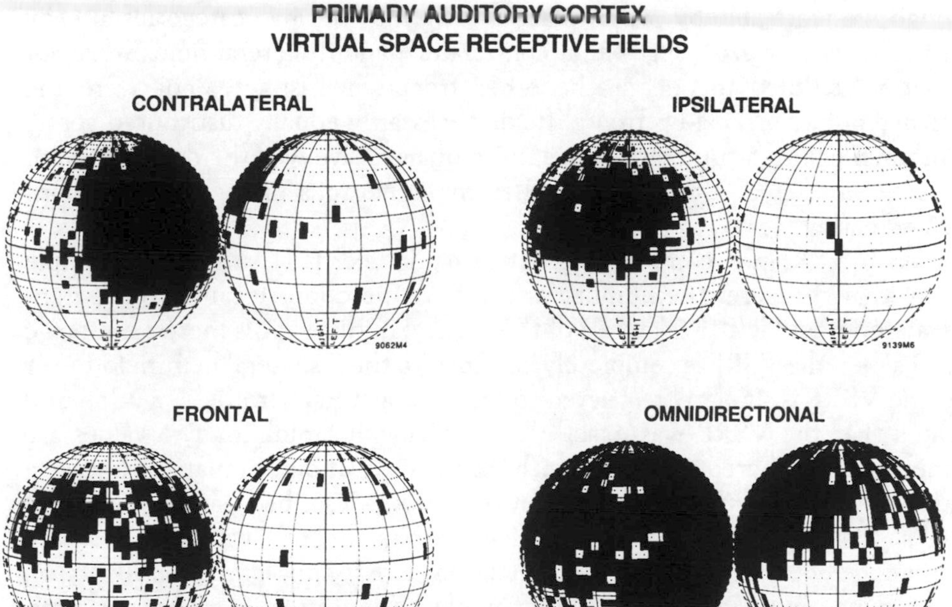

FIG. 4. VSRF classes. Four of the five categories derived from recordings of single neurons in cat AI cortex. Data are plotted on an orthographic projection of the interior surface of the coordinate sphere that has been bisected into a FRONT (left) and REAR (right) hemisphere; the rear hemisphere is shown rotated 180° as if hinged to the front hemisphere. Thus, the sphere is shown from the cat's point of view. Black squares indicate spike discharge at the virtual space locus; small filled circles indicate null points.

are plotted on the same simple orthographic projection illustrated in Fig. 3. About 15 min was required to obtain a VSRF. VSRFs were remarkably stable in configuration over several hours of recording time (Brugge *et al.*, 1994).

Different cells have VSRFs that differ from each other in location, extent, and shape, as illustrated in Fig. 4. We were able to place a VSRF into one of five classes. The majority of recorded cells (~70%) had VSRFs that were largely confined to either the contralateral (Fig. 4A) or ipsilateral (Fig. 4B) sound hemifield, and of those, contralateral VSRFs outnumbered ipsilateral VSRFs by 6 to 1. A smaller percentage (<10%) of cells had VSRFs that spanned the frontal quadrants (Fig. 4C) and hence showed little or no left–right preference. Somewhat fewer than 20% of cells were omnidirectional—that is, they showed little or no preference for any stimulus direction (Fig. 4D); effective directions represented regions in front of, behind, above, and below the animal. The remaining neurons (<10%) exhibited what, for lack of a better term, we refer to as "complex" VSRFs (not shown). A complex VSRF was often crescent or doughnut shaped, and could include regions where the discharge of the neuron appeared to be suppressed. The classes described here are in general agreement with those obtained by Middlebrooks and Pettigrew (1981) under open-field conditions and with the classes of azimuthal functions obtained by Rajan, Aitkin, Irvine, and McKay (1990), Rajan, Aitkin, and Irvine (1990), and Imig *et al.* (1990), also under open-field conditions.

VSRFs varied in both their location and size, even within a given category. Although we were able by eye to place VSRFs into the five categories already described, it is clear from Fig. 4 that contralateral and ipsilateral fields were not necessarily confined to one or the other frontal hemisphere, nor were the responsive points making up frontal fields necessarily equally distributed across the midline. Figure 5 summarizes in a more quantitative way the distribution of locations and sizes of VSRFs obtained from 76 neurons under the conditions described earlier.

For each VSRF we computed a "laterality index" (LI), which is a simple measure that compares the number of effective directions located to the right (contralateral) and left (ipsilateral) of the vertical midline. This metric can range from −1 when the VSRF is completely confined to the ipsilateral hemifield to +1 when the VSRF is similarly restricted to the contralateral hemifield; a value of 0 indicates that the VSRF was exactly bisected by the midline. The values are continuously distributed in Fig. 5A, with the majority of determinations between 0 and +1, reflecting the qualitative categorization described earlier. This contralateral bias agrees with the open-field results in both cat (Evans, 1968; Eisenman, 1974; Middlebrooks and Pettigrew, 1981; Imig *et al.*, 1990; Rajan, Aitkin, Irvine, and McKay, 1990) and monkey (Benson *et al.*, 1981; Ahissar, Ahissar, Berman, and Vaadia, 1992) and with what can be inferred from ILD data obtained under dichotic conditions (Hall and Goldstein, 1968; Phillips and Irvine, 1981, 1983; Phillips and Gates, 1982). Cells judged qualitatively to be omnidirectional had an LI around zero (−0.14 to +0.22).

The area of the VSRF can be expressed in spherical degrees. A spherical degree is that portion of a sphere enclosed by a spherical triangle with two sides each

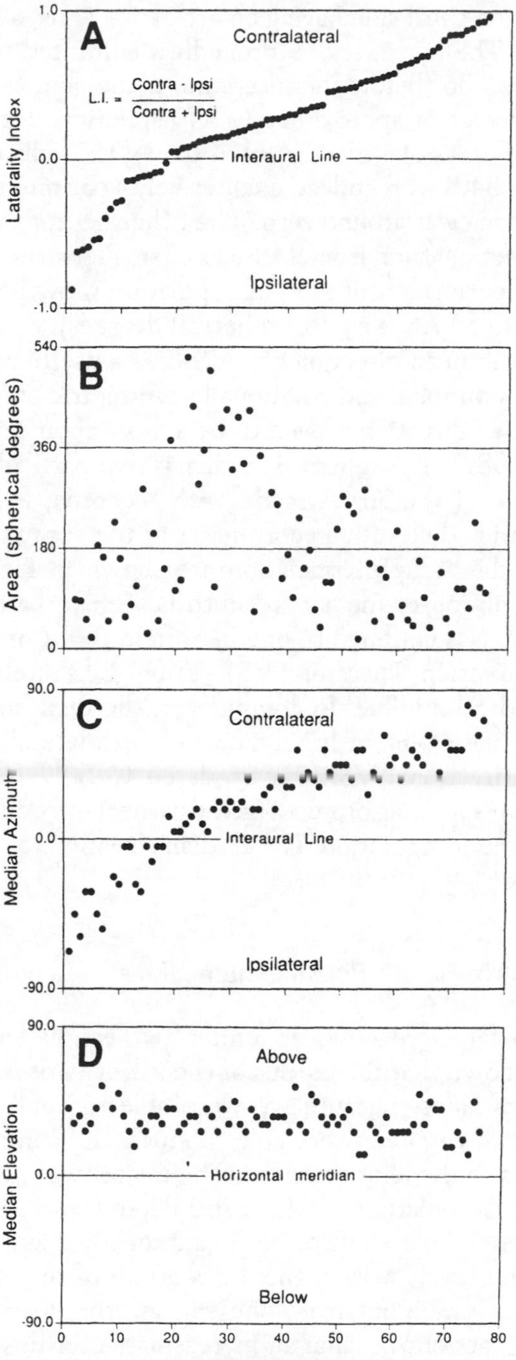

FIG. 5. Metrics of the VSRF. The abscissa in all panels represents the ordinal number of the neuron for which a VSRF was determined at a level approximately 20 dB greater than threshold. (A) LI is a measure of the degree to which the VSRF falls to the left or right of the vertical midline. A value of −1 occurs when all effective directions are to the left (ipsilateral) of the vertical midline and +1 when the VSRF is entirely to the right (contralateral) of midline. (B) The area of the VSRF was obtained by assigning each effective direction a value proportional to its nearest-neighbor distance. (C and D) Median azimuth and median elevation are measures of the VSRF direction; they were determined by computing the spherical median direction.

having arcs of 90° and the third side having an arc of 1°. Thus, a sphere contains 720 spherical degrees. The current VAS procedure is limited to sound-source directions not more than 36° below the interaural plane, and the largest VSRF possible would have an area of approximately 540 spherical degrees. Figure 5B plots the distribution of areas of VSRFs. All but one of the cells with the largest areas (between 360 and 540) were judged qualitatively to be omnidirectional; the LI for each of the neurons was around zero. The other neurons with an LI near zero represent omnidirectional and frontal VSRFs of smaller sizes. Approximately 67% of the remaining neurons in this sample population show VSRFs occupying less than a full quadrant of VAS (i.e., 180 spherical degrees).

Although the spherical mean direction of a VSRF is a useful metric when the spatial pattern appears unimodal and rotationally symmetric about some direction, the spherical median direction proved to be a more robust statistic (Fisher, Lewis, and Embleton, 1987). The spherical median is that particular direction for which the average value of the angles made with receptive field directions is minimized. The azimuth and elevation coordinates of the approximate spherical median directions for this sample population are shown in Figs. 5C and 5D, respectively. The distribution of median azimuth is seen to parallel that of LI. Thus, the more a VSRF was confined to one hemifield (right or left), the more lateral was its median direction. Therefore, VSRFs of high LI rarely have a median direction near the veridical midline. In comparison, the distribution of median elevation is rather flat, indicating little relationship with laterality. The median elevation for an omnidirectional VSRF is expected to be zero; however, the vertical asymmetry in our sampling protocol (given earlier) introduces an elevation bias that is reflected in the computation. The median elevation value of the sample population is 33°.

E. Virtual Space Receptive Fields - Binaural Interactions

The VSRFs shown so far were obtained under two-ear listening conditions. Previous studies have shown that the output of the majority of AI neurons is the result of binaural interactions. Because we were able to control the stimulus independently at the two ears, we were able to study the contributions of the left-and right-ear inputs to the joint response. The majority of neurons recorded were excited by click stimulation of the contralateral ear alone; for others stimulation of the ipsilateral ear alone or both ears together was most effective. Although at low stimulus levels, within about 20–30 dB of threshold, the VSRF was often dominated by the input from one ear, as stimulus level was raised bilaterally, binaural interactions became an increasing factor in shaping a VSRF. Figure 6 presents data from two neurons under monotic and dichotic conditions, illustrating the most common findings.

The neuron illustrated on the left (Fig. 6A–C) exhibited a "summative" interaction. For this neuron, direction-dependent clicks delivered to the left ear alone resulted in excitatory responses to signals originating mainly in the ipsilateral frontal sound field. The reverse situation obtained with monotic stimulation of

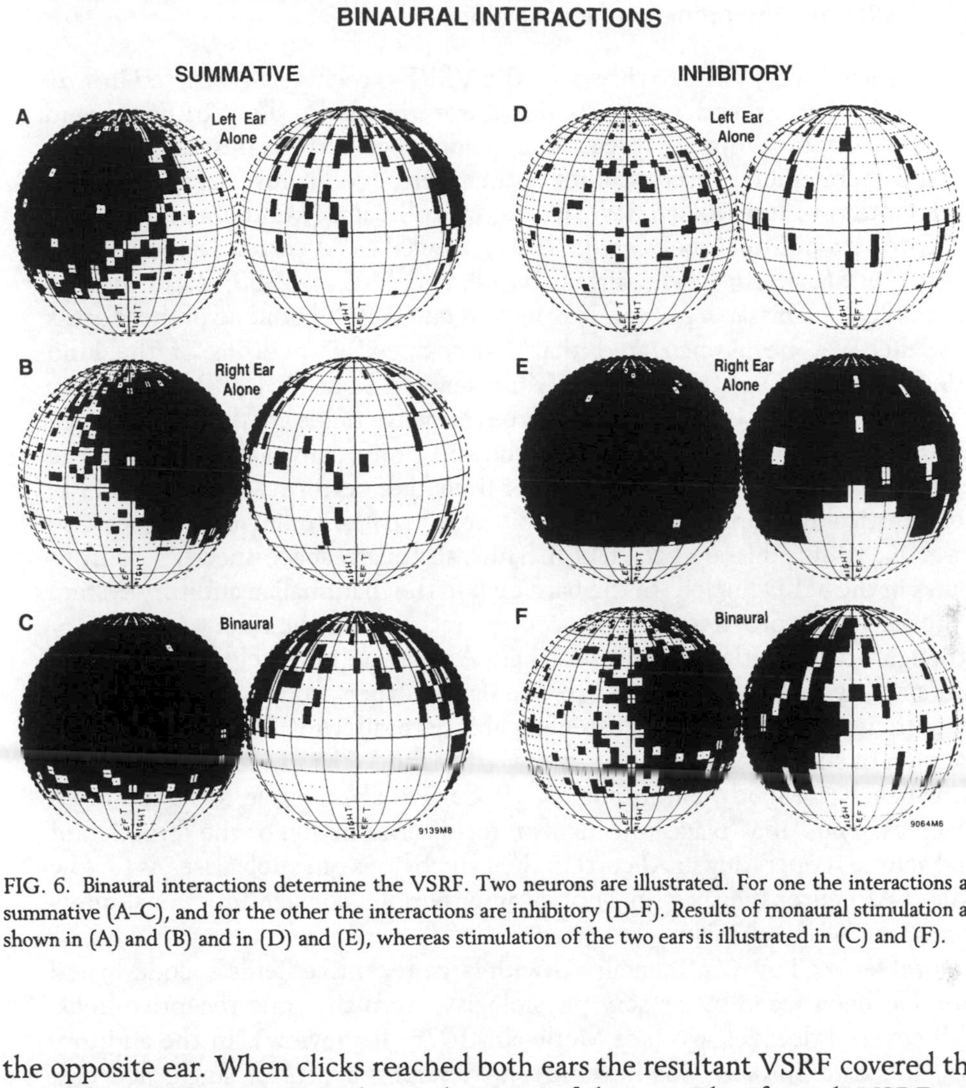

FIG. 6. Binaural interactions determine the VSRF. Two neurons are illustrated. For one the interactions are summative (A–C), and for the other the interactions are inhibitory (D–F). Results of monaural stimulation are shown in (A) and (B) and in (D) and (E), whereas stimulation of the two ears is illustrated in (C) and (F).

the opposite ear. When clicks reached both ears the resultant VSRF covered the entire frontal hemisphere and a good portion of the rear. The "frontal" VSRF was formed essentially by the simple combination of excitatory inputs from the left and right ears. For such neurons, spatial tuning *per se* is so broad as to impart little directional information, at least in the frontal hemifield.

Figure 6D–F illustrates quite a different interaction. In this case, stimulation of one ear alone (Fig. 6E, right) results in an omnidirectional excitatory response, whereas stimulation of the opposite ear (Fig. 6D, left) is without demonstrable effect on the neuronal discharge anywhere in the frontal sound field. When both ears are engaged the resultant VSRF is confined essentially to the right acoustic hemifield. We infer from this result that the left ear, although not contributing to the excitatory component of the VSRF, exerts a powerful inhibitory effect on the neuron that is confined to signals originating in the left acoustic hemifield. For this neuron, the sound was lateralized to the right (contralateral) acoustic hemifield.

F. Large VSRFs and the problem of localization

At stimulus levels very close to threshold the VSRF is relatively restricted in size, but at levels that exceed some 30 dB above threshold the VSRFs expand considerably, often occupying at least one quadrant of VAS, as described earlier. A similar picture emerges from studies of the inferior colliculus (Semple, Aitkin, Calford, Pettigrew, and Phillips, 1983), superior colliculus (Middlebrooks, 1988), and AES cortex (Middlebrooks *et al.*, 1994), as well as AI cortex (Bensen *et al.*, 1981; Imig *et al.*, 1990; Rajan, Aitkin, Irvine, and McKay, 1990; Rajan, Aitkin, and Irvine, 1990; Ahissar *et al.*, 1992; Brugge *et al.*, 1994). For none of these areas has evidence yet been uncovered that "space-specific" neurons of the kind recorded in the MLD of the barn owl (Knudsen and Konishi, 1978) exist in any substantial numbers. It is not likely that large receptive fields are the consequence of anesthesia, for Benson *et al.* (1981) showed quite convincingly that in the unanesthetized monkey, either untrained or trained to perform a localization task, auditory cortical neurons, as a rule, exhibit broad spatial tuning curves (see also Vaadia *et al.*, 1986; Ahissar *et al.*, 1992). Thus, although "space-specific" neurons are found in the MLD nucleus of the barn owl, in the mammalian auditory system their presence may prove to be the exception rather than the rule.

Although broad spatial tuning of a single AI neuron may help account for a listener's ability to localize a sound to one or the other acoustic hemifield, it is hardly sufficient to account for a listener's ability to discriminate the differences in direction of sounds, which in the cat (Martin and Webster, 1987) or monkey (Brown, Beecher, Moody, and Stebbins, 1978a, 1978b) may be to within but a few degrees. Thus, if a "place" mechanism for discrimination of the direction of a sound source is operating in AI cortex, then an obvious question arises as to how large-field AI neurons, either singly or as an ensemble, convey directional information via such a mechanism.

The problem of how central neurons with large receptive fields encode spatial location has been faced by sensory physiologists from the time receptive fields were discovered decades ago (see McIlwain, 1976, for review). In the auditory system, the issue initially was how threshold tuning curves of single neurons, which are typically very narrow only near threshold, account for a listener's capacity to make very fine frequency discriminations at suprathreshold levels (see, e.g., Whitfield, 1967). As Rose, Brugge, Anderson, and Hind (1967) once pointed out, however, frequency specificity derived from the tuning curve is essentially a negative quantity, for it provides little or no information about how the nervous system actually encodes sound frequency over a wide dynamic range. Nor does it account for inhibitory events, which may come into play both within the neuron's excitatory frequency-intensity domain and beyond its edges. For this, one has to look to the full structure of the response area. In the frequency-intensity domain, the response areas of central auditory neurons may be very complex, exhibiting in both their discharge rate and discharge timing complex interactions of excitation and inhibition (e.g., Aitkin, 1985). The same situation may obtain for localization of a sound source. A spatial tuning curve derived from an AI neuron does not reveal the gradients of discharge strength or timing within it.

G. Structure of the VSRF

Within a VSRF one can find a restricted subset of loci associated with relatively high firing probability and temporally coherent discharge. Depending on the acceptance criteria applied to stimulus loci in the VAS, the resultant "effective receptive field" may be highly focused. We illustrate this with a VSRF for which multiple (15) stimuli were delivered at each of 554 stimulus directions (Fig. 7). In the case illustrated here, we collected data for directions only in the frontal right quadrant of VAS. Figure 7A–E illustrates the structure of the VSRF when the acceptance criterion was based only on discharge probability, expressed as spike count. In the right column (Fig. 7F–J) the VSRF was constructed based on timing, expressed as first-spike latency.

When the spike-count criterion is one spike, essentially all directions within the mapped field are represented and the neuron appears broadly tuned (Fig. 7A). The VSRF in Fig. 7B is restricted to those directions for which the spike count was at least 3, a value that is greater than or equal to 25% of maximum (14 spikes). The criterion in Fig. 7C was 7–14 spikes (50% of maximum), and so on. By increasing the stringency of the criterion to 85% (i.e., 11–14 spikes) the resultant VSRF comes to occupy a relatively small region in the right frontal quadrant (Fig. 7E).

The onset latency also varied within the VSRF, and often bore a relationship to spike count. An analysis similar to that described earlier for spike count was carried out with respect to spike timing on the same set of data that was plotted in Fig. 7A. In Figs. 7F–J the VSRF was constructed by accepting those responses for which latency reached a criterion value. In this case we adopted a strategy in which the accepted latency represented a value that was less than or equal to a criterion percentage of the normalized onset minimal latency. The spatial tuning is broad (Fig. 7F) when the criterion is set to accept the full range (12.10–17.10 ms) of observed onset latencies. As the latency criterion is tightened there is a concomitant decrease in the range of latencies accepted and a gradual reduction in the size of the VSRF. The size and location of the VSRF that corresponds to acceptance of spikes with the shortest latencies (Fig. 7J) are similar to those obtained when only the highest spike count (Fig. 7E) was plotted.

From the results of this kind of analysis, carried out on a number of AI neurons, we can postulate that although a neuron may exhibit broad spatial tuning, as defined by the perimeter of the VSRF in which sounds from all directions yielding a response are given equal weight, the cell may also exhibit an "effective receptive field" consisting of a subset of directions closely coupled functionally by discharge timing and strength. The "effective receptive field" is surrounded by loci associated with low firing probability and relatively long latency. Similar mechanisms restricting a receptive field to a subset of loci may be operating in visual cortex. Receptive fields of "complex" cells in area 18 of the cat are not homogeneous in their firing probability, but exhibit "active" points. It is the clustering of these points, representing the most vigorous neural responses, that has been interpreted as representing the true shape of the receptive field (Reinis, Weiss, and Landolt, 1988). Neurons within VI also exhibit broad spatial tuning, but by applying temporal windows to the response the resultant receptive fields become re-

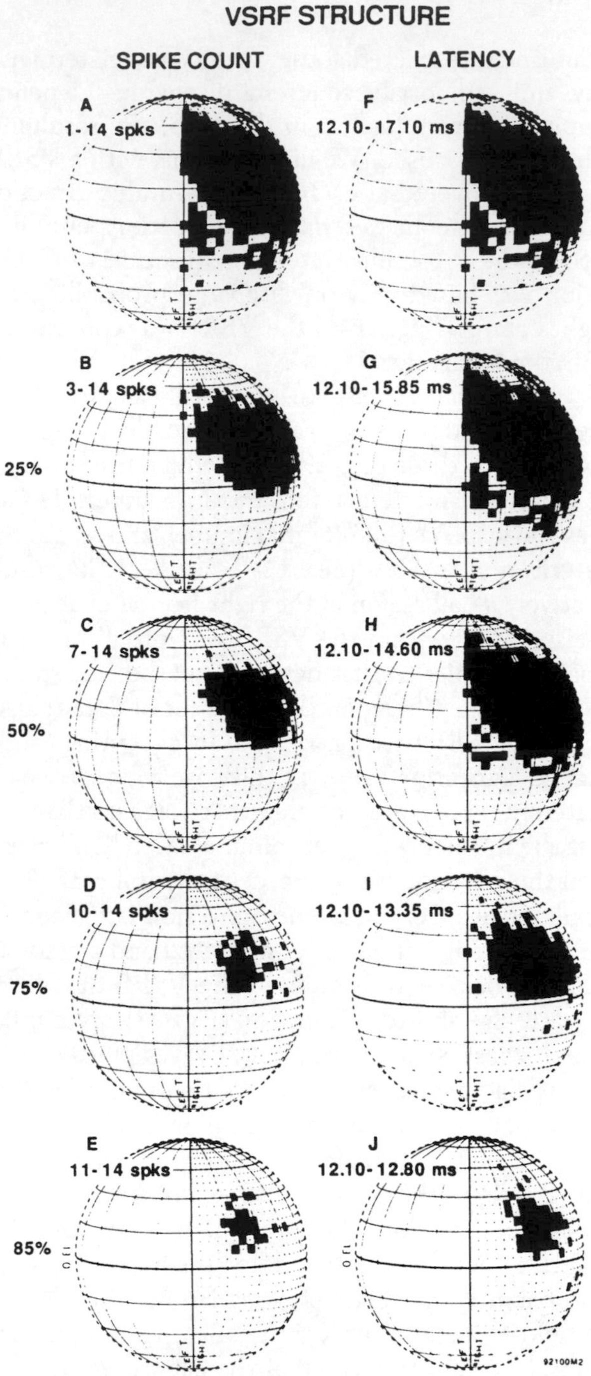

FIG. 7. Internal structure of a VSRF evaluated by either spike count (left column) or response latency (right column). The right frontal quadrant of a single cell's VSRF was studied by repeated ($N = 15$) presentations from each sound-source direction. (A–E) Spike count determines whether an effective direction is included in the VSRF. The smaller the spike count window (shown in each panel), the smaller the "effective receptive field" size. (F–J) Response latency determines whether an effective direction is included in the VSRF. The smaller the latency window (shown in each panel), the smaller the "effective receptive field" size.

stricted in size and show a high degree of spatial selectivity (see Dinse, Krüger, Mallot, and Best, 1991 for a review).

We have chosen for illustration just one way that an auditory spatial receptive field might code for direction of a sound source in space. In this case we assumed that the relevant, information-bearing part of the spatial receptive field is that cluster of directions associated with shortest latency and greatest response strength. Using other acceptance criteria, such as multiple narrow latency and spike-count windows, would also result in restricted receptive fields. Regardless of which receptive-field mechanism is actually employed, the results imply that the direction of a brief sound may be signaled by the discharge timing, the discharge strength, or some combination of the two. Moreover, because it is not likely that sound-source direction is coded by a single neuron acting alone, such a timing mechanism could result in synchronous impulse activity in a population of AI cells for a sound originating from a single source or closely grouped sources. AI neurons project to a wide variety of targets in the forebrain and midbrain. Thus, it may be the synchronous impulse activity in a population of AI cells converging on postsynaptic target neurons that determines the postsynaptic responses, thereby transmitting relatively precise information pertaining to sound-source direction.

That sound direction may be encoded in the temporal discharge patterns of cortical cells was recently reported by Middlebrooks and his colleagues (1994). They found that neurons in field AES of the chloralose-anesthetized cat, as a rule, responded to sounds at any location in the horizontal plane, and that if spike rate were the criterion used to describe spatial tuning, then such neurons would be essentially omnidirectional. Training an artificial neural network to classify temporal spike patterns according to azimuthal location, they found that for a high proportion of cells temporal discharge patterns carried more directional information than did spike counts alone.

Alternatively, of course, we need to consider the possibility that sound-source direction is encoded by punctate spatial receptive fields that are the property of AI neurons that we failed to sample, or that such cells exist in abundance in other auditory centers or in cortical fields that are yet to be explored. As mentioned earlier, however, narrow spatial tuning functions have yet to be shown in any number in the mammalian auditory system.

In the visual system, ensemble coding and feature detection have often been ascribed to large-field neurons, and similar arguments have been made for other sensory systems as well (McIlwain, 1976). Having established that a large AI spatial receptive field may contain a smaller localized region of high response strength and restricted timing (an effective receptive field) and having considered the possibility that activity restricted to this region may signal sound-source direction, we can consider how information related to other attributes of a spatial stimulus might be integrated over the large area of space to which the neuron is sensitive. After all, our auditory perceptions are based on such things as extracting (discriminating) the salient features of that acoustic object from competing background sounds from many sound sources (e.g., cocktail party effect), and sensing dynamic cues that naturally occur as one's head or the sound source or both move over considerable degrees of spatial angle. We have begun to explore these and related issues using our ability to present sounds in virtual acoustic space and control their parameters.

The neural mechanisms involved in detecting sound-source movement are poorly understood, although there is evidence that auditory cortex is involved (e.g., Sovijarvi and Hyvarinen, 1974; Ahissar *et al.*, 1992; Stumpf, Toronchuk, and Cynader, 1992). Figure 8 illustrates the use of the VAS approach to study these mechanisms. In this figure we show the frontal-hemisphere portion of a VSRF that was obtained by presenting one stimulus at each sampled direction, as described earlier. The accompanying graphs (Fig. 8A–D) show the result of presenting 30 stimuli at each azimuthal coordinate along a parallel of constant elevation (36° or 18°). The parallels are shown as white stripes stretching across the VSRF from –90° to +90° in azimuth. The plotted data were obtained using two stimulus paradigms. In one (black squares) the 30 stimuli were presented consecutively at each azimuthal locus at a rate of 2/s. Stimulation started at an azimuth of either –90° (Figs. 8A and 8B) or +90° (Figs. 8C and 8D) and proceeded until all points (4.5° separation) along the parallel were sampled. From the plots it is clear that the discharge probability is not uniform across the receptive field. For this cell maximal firing occurred around 18–36° azimuth; firing probability dropped off on either side of maximum in a nonsymmetric way. The curve may be referred to as an "azimuthal function" and is similar in form to ones reported by Rajan, Aitkin, Irvine, and McKay (1990), Rajan, Aitkin, and Irvine (1990), and Imig *et al.* (1990) in their open-field studies of AI cells in cat. The second stimulus condition (arrows) was designed to mimic the apparent ("beta" or "phi") movement perceived by listeners under dichotic conditions (Briggs and Perrott, 1972; Perrott, 1974, 1982). The apparent-motion stimulus was created by presenting

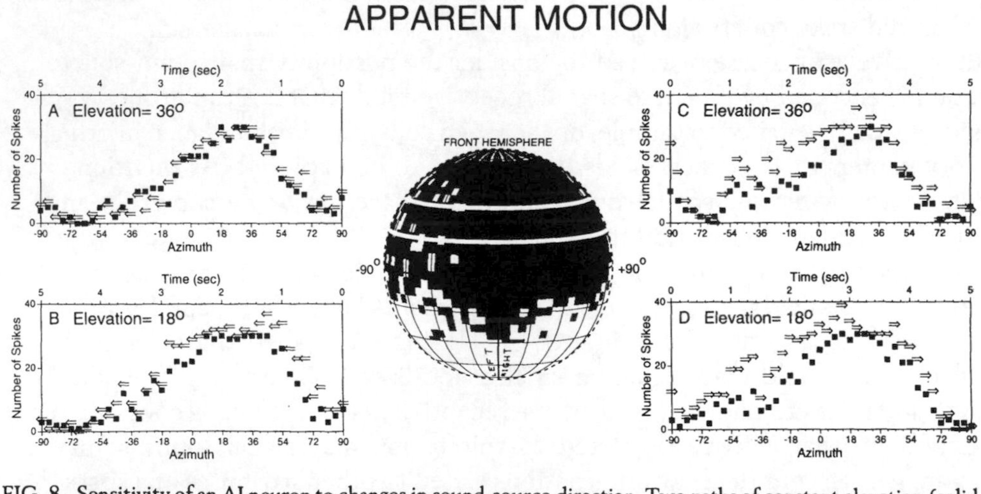

FIG. 8. Sensitivity of an AI neuron to changes in sound-source direction. Two paths of constant elevation (solid white stripes) that crossed the front hemisphere of a single cell's VSRF were studied by repeated stimulus presentations at each sound-source direction. In (A)–(D), filled squares mark the cumulative spike count resulting from 30 consecutive presentations at each azimuthal location (lower abscissa). Apparent-motion stimuli were created by presenting in an ordinal sequence the direction-dependent signals at each azimuthal coordinate along the path of constant elevation. The total time (upper abscissa) for the sequence was fixed at 5 s, which corresponds to sound velocity of 36°/s. Arrows mark the cumulative spike count at each azimuthal coordinate resulting from an apparent-motion sequence repeated 30 times. Orientation of the arrow indicates direction of the apparent motion.

the stimulus at each azimuthal coordinate along the path of constant elevation in an ordinal sequence from right to left (Figs. 8A and 8B) or from left to right (Figs. 8C and 8D). The sequence was repeated 30 times. The time interval between successive stimuli was 125 ms, which translates into a source velocity of 36°/s. The arrows on the graphs indicate both the spike count and the direction of apparent motion. It is clear from these graphs that for one trajectory (Figs. 8C and 8D) but not for the other (Figs. 8A and 8B) the azimuthal functions are quite different under static and dynamic conditions; the order of presentation of the stimulus influenced the firing probability. The extent to which this more dynamic neuronal firing behavior is related to the time and firing-probability structure of the VSRF is presently being pursued.

Our approach to understanding the role(s) played by auditory cortical circuits in spatial hearing has focused, so far, on how a single neuron encodes features of an acoustic stimulus in its firing probability, its spike timing, or both. We have emphasized the spatial receptive field and the properties inherent within it. Although results of these experiments may reveal the resolving power and feature representation of a cortical field, the cortical processing of acoustic images is likely to involve the coordinated activity of large populations of neurons, located perhaps in different auditory cortical fields: a neural code based on "cell assemblies" (Hebb, 1949). We have already suggested that the direction of an impulsive sound might be coded in the synchronous discharge of an ensemble of AI cells. Coding for direction in space may also include vector-averaging of the output of a population of neurons, as proposed for accurate movement of the arm (Georgopoulus, Taira, and Lukashin, 1993), or a mechanism in which signals remain segregated, a "winner-take-all" model, as proposed for detection of the direction of visual motion (Salzman and Newsome, 1994). In visual cortex, neural synchrony among neurons may depend on how coherent features are in the visual field, a timing mechanism that may be related to figure–ground segregation and scene segmentation (Engle, König, Kreiter, Schillen, and Singer, 1992; Singer, 1991). In this regard, multiple-neuron recording in monkey cortex has shown temporal interactions between neurons within the primary auditory field, as well as between neurons in auditory cortex and prefrontal cortex, results not predicted from recordings of single neurons in isolation (Vaadia, Ahissar, Bergman, and Lavner, 1991; Vaadia and Aertsen, 1992; Ahissar *et al.*, 1992).

In summary, spatial hearing in its broadest sense very likely involves a variety of auditory forebrain mechanisms. Some are expressed in the output of a single neuron. Typically, for many AI cells, the neuronal activity is tightly time-locked to the stimulus, and the timing and magnitude of the response are directly related to one or more acoustic parameters. Considerable information has been accumulated with respect to this aspect of cortical coding of acoustic information. Other mechanisms, only now being approached, exhibit less dependence on the stimulus parameters. Instead, they operate mainly through temporal interactions between neurons, with membership in the active population changing, depending on the stimulus conditions and behavioral context in which it is presented. Experimental techniques are now available to explore each of these mechanisms and the ways in which they interact in providing an accurate representation of acoustic space.

ACKNOWLEDGMENTS

The authors wish to acknowledge the participation of Drs. J. C. K. Chan, P. W. F. Poon, A. D. Musicant, and M. Zrull in many of the experiments related to virtual space receptive fields that are summarized here. Dr. J. Chen and Z. Wu played major roles in the development of the FIR filter approach. Ravi Kochhar was responsible for developing the software that implemented virtual acoustic space. Richard Olson, Dan Yee, and Bruce Anderson were responsible for the instrumentation. The work was supported by National Institute of Health grants DC00116, DC00398, and HD03352.

REFERENCES

Ahissar, M., Ahissar, E., Berman, H., and Vaadia, E. **(1992)**. "Encoding of sound-source location and movement: Activity of single neurons and interactions between adjacent neurons in the monkey auditory cortex," J. Neurophysiol. **67**, 203–215.

Aitkin, L. M. **(1985)**. *The Auditory Midbrain: Structure and Function in the Central Auditory Pathway* (Humana Press, Clifton, NJ).

Aitkin, L. M. **(1990)**. *The Auditory Cortex: Structural and Functional Bases of Auditory Perception* (Chapman and Hall, London).

Beitel, R. E., and Kaas, J. H. **(1993)**. "Effects of bilatral and unilateral ablation of auditory cortex in cats on the unconditioned head orienting response to acoustic stimuli," J. Neurophysiol. **70**, 351–369.

Benson, D. A., Hienz, R. D., and Goldstein, M. H., Jr. **(1981)**. "Single-unit activity in the auditory cortex of monkeys actively localizing sound sources: Spatial tuning and behavioral dependency," Brain Res. **219**, 249–267.

Benson, D. A., and Teas, D. C. **(1976)**. "Single unit study of binaural interaction in the auditory cortex of the chinchilla," Brain Res. **103**, 313–338.

Blauert, J. **(1969)**. "Sound localization in the median plane," Acoustica **22**, 205–213.

Blauert, J. **(1983)**. *Spatial Hearing* (MIT Press, Cambridge, MA).

Bregman, A. S. **(1990)**. *Auditory Scene Analysis. The Perceptual Organization of Sound* (MIT Press, Cambridge, MA).

Briggs, R. M., and Perrott, D. R. **(1972)**. "Auditory apparent movement under dichotic listening conditions," J. Exp. Psychol. **92**, 83–91.

Brown, C. H., Beecher, M. D., Moody, D. B., and Stebbins, W. C. **(1978a)**. "Localization of pure tones by Old World monkeys," J. Acoust. Soc. Am. **63**, 1484–1492.

Brown, C. H., Beecher, M. D., Moody, D. B., and Stebbins, W. C. **(1978b)**. "Localization of primate calls by Old World monkeys," Science **201**, 753–754.

Brugge, J. F., Dubrovsky, N. A., Aitkin, L. M., and Anderson, D. J. **(1969)**. "Sensitivity of single neurons in auditory cortex of cat to binaural tonal stimulation: Effects of varying interaural time and intensity," J. Neurophysiol. **32**, 1005–1024.

Brugge, J. F., and Merzenich, M. M. **(1973)**. "Responses of neurons in auditory cortex of the macaque monkey to monaural and binaural stimulation," J. Neurophysiol. **36**, 1138–1158.

Brugge, J. F., and Reale, R. A. **(1985)**. "Auditory cortex," in *Cerebral Cortex*, edited by A. Peters and E. G. Jones (Plenum, New York), pp. 229–271.

Brugge, J. F., Reale, R. A., Hind, J. E., Chan, J. C. K., Musicant, A. D., and Poon, P. W. F. **(1994)**. "Simulation of free-field sound sources and its application to studies of cortical mechanisms of sound localization in the cat," Hear. Res. **73**, 67–84.

Butler, R. A., and Belendiuk, K. **(1977)**. "Spectral cues utilized in the localization of sound in the median plane," J. Acoust. Soc. Am. **61**, 1264–1269.

Chan, J. C. K., Musicant, A. D., and Hind, J. E. **(1993)**. "An insert earphone system for delivery of spectrally shaped signals for physiological studies," J. Acoust. Soc. Am. **93**, 1496–1501.

Chen, J., Wu, Z., and Reale, R. A. **(1994)**. "Application of least-squares FIR filters to virtual acoustic space," Hear. Res. **80**, 153–166.

Clarey, J. C., Barone, P., and Imig, T. J. **(1992)**. "Physiology of thalamus and cortex," in *The Mammalian Auditory Pathway: Neurophysiology*, edited by A. N. Popper and R. R. Fay (Springer-Verlag, New York), pp. 232–334.

Dinse, H. R., Krüger, K., Mallot, H. A., and Best, J. **(1991)**. "Temporal structure of cortical information processing: Cortical architecture, oscillations, and non-separability of spatio-temporal receptive field organization," in *Neuronal Cooperativity*, edited by J. Krüger (Springer-Verlag, Berlin), pp. 68–104.

Eisenman, L. M. **(1974)**. "Neural coding of sound location: An electrophysiological study in auditory cortex (AI) of the cat using free field stimuli," Brain Res. **75**, 203–214.

Elliott, D. N., and Trahiotis, C. **(1972)**. "Cortical lesions and auditory discrimination," Psychol. Bull. **77**, 198–222.

Engle, A. K., König, P., Kreiter, A. K., Schillen, T. B., and Singer, W. **(1992)**. Temporal coding in visual cortex: New vistas on integration in the nervous system," Trends Neurosci. **15**, 218–226.

Evans, E. F. **(1968)**. "Cortical representation," in *Hearing Mechanisms in Vertebrates. A CIBA Foundation Symposium*, edited by A. V. S. DeReuck and J. Knight (Little, Brown, Boston), pp. 272–295.

Ferrier, D. **(1876)**. *The Functions of the Brain* (Smith, Elder, London).

Fisher, N. I., Lewis, T., and Embleton, B. J. J. **(1987)**. *Statistical Analysis of Spherical Data* (Cambridge University Press, Cambridge).

Georgopoulus, A. P., Taira, M., and Lukashin, A. **(1993)**. "Cognitive neurophysiology of the motor cortex," Science **260**, 47–52.

Gottlieb, Y., Vaadia, E., and Abeles, M. **(1989)**. "Single unit activity in the auditory cortex of a monkey performing a short term memory to tones task," Exp. Brain Res. **74**, 139–148.

Hall, J. L. II, and Goldstein, M. H., Jr. **(1968)**. "Representation of binaural stimuli by single units in primary auditory cortex of unanesthetized cats," J. Acoust. Soc. Am. **43**, 456–461.

Handel, S. **(1990)**. *Listening* (MIT Press, Cambridge, MA).

Hartmann, W. M. **(1988)**. "Pitch perception and the segregation and integration of auditory entities," in *Auditory Function. Neurobiological Bases of Hearing*, edited by G. M. Edelman, W. E. Gall, and W. M. Cowan (Wiley, New York), pp. 623–645.

Hebb, D. O. **(1949)**. *The Organization of Behavior* (Wiley, New York).

Hebrank, J., and Wright, D. **(1974)**. "Spectral cues used in localization in the median plane," J. Acoust. Soc. Am. **56**, 1829–1834.

Heffner, H. **(1978)**. "Effect of auditory cortex ablation on localization and discrimination of brief sounds," J. Neurophysiol. **41**, 963–976.

Heffner, H. E., and Heffner, R. S. **(1990)**. "Effect of bilateral auditory cortex lesions on sound localization in Japanese macaques," J. Neurophysiol. **64**, 915–931.

Heffner, H. E., and Masterton, R. B. **(1975)**. "Contribution of auditory cortex to sound localization in the monkey (*Macaca mulatta*)," J. Neurophysiol. **38**, 1340–1358.

Imig, T. J., Irons, W. A., and Samson, F. R. **(1990)**. "Single-unit selectivity to azimuthal direction and sound pressure level of noise bursts in cat high-frequency primary auditory cortex," J. Neurophysiol. **63**, 1448–1466.

Irvine, D. R. F. **(1985)**. "The auditory brainstem. A review of the structure and function of auditory brainstem processing mechanisms," in *Progress in Sensory Physiology 7*, edited by A. Autrum, D. Ottoson, E. R. Perl, R. F. Schmidt, H. Shimazu, and W. D. Willis (Springer-Verlag, New York), pp. 1–279.

Irvine, D. R. F., and Phillips, D. P. **(1982)**. "Polysensory 'association' areas of the cerebral cortex," in *Cortical Sensory Organization. Vol. 3. Multiple Auditory Areas*, edited by C. N. Woolsey (Humana Press, Clifton, NJ), pp. 111–156.

Jenkins, W. M., and Masterton, R. B. **(1982)**. "Sound localization: Effects of unilateral lesions in central auditory system," J. Neurophysiol. **47**, 987–1016.

Jenkins, W. M., and Merzenich, M. M. **(1984)**. "Role of cat primary auditory cortex for sound-localization behavior," J. Neurophysiol. **52**, 819–847.

Kavanagh, G. L., and Kelly, J. B. (1988). "Contribution of auditory cortex to sound localization by the ferret (*Mustela putorius*)," J. Neurophysiol. **60**, 879–888.

Knudsen, E. I., and Konishi, M. **(1978)**. "A neural map of auditory space in the owl," Science **200**, 795–797.

Kuwada, S., and Yin, T. C. T. **(1987)**. "Physiological studies of directional hearing," in *Directional Hearing*, edited by W. A. Yost and G. Gourevitch (Springer-Verlag, New York), pp. 146–176.

Martin, R. L., and Webster, W. R. **(1987)**. "The auditory spatial acuity of the domestic cat in the interaural horizontal and median vertical planes," Hear. Res. **30**, 239–252.

McIlwain, J. T. **(1976)**. "Large receptive fields and spatial transformations in the visual system," in *International Review of Physiology, Neurophysiology II, Vol. 10*, edited by R. Porter (University Park Press, Baltimore), pp. 223–248.

Meredith, M. A., and Clemo, H. R. **(1989)**. "Auditory cortical projection from the anterior ectosylvian sulcus (Field AES) to the superior colliculus in the cat: An anatomical and electrophysiological study," J. Comp. Neurol. **289**, 687–707.

Middlebrooks, J. C. **(1988)**. "Auditory mechanisms underlying a neural code for space in the cat's superior colliculus," in *Auditory Function. Neurobiological Bases of Hearing*, edited by G. M. Edelman, W. E. Gall, and W. M. Cowan (Wiley, New York), pp. 431–455.

Middlebrooks, J. C., Clock, A. E., Xu, L., and Green, D. M. **(1994)**. "A panoramic code for sound location by cortical neurons," Science **264**, 842–844.

Middlebrooks, J. C., and Pettigrew, J. D. **(1981)**. "Functional classes of neurons in primary auditory cortex of the cat distinguished by sensitivity to sound location," J. Neurosci. **1**, 107–120.

Musicant, A. D., and Butler, R. A. (1984). "The influence of pinnae-based spectral cues on sound localization," J. Acoust. Soc. Am. 75, 1195–1200.

Musicant, A. D., Chan, J. C. K., and Hind, J. E. (1990). "Direction-dependent spectral properties of cat external ear: New data and cross-species comparisons," J. Acoust. Soc. Am. 87, 757–781.

Neff, W. D. (1968). "Localization and lateralization of sound in space," in *Hearing Mechanisms in Vertebrates. A CIBA Foundation Symposium* (Little, Brown, Boston), pp. 207–243.

Neff, W. D., Diamond, I. T., and Casseday, J. H. (1975). "Behavioral studies of auditory discrimination: Central nervous system," in *Handbook of Sensory Physiology*, edited by W. D. Keidel and W. D. Neff (Springer-Verlag, New York), pp. 307–400.

Neff, W. D., Fisher, J. F., Diamond, I. T., and Yela, M. (1956). "Role of auditory cortex in discrimination requiring localization of sound in space," J. Neurophysiol. 19, 500–512.

Newman, J. D., and Lindsley, D. F. (1976). "Single unit analysis of auditory processing in squirrel monkey frontal cortex," Exp. Brain Res. 25, 169–181.

Orman, S. S., and Phillips, D. P. (1984). "Binaural interactions of single neurons in posterior field of cat auditory cortex," J. Neurophysiol. 51, 1028–1039.

Penfield, W., and Perot, P. (1963). "The brain's record of auditory and visual experience: a final summary and discussion," Brain 86, 595–696.

Perrott, D. R. (1974). "Auditory apparent motion," J. Audit. Res. 3, 163–169.

Perrott, D. R. (1982). "Studies in the perception of auditory motion," in *Localization of Sound: Theory and Applications*, edited by R. W. Gatehouse (Amphora Press, Groton, CT), pp. 169–193.

Phillips, D. P., and Gates, G. R. (1982). "Representation of two ears in the auditory cortex: A re-examination," Int. J. Neurosci. 16, 41–46.

Phillips, D. P., and Irvine, D. R. F. (1981). "Responses of single neurons in physiologically defined area AI of cerebral cortex: Sensitivity to interaural intensity differences," Hear. Res. 4, 299–307.

Phillips, D. P., and Irvine, D. R. F. (1983). "Some features of binaural input to single neurons in physiologically defined area AI of cat cerebral cortex," J. Neurophysiol. 49, 383–395.

Plenge, G. (1974). "On the difference between localization and lateralization," J. Acoust. Soc. Am. 56, 944–951.

Poirier, P., Lassonde, M., Villemure, J. G., Geoffroy, G., and Lepore, F. (1994). "Sound localization in hemispherectomized patients," Neuropsychologia 32, 541–553.

Pralong, D., and Carlile, S. (1994). "Measuring the human head-related transfer functions: a novel method for construction and calibration of a miniature 'in-ear' recording system," J. Acoust. Soc. Am. 95, 3435–3444.

Rajan, R., Aitkin, L. M., and Irvine, D. R. F. (1990). "Azimuthal sensitivity of neurons in primary auditory cortex of cats. II. Organization along frequency-band strips," J. Neurophysiol. 64, 888–902.

Rajan, R., Aitkin, L. M., Irvine, D. R. F., and McKay, J. (1990). "Azimuthal sensitivity of neurons in primary auditory cortex of cats. I. Types of sensitivity and the effects of variations in stimulus parameters," J. Neurophysiol. 64, 872–887.

Reale, R. A., and Brugge, J. F. (1990). "Auditory cortical neurons are sensitive to static and continuously changing interaural phase cues," J. Neurophysiol. 64, 1247–1260.

Reinis, S., Weiss, D. S., and Landolt, J. P. (1988). "Lack of homogeneity of receptive fields of visual neurons in the cortical area 18 of the cat," Biol. Cyber. 59, 41–48.

Rice, J. J., May, B. J., Spirou, G. A., and Young, E. D. (1992). "Pinna-based spectral cues for sound localization in cat," Hear. Res. 58, 132–152.

Rose, J. E., Brugge, J. F., Anderson, D. J., and Hind, J. E. (1967). "Phase-locked response to low-frequency tones in single auditory nerve fibers of the squirrel monkey," J. Neurophysiol. 30, 769–793.

Salzman, C. D., and Newsome, W. T. (1994). "Neural mechanisms for forming a perceptual decision," Science 264, 231–237.

Sanchez-Longo, L. P., and Forster, F. M. (1958). "Clinical significance of impairment of sound localization," Neurology 8, 119–125.

Sanchez-Longo, L. P., Forster, F. M., and Auth, T. L. (1957). "A clinical test for sound localization and its application," Neurology 7, 655–663.

Semple, M. N., Aitkin, L. M., Calford, M. B., Pettigrew, J. D., and Phillips, D. P. (1983). "Spatial receptive fields in the cat inferior colliculus," Hear. Res. 10, 203–215.

Semple, M. N., and Kitzes, L. M. (1987). "Binaural processing of sound pressure level in the inferior colliculus," J. Neurophysiol. 57, 1130–1147.

Semple, M. N., and Kitzes, L. M. (1993a). "Binaural processing of sound pressure level in cat primary auditory cortex: Evidence for representation based on absolute levels rather than interaural level differences," J. Neurophysiol. 69, 449–461.

Semple, M. N., and Kitzes, L. M. (1993b). "Focal selectivity for binaural sound pressure level in cat primary auditory cortex: two-way intensity network tuning," J. Neurophysiol. 69, 462–473.

Shaw, E. A. G. (1974a). "The external ear," in *Handbook of Sensory Physiology, Auditory System*, edited by W. D. Keidel and W. D. Neff (Springer-Verlag, New York), pp. 455–490.

Shaw, E. A. G. (1974b). "Transformation of sound pressure level from the free field to the eardrum in the horizontal plane," J. Acoust. Soc. Am. 56, 1848–1861.

Singer, W. **(1991)**. "The formation of cooperative cell assemblies in the visual cortex," in *Neuronal Cooperativity*, edited by J. Krüger (Springer-Verlag, Berlin), pp. 163–183.

Sovijarvi, A. R. A., and Hyvarinen, J. **(1974)**. "Auditory cortical neurons in the cat sensitive to the direction of sound source movement," Brain Res. **73**, 455–471.

Strominger, N. L. **(1969a)**. "Subdivisions of auditory cortex and their role in localization of sound in space," Exp. Neurol. **24**, 348–362.

Strominger, N. L. **(1969b)**. "Localization of sound in space after unilateral and bilateral ablation of auditory cortex," Exp. Neurol. **25**, 521–533.

Stumpf, E., Toronchuk, J. M., and Cynader, M. S. **(1992)**. "Neurons in cat primary auditory cortex sensitive to correlates of auditory motion in three-dimensional space," Exp. Brain Res. **88**, 158–168.

Sutherland, I. E. **(1965)**. "The ultimate display," Proc. IFIP Cong. **2**, 506–508.

Sutherland, I. E. **(1968)**. "A head-mounted three dimensional display," AFIPS Conf. Proc. **33**, 757–764.

Thompson, G. C., and Masterton, R. B. **(1978)**. "Brain stem auditory pathways involved in reflexive head orientation to sound," J. Neurophysiol. **41**, 1183–1202.

Thompson, R. F., and Welker, W. I. **(1963)**. "Role of auditory cortex in reflex head orientation by cats to auditory stimuli," J. Comp. Physiol. Psychol. **56**, 996–1002.

Vaadia, E., and Aertsen, A. **(1992)**. "Coding and computation in the cortex: Single-neuron activity and cooperative phenomena," in *Information Processing in the Cortex. Experiments and Theory*, edited by A. Aertsen and V. Braitenberg (Springer-Verlag, Berlin), pp. 81–121.

Vaadia, E., Ahissar, E., Bergman, H., and Lavner, Y. **(1991)**. "Correlated activity of neurons: A neural code for higher brain functions?" in *Neuronal Cooperativity*, edited by J. Krüger (Springer-Verlag, Berlin), pp. 249–279.

Vaadia, E., Benson, D. A., Hienz, R. D., and Goldstein, M. H., Jr. **(1986)**. "Unit study of monkey frontal cortex: Active localization of auditory and of visual stimuli," J. Neurophysiol. **56**, 934–952.

Wegener, J. G. **(1964)**. "The sound-locating behavior of brain-damaged monkeys," J. Audit Res. **4**, 227–254.

Wenzel, E. M. **(1992)**. "Localization in virtual acoustic displays," Presence **1**, 80–107.

Whitfield, I. C. **(1967)**. *The Auditory Pathway* (Arnold, London).

Whitfield, I. C. **(1977)**, "Auditory space and the role of the cortex in sound localization," in *Psychophysics and Physiology of Hearing*, edited by E. F. Evans and J. P. Wilson (Academic Press, London), pp. 1–9.

Whitfield, I. C., Cranford, J., Ravizza, R., and Diamond, I. T. **(1972)**. "Effects of unilateral ablation of auditory cortex on complex sound localization," J. Neurophysiol. **35**, 718–731.

Wightman, F. L., and Kistler, D. J. **(1989a)**. "Headphone simulation of free-field listening; I: Stimulus synthesis," J. Acoust. Soc. Am. **85**, 858–867.

Wightman, F. L., and Kistler, D. J. **(1989b)**. "Headphone simulation of free-field listening; II: Psychophysical validation," J. Acoust. Soc. Am. **85**, 868–878.

Wightman, F. L., Kistler, D. J., and Perkins, M. E. **(1987)**. "A new approach to the study of human sound localization," in *Directional Hearing*, edited by W. M. Yost and G. Gourevitch (Springer-Verlag, New York), pp. 27–48.

Winer, J. A. **(1992)**. "The functional architecture of the medial geniculate body and the primary auditory cortex," in *Springer Handbook of Auditory Research, Vol. 1, The Mammalian Auditory Pathways: Neuroanatomy*, edited by D. B. Webster, A. N. Popper, and R. R. Fay (Springer-Verlag, New York), p. 222–409.

Woolsey, C. N. **(1960)**. "Organization of cortical auditory system: a review and synthesis," in *Neural Mechanisms of the Auditiory and Vestibular Systems*, edited by G. L. Rasmussen and W. F. Windle (Charles C. Thomas, Springfield, IL), pp. 165–180.

Woolsey, C. N. **(1961)**. "Organization of cortical auditory system," in *Sensory Communication*, edited by W. A. Rosenblith (MIT Press, Cambridge, MA), pp. 235–257.

Woolsey, C. N., and Walzl, E. M. **(1942)**. "Topical projection of nerve fibers from local regions of the cochlea to the cerebral cortex of the cat," Bull. Johns Hopkins Hosp. **71**, 315–344.

Yin, T. C. T., and Kuwada, S. **(1984)**. "Neuronal mechanisms of binaural interaction," in *Dynamic Aspects of Neocortical Function*, edited by G. M. Edelman, W. E. Gall, and W. M. Cowan (Wiley, New York), pp. 263–313.

Yost, W. A. **(1991)**. "Auditory image perception and analysis: the basis for hearing," Hear. Res. **56**, 8–18.

Yost, W. A., and Hafter, E. R. **(1987)**. "Lateralization," in *Directional Hearing*, edited by W. M. Yost and G. Gourevitch (Springer-Verlag, New York), pp. 49–84.

Chapter 23

Head-Related Transfer Functions in Cat: Neural Representation and the Effects of Pinna Movement

Eric D. Young, John J. Rice
Johns Hopkins University

George A. Spirou
West Virginia University

Israel Nelken
Hebrew University, Jerusalem

Ruth A. Conley
Loyola University of Chicago

(Received November 1994; revised January 1995)

The directional dependence of the transfer function from free field to sites near the tympanic membrane is one cue for sound localization. In cat, this transfer function contains a prominent spectral notch in the frequency range 8–20 kHz. Because the notch frequency varies in an orderly fashion with both azimuth and elevation, knowledge of the notch frequencies in both ears should suffice to localize a broadband sound in the frontal field. The notch is represented in the auditory nerve by a dip in discharge rate among fibers with best frequencies (BFs) equal to the notch frequency and by an inhibitory response in dorsal cochlear nucleus (DCN) principal cells with the same BFs. When a cat moves its pinna, the mapping between sound source location and notch frequency changes; pinna movement is therefore an important auditory event because it can have substantial effects on the apparent spectra of sound sources as well as on their apparent locations. DCN principal cells receive input from the somatosensory system, which produces an inhibitory response when the pinna moves. These findings suggest the hypothesis that the DCN detects and signals, with inhibitory responses, the existence of auditory events with behavioral importance for the cat.

INTRODUCTION

The directionality of the cat external ear, as measured by the head-related transfer function (HRTF), results in spectral modifications of broadband sounds as they pass through the external ear; these spectral modifications provide cues for sound localization (Musicant, Chan, and Hind, 1990; Rice, May, Spirou, and Young, 1992). In humans, spectral cues augment binaural cues and provide the clearest information about sound source elevation and front/back position (reviewed by Middlebrooks and Green, 1991). Because the auricle of the cat's pinna is movable, the use of spectral sound localization cues by the cat is somewhat more complicated than in primates, where the pinna has a fixed relationship to the head. When a cat moves its pinna, the directionality of the external ear changes and the receptive fields of central auditory neurons move with the pinna (Phillips, Calford, Pettigrew, Aitkin, and Semple, 1982; Calford and Pettigrew, 1984; Middlebrooks and Knudsen, 1987). Thus, in order to compute source direction relative to the head, the cat has to take pinna orientation into account. The nature of this computation is not understood; presumably, the computation requires convergence of auditory information about sound localization cues and information about pinna orientation. The pinna-position information could be provided by the somatosensory system or it could be provided by the motor systems that move the pinna.

In this chapter we describe the changes that occur in HRTFs when an anesthetized cat's pinna is displaced in a fashion that resembles natural movements. We also describe the neural representation of the spectral shapes of noise filtered with HRTFs at the level of the auditory nerve (AN) and the dorsal cochlear nucleus (DCN). We show that the DCN is a site of convergence of acoustic and somatosensory information. Although current data do not suggest that the DCN is performing the corrections for pinna movement just described, this nucleus is sensitive to spectral sound localization cues and also receives somatosensory information about the pinna. Thus, the nature of the polysensory convergence in DCN is of interest to studies of spectral sound localization mechanisms.

I. THE HRTF IN THE CAT

Figures 1a and 1b show HRTFs from a cat for three different elevations at one azimuth and for three azimuths at one elevation, respectively. These data are taken from Rice *et al.* (1992) and are similar to data reported by Musicant *et al.* (1990). The horizontal dashed line shows unity gain; over most of the frequency range, the cat's pinna shows substantial pressure gain. Looking first at Fig. 1a, there is little change in the HRTF with elevation, over the narrow range of elevations used, for frequencies up to 5 kHz (the ΔL *region*). At higher frequencies, the HRTFs are quite elevation dependent. Note particularly the prominent minimum, or notch, in the HRTF at frequencies from 8 to 20 kHz; this is the *first notch* (FN). As is illustrated here, the FN moves to higher frequencies as the elevation of the

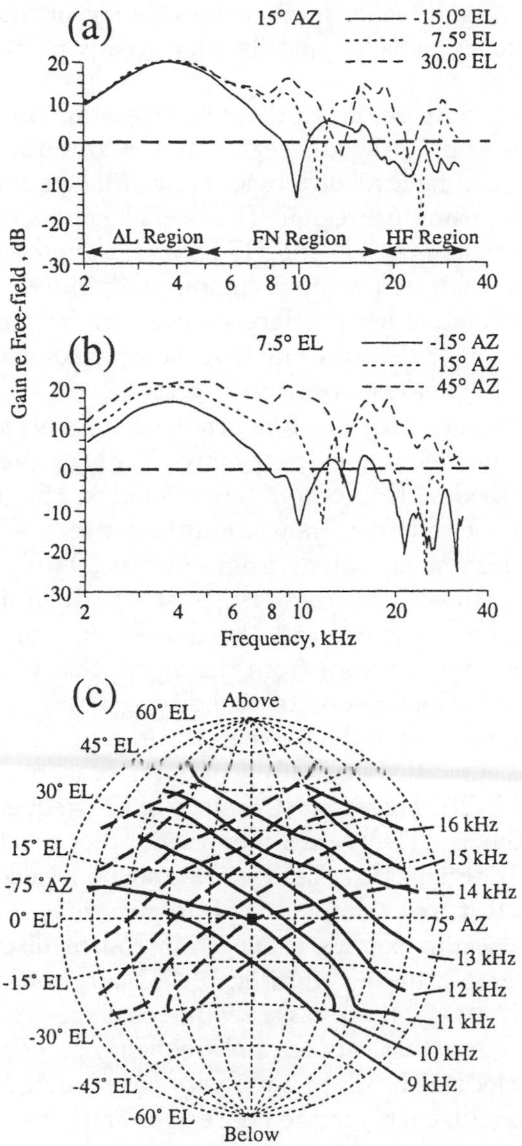

FIG. 1. (a, b) Head-related transfer functions (HRTFs) measured in a cat; only the magnitudes (gains) of the transfer functions are shown. The HRTF is defined as the ratio of the sound pressure near the eardrum to the sound pressure in free field, plotted against stimulus frequency. Measurements were made in an anesthetized cat with a probe microphone inserted in the ear canal roughly at the bony meatal ring; the sound was a click produced by a tweeter ~1 m from the cat's ear. The transfer function was computed as the fast Fourier transform (FFT) of the click recorded near the eardrum divided by the FFT of the click recorded in the free field at the same position in the soundproof room. Full details are given in Rice *et al.* (1992). Transfer functions from three directions are shown in each panel, defined by their azimuth (AZ) and elevation (EL). Azimuth is displacement along the horizon, with 0° azimuth straight ahead and positive azimuths on the right side of the animal; elevation is displacement vertically away from the horizon. Measurements were made in the right ear. Note the prominent minima, or notches, at frequencies between 8–20 kHz; these are the *first notches* (FNs). (c) Contours of constant FN frequency shown on a portion of the frontal hemisphere; the hemisphere is drawn from the perspective of the cat, with positive azimuths on the right. Dotted lines show contours of constant azimuth or elevation. Solid lines show iso-FN frequency contours for the right ear and dashed lines show mirror image contours, which are presumed to apply to the left ear. Measurements were made only in the right ear. (After Rice *et al.*, 1992.)

sound source increases. At still higher frequencies (*HF region*) the HRTFs show multiple peaks and notches, which typically vary greatly as source direction changes.

Figure 1b shows HRTFs for three azimuths at one elevation. In this case, there is an overall increase in gain in the ΔL region as the azimuth increases; this characteristic leads to interaural level differences (e.g., Phillips *et al.*, 1982), and is the justification for the name ΔL region. The overall gain increase persists to higher frequencies, although in the FN and HF regions, the presence of notches makes the interaural level difference more complicated; indeed, it is not clear that spectral cues and interaural level difference cues can be separated at high frequencies. The data in Fig. 1b demonstrate that the FN frequency also changes with azimuth, showing an increase as azimuth increases.

Figure 1c summarizes the directional dependence of FN frequency. The contours in this figure show directions in space for which FN frequency is constant at values between 9 and 16 kHz. The contours are plotted on a projection of space in front of a cat; vertical dotted curves show azimuths between –75° and 75° and horizontal dotted curves show elevations from –60° to 60°. The black square represents a sound source directly in front of the cat. The solid lines are iso-FN frequency contours for the right ear and the dashed lines are mirror-image contours for the left ear. It is apparent from this figure that FN frequency, by itself, is an adequate cue for localization of sounds originating in front of a cat; knowledge of the FN frequencies in the two ears is sufficient to uniquely specify a source direction. Of course this cue only works for broadband stimuli with substantial energy in the 8–20 kHz region (the range of FN frequencies) and only for sources in front of the cat. There are a number of other spectral features of HRTFs in the FN and HF regions that could provide sound localization cues, but none has characteristics that are as simple as FN frequency.

Cats are capable of locating sounds in elevation and of discriminating the elevation of sound sources (Martin and Webster, 1987; Masterton and Sutherland, 1994; Sutherland, 1991, 1994); these tasks require that spectral cues be used. Preliminary evidence suggests that cats use FN frequency as a cue (Huang and May, 1996), in that cats localize bands of noise with energy in the FN frequency region better than bands with energy in the HF region. Thus, it seems reasonable to investigate the neural representation of spectral notches. In the next two sections, we describe the representation of the spectral shapes of HRTFs in the AN and in the DCN.

II. REPRESENTATION OF SPECTRAL NOTCHES IN THE AUDITORY NERVE

Poon and Brugge (1993a, 1993b) showed that AN fibers provide a representation of the spectral notches in noise or click stimuli filtered with cat HRTFs. As expected, when a notch is centered over a fiber's best frequency (BF), or slightly above BF, the fiber's threshold for the signal is increased and its rate function is shifted toward higher stimulus intensities. When moving stimuli were simulated by presenting sequences of noise bursts filtered with different HRTFs, the decrease in discharge rate representing notch location was amplified, in that a fiber's discharge rate could dip below spontaneous rate as the notch passed through the fiber's tuning curve; presumably this phenomenon reflects adaptation.

The representation of the spectral shape of a typical cat HRTF is shown in Fig. 2b. Responses (discharge rate) of a population of 681 AN fibers to a stimulus whose spectrum has the shape of a HRTF (Fig. 2a) are plotted according to fiber BF; such a plot gives an estimate of the tonotopically organized array of activity carried to the brain by the AN when this stimulus is presented. Figure 2a shows the magnitude of the HRTF used to filter a flat-spectrum Gaussian noise to produce the stimulus. The lines in Fig. 2b are smoothed versions of the individual data points computed separately for the low (triangles), medium (squares), and high (x's) spontaneous rate fibers. The scatter in these data is considerable. Although it is possible to see the FN at 13.6 kHz as a dip in the smoothed rate profiles, other features of the stimulus, including the large second notch at 23 kHz, cannot be seen in the rate profiles. Indeed, there are apparently random fluctuations in the smoothed rate profiles at frequencies below 8 kHz, which do not correspond to any feature of the stimulus spectrum; these random fluctuations are about as large as the dips in the vicinity of 23 kHz.

Rate profiles like those in Fig. 2b have been analyzed for other stimulus spectra in the past; most of this work was done for speech stimuli and has been reviewed by Sachs (1984). The conclusions of that work are similar to the results in Fig. 2b in that rate profiles do not provide a clear and robust representation of stimulus spectrum. One possible explanation for the apparent poor quality of the rate representation is that differences among fibers in spontaneous rate and saturation rate produce scatter in rate profiles like Fig. 2b. This possibility can be examined by replotting the rate profile in terms of normalized rate R_{norm}, computed as follows:

$$R_{norm} = \frac{R - R_{spont}}{R_{sat} - R_{spont}},$$

where R is the average rate in response to the stimulus, R_{spont} is the spontaneous rate, and R_{sat} is the saturation rate (estimated as the rate in response to a BF tone 50 dB above threshold). Normalization expresses rate as a fraction of the unit's response range, with $R_{norm} = 0$ at spontaneous rate and $R_{norm} = 1$ at saturation rate. Normalization should eliminate the scatter in rate profiles due to differences among units in spontaneous and saturation rates. The data in Fig. 2b are plotted as normalized rate in the original paper describing these results (Rice, Young, and Spirou, 1995), with the result that the quality of the representation is little better than with simple rate. However, plotting the data as normalized rate does make it clear that the high spontaneous rate fibers are near saturation at the stimulus level used to obtain the data in Fig. 2b (passband spectrum level of approximately 20 dB re 20 $\mu Pa/Hz^{1/2}$); the fact that the fibers are near saturation partly explains the small size of the dip in the high spontaneous rate profile at the FN frequency.

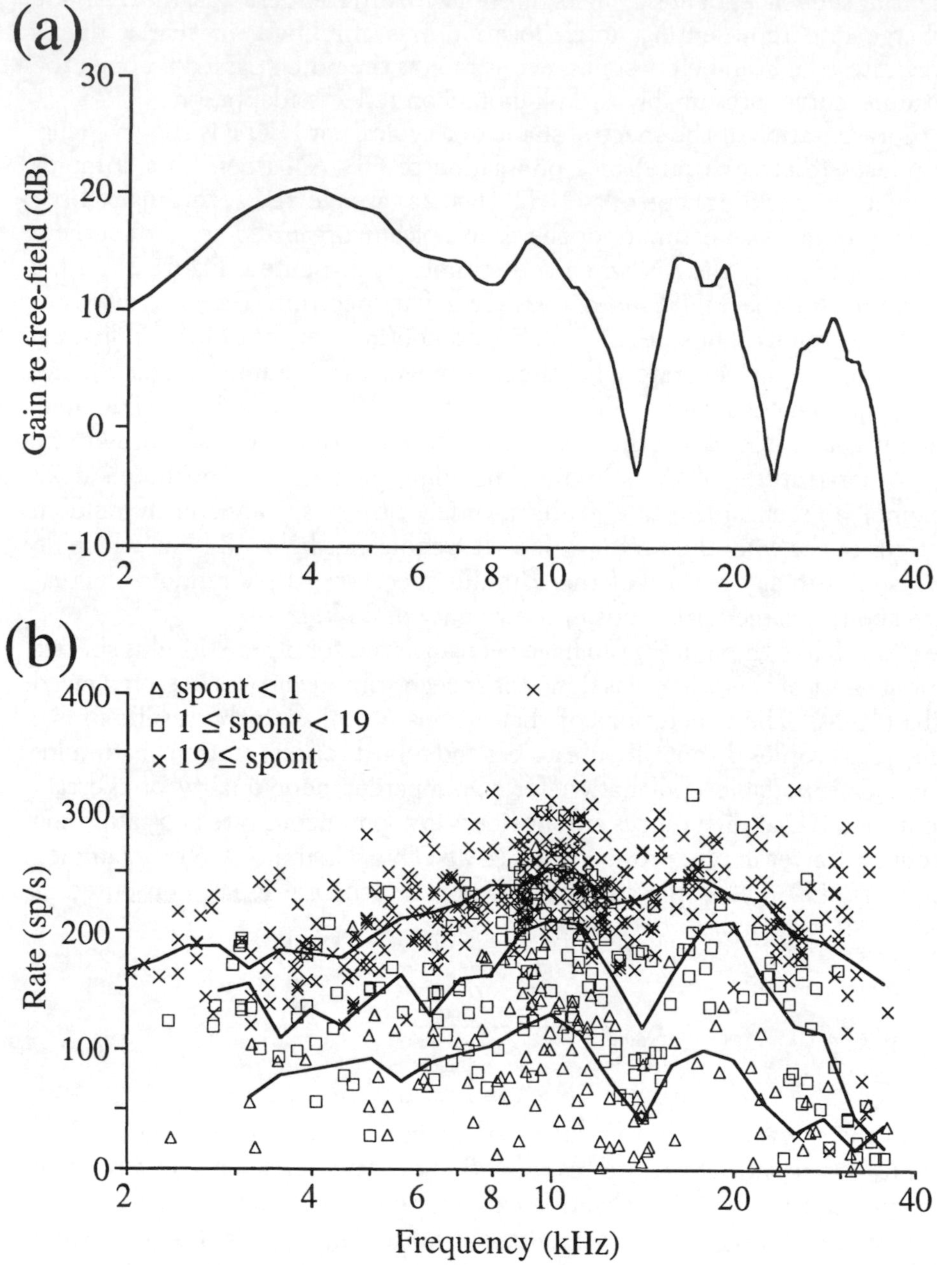

FIG. 2. (a) Magnitude of the HRTF used to generate a noise stimulus; this HRTF was obtained at 15° azimuth, 30° elevation. A 32,768-sample strip of Gaussian white noise was filtered with this transfer function to produce the stimulus used to obtain the data in (b). The actual spectrum of the stimulus deviated slightly from that shown here because of the acoustic system (see Fig. 1 of Rice *et al.*, 1995). (b) Average discharge rates of a population of AN fibers in response to the stimulus of (a). Each point shows the average rate of one fiber during 200-ms bursts of the stimulus, plotted at the fiber's BF. Data were obtained from six cats. Fibers' spontaneous rates are shown by the symbols. The lines show smoothed versions of the data computed using a triangular weighting function with a base of width 0.1 decade (~1/3 octave) on the logarithmic frequency axis. Lines are computed separately for each spontaneous rate group (378 high, 190 medium, and 113 low spontaneous rate fibers). (From Rice *et al.*, 1995.)

Figures 3a and 3b show the representation of the differences between two stimulus spectra. Figure 3a shows the decibel difference between the spectrum of the stimulus of Fig. 2a (called *E0*) and the spectrum of a second stimulus generated using a different HRTF (called *E2*). The notches in E0 appear as notches in Fig. 3a, and E2's FN (9.8 kHz) appears as a peak in the difference spectrum. Figure 3b shows the differences between fibers' discharge rates in response to these two stimuli; that is, the ordinate in Fig. 3b shows rate to E0 minus rate to E2. Data are shown in Fig. 3b for only a portion of the fiber population shown in Fig. 2b, because stimulus E2 was only presented in four of the six experiments.

The similarity of the rate-difference profile in Fig. 3b to the stimulus difference plot in Fig. 3a is striking. The peaks and valleys of the spectral difference are clearly represented by rate differences, except that the valley expected at 23 kHz is small. By comparison with Fig. 2b, there is much less scatter in the data in Fig. 3b; the rate differences clearly cluster close to the smoothed line in Fig. 3b, in contrast to the wide scatter of the rate data in Fig. 2b. The data scatter around the smoothed rate profiles was quantified by computing the standard deviation in the rates or rate differences after subtracting the smoothed profiles from the data points. Subtracting the smoothed rate profiles eliminates the trend in the data, so that the data points scatter around zero. The standard deviations calculated in this way are given in Table I, which also shows standard deviations calculated for profiles of normalized rate and differences of normalized rate.

Data are shown in Table I for E0 and E2, defined earlier, and for an additional stimulus called E1 (azimuths and elevations are given in the caption). The standard deviations in Table I were computed separately for low (<1/s), medium (1–18/s), and high (≥19/s) spontaneous rate populations combined across four experiments in which all three stimuli were presented. The standard deviations for responses to E0 from the larger set of six experiments in Fig. 2b are virtually identical to the E0 results in Table I.

TABLE I. Standard deviations of rate and rate difference (top half) and of normalized rate and difference of normalized rates (bottom half) around mean values given by the smoothed lines computed from the data with a 0.1 decade log-triangular filter. The units are *per second* in the top half, and dimensionless in the bottom half. Data are from four experiments in which three stimuli were presented at a passband spectrum level of ~20 dB re 20 μPa/Hz$^{1/2}$. Stimuli have spectral shapes of HRTFs measured at 15° AZ and three elevations: 30° EL (E0), 7.5° EL (E1), and –15° EL (E2). *N* ranges from 54 to 235 fibers. (From Rice *et al.*, 1995.)

Spontaneous Rate Group	*E0 Rate*	*E1 Rate*	*E2 Rate*	*E0 – E1 Rate Difference*	*E0 – E2 Rate Difference*
Low	37.4	40.7	37.0	12.8	15.6
Medium	43.0	44.0	44.12	18.2	16.9
High	35.4	33.2	31.6	12.2	16.2
Spontaneous Rate Group	*E0 Normalized Rate*	*E1 Normalized Rate*	*E2 Normalized Rate*	*E0 – E1 Normalized Rate*	*E0 – E2 Normalized Rate*
Low	0.133	0.140	0.134	0.052	0.074
Medium	0.137	0.144	0.144	0.065	0.062
High	0.112	0.105	0.109	0.064	0.077

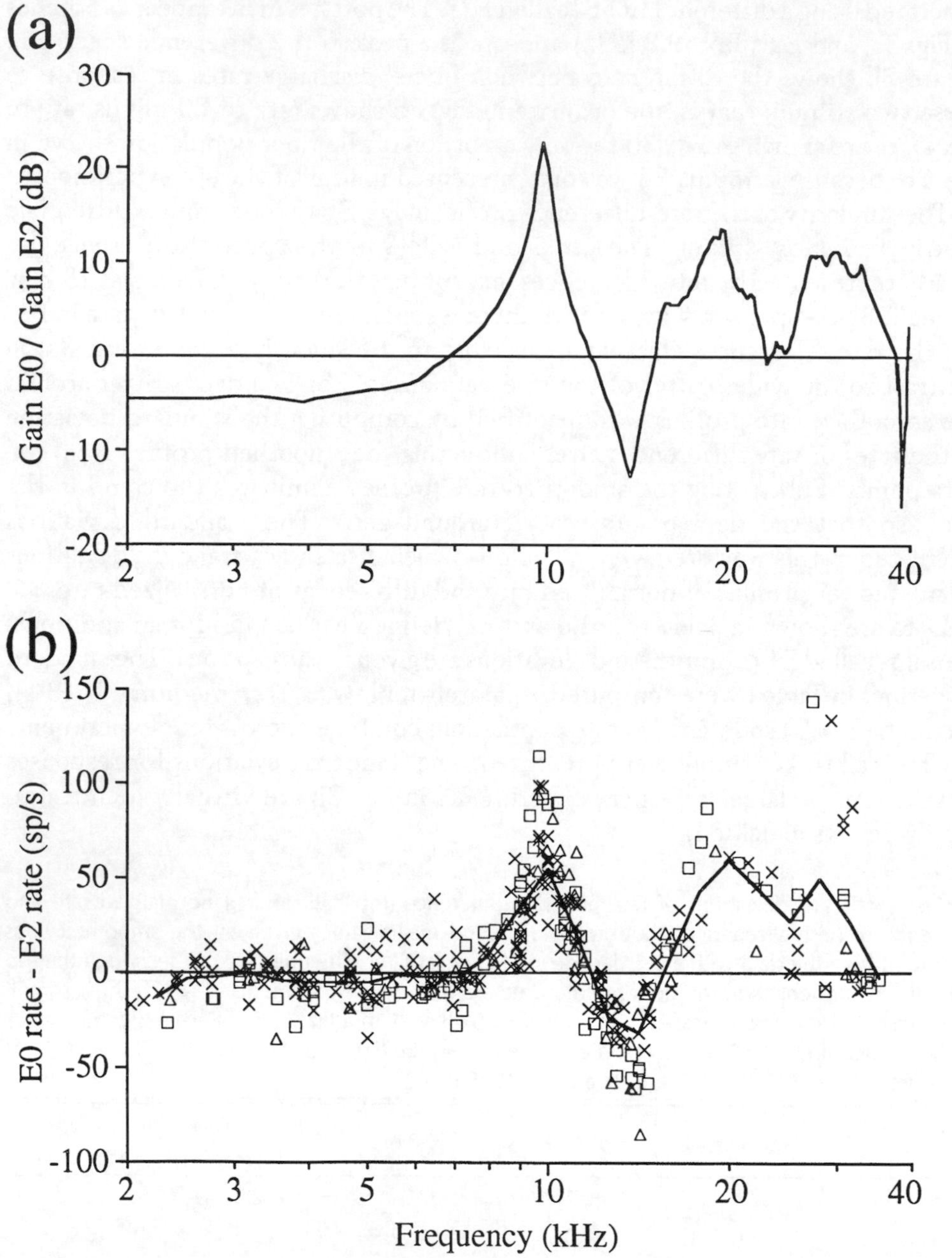

FIG. 3 (a) Ratio of two HRTFs, plotted as decibel difference in magnitudes: E0 is shown in Fig. 2a and E2 was obtained at 15° azimuth, –15° elevation; E2's FN frequency is 9.8 kHz. (b) Difference in discharge rate in response to E0 and E2 for a population of 354 fibers from four cats. Each point shows, for one AN fiber, the discharge rate in response to E0 minus the rate in response to E2, plotted at the fiber's BF. The line is a smoothed version of the data, computed using the same filter as in Fig. 2b, from all three spontaneous rate groups. (From Rice *et al.*, 1995.)

The standard deviations in Table I support the impression, gained from Figs. 2b and 3b, that the scatter in population profiles is smaller for rate differences than for rates. In each row of Table I, the standard deviations for rate differences are about half the standard deviations for rates. This result is unexpected, because computing the sum or difference of two independent noisy sets of data should increase the standard deviation (by $\sim\sqrt{2}$ if the data have equal variance) rather than decrease it. The decrease in the standard deviations shows that there is substantial variability among units, which is strongly correlated across stimuli and therefore is canceled by computing rate differences. The smaller size of the standard deviations of normalized rate differences shows that the variability among units is not in spontaneous or saturation rate.

The fact that rate-difference profiles provide such a good representation of the differences between stimulus spectra suggests that rate profiles might contain high-quality representations of absolute stimulus spectra. Furthermore, the decrease in standard deviation documented in Table I suggests that we are prevented from seeing the absolute rate representation because of the scatter among units. The next section discusses responses of neurons in DCN to spectral notches. The quality of the representation of notches in these data suggests that the DCN is capable of deriving a good representation of the stimulus spectrum from AN discharge, presumably from discharge rate. Finding a better method for analyzing rate profiles requires a more detailed analysis of the sources of the scatter, which could be differences in two-tone suppression behavior, differences in the widths of fibers' dynamic ranges, or other factors. In any case, previous conclusions about the poor quality of the rate representation of stimulus spectrum must be regarded as pessimistic (Sachs and Young, 1979).

III. RESPONSES TO NOTCHES IN THE DORSAL COCHLEAR NUCLEUS

The dorsal cochlear nucleus has the most intricate neuropil and the most complex response properties of any of the divisions of the cochlear nucleus (CN). Reviews of DCN morphology and physiology are provided by Osen, Ottersen, and Storm-Mathisen (1990) and Young, Shofner, White, Robert, and Voigt (1988). Figure 4 shows a schematic of the internal wiring of the DCN based on anatomical and physiological data. The DCN is organized by two major systems of axons forming excitatory terminals: (1) AN fibers (Osen, 1970) and axons from two types of multipolar cells in the posteroventral CN (PVCN; Oertel, Wu, Garb, and Dizack, 1990; Smith and Rhode, 1989) form tonotopically organized sheets in DCN by passing through the nucleus in a roughly parasagittal plane. The principal cells (fusiform and giant cells) contained in these sheets are shown as horizontal rows in Fig. 4. (2) Axons of granule cells run perpendicular to the tonotopic sheets, forming terminals on the dendrites of fusiform cells, but not on giant cells (Mugnaini, Warr, and Osen, 1980). Inputs to the granule cell regions originate from several sources, including type II AN fibers (Brown, Berglund, Kiang, and Ryugo, 1988), olivocochlear bundle axon collaterals (Benson and Brown, 1990; Brown, Liberman, Benson, and Ryugo, 1988), vestibular endorgans

(Burian and Gestoettner, 1988; Kevetter and Perachio, 1989), and the somatosensory system (Itoh, Kamiya, Mitani, Yasui, Takada, and Mizuno, 1987; Weinberg and Rustioni, 1987). The outputs of the DCN are the axons of fusiform and giant cells.

Each of the afferent fiber systems has an associated set of inhibitory interneurons, shown in black in Fig. 4. Two inhibitory interneurons receive AN terminals and terminate within tonotopic arrays in DCN; these are the vertical cells of DCN and one type of multipolar neuron in PVCN (assumed to be the *wideband inhibitor* in Fig. 4, discussed later). The second set of interneurons includes three cell types, only one of which (the cartwheel cell) is shown in Fig. 4. These neurons receive terminals from granule cells or mossy fibers and make inhibitory contacts on fusiform cells and possibly other targets.

DCN principal cells have complex response properties, which are dominated by inhibition (Spirou and Young, 1991; Young and Brownell, 1976). Figure 5b shows the response map of a DCN neuron whose response type (type IV) has been shown to contribute axons to the dorsal acoustic stria (Young, 1980), suggesting that it is recorded from a principal cell. The map shows responses to tones of various frequencies (abscissa) at a succession of eight sound levels separated by 10 dB. Each of the eight plots making up the response map shows discharge rate versus frequency at one level; the plots are obtained by presenting a series of 200-ms tone bursts (1/s) at frequencies that are equally spaced on a logarithmic scale. The sound level is approximately constant at the level indicated at the right in each plot. Type IV units are spontaneously active, and the horizontal line in each plot shows the unit's spontaneous discharge rate. Inhibitory responses occur when rate falls below the spontaneous rate line (hatched regions), and excitatory responses occur when rate increases above the spontaneous rate line (blackened regions).

The distribution of inhibitory and excitatory regions shown in Fig. 5b is typical of type IV neurons. In particular, there is an inhibitory region (the *central inhibitory area*) that includes the BF (11.6 kHz) of the unit. The other inhibitory and excitatory areas shown in Fig. 5b are typical of type IV units and have been described by Spirou and Young (1991). Many aspects of this complex response map can be accounted for with known properties of the DCN; these include the central inhibitory area, which is produced by inhibitory input from vertical cells (Voigt and Young, 1990). Vertical cells give strong responses to narrowband stimuli, but respond weakly or not at all to broadband stimuli, such as noise (Young and Voigt, 1982). The vertical cell inhibitory input to type IV units is quite strong and, as a result, DCN type IV units are strongly inhibited by most narrowband stimuli (such as tones or narrow bands of noise) centered on their BFs.

DCN type IV units are also inhibited by the inverse of a narrowband stimulus, that is, by a spectral notch (Nelken and Young, 1994; Spirou and Young, 1991). Figure 5a shows the spectra of three noise stimuli generated by filtering broadband noise with a HRTF. The three versions of the stimulus were produced by logarithmically shifting the stimulus spectrum along the frequency axis; this shift was accomplished by changing the sampling rate of the digital-to-analog (D/A) converter used to produce the stimuli. The noise spectra are shown on the same frequency scale as the response map of the type IV unit in Fig. 5b. The responses

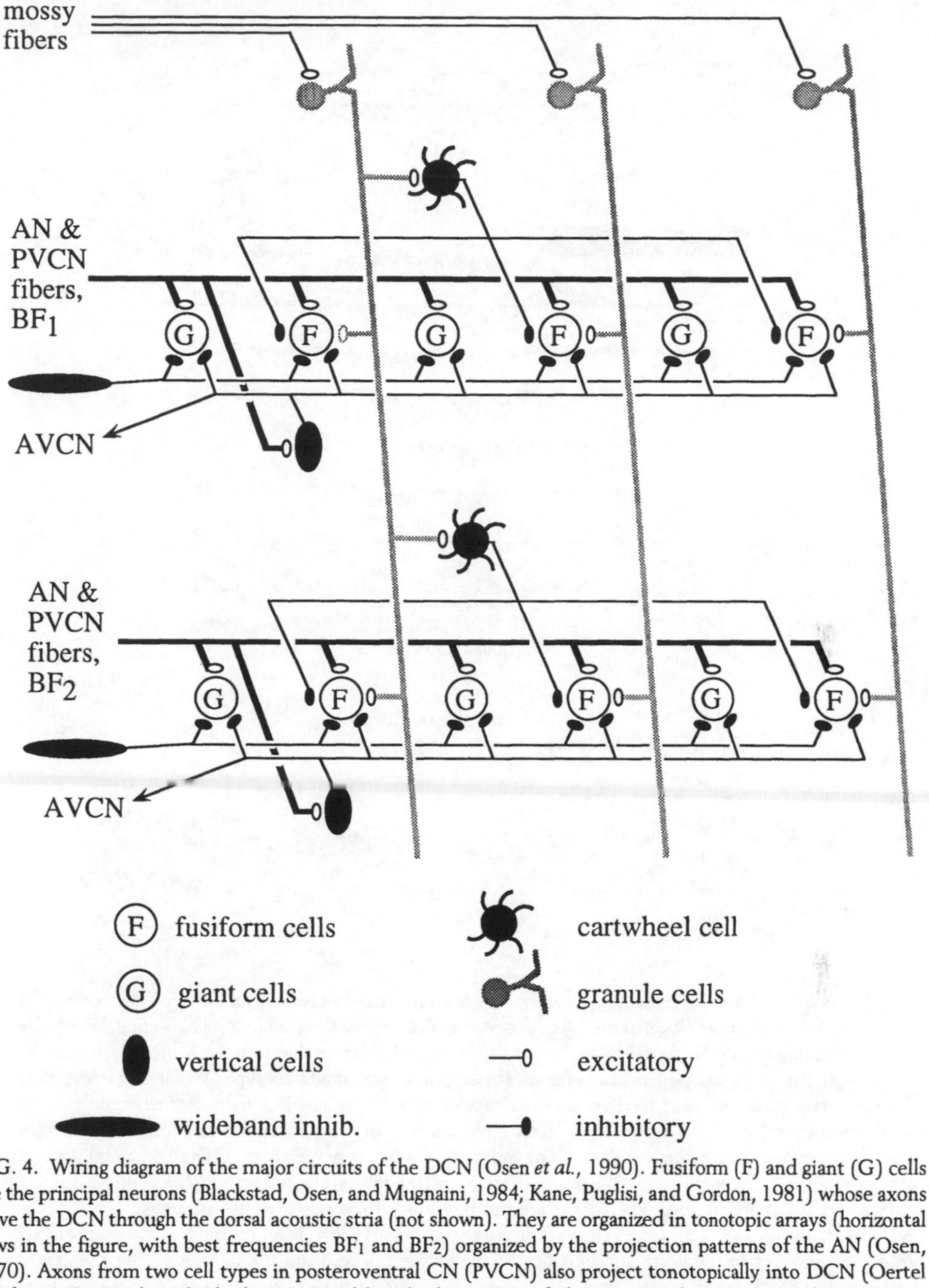

FIG. 4. Wiring diagram of the major circuits of the DCN (Osen *et al.*, 1990). Fusiform (F) and giant (G) cells are the principal neurons (Blackstad, Osen, and Mugnaini, 1984; Kane, Puglisi, and Gordon, 1981) whose axons leave the DCN through the dorsal acoustic stria (not shown). They are organized in tonotopic arrays (horizontal rows in the figure, with best frequencies BF_1 and BF_2) organized by the projection patterns of the AN (Osen, 1970). Axons from two cell types in posteroventral CN (PVCN) also project tonotopically into DCN (Oertel *et al.*, 1990; Smith and Rhode, 1989), although the nature of their terminal zones is not known. Two interneuronal circuits are shown, the vertical cell (Lorente de Nó, 1981; Saint Marie, Benson, Ostapoff, and Morest, 1991) and a postulated wideband inhibitor (Nelken and Young, 1994); the wideband inhibitor may be one of the PVCN cell types that projects to DCN (Winter and Palmer, 1995). Running orthogonal to the tonotopic sheets are axons of granule cells (Mugnaini *et al.*, 1980); these contact fusiform cells and the cartwheel cell inhibitory interneurons. Cartwheel cell axons run parallel to the tonotopic sheets and reach fusiform cells (Berrebi and Mugnaini, 1991); whether they also terminate on giant cells is not known. Mossy fiber inputs to granule cells come from a variety of sources, not including type I AN fibers, but including axons from the somatosensory dorsal column nuclei (Itoh *et al.*, 1987; Weinberg and Rustioni, 1987; Wright and Ryugo, 1995). Two additional inhibitory interneurons (stellate and Golgi cells) associated with the granule cell system are not shown. (From Young, Spirou, Rice, and Voigt, 1992.)

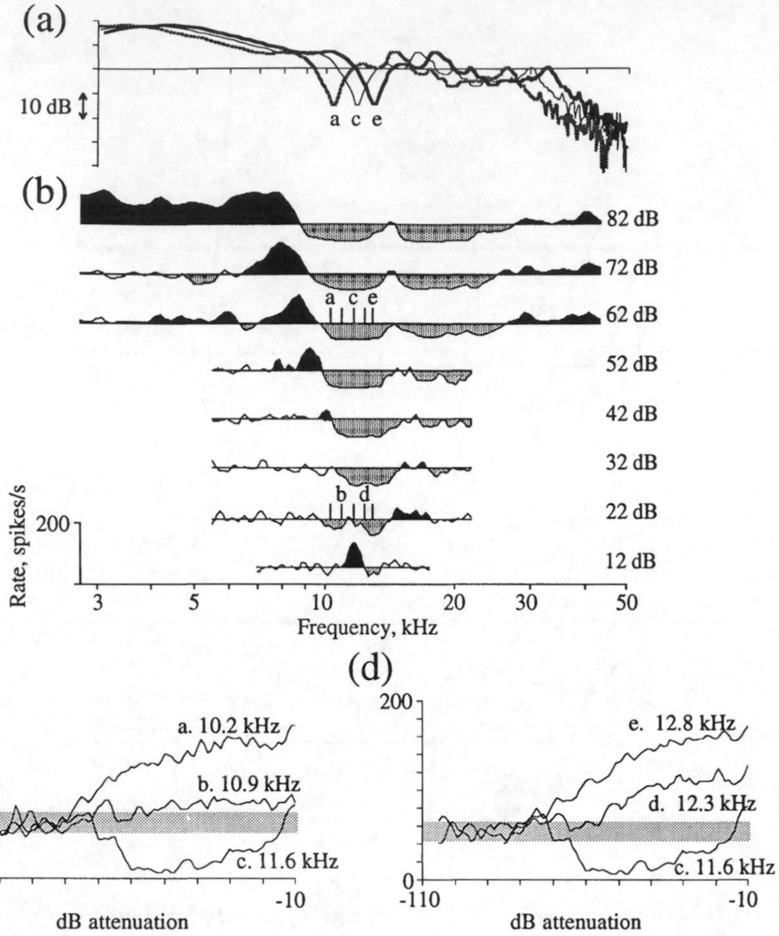

FIG. 5. (a) Spectrum of a noise signal produced by filtering broadband noise with a HRTF. The spectrum is shown at three positions on the (logarithmic) frequency axis; shifts along the frequency axis were produced by changing the sampling rate of the digital-to-analog converter used to generate the stimuli. The notch frequencies are labeled *a–e* in this and other panels of the figure. (b) Response map of a DCN type IV unit. The eight plots show discharge rate (scale at lower left) versus frequency at eight levels, given at right. Actual stimulus level varies with frequency by ±5 dB around the levels given because of the acoustic calibration. The rates are computed from responses to a single 200-ms tone burst at each frequency and level. The horizontal straight lines are spontaneous discharge rate; the hatched areas are inhibitory responses; the blackened areas are excitatory responses. Vertical lines labeled *a–e* are the positions of the notch in the stimulus of (a) for the rate-level functions in (c) and (d). (c, d) Plots of discharge rate versus sound level (given as attenuator setting) for the unit's responses to the noise stimulus of (a); the letters *a–e* and the frequencies define the center frequencies of the notch for each rate function. The unit's BF was 11.6 kHz. Note the rapid transition from excitatory to inhibitory responses as the notch frequency moves toward BF.

of this unit to these stimuli (and two others with intermediate notch frequencies) are shown in Figs. 5c and 5d. These plots show average discharge rate during 200-ms presentations of the stimuli (ordinate) plotted against stimulus level (abscissa). The shaded horizontal bar shows the range of spontaneous discharge rate in this unit. Each rate-versus-level function in Figs. 5c and 5d is identified with the center frequency of the spectral notch (10.2–12.8 kHz); these notch frequencies are identified in Fig. 5b by the vertical lines labeled *a* through *e*. These data illustrate the extraordinary sensitivity of DCN principal cells to the frequency position of a spectral notch near their BFs. When the notch is centered on BF (case *c*, notch at 11.6 kHz), the response is inhibitory, but when the notch is moved as little as 12% below (case *a*, 10.2 kHz) or 10% above (case *e*, 12.8 kHz) BF, the response is strongly excitatory. DCN principal cells vary in the strength of their inhibitory response to notches (Nelken and Young, 1994), but approximately half of the type IV units give strong inhibitory responses to spectral notches like those in HRTFs.

Some thought will convince the reader that the inhibitory response to the notch cannot be explained by the responses of this unit to tones, as summarized in the response map (Spirou and Young, 1991). In fact, to explain notch responses it is necessary to postulate the existence of a wideband inhibitor (Winter and Palmer, 1995; Nelken and Young, 1994), which is thought to be a PVCN multipolar cell whose axon terminates in DCN and makes inhibitory-type terminals (Smith and Rhode, 1989). These multipolar cells give responses of the onset-C variety (Smith and Rhode, 1989) and respond to broadband stimuli in the fashion predicted for the wideband inhibitor (Nelken and Young, 1994; Winter and Palmer, 1995). Thus, the current model of auditory processing in DCN contains two inhibitory inputs: Vertical cells inhibit principal cells for narrowband stimuli, and the wideband inhibitor inhibits principal cells for broadband stimuli containing a narrow notch.

The major problem in attempting to understand the role of the DCN in audition is that it is neither necessary nor sufficient for a variety of auditory tasks, including discriminating the elevation of sound sources, detecting a sound source at a particular elevation, and detecting tones in the presence of background noise (Masterton and Granger, 1988; Masterton, Granger, and Glendenning, 1994; Masterton and Sutherland, 1994; Sutherland, 1994). The DCN has been reported to be necessary only in one situation, which is reflex orientation to sound sources placed at various elevations in the median plane (Sutherland, 1991). This last result suggests that the DCN may play a role in reflex auditory-motor behaviors, which is consistent with the fact that the DCN is the major auditory input to a nucleus in the reticular formation that has been implicated in the startle reflex (Lingenhöhl and Friauf, 1994). However, the DCN is a major source of ascending axons to the central nucleus of the inferior colliculus (e.g., Oliver, 1984), so it must also play a role in strictly auditory analysis.

Data like those of Fig. 5 suggest a rather general hypothesis about the role of the DCN in hearing. The fact that DCN principal cells respond with inhibition either to narrowband peaks in the stimulus spectrum or to narrowband notches means that the DCN is detecting potentially interesting or important spectral features and signaling them to higher auditory centers with inhibitory responses (Nelken and Young, 1994). Information is frequently encoded in the auditory signal in the form of spectral peaks and notches. For example, spectral peaks signal the formant frequencies of speech and spectral notches carry sound localization information, as discussed earlier. Thus, an inhibitory response in a DCN output axon signals the existence of auditory information at frequencies near the BF of that axon. It is reasonable that such a mechanism should exist in the peripheral auditory system and that it should be adapted in the cat to detect the spectral notches that convey sound localization information. If the DCN is detecting important spectral features, then deficits might have been expected in some of the behavioral experiments mentioned above. But the DCN probably serves as a detector of novel stimulus features, as in the startle reflex system, which means that its role could be masked in a well-trained behavioral animal.

Questions about the role of the DCN in audition can only be answered by further behavioral and electrophysiological research. In particular, it is likely that none of the responses described earlier involve the circuitry associated with the granule cells, where much of the complexity of the DCN lies. The responses of DCN neurons to somatosensory stimuli, described in a later section, appear to pass through the granule cell system; these somatosensory inputs offer new challenges to our thinking about the DCN and also offer a new way to approach the role of the DCN.

IV. EFFECTS OF PINNA MOVEMENT ON THE HRTF

Much of the analysis already given is based on the assumption that spectral notches are an important cue to the location of sound sources. Given this assumption, it becomes important to know what effects pinna movements have on the notches. In the simplest model the movable auricle portion of the cat's external ear acts as a sound collector, so that the effect of moving the auricle is mainly to change the overall directionality of the pinna without changing the shapes of HRTFs. Under this model, for example, the map relating FN frequency to spatial position (Fig. 1c) should rotate through space with the pinna, without major changes in the organization or relative locations of FN frequencies. Although some existing evidence suggests that this simple model is not far wrong (Middlebrooks and Knudsen, 1987), changes in the pinna's frequency-dependent acoustic axes have been described that suggest more complex effects of pinna movement (Calford and Pettigrew, 1984). In any case, the effects of pinna movements on HRTFs have not been studied.

As an initial examination of the issue of pinna motion, we measured the HRTFs in anesthetized cats with the pinna in three positions. The measurement methods are essentially the same as those used in our previous study (Rice *et al.*, 1992), summarized in the caption of Fig. 1. HRTFs were determined with the pinna in three positions: (1) in the relaxed position assumed in an anesthetized cat; (2) with the pinna pulled forward in an approximation of the pinna position in an alert cat focusing on stimuli directly in front; and (3) with the pinna pulled back into a posture resembling the position of the pinna when a cat hears a stimulus to the side or behind. The pinna was moved by two sutures attached to ligaments near its base: one suture, attached to the medial side, pulled the pinna forward into an upright posture and the second, attached to the posterior edge of the base of the pinna, pulled the pinna back. The movements of the pinna between these positions are difficult to quantify: Roughly speaking, the orientation of the open face of the pinna rotated around a vertical axis through the center of the head in going from the relaxed to the pulled-back position; the open face rotated around the same axis in going from the relaxed to the forward position, but there was also a change in the orientation of the open face into a more upright posture. These three positions are probably crude approximations to the actual pinna positions adopted by an awake cat. The cat pinna is connected to over 20 muscles (Crouch, 1969; L. Populin and T. C. T. Yin, personal communication), so is likely to be under rather fine control, in terms of both shape and position.

Changes in the HRTF produced by moving the pinna are shown in Fig. 6. The solid curves show the HRTFs with the pinna pulled forward and the dashed curves shows HRTFs with the pinna in the relaxed posture. Two principal effects of moving the pinna forward can be seen in this figure. First, there is an increase in notch frequency. This increase is consistent with rotation of the pinna around the head-vertical axis; for example, such a movement should rotate the right-ear map in Fig. 1c toward the left side, increasing the FN frequency at any given azimuth. Second, the portion of frontal space in which large notches are seen moves downward. With the pinna in the relaxed posture, notches are not seen at elevations above about 60°; at higher elevations, the HRTFs are relatively flat, without sharp notches except at very high frequencies (>25 kHz). When the pinna is rotated forward, this region of relatively flat HRTFs moves down to about 30–45° elevation; the loss of significant notches in the HRTFs at 30° and 45° elevation in Fig. 6 is typical.

The data in Fig. 6 suggest that there are not major changes in the general nature of HRTFs when the pinna moves; thus, the effect of pinna movement might be as simple as a change in directionality of the external ear. The FN frequency contours shown in Fig. 1c provide a convenient way to get an overall picture of the changes produced by pinna movements. Figure 7 shows contours of constant FN frequency for the right pinna in three positions. As the pinna is moved, two changes are seen. First, the contours move toward lower azimuths as the pinna moves from back to relaxed to forward. This movement follows the direction of motion of the pinna and can be seen by looking at the relative position of the 10-kHz contour (emphasized) and the 0° azimuth, 0° elevation point (the *straight-ahead point*, shown by the heavy circle). The 10-kHz contour is to the right of the straight-ahead point with the pinna pulled back; it passes near the straight-ahead point when the pinna is relaxed, and it is to the left of the straight-ahead point with the pinna pulled forward. Second, there is a change in the orientation of the contours when the pinna is pulled forward. With the pinna forward, the iso-FN contours are almost horizontal, whereas they run at approximately a 45° angle with the pinna relaxed or pulled back. This change in orientation seems to correspond to the change in orientation of the pinna towards a more upright posture.

From the data summarized in Figs. 6 and 7, it is apparent that the cat can accomplish three aims by moving its pinna: (1) The region of space in which FN frequency is a good localization cue can be positioned to correspond to an area in which interesting sounds may be located; (2) once a sound is located, spectral notches produced by the external ear can be moved away from the direction of

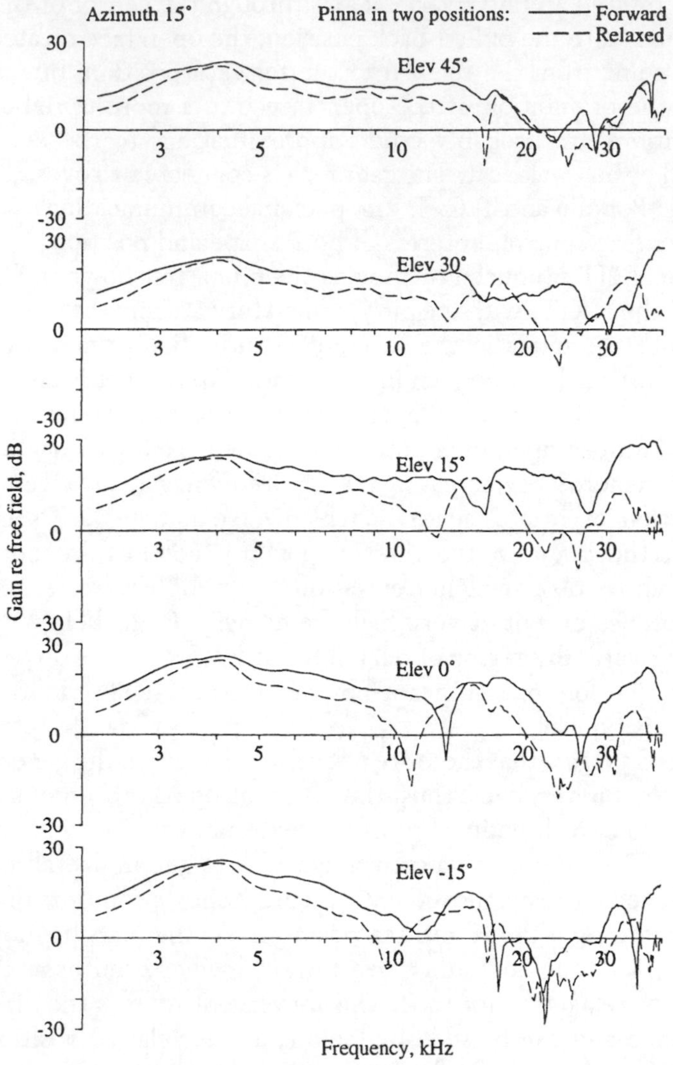

FIG. 6. HRTFs for a cat with the pinna in two positions. Data were obtained from sound sources at 15° azimuth and at elevations from –15° to 45°. Solid curves show HRTFs with the pinna pulled forward, as described in the text; dashed curves show HRTFs from the same directions (relative to the head) with the pinna in the relaxed posture assumed in an anesthetized animal. HRTFs were measured as described in the caption of Fig. 1.

the source, so as to reduce the coloring of the source spectrum by external ear acoustics; and (3) although not shown in Figs. 6 and 7, there is a broad gain maximum in the pinna transfer function for certain directions in space (Phillips *et al.*, 1982; Musicant *et al.*, 1990). By moving the pinna, this gain maximum can be positioned to provide optimal listening conditions for any particular region of space.

The data in Fig. 7 complicate the simple hypothesis put forward in Fig. 1c, that knowledge of the FN frequencies in the two ears is sufficient to localize a sound in space. Given that the cat's two ears are independently mobile, the intersection point of a particular pair of FN frequency contours can occur anywhere within a considerable region of space, perhaps as large as ±30° in both azimuth and elevation. Thus, if pinna orientation is not known, there is substantial ambiguity in the FN as a sound-localization cue. This ambiguity can be partly resolved by using other sound localization cues. Interaural time differences, for example, are probably reasonably independent of pinna position (Roth, Kochhar, and Hind, 1980); if this assumption is true, then interaural time differences can be used to uniquely determine the azimuth of the sound, leaving only the elevation subject

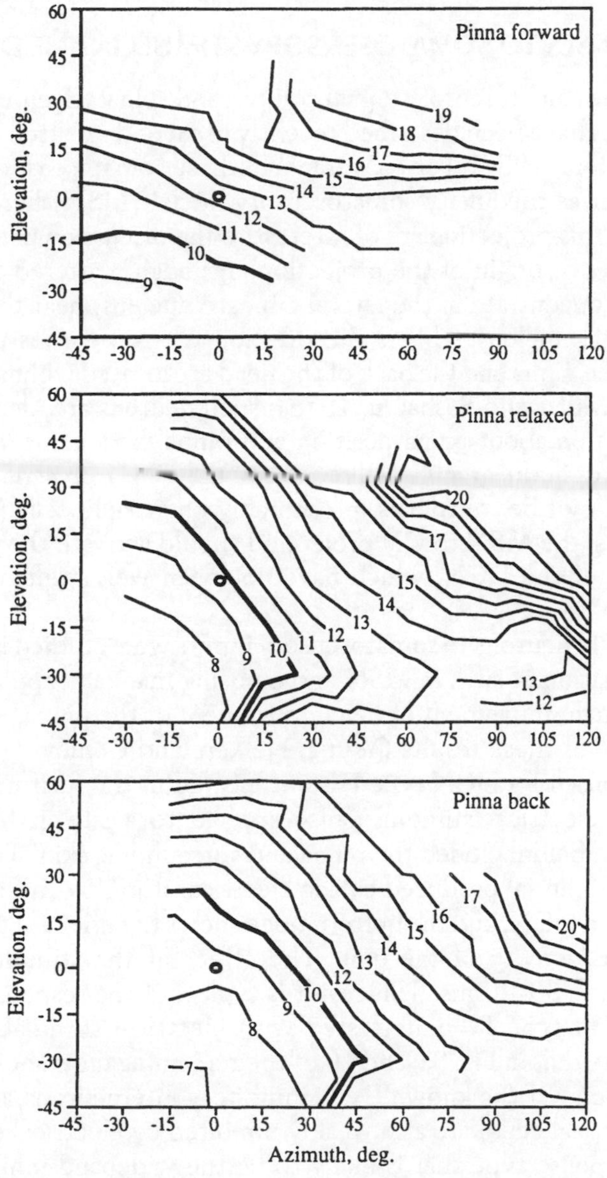

FIG. 7. Contours of constant FN frequency for the pinna in three positions. The abscissa and ordinate show the sound source's direction in space. Numbers on the contours give the FN frequencies. The heavy circle is at 0° azimuth, 0° elevation in each plot. The 10-kHz contour is emphasized to facilitate comparison.

to the uncertainties caused by pinna movement. This possibility may explain why, in human observers, interaural time differences play a dominant role in determining the azimuthal location of a sound source (Wightman and Kistler, 1992).

Thus, a full resolution of the uncertainty about the location of a sound source in the presence of pinna movements seems to require information about pinna position. It is possible that there are other acoustic cues, such as subtle changes in the shapes of HRTFs, but HRTFs with similar FN frequencies from different pinna positions appear quite similar in our data.

V. RESPONSES TO SOMATOSENSORY STIMULI IN THE DCN

Projections from the somatosensory dorsal column and spinal trigeminal nuclei to the cochlear nucleus have been described recently in cat and rat (Itoh *et al.*, 1987; Weinberg and Rustioni, 1987). For convenience, these somatosensory nuclei are referred to together as medullary somatosensory nuclei (MSN) here. Two anatomical features of this projection are of interest to the discussion in this chapter. First, the cell bodies of origin of the projection, although scattered through the MSN, do tend to concentrate in the lateral cuneate nucleus, near the border of the spinal trigeminal nucleus. This is the position where neurons that receive information from the pinna and the back of the head are located (Johnson, Welker, and Pubols, 1968; Millar and Basbaum, 1975); such neurons are ideally situated to provide information about pinna position and pinna movement. Second, the projection terminates in the granule cell regions of the CN (Itoh *et al.*, 1987) and the axons form mossy fiber terminals, presumably on granule cells (Wright and Ryugo, 1996). Thus, the MSN to CN projection should activate the granule-cell associated systems of the DCN, which have not been well studied *in vivo*, as mentioned earlier.

Responses of DCN neurons to somatosensory inputs were studied in two ways: by electrical stimulation at sites in MSN and by using manually applied somatosensory stimuli (touch, movement of hairs, movement of the pinna, etc.). Figure 8 summarizes some of these results (Young, Nelken, and Conley, 1995). Figure 8a shows the response of a DCN type IV unit located in the fusiform-cell layer to a single 50-μA electrical stimulus pulse applied to a site in MSN whose peripheral receptive field included the pinna and surrounding skin. The top trace shows the evoked potential produced by the electrical stimulus, measured at the location of the unit in DCN, and the bottom trace shows the effect of the stimulus on the spontaneous activity of the unit. The effect of the stimulus is strong inhibition, which lasts 30–40 ms. This result is typical of the responses of DCN type IV units; 20/34 type IV units tested with electrical stimulation showed strong inhibition like that in Fig. 8a, and 10 of the remaining units showed similar, but weaker inhibition. Of the known DCN inhibitory interneurons, type II units (recorded from vertical cells) are also weakly inhibited by electrical stimulation, and the PVCN response type that is likely to be the wideband inhibitor shows weak inhibition or no effect of electrical stimulation. Thus, the somatosensory inhibitory effect on DCN principal cells does not pass through the known inhibitory circuits.

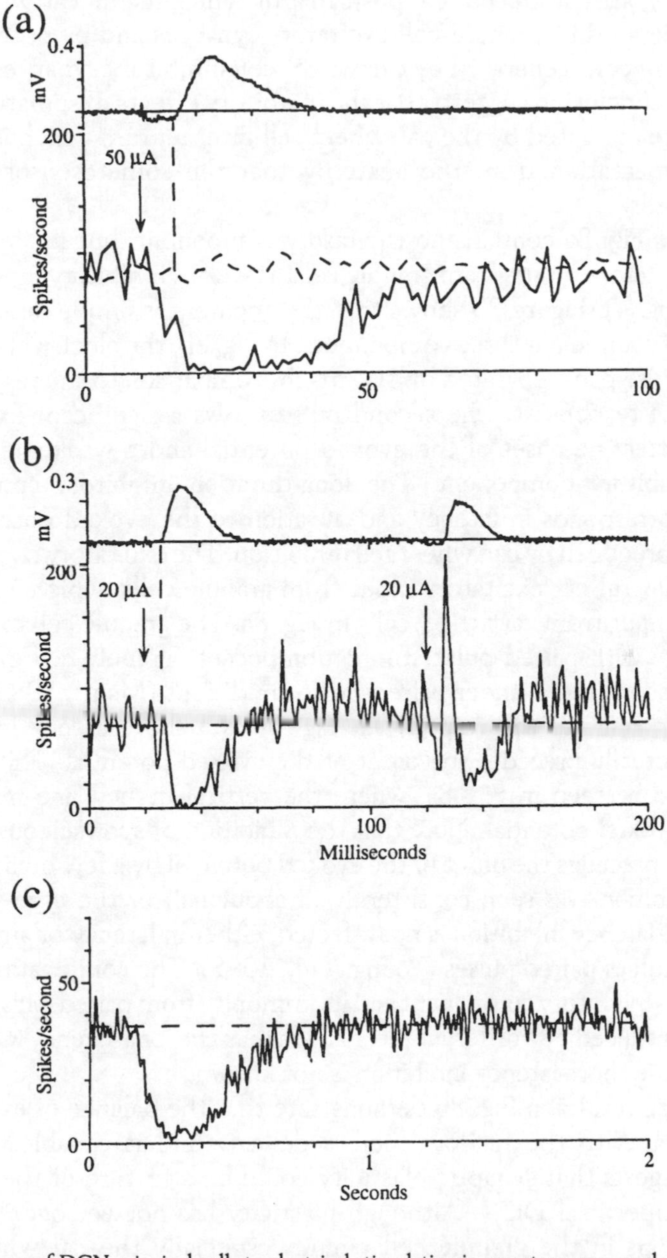

FIG. 8. Responses of DCN principal cells to electrical stimulation in somatosensory nuclei and to movement of the pinna. (a) The top trace is the evoked potential in DCN produced by a 50-µA electrical stimulus (arrow) applied to the MSN; the bottom trace shows inhibition of the spontaneous activity of a DCN type IV neuron by the same stimulus. The horizontal dashed trace is the spontaneous discharge rate from a control run without electrical stimulation. The vertical dashed line marks the approximate beginning of the evoked potential. The unit and evoked potential were recorded at the same location in DCN. (b) Same as (a), except that electrical stimuli were 20 µA and were applied in pairs separated by 100 ms (repeated every 500 ms). Note the reduction in evoked potential amplitude, the emergence of an excitatory peak, and the weakening of the inhibition in response to the second pulse. (c) Inhibition of spontaneous activity in a different type IV unit by manual movement of the pinna back and forth. The pinna movement occupied the first ~0.5 s of the 2-s data recording cycle. (From Young *et al.*, 1995.)

An analysis of evoked potentials, like the one shown in the top trace of Fig. 8a, suggests that they are produced by postsynaptic currents in cartwheel and fusiform cells generated by granule-cell excitatory synapses and by postsynaptic currents in fusiform cells generated by cartwheel-cell inhibitory synapses (Young *et al.*, 1995). This conclusion suggests that the inhibitory effects of somatosensory inputs to DCN are mediated by the cartwheel cell interneuron, which is consistent with our expectation from the anatomy that the somatosensory inputs activate granule cells.

The response in Fig. 8a contains no excitatory component, but fusiform cells should receive excitatory inputs from granule cells as well as inhibitory inputs from cartwheel cells (Fig. 4). Figure 8b shows that the apparently simple inhibition in Fig. 8a is actually a complex of three components. In Fig. 8b, the electrical stimulus was applied as a pulse pair, separated by 100 ms. In comparison to the response to the first pulse, the response to the second pulse shows a significant excitatory component just after the onset of the evoked potential and a weakening of the long-duration inhibitory component. The long-duration inhibitory component (component 1) corresponds in latency and duration to the evoked potential, so that it probably is produced by cartwheel cell inhibition. The excitatory component (component 2) may reflect excitatory input from granule cells, which is masked by the inhibitory input from cartwheel cells in Fig. 8a. The granule cell excitatory effect may emerge with paired-pulse stimulation because granule cell excitation of fusiform cells is facilitated under paired-pulse conditions (Manis, 1989).

The third component of the response in Fig. 8b is a short-latency inhibitory response, which actually precedes the onset of the evoked potential. This latency difference can also be seen in Fig. 8a, where the vertical dashed line marks the beginning of the evoked potential. Note that the inhibition of spontaneous activity in the type IV unit precedes the onset of the evoked potential by a few milliseconds. Short-latency inhibition was seen consistently in about half of the type IV units studied. The short-latency inhibition is not affected, either in latency or amplitude, by presenting stimuli as paired pulses (Young *et al.*, 1995). The combination of the short latency of this inhibitory component and its immunity from paired-pulse effects suggests that it is produced by a different mechanism than the long-latency inhibition, but the source of the short-latency inhibition is not known.

The paired-pulse results in Fig. 8b demonstrate that the balance of excitatory and inhibitory inputs to the fusiform cell is delicate and is capable of being modified; this suggests that synaptic plasticity could be a feature of the granule cell circuitry in superficial DCN. Although plasticity has not yet been demonstrated, the neurons in the granule cell circuit, especially the cartwheel cell, contain many of the molecular constituents expected in neural systems that show plasticity (Manis, Scott, and Spirou, 1993; Ryugo, Pongstaporn, Wright, and Sharp, 1995; Wright, Blackstone, Huganir, and Ryugo, 1996). Plasticity in similar circuits in the fish electrosensory and lateral line systems is used for gain control or to eliminate self-generated signals (Bastian, 1986; Bell, Caputi, Grant, and Serrier, 1993; Montgomery and Bodznick, 1994). Somatosensory inputs from the pinna may play an analogous role in the DCN, although further research is necessary to work out the role of these inputs in the auditory system.

Figure 8c shows the effect on spontaneous activity of a DCN type IV unit when the pinna is manually moved back and forth. Pinna movement occurred during the first 0.5 s or so of the data acquisition cycle and was accompanied by a significant inhibition of spontaneous activity (the dashed line is average spontaneous rate). Inhibitory effects of pinna movement were observed in 13/15 type IV units tested. Weaker inhibitory responses were produced in some units by stimulating other parts of the body, but the pinna effects were by far the strongest. Note that this response occurs during pinna movement and is not a response to pinna position; that is, the average discharge rate of type IV units does not seem to change except transiently while the pinna is moving.

VI. SUMMARY AND CONCLUSIONS

In this chapter, we have reviewed evidence that DCN principal neurons respond to sharp spectral features of stimuli, such as peaks or notches in the spectrum, which convey important information to the animal. Included in this category are spectral notches that carry sound localization information. At the same time, DCN principal cells respond to somatosensory inputs that convey information about movement of the pinna. One possibility suggested by this multisensory convergence, and by the need for information about pinna position in order to use spectral sound localization cues, is that the DCN is encoding both pinna position and spectral cues at its output. Another possibility is suggested by the idea that the DCN detects information-bearing spectral features of the acoustic signal (Nelken and Young, 1994). Pinna movement causes a response in DCN principal cells that is similar in form to the inhibitory responses to spectral peaks or notches, so that the DCN seems to report pinna movements as an important auditory event. Pinna movements are important to the auditory system for several reasons. First, when the pinna moves, the spectra of any sound sources that are present will change as the HRTFs change; the spectral modifications may include substantial changes in signal-to-noise ratio for sound sources that are spatially separated from noise sources. Second, information about sound localization will change with the HRTFs so that sound localization calculations should be redone with the pinnae in their new position. Third, cats may be able to use pinna movement in the way humans use head movement, as an aid to sound localization. This hypothesis is supported by the result that when cats are blinded they adopt scanning head and pinna movements that suggest auditory scanning of sound sources in the environment (Henning and Rauschecker, 1993).

ACKNOWLEDGMENTS

The research reported here was supported by grants DC00979 and DC00115 from the National Institute on Deafness and Other Communication Disorders and by the W. M. Keck Foundation. A number of people participated in the experiments and data analysis, including Michael Derby, Peter Kim, Roger Miller, Samuel Tong, and Wade Wan. The technical assistance of Cynthia Aleszczyk and Phyllis Taylor is appreciated.

REFERENCES

Bastian, J. (1986). "Gain control in the electrosensory system mediated by descending inputs to the electrosensory lateral line lobe," J. Neurosci. **6**, 553–562.

Bell, C. C., Caputi, A., Grant, K., and Serrier, J. (1993). "Storage of a sensory pattern by anti-Hebbian synaptic plasticity in an electric fish," Proc. Natl. Acad. Sci. USA **90**, 4650–4654.

Benson, T. E., and Brown, M. C. (1990). "Synapses formed by olivocochlear axon branches in the mouse cochlear nucleus," J. Comp. Neurol. **294**, 52–70.

Berrebi, A. S., and Mugnaini, E. (1991). "Distribution and targets of the cartwheel cell axon in the dorsal cochlear nucleus of the guinea pig," Anat. Embryol. **183**, 427–454.

Blackstad, T. W., Osen, K. K., and Mugnaini, E. (1984). "Pyramidal neurones of the dorsal cochlear nucleus: A Golgi and computer reconstruction study in cat," Neuroscience **13**, 827–854.

Brown, M. C., Berglund, A. M., Kiang, N. Y. S., and Ryugo, D. K. (1988). "Central trajectories of type II spiral ganglion neurons," J. Comp. Neurol. **278**, 581–590.

Brown, M. C., Liberman, M. C., Benson, T. E., and Ryugo, D. K. (1988). "Brainstem branches from olivocochlear axons in cats and rodents," J. Comp. Neurol. **278**, 591–603.

Burian, M., and Gestoettner, W. (1988). "Projection of primary vestibular afferent fibres to the cochlear nucleus in the guinea pig," Neurosci. Lett **84**, 13–17.

Calford, M. B., and Pettigrew, J. D. (1984). "Frequency dependence of directional amplification at the cat's pinna," Hear. Res. **14**, 13–19.

Crouch, J. E. (1969). *Text-Atlas of Cat Anatomy* (Lea & Febiger, Philadelphia).

Henning, P., and Rauschecker, J. P. (1993). "Vertical scanning movements of head and pinnae in visually deprived cats," Soc. Neurosci. Abst. **19**, 164.

Huang, A. Y., and May, B. J. (1996). "Sound orientation behavior in cats: II mid-frequency spectral cues for sound localization. J. Acoust. Soc. Am. (in press).

Itoh, K., Kamiya, H., Mitani, A., Yasui, Y., Takada, M., and Mizuno, N. (1987). "Direct projection from the dorsal column nuclei and the spinal trigeminal nuclei to the cochlear nuclei in the cat," Brain Res. **400**, 145–150.

Johnson, J. I., Welker, W. I., and Pubols, B. H., Jr. (1968). "Somatotopic organization of raccoon dorsal column nuclei," J. Comp. Neurol. **132**, 1–44.

Kane, E. S., Puglisi, S. G., and Gordon, B. S. (1981). "Neuronal types in the deep dorsal cochlear nucleus of the cat: I. Giant neurons," J. Comp. Neurol. **198**, 483–513.

Kevetter, G. A., and Perachio, A. A. (1989). "Projections from the sacculus to the cochlear nuclei in the Mongolian Gerbil," Brain. Behav. Evol. **34**, 193–200.

Lingenhöhl, K., and Friauf, E. (1994). "Giant neurons in the rat reticular formation: A sensorimotor interface in the elementary acoustic startle circuit?" J. Neurosci. **14**, 1176–1194.

Lorente de Nó, R. (1981). *The Primary Acoustic Nuclei* (Raven Press, New York).

Manis, P. B. (1989). "Responses to parallel fiber stimulation in the guinea pig dorsal cochlear nucleus in vitro," J. Neurophysiol. **61**, 149–161.

Manis, P. B., Scott, J. C., and Spirou, G. A. (1993). "Physiology of the dorsal cochlear nucleus molecular layer," in *The Mammalian Cochlear Nuclei: Organization and Function,* edited by M. A. Merchán, J. M. Juiz, D. A. Godfrey, and E. Mugnaini (Plenum, New York), pp. 361–372.

Martin, R. L., and Webster, W. R. (1987). "The auditory spatial acuity of the domestic cat in the interaural horizontal and median vertical planes," Hear. Res. **30**, 239–252.

Masterton, R. B., and Granger, E. M. (1988). "Role of the acoustic striae in hearing: Contribution of dorsal and intermediate striae to detection of noises and tones," J. Neurophysiol. **60**, 1841–1860.

Masterton, R. B., Granger, E. M., and Glendenning, K. K. (1994). "Role of acoustic striae in hearing—Mechanism for enhancement of sound detection in cats," Hear. Res. **73**, 209–222.

Masterton, R. B., and Sutherland, D. P. (1994). "Discrimination of sound source elevation in cats: I. Role of dorsal/intermediate and ventral acoustic striae," Abstr. Midwinter Res. Mtg. Assoc. Res. Otolaryngol. **17**, 84.

Middlebrooks, J. C., and Green, D. M. (1991). "Sound localization by human listeners," Annu. Rev. Psychol. **42**, 135–159.

Middlebrooks, J. C., and Knudsen, E. I. (1987). "Changes in external ear position modify the spatial tuning of auditory units in the cat's superior colliculus," J. Neurophysiol. **57**, 672–687.

Millar, J., and Basbaum, A. I. (1975). "Topography of the projection of the body surface of the cat to cuneate and gracile nuclei," Exp. Neurol. **49**, 281–290.

Montgomery, J. C., and Bodznick, D. (1994). "An adaptive filter that cancels self-induced noise in the electrosensory and lateral line mechanosensory systems of fish," Neurosci. Lett. **174**, 145–148.

Mugnaini, E., Warr, W. B., and Osen, K. K. (1980). "Distribution and light microscopic features of granule cells in the cochlear nuclei of cat, rat, and mouse," J. Comp. Neurol. **191**, 581–606.

Musicant, A. D., Chan, J. C. K., and Hind, J. E. (1990). "Direction-dependent spectral properties of cat external ear: New data and cross-species comparisons," J. Acoust. Soc. Am. **87**, 757–781.

Nelken, I., and Young, E. D. (1994). "Two separate inhibitory mechanisms shape the responses of dorsal cochlear nucleus type IV units to narrowband and wideband stimuli," J. Neurophysiol. **71**, 2446–2462.

Oertel, D., Wu, S. H., Garb, M. W., and Dizack, C. (1990). "Morphology and physiology of cells in slice preparations of the posteroventral cochlear nucleus of mice," J. Comp. Neurol. **295**, 136–154.

Oliver, D. L. (1984). "Dorsal cochlear nucleus projections to the inferior colliculus in the cat: A light and electron microscopic study," J. Comp. Neurol. **224**, 155–172.

Osen, K. K. (1970). "Course and termination of the primary afferents in the cochlear nuclei of the cat," Arch. Ital. Biol. **108**, 21–51.

Osen, K. K., Ottersen, O. P., and Storm-Mathisen, J. (1990). "Colocalization of glycine-like and GABA-like immunoreactivities. A semiquantitative study of individual neurons in the dorsal cochlear nucleus of cat," in *Glycine Neurotransmission*, edited by O. P. Ottersen and J. Storm-Mathisen (John Wiley & Sons, New York), pp. 417–451.

Phillips, D. P., Calford, M. B., Pettigrew, J. D., Aitkin, L. M., and Semple, M. N. (1982). "Directionality of sound pressure transformation at the cat's pinna," Hear. Res. **8**, 13–28.

Poon, P. W. F., and Brugge, J. F. (1993a). "Sensitivity of auditory nerve fibers to spectral notches," J. Neurophysiol. **70**, 655–666.

Poon, P. W. F., and Brugge, J. F. (1993b). "Virtual-space receptive fields of single auditory nerve fibers," J. Neurophysiol. **70**, 667–676.

Rice, J. J., May, B. J., Spirou, G. A., and Young, E. D. (1992). "Pinna-based spectral cues for sound localization in cat," Hear. Res. **58**, 132–152.

Rice, J. J., Young, E. D., and Spirou, G. A. (1995). "Auditory nerve encoding of pinna-based spectral cues: Rate representation of high frequency stimuli," J. Acoust. Soc. Am. **97**, 1764–1776.

Roth, G. L., Kochhar, R. K., and Hind, J. E. (1980). "Interaural time differences: Implications regarding the neurophysiology of sound localization," J. Acoust. Soc. Am. **68**, 1643–1651.

Ryugo, D. K., Pongstaporn, T., Wright, D. D., and Sharp, A. H. (1995). "Inositol 1,4,5–trisphosphate receptors—Immunocytochemical localization in the dorsal cochlear nucleus," J. Comp. Neurol. **358**, 102–118.

Sachs, M. B. (1984). "Speech encoding in the auditory nerve," in *Hearing Science, Recent Advances*, edited by C. I. Berlin (College-Hill Press, San Diego), pp. 263–307.

Sachs, M. B., and Young, E. D. (1979). "Encoding of steady-state vowels in the auditory nerve: representation in terms of discharge rate," J. Acoust. Soc. Am. **66**, 470–479.

Saint Marie, R. L., Benson, C. G., Ostapoff, E. M., and Morest, D. K. (1991). "Glycine immunoreactive projections from the dorsal to the anteroventral cochlear nucleus," Hear. Res. **51**, 11–28.

Smith, P. H., and Rhode, W. S. (1989). "Structural and functional properties distinguish two types of multipolar cells in the ventral cochlear nucleus," J. Comp. Neurol. **282**, 595–616.

Spirou, G. A., and Young, E. D. (1991). "Organization of dorsal cochlear nucleus type IV unit response maps and their relationship to activation by bandlimited noise," J. Neurophysiol. **65**, 1750–1768.

Sutherland, D. P. (1991). "A role of the dorsal cochlear nucleus in the localization of elevated sound sources," Abstr. Midwinter Res. Mtg. Assoc. Res. Otolaryngol. **14**, 33.

Sutherland, D. P. (1994). *Elevation Discrimination in Cats: Role of Central Auditory Structures*, PhD thesis, Florida State University, Tallahassee, FL.

Voigt, H. F., and Young, E. D. (1990). "Cross-correlation analysis of inhibitory interactions in dorsal cochlear nucleus," J. Neurophysiol. **64**, 1590–1610.

Weinberg, R. J., and Rustioni, A. (1987). "A cuneocochlear pathway in the rat," Neuroscience **20**, 209–219.

Wightman, F. L., and Kistler, D. J. (1992). "The dominant role of low-frequency interaural time differences in sound localization," J. Acoust. Soc. Am. **91**, 1648–1661.

Winter, I. M., and Palmer, A. R. (1995). "Level dependence of cochlear nucleus onset unit responses and facilitation by second tones or broadband noise," J. Neurophysiol. **73**, 141–159.

Wright, D. D., Blackstone, C. D., Huganir, R. L., and Ryugo, D. K. (1996). "Immunocytochemical localization of the mGluR1α metabotropic glutamate receptor in the dorsal cochlear nucleus," J. Comp. Neurol. **364**, 729–745.

Wright, D. D., and Ryugo, D. K. (1996). "Mossy-fiber projections from the cuneate nucleus to the dorsal cochlear nucleus in the rat," J. Comp. Neurol. **365**, 159–172.

Young, E. D. (1980). "Identification of response properties of ascending axons from dorsal cochlear nucleus," Brain Res. **200**, 23–38.

Young, E. D., and Brownell, W. E. (1976). "Responses to tones and noise of single cells in dorsal cochlear nucleus of unanesthetized cats," J. Neurophysiol. **39**, 282–300.

Young, E. D., Nelken, I., and Conley, R. A. (1995). "Somatosensory effects on neurons in dorsal cochlear nucleus," J. Neurophysiol. **73**, 743–765.

Young, E. D., Shofner, W. P., White, J. A., Robert, J. M., and Voigt, H. F. (1988). "Response properties of cochlear nucleus neurons in relationship to physiological mechanisms," in *Auditory Function: Neurobiological Bases of Hearing*, edited by G. M. Edelman, W. E. Gall, and W. M. Cowan (John Wiley & Sons, New York), pp. 277–312.

Young, E. D., Spirou, G. A., Rice, J. J., and Voigt, H. F. (1992). "Neural organization and responses to complex stimuli in the dorsal cochlear nucleus," Phil. Trans. R. Soc. Lond. B **336**, 407–413.

Young, E. D., and Voigt, H. F. (1982). "Response properties of type II and type IV units in dorsal cochlear nucleus," Hear. Res. **6**, 153–169.

Part VII

Models of Spatial Hearing

Chapter 24

Models of Binaural Perception

Richard M. Stern
Carnegie Mellon University

Constantine Trahiotis
University of Connecticut Health Center

(Received March 1995; revised July 1995)

We review some of the major trends in binaural modeling, particularly with regard to models based on the interaural cross-correlation of the auditory-nerve responses to the stimuli. Emphasis is placed on providing an intuitive understanding of cross-correlation-based binaural models, combined with an appreciation of their capabilities and limitations in describing a variety of binaural phenomena. We focus on the seminal theory of binaural processing by Jeffress and its later elaboration and quantification by Colburn. This theory describes and predicts binaural phenomena in terms of the putative activity of central units that record interaural coincidences of firing from matched pairs of auditory-nerve fibers (one from each ear). The input auditory-nerve fibers are matched in characteristic frequency with a fixed time delay inserted on one side. The response of a number of such central units at a given characteristic frequency, plotted as a function of internal delay, is an approximation to the interaural cross-correlation function of the sound as processed by the auditory periphery. We discuss predictions for many of the simple and complex binaural stimuli that are commonly used in psychoacoustical experiments. These experiments include measurements of subjective lateral position, interaural discrimination, binaural detection, and dichotic pitch.

INTRODUCTION

In this chapter we review some of the major trends of research in binaural modeling, particularly with regard to models based on the interaural cross-correlation of the auditory-nerve response to the stimuli.

The human binaural system has attracted the attention of auditory theorists since Lord Rayleigh's seminal investigations (Rayleigh, 1907). The "modern era" of binaural modeling can be said to have begun in 1948 with Jeffress's prescient paper suggesting a neural coincidence mechanism to detect interaural time differences. During that same year the original descriptions of the binaural masking level difference were provided independently by Hirsh (1948) and Licklider (1948).

A convenient starting point for this discussion is the classic review chapter of binaural models by Colburn and Durlach (1978). They described in detail models based on explicit detection of interaural differences (e.g., Jeffress, Blodgett, Sandel, and Wood, 1956; Hafter and Carrier, 1970), models based on direct comparison of the amount of the "left-sided" and "right-sided" internal response to stimuli (e.g., van Bergeijk, 1962), models based on cancellation of binaural maskers (e.g., Durlach, 1972), models based on the direct cross-correlation of the stimuli (e.g., Sayers and Cherry, 1957; Osman, 1971), and models that perform interaural comparisons of explicit descriptions of auditory-nerve activity (e.g., Colburn, 1973, 1977). These models were developed primarily to describe the results of experiments measuring binaural masking level differences (BMLDs). Domnitz and Colburn (1976) later demonstrated that, despite their apparent differences in structure, most of these models provide similar predictions for BMLDs measured with diotic maskers. In their summary, Colburn and Durlach (1978) noted that most of the contemporary models could be considered to be different implementations of the general structure shown in Fig. 1. This generic structure includes a series of peripheral processing steps including band-pass filtering and rectification, comparison of interaural timing information over a limited range of internal delays using a correlation or coincidence mechanism, consideration of interaural intensity differences of the outputs of monaural processors, and a subsequent decision-making mechanism.

Since 1978, the basic structure described by Colburn and Durlach, and especially the cross-correlation mechanism used for the extraction of interaural timing information, has formed the basis of all subsequent models of binaural hearing. Other recent trends fostering the development of a broader theory of binaural perception include an increased reliance on computational (as opposed to analytical) approaches to predicting the phenomena, and efforts to make use of head-related transfer functions in attempts to understand the relative salience of the different available cues and to mimic realistic sound fields using stimuli presented through headphones. At the same time, there has been increased attention paid to the development of models of more central physiological processing mechanisms, which may bear directly on our understanding of binaural hearing. This work has recently been summarized by Colburn (1995).

The goal of this chapter is to provide the reader with an intuitive understanding of how cross-correlation-based binaural models work, and to provide an appreciation of their capabilities and limitations in describing a variety of binaural phenomena. In contrast to other recent reviews of binaural modeling (e.g., Colburn, 1995; Stern and Trahiotis, 1995), this chapter is less comprehensive and more centered around our own efforts. Using this "narrow" approach, we show

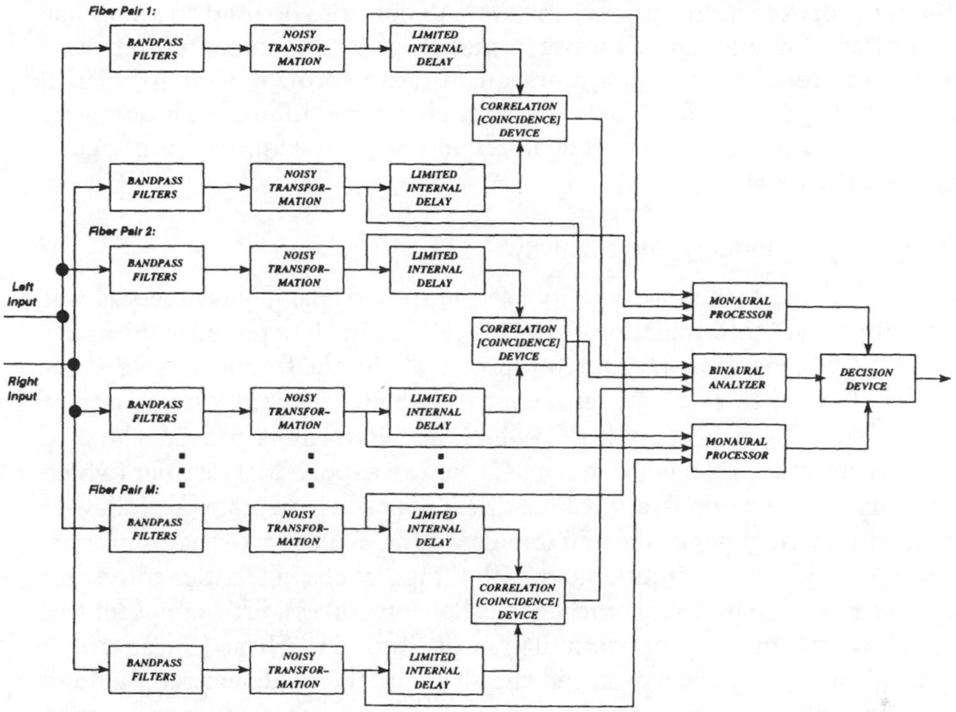

FIG. 1. Generic model of binaural processing proposed by Colburn and Durlach (1978). Three of many sets of fiber pairs are depicted.

how the same theoretical framework can be used to provide predictions spanning a wide variety of phenomena and empirical data. It should be understood that similar predictions would be provided by other cross-correlation-based models as well.

We begin by reviewing and discussing the Jeffress–Colburn model and selected extensions in Sections I and II. The response of the Jeffress–Colburn model to various kinds of simple stimuli is characterized in Section III, which also contains representative comparisons of the predictions of this kind of model to the corresponding experimental data.

I. CROSS-CORRELATION-BASED MODELS OF BINAURAL INTERACTION

A. The Jeffress–Colburn model

Modern binaural models are based on Jeffress's (1948) conception of a neural "place" mechanism that would enable the extraction of interaural timing information. Jeffress suggested that external interaural delays could be internally coded by central units that record coincidences of neural impulses from pairs of more peripheral nerve fibers. Each central unit was presumed to compare information from the two ears after a series of internal time delays. Licklider

(1959) later proposed a similar mechanism that could also be used to achieve an autocorrelation of neural signals for use in models of pitch perception. Jeffress's hypothesis was reformulated in a more quantitative form by Colburn (1973, 1977). Colburn's model consists of two parts: a characterization of auditory-nerve activity, and a central processor that analyzes and displays comparisons of neural activity from the two ears.

1. The model of auditory-nerve activity

The model of auditory-nerve activity used in the original Colburn model was adapted from an earlier formulation of Siebert (1970) and is depicted in the upper panel of Fig. 2. It consists of a bandpass filter (to depict the frequency selectivity of individual fibers), an automatic gain control (which limits the average rate of response to stimuli), a lowpass filter (which serves to limit phase-locking to stimulus fine structure at higher frequencies), and an exponential rectifier (which roughly characterizes peripheral nonlinearities). These elements were followed by a mechanism that generates neural impulses at an average rate that is proportional to the output of the rectifier and with temporal characteristics consistent with activity produced by a nonhomogeneous Poisson process. Predictions for this chapter follow the more recent formulation of Stern and Shear (Shear, 1987; Stern and Shear, 1996). They changed the shape of the nonlinear rectifier and interchanged the order of the rectifier and the lowpass filter in order to describe more accurately the response to noise stimuli and to high-frequency stimuli. Similar functional models have been used by others including Duifhuis (1973), Blauert and Cobben (1978), and Lindemann (1986a, 1986b).

Colburn used the nonhomogeneous Poisson process to characterize the response of auditory-nerve fibers to sound because it is the simplest stochastic process that can realistically be applied to model the neural firing times. Using an

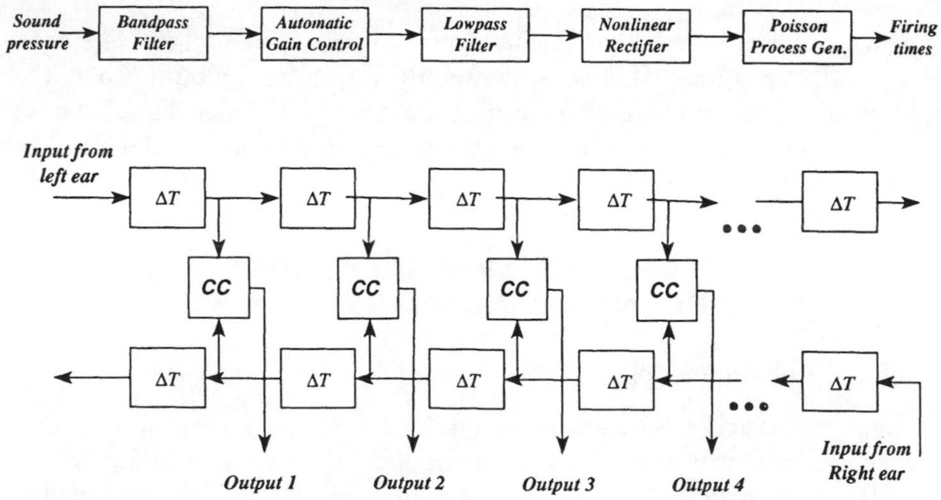

FIG. 2. Upper panel: Schematic representation of the auditory periphery. Lower panel: Schematic representation of the Jeffress place mechanism. The blocks labeled CC record coincidences of neural activity from the two ears (after the delays are incurred).

explicit analytical model like the Poisson process, one can predict discrimination and detection thresholds by application of the Cramer–Rao bound (cf. van Trees, 1968), or one can calculate means and variances of the predicted outputs of the coincidence counters and directly predict performance by assuming that the decision variable is normally distributed. The construction and evaluation of analytical models of neural activity is inevitably a compromise between faithfulness to the known physiological results and mathematical tractability. For example, it is well known that the peripheral auditory system is both time varying (e.g., due to the refractory nature of the auditory response) and nonlinear. The Poisson-process model ignores the refractoriness in the response, and the nonlinear rectifier in the model does not describe several known aspects of peripheral auditory nonlinearity. Furthermore, predictions are easily developed only for exponential and half-wave power-law rectification and only for a small set of stimuli (e.g., pure tones, tones in noise, and bandpass noise) with fixed interaural time delays (ITDs) and interaural intensity differences (IIDs).

In recent years, models of the peripheral auditory response to sound have become more computationally oriented (and more physiologically accurate) (e.g., Carney, 1993; Meddis, Hewitt, and Shackleton, 1990; Payton, 1988). These models have in turn served as front ends for binaural models. For example, the hair cell model of Meddis *et al.* has been incorporated into the binaural processing model of Shackleton, Meddis, and Hewitt (1992).

2. The model of central processing

One formulation of Colburn's quantification of Jeffress's hypothesis is depicted in the lower panel of Fig. 2. The heart of Colburn's (1973, 1977) model is an ensemble of units describing the interaction of neural activity from the left and right ears generated by auditory-nerve fibers with the same characteristic frequency (CF). The input from one side is delayed by an amount that is fixed for each fiber pair. The delay mechanism is commonly conceptualized in the form of a ladder-type delay line as in Fig. 2, but such a structure is not the only possible realization. The net interaural delay incurred by the two inputs to each fiber pair is the key parameter in the analysis of the outputs of the mechanism and is referred to using the variable τ. This ensemble of coincidence-counting units is similar in structure to the central processor of several other models including that of Blauert and Cobben (1978).

The relative number of coincidence counts of the Jeffress–Colburn model, considered as a function of the internal-delay parameter τ, is an estimate of the interaural cross-correlation of the auditory-nerve responses to the stimuli at each CF. In contrast, some previous models of binaural processing utilized the cross-correlation of the original stimuli (rather than the physiological response to the stimuli) to develop predictions (e.g., Sayers and Cherry, 1957; Osman, 1971).

Colburn and Durlach (1978) noted that the cross-correlation mechanism shown in Fig. 2 can also be regarded as a generalization of the equalization-cancellation (EC) model of Durlach (1963). Specifically, the EC model yields predictions concerning binaural detection thresholds by applying a combination of ITD and IID that produces the best "equalization" of the masker components of the stimuli presented to each of the two ears. "Cancellation" of the masker is then achieved by subtracting one of the resulting signals from the other. Predictions provided by the EC model are generally dominated by the effects of the ITD-equalization component rather than the IID-equalization component. Because the interaural delays of the fiber pairs of the Jeffress–Colburn model perform the same function as the ITD-equalizing operation of the EC model, most predictions of detection thresholds for the two models are similar.

B. Physiological plausibility of the Jeffress–Colburn model

As summarized by Kuwada, Batra, and Fitzpatrick (Chapter 20, this volume) and Yin, Joris, Smith, and Chan (Chapter 21, this volume), a number of researchers have studied neural cells that have outputs that functionally resemble those of the coincidence-counting units schematized in Fig. 2. Particularly noteworthy are the cells having a "characteristic delay" first reported by Rose, Gross, Geisler, and Hind (1966) in the inferior colliculus. Such cells are maximally sensitive to inputs that have a specific interaural delay regardless of the frequency of the stimulation. Cells with similar responses have been reported by other researchers in other sites within the central auditory system.

The anatomical origin of the internal interaural delays has been the source of some speculation. The preponderance of evidence indicates that the delays are of neural origin, caused either by slowed conduction velocity or by synaptic delays (e.g., Smith, Joris, and Yin, 1993; Carr and Konishi, 1990; Young and Rubel, 1983). It has also been suggested (without evidence) that the internal delays could come about if higher processing centers were to compare timing information derived from auditory-nerve fibers with different CFs (Schroeder, 1977; Shamma, Shen, and Gopalaswamy, 1989). The anatomical validity of the models notwithstanding, the predictions of binaural models are unaffected by whether the internal delays are assumed to be caused by neural or mechanical phenomena.

C. Temporal integration of the coincidence display

Although the binaural system is known to resolve static ITDs as small as tens of microseconds, experiments measuring responses to time-varying ITDs (e.g., Licklider, Webster, and Hedlun, 1950; Grantham and Wightman, 1978) indicate a lower degree of temporal resolution, on the order of tens of milliseconds. For this reason, the binaural system is often characterized as being "sluggish." In order to understand threshold sensitivity to stimuli with either static or time-varying ITDs, one must note that discrimination between static ITDs reflects changes in the place of activity of the coincidence-counting units along the internal-delay axis. Such resolution is limited by the density of fiber pairs with respect to internal delay at each CF. On the other hand, resolution of time-varying ITDs reflects the averaging of instantaneous responses over running time (averaged across internal delay). This type of averaging is often referred to as temporal integration and appears to be performed rather slowly.

It is helpful to think of the temporal averaging of the matrix of coincidence-counting units as resulting from a lowpass filtering of the instantaneous outputs of the coincidence counters with respect to running time. Figure 3 demonstrates how the expected number of instantaneous coincidences for fibers with a CF of 500 Hz varies as a simultaneous function of internal delay (τ) and running time (t), both with and without (running) lowpass filtering. The upper panel of Fig. 3 shows the instantaneous response of the coincidence counters depicted in Fig. 2 to a 500-Hz tone with zero ITD. Note that the peaks of activity are limited to particular intervals of the running time as well as to particular values of interaural delay. Said differently, there are areas of inactivity along both axes that reflect times for which the correlation function approaches zero. The lower panel of Fig. 3 shows the same function after temporal integration, realized by convolution with a simple lowpass filter. Note that the integration with respect to running time transforms the isolated peaks in the response of the coincidence counters to smoother ridges that are parallel to the running-time axis. We believe that such smoothing is necessary because it allows the binaural system to provide a stable spatial representation of the acoustic world.

It appears that many, if not all, of the data concerning the sluggishness phenomenon can be explained in terms of simple temporal integration of the coincidence-counter output (Grantham and Wightman, 1978; Bachorski, 1983;

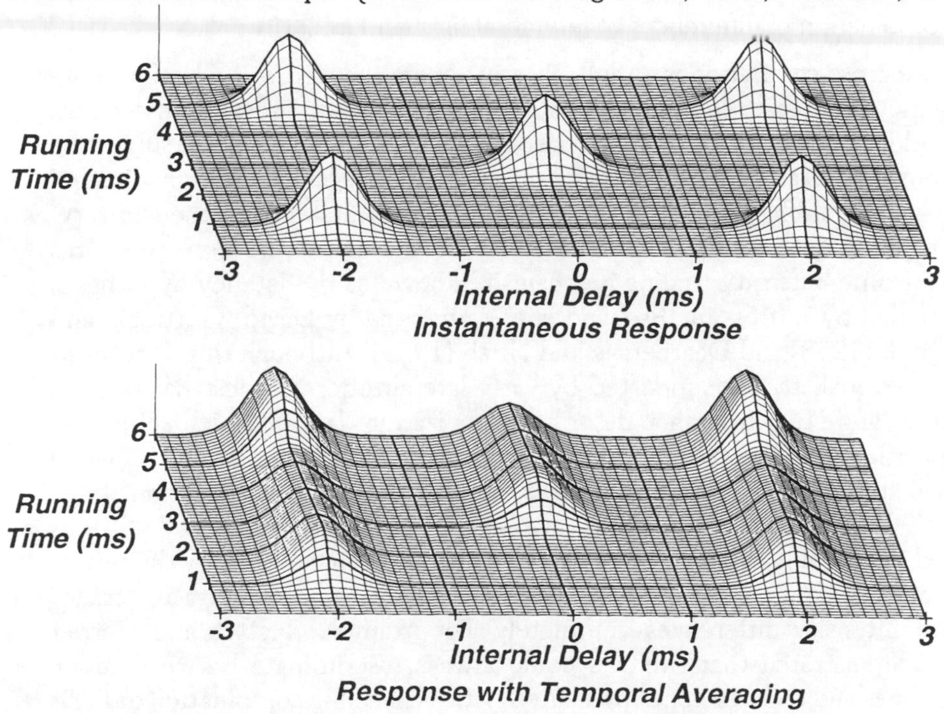

FIG. 3. Average value of the instantaneous number of coincidences as a simultaneous function of running time t and internal delay τ. The stimulus is a 500-Hz tone with zero ITD. The response is shown using no temporal integration (upper panel) and using temporal integration by an exponentially shaped temporal weighting function with an effective cutoff frequency of 5 Hz in the frequency domain.

Stern and Bachorski, 1983; Grantham, 1984). Various experimental results imply that the time constants for processing IIDs are much shorter than those that constrain the processing of ITDs (Grantham, 1984; Bernstein and Trahiotis, 1994). The necessity for including more than one time constant was also emphasized by Gabriel (1983). The type of temporal averaging that is likely to mediate binaural sluggishness also provides at least a qualitative explanation for the disappearance of binaural beats at high beat frequencies (Licklider *et al.*, 1950).

II. EXTENSIONS TO THE JEFFRESS–COLBURN MODEL

A. Extensions by Stern, Colburn, and Trahiotis

The original goal of work performed by Stern and his colleagues was to extend the Jeffress–Colburn formulation to provide predictions for the subjective lateral position of stimuli and to examine the extent to which the "position variable" could be used to describe detection and discrimination results. In order to do this, it was necessary to specify a means of combining effects produced by the ITDs and IIDs of the stimulus and to provide a way to predict subjective lateral position from the combined display. The resulting model is referred to as the position-variable model.

1. Combination of differences of interaural time and intensity

Because cross-correlation is a multiplicative operation, cross-correlation functions cannot be used to indicate which ear is receiving the more intense input. Hence, additional mechanisms are needed to describe how IIDs affect subjective lateral position. At one time it was felt that the effects of IIDs in binaural lateralization could be accounted for by the decrease in latency of the auditory-nerve response that occurs as the intensity of the signals is increased. This peripheral time–intensity trading mechanism, known as the latency hypothesis, was discussed by Jeffress in 1948 and later elaborated by David, Guttman, and van Bergeijk (1958) and Deatherage and Hirsh (1959). Although this hypothesis was at least qualitatively supported by early lateralization studies that utilized small ITDs and IIDs, it cannot describe lateralization data in which subjective lateral position is shown clearly to be a nonlinear function of ITD and IID when these two stimulus parameters are varied over a wider range of conditions (e.g., Sayers, 1964; Domnitz and Colburn, 1977; Bernstein and Trahiotis, 1985), as discussed in Sec. II.A.2. The latency hypothesis is also contradicted by the results of several interaural discrimination studies that indicate an inability to "trade" time and intensity differences completely. For example, Hafter and Carrier (1972) demonstrated that subjects could always discriminate between diotic 500-Hz tones and dichotic tones presented with a canceling combination of ITDs and IIDs that produced a centered primary image.

The position-variable model (Stern and Colburn, 1978) incorporates a more central mechanism to account for the effects of IID. The function describing the number of coincidences as a function of internal delay is multiplied by a Gaussian-shaped function with a location along the internal-delay axis that depends on the IID of the stimulus. In Sec. II.B we describe an alternative intensity-weighting mechanism that was proposed by Lindemann (1986a), which incorporates lateral inhibition of the coincidence-counting response along adjacent delays. The Stern–Colburn and Lindemann models provide similar predictions for the lateralization of 500-Hz pure tones as a joint function of ITD and IID.

2. Lateral position predictions using the coincidence display

There are several ways of predicting lateral position from the outputs of the interaural coincidence-counting units. Stern and Colburn (1978) proposed that the predicted lateral position of a stimulus, $\hat{P}$, can be obtained by computing the centroid (or center of mass) along the internal-delay axis of the intensity-weighted function describing the number of coincidences, while integrating over frequency. This definition of predicted lateral position was originally adopted by Stern and Colburn for reasons of computational simplicity, and it has been employed by Blauert and his colleagues (e.g., Lindemann, 1986a, 1986b) as well. It should be noted, however, that the centroid computation by itself produces predictions for the intracranial location of only a single image. As a result, using the centroid of activity alone one cannot explain experimental results that suggest the existence of multiple images such as the studies by Moushegian and Jeffress (1959), Whitworth and Jeffress (1961), and Hafter and Jeffress (1968).

One plausible alternative is to predict lateral position by resorting to the locations of individual peaks of the cross-correlation function. Such locations allow one to account for multiple images that can occur for tonal stimuli presented interaurally out of phase (e.g., Sayers, 1964; Yost, 1981), as well as for the secondary "time image" observed when some stimuli are presented with conflicting ITDs and IIDs (e.g., Whitworth and Jeffress, 1961; Hafter and Jeffress, 1968). Shackleton *et al.* (1992) made predictions on the basis of either the centroid or the peaks of the responses, choosing the statistic that more accurately described the results for a given experiment. Although definitely not parsimonious, this type of approach may be necessary to account for the varieties of data in all their complexity.

The function specifying the density of internal delays along the internal-delay axis plays an important (but frequently unrecognized) role in developing predictions of subjective lateral position. The form of the function $p(\tau)$ derived by Colburn (1977) and later modified by Stern and Shear (1996) specifies that there are more coincidence-counting units with internal interaural delays of smaller magnitude. This has been verified by physiological measurements (e.g., Kuwada, Stanford, and Batra, 1987). Nevertheless, in order to describe many of the detection and lateralization data, a substantial fraction of the coincidence counters must be assumed to have internal delays much greater in magnitude than the largest delays that can be physically attained using free-field stimuli.

Colburn (1969, 1977) originally assumed that the density function for internal delays, $p(\tau)$, was independent of frequency, and he fitted the shape of $p(\tau)$ to predict the relative masking level differences for two antiphasic conditions, N_0S_π versus $N_\pi S_0$. More recently, Stern and Shear (1996) made this function weakly dependent on frequency and changed its shape slightly. This allowed them to predict the lateralization of tonal stimuli with a fixed ITD as a function of stimulus frequency (Schiano, Trahiotis, and Bernstein, 1986).

The effects of the distribution of internal delay and the multiplicative intensity weighting function are illustrated in Figs. 4 and 5, which depict the representation of a 500-Hz pure tone with an ITD of +0.5 ms. Figure 4 shows the total number of coincidences recorded by the coincidence-counting units as a joint function of internal delay (along the horizontal axis) and CF (along the oblique axis). The upper panel shows the average number of coincidences per fiber pair. The center

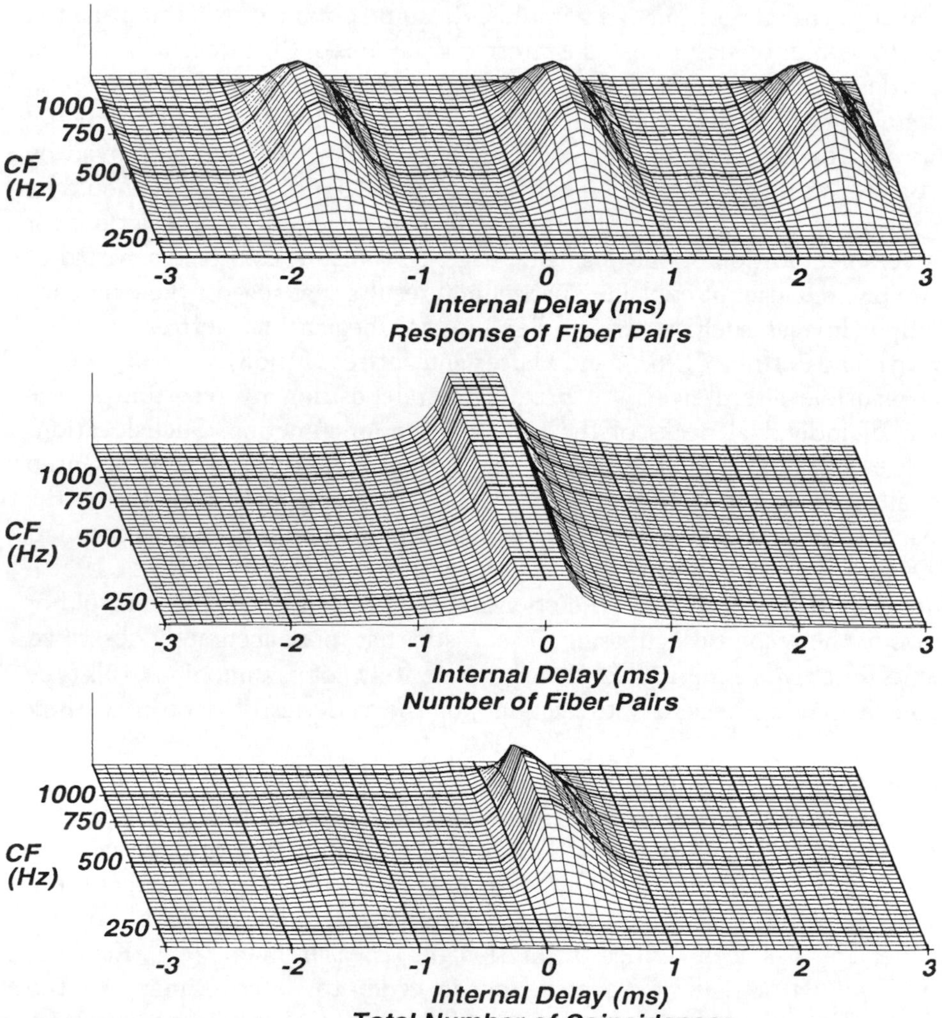

FIG. 4. Response of an ensemble of binaural coincidence-counting units to a 500-Hz pure tone with a 0.5-ms ITD. Upper panel: The relative number of coincidences per fiber pair as a function of internal delay τ (ms) and CF of the auditory-nerve fibers (Hz). Central panel: The assumed density of internal delays as a function of CF. Lower panel: The average total number of coincidences as a function of internal delay and CF, which is the product of the upper and central panel.

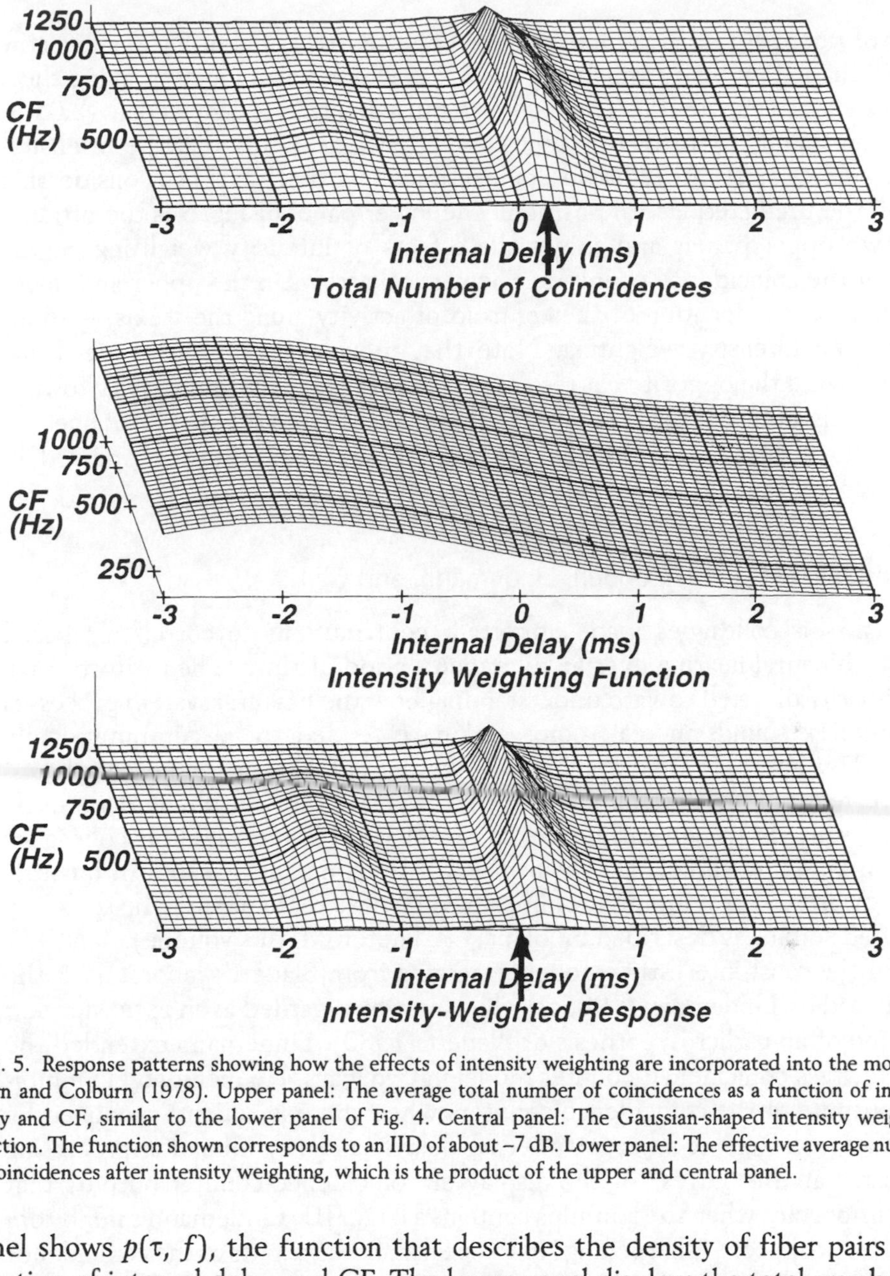

FIG. 5. Response patterns showing how the effects of intensity weighting are incorporated into the model of Stern and Colburn (1978). Upper panel: The average total number of coincidences as a function of internal delay and CF, similar to the lower panel of Fig. 4. Central panel: The Gaussian-shaped intensity weighting function. The function shown corresponds to an IID of about –7 dB. Lower panel: The effective average number of coincidences after intensity weighting, which is the product of the upper and central panel.

panel shows $p(\tau, f)$, the function that describes the density of fiber pairs as a function of internal delay and CF. The lower panel displays the total number of coincidences at each internal delay and CF. That total is the product of the number of counts per fiber pair (upper panel) and the number of fiber pairs (central panel). There is a distinct maximum in the cross-correlation function at a value of internal delay that is close to that of the original interaural delay of the stimulus and extends over a broad range of CFs.

Figure 5 demonstrates the effects of the intensity-weighting mechanism for a set of stimuli that produce time–intensity "trading." The upper panel of Fig. 5 is similar to the lower panel of Fig. 4. It depicts the total number of coincidences in response to a 500-Hz tone with a 0.5-ms ITD, after accounting for the relative number of fiber pairs at each internal delay. The central panel of Fig. 5 shows the Gaussian-shaped intensity-weighting function, which has a location along the τ axis that depends on the IID. The Gaussian pulse in Fig. 5 is centered at –2.0 ms, which corresponds to an IID of approximately –7 dB. Although the intensity-weighting function is rather broad, its location along the τ axis has considerable effect on the predicted lateral position. The lower panel of Fig. 5 is the product of the two upper panels and shows the effects of intensity weighting on the outputs of the coincidence counters. The vertical arrows in the upper and lower panels indicate the location of the centroid of activity along the τ axis, without and with the intensity weighting. Note that moving the intensity weighting function toward the opposite ear results in a shift of the resulting activity toward that ear. This outcome provides predictions consistent with data obtained in experiments utilizing conflicting ITDs and IIDs, such as those employed in "time–intensity trading" experiments.

B. Extensions by Blauert, Cobben, Lindemann, and Gaik

Blauert and his colleagues made important contributions to correlation-based models of binaural hearing over an extended period of time. Their efforts have been primarily directed toward understanding how the binaural system processes more complex sounds in real rooms and have tended to be computationally oriented. This approach is complementary to that of Colburn and his colleagues, who have focused on explaining "classical" psychoacoustical phenomena using stimuli presented through earphones. In recent years Blauert and his colleagues have been applying knowledge gleaned from fundamental research in binaural hearing toward the development of improved devices that enhance the spatiality of recorded sound, as described by Blauert (Chapter 28, this volume).

One of the most interesting models emerging from Blauert's laboratory is the one proposed by Lindemann (1986a), which may be regarded as an extension and elaboration of an earlier hypothesis of Blauert (1980). Lindemann extended the original Jeffress coincidence-counter model in two ways. He included (1) inhibition of outputs of the coincidence counters when there is activity produced by coincidence counters at adjacent internal delays, and (2) monaural-processing mechanisms at the "edges" of the display of coincidence-counter outputs that become important when the stimulus contains a large IID. Lindemann's inhibitory mechanism produces a "sharpening" of the peaks of the outputs of the coincidence counters along the internal-delay axis.

One of the very interesting properties of the Lindemann model is that it produces a time–intensity trading mechanism at the level of the coincidence-counter outputs. This occurs because the interaction of the inhibitory mechanism and the monaural processing mechanisms causes the locations of peaks of the outputs of the coincidence counters to shift along the internal-delay axis with changes in IID. The net effects of IIDs on the patterns of coincidence-counter outputs in the Lindemann model are not unlike effects produced by the intensity-weighting function used by Stern and Colburn (1978). In a sense, the time–intensity interaction of the Lindemann model is more parsimonious in that it arises naturally from the fundamental assumptions of the model rather than as the result of the imposition of an arbitrary weighting function.

Gaik (1993) extended the Lindemann mechanism by adding a further weighting to the coincidence-counter outputs that reinforces naturally occurring combinations of ITD and IID. This has the effect of causing physically plausible stimuli to produce coincidence outputs with a single prominent peak that is compact along the internal-delay axis and that is consistent over frequency. Conversely, very unnatural combinations of ITDs and IIDs presented via earphones (which tend to give rise to multiple and/or diffuse perceptual images) produce response patterns with more than one prominent peak along the internal-delay axis.

III. COMPARISONS OF THEORETICAL PREDICTIONS TO EXPERIMENTAL DATA

In this section we describe how the patterns of outputs of the coincidence counters of the Jeffress–Colburn model have been applied to describe some of the phenomena that have been important for researchers in auditory perception. In order to make the presentation easy to follow, the discussion includes both examples of responses of the coincidence counters and predictions obtained using those responses. Simultaneously, we comment on the characteristics and limitations of current models.

A. Subjective lateral position

1. Lateralization of pure tones

Figure 6 compares the predictions of the original position-variable model for the lateral position of 500-Hz tones as a function of ITD and IID (Stern and Colburn, 1978) to data obtained by Domnitz and Colburn (1977). These predictions were obtained by computing the centroid along the internal-delay axis of the intensity-weighted coincidence counts, as exemplified in the lower panel of Fig. 5. The model provides reasonably accurate predictions for a number of fundamental aspects of the lateralization of pure tones based on ongoing ITDs and IIDs. These aspects include (1) the periodicity of lateral position with respect to ITD; (2) the joint dependence of the lateralization of low-frequency pure tones on ITD and IID; and (3) the "cue-reversal phenomenon" wherein the direction of apparent motion of the image reverses at ITDs approaching half the period of the tone. Note that as IID increases, the forms of the curves for both the data and predictions are inconsistent with the latency hypothesis. This is indicated by the fact that the effect of IID is to displace the curves vertically and horizontally, rather than just horizontally.

The model was subsequently modified to allow the position variable to be a function of time (Stern and Bachorski, 1983). This enables it to account for cases where stimuli are presented with slowly varying ITD and/or IID (e.g., Grantham and Wightman, 1978; Licklider *et al.*, 1950). In addition, as noted earlier, it was also necessary to modify the $p(\tau)$ function in order to account for the fact that

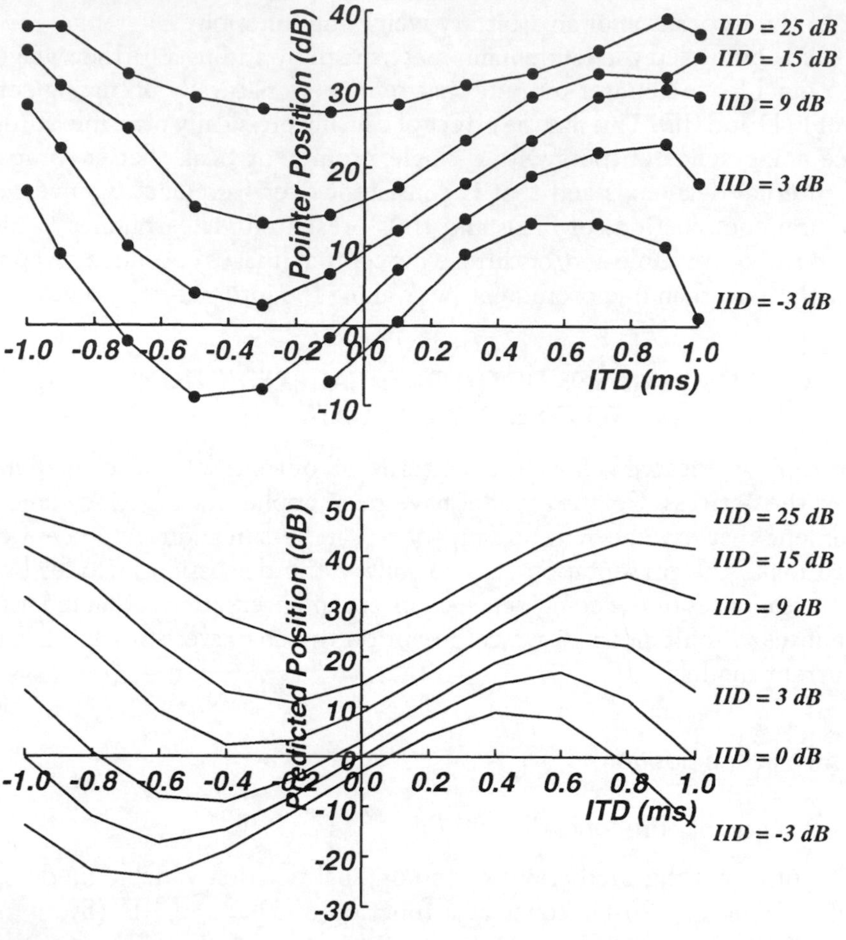

FIG. 6. Upper panel: Experimental lateralization-matching results, showing the IID of a pointer tone required to match the perceived lateral position of a 500-Hz test tone, as a function of the ITD and IID of the test tone (Domnitz and Colburn, 1977). Lower panel: Theoretical predictions for the same stimuli, from Stern and Colburn (1978).

the lateral position of pure tones with fixed ITD is approximately constant up to 1000 Hz (Schiano *et al.*, 1986).

2. Lateralization of low-frequency bandpass noise

In recent years attention has been focussed on the lateralization of spectrally and temporally complex stimuli including bandpass noise and amplitude-modulated tones. The lateralization of bandpass noise and amplitude-modulated tones are treated separately because different issues arise in understanding how they are lateralized.

Figure 7 shows the responses of the coincidence-counting units to bandpass noise presented with a center frequency of 500 Hz and two different bandwidths, 50 Hz (upper panel) and 800 Hz (lower panel). In both cases the stimuli have an ITD of –1.5 ms. The pattern of the responses for the 50-Hz-wide noise looks very similar to the pattern produced by 500-Hz pure tones presented with the same ITD. For 500-Hz tones, an ITD of –1.5 ms is equivalent to an ITD of +0.5 ms, as shown in the upper panel of Fig. 4. Consistent with this, the stimulus with the 50-Hz bandwidth is lateralized on the "wrong" side of the head, that is, the side receiving the signal that is lagging in time. For larger bandwidths, the intracranial image moves toward the left side of the head (Stern, Zeiberg, and Trahiotis, 1988; Trahiotis and Stern, 1989), indicating the true ITD. With larger bandwidths, as exemplified by the 800-Hz-wide condition in the lower panel of Fig. 7, it is obvious that the ridge at $\tau = -1.5$ corresponds to the true ITD because it is parallel to the CF axis, depicting a consistent stimulus ITD of –1.5 ms for all frequencies.

We have referred to the consistency over frequency of the maxima of the coincidence-count response (that indicates the true ITD) as *straightness*. By independently manipulating ITD, interaural phase difference (IPD), and bandwidth, it became clear that the binaural system weights more heavily the straighter components of the response to bandpass-noise stimuli.

We believe that the straightness-weighting phenomenon results from passing the outputs of the coincidence-counting units through a second level of coincidence-counting units. Each set of inputs to this second layer of temporal processing is assumed to come from first-level coincidence counters representing a range of CFs, but with a common internal delay. The effect of this type of processing is illustrated in Fig. 8, which compares the response of the original model (without

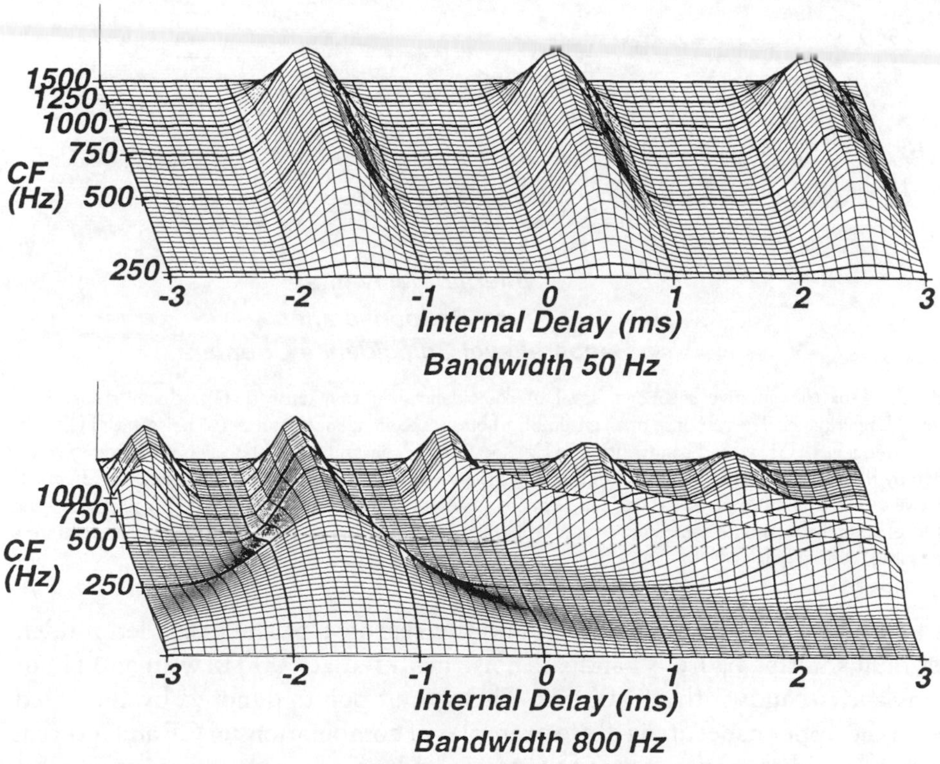

FIG. 7. Response of an ensemble of coincidence-counting units to low-frequency bandpass noise with a center frequency of 500 Hz and an ITD of –1.5 ms. Upper panel: Response to bandpass noise with a bandwidth of 50 Hz. Lower panel: Response to bandpass noise with a bandwidth of 800 Hz.

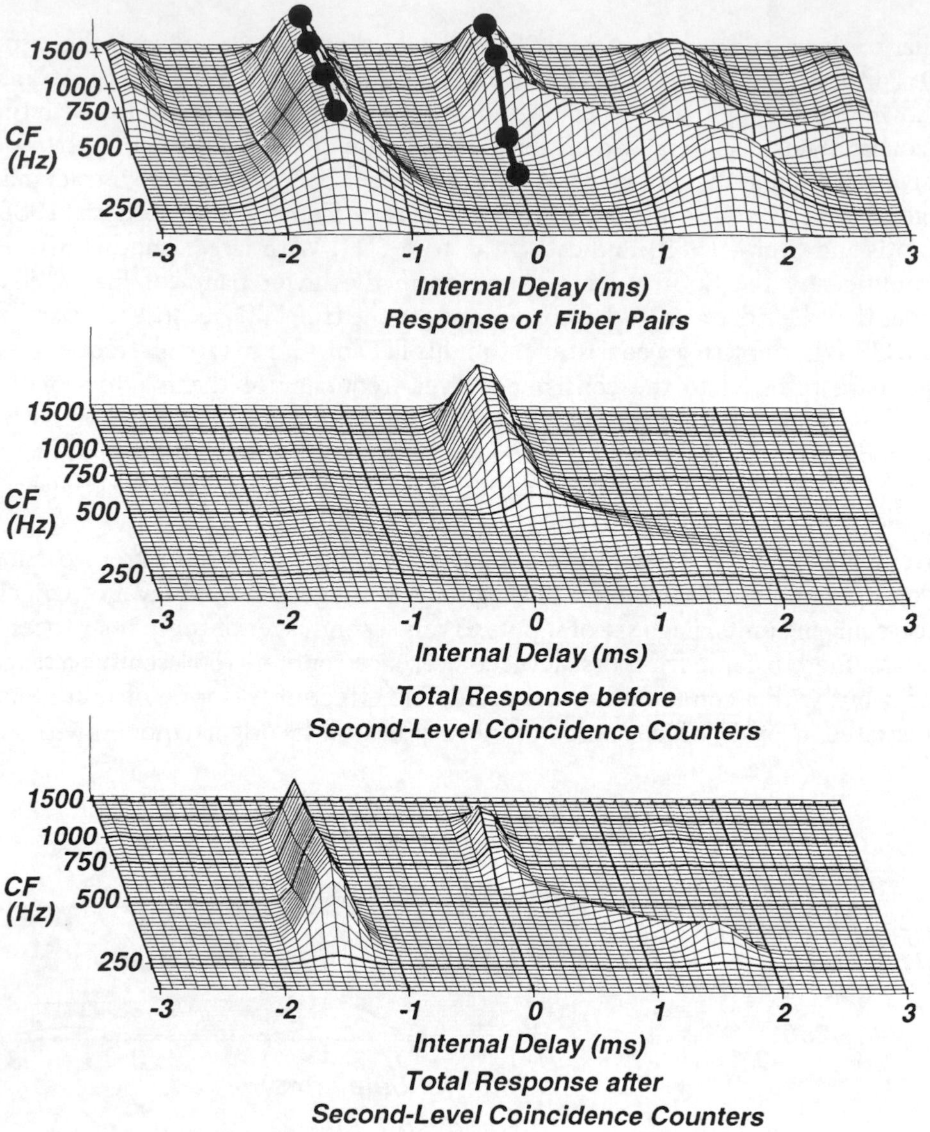

FIG. 8. Effect of the putative secondary level of coincidence-counting units that produce "straightness weighting." Upper panel: The response of an ensemble of binaural coincidence counters to noise with ITD –1.5 ms, center frequency 500 Hz, and bandwidth 400 Hz. Locations of constant internal delay but different CF are identified by filled circles joined by lines. Central panel: Same as upper panel, but incorporating the effects of the relative number of fiber pairs. Lower panel: Same as central panel, but after further processing by the second-level units that compute coincidences over frequency of the outputs of the original coincidence counters with the same internal delay.

any additional straightness weighting) and the response of the extended model. The stimulus in this figure is bandpass noise centered at 500 Hz with an ITD of –1.5 ms and a bandwidth of 400 Hz. The sets of points denoted by the filled circles in the upper panel of Fig. 8 are examples of combinations of CF and internal delay that would comprise inputs to the second-level coincidence counters. The center panel of Fig. 8 shows the effect of weighting by the relative number of fiber pairs, which suppresses the effects of the responses at the true ITD of –1.5

ms. The lower panel of Fig. 8 shows the dramatic effects of applying the second level of coincidences, which provides much greater emphasis to the straight ridge at −1.5 ms. This occurs because, for that ridge, all of the first-level coincidence counters are firing at rates that are at or near their maximum output. In contrast, the ridge closer to the midline (i.e., at an ITD of approximately zero) is attenuated because of the minimal response at characteristic frequencies below approximately 600 Hz at that ITD.

In addition to providing the weighting of straightness needed to describe the lateralization data as in Stern, Zeiberg, and Trahiotis (1988) and Trahiotis and Stern (1989), this manner of combining coincidence information across frequency also sharpens the ridges of the two-dimensional cross-correlation function along the internal-delay axis. For example, the ridges in the lower panel of Fig. 8 exhibit a smaller "width" (along the internal-delay axis) than the corresponding ridges in the upper panel of Fig. 8. The sharpening of the ridges along the internal-delay axis occurs because the rate functions of the outputs of the second-level coincidence counters are approximately proportional to the products of the rate functions of the (first-level) coincidence counters that comprise their inputs. For "straight" ridges, this has the effect of enhancing the peaks and suppressing the "valleys" in the patterns of second-level coincidence output. It is important to note that this sharpening along the internal-delay axis can occur without the explicit lateral-inhibition network proposed by Lindemann (1986a).

Figure 9 demonstrates how straightness weighting is needed to describe the lateralization of low-frequency bandpass noise. The upper panel of Fig. 9 shows the joint dependence of the lateral position of these stimuli on ITD, IPD, and bandwidth, as measured for human subjects by Stern, Zeiberg, and Trahiotis (1988). The combinations of ITD and IPD were selected because they produce maxima of the outputs of the coincidence counters at the same values of internal delay for values of CF near 500 Hz. The lateral position of noise with a 1.5-ms ITD and an IPD of 0° moves from one side of the head to the other as bandwidth increases, for the reasons discussed previously in this section. Other combinations of ITD and IPD show a similar, but weaker, effect. The central and lower panels of Fig. 9 contain predictions for the same set of data, both without and with the second-level coincidence mechanism schematized in Fig. 8 (Stern and Trahiotis, 1992). It can be seen that the second layer of coincidence-counting units is necessary for the model to describe the data. Trahiotis and Stern (1994) recently provided further evidence that a mechanism such as the second-level coincidence detectors is necessary in order to account for the position and character of intracranial images produced by multiple sinusoidally amplitude-modulated tones. That paper also contained a discussion concerning why a simple averaging, across frequency and running time, of the responses of the initial coincidence counters will not suffice.

The position-variable model as extended by Stern and Trahiotis (1992) appears to be able to describe quite well the lateralization of low-frequency bandpass noise as a joint function of ITD, IPD, and bandwidth, given that the signals are presented with equal amplitude to the two ears (e.g., Trahiotis and Stern, 1989). The model does not describe, however, some of the complex effects that occur when IIDs

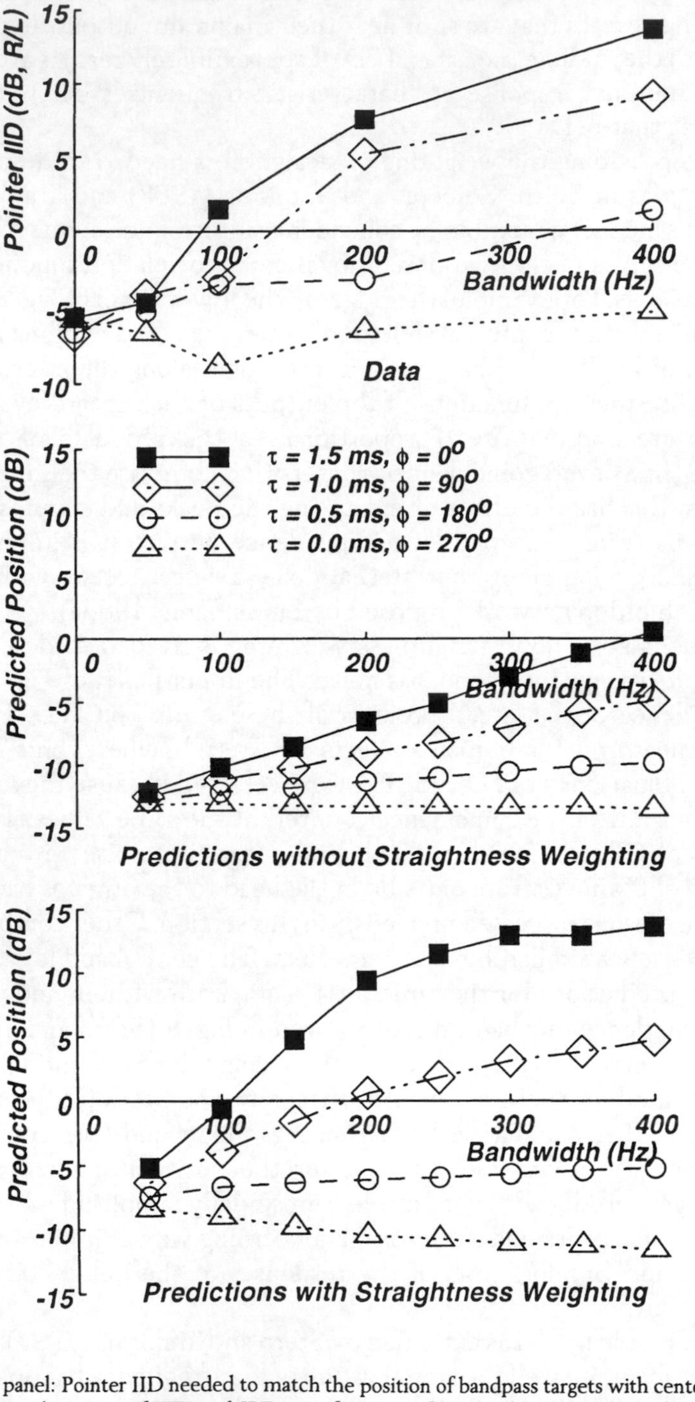

FIG. 9. Upper panel: Pointer IID needed to match the position of bandpass targets with center frequency 500 Hz and several combinations of ITD and IPD, as a function of bandwidth. Central panel: Predictions of the position-variable model without straightness weighting. Lower panel: Predictions of the position-variable model with straightness weighting. (Data from Stern, Zeiberg, and Trahiotis, 1988; predictions from Stern and Trahiotis, 1992.)

are added to these types of stimuli (Buell, Trahiotis, and Bernstein, 1994). For example, the subjective lateral position of bandpass noise presented with an ITD of 0 ms and an IPD of 270° is relatively independent of bandwidth for IIDs ranging from −10 to +10 dB. In contrast, the perceived position of similar stimuli presented with an ITD of 1.5 ms and an IPD of 0° moves toward the ear receiving the signal that leads in time as bandwidth increases from 50 to 400 Hz. To our knowledge the data of Buell *et al.* (1994) cannot be accounted for by any existing model of binaural interaction, despite concerted efforts (Tao, 1992; Tao and Stern, 1992).

3. Lateralization of low-frequency amplitude-modulated tones

It was reemphasized in the mid-1970s that the binaural system can utilize ITDs conveyed by the (low-frequency) envelopes of high-frequency stimuli (e.g., Henning, 1974; McFadden and Pasanen, 1976; Nuetzel and Hafter, 1981). In keeping with the duplex theory, many had believed that ITDs were important for low-frequency stimuli where changes in the fine structure could be utilized. For high-frequency stimuli, IID was considered to be the salient binaural cue. Using sinusoidally amplitude-modulated (SAM) 500-Hz tones, Bernstein and Trahiotis (1985) demonstrated that the lateral position of low-frequency stimuli could also be affected, albeit by a small amount, by the ITD of the envelope of the stimulus.

Figure 10 shows the response of the coincidence-counting units to a 500-Hz tone (presented without amplitude modulation, upper panel) and the response

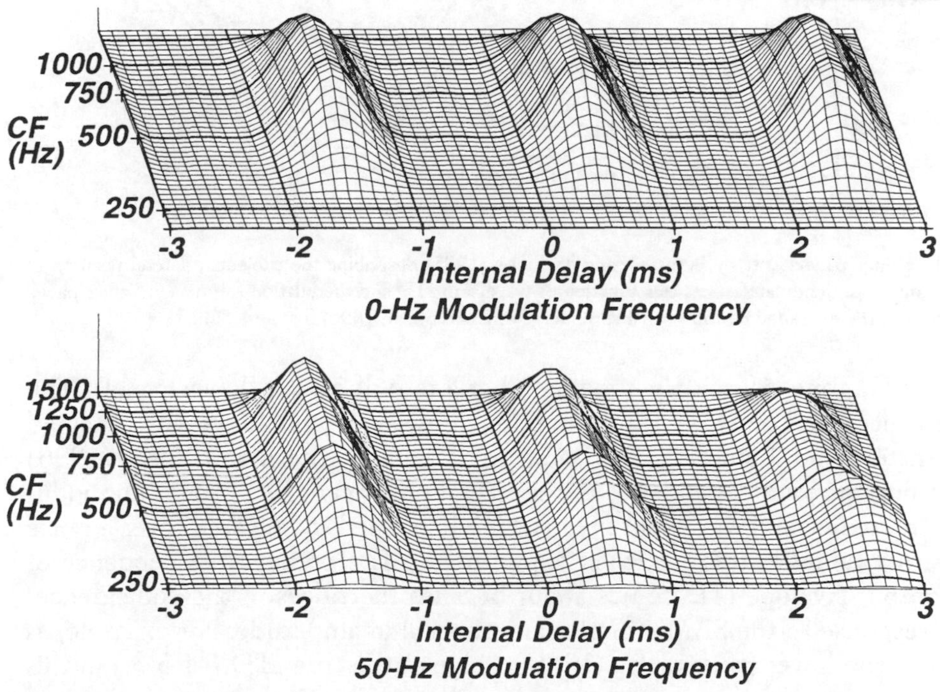

FIG. 10. Patterns of coincidence-counting activity showing the effects of amplitude modulation on low-frequency tones. Upper panel: The response to a 500-Hz tone with a waveform ITD of −1.5 ms. Lower panel: The response to a 500-Hz tone with the same waveform delay and amplitude modulated with a modulation frequency of 50 Hz.

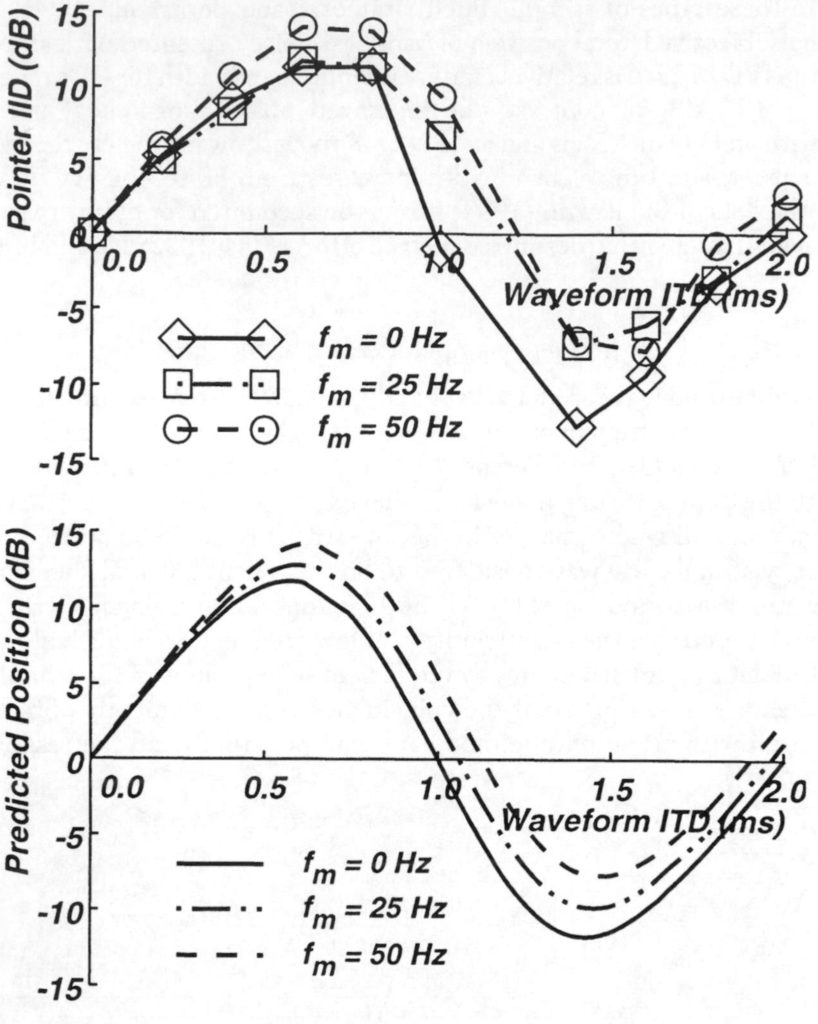

FIG. 11. Upper panel: Data by Bernstein and Trahiotis (1985) describing the subjective lateral position of 500-Hz amplitude modulated tones as a function of waveform ITD and modulation frequency. Lower panel: Predictions of the extended position-variable model (Stern and Shear, 1996) for these data.

to a 500-Hz tone sinusoidally modulated at a rate of 50 Hz (lower panel). The ongoing interaural delay is –1.5 ms in both cases. Figure 11 shows data obtained by Bernstein and Trahiotis (1985) and predictions by Stern and Shear (1996) concerning the joint dependence of the lateral position of SAM tones on modulation frequency and waveform ITD (which happened to be varied over a range of positive values in this particular experiment). The predicted dependence of position on envelope ITD comes about because the ridges in the coincidence-count response to the SAM stimulus are unequal in amplitude. For example, as shown in the lower panel of Fig. 10, the ridge at the true ITD (–1.5 ms in this case) is greater in magnitude than the other ridges. (This can be seen most clearly by comparing the height of the peaks in the lower panel to the constant response at 1500 Hz.) In contrast, the ridges of the response to the pure tone in the upper panel of Fig. 10 are all of equal magnitude. The extended model also describes other aspects of Bernstein and Trahiotis' data including the dependence of lateral position on pure modulator delay.

4. Lateralization of high-frequency amplitude-modulated tones and bandpass noise

As noted in the preceding section, the extent of laterality of high-frequency binaural stimuli such as SAM tones and bandpass-noise can be affected by the ITD of the envelope. Figure 12 illustrates how such stimuli are represented by the ensemble of coincidence-counting units. These plots were produced without the use of any envelope extraction mechanism save for the lowpass filtering incorporated in the model of auditory-nerve activity. The lowpass filter has a

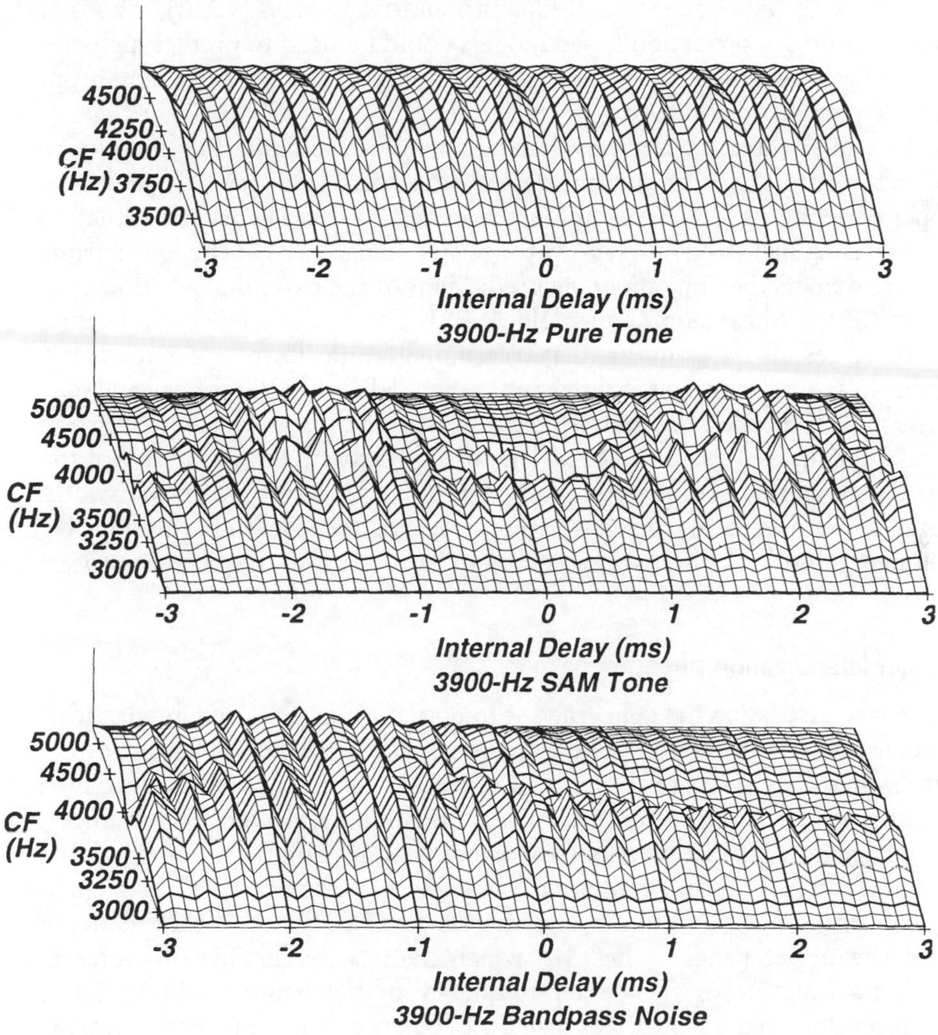

FIG. 12. The response of an ensemble of coincidence-counting units to several types of high-frequency stimuli with an ITD of –1.5 ms. Upper panel: Response to pure tones with a frequency of 3900 Hz. Central panel: Response to SAM tones with a modulation frequency of 300 Hz. Lower panel: Response to bandpass noise with a center frequency of 3900 Hz, bandwidth of 600 Hz.

frequency response that decreases linearly from 1200 to 5200 Hz, as suggested by the physiological data of Johnson (1980). The minor ripples in the plots show the effects of the residual energy at the relatively high carrier frequency after processing by the lowpass filter. The upper panel of Fig. 12 shows the relative number of coincidences observed in response to a pure tone of 3900 Hz. The central panel depicts the response to a SAM tone with a carrier frequency of 3900 Hz and a modulation frequency of 300 Hz. The lower panel of the same figure shows the response to a bandpass noise with a center frequency of 3900 Hz and a bandwidth of 600 Hz. Each stimulus has an ITD of –1.5 ms. Lateralization of the SAM tone and bandpass noise is dominated by the location along the internal-delay axis of the mode of the envelope of the response, which in Fig. 12 can be observed at an internal delay of approximately –1.5 ms. These observations are in accord with the conclusions of Colburn and Esquissaud (1976), who first suggested that cross-correlation-based models could be used to predict high-frequency binaural processing based on only the implicit envelope-extraction properties of the peripheral auditory system.

Models such as the extended position-variable model should, in principle, be able to describe most high-frequency lateralization data based on envelope delays. The upper panel of Fig. 13, for example, shows results of an ITD-discrimination experiment using high-frequency SAM tones (Henning, 1974). The lower panel of the figure depicts the corresponding predictions of the extended position-variable model (Stern, Shear, and Zeppenfeld, 1988). The model predicts the general form of these results by assuming that discrimination performance is mediated by changes in lateralization, as is discussed in Sec. III.B. On the other hand, the model is unable to predict the unexpected observation by Trahiotis and Bernstein (1986) that bandpass noise tends to be lateralized further from the center of the head than SAM tones of similar ITD, carrier frequency, and effective bandwidth. In general, there have been fewer stringent attempts to develop predictions for high-frequency binaural phenomena compared to their low-frequency counterparts.

5. Other lateralization phenomena

Thus far the discussion has concerned stimuli that have been used in "classical" psychoacoustical experiments. Several recent studies have shown that direct application of the cross-correlation-based binaural processing models described in this chapter can describe more complex phenomena as well. For example, Hafter and Shelton (1991) described the lateralization of diotic white noise that was passed through a bandpass filter and subsequently gated by brief rectangular pulses. The gating pulses themselves contained an ITD. Some of their data are shown in the upper panel of Fig. 14, which depicts percentage of "correct" response as a function of the center frequency of the bandpass filter. Some conditions produce significantly less than 50% "correct" response, indicating that the signals were lateralized toward the ear receiving the gating signal that was lagging in time. This apparently paradoxical result occurs because, for reasons discussed in Stern, Zeppenfeld, and Shear (1991), the major mode of the

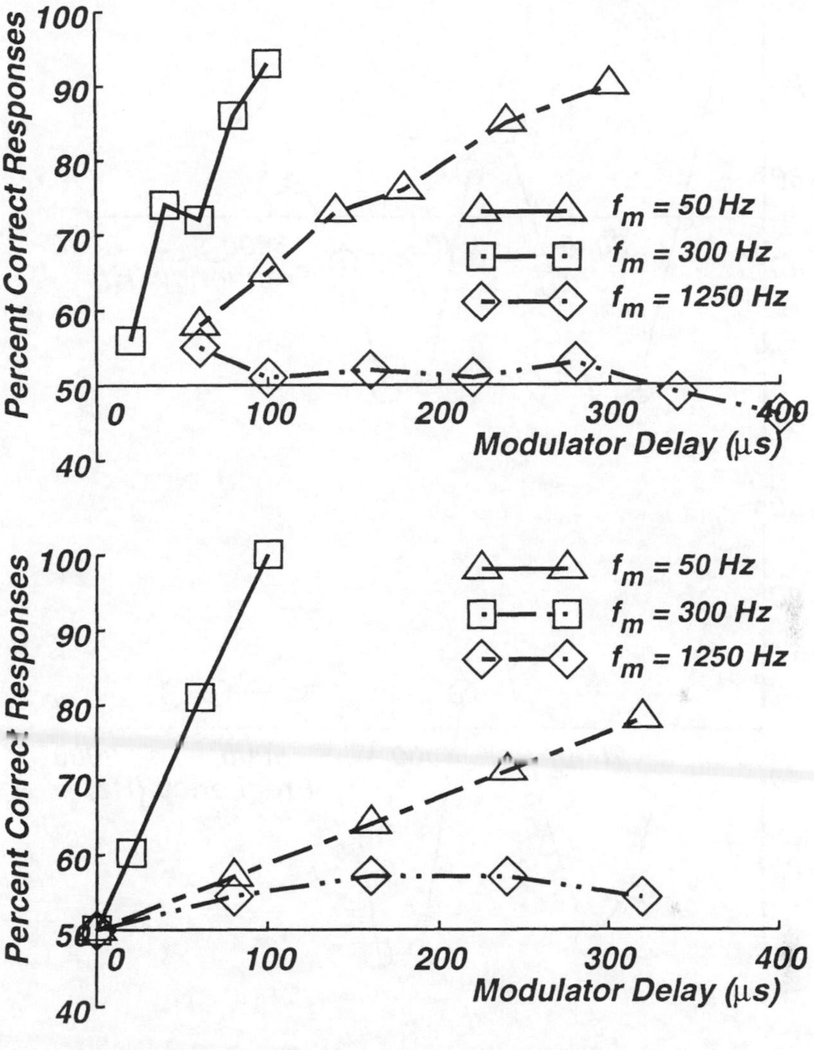

FIG. 13. Upper panel: Data by Henning (1974) describing the subjective lateral position of high-frequency SAM tones as a function of modulator delay and modulation frequency. Lower panel: Predictions of the extended position-variable model (Stern, Shear, and Zeppenfeld, 1988) for these data.

cross-correlation function of the response to these unusual stimuli is on the "wrong" (lagging) side of the internal-delay axis. The lower panel of Fig. 14 shows that the extended position-variable model does quite well in predicting the perception of such stimuli (Stern *et al.*, 1991).

Another interesting phenomenon accounted for by the model is what Bilsen and Raatgever (1973) termed the "dominant region" effect. This name refers to the fact that frequency components in the neighborhood of about 700 Hz are weighed more heavily in the lateralization of broadband noise than are frequency components in spectrally adjacent regions. Data from their experiment along with the corresponding predictions are presented in Fig. 15. The dependent variable, ΔI (dB), reflects the intensity of a narrow portion of the noise relative to the

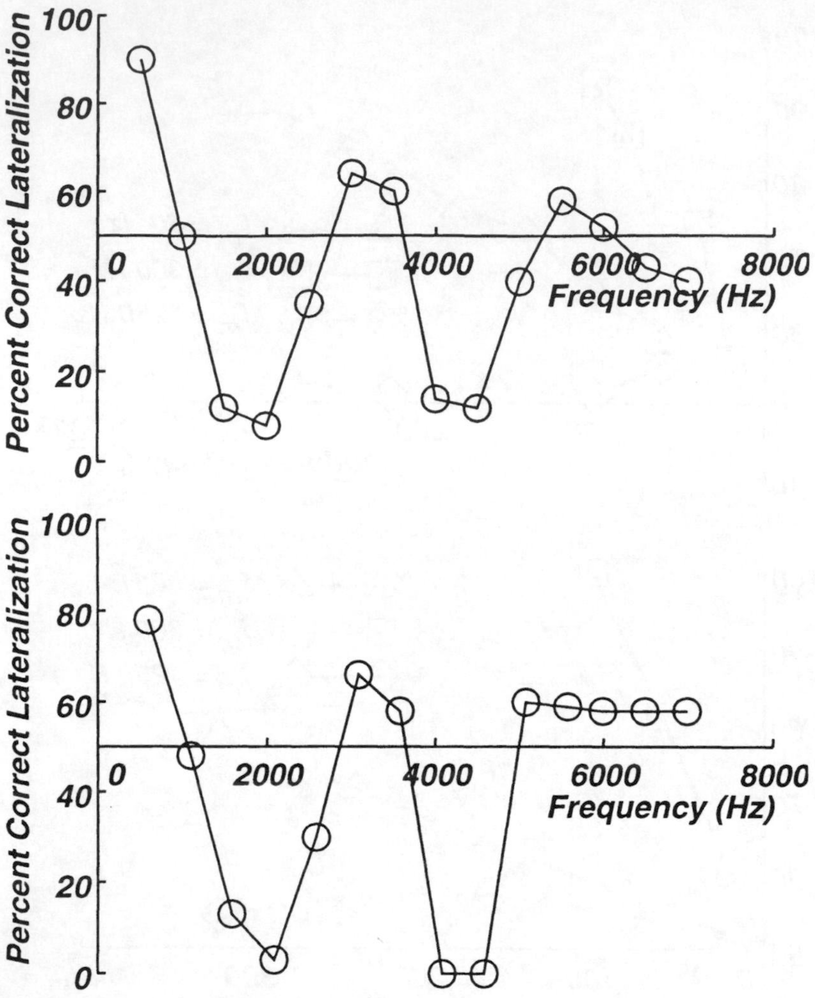

FIG. 14. Upper panel: Lateralization results by Hafter and Shelton (1991) for gated-noise stimuli as a function of center frequency. The ITD of the rectangular gating waveform is equal to 37.5 ms, the repetition period of the entire stimulus is equal to 2 ms, the noise bandwidth is equal to 1000 Hz, and the duration of the gating pulse is 400 ms. Lateralization percentages below 50% are the counterintuitive "illusory" reversals. Lower panel: Predictions of the extended position-variable model for the same stimulus conditions, except that the gating ITD was set equal to 50 ms for computational reasons. (Stern, Zeppenfeld, and Shear, 1991).

intensity of the spectral regions that surround it. The central and surrounding frequency bands were presented with conflicting ITDs and the listener's task was to adjust the level of the central band to maintain a centered image. It can be seen that the predictions of the model (in the curve without the data symbols) provide an excellent fit to the data (Stern, Shear, and Zeppenfeld, 1988; Stern and Shear, 1996). Stern and Shear (1996) have shown that the components of bandpass noise that carry the greatest weight in lateralization are those that produce patterns of activity of the coincidence-counting units that are about as wide as the major central portion of the $p(\tau, f)$ function.

B. Interaural discrimination phenomena related to subjective lateral position

The perceptual cue used by subjects in many interaural discrimination experiments is a change in the subjective lateral position of the stimuli. Models that describe the lateral position of binaural stimuli can be directly applied to discrimination experiments by computing or estimating the variance as well as the mean values of the predicted lateral positions of the stimuli. This is typically done by using optimal decision theory to estimate the best possible discrimination performance (cf. van Trees, 1968). Most of the early binaural models (e.g., Jeffress *et al.*, 1956; Hafter, 1971) implicitly assumed that intracranial position is a linear function of ITD and IID, and that the variance of the position estimate was independent of stimulus ITD and IID. These assumptions are valid if the ITD and IID of the stimuli used in an experiment are sufficiently small (Domnitz and Colburn, 1977). Models incorporating such assumptions can also predict the results of many lateralization-based detection experiments using either tonal targets and maskers or targets and maskers that are obtained by filtering, attenuating, and phase-shifting the same common noise source (e.g., Jeffress and McFadden, 1971; Yost, Nielsen, Tanis, and Bergert, 1974).

Colburn (1973) and Stern and Colburn (1985a, 1985b) provided predictions for interaural discrimination experiments using expressions for the variance of predicted position that were derived from the Poisson variability inherent in the auditory-nerve model describing the response to the stimuli. Colburn (1973) based his predictions on the amount of information in the ensemble of coincidence-counting units (without making any assumptions about the perceptual cue used by the subjects), and he predicted the dependence of just-noticeable

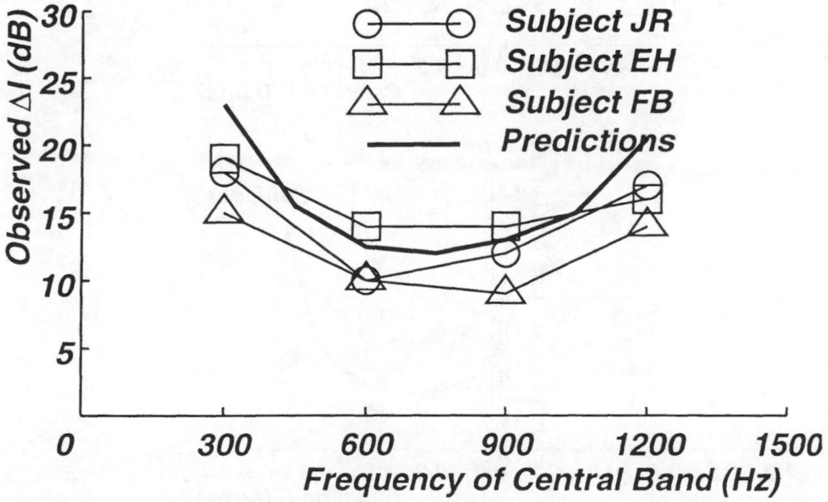

FIG. 15. Comparison of data by Bilsen and Raatgever (1973) and predictions by Stern and Shear (1996) for experiments whose results imply the existence of a "dominant frequency region" for binaural lateralization. The increment in overall intensity, ΔI, that is needed for a mid-frequency region of critical bandwidth to dominate the lateralization mechanism when frequency components in the two flanking bands are presented with a conflicting ITD is plotted as a function of frequency.

differences (JNDs) in ITD and IID on baseline ITD, IID, and overall level (Hershkowitz and Durlach, 1969). Stern and Colburn (1985b) derived an analytical expression for the variance of the predicted position variable $\hat{P}$.

As an example, Fig. 16 compares measurements of interaural JNDs in ITD by Domnitz and Colburn (1977) with predictions by Stern and Colburn (1985a, 1985b). The predictions were obtained by calculating the mean and variance of

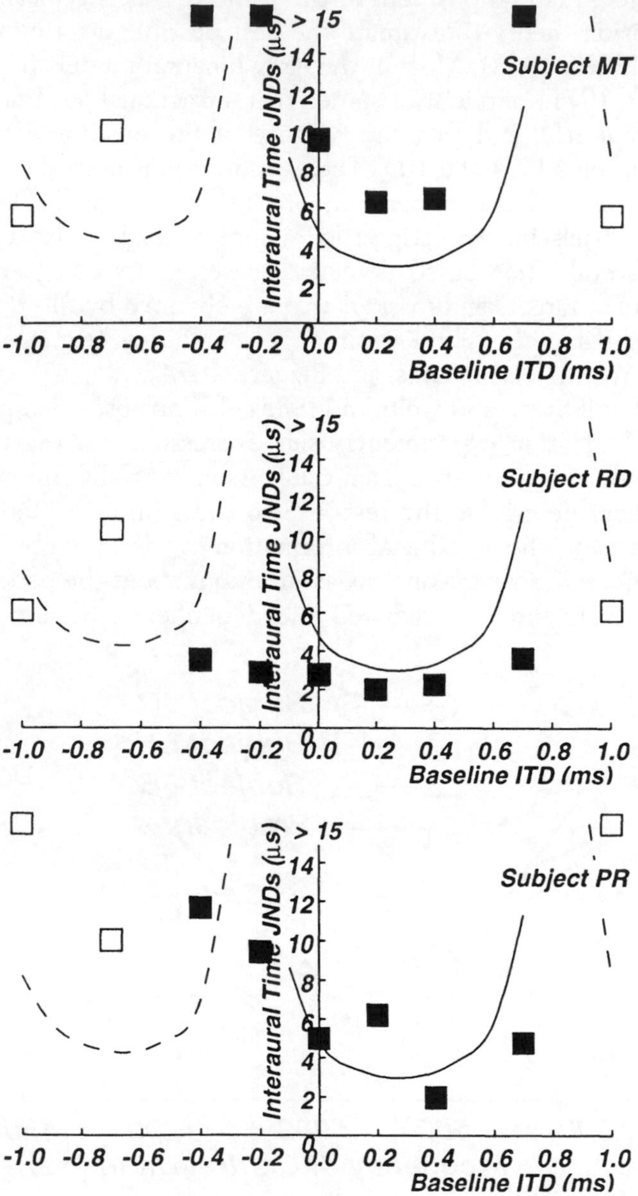

FIG. 16. Data by Domnitz and Colburn (1977) and predictions of the position-variable model (Stern and Colburn, 1985b) for interaural time JNDs as a function of baseline ITD. The stimuli were presented with an IID of +20 dB. Individual data points are plotted for each of three subjects. Filled symbols and solid curves represent conditions for which the cues are "normal"; open symbols and broken curves represent conditions for which the cues are "reversed."

$\hat{P}$ for the stimuli of each experiment and determining the value of ITD needed to produce unit value for the sensitivity index d'. The stimuli were presented with an IID of +20 dB. Filled symbols and solid curves represent conditions for which the cues are "normal" (i.e., moving in the same direction, as in time JND experiments with baseline ITDs and IIDs of small magnitude); open symbols and broken curves represent conditions for which the cues are "reversed" (i.e., moving in the opposite direction). The model correctly predicts the general increase of the magnitude of JNDs of ITD as baseline IID increases and the asymmetry with respect to baseline ITD for stimuli presented with nonzero IID. It also correctly predicts the reversal in direction reported by subjects when the baseline ITD is near 1 ms. Although the quantitative fit of predictions to data for interaural JNDs of IID is not as good, the model correctly predicts a lack of cue reversals, a weaker dependence on baseline ITD (compared to JNDs of ITD), and an overall increase of the magnitude of the JND with increasing IID.

In general, the simple position-variable model is unable to account for discrimination data in which subjects are likely to be making use of additional cues besides the lateral position of a single dominant time–intensity traded image (Stern and Colburn, 1985a, 1985b). For example, in Fig. 16, predicted interaural time JNDs are much larger than most of the observed data for baseline ITDs near the "cue-reversal" points.

A second example of this phenomenon is provided in Fig. 17, which compares data by Jeffress and McFadden (1971) for detection thresholds and "lateralization thresholds" to the corresponding theoretical predictions (Stern and Colburn, 1985b). The targets and maskers were derived from the same narrowband noise with a center frequency of 500 Hz and a bandwidth of 50 Hz. In the detection experiment subjects indicated whether or not the target stimulus was perceived to be present, as in traditional masking studies. In the lateralization-threshold experiments, the target was presented on every trial, but the signals to the two ears were randomly interchanged. Subjects in the lateralization-threshold experiments indicated the side of the head toward which the target-masker complex was perceived. Lateralization thresholds (square symbols) and detection thresholds (circular symbols) are plotted in Fig. 17 as a function of target-to-masker phase angle. Predictions (smooth curve) were obtained by adjusting model parameters to describe the relative salience of cues from ITDs and IIDs for each subject individually (Stern and Colburn, 1985b). The predictions provide a very good fit to the lateralization-threshold data, despite the sharply differing ability of the two subjects to make use of ITDs and IIDs. Nevertheless, the observed detection thresholds are much lower than predicted, implying that subjects are making use of attributes of the stimuli besides lateral position. Subjects perform similarly better than predicted in discrimination results concerning time–intensity tradability (e.g., Hafter and Carrier, 1972; Gilliom and Sorkin, 1972). Again, this occurs because the theoretical predictions are based only on the dominant time–intensity traded image of the stimuli, whereas the data reflect the use of more than one image component or some other additional cue.

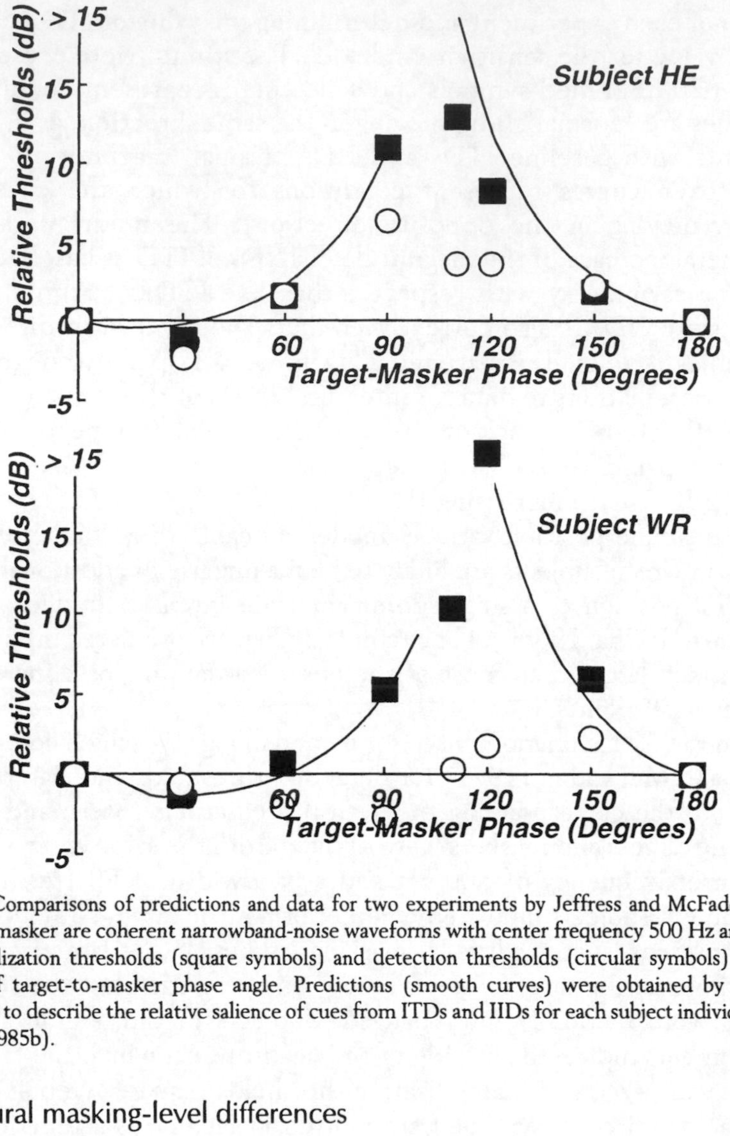

FIG. 17. Comparisons of predictions and data for two experiments by Jeffress and McFadden (1971). The target and masker are coherent narrowband-noise waveforms with center frequency 500 Hz and bandwidth 50 Hz. Lateralization thresholds (square symbols) and detection thresholds (circular symbols) are plotted as a function of target-to-masker phase angle. Predictions (smooth curves) were obtained by adjusting model parameters to describe the relative salience of cues from ITDs and IIDs for each subject individually (Stern and Colburn, 1985b).

C. Binaural masking-level differences

The binaural masking-level difference (BMLD) is an extremely well known and robust binaural phenomenon. A large number of classical measurements of BMLDs are summarized in Durlach and Colburn (1978), and several more recent results are described by Kohlrausch and Fassel (Chapter 9, this volume). Figure 18 illustrates how the ensemble of coincidence-counting units responds to typical stimuli used in classical BMLD experiments. The figure shows the patterns of activity that result when a 500-Hz tonal target and a broadband masking noise are presented in the N_0S_π (masker interaurally in phase, target interaurally out of phase) and N_0S_0 (masker and target both interaurally in phase) configurations. The plots in Fig. 18 include the effects of the relative number of fiber pairs, as specified by the function $p(\tau, f)$. Note that when the N_0 masker is presented alone (Fig. 18, lower panel), the ridge of maxima at zero internal delay has approximately constant amplitude over a broad range of frequencies. The addition of an in-phase (S_0) target to the masker at a target-to-masker intensity ratio of –20 dB has virtually no effect on the pattern of coincidence-counting activity, because the interaural time differences of the combined target and masker are unchanged (Fig. 18, central panel). On the other hand, the addition of the 500-Hz out-of-phase (S_π) target to the in-phase masker cancels masker components at that frequency, causing a "dimple" to appear in the central ridge for CFs near the target frequency (Fig. 18, upper panel). The target in the N_0S_π configuration is

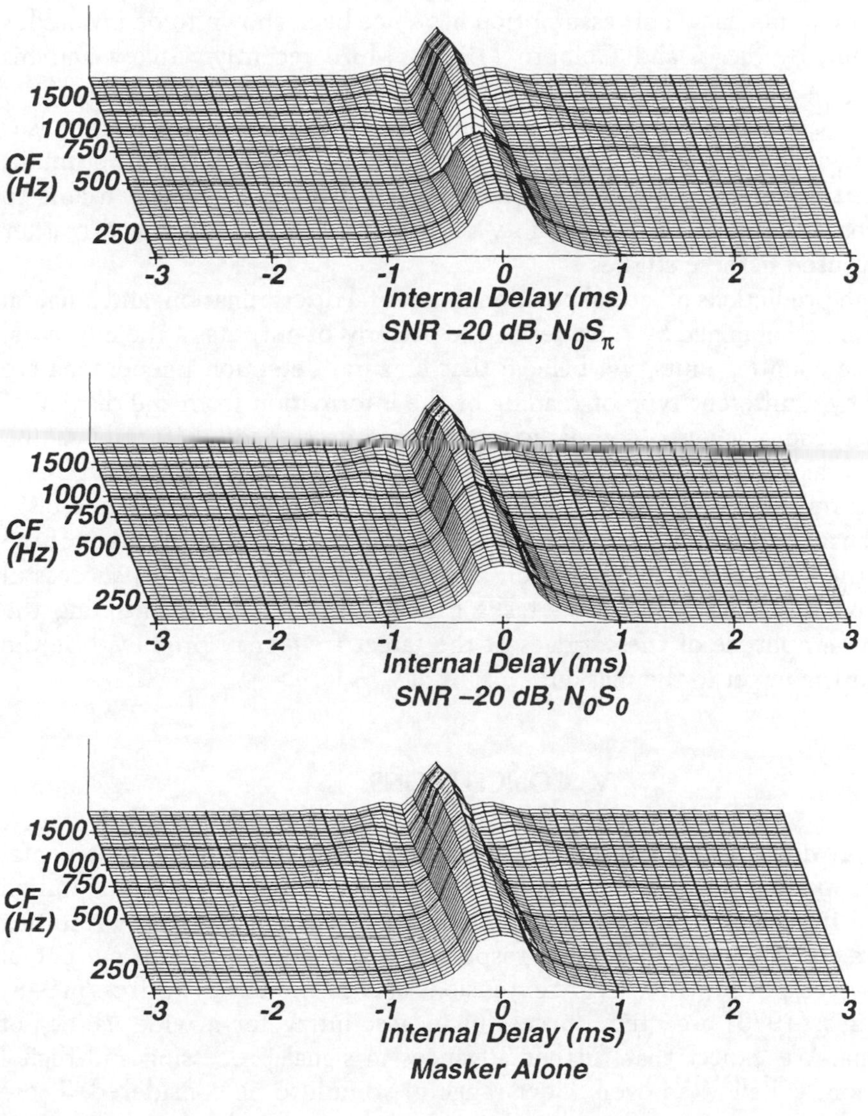

FIG. 18. Patterns of coincidence-counting activity showing the response to stimuli used in N_0S_π and N_0S_0 binaural masking level difference experiments. The target is presented at 500 Hz, either interaurally in phase or out of phase, as indicated, and the masker is broadband diotic noise. These plots include the effects of the relative number of fiber pairs, as specified by the function.

easily detected at –20 dB SNR because the pattern of responses in the upper panel of Fig. 18 is easily discriminated from that in the lower panel. The N_0S_0 stimulus is not detected because the response of the binaural system is largely unaffected by whether the target is present or absent (compare central and lower panels of Fig. 18).

Colburn (1977) was able to describe virtually all of the "classical" data obtained in experiments measuring BMLDs on the basis of the predicted outputs of the coincidence counters. His predictions were developed using the simplifying assumption that experimental performance is limited by the variability of the auditory-nerve response to the signals, as opposed to the intrinsic variability of the masker components. This assumption has since been shown to be invalid for some stimuli by Siegel and Colburn (1983). More recently, Gilkey and his colleagues (e.g., Gilkey, Robinson, and Hanna, 1985; Hanna and Robinson, 1985; Isabelle and Colburn, 1991) presented a number of results using "frozen-noise" maskers in which the actual variability of the masker component of the stimulus can be experimentally controlled. To date no binaural model has been able to account for differences of detectability associated with the individual masker waveforms used in these studies.

Although predictions of lateral position, interaural discrimination, and binaural detection are all obtained by considering the patterns of outputs of the interaural coincidence-counting units, we believe that binaural detection phenomena are mediated by a different type of reading of the information from the display of coincidence-counting units (compared to that used for subjective lateral position and interaural discrimination). Specifically, the subjective lateral position of binaural stimuli and the ability to perform certain interaural discrimination tasks based on changes in lateral position both appear to depend on the locations of the ridges of the cross-correlation function along the τ axis. In contrast, successful predictions for binaural detection tasks can be obtained by quantifying the decrease in amplitude of these ridges at the target frequency produced by the addition of the target to the masker.

IV. CONCLUSIONS

We have provided several examples illustrating how many of the fundamental data concerning binaural hearing can be predicted or explained within a unified theoretical framework. Predictions are based on the internal patterns resulting from cross-correlation of the neural responses to the stimuli by the peripheral auditory system. In our view, recent extensions of basic models by Jeffress (1948) and Colburn (1973) are quite successful in accounting for a wide variety of phenomena. We expect that further advances in signal processing and digital computation will allow an even wider range of stimuli to be considered. These advances, the recent trend toward unifying data obtained in laboratory environments with data obtained in more realistic settings, and the development of practical applications that exploit our theoretical insights make it likely that the next decade will prove to be even more fruitful.

ACKNOWLEDGMENTS

Preparation of this manuscript has been supported by National Science Foundation grant IBN 90-22080 to Richard Stern and by National Institutes of Health grant DC-00234 and Air Force Office of Scientific Research grant 89-0030 to Constantine Trahiotis. Preparation of the figures has been facilitated by the efforts of Carl Block, Wonseok Lee, Steve Palm, Glenn Shear, Sammy Tao, Xaohong Xu, Andreas Yankopolus, and Torsten Zeppenfeld.

REFERENCES

Bachorski, S. J. (**1983**). "Dynamic cues in binaural perception," MS thesis, Electrical and Computer Engineering Department, Carnegie Mellon University, Pittsburgh, PA.

Bernstein, L. R., and Trahiotis, C. (**1985**). "Lateralization of low-frequency complex waveforms: The use of envelope-based temporal disparities," J. Acoust. Soc. Am. **77**, 1868–1880.

Bernstein, L. R., and Trahiotis, C. (**1994**). "Spectral interference in a binaural detection task: Effects of masker bandwidth and temporal fringe," J. Acoust. Soc. Am. **94**, 735–742.

Bilsen, F. A., and Raatgever, J. (**1973**). "Spectral dominance in binaural lateralization," Acustica **28**, 131–132.

Blauert, J. (**1980**). "Modelling of interaural time and intensity difference discrimination," in *Psychophysical, Physiological, and Behavioral Studies in Hearing*, edited by G. van den Brink and F. A. Bilsen (Delft University Press, Delft), pp. 421–424.

Blauert, J., and Cobben, W. (**1978**). "Some consideration of binaural cross-correlation analysis," Acustica **39**, 96–103.

Buell, T. N., Trahiotis, C., and Bernstein, L. R. (**1994**). "Lateralization of bands of noise as a function of combinations of interaural intensitive differences, interaural temporal differences, and bandwidth," J. Acoust. Soc. Am. **95**, 1482–1489.

Carney, L. H. (**1993**). "A model for the responses of low-frequency auditory nerve fibers in cat," J. Acoust. Soc. Am. **93**, 401–417.

Carr, C. E., and Konishi, M. (**1990**). "A circuit for detection of interaural time differences in the brain stem of the barn owl," J. Neurosci. **10**, 3227–3246.

Colburn, H. S. (**1969**). "Some Physiological Limitations on Binaural Performance," doctoral dissertation, MIT, Cambridge, MA.

Colburn, H. S. (**1973**). "Theory of binaural interaction based on auditory-nerve data. I. General strategy and preliminary results on interaural discrimination," J. Acoust. Soc. Am. **54**, 1458–1470.

Colburn, H. S. (**1977**). "Theory of binaural interaction based on auditory-nerve data. II. Detection of tones in noise," J. Acoust. Soc. Am. **61**, 525–533.

Colburn, H. S. (**1995**). "Computational models of binaural processing," in *Auditory Computation*, edited by H. Hawkins and T. McMullin (Springer-Verlag, New York), pp. 332–400.

Colburn, H. S., and Durlach, N. I. (**1978**). "Models of binaural interaction," in *Handbook of Perception, Volume IV, Hearing*, edited by E. C. Carterette and M. P. Friedman (Academic Press, New York), pp. 467–518.

Colburn, H. S., and Esquissaud, P. (**1976**). "An auditory-nerve model for interaural time discrimination of high-frequency complex stimuli," J. Acoust. Soc. Am. **59**, S23(A).

David, E. E., Guttman, N., and van Bergeijk, W. A. (**1958**). "On the mechanism of binaural fusion," J. Acoust. Soc. Am. **30**, 801–802.

Deatherage, B. H., and Hirsh, I. J. (**1959**). "Auditory localization of clicks," J. Acoust. Soc. Am. **31**, 486–492.

Domnitz, R. H., and Colburn, H. S. (**1976**). "Analysis of binaural detection models for dependence on interaural target parameters," J. Acoust. Soc. Am. **59**, 598–601.

Domnitz, R. H., and Colburn, H. S. (**1977**). "Lateral position and interaural discrimination," J. Acoust. Soc. Am. **61**, 1586–1598.

Duifhuis, H. (**1973**). "Consequences of peripheral frequency selectivity for nonsimultaneous masking," J. Acoust. Soc. Am. **54**, 1471–1488.

Durlach, N. I. (**1963**). "Equalization and cancellation theory of binaural masking-level differences," J. Acoust. Soc. Am. **35**, 1206–1218.

Durlach, N. I. (**1972**). "Binaural signal detection: Equalization and cancellation theory," in *Foundations of Modern Auditory Theory, Volume II*, edited by J.V. Tobias (Academic Press, New York), pp. 369–462.

Durlach, N. I., and Colburn, H. S. (**1978**). "Binaural phenomena," in *Handbook of Perception, Volume IV, Hearing*, edited by E. C. Carterette and M. P. Friedman (Academic Press, New York), pp. 365–466.

Gabriel, K. J. (**1983**). "Binaural Interaction in Hearing Impaired Listeners," doctoral dissertation, MIT, Cambridge, MA.

Gaik, W. (**1993**). "Combined evaluation of interaural time and intensity differences: Psychoacoustic results and computer modeling," J. Acoust. Soc. Am. **94**, 98–110.

Gilkey, R. H., Robinson, D. E., and Hanna, T. E. (**1985**). "Effects of masker waveform and signal-to-masker phase relation on diotic and dichotic masking by reproducible noise," J. Acoust. Soc. Am. **78**, 1207–1219.

Gilliom, J. D., and Sorkin, R. D. (**1972**). "Discrimination of interaural time and intensity," J. Acoust. Soc. Am. **52**, 1635–1644.

Grantham, D. W. (**1984**). "Discrimination of dynamic interaural intensity differences," J. Acoust. Soc. Am. **76**, 71–76.

Grantham, D. W., and Wightman, F. L. (**1978**). "Detectability of varying interaural temporal differences," J. Acoust. Soc. Am. **63**, 511–523.

Hafter, E. R. (**1971**). "Quantitative evaluation of a lateralization model of masking-level differences," J. Acoust. Soc. Am. **50**, 1116–1122.

Hafter, E. R., and Carrier, S. C. (**1970**). "Masking-level difference obtained with a pulsed tonal masker," J. Acoust. Soc. Am. **47**, 1041–1047.

Hafter, E. R., and Carrier, S. C. (**1972**). "Binaural interaction in low-frequency stimuli: The inability to trade time and intensity completely," J. Acoust. Soc. Am. **51**, 1852–1862.

Hafter, E. R., and Jeffress, L. A. (**1968**). "Two-image lateralization of tones and clicks," J. Acoust. Soc. Am. **44**, 563–569.

Hafter, E. R., and Shelton, B. R. (**1991**). "Counterintuitive reversals in lateralization using rectangularly-modulated noise," J. Acoust. Soc. Am. **90**, 1901–1907.

Hanna, T. E., and Robinson, D. E. (**1985**). "Phase effects for a sine wave masked by reproducible noise," J. Acoust. Soc. Am. **77**, 1129–1140.

Henning, G. B. (**1974**). "Detectability of interaural delay in high-frequency complex waveforms," J. Acoust. Soc. Am. **55**, 84–90.

Hershkowitz, R. M., and Durlach, N. I. (**1969**). "Interaural time and amplitude jnds for a 500–Hz tone," J. Acoust. Soc. Am. **46**, 1464–1467.

Hirsh, I. J. (**1948**). "The influence of interaural phase on interaural summation and inhibition," J. Acoust. Soc. Am. **29**, 536–544.

Isabelle, S. K., and Colburn, H. S. (**1991**). "Detection of tones in reproducible narrow-band noise," J. Acoust. Soc. Am. **89**, 352–359.

Jeffress, L. A. (**1948**). "A place theory of sound localization," J. Comp. Physiol. Psychol. **41**, 35–39.

Jeffress, L. A., Blodgett, H. C., Sandel, T. T., and Wood, C. L. III. (**1956**). "Masking of tonal signals," J. Acoust. Soc. Am. **28**, 416–426.

Jeffress, L.A., and McFadden, D. (**1971**). "Differences of interaural phase and level in detection and lateralization," J. Acoust. Soc. Am. **49**, 1169–1179.

Johnson, D. H. (**1980**). "The relationship between spike rate and synchrony in responses of auditory-nerve fibers to single tones," J. Acoust. Soc. Am. **68**, 1115–1122.

Kuwada, S., Stanford, T. R., and Batra, R. (**1987**). "Interaural phase-sensitive units in the inferior colliculus of the unanesthetized rabbit: Effects of changing frequency," J. Neurophysiol. **57**, 1338–1360.

Licklider, J. C. R. (**1948**). "The influence of interaural phase relations upon the masking of speech by white noise," J. Acoust. Soc. Am. **20**, 150–159.

Licklider, J. C. R. (**1959**). "Three auditory theories," in *Psychology: A Study of a Science*, edited by S. Koch (McGraw-Hill, New York), pp. 41–144.

Licklider, J. C. R., Webster, J. C., and Hedlun, J. M. (**1950**). "On the frequency limits of binaural beats," J. Acoust. Soc. Am. **22**, 468–473.

Lindemann, W. (**1986a**). "Extension of a binaural cross-correlation model by contralateral inhibition. I. Simulation of lateralization for stationary signals," J. Acoust. Soc. Am. **80**, 1608–1622.

Lindemann, W. (**1986b**). "Extension of a binaural cross-correlation model by contralateral inhibition. II. The law of the first wavefront," J. Acoust. Soc. Am. **80**, 1623–1630.

McFadden, D., and Pasanen, E. G. (**1976**). "Lateralization at high frequencies based on interaural time differences," J. Acoust. Soc. Am. **59**, 634–639.

Meddis, R., Hewitt, M. J., and Shackleton, T. M. (**1990**). "Implementation details of a computational model of the inner hair-cell/auditory-nerve synapse," J. Acoust. Soc. Am. **87**, 1813–1816.

Moushegian, G., and Jeffress, L. A. (**1959**). "Role of interaural time and intensity differences in the lateralization of low-frequency tones," J. Acoust. Soc. Am. **31**, 1441–1445.

Nuetzel, J. M., and Hafter, E. R. (**1981**). "Discrimination of interaural delays in complex waveforms: Spectral effects," J. Acoust. Soc. Am. **69**, 1112–1118.

Osman, E. (**1971**). "A correlation model of binaural masking level differences," J. Acoust. Soc. Am. **50**, 1491–1511.

Payton, K. L. (**1988**). "Vowel processing by a model of the auditory periphery: A comparison to eighth-nerve responses," J. Acoust. Soc. Am. **83**, 145–162.

Rayleigh, Lord (J.W. Strutt, 3rd Baron of Rayleigh) (**1907**). "On our perception of sound direction," Philos. Mag. **13**, 214–232.

Rose, J. E., Gross, N. B., Geisler, C. D., and Hind, J. E. (**1966**). "Some neural mechanisms in the inferior colliculus of the cat which may be relevant to localization of a sound source," J. Neurophysiol. **29**, 288–314.

Sayers, B. M. (**1964**). "Acoustic-image lateralization judgments with binaural tones," J. Acoust. Soc. Am. **36**, 923–926.

Sayers, B. M., and Cherry, E. C. (**1957**). "Mechanism of binaural fusion in the hearing of speech," J. Acoust. Soc. Am. **29**, 973–987.

Schiano, J. L., Trahiotis, C., and Bernstein, L. R. (**1986**). "Lateralization of low-frequency tones and narrow bands of noise," J. Acoust. Soc. Am. **79**, 1563–1570.

Schroeder, M. R. (**1977**). "New viewpoints in binaural interactions," in *Psychophysics and Physiology of Hearing*, edited by E. F. Evans and J. P. Wilson (Academic Press, London), pp. 455–467.

Shackleton, T. M., Meddis, R., and Hewitt, M. J. (**1992**). "Across frequency integration in a model of lateralization," J. Acoust. Soc. Am. **91**, 2276–2279(L).

Shamma, S. A., Shen, N., and Gopalaswamy, P. (**1989**). "Binaural processing without neural delays," J. Acoust. Soc. Am. **86**, 987–1006.

Shear, G. D. (**1987**). "Modeling the Dependence of Auditory Lateralization on Frequency and Bandwidth," MS thesis, Electrical and Computer Engineering Department, Carnegie Mellon University, Pittsburgh, PA.

Siebert, W. M. (**1970**). "Frequency discrimination in the auditory system: Place or periodicity mechanisms," Proc. IEEE **58**, 723–730.

Siegel, R. A., and Colburn, H. S. (**1983**). "Internal and external noise in binaural detection," Hear. Res. **11**, 117–123.

Smith, P. H., Joris, P. X., and Yin, T. C. T. (**1993**). "Projections of physiologically characterized spherical bushy cell axons from the cochlear nucleus of the cat: Evidence for delay lines to the medial superior olive," J. Comput. Neurol. **331**, 245–260.

Stern, R. M., Jr., and Bachorski, S. J. (**1983**). "Dynamic cues in binaural perception," in *Hearing—Physiological Bases and Psychophysics*, edited by R. Klinke and R. Hartmann (Springer, Berlin), pp. 209–215.

Stern, R. M., Jr., and Colburn, H. S. (**1978**). "Theory of binaural interaction based on auditory-nerve data. IV. A model for subjective lateral position," J. Acoust. Soc. Am. **64**, 127–140.

Stern, R. M., and Colburn, H. S. (**1985a**). "Lateral-position-based models of interaural discrimination," J. Acoust. Soc. Am. **77**, 753–755.

Stern, R. M., and Colburn, H. S. (**1985b**). "Subjective Lateral Position and Interaural Discrimination," J. Acoust. Soc. Am., AIP Document No. PAPS JASMA-77-753-29, pp. 1–29.

Stern, R. M., and Shear, G. D. (**1996**). "Lateralization and detection of low frequency binaural stimuli: Effects of distribution of internal delay," J. Acoust. Soc. Am. (in press).

Stern, R. M., Shear, G. D., and Zeppenfeld, T. (**1988**). "High frequency predictions of the position-variable model," J. Acoust. Soc. Am. **84**, S60 (A).

Stern, R. M., and Trahiotis, C. (**1992**). "The role of consistency of interaural timing over frequency in binaural lateralization," in *Auditory Physiology and Perception*, edited by Y. Cazals, K. Horner, and L. Demany (Pergamon Press, Oxford), pp. 547–554.

Stern, R. M., and Trahiotis, C. (**1995**). "Models of Binaural Interaction," in *Handbook of Perception and Cognition, Volume 6: Hearing*, edited by B. C. J. Moore (Academic Press, New York), pp. 347–386.

Stern, R. M., Zeiberg, A. S., and Trahiotis, C. (**1988**). " Lateralization of complex binaural stimuli: A weighted image model," J. Acoust. Soc. Am. **84**, 156–165.

Stern, R. M., Zeppenfeld, T., and Shear, G. D. (**1991**). "Lateralization of rectangularly-modulated noise: explanations for counterintuitive reversals," J. Acoust. Soc. Am. **90**, 1901–1907.

Tao, S. H. (**1992**). "Additive versus multiplicative combination of differences of interaural time and intensity," MS thesis, Electrical and Computer Engineering Department, Carnegie Mellon University, Pittsburgh, PA.

Tao, S. H., and Stern, R. M. (**1992**). "Additive versus multiplicative combination of differences of interaural time and intensity," J. Acoust. Soc. Am. **91**, 2414(A).

Trahiotis, C., and Bernstein, L. R. (**1986**). "Lateralization of bands of noise and sinusoidally amplitude-modulated tones: effects of spectral locus and bandwidth," J. Acoust. Soc. Am. **79**, 1950–1957.

Trahiotis, C., and Stern, R. M. (**1989**). "Lateralization of bands of noise: effects of bandwidth and differences of interaural time and intensity," J. Acoust. Soc. Am. **86**, 1285–1293.

Trahiotis, C., and Stern, R. M. (**1994**). "Across-frequency interaction in lateralization of complex binaural stimuli," J. Acoust. Soc. Am. **96**, 3804–3806(L).

van Bergeijk, W. A. (**1962**). "Variation on a theme of von Bekesy: A model of binaural interaction," J. Acoust. Soc. Am. **34**, 1431–1437.

van Trees, H. L. (**1968**). *Detection, Estimation, and Modulation Theory, Part I* (Wiley, New York).

Whitworth, R. H., and Jeffress, L. A. (**1961**). "Time versus intensity in the localization of tones," J. Acoust. Soc. Am. **33**, 925–929.

Yost, W. A. (**1981**). "Lateral position of sinusoids presented with intensive and temporal differences," J. Acoust. Soc. Am. **70**, 397–409.

Yost, W. A., Nielsen, D. W., Tanis, D. C., and Bergert, B. (**1974**). "Tone-on-tone binaural masking with an antiphasic masker," Percept. Psychophys. **15**, 233–237.

Young, S. R., and Rubel, E. W. (**1983**). "Frequency-specific projections of individual neurons in chick brainstem auditory nuclei," J. Neurosci. **3**, 1373–1378.

Chapter 25

Modeling Binaural Detection Performance for Individual Masker Waveforms

H. Steven Colburn, Scott K. Isabelle, Daniel J. Tollin
Boston University

(Received October 1994; revised July 1995)

Recent studies of binaural detection are described in this chapter, and available experimental results are summarized. Attention is focused on performance measured for individual masker waveforms in the context of random selection of maskers from trial to trial. Theoretical attempts to understand these data are presented. Specific models to be discussed include interaural difference models with various assumptions about how interaural time differences and interaural level differences are combined, the equalization–cancellation (EC) model, and interaural cross-correlation models. In general, empirical results impose strong constraints on theoretical models, and the challenge of describing these data persists. We conclude that there are no satisfactory models for binaural N_0S_π detection when the dependence of detection probabilities on individual masker waveforms is considered. We suggest that the most promising approach is a physiologically based, nonlinear combination of interaural difference information.

INTRODUCTION

Binaural detection has received a lot of attention since the dramatic advantages of binaural relative to monaural detection were discovered around 1948 (Licklider, 1948; Hirsh, 1948). There have been a large number of parametric studies of the basic phenomena (see review in Durlach and Colburn, 1978) and several detailed modeling studies of binaural detection (Colburn and Durlach, 1978). In recent years, results have become available (Gilkey, Robinson, and Hanna, 1985; Isabelle and Colburn, 1991) that allow the characterization of listeners' performance for individual masker waveforms in the context of an ensemble of random waveforms that vary from trial to trial, similar to the classical detection data. These individual masker data, which have been called molecular-level data (after

Green, 1964), have presented great difficulties for classical detection models. In the present chapter, models that have been developed to predict performance averaged over the ensemble of masker waveforms are applied to results for individual masker waveforms. In Section I, classical (ensemble) data and models are summarized briefly. In Section II, the molecular-level data (i.e., results for individual masker waveforms measured within a finite ensemble of maskers) are described. In each of the remaining sections, a model that has been successfully applied to ensemble data is evaluated with respect to the molecular data.

I. SUMMARY OF CLASSICAL DATA AND MODELS

The basic reference case for binaural detection uses diotic noise (identical noise waveforms presented to each ear) as the masker and a low-frequency sinusoid as the target waveform. If we let $n(t)$ and $s(t)$ represent the masking noise and target signal at the left ear, then we can describe the best detection condition with the following equations, using $y_L(t)$ and $y_R(t)$ to represent the waveforms presented to the left and right ears, respectively,

$$\begin{aligned} y_L(t) &= n(t) + s(t) \\ y_R(t) &= n(t) + s(t). \end{aligned} \tag{1}$$

This stimulus condition is normally referred to as the N_0S_π condition. This notation is based on a code in which the subscripted symbol represents the interaural relation of the "noise" or "signal" as indicated with the preceding capital letter. Using this code, the standard comparison condition is N_0S_0. The N_0S_0 condition has the same stimulus presented to each ear, so that both ears receive the stimulus given by the equation for $y_L(t)$ just shown. Performance is often characterized by the target energy required to detect the target signal in the presence of the masking noise. The threshold is usually specified in decibels as the value of the signal energy relative to the masker spectrum level (E_s/N_0) or as the signal-to-noise power ratio (S/N) required to achieve a criterion level of performance. The threshold varies with the interaural relations of the target and masker waveforms. The difference, in decibels, between the threshold for a binaural condition, such as N_0S_π, and the threshold for the N_0S_0 condition is called a binaural masking level difference or MLD. For a wideband Gaussian-noise masker and a 500-Hz tone-burst target, E_s/N_0 is typically 10 dB for N_0S_0 and -5 dB for N_0S_π, giving an MLD of about 15 dB. For narrowband noise maskers, measured MLDs can be significantly greater, on the order of 25 dB for a 500-Hz tone in a one-third octave band of noise centered around the tone. In general, only the frequency components of the noise that are near the frequency of the target signal have significant effects on the detection threshold.

The perception of the tonal target near N_0S_π detection threshold depends on the bandwidth of the masking noise. For wideband diotic noise, the target is usually perceived as an object with distinct tonality that is located away from the primary location of the noise image, typically toward the sides of the head. For narrowband noise maskers, the target is not perceived as a separate object, but as a change in the characteristics of the noise image. In this case, the presence of the target is perceived as a widening of the noise image: The percept of the noise becomes less precisely located and more diffuse and sounds like a noise waveform that has been statistically decorrelated (e.g., by adding independent noise at one ear).

A variety of models for binaural detection have been developed, and the following paragraphs attempt to introduce the main categories of models. Each type of model emphasizes some differences between the signals at the ears, differences that are affected by the presence of the target. We introduce the models in the context of a standard masking condition, specifically, the N_0S_π condition already described. The simplest descriptions of the models are given in this section, ignoring the imperfections of the processing operations and internal noises. Both kinds of imperfections would lead to limits on performance, and specific assumptions are required to generate quantitative predictions of threshold performance. The imperfections assumed for each model are introduced in later sections of this chapter. A more extensive discussion of models of binaural interaction is available (Colburn, 1995).

Interaural difference models for detection (Webster, 1951; Jeffress, Blodgett, Sandel, and Wood, 1956; Yost, 1970; Hafter, 1971) are based on changes in the distribution of interaural time and intensity differences caused by the presence of the target. For noise-alone stimuli in the N_0S_π condition, the interaural differences in the stimulus are identically zero. When a non-diotic target is added, such as the antiphasic (S_π) tone, nonzero interaural differences in time (or phase) and intensity are generated. The sizes of these differences depend on the amplitude and phase of the target component relative to the masking noise waveform. For the usual case in which the masking noise is a Gaussian random process, the phase and envelope amplitude of the masker waveform vary in time and over the ensemble of waveforms. For the resultant target-plus-masker waveforms, the interaural time delay and the interaural intensity difference (in decibels) are random variables, both with zero mean and with variances that depend on the signal-to-noise ratio (Zurek, 1991).

The equalization–cancellation (EC) model (Duralch, 1960, 1963, 1972) is based on the idea that the subtraction (or cancellation) of the signals at the ears will cancel the masking noise components and sum the target components. The energy in the output of the subtraction operation is near zero (identically zero if there were no imperfections or internal noise) for stimuli with no target and is proportional to the target energy when the target is present. This model has been applied to a wide variety of binaural phenomena, in part because it is easy to describe and to apply. It is extremely successful in describing the basic observations for a wide variety of empirical data.

Interaural correlation models for detection (e.g., Osman, 1971) are based on the observation that the interaural correlation decreases when the non-diotic target signal is added to diotic noise. Specifically, the unnormalized cross-correlation decreases from a value equal to the energy in the masking noise, and the normalized cross-correlation decreases from a value of unity. Although correlation-based models were originally developed to describe observations of lateralization and binaural fusion (Sayers and Cherry, 1957; Licklider, 1959; Sayers, 1964), they can be successfully applied to binaural detection data. A close relationship between interaural correlation models and the EC model can be seen (Colburn and Durlach, 1978) if one expands the expression for the energy in the output of the subtractor in the EC model. Specifically, the unnormalized interaural cross-correlation is one term in the expression (the other terms are monaural energy terms).

Detection models that specifically incorporate neurophysiological data have also been proposed (e.g., Colburn, 1977). These models are similar to both the interaural correlation models and to interaural difference models. In particular, we consider a two-dimensional array of coincidence detectors with the array indices associated with an internal frequency variable and an internal interaural time delay variable. This array has been called the "internal display" or the (f,τ) display and is generally consistent with a display of neural counts from the activity of some types of brainstem neurons (Goldberg and Brown, 1969; Yin and Chan, 1990; Yin, Joris, Smith, and Chan, Chapter 21, this volume; Kuwada, Batra, and Fitzpatrick, Chapter 20, this volume). The (f,τ) display for a given f provides an approximation to the interaural cross-correlation function of bandpass filtered stimuli and can also be thought of as a mechanism for estimating the interaural time delay of the stimulus (by picking peaks from the display, for example). Because the addition of a target signal in the N_0S_π condition changes the (f,τ) display, this display can be used to predict detection judgments.

Each of these types of models has been applied to classical binaural detection data with considerable success. The successes of these models are primarily in describing the dependence of threshold on various parameters of the stimulus. Of course, by choosing the level of the internal noise, each model can be specified to predict the overall performance level. The observed dependence on the interaural parameters of the target signal is predicted by all of these models (Domnitz and Colburn, 1976). The parametric dependence on the noise parameters is a challenge for all of the models and generally depends on specific assumptions within each model.; these assumptions usually take the form of limitations in the processing capabilities, such as limitations in available internal delays. These predictions are not further discussed here. The important point is that almost all of these models are capable of describing the characteristics of the ensemble data.

II. RESULTS FOR INDIVIDUAL MASKER WAVEFORMS

By using a limited set of masker waveforms instead of samples from an infinite set (as in the classical detection experiments), it is possible to keep track of the subject's detection performance separately for each waveform. Specifically, the probability of detection P_d and the probability of false alarm P_f are measured separately for each waveform. P_d is equal to the conditional probability that the subject responds that the target is present, given that the target is actually present.

P_f is equal to the conditional probability that the subject responds that the target is present, given that the target is actually not present. In equation form,

$$\begin{aligned} P_d &= \Pr[\text{"Yes, target present."} \mid \text{target present}] \\ P_f &= \Pr[\text{"Yes, target present."} \mid \text{target not present}]. \end{aligned} \tag{2}$$

It turns out the P_d and P_f vary significantly over individual waveforms. Figure 1 shows the values of P_d and P_f measured by Gilkey *et al.* (1985) for individual waveforms. Although the axes of this graph are the same as those of a receiver operating characteristic (ROC) curve, it should be noted that these are not points on an ROC curve. The plotted values show the molecular level of the data that comprise one point on a normal ROC curve, namely, the point shown by the square near the point (0.68, 0.28). The points indicated by the numbers show that waveforms vary dramatically in the degree to which they sound like they contain the target. When P_f is large, the noise waveform sounds like it contains the target; when P_d is large, the noise-plus-target sounds like it contains the target. Of course, when P_d is small, the noise-plus-target waveform sounds like it does not contain the target, and so on. For example, the probability that this subject responds that waveform 5 contains the target is only 0.25, even when it does contain the target, whereas these subject respond that waveform 15 contains the target with probability 0.60, even when the target is not presented. The fact that P_d and P_f vary significantly provides an opportunity to test the detection models. Even though all models are successful for the ensemble data, there may be limitations in their abilities to describe the individual waveform data.

The results shown in Fig. 1 used a wideband (3-kHz bandwidth) masking noise. Later experiments (Isabelle and Colburn, 1991; Gilkey, 1990, 1992) used narrowband masking noises and found results that are comparable to those in Fig. 1. Because essentially all models of binaural hearing (including those already introduced) assume peripheral, bandpass filters that precede the binaural interactions in the waveforms, we pay little attention to the bandwidth of the masking noise stimulus in this chapter. Many of our simulations will use the narrowband (third-octave bandwidth)waveforms. The narrowband waveform set is chosen as our default set because we can avoid the assumption of a specific shape for the peripheral filter.

Models are analyzed in terms of their ability to match the P_d and P_f values for each waveform and in terms of their consistency with the general properties of the data. This exercise is meaningful only if the values of P_d and P_d show consistency over time, which is apparently true because Isabelle and Colburn (1991) obtained good correlation between their subjects' responses from the first half and second half of the experiment.

Some general properties of the data can be seen in Fig. 1. This figure (after Gilkey *et al.*, 1985) shows a large range of values for P_d and for P_f, and shows no obvious connection between P_d and P_f except that P_d is almost always greater than Pf. For the similar data of Isabelle and Colburn (1991), the correlations of

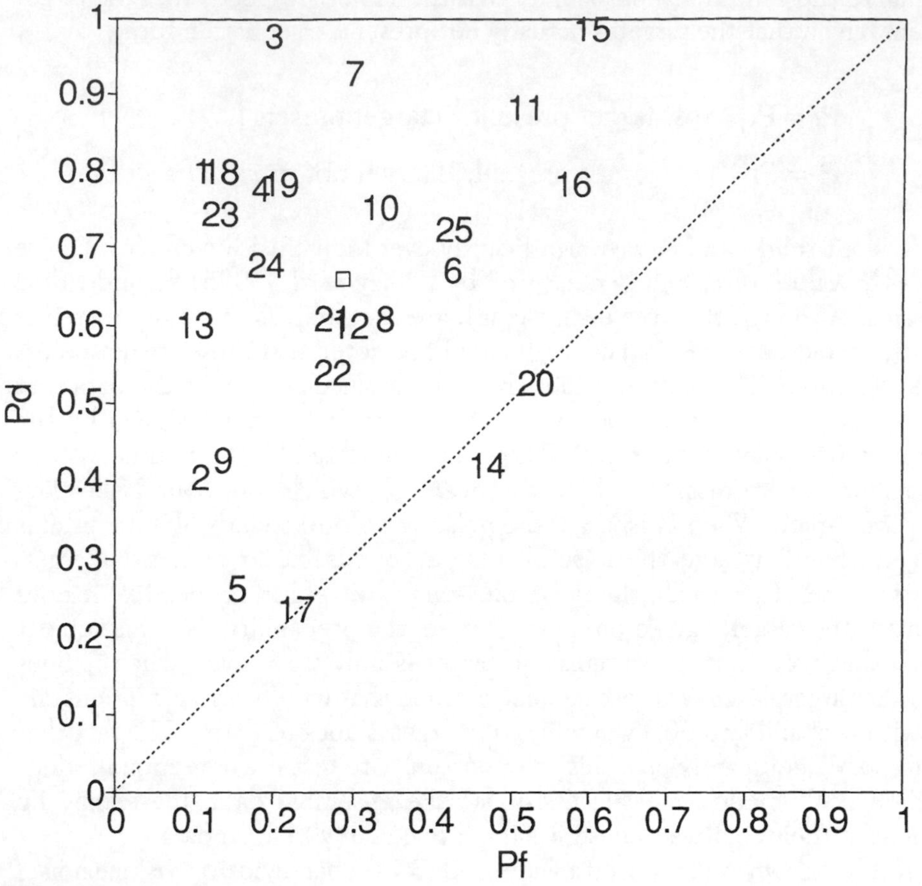

FIG. 1. Values of detection and false alarm probabilities measured for a set of 25 waveforms by Gilkey *et al.* (1985). Each number plotted corresponds to an individual waveform. The square shows the ensemble average values of P_d and P_f. (After Gilkey *et al.*, 1985, Fig. 8.)

P_d and P_f fall in the range 0.6 to 0.7. Of course, some correlation (0.5 in fact) is expected simply from the data falling above the diagonal. If there are no waveforms with simultaneously high P_d values and P_f values (corresponding to near perfect performance near the upper left of the ROC axes), the correlation expected with otherwise uniformly distributed values of P_d and P_d (with $P_d > P_d$) would be higher than 0.5. A perfectly linear relation would result in unity correlation.

Another general property is that the phase of the target signal has very little impact on performance for individual waveforms in the N_0S_π condition; in contrast, the monaural and N_0S_0 thresholds have a dramatic dependence on target phase angle for a fixed noise waveform. This has been demonstrated by Gilkey *et al.* (1985) for wideband signals and by Isabelle and Colburn (1991) for narrow-band signals. Their results show that targets differing in phase, notably sine and cosine targets, have approximately the same performance (i.e., the same values of P_d and P_f) for each masker waveform[1] in the N_0S_π condition. The lack of dependence for an individual waveform is not obvious and may be important for understanding detection.

Another interesting result has to do with the relation of the probabilities in the N_0S_π case to the corresponding probabilities in the N_0S_0 case. These probabilities are substantially correlated in the wideband data (Gilkey *et al.*, 1985) and much less correlated in the narrowband data. In the Isabelle and Colburn (1991) data the correlation was insignificant (with only 10 waveforms), and in the Gilkey (1990, 1992) data this correlation was low but significant for the narrowband data.

III. INTERAURAL DIFFERENCE MODELS APPLIED TO INDIVIDUAL MASKERS

Because of peripheral filtering, the relevant waveforms in almost all models are narrowband. Further, because narrowband waveforms can be described as amplitude- and phase-modulated sinusoids, the left and right internal signals within most models can be described as sinusoids with time-varying phases and envelopes. The interaural phase and intensity differences are thus easily defined as the differences in phases (in radians) and the decibel difference of the envelopes (the log of the ratio of the envelopes). These interaural differences vary over time and over waveforms for the target-present stimulus. Interaural differences for a specific noise waveform with a cosine target are shown in Fig. 2. The waveform in the top panel of the figure is the masker waveform with the cosine target added. For a signal-to-noise ratio near the threshold of the best-performing listeners, as indicated, the noise-alone and noise-plus-target waveforms are not visibly different. The waveform with the cosine subtracted would be presented to the other ear (in the N_0S_π condition) and would result in the interaural intensity difference (IID) and interaural time difference (ITD) waveforms plotted in the lower two panels of the figure. These difference waveforms were calculated numerically by using Hilbert transforms to create complex analytic waveforms from which the envelopes and phases are easily extracted (Oppenheim and Schafer, 1989). The interaural phase difference is plotted as the equivalent interaural time difference for the 50-Hz target frequency (which is equal to the center frequency of the noise band). For these ongoing differences in narrowband waveforms, we consider interaural time differences and interaural phase differences as equivalent descriptions. Note that the large values of interaural differences occur near the minima of the masker envelope, where the masker amplitude is comparable to the target amplitude.

Decision variables based on samples of interaural time differences or interaural intensity differences have been hypothesized as the basis for binaural detection of targets in noise. Models of this general type were introduced by Webster (1951), who considered the interaural time (or phase) difference as a cue for binaural detection and showed consistency with several binaural conditions.

[1]The observed lack of dependence on target phase for ensemble performance (performance averaged over all noise waveforms) is obvious because the ensemble average would naturally make the phase of the target irrelevant, given that all possible phases would be included in the ensemble due to the random phase variation in the waveforms.

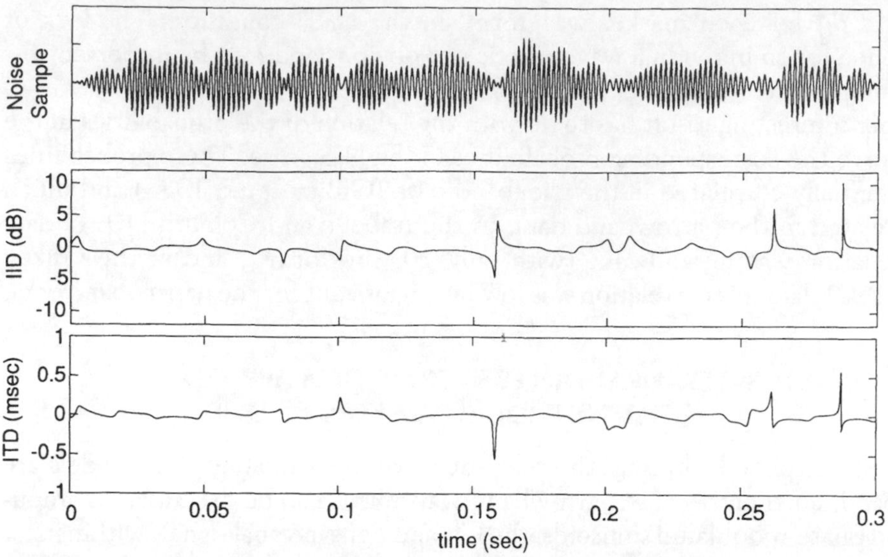

FIG. 2. Examples of interaural time differences and interaural intensity differences for the N_0S_π condition for a specific noise sample. The waveform shown in the top panel is noise sample 1 from the Isabelle and Colburn (1991) study with the cosine target added at the threshold signal-to-noise ratio of –24 dB. The two lower panels show the interaural time difference and interaural intensity difference waveforms.

Jeffress *et al.* (1956) applied this type of model to a large number of conditions, and Hafter (1971) and Yost (1970) presented extended models that included both time and intensity differences. These models are a natural means of talking about lateralization and aspects of localization as well as detection, and there is abundant physiological evidence for sensitivity to interaural parameters in brainstem neurons (e.g.., Yin *et al.*, Chapter 21, this volume; Kuwada *et al.*, Chapter 20, this volume). In a general analysis of the dependence of detection threshold on the interaural parameters of the target, Domnitz and Colburn (1976) showed that decision variables based on any combination of interaural time and intensity differences would be compatible with the observed dependence. They showed, in essence, that the details of the models are generally unimportant for the predicted dependence and that a wide class of models would make the same predictions. They generalized this result to the EC model and to other models based on interaural cross-correlation.

Gilkey *et al.* (1985) considered the application of interaural difference models to individual masker detection data and noted fundamental difficulties. These models predict a dependence on the phase of the target relative to the masker waveform, whereas their data (and all data since that time) have not shown the expected dependence on the phase. This prediction of a phase dependence for each masker holds even for models that average multiple temporal samples of interaural time or intensity (or both), as long as they are combined linearly (Kline, 1986).

If the definition of interaural difference models is extended to include non-linear combinations, the target-to-masker phase dependence may not be a problem. Specifically, we note (Isabelle and Colburn, 1987) that the sum of squares of the interaural time and intensity samples with appropriate weights have no dependence on the phase of the target relative to the masker. In addition, this statistic is of the same form as the ideal processor for the case in which the interaural time and intensity differences are statistically independent, Gaussian random variables. Perceptually, this statistic corresponds to a measure of the width of the distribution(s) of interaural differences and might logically be associated with the width of the perceived image. For narrowband maskers, this is generally consistent with the perception of an increase in the width of the acoustic image when the target is added to the diotic noise. This sum-of-squares decision variable calculated from the stimulus waveforms was correlated with the probabilities of a "yes" response in the target-present waveforms of Isabelle and Colburn (1991). A Spearman rank-order correlation coefficient of 0.7 was found (Isabelle, 1988). (There are no interaural differences in the stimulus for the noise-alone stimuli, so that some internal mechanism would be required to predict the P_f values.)

The sum-of-squares decision variable would vary inversely with the overall noise energy N, since the interaural differences caused by the addition of a given target to a noise masker would be larger when the masker energy is smaller. The narrowband data of Isabelle and Colburn (1991) show negative correlation between P_d and the noise energy (correlation's of -.577, -.348, and -.371), but the correlations are not statistically significant for two of the three subjects.

It is possible that the sum of squares is not the best measure of interaural differences, of course. Consider, for example, that the interaural difference waveforms are dominated by the large interaural differences at the minima of the masker envelope as seen in Fig. 2. It is clear that the sum of squares of the interaural differences could be strongly influenced by the relatively infrequent large values, which are determined by the minima in the specific masker envelope. These issuers deserve further study.

IV. EC MODEL APPLIED TO INDIVIDUAL MASKERS

We consider a particular formulation of the EC model (Fig. 3) in which the energy of the output of the cancellation is used as the decision variable for the model. Specifically, we assume that the decision variable Ω is generated for the diotic noise case by subtracting noisy versions of the filtered input stimuli and measuring the energy out of the subtractor. (The equalizing internal delay in the original model is not relevant for the N_0S_π condition considered here.) The internal noises are specified as random jitters, consistent with Durlach's original formulation (Durlach, 1963): Each filtered input waveform is delayed by a random time delay δ and scaled by a random amplitude factor equal to $(1 + \varepsilon)$. Mathematically, the formula for Ω is

$$\Omega = \int_0^T [(1+\varepsilon_L)x_L(t-\delta_L) - (1+\varepsilon_R)x_R(t-\delta_R)]^2 \; dt, \qquad (3)$$

where x_L and x_R are filtered versions of the input waveforms y_L and y_R.

We assume that the jitter parameters are chosen independently for each stimulus interval and independently of each other. Although a more realistic

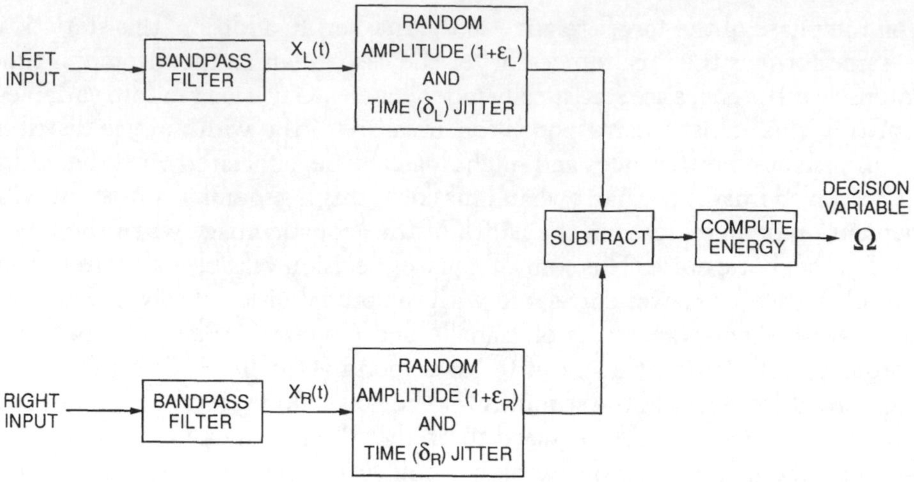

FIG. 3. Block diagram of Durlach's (1963) EC model in the decision-variable formulation suggested by Green (1966).

model would have temporal variations in these jitter values during the stimulus waveform, the complexities of this case are prohibitive and have not been considered explicitly in the literature or here.

For the specific case of identical noise (N_0) and out-of-phase signal (S_π), the expression for Ω can be rewritten in terms of the energies and correlations of the filtered masker and target waveforms. Specifically, we make the following definitions: N is the energy in the individual noise waveform; S is the energy in the signal waveform; $R_n(\tau)$ is the normalized autocorrelation of the noise waveform; R_s is defined similarly for the target signal; and $C_{ns}(\tau)$ is the unnormalized cross-correlation function of the individual noise waveform with the signal waveform. Specifically, when edge effects are ignored [so that, for example, the integral of the square of $s(t - \delta)$ is equal to S for all values of δ in the range of interest], then the expression for Ω becomes

$$\begin{aligned}\Omega = {} & (1+\varepsilon_L)^2 N + (1+\varepsilon_R)^2 N - 2(1+\varepsilon_L)(1+\varepsilon_R) N R_n(\delta_L - \delta_R) \\ & + (1+\varepsilon_L)^2 S + (1+\varepsilon_R)^2 S + 2(1+\varepsilon_L)(1+\varepsilon_R) S R_s(\delta_L - \delta_R) \\ & + 2[1+\varepsilon_L)^2 - (1+\varepsilon_R)^2] C_{ns}(0) \\ & + 2(1+\varepsilon_L)(1+\varepsilon_R)[C_{ns}(\delta_L - \delta_R) - C_{ns}(\delta_R - \delta_L)].\end{aligned} \tag{4}$$

Note that the variability in the values of Ω arises in part from the "external variability" [the variability of N and $C_{ns}(\tau)$ over the samples of the noise waveform] and in part from the "internal variability" (the variability of the time and amplitude jitters). This issue is addressed quantitatively in Sec. IV.D. For the special case of amplitude jitter only (so that all values of δ_L and δ_R are equal to zero), the expression for Ω becomes

$$\Omega = (\varepsilon_L - \varepsilon_R)^2 N + (2 + \varepsilon_L + \varepsilon_R)^2 S + 2[2(\varepsilon_L - \varepsilon_R) + \varepsilon_L^2 - \varepsilon_R^2] C_{ns}(0). \tag{5}$$

A. Distribution of decision variable Ω for individual maskers

The distributions of Ω values for two individual maskers used in the Isabelle and Colburn (1991) experiment are shown in Fig. 4. These results were computed using a pseudorandom sequence of jitter values and assuming that the peripheral (bandpass) filters have no effect on these narrowband waveforms. Specifically, for each jitter variable, values were chosen as the midpoints of 11 equally probable slices of a Gaussian distribution. For each waveform, the value of Ω was calculated for each combination of jitter values (ε_L, ε_R, δ_L, δ_R). The jitter variances are chosen so that the resulting ensemble performance is approximately equal to the observed performance: roughly just-detectable targets at a signal-to-noise ratio of -25 dB. Specifically, the standard deviation σ_δ of the time-jitter distribution is 10 μs and the standard deviation σ_ε of the amplitude-jitter distribution is 0.05. The values used by Durlach (1963) were significantly larger and would give ensemble

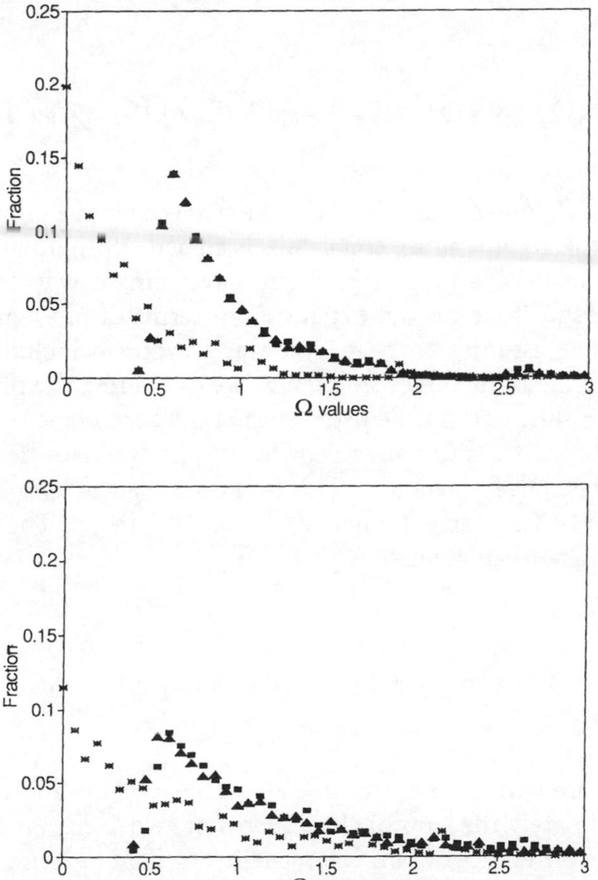

FIG. 4. Distribution of values of EC decision variable Ω for two representative waveforms from the experiment of Isabelle and Colburn (1991). The top panel is for waveform 10 and the bottom panel is for waveform 3. In each panel, the asterisks show the distribution of Ω for the noise-alone waveform and the filled symbols show the distribution for the noise-plus-target waveforms. The bin width of the distributions is chosen to be 0.0625 units. Values of Ω were scaled by a constant factor for convenience.

performance much worse that is observed in the N_0S_π case. [Green (1966) noted that his signal detection analysis resulted in smaller estimates of σ_ε than those of Durlach.]

The two panels in Fig. 4 show the distributions of Ω for two individual noise waveforms (maskers 10 and 3 from the Isabelle and Colburn experiment). The energy of masker 3 is significantly larger than the energy of masker 10 (about a factor of two), and the distribution of Ω values for the noise-alone case (the asterisks) is consequently shifted to larger values, as we expect from Eqs. 4 and 5. The distributions of Ω with target present are shown with filled symbols for two different targets, a 500-Hz sine and a 500-Hz cosine. The similarity of the distributions for the sine and cosine cases suggests that the cross-terms in the preceding equations have only a marginal effect on these distributions and therefore on performance.

We can understand the shape of the distribution for the noise-alone case by writing Ω for the noise-alone case in the form

$$\Omega = N\{2[1 - R_n(\delta_L - \delta_R)](1 + \varepsilon_L + \varepsilon_R + \varepsilon_L\varepsilon_R) + (\varepsilon_L - \varepsilon_R)^2\}. \qquad (6)$$

and then approximating $R_n(\delta_L - \delta_R)$ as a cosine and expanding it in a power series. Because the values of the argument are small, this is a good approximation, even though there will be small variations in R_n from waveform to waveform. The simplest expressions result if we do the expansion in terms of phase instead of time. Because processing assumes that the relevant waveform includes only a narrow band centered around the target frequency, we can define the phase jitter as the equivalent radian shift of the time jitter at the target frequency. That is, $\phi = 2\pi f\delta$ where f is 500 Hz. It is also convenient to use the standard deviation of the phase jitter in expressions for averages. This is of course given by $\sigma_\phi = 2\pi f\sigma_\delta$, and σ_ϕ is equal to 0.0314 (in radians) when σ_δ is equal to 10 μs. The resulting expression for Ω for the noise-alone case is given by

$$\Omega = N[(\phi_L - \phi_R)^2(1 + \varepsilon_L + \varepsilon_R + \varepsilon_L\varepsilon_R) + (\varepsilon_L - \varepsilon_R)^2]. \qquad (7)$$

Since the jitter values are small, the term $(1 + \varepsilon_L + \varepsilon_R + \varepsilon_L\varepsilon_R)$ is approximately unity, and Ω is approximately the sum of the squares of two Gaussian variables, each determined by the difference of two Gaussian jitters. For our assumed values of σ_ε and σ_δ, the jitter variances σ_ε^2 and σ_ϕ^2 are approximately equal. The sum of the squares of two Gaussian variables with equal variances has an exponential distribution, which is a reasonable characterization of the distributions in Fig. 4. The decay constant of the exponential is proportional to the product of the noise energy and the common variance of the Gaussian variables. According to Eq. 7, the effect of the individual noise waveform is simply to scale the distribution by the filtered-noise energy *N*, consistent with the differences between the two waveforms shown in the figure.[2] The fact that the distribution of Ω can be approximated without distinguishing the individual autocorrelation functions for each noise waveform reflects the fact that the dependence of $R_n(\tau)$ on the individual waveform is minimal for our range of τ.

The noise-plus-tone distributions are more complicated to describe. To a first approximation they are a shifted version of the noise-alone waveforms, and it is easy to verify that the amount of shift is approximately the same for all the waveforms, corresponding to the *S* term in Eq. 4. This term is approximately equal to 4*S* independent of the masker waveform. The fact that the noise-plus-tone distributions have values smaller than the peak of the shifted distribution is of course a reflection of both the variability in the jitter parameters and the cross-correlation terms. Recall that the cross-correlation C_{ns} varies with the noise waveform (and may be positive, negative, or zero). These terms also generate the differences in the distributions for sine and cosine targets. In general, waveforms with large $C_{ns}(0)$ values show greater differences with target phase. When the cross-correlation terms are negligible, then the performance should be approximately independent of the target phase, as is empirically observed.

B. Distribution of (P_d, P_f) pairs

With these distributions for a set of waveforms, one can calculate performance by assuming that a criterion is established and that the response "Yes, the target is present" is made whenever the value of Ω exceeds the criterion. Using the set of 10 waveforms corresponding to the experiment of Isabelle and Colburn (1991), we determined P_d and P_f values using this response rule. The specific criterion (0.67) was chosen to match the P_d calculated for a selected waveform to the measured values of 0.75 for that waveform. The values of P_d and P_f for the other waveforms can then be calculated.

The results of the application of this model to these waveforms are plotted in Fig. 5 on ROC axes for comparison to experimental results such as those in Fig. 1. The theoretical results are significantly different from the empirical results of individual subjects in two ways. First, the points lie approximately along a line, as opposed to the scatter that is apparent in the empirical data (as seen in Fig. 1). Second, the range of probabilities is more restricted than the observed data.

The fact that there is little scatter along the direction of the negative diagonal is consistent with the fact the P_d and P_f are highly correlated in the theoretical results. The values shown have a correlation coefficient of 0.87. This correlation is a direct consequence of the fact that both P_d and P_f are highly correlated with the energy in the filtered noise waveform. This correlation is equal to 0.87 for P_d

---

[2]The obvious deviations from a simple exponential at the larger values of Ω are due to the approximation of a continuous Gaussian distribution with a set of 11 discrete values (the equiprobable values) for each distribution. It can be varified, for example, that the bump in the distribution starting at Ω values around 1.9 for waveform 10 corresponds to the largest possible value of $\varepsilon_L - \varepsilon_R$ in the expression already given with the tail from that point determined by the other term in the expression, which is dominated by the φ values.

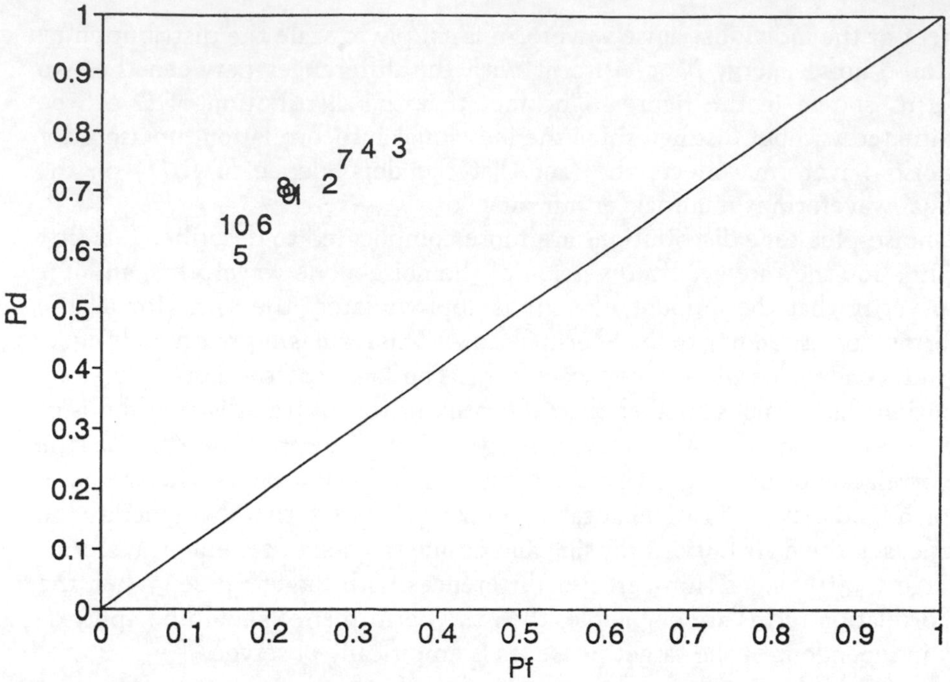

FIG. 5. Predicted values of P_d and P_f plotted in ROC space for the 10 waveforms used in the Isabelle and Colburn (1991) experiment. See text for details.

and 0.997 for P_f. This is a basic deficiency of the EC model, at least with the formulation based on the energy in the output of the subtractor. As noted, the narrowband data show negative or insignificant correlation's between P_d and energy.

This second difference seen in the plot in ROC space is related to the ratio of internal to external variability: The greater the internal variability relative to the external variability, the smaller the range of the P_d and P_f values over the waveforms. This follows from the observations that the internal variability is a measure of how much the distributions overlap for a given noise waveform and the external variability is a function of how much the distributions shift from waveform to waveform. The ratio of the internal to external variability is addressed further in Sec. IV. D.

C. Conditional mean and variance of Ω given noise waveform

The conditional expected value of Ω, given the noise waveform, is given by

$$E[\Omega|n(t)] = 2N[\sigma_\varepsilon^2 + 1 - \overline{R_n(\delta_L - \delta_R)}] + 2S\{2 + \sigma_\varepsilon^2 - [1 - \overline{R_s(\delta_L - \delta_R)}]\}, \quad (8)$$

where the symbols are defined in association with Eqs. 3 and 4 and the overbar indicates an average over the time jitter. For time or phase jitters of the size that we expect at low frequencies, we again assume that the autocorrelation of the noise can be approximated by a cosine for all noise waveforms and proceed as before. We obtain the following approximate expression for the conditional mean:

$$E[\Omega | n(t)] = 2N(\sigma_\varepsilon^2 + \sigma_\phi^2) + 2S(2 + \sigma_\varepsilon^2 - \sigma_\phi^2), \tag{9}$$

where we have again defined $\phi = 2\pi f\delta$. These expressions, which are consistent with the results for $\sigma_\phi = 0$ from Green (1966) and others, show that the change in the mean value of the decision variable when the target is added is independent of the noise waveform and that the expected value of Ω for noise alone is proportional to the energy in the noise waveform.

The conditional variance of Ω given the noise waveform is given by similar computations. This quantity depends explicitly on $C_{ns}(\tau)$, the cross-correlation function of the filtered masker and target waveforms, which can be computed for each masker waveform. For our computations, we approximated the unnormalized cross-correlation function with $C_{ns}(\tau) = C_{Max} \cos(\theta + 2\pi f\tau)$, where the parameters C_{Max} and θ vary over the set of noise waveforms. The parameter C_{Max} is the maximum value of the cross-correlation function, which takes values from 0 to about $(NS)^{1/2}/10$. The parameter θ is the phase shift observed in the cross-correlation function and takes values that appear to be uniformly distributed over a period. The cross-correlation functions of a particular noise waveform with the sine and with the cosine differ in that θ changes by a quarter period. It is straightforward to show that when x is a Gaussian random variable with variance σ^2, the expected value of $\cos(\theta + x)$ is equal to $e^{-\sigma^2/2}\cos\theta$. We can then show the following intermediate step (which arises in the computation of the conditional variance from the last line of Eq. 4):

$$\overline{C_{ns}^2(\delta_L - \delta_R)} - \overline{C_{ns}(\delta_L - \delta_R)}^2 = C_{Max}^2 \left\{ \tfrac{1}{2}\left[1 + e^{-4\sigma_\phi^2}\cos(2\theta)\right] - e^{-2\sigma_\phi^2}\cos^2\theta \right\}.$$

This expression can be simplified to $C_{Max}^2\, 2\sigma_\phi^2 \sin^2\theta$ for small values of σ_ϕ^2 when higher order terms in this jitter variance can be ignored. The resulting approximation for the conditional variance of Ω given the noise waveform is

$$\begin{aligned} Var[\Omega | n(t)] = {} & 8N^2(\sigma_\varepsilon^4 + \sigma_\phi^4) + 8S^2(4\sigma_\varepsilon^2 + \sigma_\phi^4) \\ & + 8SN\left[(2\sigma_\varepsilon^2\sigma_\phi^2 - \sigma_\phi^4) + \rho_{Max}^2(4\sigma_\varepsilon^2\cos^2\theta + 2\sigma_\phi^2\sin^2\theta)\right], \end{aligned} \tag{10}$$

where we have defined the maximum normalized cross-correlation ρ_{Max} in terms of the maximum unnormalized cross-correlation C_{Max} by dividing C_{Max} by $(NS)^{1/2}$, the geometric mean of the noise energy and the signal energy. Note that the last term in Eq. 10 is the only place in which the characteristics of the individual waveforms (other than their energies) appear. Any target-to-masker phase dependence would arise in this term via the parameters ρ_{Max} and θ. From these equations, we can see that the standard deviation for noise alone is thus proportional to the energy N in the filtered noise waveform and that the standard deviation for target plus noise is approximately (within about 10%) equal to the standard deviation for noise alone. These results are generalizations of the results presented by Green (1966), Yost (1970), and Gilkey *et al.* (1985). Green analyzed the case in which the time jitter was ignored ($\sigma_\delta = 0$); Yost derived an expression for the variance with $S = 0$ for the case of a sinusoidal masker with both time and amplitude jitter; Gilkey *et al.* presented an expression for the variance with $S \neq 0$ for sinusoidal noise with $\sigma_\delta = 0$.

D. Internal-external noise ratio

Another aspect of these results is the relative importance of the internal variability. A measure of the internal variability V_{int} is equal to the expected value (over the set of noise waveforms) of the conditional variance. The external variance V_{ext} is equal to the variance across the noise waveforms of the expression in Eq. 9 and the total variance is the sum of these two terms. Thus,

$$V_{\text{int}} = E\left[Var[\Omega \mid n(t)]\right] = 8(\sigma_n^2 + E_n^2)(\sigma_\varepsilon^4 + \sigma_\phi^4) + 8S^2(4\sigma_\varepsilon^4 + \sigma_\phi^4)$$
$$+ 8SE_n\left[2(\sigma_\varepsilon^2\sigma_\phi^2 - \phi_\phi^4) + \rho_{Max}^2(4\sigma_\varepsilon^2 \cos^2\theta + 2\sigma_\phi^2 \sin^2\theta)\right],$$
$$V_{ext} = Var\left[E[\Omega \mid n(t)]\right] = 4\sigma_n^2(\sigma_\varepsilon^2 + \sigma_\phi^2)^2,$$

and

$$\text{Var}[\Omega] = V_{\text{int}} + V_{\text{ext}}, \tag{11}$$

with $E_n = E[N]$, and $\sigma_n^2 = \text{Var}[N]$, with averages taken over the set of noise waveforms. The ratio of internal to external noise for the condition with no target present ($S = 0$) is given by

$$\frac{V_{\text{int}}}{V_{\text{ext}}} = 2\left(1 + \frac{E_n^2}{\sigma_n^2}\right)\frac{(\sigma_\varepsilon^4 + \sigma_\phi^4)}{(\sigma_\varepsilon^4 + \sigma_\phi^4 + 2\sigma_\varepsilon^2\sigma_\phi^2)}. \tag{12}$$

The size of this ratio depends to some extent on the relative sizes of the amplitude and phase jitter variances, both of which are significantly less than unity. The ratio of E_n^2 to σ_n^2 can be estimated by approximating the noise stimulus (through the peripheral filter) as a rectangular band of noise with bandwidth W and duration T. In this case, E_n is given by N_0WT and σ_n^2 is given by N_0^2WT. Thus, the ratio E_n^2/σ_n^2 is given by WT. In the detection experiments we are discussing, the stimulus frequency is 500 Hz so that W is approximately 100 Hz and T is approximately 0.3 s. Thus, the ratio E_n^2/σ_n^2 is approximately 30. If the jitter variances are of comparable magnitude, the ratio of internal to external noise is approximately equal to 31. If either jitter variance is significantly larger than the other variance, then the ratio approaches a factor of two larger, approximately 60.

Experimental values of the variance ratio for the N_0S_π condition are typically between 1 and 4, as calculated from empirical results by Siegel and Colburn (1989) and by Isabelle and Colburn (1991).

E. Summary of EC model analysis

We summarize the application of our formulation of the EC model to the individual noise detection data as follows: When the energy in the output of the subtractor in the classical EC model is taken as the decision variable Ω, the distributions of Ω (given the noise waveform) are approximately chi-squared with one or two degrees of freedom (depending on the relative sizes of the jitter variances) with a standard deviation that is proportional to the product of the energy in the noise waveform multiplied by the variance of the dominant jitter parameter. If the jitter variances are approximately equal ($\sigma_\phi^2 \cong \sigma_\varepsilon^2$, as in our cases shown), the distribution of Ω is approximately exponential and the mean is approximately equal to the standard deviation. The EC model is consistent with the minimal dependence on target phase. When the jitter parameters are chosen to be compatible with the ensemble data, the EC model is inconsistent with several aspects of the sample-level data. The model predicts a significant positive correlation between the probabilities P_d and P_f and the energy in the masker waveform. In addition, the ratio of the variance in the decision variable from internal variability relative to that from external variability predicted by the model is significantly greater than the ratios estimated empirically. We conclude that this model is not adequate to describe binaural detection performance measured separately for individual masker waveforms.

The difficulties we find with the EC model and our conclusion that this model is inadequate for the individual detection data are based on two fundamental assumptions. If these assumptions are changed, other conclusions may result. The first assumption is that the decision variable is given by the energy in the output of the subtractor in Fig. 3. If some other statistic were used, the P_d may not be correlated with the energy of the masker. The second fundamental assumption is that the jitter parameters are constant during the stimulus (and random from presentation to presentation). If the jitter parameters varied randomly during the stimulus interval, it is conceivable that the overall performance could be constrained to the values observed for ensemble performance with more variability over the waveform. In other words, it is possible that this model could predict a smaller ratio of internal to external variability. Results based on these alternative assumptions are not available.

V. INTERAURAL CORRELATION MODELS APPLIED TO INDIVIDUAL MASKERS

Another class of models that are consistent with the ensemble data comprises models based on interaural cross-correlation. Our treatment of these data here is relatively brief. We consider both unnormalized and normalized cross-correlation measures. For simplicity, we use the internal noise measures and the notation described in the previous section. The unnormalized cross-correlation decision variable CC is given by

$$CC = \int_0^T (1+\varepsilon_L)x_L(t-\delta_L)(1+\varepsilon_R)x_R(t-\delta_R)\,dt\,. \tag{13}$$

If we proceed as in the EC model analysis for the N_0S_π condition, this expression expands to

$$CC = (1+\varepsilon_L)(1+\varepsilon_R)\left[NR_n(\delta_L-\delta_R) - SR_s(\delta_L-\delta_R) + C_{ns}(\delta_L-\delta_R) - C_{ns}(\delta_R-\delta_L)\right]. \tag{14}$$

Note that the amplitude jitter is simply a multiplicative factor and that CC reduces to $N - S$ if there is no jitter. It can also be verified that the variation in CC as a consequence of variation in the filtered noise energy N is much greater than the change in CC due to the addition of a target. Because the distributions of CC are dramatically overlapping, this decision variable is inadequate for performance comparable to observed performance. In other words, fixing decision criterion and choosing "Target present" when CC is below the criterion leads to values of P_d and P_f that are approximately equal.

The conditional mean given the noise waveform is

$$E[CC\,|\,n(t)] = N(1-\sigma_\phi^2) - S(1-\sigma_\phi^2)\,. \tag{15}$$

The conditional variance given the noise waveform is given only for noise-alone stimulus conditions; specifically,

$$Var[CC\,|\,n(t)] = N^2(\sigma_\varepsilon^2 - \sigma_\phi^2)\,. \tag{16}$$

It then follows that the ration of V_{int} to V_{ext} is extremely small for reasonable values of σ_ε^2. For noise-alone the ratio is given by

$$\frac{V_{\text{int}}}{V_{\text{ext}}} = \left(1 + \frac{E_n^2}{\sigma_n^2}\right)\frac{(\sigma_\varepsilon^2 - \sigma_\phi^2)}{(1-\sigma_\phi^2)}\,. \tag{17}$$

The unnormalized cross-correlation CC is clearly too dependent on the noise waveform, as indicated by the variation for the noise-alone stimulus. [The masker energy N and the value of CC vary by a factor of 2 for the noise waveforms used by Isabelle and Colburn (1991), but the signal energy S is typically a factor of 100 smaller than N.] This would predict, contradictory to empirical data, that P_d and P_f values should be negligibly different for each waveform (relative to the variations of each over the population of waveforms). To make these notions concrete, we show in Fig. 6 the relation between $E[\text{CC}\,|\,n(t)]$ and the empirical

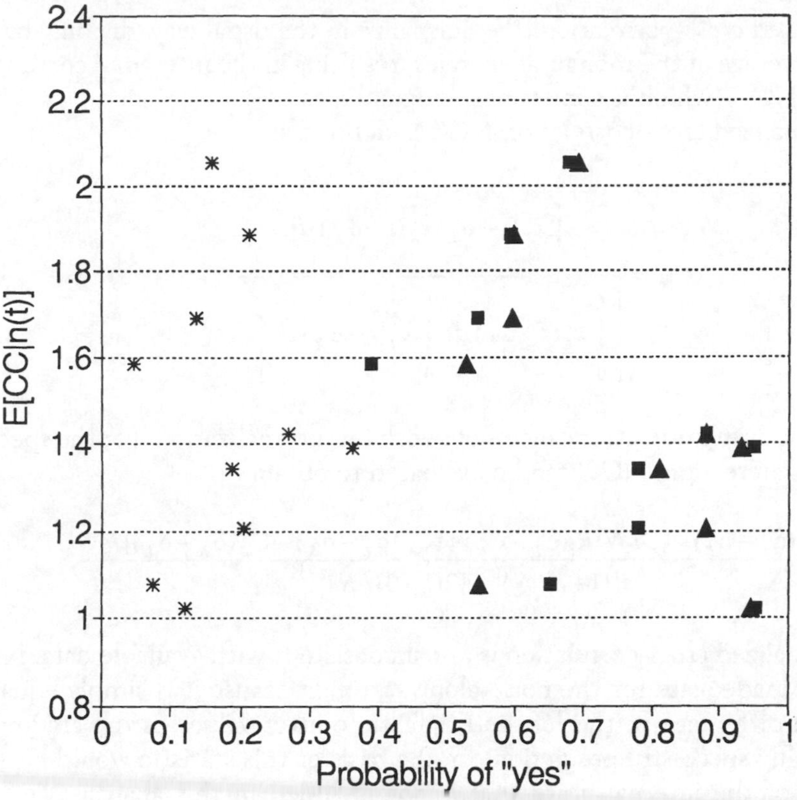

FIG. 6. Scatterplot of the expected value of the cross-correlation decision variable, $E[\mathrm{CC}|n(t)]$, and the probability of a "yes" response in the Isabelle and Colburn (1991) experiment. The probability of "yes" is P_d for noise-plus-target waveforms (filled triangles for sine and filled squares for cosine) and P_f for noise-alone waveforms (asterisks)

probability of a response "Yes, target present" for each waveform. In noise-alone cases (asterisks), the probabilities of "yes" are P_f values for specific waveforms; in the target-present case (filled symbols), the probabilities of "yes" are P_d values for specific waveforms (both sine and cosine targets). Note that values of $E[\mathrm{CC}\ |n(t)]$ come in 10 sets of three approximately equal values. Each set corresponds to an individual masker waveform. The differences from masker waveform to masker waveform are much larger than the differences over target conditions for a given masker. Thus, performance based on $E[\mathrm{CC}\ |n(t)]$ would be near chance. This model predicts a very small effect of the target relative to the variations over masker waveforms.

Previous interaural correlation models have normalized the decision variable when the model is applied to detection. In the model of Osman (1971) the correlation variable is normalized by subtracting energy terms from each ear estimated monaurally. The resulting model is mathematically equivalent to the EC model discussed in the previous section if the internal noise assumptions are the same. Although Osman assumed additive internal noise, we maintain consistency with previous sections in this chapter (and with the classic EC model) by assuming multiplicative amplitude jitter and time jitter. We next consider briefly the normalized cross-correlation. We normalize in the usual way, dividing by the geometric average of the monaural energies, resulting in the interaural correlation coefficient NCC (which is sometimes designated as ρ_{LR}).

The normalized cross-correlation NCC is defined as

$$NCC = \frac{\int_0^T x_L(t-\delta_L)x_R(t-\delta_R)\,dt}{\left[\int_0^T x_L^2(t-\delta_L)\,dt \int_0^T x_R^2(t-\delta_R)\,dt\right]^{1/2}} \; . \tag{18}$$

Note that the amplitude jitter cancels out with this normalization. For the specific case of N_0S_π detection, NCC can be evaluated to obtain

$$NCC = \frac{R_n(\delta_L-\delta_R)-(S/N)R_s(\delta_L-\delta_R)+[C_{ns}(\delta_L-\delta_R)-C_{ns}(\delta_R-\delta_L)]/N}{\{(1+S/N)^2-[2C_{ns}(0)/N]^2\}^{1/2}} \; . \tag{19}$$

The normalized cross-correlation is also inconsistent with available data. NCC is obviously inadequate for the noise-alone stimuli, because it is simply equal to R_n with the difference in the left and right time-jitter values as the argument. Therefore, any successful predictions on the basis of this statistic would have to be a result of the internal noise that is not included in this analysis. For the noise-plus-target stimulus, NCC is approximately proportional to the energy in the noise waveform and would predict that P_d is strongly negatively correlated with the energy N. The observed negative correlation is very weak.

VI. PHYSIOLOGICALLY BASED MODELS

Few predictions have been developed for binaural masked detection using models that explicitly incorporate physiological data. This is presumably related to the difficulty that inevitably arises when complex stimuli such as Gaussian random noise with and without target tones are described, particularly because the transduction from input waveform to neural firings is so complicated. This transduction includes nonlinear dynamics and transforms to a random point process with memory. The difficulties caused by this complexity have not been overcome by any models of binaural detection. We discuss here several models that might be called preliminary attempts to address this problem, and point out directions that may be promising. Essentially all of these models are formulated as information in the (f,τ) plane as described in Sec. I and most are consistent with the brilliant insights of Jeffress, as described in his place model of localization (Jeffress, 1948) and later detection models (Jeffress *et al.*, 1956). Further information about all of these models can be found in the recent chapters by Colburn (1995), Stern and Trahiotis (1995), and Stern and Trahiotis (Chapter 24, this volume).

Colburn (1973, 1977) applied a model based on auditory nerve data to binaural detection with the assumption that the internal variability (which is seen in the stochastic nature of the auditory nerve activity) dominated the external variability (which arises from the stochastic nature of the noise waveform). This assumption was required within that model because of the simplicity of Colburn's description of the auditory nerve activity. The auditory-nerve model he used had no refractory behavior and no saturation of the driving function for short-time variations in the stimulus envelope. Both of these aspects of a model would have limited the impact of stimulus variability; however, without either of these aspects, the stimulus variability was absurdly large when included. Thus, Colburn's earlier model for binaural interaction is unable to describe the variability of performance for individual stimulus waveforms without a better description of the auditory nerve activity in response to noise.

Bilsen and his colleagues (Bilsen, 1977; Raatgever and Bilsen, 1986; Frijns, Raatgever, and Bilsen, 1986) applied their central spectrum model to binaural detection data in association with binaural pitch studies. However, this model did not explicitly include internal noise and derived predictions relative to the N_0S_π condition. This model makes no explicit predictions for the individual masker waveforms.

Colburn and Isabelle (1992) pointed out in a modeling study of interaural time discrimination based on neural firing patterns observed in the MSO that models that predict interaural discrimination can be applied to binaural detection in the spirit of the interaural difference models discussed in Sec. III. In this sense, any model of discrimination that allows the processing of temporal samples of interaural time and/or intensity differences could be applied to individual masker waveforms. One of the advantages of physiologically based models in this regard is that they include explicitly internal noise that depends on the stimulus waveform and therefore have the potential for predicting variations in P_f over waveforms.

The explicit incorporation of peripheral coding of auditory signals appears to be a promising direction for understanding the dependence of performance on individual waveforms. The auditory nerve model of Carney (1993), for example, includes dynamic saturation effects and refractory effects and could be used in association with models that are sensitive to interaural differences to predict individual waveform thresholds.

VII. CONCLUSIONS

We conclude that there are no satisfactory models for binaural N_0S_π detection when the dependence of detection probabilities on individual masker waveforms are considered. We feel that there are adequate grounds for rejecting the EC model, interaural correlation models, and models based on linear combinations of interaural differences. This last category includes most models of lateral position. The most promising model that we have considered here is based on the sum of squares of interaural time and intensity differences. A general issue in modeling that has not been extensively explored is the impact of peripheral physiological transformations on the differences from waveform to waveform. It is possible that an appropriate internal noise model, perhaps physiologically based, will be able to describe both types of data. Further work is required to understand the dependence of binaural detection performance on individual masker waveforms.

ACKNOWLEDGMENT

This work was supported by a grant from the U.S. National Institutes of Health (grant no. 5 R01 DC00100).

REFERENCES

Bilsen, F. A. (**1977**). "Pitch of noise signals: Evidence for a central spectrum," J. Acoust. Soc. Am. **61**, 150.

Carney, L. H. (**1993**). "A model for the responses of low-frequency auditory-nerve fibers in cat," J. Acoust. Soc. Am. **93**, 401–417.

Colburn, H. S. (**1973**). "Theory of binaural interaction based on auditory-nerve data. I. General strategy and preliminary results on interaural discrimination," J. Acoust. Soc. Am. **54**, 1458–1470.

Colburn, H. S. (**1977**). "Theory of binaural interaction based on auditory-nerve data. II. Detection of tones in noise," J. Acoust .Soc. Am. **61**, 525–533.

Colburn, H. S. (**1995**). "Computational models of binaural processing," in *Auditory Computation*, edited by H. Hawkins, T. McMullen, R. Fay, and A. N. Popper (Springer-Verlag, New York), 332–400.

Colburn, H. S., and Durlach, N. I. (**1978**). "Models of binaural interaction," in *Handbook of Perception, Vol. IV, Hearing*, edited by E. C. Carterette and M. Friedman (Academic Press, New York), pp. 467–518.

Colburn, H. S., and Isabelle, S. K. (**1992**). "Models of binaural processing based on neural patterns in the medial superior olive," in *Auditory Physiology and Perception*, edited by Y. Cazals, L. Demany, and K. Horner (Pergamon, New York), pp. 539–546.

Domnitz, R. H., and Colburn, H. S. (**1976**). "Analysis of binaural detection models for dependence on interaural target parameters," J. Acoust. Soc. Am. **59**, 598–601.

Durlach, N. I. (**1960**). "Note on the equalization and cancellation theory of binaural masking-level differences," J. Acoust. Soc. Am. **32**, 1075–1076.

Durlach, N. I. (**1963**). "Equalization and cancellation theory of binaural masking-level differences," J. Acoust. Soc. Am. **35**, 1206–1218.

Durlach, N. I. (**1972**). "Binaural signal detection: Equalization and cancellation theory," in *Foundations of Modern Auditory Theory, Vol. II*, edited by J. V. Tobias (Academic Press, New York), pp. 371–462.

Durlach, N. I., and Colburn, H. S. (**1978**). "Binaural phenomena," in *Handbook of Perception, Vol. IV, Hearing*, edited by E. C. Carterette and M. Friedman (Academic Press, New York), pp. 365–466.

Frijns, J. H. M., Raatgever, J., and Bilsen, F. A. (**1986**). "A central spectrum theory of binaural processing: The edge pitch revisited," J. Acoust. Soc. Am. **80**, 442–451.

Gilkey, R. H. (**1990**). "The relation between monaural and binaural tone-in-noise masking," presented at the 13th Midwinter Meeting of the Assoc. Res. Otolaryngol., St. Petersburg Beach, FL, February.

Gilkey, R. H. (**1992**). "The correlation between responses under monaural and binaural conditions," J. Acoust. Soc. Am. **92**, 2298(A).

Gilkey, R. H., Robinson, D. E., and Hanna, T. E. (**1985**). "Effects of masker waveform and signal-to-masker phase relation on diotic and dichotic masking by reproducible noise," J. Acoust. Soc. Am. **78**, 1207–1219.

Goldberg, J. M., and Brown, P. B. (**1969**). "Response of binaural neurons of dog superior olivary complex to dichotic tonal stimuli: Some physiological mechanisms of sound localization," J. Neurophysiol. **32**, 613–636.

Green, D. M. (**1964**). "Consistency of auditory detection judgements," Psychol. Rev. **71**, 392–407.

Green, D. M. (**1966**). "Signal detection analysis of EC model," J. Acoust. Soc. Am. **40**, 833–838.

Hafter, E. R. (**1971**). "Quantitative evaluation of a lateralization model of masking-level differences," J. Acoust. Soc. Am. **50**, 1116–1122.

Hirsh, I. J. (**1948**). "The influence of interaural phase on interaural summation and inhibition," J. Acoust. Soc. Am. **20**, 536–544.

Isabelle, S. K. (**1988**). "Binaural narrowband-masked detection: Results for reproducible maskers and model predictions," MS thesis, Biomedical Engineering Department, Boston University, Boston.

Isabelle, S. K., and Colburn, H. S. (**1987**). "Effect of target phase in narrow-band frozen noise detection data," J. Acoust. Soc. Am. **82,** S109(A).

Isabelle, S. K., and Colburn, H. S. (**1991**). "Detection of tones in reproducible narrowband noise," J. Acoust. Soc. Am. **89**, 352–359.

Jeffress, L. A. (**1948**). "A place theory of sound localization," J. Comp. Physiol. Psychol. **41**, 35–39.

Jeffress, L. A., Blodgett, H. C., Sandel, T. T., and Wood, C. L. III (**1956**). "Masking of tonal signals," J. Acoust. Soc. Am. **28**, 416–426.

Kline, G. C. (**1986**). "A modified model of binaural hearing: Predictions for binaural masked detection with frozen maskers," MS thesis, Biomedical Engineering Department, Boston University, Boston.

Licklider, J. C. R. (**1948**). "The influence of interaural phase relations upon the masking of speech by white noise," J. Acoust. Soc. Am. **28**, 150–159.

Licklider, J. C. R. (**1959**). "Three auditory theories," in *Psychology: A Study of a Science, Vol. I*, edited by E. S. Koch (McGraw-Hill, New York), Study 1.

Oppenheim, A. V., and Schafer, R. W. (**1989**). *Discrete-Time Signal Processing* (Prentice-Hall, Englewood Cliffs, NJ), pp. 683–686.

Osman, E. (**1971**). "A correlation model of binaural masking level differences," J. Acoust. Soc. Am. **50**, 1494–1511.

Raatgever, J., and Bilsen, F. A. (**1986**). "A central spectrum theory of binaural processing: Evidence from dichotic pitch," J. Acoust. Soc. Am. **80**, 429–441.

Sayers, B. M. (**1964**). "Acoustic-image lateralization judgments with binaural tones," J. Acoust. Soc. Am. **36**, 923–926.

Sayers, B. M., and Cherry, E. C. (**1957**). "Mechanisms of binaural fusion in the hearing of speech," J. Acoust. Soc. Am. **29**, 973–987.

Siegel, R. A., and Colburn, H. S. (**1989**). "Binaural processing of noisy stimuli: Internal/external noise ratios for diotic and dichotic stimuli," J. Acoust. Soc. Am. **86**, 2122–2128.

Stern, R. M., and Trahiotis, C. (**1995**). "Models of binaural interaction," in *Handbook of Perception and Cognition, Vol. 6: Hearing*, edited by B. C. J. Moore (Academic Press, New York), 347–386.

Webster, F. A. (**1951**). "The influence of interaural phase on masked thresholds I. The role of interaural time deviation," J. Acoust. Soc. Am. **23**, 452–462.

Yin, T. C. T., and Chan, J. C. K. (**1990**). "Interaural time sensitivity in the medial superior olive of the cat," J. Neurophys. **64**, 465–488.

Yost, W. A. (**1970**). "Tone-on-tone binaural masking," PhD thesis, Department of Psychology, Indiana University, Bloomington.

Zurek, P. M. (**1991**). "Probability distributions of interaural phase and level differences in binaural detection stimuli," J. Acoust. Soc. Am. **90**, 1927–1932.

Chapter 26

Using Neural Networks to Evaluate the Viability of Monaural and Interaural Cues for Sound Localization

James A. Janko
Wright State University, Dayton, Ohio

Timothy R. Anderson
AL/CFBA, Wright-Patterson AFB, Ohio

Robert H. Gilkey
Wright State University, Dayton, Ohio
and AL/CFBA, Wright-Patterson AFB, Ohio

(Received March 1995; revised September 1995)

Artificial neural networks were trained to identify the location of virtual sound sources based on the information in head-related transfer functions (HRTFs) recorded from a human subject. The results were used to evaluate whether either a monaural representation of stimulus information or an interaural representation of stimulus information is adequate to mediate human spatial hearing performance. The simulated signals were filtered clicks presented from virtual speakers placed at 15° steps in azimuth and 18° steps in elevation. After the signals were passed through the HRTFs, quarter-octave spectra were computed. The inputs to the networks were the monaural spectra, the interaural difference spectrum, and/or the interaural time delay. Back propagation was used to train individual networks for each combination of stimulus information. Depending on the stimulus information presented to the network, performance could be much worse or much better than that of the human subject. Overall, the results indicate that the interaural time delay in combination with either monaural or interaural spectral information is sufficient to produce performance comparable to that observed for human listeners.

INTRODUCTION

As indicated in chapters throughout this volume, there is general agreement that three broad classes of acoustic cues provide the basis for human sound localization: the interaural time difference, the interaural level difference, and "spectral cues."

The interaural time difference typically refers to a broadband estimate of the delay between the proximal stimuli reaching the two ears and ignores the frequency dependence of the delay. Similarly, the interaural level difference typically refers to a broadband estimate of the difference in level between the ears. "Spectral cues" refers to across-frequency variations in the level of the proximal stimulus, typically a direction-dependent pattern of comparatively narrowband spectral peaks and notches introduced by the pinna.

There is also general agreement that the low-frequency interaural time difference plays a dominant role in determining the perceived azimuth of the sound source (actually the left/right coordinate described in Sec. II). The overall interaural level difference appears to play a similar role at high frequencies (above roughly 1.5–2.0 kHz). The "spectral cues" come in to play at still higher frequencies (above roughly 3.0–5.0 kHz) and are believed to determine the perceived elevation of the sound source (and also the front/back coordinate described in Sec. II). In addition to these primary roles, it is clear that overall interaural differences affect elevation judgments by limiting the set of possible source locations (and thus the set of possible source elevations) and that spectral cues can influence azimuth judgments (e.g., see Middlebrooks, Chapter 4, this volume; Butler, 1978, Chapter 5, this volume).

Despite these areas of agreement, there is less consensus as to how the "spectral cues" are recovered and used to determine the elevation (and the front/back coordinate) of the sound source. The spectrum of the proximal stimulus that reaches each tympanic membrane is the product of the source spectrum with the head-related transfer function (HRTF, the transfer function that describes the filtering of the torso, head, and pinna as the sound travels from the source to the tympanic membrane). In order for the auditory system to use "spectral cues" as a basis for sound localization, the direction-dependent spectral signatures of the pinnae must be recovered from the proximal stimuli.

Potentially, these pinna signatures can be recovered either through monaural processing or through interaural processing. For example, an interaural solution might "simply" compute the difference spectrum between the stimuli at the two ears; because the source spectrum will be the same at each ear and the HRTFs associated with each ear will be different, the source spectrum should cancel, leaving an interaural representation of the HRTF magnitude spectrum (i.e., the interaural level difference as a function of frequency, not the broadband interaural level difference). The most likely direction of origin could then be determined by matching this spectrum to previously learned, direction-specific interaural spectral templates.

A monaural solution is less straightforward, particularly when the source spectrum is unknown. Zakarauskas and Cynader (1993) provided one of the most quantitative discussions of the problem and suggested that if certain assumptions can be made about the form of the source spectrum, then the directional information in the HRTF can be recovered. For example, they argued that if the second derivative of the source spectrum is locally flat, good to excellent localization performance can be realized by a mechanism that computes the second derivative of the monaural input spectrum and matches that to stored representations of the second derivative of the direction-dependent monaural HRTF magnitude spectrum.

Because there are few if any data that provide a clear indication of whether the monaural solution or the interaural solution is correct, there continues to be some ambiguity in the literature. For example, different emphases on this issue can be seen in the discussion of the physical cues by Shaw (Chapter 2, this volume) as compared to the discussion by Duda (Chapter 3, this volume), and in the discussions of the psychophysical data by Middlebrooks (Chapter 4, this volume) and Butler (Chapter 5, this volume) as compared to the discussion by Wightman and Kistler (Chapter 1, this volume).

In the research described here, we used a neural-network-based model to examine whether there is sufficient information in a monaural representation of the stimulus, or in an interaural representation of the stimulus, to achieve sound localization performance comparable to that observed in a typical sound localization experiment. In our approach we use the neural network in a role much like that played by an ideal detector in other modeling efforts. That is, we constrain the stimulus representation available to the neural network, train the neural network to localize sounds based on this representation, and determine whether the asymptotic performance (assumed to be near optimal) of the network is comparable to that observed for a human listener. If the performance of the network is as good as, or better than, that of the human, this indicates that the stimulus representation is sufficient to mediate human sound localization.

A number of previous efforts have used neural-network-based models to examine spatial hearing (e.g., Palmieri, Datum, Shah, and Moiseff, 1991; Neti, Young, and Schneider, 1992; Backman and Karjalainen, 1993; Middlebrooks, Clock, Xu, and Green, 1994). However, these studies differ from the approach reported here in one or more of the following ways: (1) The analyses were based on nonhuman data, (2) the performance of models was not directly compared to the performance of actual subjects, or (3) the performance of models based on monaural information was not directly compared to the performance of models based on interaural information.

In this chapter, the stimuli are filtered with the HRTFs of a particular human subject and, in contrast to previous studies, the performance of the model is directly compared to the performance of that same subject under similar stimulus conditions. The effectiveness of monaural and interaural representations of the stimulus information is compared.

I. MODEL IMPLEMENTATION

The models investigated here were composed of two stages: a preprocessing stage and a neural-network stage. Several simplifying decisions were made in these initial investigations. The preprocessing stage provided a very crude depiction of the auditory periphery, the effects of internal noise, and the representation of interaural information within the central auditory system. The neural-network stage was intended to provide a powerful, but easily realized, pattern classifier to map the relation between the stimulus information (at the output of the preprocessing stage) and the spatial location of the source. Issues related to computational efficiency and issues concerning the similarity of these models to actual neural structures were not emphasized.

A. Preprocessing stage

Depending on the experimental question to be addressed, the preprocessing stage provided some combination of the monaural spectra, the interaural difference spectrum, and the broadband interaural time difference as input to the neural-network stage. Figure 1 shows a block diagram of the preprocessing stage. A 20-μs click served as the input signal. To simulate the acoustic effects of the torso, head, and pinnae, the signal was filtered with the HRTFs of subject SDO from Wightman and Kistler (1989a). The HRTFs corresponded to 144 virtual locations, surrounding the subject in azimuth (24 azimuths in 15° increments) and ranging from –36° to +54° in elevation (6 elevations in 18° increments).[1]

As Colburn and Durlach (1978) emphasized, the performance of any binaural model is critically dependent on the assumed form of the internal noise. For our investigations, each point on the filtered waveforms in the left channel and the right channel was multiplied by a normally distributed gain factor and subjected to a normally distributed delay, in a manner similar to that for the Equalization–Cancellation (EC) model (Durlach, 1963). The jitters in the left and right channels were independent. The standard deviation of the amplitude jitter was 0.25 and the standard deviation of the time jitter was 20 μs. [These values were chosen fairly arbitrarily; the amplitude jitter is equal to the value suggested by Colburn and Durlach (1978), based on fitting the EC model to the detection data; the time jitter is smaller than the value they suggested for the detection data, 100 μs, and perhaps slightly larger than would be needed to fit the lateralization data.]

The broadband cross-correlation function was computed between the jittered waveforms in the left and right channels. The interaural time difference, ITD, was estimated as the delay corresponding to the maximum of this cross-correlation function.

As a crude approximation of the filtering at the auditory periphery, a 1024-point fast Fourier transform was applied to the jittered waveforms in each channel, and the monaural spectra, LEFT(f) and RIGHT(f), were obtained by computing the logarithm of the energy in each of 22 rectangular quarter-octave bands, ranging in frequency from 0.375 to 17.0 kHz. A 22-point interaural difference spectrum, ILD(f), was computed as the difference between LEFT(f) and RIGHT(f).

B. Neural-network stage

Three-layer feed-forward neural networks were trained with back propagation (Rumelhart, Hinton, and Williams, 1986) to determine the location of virtual sound sources based on particular input representations of the stimuli. The

[1]Negative and positive elevations lie below and above the horizontal plane, respectively.

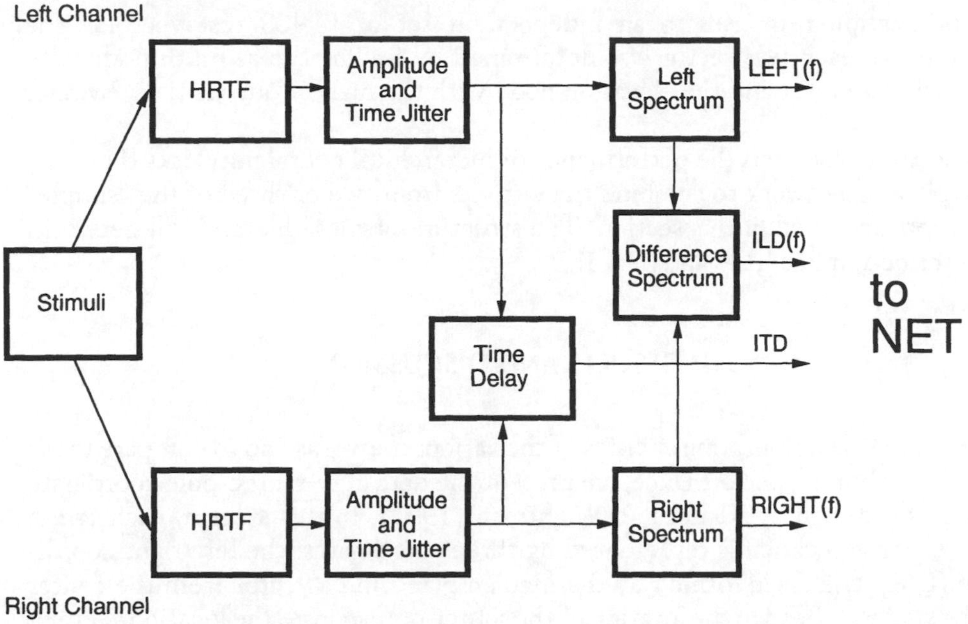

FIG. 1. Block diagram of the preprocessing stage.

neural-network stage included 1 to 23 input nodes, depending on the specific input representation; each input node corresponded to the energy at the output of one of the monaural or interaural spectral bands, or to the ITD. Each input was normalized by subtracting the expected value of that input and dividing by the estimated standard deviation of that input. (This operation placed the input values near the most sensitive range of the nodes.)

The networks contained 50 hidden nodes. Preliminary observations indicated that inferior network performance was sometimes obtained with a smaller number of hidden nodes and that a larger number of hidden nodes did not appreciably improve performance. Each hidden node computed a weighted sum of the output levels from all of the input nodes. The output level of each hidden node was determined by passing this sum through a logistic activation function.

The 30 output nodes corresponded to the 24 possible azimuths and the 6 possible elevations. Similar to the hidden nodes, each output node computed a weighted sum of the output levels from all of the hidden nodes and passed that sum through a logistic activation function to set its own output (activation) level.

The networks were trained, with the back-propagation algorithm from the Neural Shell package (Kuttuva, Little, Chen, and Ahalt, 1991), to turn on one output node indicating the azimuth of the sound source (i.e., 1 of the 24 azimuth nodes), to turn on a second output node indicating its elevation (i.e., 1 of the 6 elevation nodes), and to turn off all of the other output nodes. A learning rate of 0.0625 was used. Networks were trained for 50 epochs, with 100 presentations from each of the 144 virtual source locations within each epoch (i.e., 14 400 training vectors). Network weights were adjusted after the presentation of each training vector. The network performance reported here describes the accuracy of localization responses to an independent set of 14 400 test vectors. The response to each test vector was determined by finding the azimuth node with the highest output and the elevation node with the highest output (i.e., "winner take all").

We also considered the performance of hierarchical neural networks that used an arbitrator network to combine the outputs from two or three of the "simple" networks specified in this section. The structure of these hierarchical networks is described in Sec. II.C and Sec. II.E.

II. RESULTS AND DISCUSSION

To examine the localization abilities of the various networks and to compare those abilities to human performance, we present the data in the three-pole coordinate system described by Kistler and Wightman (1992). In this system, each target and response location is represented by three coordinates: the left/right coordinate (L/R), the angle formed by the median plane and a vector from the center of the subject's head to the location of the source or response (the location vector); the front/back coordinate (F/B), the angle between the frontal plane and the location vector; and the up/down coordinate (U/D), the angle between the horizontal plane and the location vector. Kistler and Wightman argued that the accuracy of the L/R coordinate of the subject's judgment is likely to depend on the quality of the interaural information (i.e., broadband interaural time differences and interaural level differences), whereas the accuracy of the F/B and U/D coordinates is likely to depend on spectral modulations introduced by the pinnae.

A. Human subject

Figure 2 shows the localization judgments of subject SDO (from the study of Wightman and Kistler, 1989b), replotted in the three-pole coordinate system. The results are for the condition in which SDO listened to stimuli filtered through her own HRTFs (i.e., the same HRTFs we are using in the present study) and presented through headphones. On each trial, the stimulus could arrive from any of 72 virtual locations, surrounding the subject in azimuth and ranging from −36° to +54° in elevation. Performance in the L/R, F/B, and U/D dimensions is shown in the left, middle, and right panels, respectively. Ideal performance in each panel would be represented by all of the points falling on the positive slope diagonal. As can be seen, SDO's performance in the L/R dimension is quite good, although she has a tendency to underestimate the laterality of the sounds. SDO's performance is not as accurate in the F/B dimension, as indicated by the greater spread around the positive slope diagonal. Also note that she makes some front-to-back and back-to-front reversals, that is, points falling in the lower-right and upper-left quadrants of the panel, respectively. The U/D coordinate of SDO's judgments is fairly variable, and she has a systematic tendency to overestimate the elevation of the target.

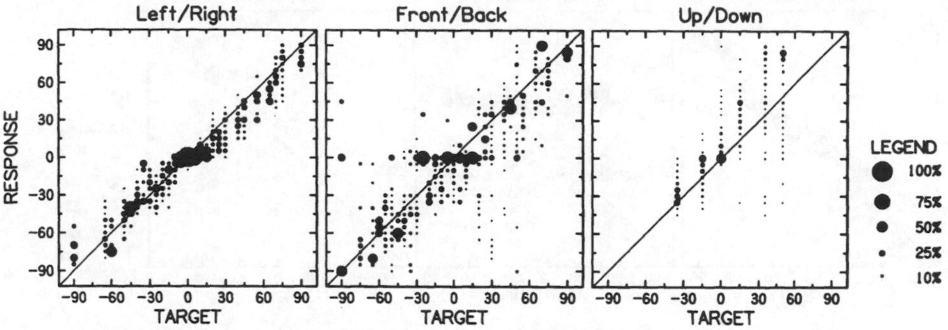

FIG. 2. Scatter plots showing the responses of subject SDO. In each panel the response angle is plotted as a function of the target angle. The size of each symbol indicates the proportion of responses in each 5°-wide target angle bin that fell within each 5°-wide judgment angle bin. Results for the left/right, front/back, and up/down dimensions are shown in the left, middle, and right panels, respectively.

B. Networks receiving only interaural cues

Traditional models of sound localization have emphasized the importance of interaural difference cues for determining the location of a sound source. In particular, interaural time differences have received considerable attention in both the empirical and theoretical literatures. Figure 3 shows the performance of a neural network that received only one input, the ITD. As can be seen, this network performs quite well in the L/R dimension, but performs very poorly in the F/B and U/D dimensions, where there is essentially no relation between the judgment and target angles. These results are compatible with the arguments of Woodworth (1938) and Mills (1972) that the ITD is sufficient to limit the set of possible source locations to the points on the surface of a cone whose central axis is the interaural axis (a "cone of confusion"; because the actual source locations in our experiment lie on the surface of a partial sphere, the ITD constrains the set of locations to two arcs). However, the ITD is not sufficient to determine which point on the cone was the actual locus of the sound source.

To quantify the performance differences between the human subject and the model, we computed the rms error between the judged and target angles in each dimension. Figure 4 shows these rms errors for subject SDO (the dashed horizontal lines) and for the ITD-only network (the open bars). These rms errors indicate that the ITD-only network actually performs slightly better than subject SDO in the L/R dimension, but much worse than SDO in the F/B and U/D dimensions.

Based on the arguments of Woodworth (1938) and Mills (1972), we might conclude that interaural level differences would lead to a similar pattern of results. Note, however, that Woodworth only considered narrowband stimuli. Because we use broadband stimuli, spectral modulations introduced by the torso, head, and pinnae create interaural level differences that vary as a function of frequency. This pattern of interaural level differences would be expected to change if the sound source is moved to a new location on the same cone of confusion and thus may provide sufficient information to determine the F/B and U/D coordinates

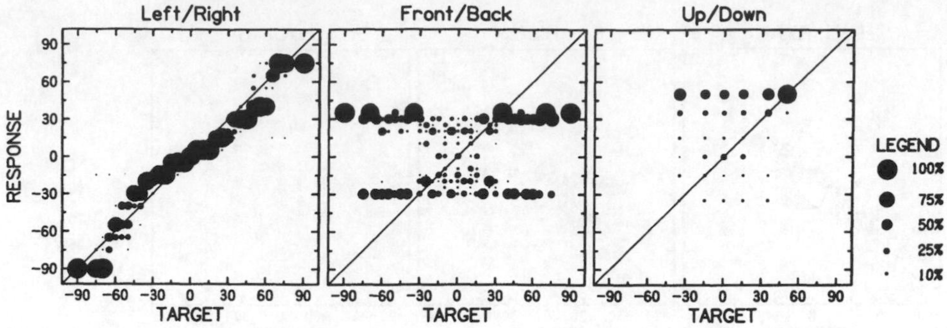

FIG. 3. Scatter plots showing the responses of the ITD network. Other details are as in Fig. 2.

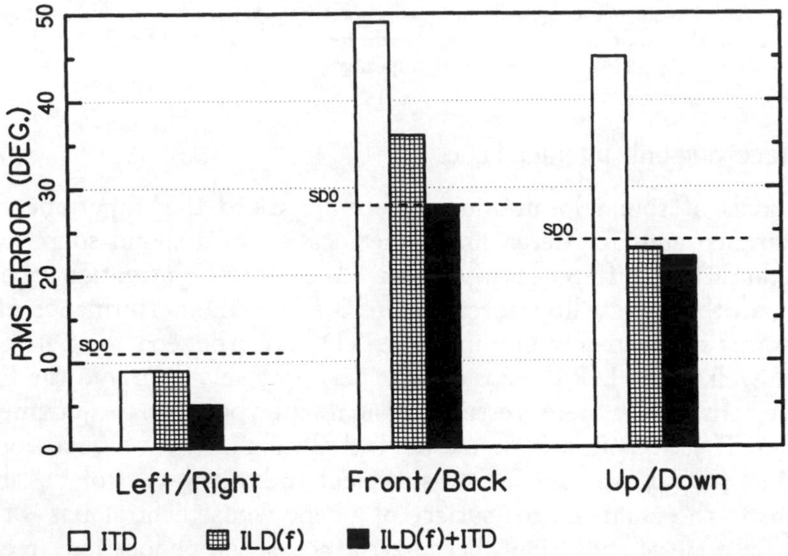

FIG. 4. Root mean square error for subject SDO (dashed lines), the ITD network (open bars), the ILD(f) network double-hashed bars), and the ITD + ILD(f) network (solid bars), in the left/right, front/back, and up/down dimensions.

of the sound source (e.g., see Duda, Chapter 3, this volume). Comparing the ITD network (open bars) to the ILD(f) network (double-hashed bars) in Fig. 4 indicates that, as expected, the two networks achieve similar performance in the L/R dimension; however, the interaural difference spectrum provides much better information about the F/B and U/D dimensions. Performance for this ILD(f) network is slightly better than that for subject SDO in both the L/R and U/D dimensions; however, performance in the F/B dimension is still worse than that for the human subject.

Somewhat surprisingly, providing both the ITD and the ILD(f) as inputs to the network substantially improves performance in the F/B dimension. As shown by the solid bars in Fig. 4, performance for this ITD + ILD(f) network is better in all three dimensions than performance for the ITD network, the ILD(f) network, or the human subject. Scatter plots showing the responses of the ITD + ILD(f) network can be seen in Fig. 5. Even though the rms errors for this model are similar to those for subject SDO, some systematic differences in the pattern of responses can be seen. Although SDO tended to underestimate the laterality of the source, the model shows little if any tendency to underestimate laterality. Although SDO makes more front-to-back reversals than back-to-front reversals (21% and 9%, respectively), the model makes approximately equal numbers of front-to-back and back-to-front reversals (12% and 13%, respectively). Finally, the model does not show the systematic tendency to overestimate the elevation of the signal that was observed for subject SDO (note, however, that the model could not respond with elevations above +54° or below −36°; SDO was not similarly constrained).

These results indicate that interaural cues provide sufficient information to produce performance comparable to that observed for the human subject. However, the analyses thus far do not demonstrate that interaural information is necessary to achieve human-like performance.

C. Networks receiving only monaural cues

Figure 6 shows the performance of a network that receives only RIGHT(f) (i.e., the monaural spectrum for the right ear) as input. As can be seen, performance looks roughly comparable to that observed for the ITD + ILD(f) network. Comparing the rms error for the RIGHT(f) network (open bars) in Fig. 7 and the ITD + ILD(f) network (solid bars) in Fig. 5 indicates that the net receiving only monaural information is worse in the L/R dimension, but better in the F/B and U/D dimensions. Moreover, the RIGHT(f) network achieves performance similar to or better than the human subject in all three dimensions.

Note, however, that the performance of the RIGHT(f) network in the L/R dimension is much better on the right side of the head. No similar asymmetry is seen for the human subject. Obviously, even if the human subject ignores interaural cues, she still has two monaural channels as potential sources of information and might, for example, base her judgment on the ear receiving the stronger signal, thereby reducing any asymmetries in her responses.

We next consider the performance of a model that receives input from both ears, but cannot utilize interaural time differences or interaural level differences. To construct such a network, we first trained two networks, like those previously

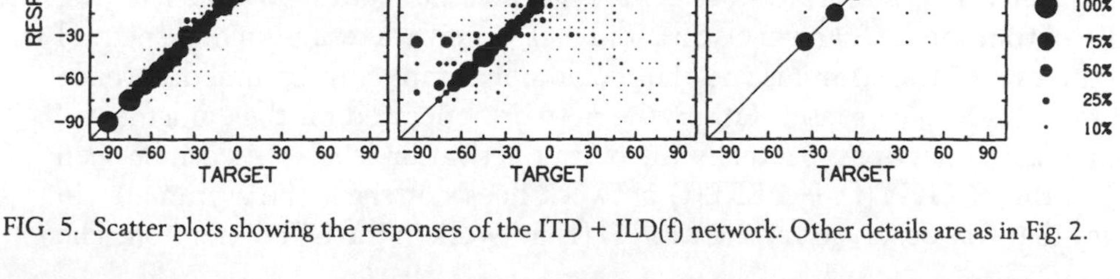

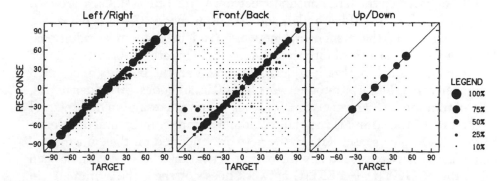

FIG. 5. Scatter plots showing the responses of the ITD + ILD(f) network. Other details are as in Fig. 2.

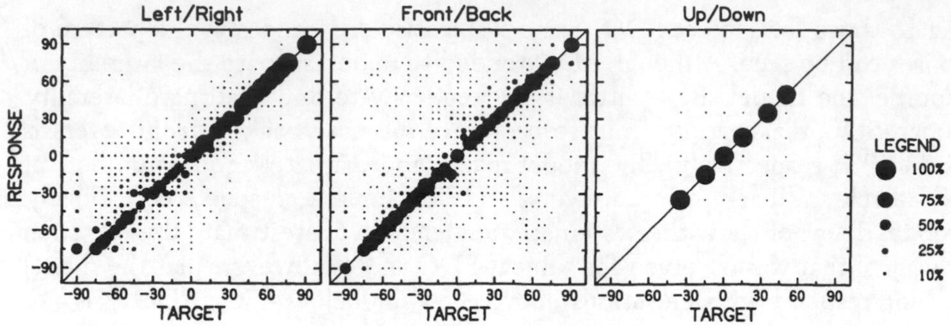

FIG. 6. Scatter plots showing the responses of the RIGHT(f) network. Other details are as in Fig. 2.

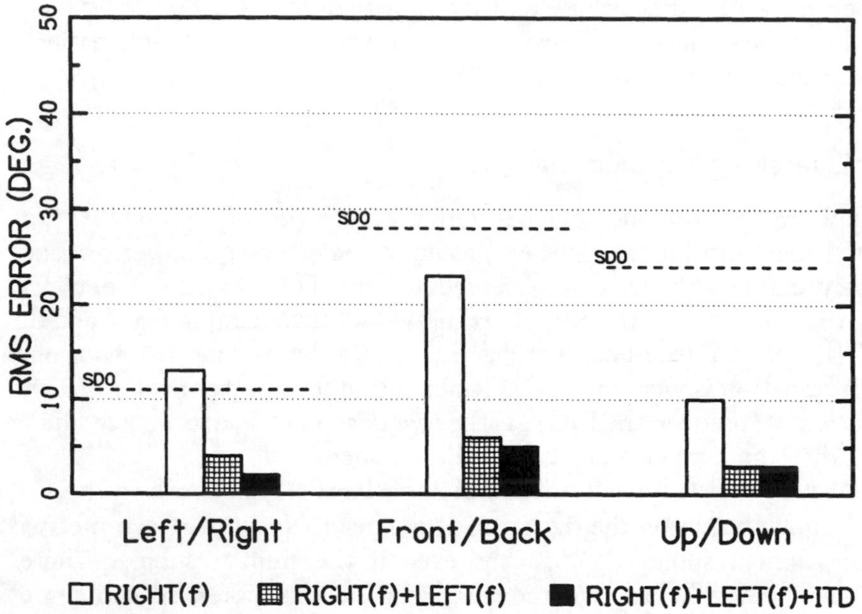

FIG. 7. Root mean square error for subject SDO (dashed lines), the RIGHT(f) network (open bars), the RIGHT(f) + LEFT(f) (double-hashed bars), and the RIGHT(f) + LEFT(f) + ITD network (solid bars), in the left/right, front/back, and up/down dimensions.

described, to localize sounds based on the right monaural spectrum alone, RIGHT(f), or based on the left monaural spectrum alone, LEFT(f). Each network had 22 input nodes, 50 hidden nodes, and 30 output nodes. After training, we fixed the weights in these monaural networks and used them as additional preprocessing stages to a third (arbitrator) network. This arbitrator network was trained to make a final localization judgment, based on the outputs of the two monaural networks. The arbitrator network had 60 input nodes, 50 hidden nodes, and 30 output nodes. This network did not receive a temporal or spectral representation of the stimulus and thus could not compute interaural difference cues in the traditional sense. Rather, the network operated on the "judgments" of the monaural networks (actually the output activation levels). As can be seen in Fig. 8, this RIGHT(f) + LEFT(f) network does not show the asymmetry in accuracy that was observed for the RIGHT(f) network in the L/R dimension. The rms errors for this network (the double-hashed bars in Fig. 7) are smaller in all three dimensions than those for any of the previously described networks or those for the human subject.

D. The influence of spectral variation in the source spectrum

The results described thus far indicate that performance similar to or better than that for the human subject can be achieved by a network that receives only interaural cues [e.g., the ITD + ILD(f) network] or by a network that is precluded from using interaural cues [e.g., the hierarchical RIGHT(f) + LEFT(f) network that combines judgments from the RIGHT(f) network and the LEFT(f) network]. It is important to note, however, that the comparisons between these models and the human subject may not be entirely fair. Although the networks "listened" to broadband flat-spectrum click stimuli, subject SDO listened to broadband noise that had been spectrally scrambled. That is, in the study of Wightman and Kistler (1989b), the level of the noise target was randomized independently in each third-octave band over a ±20-dB range. Such scrambling of the source spectrum would not be expected to alter the performance of the neural networks that use interaural cues [e.g., the ITD + ILD(f) network], because the preprocessing is linear and changes in the source spectrum will have equal effects at both ears (i.e., no effect on interaural differences). However, scrambling the spectrum might be expected to have a large effect on the performance of the networks that are based on monaural cues [e.g., the RIGHT(f) network and RIGHT(f) + LEFT(f) network].

Figure 9 shows the rms error for the "monaural" networks, when the stimuli have been spectrally scrambled over a ±20-dB range. For computational efficiency, we implement the scrambling in the preprocessing stage rather than in the stimulus. That is, we scrambled the level of each of our quarter-octave bands at the output of the filter bank. This operation does not affect either the interaural difference spectrum or the computation of the interaural delay. However, as can be seen, scrambling the spectrum dramatically degrades the performance of both the RIGHT(f) network (open bars) and the RIGHT(f) + LEFT(f) hierarchical network (double-hashed bars). That is, when the source spectrum is scrambled

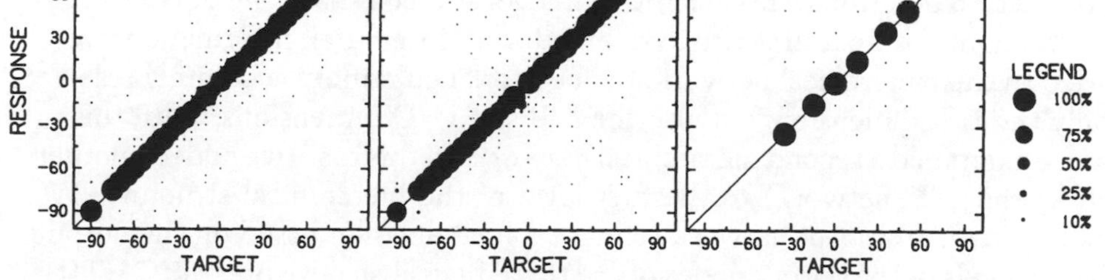

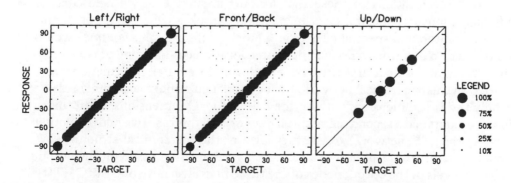

FIG 8. Scatter plots showing the responses of the RIGHT(f) + LEFT(f) network. Other details are as in Fig. 2.

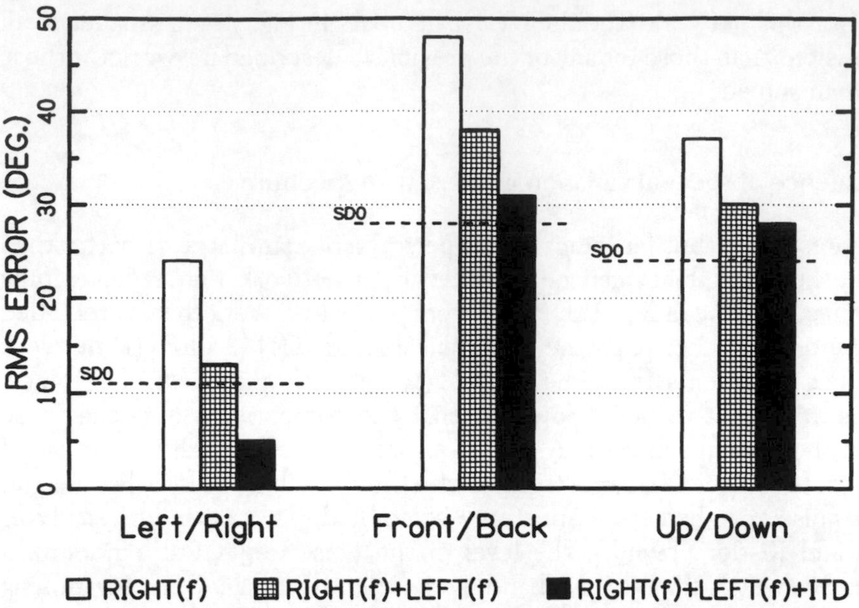

FIG. 9. Root mean square error for subject SDO (dashed lines), the RIGHT(f) network (open bars), the RIGHT(f) + LEFT(f) network (double-hashed bars), and the RIGHT(f) + LEFT(f) + ITD network (solid bars), in the left/right, front/back, and up/down dimensions. The spectra at the output of the preprocessing stage have been scrambled over a ±20 dB range.

in a manner similar to that implemented by Wightman and Kistler (1989b), the networks based on monaural information alone fail to achieve human-like performance.

E. A network based on both monaural and interaural cues

Not even the strongest advocate for the role of monaural spectral cues in human sound localization would deny that interaural cues also play a role. Thus, the models described in Sec. II.C are somewhat unrealistic at the outset. As a number of authors have suggested, a more reasonable view might be that broadband interaural difference cues are used to determine the L/R coordinate, limiting the set of possible locations to those that lie on the surface of a single cone of confusion; monaural spectral cues (e.g., Middlebrooks, 1992, Chapter 4, this volume) or interaural spectral cues (e.g., Duda, Chapter 3, this volume) would then be used to determine the specific source location on that cone of confusion. Thus, it might be that if sufficient broadband interaural information were provided to the hierarchical network, the network could more accurately resolve not only the L/R dimension, but also the F/B and U/D dimensions. With this in mind, we examined a second hierarchical network. In this case, we added another network (the ITD network) to the first level of the hierarchical structure. We then allowed an arbitrator network to make a final decision based on the output activation levels of the output nodes of the three first-level networks [RIGHT(f), LEFT(f), and ITD]. This arbitrator network had 90 input nodes, 50 hidden nodes, and 30 output nodes. Performance for this network is shown by the solid bars in Fig. 7 and Fig. 9. With no spectral scrambling (Fig. 7), this RIGHT(f) + LEFT(f) + ITD network performs better in all three dimensions than the human subject or any of the other networks. With spectral scrambling (Fig. 9), performance for this network is substantially degraded, but it is still better than the hierarchical RIGHT(f) + LEFT(f) network without ITD. The RIGHT(f) + LEFT(f) + ITD network performs slightly better than the human in the L/R dimension and slightly worse than the human in the F/B and U/D dimensions (recall that although the ITD-only network is not affected by the scrambling, by itsef it performs poorly in both the F/B and U/D dimensions). So, even with ±20-dB spectral scrambling, this RIGHT(f) + LEFT(f) + ITD network performs quite well and approaches the performance of the human subject.

III. SUMMARY AND CONCLUSION

The analyses presented here indicate that sufficient information is present in the interaural representation of the stimuli (i.e., interaural cues only) to achieve localization performance comparable to that observed for the human subject. Without spectral scrambling (i.e., with a flat source spectrum) the LEFT(f) + RIGHT(f) network can also achieve very good performance based on only monaural information. However, when the spectrum was scrambled on a band-by-band basis (a manipulation similar to that used in the experiments of Wightman and Kistler, 1989b), performance was much worse. The detrimental effects of scrambling the source spectrum can be offset to some degree by also providing information about the interaural time delay. This RIGHT(f) + LEFT(f) + ITD network, although not as good as the ITD + ILD(f) model, performed at levels near those for the human subject, even with spectral scrambling.

The fact that the ITD + ILD(f) model achieves good localization performance, which is similar to that of human subjects, is compatible with the results of Palmieri *et al.* (1991) and Duda (Chapter 3, this volume), who showed excellent performance based on only interaural information, using HRTFs from a simulated barn owl and a human subject (and also KEMAR), respectively. The good performance observed for the RIGHT(f) + LEFT(f) + ITD model is compatible with the view of Middlebrooks (1992, Chapter 4, this volume) and others that broadband interaural differences are used to determine the cone of confusion from which the stimulus arrived and that spectral modulations introduced by the pinnae are used to distinguish among sources on that cone of confusion.

Although these data indicate that a purely monaural model is inadequate to predict localization with randomized source spectra, they are unable to distinguish between two distinct classes of models: those utilizing monaural spectral cues and those utilizing interaural spectral cues. It is clear that a more constraining data set is needed. To distinguish between these models, our future modeling efforts will consider the localization of stimuli masked by noise and will examine the responses of both humans and models to specific stimulus waveforms that are likely to produce systematic localization errors.

ACKNOWLEDGMENTS

The authors thank Drs. Frederic Wightman and Doris Kistler of the University of Wisconsin for providing the HRTFs and the response information for subject SDO. We also thank Drs. Janet Weisenberger and Scott Isabelle for reading and commenting on earlier drafts of this chapter. This work was sponsored by the Air Force Office of Scientific Research (AFOSR-91-0289, F49620-95-1-0106, and AFOSR Task 2313V3) and the National Institutes of Health (DC-00786).

REFERENCES

Backman, J., and Karjalainen, M. (**1993**). "Modelling of human directional and spatial hearing using neural networks," Proc. ICASSP **93**, I125–I128.

Butler, R. A. (**1978**). "An analysis of monaural displacement of sound in space," Percept. Psychophys. **41**, 1–7.

Colburn, H. S., and Durlach, N. I. (**1978**). "Models of binaural interaction," in *Handbook of Perception, Vol. IV, Hearing*, edited by E. C. Carterette and M. P. Friedman (Academic Press, New York), pp. 467–518.

Durlach, N. (**1963**). "Equalization and cancellation theory of binaural masking-level differences," J. Acoust. Soc. Am. **35**, 1206–1218.

Kistler, D., and Wightman, F. (**1992**). "A model of head-related transfer functions based on principal components analysis and minimum-phase reconstruction," J. Acoust. Soc. Am. **91**, 1637–1647.

Kuttuva, S., Little, T., Chen, P., and Ahalt, S. (**1991**). *Neural Shell V3.0* (Department of Electrical Engineering, Ohio State University, Columbus).

Middlebrooks, J. C. (**1992**). "Narrow-band sound localization related to external ear acoustics," J. Acoust. Soc. Am. **92**, 2607–2624.

Middlebrooks, J. C., Clock, A. E., Xu, L., and Green, D. M. (**1994**). "A panoramic code for sound location by cortical neurons," Science **264**, 842–844.

Mills, A. W. (**1972**). "Auditory localization," in *Foundations of Modern Auditory Theory, Vol. II*, edited by J. V. Tobias (Academic Press, New York), pp. 303–348.

Neti, C., Young, E. D., and Schneider, M. H. (**1992**). "Neural network models of sound localization based on directional filtering by the pinna," J. Acoust. Soc. Am. **92**, 3140–3156.

Palmieri, F., Datum, M., Shah, A., and Moiseff, A. (**1991**). "Sound localization with a neural network trained with the multiple extended Kalman algorithm," in *Proc. Int. Joint Conf. on Neural Networks*, Seattle, WA, pp. I125–I131.

Rumelhart, D., Hinton, G., and Williams, R. (**1986**). "Learning internal representations by error propagation," in *Parallel Distributed Processing, Vol. 1, Foundations*, edited by D. E. Rumelhart and J. L. McClelland (MIT Press, Cambridge, MA), pp. 318–362.

Wightman, F., and Kistler, D. (**1989a**). "Headphone simulation of free-field listening. I: Stimulus synthesis," J. Acoust. Soc. Am. **85**, 858–867.

Wightman, F., and Kistler, D. (**1989b**). "Headphone simulation of free-field listening. II: Psychophysical validation," J. Acoust. Soc. Am. **85**, 868–878.

Woodworth, R. S. (**1938**). *Experimental Psychology* (Holt, New York), pp. 520–525.

Zakarauskas, P., and Cynader, M. S. (**1993**). "A computational theory of spectral cue localization," J. Acoust. Soc. Am. **94**, 1323–1331.

Part VIII

Development of Spatial Hearing

Chapter 27

Development of Binaural and Spatial Hearing in Infants and Children

Ruth Y. Litovsky
Boston University and Eaton Peabody Laboratory,
Massachusetts Eye and Ear Infirmary,
Boston, Massachusetts

Daniel H. Ashmead
Vanderbilt University Medical Center, Nashville, Tennessee

(Received February 1994; revised January 1995)

Auditory localization is a fundamental ability enabling animals to find the sources of environmental sounds. It is only since the early 1980s that auditory development has been studied systematically. In the present chapter we review recent trends in research on development of auditory localization in humans. The primary focus is on three specific issues. First, we discuss sensitivity to interaural sound localization cues. Recent work has shown that sensitivity to interaural cues is well developed during early infancy, in contrast to sound localization in free field, which matures relatively slowly. The implications of this discrepancy are discussed. Second, recent studies, which have utilized infants' reaching behavior in the dark to measure distance perception, have shown that infants are capable of discriminating distance by 6 months of age. We discuss which cues may be relevant to infants for this task. Finally, developmental changes in the precedence effect (a sound localization phenomenon related to suppression of echoes) are reviewed. The precedence effect develops slowly during infancy and childhood, and to the extent that it may reflect integrity of central auditory processing, it may be useful for detection of auditory deficits. A general theme evident in this review is that developmental work, like work with adults and lab animals, shows sound localization to be very much an active, constructive process on the part of the listener.

INTRODUCTION

Auditory localization is a fundamental ability enabling animals to find the sources of environmental sounds. Although visual development in humans and other species has been intensively studied for several decades, the development of hearing, especially spatial hearing, has received attention only since about 1980. Convincing demonstrations that infants orient their eyes (Crassini and Broerse, 1980) and head (Muir and Field, 1979) toward sound as soon as they are born led to a considerable amount of research on the development of hearing, including sound localization in infants and young children. Much of this research, especially with newborns, was reviewed by Clifton (1992). In the present chapter we briefly review recent trends in this research and then focus primarily on work reported during the past five years or so, concentrating on three specific issues: sensitivity to interaural sound localization cues, auditory distance perception, and the precedence effect (a sound localization phenomenon related to suppression of echoes). A general theme evident in this review is that developmental work, like work with adults and lab animals, shows sound localization to be very much an active, constructive process on the part of the listener.

I. OVERVIEW OF DEVELOPMENTAL TRENDS

Perhaps the most obvious and compelling sign that someone can localize a sound is that they shift their gaze toward its source. Measures of head and eye turning toward sound sources have figured prominently in studies of the development of sound localization. The first experimental demonstration that newborn infants look toward sound sources was Wertheimer's (1961) brief report. Although newborn sound localization had been included in standardized neonatal assessment scales (Brazelton, 1973), several attempts at demonstrating this ability experimentally showed mixed results (Butterworth and Castillo, 1976; McGurk, Turnure, and Creighton, 1977). Muir and Field (1979) showed convincingly that newborns turn their heads toward the hemifield containing a sound source, a finding that was soon confirmed by Clifton, Morrongiello, Kulig, and Dowd (1981). Although reliable, this orienting response was not extremely robust, for it occurred on only half the trials (with no response at all on most other trials), and its latency was typically around 8 s. Several reviews of these findings are available (Clarkson, 1992; Clifton, 1992; Muir, 1982, 1985; Muir and Clifton, 1985).

Although newborns do orient toward sound sources, the development of sound localization is far from complete at that age. Both the newborns' posture and state are important factors in their tendency to orient to sounds. In addition, stimulus characteristics are important; for example, newborns do not orient toward brief, transient sounds (see Clarkson, 1992), and conspecific stimuli are especially effective in eliciting a response in many species, including kittens (Olmstead and Villiblanca, 1980), puppy dogs (Ashmead, Clifton, and Reese, 1986), guinea pigs (Clements and Kelly, 1978), chicks (Gottlieb, 1981), and humans (Zelazo, Brody, and Chaika, 1984). But the apparent immaturity of newborns' sound localization is most dramatically illustrated by the nonmonotonic developmental trend of head orienting toward sound sources. The head orienting response is reliably elicited from the newborn period up to about 1 month, but then it "disappears" from about 1 to 3 months, reappearing at approximately 4 months (Field, Muir, Pilon, Sinclair, and Dodwell, 1980; Muir, Clifton, and Clarkson, 1989), at which time the latency of 4-month-olds' head turns toward sounds is about a second or less, much more brisk than that of newborns. Although several explanations for this "U-shaped" developmental function have been offered (including the onset of habituation and visual competition; Muir, 1985; Muir *et al.*, 1989), the most widely accepted hypothesis focuses on maturation of central (cortical) mechanisms (Muir and Clifton, 1985). According to this theory, the newborn head-orienting response is one of the neonatal subcortically mediated reflexes and is suppressed by about 1 month. It is assumed to be replaced by "higher" cortical mechanisms for sound localization, which are more volitional and less reflexive in nature. This interpretation implies that the starting point for experimental analysis of "mature" sound localization begins at around 4 months after birth. Further evidence supporting this interpretation is that at about 4 months infants first localize precedence-effect sounds (described in Sec. II.C) in an adult-like manner. Also, starting at 4–5 months of age, head turning can be used as an operant response in discrimination learning paradigms for studying auditory development. The most commonly used technique was first described by Moore, Thompson, and Thompson (1975), known as visual reinforcement audiometry. Infants are trained to turn their heads in response to an auditory stimulus and are reinforced with attractive mechanically activated toys.

A common method used to study sound localization in infants is the minimum audible angle task, which measures the smallest change in the position of a sound that can be reliably detected. The task involves a reliably correct two-alternative discrimination (usually right vs. left), where the infant's response is scored by an adult observer who watches the infant and is blind to the actual position of the sound sources. For the horizontal dimension, or azimuth, the minimum audible angle is about 1° in adults (e.g., Mills, 1958; Perrott, Marlborough, Merrill, and Strybel, 1989), and this level of precision has also recently been reported for 5-year-old children (Litovsky, 1996). During infancy, there is a dramatic change in the horizontal minimum audible angle (see Table 1 for a summary), from about 20° to 25° at 4 months to less than 5° at 18 to 24 months (Ashmead, Clifton, and Perris, 1987; Ashmead, Davis, Whalen, and Odom, 1991; Litovsky, 1996; Morrongiello, 1988a; Morrongiello and Rocca, 1990). Thus, even after "mature" sound localization emerges at about 4 months after birth, there is a protracted developmental period during which precision of localization improves. This led us to speculate on whether developmental changes in sensitivity to binaural cues for sound localization are involved, as well as on a need for perceptual calibration of the cues. These issues are particularly interesting when we consider that during this period infants' heads grow rapidly, so that the correspondence between binaural cue values and sound directions changes (Ashmead *et al.*, 1991; Clifton, Gwiazda, Bauer, Clarkson, and Held, 1988). We discuss these issues in Sec. II.A.

Finally, although the minimum audible angle identifies the limits of auditory spatial acuity, it is not very instructive regarding the development of localization accuracy, by which we mean knowing precisely where a sound is coming from. Little work has been done on the accuracy of sound localization by infants or young children, primarily due to behavioral measurement problems. Infants cannot be instructed to indicate where they perceive a sound source to be, so we

TABLE 1: Developmental trend in minimum audible angle (MAA) thresholds.

Age	*MAA*	*Study*
5 months	19.8°	Ashmead *et al.* (1991)
6 months	12.0°	Morrongiello (1988a)
	14.5°	Ashmead *et al.* (1991)
	19.0°	Ashmead *et al.* (1987)
9 months	12.0°	Morrongiello (1988a)
12 months	8.0°	Morrongiello (1988a)
	9.4°	Ashmead *et al.* (1991)
15 months	6.0°	Morrongiello (1988a)
18 months	4.0°	Morrongiello (1988a)
	5.6°	Litovsky (1996)
5 years	1.5°	Litovsky (1996)
Adult	1–2°	Mills (1958)
	< 1°	Perrott *et al.* (1989) Hartmann and Rakerd (1989) Litovsky and Macmillan (1994)

must rely on easily elicited behaviors. An obvious candidate is accurate head orientation, or pointing toward a sound source. Morrongiello and Rocca (1987) used this task and reported that accuracy improved across the age range of 6 to 18 months. However, this measure relies on a motor system, which is undergoing its own set of changes, and there are measurement problems such as uncertainty about when during a trial to assume that the infant has "decided" where the sound source is. For these reasons, we think head turning is better suited as a measure in discrimination tasks than as a graded response showing localization accuracy. Another candidate measure for investigating localization accuracy is reaching, which is inherently a spatially goal-directed behavior. This measure is discussed later under the topic of auditory distance perception.

II. SELECTED ISSUES IN THE DEVELOPMENT OF BINAURAL HEARING

In this section we review in more detail three topics that have been extensively studied in recent years.

A. Sensitivity to interaural sound localization cues

As was noted earlier, the precision of sound localization as measured by the minimum audible angle improves dramatically during infancy. Infants around 4 months old do not discriminate whether the position of a sound source changed leftward or rightward of midline unless the position change is larger than about 20°. In contrast, 18- to 24-month-olds discriminate changes smaller than 5°, and unpracticed adults and 5-year-olds easily discriminate a change of 1–2°. An obvious question is whether these age-related changes reflect improvements in perceptual sensitivity to the underlying sound localization cues. For localization in the horizontal plane, the principal cues are interaural time differences and interaural level differences. Here we summarize findings on infants' sensitivity to these cues and discuss them in the context of plasticity in the mapping of specific cue values onto actual locations of sound sources.

Only a handful of studies exist on infants' sensitivity to interaural difference cues, using presentation of signals independently to the two ears. Bundy (1980) tested infants aged 8 and 16 weeks, presenting them with large reversals in interaural time differences (+300 μs to –300 μs) or interaural level differences (+6 dB to –6 dB).

Although the infants did not look in the direction of the leading or louder sounds, a measure of overall looking time at a visual display suggested that they detected the reversals in cue values. This trend was significant on both cues for the 16-week-olds, but only on the interaural time difference cue for the 8-week-olds, showing that young infants can detect changes in interaural cues presented under dichotic conditions. However, interpretation of the study is complicated by several methodological factors, including the possibility that the level difference discrimination may not have been interaural, but could have been mediated by perception of the change in level at a single ear. Thus, the question of whether infants actually utilize interaural time and interaural intensity cues to lateralize sounds remained unanswered.

In a more recent study, Ashmead *et al.* (1991) reported sensitivity to interaural time differences in infants aged 16, 20, and 28 weeks. The procedure was similar to a minimum audible angle test, in that it involved a discrimination paradigm with a diotic click train (sounds through two earphones at the same time and presumably perceived at the "center" of the head), followed by a dichotic click train (with an interaural time difference favoring one ear). An observer, who watched the infant but did not know the side of the leading sound, voted as to which side contained the leading sound, mostly based on the infant's eye and head movements. Correct votes resulted in reinforcement for the infant, consisting of a pleasant video/audio show on the appropriate side. Threshold values for interaural time discrimination were in the range of 50–75 μs for all age groups (compare with typical adult values of 10–20 μs). For these same ages, the actual interaural time differences that correspond to minimum audible angles obtained in free field are much greater, about 100–140 μs, as shown in Fig. 1 (from Ashmead *et al.*, 1991, Fig. 3). Interestingly, Gray and Jahrsdoerfer (1986) reported a similar pattern with adult aural atresia patients who underwent surgery to eliminate the atresia. These patients had fairly precise postoperative interaural time discrimination but poor free-field sound localization.

The results from Ashmead *et al.* (1991) imply that sensitivity to interaural time differences *per se* is remarkably good during the early stages in the development of sound localization. We later discuss why it is unlikely that this sensitivity is a limiting factor in the development of sound localization precision. In a second study, Ashmead, Grantham, Murphy, Tharpe, Davis, and Whalen (1996) investigated 6-month-old infants' sensitivity to interaural level differences. They also

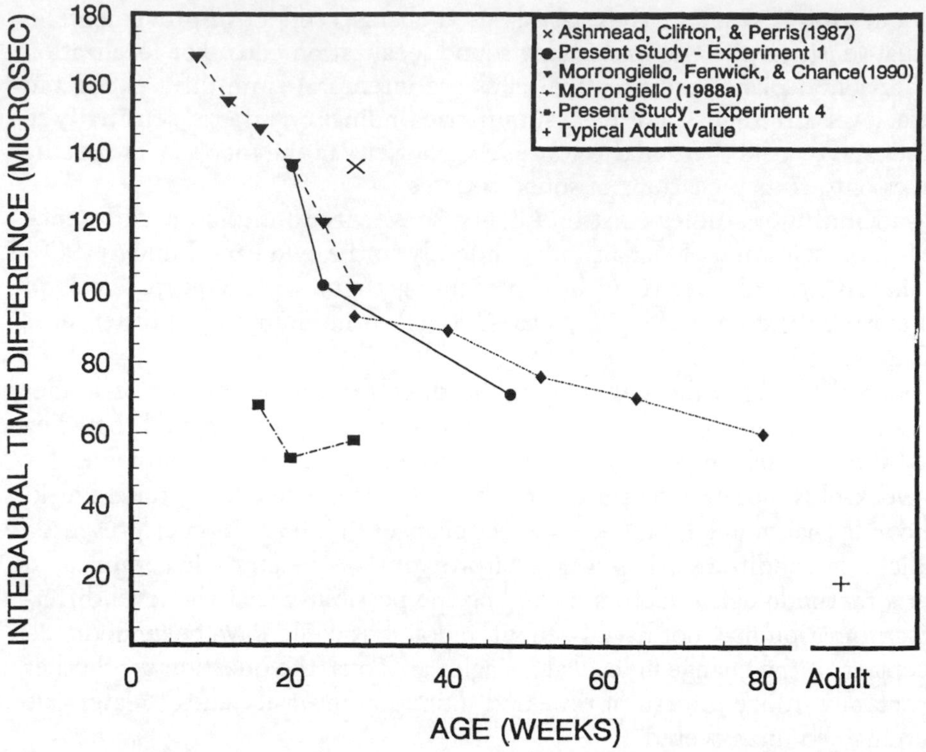

FIG. 1. Thresholds for interaural time discrimination from Ashmead *et al.* (1991, Experiment 4, triangles) compared to interaural time differences corresponding to free-field minimum audible angles (other symbols) as a function of age.

used a discrimination paradigm in which an interaural level difference of zero in the stimulus was changed abruptly to a level difference favoring one ear (overall signal levels were varied to preclude a monaural basis for the discrimination). Infants had thresholds of about 7 dB, which is considerably higher than typical adult values of 0.5 dB or so. We cannot say precisely how this 7 dB threshold value relates to the actual interaural level differences infants experience naturally in the free field. However, it seems likely that the angle changes in free field experienced by 6-month-olds with the minimum audible angle correspond to interaural level differences that are much smaller than 7 dB. This would suggest that interaural level differences probably play a minimal role in localization precision at the age of 6 months. This claim is further supported by another experiment from this study, showing that 6-month-olds did not tend to mislocalize sounds when the input to one ear was artificially attenuated, a manipulation that should have mainly affected interaural level differences. One possibility that remains to be ruled out is potential competition between interaural cues, because at all interaural level differences the interaural time difference was zero, which might have dominated over the level cue.

At this point, the findings on sensitivity to interaural cues suggest that infants are more sensitive to interaural time differences, but less sensitive to interaural level differences, than we would predict from their free-field minimum audible angles. The discrepancy between the free-field and dichotic studies led us to conclude that age-related changes in the precision of free-field sound localization cannot simply be accounted for by sensitivity to interaural time and level cues. A more likely explanation is the need for ongoing recalibration of the relation between values of sound localization cues and the actual locations of sound sources in the environment. If recalibration is constantly occurring in the nervous system, it would be reasonable to have a period during which localization is not as precise as the underlying cue sensitivity might otherwise allow, particularly if the cue values themselves are changing rapidly. Two groups of investigators have called attention to the large, rapid changes in interaural cue values that must occur during human infancy (Ashmead *et al.*, 1991; Clifton *et al.*, 1988). In neither case were the interaural cues measured directly. Rather, interaural time differences at various ages during development were estimated from measures of head circumference, using a widely accepted spherical model (Woodworth, 1938). Figure 2 shows estimated interaural time differences expressed as a percentage of a typical adult value. The rapid change in this cue value during the first year after birth suggests that if the sound localization system "locked on" to very precise relationships between cue values and sound source directions during that time, the recalibration process would be rather burdensome. An alternative approach would be to permit considerably more error in sound localization during the time when

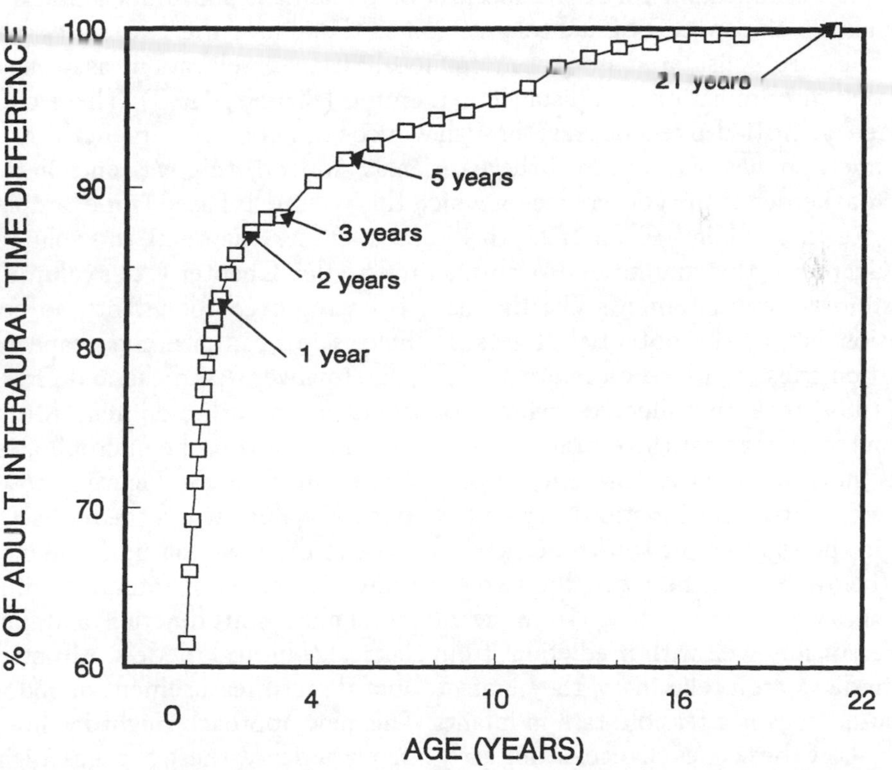

FIG. 2. Interaural time difference as a proportion of adult (21 years) interaural time difference, for ages from birth to 21 years, estimated from head circumference data of Eichorn and Bayley (1962). (From Ashmead *et al.*, 1991, Fig. 4.) Reprinted with permission.

head growth is causing rapid changes in both the binaural (interaural time, level, and spectral differences) and monaural (spectral) cues. If we consider that during infancy an organism need merely direct its attention in the general direction of important events, then from an evolutionary perspective it may be adequate to have a relatively crude sound localization system.

Evidence for this idea comes from neurophysiological work conducted in several laboratories. The superior colliculus of a variety of species is thought to contain a spatial map based on a conglomeration of visual, auditory, and somatosensory inputs (King and Moore, 1991). In fact, auditory neurons in the superior colliculus of a newborn guinea-pig are very broadly tuned for sound location, but within a few weeks after birth a refined map of auditory space emerges (Withington-Wray, Binns, and Keating, 1990). This space map, which has a similar developmental trend in other species as well, is known to be susceptible to altered localization cues during experience. For example, in barn owls (Knudsen and Knudsen, 1985) and ferrets (King, Hutchings, Moore, and Blakemore, 1988) reared with an occluded ear (producing abnormal binaural cues), normal visual input plays a major role in alignment of the auditory space map. This finding supports the notion that auditory localization is one aspect of a complex array of sensorimotor functions that play a role in an organism's ability to find the source of a sound.

In addition to interaural differences in time and level, a third interaural cue thought to be important for sound localization in humans and other animals is differences in the spectra of auditory stimuli as they enter the two ear canals. These cues are considered important for localization of elevation, as well as front/back discrimination and distance perception (Blauert, 1983). These cues have been quantified in recent years through work on direct measurement through probe microphones inserted into the ear canals. Indeed, this was one of the dominant themes at the conference on which this volume is based (for example, Brugge, Reale, and Hind, Chapter 22, this volume; Duda, Chapter 3, this volume; Shaw, Chapter 2, this volume; and Wightman and Kistler, Chapter 1, this volume). No systematic measurements like this have been reported for infants, so our conclusions about the potential effects of changes in head size and shape on localization cues are based on indirect evidence. However, Ashmead and Grantham (1994) recently collected preliminary data on a 1-month-old infant. Measurements were made at the entrance to each ear canal using probe microphones. Sounds (noise bursts) were presented from 45° or 60° to the right. Figure 3 shows the interaural transfer functions, which have positive values when the levels are higher in the right ear; it shows a clear difference in the low- to mid-frequency range (below 8 kHz) between the two locations. Estimates of interaural time differences were also computed from the interaural phase shift function, and they agree reasonably well with predictions from classical spherical models. Although these findings are preliminary, they indicate that direct measurement of sound localization cues is a feasible task in infants. This new approach might facilitate studying how these cues change during early infancy and how these changes might be related to the development of binaural hearing. These measurements might also be useful in studying the development of sound localization in the vertical plane, which has received little attention (Morrongiello, 1988b).

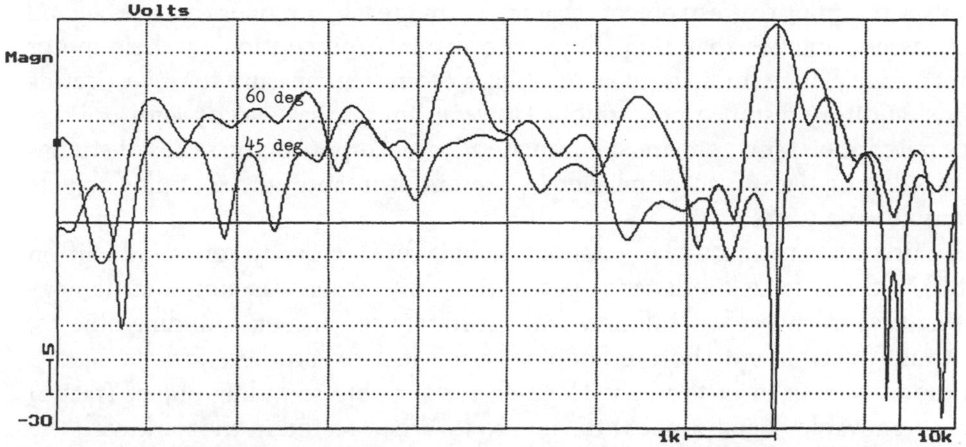

FIG. 3. Interaural transfer functions for sound sources at 45° and 60° to the right, in a 3-week-old infant. Positive values indicate a higher sound level in the right ear than in the left ear. (Ashmead and Grantham, 1994)

In summary, sensitivity to interaural cues that presumably underlie free-field sound localization is well developed early in life and is therefore probably not the limiting factor for developmental changes in free-field sound localization. Rather, the need for ongoing recalibration of the relation between cue values and sound locations may play an important role. One approach toward addressing this question is the study of sound localization abilities of congenitally totally blind individuals, because they would have no opportunity for visually based calibration. Unfortunately, we are not aware of any measures of this type performed with acceptable psychoacoustic methods.

B. Auditory distance perception

Sound localization is inherently three-dimensional in that we experience not only the horizontal and vertical directions of a sound but also its distance. Despite this everyday phenomenology, the directional aspects of sound localization have been investigated far more than those related to distance. Indeed, the acoustical bases for auditory distance perception by adults are not well understood. (For reviews, see Coleman, 1962; Blauert, 1983, pp. 116–137. For recent work, see Ashmead, Davis, and Northington, 1995; Little, Mershon, and Cox, 1992; Shaw, McGowan, and Turvey, 1991.) For developmental work on auditory distance perception there is the added question regarding what response measure might veridically reflect an infant's or young child's perceptual experience of distance. In this section we review recent findings on infants' distance perception as measured by their reaching behavior for sound-producing objects.

Anyone who has been around infants knows that they are quite proficient at reaching for objects and successfully grasping them by about 5 to 6 months after birth. A number of studies on visual depth perception have shown that infants make an impressive distinction between objects that are within versus beyond reach (see Yonas and Granrund, 1985, for a review). They display this distinction by only attempting to grasp objects that are within reach, not ones that are beyond reach, which implies that they can relate distance perception to their motor performance. These findings make reaching a promising measure for investigating infants' auditory distance perception. However, in order to study auditory distance perception *per se*, one must eliminate all visual input. In the series of studies discussed next, this was accomplished by presenting infants with sounding objects in complete darkness.

The first systematic study of infants' reaching for sounds, by Perris and Clifton (1988), did not focus on distance perception, but rather was aimed at demonstrating that infants reach willingly and accurately for unseen sounding objects, and thus it established the methodology used in later studies. Infants aged 6 months were trained in the light to reach for a visible sounding object (rattle) with a removable finger puppet attached to it. When tested in the dark with the sounding object placed in any of six directions (separated by 30°), infants touched the objects on their first reaching attempt on 77% of the trials, which was well above chance. Two subsequent studies extended this experimental paradigm to study distance perception. Clifton, Perris, and Bullinger (1991) presented 6-month-olds with sounding objects, 45° to the left or right, either within reach (10 cm from the torso) or beyond reach (100 cm). Infants reached correctly on the majority of the within-reach trials, but they did not attempt to reach at all on most of the beyond-reach trials. This study proved that by 6 months infants can rely on auditory information alone to make a dichotomous distance discrimination. It remained unclear what the effective distance information was. Recently Clifton, Rochat, Robin, and Berthier (1994) measured 6-month-olds' hand movements while reaching for objects in a lighted room, glowing objects in a dark room, and sounding objects in a dark room. They used a motion analysis system that allowed fine-grained measurement of reaching movements. Although infants were less accurate when they could not see the object (third condition just listed), they still showed a smooth deceleration of the hand movement at the end of a reach for a sounding object. Thus, rather than merely swiping at the object, they appeared to have some notion of exactly where it was located. This further reinforces the value of the reaching response as a measure of the accuracy of infants' sound localization.

Litovsky and Clifton (1992) focused on sound pressure level, a distance cue known to be relevant for adults. Sound pressure varies inversely with distance, with a change of approximately 6 dB for every halving or doubling of distance (e.g., see Coleman, 1962). In everyday language, if one assumes a sound to be constant at its source, it would be louder when in close proximity but softer when further away. In the Litovsky and Clifton study, sounds in the near and far positions (15 and 100 cm, respectively) had a natural difference of 7 dB. Unknown to the subjects, the sound pressure from the source (a small loudspeaker) could be manipulated to simulate different distances. All infants first heard and saw the sounding objects in the light, straight ahead, with the natural level cues corresponding to the near and far positions. The infants reached accurately for the near objects on virtually all trials, indicating that the near object was readily contacted. On dark trials the objects were presented 45° to the left or right. For the control group of infants, the near and far objects had their natural sound levels, louder and softer, respectively. The experimental group was presented with inconsistent combinations of sound pressure and distance. On half the near trials the sound was naturally loud, but on the other half it was reduced by 7 dB (measured from the position of the subjects' head). The reverse was true for the far trials, half of which were naturally soft and half increased by 7 dB. As is shown in Fig. 4, all infants reached more for the near than for the far objects, even when the sound pressure was misleading. In other words, the infants were not fooled by the sound pressure manipulation, and they seemed to utilize other distance cues. This contrasted sharply with findings for a group of adults run under similar conditions, who were asked to make verbal judgments about distance. The adults judged the louder objects to be near and the softer objects to be far, regardless of the actual distance. In summary, by 6 months infants have a basic capacity for discriminating between sound-producing objects that are within versus beyond reach. Because infants do not appear to rely on one distance cue, sound pressure, as strongly as adults, it seems likely that there is considerable experience-dependent development in the processes underlying auditory distance perception. In terms of methodology, the infants' reaching behavior has turned out to be a valuable tool for studying auditory distance perception.

C. The precedence effect

The precedence effect refers to an auditory illusion that occurs when two similar sounds are presented from different locations at slightly different times. Only one sound image is actually "heard," and its perceived location is dominated by the leading sound. This phenomenon is most intriguing because the second sound is above threshold, and, if presented in isolation, would be localized at its correct position. Thus, the nervous system plays an interesting trick on our experience of the world by actively shutting out prominent auditory information. Although this effect is typically studied in the laboratory by using two discrete sound sources (different loudspeakers), the underlying auditory processes presumably work in everyday life to suppress our perception of sounds reflected off surfaces such as walls, ceilings, and floors (Blauert, 1983, pp. 222–237; Zurek, 1987). Several chapters in this book focus on the precedence effect in human adults; thus we refrain from reviewing that literature in depth and focus on developmental aspects of the precedence effect.

A fundamental finding on the development of the precedence effect is that it does not appear to be present during early infancy. This has been demonstrated for human newborns (Clifton *et al.*, 1981) and young dogs (Ashmead *et al.*, 1987). In both studies, infants or puppies were presented with sounds from loudspeakers located 90° to the left and right. On "single-source" trials, the sound came from one loudspeaker only. On precedence-effect trials, the sound came from both loudspeakers with a 7 ms delay between them. With this delay, adults perceive the sound to emanate entirely from the loudspeaker having the leading sound.

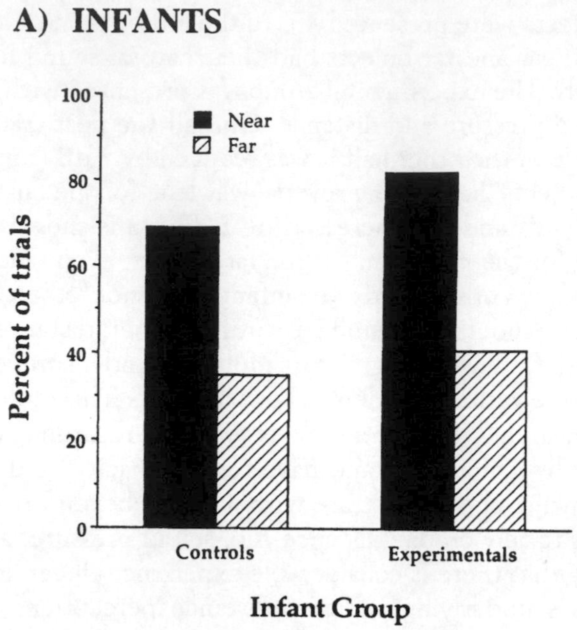

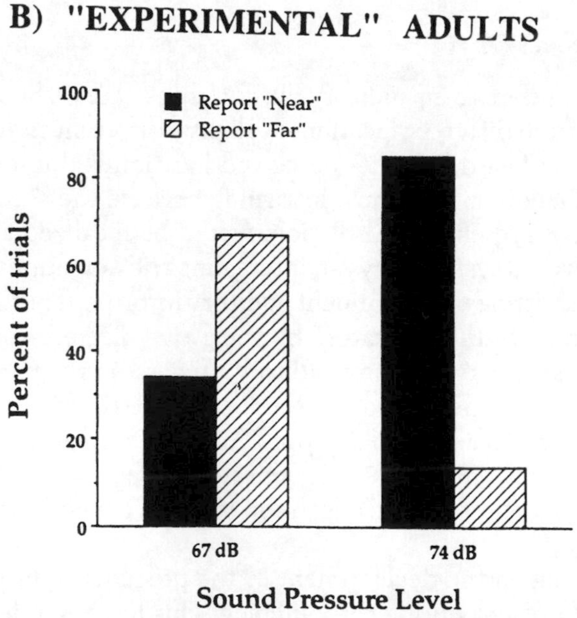

FIG. 4. (A) Infant data: Percent of Near and Far trials on which 6-month-olds reached in the dark for a sound producing object. Both Control and Experimental infants (see text for explanation) reached significantly more on the Near than on the Far trials. (B) Verbal reports of Experimental adults are plotted for Near–Far trials combined as a function of sound pressure level. Independent of the actual distance of the sound-producing object, on trials where the stimulus was at 67 dB SPL, the predominant judgment was "Near," whereas on the trials where the stimulus was at 74 dB SPL, the predominant judgment was "Far." (From Litovsky and Clifton, 1992.) Reprinted with permission.

Finally, on control trials the sound came from both loudspeakers at the same time. Infants and puppies turned reliably toward the active loudspeaker on single source trials, but on precedence-effect trials they typically did not turn at all (which was also the case on control trials). Despite the fact that infants and puppies "perk up" when they hear sounds in the precedence-effect configuration, they do not appear to localize the sound image toward the leading speaker, as adults do. It has since been shown that infants turn toward the leading side of precedence-effect sounds beginning at about 4 months of age (Muir *et al.*, 1989). The timing of appearance of the precedence effect is tightly coupled with the age at which head-turning toward single source sounds reappears (discussed earlier).

Another aspect of the precedence effect that has been investigated developmentally is the echo threshold. When the delay between the leading and lagging sounds is longer than the echo threshold, directional information from the lagging sound is no longer suppressed and the listener hears two distinct sounds at their respective locations. For adults, this value is 5–9 ms for clicks, 10–12 ms for noise, 20 ms for speech, and 40 ms for music (see Blauert, 1983, p. 231; Zurek, 1987). The echo threshold changes during development, as shown in Fig. 5. For simple stimuli such as clicks, the echo threshold is higher at 6 months (25 ms) than at 5 years or in adulthood (about 12 ms) (Clifton, 1985). For more complex stimuli of longer duration the echo threshold also differs somewhat between 5 years (30 ms) and adulthood (25 ms) (Morrongiello, Kulig, and Clifton, 1984). Burnham,

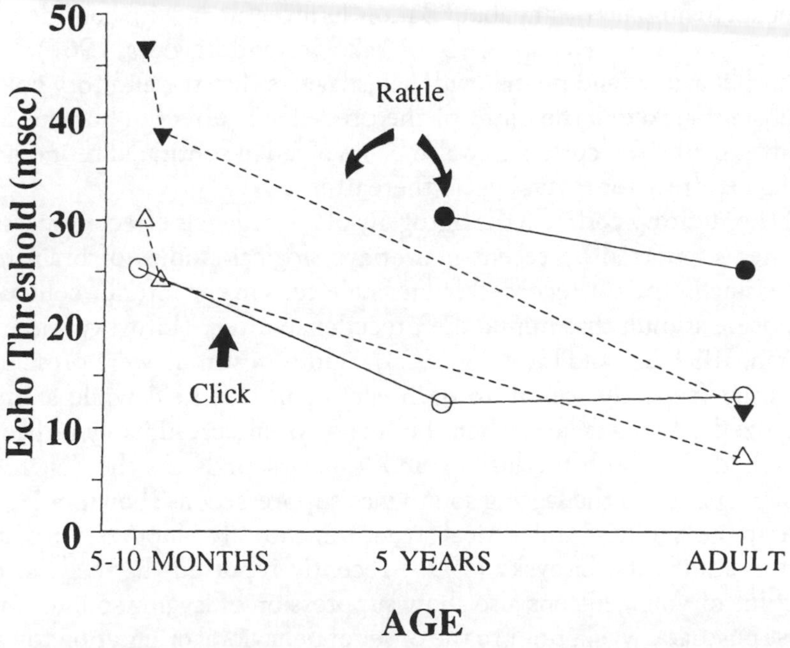

FIG. 5. Echo thresholds for precedence-effect stimuli are compared at three age ranges for two different stimulus types. For click stimuli, echo thresholds decrease between 5–10 months and 5 years, but not between 5 years and adult. Thresholds also decrease with age for the rattle stimulus between all three ages. The difference between click and rattle thresholds is noticeable at all ages as well. (Circles were redrawn with permission from Morrongiello *et al.*, 1984; triangles were redrawn with permission from Burnham, *et al.*, 1993.) Reprinted with permission.

Taplin, Henderson-Smart, Earnshaw-Brown, and O'Grady (1993) recently suggested that echo thresholds change developmentally as a function of maturation from time of conception, rather than from experience since birth. They found that the echo thresholds of preterm infants tested about 9.5 months after birth were more similar to full-term infants matched for conceptual age than to full-term infants matched for age since birth. Taken together, developmental studies of the echo threshold indicate that there is considerable age-related change in processing of sounds presented in the precedence-effect configuration, even beyond the period of infancy. It is possible that in everyday listening situations, infants and young children may experience more difficulty than older children and adults at suppressing "extra" sounds in reverberant settings. In fact, it has been shown that children's speech comprehension (Neuman and Hochberg, 1983) and sound localization (Besing and Koehnke, 1995) are diminished in a reverberant environment.

Developmental studies of the precedence effect have been motivated by the idea that it reflects maturation of the central auditory system (Clifton, 1985; Muir *et al.*, 1989). This is based on neurobehavioral evidence that cats without an intact auditory cortex do not localize stimuli presented in a precedence-effect configuration toward the leading sound (Cranford and Oberholtzer, 1976; Cranford, Ravizza, Diamond, and Whitfield, 1971; Whitfield, Cranford, Ravizza, and Diamond, 1972). Also, people with temporal-lobe lesions show deficits in performance on precedence-effect tasks (Hochster and Kelly, 1981). Finally, myelination of auditory cortex in humans begins about 3 months after birth, with considerable development up to 2 years (Dekaban, 1970; Yakovlev and Lecours, 1967). This convergence of behavioral and neural evidence suggests that the auditory cortex may play a substantial role in the onset of the precedence effect in humans at 3 to 4 months after birth. The cortex may also be involved in continued refinement of the precedence effect for several years thereafter.

The role of the auditory cortex in the ontogeny of precedence-effect processing has been further supported by recent neurophysiological studies of brainstem auditory processing in the cat recorded from single cells in the inferior colliculus of adult cats, using stimuli that mimic the precedence effect (Litovsky and Yin, 1993, 1994; Yin, 1994; Yin and Litovsky, 1993). Auditory stimuli were presented either dichotically (separate stimuli to each ear) or in free-field while animals were anaesthetized. At long delays, when the "echo" would presumably be heard, most cells responded to both the leading and lagging sounds. As the delay was decreased, the response to the lagging sound was suppressed, as shown in Fig. 6. Thus, the inferior colliculus, a subcortical structure, codes for suppression of the lagging sound in adult cats. Litovsky (1994) recently reported that cells in the inferior colliculus of young kittens also show suppression of lagging sounds, even within the first postnatal week, prior to the onset of behavioral orientation toward sounds (Olmstead and Villiblanca, 1980). Representative data from 14 kittens are compared with those of 14 adult cats in Fig. 7. The echo thresholds for individual cells (delay at which response to the lagging sound was suppressed by 50%) ranged from about 2 to 70 ms in both adult cats and kittens; however, the overall suppression was significantly weaker in kittens than cats, with respective

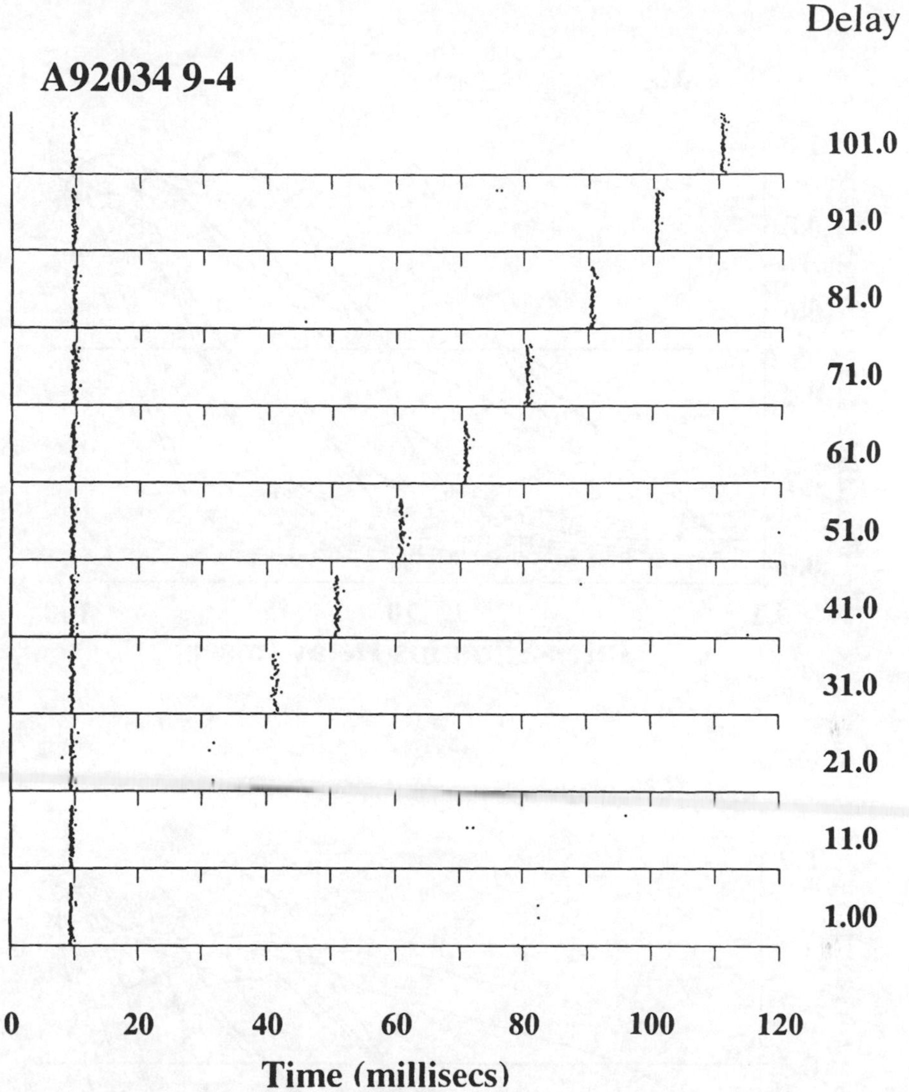

FIG. 6. The response of one neuron in the inferior colliculus of the cat. Stimuli were two dichotic pairs of clicks, both with an interaural time delay favoring the contralateral ear, where the neuron responded vigorously to the stimuli. Each set of responses represents 50 trials, with the second click pair being delayed relative to the first one. The delay was varied from 1 to 101 ms. For all delays the neuron responded to the first click pair. For delays of 41 to 101 ms the neuron also responded to the second, or lagging, click pair reliably. However, the response to the lagging stimulus was decreased at 31 ms, and disappeared at delays of 21, 11, and 1 ms (Litovsky, 1994).

means of 22.6 and 36 ms. These findings suggest that in cats the initial stages of echo suppression are processed in the inferior colliculus. The difference in mean thresholds might suggest that precedence is somewhat weaker early in life. The fact that IC neurons show precedence at all, and that newborns do not display the behavior, suggests that there is a decoupling between the capacity of the young nervous system to encode stimuli so as to suppress lagging sounds and its capacity to manifest this coding in terms of orienting toward the leading sound. The exact

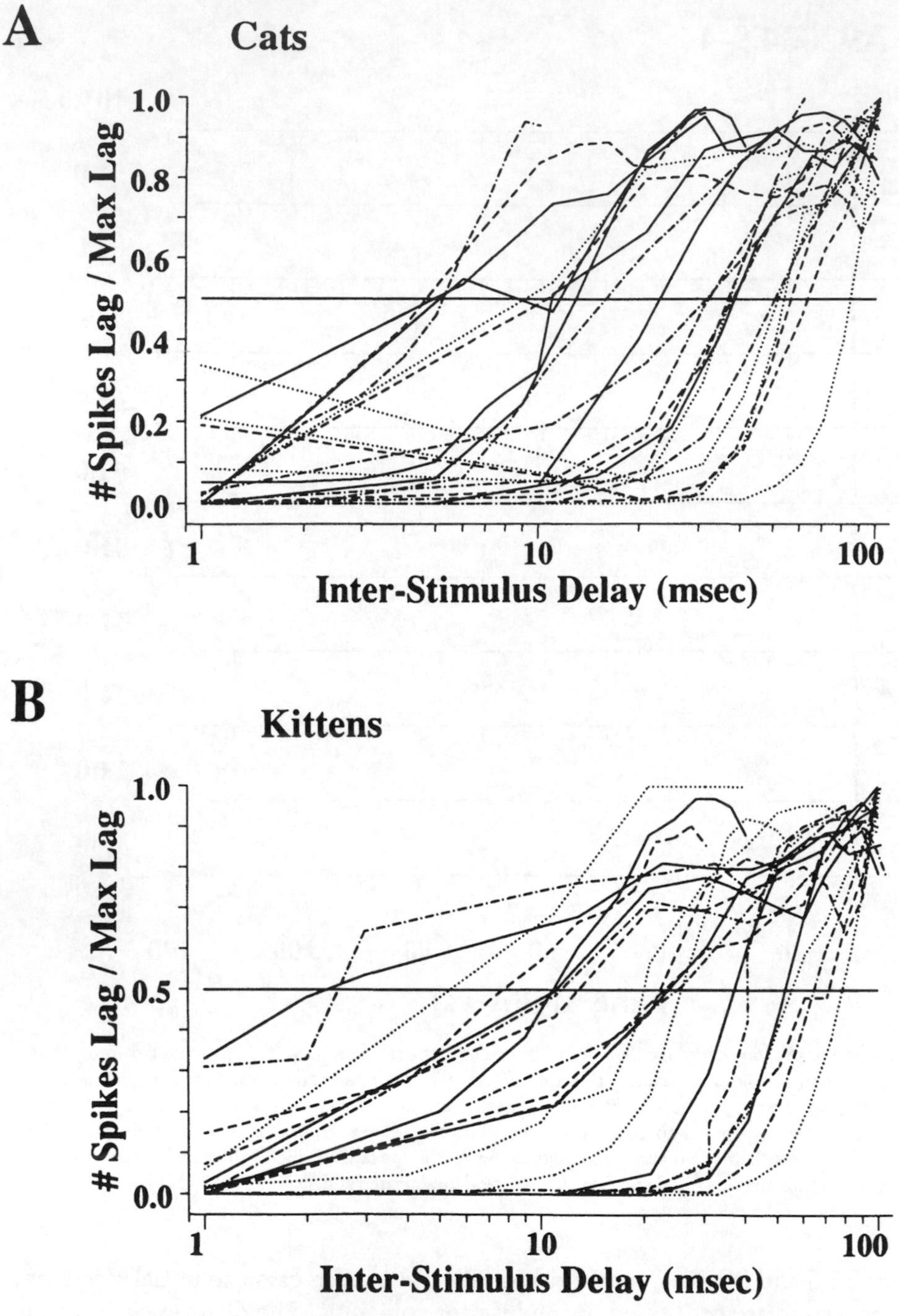

FIG. 7. The stimulus configuration from Fig. 6 was presented to a population of neurons in both adult cats and young kittens (ages 8–28 days). For each neuron the response to the lagging stimulus at every delay was divided by the "maximal lagging" response of the neuron, that is, response to the second click pair at the longest delay. Representative neurons from (A) 14 adult cats and (B) 14 kittens were then plotted as a function of delay. The point at which the functions recover to 50% of the maximal response is marked by a horizontal line in each figure, with means of 32 ms and 29 ms in cats and kittens, respectively (Litovsky, 1994).

role of the auditory cortex (or other cortical areas for that matter) in enabling overt behavioral localization is not known, but it may involve linking information that is encoded about auditory events with appropriate behavioral responses. This pattern of results is similar to the one described in Sec. II.A, where we noted that infants appear to have good sensitivity to interaural time differences yet rather imprecise sound localization. The act of localizing a sound source and making an appropriate response involves much more than sensitivity to the underlying acoustic cues.

In addition to the auditory cortex, development in other brain regions may influence some aspects of the development of the responses to precedence-effect stimuli. For example, the frontal cortex is considered critical for suppression of distracting stimuli (Guitton, Buchtel, and Douglas, 1985; Luria, 1973), an idea that has attracted much attention in recent work on perceptual-motor and cognitive development (Diamond, 1990). There is also growing evidence that the precedence effect has a cognitive component. In particular, there is a "buildup" of echo suppression while adults listen to sounds presented repeatedly (Clifton and Freyman, Chapter 12, this volume). Clifton, Freyman, Litovsky, and McCall (1994) suggested that this buildup effect depends on the listener's expectations of what types of sounds could be echoes. Presumably adults "size up" the acoustic properties of a room over the course of 5 or 10 s and adjust their suppression to the appropriate range of delays for that room. The buildup effect has not been studied in infants, but to the extent that it reflects an active cognitive process, perhaps dependent on experience, we would not expect to see it in early infancy. Supporting evidence for this prediction is that the buildup effect has not been observed in the activity of single cells in the cat inferior colliculus (Litovsky and Yin, 1993, 1994; Yin, 1994; Yin and Litovsky, 1993), so it appears to be mediated at a higher level.

So far, we have discussed work on the precedence effect as measured with echo thresholds, which reflect whether the sounds are heard as a single event or as two separate events. An alternative approach is to consider how the lagging sound can exert an effect on the leading one. This happens for sounds that are within the delay range of the precedence effect. For adults, sound localization is affected strongly by the presence of lagging sounds, even though the lagging sounds are not heard as separate auditory events (Hartmann, 1983; Rakerd and Hartmann, 1985; Litovsky and Macmillan, 1994; Wallach, Newman, and Rosenzweig, 1949). That is, we hear one "fused" sound whose perceived location is determined by a weighted sum of the leading and lagging stimuli (Shinn-Cunningham, Zurek, and Durlach, 1993). Litovsky (1996) measured this effect in 18-month-olds, 5-year-olds, and adults, using a version of the minimum audible angle procedure described earlier. Each subject was tested in three conditions. One was the classic single source test in which a sound location changed from midline to the left or right. In the other conditions the stimuli were in pairs that satisfied conditions of the precedence effect. In both conditions the first sound on each trial was a single source sound from midline. In the "lead discrimination" condition, the shifted stimulus consisted of a leading sound from the left or right and a lagging sound from midline. For "lag discrimination" the opposite occurred;

the leading sound was from midline and the lagging sound was from the left or right. The data are summarized in Fig. 8. At all ages the minimum audible angle was greater (worse) in the lead discrimination condition than the single source condition, suggesting that the lagging sound at midline interfered with the precision of localization. However, the discrepancy between the conditions decreased with age, suggesting either that the "pulling" by the lag sound is smaller in older people, or that suppression of the lagging sound is stronger in older people. In addition, at all ages lag discrimination minimum audible angles were greater (worse) than both lead discrimination and single source, but they decreased significantly between 18 months, 5 years, and adults, suggesting that with increased age listeners' ability to extract subtle directional information from an "inaudible" echo improves.

These findings can be related to the work with newborns' responses to precedence-effect stimuli discussed earlier (Clifton *et al.*, 1981). In that situation, newborns were presented with the leading and lagging stimuli on either side, and they did not orient to the leading sound, but rather, they looked straight ahead (see earlier discussion). It is conceivable that newborns "have" the precedence effect, such that they do not hear the lagging sound separately from the leading sound. However, another aspect of the precedence effect may be very weak. That is, they may be incapable of suppressing the influence of the lagging sound, thus they may perceive one sound whose location is determined almost equally by the lead and lag, and that sound appears near midline. This issue could be investigated by presenting newborns with sounds from symmetrical locations, but no such findings have been reported.

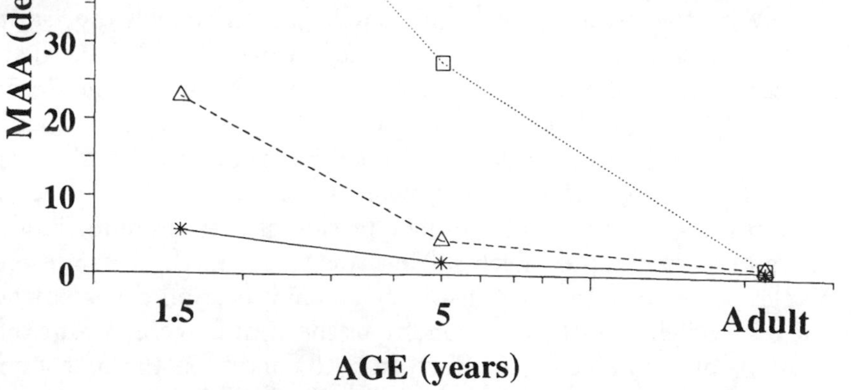

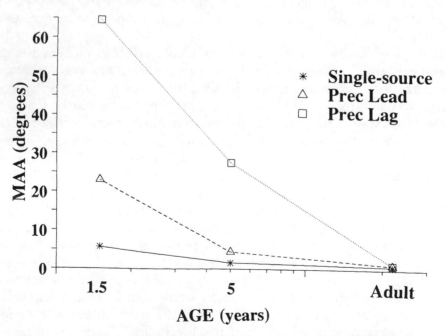

FIG. 8. Minimum audible angle thresholds at 18 months, 5 years, and adult are plotted for three stimulus conditions: single source (asterisks), precedence-lead discrimination (triangles), and precedence-lag discrimination (squares). (From Litovsky, 1995.) Reprinted with permission.

In summary, the precedence effect has proved extremely useful for investigating the development of sound localization. Mature sound localization clearly depends on processes such as the suppression of later arriving sounds. The developmental acquisition of these processes occurs over a time span of at least months and probably years, perhaps requiring considerable auditory experience and cognitive elaboration. To the extent that the precedence effect may reflect integrity of auditory processes, it may also be a useful task for detection of auditory deficits in a clinical setting.

III. SUMMARY

Perhaps the most important general point to emerge from the work described in this chapter is that the development of sound localization is very much a constructive process. Whether it be calibration of changing values of directional cues, utilization of sound level as a cue for distance, or weighting of leading and lagging sounds in the precedence effect, adult-like sound localization seems to be a constructive act on the part of the listener. We have been led to this conviction on the basis of developmental evidence, but it is very much in keeping with recent work on sound localization in adults and laboratory animals, including much of the work described in other chapters of this volume. Localization depends on integrating information across different cues, across frequency regions, and even across time (as listeners and sound sources move).

ACKNOWLEDGMENTS

This work was supported by National Institutes of Health grant DC00078 to Ruth Litovsky, grant HD23191 to D. Ashmead, and grant DC01437 to Fred Bess (with D. Ashmead and D. W. Grantham co-investigators).

REFERENCES

Ashmead, D. H., Clifton, R. K., and Perris, E. E. (1987). "Precision of auditory localization in human infants," Dev. Psychol. **23**, 641–647.

Ashmead, D. H., Clifton, R. K., and Reese, E. (1986). "Development of auditory localization in dogs: Single source and precedence effect sounds," Dev. Psychobiol. **19**, 91–104.

Ashmead, D. H., Davis, D. L., and Northington, A. (1995). "The contribution of listeners' approaching motion to auditory distance perception," J. Exp. Psychol. Hum. Percept. Perform., **21**, 239–25.

Ashmead, D. H., Davis, D. L., Whalen, T., and Odom, R. D. (1991). "Sound localization and sensitivity to interaural time differences in human infants," Child. Dev. **62**, 1211–1226.

Ashmead, D. H., and Grantham, D. W. (1994). "Direct measurement of binaural sound localization cues in a 3–week-old human infant," unpublished observations, Vanderbilt University, Nashville, TN.

Ashmead, D. H., Grantham, D. W., Murphy, W. D., Tharpe, A. M., Davis, D. L., and Whalen, T. A. (1996). "Human infants' spatial hearing: The role of interaural level differences," Child. Dev., submitted.

Besing, J. M., and Koehnke, J. (1995). "Effects of Otitis media on binaural performance in children," Ear Hear., **16**, 220–229.

Blauert, J. (1983). *Spatial Hearing* (MIT Press, Cambridge, MA).

Brazelton, T. B. (1973). *Neonatal Behavioral Assessment Scale* (Spastics International Medical Publications, London).

Bundy, R. S. (**1980**). "Discrimination of sound localization cues in young infants," Child Development **51**, 292–294.

Burnham, D., Taplin, J., Henderson-Smart, D., Earnshaw-Brown, L., and O'Grady, B. (**1993**). "Maturation of precedence-effect thresholds: Full-term and preterm infants," Infant Behav. Dev. **16**, 213–232.

Butterworth, G., and Castillo, M. (**1976**). "Coordination of auditory and visual space in newborn human infants," Perception **5**, 155–160.

Clarkson, M. (**1992**). "Infants' perception of low pitch," in *Developmental Psychoacoustics*, edited by L. A. Werner and E. W. Rubel (American Psychological Association, Washington, DC), pp. 159–188.

Clements, M., and Kelly, J. (**1978**). "Auditory spatial responses of young guinea pigs (*Cavia porcellus*) during and after ear-blocking," J. Comp. Physiol. Psychol. **92**, 34–44.

Clifton, R. K. (**1985**). "The precedence effect: Its implications for developmental questions," in *Auditory Development in Infancy*, edited by S. E. Trehub and B. Schneider (Plenum Publishing, New York), pp. 85–99.

Clifton, R. K. (**1992**). "The development of spatial hearing in human infants," in *Developmental Psychoacoustics*, edited by L. A. Werner and E. W. Rubel (American Psychological Association, Washington, DC), pp. 135–158.

Clifton, R. K., Freyman, R. L., Litovsky, R. Y., and McCall, D. D. (**1994**). "Listeners' expectations about echoes raise or lower echo thresholds," J. Acoust. Soc. Am. **95**, 1525–1533.

Clifton, R. K., Gwiazda, J., Bauer, J. A., Clarkson, M., and Held, R. (**1988**). "Growth in head size during infancy: Implications for sound localization," Dev. Psychol. **24**, 477–483.

Clifton, R. K., Morrongiello, B. A., Kulig, J., and Dowd, J. M. (**1981**). "Newborns' orientation toward sound: Possible implications for cortical development," Child. Dev. **52**, 833–838.

Clifton, R. K., Perris, E. E., and Bullinger, A. (**1991**). "Infants' perception of auditory space," Dev. Psychol. **27**, 187–197.

Clifton, R. K., Rochat, P., Robin, D. J., and Berthier, N. E. (**1994**). "Multimodal perception in the control of infant reaching," J. Exp. Psychol. Hum. Percept. Perform., **20**, 876–886.

Coleman, P. D. (**1962**). "An analysis of cues to auditory depth perception in free space," Psychol. Bull. **60**, 302–315.

Cranford, J., and Oberholtzer, M. (**1976**). "Role of neocortex in binaural hearing in the cat. II: The 'precedence effect' in sound localization," Brain Res. **111**, 225–239.

Cranford, J., Ravizza, R., Diamond, I., and Whitfield, I. (**1971**). "Unilateral ablation of the auditory cortex in the cat impairs complex sound localization," Science **172**, 286–288.

Crassini, B., and Broerse, J. (**1980**). "Auditory-visual integration in neonates: A signal detection analysis," J. Exp. Child. Psychol. **29**, 144–155.

Dekaban, A. (**1970**). *Neurology of Early Childhood* (William & Wilkins, Baltimore).

Diamond, A. (**1990**). "Developmental time course in human infants and infants monkeys, and the neural basis of inhibitory control in reaching" in *The Development and Neural Bases of Higher Cognitive Functions, Vol. 608 Annals of the New York Academy of Sciences*, edited by A. Diamond (New York Academy of Sciences, New York), pp. 637–677.

Eichorn, D. H., and Bayley, N. (**1962**). "Growth in head circumference from birth through young adulthood," Child. Dev. **33**, 257–271.

Field, J., Muir, D., Pilon, R., Sinclair, M., and Dodwell, P. (**1980**). "Infants' orientation to lateral sounds from birth to three months," Child. Dev. **51**, 295–298.

Gottlieb, G. (**1981**). "Roles of early experience in species-specific perceptual development," in *Development of Perception: Psychobiological Perspectives: Vol. 1: Audition, Somatic Perception, and the Chemical Senses*, edited by R. Aslin, J. Alberts, and M. Petersen (Academic Press, New York), pp. 5–44.

Gray, L., and Jahrsdoerfer, R. (**1986**). "Effects of congenital aural atresia on the ability to localize sounds," Otolaryngol. Head. Neck. Surg. **94** (August special issue), 46.

Guitton, D. H., Buchtel, A., and Douglas, R. M. (**1985**). "Frontal lobe lesions in man cause difficulties in suppressing reflexive glances and in generating goal directed saccades," Exp. Brain Res. **58**, 455–472.

Hartmann, W. M. (**1983**). "Localization of sound in rooms," J. Acoust. Soc. Am. **74**, 1380–1391.

Hartmann, W. M., and Rakerd, B. (**1989**). "On the minimum audible angle—A decision theory approach," J. Acoust. Soc. Amer. **85**, 2031–2041.

Hochster, M., and Kelly, J. (**1981**). "The precedence effect and sound localization by children with temporal lobe epilepsy," Neuropsychologia **19**, 49–55.

King, A. J., Hutchings, M. E., Moore, D. R., and Blakemore, C. (**1988**). "Developmental plasticity in the visual and auditory representations in the mammalian superior colliculus," Nature **332**, 73–76.

King, A. J., and Moore, D. R. (**1991**). "Plasticity of auditory maps in the brain," Trends. Neurosci. **14**, 31–37.

Knudsen, E. I., and Knudsen, P. F. (**1985**). "Vision guides the adjustment of auditory localization in young barn owls," Science **230**, 545–548.

Litovsky, R. Y. (**1994**). "Evidence for physiological correlates of the precedence effect in the inferior colliculus of kittens," J. Acoust. Soc. Am. **95**, S2843.

Litovsky, R. Y. (**1996**). "Developmental changes in minimum audible angle under conditions of the precedence effect," J. Acoust. Soc. Am., under review.

Litovsky, R. Y., and Clifton, R. K. (**1992**). "Use of sound-pressure level in auditory distance discrimination by 6-month-old infants and adults," J. Acoust. Soc. Am. **92**, 794–802.

Litovsky, R. Y., and Macmillan, N. A. (**1994**). "Minimum audible angle for clicks with simulated echoes: Effects of azimuth and standard," J. Acoust. Soc. Am. **96**, 752–758.

Litovsky, R. Y., and Yin, T. C. T. (**1993**). "Single-unit responses to stimuli that mimic the precedence effect in the inferior colliculus of the cat," presented at the meeting of the Association for Research in Otolaryngology, St. Petersburg Beach, FL.

Litovsky, R. Y. and Yin, T. C. T. (**1994**). "Physiological correlates of the precedence effect: Free-field recordings in the inferior colliculus of the cat," presented at the meeting of the Association for Research in Otolaryngology, St. Petersburg Beach, FL.

Little, A. D., Mershon, D. H., and Cox, P. H. (**1992**). "Spectral content as a cue to perceived auditory distance," Perception **21**, 405–416.

Luria, A. R. (**1973**). *Higher Cortical Functions in Man* (Basic Books, New York).

McGurk, H., Turnure, C., and Creighton, S. (**1977**). "Auditory-visual coordination in neonates," Child. Dev. **48**, 138–143.

Mills, A. (**1958**). "On the minimum audible angle," J. Acoust. Soc. Am. **30**, 237–246.

Moore, J. M., Thompson, G., and Thompson, M. (**1975**). "Auditory localization of infants as a function of reinforcement conditions," J. Speech Hear. Res. **40**, 29–34.

Morrongiello, B. (**1988a**). "Infants' localization of sounds along the horizontal axis: Estimates of minimum audible angle," Dev. Psychol. **24**, 8–13.

Morrongiello, B. (**1988b**). "Infants' localization of sounds along two spatial dimensions: Horizontal and vertical axes," Infant Behavior and Development, **11**, 127–143.

Morrongiello, B. A., Fenwick, D. K., and Chance, G. (**1990**). "Sound localization acuity in very young infants: An observer-based testing procedure," Dev. Psychol. **26**, 75–84.

Morrongiello, B., Kulig, J., and Clifton, R. K. (**1984**). "Developmental changes in auditory temporal perception," Child. Dev. **55**, 461–471.

Morrongiello, B., and Rocca, P. (**1987**). "Infants' localization of sounds in the horizontal plane: Effects of auditory and visual cues," Child. Dev. **58**, 918–927.

Morrongiello, B. A., and Rocca, P. T. (**1990**). "Infants' localization of sounds within hemifields: Estimates of minimum audible angle," Child. Dev. **61**, 1258–1270.

Muir, D. (**1982**). "The development of human auditory localization in infancy," in *Localization of Sound: Theory and Application*, edited by R. W. Gatehouse (Amphora Press, Groton, CT), pp. 220–243.

Muir, D. (**1985**). "The development of infants' auditory spatial sensitivity," in *Auditory Development in Infancy*, edited by S. E. Trehub and B. Schneider (Plenum Publishing, New York), pp. 51–83.

Muir, D., and Clifton, R. K. (**1985**). "Infants' orientation to the location of sound sources," in *Measurement of Audition and Vision in the First Postnatal Year of Life: A Methodological Overview*, edited by G. Gottlieb and N. A. Krasengor (Ablex, Norwood, NJ), pp. 171–194.

Muir, W. D., Clifton, R. K., and Clarkson, M. G. (**1989**). "The development of a human auditory localization response: A U-shaped function," Can. J. Psychol. **43**, 199–216.

Muir, D., and Field, J. (**1979**). "Newborn infants orient to sounds," Child. Dev. 50, 431–436.

Neuman, A. C., and Hochberg, I. (**1983**). "Children's perception of speech in reverberation," J. Acoust. Soc. Am. **73**, 2145–2149.

Olmstead, C. E., and Villiblanca, J. R. (**1980**). "Development of behavioral audition in the kitten," Physiol. Behav. **24**, 705–712.

Perris, E. E., and Clifton, R. K. (**1988**). "Reaching in the dark toward sound as a measure of auditory localization in 7-month-old infants," Infant Behav. Dev. **11**, 477–495.

Perrott, D. R., Marlborough, K., Merrill, P., and Strybel, T. Z. (**1989**). "Minimum audible angle thresholds obtained under conditions in which the precedence effect is assumed to operate," J. Acoust. Soc. Am. **85**, 282–288.

Rakerd, B., and Hartmann, W. M. (**1985**). "Localization of sound in rooms, II: The effect of a single reflecting surface," J. Acoust. Soc. Am. **78**, 524–533.

Shaw, B. K., McGowan, R. S., and Turvey, M. T. (**1991**). "An acoustic variable specifying time-to-contact," Ecol. Psychol. **3**, 253–261.

Shinn-Cunningham, B. G., Zurek, P. M., and Durlach, N. I. (**1993**). "Adjustment and discrimination measurements of the precedence effect," J. Acoust. Soc. Am. **93**, 2923–2932.

Wallach, H., Newman, E. B., and Rosenzweig, M. R. (**1949**). "The precedence effect in sound localization," J. Am. Psychol. **57**, 315–336.

Wertheimer, M. (**1961**). "Psychomotor coordination of auditory and visual space at birth," Science **134**, 1692.

Whitfield, I. C., Cranford, J., Ravizza, R., and Diamond, I. T. (**1972**). "Effects of unilateral ablation of auditory cortex in cat on complex sound localization," J. Neurophysiol. **35**, 718–731.

Withington-Wray, D. J., Binns, K. E., and Keating, M. J. (**1990**). "A four-day period of bimodality auditory and visual experience is sufficient to permit normal emergence of the map of auditory space in the guinea pig superior colliculus," Neurosci. Lett. **116**, 280–286.

Woodworth, R. S. (**1938**). *Experimental Psychology* (Holt, New York).

Yakovlev, P., and Lecours, A. (**1967**). "The myelogenetic cycles of regional maturation of the brain," in *Regional Development of the Brain in Early Life*, edited by A. Minkowski (F. A. Davis, Philadelphia), pp. 3–70.

Yin, T. C. T. (**1994**). "Physiological correlates of the precedence effect and summing localization in the inferior colliculus of the cat," J. Neurosci. **14**, 5170–5186.
Yin, T. C. T., and Litovsky, R. Y. (**1993**). "Physiological correlates of the precedence effect: Implications for neural models," J. Acoust. Soc. Am. **93**, 2293.
Yonas, A., and Granrud, C. (**1985**). "Reaching as a measure of infants' spatial perception," in *Measurement of Audition and Vision During the First Year of Postnatal Life: A Methodological Overview,* edited by G. Gottlieb and N. Krasengor (Ablex, Norwood, NJ), pp. 301–322.
Zelazo, P. R., Brody, L. R., and Chaika, H. (**1984**). "Neonatal habituation and dishabituation of head turning to rattle sounds," Infant Behav. Dev. **7**, 311–321.
Zurek, P. M. (**1987**). "The precedence effect," in *Directional Hearing*, edited by W. A. Yost and G. Gourevitch (Springer-Verlag, New York), pp. 85–105.

Part IX

Applications

Chapter 28

An Introduction to Binaural Technology

Jens Blauert
Ruhr-Universität Bochum, Germany

(Received November 1993; revised October 1994)

During the past decade binaural technology has become an enabling technology with a significant impact on various fields, such as information technology, human/machine interfaces, hearing aids, and advanced sound measurement techniques. In this chapter a review of the scientific foundations and generic application areas of binaural technology is presented. To this end three aspects are discussed separately, namely, the physical, psychoacoustic, and psychological aspects of binaural hearing, which together comprise binaural technology. The physical aspect is concerned with the input signals to the two ears before they reach the inner ears; the psychoacoustical aspect deals mainly with signal processing in the subcortical auditory system; and the psychological aspect focuses on cognitive brain function with respect to binaural hearing. It becomes clear that today's binaural technology rests mainly on our knowledge of the physical aspect, with an increasing use of psychoacoustics. Technology exploitation of the cognitive psychology of binaural hearing has barely begun.

INTRODUCTION

Humans, like most vertebrates, have two ears that are positioned at about equal height on the two sides of the head. Physically, the two ears and the head form an antenna system, mounted on a mobile base. This antenna system receives elastomechanical (acoustic) waves from the medium in which it is immersed, usually air. The two waves received and transmitted by the two ears are the physiologically adequate input to a specific sensory system, the auditory system.

The peripheral parts of the auditory system transform each of the two waves into neural spike trains, after having performed a running spectral decomposition into multiple frequency channels, among other preprocessing. The multichannel neural spike trains from each of the two ears are then combined in a sophisticated way to generate a running "binaural activity pattern" somewhere in the auditory system. This binaural activity pattern, most probably in combination with monaural activity patterns rendered individually by each ear's auditory channels, forms the auditory input to the cortex, which represents a powerful biologic multipurpose parallel computer with a huge memory and various interfaces and input and output ports. As an output, the cortex delivers an individual perceptual world and, eventually, neural commands to trigger and control specific motoric expressions.

It goes without saying that a number of constraints must hold for this story to be true. For example, the acoustic waves must be in the range of audibility with respect to frequency range and intensity, the auditory system must be operative, and the cortex must be in a conscious mode, ready to accept and interpret auditory information. Further, it makes sense to assume that multiple sources of feedback are involved in the processes of reception, processing, and interpretation of acoustic signals. Feedback clearly occurs between the modules of the subcortical auditory system, and between this system and the cortex. Obvious feedback from higher centers of the central nervous system to the motoric positioning system of the ears-and-head array can also be observed whenever position-finding movements of the head are induced.

Although humans can hear with one ear only—so-called monaural hearing—hearing with two functioning ears is clearly superior. This fact can best be appreciated by considering the biological role of hearing. Specifically, it is the biological role of hearing to gather information about the environment, particularly about the spatial positions and trajectories of sound sources and about their state of activity. Further, it should be recalled in this context that interindividual communication is predominantly performed acoustically, with brains deciphering meanings as encoded into acoustic signals by other brains.

In regard to this generic role of hearing, the advantage of binaural as compared to monaural hearing stands out clearly in terms of performance, particularly in the following areas (Blauert, 1983):

1. Localization of single or multiple sound sources and, consequently, formation of an auditory perspective and/or an auditory room impression.
2. Separation of signals coming from multiple incoherent sound sources, or coherent sound sources (with some restrictions), that are spread out spatially.
3. Enhancement of the signals from a chosen source with respect to further signals from incoherent sources, as well as enhancement of the direct (unreflected) signals from sources in a reverberant environment.

It is evident that the performance features of binaural hearing form a challenge for engineers in terms of technological application. In this context, a so-called "binaural technology" has evolved during the past three decades, which can operationally be defined as follows:

> Binaural technology is a body of methods that involves the acoustic input signals to both ears of the listener for achieving practical purposes, for example, by recording, analyzing, synthesizing, processing, presenting, and evaluating such signals.

Binaural technology has recently gained in economic momentum, both on its own and as an enabling technology for more complex applications. A specialized industry for binaural technology is rapidly developing. It is the purpose of this chapter to take a brief look at this exciting process and to reflect on the bases on which this technology rests, that is, on its experimental and theoretical foundations. As discussed earlier, there are basically three "modules" engaged in the reception, perception, and interpretation of acoustical signals: the ears-and-head array, the subcortical auditory system, and the cortex. Binaural technology makes use of knowledge of the functional principles of each. In the following three sections, particular functions of these three modules are reviewed in light of their specific application to binaural technology. This material has also been presented to the British Institute of Acoustics (Blauert, 1994).

I. THE EARS-AND-HEAD ARRAY: PHYSICS OF BINAURAL HEARING

The ears-and-head array is an antenna system with complex and specific transmission characteristics. Because it is a physical structure and sound propagation is a linear process, the array can be considered to be a linear system. By taking an incoming sound wave as the input and the sound pressure signals at the two eardrums as the output, it is correct to describe the system as a set of two self-adjusting filters connected to the same input. Self-adjusting, in the sense used here, means that the filters automatically provide transfer functions that are specific with regard to the geometrical orientation of the wavefront relative to the ears-and-head array.

Physically, this behavior is explained by resonances in the open cavity formed by the pinna, ear canal, and eardrum, and by diffraction and reflection of the head and torso. These various phenomena are excited differently when a sound wave impinges from different directions and/or with different curvatures of the wavefront. The resulting transfer functions are generally different for the two filters, thus causing "interaural" differences of the sound-pressure signals at the two eardrums. Because the linear distortions superimposed upon the sound wave by the two "ear filters" are very specific with respect to the geometric parameters of the sound wave, it is not far from the mark to say that the ears-and-head system encodes information about the position of sound sources in space, relative to this antenna system, into temporal and spectral attributes of the signals at the eardrums and into their interaural differences. All manipulations applied to the sound signals by the ears-and-head array are purely physical and linear. It is obvious, therefore, that they can be simulated. As a matter of fact, there is one important branch of binaural technology that attempts to do just this.

It makes sense at this point to begin the technological discussion with the earliest, and still a very important, application of binaural technology, namely, authentic auditory reproduction. Authentic auditory reproduction has been achieved when listeners hear exactly the same in a reproduction situation as what they would hear in an original sound field, the latter existing at a different time and/or location. As a working hypothesis, binaural technology begins with the assumption that listeners have the same percept in a reproduction situation as in an original sound field when the signals at the two eardrums are exactly the same during reproduction as in the original field. Technologically, this goal is achieved by means of so-called artificial heads, which are replicas of natural heads in terms of acoustics—that is, they realize two self-adjusting ear filters like natural heads.

Artificial heads, in combination with adequate playback equipment, are a basic instrumentation for a number of economically appealing applications. The playback equipment needed for this application is usually based on headphones. Yet, under specific, restricted conditions, loudspeakers can also be used. A first category of application in this context is subsumed under the following section.

A. Binaural recording and authentic reproduction

These applications exploit the capability of binaural technology to archive the sound field in a perceptually authentic way, and to make it available for listening at will, for example, in entertainment, education, instruction, scientific research, documentation, surveillance, and telemonitoring. It should be noted here that binaural recordings can be compared in direct sequence (e.g., by A/B comparison), which is often impossible for the original sound situations. Because the sound-pressure signals at the two eardrums are the physiologically adequate input to the auditory system, they are considered the basis for auditory-adequate measurement and evaluation, both in a physical and/or auditory way (Blauert and Genuit, 1993). Consequently, we have the further application category discussed next.

B. Binaural measurement and evaluation

In physical binaural measurement, physically based procedures are used, whereas in the auditory case, human listeners serve as measuring and evaluating instruments. Current applications of binaural measurement and evaluation can be found in areas such as noise control, acoustic-environment design, sound-quality assessment (e.g., in speech technology, architectural acoustics, and product-sound design), and in specific measurements on telephone systems, headphones, personal hearing protectors, and hearing aids (Blauert, Els, and Schroeter, 1980; Schroeter, 1986; Schroeter and Pösselt, 1986). For some applications, scaled-up or scaled-down artificial heads are in use, for instance, for the evaluation of architectural scale models (Els and Blauert, 1985, 1986; Xiang and Blauert, 1991, 1993).

Because artificial heads, basically, are just a specific way of implementing a set of linear filters, one may think of other ways of realizing such filters, such as electronically. For many applications this adds additional degrees of freedom, as electronic filters can be controlled at will over a wide range. This idea leads to yet another category of application, as follows.

C. Binaural simulation and displays

There are many current applications in binaural simulation and displays, with the potential of an ever-increasing number. The following list provides examples: binaural mixing (Pösselt, Schroeter, Opitz, Divenyi, and Blauert, 1986), binaural room simulation (Lehnert and Blauert, 1989, 1992), advanced sound effects (e.g., for computer games), provision of auditory spatial-orientation cues (e.g., in the cockpit or for the blind), auditory display of complex data, and auditory representation in teleconference, telepresence, and teleoperator systems.

Figure 1, by showing binaural-technology equipment in an order of increasing complexity, is meant to illustrate some of the ideas just discussed. The most basic equipment is obviously that shown in Fig. 1a. The signals at the two ears of a subject are picked up by (probe) microphones in a subject's ear canal, then recorded, and later played back to the same subject after appropriate equalization. Equalization is necessary to correct linear distortions, induced by the microphones, the recorder, and the headphones, so that the signals in the subject's ear canals during the playback correspond exactly to those in the pick-up situation. Equipment of this kind is adequate for personalized binaural recordings. Because a subject's own ears are used for the recording, maximum authenticity can be achieved.

Artificial heads (Fig. 1b) have practical advantages over real heads for most applications; for one thing, they allow for auditory real-time monitoring of a different location. One has to realize, however, that artificial heads are usually cast or designed from a typical or representative subject. Their directional characteristics will thus, in general, deviate from those of an individual listener. This fact can lead to a significant decrease in perceptual authenticity. For example, errors such as sound coloration or front/back confusion may appear. Individual adjustment is only partly possible, namely, by equalizing the headphones specifically for each subject. To this end, the equalizer may be split into two components: (1) a head equalizer and (2) a headphone equalizer. The interface between the two allows some freedom of choice. Typically, it is defined in such a way that the artificial head features a flat frequency response either for frontal sound incidence (free-field correction) or in a diffuse sound field (diffuse-field correction). The headphones must be equalized accordingly. It is clear that individual adjustment of the complete system, beyond a specific direction of sound incidence, is impossible in principle, unless the directional characteristics of the artificial head and the listener's head happen to be identical.

Figure 1c depicts the setup for applications in which the signals to the two ears of the listener are to be measured, evaluated, and/or manipulated. Signal-processing devices are provided to work on the recorded signals. Although real-time processing is not necessary for many applications, real-time playback is mandatory. The modified and/or unmodified signals can be monitored either by a signal analyzer or by binaural listening.

The most complex equipment in this context is represented by Fig. 1d. Here the input signals no longer stem from a listener's ears or from an artificial head, but have been recorded or even generated without the participation of ears or ear replicas. For instance, anechoic recordings via conventional studio microphones may be used. The linear distortions that human ears superimpose on the impinging sound waves, depending on their direction of incidence and wavefront curvature, are generated electronically via a so-called ear-filter bank (electronic head). To be able to assign the adequate head-transfer function to each incoming signal

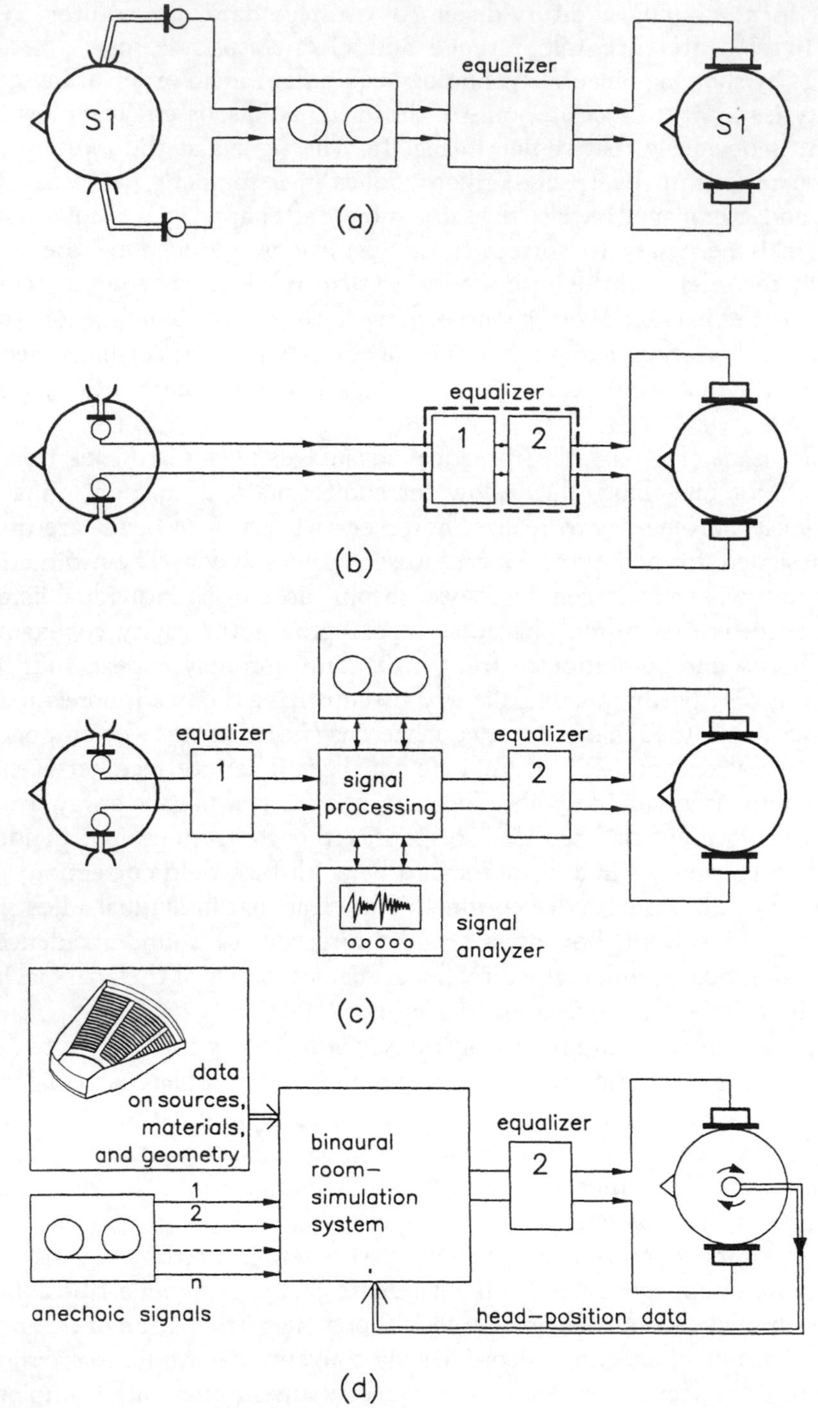

FIG. 1. Binaural technology equipment with different degrees of complexity: (a) probe-microphone system on a real head, (b) artificial head system, (c) artificial head system with signal-processing and signal-analysis capabilities, and (d) binaural room-simulation system with head-position tracker for virtual-reality applications.

component, the system needs data on the geometry of the sound field. In a typical application, such as architectural-acoustics planning, the system contains a sound-field simulation based on data of the room geometry, the absorption features of the materials implied, and the positions of the sound sources and their directional characteristics. The output of the sound-field modeling is fed into the electronic head, thus producing so-called binaural impulse responses. Subsequent convolution of these impulse responses with anechoic signals generates binaural signals as a subject would observe in a corresponding real room. The complete method is often referred to as binaural room simulation.

To give subjects the impression of being immersed in a sound field, it is important that perceptual room constancy is provided. In other words, when the subjects move their heads around, the perceived auditory world should nevertheless maintain its spatial position. To this end, the simulation system needs to know the head position in order to be able to control the binaural impulse responses adequately. Head position sensors must therefore be provided. The impression of being immersed is of particular relevance for applications in the context of virtual reality.

All of the applications discussed in this section are based on the provision of two sound-pressure signals to the eardrums of human beings, or on the use of such signals for measurement and application. They are built on our knowledge of what the ears-and-head array does, that is, on our understanding of the physics of the binaural transmission chain in front of the eardrum. The next section deals with the signal processing behind the eardrum and its possible technical applications.

II. THE SUBCORTICAL AUDITORY SYSTEM: PSYCHOPHYSICS OF BINAURAL HEARING

As mentioned earlier, the subcortical auditory system converts incoming sound waves into neural spike trains, which are then processed in a very sophisticated way. Among the things that we know from physiological experiments are the following: The signals are decomposed into spectral bands that are maintained throughout the system. Autocorrelation of the signals from each of the ears, as well as cross-correlation of the signals from both ears, are performed. Specific inhibition and excitation effects are extensively present.

Models of the function of the subcortical auditory system take our knowledge of its physiology into account, but are usually oriented primarily toward the modeling of psychoacoustic findings. Most models have a signal-driven, bottom-up architecture. As an output, a (running) binaural activity pattern is rendered that displays features corresponding to psychoacoustic evidence and/or allows for the explanation of binaural performance features. Because psychoacoustics, at least in the classical sense, attempts to design listening experiments in a "quasi-objective" way, psychoacoustic observations are, as a rule, predominantly associated with processes in the subcortical auditory system.

There seems to be consensus among model builders that a model of the subcortical auditory system must incorporate at least three functional blocks to simulate binaural performance in the areas listed above (Fig. 2):

1. A simulation of the functions of the external ear, including head (skull), torso, pinnae, ear canal, and eardrum, plus, eventually, the middle ear.
2. A simulation of the inner ears, that is, the cochleae, including receptors and first neurons, plus a set of binaural processors to identify interaurally correlated contents of the signals from the two cochleae and to measure interaural arrival-time and level differences, along with, eventually, additional monaural processors.
3. A set of algorithms for final evaluation of the information rendered by the preceding blocks with respect to the specific auditory task to be simulated.

The first block corresponds to the head-and-ears array as discussed in the preceding section, with the exception of the middle ear. As a matter of fact, detailed modeling of the middle ear is deemed unnecessary in current binaural technology. The middle ear is approximated by a linear time-invariant bandpass filter, thus neglecting features such as the middle-ear reflex. Nevertheless, more elaborate models of the middle ear are readily available from the literature, if needed (Hudde, 1983a, 1983b; Blauert, Hudde, and Letens, 1987).

The second block includes two essential modules, cochlea simulation and simulation of subcortical binaural interaction. The cochlea model simulates two primary functions, namely, a running spectral analysis of the incoming signals, and a transformation of the (continuous) mechanical vibrations of the basilar membrane into a (discrete) nerve-firing pattern: physiological analog-to-digital (A/D) conversion. In doing so, it must be considered that both spectral selectivity and A/D conversion depend on the signal amplitude, that is, behave nonlinearly. The simplest approximation for the spectral selectivity to be simulated is by means of a bank of adjacent bandpass filters, each, for example, of critical bandwidth. This realization is often used when computing speed is more relevant than precision. More detailed modeling is achieved by including the spectrally selective excitation at each point of the basilar membrane. The amplitude dependence of excitation and selectivity can optionally be included into the model by simulating active processes, which are supposed to be part of the functioning of the inner ear.

A more precise simulation of the physiological A/D conversion requires a stochastic receptor-neuron model to convert movement of the basilar membrane into neural-spike series. Such models have indeed been implemented for simulations of some delicate binaural effects. However, for practical applications, it is often not feasible to process individual neural impulses. Instead, one can generate deterministic signals that represent the time function of the firing probability of a bundle of nerve fibers. For further simplification, a linear dependence of the firing probability on the receptor potential is often assumed. The receptor potential is sufficiently well described for many applications by the time function of the movement of the basilar membrane, when half-wave rectified and fed through a first-order lowpass filter with an 800-Hz cutoff frequency. This accounts for the fact that, among other things, in the frequency region above about 1.5 kHz, binaural interaction works on the envelopes rather than on the fine structure of the incoming signals.

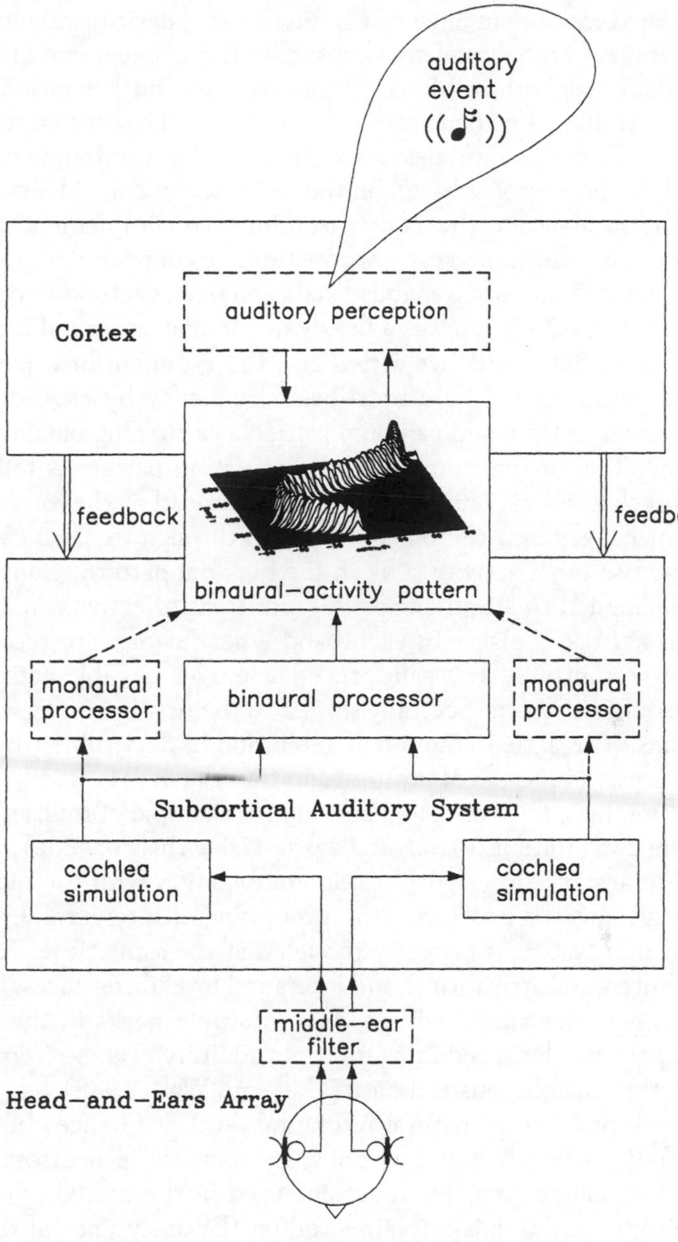

FIG. 2. Architecture for an application-oriented model of binaural hearing: Binaural signals as delivered by the ear-and-head array (or its electronic simulation) are fed into a model of the subcortical auditory system, implying simulation of the function of the cochleae and of binaural interaction as essential modules. The interface between the subcortical auditory model and the evaluation stages it is provided by a running binaural activity pattern.

With regard to the binaural processors, the following description results from work performed in the author's laboratory at Bochum (e.g., Lindemann, 1986a, 1986b; Gaik, 1993). First, a modified, interaural running cross-correlation function is computed, based on signals originating at corresponding points on the basilar membranes of the two cochlea simulators, that is, points that represent the same critical frequency. The relevance of cross-correlation to binaural processing has been assumed more than once and is, moreover, physiologically evident. A Bochum modification of cross-correlation consists of the employment of a binaural contralateral inhibition algorithm. Monaural pathways are further included in the binaural processors to allow for the explanation of monaural hearing effects.

Some details of the binaural processors are provided in the following section. The first stage of the processor is based on the well-known coincidence-detector hypothesis. A way to illustrate this is by assuming two complementary tapped delay lines—one coming from each ear—whose taps are connected to coincidence cells that fire upon receiving simultaneous excitation from each side's delay lines. It can be shown that this stage renders a family of running interaural cross-correlation functions as output. Thus, we arrive at a three-dimensional pattern (interaural arrival-time difference by critical-band frequency by cross-correlation amplitude) that varies in time and can be regarded as a running binaural activity pattern. The generation of the running cross-correlation pattern is followed by application of a mechanism of contralateral inhibition based on the following idea. Once a wavefront has entered the binaural system through the two ears, it will consequently give rise to an activity peak in the binaural pattern. Consequently, inhibition will be applied to all other possible positions of activity in each band where excitation has taken place. In each band where signals are received, the first incoming wavefront will thus gain precedence over possible activity being created by later sounds that are spectrally similar to the first incoming wavefront, such as reflections. The actual amount of inhibition is determined by specific weights, which vary as a function of position and time, such as to fit psychoacoustical data. Inhibition may, for example, continue for a couple of milliseconds and then gradually die away until it is triggered again. Using this concept, as well as a specific contralateral inhibition algorithm, in combination with the inclusion of monaural pathways into the processor, the processing of interaural level differences by the binaural system is properly modeled at the same time. For certain combinations of interaural arrival-time and interaural level differences, for example, "unnatural" ones, the model will produce multiple peaks in the inhibited binaural activity pattern, thus predicting multiple auditory events—very much in accordance with the psychoacoustical data (Gaik and Wolf, 1988).

To deal with the problem of natural interaural level differences being much higher at high frequencies than at low ones, the binaural processors must be adapted to the external-ear transfer functions used in the model. To this end, additional inhibitory weighting is implemented on the delay lines of the coincidence networks in such a way that the binaural processors are always excited within their "natural" range of operation. This additional weighting is distributed along the delay lines. The complete set of binaural processors can thus be conceptualized as an artificial neural network, more specifically, as a particular kind of time-delay neural network. The adaptation of this network to the particular set of external-ear transfer functions used is accomplished by means of a supervised learning procedure.

The output of the binaural processor, a running binaural activity pattern, is assumed to be interfaced to higher nervous centers for evaluation. The evaluation procedures must be defined with respect to the actual, specific task required.

Within the scope of our current modeling, the evaluation process is thought of in terms of pattern recognition. This concept can be applied when the desired output of the model system is a set of sound-field parameters, such as the number and the positions of the sound source, the amount of auditory spaciousness, reverberance, coloration, and so forth. Also, if the desired output of the model system is processed signals, such as a monophonic signal that has been improved with respect to its S/N ratio, the final evaluative stage may produce a set of parameters for controlling further signal processing.

Pattern-recognition procedures have so far been projected for various tasks in the field of sound localization and spatial hearing, such as lateralization, multiple-image phenomena, summing localization, auditory spaciousness, binaural signal enhancement, and parts of the precedence effect (see Blauert and Col, 1992, for cognitive components of the precedence effect). Further, effects such as binaural pitch, dereverberation, and/or decoloration are within the scope of the model.

We now consider the question of whether the physiological and psychoacoustic knowledge of the subcortical auditory system, as manifested in models of the kind described already, can be applied to binaural technology. Because we think of the subcortical auditory system as a specific front end to the cortex that extracts and enhances certain attributes from the acoustic waves for further evaluation, signal-processing algorithms as observed in the subcortical auditory system may certainly be applied in technical systems to simulate performance features of binaural hearing. Progress in signal-processor technology makes it feasible to implement some of them on microprocessor hardware for real-time operation. Consequently, a number of interesting technical applications have come into the reach of today's technology. A first category is concerned with spatial hearing, as described next.

A. Spatial hearing

Auditory-like algorithms may decode information from the input signals to the ears that allows assessment of the spatial position of sound sources. They may further be used for predictions of how humans form the positions and spatial extents of their auditory events, how they establish an auditory perspective, and how they suppress echoes and reverberance. Typical applications are source-position finders, tools for the evaluation of architectural acoustics and sound systems (e.g., spaciousness meters, echo detectors, and precedence indicators), tools for the evaluation of auditory virtual environments, and tools for psychoacoustic research. There are further perceptual features of auditory events, besides position and spatial extent, that are based on binaural rather than monaural information. Following a usage in the field of product-sound design, they may be called binaural psychoacoustic descriptors, as discussed in the next subsection.

B. Binaural psychoacoustic descriptors

Binaural psychoacoustic descriptors include binaural loudness, binaural pitch, binaural timbre, and binaural sensory consonance. Algorithms taken from binaural auditory models may be used to generate estimates of these descriptors. There is an increasing demand for such tools, such as in the area of sound-quality evaluation. The most tempting field of application for binaural auditory models, however, concerns the ability of binaural hearing to process signals from different sources selectively, and to enhance one of them with regard to the others. A key term for this area of application could be binaural signal enhancement.

C. Binaural signal enhancement

A well-known term in the context of binaural signal enhancement is the so-called "cocktail-party effect," denoting that, with the aid of binaural hearing, humans can concentrate on one talker in the presence of other competing talkers. It has further been established that with binaural hearing a desired signal and noise can be separated more effectively than with monaural hearing. Binaural auditory models may help to simulate these capabilities by providing front ends that allow for better separation of a mix of sound sources. In a specific Bochum version of a so-called cocktail-party processor, that is, a processor to enhance speech in a cocktail-party situation, the binaural processor of the auditory model is used to control a Wiener filter (Bodden and Blauert, 1992; Bodden, 1993). This is accomplished by first identifying the position of a desired talker in space and then estimating its S/N ratio with respect to competing talkers and other noise signals. The system performs its computation within critical bands. In the case of two competing talkers, the desired signal can be recovered to reasonable intelligibility, even when its level is 15 dB lower than that of the competing one. Application possibilities for this kind of system are numerous, such as tools for editing binaural recordings, front ends for signal-processing hearing aids, speech recognizers, and hands-free telephones. In general, binaural signal enhancement may be used to build better "microphones" for acoustically adverse conditions. As stated earlier, the cues provided by models of the subcortical auditory system, and contained in binaural activity patterns, must consequently be evaluated in adequate ways. The next section deals with this problem.

III. THE CORTEX: PSYCHOLOGY OF BINAURAL HEARING

Most models of the subcortical auditory system assume a bottom-up, signal-driven process up to their output, the running binaural activity pattern. The cortex, consequently, takes this pattern as an input. The evaluation of the binaural activity pattern can be conceived as a top-down, hypothesis-driven process. According to this line of thinking, cortical centers set up hypotheses, for example, in terms of expected patterns, and then try to confirm these hypotheses with appropriate means, for example, with task-specific pattern-recognition procedures. When setting up hypotheses, the cortex reflects on cognition, namely, on knowledge and awareness of the current situation and the world in general. Further, it takes into account input from other senses, such as visual or tactile information. After forming hypotheses, higher nervous stages may feed back to more peripheral modules to prompt and control optimum hypothesis testing. They may, for example, induce movement of the ears-and-head array or influence the spectral decomposition process in the subcortical auditory system.

The following two examples help to illustrate the structure of problems that arise at this point from a technological point of view. First, in a "cocktail-party" situation a human listener can follow one talker and then, immediately, switch his or her attention to another. A signal-processing hearing aid should be able to do the same thing, deliberately controlled by its user. Second, a measuring instrument to evaluate the acoustic quality of concert halls will certainly take into account psychoacoustic descriptors like auditory spaciousness, reverberance, transparency, and so on. However, the general impression of space and quality that a listener develops in a room may be codetermined by visual cues, by the specific kind of performance, by the listener's attitude, and by factors such as fashion or taste, among other things.

There is no doubt that the involvement of the cortex in the evaluation process adds a considerable amount of "subjectivity" to binaural hearing, which poses serious problems to binaural technology. Engineers, like most scientists, are trained to deal with the object as being independent of the observer (assumption of "objectivity") and prefer to neglect phenomena that cannot be measured or assessed in a strictly "objective" way. They further tend to believe that any problem can be understood by splitting it up into parts and analyzing these parts separately. At the cortical level, however, we deal with percepts, that is, objects that do not exist as separate entities, but as part of a subject–object (perceiver–percept) relationship. It should also be noted that listeners normally listen in a "gestalt" mode; that is, they perceive globally rather than segmentally. An analysis of the common engineering type may thus completely miss relevant features.

Perceiver and percept interact and may both vary considerably during the process of perception. For example, the auditory events may change when listeners focus on specific components such as the sound of a particular instrument in an orchestra. Further, the attitude of perceivers toward their percepts may vary in the course of an experimental series, thus leading to response modification.

A simple psychological model of the auditory perception and judgment process, shown in Fig. 3, can be used to elaborate on the variance of listeners' auditory events in a given acoustic setting and the variance of their respective responses. The schematic symbolizes a subject in a listening experiment. Sound waves impinge upon the two ears, are preprocessed, and are guided to higher centers of the central nervous system, where they give rise to the formation of an auditory event in the subject's perceptual space. The auditory event is a percept of the listener being tested; that is, only the listener has direct access to it. The rest of the world is only informed about the occurrence of the particular percept if the subject responds in such a way as to allow some conclusions to be made from the response to the percept (indirect access). In formal experiments the subject will usually be instructed to respond in a specified way, for example, by formal judgment on specific attributes of the auditory event. If the response is a quantitative descriptor of perceptual attributes, we may speak of measurement. Consequently, in listening experiments, subjects can serve as an instrument for the measurements of their own perception, that is, as both the object of

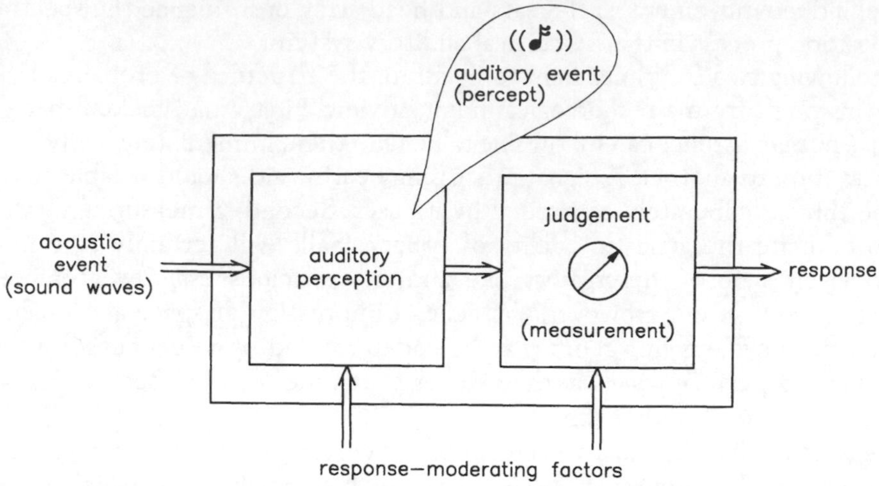

FIG. 3. Schematic of a subject in a listening experiment. Response-moderating factors influence both perception and judgment.

measurement and the "meter." The schematic in Fig. 3 features a second input into both the auditory-perception and the judgment blocks where "response-moderating factors" are fed in to introduce variance to the perception and judgment processes.

Following this line of thinking, an important task of auditory psychology can be to identify such response-moderating factors and to clarify their role in binaural listening. Many of these factors represent conventional knowledge or experience from related fields of perceptual acoustics, such as noise- and speech-quality evaluation. It is well known that the listeners' judgments of auditory events may depend on the cognitive "image" that the listeners have with respect to the sound sources involved (source-related factors). It may happen, for instance, that the auditory events evoked by sources that are considered aggressive (e.g., trucks) are judged louder than those from other sources (e.g., passenger cars)—given the same acoustical signals. The "image" of the source in the listeners' minds may be based, among other things, on cues from other senses (e.g., visual) and/or on prior knowledge. Situative factors are a further determinant in this context; that is, subjects judge an auditory event, bearing in mind the complete (multimodal) situation in which they occur. Another set of factors is given by the individual characteristics of each listener (personal factors), for example, the listener's subjective attitude toward a specific sound phenomenon, an attitude that may even change in the course of an experiment. Response-moderating factors that draw on cognition tend to be especially effective when the sounds listened to transmit specific information, that is, act as carriers of meaning. This is obvious in the case of speech sounds, but also in other cases. The sound of a running automobile engine, for instance, may signal to the driver that the engine is operating normally.

The fact that response-moderating factors do not act only on judgments but also on the process of perception itself may seem to be less obvious at a first glance, but is, nevertheless, also conventional wisdom. We all know that people in a complex sound situation have a tendency to miss what they do not pay attention to and/or do not expect to hear. For example, there is psychoacoustical evidence that the spectral selectivity of the cochlea is influenced by attention. At this point, the ability to switch at will between a global and an analytic mode of listening should also be noted. It is commonly accepted among psychologists that percepts are the result both of the actual sensory input at a given time and of expectation.

If we wish to build sophisticated binaural technology equipment for complex tasks, there is no doubt that psychological effects must be taken into account. Let us consider, as an example, a binaural surveillance system for acoustic monitoring of a factory floor. Such a system must know the relevance and meaning of many classes of signals and must pay selective attention to very specific ones, when an abnormal situation has been detected. A system for the evaluation of acoustic qualities of spaces for musical performances must detect and consider a range of different shades of binaural signals, depending on the kind and purpose of the performances. It might even need to take into account the taste of the local audience or that of the most influential local music reviewer. An intelligent binaural hearing aid should know, to a certain extent, which components of the incoming acoustic signals are relevant to its user, for example, track a talker who has just uttered the user's name.

As a consequence, we shall see in the future of binaural technology that psychological models will be exploited and implemented technologically, although perhaps not immediately, in the form of massively parallel biologic computing elements, as in the cortex. There are already discussions about and early examples of combinations of expert systems and other knowledge-based systems with artificial heads, auditory displays, and auditory-system models. When we think of applications like complex human/machine interfaces, multimedia systems, interactive virtual environments, and teleoperation systems, it becomes obvious that conventional binaural technology must be combined with, or integrated into, systems that are able to make decisions and control actions in an intelligent way. With this view in mind it is clear that binaural technology is still in an early stage of development. There are many relevant technological challenges and business opportunities ahead.

ACKNOWLEDGMENTS

Many of the ideas discussed in this chapter have evolved from work at the author's lab. The author is especially indebted to his doctoral students over the years, who have helped to provide a constant atmosphere of stimulating discussion. A list of completed doctoral dissertations that are related to this chapter, along with references to tagged publications in English, is given in the following:

Bodden, Markus: Binaurale Signalverarbeitung: Modellierung der Richtungserkennung und des Cocktail-Party-Effektes (Binaural signal processing: Modeling of direction finding and of the cocktail-party effect), Bochum, 1992 (Bodden and Blauert, 1992; Bodden, 1993; Blauert, Bodden, and Lehnert, 1993).

Col, Jean-Pierre: Localisation auditiv d'un signal et aspects temporels de l'audition spatiale (Auditory localization of a signal and temporal aspects of spatial hearing), Marseille, 1990 (Blauert and Col, 1992).

Els, Hartmut: Ein Meßsystem für die akustische Modelltechnik (A measuring system for the technique of acoustic modeling), Bochum, 1986 (Els and Blauert, 1985, 1986).

Gaik, Werner: Untersuchungen zur binauralen Verarbeitung kopfbezogener Signale (Investigations into binaural signal processing of head-related signals), Bochum, 1990 (Gaik and Wolf, 1988; Gaik, 1993).

Hudde, Herbert: Messung der Trommelfellimpedanz des menschlichen Ohres bis 19kHz (Measurement of eardrum impedance up to 19 kHz), Bochum, 1980 (Hudde, 1983a, 1983b).

Lehnert, Hilmar: Binaurale Raumsimulation: Ein Computermodell zur Erzeugung virtueller auditiver Umgebungen (Binaural room simulation: A computer model for generation of virtual auditory environments), Bochum, 1992 (Lehnert and Blauert, 1989, 1992; Blauert, Bodden, and Lehnert, 1993).

Letens, Uwe: Über die Interpretation von Impedanzmessungen im Gehörgang anhand von Mittelohr-Modellen (Interpretation of impedance measurements in the ear canal in terms of middle-ear models), Bochum, 1988 (Blauert, Hudde, and Letens, 1987).

Lindemann, Werner: Die Erweiterung eines Kreuzkorrelationsmodells der binauralen Signalverarbeitung durch kontralaterale Inhibitionsmechanismen (Extension of a cross-correlation model of binaural signal processing by means of contralateral inhibition mechanisms), Bochum, 1985 (Lindemann, 1986a, 1986b).

Pompetzki, Wulf: Psychoakustische Verifikation von Computermodellen zur binauralen Raumsimulation (Psychoacoustical verification of computer-models for binaural room simulation), Bochum, 1993.

Pösselt, Christoph: Einfluß von Knochenschall auf die Schalldämmung von Gehörschützern (Influence of bone conduction on the attenuation of personal hearing protectors), Bochum, 1986 (Schroeter and Pösselt, 1986).

Schlichthärle, Dietrich: Modelle des Hörens—mit Anwendungen auf die Hörbarkeit von Laufzeitverzerrungen (Models of hearing—Applied to the audibility of arrival-time distortions), Bochum, 1980.

Schroeter, Juergen: Messung der Schalldämmung von Gehörschützern mit einem physikalischen Verfahren—Kunstkopfmethode (Measurement of the attenuation of personal hearing protectors by means of a physical technique—Dummy-head method), Bochum, 1983 (Blauert, Els, and Schroeter, 1980; Schroeter, 1986).

Slatky, Harald: Algorithmen zur richtungsselektiven Verarbeitung von Schallsignalen mittels eines binauralen Cocktail-Party-Prozessors (Algorithms for direction-selective processing of sound signals by means of a binaural cocktail-party processor), Bochum, 1993.

Wolf, Siegbert: Lokalisation von Schallquellen in geschlossenen Räumen (Localization of sound sources in enclosed spaces), Bochum, 1991.

Xiang, Ning: Mobile Universal Measuring System for the Binaural Room-Acoustic-Model Technique, Bochum, 1991 (Xiang and Blauert, 1991, 1993).

REFERENCES

Blauert, J. (**1983**). "Psychoacoustic binaural phenomena," in *Hearing—Psychological Bases and Psychophysics,* edited by R. Klinke, and R. Hartmann (Springer-Verlag, Berlin), pp. 182–199.

Blauert, J. (**1994**). "Scientific foundations and generic application areas of binaural technology," Ray-Stevens Lecture, Spring Meeting Inst. of Acoustics, Great Britain-Salford.

Blauert, J., Bodden, M., and Lehnert, H. (**1993**). "Binaural signal processing and room acoustics," IEICE Transact. Fundam. **E75** (Japan), 1454–1458.

Blauert, J., and Col, J.-P. (**1992**). "A study of temporal effects in spatial hearing," in *Auditory Psychology and Perception,* edited by Y. Cazals, K. Horner, and L. Demay (Pergamon Press, Oxford), pp. 531–538.

Blauert, J., Els, H., and Schroeter, J. (**1980**). "A review of the progress in external ear physics regarding the objective performance evaluation of personal ear protectors," *Proceedings of Inter-Noise '80, Vol. II* (Noise-Control Foundation, USA, New York), pp. 653–658.

Blauert, J., and Genuit, K. (**1993**). "Sound-environment evaluation by binaural technology: Some basic considerations," J. Acoust. Soc. Jpn. **14**, 139–145.

Blauert, J., Hudde, H., and Letens, U. (**1987**). "Eardrum-impedance and middle-ear modeling," *Proceedings Symp. Fed. Europ. Acoust. Soc. (FASE;* Sociedade Portugueasa de Acùstica, Lisboa), 125–128.

Bodden, M. (**1993**). "Modeling human sound source localization and the cocktail-party-effect," Acta Acustica **1**, 43–55.

Bodden, M., and Blauert, J. (**1992**). "Separation of concurrent speech signals: A cocktail-party processor for speech enhancement," in *Proceedings of ESCA Workshop on Speech Processing in Adverse Conditions* (Cannes Mandliev, France), pp. 147–150.

Els, H., and Blauert, J. (**1985**). "Measuring techniques for acoustic models—Upgraded," *Proceeding of InterNoise '85, Schriftenr. Bundesanst. Arbeitsschutz Tb 39/II,* Wirtschaftsverlag NW, D-Bremerhaven, pp. 1359–1362.

Els, H., and Blauert, J. (**1986**). "A measuring system for acoustic scale models," *12th Int. Congr. Acoust. Proc. Vancouver Symp. Acoustics and Theatre Planning for the Performing Arts,* pp. 65–70.

Gaik, W. (**1993**). "Combined evaluation of interaural time and intensity differences: Psychoacoustic results and computer modeling," J. Acoust. Soc. Am. **94**, 98–110.

Gaik, W., and Wolf, S. (**1988**). "Multiple images: Psychological data and model predictions," in *Basic Issues of Hearing,* edited by H. Duifhius, J. W. Horst, and H. P. Wit (Academic Press, London), pp. 386–393.

Hudde, H. (**1983a**). "Estimation of the area function of human ear canals by sound-pressure measurements," J. Acoust. Soc Am. **73**, 24–31.

Hudde, H. (**1983b**). "Measurement of eardrum impedance of human ears," J. Acoust. Soc. Am. **73**, 242–247.

Lehnert, H., and Blauert, J. (**1989**). "A concept for binaural room simulation," in *Proceedings IEEE-ASSP Workshop on Application of Signal Processing to Audio and Acoustics,* New Paltz, NY (IEEE, New York).

Lehnert, H., and Blauert, J. (**1992**). "Principles of binaural room simulation," J. Appl. Acoust. **36**, 259–291.

Lindemann, W. (**1986a**). "Extension of a binaural cross-correlation model by means of contralateral inhibition. I. Simulation of lateralization of stationary signals," J. Acoust. Soc. Am. **80**, 1608–1622.

Lindemann, W. (**1986b**). "Extension of a binaural cross-correlation model by means of contralateral inhibition. II. The law of the first wave front," J. Acoust. Soc. Am. **80**, 1623–1630.

Pösselt, C., Schroeter, J., Opitz, M., Divenyi, P. L., and Blauert, J. (**1986**). "Generation of binaural Signals for research and home entertainment," *Procedings 12th Int. Congr. Acoust. Vol. I* (Beauregard Press Ltd., Toronto), pp. B1–6.

Schroeter, J. (**1986**). "The use of acoustical test fixtures for the measurement of hearing-protector attenuation, Part I: Review of previous work and the design of an improved test fixture," J. Acoust. Soc. Am. **79**, 1065–1081.

Schroeter, J., and Pösselt, C. (**1986**). "The use of acoustical test fixtures for the measurement of hearing-protector attenuation, Part II: Modeling the external ear, simulating bone conduction, and comparing test fixture and real-ear data," J. Acoust. Soc. Am. **80**, 505–527.

Xiang, N., and Blauert, J. (**1991**). "A miniature dummy head for binaural evaluation of tenth-scale acoustic models," J. Appl. Acoust. **33**, 123–140.

Xiang, N., and Blauert, J. (**1993**). "Binaural scale modelling for auralization and prediction of acoustics in auditoria," J. Appl. Acoust. **38**, 267–290.

Chapter 29

Auditory Displays

Barbara Shinn-Cunningham
Massachusetts Institute of Technology

Hilmar Lehnert
Ruhr-Universität Bochum, Germany

Gregory Kramer
Clarity/Santa Fe Institute, Garrison, New York

Elizabeth Wenzel
NASA Ames Research Center, Moffett Field, California

Nathaniel Durlach
Massachusetts Institute of Technology

(Received September 1994; revised October 1994)

Many factors must be considered in designing spatial acoustic displays, including the technology used to generate the sensory cues as well as the perceptual factors that affect how much information is received by the listener. After discussing auditory displays in general, this chapter reviews the psychophysical cues that affect auditory spatial processing, including how acoustic cues can be influenced by spatial cues from other modalities. Methods for simulating acoustic spatial cues are then discussed, followed by a more detailed examination of factors affecting the design of a virtual environment (which includes the dynamic simulation of acoustic spatial cues). Finally, some experimental results are presented that address how human performance on auditory spatial tasks may be limited by perceptual factors as well as by the chosen method of display.

INTRODUCTION

In this chapter, we review past and current work on the display of information to human observers via the auditory system, that is, on auditory displays. In general, the sources of the information need not be acoustic, and there is no constraint on how the information is encoded in terms of acoustic signals; all that is required is that the information be displayed acoustically.

In accordance with the main thrust of this book, most of the discussion in this chapter is concerned with the spatial aspects of auditory displays. However, before focussing on these aspects, we consider auditory displays from a more general point of view in order to provide a display-oriented context for the subsequent discussion of spatial features.

After discussing some general issues associated with auditory displays (Sec. I), we review briefly the psychophysics of auditory localization (Sec. II). We then focus on simulation of auditory space and on spatial auditory displays (Sec. III), and on the implementation of such displays in virtual environments (Sec. IV). Finally, we discuss briefly some recent work directed toward the development of displays that provide supernormal localization (Sec. V).

No attention is given in this chapter to speech sounds or to physical modeling for the computer generation of sounds.

I. GENERAL ISSUES IN AUDITORY DISPLAYS

The major goal of research on auditory displays is to develop improved displays for human–machine interfaces by making use of knowledge about how we hear, about how we use sound in everyday life, about how we adapt to new uses of sound, and about how we organize and interpret various types of sound streams. Within this field of research, there are two major foci: audification and sonification. In audification, the acoustic stimulus involves direct playback of data samples (Kramer, 1994), with frequency shifting employed, if necessary, to bring the signals into the audible frequency range. Examples in this category are the display of very-low-frequency seismic data (Hayward, 1994) and of very-high-frequency radiotelescope data (Terenzi, 1988). In sonification, data are used to control various parameters of a sound generator in such a manner that a person listening to the output sound is able to extract some meaning about the controlling data. Although sonification is generally much more abstract than audification, in both sonification and audification, various acoustic features (e.g., temporal onsets and offsets, timbre, pitch, intensity, and rhythm) are used to convey information to the listener.

In the following subsections, we consider briefly some of the advantages and disadvantages of auditory displays, some of the tasks and applications for which auditory displays are likely to prove useful, and some questions related to future research. As already indicated, in the later sections of this chapter attention is confined exclusively to spatial aspects of the displays.

A. Advantages and disadvantages of auditory displays

The advantages and disadvantages of using an auditory display depend on the specific task under consideration. Nevertheless, there are certain basic features of the auditory channel and its relation to the visual channel that are worth considering when designing an auditory display.

When the visual channel is being heavily used and the auditory channel is relatively free (in particular, when the speech communication load is light or nonexistent), it obviously makes sense to supplement the visual display with an auditory display. Whether or not such supplementation is appropriately described as sensory substitution depends on whether the information presented via the auditory display is normally presented to the visual system.

Two task components that are particularly well suited to auditory displays are monitoring and alerting, because the auditory system is able to ignore expected sounds, while rapidly detecting and attending to unexpected sounds. Within the general alerting category, spatially directing attention and orienting are intimately related to the natural function of the auditory system.

A closely related advantage of the auditory system is its ability to monitor (or listen in parallel to) multiple data streams simultaneously. This ability depends in part on the perceptual segregation of the streams and in part on the ability of the listener to selectively attend to significant events within any one of the streams at will. Thus, it is also important to consider the topics of auditory Gestalt formation and auditory scene analysis in the design of auditory displays.

Auditory displays are also well suited to the task of making temporal comparisons. The auditory system not only provides acute temporal resolution, but it can also perceive temporal patterns over a broad range of time scales. Thus, auditory displays are extremely useful for presenting streams of time-sequenced data of broad dynamic range.

Affective features of the auditory channel that are relevant to the use of auditory displays concern the general ability of auditory displays to engage the subject and to cause strong emotional responses (as in music).

Use of multimodal displays that include both auditory and visual channels can increase the subjective quality of the displays, as well as the objective amount of information transferred to a user. When correlated visual and auditory information is presented, the user often fuses the information from the two modalities into a single perceptual event, and the information within each channel is reinforced. When correlated multimodal displays are immersive and interactive (e.g., in a multimodal virtual environment) they more accurately simulate real-world experience and allow the user to explore information using already well-developed skills; however, information transfer from one modality can be decreased when disparate information from two modalities is fused into one event. For example, visual spatial information may totally dominate judgments of a fused source's position and thus destroy auditory spatial information (see Sec. II.B).

Many of the limitations on the usefulness of auditory displays are similar to those that occur with displays in other modalities. Thus, for example, the amount of information that can be transmitted via an auditory display is limited by the very restricted ability to transfer information to human observers using one-dimensional stimulus sets (Miller, 1956) and by the lack of perceptual orthogonality among many objective stimulus dimensions (e.g., intensity and frequency, or intensity and duration).

Limitations that are uniquely relevant to the auditory channel (as compared to the visual channel) include relatively poor spatial resolution and the inability to shut off annoying sounds (we are sensitive to sounds from all directions and have no ear-lids). The greatest drawback, however, concerns the transitory nature of sounds and the associated difficulties inherent in scanning artificially stored sounds. One need only consider the problems of interfacing with a computer using only audio (e.g., see Arons, 1991, 1993) to appreciate the problems associated with this feature of auditory displays.

B. Task types and applications

There are two types of tasks that seem to require somewhat different approaches to the design of the associated auditory displays: monitoring and data exploration.

Monitoring tasks generally involve listening for known patterns in the sound. Examples of common auditory monitoring tasks are listening to the cadence of a heart monitor for irregularities or attending to an auditory signal representing seismic information in order to identify important events. Such tasks usually employ some form of template matching and thus require a limited but unambiguous display of the data. In general, such tasks require that the user be trained to recognize a known universe of possible sounds and to know what such sounds indicate in the data. In data-exploration tasks, although some such template matching may also be required, the need to search and to test various hypotheses requires greater flexibility and tolerance of ambiguity. These tasks thus favor use of a "soft-wired" and interactive user interface that allows users to scale, reroute, and preprocess data, to select regions of interest, to perform statistical analysis, and to undertake other operations.

To date, most of the applications of auditory displays have been experimental. The exceptions tend to consist of real-time monitoring tasks in games, alarm systems, speech interfaces, and devices for the blind (e.g., thermometers). Other examples of commonly used rudimentary auditory displays include the tones used in electronic circuit testers and the notification tones used in automobiles, planes, and boats. The use of auditory displays in entertainment has been taken for granted ever since the introduction of background music in movies. Sound effects in games, and now in toys, are becoming standard. Similarly, simple auditory displays, including the beeps of the heart monitor and alarms in intensive care units, have been used in medical monitoring for years. In these applications, auditory displays convey the status of a system in rather elementary terms. The monitoring tasks undertaken to date are sufficiently simple that little training is necessary and displays are capable of presenting the cues in a relatively straightforward manner.

More sophisticated auditory displays for medical monitoring, such as those included in the anesthesiologist's workstation (Fitch and Kramer, 1994), are now being studied. Tasks demanding heightened attention in complex environments are driving the development of auditory displays in aircraft flight decks (Patterson, 1982), air traffic control (Wenzel, 1994; Begault and Wenzel, 1992), financial trading desks (Kramer, 1994), and, of course, sonar. Several recent papers have described the use of auditory displays for debugging software (Jameson, 1994) and analyzing processor performance in parallel computers (Francioni, Albright, and Jackson, 1991; Madhyastha and Reed, 1994). Factories with human process control monitors, such as paper and steel mills, and assembly lines also stand to benefit from auditory display technology (Gaver, Smith, and O'Shea, 1991).

Some relatively complex tasks already employ auditory displays because such displays, although imperfect, are still superior to other types of displays. Some examples of more complex auditory-display applications include the use of instrumentation designed for vision-impaired users, such as the Lunney chromatograph (Lunney and Morrison, 1981), the Smith Kettlewell Auditory Oscilloscope (Scadden, 1978), the Loomis navigation system (Loomis, Hebert, and Cicinelli, 1990), and the acoustic interface of Edwards (1989). More complex auditory displays for sighted users, such as the Geiger counter and metal detector, center around eyes-busy tasks.

In contrast to the use of auditory displays for monitoring, effective data exploration often requires extensive training and more sophisticated tools than are currently available. However, the use of auditory displays is currently under investigation for the exploration of data from a wide variety of fields, including computer science (Brown, 1992), mathematics (Mayer-Kress, Bargar, and Choi, 1994; Kramer and Ellison, 1991), physics (Rabenhorst, Farrell, Jameson, Linton, and Mandelman, 1990), finance (Mezrich, Frysinger, and Slivjanovski, 1984; Kramer, 1994), and medicine (Smith, 1991). Other types of data targeted for auditory exploration, inspection, and analysis include seismic (Hayward, 1994), census (Smith, 1991; Madhyastha and Reed, 1994), environmental (Scaletti and Craig, 1991), astrophysical (Terenzi, 1988), geographical (Blattner, Glinert, and Papp, 1994), cartographic (Weber, 1993; Krygier, 1992), and neurological (Witten, 1992). In addition, auditory displays may be used to understand simulation results, including those of artificial hearts and rotors (McCabe and Rangwalla, 1994) and predator/prey models (Kramer, 1990).

Multimodal systems that include auditory displays have been used for many years in the area of teleoperation (e.g., Johnsen and Corliss, 1967; Vertut and Coiffet, 1986; Sheridan, 1992) and are now also being used extensively in the area of virtual environments (e.g., Wenzel, Stone, Fisher, and Foster, 1990; Cruz-Neira, Sandin, and DeFanti, 1993; Hodges, Bolter, Mynatt, Ribarsky, and van Teylingen, 1993; Zyda, Pratt, Falby, Barham, and Kelleher, 1993; Cohen and Wenzel, 1995). Examples of specific applications (beyond the many applications centered on speech communication) include architectural design (Persterer, 1989; Foster and Wenzel, 1991; Foster, Wenzel, and Taylor, 1991; see also Applied Acoustics, **36**, 1992), shared electronic workspaces (Fisher, Wenzel, Coler, and McGreevy, 1988; Gaver *et al.*, 1991), and aeronautics displays (Begault and Wenzel, 1992). A more complete review of auditory virtual environment work can be found in the National Academy of Sciences review (Durlach and Mavor, 1994).

C. Future work

The use of auditory displays for complex tasks is a relatively new field. Historically, most of the work in psychoacoustics has focused on the perception of relatively simple sounds. Only recently has work been undertaken that investigates the perception of complex, multivariate sounds, for instance, in the perception of environmental sounds (Ballas, 1994), music (Deutsch, 1982), and multiple sound streams (Bregman, 1984, 1990; Blattner, Sumikawa, and Greenberg, 1989; Buxton, Gaver, and Bly, 1989).

Auditory display of high-dimensionality data will depend on the use of multiple acoustic cues; however, as yet very little work has been done in this field. Questions to be addressed include identifying the most salient acoustic cues available, quantifying the usefulness of different cues, learning how to compare different cue dimensions, exploring how total information transfer is affected by increasing the number of acoustic cues present, determining how multiple cues interact and either interfere or augment each other, and finding optimal strategies for choosing acoustic cues to encode information for a given application.

A related set of questions arises from the emotional associations many acoustic percepts cause. For instance, musical attributes such as tempo, harmonicity, and similar variables are easily perceived; however, such cues may be unsuitable for the display of certain quantitative information simply because of their emotional impact. On the other hand, these attributes of acoustic cues may be beneficial for many applications. Another area to be investigated is how qualitative differences between display techniques may make a particular display strategy advantageous for certain applications (e.g., there are indications that certain individuals learn more effectively from auditory rather than visual information; Hunter and McCants, 1977; Gardner, 1985).

As auditory display techniques mature, the need for a common protocol for data formatting will become more and more pressing. Sonification is at the point that data visualization was a decade ago. Substantial progress is likely in a number of areas, including development of effective architectures for providing flexible sound synthesis and increased understanding of the effectiveness of various sonification techniques.

II. PSYCHOPHYSICS OF AUDITORY LOCALIZATION

Although the previous section discussed general issues concerning the use of auditory displays, the remainder of this chapter focuses on the display of one specific class of cues, namely, cues related to the perceived location of a sound source. The current section examines some of the psychophysical bases for the perception of sound source location, reviewing first some basic results in spatial hearing and then studies of how information from other spatial modalities affects auditory localization.

A. Overview of spatial hearing

The utility of a spatial auditory display depends greatly on the user's ability to localize the various sources of information in auditory space. Thus, designers of such interfaces must carefully consider the acoustic cues needed by listeners for accurate localization and ensure that these cues will be faithfully (or at least adequately, in a human performance sense) transduced by the synthesis device. When psychophysical results are included in design considerations, the designs can make optimal use of computational resources, and thereby achieve the best possible overall performance.

Much of the research on human sound localization has derived from the classical "duplex theory" (Lord Rayleigh, 1907), which emphasizes the role of two primary cues: interaural intensity differences (IIDs), mainly used for high-frequency components, and interaural time differences (ITDs), used primarily for low-frequency components. Binaural research over the last few decades, however, points to serious limitations with this approach. For example, ITDs in the envelopes of high-frequency sounds with significant bandwidth also provide localization cues (e.g., Henning, 1974). A further set of acoustic cues not included in the duplex theory concerns the direction-dependent spectral information that occurs when incoming sound waves impinge on the listener's head, particularly his or her pinnae (Blauert, 1969; Butler and Belendiuk, 1977; Oldfield and Parker, 1986). Experiments have shown that spectral shaping by the pinnae is highly direction dependent (Shaw, 1974, 1975), that the absence of pinna cues degrades localization accuracy (Gardner and Gardner, 1973; Oldfield and Parker, 1984b), and that pinna cues aid in externalization or the "outside-of-the-head" sensation (Plenge, 1974), as well as in determining the elevation of a source. These spectral cues enable the listener to gain localization information monaurally provided he or she has adequate *a priori* information on the spectrum of the transmitted signal. The importance of these monaural cues is well demonstrated by results on the localization capabilities of subjects who are unilaterally deaf (Hausler, Colburn, and Marr, 1983).

In many headphone localization studies or localization studies in which the listener's head is restrained, localization "reversals" occur. Front-to-back reversals (where a sound simulated in the front hemisphere of the listener is heard at the mirror-image position in the rear hemisphere) are the most common type observed, although back-to-front (e.g., Oldfield and Parker, 1984a), up-to-down, and down-to-up (Wenzel, Arruda, Kistler, and Wightman, 1993) reversals have also been reported. These reversals are generally predictable by assuming that the head is a rigid sphere with two receivers at opposite ends of a diameter and noting that the surface over which interaural differences are constant can be approximated by a family of cones ("cones of confusion") whose axes are collinear with the interaural axis (Mills, 1972). Kuhn (1977) has shown that interaural delays can be predicted from the rigid-sphere model for frequencies below 4 kHz, whereas Middlebrooks and Green (1990) observed a similar phenomenon for interaural envelope delays in narrowband signals ranging from 3 to 16 kHz. The situation for IIDs appears to be more complex. Middlebrooks, Makous, and Green (1989) observed iso-IID contours that increased monotonically with increasing azimuth for frequencies below 8 kHz as predicted by the model, but for higher frequencies, the regions of constant IID were dependent on both the azimuth and elevation of the source in a complicated manner (also see Duda, Chapter 3, this volume).

Several cues are thought to help to disambiguate the cones of confusion. One is the complex spectral shaping of the received signal as a function of location that was described above (e.g., see Blauert's 1983 discussion of "boosted bands," pp. 107–116). A cue that is more robust (because it does not depend on the availability of adequate *a priori* information about the source spectrum) occurs when the listener is free to move his or her head. Head movements have been shown to influence the apparent source position and to reduce the probability of reversals in a wide variety of circumstances (e.g., Wallach, 1939, 1940; Thurlow, Mangels, and Runge, 1967; Thurlow and Runge, 1967; Fisher and Freedman, 1968; Wightman, Kistler, and Anderson, 1994).

The accuracy with which single sources in anechoic environments can be localized depends on their location relative to the listener's head. Source azimuths directly in front of the listener can be discriminated when they differ by about a degree; however, the just-noticeable-difference (JND) in source azimuth to the extreme left or right of a subject is roughly 5–10 times this size (Blauert, 1983, pp. 37–50; Mills, 1958). The JND in elevation is on the order of 10–15° (Blauert, 1983, pp. 44–46).

Other perceptual effects influence performance when multiple sources are to be localized. When sources from different positions in space are played concurrently, their spatial information is often combined by the listener, even when the sources do not overlap in frequency content (Dye, 1990; Stellmack and Dye, 1993; Buell and Hafter, 1990). This perceptual integration decreases the accuracy with which each source can be localized. In addition, hearing simultaneous sources can interfere with the reception of the content of the sounds as well. The amount of interference decreases with the spatial separation of the sources (the "cocktail-party effect"; Durlach and Colburn, 1978; Colburn and Durlach, 1978; Cherry, 1953; Bronkhorst and Plomp, 1988). Sources need not be simultaneous to affect each other. If two sources are presented within 1–10 ms of each other, the apparent position of both sources is dominated by the position of the source reaching the ears first (the precedence effect or, alternatively, the law of the first wavefront or the Haas effect; see Wallach, Newman, and Rosenzweig, 1949; Blauert, 1971; Zurek, 1979, 1980, 1987; Gaskell, 1983; Divenyi, 1992), and the ability to determine the location of the later arriving source is seriously compromised. As the onset delay between the sources increases, the relative dominance of the initial source decreases; however, the location information from the two sources continues to be combined perceptually so that the apparent locations of each source are biased by the location of the other source (Wallach *et al.*, 1949; Zurek, 1979, 1980, 1987; Shinn-Cunningham, Zurek, and Durlach, 1993). Thus, even under circumstances in which the location of single sound sources can be reliably discriminated, discrimination of source position for multiple sources can be difficult or impossible.

The cues discussed so far encode two out of the three spatial dimensions: azimuth and elevation. The third spatial dimension, that of distance, is a much less salient percept for human listeners. Humans are rather poor at judging the absolute distance of sound sources and relatively little is known about the parameters that determine distance perception (Coleman, 1963; Laws, 1972).

Some information on distance can be obtained from loudness by exploiting *a priori* information about the intensity of the source (Mershon and King, 1975; Mershon and Bowers, 1979) or by exploiting the change in loudness with motion (Ashmead, LeRoy, and Odom, 1990; Speigle and Loomis, 1993). Information on distance can also be obtained from spectral shape (because high frequencies tend to be attenuated with distance more than low frequencies) and by exploiting *a priori* information about the spectrum of the source (Coleman, 1968; Gardner, 1968b; Little, Mershon, and Cox, 1992). Finally, an additional cue arises from estimating the ratio of reflected to direct energy when localizing in echoic environments (Mershon and King, 1975; Mershon, Ballenger, Little, McMurtry, and Buchanan, 1989).

The perception of distance is closely related to the externalization of a sound source. Either when listening in an anechoic space with head restrained or when listening over headphones, sound sources often fail to be perceived as external to the listener's head (Toole, 1969; Plenge, 1974). The tendency to localize sound sources inside the head is increased if the signals are unfamiliar (Coleman, 1963; Gardner, 1968b). Thus, the use of familiar signals in the presence of cues that provide a sense of distance and environmental context (such as the ratio of reflected to direct energy and other characteristics specific to echoic spaces) may help to enhance the externalization of images (Coleman, 1963; Gardner, 1968a; Laws, 1972, 1973; Plenge, 1974; Borish, 1984; Begault, 1987). A recent review of the factors influencing externalization can be found in Durlach, Rigopulos, Pang, Woods, Kulkarni, Colburn, and Wenzel (1992).

This overview is necessarily brief, ignoring all but some of the most important acoustic cues in auditory localization. In addition, cognitive factors and other more complex acoustic cues may affect localization performance (e.g., expectations of source level and character can affect the apparent distance of a source; Gardner, 1968b, 1969a). For more extensive discussions of spatial hearing, the reader is referred to the in-depth reviews by Blauert (1983) and Yost and Gourevitch (1987), as well as to many of the other chapters in this volume.

B. Intersensory bias and adaptation of audition

Although acoustic cues determine much of how sound sources are localized, spatial cues from other modalities also affect sound localization. These interactions among the senses have been studied under the guise of sensorimotor-bias and sensorimotor-adaptation experiments.

In typical studies of sensorimotor adaptation and bias, sensory relationships are rearranged such that different modalities give discordant information about the observers environment, and the subject's resultant spatial perceptions are measured. These studies can be broken into two different categories (as in Welch and Warren, 1986): initial bias effects (reviewed in Welch and Warren, 1980, 1986) and adaptation (reviewed in Welch, 1978, 1986). Studies of initial bias typically examine which spatial modality dominates localization judgments when intermodal discrepancies are first presented to a subject. In studies of sensorimotor adaptation, subjects are exposed to intermodal discrepancies for more extended time periods in order to measure how they learn to compensate for the discrepancies (by examining how response bias changes with exposure). In adaptation studies, true adaptation is said to occur if subjects correct for discrepancies via some automatic, unconscious process, rather than a purely conscious process. If subjects show negative after-effects in their response bias when the discrepancy is removed (errors opposite to the errors originally induced by the intermodal discrepancy), adaptation is indicated.

1. Intersensory bias

A number of studies have examined how perceived body position and perceived body motion bias auditory spatial perception. When vestibular cues give rise to illusory perceptions, exocentric auditory localization judgments are biased (Arnoult, 1950, 1952; Thurlow and Kerr, 1970; Graybiel and Niven, 1951; Lackner, 1973b, 1974a, 1974b, 1983; Lackner and Levine, 1979; Lackner and Shenker, 1983; Clark and Graybiel, 1963; Mann and Passey, 1951; Teuber and Diamond, 1956; Teuber and Liebert, 1956). Under some conditions, visual rearrangement alters perceived body or limb position. When subjects then are asked to localize exocentric auditory targets, their responses are affected by the perceived positions of their bodies (Lackner, 1973a, 1973b; Freedman and Rekosh, 1965; Cohen, 1974).

Auditory spatial judgments can be strongly biased by discrepant visual or proprioceptive spatial information, such that auditory sources are perceptually displaced towards the location of the visual or proprioceptive stimulus. In fact, when visual and acoustic spatial cues are in conflict, the bias is so strong that subjects sometimes perceive the auditory stimulus as arising from the same point as the visual stimulus. This is known as the ventriloquism effect (see, e.g., Thomas, 1941; Radeau and Bertelson, 1974). Although strong, the ventriloquism effect is usually not complete: Auditory localization judgments are typically displaced by about 50–80% of the difference between visual and auditory source positions. In addition, auditory spatial cues often bias visual spatial perception, but to a much smaller degree than visual cues bias auditory perception, on the order of 6% of the discrepancy (e.g., Pick, Warren, and Hay, 1969; Warren and Pick, 1970; Canon, 1971; Warren, Welch, and McCarthy, 1981). A similar result is found when proprioceptive and acoustic spatial cues are in opposition (Pick *et al.*, 1969; Willot, 1973; Warren and Pick, 1970).

Although vision and proprioception always have stronger effects on auditory spatial perception than auditory cues have on either of these other spatial senses, experimental conditions can alter the relative strengths of these interactions. Generally, when exposure conditions give the subject less complete information about his or her environment, less interaction is found between modalities. For example, vision-induced immediate bias and postexposure after-effects on audition are decreased when subjects view isolated visual targets compared to situations where a "visual reference frame" is available (Radeau and Bertelson, 1976). Similarly, visual influence on auditory judgments and auditory influence on visual judgments are both weaker when subjects are exposed to discrepant stimuli while their heads are fixed compared to when they are free to move (Canon, 1970).

A number of experiments have shown that visual and auditory cues that are less likely to arise from a single source cause weaker bias in both directions. Interaction decreases with the decreasing temporal correlation of auditory and visual cues (Thomas, 1941), with increasing intersensory delay (Jack and Thurlow, 1973; Radeau and Bertelson, 1977), and with increasing spatial discrepancy of the cues (Jack and Thurlow, 1973; Warren, McCarthy, and Welch, 1983). If subjects are told to attend to one modality (either vision or audition) and to ignore the other, each modality is biased less when it is attended to than when it is ignored (Canon, 1970). When subjects are explicitly told that discrepancies between sensory modalities may exist, bias still occurs in both directions but the magnitude of the interactions is decreased (Radeau and Bertelson, 1974; Warren, 1980; Warren *et al.*, 1983). Finally, a factor variously described as "compellingness" (Warren *et al.*, 1983), "realism" (Radeau and Bertelson, 1977), and "degree of correspondence" (Jack and Thurlow, 1973) has been shown to be positively correlated with the strength of bias effects.[1]

One final, important factor that affects the relative perceptual strengths of different modalities is the developmental age of the subjects. Most studies that directly compared the relative perceptual strengths of spatial cues from vision, proprioception, and audition found that vision carries the most weight, proprioception an intermediate amount, and audition the least (e.g., Pick *et al.*, 1969; Warren and Pick, 1970; Willot, 1973). However, for grade school children, proprioceptive cues are the most strongly weighted (Warren and Pick, 1970). In the same study, blind subjects weighed proprioception more strongly than vision or audition, similar to the pattern seen in normal-sighted grade school children; subjects who had some vision impairment exhibited relative weightings that fell between those shown by normal-sighted and those shown by blind subjects. This study emphasizes the important role vision plays in spatial perception for normal, adult subjects.

The importance of vision in spatial perception is further supported by studies of visual facilitation. In these studies, visual cues give no obvious spatial information to subjects, but subjects are able to make more accurate auditory spatial judgments with visual cues than without. Eye movement toward the source causes a facilitating effect over having the eyes fixated or moving the eyes in the direction opposite the sound source (Jones and Kabanoff, 1975; Platt and Warren, 1972; Ryan and Schehr, 1941). In addition, facilitation provided by eye movements is greater in the light than in the dark (Warren, 1970; Platt and Warren, 1972; Mastroianni, 1982). When both eye movements and a lit visual frame are present, a statistically significant facilitation can generally be found. Finally, visual facilitation effects depend on the age of subjects; second graders show no visual facilitation, whereas sixth graders and adults do (Warren, 1970).

2. Adaptation to auditory rearrangement

A number of investigators have studied adaptation to different rotational acoustic cue rearrangements using pseudophones (a pseudophone is an acoustical

[1]For example, a video of someone speaking has a much stronger biasing effect on the apparent location of a voice than does the picture of a simple cube.

hat containing microphones and earphones arranged in a manner that transforms the acoustical stimuli to the eardrums in some desired manner). In the most severe cases (Young, 1928; Willey, Inglis, and Pearce, 1937), where 180° rotations were used, little adaptation was found after days of exposure. Studies in which smaller pseudophone-induced rotations (from 20° to 30°) were employed show adaptation can occur under a broad range of experimental conditions and localization measures (e.g., Freedman, Wilson, and Rekosh, 1967; Freedman and Stampfer, 1964a, 1964b; Freedman and Gardos, 1965; Freedman and Wilson, 1967; Craske, 1966). In some cases, subjects who were trained with hand movement tasks using only one hand showed shifts when pointing to both auditory and visual targets with the exposed hand (Freedman and Gardos, 1965; Rekosh and Freedman, 1967; Freedman and Rekosh, 1965; Lackner, 1974b; Craske, 1966; Mikaelian, 1969), but little or no adaptation to auditory or visual targets when tested with the unexposed hand (Mikaelian, 1972, 1974; Mikaelian and Russotti, 1972), implying that in at least some of these studies, auditory rearrangement caused changes in proprioceptive perception, not in auditory perception.

The amount of adaptation was never complete in the foregoing studies. Typically, changes in localization judgments increased with exposure time (Freedman and Stampfer, 1964a, 1964b), and greater, faster adaptation occurred when subjects were allowed free motion versus cases where they sat still or were passively moved (Held, 1955; Freedman and Zacks, 1964). In comparing conditions, larger shifts occurred when subjects had more information available for otherwise similar exposure conditions [e.g., in one experiment, shifts of 40% were found when subjects could view their surroundings (Freedman and Gardos, 1965); however, only a 27% shift was found for similar conditions when subjects were blindfolded (Freedman, Hall, and Rekosh, 1965)].

Wien (1964) performed pseudophone experiments in which the headwidth was effectively expanded to roughly three times the normal size. Although localization bias did not decrease for all the subjects while wearing the pseudophone, all subjects showed a negative after-effect following exposure when tested without the pseudophone.

A few studies have examined how subjects adapt to auditory location information underwater, where acoustic cues are decreased because the speed of sound is increased relative to in-air localization. In these studies, localization resolution is reduced for both humans (Feinstein, 1966) and other mammals (Terhune, 1974), as might be expected from the decrease in cue salience. The only study that examined whether localization judgment bias is affected by underwater exposure showed only weak after-effects (Wells and Ross, 1980).

The majority of studies of localization by hearing-impaired subjects have measured either resolution or overall error (which confounds response bias with response variability), rather than employing direct measures of response bias. Florentine (1976) demonstrated that unilaterally impaired subjects show significant bias in localization toward the unimpaired ear (in the direction that a normal listener would perceive a source with large interaural level differences), even though subjects had been impaired for over three years. For subjects who wear hearing aids most of the time, some subjects actually localize better without the aid than with it (Hausler, Colburn, and Marr, 1983). These studies imply that impaired subjects do not fully adapt to their permanent "rearrangement." Other studies have simulated unilateral (Bauer, Matuzsa, and Blackmer, 1966; Florentine, 1976) or bilateral (Russell, 1977; Mershon and Lin, 1987) hearing impairment in order to observe how localization performance changes with time. Partial adaptation occurred gradually, for some subjects taking up to 20 days to stabilize. Most surprisingly, some subjects took even longer to readjust to normal listening than they did to adapt (Florentine, 1976). One aspect of adaptation to simulated or actual hearing impairments is that cues are not simply rearranged; they are often degraded. A number of studies show that hearing impairment decreases resolution (Russell, 1977; Hausler *et al.*, 1983), in addition to increasing localization bias.

3. Adaptation to sensory substitution

Auditory localization cues have been used as a way of presenting information that is normally interpreted by sensory organs other than the ears. One of the most systematic studies of such sensory substitution investigated the use of the Binaural Sensory Aid (Kay, 1974), a device that uses ultrasound echo location to determine the distance and direction of objects. With this system, distance was coded by the frequency of the carrier signal presented, and interaural intensity differences were used to represent directional information. Warren and Strelow (1984, 1985) showed that blindfolded subjects are able to adapt and use these cues accurately when trained using a simple correct-answer feedback paradigm on a 25-position identification task (where the positions made up a five-distance, five-azimuth grid). Training effectiveness did not depend on the order of presentation of the training trials, but decreased significantly when subjects were trained on each dimension separately. Performance asymptoted more quickly for distance cues than for azimuth cues, an effect that the investigators attributed to the fact that resolution of distance cues was much better than resolution of azimuth cues for the ranges employed. Training effectiveness decreased monotonically as feedback was delayed from no delay up to 30 s (Warren and Strelow, 1985).

Another example of sensory substitution is found in the work of Gescheider (1965, 1966, 1968), who performed experiments in which acoustic localization cues were presented cutaneously via vibrators. In both this work and the work on bilocal cutaneous unmasking by Braida (1964), as well as the earlier work by von Bekesy (e.g., von Bekesy, 1957), the cutaneous system was stimulated by the use of two vibrators and the stimuli were structured in a manner similar to that used in stimulating the auditory system. In other words, no attempt was made to code the information by the use of an array of vibrators and a transformation that maps various signal characteristics (e.g., frequency spectrum) onto the array (as is frequently done in work on the tactile reception of speech). Although the results on cutaneous analogs of binaural hearing by such investigators as Gescheider, Braida, and Bekesy are not entirely consistent, many of these results suggest strong analogs between binaural auditory perception and bilocal cutaneous reception.

4. Modeling

Although many studies of intersensory interaction have been undertaken, a relatively small amount of work has been done to model these results. What modeling has been performed has not been quantitative, but rather describes in general terms what conditions lead to more complete immediate bias or adaptation (e.g., Welch and Warren, 1980; Welch, 1978, p. 280). A great deal of work will still be required to develop a quantitative model of how discrepant information is integrated across modalities. Such models may ultimately lead to insights into both auditory spatial perception and integration of information across spatial modalities.

III. SPATIAL AUDITORY DISPLAYS

One great benefit of spatial auditory displays is that they allow users to monitor and identify sources of information from all possible locations, not just the direction of gaze. This characteristic of the auditory channel is especially useful in inherently spatial tasks, particularly when visual cues are limited and workload is high. For example, recent research at NASA Ames has investigated the utility of spatial acoustic displays for use in air traffic control and aviation warning systems, both in the tower and in the cockpit (Begault and Wenzel, 1992; Begault, 1993; Begault and Erbe, 1993; Begault and Pittman, 1994). Although visual spatial resolution is an order of magnitude better than auditory spatial resolution, the omnidirectionality of acoustic displays can enhance the utility of a spatial visual display. In fact, Perrott, Sadralodabai, Saberi, and Strybel (1991) recently reported that aurally guided visual search for a target in a cluttered visual display is superior to unaided visual search, even for objects in the central visual field.

Spatial acoustic displays can also enhance the auditory system's ability to segregate, monitor, and switch attention among simultaneous streams of sound (Mowbray and Gebhard, 1961) because one of the most important determinants of acoustic segregation is an object's location in space (Kubovy and Howard, 1976; Bregman, 1981, 1990; Deutsch, 1982). This ability is related to the "cocktail-party effect" discussed previously (Durlach and Colburn, 1978; Colburn and Durlach, 1978; Cherry, 1953; Bronkhorst and Plomp, 1988). These enhancements can be critical in applications involving simultaneous speech channels, as in aviation communication systems, or combinations of speech signals and the kind of encoded nonspeech cues proposed for scientific visualization.

The success of different approaches to simulating spatial auditory cues is determined by the psychophysical validity of the method. The following subsection reviews various approaches to creating spatial auditory displays and discusses some of the advantages and drawbacks of the various approaches.

A. Simulation techniques

1. Simulation using speakers

One of the simplest approaches to simulating veridical auditory localization cues is to place speakers at those locations around the listener from which sources are to be simulated. This approach, although effective perceptually, requires considerable space and is extremely inflexible. A variant on this approach uses a small number of speakers to simulate the sound field for a listener seated at a particular location in the room (e.g., see Meares, 1992; Miyoshi and Koizumi, 1992; Gierlich, 1992). This type of simulation has been used extensively for home audio systems, as well as in applications concerned with room acoustics and telecommunications. Often, however, because of space requirements or because of the need to have more precise stimulus control, spatial acoustic stimulation is achieved by using earphones and synthesized spatialization.

2. Binaural recordings

One of the easiest ways to generate auditory localization stimuli for playback over headphones is to make binaural recordings of signals by placing microphones in the ears of a manikin (Plenge, 1974; Doll, Gerth, Engelman, and Folds, 1986) or of a human (Butler and Belendiuk, 1977) and to present these recordings to listeners over headphones. Such recordings can give an immediate and essentially veridical perception of three-dimensional auditory space (Plenge, 1974; Butler and Belendiuk, 1977; Blauert, 1983; Doll *et al.*, 1986; Durlach, Rigopulos, Pang, Woods, Kulkarni, Colburn, and Wenzel, 1992). The naturalness of such recordings is not surprising: These recordings include all localization cues normally available to a listener except those dynamic changes in cues that would occur for real external sources when the listener moves his or her head. Although such recordings are extremely effective, their utility for general display purposes is limited by their inflexibility: Recordings must be made for every source to be displayed at every possible position around the listener in every environment to be simulated. Even so, the use of manikins (e.g., KEMAR by Knowles Electronics, Inc., or other artificial heads developed by Hudde and Schroeter, 1981, or Gierlich and Genuit, 1989) has proven extremely useful for architectural acoustics applications, such as assessing concert-hall acoustics and making spatially realistic recordings of music (see Blauert, 1983).

3. Teleoperator systems

One of the earliest kinds of systems in which spatial acoustic cues were made available in signals presented through earphones was teleoperator systems. In these kinds of systems, natural acoustic signals are sensed by a pair of microphones (telerobotic ears) and presented directly to the listener through earphones in real-time. In the event that the position of the listener's head is tracked and used to control the position of the telerobotic ears, dynamic cues can also be represented in such a system.

Examples of such auditory teleoperator systems include a system used in World War I to help detect and localize hostile aircraft (see Fig. 4 in Wenzel, 1992), the work by Doll at the Georgia Institute of Technology (Doll *et al.*, 1986), and the system developed for the Super Cockpit Project at Wright-Patterson Air Force Base (Gehring AL100, discussed in Calhoun, Valencia, and Furness, 1987). In many such teleoperator systems, listeners hear binaural signals sensed by microphones in an artificial head, the orientation of which is mechanically coupled to the orientation of the listener's head. To the extent that these systems make use of high-fidelity components, they provide all the static and dynamic cues that would have been available to a listener positioned in the environment where the sensors are located. Of course, only the remote environment in which the sensors reside can be represented in such displays.

4. Synthesis using head-related transfer functions

Although binaural recording and playback techniques do not themselves permit the simulation of arbitrary signals in arbitrary spaces, their perceptual effectiveness suggests that perceptually veridical spatialization over headphones is possible if the interaural difference cues and the spectral shape cues are adequately reproduced. All such effects can be described by linear, time-invariant filters that depend on the position of the source, the position of the listener, and the acoustic environment. Such filters can be estimated from binaural recordings if a known signal from a known position is presented during binaural recording. Once such filters (also referred to as binaural room transfer functions) are estimated, arbitrary sources can be simulated from any position in the room by filtering the source signal with the appropriate left- and right-ear filters, and then presenting the results over headphones.

Filters measured in this manner include both the effects of the room and the direction-dependent effects of the listener's head. Further simulation flexibility can be gained by separating the room effects from the directional effects of the head. This can be achieved by measuring responses in an anechoic space, where room reflections are insignificant. The resulting filters are referred to as head-related transfer functions (HRTFs) because they depend only on the position of the acoustic source relative to the listener's head. By combining acoustic room models with empirically measured HRTFs, sources can be simulated from arbitrary positions around the listener in arbitrary acoustic environments.

Fine details in the HRTFs vary from subject to subject, particularly the details present at high frequencies. The question of how important these intersubject differences are in simulating realistic sound sources is an area of current interest and debate. In general, data suggest that most listeners can obtain useful directional information from an auditory display without requiring the use of individually tailored HRTFs, particularly for the dimension of azimuth. However, the rate of reversals is higher and localization in elevation is less precise when using nonindividualized HRTFs than it is when using individualized HRTFs (Wenzel, Wightman, Kistler, and Foster, 1988; Wenzel, Wightman, and Kistler, 1991; Wenzel *et al.*, 1993). Such problems may decrease, however, when subjects are given sufficient training to adapt to new HRTFs. Questions of this type are currently being explored at a number of laboratories (e.g., NASA Ames, MIT, University of Wisconsin, etc.).

HRTF measurement is a lengthy and difficult process. Thus, the question of whether HRTFs must be individualized to each subject is important for practical as well as theoretical reasons. Although HRTFs are now usually determined empirically (by acoustic measurement), the possibility of generating HRTFs from physically based acoustic models of the head and pinnae has also been explored. In Genuit's work (e.g., Genuit, 1986) in this area, individualized HRTFs are derived mathematically using simplified representations of the head and pinnae and a relatively small number of physical measurements of these structures.

B. Real-time systems

Some early displays synthesized very simple localization cues in real time. An early example of a simple spatial acoustic display is the FLYBAR system (FLYing By Auditory Reference) developed by Forbes (1946) just after World War II. Rather than transducing and transforming real-world sources, this display used only crude left/right intensity panning along with pitch and temporal pattern changes to represent turn, bank, and air speed in a symbolic acoustic display for instrument flying.

With the advent of powerful new digital signal-processing (DSP) chips, real-time auditory spatial display systems based on filtering by HRTFs appeared in Europe and the United States. In general, these systems are intended for headphone delivery and use time-domain convolution to achieve real-time performance. Examples of such systems include the binaural mixing console (CAP 340M creative audio processor) developed by AKG in Austria and based at least partially on work by Blauert (1984, personal communication). The system is aimed at applications like audio recording, acoustic design, and psychoacoustic research (Persterer, 1989; Richter and Persterer, 1989). The system (which uses a 50-kHz sampling rate and 16-bit floating-point computation, and is capable of up to 340-Mflops peak computation speed) is rather large, involving an entire rack of digital signal processors and related hardware, but it can spatialize up to 32 channels in azimuth and elevation along with variable simulation of room response characteristics. A collection of HRTFs is offered, derived from measurements taken in the ear canals of both manikins and individual subjects. A more recent system from the same group is known as the binaural audio processor (BAP). This system simulates an ideal control room for headphone reproduction and the user has the option of having his or her individual transforms programmed onto a PROM card (Persterer, 1991). The BAP is also capable of simulating a source and two identical reflections in real time. So far, neither system has been integrated with interactive head-tracking.

Other projects in Europe include the most recent efforts of Jens Blauert and his colleagues at the Ruhr University at Bochum (Boerger, Laws, and Blauert, 1977; Lehnert and Blauert, 1989; Poesselt, Schroeter, Opitz, Divenyi, and Blauert, 1986). The group at Bochum has been working on a prototype PC-based DSP system, again a kind of binaural mixing console, which performs real-time convolution of HRTFs for up to four sources, interpolation between transforms to simulate motion, and room modeling. Another researcher in Germany, Klaus Genuit, worked at the Institute of Technology of Aachen and later went on to form HEAD Acoustics. Genuit and his colleagues have also produced a real-time, four-channel binaural mixing console using anechoic simulations (Gierlich and

Genuit, 1989). For a review of more recent work by these researchers and others in Europe, see also Applied Acoustics, **36**, 1992.

A final example of a real-time synthesis system is the Roland sound space processing system (RSS; Chan, 1992). This system is designed to simulate spatial cues either for headphone playback or for presentation over speakers. Up to four sources can be simulated in the RSS, which can use either a 44.1- or 48-kHz sampling rate. Time domain processing is performed using 24-bit arithmetic. This system, when used to simulate cues over speakers, includes cross-talk cancellation techniques to improve the veridicality of the simulation.

C. Auditory virtual environments

Although many researchers have developed systems capable of real-time simulation of binaural spatial signals, few have incorporated head-tracking into the display system in order to make a true auditory virtual environment that incorporates dynamic cue changes dependent upon user motion.

One example of a simplistic auditory virtual environment (VE) is that of Loomis et al. (1990), developed as a navigation aid for the blind. In this analog system, which worked well in an active tracking task, spatial cues were approximated using simple interaural time and intensity differences dynamically linked to head motion. The display also included simple distance and reverberation cues such as an intensity rolloff with distance and a fixed ratio of direct-to-reflected energy.

In the United States, a number of projects are currently underway that use real-time DSP systems to simulate localization cues and that include dynamic cues through the incorporation of head-tracking information. For example, the spatialization system developed by McKinley and his associates in the Bioacoustics and Biocommunications Branch of the Armstrong Laboratory at Wright-Patterson Air Force Base was created in order to present three-dimensional audio cues to pilots (McKinley and Ericson, 1988; McKinley, Ericson, and D'Angelo, 1994). The HRTFs incorporated into this system, derived from measurements using the KEMAR mannikin, are sufficiently dense in azimuth (HRTFs are measured every degree in azimuth) to eliminate the need for interpolation in azimuth. In elevation, the measurements are much less dense and linear interpolation is employed. Kendall's group, currently at Northwestern University, has also been working on a real-time system aimed at spatial room modeling for recording and entertainment (e.g., Kendall and Martens, 1984). Gehring Research offers similar systems for real-time anechoic simulation using off-the-shelf DSP cards. This family of systems, known as FocalPoint, uses a 44.1-kHz sampling rate with 16-bit resolution. The HRTFs currently used in the FocalPoint system are from an unspecified source and are described as providing a neutral timbre, suitable for music, entertainment, and virtual reality applications. This family of products can work with a variety of host computer platforms; the systems run independent of the host, except for receiving control messages (e.g., when sources change positions).

The most widely used and commercially successful auditory virtual environment system was developed by a collaborative effort involving researchers at NASA Ames, the University of Wisconsin, and Crystal River Engineering of

Groveland, CA. In the Convolvotron (the commercial product that resulted from this collaboration), a map of HRTFs [represented as finite impulse response (FIR) filters] is downloaded from a host computer to dual-port memory in a special-purpose digital signal processor. The Convolvotron converts monaural analog inputs to digital signals at a rate of 50 kHz with 16-bit resolution. After being filtered by the appropriate HRTFs, the resulting data streams are mixed, converted to left and right analog signals, and presented over headphones. The Convolvotron allows up to four independent and simultaneous anechoic sources to be simulated and has an aggregate computational speed of more than 300 million multiply-accumulates per second. This processing speed is also sufficient for interactively simulating a single source in relatively small reverberant environments (i.e., with head-tracking; Foster and Wenzel, 1991; Foster *et al.*, 1991).

Motion trajectories and static locations at greater resolution than the HRTFs stored in the Convolvotron are simulated by selecting the four measured positions nearest to the desired target location and interpolating with linear weighting functions. The interpolation algorithm effectively computes a new coefficient at the sampling interval (every 20 μs), so that changes in position are free from artifacts like clicks or switching noises. When integrated with one of the fastest, common magnetic head-tracking systems (e.g., Polhemus Fastrak), the listener's head position can be monitored in real-time so that the four simultaneous sources are stabilized in fixed locations or in motion trajectories relative to the user (i.e., simulation of the direct path plus six early reflections with head-tracking).

As with any system required to compute data "on the fly," the term real-time is a relative one. The Convolvotron, including the host computer, has a computational delay of about 30–40 ms, depending on such factors as the number of simultaneous sources, the duration of the HRTFs used as filters, and the complexity of the source geometry. An additional latency of about 10 ms is introduced by the head-tracker. This accumulation of computational delays has important implications for how well the system can simulate realistic moving sources or realistic head motion. At the maximum delay, the system can only update to a new location about every 50 ms. As is discussed in the later section entitled Head-Tracking, these delays imply that moderate relative velocities can be adequately represented by the Convolvotron, while speeds approaching 360°/s should begin to result in perceptible delays, especially when multiple sources or larger filters (e.g., simulations of reverberant rooms) are being generated.

In addition to the Convolvotron, Crystal River Engineering offers two other systems: the Beachtron and the Acoustetron. The Beachtron is a relatively inexpensive system capable of simulating up to two sources in anechoic space using relatively short-impulse-response HRTFs. However, the Beachtron also includes a MIDI interface and digital source inputs. The Acoustetron (made up of four Convolvotrons in a single system) comes with software that contains a relatively simple echoic-space sound-field model that allows simulation of echoic rooms with programmable reflectivity of surfaces, Doppler shift of moving sources, and atmospheric absorption of propagating sources.

More recently, Tucker-Davis Technologies of Gainesville, FL, has produced a new, commercially available, time-domain processor. This machine will contain more memory than has been available on any auditory spatialization system to date. In addition, the product is being designed to maximize the flexibility of the system, allowing researchers to allocate the available processing power as necessary for the individual application.

Frequency-domain filtering will be employed in the Newtron, a next-generation spatialization device under development at Crystal River Engineering. By performing frequency-domain filtering, the Newtron will be capable of greater throughput for relatively low cost. In addition, because the Newtron will be built from general-purpose, mass-produced DSP boards, the system will be completely modular and easily upgraded, providing even more inexpensive computational power than has previously been available for auditory spatialization systems. Another product currently under development at Crystal River Engineering is a relatively low-cost portable system for measuring HRTFs known as Snapshot. This system will allow quick and convenient measurement of HRTFs in any acoustic space and is the first system for HRTF measurement that will not require the use of an anechoic chamber for measurement.

D. Comments on the psychophysical validity of simulations

Current simulation techniques achieve a fair degree of realism, and tests show that HRTF simulation causes psychophysical performance much like that achieved in free field (Wightman and Kistler, 1989b). There are a number of issues relevant to the question of how well spatial auditory displays simulate sources around the listener, and only a few researchers (most notably, Wightman, Kistler, Wenzel, and their associates) are actively investigating these questions. Most psychophysical tests of auditory simulation have used simple anechoic simulations, which did not include head-tracking. Perhaps for these reasons, even though localization performance was roughly similar to performance in free field, some degradations occur: More localization reversals occur and elevation cues are somewhat less salient when listening to HRTF simulations (Wightman and Kistler, 1989b). In addition, even though sources can be localized with some accuracy, they do not always sound externalized in these simulations. A number of factors may prove important in reducing reversals and improving externalization. First, preliminary observations from a number of labs (e.g., Wightman *et al.*, 1994; Boston University, MIT, NASA Ames) hint that with the inclusion of head-tracking, fewer reversals will occur and sources are more likely to be externalized. Similarly, anechoic simulation is far more likely to cause poor externalization, because studies of free-field localization can also result in in-head localization (but only in anechoic listening conditions).

The importance of individualized HRTFs is also under investigation. Studies show that some subjects using nonindividualized HRTFs can localize relatively well in azimuth with only slight increases in reversals and errors, whereas other subjects may show rather large increases in reversal rates compared to real-source localization (e.g., all locations in the front may be heard as though they were in the rear). All subjects tended to show some performance degradation in elevation (Wenzel, 1992; Wenzel *et al.*, 1993). This pattern of results probably reflects the fact that details in high-frequency spectra (which are primarily responsible for elevation and front/back discrimination) account for the largest intersubject differences in HRTFs. It is unclear whether performance using nonindividualized HRTFs can improve if appropriate training is used and subjects are given the opportunity to adapt to new HRTFs.

Finally, in realizing auditory VEs, technical limitations decrease the veridicality of cues presented. The need for spatial interpolation of HRTFs (because only a finite number of HRTFs can be measured and stored) is one such limitation. The psychophysical impact of HRTF interpolation has been investigated by a few researchers (e.g., a pilot study by Wightman and Kistler, referred to in Wenzel, 1992; Wightman, Kistler, and Arruda, 1992; Wenzel and Foster, 1993; Kulkarni, 1993); results show that the Convolvotron interpolation scheme disturbs azimuthal localization very little, particularly when minimum phase representations of the HRTFs are used (see note 3). In fact, for nonindividualized HRTFs, performance is essentially equivalent for interpolated and uninterpolated stimuli (Wenzel and Foster, 1993). Other simulation problems include limited frame rates and system delays, and the somewhat simplified acoustic models that can currently be simulated in real time.

Overall, the results just reviewed suggest that the main difficulties in synthesizing spatial information are in providing reliable elevation discrimination, eliminating or at least minimizing the number of reversals, and achieving externalization of source images. It is probable that higher level cognitive factors like visual dominance play a substantial role in auditory localization (as discussed in Sec. IV.B.1, Intersensory Bias), and these effects may help explain the reversals observed in auditory virtual environments. No doubt, the addition of correlated visual cues and dynamic acoustic cues coupled with head motion will do much toward restoring the ability to resolve these ambiguities in virtual acoustic displays. Systematic investigations of such effects will be a next step in the work at NASA Ames.

Whether distance, the third dimension in a virtual acoustic display, can be reliably controlled beyond mere externalization also awaits further research. Attempting to enhance the ability to make relative, rather than absolute, distance judgments may be a more fruitful approach, and at least crude manipulations of relative distance should be possible in a virtual acoustic display. Further understanding of the role of environmental cues, and the ability to synthesize such cues interactively, may eventually improve the reliable discrimination of source distances. Additionally, the success of any reasonably complex spatial display will depend on our understanding of localization masking, or the stimulus parameters that affect the identification, segregation (e.g., Bregman, 1990), and discrimination (e.g., Perrott, 1984a, 1984b) of multiple sources. Surprisingly, little or no research has been done on the localization of more than two simultaneous sources.

Other important research will be related to further refinements in the techniques for the measurement, manipulation, and perceptual validation of HRTFs, including practical signal-processing issues such as determining optimal techniques for interpolation between measured or modeled transforms to ensure veridical motion, and determining more efficient HRTF coding techniques and computational approaches to spatialization (e.g., Kistler and Wightman, 1991).

The simulation techniques described here provide both a means of implementing a virtual acoustic display and the ability to study features of human sound localization that were previously inaccessible due to a lack of control over the stimuli. The availability of real-time control systems (e.g., Wenzel, Wightman, and Foster, 1988a, 1988b) further expands the scope of possible research, allowing the study of dynamic, intersensory aspects of localization, which may help to alleviate the problems encountered in producing the reliable and veridical perception that is critical for many applications.

IV. IMPLEMENTATION ISSUES IN AUDITORY VIRTUAL ENVIRONMENTS

Most existing spatial auditory displays either (1) do not incorporate listener movements in the system, or (2) simulate anechoic or relatively simple echoic environments. This section focuses on implementation issues that arise in the development of auditory virtual environment systems that include realistic modeling of complex acoustic spaces, incorporate user motion, and allow for multimodal displays. Any implementation of an auditory virtual environment has to be assembled from components, the behaviors of which are determined by the current state of technology. Difficulties are encountered that do not result from theoretical, physical, or psychophysical problems, but rather from practical limitations. The purpose of this section is to discuss the types of implementation problems that can arise when a multimodal VE generator is being assembled. In particular, head-tracking, communication issues, event handling, sound-field modeling, and auralization are discussed, taking into account the two basic requirements of any interactive simulation system: smoothness and responsiveness. Performance of a system will depend on architectural issues, synchronization procedures, and the limited capabilities of software and hardware components, such as limits in computational power and communication bandwidth.

First, the real-time requirements of an auditory VE are discussed; then the auditory processing pipeline is described. Finally, modules in the pipeline that are particularly important for the performance of the system are analyzed in greater detail. Most of the designs discussed in this section have been taken from the ESPRIT (European Strategic Program for Research and Development in Information Technology) basic research project SCATIS (Spatially Coordinated Auditory/Tactile Interactive Scenario), where a real-time multimodal VE is currently under development. However, the problems encountered in SCATIS are very typical for VE systems in general and the issues raised may be universally applied.

A. Real-time requirements

In a VE, the simulation system must react in real-time to the actions of the user. The issues of exactly what "real-time" means and of what kind of real-time behavior is required are especially important because real-time behavior is, at least from a technical point of view, the most challenging design criteria for any VE generator.

In this context, the requirement that the system respond in real-time actually refers to two different conditions:

Time lag: The total delay between the physical action of the subject and the corresponding changes of the displayed sound pressure signal at the eardrums must be below the perceptual threshold.

Frame rate: The rate of display updates must be so high that all changes in the VE are perceived as being smooth and continuous.

For both conditions, a psychophysical quantity can be found that determines the necessary criteria for the physical quantity. Time lag contributes mainly to "responsiveness" and frame rate to the "smoothness" of the simulation (see Appino *et al.*, 1992). As shown later, these two attributes call for contradictory strategies for the design of auditory VE systems, making design compromise necessary.

B. Overview of the auditory processing pipeline

There are a number of considerations that make implementation of a virtual environment system difficult. Such systems must incorporate multiple sensors and multiple displays, combine both computer-generated and user-generated events in the data being displayed, and work in real-time. The high computational and communication demands of such systems make the architectural design of such systems extremely important. This section describes the various stages in the pipeline of a typical auditory VE system, pointing out some of the considerations that must be taken into account in creating an efficient real-time display system.

The complete auditory processing pipeline of an interactive auditory VE system is shown in Fig. 1. The figure shows all modules that are likely to introduce time lag and/or affect the frame rate. The indicated communication mechanisms (RS-232, ethernet, local communication, etc.) are taken from the practical implementation within SCATIS and may be different in other systems. First the six degrees of freedom describing the position of the subject's head are measured (head-tracking). These data are then transferred to a host computer (communication) and are transformed into the coordinate system of the virtual world. A "head-movement" event is produced and sent to the control level, where the event is evaluated and the reaction of the system (e.g., the change in information displayed to the user) is decided on according to the result of this event (event-handling layer, discussed in Sec. IV.E). As far as the auditory domain is concerned, the event will, in most cases, be sent unmodified to a module capable of modeling sound propagation in an acoustic virtual environment. From the results of this sound-field simulation, a new set of control parameters for the auralization processors is derived and transmitted. These processors can simulate both the acoustics of the virtual space and the direction of incidence of sound waves reaching the listener. After receiving a new parameter set, the auralization processor updates the signals output by the displays. It should be noted that the event-handling layer of the system is not mandatory for a "pure" auditory display

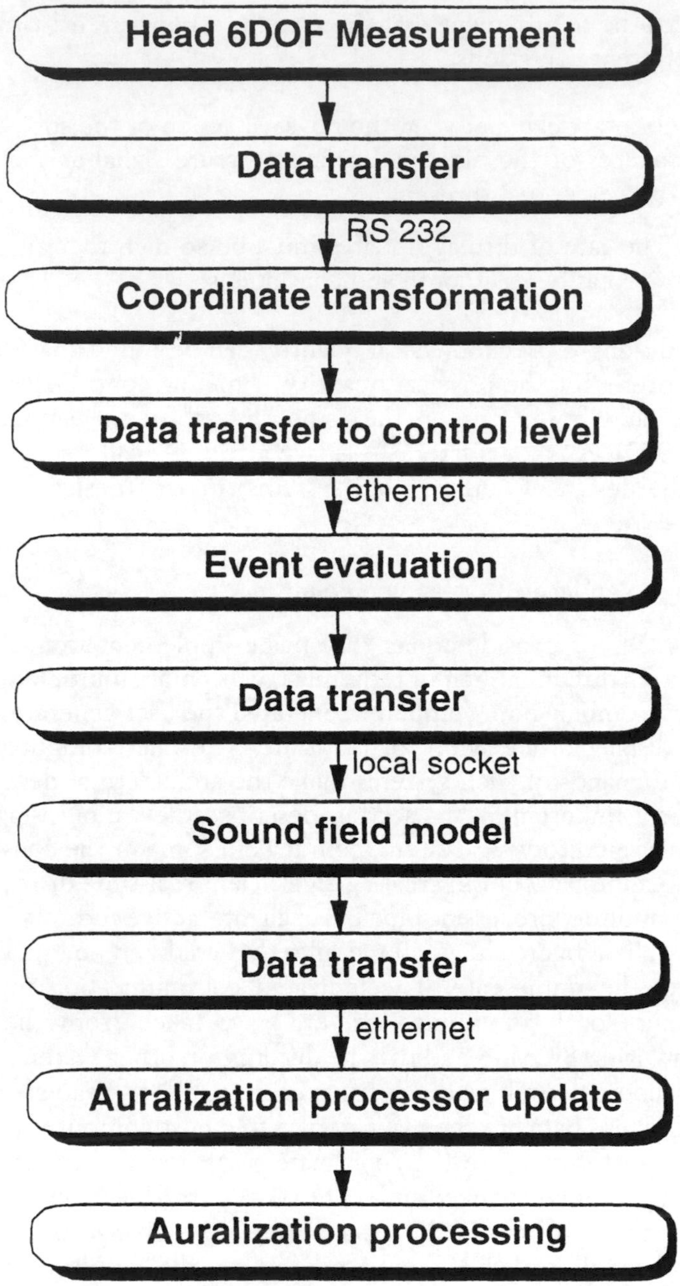

FIG. 1. The processing pipeline of an auditory virtual environment system.

system. However, if the system is used as a general VE interface, the actions of the subject may have to trigger tasks that depend on the subject's actions. Moreover, for a multimodal VE, it seems reasonable to assume an event-handling/evaluation layer in the system to aid in synchronizing and maintaining cross-modal consistency in the displays. The main modules in the pipeline are analyzed in the following sections.

C. Head-tracking

The measurement of the position and orientation of the human head (or sometimes the wrist) is a task frequently performed by VE systems. To this end, several systems of various types (e.g., mechanical, optical, acoustical, or magnetic) have been developed, some of which are commercially available. A thorough survey of the underlying principles and the history of development, as well as an analysis of state-of-the-art position trackers, can be found in Meyer, Applewhite, and Biocca, (1993), where nearly 50 different implementations of position-tracking systems are listed. The trackers most commonly found in VE applications are magnetic-field or mechanical systems, both of which offer reasonable accuracy at a relatively low cost.

When choosing a specific system one has to look at the required workspace, the translational and angular accuracy/resolution, and the time lag and update rate of the tracker. The workspace required always depends on the specific application. On the other hand, the necessary translational and angular accuracy and the resolution and dynamic behavior of the tracker depend on the corresponding human perceptual thresholds.

The human auditory system is most sensitive to changes in the azimuthal position of acoustic objects located in front of the listener, so that the necessary angular resolution and accuracy of a tracker are determined by the JND in azimuth for sources directly in front of the listener. This localization blur (Blauert, 1983) is dependent to some extent on the nature of the signal, but is never less than about 1°. The angular accuracy of today's state-of-the-art trackers is on the order of 0.5°, and thus meets this requirement. The necessary translational accuracy of trackers depends on the distances of the objects to be simulated: Because perception of source distance itself is very poor, the permissible translational error of the head tracker (left–right) is not bound by error in simulated source distance, but rather by error in simulated source angle. Again considering sources in front of the listener, source distance must be large enough that the maximum angular positional error (equal to the angular tracker error plus the error in angular position due to translational tracker error) is smaller than the JND in angular position. As long as translational error causes no greater than about 0.5° of angular error, it will be perceptually insignificant. For a given translational accuracy, sources above some minimum distance (d_{min}) from the listener can be simulated without perceptual error. The value of d_{min} is given by:

$$d_{min} = \frac{\varepsilon}{2\tan\left(\frac{\alpha}{2}\right)},$$

where α is the allowable angular error due to translational error (0.5°) and ε is the translational accuracy of the tracker. For an accuracy of $\varepsilon = 1$ mm, d_{min} is about 12 cm, a value that seems sufficient for all practical cases. It should be noted that the limited accuracy of the tracking device will, in most cases, cause no audible effects even if the objects are somewhat closer to the subject, because the localization blur is larger than 1° for most kinds of signals and is considerably larger for directions of incidence other than straight ahead.

The questions of what latency and what update rates are required to create natural virtual auditory environments are still unresolved. Some relevant perceptual studies include the work of Perrott and his colleagues (e.g., Perrott and Marlborough, 1989) and Grantham and his colleagues (e.g., Grantham, 1986, 1989, 1992; Chandler and Grantham, 1992). For example, for source speeds ranging from 8°/s to 360°/s, minimum audible movement angles ranged from about 4° to 21°, respectively, for a 500-Hz tone-burst (Perrott, 1982; Perrott and Tucker, 1988). Given the delays found in fairly simple auditory VEs (e.g., positional update rates of about 50 ms as found in the Convolvotron system discussed earlier), the change in angular position on subsequent position updates can be estimated as about 18° when the relative source-listener speed is 360°/s, 9° at 180°/s, and so on. The recent work on the perception of auditory motion by Perrott and others using real sound sources (moving loudspeakers) suggests that these computational latencies are acceptable for moderate velocities. As yet, no relevant studies have been performed that investigate what delays may be tolerable in rendering dynamic cues when subjects actively move their heads, although such questions are being investigated in the SCATIS project and in the United States at NASA Ames. In any event, the overall update rate in a complex auditory VE will depend not only on tracker delays (nominally 10 ms for the Polhemus Fastrak), but on communication delays and delays in event processing/handling as well. The tracker delays in such systems probably contribute only a small fraction of the overall delay.

D. Communication

The hardware mechanisms used for communication in different VE systems have widely different performance characteristics. In the following analysis, an attempt is made to list different hardware mechanisms and to comment on their suitability for the task. There are two different requirements for a communication link: (1) low delay between sending and receiving data, and (2) high data throughput. The following three classes of communication mechanism can be identified. In the definition of the classes, the operator "↔" is used to denote "receives and sends data to/from."

1. External hardware ↔ process

In this type of communication, external hardware devices such as trackers or convolution processors are accessed by a controlling process. Most popular, although remarkably slow, is the RS-232 serial interface found in almost every computer today. Another widely used class of interfaces with much higher bandwidth uses direct connections to the system bus of the host computer of the controlling process. The major disadvantage of this type of communications is the large variety of bus systems available (VME, EISA, S-Bus, VL, PCI, Microchannel, etc.); compatibility in both hardware and software is nearly impossible across different platforms. One reasonable alternative is the use of a standard interface for a mass storage connection like the SCSI interface (which has wider bandwidth than does the RS-232 serial port and which is common on a wide variety of computer systems).

2. Process ↔ process (network)

If the VE system is distributed over several hardware nodes, these nodes are generally connected by a local area network (LAN). LAN communications depend greatly on both the operating system running on the nodes and the hardware connections between nodes. Ethernet connections under a UNIX operating system are probably the most common combination of operating system and hardware network used. There are two standard software connection mechanisms under UNIX: sockets and transport layer interface (TLI).

3. Process ↔ process (local)

Processes sharing the same CPU (central processing unit) can communicate even faster than can processes distributed on a LAN, because no network transfers are required. Standard UNIX procedures for local communication include sockets, TLI, message queues (named pipes), shared memory in combination with semaphores, and so on.

In SCATIS, informal tests were carried out on both network and local process-to-process communications for a system comprised of SUN 10 and Silicon Graphics IRIS Indigo workstations. Measurements were made by sending a large number of messages of fixed length in full duplex mode and measuring the elapsed time for the transfer. The average duration for sending or receiving a single message over a network is about 2 ms for a 1024-byte message and about 1 ms for a 200-byte message. For local message passing, communication delays of less then 0.5 ms are possible. In local interprocess communication, delay is probably caused by process switching rather than by the actual communication procedure.

4. Multiple processes versus a single process

Provided that the operating system permits, tasks to be performed on a single hardware node can be realized either as a number of different processes or as a single one. The advantages of a single process seem obvious. No local communication mechanism needs to be implemented, and both synchronization and data transfer can easily be realized. However, there is a significant drawback. When any I/O (input/output) operation is performed, for instance, when accessing external hardware, most of the work is done by subcomponents of the system while the CPU remains idle. This may lead to a significant waste of computational resources. When I/O operations occur in a multiprocess system, a new process is activated while the I/O is performed for the requesting process, and the CPU usage remains high. Another advantage of multiprocessing is its increased modularity because other modalities or functionalities can be added easily. With multiprocessing, processes can also be distributed among available hardware nodes to optimize the system performance for a given task. External synchronization can be achieved by building a client–server architecture in which each hardware node has only one client (see Appino *et al.*, 1992). In a client–server architecture, each server processes requests (for information, storage, display, or computations) from one or more clients.

E. Event-handling layer

The task of the event-handling layer is to collect incoming events that are produced by sensors that monitor the users actions (or that are generated by the virtual world itself), to evaluate these events, to decide the system's reaction to these events, and to realize the reaction by sending corresponding control events to the displays. Furthermore, the event-handling layer may be used to monitor the subject's behavior, to evaluate subject performance for a given task, and to modify the VE while taking into account both the subject's actions and any specific rules governing the virtual tasks. In the most simple case of a pure auditory display, "head-movement" events coming from the head tracker would simply be forwarded to the auditory display.

A less obvious task of this layer is to synchronize all of the system components. There are different strategies for causing events to be triggered. The choice of event-triggering strategy has a significant influence on both frame rate and time lag. To illustrate this point, we examine a simple example. Assume that the event-handling layer is the only client in a client–server architecture, and that all attached sensors and displays are servers. Further, for simplicity, assume that only the head-tracker and the auditory display are connected.

The first strategy is to operate in a fully sequential mode. Using this strategy, the event-handler requests a head-movement event from the tracker, which then measures the head position and reports to the handler. The resultant event is passed on to the display, which is then updated. Once the display is updated, it sends a "ready" message to the event-handler and the cycle restarts. This sequential procedure minimizes time lag, because the head measurement is immediately transferred to the display. However, the frame rate is not optimal because only one component (either the sensor or the display) is active at a time and each device is idle as long as the other one is active.

Using an alternative strategy, the tracker does not start a measurement when triggered, but instead reports an already measured set of data when it is requested. After reporting the previously stored data, the next position is automatically measured and stored. The advantages of this method are that both sensor and display can work simultaneously because the display processes a previous measurement while the sensor takes the current measurement, thus optimizing frame rate. In cases where the speed of the display is faster or equal to that of the sensor, time lag is still close to optimal for this strategy. However, in the more likely case where the sensor is faster than is the processing of sensor data, the time lag is not optimal because a measurement will be stored for some time before it is requested. Methods that improve time lag can be found for this situation, but they all require a significant administrative overhead and depend on specific implementation details. A general solution for achieving optimal performance is not easily found. Further, the situation becomes even more complicated as the number of sensors and displays attached to an event-handling layer increases, especially when the sensors and displays may all operate at different speeds. It should also be noted that the one-client, all-server model considered here is not necessarily the optimal solution. For instance, either all sensors (spontaneous event creation in which the sensors update the displays) or all displays (request-driven event creation in which the displays request new information from the sensors) can be clients, where in each case the remaining modules of the system are servers. The only general conclusion that can be made is that the architecture of the event-handling layer can vary widely and that the choice of architecture has a severe impact on the overall system performance.

F. Sound-field model

The task of the sound-field modeling stage is to compute the temporal, spectral, and spatial properties of the sound field at the subject's position for a given virtual world model, taking into account all the physical parameters that may influence the sound field in the physical reality. The most common approach to sound-field modeling is to generate a spatial map of secondary sound sources (Kendall and Martens, 1984; Lehnert and Blauert, 1989; Foster *et al.*, 1991). In this method, the sound field due to a source in echoic space is modeled in an anechoic environment as a single primary source and a cloud of discrete secondary sound sources (which correspond to the reflections in the echoic space). The secondary sources can be described by three major properties (Lehnert, 1993b):

(1) Distance (delay).
(2) Spectral modification with respect to the primary source (air absorption, surface reflectivity, source directivity, and propagation attenuation).
(3) Direction of incidence (azimuth and elevation).

These properties may be considered to represent the (1) temporal, (2) spectral, and (3) spatial properties of the sound field. Although distance is also a spatial property, in this context it is reasonable to consider distance in terms of delay rather than in terms of spatial position.

Most of the present approaches to determining the attributes of secondary sources are based on geometrical-acoustics methods, which approximate the exact solution. Two methods are commonly used in this modeling: the mirror-image method (Allen and Berkely, 1979; Borish, 1984), and variants of ray tracing (Krokstadt, Strom, and Sorsdal, 1968). Although in its original form ray tracing is not suitable for the computation of secondary sources, it has been shown (Lehnert, 1993a) that the results of a ray-tracing procedure can be postprocessed such that they are identical to those found by the mirror-image method.

Computer models have been applied to a wide variety of room-acoustics problems. An overview of the current state of the art, particularly in Europe, and a representative collection of contemporary papers may be found in Applied

Acoustics, **36**(3-4), 1992, "Special Issue on Auditory Virtual Environments and Telepresence," and **38**(2-4), 1993, "Special Issue on Computer Modelling and Auralization of Sound Fields in Rooms." Despite their broad usage, these complex acoustic environment models have as yet never been used to simulate nontrivial environments in real-time systems. Issues of real-time realization have been discussed by a number of researchers (Kendall and Martens, 1984; Lehnert and Blauert, 1991; Foster *et al.*, 1991; Jot, Warusfel, Kahle, and Mein, 1993). Recently, Lehnert and Blauert (1991) proposed the following procedure:

- Sources corresponding to direct sound and early reflections are computed in real time.
- Late reflections are modeled as reverberation, where the parameters of the reverberation algorithm are extracted in real-time from the world model. If the reflective surfaces of the world model are static (i.e., their shape and their properties do not change in time), the parameters need to be extracted only once.

Many existing models of complex rooms use the binaural room impulse response as the basis of the simulation. This is only valid for time-invariant rooms. If the simulation is to be fully interactive, room changes (such as movement of objects in the room or opening or closing of windows, doors, or even curtains in the room) can occur in intervals that are small compared to the length of the room impulse response. Thus, the concept of the room impulse response is no longer valid. However, this is not the case for the spatial map of secondary sound sources. Here the length of the impulse responses assigned to individual sources in the simulation may be small compared to the time over which the acoustic environment can change, so the system can be considered to be time-invariant by piece.

1. Comparison of sound-field modeling techniques

In contrast to the digital generation of reverberation (which has a long history, e.g., Schroeder 1962), very few people have experience with real-time sound-field modeling. The use of detailed sound-field models for VE simulation has been limited to date by the computational resources required.

The efficiency of ray-tracing (in which the paths of waves from each source are traced as they are reflected around a room) and mirror-image methods (in which reflections from each original source are treated as virtual sources in an anechoic space) has frequently been compared (Hunt, 1964; Stephenson, 1988; Vorlander, 1988). However, these results cannot easily be applied to the current problem, because only the early reflections have to be considered. Also, a wide variety of ray-tracing dialects exist, and the papers just cited do not deal with dialects suitable for the calculation of secondary sources.

Because computational efficiency is a prerequisite for any VE application, the two methods have been compared with respect to their achievable frame rate and their real-time performance. To this end, benchmarks have been performed for the SCATIS project on a Sun 10/30 workstation with 10 Mflops of computational power. The test scenario was a room of moderate complexity with 24 surfaces. Eight first-order and 19 second-order reflections were calculated for a specific sender–receiver configuration giving a total of 28 reflections including the direct sound. The resulting computation time t_r for the ray tracing could be approximated by

$$t_r = (0.1)N\eta \text{ ms},$$

where N is the number of rays used and η the maximum order of the reflections to be simulated. For the mirror image method the computation time t_m can roughly be expressed as

$$t_m = 12(\eta - 1) \text{ ms}$$

If direct sound, first-order reflections and second-order reflections are to be computed, the resulting processing times are 12 ms for the image method and 60 ms for the ray-tracing method, where 300 rays are necessary to find all 28 reflections in the ray-tracing method. However, if only 24 rays are traced, the resulting processing time is less than 5 ms and 16 out of 28 reflections can still be found. The results of these pilot experiments can be summarized as follows:

> In the test scenario, the mirror-image method showed better performances than the ray-tracing method. It is also safer as it will find all the geometrically correct sound paths, whereas this can not be guaranteed for the ray-tracing method. In the ray-tracing method, it is difficult to predict the required number of rays to find all desired reflections. On the other hand, the ray-tracing method has the advantage that it produces reasonable results even when very little processing time is available, and it can easily be adapted to work at a given frame rate by adjusting the number of rays used. The mirror-image method cannot be scaled back easily because the algorithm is recursive. Ray tracing will yield better results in more complex environments because the dependency of the processing time on the number of surfaces is linear, not exponential as is the case for the mirror-image method. In conclusion, there will probably be some scenarios in which the mirror-image method is superior and others where the ray-tracing method offers better performance.

2. Events relevant to the sound-field model

The events handled in the sound-field model and the corresponding reactions of the system are described as follows:

(a) Rotation of the subject. Head rotation changes only the spatial characteristics of the sound field. Accordingly, only the choice of HRTFs in the auralization stage of the pipeline need to be updated.

(b) Translation of the subject. In principle, all of the secondary sources must be recalculated, making it necessary to recalculate the sound-field model.

(c) Rotation of sound source. Source rotations affect the model only if the source is not omnidirectional, in which case "directivity filters" in the auralization stage must be updated.

(d) Translation of sound source. Translations of the sound source require the sound-field model to be recalculated.

(e) Modification of sound source directivity. These modifications require both the choice of directivity filters and the directivity-filter data base in the auralization processor to be updated.

(f) Modification of a surface property. "Reflectivity filters" in the auralization stage must be updated when the properties of surfaces are changed.

(g) Modifications of the geometry of the VE. These modifications include changes in shape and movement, creation, and deletion of virtual objects (such as walls). In general, a recalculation of the sound field is required for such changes.

Events of type e, f, and g are modifications of the sound-field model itself. If such events are not allowed and the virtual environment cannot change, or if the set of all possible changes is known in advance (restrictions that are acceptable for many applications), a lot of optimization can be performed.

It should be noted that the sound-field model has to be able to delay events and synchronize them to overcome the time difference between the occurrence of the event and the time when the effects of the event lead to a physical change in the sound pressure signals in the listener's eardrums. For example, a source rotation causes an update of the corresponding directivity filter. However, this change in the directivity should be delayed, dependent on the time it takes the sound to travel from source to receiver.

3. Further optimization

Because the sound-field model can be assumed to be the most time-consuming part of the auditory pipeline, any kind of optimization of this portion of the simulation is worthwhile.

Treating translational and rotational movements as separate events in the sound-field model is somewhat arbitrary because the tracking device will always deliver all six degrees of freedom at once. However, great computational savings can be made by separating rotational from translational movement, because in the former case only the final stage of processing is affected, whereas in the latter the whole sound-field model must be recomputed. Unfortunately, the head makes very small translations even if the subject tries not to move. Recalculation of the entire sound-field model can be avoided in many cases using the following approach. First, a translation threshold value can be specified. Translations below that threshold can simply be ignored. Second, a simple approximation for small translations (such as might occur for a seated subject) can be used, as explained next.

The positions of all secondary sources are determined by the position of the sound source and the geometry of any reflecting surfaces. The position of the receiver does not affect the position of secondary sources, but rather determines whether a given secondary source is valid or not (by the so-called visibility and obstruction tests). For small translations it can be assumed that the validity of secondary sources is unchanged. Then small translations can be modeled by simply recalculating the delays and the directions of incidence for the already known set of secondary sources. A similar approximation is possible for small translations of the sound source. Assuming that the visibility of the current set of secondary sources is not influenced by small translations, the new positions of the secondary sources can be calculated from the trajectory of the primary source, a procedure that is relatively easy to perform.

For larger translations, these approximations do not hold and a complete recalculation of the sound-field model is required. If the recalculation of the sound field is so time-consuming that the smoothness of the simulation would be severely disturbed, the model can be updated across several frames. In this approach, only a part of the sound field is modeled during one frame and the approximation method is used for the remaining part. Updates are performed as soon as new results become available. Using this method, the frame rate can be higher than is the rate at which the sound-field model is recalculated, although secondary source position updates are delayed by one or more frames. The perceptual effects of these errors can be kept small by prioritizing the updates according to the perceptual relevance of each sound-field component.

G. Auralization

The main task inside the auralization module is to perform binaural filtering of sound sources to produce the appropriate directional cues. In addition to performing HRTF filtering, the auralization stage has to perform filtering due to source directivity and surface reflectivity, and to delay signals as appropriate. In the SCATIS project, auralization is done in three steps. First, the signal is delayed. Second, any spectral modification of the direct sound due to the effects of reflective surfaces is accomplished by means of appropriate FIR or IIR filtering (referred to as prefiltering). Third, the resulting signals are spatially imaged by convolution with the HRTFs for the corresponding direction of incidence. Finally, the resulting contributions of all primary sources and reflections are added up and played to the listener over headphones. The three main processing steps correspond to the three properties of the secondary sources already listed, namely, the temporal, spectral, and spatial pattern of the sound field.

In recent investigations (Sandvad and Hammershoi, 1994), IIR filter representations were compared to FIR representations and the FIR representation was shown to be superior. FIR filtering can be performed either in the frequency domain, using one of the well-known fast Fourier transform methods (e.g., the overlap-add algorithm), or in the time domain using direct convolution. The relative efficiency of each method depends on the number of filter coefficients, as well as on the processing hardware. In any case, the direct convolution has the advantage of being delay free, whereas frequency-domain algorithms introduce a delay of about two times the filter length. Additionally, in the frequency-domain approach, filters may only be updated at time intervals that are multiples of the filter length. Because the length of the binaural filters is of an order where direct convolution and overlap-add are of about the same computational efficiency for most current processing devices, direct convolution is often preferred to frequency-domain processing. In most existing spatialization systems, digital signal processing chips (DSPs) are used for convolution. Other hardware solutions include hardwired, discrete multipliers/adders or very fast FIR chips operating in time-multiplexed mode.

Figure 2 shows the general schematic overview of a single auralization unit. In this example three separate prefilters (PRF) are used to perform the prefiltering, and two FIR filters perform the HRTF processing. In the example with three prefilters, it would be possible to model the influence of the source directivity (PRF-1), as well as the reflectivity at two walls (PRF-2 and PRF-3).

The structure shown in Fig. 2 allows assignment of computational resources to each block according to its psychoacoustical significance. If, for example, a primary source is to be auralized, no reflection filters are required. Consequently, the blocks PRF-2 and PRF-3 can be skipped, and more resources (i.e., more FIR filter coefficients) can be assigned to the HRTFs to obtain more precise spatial imaging. For a second-order reflection, all prefilters are involved, but because the directivity of the delayed reflection is less salient psychoacoustically (e.g., see the body of psychophysical literature on the precedence effect, including Wallach *et al.*, 1949; Blauert, 1971; Zurek, 1979, 1980, 1987; Yost and Soderquist, 1984; Saberi and Perrott, 1990; Shinn-Cunningham *et al.*, 1993; Hartman, Chapter 10, this volume), less accuracy needs to be used for the binaural filtering. Thus, the structure of the auralization unit provides task adequate assignment of resources.

If the number of auralization units is very high, it may become more efficient to use an array of binaural processors, each of which spatializes sources from a fixed direction instead of using individual binaural processors for each source. In this case, the output of the prefilters can be routed to that binaural processor whose direction corresponds best to that of the sound source. Alternatively, the output can be distributed to each of several binaural processors that generate sources near the desired source position, taking advantage of the psychoacoustical effect known as summing localization (Blauert, 1983, pp. 204–222).

H. Summary

Implementation of virtual auditory displays cannot be done in a straightforward manner. Each component must be examined, and its influence on overall time lag and overall frame rate considered. In addition, the mechanisms by which compo-

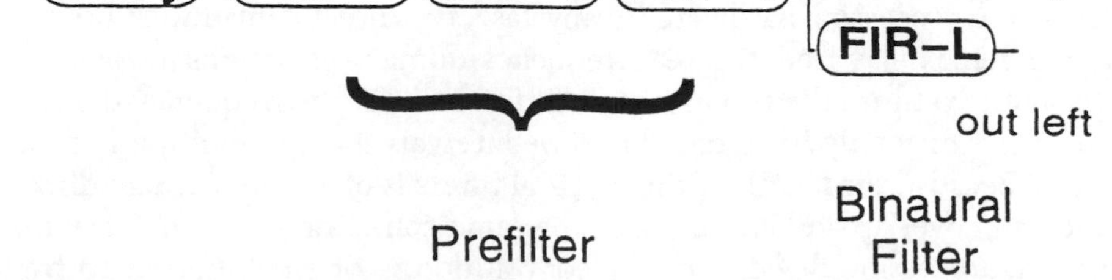

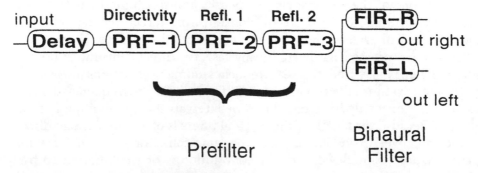

FIG. 2. General operation of a single auralization unit.

nents communicate with each other and the method by which this communication is controlled are important to the efficiency of the system as a whole.

State-of-the-art magnetic tracking devices appear to be adequate for measuring the six degrees of freedom of the subject's head. Major computational demands arise from the sound-field model (which generates realistic room simulations) and from the auralization processor (which spatializes primary and reflective sources). The sound-field model can be realized on a multipurpose workstation; however, the auralization processor requires dedicated (often special-purpose) hardware.

Although this section has mainly dealt with technical issues, it should be noted that the most promising avenue for improving the quality of auditory VEs is neither development of fast hardware, software optimization, nor clever algorithms, but rather in further psychophysical study. There is hope that higher quality auditory VE displays can be implemented at lower expense as we gain better understanding of the most powerful auditory signal processor presently known: the human brain.

V. SUPERNORMAL SPATIALIZATION

The final section in this chapter discusses some ongoing work in the Research Laboratory of Electronics at MIT that illustrates both how auditory spatial displays can be used in studies of psychophysical phenomena and in studies of how knowledge of sensorimotor performance can help improve the design of human–machine interfaces (Durlach, 1991; Durlach, Held, and Shinn-Cunningham, 1992; Durlach, Shinn-Cunningham, and Held, 1994; Shinn-Cunningham, 1994).

When auditory localization is considered in the context of human–machine interfaces, such as those employed in teleoperator or virtual-environment systems, there is an opportunity to recode source locations in a manner that improves localization. In other words, one can transform the acoustical cues available to the listener for determining source location in such a way that the listener may achieve "supernormal" auditory localization. Although such enhanced performance should be of value in essentially all systems that make use of auditory localization for conveying information to the human user, the application area of primary interest in this work is that of human–machine interfaces for teleoperator and virtual-environment systems. Thus, for example, one can simulate the effects of an enlarged head and enlarged ears to increase the dependence of interaural differences and monaural spectral characteristics on source direction. As mentioned previously, this approach has been tried before to achieve better than normal localization of enemy aircraft during World War I (see Fig. 4 in Wenzel, 1992). The question of whether subjects can adapt to such changes was investigated in a preliminary study by Wien (1964).

The overall, long-term objectives of the current research are to (1) determine, understand, and model the perceptual effects of altered auditory localization cues, and (2) design, construct, and evaluate cue alterations that can be used to improve performance of human–machine interfaces in virtual-environment and teleoperator systems. This research differs from most other research concerned with spatial localization in auditory displays in its concern with supernormal performance and adaptation to altered cues. It differs from most other research on perceptual rearrangement and adaptation in its focus on improving performance and its concern with resolution as well as response bias.

A. Improving resolution in source position

Perhaps the most obvious approach to increasing directional resolution is to simulate the results that would be obtained in field listening with a larger head. As pointed out by Clifton, Gwiazda, Bauer, Clarkson, and Held (1988), adaptation to small changes in head size is already required in connection with natural development in infants. Simulating a larger than normal headsize would result in larger than normal localization cues and might be easily accommodated by listeners because such changes occur naturally.

One method of achieving such a simulation is by frequency scaling the HRTFs (e.g., see Rabinowitz, Maxwell, Shao, and Wei, 1993). Transformations that do not truly simulate an enlarged head in the sense achieved by frequency scaling, but that nevertheless capture certain aspects of head enlargement and may be quite useful for special purposes, have previously been discussed by Durlach and Pang (1986) and Van Veen and Jenison (1991).

A very different approach for altering directional resolution involves retention of the same (natural) set of HRTFs, but introduction of a new mapping between these filters and the directions of azimuth and elevation (see Durlach *et al.*, 1994). With this approach, no new HRTFs are created; instead, the old filters are reassigned to different angles. Moreover, they are assigned consistently to the two ears so that not only are the same set of space filters used for each ear, but the same set of interaural ratios is preserved. In general, the use of such a remapping transformation will increase resolution in some regions of space and decrease it in others. In fact, a remapping transformation similar to that in the experiment reported here was recently applied successfully in a study of a simplified spatial acoustic display for traffic collision avoidance systems in commercial cockpits (Begault, 1993). Transformations of this type may present less of a challenge to sensorimotor adaptation mechanisms than those that use unnatural HRTFs in that no new auditory stimuli are introduced in the remapping transformations. For this reason (and the practical issues discussed later), this type of supernormal transformation was used in the current study.

B. Adaptation to supernormal localization cues

The goal of supernormal localization is to see if subjects can achieve better than normal auditory localization performance when auditory localization cues are enhanced. However, because the relationship between a particular localization cue and the position of the source changes when cues are enhanced, subject response bias will also be affected. The experiments undertaken thus ask two questions: Can subjects (1) achieve better-than-normal resolution on auditory tasks using supernormal (enhanced) auditory cues, and (2) can they adapt to any bias induced by the use of the supernormal cues? To answer these questions, localization performance was measured by two metrics, a resolution measure and a bias measure. The question of how bias changes with exposure to altered auditory cues has been examined previously in studies of sensorimotor adaptation, a topic that was reviewed in Sec. II. In addition, the current study examines resolution in order to learn how information transfer is affected by the process of sensorimotor adaptation.

1. Practical issues

In theory, an auditory VE is the perfect tool for investigating adaptation to auditory rearrangement. The auditory VE allows precise control of the spatial cues presented to the subject, allowing these spatial cues to be arbitrarily rearranged. In particular, simulating cues for a larger than normal head is theoretically no more difficult than simulation of normal cues in such a system. Practical limitations like those discussed in Sec. IV, however, do limit the flexibility and usefulness of investigations that present cues using an auditory VE.

The two main differences between an auditory VE and more traditional psychophysical tools is (1) the degree of veridicality achieved, and (2) the real-time capability of the auditory VE. Unfortunately, the simulation is limited in most existing systems by the speed and working volume of the position trackers used. In our system, tracker delays were on the order of tens of milliseconds. Because delays have been shown to affect the strength of adaptation (e.g., see Held and Durlach, 1987; Held, Efstathiou, and Greene, 1966), this delay is as troublesome as it is unavoidable. Similarly, other studies have shown that allowing a user to actively move about while experiencing a rearrangement can enhance adaptation (Pick and Hay, 1965; Held and Hein, 1958; Freedman and Zacks, 1964). Again, the working volume of our trackers made any significant translational movement impractical in the study reported here.

It is likely that anything that reduces the naturalness of sensory cues also reduces the amount of adaptation found with exposure to such cues (Warren *et al.*, 1981; Radeau and Bertelson, 1977). Thus, to the extent that sources simulated by the auditory VE are distinguishable from real auditory events, exposure to rearrangements using an auditory VE will probably cause less adaptation than could be achieved under ideal circumstances. The presentation over our VE system of localization cues that are "normal" (i.e., not rearranged) still does not result in completely natural-sounding, externalized sound images. Many of the issues already mentioned in previous sections are likely contributors to this failure; the sound-field model used in our simulations assumed that all sources were omnidirectional, in an anechoic space, and in the acoustic "far-field" (i.e., more than 3 or 4 ft from the listener). The resulting unnaturalness of the display is troublesome, but again, the best that could be realized, given the limitations of our system. Even though the simulation is not completely natural, subjects can make accurate localization judgments of the simulated sources.

Although an auditory VE is extremely flexible in theory, in practice, additional problems limited our approach. In particular, the software and hardware used in our auditory VE (the Convolvotron and associated code from Crystal River Engineering) were designed to simulate normal localization cues. Simulation of larger than normal head HRTFs proved impractical on this system for a variety of reasons. The simplest approach to simulating HRTFs for a larger than normal head would be to frequency-scale the HRTFs (Rabinowitz *et al.*, 1993). If one ignores the problem of how to define the HRTFs for the higher frequencies and assumes that the impulse response sampling rate is the same for both normal and larger than normal head HRTFs, then simulation of HRTFs by this method increases the memory and computational requirements of the auditory display hardware by a factor of *k* for a head *k* times the normal size. The existing system was not designed to make use of the resulting long impulse responses and could neither store such filters nor process sources with them in real time. Similarly, larger than normal interaural delays could not be generated using the system as originally designed. Even if low-level code was rewritten to allow the simulation of a single source using enlarged-head HRTFs, the processing done by the Convolvotron would be less accurate than when using normal HRTFs due to spatial interpolation error. The interpolation errors resulting from this processing have been investigated for normal cue HRTFs and are thought to be perceptually negligible (e.g., Kulkarni, 1993; Wightman, Kistler, and Arruda, 1992; Wenzel, 1992; Wenzel and Foster, 1993); however, the errors introduced by interpolation of supernormal HRTFs would be larger.

Other difficulties in investigating adaptation to larger than normal head HRTFs do not involve equipment, but rather perceptual issues. For example, if, as many theories assume (e.g., see Colburn and Durlach, 1978, or Jeffress, 1948), interaural delays in the stimulus are estimated by means of compensating internal interaural delay lines, perception of larger than normal interaural delays might require the creation of longer internal interaural delay lines.[2] In addition, scaling the head will cause interaural intensity differences for frequencies that never have significant differences normally; again, it is not clear how useful such cues would be. Finally, because interaural time differences are simply scaled up, whereas intensity differences (as well as monaural spectral cues) are shifted in frequency, enlarging the head is not equivalent to simply emphasizing spatial position cues. Intensity and time cues may be inconsistent with each other, and subjects may hear a more diffuse, broader source image, which is difficult to localize.

Because of the practical limitations of both the simulation system and the approach, supernormal HRTFs were not generated by simulating a larger-than-normal head in our study, but were drawn from the pool of normal HRTF impulse responses. Cue alterations were achieved by changing the mapping between HRTFs and the direction of the source relative to the head. This approach ensured that the Convolvotron would perform as well as with normal cues: Interpolation errors were no worse than in the normal simulation, and the source images presented to our subjects were as natural-sounding and as compact as the system could generate.

---

[2]Although some studies indicate that subjects can discriminate very long interaural delays, the sensitivity to such delays has not been explored in any detail.

2. Methods

Adaptation to altered auditory localization cues was investigated by presenting simulated acoustic cues and real visual cues. Acoustic sources were "spatialized" by the Convolvotron, using HRTFs from subject SDO (measured and reported by Wightman and Kistler, 1989a). The Convolvotron takes as inputs the source signal to be spatialized and the instantaneous position of the source relative to the listener's head, from which it generates the binaural signals appropriate for a source from the specified position. In our system, the relative source position was calculated by a PC from the absolute position of the source to be simulated and the instantaneous orientation of the listener's head (reported to the PC by the Ascension Bird, a commercial head-tracking system).

This auditory VE was used to simulate sources from 1 of 13 positions around the listener at 0° elevation, from –60° to +60° in azimuth. These positions were indicated visually by a 3-ft-diameter arc of lights, which were clearly labeled (1 to 13) from left to right. These lights constituted our "real" visual display and were used to present visual spatial information about the simulated auditory sources to our subjects.

Auditory localization cues were transformed in this project by remapping the relationship between source position and HRTFs. The mapping function used is given by

$$f_n(\theta) = \frac{1}{2}\tan^{-1}\left[\frac{2n\sin(2\theta)}{1-n^2+(1+n^2)\cos(2\theta)}\right], \qquad (1)$$

where the HRTF used for presenting a stimulus at azimuth θ was simply the normal HRTF for azimuth $f_n(\theta)$. The parameter n is equal to the slope of remapping function for a source directly in front of the listener, and thus reflects the extremity of the remapping. This mapping is shown in Fig. 3 for different values of n. The only member of this family of functions that we have used in the results reported here is the function $f_3(\theta)$. With this function, source positions are displaced laterally relative to the position heard using normal cues. The differences in localization cues for two sources in the frontal region (from –30° to +30° in azimuth) are larger than normal with this remapping, whereas the differences for two locations off to the side are smaller than normal. As a result, subjects were expected to show better than normal resolution in the front and reduced resolution on the side, creating an enhanced "acoustic fovea" in which supernormal auditory localization could occur. In addition to affecting resolution, however, this transformation was also expected to cause a bias whereby sources were perceived farther off-center than were their actual locations. The main questions of the study were whether (1) bias could be overcome by subjects over time, so that they interpreted the new acoustic mapping of source position accurately, and (2) resolution was enhanced as expected in the "acoustic fovea."

In most of our experimental work to date, we focused on the identification of source azimuth. Although a number of experimental conditions have been tested,

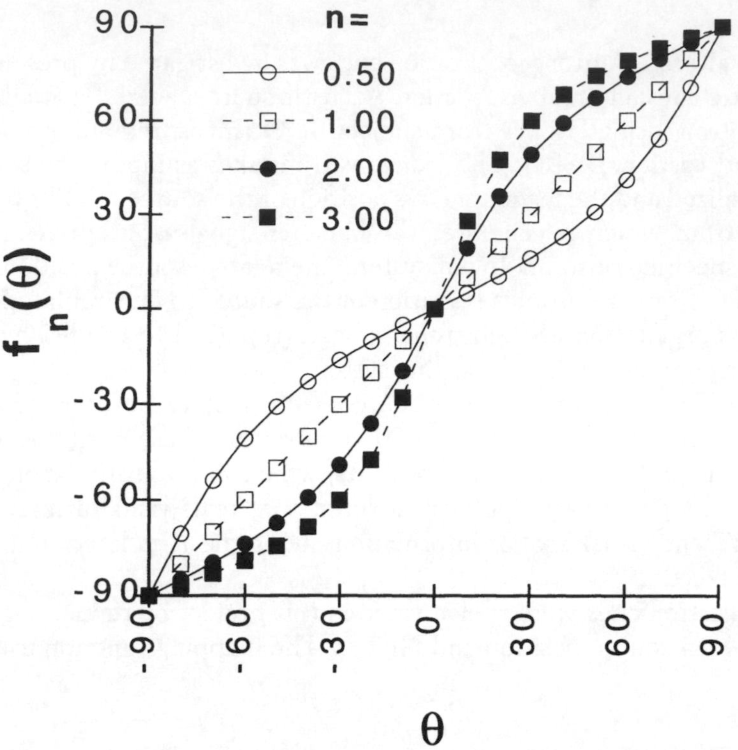

FIG. 3. A plot of the transformations specified by Eq. 1. The parameter *n* reflects the slope of the transformation when q is zero.

we report only one case here, for illustrative purposes. Variations on the basic experiment reported here will be discussed in a paper currently in preparation.

The basic experimental protocol consisted of a sequence of interleaved training and test runs. Each test run in the sequence consisted of 26 trials of a 13-alternative angle identification experiment. Test stimuli consisted of a 500-ms click-train from one of 13 azimuthal positions separated by 10° (ranging from –60° to +60°). These positions corresponded to the positions of the lights, which were clearly numbered from left to right in an arc around the subject. Subjects had to face forward during each test stimulus or the trial was discarded. No correct-answer feedback was given and the lights were not used during the test runs. After each source was presented, the subject entered the number of the source position on a laptop keyboard.

During training runs, the subject was asked to track the source (whose position was chosen randomly on each trial from the set of 13 positions) by turning to point his or her nose to the correct location. During training, the light at the simulated acoustic location was turned on simultaneously with the acoustic source. This light/sound source remained on until the subject turned to face the position, at which time it was turned off and, after a brief pause, a new random position was turned on. In this manner, the subject became familiar with the mapping between source position, acoustic cues, head orientation, and the dynamic changes of these cues with movement.

Subjects completed eight identical, 2-h sessions in which they were first tested and trained with normal localization cues [i.e., using the identity mapping function $f_1(\theta)$], then tested and trained with the supernormal localization cues [using the mapping function $f_3(\theta)$], and finally retested and retrained with normal localization cues [with the mapping function $f_1(\theta)$]. This order of runs allowed the subjects' performance to be tracked over the course of the session, and provided "normal" control results against which performance with the supernormal localization cues could be compared. Ten test runs were performed per session; however, results from only four of these runs are presented here: (1) the first run using normal cues, (2) the first run using altered cues, (3) the final altered cue run, and (4) the first normal cue run following exposure to altered cues.

3. Preliminary results

Results from each subject were found by combining responses for each of the four runs across sessions. For each subject and run the average response and the standard deviation in response were found for each of the 13 possible locations. Because the standard deviation did not vary systematically with position, the 13 measures of standard deviation were further averaged across position to yield an overall estimate of response variability. These two statistics (average response and standard deviation in response) were then used to estimate resolution and bias for each run during the course of a session. Resolution between adjacent pairs of positions was estimated as the difference in mean responses, normalized by the average standard deviation across positions (similar to the standard sensitivity measure d'). Bias (which is traditionally used to measure adaptation) was estimated as the difference between mean response and correct response, again normalized by the average standard deviation.[3] Because the initial bias using normal cues should be approximately equal to zero (and because any systematic deviations from zero bias probably arise from effects of the simulation method, constant in all runs and experiments), each subject's bias results were normalized by subtracting the initial, normal-cue run bias results. Thus, initial, normal-cue bias results are always identically equal to zero with this processing method. Finally, the resulting bias and resolution metrics were averaged across subjects to generate a concise summary of results for each run.

The first test using normal cues provided a baseline against which later results could be measured. When first tested using the supernormal cues, a strong bias was predicted from the transformation: Subjects should hear sources to be farther off center than they were. If subjects adapt with exposure, bias should be reduced in the final test using supernormal cues. Finally, when tested with the normal cues following exposure to the supernormal cues, any negative after-effect will be seen as a change in bias compared to the first (preexposure) normal-cue bias results.

---

[3]The relation between the resolution and bias metrics reported here and resolution and bias as typically discussed in detection-theory models of similar psychophysical tasks is fairly complex. From the confusion matrices of the responses for each stimulus, more precise estimates of the resolution and bias in the underlying decision space can be made (see Durlach and Braida, 1969; Braida and Durlach, 1972; Lippmann, Braida, and Durlach, 1976); however, for the purposes of the current, preliminary report, these rough estimates were deemed sufficient.

If results show that bias decreased with exposure when testing with supernormal cues, but that no negative after-effect occurred, it is likely that subjects consciously corrected for the bias induced by the remapping function. On the other hand, if a negative after-effect is found, it implies that true (unconscious) adaptation occurred in some form. For the first test using supernormal cues, resolution should be enhanced in the center region and decreased at the edges of the range of positions tested. If the state of the subject does not affect resolution, resolution should remain unchanged from the first supernormal-cue test to the final supernormal-cue test. Finally, in the first normal-cue test after exposure, resolution results are not expected to differ from the initial normal-cue test unless the adaptive state of the subject affects resolution performance. No special attention was given in these experiments to the issues of conditional or dual adaptation (e.g., Welch, 1978; Welch, Bridgeman, Anand, and Browman, 1993).

Figure 4 shows bias results for the four runs analyzed as a function of source position. Normal-cue runs are plotted with circles, and supernormal-cue runs with squares. The open symbols represent runs prior to supernormal-cue training exposure, whereas filled symbols correspond to the "adapted" results. A strong bias occurred in the first supernormal-cue test (open squares) in the direction predicted by the transformation (subjects heard sources farther off-center than they were, except for the leftmost and rightmost positions). Results for super-

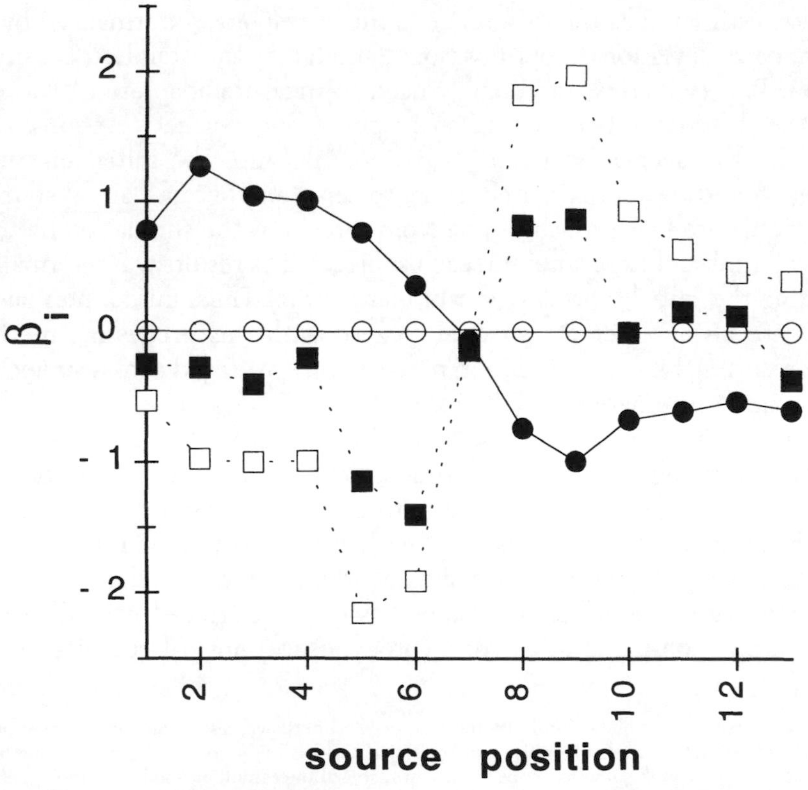

FIG. 4. Bias results. Normal-cue tests are shown with circles, supernormal-cue tests with squares. Open symbols represent tests prior to supernormal-cue exposure, filled symbols tests after exposure.

normal-cue testing after training (filled squares) showed a clear reduction in bias over the whole range of positions tested; however, this adaptation was not complete. Bias was reduced by roughly 50% with this experimental protocol. Finally, a negative after-effect is seen in the results from the first normal-cue test following exposure (filled circles), where a strong bias was found in the direction opposite that induced by the supernormal cues.

Resolution results are shown in Fig. 5. Resolution for normal-cue runs showed a systematic pattern (which may be due to systematic dependencies of the accuracy of the simulation on source position[4]), which was consistent for pre- and postexposure runs. Of more interest is the comparison between normal- and supernormal-cue results. As expected for the transformation employed, resolution was enhanced for positions in the central region and degraded at the edges of the range for the first run using supernormal cues. Most interesting is the fact that resolution decreases as subjects adapt (compare filled to open squares). One possible explanation for this effect has to do with the range of stimuli attended by subjects. It is well understood that the resolution between two stimuli depends not only on the stimulus values, but also on the number and distribution of stimuli presented (e.g., resolution on JND tasks is always better than is resolution on identification tasks with many stimuli; for example, see Durlach and Braida, 1969). Because changing from normal cues to supernormal cues also increases the range of physical stimuli to be attended, resolution between the same physical stimuli may decrease as subjects adapt to the change in cues and to the change in stimulus range (see Shinn-Cunningham, 1994). Finally, a similar decrease in resolution is seen when comparing the first test using normal cues after training with the supernormal cues (filled circles) compared to the initial run with normal cues (open circles). Again, this difference may depend on the range of stimuli being attended by the subject during each test. Overall, resolution using the supernormal cues is better than that achieved using normal cues, even though the increase in resolution depends on the adaptive state of the subject.

C. Discussion

In the experiment described here, introduction of the transformation $f_3(\theta)$ produced the anticipated changes in resolution and, in particular, increased resolution in the center of the field. Furthermore, results showed clear evidence of adaptation. Not only did the subjects show a reduction in bias (and localization

[4]The simulation employed in this experiment used the earliest version of the Convolvotron processing scheme. This processing scheme interpolated HRTFs that contained both spectral and phase information (e.g., that included the left-to-right-ear group delay). Although the mean subjective position of a stimulus generated by this method was near to the desired position, the interaural cross-correlation functions of such stimuli are quite complex. Instead of generating stimuli that have a single peak in the interaural cross-correlation, the stimuli have four small peaks. The apparently systematic variations in both bias and resolution with position in the experiment reported here may be a result of this processing scheme. More recent Convolvotron code performs a spectral interpolation of minimum-phase versions of the spectra of the four nearest neighbor HRTFs. After this minimum-phase filtering (which approximates the appropriate monaural and interaural spectral characteristics), a separate interpolation of the interaural group delay for the four nearest neighbors is used to approximate the group delay for the desired position. Thus, in the current scheme, the cross-correlation has only a single peak, as desired.

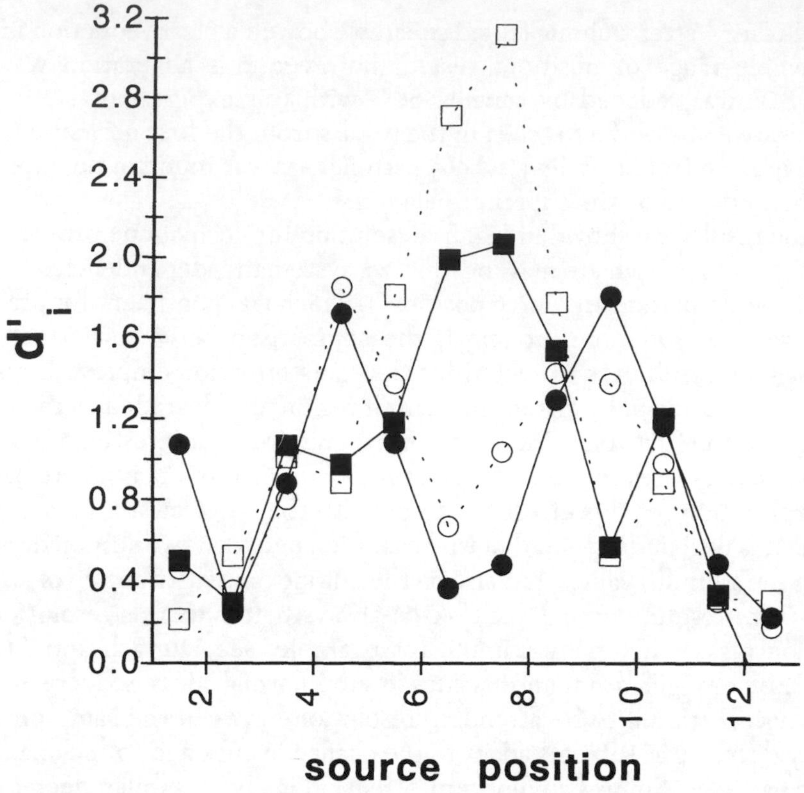

FIG. 5. Resolution results. Normal-cue tests are shown with circles, supernormal-cue tests with squares. Open symbols represent tests prior to supernormal-cue exposure, filled symbols tests after exposure.

error) with exposure to the supernormal cues, but also an increase in bias (and localization error) in the opposite direction when tested with normal cues following supernormal-cue exposure (the negative after-effect). It is important to note that although bias decreased over time when testing with supernormal cues, adaptation was not complete: Some bias remained. This is typical for adaptation results; in particular, only a tiny percentage of adaptation studies have found complete or nearly complete adaptation. Although it is possible that adaptation could be made more complete by longer exposure (total training time in the experiment reported here was 40 min), for many applications it is equally important that adaptation be swift as well as being as complete as possible. As pointed out earlier, numerous imperfections exist in our experimental setup, reducing the salience of training during our experiments; however, even with short exposure times and imperfect equipment, the results reported here demonstrate that supernormal localization may be achievable. Further, this work demonstrates that auditory virtual environments, even with their current limitations, are powerful tools for investigating psychophysical phenomenon.

VI. CONCLUDING REMARKS

Many applications in a wide variety of fields are using or investigating the use of auditory displays to present information that has previously been presented via other modalities. Many theoretical issues still need to be explored to further the development of future auditory displays, especially questions involving the display of highly dimensioned, complex information.

One area that has already received a great deal of attention is the development of spatial auditory displays. Such displays, especially those that include interactive monitoring of user motion, allow the presentation of spatial information in natural and intuitive ways, and allow the user to make use of well-developed skills to interpret the synthesized spatial information. In the design of these auditory virtual environments, many real-world implementation issues affect the ultimate usefulness of the display. Careful consideration must be given to both technological and perceptual issues in order to design systems for optimal performance. Such systems are already proving useful both in practical applications and in psychophysical studies of the processes of human auditory localization. Indeed, the flexibility of these systems allows the presentation of cues that may actually improve performance over that achievable with naturally occurring auditory cues (e.g., achieving supernormal resolution). Future work must continue to address both technical and perceptual issues in order to create more cost-effective, efficient systems.

REFERENCES

Allen, J. B., and Berkely, D. A. (1979). "Image method for efficiently simulating small-room acoustics," J. Acoust. Soc. Am. **65**, 943–950.

Appino, P. A., Lewis, J. B., Koved, L., Ling, D. T., Rabenhorst, D. A., and Codella, C. F. (1992). "An architecture for virtual worlds," Presence **1**, 1–17.

Arnoult, M. D. (1950). "Post-rotary localization of sound," Am. J. Psychol. **63**, 229–236.

Arnoult, M. D. (1952). "Localization of sound during rotation of the visual environment," Am. J. Psychol. **65**, 48–58.

Arons, B. (1991). "Hyperspeech: Navigating in speech-only hypermedia," in *Proceedings of Hypertext*, San Antonio, TX (ACM, New York), pp. 133–146.

Arons, B. (1993). "SpeechSkimmer: Interactively skimming recorded speech," in *Proceedings of UIST 93, ACM Symposium on User Interface Software and Technology*, Atlanta, GA (ACM Press, New York), pp. 187–196.

Ashmead, D. H., LeRoy, D., and Odom, R. D. (1990). "Perception of the relative distances of nearby sound sources," Percept. Psychophys. **47**, 326.

Ballas, J. A. (1994). "Delivery of information through sound," in *Auditory Display: Sonification, Audification, and Auditory Interface, SFI Studies in the Sciences of Complexity, Proc. XVIII*, edited by G. Kramer (Addison-Wesley, Reading, MA).

Bauer, R. W., Matuzsa, J. L., and Blackmer, R. F. (1966). "Noise localization after unilateral attenuation," J. Acoust. Soc. Am. **40**, 441–444.

Begault, D. R. (1987). "Control of auditory distance," unpublished doctoral dissertation, University of California, San Diego.

Begault, D. R. (1993). "A head-up auditory display for traffic collision avoidance system advisories: A preliminary investigation," Hum. Factors **35**, 707–717.

Begault, D. R., and Erbe, T. R. (1993). "Multi-channel spatial auditory display for speech communications," 95th Audio Engineering Society Convention, Preprint No. 3707 (Audio Engineering Society, New York).

Begault, D. R, and Pittman, M. T. (1994). "3–D audio versus head-down TCAS displays," Technical report 177636 (NASA Ames Research Center, Mt. View, CA).

Begault, D. R., and Wenzel, E. M. (1992). "Techniques and applications for binaural sound manipulation in man-machine interfaces," Int. J. Aviat. Psychol. **2**, 1–22.

Bekesy, G. von. (1957). "Neural volleys and the similarity between some sensations produced by tones and by skin vibrations," J. Acoust. Soc. Am. **29**, 1059–1069.

Blattner, M. M., Glinert, E., and Papp, A. (1994). "Sonic enhancements for 2–D graphic displays," in *Auditory Display: Sonification, Audification, and Auditory Interface, SFI Studies in the Sciences of Complexity, Proc. XVIII*, edited by G. Kramer (Addison-Wesley, Reading, MA).

Blattner, M. M., Sumikawa, D. A., and Greenberg, R. M. (**1989**). "Earcons and icons: Their structure and common design principles," Hum.-Computer Interact. **4**, 11–44.
Blauert, J. (**1969**). "Sound localization in the median plane," Acustica **22**, 205–213.
Blauert, J. (**1971**). "Localization and the law of the first wavefront in the median plane," J. Acoust. Soc. Am. **50**, 466–470.
Blauert, J. (**1983**). *Spatial Hearing* (MIT Press, Cambridge, MA).
Blauert, J. (**1984**). "Psychoakustik des binauralen Horens [The psychophysics of binaural hearing]," invited plenary paper presented at DAGA '84, Darmstadt, Germany.
Boerger, G., Laws, P., and Blauert, J. (**1977**). "Stereophonic reproduction by earphones with control of special transfer funtions through head movements," Acustica **39**, 22–26.
Borish, J. (**1984**). "Extension of the image model to arbitrary polyhedra," J. Acoust. Soc. Am. **75**, 1827–1836.
Braida, L. D. (**1964**). "Bilocal cutaneous unmasking," unpublished master's thesis, Department of Electrical Engineering, MIT, Cambridge, MA.
Braida, L. D., and Durlach, N. I. (**1972**). "Intensity perception. II. Resolution in one-interval paradigms," J. Acoust. Soc. Am. **51**, 483–502.
Bregman, A. S. (**1981**). "Asking the what for question in auditory perception," in *Perceptual Organization*, edited by M. Kubovy and J. R. Pomerantz (Lawrence Erlbaum Associates, Hillsdale, NJ), pp. 99–118.
Bregman, A. S. (**1984**). "Auditory scene analysis," in *Proceedings of the Seventh International Conference on Pattern Recognition* (IEEE Computer Society Press, Silver Spring, MD).
Bregman, A. S. (**1990**). *Auditory Scene Analysis* (MIT Press, Cambridge, MA).
Bronkhorst, A. W., and Plomp, R. (**1988**). "The effect of head-induced interaural time and level differences on speech intelligibility in noise," J. Acoust. Soc. Am. **83**, 1508–1516.
Brown, M. H. (**1992**). "An introduction to Zeus: Audiovisualization of some elementary sequential and parallel sorting algorithms," in *Proceedings of the CHI '91, ACM Conference on Computer-Human Interaction*, New Orleans (ACM, New York), pp. 663–664.
Buell, T. N., and Hafter, E. R. (**1990**). "Combination of binaural information across frequency bands," J. Acoust. Soc. Am. **90**, 1894–1900.
Butler, R. A., and Belendiuk, K. (**1977**). "Spectral cues utilized in the localization of sound in the median sagittal plane," J. Acoust. Soc. Am. **61**, 1264–1269.
Buxton, W., Gaver, W., and Bly, S. (**1989**). "The use of non-speech audio at the interface," Tutorial #10, CHI 89 (ACM, Press New York).
Calhoun, G. L., Valencia, G., and Furness, T. III (**1987**). "Three-dimensional auditory cue simulation for crew station design/evaluation," Proc. Hum. Factors Soc. **31**, 1398–1402.
Canon, L. K. (**1970**). "Intermodality inconsistency of input and directed attention as determinants of the nature of adaptation," J. Exp. Psychol. **84**, 141–147.
Canon, L. K. (**1971**). "Directed attention and the maladaptive adaptation to displacement of the visual field," J. Exp. Psychol. **88**, 403–408.
Chan, C. J. (**1992**). "Sound localization and spatial enhancement with the Roland Sound Space Processor," in *CyberArts: Exploring Art and Technology*, edited by L. Jacobson (Miller Freeman, San Francisco).
Chandler, D. W., and Grantham, D. W. (**1992**). "Minimum audible movement angle in the horizontal plane as a function of stimulus frequency and bandwidth, source azimuth, and velocity," J. Acoust. Soc. Am. **91**, 1624–1636.
Cherry, E. C. (**1953**). "Some experiments on the recognition of speech with one and two ears," J. Acoust. Soc. Am. **22**, 61–62.
Clark, B., and Graybiel, A. (**1963**). "Perception of the postural vertical in normals and subjects with labyrinthine defects," J. Exp. Psychol. **65**, 490.
Clifton, R. K., Gwiazda, J., Bauer, J. A., Clarkson, M. G., and Held, R. M. (**1988**). "Growth in head size during infancy: Implications for sound localization," Dev. Psychol. **4**, 477–483.
Cohen, M. M. (**1974**). "Changes in auditory localization following prismatic exposure under continuous and terminal visual feedback," Percept. Motor Skills **38**, 1202.
Cohen, M., and Wenzel, E. M. (**1995**). "The Design of Multidimensional Sound Interfaces," in *Virtual Environments and Advanced Interface Design*, edited by W. Barfield and T. Furness III (Oxford University Press, New York), pp. 291–346.
Colburn, H. S., and Durlach, N. I. (**1978**). "Models of Binaural Interaction," in *Handbook of Perception, Vol. IV, Hearing*, edited by E. C. Carterette and M. P. Friedman (Academic Press, New York), pp. 467–515.
Coleman, P. D. (**1963**). "An analysis of cues to auditory depth perception in free space," Psychol. Bul. **60**, 302–315.
Coleman, P. D. (**1968**). "Dual role of frequency spectrum in determination of auditory distance," J. Acoust. Soc. Am. **44**, 631–632.
Craske, B. (**1966**). "Intermodal transfer of adaptation to displacement," Nature **210**, 765.
Cruz-Neira, C., Sandin, D. J., and DeFanti, T. A. (**1993**). "Surround screen projection based virtual reality: The design and implementation of the CAVE," in *Computer Graphics Proceedings of SIGGRAPH* (ACM, New York), pp. 135–142.
Deutsch, D. (**1982**). *The Psychology of Music* (Academic Press, New York).

Divenyi, P. L. (**1992**). "Binaural suppression of nonechoes," J. Acoust. Soc. Am. **91**, 1078–1084.
Doll, T. J., Gerth, J. M., Engelman, W. R., and Folds, D. J. (**1986**). *Development of simulated directional audio for cockpit applications*, Report No. AAMRL-TR-86-014 (Wright-Patterson Air Force Base, Dayton, OH).
Durlach, N. I. (**1991**). "Auditory localization in teleoperator and virtual environment systems: Ideas, issues, and problems," Perception **20**, 543–554.
Durlach, N. I., and Braida, L. D. (**1969**). "Intensity perception. I. Preliminary theory of intensity resolution," J. Acoust. Soc. Am. **46**, 372–383.
Durlach, N. I., and Colburn, H. S. (**1978**). "Binaural Phenomena," in *Handbook of Perception, Vol. IV, Hearing*, edited by E. C. Carterette and M. P. Friedman (Academic Press, New York), pp. 365–466.
Durlach, N. I., Held, R. M., and Shinn-Cunningham, B. G. (**1992**). "Super Auditory Localization Displays," in *Society for Information Displays International Symposium Digest of Technical Papers, XXIII* (Society for Information Displays, Boston), pp. 98–101.
Durlach, N. I., and Mavor, A. (**1994**). *Virtual Reality: Scientific and Technical Challenges* (National Academy of Sciences, Washington, DC).
Durlach, N. I., and Pang, X. D. (**1986**). "Interaural magnification," J. Acoust. Soc. Am. **80**, 1849–1850.
Durlach, N. I., Rigopulos, A., Pang, X. D., Woods, W. S., Kulkarni, A., Colburn, H. S., and Wenzel, E. M. (**1992**). "On the externalization of auditory images," Presence **1**, 251–257.
Durlach, N. I., Shinn-Cunningham, B. G., and Held, R. M. (**1994**). "Super Auditory Localization. I. General Background," Presence **2**, 89–103.
Dye, R. H. (**1990**). "The combination of interaural information across frequencies: Lateralization on the basis of interaural delay," J. Acoust. Soc. Am. **88**, 2159–2170.
Edwards, A. D. N. (**1989**). "Soundtrack: An auditory interface for blind users," Human-Computer Interaction **4**, 45–66.
Feinstein, S. H. (**1966**). "Human hearing under water: Are things as bad as they seem?" J. Acoust. Soc. Am. **40**, 1561–1562.
Fisher, H. G., and Freedman, S. J. (**1968**). "The role of the pinna in auditory localization," J. Audit. Res. **8**, 15–26.
Fisher, S. S., Wenzel, E. M., Coler, C., and McGreevy, M.W. (1988). "Virtual interface environment workstations," Proc. Hum. Factors Soc. **32**, 91–95.
Fitch, T., and Kramer, G. (**1994**). "Sonifying the body electric: Superiority of an auditory over a visual display in a complex, multi-variate system," in *Auditory Display: Sonification, Audification, and Auditory Interface, SFI Studies in the Sciences of Complexity, Proc. XVIII*, edited by G. Kramer (Addison-Wesley, Reading, MA).
Florentine, M. (1976). "Relation between lateralization and loudness in asymmetrical hearing losses," J. Audiologic Soc. **1**, 243–251.
Forbes, T. W. (**1946**). "Auditory signals for instrument flying," J. Aeronautical Soc., May, 255–258.
Foster, S. H., and Wenzel, E. M. (**1991**). "Virtual acoustic environments: The Convolvotron," Demonstration system presented at the Tomorrow's Realities Gallery, SIGGRAPH '91, 18th ACM Conference on Computer Graphics and Interactive Techniques, Las Vegas, NV (ACM Press, New York).
Foster, S.H., Wenzel, E.M., and Taylor, R.M. (**1991**). "Real-time synthesis of complex acoustic environments [Summary]," in *Proceedings of the IEEE Workshop on Applications of Signal Processing to Audio and Acoustics*, New Paltz, NY (IEEE, New York).
Francioni, J. F., Albright, L., and Jackson, J.A. (**1991**). "Debugging parallel programs using sound," in *Proceedings of the ACM/ONR Workshop on Parallel and Distributed Debugging*, pp. 68–73.
Freedman, S. J., Hall, S. B., and Rekosh, J. H. (**1965**). "Effects on hand-eye coordination of two different arm motions during adaptation to displaced vision," Percept. Motor Skills **20**, 1054–1056.
Freedman, S. J., and Wilson, L. (**1967**). "Compensation for auditory rearrangement following exposure to auditory-tactile discordance," Percept. Motor Skills **25**, 861–866.
Freedman, S. J., and Gardos, G. (**1965**). "Compensation for auditory re-arrangement and transfer to hand-eye coordination," paper read at MIT Conference on Adaptation, Cambridge, MA, June.
Freedman, S. J., and Rekosh, J. H. (**1965**). "Auditory effects of visual rearrangement," paper read at MIT Conference on Adaptation, Cambridge, MA, June.
Freedman, S. J., and Stampfer, K. (**1964a**). "The effects of displaced ears on auditory localization," Technical Report 64–0938 (AFOSR).
Freedman, S. J., and Stampfer, K. (**1964b**). "Changes in auditory localization with displaced ears," paper presented to the Psychonomic Society, Niagara Falls, Ontario, October.
Freedman, S. J., Wilson, L., and Rekosh, J. H. (**1967**). "Compensation for auditory re-arrangement in hand-ear coordination," Percept. Motor Skills **24**, 1207–1210.
Freedman, S. J., and Zacks, J. L. (1964). "Effects of active and passive movement upon auditory function during prolonged atypical stimulation," Percept. Motor Skills **18**, 361–366.
Gardner, H. (**1985**). *Frames of Mind, The Theory of Multiple Intelligences* (Basic Books, New York).
Gardner, M. B. (**1968a**). "Proximity image effect in sound localization," J. Acoust. Soc. Am. **43**, 163.
Gardner, M. B. (**1968b**). "Lateral localization of 0–degree or near 0–degree-oriented speech signals in anechoic space," J. Acoust. Soc. Am. **44**, 797–802.

Gardner, M. B. (**1969a**). "Distance estimation of 0-degree or apparent 0-degree-oriented speech signals in anechoic space," J. Acoust. Soc. Am. **45**, 47–53.
Gardner, M. B. (**1969b**). "Image fusion, broadening, and displacement in sound localization," J. Acoust. Soc. Am. **46**, 339–349.
Gardner, M. B., and Gardner, R. S. (**1973**). "Problem of localization in the median plane: Effect of pinnae cavity occlusion," J. Acoust. Soc. Am. **53**, 400–408.
Gaskell, H. (**1983**). "The precedence effect," Hear. Res. **11**, 277–303.
Gaver, W. W., Smith, R. B., and O'Shea, T. (**1991**). "Effective sounds in complex systems: The ARKola simulation," in *Proceedings of CHI '91, ACM Conference on Computer-Human Interaction*, New Orleans (ACM, New York), pp. 85–90.
Genuit, K. (**1986**). "A description of the human outer ear transfer function by elements of communication theory," in *Proceedings of the 12th International Congress on Acoustics*, Paper B6–8, Toronto, Ontario.
Gescheider, G. A. (**1965**). "Cutaneous sound localization," J. Exp. Psychol. **70**, 617–625.
Gescheider, G. A. (**1966**). "The resolving of successive clicks by the ears and skin," J. Exp. Psychol. **71**, 378–381.
Gescheider, G. A. (**1968**). "The role of phase-difference cues in the cutaneous analog of auditory sound localization," J. Acoust. Soc. Am. **43**, 1249–1254.
Gierlich, H. W. (**1992**). "The application of binaural technology," Appl. Acoust. **36**, 219–243.
Gierlich, H. W., and Genuit, K. (**1989**). "Processing artificial-head recordings," J. Audio Eng. Soc. **37**, 34–39.
Grantham, D. W.(**1986**). "Detection and discrimination of simulated motion of auditory targets in the horizontal plane," J. Acoust. Soc. Am. **79**, 1939–1949.
Grantham, D. W. (**1989**). "Motion aftereffects with horizontally moving sound sources in the free field," Percept. Psychophys. **45**, 129–136.
Grantham, D. W. (**1992**). "Adaptation to auditory motion in the horizontal plane: Effects of prior exposure to motion on motion detectability," J. Acoust. Soc. Am. **52**, 144–150.
Graybiel, A., and Niven, J. I. (**1951**). "The effect of a change in direction of resultant force on sound localization: The audiogravic illusion," J. Exp. Psychol. **42**, 227–230.
Hausler, R., Colburn, H. S., and Marr, E. (**1983**). "Sound localization in subjects with impaired hearing," Acta Otolaryngol. Suppl. 400.
Hayward, C. (**1994**). "Listening to the earth sing," in *Auditory Display: Sonification, Audification, and Auditory Interface, SFI Studies in the Sciences of Complexity, Proc. XVIII*, edited by G. Kramer (Addison-Wesley, Reading, MA).
Held, R. M. (**1955**). "Shifts in binaural localization after prolonged exposure to atypical combinations of stimuli," Am. J. Psychol. **68**, 526–548.
Held, R. M., and Durlach, N. I. (**1987**). "Telepresence, time delay, and adaptation," NASA conference publication 10032.
Held, R. M., Efstathiou, A., and Greene, M. (**1966**). "Adaptation to displaced and delayed visual feedback from the hand," J. Exp. Psychol. **72(6)**, 889–891.
Held, R., and Hein, A. (**1958**). "Adaptation to disarranged hand-eye co-ordination contingent upon re-afferent stimulation," Percept. Motor Skills **8**, 87–90.
Henning, G. B. (**1974**). "Detectability of interaural delay in high-frequency complex waveforms," J. Acoust. Soc. Am. **55**, 84–90.
Hodges, L. F., Bolter, J., Mynatt, E., Ribarsky, W., and van Teylingen, R. (**1993**). "Virtual environment research at the Georgia Tech GVU Center," Presence **2**, 234–243.
Hudde, H., and Schroeter, J. (**1981**). "[Improvements in the Neumann artificial head system], in *Runkfunk-technische Mitteilungen [Radio Technology Reports]*, Federal Republic of Germany (in German).
Hunt, F. V. (**1964**). "Remarks on the mean free path problem," J. Acoust. Soc. Am. **36**, 556–564.
Hunter, W. E., and McCants, L. S. (**1977**). "The new generation gap: Involvement vs. instant gratification," National Institute of Education Topical Paper No. 64 (U.S. Department of Health, Education, and Welfare, Washington, DC).
Jack, C. E., and Thurlow, W. R. (**1973**). "Effects of degree of visual association and angle of displacement on the ventriloquism effect," Percept. Motor Skills **37**, 967–979.
Jameson, D. (**1994**). "Sonnet: audio enhanced monitoring and debugging," in *Auditory Display: Sonification, Audification, and Auditory Interface, SFI Studies in the Sciences of Complexity, Proc. XVIII*, edited by G. Kramer (Addison-Wesley, Reading, MA).
Jeffress, L. A. (**1948**). "A place theory of sound localization," J. Comp. Physiol. Psychol. **61**, 468–486.
Johnsen, E. G., and Corliss, W. R. (**1967**). "Teleoperators and human augmentation," NASA SP-5047 (NASA Office of Technology Utilization, Washington, DC).
Jones, B., and Kabanoff, B. (**1975**). "Eye movements in auditory space perception," Percept. Psychophys. **17**, 241–245.
Jot, J. M., Warusfel, O., Kahle, E., and Mein, M. (**1993**). "Binaural concert hall simulation in real time," Presented at the IEEE Workshop on Applications of Signal Processing to Audio and Acoustics, New Paltz, NY, October.
Kay, L. (**1974**). "A sonar aid to enhance spatial perception of the blind: Engineering design and evaluation," Radio and Electronics Engineer **44**, 40–62.

Kendall, G. S., and Martens, W. L. (**1984**). "Simulating the cues of spatial hearing in natural environments," in *Proceedings of the 1984 International Computer Music Conference*, Paris, France.

Kistler, D. J., and Wightman, F. L. (**1991**). "A model of head-related transfer functions based on principal components analysis and minimum-phase reconstruction," J. Acoust. Soc. Am. **91**, 1637–1647.

Kramer, G. (**1990**). *Audification of the ACOT Predator/Prey Model*, unpublished research report prepared for Apple Computer's Advanced Technology Group, Apple Classrooms of Tomorrow.

Kramer, G. (**1994**). "Some organizing principles for auditory display," in *Auditory Display: Sonification, Audification, and Auditory Interface, SFI Studies in the Sciences of Complexity, Proc. XVIII*, edited by G. Kramer (Addison-Wesley, Reading, MA).

Kramer, G., and Ellison, S. (**1991**). "Audification: the use of sound to display multivariate data," in *Proceedings of the International Computer Music Conference*, pp. 214–221.

Krokstadt A., Strom S., and Sorsdal S. (**1968**). "Calculating the acoustical room response by the use of a ray tracing technique," J. Sound Vib. **8**, 118–125.

Krygier, J. B. (**1992**). "Sound variables, sound maps, and cartographic visualization," unpublished thesis, Department of Geography, Pennsylvania State University, University Park.

Kubovy, M., and Howard, F. P. (**1976**). "Persistence of a pitch-segregating echoic memory," J. Exp. Psychol. Hum. Percept. Perform. **2**, 531–537.

Kuhn, G. F. (**1977**). "Model for the interaural time differences in the azimuthal plane," J. Acoust. Soc. Am. **62**, 157–167.

Kulkarni, A. (**1993**). "Auditory imaging in a virtual acoustical environment," unpublished master's thesis, Department of Biomedical Engineering, Boston University, Boston.

Lackner, J. R. (**1973a**). "Visual rearrangement affects auditory localization," Neuropsychologia **11**, 29–32.

Lackner, J. R. (**1973b**). "The role of posture in sound localization," J. Exp. Psychol. **26**, 235–251.

Lackner, J. R. (**1974a**). "Influence of visual rearrangement and visual motion on sound localization," Neuropsychologia **12**, 291–293.

Lackner, J. R. (**1974b**). "Changes in auditory localization during body tilt," Acta Otolaryngol. **77**, 19–28.

Lackner, J. R. (**1983**). "Influence of posture on the spatial localization of sound," J. Audio Eng. Soc. **31**, 226–233.

Lackner, J. R., and Levine, M. S. (**1979**). "Changes in apparent body orientation and sensory localization induced by vibration of skeletal muscles: Vibratory myesthetic illusions," Aviat. Space. Environ. Med. **50**, 346–354.

Lackner, J. R., and Shenker. (**1983**). "Proprioceptive influences on auditory and visual spatial localization," J. Neurosci. **5**, 579–583.

Laws, P. (**1972**). "Zum Problem des Entfernungshorens und der Im-Kopf-Lokalisiertheit von Horeregnissen [On the problem of distance hearing and the localization of auditory events inside the head]," unpublished doctoral dissertation, Technische Hochschule, Aachen, Federal Republic of Germany.

Laws, P. (**1973**). "Entfernungshoeren und das Problem der Im-Kopf-Lokalisiertheit von Hoerereignissen. [Auditory distance perception and the problem of in-head localization of sound images]," Acustica **29**, 243–259.

Lehnert, H. (**1993a**). "Systematic errors of the ray-tracing algorithm," Appl. Acoust. **38**, 207–221.

Lehnert, H. (**1993b**). "Auditory spatial impression," In *Proceedings of the 12th International AES Conference*, Copenhagen, Denmark, pp. 40–46.

Lehnert, H., and Blauert, J. (**1989**). "A concept for binaural room simulation [Summary]," In *Proceedings of the IEEE Workshop on Applications of Signal Processing to Audio and Acoustics*, New Paltz, NY (IEEE, New York).

Lehnert, H., and Blauert, J. (**1991**). "Virtual Auditory Environment," Proc. 5th Int. Conf. Advanced Robotics IEEE-ICAR **1**, 211–216.

Lippmann, R. P., Braida, L. D., and Durlach, N. I. (**1976**). "Intensity perception. V. Effect of payoff matrix on absolute identification," J. Acoust. Soc. Am. **59**, 129–134.

Little, A. D., Mershon, D. H., and Cox, P. H. (**1992**). "Spectral content as a cue to perceived auditory distance," Perception **21**, 405–416.

Loomis, J. M., Hebert, C., and Cicinelli, J. G. (**1990**). "Active localization of virtual sounds," J. Acoust. Soc. Am. **88**, 1757–1764.

Lunney, D., and Morrison, R. (**1981**). "High technology laboratory aids for visually handicapped chemistry students," J. Chem. Educ. **58**, 228.

Madhyastha, T. M., and Reed, D. A. (**1994**). "A framework for sonification design," in *Auditory Display: Sonification, Audification, and Auditory Interface, SFI Studies in the Sciences of Complexity, Proc. XVIII*, edited by G. Kramer (Addison-Wesley, Reading, MA).

Mann, C., and Passey, G. (**1951**). "The perception of the vertical: V. Adjustment to the postural vertical as a function of the magnitude of postural tilt and duration of exposure," J. Exp. Psychol. **41**, 108.

Mastroianni, G. R. (**1982**). "The influence of eye movements and illumination on auditory localization," Percept. Psychophys. **31**, 581–584.

Mayer-Kress, G., Bargar, R., and Choi, I. (**1994**). "Musical structures in data from chaotic attractors," in *Auditory Display: Sonification, Audification, and Auditory Interface, SFI Studies in the Sciences of Complexity, Proc. XVIII*, edited by G. Kramer (Addison-Wesley, Reading, MA).

McCabe, R. K., and Rangwalla, A. A. (**1994**). "Auditory display of computational fluid dynamics data," in *Auditory Display: Sonification, Audification, and Auditory Interface, SFI Studies in the Sciences of Complexity, Proc. XVIII*, edited by G. Kramer (Addison-Wesley, Redaing, MA).
McKinley, R. L., and Ericson, M. A. (**1988**). "Digital synthesis of binaural auditory localization azimuth cues using headphones," J. Acoust. Soc. Am. **83**, S18.
McKinley, R. L., Ericson, M. A., and D'Angelo, W. R. (**1994**). "3–Dimensional auditory displays: Development, applications, and performance," Aviat. Space. Environ. Med., May, A31–A38.
Meares, D. J. (**1992**). "Multichannel sound systems for HDTV," Appl. Acoust. **36**, 245–258.
Mershon, D. H., Ballenger, W. L., Little, A. D., McMurtry, P. L., and Buchanan, J. L. (**1989**). "Effects of room reflectance and background noise on perceived auditory distance," Perception **18**, 403–416.
Mershon, D. H., and Bowers, J. N. (**1979**). "Absolute and relative cues for the auditory perception of egocentric distance," Perception **8**, 311–322.
Mershon, D. H., and King, L. E. (**1975**). "Intensity and reverberation as factors in the auditory perception of egocentric distance," Percept. Psychophys. **18**, 409–415.
Mershon, D. H., and Lin, L.-J. (**1987**). "Directional localization in high ambient noise with and without the use of hearing protectors," Ergonomics **30**, 1161–1173.
Meyer, K., Applewhite, H. L., and Biocca, F. A. (**1993**). "A survey of position trackers," Presence **1**, 173–200.
Mezrich, J. J., Frysinger, S. P., and Slivjanovski, R. (**1984**). "Dynamic representation of multivariate time-series data," J. Am. Statist. Assoc. **79**, 34–40.
Middlebrooks, J. C., and Green, D. M. (**1990**). "Directional dependence of interaural envelope delays," J. Acoust. Soc. Am. **87**, 2149–2162.
Middlebrooks, J. C., Makous, J. C., and Green, D. M. (**1989**). "Directional sensitivity of sound-pressure levels in the human ear canal," J. Acoust. Soc. Am. **86**, 89–108.
Mikaelian, H. H. (**1969**). "Adaptation to rearranged ear-hand coordination," Percept. Motor Skills **28**, 147–150.
Mikaelian, H. H. (**1972**). "Lack of bilateral generalization of adaptation to auditory rearrangement," Percept. Psychophys. **11**, 222–224.
Mikaelian, H. H. (**1974**). "Adaptation to displaced hearing: a nonproprioceptive change," J. Exp. Psychol. **103**, 326–330.
Mikaelian, H. H., and Russotti, J. S. (**1972**). *Lack of bilateral generalization of adaptation to auditory rearrangement*, Report Number 715 (Naval Submarine Medical Research Laboratory, Groton, CT).
Miller, G. A. (**1956**). "The magical number seven, plus or minus two: Some limits on our capacity for processing information," Psych. Rev. **63**, 81–96.
Mills, A. W. (**1958**). "On the minimum audible angle," J. Acoust. Soc. Am. **30**, 237–246.
Mills, A. W. (**1972**). "Auditory localization," in *Foundations of Modern Auditory Theory, Vol. II*, edited by J. V. Tobias (Academic Press, New York), pp. 301–345.
Miyoshi, M., and Koizumi, N. (**1992**). "NNTs research on acoustics for future telecommunication services," Appl. Acoust. **36**, 307–326.
Mowbray, G. H., and Gebhard, J. W. (**1961**). "Man's senses as informational channels," in *Human Factors in the Design and Use of Control Systems*, edited by H. W. Sinaiko (Dover, New York), pp. 115–149.
Oldfield, S. R., and Parker, S. P. A. (**1984a**). "Acuity of sound localisation: A topography of auditory space. I. Normal hearing conditions," Perception **13**, 581–600.
Oldfield, S. R., and Parker, S. P. A. (**1984b**). "Acuity of sound localisation: A topography of auditory space. II. Pinna cues absent," Perception **13**, 601–617.
Oldfield, S. R., and Parker, S. P. A. (**1986**). "Acuity of sound localisation: A topography of auditory space. III. Monaural hearing conditions," Perception **15**, 67–81.
Patterson, R. D. (**1982**). "Guidelines for auditory warning systems on civil aircraft," Paper No. 82017 (Civil Aviation Authority, London).
Perrott, D. R. (**1982**). "Studies in the perception of auditory motion," in *Localization of Sound: Theory and Applications*, edited by R.W. Gatehouse (Amphora Press, Groton, CT), pp. 169–193.
Perrott, D. R. (**1984a**). "Concurrent minimum audible angle: A re-examination of the concept of auditory spatial acuity," J. Acoust. Soc. Am. **75**, 1201–1206.
Perrott, D. R. (**1984b**). "Discrimination of the spatial distribution of concurrently active sound sources: Some experiments with stereophonic arrays," J. Acoust. Soc. Am. **76**, 1704–1712.
Perrott, D. R., and Marlborough, K. (**1989**). "Minimum audible movement angle: Marking the end points of the path traveled by a moving sound source," J. Acoust. Soc. Am. **85**, 1773–1775.
Perrott, D. R., Sadralodabai, T., Saberi, K., and Strybel, T. Z. (**1991**). "Aurally aided visual search in the central visual field: Effects of visual load and visual enhancement of the target," Hum. Factors **33**, 389–400.
Perrott, D. R., and Tucker, J. (**1988**). "Minimum audible movement angle as a function of signal frequency and the velocity of the source," J. Acoust. Soc. Am. **83**, 1522–1527.
Persterer, A. (**1989**). "A very high performance digital audio signal processing system [Summary]," in *Proceedings of the IEEE Workshop on Applications of Signal Processing to Audio and Acoustics*, New Paltz, NY (IEEE, New York).
Persterer, A. (**1991**). "Binaural simulation of an ideal control room for headphone reproduction." Preprint 3062 (K-4), 90th Convention of the Audio Engineering Society, Paris.

Pick, H. L., and Hay, J. C. (**1965**). "A passive test of the Held reafference hypothesis," Percept. Motor Skills **20**, 1070–1072.
Pick, H. L., Warren, D. H., and Hay, J. C. (**1969**). "Sensory conflict in judgements of spatial direction," Percept. Psychophys. **6**, 203–205.
Platt, B. B., and Warren, D. H. (**1972**). "Auditory localization: the importance of eye movements and a textured visual environment," Percept. Psychophys. **12**, 245–248.
Plenge, G. (**1974**). "On the difference between localization and lateralization," J. Acoust. Soc. Am. **56**, 944–951.
Poesselt, C., Schroeter, J., Opitz, M., Divenyi, P., and Blauert, J. (**1986**). "Generation of binaural signals for research and home entertainment," in *Proceedings of the 12th International Congress on Acoustics*, Paper B1–6, Toronto, Ontario.
Rabenhorst, D. A., Farrell, E. J., Jameson, D. H., Linton, T. D., and Mandelman, J.A. (**1990**). "Complementary visualization and sonification of multidimensional data," in *Extracting Meaning from Complex Data: Processing, Display, Interaction*, edited by E. J. Farrel, Proc. SPIE **1259**, 147–153.
Rabinowitz, W.M., Maxwell, J., Shao, Y., and Wei, M. (**1993**). "Sound localization cues for a magnified head: Implications from sound diffraction about a rigid sphere," Presence **2**, 125–129.
Radeau, M., and Bertelson, P. (**1974**). "The after-effects of ventriloquism," J. Exp. Psychol. **26**, 63–71.
Radeau, M., and Bertelson, P. (**1976**). "The effect of a textured visual field on modality dominance in a ventriloquism situation," Percept. Psychophys. **20**, 227–235.
Radeau, M., and Bertelson, P. (**1977**). "Adaptation to auditory-visual discordance and ventriloquism in semirealistic situations," Percept. Psychophys. **22**, 137–146.
Rayleigh, Lord (J. W. Strutt, 3rd Baron of Rayleigh) (**1907**). "On our perception of sound direction," Philos. Mag. **13**, 214–232.
Rekosh, J. H., and Freedman, S. J. (**1967**). "Errors in auditory direction-finding after compensation for visual re-arrangement," Percept. Psychophys. **2**, 466–468.
Richter, F., and Persterer, A. (**1989**). "Design and applications of a creative audio processor," 86th Convention of the Audio Engineering Society, Preprint 2782 (U-4), Hamburg, Germany.
Russell, G. (**1977**). "Limits in behavioral compensation for auditory localization in earmuff listening conditions," J. Acoust. Soc. Am. **61**, 219–220.
Ryan, T. A., and Schehr, F. (**1941**). "The influence of eye movement and position on auditory localization," Am. J. Psychol. **54**, 243–252.
Saberi, K., and Perrott, D. R. (**1990**). "Lateralization thresholds obtained under conditions in which the precedence effect is assumed to operate," J. Acoust. Soc. Am. **87**, 1732–1737.
Sandvad, J., and Hammershoi, D. (**1994**). "Binaural auralization: Comparison of FIR and IIR filter representation of HIRs," 96th AES Convention, Amsterdam, the Netherlands.
Scadden, L. A. (**1978**). *Annual Report of Progress* (Rehabilitation Engineering Center of the Smith-Kettlewell Institute of Visual Sciences, San Francisco).
Scaletti, C., and Craig, A. B. (**1991**). "Using sound to extract meaning from complex data," in *Extracting Meaning from Complex Data: Processing, Display, Interaction*, edited by E. J. Farrel, Proc. SPIE **1459**, pp. 207–219.
Schroeder M. R. (**1962**). "Natural sounding artificial reverberation," J. Audio Eng. Soc. **10**, 219–223.
Shaw, E. A. G. (**1974**). "The external ear," in *Handbook of Sensory Physiology, Vol. V/1, Auditory System*, edited by W. D. Keidel and W. D. Neff (Springer-Verlag, New York), pp. 455–490.
Shaw, E. A. G. (**1975**). "The external ear: New knowledge," in *Earmolds and Associated Problems. Proceedings of the 7th Danavox Symposium*, edited by S. C. Dalsgaard, Scand. Audiol. Suppl. 5, 24–50.
Sheridan, T. (**1992**). *Telerobotics, Automation, and Human Supervisory Control* (MIT Press, Cambridge, MA).
Shinn-Cunningham, B. G. (**1994**). *Adaptation to Supernormal Auditory Localization Cues in an Auditory Virtual Environment*, PhD dissertation in Electrical Engineering and Computer Science, Massachusetts Institute of Technology, Cambridge, MA.
Shinn-Cunningham, B. G., Zurek, P. M., and Durlach, N. I. (**1993**). "Adjustment and discrimination measurements of the precedence effect," J. Acoust. Soc. Am. **93**, 2923–2932.
Smith, S. (**1991**). "An auditory display for exploratory visualization of multidimensional data," in *Workstations for Experiment*, edited by G. Grinstein and J. Encarnacao (Springer-Verlag, Berlin).
Speigle, J. M., and Loomis, J. M. (**1993**). "Auditory distance perception by translating observers," in *Proceedings of the IEEE 1993 Symposium on Research Frontiers in Virtual Reality*, San Jose, CA (IEEE Computer Society), pp. 92–99.
Stellmack, M. A., and Dye, R. H., Jr. (**1993**). "The combination of interaural information across frequencies: The effects of number and spacing of components, onset asynchrony," J. Acoust. Soc. Am. **93**, 2933–2947.
Stephenson, U. (**1988**). "Schallteilchen-contra Spiegelquellenmethode-Methode," *Fortschritte der Akustik-DAGA '88* (DPG-GmbH, Bad Honnef), pp. 741–747.
Terenzi, F. (**1988**). "Design and Realization of an Integrated System for the Composition of Musical Scores and for the Numerical Synthesis of Sound (Special application for translation of radiation from galaxies into sound using computer music procedures)," Physics Deptartment, University of Milan.
Terhune, J. M. (**1974**). "Directional hearing of a harbor seal in air and water," J. Acoust. Soc. Am. **56**, 1862–1865.

Teuber, H.-L., and Diamond, S. (**1956**). "Effects of brain injury on binaural localization of sounds," paper read at Eastern Psychological Association, Atlantic City, NJ, as reported in Lackner (**1983**).

Teuber, H.-L., and Liebert, R. (**1956**). "Effects of body tilts on auditory localization," Am. Psychol. **11**, 430A.

Thomas, G. J. (**1941**). "Experimental study of the influence of vision on sound localization," J. Exp. Psychol. **28**, 163–177.

Thurlow, W. R., and Kerr, T. P. (**1970**). "Effect of a moving visual environment on localization of sound," Am. J. Psychol. **83**, 112–118.

Thurlow, W. R., Mangels, J. W., and Runge, P. S. (**1967**). "Head movements during sound localization," J. Acoust. Soc. Am. **42**, 489–493.

Thurlow, W. R., and Runge, P. S. (**1967**). "Effects of induced head movements on localization of direction of sound sources," J. Acoust. Soc. Am. **42**, 480–488.

Toole, F. E. (1969). "In-head localization of acoustic images," J. Acoust. Soc. Am. **48**, 943–949.

Van Veen, B. D., and Jenison, R. L. (**1991**). "Auditory space expansion via linear filtering," J. Acoust. Soc. Am. **90**, 231–240.

Vertut, J., and Coiffet, P. (**1986**). *Robot Technology, Volume 3B: Teleoperation and Robotics: Applications and Technology* (Prentice-Hall, Englewood Cliffs, NJ).

Vorlander, M. (1988). "Die Genauigkeit von Berechnungen mit dem raumakustischen Schallteilchenmodell und ihre Abhngigkeit von der Rechenzeit," Acustica **66**, 90–96.

Wallach, H. (**1939**). "On sound localization," J. Acoust. Soc. Am. **10**, 270–274.

Wallach, H. (**1940**). "The role of head movements and vestibular and visual cues in sound localization," J. Exp. Psychol. **27**, 339–368.

Wallach, H., Newman, E. B., and Rosenzweig, M. R. (1949). "The precedence effect in sound localization," Am. J. Psychol. **62**, 315–336.

Warren, D. H. (**1970**). "Intermodality interactions in spatial localization," Cognit. Psychol. **1**, 114–133.

Warren, D. H. (**1980**). "Response factors in intermodality localization under conflict conditions," Percept. Psychophys. **27**, 28–32.

Warren, D. H., McCarthy, T. J., and Welch, R. B. (**1983**). "Discrepancy and nondiscrepancy methods of assessing visual-auditory interaction," Percept. Psychophys. **33**, 413–419.

Warren, D. H., and Pick, H. L. (**1970**). "Intermodality relations in localization in blind and sighted people," Percept. Psychophys. **8**, 430–432.

Warren, D. H., and Strelow, E. R. (**1984**). "Learning spatial dimensions with a visual sensory aid: Molyneaux revisited," Perception **13**, 331–350.

Warren, D. H., and Strelow, E. R. (**1985**). "Training the use of artificial spatial displays," in *Electronic Spatial Sensing for the Blind*, edited by D. H. Warren and E. R. Strelow (Martinus-Nijhoff, Dordrecht, the Netherlands), pp. 201–216.

Warren, D. H., Welch, R. B., and McCarthy, T. J. (**1981**). "The role of visual-auditory compellingness in the ventriloquism effect: Implications for transitivity among the spatial senses," Percept. Psychophys. **30**, 557–564.

Weber, C. R. (**1993**). "Sonic enhancement of map information: Experiments using harmonic intervals," unpublished dissertation, Department of Geography, State University of New York at Buffalo, Buffalo.

Welch, R. B. (**1978**). *Perceptual Modification: Adapting to Altered Sensory Environments* (Academic Press, New York).

Welch, R. (**1986**). "Adaptation of Space Perception," in *Handbook of Perception and Human Performance, Vol. I*, edited by K. R. Boff, L. Kaufman, and J. P. Thomas (John Wiley and Sons, New York), Chapter 24.

Welch, R. B., Bridgeman, B., Anand, S., and Browman, K. E. (**1993**). "Alternating prism exposure causes dual adaptation and generalization to a novel displacement," Percept. Psychophys. **54**, 195–204.

Welch, R. B., and Warren, D. H. (**1980**). "Immediate perceptual response to intersensory discrepancy," Psychol. Bull. **88**, 638–667.

Welch, R., and Warren, D. H. (**1986**). "Intersensory interactions," in *Handbook of Perception and Human Performance, Vol. I*, edited by K. R. Boff, L. Kaufman, and J. P. Thomas (John Wiley and Sons, New York), Chapter 25.

Wells, M. J., and Ross, H. E. (**1980**). "Distortion and adaptation in underwater sound localization," Aviat. Space. Environ. Med. **51**, 767–774.

Wenzel, E. M. (**1992**). "Localization in virtual acoustic displays," Presence **1**, 80–107.

Wenzel, E. M. (**1994**). "Spatial sound and sonification," in *Auditory Display: Sonification, Audification, and Auditory Interface, SFI Studies in the Sciences of Complexity, Proc. XVIII*, edited by G. Kramer (Addison-Wesley, Reading, MA).

Wenzel, E. M., Arruda, M., Kistler, D. J., and Wightman, F. L. (**1993**). "Localization using nonindividualized head-related transfer functions," J. Acoust. Soc. Am. **94**, 111–123.

Wenzel, E. M., and Foster, S. H. (**1993**). "Perceptual consequences of interpolating head-related transfer functions during spatial synthesis," in *Proceedings of the IEEE Workshop on Applications of Signal Processing to Audio and Acoustics*, New Paltz, NY (IEEE, New York).

Wenzel, E. M., Stone, P. K., Fisher, S. S., and Foster, S. H. (**1990**). "A system for three-dimensional acoustic visualization in a virtual environment workstation," in *Proceedings of the IEEE Visualization 90 Conference*, San Francisco. (IEEE, New York), pp. 329–337.

Wenzel, E. M., Wightman, F. L., and Foster, S. H. (**1988a**). "Development of a three-dimensional auditory display system," SIGCHI Bull. **20**, 52–57.

Wenzel, E. M., Wightman, F. L., and Foster, S. H. (**1988b**). "A virtual display system for conveying three-dimensional acoustic information," Proc. Hum. Factors Soc. **32**, 86–90.

Wenzel, E. M., Wightman, F. L., and Kistler, D. J. (**1991**). "Localization of non-individualized virtual acoustic display cues," in *Proceedings of the CHI '91, ACM Conference on Computer-Human Interaction*, New Orleans, LA (ACM, New York), pp. 351–359.

Wenzel, E. M., Wightman, F. L., Kistler, D. J., and Foster, S. H. (**1988**). "Acoustic origins of individual differences in sound localization behavior," J. Acoust. Soc. Am. **84**, S79.

Wien, G. E. (**1964**). "A preliminary investigation of the effect of head width on binaural hearing," unpublished master's thesis, Department of Electrical Engineering, Massachusetts Institute of Technology, Cambridge, MA.

Wightman, F. L., and Kistler, D. J. (**1989a**). "Headphone simulation of free-field listening I: stimulus synthesis," J. Acoust. Soc. Am. **85**, 858–867.

Wightman, F. L., and Kistler, D. J. (**1989b**). "Headphone simulation of free-field listening II: Psychophysical validation," J. Acoust. Soc. Am. **85**, 868–878.

Wightman, F. L., Kistler, D. K., and Anderson, K. (**1994**). "Reassessment of the role of head movements in human sound localization," J. Acoust. Soc. Am. **95**, 3003–3004.

Wightman, F. L., Kistler, D. J., and Arruda, M. (**1992**). "Perceptual consequences of engineering compromises in synthesis of virtual auditory objects," J. Acoust. Soc. Am. **92**, 2332.

Willey, C. F., Inglis, E., and Pearce, C. H. (**1937**). "Reversal of auditory localization," J. Exp. Psychol. **20**, 114–130.

Willot, J. F. (**1973**). "Perceptual judgements with discrepant information from audition and proprioception," Percept. Psychophys. **14**, 577–580.

Witten, M. (**1992**). "Increasing our understanding of biological models through visual and sonic representations: A cortical case study," Int. J. Supercomputer Applications **6**, 257–280.

Yost, W. A., and Gourevitch, G. (Eds.). (**1987**). *Directional Hearing* (Springer-Verlag, New York).

Yost, W. A., and Soderquist, D. R. (**1984**). "The precedence effect: Revisited," J. Acoust. Soc. Am. **76**, 1377–1383.

Young, P. T. (**1928**). "Auditory localization with acoustic transposition of the ears," J. Exp. Psychol. **11**, 399–429.

Zurek, P. M. (**1979**). "Measurements of binaural echo suppression," J. Acoust. Soc. Am. **66**, 1750–1757.

Zurek, P. M. (**1980**). "The precedence effect and its possible role in the avoidance of interaural ambiguities," J. Acoust. Soc. Am. **67**, 952–964.

Zurek, P. M. (**1987**). "The Precedence Effect," in *Directional Hearing*, edited by W. A. Yost and G. Gourevitch (Springer-Verlag, New York), pp. 85–105.

Zyda, M., Pratt, D., Falby, J., Barham, P., and Kelleher, K. (**1993**). "NPSNET and the Naval Postgraduate School Graphics and Video Laboratory," Presence **2**, 244–258.

Chapter 30

Binaural Measurements and Applications

Mahlon D. Burkhard
Sonic Perceptions, Inc., Norwalk, Connecticut

(Received November 1994; revised May 1995)

Measurements in a sound field with equipment based on use of single microphones give incomplete indications of what a person may experience in that sound field. The torso, head, pinnae, and ear canal alter substantially the spectral shape of the sound experienced by a person as compared to that evaluated by instruments having responses that are flat over frequency. Binaural measurement systems incorporate an artificial head for capturing the sound at the ear entrance location on the head as two separate signals. The artificial head reproduces the diffractions and external ear resonances that contribute to perceptions. Analyzing and quantifying of the sound is done binaurally in an analyzer that combines superior signal analysis and display with simultaneous listening to the sound being analyzed. The human ear is unsurpassed as an analyzer and interpreter of sound. Three application examples are included in the discussion. Competitive pressure is causing product developers to use binaural measurements to obtain a better understanding of how product noise is perceived and thus to identify refinements that will make products more acceptable to users. In the field of architectural acoustics binaural measurements give a better understanding of the properties of existing halls and new or renovated spaces and how they can be improved for the benefit of performers and patrons. There is growing evidence that binaurally presented and perceived sound stimuli affect subliminal physiological responses to sounds.

INTRODUCTION

The traditional method of measuring sound was with a single microphone, but the majority of people listen, interact, and respond to sound based on the perceptions and impressions obtained binaurally. Although many regulations and even many psychoacoustic experimental results are based on the single-microphone detection of sound, experience has shown that many measurements with this method often relate poorly to a wide variety of everyday experiences. There is a need to sense and analyze binaurally the noise and sound produced in the workplace, by products, for personal and public entertainment, and in many other situations. Measurement methods are evolving that combine the best features of signal processing and analysis with the superior capabilities of the human hearing mechanisms to create a highly efficient system capable of searching for and quantifying important features of a sound or noise situation.

In this chapter, the basis of binaural measurement is discussed, and a brief description of equipment and methods for binaural measurement as it is currently implemented is presented. Calibration of the measurement system is necessary to quantify binaural measurements and observations and relate them to more familiar and conventional measurements. Three problem areas that make use of binaural measurements are used to illustrate practical applications of this measurement technology. One area is environmental noise, and an example is taken from experiments studying the role of binaural hearing in human physiological responses to noise. Another application is an architectural acoustics problem where intelligible communication among performing musicians is important. The third application is in product engineering, especially in the automotive industry. Many potentially annoying noise sources are present in vehicles and can be found with binaural measurement and analysis methods that more closely simulate human perceptions. The conclusion mentions briefly the goals of binaural measurement development.

I. ATTRIBUTES OF BINAURAL HEARING AND MEASUREMENT

One way binaural measurement methods differ from single-microphone methods is illustrated by a simple masking experiment. When a signal and a masker are located at different positions, the output from a single measurement microphone such as in a sound level meter is no different from what would be measured if the signal and masker were at the same position. That is, a single measurement microphone gives no information about direction and distance and is unable to show that two or more sound sources may be active. Figure 1 shows an example of two sounds recorded with a single microphone and the same sounds recorded with a binaural head measurement microphone system. One sound is a one-third octave band of noise centered at 4 kHz, located 45° to the left; the other is a pulsed 4-kHz sine wave at a level 20 dB lower, located 45° to the right. Because of head shadow and directional response of ears, the pulsed sound can readily be shown in the binaural display as well as being audible to a listener either in the live situation or in a binaural playback.

The physical basis for the head shadow effect (as well as other head, ear, and torso spectrum shaping and the resulting ear sound) is evident in the directional frequency response curves in Fig. 2. For a sound source emitting a constant level as a function of frequency in an anechoic space, both ears receive quite similar sound levels for low-frequency sounds independent of direction. At higher frequencies, as in the 4-kHz range shown in Fig. 1, the sound level at the ear facing a source increases on the order of 7 dB relative to free field, whereas the level at the remote ear decreases by more than 20 dB. The lower-level pulsed 4-kHz sound

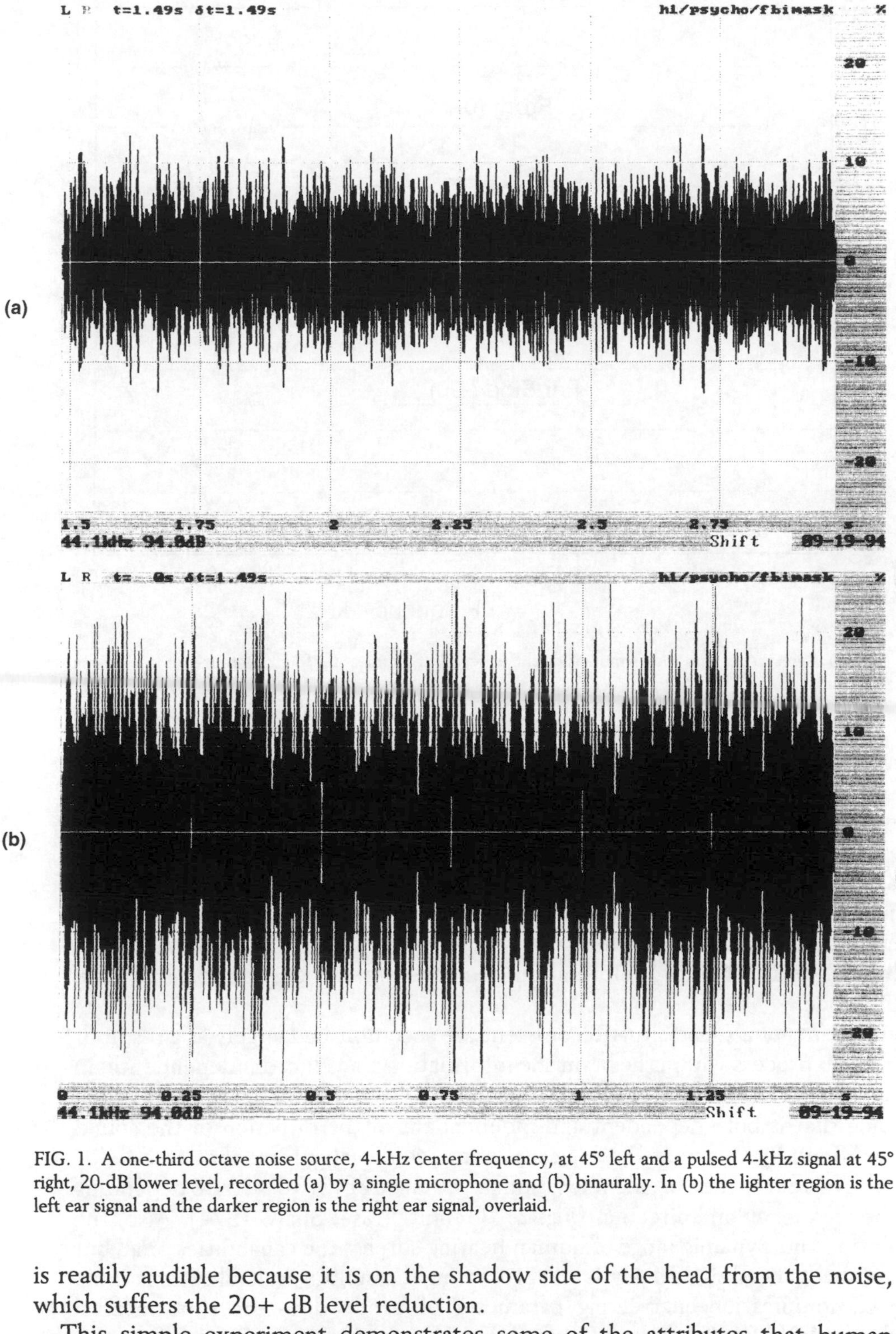

FIG. 1. A one-third octave noise source, 4-kHz center frequency, at 45° left and a pulsed 4-kHz signal at 45° right, 20-dB lower level, recorded (a) by a single microphone and (b) binaurally. In (b) the lighter region is the left ear signal and the darker region is the right ear signal, overlaid.

is readily audible because it is on the shadow side of the head from the noise, which suffers the 20+ dB level reduction.

This simple experiment demonstrates some of the attributes that human hearing uses to recognize direction and to select and identify a particular sound

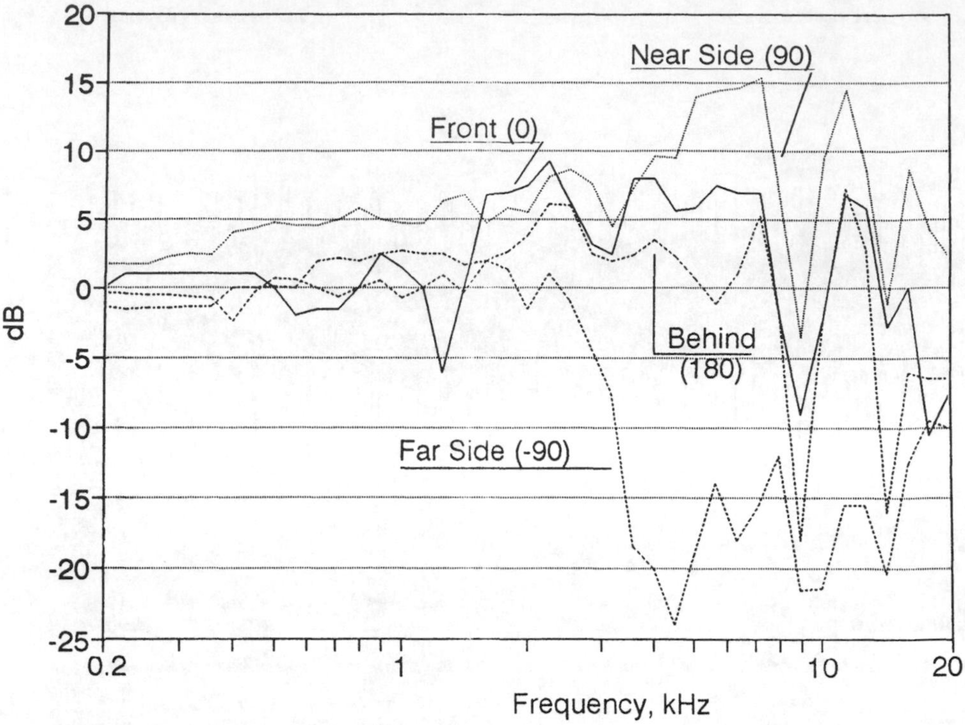

FIG. 2. Sound pressure at a position 4 mm inside the ear canal of a subject for four different source locations in the horizontal plane.

from among a number of competing sounds. In doing so, human hearing suppresses irrelevant noise or sounds and performs evaluation or interpretation of relevant sound. Masking and unmasking of sounds are two of a number of characteristics of hearing that are not recreated with the single microphone measurement technique or in many analyzers. Also note that detection in such a sound situation with two microphones by themselves, without benefit of the filtering of the external ear, head, and torso, provides only a small amount of additional useful auditory information compared to the observation with one microphone.

Judgments of a sound situation or event are accomplished largely as a result of learning to process within the brain the information transduced independently in the cochlea of each ear. To reach the cochlea, the sound stimulus has undergone filtering that is both dependent and independent of the direction of the sound source. Sound pressure at the ear canal entrance deviates from the "free-field" sound levels at the measurement location over a range of –30 to +15 dB depending on the frequency and direction (Fig. 2) (Genuit, 1984; Shaw, 1974). Also, the resolution and dynamic range of human hearing surpass the capabilities of all but the most advanced signal analysis and processing technology available at this time. The communication engineering parameter of bandwidth—the time interval product, $(\Delta f)(\Delta t)$—is less than 0.3 for human hearing compared to 1.0 for most instruments. As frequency resolution increases, time resolution decreases, and *vice versa.* The trade-off rate is slower in human hearing, resulting in better overall discrimination. It should also be noted that the dynamic range from the threshold of hearing to the pain limit of the ear is more than 120 dB. Only the most carefully engineered acoustical measurement equipment can match this range.

II. MODEL FOR BINAURAL MEASUREMENT AND ANALYSIS

A model for binaural hearing, which is the basis for binaural measurement and analysis of sound, is shown in Fig. 3. Typically, there are a number of sources contributing to the sound, which the hearing system processes to make one or more conclusions or decisions. The result is a subjective "hearing event" arising from a subjective impression. Each internal ear mechanism receives the sound filtered by the various external ear features. The inner ear signals enter a binaural processor in the brain where the bits of information are evaluated relative to the known or learned features of sounds. At the present time, our instrumentation and physical models only carry us to the filter system of the inner ear. Each ear signal can be processed independently, for example, for psychoacoustic parameters. To bridge the big gap between what can be done with instrumentation and what is heard, recent binaural measurement systems for critical assessment of sounds combine instrument analysis capability with the still unsurpassed capability of human hearing to detect significant time, spectral, and amplitude variations. It is these measurable details that contribute to a pleasing or annoying sound or noise, but are difficult to identify without actually listening to the sound, as it existed, while it is being analyzed.

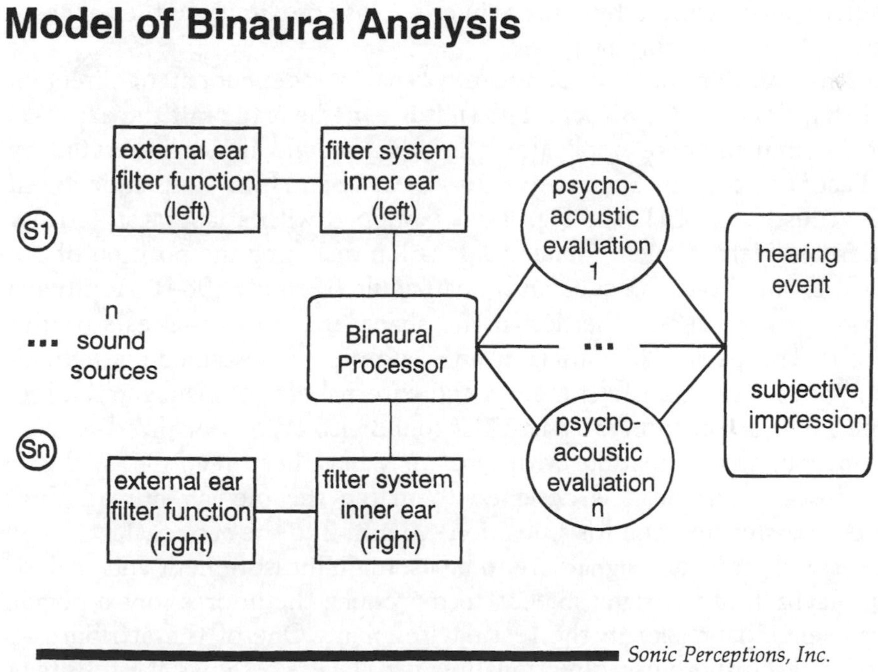

FIG. 3. Model of human hearing and signal processing. Reprinted with permission of Sonic Perceptions, Inc.

Once the transduced information reaches the brain, many judgments about the sound may be made. Signals at the two ears (i.e., two inputs) can be, and usually are, different so as to contribute to directional hearing sensations. This difference also affords selectivity among sources, suppression of noise, and other subjective responses such as estimation of distance, number of sound sources, identification of one source among many, source location, characterization of the environment or space as a small or large room, and so forth.

Such psychoacoustic parameters as loudness, sharpness, roughness, tonality, and fluctuation strength are measurable quantities that have been studied and for which binaural hearing contributes to impressions. These parameters are primarily derived quantities and at this time, unfortunately, are based mostly on correlation of single microphone measurements to subjective responses obtained through binaural listening or earphone listening (Zwicker and Fastl, 1990).

III. RECORDING BINAURALLY

Typically, a sound event is recorded with a binaural head measurement microphone system (HMMS). The dimensions, shape, and external ear acoustical response of an HMMS duplicate a median or typical adult human. An example is the KEMAR manikin (Knowles Electronics Manikin for Acoustic Research) (Burkhard and Sachs, 1975). It provides diffraction, external ear, ear canal, and eardrum simulation for replication of the acoustical response or transfer function of sound from the surroundings to a microphone at the equivalent eardrum location. The ear canal and eardrum simulation are important when the measurements involve sounds created by sources in or in close proximity to the ear (e.g., the insertion gain of a hearing aid).

Because the transfer function of the ear canal is independent of direction (Genuit, 1984; Shaw, 1974; Blauert, 1983), it is expedient to omit the ear canal and eardrum simulation for applications in which sound is not generated by sources adjacent to the ear. For example, each ear of an HMS II, manufactured by HEAD acoustics GmbH (see Fig. 4), is equipped with a laboratory-quality measurement condenser microphone at a location matching the position of the ear entrance on the head of a median human adult (Genuit, 1984). Additional simplification can be seen in the design and shape of the external ears on this artificial head. This particular artificial head is completely described mathematically, including its head transfer function and external ear resonance and directional response. If one convolves a particular sound into a directionalized version, the resulting sound is compatible with what may have been recorded with the HMS II. This artificial head is designed to match the median human adult head-related transfer function for a position 4.0 mm into the ear canal.

If the binaurally recorded signals are to be useful in measurement and analysis processes, playback of the signals needs to reproduce the impressions a person would experience if present in the real environment. One of the attributes is correct sound level; another is directional realism. Figure 5 shows the results of a test (Genuit, Gierlich, and Künzli, 1992) to assess the ability of listeners to

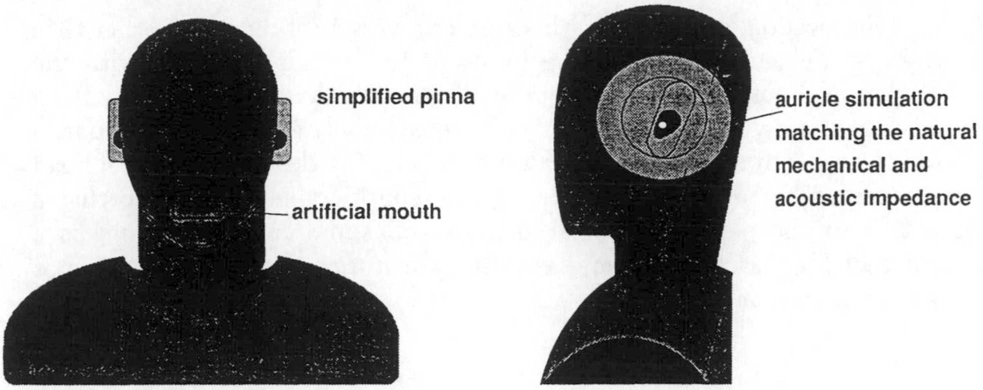

FIG. 4. HMS II artificial head manufactured by HEAD acoustics GmbH.

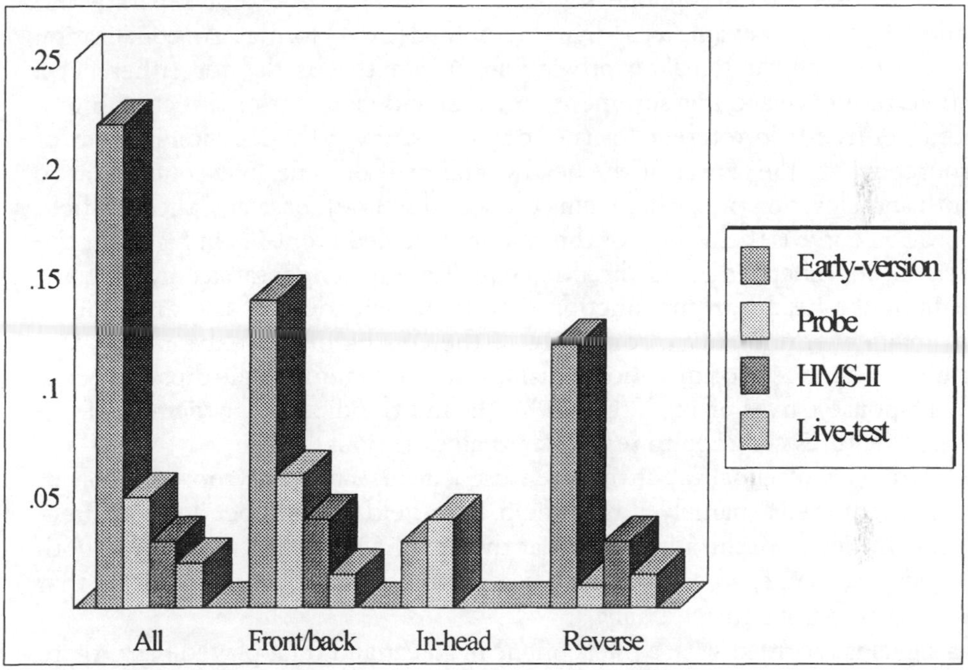

FIG. 5. Fraction of responses in which subjects identify sound source locations incorrectly in the horizontal plane for binaurally recorded sounds reproduced with headphones and for direct listening in a free field. Errors for all responses, front-to-back confusion, in-head localization, and other errors of location are shown for four source materials.

locate sources of sound in the horizontal plane when produced by each of several methods. Sounds played to listeners from recordings made by each of three methods were compared to live listening: (1) an early design of binaural measurement head, (2) probe tube microphones in the ear canals of test subjects, and (3) the HMS II. Twelve loudspeakers placed 30° apart around the listening position produced sound. Observers were asked to identify the source location of each sound as it was presented. The figure gives the fraction of responses incorrect for all test conditions, incorrect because of front-to-back confusion, incorrect because of in-head localization, and incorrect because of reversals of direction other than front-to-back. Subjects identified the locations for sounds recorded with the HMS II system almost as well as when they listened to the sounds directly from the loudspeaker array in the anechoic room. Substantially all of the directionally important features of a sound as recorded by a carefully designed artificial head can be detected by most persons, thus giving considerable confidence that a combination of the electronic signal analysis and simultaneous listening is a powerful tool for searching for and evaluating features of sound that are not otherwise identified and measured.

IV. EQUALIZATION

In use, the two ear microphone signals of an HMS II are kept separate and recorded digitally, for example, in digital audiotape (DAT) format. An equalization is applied to each ear signal to provide an output that is flat for either (1) a free-field reference and measurement, or (2) an independent-of-direction measurement. A free-field reference is the sound pressure at the location in front of the source where the center of the head would be if present. The source is at 0° azimuth and elevation (i.e., head facing the sound source). Basically, the free-field equalization curve is the inverse of the response labeled Front (0) in Fig. 2 for the artificial head. Independent-of-direction equalization compensates only for components of the head transfer function that are independent of the direction of sound incidence, primarily a resonance in the concha of the external ear. For example, independent-of-direction equalization would remove the dips and peaks in the response curves of Fig. 2 above 7 kHz and the dips in the vicinity of 3.5 kHz (i.e., features common to responses in all directions).

A third type of equalization is often used in research and reproduction of entertainment media, namely, diffuse field. Free-field and independent-of-direction equalization have the advantage that they can be described uniquely in both magnitude and phase, whereas diffuse field is a statistically based condition that is characterized in magnitude only.

If a signal is recorded with a microphone in an ear and then played back, there will be two head and ear transfer functions affecting what is heard. In addition, there may be a modification to the sound spectrum by the response of the playback device (e.g., earphone). In a dedicated system that has an HMMS essentially hardwired to a reproduction device, equalization to remove one of the transfer functions and to compensate for the reproduce or playback (earphone) response can be combined into one equalization filter. To be more generally useful, a recorded signal that is compatible with and can be reproduced through a wide variety of playback devices is needed. By dividing equalization into two parts, one associated with the binaural recording and measurement, and one associated with the playback, as shown in Fig. 6, the HMMS signals can be used with a variety of reproduction systems. Equalization in the HMMS ensures that sound level data for the reference condition, that is, facing the source, have a high correlation with data obtained by conventional and standardized single-microphone instrumenta-

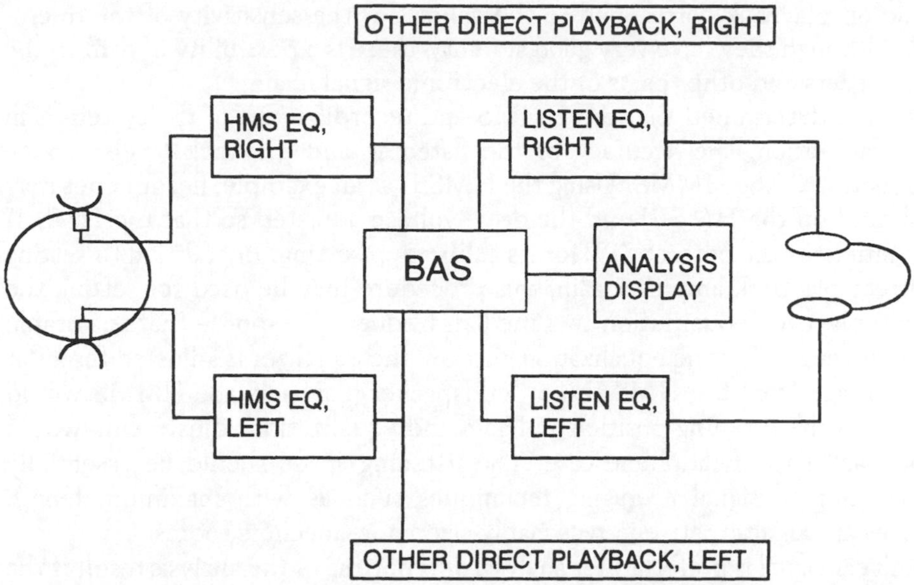

FIG. 6. System of binaural recording and analysis, including reproduction showing the separate equalization for HMS II and for analysis listening, as well as for other applications such as direct listening to a binaurally recorded signal.

tion. Because equalization reduces the range between maximum and minimum microphone output voltage levels that are common to signals from various source directions (i.e., produces a flat output with frequency for the reference condition), the nominal record level can be set closer to the record clip level and further from the record noise floor. This results in an effective increase in the dynamic range of signals that will be presented on playback or will be available for analysis.

V. CALIBRATION

Calibration of an HMMS is essential for at least two reasons. The first is to ensure that the playback levels will be set the same as in the actual situation. If good judgments of the nature of a sound are to be made, the signals must be evaluated at the levels that occurred in the original environment. The second reason for calibration is so that levels obtained binaurally will correlate with those that would have been obtained in standard single-microphone techniques (i.e., so they can be related to existing measurement procedures). The HMS II system, for example, includes precision gain-setting so that the voltage at its output and recorded on a DAT tape is known to represent a specific sound pressure level at the ear entrance. This information becomes part of the recorded record so that compatible analysis and playback equipment will set itself to the correct level automatically.

Means should be available for calibration of the whole system, beginning at the microphone with a piston phone or equivalent standard signal generator. With the standard input, it should be determined that the signal voltages recorded and available on playback correspond to the values for the sensitivity of the microphone. Although they have very good stability, there is a possibility of drift in the DAT recorders and other parts of the electronic signal chain.

After it is determined that the HMMS and recording part of the system is in correct calibration, the accuracy of the listening and playback levels can be determined with the HMMS. Using the HMS II as an example, headphones may be mounted on the HMS II and the drive voltage adjusted so that the HMS II output indicates the correct SPL for its calibration setting. In addition to setting the correct playback amplifier gain, this procedure may be used for setting the earphone playback equalization to a median frequency response that is suitable for most listeners. For the equalization portion, the equalizer is adjusted for a flat output voltage from the HMS II. For loudspeaker playback, the HMMS would be placed in the listening position and gain and equalization adjustments would be made as in the headphone case. The listening space should be essentially anechoic. Digital signal averaging techniques such as with maximum length sequences are an alternative in reasonably sized non-anechoic rooms.

Which ear signal is preferred for analysis or reporting of the analysis result if the level of sound at the two ears is different? This is often the case in actual situations. Although somewhat arbitrary, it is recommended that the ear signal with the higher level should be reported when a single number is desired. Persons tend to respond first to the loudest sounds and then to adjust their attention to the lower level sounds as they become accustomed to the situation and environment.

VI. ANALYZING BINAURALLY

The recorded signals are entered into the memory of a computer (i.e., an analyzer) for analysis and measurement. Analysis provides for the extraction, binaurally, of a number of conventional sound and noise rating parameters: dBA, octave and one-third octave spectra, narrowband spectra, impulse and parameter, as well as a number of psychoacoustic metrics (loudness, sharpness, roughness, and fluctuation strength). Displays available include spectra, spectrograms, filtered signal displays, octave and fractional octave levels, dependence of level on frequency or bark, specific loudness, specific roughness, impulse responses, and time history. Segments of a sound sample can be selected for more detailed analysis. As the sound is being analyzed, the experimenter listens to the sound binaurally in real time while it is being manipulated by filters or other processes. By making the hearing acuity of the person doing the analysis a part of the process, much useful information about the properties of a sound can be uncovered that is completely obscured in single or monaural microphone techniques or is not identifiable *a priori* as being subjectively significant, but that may be very important to human responses (Genuit and Burkhard, 1992).

Listening is typically done with earphones, although many useful results may be obtained with a two-loudspeaker playback system in a treated listening room. The primary difference between these two playback schemes is that loudspeaker playback recreates well only the front hemisphere of sound impressions, whereas high-quality equalized earphone playback recreates, for most listeners, the full 4π steradians of sound impression or image. In either playback method, listening to the sound while it is being analyzed provides a means for correlation of the physical displays and features of a response curve with what is either a unique, an annoying, or a pleasant feature of the sound. It is possible, for example, to move narrowband rejection filters smoothly through a frequency spectrum, listen to the resulting changes, and find that equal level peaks in a response curve have markedly different effects subjectively. Conversely, this also provides the possibility to tailor or synthesize sounds by addition or elimination to accomplish particular goals.

The next three sections discuss applications in which it has been of value to assess sound binaurally and in which there are subjective reactions and impressions that need to be taken into account in a more quantitative way.

VII. RESPONSE TO INDUSTRIAL NOISE

It has been demonstrated that people exposed to sound may exhibit subconscious physiological responses. These responses may appear as changes in blood pressure, galvanic skin resistance, electroencephalogram (EEG), electrocardiogram (EKG), nystagmus, or pulse rate, for example. A recent study conducted for the German government addressed the question of whether these responses were influenced by binaural listening to various factory and industrial noise environments (Genuit and Burkhard, 1993; Bodden, 1993). The sound of industrial machines was recorded independently with a single microphone. Physiological reactions to playback of the machine noise when the machines were placed at different locations around a subject were observed. In the example included here, two sources were colocated for one test and placed on opposite sides of the subject for a second test. For the single-location sound presentation, the two sound signals were placed at 60° azimuth and summed. For the two-location or separated source sound presentation, the sound signal for one machine was on the right, 70° from the front; the sound signal for the other machine was on the left, –40° from the front. The synthetic placement was accomplished by convolution of head transfer impulse responses for the particular directions with the recorded sounds using a HEAD acoustics binaural mixing console (BMC). Figure 7 shows the amplitudes as a function of time for short segments of the sound signals at each ear for the case of colocated source presentation and for the spatially separated source presentation. One-third octave spectra are also shown for the two test conditions. In both tests, the sound was presented at 84 dBA as measured at the listening reference position, namely, the center of the head with the head absent. The sound levels at the two ears are different in both cases, but can be readily distinguished by binaural analysis as well as by the subjects. Although not evident in the black-and-white time display for the separated sources, at times the level at the right ear was higher and at other times the level at the left ear was higher. However, the binaural spectra are very similar for both signal presentations.

Figure 8 shows the effect of a sudden exposure to these test signals on finger blood pressure pulse amplitude. For both stimuli, there was an abrupt decrease in the amplitude, but the pressure drop was about two times as large and the

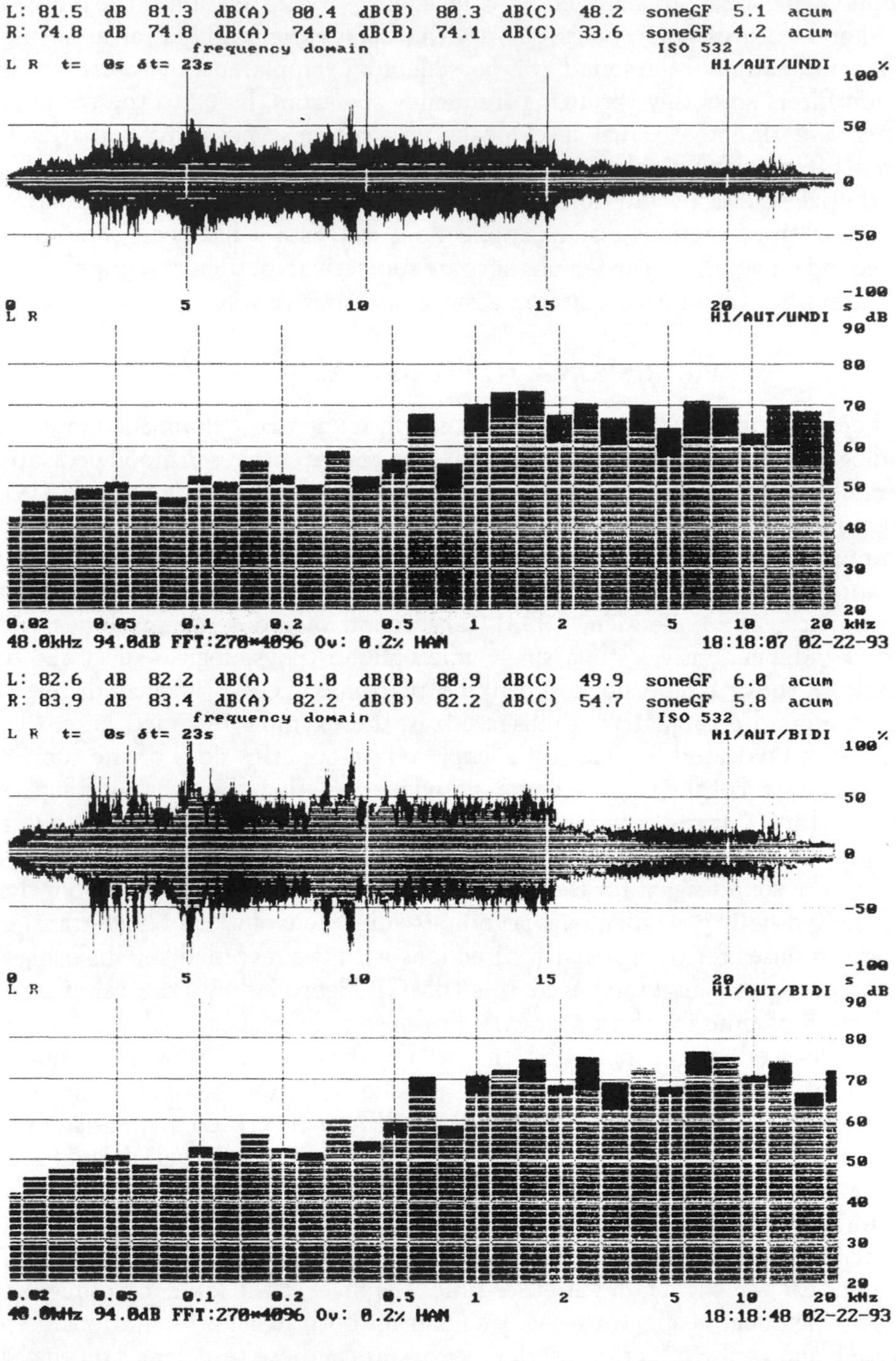

FIG. 7. Binaural time history and one-third octave analysis of sound test signals for two industrial machines when the machines are located at the same position (colocated) 60° to the left (upper set) and when they are separated and on opposite sides of the artificial head. Upper set: the left ear signal is the darker region, the right ear the lighter region. Lower set: either ear may be higher level as would be shown by color.

recovery was much slower for the spatially separated sounds. Other physiological responses were also more pronounced when the sounds were at separated locations. Even though the levels observed with a single microphone are similar, the effect on a person working in the environment may vary widely because of the relative positions of the sound sources. The separation of the sources seems to have significant influence on physiological responses and stress. More study of the effects of noise on workers is needed.

VIII. ORCHESTRA PERFORMANCE

Musicians, conductors, and acoustical consultants are very aware of the contribution of good listening conditions on the stage to the quality of a concert. Musicians depend on the binaural information provided by their ears to adjust tempo, tonal balance, and so forth. Many stages provide a poor environment for performance. Musicians and conductors often complain and may even refuse to perform on them. A hall experiencing this type of complaint was investigated with the aid of binaural artificial head recording and signal analysis (Scarbrough, 1992). The objective of the experiment was to capture the sounds in a manner closely simulating what the musicians heard so that they, as well as the management, could judge the effectiveness of several proposed solutions in simple A/B comparisons, without the intervening time gaps that would be necessary for making physical and temporary structural changes. This approach also provided recorded signals that could be analyzed for particular features that were important to binaural perceptions but were missed or buried in previous monaural or single-microphone measurements taken in the hall.

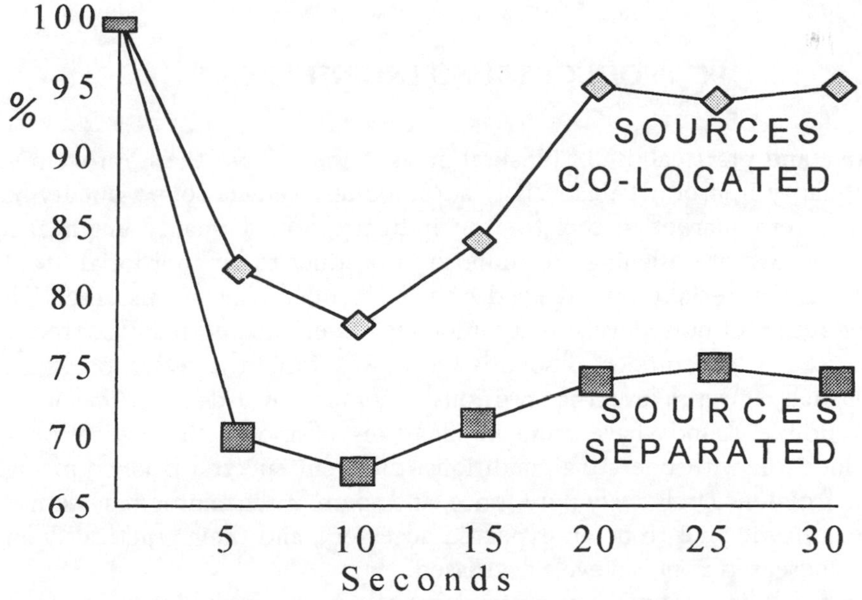

FIG. 8. Finger pulse amplitude change from rest condition as a function of time after abrupt exposure of subjects to the machine sounds shown in Fig. 7.

With the help of the orchestra and hall management, binaural recording and analysis of the conditions were made on the stage and in the audience seating area before and after a temporary proposed acoustic treatment. Artificial heads were located in the orchestra area and in the main seating area so that recordings during rehearsals could be made under various acoustical treatment conditions. Diffuser and reflecting panels were mounted along the side walls and over the musicians for the changes. Stop chords and passages from orchestral works were recorded and analyzed with the different stage and hall acoustical treatments.

An example of the problem for the first violin position was visible in impulse responses recorded binaurally at that location. A sound burst on the stage created a burst 50 ms later at the left ear due to reflection from the rear wall of the stage, then an unexpectedly large burst after approximately 300 ms reflected from the rear wall of the hall at the right ear, and another secondary rear-wall reflection at the left ear after 350 ms. After treatment, these reflections were substantially reduced in amplitude and spread in time so as to mitigate confusion in the timing of musical events in a performance. Smaller difference between the sound levels at the two ears is indicative of a more uniformly distributed sound on the stage, which leads to better musician performance. Spectrograms of various musical passages confirmed that musicians indeed could improve their coordination after the treatments.

Samples of the binaurally recorded material closely replicating the original test conditions and levels were presented to representatives of the orchestra and hall management so they could judge the effectiveness of the proposed alterations. As a result, a much clearer understanding of the deficiencies and potential improvements was achieved, in a way that could be related more objectively and quantitatively to subjective impressions.

IX. PRODUCT SOUND ENGINEERING

An effective and practical use of binaural measurement is for the improvement of sound quality in products, especially automobiles. Vehicle sound quality has become a potent marketing tool for the industry. Sound quality engineering addresses the task of designing the sound of a product to be appropriate to its purpose or use, especially as perceived by the intended user or customer. The general reduction of noise levels in automobiles has eliminated many sources of sound. As a result, a number of sounds are now audible that were previously masked. Usually lower in level than previously measured broad spectrum sounds, the now audible sounds have annoying features of modulation, variation of apparent location with operating conditions, different spectral balance of high versus low frequency, relatively pure tones, and so on. Entertainment systems in automobiles have come to be an expected accessory, and their practicality and popularity increased as noise levels decreased.

Binaural recording and measurement play a role in automobile product development and engineering in a number of ways.

First, sounds of the operating vehicle are recorded binaurally. Experience has shown that binaurally recorded signals when played back provide most of the auditory impression that a person experiences in the actual situation. Thus, one recording can be used to obtain a consensus among listeners as to the nature of the sound rather than having many persons drive the vehicle. Economy is achieved and there are fewer confounding variables with which to contend because all judgments are made for the same operating condition.

As in previous examples, sound is recorded binaurally with one or more artificial heads in a vehicle. The vehicle is operated over standardized road surfaces, in wind tunnels, and in other environments at various speeds. Recordings are then fed into the binaural analysis system where engineers and technicians simultaneously view the physical features of both channels while they listen through earphones. Various resonances in the structure of a vehicle may be excited at different operating conditions in the course of a recording. The result may be varying sound levels, varying standing wave patterns, varying sound radiation sites, and varying frequency composition. The analyzer includes capability to relate these features to each other and to what is heard. Typically, rejection (i.e., band cut) or bandpass filters are applied to various parts of a spectrum while listening binaurally through headphones. Segments of recordings may be extracted to produce test material for comparative evaluation by juries.

Second, noise from undesired sources can be identified through the binaural recorded signals as effectively as in the live situation. The binaural listening acuity of persons enables identification of sound peculiarities and sources that are not audible with single-microphone methods.

Third, because the two ear signals are maintained distinct, the relative importance of sound level at each ear to a noise situation can be identified and possibly compensated in the design of the vehicle. As mentioned earlier, a critical component of sound annoyance is the changing level differences at the two ears.

Fourth, with the combination of analysis equipment incorporating comprehensive signal processing capability and listening to the signal as it is being analyzed and manipulated, design engineers are able to identify and quantify the sounds. From this information, the mechanical or design features contributing to a particular sound can be identified more quickly.

Fifth, the sound of the product can be adapted to customer tastes. An aficionado of high performance sports cars desires a particular sound, while the buyer of an expensive prestige sedan expects quite a different sound. The sound of the automobile needs to be compatible with the market and expectations of the buyer for both quality and performance. Binaural measurement and analysis enable designers and engineers to match the sound to the expectations of their customers in a more direct and efficient way.

SUMMARY

Binaural measurement is a combination of several basic measurement concepts: recording sound with carefully designed and constructed artificial heads, comprehensive signal analysis with a fast Fourier transform (FFT) and discrete Fourier transform (DFT) dual-channel analyzer, signal manipulation in real time, and use of human hearing acuity to identify features of a sound that may be either beneficial or detrimental. Because overall levels of sound emitted by many products have been significantly reduced, new sources of sound need to be investigated, and eliminated or ameliorated. Awareness of customer and user perceptions is increasing. These measurement tools enable engineers and designers to delve more deeply into features and sources of sound that annoy or please. These tools have become increasingly valuable in a variety of investigations and problem solutions requiring much more than the simple observation of noise and sound levels. They play an important role in the field of acoustic measurements because they provide data and results that more closely agree with what a person experiences in the real situation. The techniques have been applied in a variety of situations with both relatively high and very low sound levels. Because of economic and marketing pressures, binaural measurement and analysis have been applied effectively in the automotive industry. Environmental noise in the work place appears to produce physiological effects that depend on binaural hearing and that are not apparent in conventional single-microphone measurement technology.

Other applications, not mentioned previously, include measurement of telecommunication equipment. Hands-free telephones and teleconferencing depend on a person's ability to communicate binaurally. Binaural measurement and analysis provide information that in turn leads to improvements in the quality of communication.

Binaural measurement applications to the entertainment industry have been limited. However, many of the concepts involved in binaural measurement and instrumentation are being applied to the creation or synthesis of spatial acoustic images, which is a very active field and part of "virtual reality." Detailed knowledge of head transfer functions is required for accurate binaural recording and for precise impulse functions used in convolving recorded or artificial sounds. As these technologies mature, the tools of binaural measurement and analysis can be expected to play an important role.

ACKNOWLEDGMENTS

In addition to the specific references throughout this chapter, reports and papers prepared by the staff of HEAD acoustics, Dr. K. Genuit and Dr. H. Gierlich in particular, were the basis for much of the material and discussion herein.

REFERENCES

Blauert, J. (1983). *Spatial Hearing* (MIT Press, Cambridge, MA).

Bodden, M. (1993). "The importance of binaural hearing for noise validation," in *Contributions to Psychological Acoustics, Sixth Oldenburg Symposium on Psychological Acoustics* (Carl von Ossietzky Universität Oldenburg, Oldenburg, Germany), pp. 537–554.

Burkhard, M. D., and Sachs, R. M. (1975). "Anthropometric manikin for acoustic research," J. Acoust. Soc. Am. **58**, 214–222.

Genuit, K. (**1984**). "Ein Modell zur Beschreibung von Aussenohrübertragungseigenschaften," Dissertation, Rheinisch-Westfälischen Technischen Hochschule Aachen, Germany.
Genuit, K., and Burkhard, M. (**1992**). "Artificial head measurement systems for subjective evaluation of sound quality," Sound and Vibration (March), 18–23.
Genuit, K., and Burkhard, M. (**1993**). "The significance of binaural measurement and analysis technique for aurally-adequate sound evaluation," in *Proceedings of Noise-Con 93* (Noise Control Foundation, Poughkeepsie, NY), pp. 497–502.
Genuit, K., Gierlich, H. W., and Künzli, U. (**1992**). "Improved possibilities of binaural recording and playback techniques," Preprint 3332, Audio Engineering Society 92nd Convention, Vienna.
Scarbrough, P. (**1992**). "The use of binaural techniques in the evaluation of concert hall acoustics," *Proceedings of the Institute of Acoustics: Reproduced Sound 8* (Windermere, UK).
Shaw, E. A .G. (**1974**). "Transformation of sound pressure level from the free field to the eardrum in the horizontal plane," J. Acoust. Soc. Am. **56**, 1848–1861.
Zwicker, E., and Fastl, H. (**1990**). *Psychoacoustics Facts and Models* (Springer-Verlag, New York).

Chapter 31

Flight Demonstration of a 3-D Auditory Display

Richard L. McKinley and Mark A. Ericson
Crew Systems Directorate, Armstrong Laboratory, Wright-Patterson Air Force Base, Ohio

(Received November 1994; revised September 1995)

Virtual or three-dimensional (3-D) audio display technology has advanced to a form suitable for flight demonstrations. Three-dimensional audio display systems have the capability of synthesizing signals presented over headphones that give the user the illusion that the sound is emanating from some external location. The development of this technology, its applications, and its performance in both laboratory and flight test situations are presented. Potential fighter aircraft applications include threat location warning, wingman location indication, spatially separated multi-channel communications, and audio target-location indication. The laboratory performance data show an average localization error in azimuth of approximately 5°, a minimum audible angle of approximately 5°, and a speech intelligibility improvement of up to 28%. Flight demonstration results show successful audio-cued target acquisition, a subjective decrease in target acquisition times, a subjective improvement in speech intelligibility, a subjective increase in situational awareness, and a subjective decrease in pilot workload. A summary of both laboratory and flight demonstration results is presented in addition to recommendations for future research.

INTRODUCTION

The auditory system is the only human sensory system that is three-dimensional (3-D) with complete coverage. Auditory perception dimensions include azimuth, elevation, and distance over 4π steradians. The visual system, although including azimuth, elevation, and distance, only covers approximately ±90° in azimuth and +50° and –40° in elevation. However, these two sensory systems are tightly integrated with the motor control system.

The interactions among the visual, auditory, and psychomotor systems are especially active in complex operating environments such as those found in aviation. The visual system is capable of giving a pilot the majority of the information required to fly an aircraft safely in normal environments. However, in many flight environments, particularly those where other aircraft and/or targets are present, the visual system is loaded beyond the limits of human capability.

Some researchers, such as Perrott (1988), have proposed that the integration of the visual and auditory systems is such that the auditory system acts as a spatial controller/locator for the visual system. When an auditory event is outside the visual field of view, the natural reaction is for the human motor system to perform whatever motor actuations are necessary to focus the visual system on the location of interest as quickly as possible. In this function, the auditory system seems to act as a servocontroller for the visual system.

This is a basic and natural use of spatial auditory information. The applications of this type of information extend to almost all aspects of human interaction. One of the most complex tasks accomplished by humans is the piloting of a high-performance modern military fighter aircraft. The task loading in this type of aircraft is very high, and it is easy for a pilot to become overloaded. The visual system is normally the first sensory system to be overloaded. As aircraft operations become increasingly complex, the probability of visual overload significantly increases.

Typically, spatial information is presented (to the pilot of a high-performance aircraft) on a two-dimensional visual screen. This display method, by definition, ignores at least one dimension in spatial information. In addition, some visual vigilance is required to detect and discriminate the relative location of items displayed. The logical alternative is to present information via the auditory system. However, in current aircraft cockpits, spatial auditory information is not available to the pilot. The source location of all audio information presented to the pilot over a headset appears to be somewhere in the center of the head. This lack of spatial auditory information deprives the pilot of the natural cues used to monitor and react to spatial auditory events.

Several visual technologies, such as heads-up-displays (HUDs) and helmet-mounted-displays (HMDs), have attempted to reduce overload of the visual system by displaying symbology that is tailored for the specific applications. Although these systems have proven to be partially effective, they are not a cure-all for providing spatial information to a pilot. When a production cockpit 3-D audio display system is implemented, it will provide spatial auditory cues that allow the visual and auditory systems to function together. This will allow a pilot to take advantage of the natural human ability to monitor the location of targets both inside and outside the field of view. This ability is demonstrated in several team sports such as soccer, basketball, and ice hockey. In these sports and others, team players use a combination of auditory and visual information to maintain awareness of the location of other players on their team and on the opposing team. Removal of this auditory information has significant negative impact on team interaction and individual performance (e.g., try playing basketball with reduced spatial auditory cues as found when wearing earplugs/earmuffs). Providing this spatial audio information to a pilot in the cockpit should increase situational awareness, reduce the time required to find targets, and increase the rate of information transmission, without increasing workload.

A. Background

In the early 1980s, Dr. Thomas Furness, of the Human Engineering (HE) Division of what was then the Air Force Aerospace Medical Research Laboratory (AFAMRL), had a vision of an integrated virtual cockpit system called "Super Cockpit." One basic problem to be solved was cueing a pilot to look outside the current field of view. The Bioacoustics Branch (BBA) of AFAMRL suggested that a 3-D audio system could provide the desired cueing. The 3-D audio system was envisioned to be integrated with a helmet-mounted display to provide the pilot with a natural but "virtual" interface for the visual and auditory sensory systems. The Bioengineering Division (BB) of AFAMRL began in-house work in 1985 to develop laboratory demonstration hardware of a 3-D audio system to provide natural auditory spatial information to a pilot wearing headphones in a cockpit. The goal was to increase the amount of information provided to the pilot (i.e., increase situational awareness) while decreasing workload.

An effective 3-D audio display must generate auditory signals over headphones that can be localized by the user. Prior to the mid 1980s, the perception that could be generated via headphones was lateralization; that is, the sound appears to be radiating from the left ear, the right ear, or somewhere inside the head. Many experts believed that auditory signals presented via headphones could not elicit the perception of localization.

For over 100 years, the scientific community interested in audition has been attempting to converge on a unifying model of human auditory localization. Fechner (1860) was one of the earliest researchers to study the mechanism of human auditory localization. Batteau, Plante, Spencer, and Lyle (1963) reported on a time delay theory of auditory localization. Blauert (1969/1970) found that sounds falling on the pinna, head, and ear canal were modified according to the angle of arrival of the sound to the ear and that these changes were frequency dependent. This resulted in a model of localization based on timbre differences. Shaw (1974a, 1974b) has probably done the most extensive work on understanding the effects of pinna structure on auditory localization. In the duplex theory, it is proposed that the listener uses both interaural time differences and interaural intensity differences to determine the sound source location.

Burkhard and Sachs (1975) designed an acoustic manikin in an attempt to accurately simulate the acoustic diffraction of the head and torso, and the effect of the pinna and eardrum. The Knowles Electronic Manikin for Acoustic Research (KEMAR) has been extensively used by researchers investigating auditory localization. However, listening to binaural auditory signals from an acoustic manikin (i.e., a binaural recording) does not provide dynamic acoustic cues that help the listener to localize the sound source in exocentric space. Lambert (1974) proposed a dynamic theory of auditory localization based on the effects of head movement. Doll, Gerth, Engelman, and Folds (1986) used a KEMAR manikin surrounded by an array of loudspeakers in the horizontal plane. With this apparatus and adjustment of the position of sound relative to the manikin to match the head motions of the listener, Doll was able to demonstrate auditory localization over headphones. Doll reported that, for localization in azimuth, interaural time delays and head motion were the two critical parameters.

McKinley (1988) described a concept for a localization cue synthesizer that included all three parameters: head movement; interaural time delays; and pinna, head, torso, and ear canal transforms (head-related transfer functions, or HRTFs, as described by Blauert, 1983). Work on the system started in 1985, and a laboratory demonstration prototype was completed in February 1987.

About the same time period, Dr. Elizabeth Wenzel of NASA–Ames Research Center began development of a system with many of the same objectives as the Armstrong Laboratory system. This development effort resulted in a system known as the Convolvotron, produced by Scott Foster at Crystal River Engineering. Improvements in performance and applications continue to be pursued for both the NASA–Ames system and the Armstrong Laboratory system.

Much of the recent research has focused on the HRTFs and interaural time delays measured by Wightman and Kistler (1989). These researchers, working at the University of Wisconsin under sponsorship of NASA–Ames and the Armstrong Laboratory (AL), found that the interaural time information is most critical for localization in azimuth, whereas the HRTF information is most critical for elevation. In addition, the HRTF information seems to vary noticeably between subjects, and therefore synthetic generators of 3-D audio displays need to be able to model individual HRTFs to optimize individual performance, as reported by Wenzel, Arruda, Kistler, and Wightman (1993).

The Armstrong Laboratory received funding from the Defense Advanced Research Projects Agency (DARPA) to design and develop an integrated audio demonstration helmet that included 3-D audio displays, active noise reduction, advanced noise-canceling microphones, head-tracking sensors, and physiological monitoring. This integrated helmet was to be used for demonstrations and performance data collection in high-fidelity flight simulators. This DARPA-sponsored effort was very successful. In 1992, DARPA proposed a flight demonstration of this system on a U.S. Marine Corps AV-8B Harrier, a two-place cockpit aircraft that had been previously modified to include a militarized head-tracking system. Through a cooperative effort sponsored by DARPA and executed by USAF Armstrong Laboratory, USN Naval Air Warfare Center, McDonnell Aircraft, and Systems Research Laboratories, the Armstrong Laboratory 3-D audio display system was integrated with the AV-8B for flight demonstrations.

B. Objective/approach

The objective of this chapter is to describe the flight demonstration of the 3-D audio display system and the laboratory developments and performance measures that led to the flight demonstration. The objective of the development of the Armstrong Laboratory's 3-D audio display system is to provide spatial–audio information to a pilot in the cockpit in order to increase situational awareness, to reduce the time required to find targets, and to increase the rate of information transmission, without increasing workload. The approach is to develop 3-D audio display laboratory demonstration and flight-test hardware and to quantify the performance of these systems under a wide range of candidate applications. These performance experiments have been and will continue to be conducted in laboratory, simulator, and flight-test environments. The candidate applications include, but are not limited to, radar-warning receiver cueing of threat location, wingman-location cueing, missile-warning system cueing, target-location cueing, multiple-channel communications spatial separation, collision avoidance cueing, auditory spatial orientation, auditory-navigation aides, and command and control spatial-communications enhancement.

I. METHODS

A. Equipment

The Armstrong Laboratory's Biocommunications Facilities at Wright-Patterson Air Force Base were used to conduct the laboratory studies. The primary facility used was the Auditory Localization Facility (ALF). This facility is housed in a large anechoic chamber of approximately 8000 ft^3 with the six inside walls covered with 1.33-m fiberglass wedges. This chamber has a noise floor 10 dB below the average minimum audible field. A horizontal ring inside the anechoic chamber (4.3 m in diameter with 24 matched 11.4-cm diameter loudspeakers spaced at 15° increments) was used for a series of azimuth studies conducted by Ericson (1989). When the free-field azimuth localization performance studies were complete, the ring was replaced with a geodesic sphere also 4.3 m in diameter. The sphere has 272 matched loudspeakers, one at each of the vertices of the sphere with a maximum spacing of 15° along any one of the sphere struts. A major use of the facility is to measure HRTFs in azimuth and elevation. The measured HRTFs are processed for implementing digital filters generating synthetic-audio localization cues.

The Armstrong Laboratory's auditory localization cue synthesizer (ALCS) was used for the laboratory studies of synthetic localization performance in azimuth. The ALCS utilizes digital signal processing chips implementing finite impulse response (FIR) digital filters that simulate KEMAR HRTFs and delay lines that simulate KEMAR interaural time delays. The filter sampling rate was 40 kHz with a 10-kHz audio bandwidth and 179 tap FIR filters. The ALCS was interfaced to a standard IBM-compatible PC and a Polhemus 3-Space or Iso-Tracker head-position tracker. The circumaural headphones used were Sennheisser HD-230s. These headphones have a usable bandwidth greater than 10 kHz and provide essentially no attenuation of ambient noise.

The Armstrong Laboratory's 3-D audio display system was used for the in-flight localization tests, and was based on digital signal processing chips implementing FIR digital filters simulating KEMAR and individual HRTFs, and delay lines simulating KEMAR and individual interaural time delays. The sampling rate was 42.6 kHz with a 10-kHz audio bandwidth, and 139 tap FIR filters for target indications and 61 tap FIR filters for communication separation. The target indication mode and spatial communication mode on this system were switch selectable via a 3-D audio control panel in the aft cockpit of the AV-8B.

Armstrong Laboratory's Voice Communication Research and Evaluation System (VOCRES) described by McKinley (1986) was used to conduct the voice communication performance studies. This system is housed in a 233-m^3 reverberation chamber driven by a 10,000-W sound system to duplicate the noise environments found in such operational locations as fighter aircraft cockpits. Inside the chamber are 10 human-subject stations with 4-lines-by-32-character alphanumeric plasma displays and response buttons. This system is used for the automatic collection of speech intelligibility data.

The flight demonstrations were a joint effort involving both Air Force and Navy organizations. Flight tests were conducted at the Naval Air Warfare Center (NAWC), Weapons Directorate at China Lake, CA. The T-1 AV-8B Harrier vertical take-off and landing attack aircraft was provided and modified to incorporate the 3-D audio system by NAWC Strike Directorate at Patuxent River Naval Air Station, MD. The Armstrong Laboratory's flight-worthy 3-D audio system was integrated by McDonnell Aircraft, St. Louis, MO, with the AV-8B's mission computer via a digital bus. The 3-D audio system used a Navy Standard Polhemus head-tracking system for head-orientation information. The head-tracking system had been installed in the AV-8B as part of a previous project. The 3-D audio information was presented over a binaural Bose PRU-57 military active noise reduction (ANR) headset integrated with the head-position sensor inside a modified Gentex HGU-53/P flight helmet. This ANR headset has a minimum 10-kHz audio bandwidth and approximately 15 dB of active attenuation of ambient noise.

B. Subjects

Laboratory test subjects were paid volunteers and all had normal hearing thresholds (less than or equal to 15-dB hearing threshold level) at each of the standard audiometric test frequencies of 500 Hz to 8 kHz. They were paid minimum wage plus a bonus for completing the study. In all experiments, the number of male and female subjects was equal. The test subjects used in these studies had significant experience in psychoacoustic experiments, participating as subjects in these types of experiments approximately four test sessions per day of 45 min each with a 15-min rest period, 5 days per week.

Four Navy and Marine test pilots were selected as test subjects for the flight demonstrations. Additional flight demonstrations were conducted using volunteer Navy and Marine test pilots. During the flight demonstrations, all pilots were rated in one or more of the following aircraft: AV-8B, F-18, and A-6. Most test pilots used in this study were stationed at NAWC, Weapons Directorate, China Lake, CA, except for two AV-8B test pilots who were stationed at NAWC, Strike Directorate, Patuxent River Naval Air Station, MD.

C. Procedures

1. Laboratory localization studies

Synthetic 3-D audio cues were generated using the Armstrong Laboratory ALCS. Three separate procedures were used by the subjects to quantify the accuracy and resolution of the synthetic 3-D audio cues in the horizontal plane (azimuth). The procedures were head pointing, head pointing in noise, and minimum audible angle.

The stimuli for the head-pointing experiments were broadband pink noise from 100 Hz to 10 kHz; octave-band pink noise centered at 125, 250, 500, 1k, 2k, 4k, and 8k Hz; male speech with 3.5 kHz bandwidth; and female speech with 6 kHz bandwidth. Three blocks of 24 pseudo-randomized stimuli were presented at a 2-Hz rate with a 50% duty cycle. Each stimulus was presented for a total of 72 trials for each of the 10 subjects. Subjects responded by pointing their heads to the apparent direction of the sound source and pushing a response button.

Using the same head-pointing technique, localization performance was measured in high levels of ambient acoustic noise in the VOCRES facility. Ambient acoustic noise levels up to 115 dB of pink noise were generated, replicating the acoustic levels found in high-performance aircraft cockpits. The target stimuli were gated pink noise at a 2-Hz rate and 50% duty cycle, which was spectrally similar to the continuous ambient pink noise. The target stimuli were presented over Bose PRU-57 ANR headsets.

Minimum audible angles (MAAs) were measured using a modification of a procedure described by Hartmann and Rakerd (1989). A 500-Hz pure tone was presented at a randomly selected angle of 0°, 30°, 60°, or 90°. Immediately following the primary signal, a second signal was presented offset from the primary signal by 0° to ±15°. The subject was asked to indicate whether the apparent change in location of the sound source was to the left or to the right. The MAA was selected as the angle at which the subjects achieved 75% correct response criterion.

2. In-flight localization tests

Synthetic 3-D audio cues for the flight demonstrations were generated using the Armstrong Laboratory flight-worthy 3-D audio display system. The 3-D audio display system was used to generate target location cues relative to the earth. The aircraft inertial navigation system was used to correct for the attitude and location of the aircraft relative to the earth, and the head-tracker was used to correct for the attitude and location of the pilot's head in the cockpit.

The combined azimuth and elevation performance of the flight-worthy 3-D audio display system was measured under four conditions: straight and level flight/target identification, straight and level flight/target discrimination, 4-G maneuvering flight/target identification, and 4-G maneuvering flight/target discrimination. Prior to the test flights, the exact latitude and longitude of test targets were measured using a ground-based global positioning system (GPS) receiver giving an approximate average error of less than 30 m. In some cases, multiple targets in the same area were surveyed for use in the target discrimination portion of the tests. An example is three targets: a tower, a bull's-eye, and an F-4 bunker. Two separate decision points were also geographically located using the GPS surveying method. These decision points corresponded to angular separations of the targets of 12° and 20°.

Typically the aircraft approached the target area at altitudes from 200 to 1000 ft above ground level and airspeeds from 360 to 450 knots (415–520 mph). Upon selection of the next navigation way-point or target, the 3-D audio system produced a 3-D audio beacon for 5 s. The test pilot in the aft cockpit could also receive an additional cue for as long as desired by selecting the "track" position on the 3-D audio panel. At each of the decision points, the test pilot in the aft cockpit verbally identified the target indicated by the 3-D audio system. The flight control and verbal responses of the test pilots in the aft cockpit were recorded by HUD video tapes and cockpit audio tapes. The tapes were analyzed postflight by the experimenters at China Lake, NAWC.

3. Laboratory communication studies

Virtual audio locations at several spatial separations were generated using the Armstrong Laboratory's ALCS. The intelligibility as quantified by the coordinate response measure (CRM) was used in the competing messages experiments as the performance metric. The CRM test involves the transmission of a call sign (Ringo or Baron), a color (red, white, blue, or gray), and a number (1 to 8). CRM performance was measured using stimuli generated by a single talker, two talkers, and four talkers in a quiet environment. Listeners were in high levels of ambient pink noise (up to 115 dB) and responded to the stimulus by pressing the appropriate color and number response button if the stimulus included their call sign. VOCRES was used to automatically score all subject responses and did not include correction for guessing.

4. In-flight communication tests

Virtual audio locations at ±45° in azimuth relative to the aircraft centerline were generated using the flight-worthy 3-D audio display system. Ground controllers simultaneously read two different types of voice communications, a close air support (CAS) simulation and an emergency procedures checklist, over two different radio channels. The test pilot in the aft seat attempted to copy both sets of spatially separated instructions. The in-flight voice communication effectiveness was measured using subjective ratings by the test pilots.

II. RESULTS

A. Laboratory data

All three laboratory measures of localization error and resolution should be considered in describing the performance of a 3-D audio system. Laboratory head-pointing error in azimuth collapsed over the 10 subjects for each of the stimuli types is shown in Fig. 1. The subject responses for octave-band noise stimuli centered from 125 Hz to 8 kHz vary in mean magnitude error from 4.4° to 5.9°, with the subject responses for the 4-kHz octave band having the highest average error of 5.9°. Without the 4-kHz octave band, the highest subject response mean magnitude error is 5.3°.

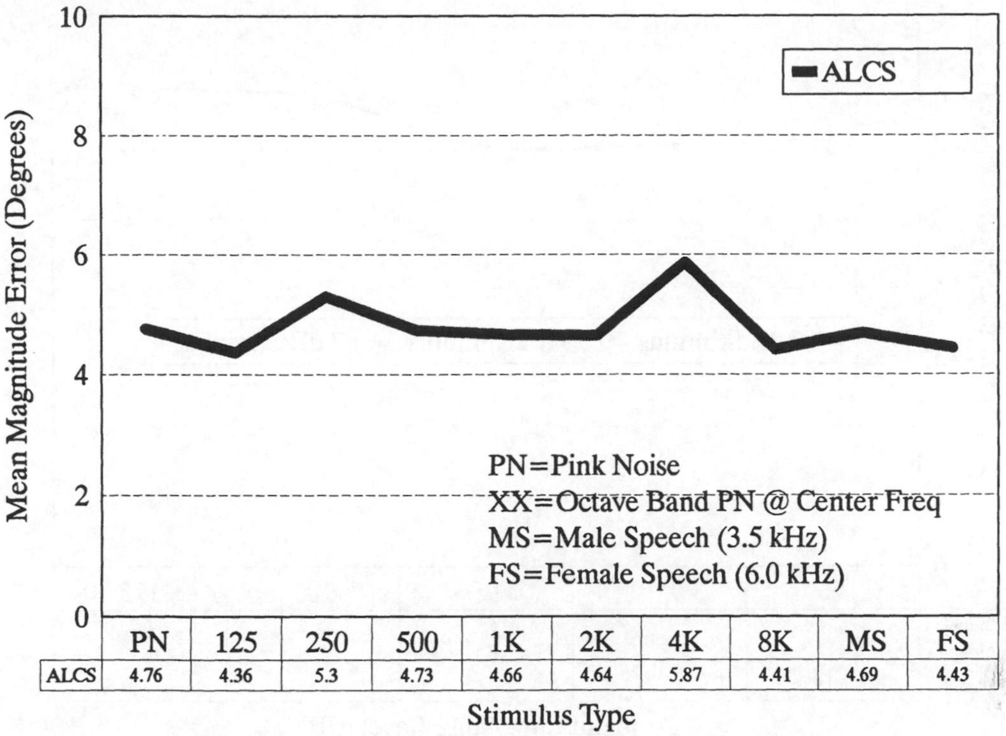

FIG. 1. Human auditory localization performance in mean magnitude error by stimulus type for 10 subjects in quiet.

Head-pointing error for pink noise in noise environments from 95 to 115 dB is shown in Fig. 2. The mean magnitude head-pointing error in azimuth is approximately 6° to 7° with little subject response variation due to the presentation level of the stimuli.

The minimum audible angles data are for 500-Hz pure tone stimuli. MAA data in the horizontal plane are shown in Figs. 3 through 6. The MAAs were calculated for a 75% correct decision threshold. The lowest MAA in the horizontal plane using the synthetic 3-D audio cue is 4° to 5° for the 0° target location as shown in Fig. 3. The mean MAA in the horizontal plane for the 30° target location is shown in Fig. 4. Figure 5 shows the mean MAA for the 60° target location. Mean MAA data are presented for the 90° target location in Fig. 6; however, as can be seen, the response measure used became very confusing at this location. The subjects no longer had a left–right decision as the target moved behind them; that is, what was moving "right" seemed to move left when behind the subject. Figure 7 summarizes the mean MAA data for each presentation location.

Speech intelligibility data described in detail by Ericson and McKinley (Chapter 32, this volume) are shown in Fig. 8. Three pairs of talkers are presented: a female–female pair, a female–male pair, and a male–male pair. In a high ambient noise environment of 115 dB the female–female pair shows the largest effect of the spatial presentation of the simultaneous speech. Significant benefits are seen

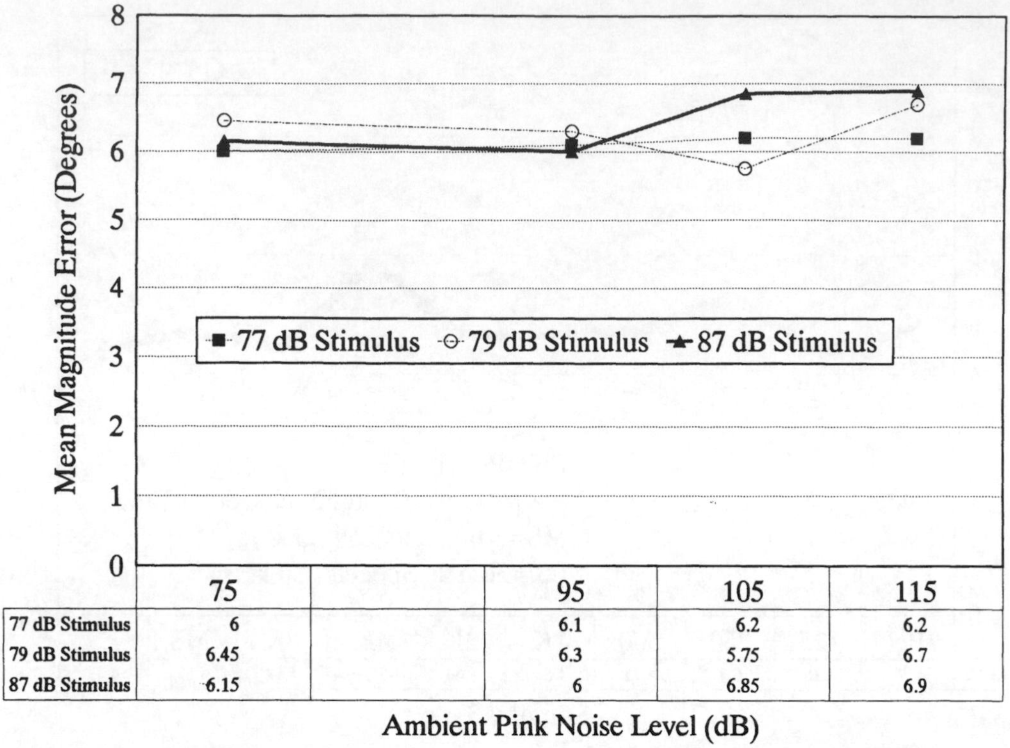

	75		95	105	115
77 dB Stimulus	6		6.1	6.2	6.2
79 dB Stimulus	6.45		6.3	5.75	6.7
87 dB Stimulus	6.15		6	6.85	6.9

FIG. 2. Human auditory localization performance in mean magnitude error with pulsed pink-noise signal for 10 subjects in high-level ambient pink noise.

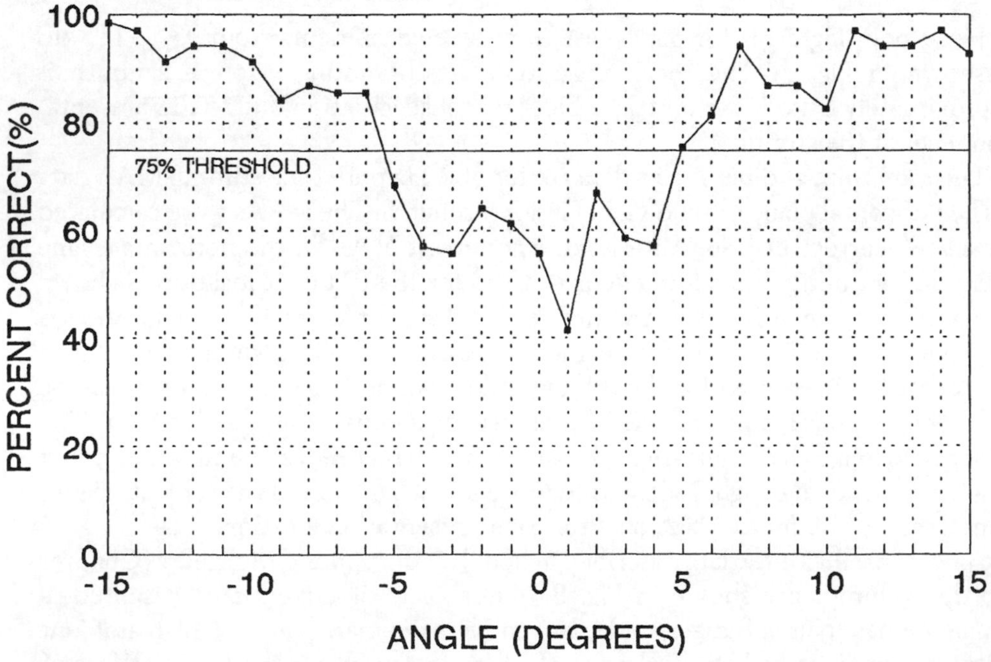

FIG. 3. Minimum audible angle for target at 0° azimuth for 7 subjects, 10 blocks of data per subject, 500-Hz pure-tone stimuli.

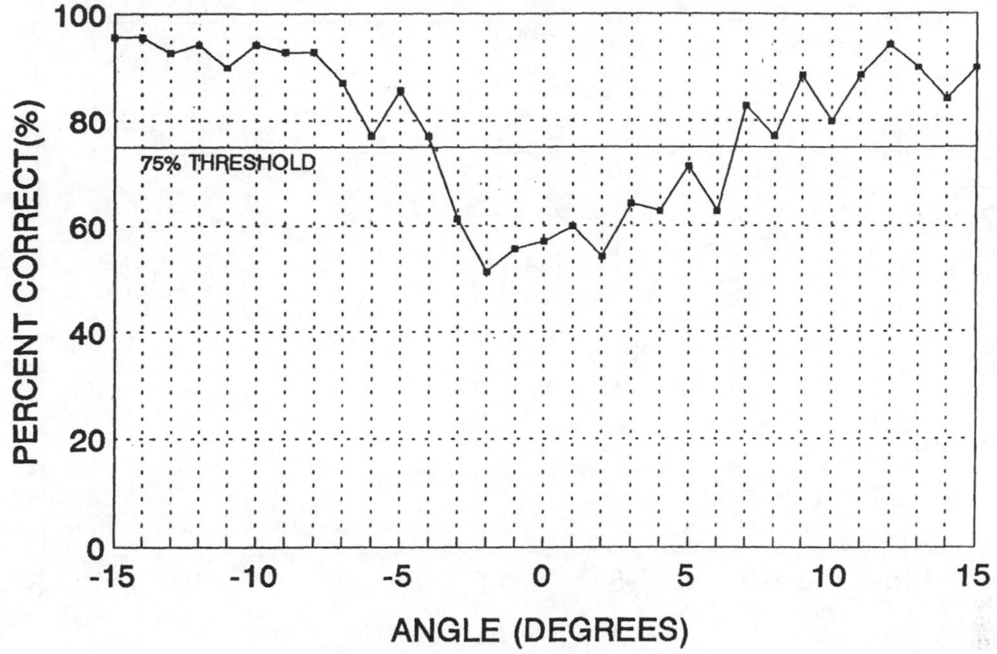

FIG. 4. Minimum audible angle for target at 30° azimuth for 7 subjects, 10 blocks of data per subject, 500-Hz pure-tone stimuli.

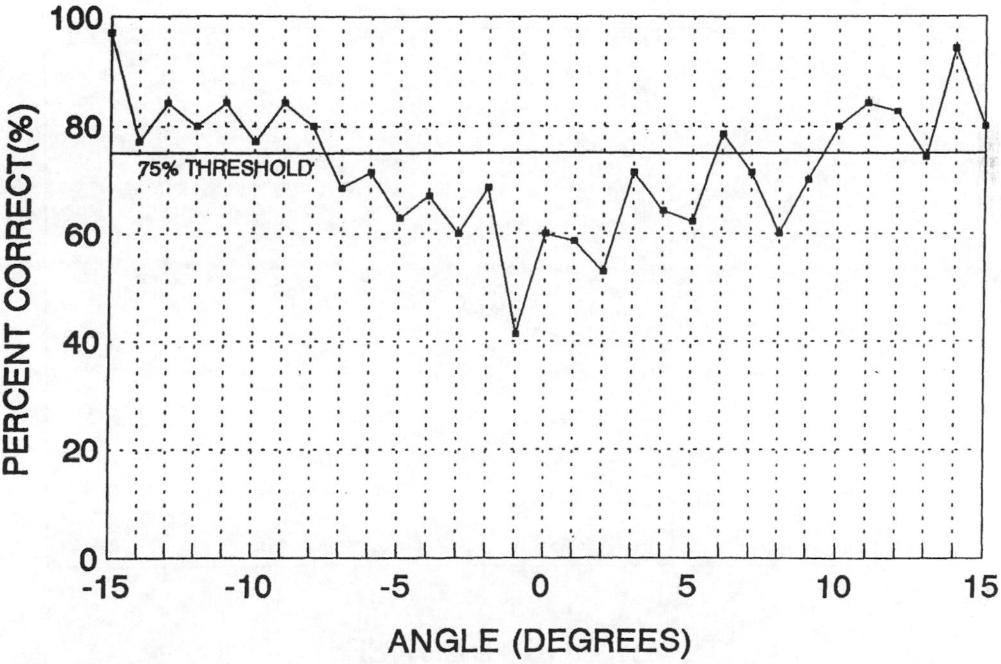

FIG. 5. Minimum audible angle for target at 60° azimuth for 7 subjects, 10 blocks of data per subject, 500-Hz pure-tone stimuli.

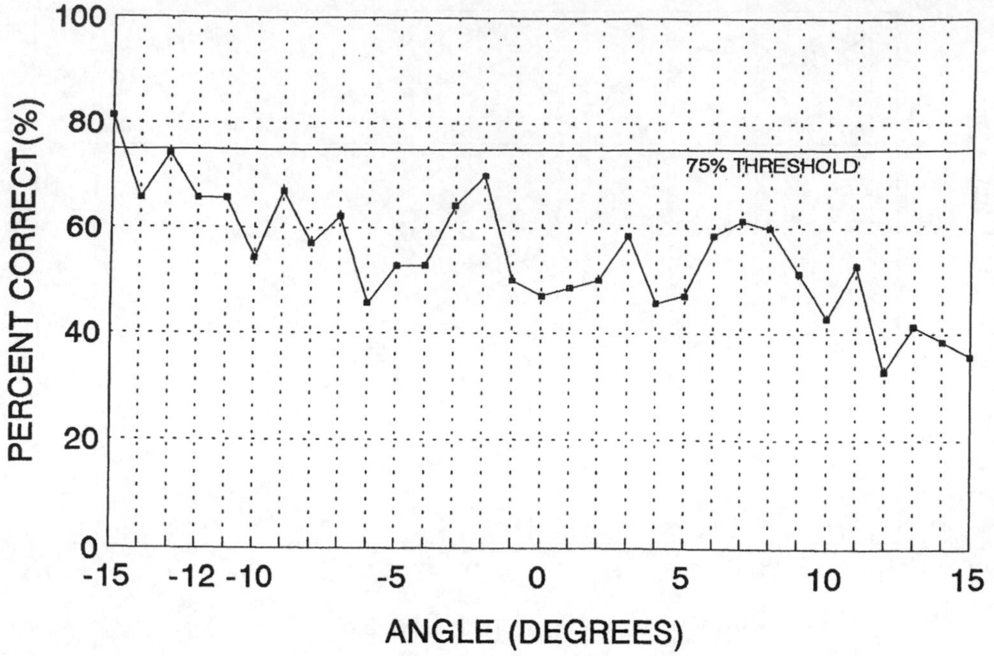

FIG. 6. Minimum audible angle for target at 90° azimuth for 7 subjects, 10 blocks of data per subject, 500-Hz pure-tone stimuli.

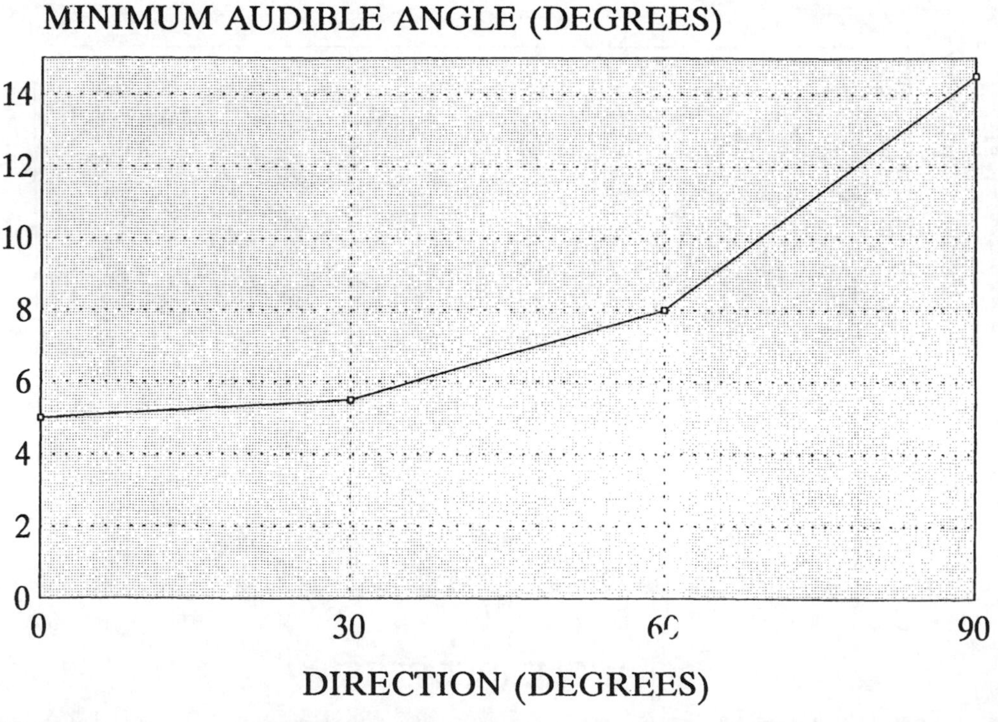

FIG. 7. Mean minimum audible angle in azimuth for multiple target locations of 0°, 30°, 60°, and 90° for 7 subjects, 10 blocks of data per subject, 500-Hz pure-tone stimuli.

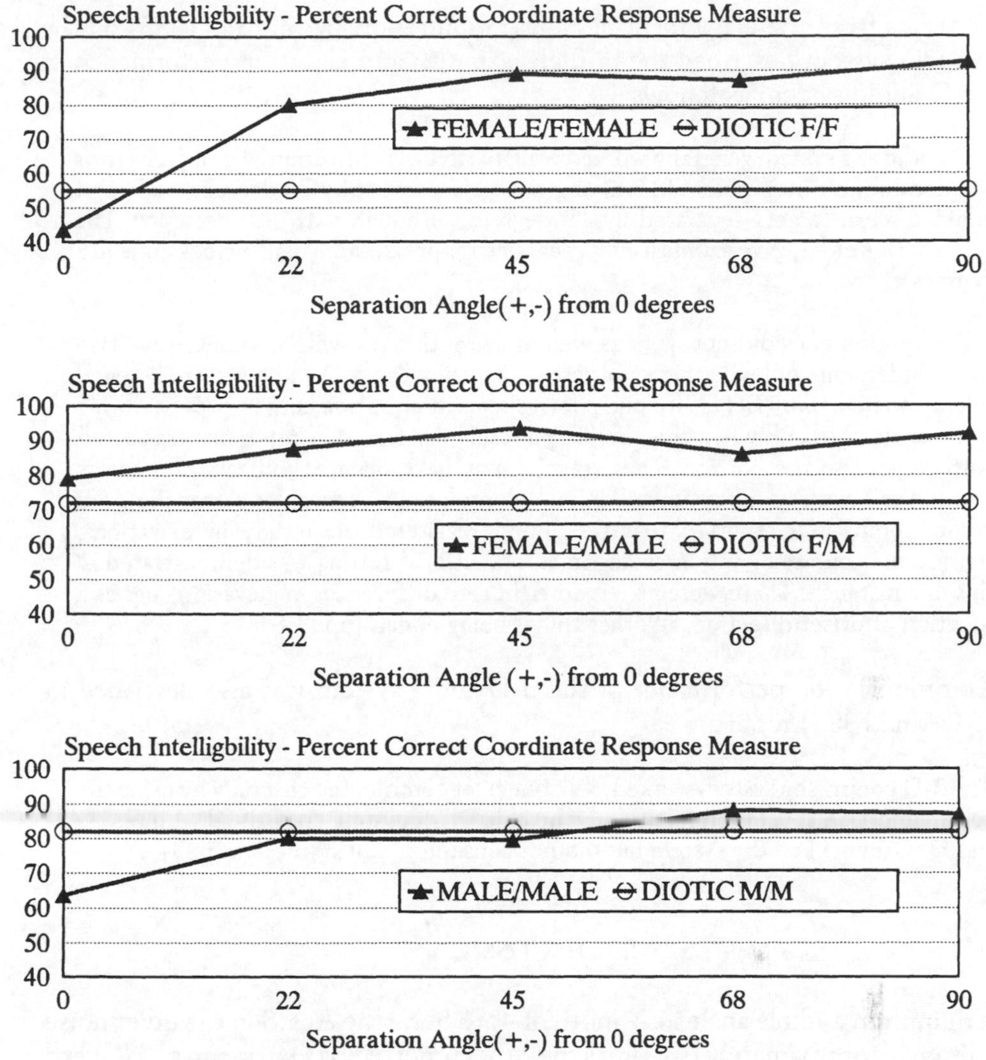

FIG. 8. Average (3 pairs of 2 talkers × 4 listeners) coordinate response measure intelligibility for two competing messages in 115-dB ambient SPL pink noise for directional (spatially separated) with head motion versus diotic speech presentation at multiple angles of separation in azimuth.

in the female–male pairing, whereas only marginal benefits are seen in the male–male pairing. Performance using spatially separated sources averaged approximately 25–28% better than diotic presentation for two talkers as shown in Fig. 8.

B. Flight test data

The flight demonstration data collected were only qualitative data due to funding constraints. The objective of the flight-demonstration project was to demonstrate the operation of the 3-D audio system in a flight environment. Future efforts will focus on collection of quantitative in-flight performance data.

Excerpts from the Navy flight demonstration report by Martin (1993) on the 3-D audio system described the in-flight azimuth and elevation performance of the 3-D audio system as follows:

> 3-D audio as a system generally worked well, particularly in azimuth cueing. Aviators seemed to have no problem identifying targets separated by 20 degrees; and most could discern targets separated by 12 degrees, although with less accuracy. The system, therefore, gave azimuth cues reliably to approximately half a clock code (15 degrees).
>
> 3-D elevation cues did not work as well as azimuth cues, with certainty gave two rough judgments of low or high. All test pilots using the 3-D audio system listened to only one custom HRTF's for one pilot. Apparent elevation cues improved during steep angles of bank when the aircraft/pilot angular frame of reference translated with respect to the horizon. These results may have been an indication of errors within the headtracking system. One pilot completed a vertical loop over the cued ground point and reported that the sound registered accurately in elevations; therefore, accurate elevation cueing in an operational setting was demonstrated in this one instance. There were no left-to-right side differences in elevation cues as a function of offset direction, all other things being equal. (pp. 8–9)

Communication performance of the 3-D audio system was also described in the Martin (1993) report:

> The 3-D comm-sep system worked well; one pilot commented that only by using the communication separation feature was he able to accurately copy the dual message traffic. Others liked the system but did not consider it a high priority. (p. 9)

III. DISCUSSION

The minimum audible angle in azimuth of 4° to 5° by the ALCS in the quiet noise condition is approximately two times the MAA reported by Hartmann and Rakerd (1989), using a similar but simpler paradigm in a free field. This average 4° to 5° error also is shown in the head-pointing data. These average errors are a combination of localization error, response error, 3-D audio synthesis error, and head-tracker error. This average error is consistent across both the MAA paradigm and the head-pointing paradigm. The addition of high levels of ambient (noncorrelated) noise, such as found in high-performance military aircraft, increased the mean magnitude error to 6° to 7°. The flight test aircraft cockpit noise levels have been measured up to 130 dB. No calibrated noise levels were available from this specially modified aircraft, although the levels were estimated to be at least 120 dB. The test flight data were reported in a different format: "Most subjects could discern targets separated by 12 degrees." This gradual degradation in performance, from laboratory in quiet to laboratory in noise to aircraft in higher level noise, demonstrates the effects of increasing environmental factors on 3-D audio applications. This environmental degradation is less than was expected, but still leaves room for performance improvement. It is expected that future systems could reduce the average error by a factor of two, but current performance is satisfactory for aircraft applications.

The MAA in elevation using KEMAR HRTFs and interaural time delays is approximately 30° to 35° as reported by McKinley, Ericson, and D'Angelo (1994). This corresponds well with the flight test pilot reports of being able to reliably discern high and low. One point of note is that the pilots reported better elevation perception when banking the plane than when moving their heads. This points out a potential problem in some applications. The head-tracker installation in the AV-8B required an unavailable collimated-light source to bore-sight the head-tracker. The alternate bore-sight procedure used in the flight test resulted in significant head elevation and roll errors from the head-tracking system due to the bore-sighting procedure. Additionally, the azimuth and elevation performance were measured independently in the laboratory environment but simultaneously in the flight environment.

The spatial-communication feature, which demonstrated up to 37% improvement (female-female at 90°) in intelligibility in the laboratory, was corroborated by the pilot reports of ability to copy the two simultaneous messages. An additional factor was noted on the individual pilot responses but not listed in the final report. The pilots reported that the apparent location of the indicated targets, even when the targets could not be seen, was significantly external to the aircraft at the approximate location of the target, whereas the apparent location of the spatially separated voice communications appeared to be just inside or outside the aircraft canopy. One possible explanation is that, just as the human system interprets sounds that move in coordination with head movement as being on the head, the pilots interpreted the communications that were relative to the aircraft centerline as being on the aircraft, whereas the target cues that were relative to the ground were interpreted as being external to the aircraft.

Several pilots also informally indicated that the targets were acquired more rapidly with the 3-D audio system than with the HUD and that, even though they were getting additional information, their workload actually decreased. This is conjectured to be due to the nature of the human response to 3-D audio cues and the corresponding reaction of the visual system. The pilots viewed 3-D audio displays as offering an increase in situational awareness without an increase in workload.

IV. SUMMARY

The flight demonstration performance of a 3-D audio display system has been presented. In addition, laboratory performance of 4° to 5° in azimuth in quiet and 6° to 7° in azimuth in noise demonstrated that the concept was viable for flight demonstration. The in-flight data demonstrated 12° performance under the most demanding conditions of low-level high-speed flight and clearly show that the technique is viable for the applications tested. Additional applications described by Ericson and D'Angelo (1993) that are being investigated include an auditory display for threat warning location, wingman location, collision avoidance, spatial communications separation, air and ground target location, and navigation aids. The flight test pilots reported decreased target acquisition times, increased communication capability, increased situational awareness, and decreased workload.

V. FUTURE DIRECTIONS

Future efforts within the Armstrong Laboratory will focus on collecting additional quantitative performance data in the laboratory, in high-performance simulators, and in flight-test aircraft. Laboratory studies will concentrate on elevation performance with a number of individual HRTFs, the optimization of distance cueing algorithms, and auditory/visual interaction. High-performance flight-simulator studies, conducted cooperatively with other Department of Defense laboratories and major aircraft manufacturers, will focus on quantitative performance measures of 3-D audio technology in a number of simulated applications. The flightworthy 3-D audio system was installed in a NASA OV-10 flight test aircraft in late 1993 for collection of in-flight quantitative-flight performance data in a number of applications. These applications include multichannel communications intelligibility (up to four channels), threat-avoidance performance, wingman-location performance, collision avoidance at a variety of approach angles, and auditory-navigation aids. Flight test data collection on the OV-10 is expected to be completed in late 1995. The objectives of these laboratory, simulator, and flight-test studies are to establish the performance basis for the application of 3-D audio technology in both military and civilian environments, to improve user performance, and to increase safety by use of this unique technology to improve the human/machine interface.

ACKNOWLEDGMENTS

The authors would like to acknowledge the very significant contributions to the 3-D audio system development, fabrication, and integration by David Ovenshire, hardware; Ronald Dallman, software; and Douglas Brungart, software; all with Systems Research Laboratories. Also acknowledged are the contributions of John Martin, US Navy; Robert Tock, McDonnell Aircraft; and William McGarity, DCS Corp., to the accomplishment of the 3-D audio flight demonstrations. Finally, the authors would like to thank Drs. Charles W. Nixon, Thomas J. Moore, and Henning E. von Gierke for their support, guidance, and mentoring.

REFERENCES

Batteau, D. W., Plante, R. L., Spencer, R. H., and Lyle, W. E (**1963**). *Localization of Sound: Part 3. A New Theory of Human Audition*, Report No. TP3109, Part 3 (U.S. Naval Ordnance Test Station, China Lake, CA).

Blauert, J. (**1969/1970**). "Sound localization in the median plane,"Acustica **22**, 205–213.

Blauert, J. (**1983**). *Spatial Hearing* (MIT Press, Cambridge, MA).

Burkhard, M. D., and Sachs, R. M. (**1975**). "Anthropometric manikin for acoustic research," J. Acoust. Soc. Am. **58**, 214–222.

Doll, T. J., Gerth, J. M., Engelman, W. R., and Folds, D. J. (**1975**). *Development of Simulated Directional Audio for Cockpit Applications*, AAMRL-TR-86-014 (Armstrong Aeromedical Research Laboratory, USAF, Wright-Patterson AFB, OH).

Ericson, M. A. (**1989**). "Auditory localization and cue synthesis and human performance," NAECON, Dayton, OH, pp. 718–725.
Ericson, M. A., and D'Angelo, W. R. (**1993**). "Applications of virtual audio," NAECON, Dayton, OH, pp. 604–611.
Fechner, G. T. (**1860**). *Elemente der Psychophysics [Elements of Psychophysics]* (Breitkopk und Hartel, Leipzig).
Hartmann, W. M, and Rakerd, B. (**1989**). "On the minimum audible angle—A decision theory approach," J. Acoust. Soc. Am. **85**, 2031–2041.
Lambert, R. M. (**1974**). "Dynamics theory of sound-source localization," J. Acoust. Soc. Am. **56**, 165–171.
Martin, J. J. (**1993**). *Airborne Demonstration of a 3-D Audio Display*, NAWCWPNS TP 8138 (Naval Air Warfare Center Weapons Division, China Lake, CA).
McKinley, R. L. (**1986**). *Voice Communications Research and Evaluation System*, AFAMRL-TR-012-86 (Armstrong Aeromedical Research Laboratory, USAF, Wright-Patterson AFB, OH).
McKinley, R. L. (**1988**). Concept and Design of an Auditory Localization Cue Synthesizer, master's thesis, AFIT/GE/ENG/88D-29, Air Force Institute of Technology, Wright-Patterson AFB, OH.
McKinley, R. L., Ericson, M. A., and D'Angelo, W. R. (**1994**). "3-Dimensional auditory displays: Development, applications, and performance," J. Aviation Space Environ. Med. **65**(5, suppl.), A31–A38.
Perrott, D. R. (**1988**). "Auditory psychomotor coordination: Auditory spatial information can facilitate the localization of visual targets," presented at the Sound Localization by Human Observers Symposium, Washington, DC, October.
Shaw, E. A. G. (**1974a**). "The external ear," in *Handbook of Sensory Psychology, Vol. 5*, edited by W. D. Keidel and W. D. Neff (Springer-Verlag, New York), pp. 455–490.
Shaw, E. A. G. (**1974b**). "Transformation of sound pressure level from the far field to the eardrum in the horizontal plane," J. Acoust. Soc. Am. **56**, 1848–1861.
Wenzel, E. M., Arruda, M., Kistler, D. J., and Wightman, F. L (**1993**). "Localization using nonindividualized head-related transfer functions," J. Acoust. Soc. Am. **94**, 111–123.
Wightman, F. L., and Kistler, D. J. (**1989**). "Headphone simulation of free-field listening. II: Psychophysical validation," J. Acoust. Soc. Am. **85**, 868–878.

Chapter 32

The Intelligibility of Multiple Talkers Separated Spatially in Noise

Mark A. Ericson and Richard L. McKinley
Crew Systems Directorate, Armstrong Laboratory,
Wright-Patterson Air Force Base, Ohio

(Received December 1994; revised August 1995)

Speech communications are seldom isolated auditory events in quiet environments. Frequently, the desired speech signal is confounded with other speech signals and noises. Real-world environments often degrade the intelligibility of the desired speech signal. In this chapter, the literature on the speech intelligibility of competing messages and the masking of speech is reviewed. The literature on the detection of speech is included to describe factors that can affect speech intelligibility. Following the review, several experiments are presented in which the effects of various conflicting signals on speech communications are measured. Virtual audio over headphones is used to investigate the effects of directional separation of talkers, the quantity and gender of talkers, the degree of masker interaural correlation, masking level, and selective attention. The results are discussed and compared with the previous literature.

INTRODUCTION

Many real-life listening environments have a myriad of simultaneous competing auditory signals, much like in a cocktail party. One situation in which voice communication in poor listening environments is critical is in aircraft cockpits. In this situation, voice communication is sometimes difficult due to competing voice messages over the radio and/or intercom, low-fidelity speech signals, and high ambient noise levels. Many pilots monitor several radio channels simultaneously to navigate, to receive commands and clearances, and to maintain awareness of other nearby aircraft. Aircraft radios typically have limited bandwidth (approximately 3.5 kHz) and marginal speech-to-noise ratios (0 to 10 dB). Civilian commercial aircraft cockpit noise levels range from 85 to 100 dB SPL for most aircraft types, with some approaching the military aircraft noise levels of 95 to 115 dB SPL under normal operating (cruising) conditions. The safety of the pilot, the crew, the passengers, and people on the ground depend on the timely and accurate reception of voice information in an environment that is less than ideal.

A new technology has been developed that may have the capability of improving speech intelligibility, information transfer, and situational awareness in complex listening environments. Virtual or 3-D audio is a technology that can improve speech communication when there are competing messages. Virtual audio is realized by electronically simulating the natural binaural cues and creating the illusion of spatial auditory images. The effect can be created over headphones or loudspeakers, although only headphone presentations are considered in this chapter. Audio signals can be encoded with natural spatial cues to create the illusion of a sound appearing somewhere around the listener. The process causes the listener to perceive the sound to originate from a particular location outside his or her head. Without the spatial encoding process a listener hears diotic sounds as if they originate halfway between the two ears. Spatial or 3-D audio displays can be manipulated in azimuth, elevation, and distance. Virtual audio technology provides a flexible system for generating a virtual "cocktail party" presented via headphones. This development has enabled research on the cocktail-party effect and parameters affecting communication capability and performance. Previously, such research was cumbersome or impossible to accomplish with a physical sound system.

The focus of this chapter is to review the pertinent literature on speech intelligibility with competing messages, to quantify the effects of directional encoding on speech intelligibility, and to identify parameters affecting directional speech intelligibility. Directional speech intelligibility with multiple talkers is compared with diotic presentations of speech in quiet and in high-noise environments.

I. BACKGROUND

The following literature review is grouped into six general areas: (1) monaural aspects of speech intelligibility, (2) multichannel (left-eared and right-eared) presentations over headphones, (3) lateralized speech signals, (4) free-field talkers and maskers, (5) multipath interference, and (6) headphone presentations via manikins and synthesizers. Although some overlap does exist across these six categories, the grouping should enable discussion of several factors related to the cocktail-party effect. The review is intended to consolidate research findings of masking and binaural hearing with respect to their roles in understanding speech in real-world environments.

A. Monaural speech intelligibility

Before delving into the binaural aspects of listening to multiple talkers, a few comments should be made on the monaural aspects. A broad review on the masking of speech was written by Miller in 1947 and still is relevant today. The masking of speech by speech, noise, and tones was discussed. Monaural factors included intensity, spectrum, and temporal pattern of sound. Interruptions in the continuity of the masker's temporal pattern were found to decrease its effectiveness. Regardless of the type of sound, the spectra of the speech and noise were the primary factors in the amount of masking. Based on this and other findings, the articulation index (Kryter, 1962) was developed to predict the percentage of speech intelligibility based only on the spectra of the speech and masker. Since this early work, other monaural and binaural effects on speech intelligibility have been investigated.

B. Multi-channel listening

Many everyday sounds interfere with speech communication. Cherry (1953) coined the term "cocktail party" to describe a typical situation in which speech can be understood despite several other sound sources. The interference may include other speech signals, music, mechanical noise, and transient auditory events. If a single microphone were immersed in the din of a cocktail party and recorded the sounds in the room, individual sources would be difficult to discern from one another when played back. If a manikin with a microphone in each ear were placed in the same location as the single microphone, then the individual talkers in the binaural representation would be more intelligible. Temporal and spectral information encoded by the manikin onto the speech signals would enable a listener to pay more attention to one auditory source of interest and suppress the others. Listeners in cocktail-party situations use monaural and binaural cues to attend to various audio signals (Miller, 1947; Cherry, 1953).

Cherry (1953) published his classic article on the improvements in speech intelligibility due to the separation of talkers into left and right channels. Several interesting observations were made. Contextual information facilitated the ability to follow a speech message that was heard among other messages. While following a particular message in one ear, unwanted speech or signals from the other ear could be more easily rejected than while following a string of words with no connected meaning. When asked to recall information about sounds heard in the ear opposite the speech message, only statistical information could be remembered. For example, the listener may recall the signal being speech, or noise, or a pure tone, but no other information. Cherry found that subjects could switch attention between talkers very quickly (up to seven times per second) without degrading understanding of the message. Although no spatial or directional properties were added to the speech signals, aspects of two-channel (two-eared) listening abilities in cocktail-party situations were examined.

Many other researchers began investigating other two-channel (two-eared) phenomena. Egan, Carterette, and Thwing (1954) found that equal intensities of speech in the two ears led to 50% intelligibility for a talker masked by himself. However, intelligibility values above and below 50% were found with two different talkers. Qualitative differences between the talkers would alter intelligibility levels due to pitch, dialects, and clarity of individual talkers.

Webster and Solomon (1955) varied the response complexity and applied information theory to quantify the benefits of two-eared listening. At low information-transfer rates large benefits for two-eared listening were found. However, at high transfer rates, the channel bandwidth limited the information going to each ear and little additional benefit was found for two-eared listening.

Broadbent and Ladefoged (1957) measured vowel recognition in the presence of other signals. Little additional advantage was found by separating the speech signals into two channels. They inferred from these results that the correlation in the binaural system was mostly effective with random or noncontextual signals. In other words, the peripheral signals of each ear were correlated with stored patterns in memory. The peripheral to central correlation was often more salient than left ear to right ear correlation. However, Broadbent and Ladefoged cautioned that generalizations of the experimental results to localizing speech in real environments would not necessarily be fruitful.

The two-channel listening experiments were important in evaluating factors involved in multitalker communications. In real-life situations, sounds aren't separated into two channels but overlap and blend across the two ears. Actual listening performance in everyday situations is degraded by the presence of sounds from different auditory events being simultaneously present in each ear.

C. Headphone presentation of lateralized speech signals

Lateralization experiments have demonstrated the relative effects of interaural level differences (ILDs) and interaural time differences (ITDs) on speech intelligibility. The perceived location of a lateralized sound is inside the head and along the interaural axis. Many researchers have investigated the effects of lateralization on speech intelligibility, beginning with Licklider (1948). In general, combined time and level differences were found to provide higher intelligibility level differences than either ITD or ILD alone. An ILD is usually described by a single value in decibels and is independent of frequency. Corbett (1986) spectrally filtered speech and noise signals into various frequency bands and presented the signals over headphones to a listener. Corbett found improvements in speech intelligibility using this technique. A variation on the ITD parameter was made by amplifying the time differences to greater than normal differences of about 800 μs. Kollmeier and Peissig (1990) found slight improvements in speech intelligibility using this technique. One advantage of lateralization experiments is the ability to individually control ITD and ILD parameters via headphone presentation. When sounds are generated away from a listener's head as in free-field conditions, the ILD and ITD cannot be individually controlled. The next section contains descriptions of speech intelligibility of multiple talkers in free-field environments.

D. Free-field listening

Free-field listening incorporates the monaural factor of the best ear signal-to-noise ratio (SNR) and the binaural factors of interaural time and interaural level differences. Compared to two-channel listening, absolute speech intelligibility performance in free-field listening is slightly degraded due to signal and noise being heard in both ears simultaneously. Relative performance within the free-field condition was found to be a function of spatial separation and frequency content.

Spieth, Curtis, and Webster (1954) found an increase in speech intelligibility with horizontal spatial separation and with shaping filters, for responding to one of two simultaneous competing messages. Spieth *et al.* also investigated the effects of context in which messages were presented. Clichés were used to couch speech information within meaningful fragments. Speech intelligibility was higher when left and right signals were switched between a cliché, so that the entire cliché was heard intact by the same ear, than when randomly switched within a cliché. One possible inference is that higher order cognitive processing was being incorporated when listening to meaningful phrases. Bregman and Campbell (1971) developed a theory of auditory streaming and auditory scene analysis related to the cocktail-party effect. Recently, Bregman (1990) expounded on the theory of auditory streaming.

Webster and Thompson (1954) investigated responding to both of two overlapping messages. On average, 20% of the time messages overlapped. Leading messages prevailed over lagging messages as measured by number of phrases correct. Total information transfer was increased if messages had low information content. These findings agreed with results of a later experiment by Webster and Solomon (1955).

In a series of five experiments, Dirks and Wilson (1969) measured speech intelligibility in the free field and via a Kunstkopf. Competing noises and competing messages were used to mask the speech signal. This article contained an excellent review of the literature at that time. Unfortunately, measurement of the cocktail-party effect has not progressed very much since then. Some recent work by Yost, Sheft, and Dye (1994) and Yost (1995) should provide some valuable, quantitative data to the literature.

E. The effects of multipath signals on speech detection

Adding reverberation to the competing message experiments as described in the previous free-field section provides another factor of the "cocktail-party" effect described by Cherry. The reflections from a listening environment have long been known to reduce the level of speech intelligibility (Haas, 1951). The precedence effect, as described by Haas, had a maximum echo suppression of about 10 dB at 15 ms after the first wavefront. The most degrading effect on speech intelligibility from a single reflection occurred after the maximum echo-suppression delay, at about 30 ms after the first wavefront. These experiments were conducted with a single talker's voice and only a single reflection. The inclusion of other reflections in reverberant environments successively degrades speech intelligibility by reducing the interaural correlation and the SNR.

Hirsh (1950) found that thresholds of speech intelligibility were raised when listeners were moved from an anechoic environment (61 dB) to a reverberant environment (66 dB). The latter condition is the worst case situation for a single talker in a highly reverberant environment. Head motion cues seemed to improve (lower) the threshold of speech intelligibility from 63 dB with a fixed head condition to 59 dB with the head motion condition. Multiple talkers tend to degrade speech communication performance even further than random noise, due to the similarity of speech signal spectra and modulations.

Tobias (1972) simulated an airborne "cocktail party" with speech presented over an array of three loudspeakers in a small aircraft. Competing messages were presented either over a single center loudspeaker or over two separate loudspeakers, either in phase or out of phase. Only a small benefit of 2 dB was measured for the out-of-phase separate loudspeakers compared to the single in-phase loudspeaker condition.

In general, speech discrimination is better with binaural hearing than with monaural hearing in reverberant environments. The binaural system serves to reduce the deleterious effects of reverberation on localization, as reported by Wallach, Newman, and Rosenzweig (1949). The "squelch effect" as observed by Koenig (1950) is a decrease in the perceived amount of reverberation when listening binaurally as compared to listening monaurally or diotically. Later, Koenig, Allen, and Berkley (1977) measured masking level differences of about 3 dB for both coherent and incoherent maskers in a reverberant environment. Mackeith and Coles (1971) measured the effects of reverberation on binaural and monaural speech discrimination. This work was mostly motivated by hearing aid research as to the benefit of two-eared versus one-eared listening. They found changes in the speech-to-noise ratio from 0 to 4 dB for the squelch effect depending on the locations of the speech and masker and degree of reverberation. As noted before, the binaural hearing system tends to provide its greatest advantage over the monaural system when listening conditions are degraded by competing sounds.

F. Headphone presentation of free-field directional cues

Schubert and Schultz (1962) conducted two experiments in which masked speech signals were more easily understood by listening binaurally than monaurally. In the first experiment, the speech was masked by broadband random noise. Three speech ranges were filtered and presented to the listener. Each of the three frequency ranges was presented at three interaural time differences. The interaural time difference conditions included homophasic, antiphasic, and a 0.5-ms delay. The low-frequency speech was observed to provide the highest intelligibility percent improvement over the homophasic condition. From these data, the auditory system was inferred to make use of longer periods (6–15 Hz modulation) in the speech waveform when masked by broadband random noise. Binaural fusion was conjectured to operate peripherally by extraction of the low-frequency modulation envelope of speech waveforms.

In the second experiment, speech of a single talker was masked by speech signals from various sets of talkers. The same interaural time difference conditions as in the first experiment were used. The antiphasic condition yielded slightly higher masking level differences than the delayed speech condition. Although, significant ($p < 0.01$) MLDs (masking level differences) were found for maskers of five simultaneous talkers, multiple random talkers, and the talker's own voice for both anti-phasic and delayed speech conditions, generally, the binaural system was less efficient at extracting speech information from speech-like maskers than from random noise maskers.

Schubert and Schultz (1962) hypothesized that one might expect the largest differences between monaural and binaural hearing for signal detection, next for localization, and least for identification of a signal. However, they noted that factors such as contextual information play a role in localization and identification due to pattern matching and fusing of harmonically coherent portions of the monaural spectrum. Therefore, data from signal detection experiments may not always coincide with speech intelligibility data.

Bronkhorst and Plomp (1988) used speech reception thresholds (SRTs) to measure effects of ITD, ILD, and a combination of these two factors for speech presented from a virtual location directly in front of the subject (0° azimuth) and noise presented at various virtual directions in azimuth. When the noise was synthesized with both ITDs and ILDs, thresholds were lower than when the noise contained only ILDs or only ITDs. The data were converted to binaural intelligibility level differences (BILDs) in decibels by subtracting the mean SRT for each condition from the mean SRT for 0° free-field noise. The sum of the BILDs for the ILD only (5.5 dB) and ITD only (4.6 dB) noise masking conditions was higher than that for the combined free-field (both ILDs and ITDs) condition (8.1 dB). An ILD effectively reduced the overall release from masking when it was introduced into the ITD-only noise masker. That is, a simple linear combination of ILD and ITD effects would have produced a 10.1-dB BILD, instead of the measured 8.1-dB BILD. Previous experiments in the free field (Plomp and Mimpen, 1981) agreed with the combined threshold data.

Bronkhorst and Plomp (1992) measured the effects of multiple speech-like maskers on SRTs for normal and hearing impaired listeners. Interfering noise was modulated by speech waveform envelopes and spectrally matched to the long-term average spectrum of speech. On average, a 3-dB advantage was found for the binaural over the monaural mode. The monaural contribution was observed to be considerable when compared to the binaural advantage. However, the monaural and binaural contributions were strongly dependent on the number and azimuthal positions of the maskers.

Ricard and Meirs (1994) measured the intelligibility of speech from virtual directions in azimuth. Stimuli included synthetic speech and a 5-kHz white-noise masker without modulation. Thresholds for masking of speech were found by linear extrapolation to the 70% speech intelligibility level. On average, thresholds were reduced by 4–5 dB for speech presented at various directions in azimuth with the interference always straight ahead.

A model of the binaural advantages in speech intelligibility was developed by Zurek (1993). The model accounts for a single interfering sound source in azimuth located in an anechoic environment. Zurek's model distinguishes itself from other models by taking into account interactive effects found in binaural hearing. As data become available, other variables, such as multiple maskers, elevation angle, distance, and reverberation, will hopefully be included in future models. The current model and inclusion of other factors will help to predict speech intelligibility in real-life environments.

Overall the cocktail-party effect literature contains several consistent findings. Large advantages are found for binaural speech intelligibility when speech and noise signals are presented from different directions in azimuth. The absolute contribution of the monaural cues is much larger than the absolute contribution of the binaural cues. The greatest monaural cue is the relative energies in the spectra of the speech and noise waveforms. Binaural hearing provides a relatively large advantage to speech intelligibility in low speech-to-noise ratio conditions. Contextual information tends to improve speech intelligibility but not speech detection. Binaural hearing in reverberant environments is more robust than monaural hearing due to the "squelch effect." Multiple speech-like maskers are more effective than broadband, random noise maskers due to low-frequency modulations of the speech waveform envelope.

II. METHODOLOGY

A. Facilities and equipment

Speech intelligibility performance was measured using either the coordinate response measure (CRM) (Moore, 1981) or the voice communications effectiveness test (VCET) (McKinley and Moore, 1989). Experiments were conducted in the voice communications research and evaluation system (VOCRES) (McKinley, 1979) and in the performance and communications research and technology (PACRAT) facility.

VOCRES includes a control room, a reverberation chamber, and 10 subject stations in the chamber. VOCRES's sound generation system is capable of producing up to an overall 130 dB (SPL) of broadband noise from 100 to 10 000 Hz. The chamber is 8000 ft^3 in volume with a reverberation time (RT_{60}) of 6 s at 500 Hz. Listening stations are equipped with individual AIC-25 intercommunication systems, compressed air regulators, alphanumeric displays, and response panels. Visual presentation of the sentences to the talker and collection of the listeners' responses are automated by an HP-9845 computer. Talkers wore an HGU-26/P helmet and an MBU-12/P oxygen mask, equipped with an M-169 microphone. The output from the microphone was transmitted by an AIC-25 intercommunication set to the input of Armstrong Laboratory's auditory localization cue synthesizer (ALCS) (McKinley, 1988).

ALCS units were installed in VOCRES to produce the azimuthal auditory display over headphones. The ALCS contained HRTFs from a KEMAR manikin measured at 1° spacings at 7 ft of radius. The ALCS operated in conjunction with a computer, head tracker, external audio source, and two-channel headphones. A Polhemus electromagnetic head tracker monitored the orientation of the listener's head, which was used to maintain a constant direction of the sound source with respect to the chamber. ALCS outputs were displayed over Bose AH-1A active noise-reducing headphones, configured for binaural operation.

PACRAT, like VOCRES, includes a control room, reverberation chamber, and 10 subject stations. PACRAT's sound system is capable of producing up to 137 dB of broadband noise from 16 to 10 000 Hz. The chamber is about 20 000 ft^3 in volume and with a reverberation time (RT_{60}) of 12 s at 250 Hz. Subject stations were equipped with the same equipment as in VOCRES plus three multifunction CRT displays to enter responses during the VCET task.

B. Subjects

A panel of 12 paid volunteer subjects, 6 male and 6 female, participated in the experiments. All subjects exhibited hearing sensitivities equal to or better than 15 dB hearing threshold level for audiometric frequencies from 125 to 8000 Hz. In addition, all subjects had normal middle ear function. All talkers were from the same geographic location and had the same Midwestern regional accent.

C. Procedure

Speech was either presented diotically, dichotically, or directionally over headphones. Diotic presentations were realized by mixing all signals together and presenting them equally to each earphone; these auditory images appeared to originate in the center of one's head. Dichotic displays of two talkers were made by passing one talker's voice to one earphone and the other talker's voice to the other earphone. Directional presentations of two-talker displays were achieved with one ALCS, and four-talker displays were achieved with two ALCS units. The speech signals were encoded for various directions around the listener in azimuth. Elevation angle was held constant at the horizontal plane. Distance cues were essentially absent. All signals were encoded with a constant gain term without multipath cues. Subjects were allowed to freely move their heads during testing; however, no gross amount of motion was visually observed during testing. The criterion measure was speech intelligibility as measured by either the CRM or the VCET.

The CRM is a nonstandardized test to measure the speech intelligibility of simultaneous talkers. Each test phrase contains a call sign, a color, and a number. Two call signs, "ringo" and "baron," were used. Talker call signs were randomized so that half (25/50) were for "ringo" and half were for "baron." Individual listeners were instructed to respond to either "baron" or "ringo" for each 50-phrase session. One of four possible colors included "red," "white," "blue," and "grey." Numbers ranged from "one" to "eight." A typical sentence embedded in a phrase might be "Ready Ringo, go to blue eight, now." If any one part of the response was wrong, then the entire phrase was scored as incorrect. There was no correction for guessing. Presentation of the test words was randomized. Talkers spoke equal numbers of the call signs "ringo" and "baron" within each session.

VCET was designed to measure the amount of information transfer in typical airborne communications. Words and phrases were based on typical radio communications aboard military aircraft. Phrases were generated by computer for each session from a 200-word vocabulary. Phrases were six words in length and formed meaningful, sensible thoughts. Information in bits for each transmitted phrase was predetermined. The average number of bits per received phrase was predetermined for each 44-phrase session. The information rate in bits per second was found after each session. Speech intelligibility scores were based on entire phrases being correct. Any portion of the phrase being incorrect made the scoring of that phrase incorrect. Talkers read the phrases once, without repetition. No correction for guessing was made.

In the first experiment, listening levels were predetermined and held constant through all sessions. The gain of the intercom was set to a constant level to provide the same speech-to-noise ratios across all presentation modes. To calibrate the gain, a 1-kHz, 1-V peak–peak sinusoid was input to the headphone amplifier. The sound pressure level under the earcup was adjusted to a fixed level (73 dB SPL) using a B&K 2131 spectrum analyzer, a flat plate coupler, a B&K 523 artificial ear, and a B&K 4145 pressure microphone. Sound pressure levels under each earcup were calibrated to within ±0.5 dB of each other.

In the other four experiments, listening levels were individually adjusted by the listeners to most comfortable levels. Each subject had a knob that adjusted the gain of the sidetone presented over a headset. A typical level was set 5–10 dB above the background noise. However, more experienced listeners tended to set their levels several decibels lower than the less experienced listeners.

III. EXPERIMENT 1: SPEECH INTELLIGIBILITY IN DIFFERENT DIRECTIONS

A. Method

Ten subjects from the 12-member panel were used. Either a pair of two males, two females, or a mixed male and female pair was chosen as talkers. A male and a female were assigned to each of the two (diotic and directional) listening conditions. All listeners participated in all conditions of the study.

Signals and maskers were set to predetermined levels. The speech-to-noise ratio was chosen to achieve speech intelligibility levels from near 100% to below 50%. Speech spectra from the three pairs of talkers and the noise spectra are shown in Figs. 1, 2, and 3. Peak speech energy is about 20 dB above the long term average speech spectra. The male and female speech spectra are the most

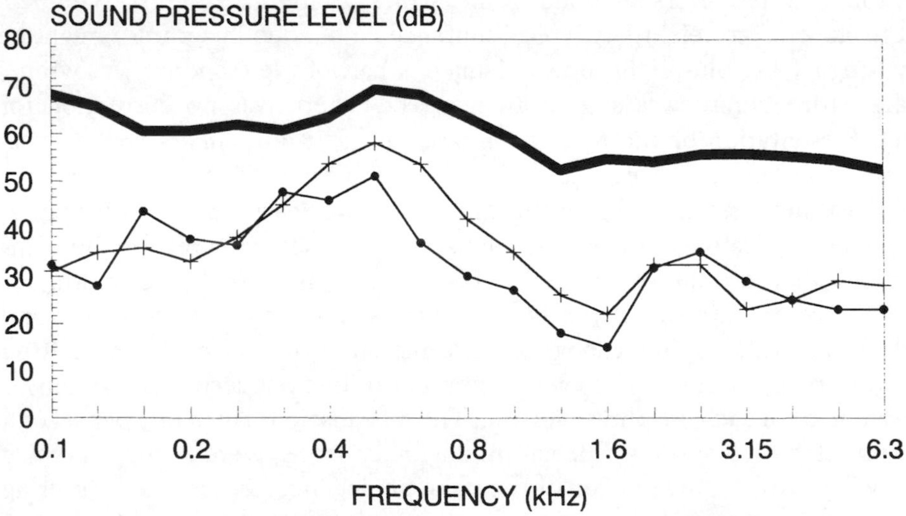

FIG. 1. Long-term average (32 s) of male speech (+), female speech (•), and 105 dB SPL noise (thick line) spectra.

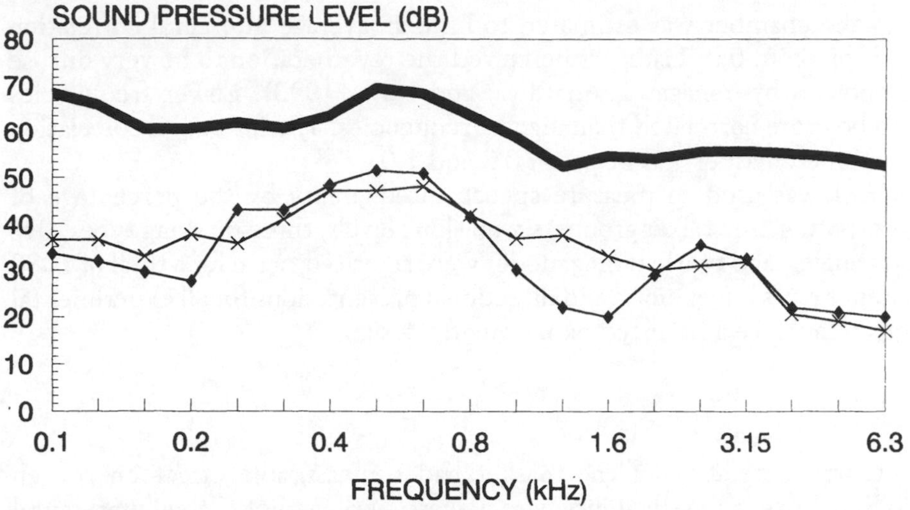

FIG. 2. Long-term average (32 s) of male speech (♦), male speech (x), and 105 dB SPL noise (thick line)

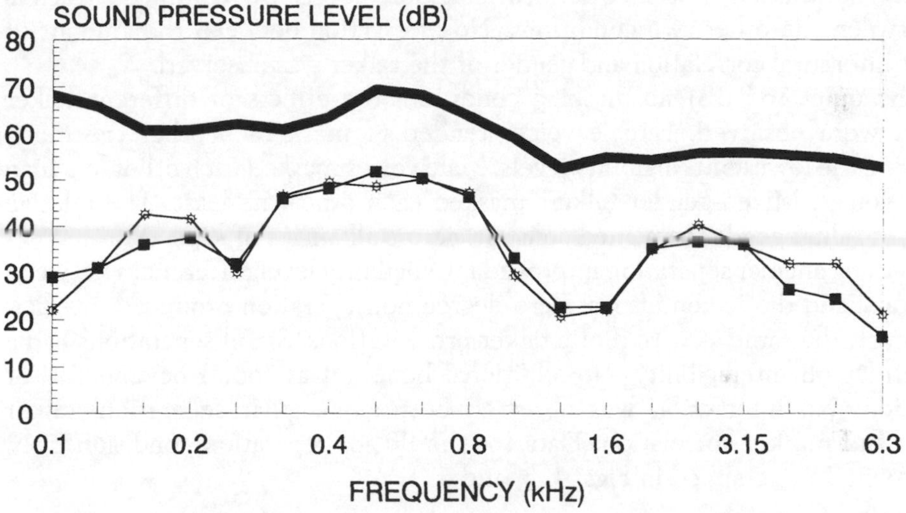

FIG. 3. Long-term average (32 s) of female speech (■), female speech (✪), and 105 dB SPL noise (thick line) spectra.

dissimilar of the three pairs. The male speech spectra are very closely matched, except for between 1 and 2 kHz. The female speech spectra are the most closely matched of the three talker pairs.

The six noise levels included quiet (65), 85, 95, 105, 110, and 120 dB SPL. The spectrum and level of the noise under the headset were matched with a JBL one-third octave band graphic equalizer to the spectrum and level of the pink noise in the chamber. In this manner, the same signal-to-noise levels were realized for diotic and ambient maskers, although the interaural correlation of the maskers differed dramatically. Masking conditions of diotic, ambient, and a simultaneous combination of these two maskers were used to mask the talkers' voices. The diotic headphone masker had a correlation coefficient equal to 1.0. The ambient masker in the chamber was estimated to have an average interaural correlation coefficient of about 0.3. Listeners perceived the reverberation to be very diffuse as also reported by Yanagawa, Anazawa, and Itow (1990). Lower frequencies tended to be more correlated than higher frequencies. The interaural correlation of the combined masker was between 0.3 and 1.0.

The CRM was used to measure speech intelligibility by the percentage of phrases correct. Three talker groups, six masking levels, three masking types, five separation angles, and two listening modes were repeated twice for a total of 1080 runs. Listener pairs ran in diotic and directional presentations for all experimental conditions to achieve a balanced experimental design.

B. Results

The interaural correlation of the masker had a measurable effect on speech intelligibility. Speech intelligibility was lowest with a diotic (high interaural correlation) masker. Speech intelligibility was highest with an ambient (low interaural correlation) masker. Speech intelligibility levels with combined maskers fell between the other two conditions. No interaction between the amount of masker interaural correlation and gender of the talker was observed.

In the quiet (65 dB) no masking condition, the effects of different talker genders were observed. Female voices tended to mask each other the most, producing the lowest intelligibility levels. Male voices masked each other less than female voices. Mixed-gender talkers masked each other the least. The relative effects of talker gender remained constant across all angles of separation.

Increasing angular separation improved intelligibility level differences between directional and diotic conditions. Zero degree nonseparation produced intelligibility levels the same as with diotic talker presentations. Small separations had a large effect on intelligibility. No additional benefit was found beyond 90° of separation. No interaction was observed between angular separation, talker gender, and masker correlation. Data for the 90° of separation condition from experiment 1 are graphed in Figs. 4, 5, and 6.

C. Discussion

In the first experiment, broadband noise maskers of three levels of interaural correlation were examined. The diotic masker, with high interaural correlation, was consistently observed to be the most effective masker of speech. Alternately, the ambient masker, with a relatively low interaural correlation, was consistently observed to mask speech the least. The masker correlation effect was seen within the three directional presentations and within the three diotic presentations. These differences were most prominent at the poor speech-to-noise ratios, that is, around the 50% intelligibility levels. Durlach (1964) measured the binaural masking level differences for different interaural correlations. The rank order of the intelligibility data agreed with the relative amount of masking for the various interaural correlations. Doll, Hanna, and Russotti (1992) measured improvements in masking thresholds when the background noise was uncorrelated with

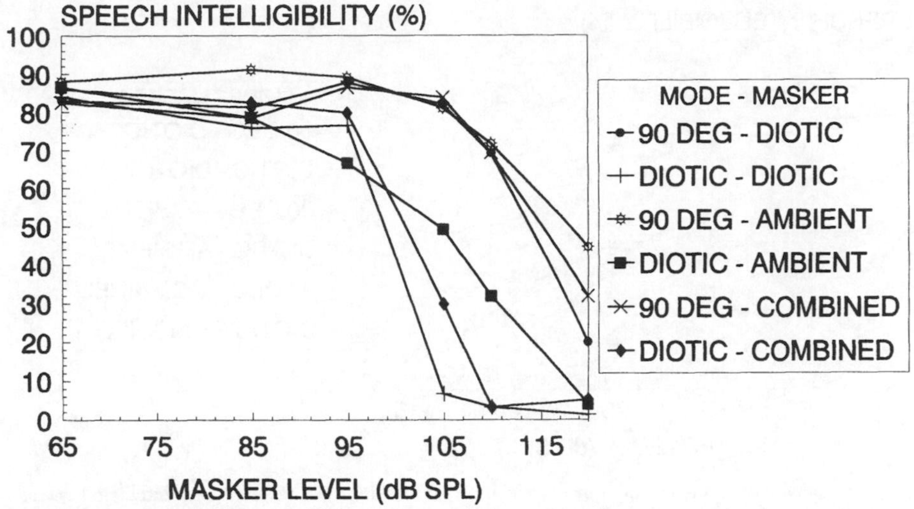

FIG. 4. Speech intelligibility of male and female speech versus masking noise level. Speech intelligibility was measured by the CRM at fixed presentation levels.

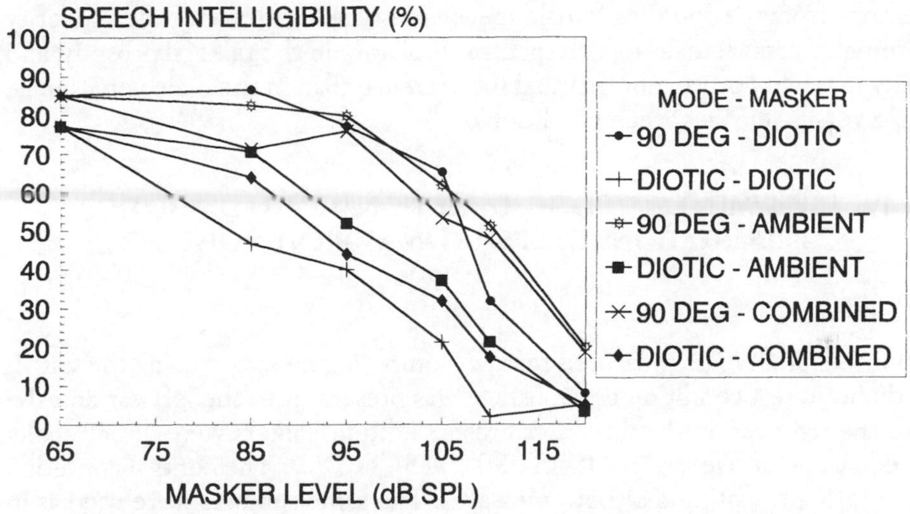

FIG. 5. Speech intelligibility of male and male speech versus masking noise level. Speech intelligibility was measured by the CRM at fixed presentation levels.

the signal and when angular separation increased. As are most factors observed in the cocktail-party effect, the degree of interaural correlation is a second-order effect after the primary factor, the speech-to-noise ratio at the better of the two ears.

Directional presentation of speech messages at 90° separation provides generally much higher intelligibility levels than with the diotic presentation. The binaural cues help to unmask the desired speech message from the interfering speech message and interfering noise. Within each presentation mode, the lowest intelligibility levels are measured with the diotic masker and the highest intelligibility levels are measured with the ambient masker. In Fig. 6, the intelligibility

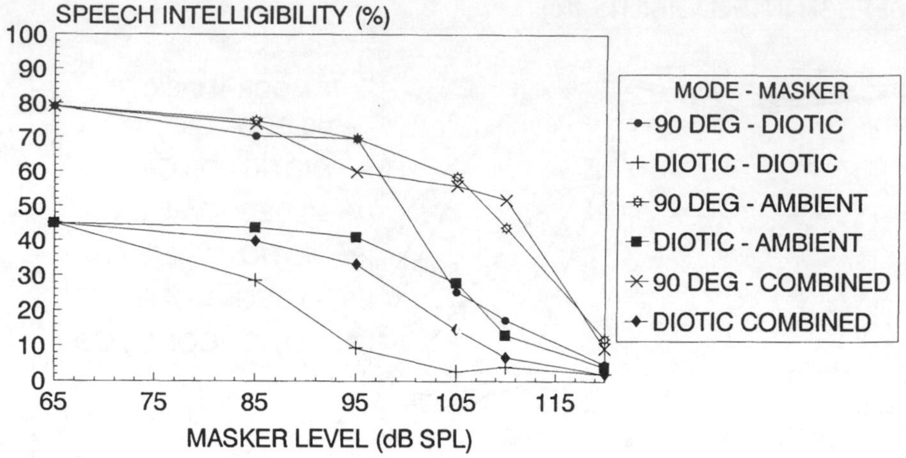

FIG. 6. Speech intelligibility of female and female speech versus masking noise level. Speech intelligibility was measured by the CRM at fixed presentation levels.

levels in the diotic presentation mode are lower than in Figs. 4 and 5 due to interference from the opposing female speech message. Presumably, the similarity of the female versus female speech spectra, similarity in the talkers' prosody, and similarity in quality cause more mutual interference than in the male versus male and male versus female speech conditions.

IV. EXPERIMENT 2: DIOTIC, DIRECTIONAL, AND DICHOTIC PRESENTATIONS OF SPEECH IN AMBIENT NOISE

A. Method

Speech intelligibility was measured for two competing messages using the CRM. In the dichotic test condition one message was presented to the left ear and the other to the right ear. In the directional test condition, talkers were directionally separated at one of five angles: 0°, 45°, 90°, 135°, or 180°. The control condition was the diotic presentation of both messages. The same subjects were used as in the first experiment.

Unlike experiment 1, the listener set talker voice amplifications to a most comfortable level. However, amplification of each talker channel was set to the same gain. No adjustments for different talker pairs were made. Talker pairs were chosen so that competing talkers spoke at similar loudness levels. One ambient, pink-noise masking level (105 dB SPL) and one quiet (65 dB SPL) level were used in VOCRES to provide speech-to-noise ratios representative of best and worst listening conditions.

A balanced repeated-measures design was employed. Three talker pairs, two masking levels, and seven listening conditions were repeated twice for a total of 84 runs. Listener pairs participated in diotic, directional, and dichotic presentations. Speech intelligibility levels for dichotic, directional, and diotic presentation modes were calculated for the two masking levels.

B. Results

Data for the second experiment are shown in Figs. 7 and 8 for 65 and 105 dB SPL ambient masking levels, respectively. Dichotic presentation of the competing messages was always more intelligible than the diotic presentation, and also more intelligible than 0° or 45° directional presentations. As was expected, speech intelligibility levels in the directional presentation condition at 0° were similar to levels in the diotic condition. However, a small angular separation of the messages (45°) greatly improved speech intelligibility. At 90° of separation, speech intelligibility levels were maximized and further separation did not yield higher intelligibility levels.

In quiet, female talkers tended to mask each other more than the male and mixed gender pairs. In ambient noise, the intelligibility of the dichotic presentation remained high (above 90%) compared to the levels in the diotic condition (62–84%). The speech intelligibility levels in the directional presentation condition at maximum separation approached those of the dichotic presentations.

C. Discussion

As shown again by the data of experiment 2, directional presentations of speech are more intelligible than diotic presentations, especially in low speech-to-noise environments. The same effects of angular separation and talker gender were observed in experiments 1 and 2. In practical situations, such directional presentations over headphones may improve speech communications when the signal is weak compared to the interfering noise, and the listener does not want to or cannot increase the signal level.

The dichotic (separate signals to the left and right ears) presentations provided higher levels of intelligibility than the small (45°) directional presentations. The left ear signal did not interfere with the right ear signal, or vice versa, in the

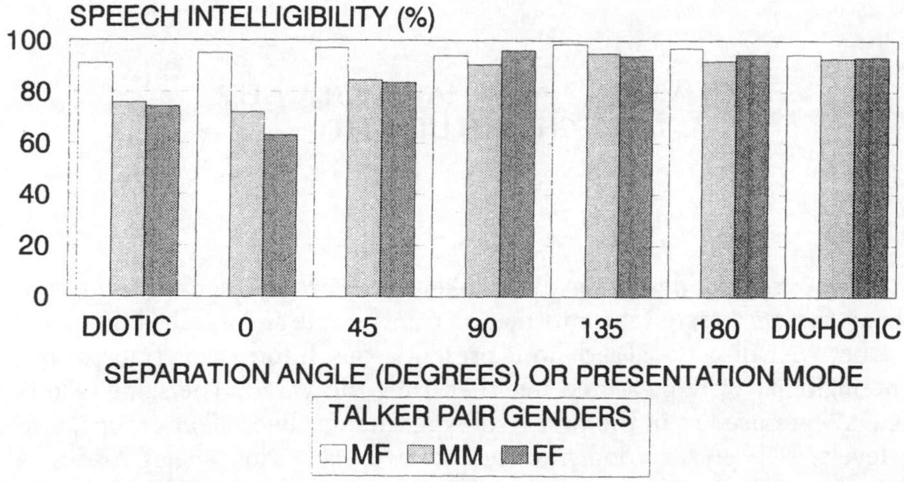

FIG. 7. Speech intelligibility for diotic, dichotic, and directional presentations of two talkers in quiet (65 dB SPL of ambient noise). Speech intelligibility was measured by the CRM with talker presentation levels set to most comfortable levels.

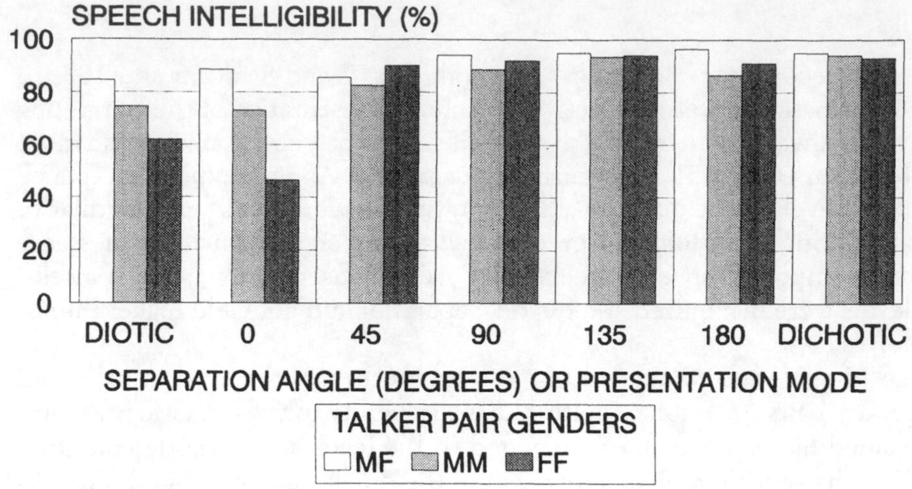

FIG. 8. Speech intelligibility for diotic, dichotic, and directional presentations of two talkers in 105 dB SPL of ambient pink noise. Speech intelligibility was measured by the CRM with talker presentation levels set to most comfortable levels.

dichotic presentation. However, the 45° directional presentation did contain these cross-talk signals, which produced lower intelligibility levels. The deleterious effects of the combined ITD and ILD cues were the same as measured by Bronkhorst and Plomp (1988) using speech reception thresholds. As conjectured much earlier by Cherry (1953), the ear closest to the sound source in free-field environments receives a greater signal than the ear away from the sound source. When there are several sound sources around a listener, these multiple signals reduce the speech-to-noise ratio at the ear closest to the desired talker. Thereby, the overall intelligibility level is reduced by the unwanted but necessary binaural signals. The potentially best benefit of directional over dichotic presentations should be found in displays that contain more than two talkers, because we only have two ears.

V. EXPERIMENT 3: INFORMATION TRANSFER AND SPEECH INTELLIGIBILITY

A. Method

A factorial experimental design for each talker group was chosen to determine which, if any, factors affected the information transfer rate and intelligibility level difference between directional and diotic presentations. Information transfer and speech intelligibility were measured together using the VCET. The same talkers and listeners were used as in the first two experiments. Two talker groups, two masking levels, two presentation modes, and two separation angles made 24 sessions in the study. Separation angles included no separation (0°) and 180° (±90°) of separation. The control condition was the diotic presentation of talkers. Noise levels included quiet (65 dB SPL) and 105 dB SPL of ambient pink noise.

B. Results

Directionally separated and diotic presentations of VCET yielded similar response times, 8.16 and 8.20 s, respectively. On average, a set of 44 phrases had 33 bits per phrase. In the directionally separated condition, 4.04 bits per second were communicated between talker and listener. Similarly, 3.86 and 4.02 bits per second were communicated in the diotic and 0° conditions, respectively.

Speech intelligibility percentages are graphed in Fig. 9 for quiet and in Fig. 10 for 105 dB SPL of noise. Speech intelligibility percentages were about the same with the VCET in experiment 3 as with the CRM in experiment 2 using the coordinate response measure. Speech intelligibility averaged about 85% with 180° angular separation in azimuth, and ranged from 55 to 85% with the diotic presentation. No practical difference was found between the 0° separation and the diotic condition.

C. Discussion

In experiment 3, response times for diotic and directional modes were the same, although intelligibility levels were higher for the directional presentations. Because subjects were not allowed to repeat messages, the average number of bits per second would actually be higher with the directional presentation compared to the diotic presentation condition if talkers repeated messages until all the information was transferred. An advantage for directional over diotic presentations may exist as a reduced number of times a talker has to communicate. Such an advantage would be important in time-critical situations.

Webster and Solomon (1955) observed that complex tasks tended to reduce the additional benefit of binaural presentations. Because the percent intelligibility levels were similar for both the CRM and VCET tasks, then listeners were

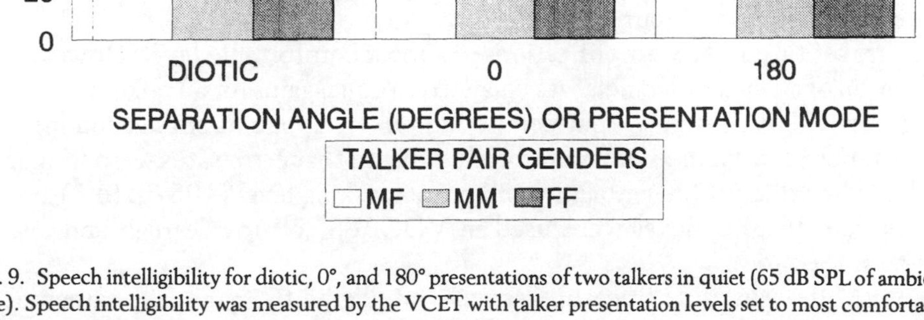

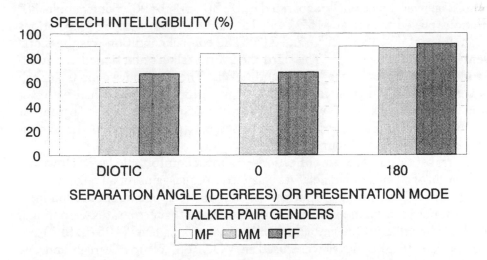

FIG. 9. Speech intelligibility for diotic, 0°, and 180° presentations of two talkers in quiet (65 dB SPL of ambient noise). Speech intelligibility was measured by the VCET with talker presentation levels set to most comfortable levels.

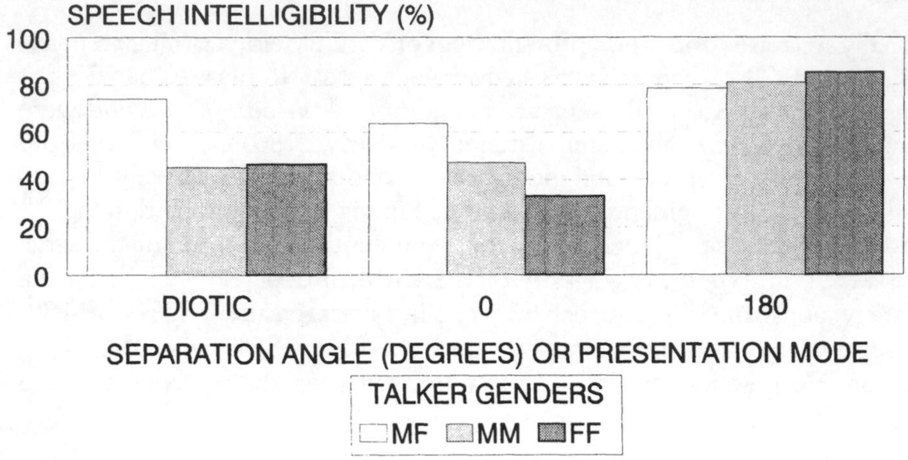

FIG. 10. Speech intelligibility for diotic, 0°, and 180° presentations of two talkers in 105 dB SPL of ambient pink noise. Speech intelligibility was measured by the VCET with talker presentation levels set to most comfortable levels.

probably not overtasked by the six word phrases in the VCET task. In other words, the binaural advantage was probably not limited by the width of the information channel.

VI. EXPERIMENT 4: FOUR COMPETING MESSAGES

A. Method

Speech intelligibility was measured for four competing messages using the coordinate response measure with two additional talkers. In the test condition each message was directionally separated by 0°, 30°, 60°, or 90°. For example, 30° separations placed talkers at 315°, 345°, 15°, and 45°. Likewise, 90° separations placed talkers at 45°, 135°, 225°, and 315°. The control condition was the diotic presentation of four messages. The third and fourth talkers functioned as distracters and went by the call signs "alpha" and "laker." The first and second talker call signs were randomized so that half (25/50) were for "ringo" and half were for "baron." Individual listeners were instructed to respond to either "baron" or "ringo" for each 50-phrase session. Twelve subjects participated in the experiment, eight as talkers and four as listeners.

Listeners set talker voice amplifications to a most comfortable level. However, amplification of all talker channels was balanced to equal gains for all talker groups. Talker groups were chosen so that competing talkers spoke at similar loudness levels. Listener performance was monitored to ensure that error rates were similar for each of the talkers. One ambient, pink-noise masking level (105 dB SPL) and one quiet (65 dB SPL) level were used in VOCRES to provide high and low speech-to-noise ratios.

The CRM was used to measure speech intelligibility in all experimental conditions. Three talker groups, three masking levels, four separation angles, and two listening conditions were repeated twice for a total of 144 runs. Listener pairs participated in diotic and directional presentation modes to balance the experimental design.

B. Results

The same relative intelligibilities were found with four talkers as with two talkers. Overall levels were decreased due to the mutual interference of the competing three talkers. Only marginal intelligibility levels were achieved in the most optimal conditions (75% for MFMF at 90° in quiet). The addition of ambient pink noise greatly reduced speech intelligibility of the four talkers to barely intelligible levels. Data are plotted in Figs. 11 and 12.

C. Discussion

Data from experiment 4 showed little advantage for directional over diotic presentations of four simultaneous talkers. However, initial capture of the call sign may have been made easier by directional separation. The length of phrases made it more difficult to gain any advantage from initial capture. Yost *et al.* (1994) showed a benefit with single-word, multitalker experiments. Previous experiments showed benefit when less than seven talkers spoke unsynchronized phrases of different content (Bronkhorst and Plomp, 1992).

Less degradation in intelligibility would have been observed if the phrases had overlapped and had not been simultaneous. Four simultaneous talkers is an extremely difficult and unusual situation. There are not many situations in which one encounters monitoring four constant communications.

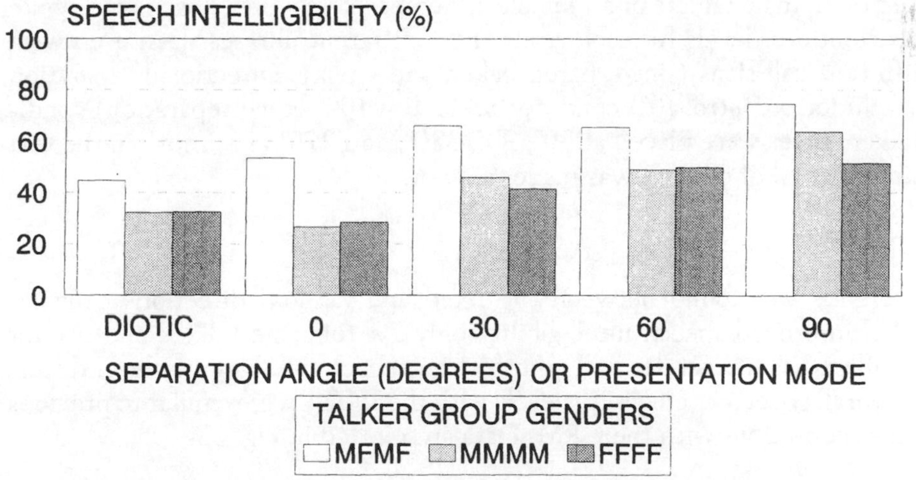

FIG. 11. Speech intelligibility for diotic and directional presentations of four talkers in quiet (65 dB SPL of ambient noise). Speech intelligibility was measured by the CRM with talker presentation levels set to most comfortable levels.

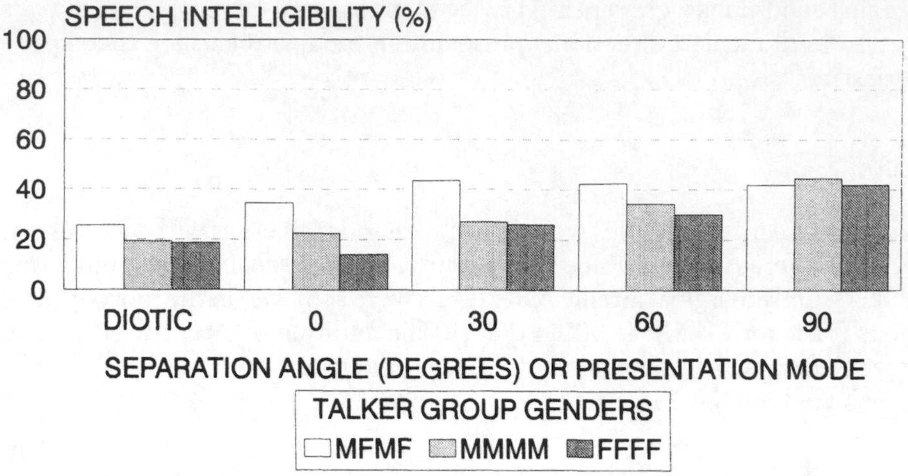

FIG. 12. Speech intelligibility for diotic and directional presentations of four talkers in 105 dB SPL of ambient pink noise. Speech intelligibility was measured by the CRM with talker presentation levels set to most comfortable levels.

VII. EXPERIMENT 5: SELECTIVE ATTENTION (TALKER LOCATION) AND SPEECH INTELLIGIBILITY

A. Method

The CRM was used to measure speech intelligibility for fixed versus random talker directions. In the fixed talker direction condition, listeners always heard the same talker's voice coming from the same direction. In the random talker direction, listeners did not know *a priori* from which direction a particular talker's voice would be heard. In this manner, the ability of the listeners to selectively attend to one direction could be measured. Two groups of talkers were used. Each group consisted of all male talkers or all female talkers. Talkers were chosen who spoke at similar loudness levels for each group. Four different phrases were used with four different call signs (ringo, baron, laker, and alpha). Directional separation angles included a control (0°) condition and a test (60° equal separation) condition. Talker voices were placed at 30°, 90°, 330°, and 270° in azimuth in the test condition. A total of 64 runs was made in quiet.

B. Results

No difference was found between the fixed and random directions. Angular separation improved speech intelligibility only 7% for male talkers and 5% for female talkers. Talker gender had no effect on speech intelligibility level differences. Overall speech intelligibility levels with the VCET were similar to previous four-talker conditions with the CRM. Data are plotted in Fig. 13.

C. Discussion

Selective attention to audio signals may be a fragile resource, one easily destroyed by multiple, simultaneous talkers. In other words, equal weighting may be assigned to the start of every new message. Most data as described in the background section are on two talkers, as is often found in every day situations. Yost *et al.* (1994) observed a benefit of binaural displays with up to three talkers, but did not measure with four talkers. Bronkhorst and Plomp (1990) observed a benefit with up to six talkers, but the talkers spoke with pauses in an overlapping manner. The fifth experiment in this chapter was different from the others in that messages from four simultaneous talkers were heard by the listeners. Several simultaneous messages may overload the auditory system and prevent it from capturing the desired message from a particular direction.

VIII. GENERAL DISCUSSION

The cocktail-party effect cannot be measured by just one experiment. Unfortunately, one may infer from the name that there is a single cause, such as having two ears instead of one, that creates the effect. Hidden within the phenomenon are several factors that contribute to the overall ability to understand conversations in poor listening environments. Some of these include reflections in the listening environment, contextual information, prior knowledge of sounds, and quality of voices. The summation of all contributing factors may not add linearly, but interact, to provide an overall advantage greater than predicted.

A nonlinear relationship exists between speech intelligibility level and angular separation of talkers. The underlying reasons may be related to the way humans process binaural cues and the nonlinearity of the ILD and ITD functions in azimuth. The improvement seems to be most evident at low speech-to-noise ratios and in front of the listener where the ITD is at its steepest rate of change, about 10 μs per degree. Even a small talker separation (22°) centered in front of the

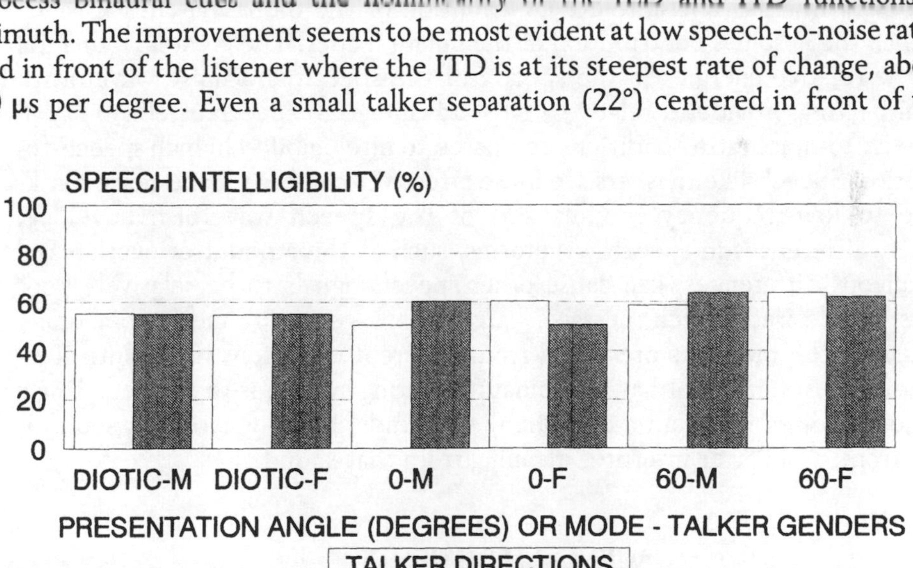

FIG. 13. Speech intelligibility for diotic, 0°, and 60° presentations of four talkers in quiet (65 dB SPL of ambient noise). Speech intelligibility was measured by the VCET with talker presentation levels set to most comfortable levels. In the 60° directional condition, talker messages were presented either from the same direction within each test session or from one of four random directions each time.

listener has a large effect on intelligibility. Talker separations centered at the side of the listener did not have as great an improvement for the same amount of separation.

Unwanted speech signals can act as maskers just as random noises do in the cocktail-party effect. Several attributes of speech signals affect the amount of disturbance on other desired sounds. The spectra of the speech signals are generally considered the most important factor in the mutual masking of speech. Pitch similarities across talkers play a role in the amount of masking. The female talker pairs in the experiments were observed to have very similar pitches and somewhat annoying timbre in their voices. In addition to their similar spectra, these factors reduced intelligibility, as is seen by comparing the data of the diotic presentations of the three talker pairs in quiet.

IX. SUMMARY AND CONCLUSIONS

The pertinent literature on speech intelligibility with competing messages was reviewed. The effects of directional encoding on speech intelligibility was measured and compared to speech intelligibility with diotic presentations. Several experiments were conducted in quiet, with maskers presented over headphones, and in high levels of reverberant noise.

Several parameters affecting directional speech intelligibility were identified. Overall the cocktail-party literature contains several findings consistent with the current experiments. The absolute contribution of the monaural cues is much larger than the absolute contribution of the binaural cues. The greatest monaural cue is the relative energies in the spectra of the speech and noise waveforms. Binaural hearing provides a relatively large advantage to speech intelligibility in low speech-to-noise ratio conditions compared to intelligibility in high speech-to-noise ratios. Speech-like maskers are more effective than broadband noise maskers due to low-frequency modulations of the speech waveform envelope. However, differences in speech waveforms, such as the amount of overlap and instantaneous differences, can cause other speech signals to be relatively poor maskers of a desired speech message. Large advantages are found for binaurally separated speech messages presented from different directions in azimuth. Perhaps the clearest benefit of having a binaural hearing system is to extract a single sound source direction from a cacophony of sounds, know where that sound is coming from, and better interpret meaning from that sound.

ACKNOWLEDGMENTS

The authors acknowledge the support and guidance of Drs. Charles W. Nixon and Thomas J. Moore during the development of this technology and the conduction of these experiments. The authors also acknowledge the efforts of Michael Ward, David Ovenshire, and Ronald Dallman during the data collection.

REFERENCES

Bregman, A. S., and Campbell, J. (**1971**). "Primary auditory stream segregation and perception of order in rapid sequences of tones," J. Exp. Psych. **89**, 244–249.

Bregman, A. S. (**1990**). *Auditory Scene Analysis: The Perceptual Organization of Sound* (MIT, Cambridge, MA).

Broadbent, D. E., and Ladefoged, P. (**1957**). "On the fusion of sounds reaching different sense organs," J. Acoust. Soc. Am. **29**, 708–710.

Bronkhorst, A. W. and Plomp, R. (**1988**). "The effect of head-induced interaural time and level differences on speech intelligibility in noise," J. Acoust. Soc. Am. **83**, 1508–1516.

Bronkhorst, A. W., and Plomp, R. (**1990**). "A clinical test for the assessment of binaural speech perception in noise," Audiology **29**, 275–285.

Bronkhorst, A. W., and Plomp, R. (**1992**). "Effect of multiple speech like maskers on binaural speech recognition in normal and impaired hearing," J. Acoust. Soc. Am. **92**, 3132–3139.

Cherry, E. C. (**1953**). "Some experiments on the recognition of speech, with one and with two ears," J. Acoust. Soc. Am. **25**, 975–979.

Corbett, C. R. (**1986**). "Filtering competing messages to enhance mutual intelligibility," M.S. thesis, MIT, Cambridge, MA.

Dirks, D. D., and Wilson, R. H. (**1969**). "The effect of spatially separated sound sources on speech intelligibility," J. Speech Hear. Res. **12**, 5–38.

Doll, T. J., Hanna, T. E., and Russotti, J. S. (**1992**). "Masking in three-dimensional displays," Hum. Factors **34**, 255–265.

Durlach, N. I. (**1964**). "Note on the binaural masking level differences as a function of the interaural correlation of the masking noise," J. Acoust. Soc. Am. **36**, 1613–1617.

Egan, J. P., Carterette, E. C., and Thwing, E. J. (**1954**). "Some factors affecting multi-channel listening," J. Acoust. Soc. Am. **26**, 774–782.

Haas, H. (**1951**). "Uber den Einfluss eines Einfachechos auf die Horsamkeit von Sprache [On the influence of a single echo on the intelligibility of speech]," Acustica **1**, 49–58.

Hirsh, I. J. (**1950**). "The relation between localization and intelligibility," J. Acoust. Soc. Am. **22**, 196–200.

Koenig, W. (**1950**). "Subjective effects in binaural hearing," J. Acoust. Soc. Am. **22**, 61–62(L).

Koenig, A. H., Allen, J. B., and Berkley, D. A. (**1977**). "Determination of masking level differences in a reverberant environment," J. Acoust. Soc. Am. **61**, 1374–1376.

Kollmeier, B., and Peissig, J. (**1990**). "Speech intelligibility enhancement by interaural magnification," Acta Otolaryngol. Suppl. **469**, 215–223.

Kryter, K. D. (**1962**). "Methods for the calculation and use of the Articulation Index," J. Acoust. Soc. Am. **34**, 1689–1697.

Licklider, J. C. R. (**1948**). "The influence of interaural phase relations upon the masking of speech by white noise," J. Acoust. Soc. Am. **20**, 150–159.

MacKeith, N. W., and Coles, R. R. A. (**1971**). "Binaural advantages in hearing of speech," J. Laryngol. Otol. **85**, 213–232.

McKinley, R. L. (**1979**). "Voice communications research and evaluation system," *Proceedings IEEE, National Aerospace and Electronics Conference, NAECON 79*, Vol. 1, p. 212.

McKinley, R. L. (**1988**). "Concept and design of an auditory localization cue synthesizer," master's thesis, AFIT/GE/ENG/88D-29, Air Force Institute of Technology, Wright-Patterson AFB, OH.

McKinley, R. L., and Moore, T. J. (**1989**). "An information theory based model and measure of speech communication effectiveness in jamming," *Proceedings of Speech Tech '89* (Media Dimensions, New York), pp. 101–105.

Miller, G. A. (**1947**). "The masking of speech," Psychol. Bull. **44**, 105–129.

Moore, T. J. (**1981**). "Voice communication jamming research," Advisory Group for Aerospace Research and Development (AGARD) Conference Proceedings No. 311, Aural Communication in Aviation, **CP311**, 2-1–2-6.

Plomp, R., and Mimpen, A. M. (**1981**). "Effect of the orientation of the speaker's head and the azimuth of the noise source on speech reception thresholds for sentences," Acustica **48**, 325–328.

Ricard, G. L., and Meirs, S. L. (**1994**). "Intelligibility and localization of speech from virtual directions," Hum. Factors **36**, 120–128.

Schubert, E. D., and Schultz, M. C. (**1962**). "Some aspects of binaural signal selection," J. Acoust. Soc. Am. **34**, 844–849.

Spieth, W., Curtis, J. F., and Webster, J. C. (**1954**). "Responding to one of two simultaneous messages," J. Acoust. Soc. Am. **26**, 391–396.

Tobias, J. (**1972**). "Binaural processing of speech in light aircraft," FAA-AM-72-31, September.

Wallach, H., Newman, E.B., and Rosenzweig, M.R. (**1949**). "The precedence effect in sound localization," Am. J. Psychol. **62** (3), 315–336.

Webster, J. C., and Thompson, P. O. (**1954**). "Responding to both of two overlapping messages," J. Acoust. Soc. Am. **26**, 396–402.

Webster, J. C., and Solomon, L. N. (**1955**). "Effects of response complexity upon listening to competing messages," J. Acoust. Soc. Am. **27**, 1199–1203.
Yanagawa, H., Anazawa, T., and Itow, T. (**1990**). "Interaural correlation coefficients and their relation to the perception of subjective diffuseness," Acustica **71**, 230–232.
Yost, W. A., Sheft, S., and Dye, R. (**1994**). "Divided auditory attention with up to three sound sources: A cocktail party," J. Acoust. Soc. Am. **95**, 2916.
Zurek, P. M. (**1993**). "Binaural advantages and directional effects in speech intelligibility," in *Acoustical Factors Affecting Hearing Aid Performance*, edited by G. A. Studebaker and I. Hochberg (Allyn and Bacon, Boston), pp. 255–276.

Chapter 33

Binaural Performance in Listeners With Impaired Hearing: Aided and Unaided Results

Janet Koehnke and Joan Besing
University of South Alabama, Mobile

(Received June 1994; revised October 1994)

It is well known that listeners with impaired hearing have difficulty understanding speech in noise and localizing sound sources. These difficulties are believed to be due, at least in part, to binaural processing problems. This chapter describes selected results of two studies designed to determine the extent and the basis of these problems and to determine the amplification configuration most appropriate for alleviating these difficulties. The first set of experiments includes unaided measurements of N_0S_π detection and just noticeable differences in interaural time delay and interaural intensity difference. The second set of experiments includes measurements of binaural interaction (N_0S_π vs. N_0S_0), contralateral interference (N_uS_m vs. N_mS_m), and virtual localization with and without simulated monaural and binaural amplification. Data are presented for selected subjects from each study, with emphasis on cross-study comparison for listeners who participated in both studies. Overall, results indicate that the effects of hearing impairment on binaural processing and the benefits obtained from binaural amplification vary widely across listeners, even those with similar degree and configuration of hearing loss. It is remarkable that for the listeners participating in both studies, performance measured without amplification is quite similar to performance measured with amplification, particularly binaural amplification.

INTRODUCTION

Over the past 10 to 20 years there has been slow but steady progress in the study of binaural performance in listeners with hearing impairments. However, much remains to be studied in attempting to understand the effects of hearing impairment on binaural processing and in pursuing ways to remediate these effects. This chapter provides a brief summary of previous work and a description of selected results from two investigations designed to (1) evaluate the effects of hearing impairment on basic binaural performance and (2) assess the effects of amplification on binaural performance in listeners with impaired hearing. The results described in this chapter are particularly novel for two reasons. First, they represent a survey of binaural performance on a variety of binaural tasks, including basic detection and discrimination as well as the more complex task of localization. Second, much of the data presented in this chapter were obtained for *the same subjects* in both studies. Thus, the effects of monaural and binaural amplification on binaural performance can be evaluated for the same subjects with knowledge of their basic binaural detection and discrimination abilities.

An entire chapter might easily be written to provide a comprehensive review of the literature on binaural performance in listeners with impaired hearing. Here only a brief overview of the topic is presented, including references to a number of review papers that provide a much more thorough summary of the individual studies of hearing-impaired listeners' performance on various binaural tasks (Durlach, Thompson, and Colburn, 1981; Colburn, 1982; Colburn, Zurek, and Durlach, 1987; Colburn and Trahiotis, 1992). Also, there have been a number of studies of binaural performance with monaural and binaural amplification, which are discussed briefly (e.g., Dermody and Byrne, 1975; Markides, 1977, 1982; Hawkins and Yacullo, 1984; Festen and Plomp, 1986).

The majority of the studies of binaural performance in hearing-impaired listeners conducted in the last two decades have focused on basic psychophysical measures of masking level differences (MLDs), interaural time just noticeable differences (JNDs), and interaural intensity JNDs (e.g., Olsen, Noffsinger, and Carhart, 1976; Hawkins and Wightman, 1980; Hall and Fernandes, 1983; Hall, Tyler, and Fernandes, 1984; Smoski and Trahiotis, 1986; Staffel, Hall, Grose, and Pillsbury, 1990; Gabriel, Koehnke, and Colburn, 1992). A few have also included measures of localization or angle discrimination (Hausler, Colburn, and Marr, 1983; Abel, Birt, and McLean, 1978). Most of these studies have been limited to measuring performance on a single binaural task. However, at least a few of the studies have investigated binaural performance across a number of tasks for the same listeners (Hausler *et al.*, 1983; Hall *et al.*, 1984; Koehnke and Besing, 1991; Gabriel *et al.*, 1992).

Studies of binaural performance in listeners with impaired hearing have also included subjects with conductive hearing losses and sensorineural hearing losses, of cochlear and retrocochlear origin (e.g., Olsen *et al.*, 1976; Olsen and Noffsinger, 1976; Abel *et al.*, 1978; Hausler *et al.*, 1983; Gabriel *et al.*, 1992) although the majority have focused on sensorineural hearing loss of cochlear origin (e.g., Hawkins and Wightman, 1980; Hall and Fernandes, 1983; Hall et *al.*, 1984; Hall and Harvey, 1985; Smoski and Trahiotis, 1986; Staffel *et al.*, 1990; Koehnke and Besing, 1991). Most of these studies have included only subjects with bilateral, symmetrical hearing losses, but a few have included subjects with unilateral or asymmetrical hearing losses (e.g., Abel *et al.*, 1978; Hausler *et al.*, 1983; Wilson, Civitello, and Margolis, 1985). The present review describes results obtained from listeners with sensorineural hearing loss of cochlear origin, because almost all of the subjects in the investigations described in this chapter had this type of hearing impairment.

Although previous studies of binaural performance in listeners with impaired hearing have included a number of different procedures and stimuli with various parameters, there are some general results that are found in most, if not all, of these investigations. First, it is clear that overall performance of the listeners with impaired hearing is usually poorer than performance of the listeners with normal hearing (e.g., Hawkins and Wightman, 1980; Hausler *et al.*, 1983; Hall *et al.*, 1984; Smoski and Trahiotis, 1986; Koehnke and Besing, 1991; Gabriel *et al.*, 1992). However, as most of the authors point out, a wide range of performance is obtained from the hearing-impaired listeners for each of the binaural tasks measured in these investigations; some of the subjects have binaural performance comparable to normal hearing listeners, whereas others apparently have no ability to use the binaural information being presented to them. The majority of the subjects tested in these studies fall somewhere between these two extremes of binaural performance.

Another finding reported by a number of these investigators is the lack of any relationship between binaural performance and the audiogram (e.g., Hawkins and Wightman, 1980; Hausler *et al.*, 1983; Gabriel *et al.*, 1992). It is evident from these and other studies that two (or more) listeners with virtually the same degree, type, and configuration of hearing loss are likely to have very different binaural performance on one or more binaural tasks (e.g., Durlach *et al.*, 1981; Hausler *et al.*, 1983; Colburn *et al.*, 1987; Gabriel *et al.*, 1992). At the same time, similar binaural performance might be observed for a listener with a bilateral, moderate-to-severe, flat, sensorineural hearing loss and a listener with a unilateral, high-frequency sensorineural hearing loss. Hall *et al.* (1984) obtained monaural measures of intensity discrimination, temporal resolution, and frequency resolution, along with binaural measures of MLDs and interaural time discrimination. They failed to find any significant correlation between performance on the monaural and binaural tasks when the effects of threshold were partialled out.

One relationship was noted by Hausler *et al.* (1983) between monaural, audiometric speech discrimination scores and binaural performance on tests of interaural discrimination and horizontal and vertical minimum audible angle discrimination. Specifically, they found that for listeners with bilateral, symmetric, sensorineural hearing loss, those with good speech discrimination (91% or better) had essentially normal binaural performance, whereas those with poor speech discrimination (73% or poorer) had poor binaural performance.

Another result reported in a few of these studies that also points to the lack of any relationship between binaural performance and audiometric thresholds is the poor binaural performance often measured for low-frequency stimuli in listeners with high-frequency sensorineural hearing losses (Smoski and Trahiotis, 1986; Gabriel *et al.*, 1992). That is, many subjects with normal audiometric thresholds at 500 Hz have considerably poorer than normal binaural performance (N_0S_π detection and/or interaural discrimination) for 500-Hz stimuli.

Although performance on more than one binaural task was measured for the same listeners in some of these studies (Hausler *et al.*, 1983; Hall *et al.*, 1984; Koehnke and Besing, 1991; Gabriel *et al.*, 1992), and two studies included some binaural measurements with interaural level differences (Hausler *et al.*, 1983;

Wilson *et al.*, 1985), none of these studies investigated the possibility of compensating for internal interaural asymmetries in intensity or phase by externally imposing these interaural differences. Because the signals used in these studies were clearly at intensity levels well above the subjects' thresholds, poor binaural performance cannot be attributed to the audibility of the signals. It is possible, however, that performance on some or all of the binaural tasks measured in these studies was affected by internal interaural asymmetries in phase and/or level. Therefore, the first experiment described in this chapter includes a systematic investigation of binaural performance for the same subjects on a number of tasks when the external interaural differences are varied systematically.

The second experiment described in this chapter compares the effects of monaural and binaural amplification on the performance of listeners with sensorineural hearing loss on basic tests of signal detection in noise and the complex task of sound source localization. There have been a number of recent studies comparing monaural and binaural amplification, although almost all of them were limited to the measurement of performance on a single task. Most of them were concerned with the effects of amplification on speech discrimination in noise (e.g., Tonning, 1975; Cox and Bisset, 1984; Hawkins and Yacullo, 1984; Festen and Plomp, 1986), whereas a few included measures of localization (e.g., Dermody and Byrne, 1975; Markides, 1977; Byrne, Noble, and LePage, 1992). Reviews describing some of these and other, earlier, studies can be found in Markides (1977) and Libby (1980).

In general, these studies demonstrate a definite and substantial benefit from binaural amplification, at least in some listening situations, for subjects with bilateral, symmetrical, mild-to-moderate hearing losses, with either flat or sloping configurations. However, even with binaural amplification, localization and/or speech intelligibility in noise for the listeners with impaired hearing was often poorer than for normal hearing listeners (e.g., Dermody and Byrne, 1975; Tonning, 1975; Markides, 1977). With a few exceptions, speech intelligibility in noise was better with binaural hearing aids than with monaural hearing aids when the signal and noise sources were in different locations (e.g., Tonning, 1975; Cox and Bisset, 1984); however, with no background noise present, speech intelligibility was not usually improved with binaural hearing aids (e.g., Markides, 1977). In contrast, Festen and Plomp (1986) found an advantage with binaural amplification only when speech reception was limited by absolute threshold, not by external noise. It is important to note however, that in most of these studies (e.g., Markides, 1977; Cox and Bisset, 1984; Hawkins and Yacullo, 1984) the unaided ear was plugged and/or muffed in the monaural condition. Thus, what was actually being compared was monaural and binaural listening, not monaural and binaural amplification.

Binaural amplification often results in better localization performance than monaural amplification (Dermody and Byrne, 1975; Markides, 1977; Byrne *et al.*, 1992), especially for listeners with moderate and severe hearing impairments (Byrne *et al.*, 1992). However, listeners with mild hearing losses may localize as well, or even better, with monaural amplification as with binaural amplification (Byrne *et al.*, 1992). In one study, none of the subjects with bilateral, symmetrical hearing losses were able to localize as well as the normal-hearing listeners, and about half of the subjects had poorer localization with binaural aids than with monaural aids in some of the experimental conditions (Dermody and Byrne, 1975). In some instances, directional hearing with two hearing aids was found to be worse than without aids (Tonning, 1973; Dermody and Byrne, 1975), a result that is probably due to the elimination of pinna effects and the limited bandwidth of the hearing aids. Also, in most of these studies (as in the studies of speech intelligibility), one ear was plugged and/or muffed in the monaural conditions, making the results difficult to interpret for normal monaural hearing aid use (Tonning, 1973; Dermody and Byrne, 1975; Markides, 1977).

Although plugging and/or muffing one ear does create a monaural listening situation, it is certainly not a situation typically encountered by hearing-impaired listeners in their everyday experiences. On the other hand, although testing in a free field with one ear aided and the other ear open and unaided is more realistic, it is difficult to be certain of the characteristics of the signals that are actually reaching the listeners' aided and unaided ears. Therefore, in the study of binaural versus monaural amplification to be described here, all of the hearing aids, monaural and binaural, are simulated using digital signal processing techniques, and the signals are presented to the listeners through headphones. Thus, the characteristics of the signals presented to each ear in the different listening conditions are known.

Despite the limitations of some of these previous studies, they do provide important information concerning the effects of monaural and binaural amplification on the complex tasks of localization and speech intelligibility in noise. However, none of these investigations examined performance with monaural and binaural amplification across both basic and complex binaural tasks. According to the models of Levitt and Rabiner (1967) and Zurek (1993), improvements in speech intelligibility can be predicted by performance on binaural detection of tones in noise. Levitt and Rabiner (1967) demonstrated that binaural intelligibility level differences measured under headphones can be predicted from binaural detection thresholds. They assumed only that the masking level difference improved the signal-to-noise ratio at one ear in each frequency band, depending on the interaural phase and amplitude in each band. Zurek (1993) extended this model to predict the improvement in speech intelligibility in the free field. In addition to the assumption made by Levitt and Rabiner, Zurek assumed that the subject listens to the signal at the ear that, due to the head-shadow effect, has the better signal-to-noise ratio. This model predicts many of the available experimental data comparing monaural and binaural performance for listeners with normal hearing for various locations of the target and interference (Zurek, 1993). However, in most of the studies, basic binaural detection data and speech intelligibility data are not available for the same listeners with normal hearing, nor are there any such data available for listeners with hearing impairments.

Nonetheless, based on the models of Levitt and Rabiner (1967) and Zurek (1993), it is expected that speech intelligibility in noise and possibly also localization can be predicted using basic binaural detection measures of masking level differences and the head-shadow effect. Therefore, the second study described in this chapter was designed to compare various amplification configurations based on measures of both basic binaural detection and a more complex localization test.

I. EXPERIMENT 1: EFFECTS OF REFERENCE INTERAURAL DIFFERENCES ON BINAURAL PERFORMANCE

This study in its entirety includes a survey of binaural performance for 11 listeners with impaired hearing and 9 listeners with normal hearing. Here, we illustrate the major findings and present only a sample of the data. A complete description of the study can be found in Koehnke, Colburn, Hawley, and Culotta (1995). Some of these data can also be found in Koehnke and Colburn (1986), Passaro, Koehnke, and Colburn (1986), and Koehnke, Colburn, and Owen (1988).

In contrast to the majority of the studies of binaural performance of listeners with impaired hearing described earlier, this study was designed with several goals in mind: (1) to relate binaural performance across a number of tasks for individual hearing-impaired listeners, (2) to determine whether internal interaural imbalances (internal interaural delay or asymmetrical hearing loss) experienced by listeners with impaired hearing can be compensated for by certain combinations of externally imposed interaural differences, and (3) to compare binaural performance of listeners with impaired hearing both to listeners with normal hearing and to other listeners with impaired hearing.

A. Method

Two sets of tests were conducted for each subject, baseline tests and primary binaural tests. The baseline tests were done prior to the primary tests and were designed for two purposes. First, they served to characterize monaural processing of the subjects; second, they helped in establishing the base intensity levels[1] to be used in the primary binaural tests. There were six baseline tests: (1) quiet monaural thresholds, (2) discomfort levels, (3) monaural masked thresholds (N_mS_m), (4) monaural intensity JNDs, (5) equal loudness levels, and (6) centered-image levels.

The primary binaural tests described in this chapter include three tasks: N_0S_π detection thresholds, interaural intensity difference (IID) JNDs, and interaural time delay (ITD) JNDs. These measurements were made for a range of externally imposed reference interaural time delays and interaural intensity differences. The reference ITDs ranged from +600 μs to –600 μs, and the reference IIDs ranged from +24 dB to –46 dB. By convention, a positive IID or ITD indicates that the time delay and/or intensity difference favors the right ear; a negative IID or ITD indicates that the time delay and/or intensity difference favors the left ear. Thus, when both the reference IID and ITD have the same sign they are said to be *reinforcing*, and when they have the opposite sign they are *canceling*. A number of reference conditions were used when measuring binaural detection and discrimination for each subject, as indicated on the individual subject graphs. In the IID test, a 10-dB overall roving level was used to limit the ability of the subjects to use monaural intensity cues to complete the task. In the N_0S_π detection test, the reference ITD and IID were imposed so that the signal-to-noise ratio at each

[1]The base intensity refers to the level of the stimuli before any reference or test interaural intensity differences were introduced.

ear was the same, the noise alone was the same as the reference stimulus in the ITD and IID tests, and the largest ITDs and IIDs occurred when the target was present.

The stimuli for both the primary and baseline tests were ⅓-octave noise bands geometrically centered at 500 or 4000 Hz. In the masked detection tests, N_mS_m and N_0S_π, the target was a pure-tone centered in the ⅓-octave noise, which served as the masker. The base intensity for the stimuli was 75 dB SPL for listeners with normal hearing and with hearing impairments when their quiet thresholds for the target stimuli were 55 dB SPL or better. For subjects with thresholds poorer than 55 dB SPL, the base level was set at 20 dB above the threshold in the poorer ear. The levels actually used for the individual subjects are provided in the figures with their data.

A two-cue, two-interval, two-alternative, forced-choice procedure with feedback was used in all of the masked detection and interaural discrimination tests. A two-down, one-up adaptive tracking procedure (Levitt, 1971) was used, with each experimental run consisting of 14 reversals. Threshold was defined as the average level of the last 10 reversals. To ensure relatively stable performance, the interquartile range of the levels presented that constituted an acceptable run was constrained. If the interquartile range of the levels for all trials of the last ten reversals was greater than the difference between the levels one step above and below the threshold, the data were considered invalid and the experimental condition was tested again. For most conditions only one valid data point was obtained, but in a few conditions two valid runs were completed. A detailed description of the experimental procedures is provided in Koehnke *et al.* (1995).

Although the entire study included 11 subjects with impaired hearing and 9 subjects with normal hearing, the results presented here focus on 3 subjects with bilateral, symmetrical, moderate-to-severe, flat sensorineural hearing losses. All of them have had some hearing impairment since birth and all have worn bilateral hearing aids for at least 8 years. Selected results for 2 other subjects with unilateral, high-frequency, sensorineural hearing losses are also presented.

B. Results

Before examining the results for the individual subjects across tasks and reference interaural conditions, a sample of the results for all the subjects is presented for the diotic reference interaural condition, 0 μs, 0 dB, in Fig. 1 (for listeners with normal hearing this condition produces a sound image in the center of the head). These data provide results both for comparison of performance of listeners with normal and impaired hearing and for comparison between the present study and previous studies of listeners with impaired hearing.

Figure 1 includes data for three binaural tasks: N_0S_π detection (Fig. 1a), interaural intensity difference discrimination (Fig. 1b), and interaural time delay discrimination (Fig. 1c). Each panel includes data from the present study and from previous studies using the same ⅓-octave stimuli for listeners with normal hearing (NH) and impaired hearing (IH).

The data plotted in Fig. 1 illustrate two important points. First, for all three tasks, there is substantial overlap in the range of thresholds and JNDs for the listeners with normal and impaired hearing in this study. But clearly, the range of

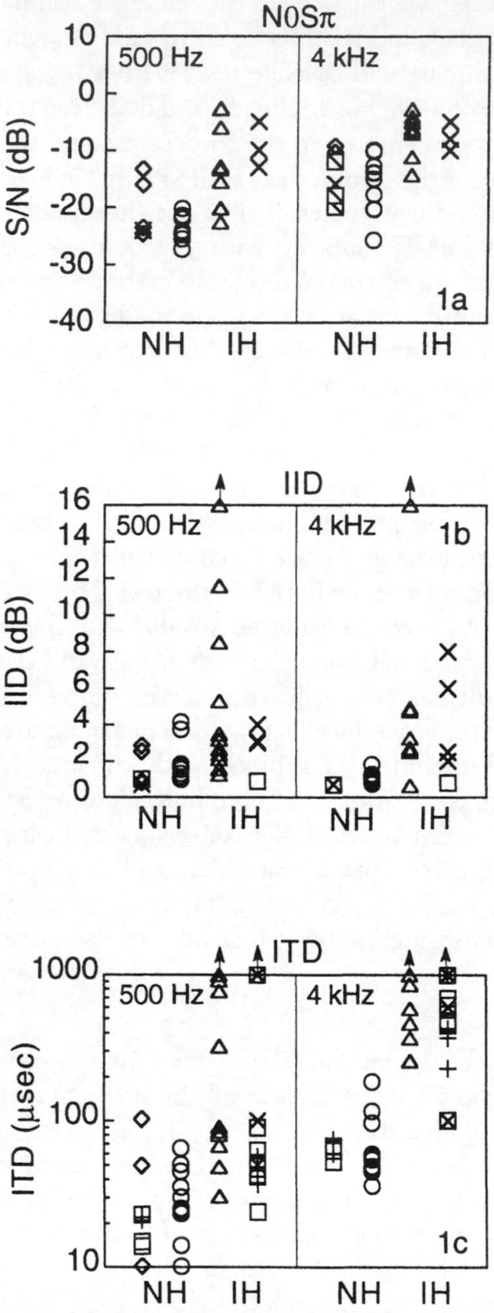

FIG. 1. Binaural detection and discrimination results for the diotic reference condition. Results for 11 hearing-impaired subjects (Δ) and 9 normal-hearing subjects (O) are in the center columns of each panel. The results from other studies are plotted in the outside columns with different symbols: ❑, Hawkins and Wightman (1980); ◇, Koehnke *et al.* (1986); +, Smoski and Trahiotis (1986); ⧅, Zurek and Durlach (1987); X, Gabriel *et al.* (1992)]. The top panel (a) is for N_0S_π detection, the middle panel (b) is for interaural intensity discrimination, and the bottom panel (c) is for interaural time discrimination. The right side of each panel shows the results for the 4000-Hz stimulus and the left side shows the results for the 500-Hz stimulus. For N_0S_π detection, the threshold signal-to-noise ratio in dB is plotted as a function of subject group. For interaural discrimination the interaural intensity JND (dB) and the interaural time delay JND (μs) are plotted as a function of subject group.

listeners with normal and impaired hearing in this study. But clearly, the range of performance for the listeners with impaired hearing is larger than the range for listeners with normal hearing, and in many cases the thresholds and JNDs of the hearing-impaired listeners are poorer than those of the normal-hearing subjects. Second, despite some differences between the procedures and stimulus levels used in this study and previous studies in the literature, the results are similar when the listeners with normal hearing are compared to each other and when the listeners with impaired hearing are compared to each other.

The results obtained for three subjects with moderate-to-severe, bilateral, symmetrical, sensorineural hearing losses are shown in Figs. 2, 3, and 4. Each figure includes the audiogram (panel a), IID JNDs (panel b), ITD JNDs (panel

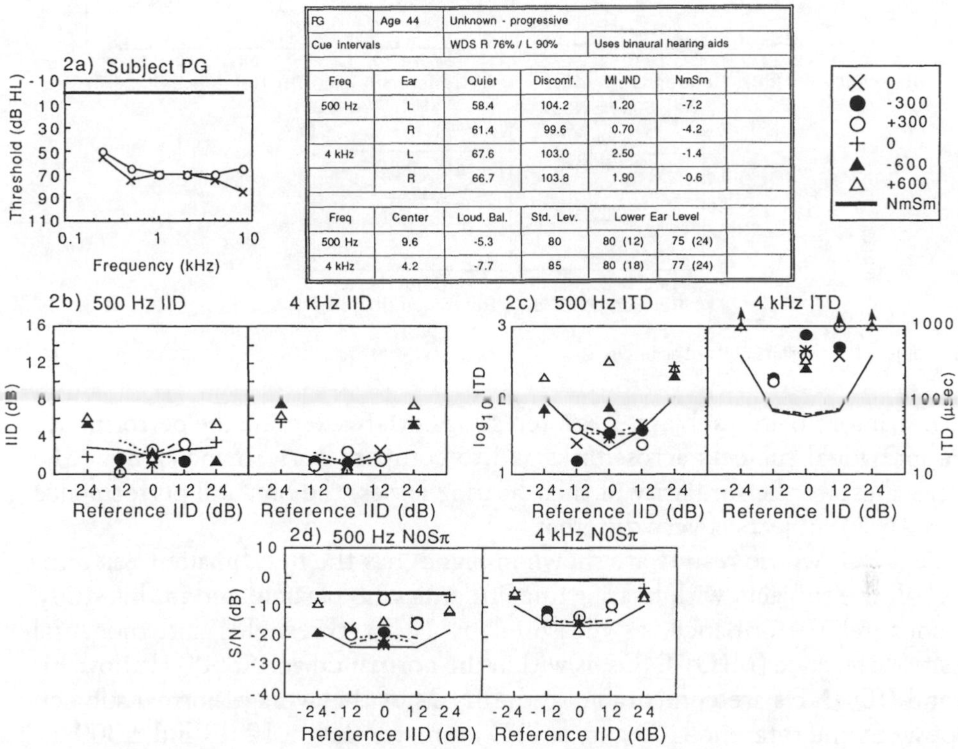

PG	Age 44	Unknown - progressive			
Cue intervals		WDS R 76% / L 90%		Uses binaural hearing aids	
Freq	Ear	Quiet	Discomf.	MI JND	NmSm
500 Hz	L	58.4	104.2	1.20	-7.2
	R	61.4	99.6	0.70	-4.2
4 kHz	L	67.6	103.0	2.50	-1.4
	R	66.7	103.8	1.90	-0.6
Freq	Center	Loud. Bal.	Std. Lev.	Lower Ear Level	
500 Hz	9.6	-5.3	80	80 (12)	75 (24)
4 kHz	4.2	-7.7	85	80 (18)	77 (24)

FIG. 2. Subject PG. The audiogram is in the upper left panel (a). The table includes information about the etiology of the loss, hearing aid use, and word discrimination scores at the top. In the center of the table are the quiet thresholds, discomfort thresholds, and monaural intensity difference JNDs for the 1/3-octave stimuli, and monaural masked thresholds for pure-tones masked by 1/3-octave noise for each ear. At the bottom of the table are the interaural differences needed for a centered image (Center) and for equal loudness (Loud Bal.), the base or standard intensity level (Std. Lev.) for each stimulus, and the lower ear level for each reference IID (in parentheses). IID and ITD JNDs are plotted in the two middle panels (b and c) as a function of the reference IID (dB), and N_0S_π threshold signal-to-noise ratios (S/N; dB) are plotted in the bottom panel (d). The straight, solid line in the N_0S_π panel indicates the average N_mS_m threshold. Data for the 500-Hz stimulus are on the left and data for the 4000-Hz stimulus are on the right side of each panel. Each symbol represents the data for a different reference ITD. If subjects were unable to discriminate at the maximum interaural differences presented, points are plotted at those values with an upward-pointing arrow. Each panel also includes a set of lines indicating symmetrically averaged results for the listeners with normal hearing. The solid, dotted, and dashed lines indicate 0 μs, –300 μs, and +300 μs ITD, respectively.

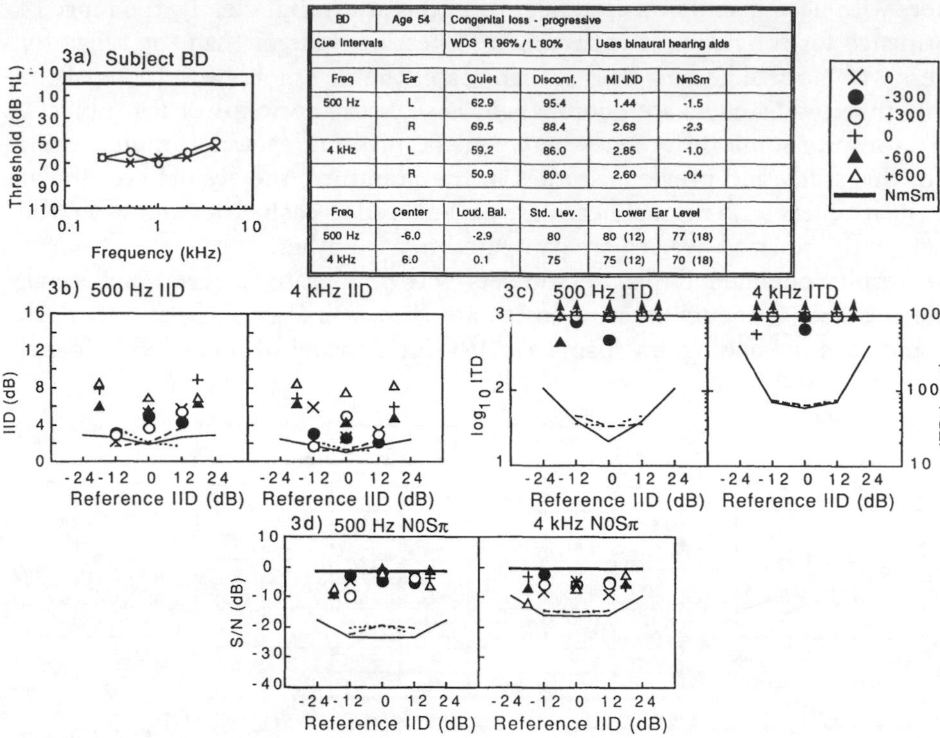

BD	Age 54	Congenital loss - progressive			
Cue Intervals		WDS R 96% / L 80%		Uses binaural hearing aids	
Freq	Ear	Quiet	Discomf.	MI JND	NmSm
500 Hz	L	62.9	95.4	1.44	-1.5
	R	69.5	88.4	2.68	-2.3
4 kHz	L	59.2	86.0	2.85	-1.0
	R	50.9	80.0	2.60	-0.4
Freq	Center	Loud. Bal.	Std. Lev.	Lower Ear Level	
500 Hz	-6.0	-2.9	80	80 (12)	77 (18)
4 kHz	6.0	0.1	75	75 (12)	70 (18)

FIG. 3. Subject BD. Results plotted as in Fig. 2.

single hearing-impaired subject. It is interesting both to examine the performance of the individual subjects across tasks and to compare performance among the subjects. Despite the similarity of their hearing losses, the binaural performance of these three subjects is very different.

Subject PG, whose results are shown in Fig. 2, has the best binaural performance of all the subjects with hearing impairments who participated in this study. His monaural performance, as measured by N_mS_m thresholds and monaural intensity difference (MID) JNDs, is within the normal range. At 500 Hz both his ITD and IID JNDs are comparable to the JNDs of the average normal subject, except when the reference IID and/or ITD is greater than ± 12 dB and ± 300 µs; then his performance is often considerably degraded relative to normal and relative to his own performance for the smaller reference interaural conditions. At 4000 Hz his ITD JNDs are much poorer than normal for all the reference conditions. PG's N_0S_π thresholds at 500 and 4000 Hz are generally normal or near the normal range, although in some conditions they are considerably poorer than normal. This subject is a clear example of someone who can have both IID discrimination and N_0S_π detection comparable to normal with ITD discrimination much poorer than normal. However, there is no consistent or systematic effect of reference interaural condition on PG's binaural performance for any of the tasks measured here. That is, binaural performance is not consistently improved or degraded across frequency or task by any specific reference interaural condition.

In contrast to PG, subject BD, whose results are shown in Fig. 3, has limited binaural abilities. Her monaural performance, however, is normal or just slightly poorer than normal for both MID discrimination and N_mS_m detection. BD's ITD JNDs were beyond the range of measurement in almost every condition at 500 and 4000 Hz. Her IID JNDs were also much larger than normal in all but a few conditions. Because the overall roving level used in these measurements was 10 dB, JNDs greater than 5 dB, which account for more than half of her JNDs, are likely due to monaural listening. Finally, her N_0S_π thresholds are close to the N_mS_m thresholds in many conditions (negligible MLDs), but in other conditions (such as +12 dB IID at 4000 Hz) BD has MLDs of 8 to 10 dB. Like PG, there is no reference interaural condition that systematically improves or degrades binaural performance for subject BD.

Subject AL, whose results are shown in Fig. 4, is not able to do any of the binaural tasks at either test frequency. Although it is common for individuals with hearing impairments to have varying degrees of binaural impairment, it is unusual, in our experience, for subjects to have no measurable binaural abilities on any binaural test. For the IID discrimination test, AL is unable to discriminate 10-dB differences at 500 Hz and 16-dB differences at 4000 Hz whether or not an overall roving level was used. She is able to discriminate monaural intensity differences, but even monaurally her JNDs are unusually large, roughly three times larger than

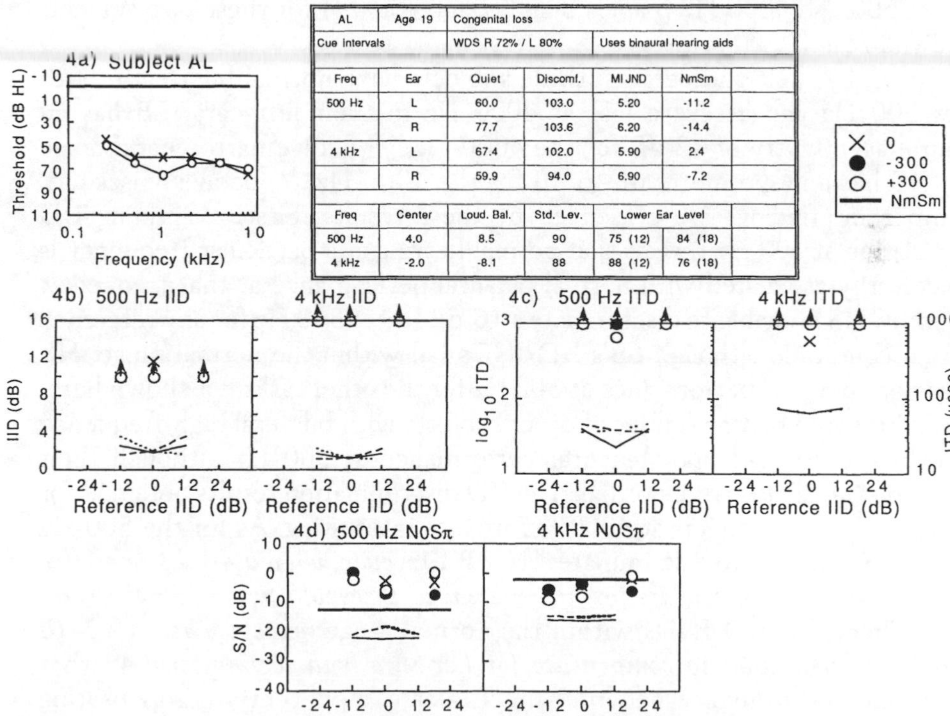

AL	Age 19	Congenital loss				
Cue intervals		WDS R 72% / L 80%		Uses binaural hearing aids		
Freq	Ear	Quiet	Discomf.	MI JND	NmSm	
500 Hz	L	60.0	103.0	5.20	-11.2	
	R	77.7	103.6	6.20	-14.4	
4 kHz	L	67.4	102.0	5.90	2.4	
	R	59.9	94.0	6.90	-7.2	
Freq	Center	Loud. Bal.	Std. Lev.	Lower Ear Level		
500 Hz	4.0	8.5	90	75 (12)	84 (18)	
4 kHz	-2.0	-8.1	88	88 (12)	76 (18)	

FIG. 4. Subject AL. Results plotted as in Fig. 2.

those of either PG or BD. In contrast to this, AL's monaural masked thresholds were at least as good, or slightly better than, the normal-hearing listeners' N_mS_m thresholds and better than the other hearing-impaired subjects' monaural masked thresholds. No combination of reference IID and ITD improves her binaural performance.

The results of these three subjects clearly demonstrate (1) the range of binaural performance that can be found in listeners with hearing impairments and (2) that binaural performance is not apparently related to monaural performance as measured by the audiogram or by measures of MID JNDs or monaural masked thresholds. Also evident in these results is the lack of any systematic or consistent effect of reference IID and/or ITD. Apparently internal interaural differences cannot be compensated for by simply introducing external interaural differences.

The three subjects just discussed have bilateral, symmetrical hearing losses, and their hearing losses span the audiometric frequencies (including the test stimulus frequencies). Thus, neither the effect of an asymmetrical hearing loss nor the effect of normal hearing at some frequencies on binaural performance can be ascertained from their data. However, two of the other subjects who participated in this study have high-frequency, unilateral sensorineural hearing losses. Their results are quite interesting and provide an opportunity to examine (1) the effect of an asymmetrical hearing loss on binaural performance and (2) binaural performance in a frequency region where audiometric thresholds in both ears are within the normal range. The audiograms (panels a and d) and IID discrimination results at 500 and 4000 Hz (panels b and c, and e and f) for these two subjects are shown in Fig. 5.

As shown by their audiograms, these subjects have normal hearing in both ears at 500 Hz and a severe loss at 4000 Hz in their left ears. LB has an interaural asymmetry of 42 dB for the 4000-Hz, 1/3-octave narrowband noise signal; HS has an asymmetry of 46 dB for the 4000-Hz, 1/3-octave noiseband. Two important findings are evidenced by these results. First, examining IID discrimination at 500 Hz reveals that normal hearing at a particular frequency is not necessarily associated with normal binaural performance at that frequency. Specifically, HS is unable to discriminate a 16-dB IID at 500 Hz for any reference interaural condition, although LB's IID JNDs fall within the normal range. HS also has poor binaural performance at 500 Hz for the other tasks not shown here. It should be noted that a number of other subjects with bilateral high-frequency hearing losses also had poor binaural performance at 500 Hz although their audiometric thresholds were normal. The IID discrimination results obtained for these unilateral loss subjects at 4000 Hz are also interesting. As for the 500-Hz stimulus, HS is unable to discriminate a 16-dB IID, *even when a 46 dB reference IID was present to compensate for his interaural threshold asymmetry!* LB on the other hand has IID JNDs within the normal range, *except when a 42-dB reference IID was used to compensate for her threshold asymmetry!* In that condition her performance becomes much worse. Apparently compensating for an internal threshold asymmetry with an external IID does not benefit either of these subjects.

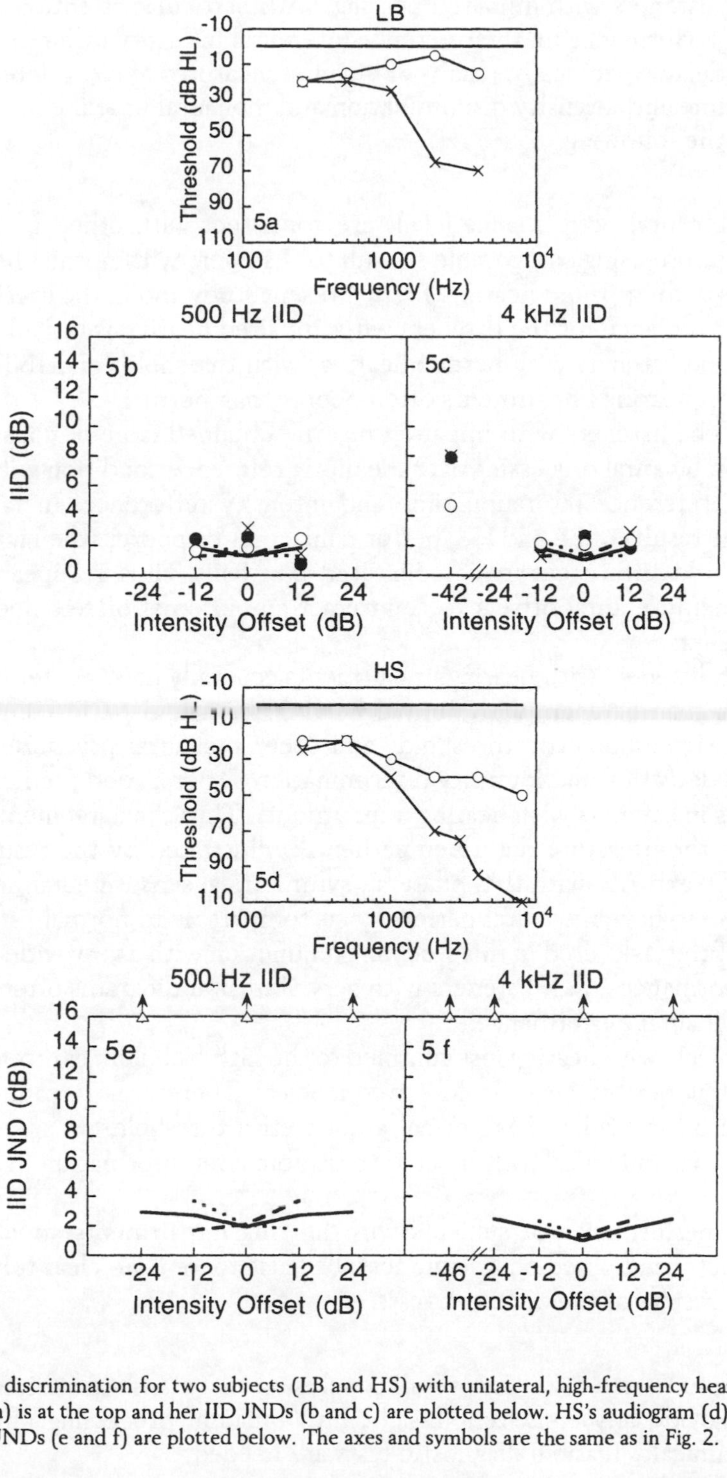

FIG. 5. IID discrimination for two subjects (LB and HS) with unilateral, high-frequency hearing losses. LB's audiogram (a) is at the top and her IID JNDs (b and c) are plotted below. HS's audiogram (d) is in the center and his IID JNDs (e and f) are plotted below. The axes and symbols are the same as in Fig. 2.

C. Summary of experiment 1

This study illustrates a number of interesting findings concerning the binaural performance of listeners with impaired hearing, with particular attention to the dependence of performance on the reference interaural intensity difference and interaural time delay. Specifically, results of binaural measures of N_0S_π detection, and interaural time and intensity discrimination and monaural baseline measurements indicate the following:

(1) Overall binaural performance levels are consistent with other investigations in the literature using comparable stimuli for listeners with normal hearing and for listeners with impaired hearing. In the present study and in the literature, the range of performance for the listeners with impaired hearing is considerably wider than for the listeners with normal hearing, with thresholds and JNDs for the listeners with hearing impairments often poorer than normal.

(2) None of the listeners with impaired hearing obtained large or consistent improvements in binaural processing over the diotic reference condition with *any* combination of reference interaural time and intensity difference. In fact, as illustrated by the results of LB and HS, performance may be poorer when internal interaural threshold differences are compensated externally. Thus, it appears that imposing external interaural offsets to counteract any internal offsets does not assist these listeners.

(3) Although listeners with hearing impairments generally have poorer binaural performance than listeners with normal hearing, monaural performance, as measured by basic audiometric thresholds and other monaural psychophysical tests of masked detection and intensity discrimination, is not a good predictor of binaural abilities in listeners with hearing impairments. This is in agreement with other studies in the literature described earlier. As illustrated by the results of subjects PG, BD, and AL, with flat, bilateral, symmetrical sensorineural hearing loss, it is possible to have monaural performance comparable to normal listeners on some or all of the tasks used in this study in conjunction with a very wide range of binaural performance. Also, listeners with very similar audiograms often have very different binaural performance.

(4) Even subjects with hearing loss confined to the high frequencies often have impaired binaural performance at low frequencies. Therefore, it cannot be assumed that if an individual has normal audiometric thresholds in some frequency regions that individual will be able to use binaural information in those regions.

(5) Binaural performance of subjects with hearing impairments apparently cannot be characterized based on a single test, because there is no clear relationship among the results of the different tests.

All of these results lead us to the overall conclusion that standard audiometric tests do not provide any consistent insight into binaural processing abilities. Clearly, other clinically feasible diagnostic tests are needed.

II. EXPERIMENT 2: EFFECTS OF AMPLIFICATION ON BINAURAL PERFORMANCE

This is an ongoing study, which to date includes measurements of binaural detection, localization, and speech intelligibility for 14 listeners with hearing impairments and 4 listeners with normal hearing. In this chapter, only results for 3 subjects on a subset of these binaural tests are presented. These subjects were selected because they are the same individuals whose results for the study on the effects of reference interaural differences on binaural performance were presented earlier in the chapter. A complete description of the procedures and the results of this study of the effects of amplification on binaural performance can be found in Koehnke, Besing, and Zurek (1996). Some of the results can also be found in Koehnke and Zurek (1990) and Koehnke, Besing, Goulet, Allard, and Zurek (1992).

Although the binaural survey study was still underway when this project began, it was already clear that the binaural processing ability of individuals with hearing impairments could not be predicted based on audiometric results and that no one test of binaural performance could be used to characterize overall binaural ability. Thus, with these facts in mind, the study of the effects of amplification on binaural performance was designed to investigate the following: (1) performance of listeners with hearing impairments using different simulated amplification configurations on basic binaural detection tests and more complex binaural tasks encountered in everyday activities, (2) the effectiveness of binaural amplification fit to each ear individually (best monaural) and to both ears simultaneously (true binaural), and (3) the relationship between performance on the basic binaural detection tests and more complex binaural tasks, such as localization.

A. Method

A three-step measurement protocol was used to obtain the results presented here. First, individual frequency-gain characteristics (FGCs) were obtained for each subject. Then, using these FGCs, performance was measured for two binaural detection tests. Finally, localization ability was measured, again using the individual FGCs. Each step is described here briefly.

Frequency-gain characteristics were measured using an octaves-at-most-comfortable-loudness (OMCL) procedure (DeGennaro, 1982). In this procedure, the level of octave bands of speech is adjusted to the most comfortable loudness (MCL) level. There are three listening conditions: monaural right, monaural left, and binaural. In the first two, the level is adjusted in one ear with the level in the nonadjusted ear presented at a normal conversational level. In the binaural condition, the level is adjusted in each ear individually, but can be adjusted in both ears simultaneously. After obtaining MCLs for the individual octave bands, the bands are combined (keeping the relative levels set according to the OMCL results), and the overall level is adjusted to the MCL for each condition. Five different amplification configurations are constructed based on these FGCs: (1) unaided (UA), (2) monaural right (MR), (3) monaural left (ML), (4) combined monaural (CM), and (5) true binaural (BN). The resulting frequency gain characteristic for each ear in each amplification condition is shown in Table I.

Table I. Amplification Configurations for Binaural Detection and Localization

Amplification condition	Frequecy Gain Characteristic	
	Right ear	Left ear
Unaided (UA)	No gain	No gain
Monaural right (MR)	OMCL (R)	No gain
monaural left (ML)	No gain	OMCL (L)
Monaural right + left (CM)	OMCL (R)	OMCL (L)
Binaural (BN)	OMCL (BR)	OMCL (BL)

The second step in the protocol includes two binaural detection tests, MLDs and contralateral interference (CLIF). Both of these tests are included in order to obtain measures of binaural interaction ability (MLD) and the ability to take advantage of the head-shadow effect and listen with the more favorably placed ear (CLIF). Although MLDs have been measured in a number of studies of listeners with normal hearing and impaired hearing (e.g., Durlach and Colburn, 1978; Durlach *et al.*, 1981), CLIF has not been measured previously for listeners with impaired hearing. However, these two tests were included in this study because both binaural interaction and the head-shadow effect have been shown to underlie the overall binaural advantage (e.g., Markides, 1977; Byrne, 1980).

For both tests, the targets are octave bands of speech-spectrum noise centered at 175, 350, 700, 1400, 2800, and 5600 Hz. The masker is a wideband speech spectrum noise. All these tests are conducted under headphones, with the amplification configurations simulated using digital filters to process the stimuli for each subject for each condition. The masker at the input to the simulated hearing aids is at the same conversational level of 70 dB SPL used in the OMCL procedure. An adaptive, two-interval, two-alternative, forced-choice procedure with feedback (Levitt, 1971) was used for these measurements.

To obtain MLDs, N_0S_0 and N_0S_π thresholds were measured for each of the six octave-band targets for all five amplification configurations. To determine whether subjects could take advantage of the head-shadow effect and ignore CLIF, monaural and dichotic listening conditions were also compared. Specifically, monaural (N_RS_R and N_LS_L) and dichotic (N_uS_R and N_uS_L) masked detection thresholds were measured for the same octave-band targets used to measure MLDs. CLIF was measured for the binaural amplification condition with a 20-dB interaural level imbalance imposed by raising the overall level in the contralateral ear 10 dB and lowering the overall level in the signal ear 10 dB. This always resulted in a higher intensity masker in the contralateral ear than the signal ear. The exact interaural level difference for each subject varied depending on the gain selected for each ear in the binaural amplification configuration with the OMCL procedure.

The final step in the measurement protocol to be described here was the localization test. Localization was measured in the horizontal plane in both an anechoic and reverberant environment for each of the amplification configurations. There were nine sources, 22.5° apart, located from –90° (at the left ear) to

+90° (at the right ear). The stimuli were three-word phrases such as "mark the spot." Like the detection measurements, localization was tested under earphones. The amplification configurations were simulated using digital filters and the listening environments were simulated by convolving impulse responses obtained from KEMAR (Burkhard and Sachs, 1975) for each of the source locations in both environments with the speech stimuli. A single-interval procedure was used in which the task of the subject was to identify the source location by selecting a number from 1 through 9 on the computer keyboard. A complete description of the localization test procedure can be found in Besing and Koehnke (1995).

B. Results

Binaural detection and localization data for four listeners with normal hearing are shown in Fig. 6. Average results for the four subjects are plotted since performance of all the subjects was similar. For the MLD (Fig. 6a) and localization (Fig. 6c) tests, results are shown for all five amplification configurations. For the CLIF test (Fig. 6b), data are plotted only for a single condition in which the subjects listened through their binaural amplification with the level of the masker in the contralateral ear raised 10 dB and the level of the masker in the signal ear lowered 10 dB. Thus, the level of the masker in the nonsignal ear was at least 20 dB more intense than in the signal ear. CLIF was measured with the right ear receiving the signal (Int Left +) and with the left ear receiving the signal (Int Right +).

Although they are not shown in this figure, the FGCs for the subjects with normal hearing were very similar to one another and were also similar across all the amplification conditions. As expected, these subjects selected overall levels near the normal conversational speech level of 70 dB SPL, but tended to increase the level in the highest and lowest frequency bands relative to the long-term speech spectrum representative of the unaided condition.

The MLDs shown in Fig. 6a indicate, not surprisingly, that performance of the subjects with normal hearing is not affected by amplification configuration. That is, regardless of amplification, these subjects have larger MLDs for the low frequency signals, and smaller MLDs for the high frequency signals. These results are consistent with other studies measuring MLDs for similar signals and maskers but with no amplification (e.g., Gabriel *et al.*, 1992; Zurek and Durlach, 1987; Koehnke, Colburn, and Durlach, 1986; Durlach and Colburn, 1978). The results of the CLIF test for these subjects (Fig. 6b) show no large or consistent interference in the presence of a high-level noise in the nonsignal ear. This indicates that the normal listeners are able to take advantage of the head-shadow effect and listen with the more-favorably-placed ear. Localization data (Fig. 6c) for the subjects with normal hearing reveals no effect of listening environment and no effect of amplification configuration. Average root mean square (rms) errors are 10° to 20° (less than the 22.5° separating the sources) for all conditions.

The effects of amplification on binaural performance of three subjects with bilateral, symmetrical, flat, moderate-to-severe, sensorineural hearing losses can be seen in Figs. 7, 8, and 9. These are the same subjects whose results were shown

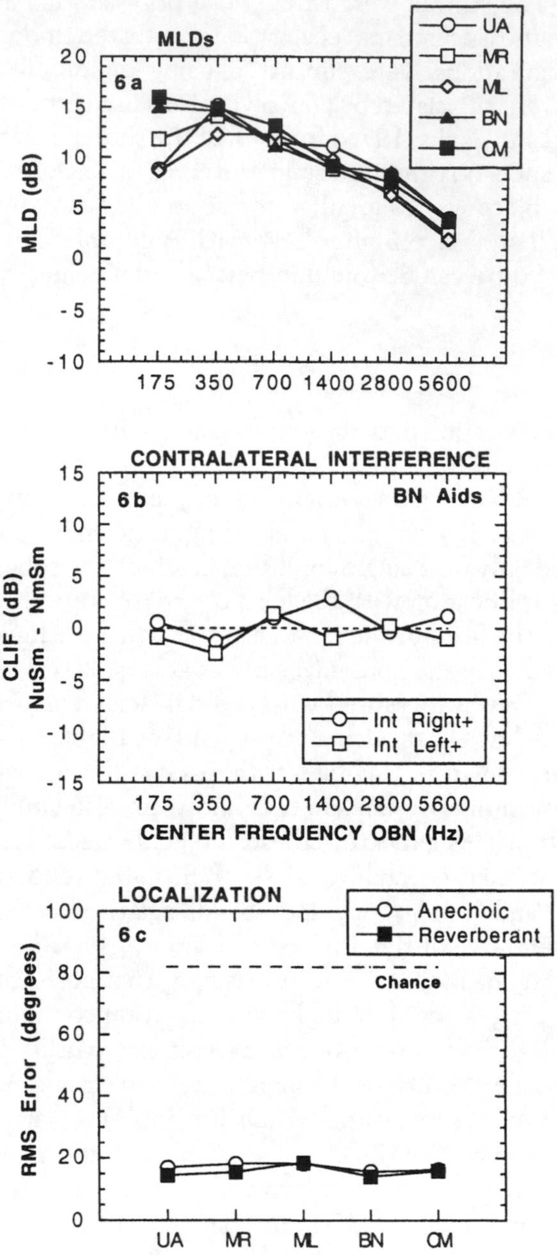

FIG. 6. Binaural performance for listeners with normal hearing. Average MLDs in dB for 4 subjects are plotted as a function of the center frequency of the octave-band noise signal (panel 6a). Each amplification condition is represented by a different symbol: O, UA; ❑, MR; ◇, ML; ▲, BN; ■, CM. Contralateral interference (CLIF) in dB is plotted as a function of the center frequency of the octave-band noise signal for the binaural amplification condition (b). Circles represent CLIF when the interference in the right ear is at least 20 dB more intense than the left, and squares represent CLIF when the left ear interference is at least 20 dB more intense than the right. The dashed line is plotted at zero; CLIF greater than 0 indicates the subject is not able to listen with the more favorably placed ear. The rms localization error in degrees is plotted as a function of the amplification configuration (c). The dashed line plotted at 82° indicates the rms error corresponding to chance performance. Performance in the anechoic environment is indicated by the open circles, and performance in the reverberant environment is indicated by the filled squares.

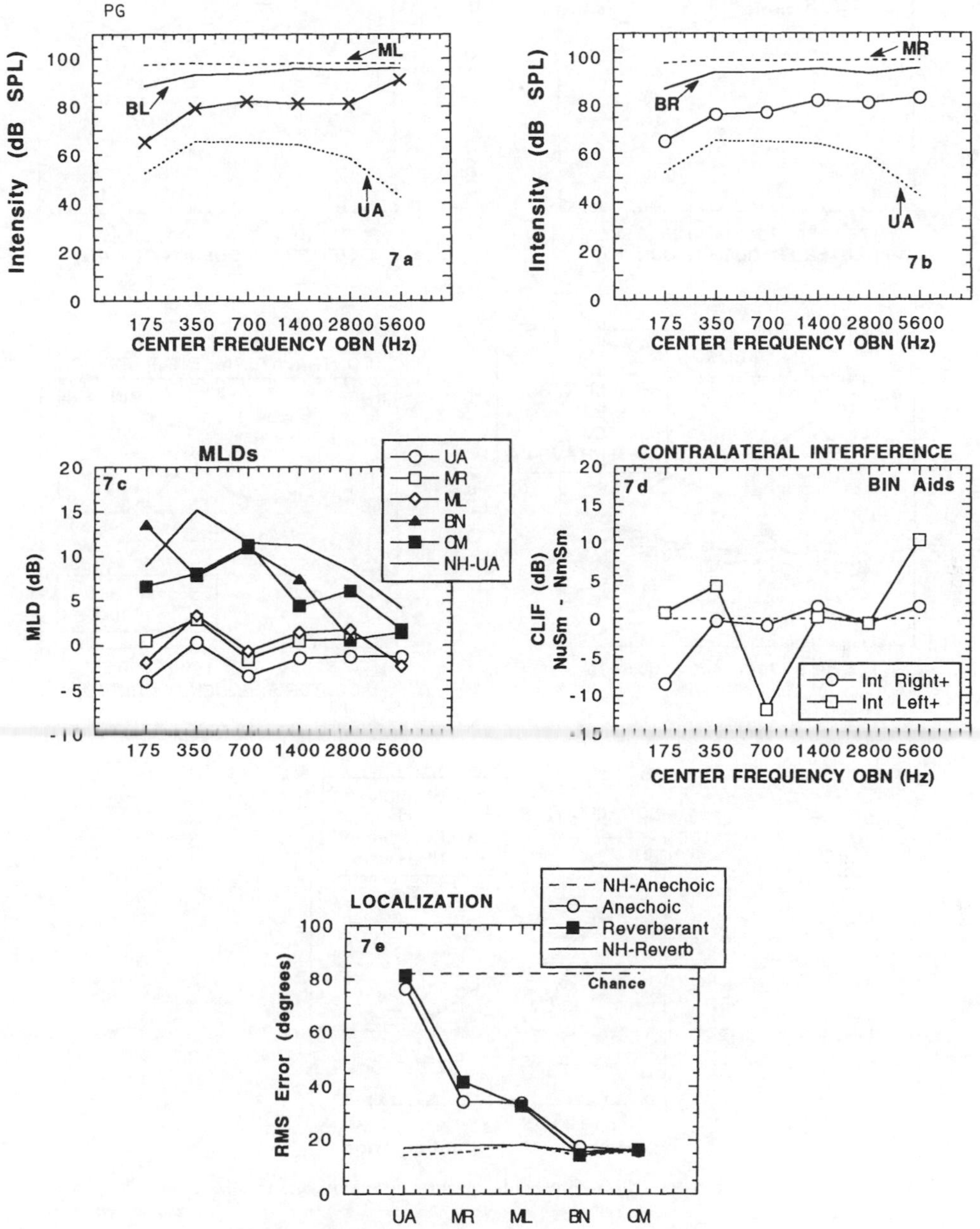

FIG. 7. Subject PG. The top two panels (a and b) include thresholds and frequency characteristics for the different amplification configurations as a function of the center frequency of the octave-band signals. Right ear information is plotted in the right panel (O's indicate thresholds) and left ear information in the left panel (X's indicate thresholds). The middle panels (c and d) indicate results for the MLD and CLIF tests and are plotted as in Fig. 6. In the MLD panel, the average MLDs for the listeners with normal hearing for the unaided (UA) condition are indicated by the solid line. Localization data are plotted at the bottom (e) as in Fig. 6, with the average results for the listeners with normal hearing for the anechoic and reverberant conditions indicated by the dashed and solid lines, respectively.

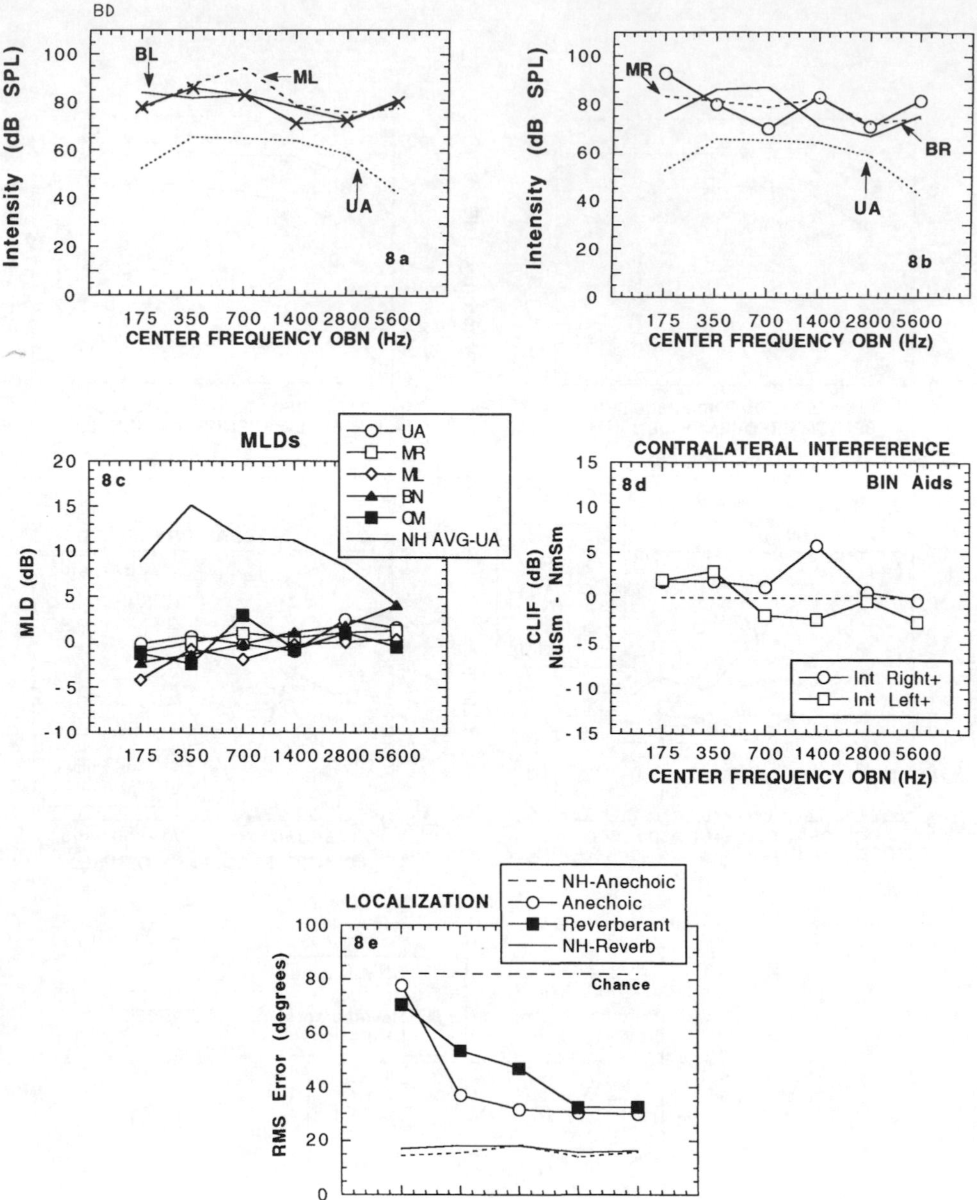

FIG. 8. Subject BD. Frequency characteristics, thresholds, binaural detection, and localization results plotted as in Fig. 7.

in Figs. 2, 3, and 4 for binaural detection and discrimination as a function of the reference interaural time and intensity. Recall that these subjects were binaural hearing aids users at the time of these experiments and had worn two hearing aids for at least 8 years. Despite the similarity of their hearing losses, these figures indicate very different binaural performance for these three subjects with amplification. Results are shown for the MLD and CLIF detection tests and for the localization test. These figures also show the subjects' thresholds for the octave-band noise signals and the frequency characteristics they chose for the different amplification configurations.

Overall, these figures show a wide range of performance for the tasks measured here. One of the subjects obtains large and consistent benefit from binaural amplification, the second shows some benefit for some tasks and conditions, and the third shows no measurable benefit from binaural amplification.

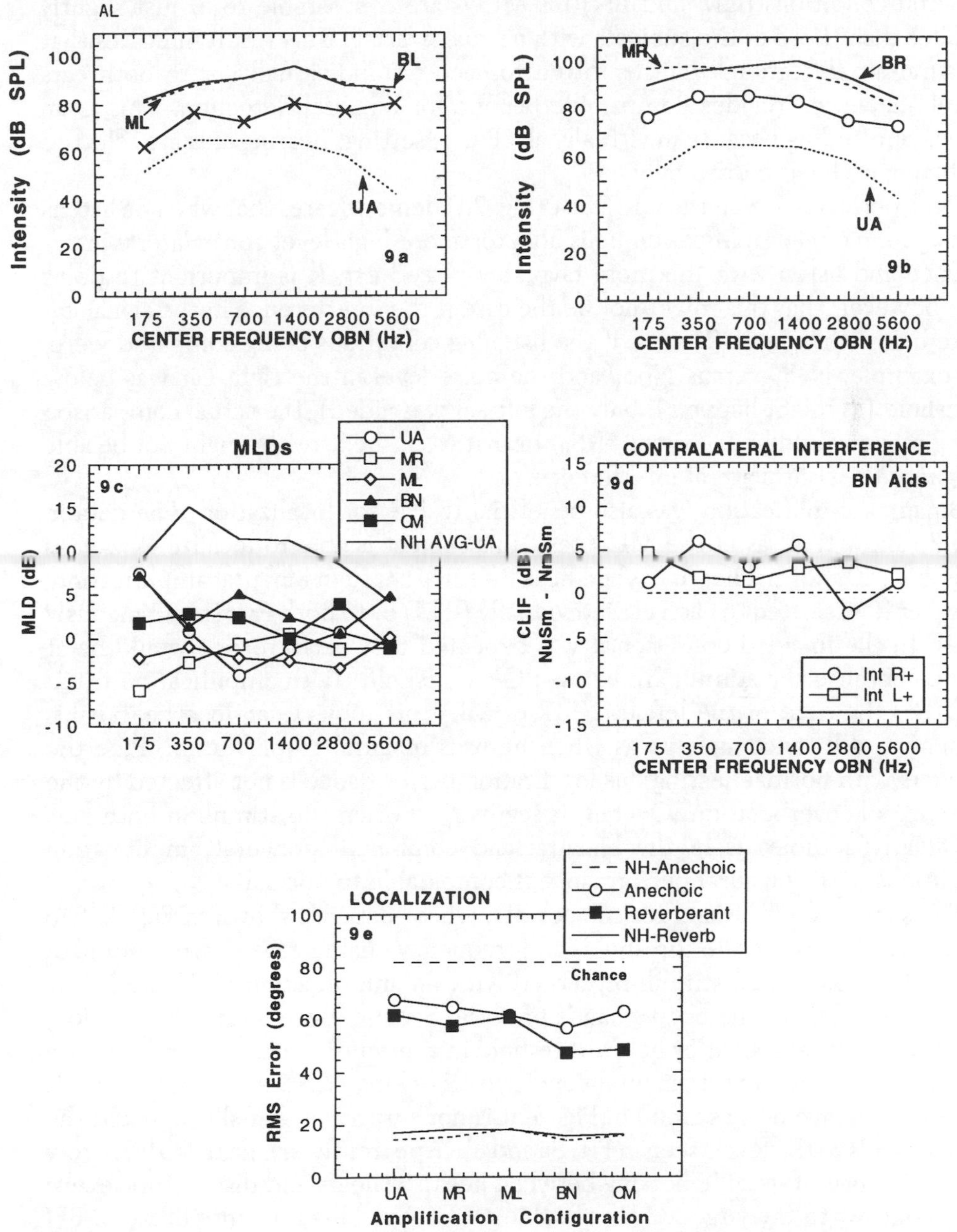

FIG. 9. Subject AL. Frequency characteristics, thresholds, binaural detection, and localization results plotted as in Fig. 7.

Looking first at the thresholds and frequency characteristics for subject PG in Fig. 7a and 7b, it is immediately apparent that, due to the severity of his hearing loss, stimuli presented in the unaided condition are not audible to him. Thus, it is not surprising that his binaural performance in this condition is extremely poor. However, PG does appear to obtain significant benefit from binaural amplification, as evidenced by the results of the MLD (Fig. 7c) and localization (Fig. 7e) tests. In the monaural and unaided conditions he has no MLDs, but in both binaural conditions (CM and BN) his MLDs are comparable to or just slightly smaller than those of the subjects with normal hearing. This result indicates that binaural amplification, whether fitted to each ear individually or to both ears simultaneously, provides comparable benefit for binaural detection. This is an important finding because in virtually all clinical settings hearing aids are selected by fitting each ear individually.

PG's performance on the CLIF test (Fig. 7d) demonstrates that when he listens through binaural amplification he is able to ignore high-level contralateral interference and listen with the more-favorably-placed ear. It is important to point out, however, that this might not be the case if the interference in the signal ear were below threshold. That is, if the listening conditions being compared were, for example, N_RS_R versus N_US_R and the noise level in the right ear was below threshold (as might happen if only the left ear was aided), the actual comparison being made would be S_R versus N_LS_R. In that case, the listener might not be able to ignore the contralateral interference.

Binaural amplification was also beneficial to PG for localization. The data in Fig. 7e show that, as in the MLD test, this subject is able to localize as well as listeners with normal hearing when he is listening through binaural amplification, whether it was fitted to each ear individually (CM) or to both ears simultaneously (BN). In the unaided condition it was expected that performance would be at chance because the stimuli are below PG's threshold. With amplification fitted to either the right or the left ear (MR or ML) this subject can localize, but his errors are still twice as large as when he uses binaural amplification. Like the listeners with normal hearing, his localization performance is not affected by the presence of reverberation. Overall, it seems that when the stimuli in both ears are clearly audible, as in the binaural and combined monaural amplification conditions, PG's binaural performance is comparable to normal.

The same cannot be said for subject BD, whose data are shown in Fig. 8. Two things are clear when the thresholds and frequency characteristics are examined. First, like subject PG, stimuli presented with no amplification (UA) are below BD's thresholds for the octave bands of noise. Second, even with amplification, the stimulus levels fall at or below threshold in a number of octave bands in both ears in the monaural and binaural conditions. Looking at BD's discomfort levels for the $^1/_3$-octave noise stimuli in Fig. 3, it is not surprising that she adjusted the octave bands to the levels seen in Fig. 8a and 8b. Apparently, she has a fairly narrow dynamic range of useable hearing between her thresholds and discomfort levels.

In contrast to the large MLDs of subject PG with binaural amplification, BD has no MLDs for any amplification configuration (Fig. 8c). Perhaps this is because the masker level is at or even below her threshold in the individual octave bands.

In other words, the masker level may not be sufficient to show a release from masking. BD's CLIF results (Fig. 8d) indicate that she may be able to take advantage of the head-shadow effect. That is, BD experiences little or no interference with her binaural amplification.

This subject also obtains some benefit in localization with binaural amplification (Fig. 8e), although even in the best case her errors are still twice as large as normal. Like PG, she obtains some benefit with monaural amplification, but more benefit with binaural amplification. BD also has comparable performance with binaural amplification whether it is fitted to each ear individually (CM) or to both ears simultaneously (BN). So, although BD does not obtain consistent binaural benefit with binaural amplification, and does not generally have binaural performance comparable to normal, she does obtain a measurable benefit from binaural amplification for some tasks.

In contrast to both of the subjects just described, AL, whose data are shown in Fig. 9, demonstrates no measurable benefit to binaural performance with monaural or binaural amplification. Although her frequency characteristics and thresholds indicate that the stimuli are well above threshold in all the aided conditions, she has very small (2–4 dB) or no MLDs for all the amplification conditions (Fig. 9c). Unlike subjects PG and BD, she also experiences consistent contralateral interference in the CLIF test (Fig. 9d), indicating that she cannot listen with the more-favorably-placed ear when using binaural amplification. Finally, not even AL's localization performance (Fig. 9e) is appreciably improved with amplification. The only condition in which she shows any improvement at all is with binaural amplification in the reverberant condition where she shows a small improvement. Thus, it would appear that, at least for the tasks measured in this experiment, binaural amplification is not beneficial to AL.

C. Summary of experiment 2

The aided and unaided measurements of these three subjects with bilateral, symmetrical, moderate-to-severe sensorineural hearing loss reveal a number of interesting findings. In particular, the results of binaural detection and localization tests with monaural and binaural amplification indicate the following:

(1) Subjects with bilateral, sensorineural hearing loss generally perform more poorly than subjects with normal hearing, especially without amplification, and exhibit greater variability than subjects with normal hearing.

(2) The audiogram is not a good predictor of binaural abilities, because these three listeners with similar audiometric results show very different benefits to binaural processing from amplification.

(3) Based on this limited set of results, performance with binaural amplification on binaural detection and localization tests is comparable whether the amplification is fitted to each ear individually, as in the CM condition, or to both ears simultaneously, as in the BN condition.

(4) There is apparently not a simple relationship between binaural detection and localization for these subjects, because good performance on one of the binaural detection tests is not necessarily associated with good performance on the other binaural tests.

III. COMPARISON BETWEEN STUDIES

Each of these studies alone reveals interesting results concerning binaural performance in listeners with impaired hearing and the effects of amplification on binaural performance of listeners with impaired hearing. However, of greater interest for the purpose of this chapter is the comparison of performance of the three subjects who participated in both experiments. Results of monaural and binaural tests, with and without amplification, have been presented for three listeners with bilateral, symmetrical, moderate to severe sensorineural hearing loss. These listeners represent a wide range of binaural performance as evidenced by their data from both of these studies.

It is remarkable that *for each of the three subjects*, performance measured without amplification on basic tests of interaural discrimination and binaural detection is quite similar to performance measured with amplification, particularly binaural amplification, on basic tests of binaural detection and a more complex test of localization. Although the stimuli used in the unaided experiments were ⅓-octave noise bands compared to octave-band and wide-band stimuli used in the aided experiments, and the tests were all different except for binaural detection, the overall results obtained for these subjects across experiments are strikingly similar. One subject, PG (see Figs. 2 and 7), has normal or near-normal binaural performance on most of the basic tests of interaural discrimination and binaural detection; this subject also receives consistent and substantial benefit from binaural amplification for both binaural detection and localization tasks. This is despite the fact that for PG the stimulus levels used in the aided experiments were about 10 or 15 dB higher than the levels used in the unaided experiments.[2] Another subject, BD (see Figs. 3 and 8), is able to perform some basic binaural tasks, but certainly does not have the same sensitivity as normal listeners. When provided with binaural amplification her localization ability improves considerably relative to her unaided performance, and she is able to take advantage of the head-shadow effect (measured with the CLIF test), although her N_0S_π detection is still very poor. Unlike subject PG, however, BD's overall stimulus levels in the aided experiments are not consistently or appreciably higher than the stimulus levels in the unaided experiments. It is likely that her sensitivity to interaural intensity differences, as measured in the first experiment, is the basis for her ability to localize reasonably well and to take advantage of the head-shadow effect. The third subject, AL (see Figs. 4 and 9), is unable to do any of the basic binaural tasks in any of the experimental conditions; she also receives no measurable benefit from binaural amplification.

Thus, it would appear that for each of these hearing-impaired listeners, a general idea of the relative benefit likely to be obtained from binaural amplification can be estimated based on the results of basic binaural tests. However, as mentioned in the summary of results, there is not a simple relationship among these binaural tasks that would enable a specific prediction of the expected benefit

[2]This level comparison is in reference to the diotic condition in the unaided experiments, with 0-dB and 0-μs interaural reference differences.

these binaural tasks that would enable a specific prediction of the expected benefit from amplification. Listeners performing well on basic binaural tests would be expected to obtain significant benefit from binaural amplification for binaural tasks, whereas listeners unable to do basic binaural tasks would be unlikely to obtain consistent, measurable benefits from binaural amplification for binaural tasks. Obviously, the results presented here represent a very small group of subjects, all of whom have moderate-to-severe sensorineural hearing losses with a flat configuration. Whether even this general relationship between aided and unaided performance would be observed for listeners with other degrees and configurations will be investigated in our future experiments.

IV. SUMMARY

The results of these studies provide us with a better understanding of the effects of hearing impairment on binaural processing. It is clear from these and other studies reported in the literature (e.g., Smoski and Trahiotis, 1986; Gabriel *et al.*, 1992) that the ability to use binaural information cannot be predicted based on audiometric thresholds or other measures of monaural sensitivity such as monaural intensity JNDs. It also appears that the binaural processing problems experienced by these listeners are not due to "simple" internal interaural time and/or intensity differences, because imposing external differences does not improve performance consistently or substantially for any of the impaired listeners. Nonetheless, the data obtained in the two studies discussed in this chapter suggest that when we consider individual listeners with impaired hearing, performance without amplification on tests of basic binaural processing (such as binaural detection and interaural time and intensity discrimination) is generally related to performance with amplification on basic and complex tests of binaural performance (such as binaural detection and localization). Specifically, the subject that had normal or near normal performance on tests of interaural discrimination and binaural detection also obtained a clear and consistent benefit from binaural amplification; the subject that had very poor and limited ability to perform on tests of interaural discrimination and binaural detection also obtained no measurable benefit from binaural (or monaural) amplification.

This information is important to consider in the development of a diagnostic test of binaural performance, which is one of our primary long-term goals. Although it is unfortunate that binaural performance apparently cannot be predicted based on the traditional diagnostic audiological tests, it is encouraging that binaural performance with and without amplification is similar. Thus, we plan to use the results obtained in these studies in the development of a test that is easy to administer, score, and interpret in a clinical setting, as well as being a straightforward task for the listener. Ideally, the test will be able to be administered with or without amplification, so that the potential success with binaural amplification can be predicted, *and* the expected benefits to binaural performance from amplification presently being used can be assessed.

Great advances have been made in our understanding of binaural processing in listeners with impaired hearing during the past decade. The data described here provide further insight into the effects of hearing impairment on basic binaural processing and the relationship of these results to binaural performance with amplification. Nonetheless, although hearing impairment always has some effect on binaural performance, we are not yet able to clearly and easily predict the extent of these effects on binaural hearing, nor can we specifically predict the magnitude of the benefits to be expected from amplification. There is clearly a need for further investigation of binaural processing in hearing-impaired listeners with and without amplification. The results of such studies will further our understanding of the problems encountered by hearing-impaired listeners on a daily basis and provide us with information to develop better diagnostic tools and improve remediation for these individuals.

ACKNOWLEDGMENTS

We thank Steve Colburn and Pat Zurek, who were integrally involved in all aspects of this work, and Monica Hawley for her assistance with the figures. This research was supported by National Institute on Deafness and Other Communication Disorders (NIDCD) grants DC00428 and DC00100.

REFERENCES

Abel, S. M., Birt, B. D., and McLean, J. A. G. (1978). "Sound localization: Value in localizing lesions of the auditory pathway," J. Otolaryngol. 7(2), 132–140.

Besing, J., and Koehnke, J. (1995). "A test of virtual auditory localization," Ear. Hear. **16**(2), 220–229.

Burkhard, M. D., and Sachs, R. M. (1975). "Anthropometric manikin for acoustic research," J. Acoust. Soc. Am. **58**, 214–222.

Byrne, D. (1980). "Binaural hearing aid fitting: Research findings and clinical applications," in *Binaural Hearing and Amplification*, edited by E. Libby (Zenetron, Chicago), pp. 23–75.

Byrne, D., Noble, W., and LePage, B. (1992). "Effects of long-term bilateral and unilateral fitting of different hearing aid types on the ability to locate sounds," J. Am. Acad. Audiol. **3**, 369–382.

Colburn, H. S. (1982). "Binaural interaction and localization with various hearing impairments," in Scand. Audiol. Suppl., edited by O. J. Pederson and T. Poulsen, **15**, pp. 27–45.

Colburn, S., and Trahiotis, C. (1992). "Effects of noise on binaural hearing," in *Noise-Induced Hearing Loss*, edited by A. Dancer, D. Henderson, R. Salvi, and R. Hamernik (Mosby Year Book, St. Louis), pp. 293–302.

Colburn, S., Zurek, P., and Durlach, N. (1987). "Binaural directional hearing—Impairments and aids," in *Directional Hearing*, edited by W. Yost and G. Gourevitch (Springer-Verlag, New York), pp. 261–278.

Cox, R., and Bisset, J. D. (1984). "Relationship between two measures of aided binaural advantage," J. Speech Hear. Dis. **49**, 399–408.

DeGennaro, S. V. (1982). "An analytic study of syllabic compression for severely impaired listeners," Unpublished doctoral dissertation, MIT, Cambridge, MA.

Dermody, P., and Byrne, D. (1975). "Auditory localization by hearing-impaired persons using binaural in-the-ear hearing aids," Br. J. Audiol. **9**, 93–101.

Durlach, N. I., and Colburn, H. S. (1978). "Binaural phenomena," in *Handbook of Perception, Vol. IV, Hearing*, edited by E. C. Carterette and M. P. Friedman (Academic Press, New York), pp. 364–466.

Durlach, N. I., Thompson, C. L., and Colburn, H. S. (1981). "Binaural interaction in impaired listeners—A review of past research," Audiology **20**, 181–211.

Festen, J. M., and Plomp, R. (1986). "Speech-reception threshold in noise with one and two hearing aids," J. Acoust. Soc. Am. **79**, 465–471.

Gabriel, K. J., Koehnke, J., and Colburn, H. S. (1992). "Frequency dependence of binaural performance in listeners with impaired binaural hearing," J. Acoust. Soc. Am. **91**, 336–347.

Hall, J., and Fernandes, M. A. (1983). "Monaural and binaural intensity discrimination in normal and cochlear-impaired listeners," Audiology **22**, 364–371.

Hall, J., and Harvey, A. (**1985**). "The binaural masking level difference as a function of frequency, masker level and masking bandwidth in normal-hearing and hearing-impaired listeners," Audiology **24**, 25–31.

Hall, J., Tyler, R., and Fernandes, M. A. (**1984**). "Factors influencing the masking level difference in cochlear hearing-impaired and normal-hearing listeners," J. Speech Hear. Res. **27**, 145–154.

Hausler, R., Colburn, S., and Marr, E. (**1983**). "Sound localization in subjects with impaired hearing. Spatial-discrimination and interaural-discrimination tests," Acta Otolaryng. Suppl. 400.

Hawkins, D. B., and Wightman, F. L. (**1980**). "Interaural time discrimination ability of listeners with sensorineural hearing loss," Audiology **19**, 495–507.

Hawkins, D., and Yacullo, W. (**1984**). "Signal-to-noise ratio advantage of binaural hearing aids and directional microphones under different levels of reverberation," J. Speech Hear. Dis. **49**, 278–286.

Koehnke, J., and Besing, J. (**1991**). "Monaural detection with a contralateral cue in normal-hearing and hearing-impaired listeners," J. Acoust. Soc. Am. **89**, 2009.

Koehnke, J., Besing, J., Goulet, C., Allard, M., and Zurek, P. (**1992**). "Speech intelligibility, localization and binaural detection with monaural and binaural amplification," J. Acoust. Soc. Am. **92**, 2434.

Koehnke, J., Besing, J., and Zurek, P. (**1996**). Effects of amplification on binaural performance in hearing-impaired listeners (in preparation).

Koehnke, J., and Colburn, S. (**1986**). "Binaural detection and discrimination: Impaired listeners," J. Acoust. Soc. Am. **79**(S1), S22.

Koehnke, J., Colburn, S., and Durlach, N. (**1986**). "Performance in several binaural-interaction experiments," J. Acoust. Soc. Am. **79**, 1558–1562.

Koehnke, J., Colburn, S., Hawley, M., and Culotta, C. (**1995**). "Effects of reference interaural time and intensity differences on binaural performance in listeners with normal and impaired hearing," Ear Hear. **16**(4), 331–353.

Koehnke, J., Colburn, S., and Owen, G. (**1988**). "Binaural detection and discrimination for listeners with high-frequency sensorineural hearing losses," J. Acoust. Soc. Am. **84**, S74.

Koehnke, J., and Zurek, P. (**1990**). "Localization and binaural detection with monaural and binaural amplification," J. Acoust. Soc. Am. **88**(S1), S169.

Levitt, H. (**1971**). "Transformed up-down methods in psychoacoustics," J. Acoust. Soc. Am. **49**, 467–477.

Levitt, H., and Rabiner, L. (**1967**). "Predicting binaural gain in intelligibility and release from masking for speech," J. Acoust. Soc. Am. **42**, 820–829.

Libby, E. (**1980**). *Binaural Hearing and Amplification. Volume II: Binaural Amplification* (Zenetron, Chicago).

Markides, A. (**1977**). *Binaural Hearing Aids* (Academic Press, New York).

Markides, A. (**1982**). "Reactions to binaural hearing aid fitting," in Scand. Audiol. Suppl. 15, edited by O. J. Pederson and T. Poulsen, pp. 197–205.

Olsen, W., and Noffsinger, D. (**1976**). "Masking level differences for cochlear and brain stem lesions," Ann. Otol. Rhinol. Laryngol. **85**, 820–826.

Olsen, W., Noffsinger, D., and Carhart, R. (**1976**). "Masking level differences encountered in clinical populations," Audiology **15**, 287–301.

Passaro, C., Koehnke, J., and Colburn, S. (**1986**). "Binaural detection and discrimination: Normal listeners," J. Acoust. Soc. Am. **79**, S22.

Smoski, W., and Trahiotis, C. (**1986**). "Discrimination of interaural disparities by normal-hearing listeners and listeners with high-frequency, sensorineural hearing loss," J. Acoust. Soc. Am. **79**, 1541–1547.

Staffel, J. G., Hall, J. W., Grose, J. H., and Pillsbury, H. C. (**1990**). "N_0S_0 and N_0S_π detection as a function of masker bandwidth in normal-hearing and cochlear impaired listeners," J. Acoust. Soc. Am. **87**, 1720–1727.

Tonning, F. M. (**1973**). "Directional audiometry VIII. The influence of hearing aids on the localization of white noise," Acta. Otolaryngol. **76**, 114–120.

Tonning, F. M. (**1975**). "Auditory localization and its clinical applications," Audiology **14**, 368–380.

Wilson, R. H., Civitello, B. A., and Margolis, R. H. (**1985**). "Influence of interaural level differences on the speech recognition masking level difference," Audiology **24**, 15–24.

Zurek, P. M. (**1993**). "Binaural advantages and directional effects in speech intelligibility," in *Acoustical Factors Affecting Hearing Aid Performance*, edited by G. A. Studebaker and I. Hochberg (Allyn and Bacon, Boston), pp. 255–277.

Zurek, P., and Durlach, N. (**1987**). "Masker-bandwidth dependence in homophasic and antiphasic tone detection," J. Acoust. Soc. Am. **81**, 459–464.

Chapter 34

Signal Processing for Hearing Aids Employing Binaural Cues

Birger Kollmeier
Fachbereich Physik, Universität Oldenburg, Germany

(Received December 1993; revised October 1994)

Hearing-impaired and elderly persons often suffer from impaired loudness perception, as well as a reduced ability to separate speech from background noise. This chapter reviews the principles and applications of digital hearing aid algorithms that aim at restoring these auditory functions. Because binaural and spatial hearing is essential for impaired listeners, a special emphasis is given to "true" binaural algorithms that operate on the two input signals to both ears and simulate or enhance binaural auditory processing. At first, dynamic range compression algorithms are described that try to restore the impaired listeners' loudness percept to that of normal listeners. Incorporating a binaural loudness model in these algorithms appears promising. In the second section, the binaural system's noise reduction performance in simulated "cocktail-party" situations is examined. To a first approximation, the binaural system operates like a two-sensor system that efficiently switches the spatial direction of maximum attenuation to optimize the signal-to-noise ratio. In the third section, several algorithms operating in the frequency domain are described and evaluated that are based on these results. These algorithms attempt to enhance or simulate binaural noise suppression by exploiting binaural cues (such as interaural time and intensity differences and interaural correlation). A combined algorithm that suppresses lateral noise sources and reverberation yields encouraging results. In the fourth section, a more elaborate binaural signal processing algorithm is proposed that operates on the "modulation spectrogram," that is, the two-dimensional signal representation in the frequency and modulation frequency domain. This algorithm produces an improvement of about 2 dB in signal-to-noise ratio and appears to be very robust against reverberation and noise. Although these algorithms cannot yet be implemented in in-the-ear hearing aids, they should be considered for future "intelligent" and "true binaural" hearing aids.

INTRODUCTION

The fact that human beings have two ears and benefit from the interaction of the input to both ears in daily life is an important but often neglected factor in the rehabilitation of hearing-impaired patients. Although traditionally only one hearing aid has been fitted to the individual impaired listener, the use of two hearing aids fitted individually for each ear has become popular in recent years. However, bilaterally worn hearing aids do not necessarily restore the impaired listener's abilities in binaural listening. Instead, a "true" binaural hearing aid would include a mutual interaction and exchange of information between the signals recorded at the two ears before transmitting them in a modified form to the impaired ears. The following chapter therefore is devoted to "true" binaural hearing aids, which until now have only been developed and tested in laboratory experiments.

The most common complaints of sensorineurally hearing-impaired patients are their reduced abilities to understand speech in a noisy environment and their impaired mapping between the sound pressure level of natural acoustical signals and the perceived loudness of these signals. Impaired loudness perception is often associated with the so-called "recruitment phenomenon," that is, the patient's inability to perceive any sound at low to moderate sound pressure levels, and the steep increase of perceived loudness as the level increases from moderate to high values. Therefore, dynamic compression circuits have traditionally been incorporated in hearing aids (CHABA, 1991). They operate on the full input frequency range or in several independent frequency bands in order to account for the frequency dependence of the hearing dysfunction.

In the literature, however, there has been a controversial discussion about the benefit of multichannel compression algorithms (especially if short time constants are involved) in comparison to linear or broadband compression systems (Bustamante and Braida, 1987; Villchur, 1987; Plomp, 1988; Hohmann and Kollmeier, 1995). Unfortunately, due to the computational expense involved in multiband algorithms, only short speech samples have so far been used to evaluate these systems empirically and to compare their performance with other systems. In addition, most of the compression systems developed so far only operate monaurally, that is, on the signal for one ear. Thus, they can distort the spatial auditory impression, which is primarily determined by binaural hearing, that is, by listening with both ears. The first section of this chapter therefore describes a real-time binaural multiband dynamic compression algorithm that introduces interaction between both binaural channels to preserve interaural intensity cues (Hohmann, 1993; Kollmeier, Peissig, and Hohmann, 1993).

Binaural hearing also contributes significantly to the so-called "cocktail party effect," that is, to normal listeners' abilities to suppress disturbing noise and to enhance the signal coming from a "desired" direction. In addition, the auditory processing of normal listeners appears to reduce the negative impact of reverberation on speech intelligibility. Normal listeners are able to exploit binaural cues (i.e., interaural time and intensity differences) with sophisticated signal-processing strategies in the central auditory system (cf. Durlach, Thompson, and Colburn, 1981, for a review). The second part of this chapter therefore reviews some findings about speech intelligibility in spatially distributed interfering noise arrangements.

To restore the impaired listener's speech perception abilities in noisy and reverberant environments, the evaluation and processing of interaural differences might be performed by a "binaural" hearing aid using an intelligent processing scheme that operates on two input signals and provides one or two output signals. Although not necessarily intended for use in hearing aids, several algorithms of this type have been proposed in the literature (i.e., Allen, Berkley, and Blauert, 1977; Strube, 1981; Gaik and Lindemann, 1986; Koch, 1990; Kollmeier, 1990; Peterson, Wei, Rabinowitz, and Zurek, 1990; Kompis, 1992; Bodden, 1993). However, they tend to be very sensitive to small alterations in the acoustic transfer functions, have a high computational complexity, or introduce disturbing processing artifacts. The third section of this chapter therefore reviews the properties of binaural algorithms operating in the frequency domain, as proposed by Kollmeier *et al.* (1993).

To overcome some of the problems encountered in these algorithms, namely, the sensitivity to reverberation, a more complex binaural processing scheme was investigated, which incorporates processing in the modulation frequency domain. The basic properties of this kind of algorithm and the main findings from its application are reviewed in the fourth section of this chapter. In the last section, some conclusions and final remarks are presented.

I. DYNAMIC COMPRESSION IN BINAURAL HEARING AIDS

A typical and common complaint of sensorineurally impaired listeners is their inability to understand speech at low levels, combined with an excessively loud percept when the speech level is increased even by a small amount. This pathological increase of perceived loudness, or the "recruitment phenomenon," is caused by the distorted active undamping of the basilar membrane at low input levels. Thus, the range of perceivable oscillations of the basilar membrane is limited in impaired listeners to the range from intermediate to very high levels of the acoustic input signal. The full range of loudness sensations between nearly inaudible and very loud is mapped into this limited range of input levels. One commonly employed method of determining the degree of recruitment is the loudness scaling method (Würzburger Hörfeldskalierung after Heller, 1985; Hellbrück and Moser, 1985). A similar method has been used by Pascoe (1978) and Allen, Hall, and Jeng (1990): Short segments of narrowband noise are presented to the subject with a randomly selected presentation level. The subject's task is to judge the perceived loudness on a categorical scale with subdivisions between 0 (inaudible), very soft (1–10), soft (11–20), neither loud nor soft (21–30), loud (31–40), and very loud (41–50). The average result for normal listeners for 1-kHz narrowband noise is plotted in Fig. 1 as the dotted line. Normal listeners exhibit a continuous, almost linear increase in perceived loudness with increasing input level. On the other hand, the range of perceived loudness for cochlearly impaired listeners begins at intermediate levels and reaches the same loudness as normal listeners at high input levels. In Fig. 1 the data of one

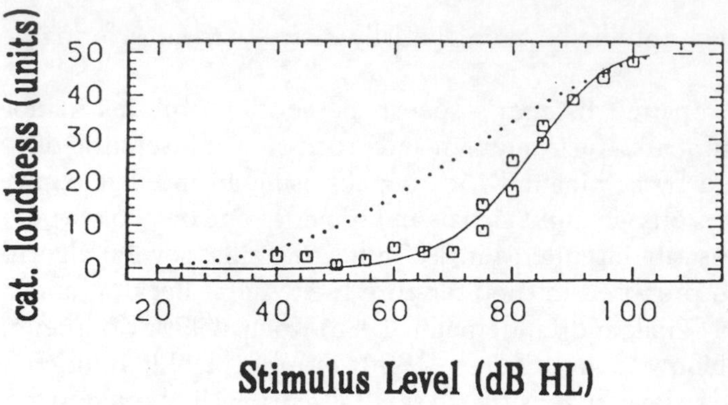

FIG. 1. Results of the categorial loudness scaling for a narrowband noise centered around 1 kHz averaged for normal listeners (dotted line) and a single sensorineurally impaired listener (squares with fitted solid line). Loudness categories (including 10 subdivisions for each category) range from very soft (5) to very loud (45).

individual cochlearly impaired subject with a high-frequency hearing loss are plotted as squares. The details of this method have been investigated by Hohmann (1993) and Kollmeier and Hohmann (1995). If the scaling method is performed for several center frequencies of narrowband noise, iso-loudness contours can be derived for each loudness level as a function of frequency.

The basic principle of fitting hearing aids is to match the impaired listener's loudness perception to that of a normal listener with the same input signal. Thus, the amplification of the "ideal" hearing aid is dependent on the input level and the spectral shape of the input signal. The fitting procedure of a multiband dynamic compression algorithm would attempt to restore the loudness in each individual frequency band. In commercial hearing aids, only wideband amplification with some frequency shaping, or amplification in up to three separate frequency bands, is provided. However, several attempts have been made to perform a multiband dynamic compression based on different fitting rationales (see CHABA, 1991, for a review).

The approach used by Hohmann (1993) and Kollmeier *et al.* (1993) is based on the already described loudness scaling method and was tested with the algorithm depicted in Fig. 2 (see Kollmeier *et al.*, 1993, for details). Successive short-term spectra are calculated in both binaural channels and the subsequent processing is performed in the frequency domain. For each ear, linear frequency shaping is provided with a high spectral resolution. A dynamic nonlinear weighting of the frequency channels is performed in 24 nonoverlapping bands, with bandwidths corresponding to the ear's critical bandwidth. Thus, the nonlinear level adjustment is performed with less spectral resolution than the linear frequency shaping. The entire algorithm was implemented in real-time on a multiple-signal-processor setup (Peissig, 1993). The attack and release time (i.e., the decay of the impulse response of the energy detector to $1/e$) were both set to 7 ms for all frequency bands and were not adjusted individually.

The algorithm was tested with six sensorineurally hearing-impaired listeners using both subjective quality assessment methods and speech intelligibility measurements in different acoustical situations. For most subjects, linear frequency

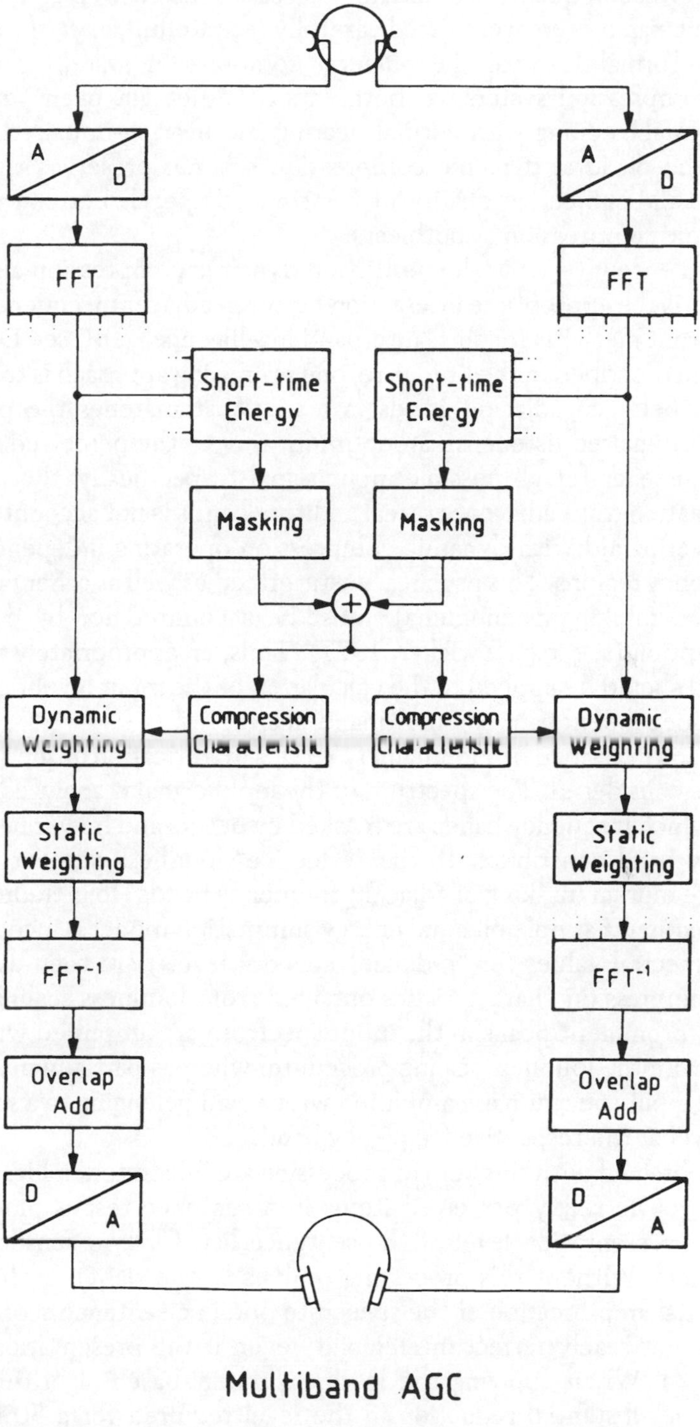

FIG. 2. Block diagram of the multiband dynamic range compression algorithm operating on both binaural channels. (From Kollmeier *et al.*, 1993.) Reprinted with permission.

shaping was subjectively assessed to have a negative effect on quality, although speech intelligibility improved in noise. Additional compression was assessed to have a positive effect on quality, and did not decrease speech intelligibility as long as the processing parameters were fitted carefully (see Kollmeier *et al.*, 1993, for more details). Formal tests of the binaural compression system versus two independent compression systems at both ears have not yet been performed. However, informal listening with normal-hearing and hearing-impaired listeners suggests that the binaural dynamic compression scheme preserves the spatial auditory image and subjective quality of transmitted speech better than independent dynamic compression at both ears.

One problem encountered in the multiband dynamic compression algorithms described so far is the appropriate interaction between adjacent frequency bands. Although different methods for this "interband intelligence" (IBI, see Dreschler, 1993) have been described in the literature, one promising approach is to perform the interaction between adjacent bands in a way that matches the perceived loudness of the impaired listener in an optimum way to the perceived loudness of the normal listener for all possible input signals. Specifically, the nonlinear loudness summation from adjacent critical auditory bands is not accounted for by a multiband hearing aid with dynamic compression operating independently in adjacent frequency regions. This psychoacoustic effect, as well as other properties of the ear (e.g., masking phenomena), must be accounted for by models of loudness perception (see, e.g., Zwicker, 1977). Thus, an appropriately modified loudness model should be applied to the calculation of the input level-dependent and frequency-dependent gain of a multiband hearing aid.

In the approach described by Hohmann (1993), a modification of the algorithm from Fig. 2 was considered: The spectrum of the input signal is analyzed in order to determine which frequency bands are masked by others and how much energy each frequency band contributes to the "effective" loudness percept after accounting for the mutual masking of adjacent frequency bands. To include binaural loudness summation, a simple binaural energy summation model is incorporated. The "kernel" spectral values (or "reduced" spectral levels) are then used as an input to the compression characteristics obtained from loudness scaling experiments. Hence, prominent peaks in the input spectrum are amplified with a gain as prescribed from the loudness scaling procedure, whereas partially masked flat portions of the input spectrum are amplified with a gain belonging to a somewhat lower input level at the respective frequency band.

The results obtained with this kind of processing are illustrated in Fig. 3, where the percentage of correctly perceived items in a sentence test is plotted as a function of the presentation level of the sentence list, for two sensorineurally impaired listeners. Without this processing (curves to the right), both subjects need a substantial amplification of the speech to obtain a sentence score of 50% correct and do not reach perfect intelligibility even if the presentation level is further increased. When applying the loudness model-based algorithm as described earlier, a substantial reduction in the level required for a 50% correct sentence score is observed, as well as a nearly perfect sentence score with a sufficient increase in presentation level. Thus, the current algorithm still under-

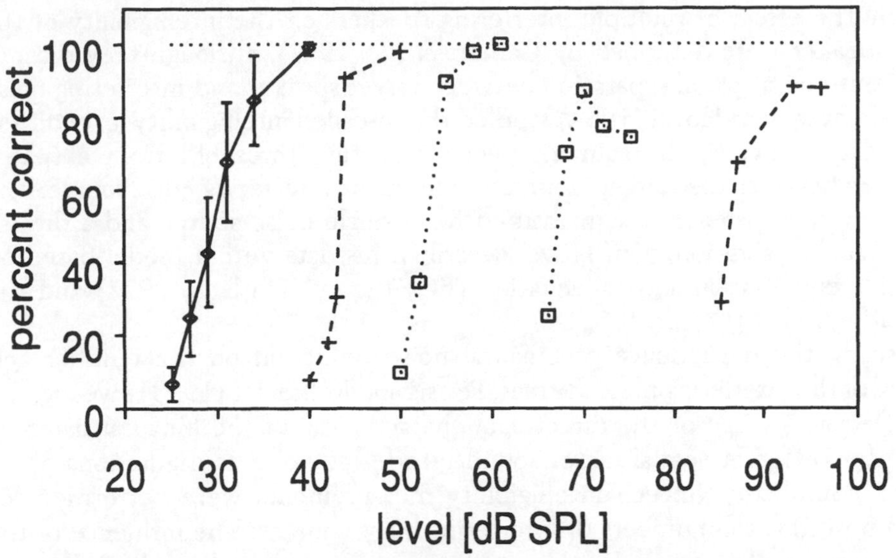

FIG. 3. Performance–intensity curve for the Göttinger sentence test (Wesselkamp *et al.*, 1992) in quiet for normal listeners (mean values and standard deviations denoted by diamonds) and for the two sensorineurally impaired subjects GS (crosses) and JS (squares) in the unaided and aided condition. In the latter case, a loudness model was incorporated in the dynamic range compression algorithm. (From Kollmeier and Hohmann, 1995.) Reprinted with permission.

estimates the "attenuation" component of the hearing loss, that is, the amount of global amplification required to shift the performance–intensity curve of impaired listeners to that of normal listeners. However, the loudness model-based algorithm also seems to enhance the maximum intelligibility of speech and thus minimizes the "distortion" component of the hearing loss, which prevents impaired listeners from obtaining a perfect sentence score for high input levels. Although these results look very promising, a better loudness model for each individual impaired listener would be required for a better compensation of the hearing loss. In addition, further tests of the algorithm should be performed with a larger number of impaired listeners.

II. SPEECH INTELLIGIBILITY IN NOISE

In a noisy environment, the normal hearing system is capable of enhancing a "target" speaker and suppressing several interfering noise sources. In normal listeners, this so-called "cocktail-party effect" is largely supported by binaural listening. The amount of noise reduction that can occur depends on the acoustical environment and on the number, position, and spectral–temporal properties of the target and the interfering sound sources. Several studies have been performed in the literature to measure the performance of the "cocktail-party processor" in simple and complex acoustical configurations (Carhart, Tillman, and Greetis, 1967; Plomp and Mimpen, 1981; vom Hövel, 1984; Peissig, 1993; Peissig and Kollmeier, 1993; a review is provided by Kollmeier, 1990). Some early attempts to study the effect of multiple interfering speakers on the intelligibility of the target speaker were described by Carhart *et al.* (1967), although they did not concentrate on a spatial separation between target speaker and interfering noise sources. Later, vom Hövel (1984) studied the so-called intelligibility level difference (ILD[1]), that is, the gain in speech reception threshold from a spatial separation between the "target" sound source and an interfering noise source. The ILD for normal listeners was measured for a single noise source and a diffuse sound field. In addition, vom Hövel described his data with a model based on Durlach's equalization and cancellation (EC) theory (Durlach, 1972) and the articulation index (Kryter, 1962).

To study the dependence of binaural noise reduction on the number and position of the interfering noise sources, Peissig and Kollmeier (1993) investigated the "effective" shape of the directional characteristic of the binaural listening system for different spatial target sound/interfering noise configurations of increasing complexity. Speech intelligibility measurements were performed for various positions and numbers of interfering noise sources. The influence of the spectral–temporal properties of the interfering noise on speech intelligibility was studied both with speech-simulating noise and with several interfering talkers. So that measurements could be obtained within a reasonable amount of time, subjective judgments of speech intelligibility were used, in which subjects adjusted the level of the target speech until they thought that 50% of the target speech was intelligible. The spatial distributions of the different sound sources were simulated with a real-time convolution of the original signals with outer ear impulse responses (see Peissig, 1993, for details).

Figure 4 gives the ILD for normal listeners in the situation with one target talker in front of the listener and an increasing number of continuous interfering noise sources. The signal-to-noise ratio (S/N) for 50% subjective speech intelligibility is plotted as a function of the azimuthal angle of incidence for one interfering noise source. Because the dB scale on the ordinate relates to the S/N for 0° azimuth, the ILD is reported as the negative S/N value. If only one interfering noise source is present (upper panel), a maximum ILD value of 9–10 dB is attained when the interfering noise is at 105° or 255° azimuth. The slight decrease of the ILD for noise incidence directly from the side (±90°) is caused by diffraction effects at the head, which lead to a high interaural cross-talk for direct incidence from the side.

The middle panel of Fig. 4 gives the configuration as before, but with one additional continuous noise source fixed at 105° azimuth. If both interfering noise sources are close to each other, the average adjusted intelligibility threshold is nearly identical with the threshold given in the upper panel, where only one noise source was present. However, if the two interfering noise sources differ considerably in their azimuthal angle of incidence (i.e., 180° to 360° incidence angle of

[1]The term ILD as it is used here in accordance with literature should not be confused with the abbreviation used commonly for the interaural level difference. To avoid this confusion, the abbreviation IID (i.e., interaural intensity difference) should be used instead.

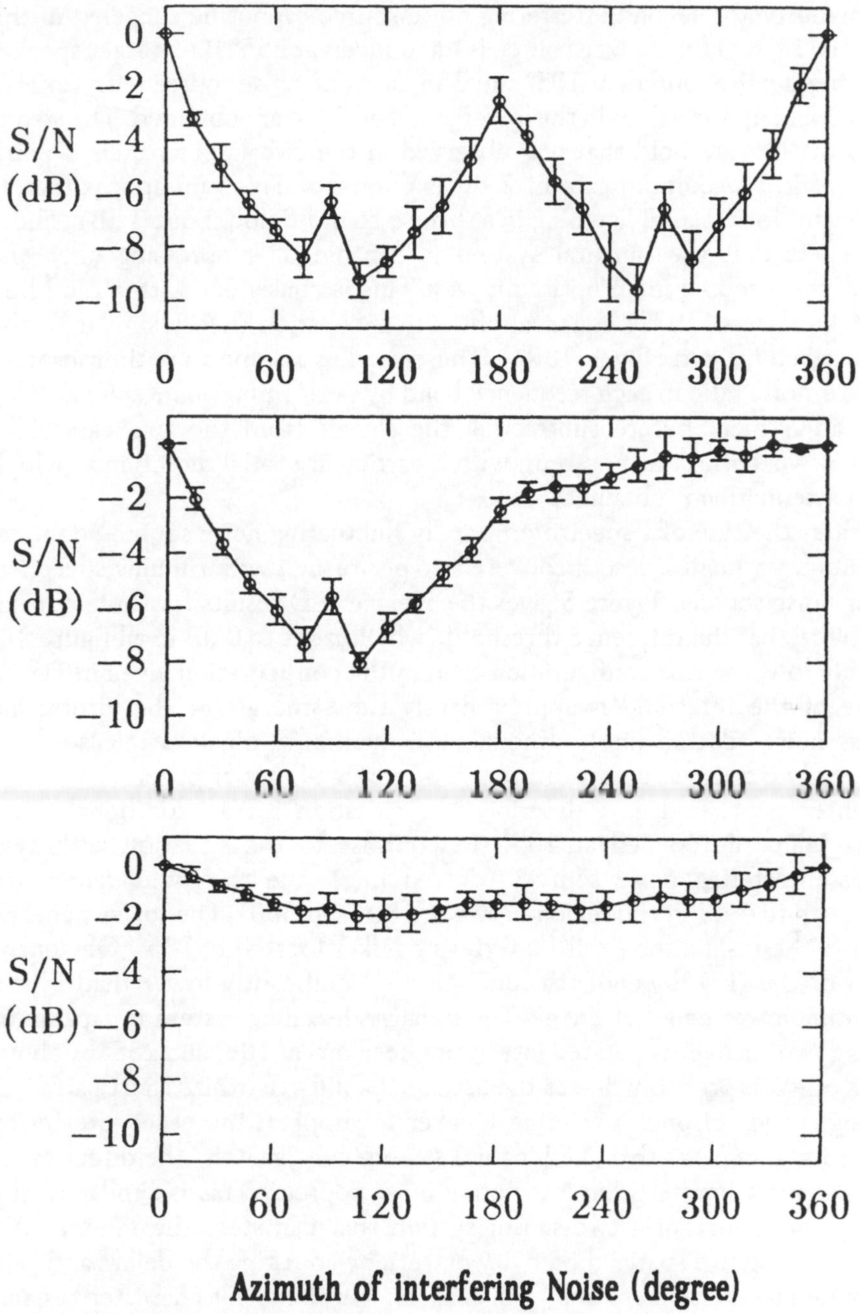

FIG. 4. Intelligibility level difference (ILD) for eight normal listeners (average values and standard deviations of subjectively adjusted thresholds) as a function of the azimuth of an interfering continuous speech-simulating noise source. The target talker is always located in front of the listener (0°). The upper panel gives the situation with one target talker and one variable interfering noise source. The center panel gives the situation with one additional interfering noise source fixed at an azimuthal angle of 105°. The bottom panel gives the situation with two additional interfering noise sources at angles of 105° and 255°, respectively. At the ordinate 0 dB marks the reference condition where the variable interfering noise source has 0° azimuth. (After Peissig and Kollmeier, 1993.) Reprinted with permission.

the variable noise source), no significant ILD is observed, as opposed to the upper panel. Obviously, the second interfering noise source cannot be canceled in this situation. If a second fixed noise source is introduced at 255° (i.e., target speaker at 0°, two fixed noise sources at 105° and 255° and one noise source with variable angle of incidence), the values in the lower panel of Fig. 4 are obtained. The strong directivity of the threshold that was observed in the two upper panels is completely lost and a maximum gain of 2 dB is obtained. This gain approximately equals the gain for binaural listening in a diffuse sound field (about 3 dB). These results suggest that the binaural system is capable of suppressing only one broadband noise source in an optimum way. This is consistent with a modified version of Durlach's (1972) equalization and cancellation theory similar to the model described by vom Hövel (1984). These models assume an optimization of the signal-to-noise ratio in each frequency band by performing an interaural delay and level adjustment before subtracting the signals from the two ears. This resembles a two-sensor radar system, with a particular spatial direction at which maximum attenuation is obtained.

To consider the case of a spectrotemporally fluctuating noise source, identical experiments to those just described were also performed with running speech as interfering noise sources. Figure 5 gives the average ILD results for three normal subjects. Note that the reference threshold (which is set to 0 dB in all figures) is considerably lower in this configuration than in the configuration given in Fig. 4. The shape of the threshold is approximately the same as for the interfering continuous noise (dotted line), although the maximum binaural release from masking is only 6.5 dB, as compared to 9.5 dB in Fig. 4, upper panel.

The center panel in Fig. 5 describes the situation for an additional fixed interfering talker introduced at 105°. In contrast to the situation with two continuous interfering noise sources (dotted line), the threshold values are reduced by up to 4 dB in the region between 180° and 360°. The lower panel of Fig. 5 shows the results for a third interfering talker located at 255°. Obviously, both sides of the ILD dependence function are significantly lower than in the corresponding lower panel of Fig. 4. The binaural listening system is capable of suppressing two spatially separated interfering speakers at 105° and 255° by about 4 dB. This effect is probably due to the listener's ability to utilize short pauses in the running speech of one interfering speaker to suppress the other interfering speaker. Thus, it appears that the binaural system can "switch" the direction of maximum attenuation between interfering noise sources. This is similar to the optimum performance of a two-sensor system that can steer the minima and maxima of its effective spatial directivity pattern by adjusting the delays and gain factors applied to the signals from both sensors. This behavior characterizes and limits the listener's performance in a complex spatial arrangement, which might be typical of a cocktail-party situation.

Preliminary results with impaired subjects show that the maximum effect of binaural unmasking is very limited in this group of listeners and that their binaural systems' ability to "switch" the direction of maximum attenuation between different interfering speakers is severely impaired (Peissig, 1993). Thus, a "binaural" hearing aid should try to simulate the performance of the human auditory

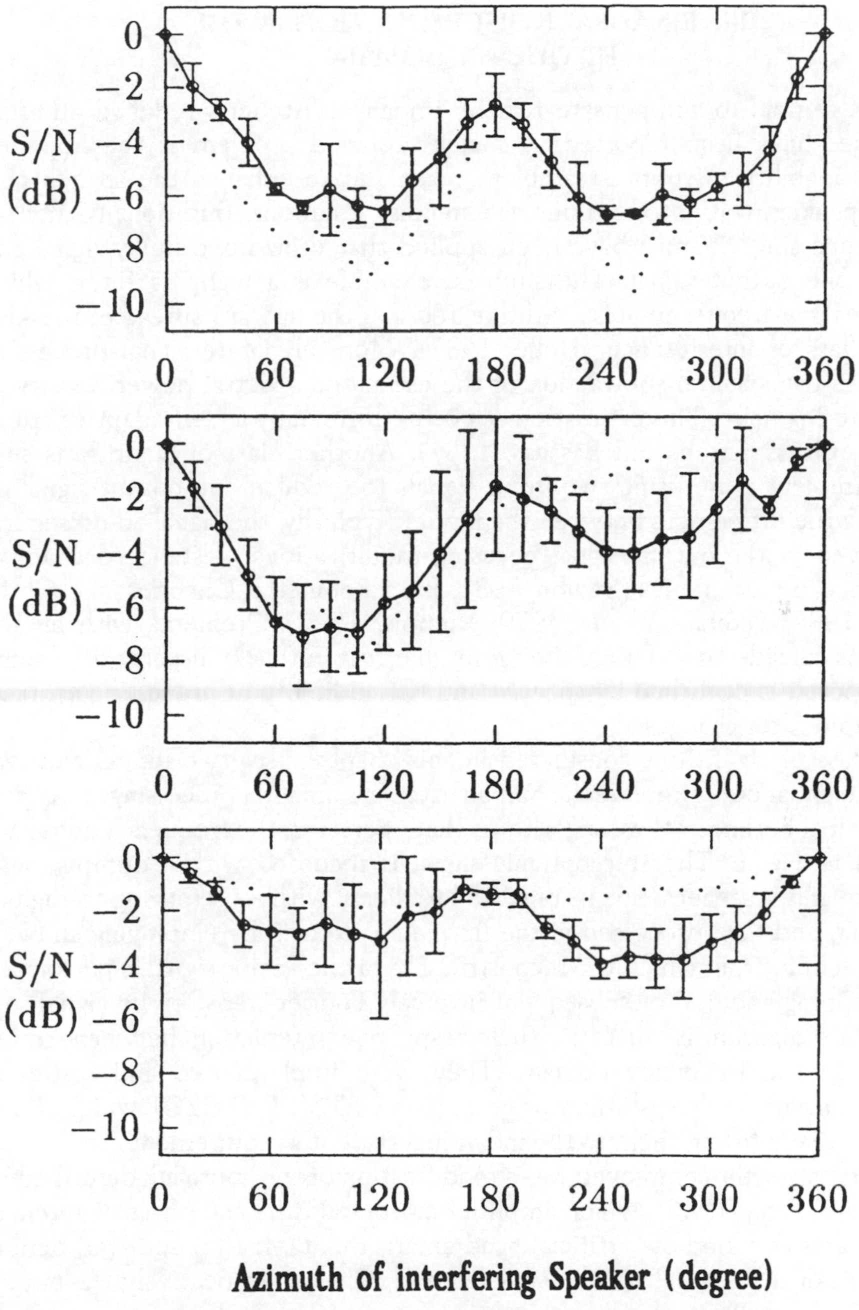

FIG. 5. Same as Fig. 4 with continuous discourse of one male talker (interfering from up to three spatial directions) employed instead of continuous interfering noise source(s). For comparison, the respective curves from Fig. 4 are plotted as dotted lines.

system by canceling the sounds from "undesired" directions, which are typically to the side of the listener. In addition, the spatial directivity pattern should vary across time and frequency. The next section reviews hearing aid algorithms of this type.

III. BINAURAL NOISE REDUCTION IN THE FREQUENCY DOMAIN

Several attempts to compensate for the impaired listener's reduced auditory capabilities have been reported. A major unsolved problem is the impaired listener's inability to suppress ambient noise and to enhance the speech of a desired speaker in order to communicate in noisy situations. Traditionally, monaural preprocessing schemes have been applied that utilize one input signal and produce one output signal. The simplest example is a highpass filter, which suppresses low-frequency noise and thus reduces the upward spread of masking by this class of interference (Helle, 1987). More elaborate signal processing techniques use spectral subtraction of the estimated spectral power density of the interfering noise. This estimation can be performed by a "self-adaptive" filter (Graupe, Grosspietsch, and Basseas, 1987). Another class of algorithms suppresses ambient noise using two input signals to produce one output signal by exploiting the differences between the inputs. Typically, the signal-to-noise ratio is improved in the output signal by using modifications of standard adaptive noise-canceling techniques (Strube, 1981; Brey, Robinette, Chabries, and Christiansen, 1987; Peterson *et al.*, 1990; Kompis, 1992). Problems with all the algorithms considered so far are their limited effect in "cocktail-party situations" (i.e., if speech is disturbed by speech) and the audibility of processing artifacts due to rapid filter changes.

The class of algorithms considered in this chapter uses two inputs and two outputs to enhance or simulate the human listener's binaural processing strategies. The principal outline of these algorithms that operate in the frequency domain is sketched in Fig. 6. The stereophonic signal is recorded with a dummy head (Damaske and Wagener, 1969), converted to digital with A/D (analog-to-digital) converters, and then processed in the frequency domain by employing an overlap-add technique, in which the reconstruction of the analog signal is performed by overlapping addition of subsequent inversely Fourier-transformed signal segments. The algorithms differ in their respective interaction between stereo channels in the frequency domain. They were implemented and tested in real-time on a multi-signal-processor setup (three AT&T DSP 32C), which allows for interactively fitting them to the individual patient's requirements.

The first algorithm employed was a modification of the approach described by Durlach and Pang (1986), which amplifies interaural time and phase differences and thus acts as a kind of "artificial head enlargement". If $l(\omega)$ and $r(\omega)$ denote the spectra of the original signals at the left and right ear, respectively, the output signals $l'(\omega)$ and $r'(\omega)$ are calculated as

$$l'(\omega) = l(\omega)\left(\frac{l(\omega)}{r(\omega)}\right)^{\alpha}$$

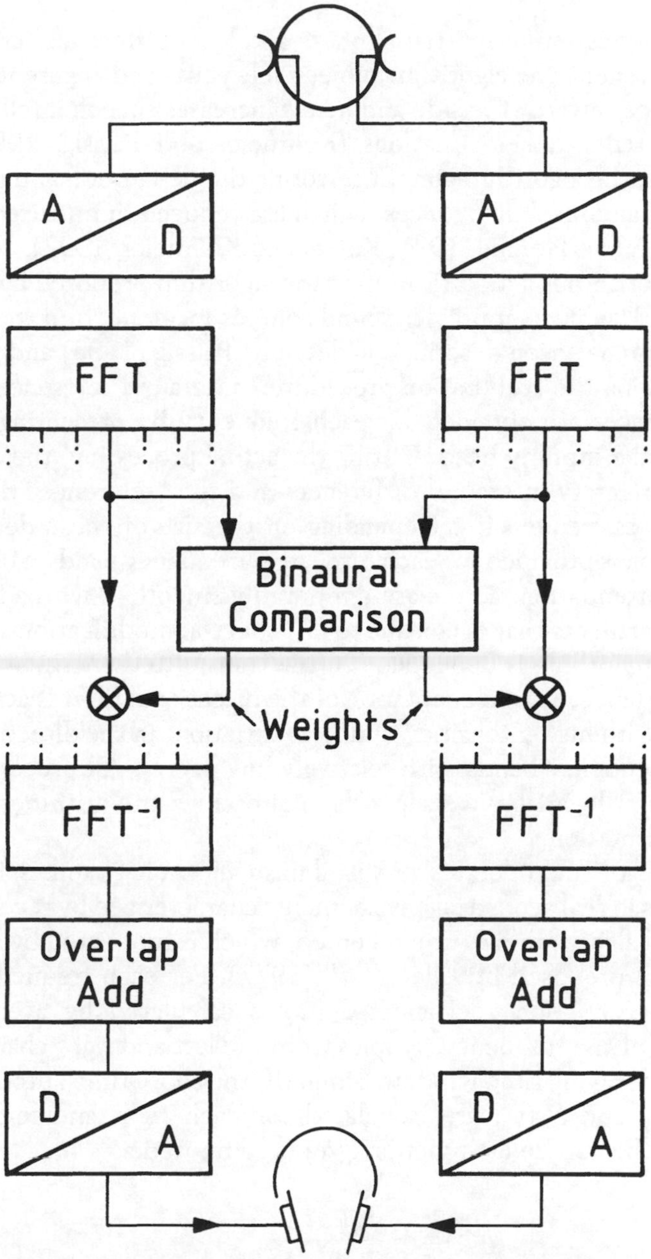

FIG. 6. Schematic diagram of the algorithms employed to enhance or simulate binaural interaction in impaired listeners. A dummy-head recorded stereo signal serves as input signal and the output is presented to the subjects via headphones. The algorithms, described in the text, differ in the block "binaural comparison," where an appropriate weight is calculated for each frequency, each stereo channel, and each time frame.

and

$$r'(\omega) = r(\omega).\left(\frac{r(\omega)}{l(\omega)}\right)^{\alpha},$$

where the amplification of interaural phase and level differences equals (1 + 2α). In normal listeners, the algorithm subjectively shifts the apparent direction of the sound source towards the side and hence increases speech intelligibility in certain spatial listener–talker situations (Kollmeier and Peissig, 1990). With impaired listeners, the algorithm aims at restoring the perception and processing of interaural time and level differences, which are reduced in impaired listeners (Kinkel, Kollmeier, and Holube, 1991; Kinkel and Kollmeier, 1992).

The second algorithm is a modification of the algorithm proposed by Gaik and Lindemann (1986), which suppresses sound sources incident from the subject's side. This algorithm has been described in detail by Peissig (1993) and Kollmeier *et al.* (1993). During the "calibration procedure," interaural reference intensity and phase differences are obtained for each frequency by presenting a speech signal in front of the dummy head. During the actual processing, the deviations between the momentary interaural differences and the "reference" differences are evaluated across frequencies. Depending on the size of these deviations, a variable attenuation is provided for each respective frequency band on both stereo channels. These attenuation factors are temporarily smoothed with a first-order filter to suppress artifacts that occur due to fast spectral modifications. The time constant of this smoothing is dependent on the transmitted energy within each frequency band. Hence, a rapid adaptation of the directional filter is achieved for frequency bands with high intensities, and slow variations in the directional filter are obtained in frequency bands with relatively low energy. All processing steps are performed on a logarithmic scale, which simplifies the arithmetic for the real-time implementation.

Although this algorithm operates very well in an anechoic chamber, it tends to introduce artifacts in real acoustical environments characterized by reverberation. Therefore, a third algorithm was implemented, which is motivated by a dereverberation algorithm proposed by Allen *et al.* (1977). For each frequency ω, the short-time cross-correlation coefficient $S_{lr}(\omega)$ is calculated by averaging the complex product of the frequency samples from the left and right channels with an exponentially decaying time window. Similarly, the short-time autocorrelation coefficients $S_{ll}(\omega)$ and $S_{rr}(\omega)$ are calculated for each right and left channel, respectively, and the coherence function $g(\omega)$ is computed as

$$g(\omega) = \frac{S_{lr}(\omega)}{S_{ll}(\omega)S_{rr}(\omega)}.$$

The absolute value of $g(\omega)$ is used to suppress reverberation, because a low interaural coherence is an indicator for a reverberant part of the signal. The phase of $g(\omega)$ is used to estimate the momentary interaural phase difference. In addition, the ratio $S_{ll}(\omega)/S_{rr}(\omega)$ estimates the momentary interaural level difference. As shown earlier, estimates of both interaural phase and level differences are used to control the attenuation performed in each frequency channel. Hence, the directional filtering properties of this algorithm are comparable to the second algorithm, although the interaural parameters are estimated on the envelope rather than the fine structure of the signal. However, the subjective quality of processed speech recorded in reverberant acoustical conditions is significantly improved. A detailed description of the algorithm, which is sketched in Fig. 7, is provided by Peissig (1993) and Kollmeier *et al.* (1993).

Figure 8 shows speech intelligibility results with five normal listeners using a German sentence test for each algorithm. The target speech was always presented in front of the dummy head, which was located in a 2 m by 2 m listening chamber. Several chapters of L. Carroll's *Alice in Wonderland* were presented, from 60° to the right (female interfering talker), and from 15° to the right and 30° to the left (male interfering talkers), at the same average level and the same distance (0.8 m) from the dummy head as the target speech. The signal-to-noise ratio was about –4 dB. As can be seen from the figure, a significant improvement in speech intelligibility is obtained by binaural listening, that is, when comparing the unprocessed binaural situation with the unprocessed "diotic" situation, where the sum of both ear signals is presented to both ears of the subject. The additional benefit provided by algorithm 1 (interaural magnification) is considerably less than the benefit to speech intelligibility obtained by algorithm 2 (suppression of lateral noise sources). Note that algorithm 2 provides even better noise reduction than the normal listener's binaural system, with or without interaural magnification. In addition, algorithm 2 appears to exploit nearly all binaural information available for human listeners, because no large increase is observed between diotic and binaural presentation of the output of algorithm 2. Similarly, the combination of algorithms 1 and 2 (i.e., lateral noise suppression applied to the output of the interaural magnification algorithm) provides no additional benefit. On the contrary, the increase of artifacts actually results in a deterioration of the intelligibility.

To evaluate the performance of the third algorithm in suppressing lateral noise sources and reverberation simultaneously, an acoustic situation was simulated by dummy head recordings in a reverberant room (approximate 5 s reverberation time) with one target talker and one interfering talker (see Kollmeier *et al.*, 1993, for more details). Figure 9 shows the results of the speech intelligibility tests as the percentage of words correctly repeated in a sentence test. The first two bars for each sensorineurally impaired subject show the results for the unprocessed, linear frequency shaped material presented monaurally (first bar) or binaurally (second bar). Subject HS was only tested in the binaural conditions. Three out of the remaining five subjects exhibit a binaural gain in intelligibility as compared to the monaural unprocessed version. The binaural system of these subjects obviously manages to suppress parts of the interference caused by reverberation and interfering speech. However, subjects RP and JS exhibit a decrease in intelligibility if speech is also presented to the "worse" ear. This suggests that the distorted internal representation of the input signal provided by this ear causes "binaural confusion," rather than binaural enhancement. The third and fourth bars

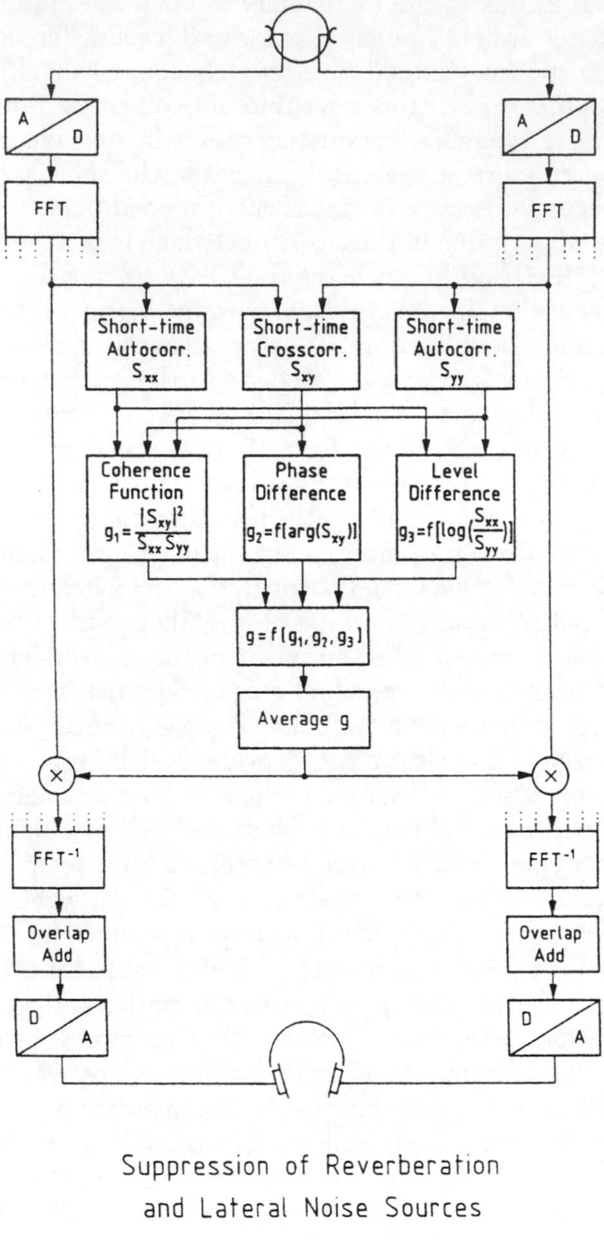

FIG. 7. Block diagram of the algorithm for suppressing reverberation and lateral incident sound sources. (After Kollmeier *et al.*, 1993.) Reprinted with permission.

in Fig. 9 denote the intelligibility score for the dereverberation algorithm, where the output signal is presented monaurally or binaurally to the subject, respectively. Obviously, no significant improvement in speech intelligibility (but marked improvement in speech quality) is obtained if the third algorithm is used as a pure dereverberation algorithm.

However, after adding the directional filter to the third algorithm, all subjects (except subject JJ) achieved higher intelligibility for the monaural presentation than the for the unprocessed version (fifth bar vs. first bar). For the binaural presentation, however, no unambiguous conclusion can be drawn (cf. sixth bar vs. second bar): Three subjects exhibited only a small change in intelligibility, which was not significant. Only two subjects obtained a significant gain in speech intelligibility of 25% with the combination of dereverberation and directional filtering. The overall results from these subjects with various degrees of hearing impairment imply that the benefit from the preprocessing strategy of algorithm 3 obtainable for each individual listener depends on the individual's hearing loss, the residual dynamic range in the high-frequency region, and the S/N of the test situation. A more detailed evaluation of algorithm 3 is provided by Peissig (1993).

The general conclusion from this evaluation is that the third algorithm for suppressing lateral noise sources and reverberation by exploiting binaural cues appears to operate quite effectively even under adverse acoustical conditions (i.e., a reverberant environment). It produces a larger benefit than the algorithm for interaural magnification and seems to operate well under reverberant conditions,

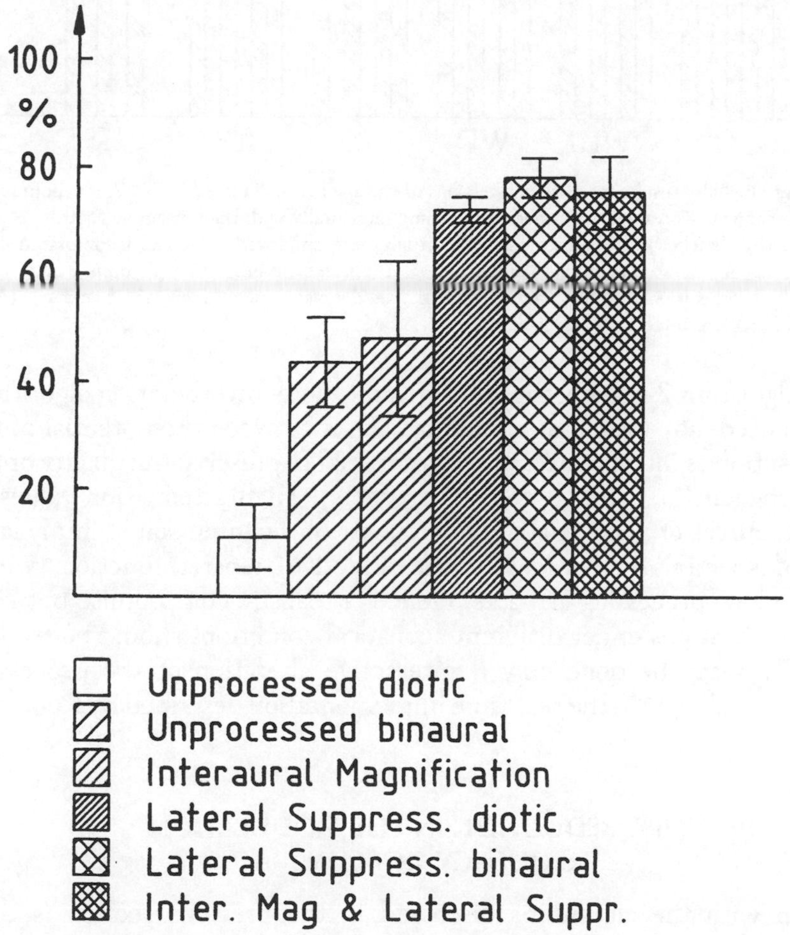

FIG. 8. Average sentence intelligibility scores and standard deviations for five normal listeners in a spatial configuration with one target speaker in front and three interfering speakers at –30°, +15°, and +60° azimuth. In the "diotic" conditions, the stereo signals are summed up and are identically presented to both ears.

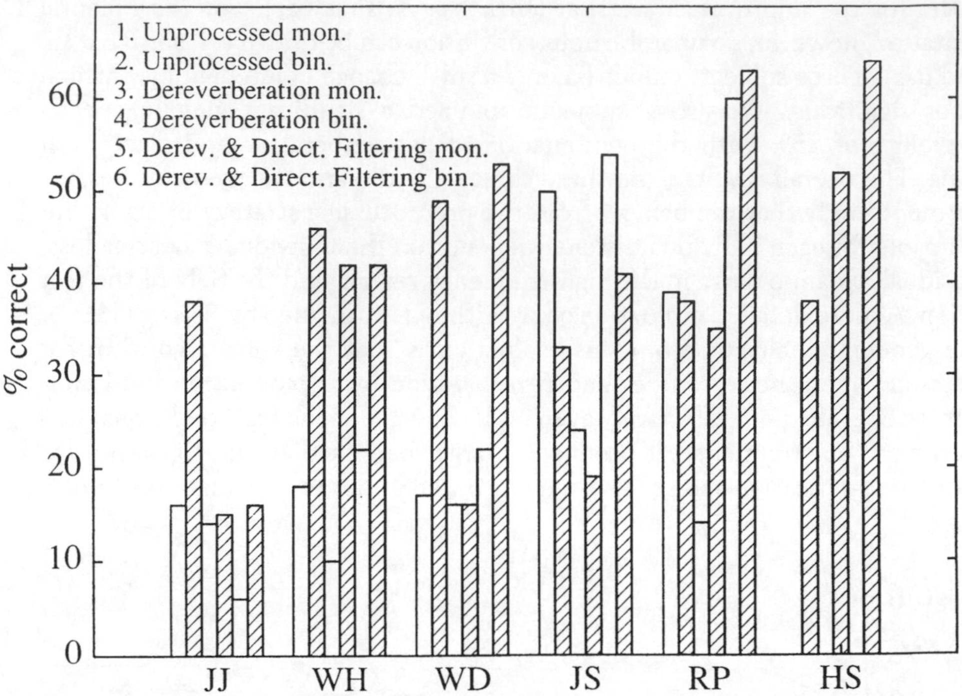

FIG. 9. Speech intelligibility results for different versions of the algorithm depicted in Fig. 7, for six impaired listeners. For each subject, scores were obtained for listening monaurally with the respective "better" ear and for listening binaurally (hatched). Three processing conditions were employed, which all incorporated linear frequency shaping: (a) unprocessed (columns 1 and 2), (b) suppression of reverberation (columns 3 and 4), and (c) suppression of reverberation including suppression of lateral noise sources (columns 5 and 6). (After Kollmeier *et al.*, 1993.) Reprinted with permission.

better than algorithm 2, which does not include the dereverberation algorithm. It should be noted, however, that a trade-off exists between the potential of the algorithm to suppress interferences and its potential to preserve the quality of the transmitted speech (i.e., the absence of artifacts). High attenuation values of lateral sound sources or uncorrelated components of the input sound imply large temporal and spectral fluctuations of the effective transfer function, which inevitably produce processing artifacts. Hence, a realistic compromise between these two specifications under different acoustical conditions should be studied empirically. This can be done only if interactive alteration of the processing parameters is possible, as in the real-time implementation described by Kollmeier *et al.* (1993).

IV. NOISE REDUCTION IN THE MODULATION FREQUENCY DOMAIN

The problem with the algorithms discussed in the previous section is their decrease in performance with increasing complexity of the spatial arrangement of the interfering noise sources and the target sound source, as well as with increasing reverberation. Specifically, interaural level and interaural phase cues are relatively good estimators of the incidence angle of a sound source in an anechoic environment. In a reverberant environment, however, the interaural parameters lose their more or less unambiguous relationship with the incidence angle and hence can no longer be used as good estimators. One acoustical cue that remains comparatively stable even in a reverberant environment is the envelope of a signal. Thus, it appears promising to consider not only the interaural parameters of the fine structure of a signal, but also the interaural parameters of a signal's envelope.

This novel approach for analyzing and filtering speech based on interaural envelope cues and their processing in the modulation frequency domain was investigated by Koch (1992) and Kollmeier and Koch (1994). They utilized the "modulation spectrogram," that is, the two-dimensional representation of modulation frequencies versus center frequency as a function of time. This approach is based on physiological findings of a periodotopical organization of modulation frequencies perpendicular to carrier frequencies as well as psychoacoustical findings of "modulation tuning curves" (Fassel and Püschel, 1993). In addition, an interaction is assumed between the representation of modulation frequencies and the representation of auditory space, as described by physiological and psychological models of binaural hearing. A noise-reduction algorithm based on this approach was implemented and tested, which enhances or suppresses each combination of modulation frequency and center frequency according to the phase and intensity relations between the two input signals (i.e., both stereo channels of a dummy-head recording).

A sketch of this algorithm is shown in Fig. 10 (Kollmeier and Koch, 1994). Because the processing in both binaural channels is very similar, only the processing for the left channel is completely represented. As before, an overlap-add technique was used with much smaller temporal windows (2.56-ms duration) and progression steps (0.16 ms) than for the algorithm described previously. The Fourier-transformed samples are considered as a function of time (i.e., as bandpass-filtered complex time signal, B). The envelope spectra of these time signals are calculated. They represent the complex modulation spectra (M). To compute a weighting function for each combination of center frequency and modulation frequency, the interaural level and phase difference for each of these combinations is extracted. These differences are compared with the range of "desired" differences, in order to find an appropriate weighting factor for the combination of modulation frequency and center frequency. A moving average (and standard deviation) is calculated across each submatrix (consisting of five adjacent modulation frequencies by five adjacent center frequencies), in order to obtain a more stable estimate of the actual weighting factor (see Kollmeier and Koch, 1994, for details). To reconstruct the signal, a smoothed version of the weighting function is applied to the modulation spectrum. The modulation spectrum is inversely transformed to yield the filtered envelope function (E'). The original bandpass-filtered time signals B are multiplied with a correction factor K, which in turn was obtained by dividing the "desired" envelope function E' by the original envelope function E. The output signal is reconstructed by an inverse Fourier transform and overlapping addition of the filtered bandpass signals B'. This process can also be viewed as first separating the original envelope from the bandpass-filtered time signals and then shaping the signals with the "desired" envelope.

This algorithm was tested in several situations with one continuous interfering noise source, two interfering talkers, and four interfering talkers as background, in both an anechoic and a reverberant environment (reverberation time 1.3 s). Figure 11 gives the average results for a sentence intelligibility test (Wesselkamp, Kliem, and Kollmeier, 1992) with 13 normal subjects both for the original signal and processed signal in three different acoustical situations with and without reverberation (Kollmeier and Koch, 1994). Obviously, the algorithm provides a small but very robust increase in speech intelligibility, which corresponds to approximately 2 dB in signal-to-noise ratio. Because the algorithm effectively increases the signal-to-noise ratio, it can be assumed that it provides a similar benefit for impaired listeners who typically benefit from a noise suppression algorithm even at higher signal-to-noise ratios. However, it remains to be seen whether the additional computational complexity of the algorithm (which includes one further spectral transformation and inverse transformation) is justifiable by the enhanced performance of the algorithm in reverberation and in complex acoustical conditions. Nevertheless, the goal of the algorithm, to mimic the human auditory system by incorporating the processing of modulation frequencies, appears to be promising. A further simplification of the algorithm and its application as a noise-reduction hearing aid or preprocessor for a speech recognition machine should be considered.

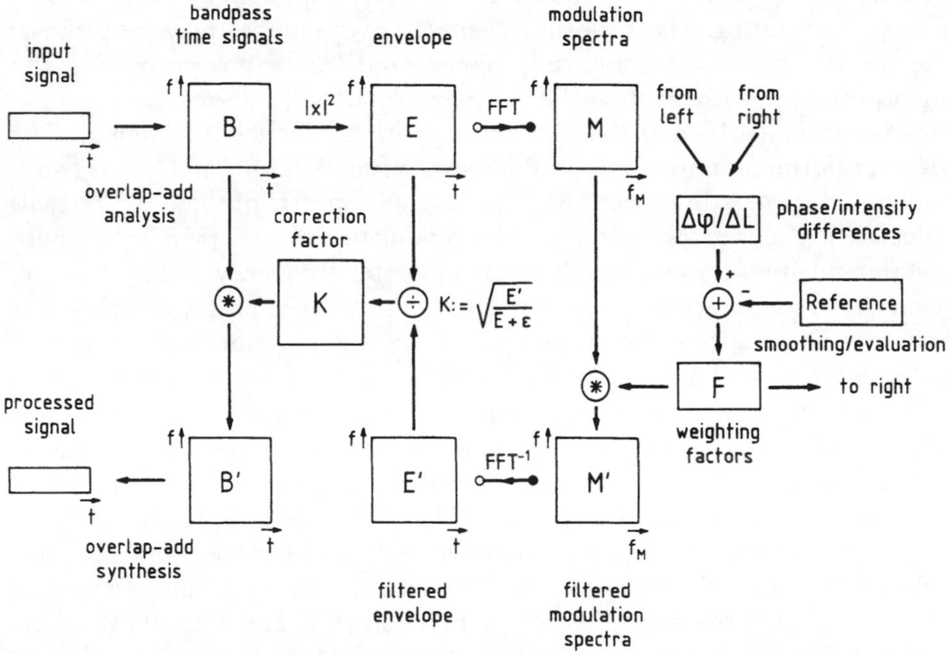

FIG. 10. Block diagram of the algorithm operating in the modulation frequency domain employed for suppressing noise emanating from "undesired" directions. Only the left stereo channel is plotted. See text for details. (After Kollmeier and Koch, 1994.)

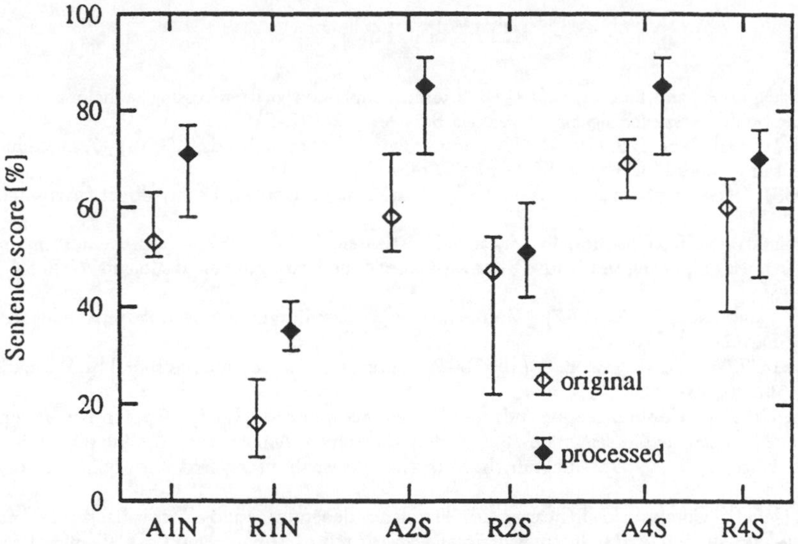

FIG. 11. Sentence scores (median values and interquartile ranges for 7 normal subjects) for several acoustical configurations with increasing number of interfering noise sources. Results are shown for the unprocessed and processed version: A1N/R1N, anechoic/reverbant condition with one interfering noise source; A2S/R2S, anechoic/reverbant condition with two interfering talkers; and A4S/R4S, anechoic/reverbant condition with four interfering speakers. (After Kollmeier and Koch, 1994.)

V. GENERAL CONCLUSION AND REMARKS

In conclusion, several algorithms suitable for binaural hearing aids have been reviewed, all of which appear to be beneficial in certain aspects for certain listeners. The general principle underlying all these algorithms appears to be very promising, that is, to incorporate characteristics of the normal auditory system (such as loudness perception and binaural listening) into hearing aids that ideally should permit impaired listeners to approximate normal performance. However, we are still far from being able to devise an "intelligent" binaural hearing aid that provides benefits for nearly all users in nearly all situations. This is partly due to the fact that the human auditory system and the alterations that hearing impairment imposes on it are still not very well understood. Another issue is that most algorithms under consideration are still too complex to be implemented in a wearable device that could be used for testing the algorithms under daily life conditions. In particular, the combination of several of the described algorithms in a practical, general purpose hearing aid is even more difficult to implement in a wearable form. However, because technological achievements are proceeding rapidly, the era of "true" binaural hearing aids may actually begin within the next few years.

ACKNOWLEDGMENTS

Thanks to the members of the "Arbeitsgruppe Medizinische Physik" for their contributions and to Robert H. Gilkey for his invitation to the conference and his guidance in earlier days. Thanks to A. Sievers for typing the manuscript. This work was supported by BMBF PT-FDG.

REFERENCES

Allen, J. B., Berkley, D. A., and Blauert, J. (**1977**). "Multimicrophone signal-processing technique to remove room reverberation from speech signals," J. Acoust. Soc. Am. **62**, 912–915.

Allen, J. B., Hall, J. L., and Jeng, P. S. (**1990**). "Loudness growth in ½-octave bands (LGOB)—A procedure for the assessment of loudness," J. Acoust. Soc. Am. **88**, 745–753.

Bodden, M. (**1993**). "Modeling human sound-source localization and the cocktail-party-effect," Acta Acustica **1**, 43–56.

Brey, R. H., Robinette, M. S., Chabries, D. M., and Christiansen, R. W. (**1987**). "Improvement in speech intelligibility in noise employing an adaptive filter with normal and hearing impaired subjects," J. Rehab. Res. Dev. **24**, 75–86.

Bustamante, D. K., and Braida, L. D. (**1987**). "Multiband compression limiting for hearing-impaired listeners," J. Rehab. Res. Dev. **24**, 149–160.

Carhart, R., Tillman, T. W., and Greetis, E. S. (**1967**). "Perceptual masking in multiple sound backgrounds," J. Acoust. Soc. Am. **45**, 694–703.

CHABA Working Group on Communication Aids for the Hearing-Impaired. (**1991**). "Speech-perception aids for hearing-impaired people: Current status and needed research," J. Acoust. Soc. Am. **90**, 637–685.

Damaske, P., and Wagener, B. (**1969**). "Richtungshörversuche über einen nachgebildeten Kopf," Acustica **21**, 30–35.

Dreschler, W. A. (**1993**). "Compression in hearing aids: Frequency dependence and effect in background noise," in *Recent Developments in Hearing Instrument Technology*, edited by J. Beilin and G. R. Jensen (Danavox Foundation, Copenhagen), pp. 253–272.

Durlach, N. I. (**1972**). "Binaural signal detection: Equalization and cancellation theory," in *Foundations of Modern Auditory Theory, Vol. II*, edited by J. V. Tobias (Academic Press, New York), pp. 363–462.

Durlach, N. I., and Pang, X. D. (**1986**). "Interaural magnification," J. Acoust. Soc. Am. **80**, 1849–1850.

Durlach, N. I., Thompson, C. L., and Colburn, H. S. (**1981**). "Binaural interaction in impaired listeners. A review of past research," Audiology **20**, 181–211.

Fassel, R. and Püschel, D. (**1993**). "Form de Modulationsfilter im Gehör," in *Fortschritte der Akustik—DAGA '93* (DPG-Verlag, Bad Honnef), pp. 812–815.

Gaik, W., and Lindemann, W. (**1986**). "Ein digitales Richtungsfilter, basierend auf der Auswertung interauraler Parameter von Kunstkopfsignalen," in *Fortschritte der Akustik—DAGA '86* (DPG-Verlag, Bad Honnef), pp. 721–724.

Graupe, D., Grosspietsch, J. K., and Basseas, S. P. (**1987**). "A single-microphone-based self-adaptive filter of noise from speech and its performance evaluation," J. Rehab. Res. Dev. **24**, 119–126.

Hellbrück, J., and Moser, L. M. (**1985**). "Hörgeräte-Audiometrie: Ein computerunterstütztes psychologisches Verfahren zur Hörgeräteanpassun," Psycholog. Beiträge **27**, 494–508.

Helle, R. (**1987**). "Fortschritte bei der Miniaturisierung des Hörgeräte," in *Fortschritte der Akustik—DAGA '87* (DPG-Verlag, Bad Honnef), pp. 115–136.

Heller, O. (**1985**). "Hörfeldaudiometrie mit dem Verfahren der Kategorial-Unterteilung (KU)," Psychol. Beitr. **27**, 478–493.

Hohmann, V. (**1993**). "Dynamikkompression für Hörgeräte—Psychoakustische Grundlagen und Algorithmen," *Fortschr.-Ber. VDI Reihe 17 Nr.93* (VDI-Verlag, Düsseldorf).

Hohmann, V., and Kollmeier, B. (**1995**). "The effect of multichannel dynamic compression on speech intelligibility," J. Acoust. Soc. Am. **97**, 1191–1195.

Kinkel, M., and Kollmeier, B. (**1992**). "Binaurales Hören bei Normal- und Schwerhörigen II: Analyse der Ergebnisse," Audiol. Akustik **31**, 22–33.

Kinkel, M., Kollmeier, B., and Holube, I. (**1991**). "Binaurales Hören bei Normal- und Schwerhörigen I: Methoden und Ergebnisse," Audiol. Akustik **30**, 192–201.

Koch, R. (**1990**). "Störgeräusch-Unterdrückung für Hörhilfen—ein adaptiver Cocktail-Party-Prozessor," in *Fortschritte der Akustik—DAGA '90* (DPG-Kongreß GmbH, Bad Honnef), pp. 1019–1022.

Koch, R. (**1992**). "Gehörgerechte Schallanalyse zur Vorhersage und Verbesserung der Sprachverständlichkeit," dissertation, Universität Göttingen, Göttingen, Germany.

Kollmeier, B. (**1990**). "Meßmethodik, Modellierung und Verbesserung der Verständlichkeit von Sprache," Habilitationsschrift, Universität Göttingen, Göttingen, Germany.

Kollmeier, B., and Hohmann, V. (**1995**). "Loudness estimation and compensation for impaired listeners employing a categorical scale," in *Advances in Hearing Research, Proc. 10th Intl. Symp. on Hearing*, edited by G. A. Manley (World Scientific Publishers, Singapore), pp. 441–453.

Kollmeier, B., and Koch, R. (**1994**). "Speech enhancement based on physiological and psychoacoustical models of modulation perception and binaural interaction," J. Acoust. Soc. Am. **95**, 1593–1602.

Kollmeier, B., and Peissig, J. (**1990**). "Speech intelligibility enhancement by interaural magnification," Acta Otolaryngol. Suppl. **469**, 215–223.

Kollmeier, B., Peissig, J., and Hohmann, V. (**1993**). "Real-time multiband dynamic compression and noise reduction for binaural hearing aids," J. Rehab. Res. **30**, 82–94.

Kompis, M. (1992). "Der adaptive Beamformer: Evaluation eines Verfahrens zur Störgeräuschunterdrückung für Hörgerät," dissertation, ETH Zürich, Zürich, Switzerland.

Kryter, K. D. (1962). "Methods for the calculation and use of the articulation index," J. Acoust. Soc. Am. **34**, 1689–1697.

Pascoe, D. P. (1978). "An approach to hearing aid selection," Hear. Instrum. **29**, 12–16.

Peissig, J. (1993). "Binaurale Hörgerätestrategien in komplexen Störschallsituationen," *Fortschr.-Ber. VDI Reihe 17, Nr. 88.* (VDI-Verlag, Düsseldorf).

Peissig, J., and Kollmeier, B. (1993). "Richtcharakteristik des binauralen Hörsystems bei Normal- und Schwerhörige," in *Fortschritte der Akustik—DAGA '93,* (DPG-Verlag, Bad Honnef), pp. 744–747.

Peterson, P. M., Wei, S. M., Rabinowitz, W. M., and Zurek, P. M. (1990). "Robustness of an adaptive beamforming method for hearing aids," Acta Otolaryngol. Suppl. **469**, 85–90.

Plomp, R. (1988). "The negative effect of amplitude compression in multichannel hearing aids in the light of the modulation transfer function," J. Acoust. Soc. Am. **83**, 2322–2327.

Plomp, R., and Mimpen, A. M. (1981). "Effect of the orientation of the speaker's head and the azimuth of a noise source on the speech-reception threshold for sentences," Acustica **48**, 325–328.

Strube, H. W. (1981). "Separation of several speakers recorded by two microphones (cocktail-party-processing)," Signal Processing **3**, 355–364.

Villchur, E. (1987). "Multiband compression processing for profound deafness," J. Rehab. Res. Dev. **24**, 135–148.

vom Hövel, H. (1984). "Zur Bedeutung der Übertragungseigenschaften des Außenohres sowie des binauralen Hörsystems bei gestörter Sprachübertragung," dissertation, RWTH Aachen, Germany.

Wesselkamp, M., Kliem, K., and Kollmeier, B. (1992). "Erstellung eines optimierten Satztestes in deutscher Sprache," in *Moderne Verfahren der Spachaudiometrie,* edited by B. Kollmeier (Heidelberg), pp. 330–343.

Zwicker, E. (1977). "Procedure for calculating loudness of temporally variable sounds," J. Acoust. Soc. Am. **62**, 675–682.

Author Index

Subject Index